+HF5467 .S4 E5

HF
5467
S4
E5

Emmet, Boris, 1885-
   Catalogues and
counters

DATE DUE

COLLEGE FOR HUMAN SERVICES
LIBRARY
345 HUDSON STREET
NEW YORK, N.Y. 10014

Catalogues and Counters

Catalogues and Counters

A History of Sears, Roebuck and Company

By

BORIS EMMET & JOHN E. JEUCK

THE UNIVERSITY OF CHICAGO PRESS
CHICAGO & LONDON

THE UNIVERSITY OF CHICAGO PRESS, CHICAGO 60637
The University of Chicago Press, Ltd., London

*Copyright 1950 by The University of Chicago. All rights reserved
Published 1950. Fifth Impression 1974
Printed in the United States of America*

*International Standard Book Number: 0-226-20710-2
Library of Congress Catalog Card Number: 50-7387*

Foreword

THE importance of business enterprises in American society is out of all proportion to the scant attention thus far given them by professional historians. Their comparative neglect of business concerns as material for histories probably results from several factors. Among these, three seem fairly clear. One is the greater prestige enjoyed for centuries by religious, military, and political institutions and their leaders. A second is that economic historians have preferred to deal with general trends rather than with the development of specific business concerns. A third reason has been the inaccessibility, often the inadequacy, of business records.

For business enterprises that have grown large the business records are usually formidable in amount, but the choice of materials retained and the methods of storing have seldom been influenced by any thought of their usefulness to scholars. Also, since business is competitive and since many of the decisions of a firm have seemed to its executives to be private matters, there has been a natural reluctance to open to outsiders the records of a business concern still in the prime of its life. There may also be doubt that an outsider will acquire sufficiently accurate knowledge of the business, or form sufficiently valid judgments of its policies, to justify the opening to him of its archives.

Fortunately a few competent investigators have turned their talents to the writing of histories of individual business corporations. It is to be hoped that their numbers will increase. Happily, too, the managements of a growing number of business concerns are showing a willingness to have the histories of their respective enterprises competently and objectively told. The results should be of increasing value to students, to business executives, and to shapers of public policy toward business. It seems probable that the stories awaiting the telling are on balance and in most instances creditable ones. If this proves so, then a by-product of a policy of frankness on the part of business managements may be a greater measure of public confidence in private enterprise.

The present volume deals with the history of a remarkably successful business concern. Few corporate names are as familiar to Americans as that of Sears, Roebuck and Company. This study of its development was made possible by a grant from the Rockefeller Foundation to the School of Business of the University of Chicago. To help finance completion of the project, Sears, Roebuck and Company later made a supplementary grant.

The authors of the study were well qualified for their task. In addition to experience as government economist and university professor, Dr. Emmet served some ten years as a department-store executive before becoming retail merchandise manager for Sears, Roebuck and Company. After ten years' service in that capacity, he retired in 1946 before beginning work upon this history. He is now chairman of the board of directors of a large department store in Philadelphia. He thus had the benefit of considerable firsthand knowledge of men, methods, and policies of the company, yet had become far enough removed from that experience to gain in objectivity. Dr. Jeuck, assistant professor in the School of Business of the University of Chicago and assistant director of its Executive Program, came to the undertaking with the detachment of a student of marketing and of industrial relations. From the beginning of their work the authors availed themselves of the counsels of an advisory committee composed of six members of the faculty of the University of Chicago.

This study traces the way in which the company's management met internal problems and adjusted its business to the tides of external developments. It is a competent account of the men and methods by which this enterprise has risen in sixty years to its present eminence. It thus holds much of interest to business managers, to government officials, and to students. Though the authors have not attempted to write a popular book, the general reader should find the volume a rewarding experience.

GARFIELD V. COX
Dean of the School of Business
University of Chicago

CHICAGO
September, 1949

Acknowledgments

SPACE limitations preclude listing all those for whose assistance in preparing this study the authors are indebted. Our largest, and initial, expression of gratitude goes rightfully to the Rockefeller Foundation, without whose grant this study would not have been possible. Thanks are due also to Sears, Roebuck and Company for a supplementary grant to see the project completed; and to the officers, directors, and many employees of the company who extended active aid in securing the original material herein contained.

Of those who have been in the past associated with Sears, Roebuck in various capacities, the authors are particularly in debt to Lessing J. Rosenwald, Donald M. Nelson, Elmer Scott, Otto C. Doering, Robert P. Sniffen, Waddill Catchings, Arthur Price, John C. Higgins, and Emil J. Pollock. Sidney Weinberg and others of Goldman, Sachs and Company, the office of Nathan W. Levin, and various officials of Lehman Brothers have made available old records not otherwise accessible.

The authors have received valuable assistance from William C. Pettigrew, former catalogue editor of Sears, Roebuck and Company, in collecting old documents and in helping to interview retired employees of the company. Mr. Pettigrew's personal recollections and firsthand knowledge of the company, dating back to the heyday of Richard Sears, have been a fruitful source of much important material.

We also owe a sizable debt to the late Louis E. Asher, former general manager of Sears, Roebuck, close associate of Richard Sears, and coauthor of *Send No Money*. Mr. Asher gave generously of his time for interviews and made available a wealth of material from his personal files, including old documents, photographs, correspondence with Richard Sears and others, and an abundance of notes prepared in connection with his own book. All this material provided primary sources nowhere else available.

Modie J. Spiegel, president of Spiegel, Inc., gave freely of his own time and that of members of his staff for several interviews and access to much confidential information, which provided valuable background material on the rise of some of Sears, Roebuck's chief competitors.

Florence Kiper Frank has been most gracious in giving us access to, and permission to quote from, her unpublished manuscript on the life of Julius Rosenwald. She has also been generous and patient in supplementing that material in personal conferences.

More than mere assistance has been rendered by John Page Tolbert, who drafted much of the manuscript and performed invaluable editorial work through all stages of its preparation. But for his intelligence, initiative, industry, and verbal facility, the composition of the work would have come along more slowly.

Our greatest collective assistance in the preparation of the manuscript came from a faculty committee of the University of Chicago, under whose general supervision the project was carried out. The authors wish especially to express their gratitude to Garfield V. Cox, dean of the School of Business, and to Professors George H. Brown, Everett C. Hughes, Neil H. Jacoby (now at the University of California at Los Angeles), Raleigh W. Stone, and Chester Wright. This committee patiently examined various proposed outlines for the study and reviewed the entire manuscript. Their valuable suggestions helped materially in orientation and approach. Whatever errors of fact and judgment there be remain, of course, the responsibility of the authors.

Boris Emmet
John E. Jeuck

New York City
September 23, 1949

Table of Contents

LIST OF ILLUSTRATIONS	xi
LIST OF CHARTS	xiii
LIST OF TABLES	xv
I. INTRODUCTION: SEARS, ROEBUCK AS MASS DISTRIBUTOR	1

FOUNDING A MAIL-ORDER BUSINESS, 1886–1908

II. AMERICAN ECONOMIC EXPANSION	9
III. ORIGINS: BUILDING A BUSINESS	23
IV. CAPITAL AND TRANSITION: GROWING PAINS AND FINANCIAL PANIC	47
V. SALES PRESSURE AND PROMOTION	59
VI. CATALOGUE APPEALS AND POLICIES	85
VII. MAIL-ORDER MERCHANDISE	100
VIII. MANAGEMENT AND METHODS: ORDER OUT OF CHAOS	123
IX. WORKING CONDITIONS, WELFARE, AND WAGES	137
X. OPPOSITION AND COMPETITION	150
XI. END OF AN ERA	169

THE MATURITY OF MAIL ORDER, 1908–25

XII. THE MAIL-ORDER MARKET	187
XIII. THE DEBACLE OF 1921	196
XIV. REORIENTATION OF MERCHANDISING	216
XV. CHANGES IN CATALOGUE SELLING	245
XVI. SELLING ON INSTALMENTS	264
XVII. OPERATING METHODS AND EMPLOYEE WELFARE	276
XVIII. THE PERIOD IN REVIEW	293

DEVELOPMENT OF RETAIL STORES, 1925–48

XIX. URBAN AMERICA	313
XX. THE NEW MANAGEMENT: ASCENDANCY OF ROBERT E. WOOD	324
XXI. LEARNING ANEW: THE RETAIL STORES	338
XXII. NEW PATTERNS OF ORGANIZATION	358
XXIII. SOME ASPECTS OF CENTRAL BUYING	374

TABLE OF CONTENTS

XXIV.	Merchandising Influences and Adventures	421
XXV.	New Techniques of Mail-Order Selling	450
XXVI.	Expanding Over-the-Counter Sales	482
XXVII.	Easy Payments and "Modern Homes"	505
XXVIII.	Store Planning and Design	531
XXIX.	Personnel Management Matures	547
XXX.	The New Opposition	604
XXXI.	Public Relations: Scholarships and Special Services	622
XXXII.	The Period in Review	648
XXXIII.	In Retrospect	668

APPENDIXES

A.	Sharing Profits with Employees	679
B.	Method for Calculating the Capital Base	715

NOTES

Notes 719

BIBLIOGRAPHY

Bibliography 755

INDEX

Index 777

List of Illustrations

Richard Warren Sears, Founder	7
Minnesota Station from Which Richard Sears Sold His First Watches	26
Alvah Curtis Roebuck, Cofounder	27
Front Cover of the 1894 Catalogue	38
The Company's Plant, 1895, Adams Street Near Halsted, Chicago	39
Sears, Roebuck and Company Balance Sheet for August 19, 1895	48
Some Early Sears, Roebuck and Company Advertisements in Periodicals	60
"Our $4.98 Leader" from the 1895 Catalogue	66
Catalogue Copy on the "Economy" Separator, Fall, 1906	67
Customers' Profit-sharing	76
"Simple Rules for Ordering" from the Spring 1906 Catalogue	86
Sears, Roebuck and Company Headquarters, Chicago	170
Julius Rosenwald	185
An Early Retail Store, Houston, Texas, 1929	542
A Modern Retail Store, Houston, Texas, 1947	542
Pico Boulevard Store, Los Angeles, California, Opened November 2, 1939	543

List of Charts

I.	Top Management Organization	366
II.	Midwestern Territory Organization	facing 367
III.	Group Organization	368
IV.	Zone Office Staff	370
V.	Parent Merchandising Organization	facing 380
VI.	Mail-Order Executive Organization	480
VII.	Independent "A" Store Organization	483
VIII.	Medium "B" Store Organization	484
IX.	"C" Store Organization	486
X.	Personnel Department Organization, 1931	550
XI.	"A" Store Personnel Functional Chart	552
XII.	Staff Organization (Personnel Department)	591
XIII.	Public Relations Organization	645

APPENDIX

A. Company Contributions, Employee Deposits, and Company Sales, 1916–47 690

List of Tables

1. Net Sales Related to Various Measures of Retail Trade in the United States, 1929–48 5
2. United States Population and Income, 1879–1910 . . . 12
3. Stocks of Companies Owned, 1906 55
4. Electric-Belt Sales, 1901–5 73
5. General Catalogue Circulation, 1902–8 93
6. Indiana Freight Catalogue Distribution, 1906 95
7. Sales and Profits by Major Merchandise Divisions, 1902 . 111
8. Sales and Profits by Major Merchandise Divisions, 1907 . 111
9. Cream-Separator Sales, 1902–8 112
10. Inventory Data, 1897–1908 117
11. Sales, Capital, Assets, and Profits, 1889–1908 172
12. Measures of Success, 1889–1908 172
13. Operating Expenses as Percentage of Net Sales, 1902–5 . 175
14. Comparison of R. H. Macy and Company and Sears, Roebuck and Company Operating Expense, Gross Margin, and Operating Income, 1902–5 175
15. Farm Income and Prices 192
16. Population of the United States, Urban and Rural, 1880–1930 . 194
17. Percentage of Urban to Total United States Population by Geographic Divisions, 1880–1930 194
18. Yearly Sales of Leading Mail-Order Concerns, 1913–25 . 204
19. Retail Sales Index Numbers 205
20. Comparison of Sales, Year Ending December 31, 1920 . 206
21. Comparison of Sales, Year Ending December 31, 1921 . 207
22. Comparison of Sales, Year Ending December 31, 1922 . 208
23. Changes in Selling Prices of Certain Commodities, 1920, 1921, and 1922 210
24. Number of Orders Received in Chicago Mail-Order Plant, 1910–22 211
25. Factories Wholly and Partly Owned, 1918 243
26. General Catalogue Circulation, 1908–25 263
27. Sales on Credit, 1911–16 267

LIST OF TABLES

28. Credit Terms, 1919–21 270
29. Credit Experience by Merchandise Items, 1917–21 . . . 271
30. Collection Experience on Instalment Sales, 1917–24 . . . 271
31. Credit Workout, 1913, 1917–20, and 1924 273
32. Anniversary Checks, 1912–23 282
33. Profit-sharing Fund Program, 1916–28 283
34. Employees' Average Weekly Earnings, 1907–27 285
35. United States and Sears, Roebuck and Company Employees' Average Weekly Earnings, 1907–22 285
36. Philadelphia Mail-Order Hiring Rates, 1920 and 1929 . . . 286
37. Average Number of Employees, 1909–25 290
38. Sales and Profits, 1908–25 294
39. Net Profit as Percentage of Sales, Sears, Roebuck and Company, Montgomery Ward and Company, and R. H. Macy and Company, 1909–25 294
40. Relative Position of Sears, Roebuck and Company and Montgomery Ward and Company Sales, 1913–25 295
41. Merchandise Inventories, Sears, Roebuck and Company and Montgomery Ward and Company, 1909–25 296
42. Employee Productivity, 1908–25 296
43. Merchandise Returns—Mail Order, 1912–25 297
44. Indexes of Growth, 1908–25 301
45. Sales and Profits by Decades, 1896–1925 302
46. Rate of Return on Investment, Sears, Roebuck and Company and Montgomery Ward and Company, 1909–15 . . . 303
47. Stock and Dividend Record, 1907–25 305
48. Proportion of Net Income Paid in Cash Dividends, 1908–25 . 306
49. Dividend Record and Stock Increases, 1906–26 306
50. Percentage of Farm Cash Income Represented by Company Mail-Order Sales, 1910–25 308
51. Farm Income and National Income, 1919–29 315
52. Farm Income as Percentage of National Income, 1929–47 . . 316
53. Automobile Registrations in the United States, 1900–1942 . 318
54. Progress of Certain Chain-Store Organizations, 1902–28 . . 321
55. Pay Roll for Laboratories, 1929–44 377
56. Distribution Costs of Manufacturers in Selected Industries Expressed as Percentage of Manufacturers' Net Sales, 1939 401
57. Length of Service of Sources, 1946 405
58. Length-of-Service Breakdown of Sources, 1946 406

LIST OF TABLES

59.	Merchandise Purchases, 1929–43	407
60.	Brand Names Proposed in 1945	418
61.	Sales Trends in Dollar Volume, 1932–45	431
62.	Circulation of the General Catalogue, 1942–45	432
63.	Premiums Written and Admitted Assets of the Allstate Insurance Company and the Allstate Fire Insurance Company, 1931–45	441
64.	Encyclopaedia Britannica, Inc., Gross Sales and Net Profit Analysis, 1933–42	444
65.	Principal Retail Merchandise Departments	486
66.	Number of Retail Stores by Years, 1925–48	487
67.	Retail Stores by State and Type, 1948	488
68.	Newspaper Advertising Expenditures, 1930–47	491
69.	Years of Service Prior to Appointment to Store Management	502
70.	Educational Background of Retail-Store Managers by Period of First Appointment to Store Management	503
71.	"Cash Merchandise" as Percentage of Total Credit Sales, 1937–41	513
72.	Instalment Credit Experience, Total Instalment Accounts All Stores (Mail Order and Retail), 1911–39	514
73.	Percentage Credit Sales to Total Sales, 1928–41	515
74.	Distribution of Instalment Sales by Customer's Occupation	517
75.	Average Instalment Sale by Customer's Occupation	517
76.	Analysis of Easy-Payment Customers Based on Contracts Approved in Twenty-one Stores, Spring, 1944	518
77.	Construction Activity in the United States, 1910–29	521
78.	Length of Service of Present Store Managers at Time of First Assignment to Management	558
79.	Retail Executive Training	560
80.	Number of Employees, 1939–47	565
81.	Percentage Annual Personnel Turnover, Regular Retail Time-Card Employees, 1940–47	565
82.	Expenditures for Training Materials	566
83.	Cost of Voluntary Employee Benefits, 1939–48	579
84.	Regular Employees on Military Leave, 1940–46	580
85.	Costs of Military Benefits, 1940–46	582
86.	Personnel Turnover Rates, 1939–45	584
87.	Reasons for Leaving, Retail Regular Time-Card Employees, 1939–45	585
88.	Average Number of Employees, 1924–45	595

LIST OF TABLES

89. Percentage Change in Chain-Store Sales, 1927–31 . . . 605
90. State Chain-Store Legislation, 1925–48 607
91. Chain-Store Taxes Paid by Sears, Roebuck and Company, 1932–47 613
92. Sears, Roebuck and Company Tire Sales, 1925–33 . . . 619
93. Some Indexes of Business Efficiency, 1925–47 649
94. Measures of Growth, 1925–47 650
95. Gross Sales, Mail Order versus Retail, 1925–41 . . . 653
96. Capital Expenditures, 1925–47 654
97. Stock and Dividend Record, 1925–47 657
98. Depreciation Reserve and Other Reserves, 1932–47 . . . 657
99. Sears, Roebuck and Company, Montgomery Ward and Company, and Department-Store Net Profits (after Income Taxes) as Percentage of Sales, 1925–47 658
100. Percentage Rate of Return on Capital Investment, Sears, Roebuck and Company and Montgomery Ward and Company, 1925–47 659
101. State, Local, and Federal Taxes, 1925–47 660
102. Tax Burden, 1925–48 661
103. Sales and Profits by Decades, 1926–45 662
104. Dividend Record and Stock Increases, 1925–47 . . . 663
105. Sears, Roebuck and Company Sales and Department-Store Sales, 1929–47 664
106. Relative Position of Sears, Roebuck and Company and Montgomery Ward and Company Sales, 1925–47 664
107. Mail-Order Sales Relative to Farm Cash Income, 1925–41 . 665
108. Ratio of Net Sales to National Personal Consumption Expenditures for Sears-Type Products, 1929–47 666

APPENDIX

A. Value of Shares in Profit-sharing Fund, 1916–47 . . . 684
B. Percentage of Total Outstanding Company Common Stock Held by the Profit-sharing Fund, 1916–47 687
C. Profit-sharing Fund Stock Purchases, 1916–47 . . . 688
D. Annual Average Price of Shares, 1916–47 689
E. Profit-sharing Fund Earnings, 1917–40 691
F. Distribution Price, Dividends, and Return, 1916–47 . . 692
G. Profit-sharing Fund Membership, 1916–47 694

LIST OF TABLES

H. Profit-sharing Fund Withdrawals, by Length of Service and by Sex, 1937 697
I. Profit-sharing Fund Withdrawals, by Groups and by Sex, 1940–47 698
J. Profit-sharing Fund Withdrawals, by Reasons, 1940–47 . . 698
K. Employee Contributions (Deposits), Profit-sharing Fund, 1916–47 700
L. Contract Rates of Company Contributions 702
M. Company Contributions, 1916–47 702
N. Company Contributions per Dollar of Member Deposits, 1916–47 706
O. Summary of Closed Accounts, Profit-sharing Fund, by Periods, 1916–40 709
P. Hypothetical Accounts, 1945 710
Q. Value of Holdings at Various Market Prices 710
R. Profit-sharing Records of Retired Employees by Years of Service 712

CHAPTER I

Introduction: Sears, Roebuck as Mass Distributor

OVER the counters of nearly two million retail stores in the United States pass virtually all the goods and services used by some 147,000,000 customers—in the amount of one hundred and thirty billion dollars in 1948. Of all economic agencies, retailers are probably the most familiar to consumers, for through the retail market each day pass the shoppers of America to buy the products that characterize the American standard of living.

With the increasing complexity of the production process, and changes in consumer habits and income, retailing has taken on an increasingly variegated appearance. The nature of the retailer's place in the economic pattern leads him (if he is to survive and prosper) to make adjustments to two spheres of influence—manufacturing and intermediate distributive changes, and, more important, shifts in the character of consumer demand. Thus it is clear that the retailer is at once in the position of acting as purchasing agent for the consumer and as selling agent for the manufacturer. Closer to the ultimate consumer than any other agency, the retailer wields peculiar influence.

The services or activities of retail agencies are numerous and vary, of course, with the particular institution with which one may be concerned. There are, for example, the differences associated with the type of retailing—whether the seller seeks to contact his customers through door-to-door canvassing, automatic vending machines, mail-order catalogues, or the more conventional retail store. But, no matter how different the method of operation, certain activities are common to all retail institutions, from the tiny, family-operated neighborhood grocery store, to the de luxe salon that caters to the preferences of the upper reaches of the "carriage trade," to the great department store which seeks to cut across lines of both income and geography.

The retailer must calculate in advance what his customers will buy—the products, qualities, quantities, and the prices of goods to be offered for sale. He must arrange to buy these goods, usually from many different suppliers, and he must provide storage facilities so that goods will be available to customers when they wish to take possession of them. And perhaps most characteristic of retailing is "bulk-breaking"; indeed, the word "retail" itself is derived from the French equivalent for "cutting up" —the process of reducing the wholesale lot to the smaller units in which consumers prefer to buy. Finally, by one means or another, goods must be presented to customers; buyers must be made aware of the availability of merchandise and the terms on which it is available. These are but a minimum list of retailing activities, the scope of which is almost indefinitely expansible depending upon the markets to which the particular retailing establishment chooses to cater.

In the course of adapting to different market situations, numerous retail forms have arisen to serve the consumer. Retailing has evolved in America from the elemental trading post of a frontier civilization through a host of forms until there exists now a great variety of functioning types of varying degrees of strength, as well as vestigial remnants of institutions surviving from earlier trading conditions. Accompanying the evolution of trading methods has been a marked change in the attitude of society toward retail merchants. In the America of the 1940's the names of Marshall Field, John Wanamaker, Sears, Roebuck, and J. C. Penney are at once well known and well thought of in the business civilization of the United States. But it was not more than a century ago—and perhaps less—that the retail merchant carried some of the opprobrium that supported Plato's advice. As a part of his plan for the ideal state, the Athenian said in *The Laws:*

> In the first place they must have as few retail traders as possible; and in the second place, they must assign the occupation to that class of men whose corruption will be the least injury to the state; and in the third place, they must devise some way whereby the followers of these occupations themselves will not readily fall into the habits of unbridled shamelessness and meanness.[1]

The development of an economy characterized by a high degree of specialization of labor and mass-production methods brought with it an increasingly complex distributive organization. To a large extent, the dramatic cost reduction which has typified modern manufacturing was achieved largely at the expense of higher proportionate costs of distribution. Retailing has come to absorb increasing amounts of resources in the task of serving as intermediary between the production centers and the consuming public. As the Twentieth Century Fund demonstrated in one of its publications of ten years ago, it costs more to distribute goods than to manufacture them. And the largest part of the cost of distribution is incurred in the retailing process.[2]

One of the notable attempts to lower the high cost of retailing was mail-order selling, which, while known in America since the earliest Colonial days, did not attain any real stature until after Aaron Montgomery Ward established his mail-order firm in 1872. While mail-order selling has, before and since then, attracted a host of entrants, this type of retailing accounts for but a very small proportion of total retail volume. In 1939 the Census of Business reported that the aggregate of 434 firms it classified as "mail order" transacted but 1 per cent of total retail-trade volume. (The figure of 434 mail-order sellers did not include large department stores doing the bulk of their business over the counters while accepting orders by mail as an incidental aspect of their selling.) When it is recalled that Sears, Roebuck and Montgomery Ward between them account for the great preponderance of all mail-order sales, with their next two principal competitors—Spiegel's and Alden's—accounting for a not inconsiderable portion of the remainder, the mail-order business for which the other 430 firms must compete is relatively small. Yet the mail-order business continues to attract countless vendors of such items as jewelry, books, food, clothing, furniture, cosmetics, stationery, fish (both live and dead), canaries, flowers, shrubbery, and a wealth of others. Even such a sophisticated publication as the *New Yorker* magazine abounds with "mail-order" advertisements.

It was, of course, in the mail-order field that Sears, Roebuck and Company achieved its first great success, before marrying that venture to retail stores. Through this dual system of distribution Sears, Roebuck has come to be America's largest retailer of general merchandise, having sold, in 1948, $2,290,000,000 worth of goods through its catalogues and over its counters—a task which demanded the services of more than 150,000 employees in the company's 632 retail stores, 11 mail-order plants, and 341 order offices.

Sears, Roebuck is an example, perhaps the outstanding example, of mass merchandising—the mass distributor that has evolved almost contemporaneously with the great mass production industries. Serving many millions of customers across—and sometimes beyond—a continent, a mass merchandiser such as Sears, Roebuck and Company works to co-ordinate the output of thousands of manufacturers with the buying needs of the millions of customers. Accommodating itself to the achievements of mass production, the mass distributor seeks to capture corresponding economies in the distribution of goods, motivated not so much by the desire to achieve a public benefaction as by a desire to realize profits that may accrue to a seller whose costs of operation are sufficiently low to permit lower selling prices and an increased volume of trade. What is really the distinguishing hallmark of Sears, Roebuck, over and above its large volume of business and the legend and lore that have come to surround the firm's name, is its *character*—as distinguished from merely its *position*—as a mass distributor.

Originally making a place for itself by a combination of low prices and sensational promotional strategy in a rural market where retailing facilities were limited, Sears has, in its constant search for greater efficiency, come to be an aggressive champion of new methods of merchandising. From a position where the flamboyant mail-order business was more or less passive, simply selecting from the available merchandise offerings of suppliers, Sears, Roebuck has come to take the initiative in product-planning, which enables the company to hold a strategic place between its suppliers and its customers. The Sears view of the company's place in distribution can be seen in the remarks of one of its officers, who has outlined the role of mass distribution in these terms:

> In recent years we have seen . . . the concentration of money, organization, and brains in the distribution field, and, paralleling that, the growth of efficiency of the small manufacturer. The small manufacturer standing alone has often lacked what it takes to duplicate the progress of his large competitor. He has lacked engineering and research talent—money for advertising and sales expense to displace some of his big competitor's goods from dealers' shelves. Probably, most difficult of all, his manufacturing costs have been high because of the uncertain and spasmodic production schedules this situation forces on him. Just as the small dealer needs a powerful ally, which he finds in the large manufacturer, to complete the sequence, so the small manufacturer needs an ally who can furnish what he lacks—acceptance by the public, expert product leadership, and assured volume. So . . . we are developing two parallel systems, each having its place in the total economy of the country. On the one hand, the dominant, large manufacturers with their own branded lines, distributing their products through thousands of independent dealers; on the other hand, the mass distributor with his many and various branded lines, buying each of these lines from smaller manufacturers. You can see that in each case the production of the goods is in the factory and the retail sale to the public is in a store, but in one case the manufacturer determines the character of product (i.e., its design, quality, prices, and production schedules), while in the other case these functions are assumed by the mass distributor.

However large the distributor, and Sears, Roebuck is very nearly the largest, it should be noted that retailing is essentially an industry characterized by small-scale business. The total volume of retail trade is so immense that even the largest firms account for but a small proportion of retail sales. In 1948, for example, Sears's sales accounted for something less than 2 per cent of all retail-store sales. Since food stores constitute the most important group of retail stores in terms of both numbers and volume and since Sears does not sell groceries (except through a concessionaire in a very few of its stores), it is more appropriate to consider Sears's portion of the general merchandise market. Of calculated general merchandise sales of some $47,500,000,000 in 1947, Sears sold about 4.5 per cent. Other measures of the company's place in retail distribution are indicated in Table 1.

Compared to United States Steel Corporation's share of the steel industry's sales, or General Motors' share of the automobile industry, Sears, Roebuck's share of the volume of trade available in the retail marts may not seem impressive. But viewed as an agency surrounded by characteristically much smaller firms, the true status of the company is more apparent. The 1939 Census of Business demonstrates how very small most retailing establishments are, for more than half of them had an annual sales volume averaging less than $10,000, and but 0.7 per cent recorded sales volume of $300,000 or more. In an industry peopled by small-scale enterprise, the

INTRODUCTION 5

achievement of an annual volume exceeding two billion dollars and more than 4 per cent of the general merchandise sales of the nation is indeed impressive.

But Sears is an interesting case study not alone on account of its size but as well for its method, for the firm has stood unequaled for years as the most successful mail-order seller in America and has pioneered in the development of that method of retailing, even though the company did not invent the method. Sears, Roebuck came to be synonymous with cata-

TABLE 1*

NET SALES RELATED TO VARIOUS MEASURES OF RETAIL TRADE
IN THE UNITED STATES, 1929-48

Year	Sears's Net Sales (000,000)	Consumption Expenditures (000,000)	Total Retail Sales (000,000)	Department-Store Sales (000,000)	Sears's Net Sales as Percentage of— Consumption Expenditures	Total Retail Sales	Department-Store Sales†
1929	$ 415	$ 78,761	$ 48,450	$ 4,350	0.53	0.86	9.54
1933	273	46,346	24,517	2,538	0.59	1.11	10.76
1935	392	56,215	32,791	3,311	0.69	1.20	11.84
1939	617	67,466	42,042	3,975	0.91	1.47	15.52
1940	704	72,052	46,388	4,266	0.98	1.52	16.50
1941	915	82,255	55,490	5,027	1.11	1.65	18.20
1942	868	90,835	57,552	5,566	0.96	1.51	15.59
1943	853	101,626	63,680	6,132	0.84	1.34	13.91
1944	989	111,401	69,484	6,764	0.89	1.39	14.62
1945	1,045	122,830	76,572	7,428	0.85	1.36	14.06
1946	1,013	147,363	100,787	9,621	1.09	1.60	16.77
1947	1,982	164,755	118,328	10,615	1.20	1.67	18.67
1948	2,296	177,700	129,923	11,322	1.29	1.77	20.28

* Source: United States Department of Commerce and annual reports of Sears, Roebuck and Company.
† Including mail order.

logue selling. So successful did it become and so effective were its techniques that few commercial enterprises have inspired the lore and legend that surround the name "Sears, Roebuck."

This, then, is a chronicle of the growth of a business enterprise once uncertain and halting, flamboyant and aggressive, that has emerged as one of the great commercial endeavors of America. This is a study of the evolution of a method of distribution—of the problems that beset one mercantile establishment in its efforts to identify and cultivate a market that was constantly changing and of the men and methods employed to adapt to the shifting bases of prosperity, in the course of which the business was itself transformed.

RICHARD WARREN SEARS, FOUNDER
President, 1886–1908

Founding a Mail-Order Business, 1886–1908

CHAPTER II

American Economic Expansion

THE mail-order business is very nearly indigenous to America. Nowhere else in the world has the catalogue house assumed the unique status it enjoys in the United States, where "Sears, Roebuck" has become a household term as well as the country's largest purveyor of general merchandise. While this is a study of the development of Sears, Roebuck and Company, it is impossible to explain the remarkable growth of this company without examining the soil in which Richard Warren Sears rooted his business. The plot of the mail-order story is reasonable only in terms of the settings that give it life and bring it within the perspective of American culture in the period of Sears, Roebuck's incubation.

When the Confederate cannon sounded at Fort Sumter in 1861, the bulk of the population of the United States was concentrated in the region east of the Mississippi River. Of a total population of 31,443,321, only a little over 14 per cent resided west of the Mississippi. The period between the end of the Civil War and the opening of the twentieth century saw a powerful migration of Americans to the Far West. New immigrants from Europe added to the swell of older Americans pushing the frontier to the Pacific Coast and, in fact, bringing an end to the frontier. By 1890 nearly 27 per cent of the people of the United States were living west of the Mississippi River, the overwhelming majority of them engaged in wresting their livelihood from the soil.

Encouragement of westward migration had, of course, begun before the Civil War. The Pre-emption Act of 1841, implementing legislation passed two decades earlier, protected "squatters' rights" by allowing a settler to purchase from the national government a quarter-section of 160 acres of land at the price of $1.25 per acre.[1] Some three years before Lee surrendered to Grant at Appomattox Court House, the Congress of the United States catalyzed the westward movement with the Homestead Act of 1862 and laid the groundwork for postwar agricultural reconversion with the Morrill Act of the same year.

In the eighteen years following passage of this and of subsequent amending legislation, 65,000,000 of the more than a billion acres of public land were pre-empted by settlers pushing out to the West.[2] In addition, huge acreage was sold to settlers from the lush land grants given the railroads by the state and federal governments.

The Hatch Act of 1887 provided federal appropriations to support experiment stations connected with agricultural colleges. Direct federal money subsidy of these colleges began with the annual congressional appropriation of $25,000 to each college in 1890.[3] The national concern with agriculture was writ bold when in 1890 cabinet status was bestowed on the executive office of the Department of Agriculture, first established in 1862.

The reasons for the lawmakers' interest in the farmers were obvious. Agricultural wealth constituted 56 per cent of the nation's wealth in 1850 (this figure was to drop to 21.8 per cent by 1912), and even as late as 1880 agriculture still represented the principal source of wealth.[4] The population of the United States in the year 1880 was 71.8 per cent rural; specifically, the rural population in that year stood at 36,026,048.[5] The rise of the great cities was still to come. In 1870 there were only seven cities with as many as 200,000 inhabitants, and the combined population of the seven was less than 9 per cent of the country's total. (By 1900 there were to be nineteen cities in this category, aggregating 15.5 per cent of the country's inhabitants; and, whereas Boston grew by only 124 per cent in those three decades, and Baltimore only 90 per cent, Chicago gained 470 per cent, Minneapolis 1,460 per cent, and Omaha 536 per cent.)[6]

The bulk of the population and much of the wealth in the last half of the nineteenth century, then, were still on the farms and in small rural communities. This fact alone, from the political point of view, might have been sufficient to account for much of the legislative interest in the farmer—such interest, that is, as was shown. But there were still other factors. England had repealed its corn laws in 1846 and had embarked upon an industrial, mercantile economy, determined to buy its food with the products of its factories. And manufacturing cities were rising in the United States; their workers had to be fed by the American farmers.[7]

In the last five decades of the nineteenth century the value of agricultural products in the United States tripled.[8] Between 1860 and 1900 the farm area of the nation increased from 407,213,000 to 838,592,000 acres—an average annual increase of more than 10,750,000 acres.[9] The number of farms grew from about 2,000,000 in 1860 to 5,737,000 in 1900, and the value of farm implements and machinery rose from $246,000,000 in 1860 to $761,-000,000 in 1900.[10] The value of the farm property of the country, in land, buildings, implements, and livestock, rose from $8,000,000,000 in 1860 to a little more than $20,000,000,000 by 1900.[11] In the decade from 1890 to 1900 the country's total wealth increased from $78,500,000,000 to $126,-700,000,000—according to Tarbell, "the greatest gain ever made in a single decade."[12]

The mail-order companies were not the only ones to feed on (and at once to nourish) the great expansion and growth of the western producers. Where the catalogues went, so went the agents of great urban industries.[13]

The farmers steadily increased their output of farm produce not only by opening up new land but also by mechanizing their operations through more and better farm implements; when the Industrial Revolution reached the farm, it wreaked a minor revolution of its own. The "Marsh Harvester," patented in 1858, doubled the amount of grain which could be harvested in a given time, but John F. Appleby's "twine-binder," patented in 1878, increased eightfold the speed in harvesting and more than any other factor enabled the country to increase its production of grain.[14]

By 1899, patents on farm machinery had been issued in the following numbers (to indicate only a few of the most important implements): thrashers, 5,319; harrows and diggers, 5,801; seeders and planters, 9,156; harvesters, 12,519; and plows, 12,652.[15] Advances in refrigeration techniques by the great meat-packers effected a revolution in meat distribution and in the nation's eating habits and created an ever greater demand for meat.[16]

The output of corn rose from almost 839,000,000 bushels in 1860 to some 2,500,000,000 bushels by 1900. In the same period, wheat production increased from 173,105,000 bushels to 602,708,000, while cotton jumped from 3,841,000 bales to 10,123,000.[17] The increase in agricultural wealth in those decades was due to the increasing numbers of farmers and the increasing acreage under cultivation and improved yields. The individual farmer, nonetheless, sometimes felt that his lot was worsening instead of improving. Between 1885 and 1890 the value of the corn crop shrank by more than $70,000,000; the price was so low (15 cents in Iowa; $1.00 in New York) that farmers burned the grain for fuel.[18]

During this same period the country moved toward a steadily higher degree of urbanization, and the value of manufactured products increased eleven fold, from $1,886,000,000 in 1859 to $11,407,000,000 in 1899. (The value of agricultural products only tripled in the same period.) By 1900 the United States was the first manufacturing country of the world, producing twice as much as England and half the amount of all Europe combined. Thus agriculture, while making considerable absolute gains, suffered a relative decline in relation to manufactures.[19] The growth of population and income which formed the market base is summarized in Table 2.

To connect the growing communities of the sprawling country and to carry the grain and fatted calves—and incidentally, in the process, to lay the physical minimum of communications necessary to any national mail-order business—late-nineteenth-century America built the railroads and the postal system.

From 1860 to 1910, railroad construction in this country averaged over four thousand miles per year until, at the end of the first decade of this century, the United States had one-third of the world's railroad mileage. By the end of the century there were virtually two hundred thousand miles of track, and in the following decade this figure jumped by 25 per cent. The growth was explosively rapid but ill planned and often exploited with little attention to the country's actual needs. This haphazard expansion culminated logically in the fact that, since 1916, more mileage has been abandoned than has been built; requests to build new lines are rare indeed, whereas requests to the Interstate Commerce Commission for permission to abandon mileage are routine.[20]

There were many reasons for this mushroom growth. Overland treks of settlers by wagon trains and stagecoach were uncomfortable, expensive, and dangerous, yet the land was ripe for settlement. The many thousands of people eager to recoup their war-torn fortunes by moving to virgin land were augmented by immigrants pouring in by the hundreds of thousands. And, as always, trade followed settlement.

TABLE 2*

UNITED STATES POPULATION AND INCOME, 1879–1910

YEAR	POPULATION Rural	POPULATION Urban	AGRICULTURAL INCOME (000,000)	NATIONAL INCOME (000,000)
1879			$1,371	$ 7,227
1880	36,026,048	14,129,735		
1889			1,517	10,701
1890	40,841,449	22,106,265		
1899			2,933	15,364
1900	45,834,654	30,159,921	3,034	16,158
1905			3,678	21,428
1906			4,029	23,165
1907			4,214	24,403
1908			4,621	23,458
1909			5,311	28,700
1910	49,973,334	41,998,932		30,400

* Source: population, *Sixteenth Census of the United States, 1940, Population*, I, 18; agricultural income, R. F. Martin, *National Income in the United States, 1799–1938* (New York: National Industrial Conference Board, Inc., 1939), p. 65; national income, 1879–1908, *ibid.*, p. 6; 1909–10, J. F. Dewhurst and Associates, *America's Needs and Resources* (New York: Twentieth Century Fund, 1947), p. 696.

The boom in railroad-building after the Civil War undoubtedly contributed strongly to industry's burgeoning. Better, truer, stronger tracks were needed, as well as coupling devices, locomotives, freight and passenger cars, roundhouses, switches, marshaling yards, and all the myriad related devices to pour into the gaping maw of the iron horse. And, perhaps more important to the mail-order business, the rail links opened up the entire country to the products of the manufactories; farmers in California wanted plows made from Pittsburgh steel; Toledo baling wire was needed in Montana; and so it went. New inventions and discoveries created new wealth; much of this was poured as capital into still further developments. The economy had received a tremendous injection of industrial adrenalin, so to speak; the railroads' share in that was considerable.

As the railroads stretched their iron fingers over the entire country, additional settlers spilled out into the great, virtually untapped West. A relatively high birth rate and heavy immigration from Europe combined to effect the great increases in population. The total population of the country increased from 31,513,114 in 1860 to 92,406,536 in 1910.[21] As previously indicated, the overwhelming majority of the people were located on farms or in communities of less than 2,500 population. Large circulations of magazines, newspapers, and books attested to a relatively high degree of literacy.

In short, the United States in the latter half of the previous century contained many millions of people, located in widely scattered and often relatively isolated areas, able and eager to read and write and still habituated to making demands upon their government. Those demands culminated in, among other things, a postal system which extended its services as the country's need for those services grew. And just as those people who most needed and demanded such postal services were the logical customers of the mail-order houses, so did the mail-order business benefit from the postal system. In fact, the mail order houses soon became the largest individual users of the mail.[22] Nystrom points out:

> The one-cent postal card came into use in 1873, the two-cent postal rate on first-class letters was established in 1883. For many years during the early stages of the development of the mail order business they were permitted to ship their catalogs and other advertising matter as second-class mail at the very low second-class mail rates.[23]

Postal regulations which classified "mail-order" publications as aids in the dissemination of knowledge, and thus entitled the magazines to a postage rate of one cent per pound, were a great indirect boon to mail-order houses and particularly to Sears, Roebuck and Company. Those policies made possible the very existence of the mail-order magazines and thus in turn opened a potent advertising medium to Richard Sears.

The rates referred to above as being directly and indirectly beneficial to the mail-order houses were specified in legislation passed in 1879, setting up the classes of mail matter: (1) written (including typewritten) and sealed matter; (2) periodical publications complying with the law governing second-class mail privilege; and (3) miscellaneous printed matter. By 1871 the number of post offices had reached 30,000. Subsequently, the establishment of post offices proceeded with great rapidity until by 1901 they numbered 76,945—the high-water mark.[24]

A system of rural free delivery was first officially suggested in 1891 by Postmaster-General John Wanamaker, the "merchant king" and department-store owner. Initial appropriations made a few years later were deemed inadequate to inaugurate a trial of the plan, but by 1896 a backlog of $80,000 in congressional appropriations had been amassed. Roper says:

> By 1896 education was universal, and personal and business correspondence became a necessity on the farm. The rising interest of the American farmer in

state and national politics made him an earnest reader of daily and weekly newspapers and the national magazines. His increasing prosperity and his dependence on machinery made him an important market which the manufacturers desired to reach with their advertising.[25]

Rural free delivery was successful and widely popular from the start. Postmaster-General Smith in 1901 enthusiastically commended the new service as a great public welfare project:

> It has been made plain that this service is a potent educational force; that it brings agricultural life into far closer relationship with the business world; that it keeps the farmer in daily touch with markets and prices; that it advances general intelligence through the increased circulation of legitimate journals and periodicals, stimulates correspondence, quickens all interchanges, promotes good roads, enhances farm value, makes farm life less isolated and more attractive. The national value of these advantages is incalculable.[26]

Smith might well have added that RFD was also of incalculable value to the mail-order business. Rural free delivery contributed to the mitigation of the loneliness that the open-handed character of the whole system of land grants had done much to establish—physical isolation of the settlers, an isolation that must be given an important weight in accounting for the farmer's eagerness to make literature of the huckstering cries of the mail-order catalogues.

Country life was often tedious, neighbors distant, and amusements limited. Even of the villages in the well-settled northeastern United States, Egleston remarks, "It has been said of New England villages particularly that their only recreation are their funeral occasions."[27] Specifically noting the relationship of the national land policy to rural isolation, Professor Schlesinger has written:

> At least since the adoption of a national land policy in 1785, isolation and loneliness had been the almost inescapable conditions of country existence, for by the ordinance of that year the government rejected the New England system of farmer communities and provided for large, scattered, individual holdings. These tendencies were confirmed and strengthened by the homestead law of 1862. Thus in the less developed parts of the Middle West such as Minnesota and Wisconsin, or in the near-by territory of Dakota, country neighbors dwelt too far apart for friendly intercourse, being but four to the square mile when land was held in quarter sections and even farther away if the homesteads were larger or tracts remained unoccupied. Even in the older farming districts families generally lived out of sight of other habitations; they had no mail deliveries; and the balm of a telephone was denied to all but a tiny minority.[28]

This life in isolation was in marked contrast to the community life possible in the village society characteristic of the agricultural countries of Europe. In the last decade of the nineteenth century the *Atlantic Monthly* published an article attacking the contemporary organization of American farming and recommending that the people come together in villages.[29]

The growing farm population, increasing (though not without pause) wealth on farms, and the completion of transportation and communication facilities supplied the basis for improved trade conditions. If an expanding agriculture and rail network were auspicious circumstances for mail-order techniques, they were no less hospitable to rural retailers. As much as anything else, the successful exploitation of the rural market by the mail-order protagonists was a function of the state of rural retailing and the farmer's resentment of the middleman.

As thousands upon untold thousands of farmers spilled into the West—as many as 100,000 settlers moved west of the Mississippi in a single year—and began to grow the produce wanted by the East and by foreign countries, they began perforce to create a wider market for manufactured products which were beginning to pour out of the East in increasing quantities. The density of population of the United States rose from 10.6 persons per square mile in 1860 to 25.6 in 1900 and to 30.9 in 1910.[30]

The purchasing power, much as it might fluctuate, was there to be satisfied. Cash crops started to move toward replacement of "self-sufficient," diversified farming; and farmers sowing scores and hundreds of acres in wheat, corn, and other foods found progressively less time in which to make their own clothing, tools, shingles, and other artifacts. They preferred to buy them. But their sources of purchase were limited, crude, and costly. The farmer's chief—and often his only—recourse was to the small, ill-supplied general store stocked with prosaic necessities.[31]

Shopping opportunities were further limited, of course, by conditions of geography and transportation that helped define the trading areas. While the last two decades of the nineteenth century brought the development of nation-wide markets for producers, consumers' marketing was contained within a small radius. Indeed, one writer finds in geographic factors the explanation for the rise of the mail-order business.[32]

Except for the occasional visits of the Yankee peddler, and manufacturers' agents, the general store constituted the nexus between the wants of farmers and villages and the "manufactories." Cataloguing its wares, Nystrom states:

> The old-time general merchandise store supplied its customers with dry goods like cotton, woolen and linen yard goods, notions, sewing supplies, handkerchiefs, skeins of cotton, wool and silk yarns, buttons, ribbons, and laces. Such stores also handled the common groceries. ... It also dealt in hardware including the ordinary tools. ... Finally, it provided such drugs and medicines as were in common use during the early and middle parts of the nineteenth century, including many which have ... passed out of use. On the old order sheets ... one may find ... Church's Cough Drops, Turlington's Balsam of Life, Bateman's Drops ... Steer's Opodildoc. ... .[33]

The merchant was often a man of considerable local power, but that power was based to a great extent on the farmers' prosperity, in which the merchant held a vital stake and which he had to estimate in advance in order to determine how much credit he could safely advance to any farmer. Credit was the basis of most purchases. For most of the year the farmer would draw against his expected income in buying from his local merchant; after the harvest, he would settle with the merchant and then dig in for another protracted period of buying on credit.[34]

The merchant, in turn, found himself squeezed on both sides. His turnover was slow, his sources of supply often uncertain, and his cost of goods high. The wholesaler and the jobber added their margins before the small retail merchant could add his own markup. And since many farmers had to buy on credit, the merchant was also often forced to purchase the same way, which further raised the price of goods to the ultimate consumer. Since some of the credit risks turned out poorly, the good risks had naturally to absorb the losses the merchant took on the poor. Everything seemed to conspire to make prices relatively high.

Yet a farmer's own particular merchant was the source of many things good and pleasant. His store was the rendezvous, the oasis, the mecca, where farmers gathered to exchange crop intelligence, gossip, and questions, to berate politicians and railroads and trusts, to enjoy a friendly drink of whiskey, and to swap earthy jokes. Nystrom notes the community center aspect of the general store as follows:

> The general . . . store served as the village social center for the men. The old box stove, the rickety chair or two, the flour barrel and the sawdust spit box were the almost universal furnishings that equipped it for its social services. Here politics, religion, and neighbors were discussed. It may not be too much to say that here the tariff question, government bank, internal improvements, foreign policies, and other important national matters were ultimately settled. American statesmen for many years had to reckon with the force of public opinion generated and cultivated around the stove of the country store.[35]

In many cases the country store was the equivalent of the local newspaper. Passing travelers kept the merchant posted on state and national news, which he in turn passed on to his customers. The merchant knew from the orders he filled just who was sick, who was expecting a baby, who had relatives coming for a visit. He was, in addition, the business adviser to the community and usually a pillar of the church (which was in many cases located in the attic over his store, often sharing the space with some fraternal order). Not infrequently the storekeeper was also the local postmaster. He read and wrote letters for the illiterate and semiliterate; he made out money orders; he even supplied stamps on credit. He was, in short, all things to all men—things good and things less good.

Despite the often inadequate if large stock carried in many stores and the high prices of the goods, there was one pleasant aspect of shopping there: the customer could spend months looking over goods at intervals before making his mind up to buy. And most of his buying was on the basis of need, not mere desire. His primary purchases were of necessity the goods he needed to farm and to feed his family: plows and harness, fatback and flour, meal and molasses.

The clothes he bought were almost entirely utilitarian; they were designed to afford whatever warmth might be necessary and to meet the minimum standards of modesty and decency. Appearance and fit were allowed wide latitude. Clothes simply had to be durable and comfortable enough to stand up under work on the farm and in the kitchen or to present an acceptable appearance at church.

Even with these low standards, however, the farmer was dissatisfied with many phases of retailing. Especially in sparsely settled parts he often found himself forced to ride miles by horseback to reach the nearest store. He was frequently unable to leave his farm chores to go himself; he was compelled to send some other member of his family or a hired hand, and the results of this indirect purchasing were not always happy.

Another source of great annoyance and public outcry was the wide discrepancy between wholesale and retail prices. In the South, which was not too dissimilar from the West, it is said that a barrel of flour in 1894 sold wholesale for $3.47 but that before it reached a customer's hands the price was as least $7.00—a 100 per cent increase.[36] Clark goes on to assert:

> Thus it was that country merchants were charged with usury in its grossest form, and on the strength of individual cases they were guilty as charged. The customer not only paid a published interest charge of twelve and a half per-cent, but a markup of twenty-five percent and more for credit plus a profit charge of ten to fifty percent. Interest rates were always based upon a period of twelve months, or, as one merchant said, "from gin whistle to gin whistle." Actually the carrying period seldom averaged longer than seven or eight months.
>
> When customers depended upon stores to credit them for everything they bought, liability for merchants was great . . . he had to spread his liabilities to all his trade. A hundred credit customers who religiously settled their accounts at the end of each crop season were often forced to pay the accounts of another hundred who did not. . . . Both merchant and customer were clear on the point that good risks had to be responsible for the bad ones. . . .
>
> Always there was an element of secrecy involved in price quotations. Brogan shoes could be bought wholesale for seventy-five cents a pair, but they retailed at prices from $1.25 to $2.25. Suits of woolen clothes were bought for $3.25 to $15.00 but sold for $10.00 to $25.00. Meat was five to seven cents a pound, flour $3.00 to $5.00 per barrel and sugar from four to six cents a pound. But before any of these commodities were loaded onto a customer's wagon the price was practically doubled.[37]

Yet the farmer had little choice. There was no mail-order business of any real consequence until 1872 (though mail order had operated in New England on a minuscule scale as early as 1830), no rural free delivery until 1896, and no parcel post until 1913.

The following lengthy passage from Buck's classic study of the Granger movement effectively summarizes significant aspects of rural trade and sentiment:

> Like the physiocrats, the farmers were wont to look upon agriculture and land as the source of all wealth and to divide society into the two classes of producers and non-producers, including in the latter all those engaged in the distribution

of the products of the former. . . . Next in importance to transportation among [the distributive factors] were the middlemen who served as agents for the distribution of commodities between producer and consumer; and it was against the exaction of these middlemen that much of the wrath of the farmers was directed. From the standpoint of the farmer the middlemen were of two principal classes: the commission merchants and produce buyers through whom he disposed of his products, and the numerous agents and retail dealers through whom he purchased his supplies.[38]

When the farmer found himself virtually compelled to sell his produce to commission men at what he thought were unconscionably low prices, he felt that these commission men were his natural enemies, so controlling the situation that they could fix prices at will. The lack of competition among merchants and of organization among farmers appeared to combine to keep the farmer's return low:

Just as the price which the farmer received for the commodities he sold seemed to him to be fixed by those to whom he sold, so also, he felt that the price of his supplies was fixed by those from whom he bought. The retail dealers, like the commission men, were comparatively few in number and usually able to prevent serious competition among themselves. Then in many parts of the country and especially in the newly settled areas of the western states there prevailed a credit system somewhat similar to that . . . [in] the southern states. The feature of crop mortgages was usually absent in the West but otherwise the system was very much the same; the farmer lacked ready money and was forced to buy on credit; and an account having been begun, he was practically placed at the mercy of the dealer until he could square himself on the books. A large part of the farmers' supplies were purchased, however, not from retail dealers, but from agents who handled the articles on a commission for the manufacturer; this was particularly true of all sorts of farm machinery, of sewing machines, and other patented devices. The complaints against these agents were that their large commissions unduly increased their prices, that they frequently persuaded farmers to purchase machinery which they did not need or could not afford, and that they sold on credit and in addition charged exorbitant rates of interest.[39]

It is important in following the rise of mail-order selling to note the role of agrarian discontent, for it was this dissatisfaction—almost universally articulated in terms of middlemen's abuses—that did much to lead to accepting the intrusion of a new institution despite the strong social attraction of the general store and the strategic credit ties that bound the grower to his storekeeper. Thus into the vacuum of rural trading facilities poured the general mail-order business, aided by the physical facilities of auxiliary industries and abetted by the wells of agricultural discontent in the midst of improving economic circumstances.

Mail-order firms were slow to develop fully, but they had roots of a sort in America from Colonial days. There were, obviously, almost no manufactures in the earliest settlements in the thirteen colonies. Even up to the Revolution, such figures as Thomas Jefferson and George Washington and many lesser-known citizens ordered goods by mail from the mother-country. After the Revolution, "mail-order" business continued, though the colonists were then trading more with France.

As the Industrial Revolution began to exert its impact upon the United States, abetted perhaps by the protective tariff passed after the War of 1812 to assist "infant" industries, manufactures grew apace here. Retail and wholesale outlets of various kinds arose to distribute the goods so produced as well as the merchandise still imported. By the close of the Civil War the practice of buying goods by mail was plainly evident, for such periodicals as the *American Agriculturist* and the *Cultivator and Country Gentleman* contained many advertisements of mail-order firms selling seed and nursery products, sewing machines, dry goods, farm implements and wagons, books, medicines, jewelry and watches, musical instruments, toys, and other lines. Significantly, however, each such firm almost invariably sold only a single line of goods, and few of them sold exclusively by mail.[40]

The earliest known effort to promote sales exclusively by mail, aggressively and on a broad scale, appears to have been made by E. C. Allen of Augusta, Maine:

[Allen] started national advertising on specialities such as recipes for washing powder, engravings, chromos, and novelties, as early as 1870. Allen's success led to rapid imitation close at hand. Augusta, Maine, became and for many years continued to be the most important mail order center in the United States. Several so-called "mail order periodicals" were established, such as the household magazine, "Comfort," and a list of periodicals published by Vickery and Hill, carrying mail order advertising, and sent to patrons of mail order concerns all over the country.[41]

The horde of "mail-order" magazines which arose to compete with Allen's *People's Literary Companion*, established in 1869, included P. O. Vickery's *Fireside Visitor*, launched in 1874; True and Company's *Our Fireside Journal*, begun in 1875; and a host of others in Augusta, Maine, which were the forerunners of groups later to be listed together for the benefit of advertisers. These groups came to include Vickery and Hill's list, Lane's list, Ellis' list, and more. While Augusta remained the center of the mail-order magazines or "papers"—so called because they all came to depend chiefly or wholly upon mail-order advertising—publishers in other cities imitated the success of those publications: the *Fireside Companion* of New York, the *New York Weekly*, and the *Chicago Fireside Friend*. Allen's *Companion*, priced variously at fifty cents yearly to individuals and lesser amounts to clubs, and often distributed free, attained a circulation of some 500,000 in its second year. The combined circulations of the mail-order papers ran into the untold millions.[42]

In 1872 there appeared in Chicago the first large concern to sell a wide variety of goods exclusively by mail. It bore the name of (Aaron) Montgomery Ward, former general-store manager, dry-goods salesman, and traveling salesman. Ward had worked and lived among the farmers for many years. He knew their living habits, their likes and dislikes, their complaints about the high cost of goods bought at retail from the inefficient, obsolescent general store. And he knew, too, of the organization they had recently formed, the Patrons of Husbandry, better known as the Grange, among the basic tenets of which was co-operative purchasing to save farmers money by "eliminating the middleman."

Ward's idea was, in simplest terms, to buy directly from manufacturers for cash and to sell to farmers directly for cash, with the hope of eliminating the expenses and profits of middlemen as well as eliminating credit risks. And the greater the quantities he could buy, the cheaper would be the unit cost to him and to his customers. A small profit on each transaction would aggregate a considerable volume if the transactions could be made numerous enough. In Ward's own words, "Having had experience in all classes of merchandise, and traveling salesman, and a fair judge of human nature, saw a great opening for a house to sell direct to the consumer and save them the profit of the middle man."[43]

By 1872 Ward and his brother-in-law, George R. Thorne, had amassed $2,400 of their own funds for capital, $1,600 of this amount being supplied by Ward. In that year the fledgling firm established a mail-order business at Clark and Kinzie streets in Chicago, in a room 12 by 14 feet. They issued a single sheet, 8 by 12 inches, listing the articles for sale and their prices and explaining how to order.

By 1874 the price sheet had grown to an eight-page booklet. Later in that same year it increased to seventy-two pages. The title-page proclaimed Montgomery Ward and Company the cheapest cash house in the country and, perhaps more important, "The Original Grange Supply House," selling to grangers, other farmers, and mechanics at "the lowest wholesale prices." The catalogue claimed that "by purchasing with us you save from 40 to 100 per cent which are the profits of the middle men." All goods were sent by express, subject to examination, the customer paying the shipping expenses and the cost of the goods only if satisfied. The merchandise line included notions, hose and gloves, hat trimmings, toilet goods, letter paper, needles, cutlery, jewelry and watches, fans and parasols, stereoscopes and albums, trunks and traveling bags, harness, Grange regalia, dry goods, clothing, hats and caps, boots and shoes."[44]

By the early 1880's almost every item in the Ward catalogue was illustrated by a woodcut, and the 1883 catalogue stated that a half-million dollars' worth of merchandise was carried in stock. In the following year the catalogue's 240 pages listed nearly 10,000 items of merchandise. Two years later Montgomery Ward and Company began construction of its own building to house its rapidly expanding business; the structure, occupied in August, 1887, provided about 120,000 square feet of space. By the early nineties the 8-by-11-inch catalogue numbered 540 pages and listed 24,000 items; it brought an annual volume of business in excess of one million dollars.[45]

Ward's, then, was very much a going concern by the time Richard Sears started selling watches in 1886. Over and above the general conditions making possible the rise of mail order, several other factors account in large part for the success of this first company to sell a wide variety of goods exclusively by mail. First, of course, at least in chronology, was Ward's status as the official supply house of the Grange. From his earliest "catalogue" (i.e., price list), in 1872, until well into the eighties, Ward's catalogue bore on its cover "The Original Grange Supply House" or "The Wholesale Grange Supply House." Grangers initially enjoyed special privileges: orders sent via a grange official or countersigned with the grange seal or the grangemaster's signature did not have to be paid for upon receipt but received instead a ten-day period of grace in which to make payment. Ward's awareness of the importance of his arrangement with the Grange was reflected not only on the covers of his catalogues but also in the use of testimonials from grange officials and the display of his goods at grange meetings. Some granges even sent delegations to Chicago to inspect his supply house and to report on its prices and quality.[46]

No less significant than the designation as the Grange purchasing house, and certainly far more important in the long run, was Ward's guaranty. The 1874 catalogue assured buyers that mistakes would be corrected if reported and stressed the fact that goods were sent by express "subject to examination." The phrasing of the guaranty changed through the years, but from the outset it was made clear that any goods could be returned to the company, which would also pay transportation charges both ways, if the customer were dissatisfied. The importance of the guaranty in first inducing people to buy from afar can hardly be overestimated.

Ward's also advertised in mail-order periodicals and other publications in the 1870's. *Among Ourselves*, a Ward house organ, reprinted in 1907 some ads which had appeared in the *Farmer's Review* and the *Women's Farm Journal* in 1878.[47] Ward's continued to advertise in such publications for many years, usually employing institutional ads which also urged readers to send for the big catalogue. Montgomery Ward and Company also mailed farmers almanacs containing reading and pictorial matter interlarded with merchandise advertisements. Finally, Ward's sent out barnstorming railroad cars for several years in the nineties to display the firm's goods. The "act" included entertainment of a minstrel variety not radically unlike the "snake-oil" salesmen of the time.[48] This scheme was probably one of Ward's ways of meeting the bitter opposition of retail merchants to mail-order houses.

Always, of course, there was an effort at friendliness in the Ward catalogues; the attempted camaraderie never attained the heights to which Richard Sears was later to carry it, but the effort was always made. Customers were invited to visit the company's plant in Chicago, and during the Columbian Exposition 285,000 visitors thronged through the Ward plant.[49]

These, in brief, were some of the elements which made Montgomery Ward's mail-order business a success even before Richard Sears made his beginnings in that field. They were also the factors which were to keep Ward's ahead of Sears, Roebuck in annual volume of sales until after the turn of the century.

While Montgomery Ward and Company was the earliest of the great mail-order concerns still in existence, and while Sears, Roebuck and Company was to be the next, and eventually the largest, of the mail-order "giants," mail order attracted many other firms before 1900, including Spiegel, May, Stern Company founded in 1882 in Chicago. The National Cloak and Suit Company (later National Bellas Hess) was established in 1888. In 1885 the Larkin Company, a soap manufacturer since 1875, entered the mail-order business, offering its line of soaps and supplementary lines of tea, coffee, and extracts on "Thirty Days' Trial and Pay if Pleased."[50]

Almost simultaneously with the appearance of the general mail-order business, America witnessed the rise of the department store catering to city trade. But these new stores almost invariably gave some attention to mail-order business as well.[51] The importance attached to this business by department stores is illustrated in a book written at the turn of the century by a department-store executive.[52] The author, claiming "several years' experience . . . in running one of the largest Department Stores on this continent," devoted eight of his thirty-four chapters to various aspects of mail-order operations of department stores.

Among the earliest department stores to enter the mail-order field seriously was R. H. Macy and Company of New York, which embarked on mail order in 1874. Macy's 1881 catalogue, the first now available for perusal, was a small booklet of 127 pages with a single-page index on the inside of the back cover. The cover itself was sedate (as the covers of all its subsequent catalogues were to be), and the conservative tone of all Macy's catalogues indicates that the company was seeking urban rather than rural trade, and this evidence is reinforced by many of their derogatory catalogue allusions to the rural element.

John Wanamaker also ran a mail-order department, and there were many others throughout the land. Tiffany advertised "superior service by mail" as early as 1870.[53] But around 1910 some of the department stores that had pushed their mail-order business began to question whether such promotion was profitable.[54]

While the department stores, essentially urban institutions, were soon to abandon (for a time at least) the mail-order field in favor of their "home markets," the expanding parameters of farm population and income were not to be contained within the trading system of the peddler and the general store. Montgomery Ward was finding great success catering to a market beyond the reach of city stores. Hundreds of other advertisers were nibbling at the mail-order market by the time Richard Sears turned to its systematic exploitation.

CHAPTER III

Origins: Building a Business

THE career of Richard Warren Sears provides a nearly classic example of the "triumph over humble origins" so prominent in American fiction. Many details in Sears's career are lost in confusion and contradiction. One such is the date and place of his birth. The *Dictionary of American Biography* lists December 7, 1863, as the date, and Stewartville, Minnesota, as the place.[1] There is some divergence of opinion on Sears's parentage. But it seems generally agreed that his father, James Warren Sears, was of English descent, and his mother, Eliza, either Scotch-Irish or English. One thing seems certain. Richard Sears probably never concerned himself over such details, as he apparently never left any genealogical data about himself.

As Richard Sears's parents were in modest circumstances, he had to start working for a living at an early age. His father went off to a Civil War in which he had little interest, leaving his nineteen-year-old bride in territory where the Indians outnumbered the whites. James Sears wrote his father-in-law: "I would not expose myself one minute to save the whole government. I have got enough of the government; there is nothing but roguery and rascality from one end to the other, which you can see is the only thing that has protracted this war."[2]

That war was a bitter draught for the young man who had gone to California in the Gold Rush of 1849 and had returned from that unsuccessful venture by sailing vessel around Cape Horn. He returned to his family after the war, nursing a bothersome leg wound and sore distraught in spirit. He withdrew more and more from his family, turning in upon himself. Eliza Sears, in turn, devoted herself increasingly to her son, and there developed between the two an attachment which was never to slacken.[3]

When young Richard was about six, the family moved to Spring Valley, Minnesota, where James pursued his trade as a blacksmith and wagon-maker. (According to Asher, the Sears family, before going to Spring Valley, lived for a while in Rochester, where James made some of Dr. William Mayo's first surgical instruments.)[4]

A. C. Roebuck says that James Sears accumulated about fifty thousand dollars—a questionably large sum of money for a blacksmith to make at that time—in Spring Valley and then lost the entire sum in a stock-farm venture.[5] Werner gives the date of the stock-farm failure as 1878,[6] at which time Richard would have been fourteen or fifteen years old. The stage was set for Richard to assume the role of family breadwinner.

When he was four, Richard was allowed to cross a vacant lot to the house of the neighbor next door to buy milk and to make his own change. He started grammar school when six and Sunday school the following year, although the influence of his family's free-thinking background was to prevent his ever becoming an active churchman. When he was seven, Richard took a job for a wage of twenty-five cents a day carrying water to field hands gathering the harvest. His father, maintaining that he was still able to support his family, put a halt to that enterprise.[7]

Richard entered high school in Spring Valley and later had a year of high school in Mankato, Minnesota, where the family had moved from Spring Valley. In his early teens the youngster amused and astounded his family by constantly answering advertisements offering free booklets and other enticements. He ordered trinkets and notions of all sorts and traded them to other boys in the neighborhood.[8] While Richard was about nine when Montgomery Ward established his mail-order business in Chicago, there is no evidence that young Richard saw Ward's price lists or catalogues at that time or that he was influenced then (though he was profoundly influenced later) by the company which he was later to outstrip with a mail-order house of his own.[9]

When young Sears was about sixteen, the necessity of assisting his family called for more decisive action than a boyish interest in advertisements and trinket-trading. He set out to learn telegraphy, performing manual labor around the railroad station in return for instruction. When fully qualified as an operator, he went to work and from then on was the chief financial bulwark of his family.

The first station at which he served was Wolsey, South Dakota, according to Roebuck;[10] North Branch, Minnesota, according to Asher.[11] A fellow station agent reported in later years that Sears was also employed for a time in Mitchell, South Dakota. Eventually he was transferred to the general offices of the Minneapolis and St. Louis Railroad in St. Paul. He is reputed to have worked for a time in the auditing department there, but working for a straight salary was not to his liking. He requested, and received, an assignment to manage the railroad and express office at North Redwood, Minnesota, where he would have time to make additional money by trading on the side.

North Redwood, consisting at that time of a station and two or three houses, was two miles north of Redwood Falls, county seat of Redwood County. The North Redwood station, to which Richard Sears went, was the Minneapolis and St. Louis Railroad's nearest station to Redwood Falls, a somewhat larger town. As the railroad received very little business from Redwood Falls, it gave young Sears special rates on wood, coal, and other products to enable him to compete with local merchants. The new station agent also received discretionary power to grant his own low rates to other merchants to secure additional business for the railroad. Sears's duties as freight and express agent occupied only a few hours of his time daily. He utilized his free time, and his special freight rates, to develop a fairly extensive trade with farmers and Indians in the community, to his own profit and to the increased freight traffic of the railroad. He sold lumber, coal, and other products to the townfolk; and from those customers he in turn purchased meat and berries, which he shipped to other localities.[12]

Even in these mundane chores, Sears displayed some of the perception he was later to demonstrate to the nation. He went out of his way to give full measure to all who bought from him; he would insist to a farmer buying a wagonload of wood that he could get a few more pieces on the wagon and welcome to them.[13] He made himself available at all hours to anyone who wished to trade or ship.

As station agent, Sears had ample opportunity to read the trade catalogues which revealed both wholesale and retail prices on jewelry and other items. From packages received for delivery to local residents, he learned of parties in the East who were doing a mail-order business in watches.[14] The possibilities of profit struck a responsive chord. One day in 1886 a package of watches shipped by a Chicago jewelry company was refused by a retail jeweler in the neighboring community of Redwood Falls. It was a common practice of the time for wholesalers to ship on consignment to retailers—frequently even to ship goods which had not been ordered by the retailer.[15] Another device was shipping goods to fictitious addressees; when the stationmaster would write that the goods could not be delivered, the wholesaler would reply that, to avoid the cost of returning the goods, the agent could purchase them at "half-price" and resell them at a considerable profit.

The Chicago company in this specific instance offered Sears the watches at $12 each. They were the so-called "yellow watches," of the gold-filled, hunting-case type, much in demand as a symbol of urban sophistication. Sears proceeded to write other agents along his line a description of the watches. He offered them to the agents at $14 each; they would be sent C.O.D., subject to examination, and the local agent could keep all the profit over the $14 he was to pay Sears. With watches of a similar type retailing for $25 generally, the agents were able to undersell their local jewelers and still make a profit for themselves—and for Richard Sears, so long as they continued such business as a side line.[16]

Sears's profit was ample enough to interest him in continuing this type of transaction on a basis which also reveals his early astuteness in obtaining working capital. Apparently a short time after disposing of the first consignment of watches at a satisfactory return, Sears wrote station agents that he had some watches to dispose of and requested permission to send one to each agent C.O.D. The watch would be sent subject to examination, and the agent would be allowed to retain as his profit all he could realize over Sears's asking price. Sears had ordered a number of watches C.O.D. from a Chicago wholesale house. He held the invoice himself, reshipped the watches C.O.D. to the various interested express agents, and, after receiving payment from them, settled the C.O.D. on himself.

In other words, the Chicago wholesale house which shipped the watches C.O.D. to Station Agent Richard Sears actually supplied his working capital. As a bonded agent, he was a comparatively safe risk; and, as all the other agents were likewise bonded, Sears himself ran little risk. Interestingly, he apparently sometimes accepted payment by the other agents in merchandise in lieu of cash, possible testimony to the trading business he had developed before selling watches.[17]

The young entrepreneur developed still another approach, modeled after that of the wholesale companies. He would send out watches to fictitious names, and the old pattern would repeat itself. Sears would offer the station agent a commission of two dollars if the agent would sell the watch at a certain price. If this proved unsuccessful, Sears was prepared to raise the commission to five dollars. Some of Sears's admirers have denied that he ever resorted to this device of shipping to fictitious names, but it seems certain that he did. Roebuck admits and defends this method of doing business.[18]

Within six months the trade in watches netted around five thousand dollars, and Sears abandoned railroading and moved to Minneapolis to found the R. W. Sears Watch Company in 1886. His office there consisted of a kitchen table, a fifty-cent chair, and some record-books and stationery, plumped down in a room for which he paid ten dollars a month rent.[19] His assets, over and above the five thousand dollars he had accumulated, consisted solely of his teeming brain, which was already beginning to show a flair for writing copy that would appeal to the common man. His staff consisted of himself; Arthur Lawrence, an older man with experience in bookkeeping and correspondence, who had entered Sears's employ in North Redwood; a Mr. Cook, former schoolmate and then stenographer; and some assistance from Eva and Kate Sears.[20]

It was apparently while Sears was still in Minneapolis, in the fall of 1886 or early winter of 1887, that he first began to advertise in newspapers.[21] This was a radical, if logical, departure, as his earlier advertising seems to have been directed almost entirely to station agents.

Minneapolis proved a fertile soil for the watch business—so fertile that the enterprise soon outgrew that city. Sears discovered in a few months' time that Minneapolis was poorly suited to serve the entire country. He resolved to seek a more nearly central location, with a rail network which would facilitate speedy and less costly service to the whole country. History had already made the decision for him. It was Chicago, already be-

MINNESOTA STATION FROM WHICH RICHARD SEARS SOLD HIS FIRST WATCHES

ALVAH CURTIS ROEBUCK, COFOUNDER

come the rail hub of the United States, a great fresh-water port, a rapidly growing city.

The move was made around March 1, 1887, and the company established on Dearborn Street, north of Randolph and a block west of the main retail section. Sears proceeded in his usual fashion. He sat down at a table and began to write advertisements for newspapers, offering to send his watches with a deposit of fifty cents to a dollar required.[22]

In Hammond, Indiana, meanwhile, a young watchmaker named Alvah Curtis Roebuck was plodding along at his trade, receiving room and board and $3.50 a week from the delicatessen owner in whose store he repaired watches.[23] He was about the same age as Sears, having been born on January 9, 1864, in Lafayette, Indiana, of English parentage. Like Sears, he had struck out on his own at the age of sixteen; but, even before this, he had developed a modest business repairing watches, clocks, jewelry, sewing machines, and other items for neighbors. He loved to tinker; his library was built around Saunier's *Complete Treatise on Modern Horology* and the *Watchmakers' Handbook*, augmented by catalogues and trade journals.

At seventeen Roebuck bought a used printing press with type. When writing to factories to buy parts for repairing watches, he had often been asked for his business card; he decided to print his own cards and then developed a small job-printing business on the side. He learned telegraphy and built a telegraph line to a neighborhood chum's home about half a mile away. He picked up the art of engraving upon metal. He tinkered endlessly. But his real love was watch-repairing. When he obtained his position with the delicatessen operator, Roebuck felt that he was on the way.

Richard Sears was at about the same time encountering some difficulties in his business in Chicago. He had increased his staff by adding a stenographer, but he found that many customers wanted him to repair watches, most of them purchased elsewhere. He had also concluded that he could operate more profitably by buying components and assembling the parts himself than by purchasing already assembled watches. But Sears was an entrepreneur, not a watchmaker. On April 1, 1887, he inserted the following advertisement in the *Chicago Daily News:*

> WANTED—Watchmaker with reference who can furnish tools. State age, experience and salary required.
> ADDRESS T39, Daily News.[24]

Roebuck saw the ad and wondered. He had been planning to go west; should he abandon that cardinal direction and go north instead? He laid the ad aside—and got up from bed hours afterward to answer it. Two days later a letter came from Sears inviting Roebuck to Chicago for an interview.

Florence Kiper Frank describes Roebuck as "a gentleman who might have been a bank president or a Methodist minister—a tall man, thin to emaciation, in a black suit, high standing collar and black bow tie."[25] Pictures taken around that time show the young watchmaker with long sideburns, a man of distinguished mien.

He submitted a sample of his finest and most intricate repair work to Sears, who held it up with both hands, turned it this way and that, examined it solemnly with a professional eye, and then said, in effect: "I don't know anything about watchmaking, but I presume this is good, otherwise you wouldn't have submitted it to me. You look all right, and you may have the position."[26]

In the first weeks of his employment Roebuck frequently assisted in assembling and mailing advertising matter, since there was not enough repair work to keep him busy. The chief reason for his free time at first, Roebuck asserted, was the fact that sales had dropped sharply after the move to Chicago, with the result that there was "but a small amount of business."[27] This decline in business may have been the main stimulus to Sears to advertise heavily. The advertising must have been effective, for in less than a year Roebuck was so busy that he was working seven days a week at watch-repairing and had eight watchmakers under his supervision.

Sears was buying up discontinued lines of watch movements offered by manufacturers at less than standard wholesale prices in order to close them out. The fact that they were being discontinued did not lessen their value to Sears; on the contrary, this buying tactic enabled him to offer great values to prospective customers while making a profit for himself and for the express agents when they consummated the sale. The agent was, in fact, enabled to sell the watches for little if any more than the cost of such goods to retail jewelers.[28] There were some twenty thousand express agents then; how many of them Sears dealt with at that time it is impossible to say.

The task of assembling these movements and incasing them kept Roebuck and his staff busy. And, in addition to the lines of discontinued watches, Sears sold large quantities of regular lines of American watches. He began to sell watches to express agents on the instalment plan: one-quarter to one-third down in cash, the remainder in promissory notes payable monthly. This arrangement applied largely to watches selling at from twelve to fifty dollars and up. It was successful because the agents, all bonded, were generally responsible men. This device allowed the agents to resell the watches on a deferred-payment plan, which increased sales for the R. W. Sears Watch Company.[29]

In 1888 Sears heard of a competitor who was selling watches on a "club plan" whereby thirty-eight men would each pay a dollar a week into a pool. They would draw by lot, one man "winning" a watch each week until all thirty-eight members had received watches—for which, of course, each had paid thirty-eight dollars. Sears promptly adopted this scheme, with variations of his own, one of which was to get the money in advance each week.[30]

The low prices at which Sears was able to offer his watches gave him a ready market for them, and, even after his profit and that of the station agent who sold the watch direct to the customer, the price was low enough to make the customer feel that he had purchased the item well below the generally high prices being asked for watches at the time. It is of some significance that the years of Richard Sears's early ventures were ones in which combinations in the watch industry sought to maintain prices. As Charles Moore has observed:

> By the year 1885 the Waltham Company, and the watch industry in general had reached the conclusion that lethal competition could not be avoided by expanding output, by cutting wages, or by competitive merchandising. The best efforts along those lines led only to a faster competitive race toward the ultimate goal of bankruptcy for marginal producers. . . .
> Waltham officials followed the usual procedure. Every possible alternative to industrial combination was tried. . . . They were tried and failed failed to pro duce any significant advantage. It was at this point that Waltham officials turned to horizontal combination as the last resort, the forlorn hope. Neglecting such strong and forthright methods as the consolidation, the merger, or the trust company, they took refuge in the weak and furtive device of trade association.
> A crisis developed in the depression year of 1885 which resulted in the formation of the National Association of Jobbers in American Watches. For the next seven years the association led a stormy career. . . . Internal intrigue and dissension created gaps in the ranks of the association, and the threat of punitive action under the State anti-trust laws finally resulted in voluntary dissolution.[31]

A. C. Roebuck, who was familiar with the watch business even before joining Sears, described the ingenious method evolved by the trade association for policing its rules and for punishing offenders. Each member was compelled to make a cash deposit with the organization, from which any fines levied could be deducted. If a member persistently disobeyed the rules, he could be (and some were) expelled. Members in good standing were prohibited from trading with an expelled member. Prices were set at a fairly uniform level.

Only when a certain line of movements or cases was being discontinued was a manufacturer allowed by the association to reduce his price below the established scale. Sears was able not only to make a practice of buying up large lots of such discontinued lines but also often to persuade the manufacturer to continue, *sub rosa,* to manufacture them for him at the reduced price. Sears thus frequently obtained watches at as much as 25 per cent less than the established wholesale price. And by buying up the stocks of bankrupt watch companies, Sears was able on occasion to sell a complete watch for no more than the wholesale price of the movement alone.[32]

Another factor in keeping watch prices high was the slow turnover experienced by most retail merchants. Also, the general practice was to sell on open account, settling every few months or once a year; Sears, on the other hand, paid his bills on the first and fifteenth of each month, making his account more attractive to wholesalers and to manufacturers. Whereas most retailers sold watches and jewelry at twice the cost to themselves, Sears's large volume of business enabled him to take a smaller unit profit, which in turn further increased his volume; he fed handsomely on this far from vicious circle.[33]

He also capitalized upon the farmers' hostility to combines in any form, seeking to win them to his business by attacking their own bête noire. (This technique, revealed in some of his earliest catalogues, reached its apogee in Sears's 1895 book. Under the caption, "War to the Knife," that catalogue asserted, "We are Waging War against Combinations, Associations, Trusts and High Prices.")

In late 1887 and early 1888, Sears continued to advertise in country weeklies, the circulation of some of which spilled over into Canada and created business there. He also began around this time to advertise in other publications, mostly periodicals designed for rural consumption. As the watch business continued to boom, Sears added a line of diamonds, watch chains, and general jewelry, selling the diamonds also on an instalment basis.

Mail-order business appeared eminently profitable—at least in certain lines and items—but Richard Sears had grave doubts about its staying power that he was to retain as long as he was in that business. Roebuck wrote his mother on May 18, 1887: "Mr. Sears is well pleased with me and said I must stay with him. . . . 'We will not stay here much more than a year. I'll sell out, we'll go to some town in Iowa, and start a big retail store, and you will be my best and first man.'"[34] That dream of settling down to a quiet life in Iowa remained a will-o'-the-wisp in Richard Sears's mind for years to follow. He was indeed to sell out, and he did go to Iowa, but this retirement from the hurly-burly of mail order was to be short lived.

Carrying on his expanding business at that time was taxing enough to make almost any man yearn for the bucolic pleasures of Iowa in lieu of the blistering pace of Chicago mail order. Sears's working day at the office was usually from around seven in the morning until ten or eleven at night.[35] But he could leave his office far more easily than he could leave the business itself; he would appear almost every morning with all his pockets bulging with ideas he had scribbled down, advertisements he had written, plans he had outlined.[36]

By December, 1888, the number of letters received from Canada, where Sears's advertisements had spread through "slop-over" circulation of American publications, appeared to justify opening an office in that country. Toronto was selected as the best location. Sears's assistant, Arthur Lawrence, was placed in charge of the branch office.

As Sears began to extend the base of his clientele and to sell to the general public instead of merely to railroad station agents, he began to amass a fund of experience. In the process of developing that reservoir of knowledge, he found that attracting customers in large numbers to his mail-order business required at least three things: (1) assurance that the merchant with whom one dealt was honest, dependable, and financially reliable; (2) a method by which the customer could see the goods before deciding to buy; and (3) prices so attractively low that potential customers could not resist buying in what was still a somewhat unconventional way.

These three factors proved much more cogent in dealing with the public at large than they had when station agents constituted Sears's only customers (even though they were, in actuality, only his "retail" outlets). All three factors operated easily in his first watch-selling days. There was every reason, in the absence of proof to the contrary, for each express agent to assume that every fellow-agent with whom he dealt was honest and dependable. The agents always saw the goods before they bought; as a matter of fact, the agents' customers also usually saw and approved before the agent remitted to Sears on the C.O.D. And Sears's low prices were made to seem even lower through his merchandising technique of appearing willing to continue reducing his asking price until he dropped to the originally planned price, which he had padded sufficiently to permit serious reduction without destroying the profit he had envisaged.

As the watch and jewelry business expanded to include "strangers," Richard Sears had to devise additional techniques of meeting the three requirements he had concluded were essential. He realized early that, of all the weapons he might employ, one was basic to the success of his business: some sort of warranty of the merchandise, some kind of guaranty that, if the goods were not satisfactory, one's money would be refunded. Sears seems to have realized the necessity of this element almost as a matter of course. A catalogue issued by the R. W. Sears Watch Company in the fall of 1887 contained this statement on page 4 under "Terms and Discounts":

Every article is warranted exactly as represented and every American movement is accompanied by a special Certificate of Guarantee for six years.

Within two years that statement of the guaranty was reworded and refined in these terms:

We guarantee every watch we sell to be exactly as represented and if not found so, they can be returned at any time and we will refund all the money paid.

The text accompanying the listing of almost every watch in that 1889 catalogue went out of its way to include such a phrase as "We guarantee it in every respect."

Some chroniclers have sought to establish that Richard Sears preceded Montgomery Ward with a general guaranty of merchandise.[37] There is stronger evidence, however, to show that Ward's announced its guaranty in 1872, its first year in business, and in words very close to those enunciated by Sears fifteen years later.[38] The controversy seems academic; what appears more important is the fact that Sears early recognized the importance of stating his guaranty unequivocally and of making good on it throughout his mail-order career. Sears perhaps dramatized his guaranty better than did Ward's; in some of his catalogue copy and advertisements he even went to the extent of going through a piece of merchandise part by part and guaranteeing each part to perform its allotted function.

Sears also sought to bolster his guaranty through the liberal use of bank references and testimonials from customers. To establish his financial reliability, he stated in his 1889 catalogue:

> To those unacquainted with our reputation for fair and honorable dealings, on application we will be pleased to furnish reference in any State in the Union; or will refer you to the managers of any Express Company doing business in this city; the Fort Dearborn National Bank, or any old reliable business house in Chicago.

It was on sensationally low prices that Sears placed his chief reliance, for this was the requirement which he met first—and met decisively and dramatically. One of the primary reasons he realized the importance of outstandingly low prices was his own deep conviction, which he was never fully to lose, that mail order was but a fleeting phenomenon in the merchandising world and that it would survive only so long as it was constantly dramatized and exploited with electrifying schemes.[39]

There were, of course, additional factors shaping Sears's attitude toward the importance of low prices. As a station agent, and then as a station agent selling watches on the side, he had early discovered the high gross margin inherent in the watch and jewelry business of that day. Sears was struck with the notion that the margin was large enough to be whittled down well under the prevailing prices for similar goods and still leave ample profits for a man who could transact a sufficient volume of business. Low prices, a relatively low profit margin, and heavy advertising of goods for a fast turnover early loomed as the bases of Richard Sears's merchandising.

Acting in accordance with these policies, and driven by his restless and irresistible urge for expansion, Sears early in 1889 placed an order for sixty thousand "Silverine" watches with a manufacturer. The price was low, but the move left him with heavy inventories and too little capital at the time. Sears was frankly worried about the financial condition of his business, although he seemed to feel that he would manage to ease through the tight spot. At the same time, however, the placid towns and rolling hills of Iowa became hourly more enticing. Sears had come more and more to plan on entering the banking business in that state and settling down to a quiet life.[40]

In March, 1889, he sold out the R. W. Sears Watch Company to a Chicago concern which later became the Moore and Evans Company. Some chroniclers have since variously recorded the purchase price as $60,000 and as an even $100,000. According to Roebuck, it was actually $72,000.[41] Sears further enhanced his cash position by selling Roebuck and Lawrence together a half-interest in the Toronto branch, not included in the sale of the R. W. Sears Watch Company, for one-half the inventory value of $2,950, keeping a half-interest in the Canadian business himself.[42]

At twenty-five years of age, Richard Sears retired from the mail-order business with a fortune possessed by few men of his age at that period. It took him little time to decide that banking was too placid an existence for his temperament. He invested some $60,000 in Iowa farm mortgages— in his mother's name. A secret document transferred title from his mother back to himself.[43] Apparently realizing his own flair for spectacular schemes which might end in bankruptcy, Sears was taking no chances on having his nest egg taken over by creditors.

The question facing him was, "What to do now?" As part of the terms of sale of his watch company, he had agreed not to re-enter that business under his own name for a period of three years.[44] Sears hurdled this obstacle by establishing a watch business under the name of Henry Hoverson and Company, Hoverson being the name of Sears's former bookkeeper. It was back to Chicago's Dearborn Street for Sears, but not for long.

By the fall of 1889 Sears's family persuaded him to return to Minneapolis. They had never liked Chicago. Coincidental with the moving, Sears adopted a new business name: The Warren Company. The name was, of course, his own middle name. He incorporated in Minnesota.

His merchandise line consisted largely of watches and jewelry. The 80 pages of his 1889 catalogue were top-heavy with watches, predominantly men's. While diamond jewelry occupied the first 3 pages after a 4-page introduction, men's watches held sway for 38½ pages. Ladies' watches took 18½ pages, followed by men's and ladies' watch chains with 12 pages, and charms with 4 pages. The diamond jewelry comprised rings, earrings, bar pins, men's studs, and a page each of men's and ladies' watches set with diamonds.

That 1889 catalogue also revealed that Sears was still thinking of how he could further overcome the farmer's understandable reluctance to part with his money before seeing the goods. That book, under "Conditions of C.O.D. Shipments," made a slight alteration in the demand for a deposit of fifty cents to a dollar as a token of good faith:

Strangers ordering goods sent C.O.D. subject to examination must enclose at least 50 cents (postage stamps accepted to the amount of $5.00) with their order to cover cost of express charges and save us from loss.

We will fill C.O.D. orders for any of our regular customers without cash with order, provided an agreement accompanies the order to the effect that the C.O.D. will be paid or goods returned within 15 days without expense to us. (Consignee paying all express charges.)

A photostat of one particular page from a catalogue of the Warren Company is interesting for several reasons. The page was decorous, the typography chaste, the white space abundant; but the punch line was typical of what would long characterize Richard Sears: "Best on Earth. We recommend this machine above all others." The item was a sewing machine, priced at twenty dollars but blandly identified as a sixty-dollar machine. At the bottom of the page appeared this: "Remember, when cash accompanies the order, we pay the freight."

The Warren Company flourished, but, even so, the bloom began to fade again. Sears wrote to Roebuck in Toronto some ten months after his return to Minneapolis, "You will probably be surprised when I tell you I am going to close out this business here forever and for good, notwithstanding I have made a great deal of money."[45] Competition, he added, was stiff. Roebuck in turn asked to be kept in mind in whatever steps Sears took, and at about the same time he started negotiating with Sears to purchase the latter's half-interest in the Canadian business. Since Lawrence was preparing to leave Toronto, that would place the business entirely in Roebuck's hands. This arrangement was worked out late in 1890. Roebuck paid Sears $5,190.18 for his half-interest.[46]

Sears's 1890–91 catalogue eliminated the deposit on goods ordered, with this message on the inside of the front cover:

> There have been so many cheap watches sold by irresponsible houses, who invariably require you to send cash with your order, or at least make a cash deposit——. *We propose to make a new departure—sell none but the better grades of watches,* such as we can warrant in every respect, put the price *below* all competitors (for the same quality) and then *without requiring ONE CENT* we will send any watch to any address by express, C.O.D. subject to examination.

The message went on to point out that the company paid all express charges and that the customer did not pay a cent until he saw the watch and unless it satisfied him.[47]

A watch advertisement of the Warren Company reveals that Sears was using periodicals as a medium at that time; it further shows that he was even then scheming to use any device which would attract attention to his ads. That one showed a large illustration of a man's pocket watch with the price, $3.98, and, in all-capital letters: "FREE! FREE!" The next line of type—Sears's usual agate body type—continued, "to see and thoroughly examine at the express office." Below the name of the Warren Company at the bottom of the ad there appeared a crude keying device: "Please state what periodical you saw our advertisement in."

In March, 1891, Sears kept his vow to pull out of the Minneapolis business; he sold the Warren Company, which had a net worth of $14,614.65, to Roebuck, who seemed happy to buy up businesses founded by Sears. Roebuck, in turn, disposed of the Toronto business on August 24, 1891, and changed the name of the Warren Company to "A. C. Roebuck," on Sears's suggestion.[48]

At less than twenty-seven years of age, Richard Sears had retired again. This withdrawal lasted a week, after which he persuaded Roebuck to allow him a half-interest in the business.[49] Persuading Roebuck seems to have been among Sears's most easily come-by accomplishments; in July or August of 1891 Roebuck was persuaded to increase Sears's half-interest to two-thirds. According to Roebuck, Sears was given the two-thirds interest in the business on his promise to invest considerable additional capital in it. Roebuck holds that Sears never did so invest, not even in 1895, when the company faced a critical financial situation and heavy liabilities in excess of that authorized by the charter of incorporation.[50]

In that same year of 1891 Sears issued the new company's first catalogue. It contained thirty-two pages, with a format which was designed to fit into a business envelope, and was accompanied by an eight-page insert. The catalogue proper listed only watches; the folder featured general jewelry and sewing machines. All items were offered on a C.O.D. basis, with a dollar deposit to show good faith. Sometime in 1891 the firm moved to the Globe Building, pictured in so many of the company's catalogues and other advertising matter for the following four years; there it occupied initially only a few rooms.

"A. C. Roebuck" maintained that title until April 6, 1892, when it became A. C. Roebuck, Inc.[51] Under the incorporation, Roebuck held 250 shares of $100 each.[52] Sears had 499, and his sister Eva had one share, which allowed her to sit on the board of directors. Richard Sears was president and a director; Roebuck, secretary, treasurer, and a director; Eva Sears completed the board of directors.[53]

The company issued a much larger catalogue then, including fifty-five pages of testimonials. Sears was to rely heavily upon testimonials for years to come. The adulation of his customers was to his liking. And he seemed convinced that his customers, located almost entirely in rural areas, lent great credence to expressions of satisfaction from their neighbors and other folk in similar circumstances.

That general catalogue reveals that the merchandise line was still dominated by jewelry and allied goods. Watches occupied 63 pages; watch chains, 21; diamonds, 18; charms, rings, and miscellaneous jewelry, 14 pages; and silverware, 6 pages. Clocks followed, with 4 pages, while revolvers (Smith and Wesson "automatic" type) trailed with 1 page, and miscellaneous small items filled 12 pages. But the copy was still largely institutional, as indicated by the amount of space devoted to testimonials and the 8 pages devoted to photographs of various departments and warehouses. This latter may well have represented an attempt to indicate the solidity and size of the company.

In 1892 watch chains rose to a position important enough to merit a separate catalogue, as did diamonds. The diamond catalogue sought further to dramatize the guaranty by reproducing "Our Binding Guarantee and Refund Certificate":

With every diamond sold we send the following Guarantee and Refund Certificate:
We guarantee the diamond sold this day to Mr.----for----dollars to be a genuine diamond and absolutely perfect stone, free from any flaw or imperfection whatsoever; and we hereby bargain and agree to take back the diamond any time within *one year* and refund the purchase price less ten per cent.

Sears, as always, moved on to new schemes. Hearing of a Chicago firm which was successfully selling baking powder house to house through school children, he decided to enter that field. Roebuck convinced him that another item would obviate direct competition with the company already operating that plan; as a result, Sears decided to experiment with toilet soap. An office was opened in Minneapolis under the name "A. Curtis Company"; soon, like Sears's earlier ventures, it moved to Chicago. House-to-house and mail-order selling proved, however, to be two different things. The soap venture was closed out after taking a $20,000 loss, but in its brief life it spawned a subsidiary known as the Alvah Company for the sale of sewing machines.[54]

On September 16, 1893, "A. C. Roebuck, Inc.," was changed to "Sears, Roebuck and Company" through an amendment in the articles of incorporation, the only change being the name.[55] Corporate liability fixed by the charter remained at $25,000.[56]

The new title—one that was to withstand Sears's capacity for juggling nomenclature—also resulted in a new catalogue of 196 pages. In addition to watches, jewelry, and sewing machines, it listed furniture, dishes, clothing (a single page), harness, saddles, firearms (now up to 7 pages), wagons, buggies, bicycles, shoes, baby carriages, and musical instruments. The company was moving away from narrow specialization to mail order on a broader merchandise base. It was also still hammering at the guaranty, this time emphasizing more than merely the quality of the product or its conformity to the claims made for it in the sweeping generalization that appeared on the page of the 1893 catalogue introducing jewelry:

We GUARANTEE our prices below all others for the same grade of goods and if you do not find them so at all times, we will cheerfully refund your money.
We guarantee everything and always refund money when goods do not prove satisfactory.

The 1893 catalogue also attested to the elimination of the deposit, blaring in large type:

IT COSTS YOU NOTHING to see any watch we advertise. WE DON'T WANT A CENT until after you have seen the watch and become thoroughly convinced that the

ORIGINS

watch is exactly as represented and you are perfectly satisfied. . . . If you don't want it, the express agent will return it at OUR EXPENSE.

A special 64-page catalogue issued in August, 1893, listed little other than the old stand-by lines, watches and jewelry. Men's watches filled 22 pages, while half that much space went to ladies' watches. Silverware and revolvers were the only other lines. The 6 pages of testimonials included one from a representative in the Minnesota state legislature. Possibly the most significant feature of the abridged book was its back cover, which urged customers to write for the company's 196-page catalogue—"Mailed Free on receipt of 5 cents to pay postage."

The stay in Minneapolis also produced another significant, though short-lived, innovation. During 1893 and 1894 Sears, Roebuck and Company used a room on the sixth floor of the Globe Building in Minneapolis for a city sales department. (By 1894 the business' few rooms in the Globe Building had expanded to include two floors, with total floor space of about 7,450 square feet.) Merchandise offered to the local trade included watches, diamonds, jewelry, clocks, silverware, and related items. Advertisements were placed in the Minneapolis papers, and the venture produced a considerable volume of business. It was Sears's first attempt at over-the-counter retailing, but there is no evidence that the volume of business in this undertaking was sufficient to divert him from his main course of selling by mail.[57]

Then the pattern of 1887 began to reassert itself. Minneapolis proved to be a disadvantageous shipping point. The bulk of the firm's business was coming from Pennsylvania, Georgia, Texas, and Iowa. Minneapolis was an inadequate railhead; Chicago, on the other hand, was even better equipped in this respect than when Sears had first moved there. It was reluctantly decided to establish a branch office in Chicago on an experimental basis. This step was taken in December, 1893.[58] The office and shipping warehouse on West Van Buren Street in Chicago provided approximately 3,600 square feet of floor space.

Additional catalogues were issued while the firm was occupying dual headquarters. A 322-page book, dated 1894, was actually issued late in 1893 for use in the following year, according to Roebuck.[59] Men's watches constituted the first offering, spread over 49 pages; ladies' watches came next, with 18 pages. Related jewelry and silverware lines ran this section to 152 pages. Revolvers and other firearms, with ammunition, appeared almost at the end of the book, but this department now occupied 53 instead of 7 pages. Sewing machines and bicycles were up near the front, but with only 8 and 5 pages, respectively. Men's and boys' clothing jumped to 11½ pages. Organs and pianos filled 5 pages, with other musical instruments spread over an additional 22½ pages. Tennis, football, baseball, and gymnasium supplies closed out the book with 5½ pages of space.

The 1894 catalogue said: ". . . in all cases, unless otherwise specified, CASH IN FULL MUST ACCOMPANY YOUR ORDER." Under the exceptions to this policy came watches, diamonds, and jewelry (no money in advance; sent C.O.D. with express charges prepaid); pianos and organs, ten days' free trial; guns and revolvers, a deposit of fifty cents to three dollars as a guaranty of good faith; a dollar deposit on harness and bicycles, and twice that amount on baby carriages; and a few other, similar, exceptions. The 1894 catalogue also stated: "Our daily average sales of Watches have been over 400, Jewelry and Silverware in proportion, while in the diamond business our sales have almost from the very start exceeded that of any firm in America selling direct to the consumer."

The spring of 1894 saw still another booklet bearing the company's name. Its 58 pages represented simply a condensed version of the 322-page general catalogue, to which it called attention. One of the big leaders in this abridged catalogue was men's suits at $9.95, with complete rules for taking one's own measurements. The orders were, however, almost invariably filled from stock, except in the case of exceptionally large men; the actual tailoring was confined to making alterations on stock garments to obtain something akin to a fit.[60]

In the fall of 1894 there appeared the most ambitious catalogue thus far, containing 507 pages and dated 1895 for use in that year. This 1894–95 book offered shoes, women's garments and millinery, wagons, fishing tackle, stoves, furniture, china, and glassware, in addition to the usual items. Watches and related goods still led the list, occupying 208 pages. The second most important space allocation went to weapons and fishing equipment, which filled 83 pages. The new line of men's clothing received 16 pages—less than half the space allotted harness and saddles. That catalogue also referred to a discount of 3 per cent when cash in full accompanied the order.

Seeds and books were added to Sears's offerings around this time, only to be dropped from the catalogue in 1896 as being unprofitable. Seeds and books were to go back into the general catalogue in 1897, after it had become apparent that their absence contributed to a decline in sales of other goods.

Sears, Roebuck sales increased under its dual location, but it soon was evident that the tail was wagging the dog. Chicago proved eminently desirable for the shipping needs of the business, and maintaining two offices likewise proved a hindrance. In January, 1895, Sears, Roebuck and Company left Minneapolis for good (except for the mail-order plant and retail stores established there much later) and rented a five-story building with basement on West Adams Street in Chicago. These quarters appeared too spacious for the company's requirements; the company sought vainly to rent the top two floors to another concern. A city sales department—their second timid venture in retail, if Minneapolis is counted—was opened on

FRONT COVER OF THE 1894 CATALOGUE
(ORIGINAL 6×9 INCHES)

THE COMPANY'S PLANT, 1895, ADAMS STREET
NEAR HALSTED, CHICAGO

the ground floor. Sears, Roebuck and Company numbered about eighty employees on its pay roll.[61]

It was only a matter of months until the growing business urgently needed all the 38,040 square feet of floor space in that structure, including its top two floors. Orders poured in by the thousands; goods streamed out in profusion and confusion.

Through it all stalked the solid figure of Richard Sears, smiling away or ignoring the chaos around him, working around the clock to write his advertisements which continued to bring in new business even before old orders could be filled in an orderly fashion, or, indeed, in any fashion at all. Sears was happy—and plainly determined—to leave the turmoil to his subordinates. New business, new schemes, unorthodox advertising pyrotechnics—these were his interests. The confusion grew, and so did the volume of sales. Sears, Roebuck and Company did more than three-quarters of a million dollars of business in 1895. Even during the depression years of 1893-94 the company had managed to increase its sales. Gross sales rose from $296,368 in 1892 to $415,656 the following year and to $420,855 in 1894; net sales for these years were, respectively, $276,980, $388,464, and $393,323.[62]

The rapid expansion of the United States in the last half of the past century created a great market for goods. And the cumbersome, costly system of rural retail distribution likewise created opportunities for businesses like Montgomery Ward and Sears, Roebuck. Richard Sears's rise epitomized the historical confluence of a man and a situation.

But the company's success was due to far more than merely the environment. It may have been true that rural folk needed a system of distribution like Sears's; but making them realize that they needed it was something else. The great task was to win their confidence in numbers and to manage to retain that confidence by keeping enough customers satisfied to offset the number who were dissatisfied. Sears the man was perfectly equipped for the job. His spellbinding advertisements exerted a telling effect on farm readers. His compelling messages pulled the reader into his copy and kept that reader's attention to the end. That end was usually the dispatching of an order to Richard Sears for merchandise.

From his own rural and small-town background, Richard Sears knew the farmer's mind. He understood the farmer's needs and his desires—and he knew what the farmer could afford to pay for goods. It was this knowledge that enabled the entrepreneur to make farmers read those advertisements which were the horror of advertising men. By the same token, Sears developed a knack for knowing what merchandise would lend itself to intensive sales promotion. This knowledge, this intuition, and the business of translating it into action were meat and drink to him.

Even though Montgomery Ward had been issuing its catalogue for fourteen years before Sears sold his first watch, Sears had made several thousands of dollars through mail-order selling before he issued a catalogue. In his initial experiments he used handwritten letters to express agents soliciting watch sales. He was well intrenched in Minneapolis and already using newspaper advertising by the time he issued his first catalogue in 1887. And not until 1889, when he was settled in Chicago, did Sears make his first effort at a really comprehensive catalogue listing everything he had to sell.

The covers of that 1889 book, which numbered eighty pages, were printed in a simulated leather pattern imparting a tone of bucolic swank. Like most of Sears's early catalogues, it opened on a sales talk; but, in view of Sears's subsequent sky's-the-limit tactics, the 1889 sales talk was a model of dignity and modesty. The introductory note "To Our Patrons" read in part:

> We have studied carefully to avoid all exaggerations, honestly representing everything, and any statement made concerning any article in this book is a correct one and fully guaranteed by us.
>
> We do not claim, as some do, to be the only honorable dealers in existence, or endowed with more power than other men, but we have a very extensive trade and buy in large quantities from the manufacturers at cost and we offer you every advantage that capital, skill and experience combined will command. A close comparison of our prices with those of other reliable houses, will fully satisfy you that you can save money by placing your orders in our hands. We warrant every American watch sold by us, with fair usage, an accurate timekeeper for six years —during which time, under our written guarantee we are compelled to keep it in perfect order free of charge.

Incidentally, both the cover and an inside page of the 1889 catalogue showed the date of the founding of the business as 1884 (in Roman numerals). This catalogue was intended for individual customers. When it was sent to dealers and station agents, however, it was accompanied by a "confidential" price list showing a flat 50 per cent reduction on all watches.

The catalogues which followed that of 1889 were for several years to hew to the original line in many respects: the descriptive text and messages to the reader were set in very small type, and woodcuts exclusively were used for illustrations. All space was utilized; Sears was content to leave the lavish use of "white space" to his competitors, and his later catalogues were to be even more crowded. Most of the catalogues of the years up to 1895 (and afterward) contained pictures of the firm's buildings and its officers. The keynote of all the catalogues was friendliness beyond the call of business duty. Customers were invited to visit the plant whenever they happened to be in town, to check parcels, and to write letters there. The 1894 catalogue stated: "If you don't find what you want in this book, write us. We may have the very thing in stock; if we haven't, we can no doubt get it for you at a great saving. Don't hesitate to write to us at any time. We are always at your service."

The 1895 book asserted: "We will furnish you anything not listed in this catalogue (except spirituous liquors) on application and always at wholesale rates or lower. Give us a trial order...."

Some of the catalogues in the early years were not even dated. Sears apparently feared that a customer might hesitate to order if he thought the catalogue he had was out of date. But all the catalogues in this period seemed to reflect a belief that the book would—and must—be so interesting that every reader would study every page. Little attention was paid to the index or to the customer who might be interested in finding the page which contained the one article he wanted at that time. Richard Sears himself may well have felt that any well-worked-out index might have defeated his purpose of making every reader a cover-to-cover reader. The index in the 1894 book occupied one page—the last in the catalogue. It was printed on regular catalogue paper, and little was done to call attention to it.

There was no set routine for catalogue publication up to 1895. Sears issued one whenever he felt that he had added enough additional lines to justify the expense of publishing another book, or when price changes dictated such a course. In addition to issuance of general catalogues at irregular intervals, special catalogues or booklets were often published to push a particular line of goods. The copy for these books was usually a reprint from the general catalogue, with special introductory messages and a few other embellishments.

At first there was no charge for the catalogue. Anyone who ordered a watch or some jewelry received the catalogue free; so did anyone else who wrote in merely to inquire.[63] Since Sears began to advertise in newspapers and magazines shortly after entering business, he received a fair number of inquiries to serve as the nucleus for some kind of mailing list. At some stage, however, owing possibly to the increasing cost as the book steadily grew in size, the firm began charging five cents for it "to help cover cost of postage." This was the price in 1893, but that charge was not sufficient even to pay postage. One object of charging for the book was to discourage children and the simply curious (and possibly impecunious) from requesting catalogues which would not result in orders. It was felt that any small charge would virtually eliminate those who had no serious intention of placing an order. According to a Sears, Roebuck ad in the *Fireside Visitor* in 1894, however, the big catalogue was free for the asking; it would be sent to anyone who requested it. One had but to mail a postal card saying, "Send me your big free catalogue." And the Sears, Roebuck and Company letterhead on a communication written by Richard Sears in March, 1894, stated clearly, "Catalog Free." But subsequent years were to see the price of the catalogue rise much higher even than five cents.

Just as the date of issuance of a catalogue was a matter of Richard Sears's own judgment, so was the physical production casual and unsystematized. The early catalogues represented simply a job-printing assignment and probably not a particularly lucrative one at that. Sears submitted about as much copy as, augmented with illustrations, he thought he would need for his book. When the proofs came back, he set about making things fit. He operated on the old principle that one can adapt to any space with a pencil and a pocketknife—the former to write additional copy when required, the latter to cut lines of type to fit even the tightest spaces. Many special pages were of course planned from the start, usually by Sears himself. Otherwise, it was largely a matter of cutting the proofs and pasting them onto the dummy, without wasting an iota of space. The artwork consisted entirely of woodcuts.

In the early 1890's Sears made a contract with Charles C. Spangler, who operated a type composition plant in Chicago, to set up his ads, and another contract with W. B. Conkey, of Hammond, Indiana, to set up the catalogue pages and print and bind the book. It was in no way a happy arrangement. It is said that there was one period of rebellion by Sears, Roebuck when it rejected and returned three-quarters of the several carloads of one particular issue of the catalogue delivered by Conkey.[64]

And a letter from Richard Sears to Asher, dated January 30, 1892, indicates that Sears himself could bargain effectively. After telling of a discussion with Conkey the previous evening, Sears went on to say:

> I endeavored to impress Conkey with the importance of our having as near 10,000 per day of these catalogues as possible and I believe I made him understand and believe that subsequently and for future seasons, if necessary at least for a year or two, that we could cut down our editions to a comparatively small number where it would not overtax his manufacturing capacity on the perfecting machines, and I fancy I could see at once that Mr. Conkey would be very much disappointed if he did not get additional work from us on which to run his flat machines, and I candidly believe if we will change places with him somewhat as to dictatorship that he will be very glad to have the opportunity to run his flat presses to make us an excess number of catalogues and this without any excess charge or bonus. . . .[65]

As Sears acquired experience in the mail-order business, he abandoned the modest and cautious tone manifested in his 1889 catalogue. He came more and more to depend upon the pulling power of his low-price policy, and he began to stress price over quality and service. He came increasingly to bill his goods as "the best in the world" and frequently promised that they would "last forever." Within a relatively short time he developed a genuine ease and facility in writing advertising copy, in carrying on a friendly if compelling monologue with his readers. And advertising was all of a package to Sears; he drew little if any line between his catalogue copy and copy for newspaper or periodical advertising. The chief difference lay in his tendency toward even greater exaggeration in the latter, which he frankly admitted was designed as much to stimulate requests for his catalogues as to pull immediate orders.

As pointed out earlier, he was convinced that the mail-order pot could be kept boiling only with a red-hot fire. As the fagots he heaped on the flames were found to produce an astonishing degree of heat, as he developed and became increasingly aware of his skill as the tender of the fire, he tossed caution to the winds—and a full load of fuel on the mail-order bonfire.

For Richard W. Sears was born, he lived, he died, in an age of schemes. It was the grand era of the unfettered entrepreneur. Stories of gullible farm folk being duped by city slickers are today a very minor ingredient of American humor; but in Sears's time the stories were more often not merely jokes but also blunt and frequently bitter truth. Long before he entered the watch business in 1886, the rural populace had developed a healthy skepticism of all things distant and in any way alien; most "strangers" were suspect. City folk in particular were, to the farmers, evil, unscrupulous, immoral, and untrustworthy—a point of view which still persists quite widely.

Richard Sears set about to breach this wall of suspicion. His campaign was not well thought out at the beginning. It was halting and stumbling and contradictory, and the deed frequently tended to belie the word. He relied upon his low prices and the exciting effect of the honeyed words which were his advertisements. What matter if performance sometimes failed to comport with claim? Yet Sears was by no means atypical of his times. His merchandising and advertising tactics were certainly no worse—and often possibly a shade better—than those of most of his competitors, as even a casual perusal of advertising in the periodicals of that day will show.

Presbrey quotes Manly M. Gillam, advertising manager of John Wanamaker's, as saying in the 1880's:

> Even if it is crude in form, awkward in expression, ragged in get up, so there's a streak of honest thought and good intent running through it, all else is overlooked. Today I'd rather have for a venture of my own a rugged, rocky, backwoodsy advertisement that shone with truthfulness and business point than a model of composition and display that was cynical and hollow. There must be a big slice of human feeling in the successful advertiser. A bright, sparkling roundup of words without heart—cold, pharisaical—may attract by its flash, but it doesn't win in the long run. I've known work that limped along on every foot except sincerity to bring very satisfactory results.[66]

Gillam's stated concept of his ideal advertisement applied in great measure to Richard Sears's ads. To what extent Sears's ads "shone with truthfulness," it is difficult to know, although the gleam appears often to have been faint, at least in his early days. But when it came to being "crude in form, awkward in expression, ragged in get up"—when it came to being "rugged, rocky, backwoodsy"—Sears's ads were just that. And, as for sincerity, Richard Sears managed to give his product the ring of authenticity, no matter what he himself may have felt.

Sears's advertising paid; just how well, it is hard to say exactly, because he kept almost no records and at first did not even "key" his ads to determine the response from each publication in which he purchased space.[67] While Sears may not have keyed his ads at the very outset, it is hard to believe he could have failed for very long to adopt this elementary device. Roebuck said:

> While enormous quantities of advertising space were used even in the early days, it was not used without discretion, because in connection with each article advertised, tests were made, first on a small scale to determine the drawing power of the ad, then if the records showed encouraging results had been obtained, the ad would be continued as long as it continued to draw a satisfactory percentage of orders.
> If a new ad did not draw as it should, or when an ad that had been satisfactory failed later to draw enough orders the ad might be changed in an effort to bring about proper drawing power or it would be discontinued.[68]

But the results of his advertising must have been encouraging from the very beginning, for, when Sears moved to Chicago in 1887, he began to advertise in periodicals as well as in newspapers. It was primarily through those periodicals, known as "mail-order" magazines and designed almost solely for rural consumption, that Richard Sears unveiled his great promotion schemes and intrenched his business firmly. It was largely through those magazines that he sought to make his firm's name a household byword throughout the land, to pre-empt large markets for himself. And his advertisements in the mail-order publications were almost invariably keyed to his catalogues; the attack was concerted and consistent.

In 1889, when Sears was still using newspapers to a greater extent than mail-order publications, he uncorked an advertisement for rural weeklies captioned "An Astonishing Offer." The ad contained illustrations of a sofa and two chairs. The text which followed announced that "as an advertisement only" that beautiful set of furniture, for the next sixty days only, would be sent to anyone who furnished ninety-five cents "to pay expenses, boxing, packing, advertising, etc." The furniture was made of "fine, lustrous, metal frames, beautifully finished and decorated, and upholstered in the finest manner with beautiful plush."[69] In agate type in the first line of the copy was the word "miniature." The furniture proved upon arrival to be doll's furniture. The joke was on the customer for not being sharp enough to detect and understand that key word "miniature." It is, of course, impossible to know whether Sears thought readers would be able to detect and understand. But most of the copy certainly would have led one to believe that the goods were real, full-size, serviceable household furniture.[70]

There are other stories, probably apocryphal, that Sears advertised for one dollar a "sewing machine" which proved upon receipt to be a needle and thread. So many crude jokes and so much venomous rumor was circulated about Sears (and about Montgomery Ward as well) that it is virtually impossible to separate fact from fabrication.

By 1892 Sears had moved away from such schemes as miniature furniture. That year found him still working on express agents, his original outlets, for further business. In April, 1892, he sent out eight thousand postal cards in imitation handwriting (from zinc plates) soliciting repeat orders on the $8.95 and $9.95 watches. The cost of the cards, printing, and postage was $90; two thousand orders came in, at an average cost of about 4½ cents per order.[71] Sears at this time and for some time thereafter insisted that his own letters and all others sent out from the company be in longhand, in order to inject the presonal touch. When the volume of correspondence prohibited this, imitation handwriting was employed. Typewriters were still suspect, and Sears hesitated to wound a customer's sensitivities with a cold, "machine-made" letter.[72]

Sears's attitude toward his associates reflected the same consideration he displayed toward correspondence with customers. While he remained aloof to the extent that he never called some of his associates by first name even after decades of friendship,[73] he usually avoided flat orders. He preferred suggestion, request, moral suasion. Instead of summoning staff members to his office, he was far more likely to walk up to them to talk over a scheme. It was always "Will you?" or "What do you think?"; seldom "You will." Sears was quick to bestow praise for good work well done; he was free with pats on the back, which must have been an important morale factor in a period when confusion and overwork reigned supreme.[74]

In 1893 Richard Sears decided further to exploit the market through express agents, in a grand enveloping movement. He sent an unordered watch to a businessman in the vicinity of each of the twenty thousand express offices in the country. Most of the watches were, of course, rejected by the addressees. The old pattern unfolded then; Sears wrote the station agents asking that they seek to dispose of the watches and offering to cut the price. The agent could keep whatever he received over the new "reduced" price. The agent could further show the original bill to prospective customers to help clinch the sale. And Sears lost nothing; the watch had been marked up enough to allow for a predetermined reduction without impairment of the profit he expected to realize.[75]

Sears also had a penchant for offering prizes for the first order sent in from any given state or county in any particular advertising campaign of his. This and his predilection for using handwritten letters are graphically revealed in a letter to one J. W. Bull, of West Virginia, dated March 24, 1894, and written on a Minneapolis letterhead of Sears, Roebuck and Company:

DEAR SIR:

About three weeks ago we sent out a special offer, offering as a present a $100.00 organ to the first one to order our $5.95 watch, and a $50.00 gold filled watch, as a present, to the first order received from each state. Up to the present time we have received no order from your state, so we write you confidentially under two cent stamp. If you will fill out the enclosed order blank immediately, and send to us, with $5.95 for watch described, we will see that you get "at least" *a very nice present at once.*

Very truly,
SEARS, ROEBUCK & CO.
By [signed] R. W. SEARS, *President*

The signature appears to be that of Sears himself, but the handwriting of the remainder of the letter does not. The addressee, Bull, was probably a West Virginian who had at some time ordered from the company; how many more of similar status may have received that same "confidential" letter, there is no way of knowing. But, at Richard Sears's state of development in the year 1894, it is a reasonable assumption that if Bull sent in that order with $5.95, he very probably received not the $100 organ or the $50 watch, but instead the "very nice present."

And just as Sears did not believe in wasting space in his catalogues and advertisements, so he did not waste any in his stationery. The reverse side of the letter just quoted heralded, in 48-point type, the "Grandest Offer Made!" A four-piece tea set of silver plate, which retailed at $20 and wholesaled at $10 to $15, according to Sears, could be had for only $5.25. All four pieces were pictured. The set would be sent to anyone C.O.D., no money in advance. "NEVER AGAIN" would that set be offered for less than $10; it was simply a "SPECIAL OFFER TO EXPRESS AGENTS to close out a lot we bought at a forced sale at a low price."

By August, 1895, Sears's powers of promotion had racked up a truly impressive accomplishment: he had carried the business through the depression of 1893–94 with expanding sales aided by the addition of many new lines of merchandise. Advertising was expanded. After moving to Chicago, he had begun to build a name throughout the rural regions. The expansion of merchandise departments and further increased advertising were expensive stratagems. In the year from July, 1894, to the same month of the following year, net worth had been reduced from $79,149.57 to $54,570.76. Total liabilities had risen to $78,163.78—more than three times the amount permitted by the company's Minnesota charter.[76]

Sears thrived on a twelve-hour day and a seven-day week, but Roebuck was in ill-health and under a doctor's care.[77] Roebuck began to wonder how long he could stand the pace. And it is reasonable to assume—from the state of finances, the general confusion of the business, the lack of a firm administrative hand, and from the infusion of new blood which was soon to follow—that Richard Sears must have wondered how long his business could continue to careen along. He surely must have known that, in the absence of adequate working capital, he could not have continued to expand his volume of business yearly and that, in the absence of top-level assistance in conception and execution of policy, he could not consolidate his gains advantageously and push on toward his goal.

CHAPTER IV

Capital and Transition: Growing Pains and Financial Panic

ALVAH CURTIS ROEBUCK was beginning in the dog days of August, 1895, to feel the strain of long hours at the firm which bore his name. He and Richard Sears were still often working from early morning until nearly midnight, seven days a week. The long-term prospects of the company were in many ways promising, if the experience of the past decade could be believed. In the short view, however, the outlook was less pleasing.

With the liabilities of the firm standing at more than three times the $25,000 limitation on corporate liability imposed by the company's charter of incorporation, Roebuck was seriously worried over the possibility of his personal liability in connection with the excess. He was a man in whom the gambling instinct was hardly discernible, and his financial resources were very limited. All this, plus his concern over his health, led Roebuck on the seventeenth of August to make the decision that was to remove him as an officer and stockholder of record. He decided to sell out and eventually (in 1897) realized $25,000 for an interest which in a few years—hindsight is so much better than foresight—would be worth millions.[1]

Richard Sears agreed to hold his cofounder's interest in trust, to be disposed of as soon as a satisfactory opportunity should arise.[2] Apparently no specific sum was mentioned. Roebuck at that time held a one-third interest in the business.[3]

In the summer of 1895 Sears had had a visit from Aaron E. Nusbaum, who had amassed $150,000 from his soda-pop and ice-cream concession at the Chicago Columbian Exposition in 1893.[4] Part of this money he had invested in a company making pneumatic tubes to expedite movement of cash and vouchers in department stores. Nusbaum paid a call on Richard Sears to sell him the pneumatic-tube system—and to get a closer look at the president of the mail-order business about whom he had heard so much.[5]

Nusbaum failed to sell Sears any pneumatic tubes, but Nusbaum was sold on Richard Sears—so thoroughly sold, in fact, that he consented to invest some of his money in Sears, Roebuck and Company. On August 7, 1895, negotiations had proceeded far enough that Sears wrote Nusbaum a letter outlining the actual terms of the deal. The arrangement was apparently arrived at over coffee cups; the communication was penciled on stationery of the Chicago Stock Exchange Restaurant and Buffet. R. W. Sears submitted this proposition:

I will admit you into the firm of Sears, Roebuck and Company on the basis of $15,000.00 for the good will or in other words, the business to be based on $15,000.00 more than the net assets which at present is [sic] about $50,000.00, the understanding is that the money be used to increase the capital, and the firm be reorganized with the new capital added, you to take one-half interest in the business and immediately assume an active part in the management, the capitalization to be approximately $135,000.00 paid in full. I will guarantee the correctness of the inventory and become responsible for same in every way. I hold this proposition open until Aug. 17th, 1895.[6]

Just when Roebuck first knew that negotiations were in progress, it is difficult to determine.[7] In any case, he did not take any active part in the discussions that were to bring a new interest into the business.

Nusbaum quickly accepted Sears's proposition. A letter to him from Sears on August 13 acknowledged Nusbaum's acceptance of the proposal.[8] But Nusbaum was not ready to provide the $75,000 for a half-interest entirely from his own funds. He began canvassing his family to find someone to assume half his commitment. After two or three of his relatives and friends declined, Nusbaum approached his brother-in-law, Julius Rosenwald.[9]

Rosenwald already knew Richard Sears and something of his business. As Florence Kiper Frank states:

One day a new customer entered the offices of Rosenwald and Company. He was tall and handsome. His lank black hair was parted smoothly in the middle and brushed back from a high, square forehead. His thick black moustache curled smartly at the corners. His finely shaped eyes were alive and eager. Something in his manner and carriage gave a flamboyance to his conventional good looks. A theatre audience of the nineties, seeing him walk upon the stage would have known him at once for the Hero of the piece. . . . he towered above the stout, genial salesman who stepped forward, courteously ready to display the wares of Rosenwald and Company.

But the new customer scarcely took time to look at the suits. He could not wait to finger the fabrics, examine them expertly, or enter into leisurely discussion of weights and weaves. He appraised them with one shrewd glance, ignoring the established rituals of purchase. Nor did the usual fear of overbuying seem to check this novel person in the slightest. When could the suits be delivered? When would more be available? It was, oddly enough, the salesman who suggested caution. Was Mr. Sears sure he could sell so many suits? Sell them! They were sold already! His customers were clamoring for delivery. He would be back for further purchases.[10]

Sears's contagious vitality had dramatized an order for fifty men's suits. In a few minutes' time he had purchased the clothing and sold himself, all in almost one sweeping motion. And, as predicted,

Sears returned, not once but often. He was always in a hurry, always driven by anxiety and the pressure of time. It was a unique anxiety in those dull days that plodded in the rear of the World's Fair. This man was not fretted by doubts of

SEARS, ROEBUCK AND COMPANY BALANCE SHEET
FOR AUGUST 19, 1895

CAPITAL AND TRANSITION

disposal of stock but by need of keeping pace with his mysteriously mounting sales.

Thus, in the early relationship between Julius Rosenwald and Richard Sears the familiar American pattern was reversed. It was the customer who sold himself and his ideas; the unaggressive salesman whose interest was captured.

Sears' orders jumped crazily from fifty to five hundred suits for a single shipment. The Minneapolis house of Sears, Roebuck and Company which he represented seemed to have tapped an inexhaustible market. Rosenwald, amazed by the ravening appetite of this market, saw that Sears seemed also mystified. Indeed, Sears was breathless in the current that was sweeping him on to success. . . . Out of his phantasy he had created this phenomenal business. He was incapable of believing it was fact now, not fiction.[11]

Rosenwald felt that the mail-order business was definitely fact. He was intrigued by the business which Richard Sears had developed into a going concern. He was convinced that it had a profitable future if only Sears could be somewhat restrained in his daring promotion campaigns and if the organization could be made to operate on a more business-like, more systematized basis. Rosenwald's interest was therefore great from the moment Nusbaum broached the proposition that the two buy into Sears, Roebuck and Company.

His interest, however, outstripped his finances; he was forced to arrange for the required funds through his clothing concern, Rosenwald and Company, from that concern's parent-organization in New York, Newborg, Rosenberg and Company. This transaction, however, involved no cash but instead simply reduced the current liabilities of Sears, Roebuck. The mail-order firm owed a large sum of money to Rosenwald and Company, a subsidiary of Newborg, Rosenberg and Company, for merchandise received. Newborg, Rosenberg agreed to an arrangement whereby Julius Rosenwald held his shares of the capital stock of Sears, Roebuck in trust for the benefit of Rosenwald and Company.[12]

It was agreed that Nusbaum should join the mail-order house immediately, with Rosenwald to follow as soon as he could conveniently liquidate his affairs at Rosenwald and Weil and at Rosenwald and Company. Nusbaum, in fact, joined the firm on August 17, 1895—the date on which Roebuck said he resigned and placed his stock in trust with Richard Sears.

On August 23 Sears, Roebuck and Company was reincorporated under the laws of Illinois with a capitalization of $150,000. Richard Sears as president held 800 shares, worth $80,000. Julius Rosenwald as vice-president held 350 shares, valued at $35,000; and Nusbaum as treasurer and general manager likewise held 350 shares of the same value.[13] The articles of incorporation were filed with the Illinois secretary of state on September 7, 1895.

The very process of the new incorporation was a dramatic story; and, like many aspects of the rise of the great mail-order house, it is hedged about with contradictions. Shortly after Nusbaum and Rosenwald jointly accepted Sears's offer to invest in the firm, Nusbaum and Sears called upon a young lawyer named Albert Loeb. Some accounts have it that Loeb was called on early one afternoon, only because the lawyer the two men had in mind was out to a late and protracted lunch, while young Loeb happened to be at work in his office.[14] Another version holds that the meeting took place early one morning, when few lawyers could be found in their offices; this story also maintains that a mutual friend of Nusbaum and Loeb recommended the latter.[15]

On September 6 Rosenwald joined the other two partners for another meeting in Loeb's office. The papers of incorporation drafted by Loeb were agreed upon. Stock was issued on the spot. Loeb was appointed the company's attorney. Four shares of stock were placed in escrow with Loeb and Adler's law firm (two contributed by Sears, and one share each by the other two partners). Worth $400 then, the four shares would be worth $400,000 in 1918.[16]

Cofounder Roebuck was, to all practical purposes, out of the business, although he agreed to the company's continued use of his name. An era had ended and a new one was beginning. Nusbaum assumed his new duties forthwith, and Rosenwald came to the company the following year. Roebuck remained as a trouble-shooter, utilizing his mechanical talent, and later served as head of the watch and jewelry department.[17]

The reorganized mail-order house moved ahead rapidly. Stockholdings were revised to make Sears, Nusbaum, and Rosenwald equal stockholders. On September 25, 1895, Sears sold the other two 25 shares each.[18] On April 12, 1898, he sold each of them 125 shares,[19] which resulted in each partner's holding 500 of the 1,500 shares in the firm.

On December 10, 1896, Julius Rosenwald moved into his office at Sears, Roebuck and Company.[20] It was the quiet and unheralded beginning of a great fortune which was to become a significant philanthropic venture and of an era of more cautious advertising and systematic merchandising which was to transform the mail-order company considerably.

Rosenwald was slightly older than Richard Sears. He was born on August 12, 1862, the son of Samuel Rosenwald, who had reached Baltimore eight years earlier as a twenty-six-year-old "merchant"[21] ("peddler" would have been a more accurate description). Four years after arriving in this country, Samuel Rosenwald joined the Baltimore clothing concern of the Hammerslough Brothers. In about a year he married their sister and shortly afterward was placed in charge of their Peoria, Illinois, store. After some wandering around the country, Samuel Rosenwald took over the management of the Springfield, Illinois, branch of Hammerslough to handle the booming business in supplying uniforms to the Federal forces. In that city, one block from the home of Abraham Lincoln, Julius was born.

After two years of high school there, young Julius went to New York to make his way through an apprenticeship with his Hammerslough uncles.

His weekly salary was $5.00, which he supplemented by night work at other clothing establishments. Among his young friends were Henry Morgenthau, Henry Goldman (later of Goldman, Sachs), and Moses Newborg.[22] He learned the clothing business from the ground up.

In 1885 he and his cousin, Julius Weil, opened the Chicago company of Rosenwald and Weil to manufacture men's clothing. Like their competitors, Rosenwald and Weil farmed out their orders to sweatshop operators who, in turn, subcontracted the work to immigrant men, women, and children.[23] Most of these workers put in from ten to eighteen hours daily, six days a week, for wages ranging from $2.00 a week for children to about $6.00 or $8.00 for men. They worked in poorly lit, ill-ventilated, unsanitary tenements, and competition to drive wages lower and lower was strong and often savage. This was the arena in which Julius Rosenwald began to grow to maturity as a merchant.

In 1890 Julius married Augusta Nusbaum, sister of Aaron E. Nusbaum. Their first son, Lessing, later to be chairman of the board of Sears, Roebuck and Company, was born on February 10, 1891. The dynasty was taking form.

In the first half of that decade of the nineties, Julius Rosenwald lived a life pretty generally typical of a moderately successful clothing merchant. He managed to weather the depression of 1893–94 and to support his family comfortably. His expressed ambition then was to attain an income of $15,000 a year: "$5,000 to be used for my personal expenses, $5,000 to be laid aside, and $5,000 to go to charity."[24] Before the stock-market crisis of 1929, his fortune—even after some $63,000,000 in charitable donations—was estimated at as much as half a billion dollars.

When Rosenwald assumed his duties in 1896, Nusbaum and Sears had already ceased to get along harmoniously. Julius Rosenwald soon found himself clashing with both of them. Nusbaum was an excellent administrator and a good improviser, but he was reputedly an intellectual of the Prussian Junker type with a faculty for rubbing people the wrong way. He often concluded a discussion with a suave, almost smug, "I told you all the time you were wrong."[25] Louis Asher described him in these terms:

> It is the opinion of two of the former high executives whom I have interviewed recently and it is also my impression from the few times I met A. E. Nusbaum in 1898, that he was a very capable and high-grade man. He was very gentlemanly, aristocratic in his appearance and manner, dressed in perfect fashion, elegantly, was good looking with very expressive eyes, rather distinguished in fact. Quick to make decisions. The temperament of Nusbaum clashed with that of Sears and Rosenwald. One of the inside men of that period reports that Nusbaum in discussions with his partners, did not like to commit himself on any important matter and thus was left in a position to say: "I told you so," no matter what the outcome. The same man says that Nusbaum was fault-finding and nagging and did not believe in praising a man for good work. He believed an employee was kept on his toes by criticism rather than by praise.[26]

When bills had to be paid on time and the company's bank balance was negligible, Nusbaum found a way. He simply picked up the pay-roll cards and went through them, saying, "Lay off this man, and rehire him in about two weeks. Lay off this man."[27] The pay roll was always pared to a point where the company could somehow pay its bills when they fell due.

But, despite Nusbaum's abilities, the friction between him, on the one hand, and Rosenwald and Sears, on the other, continued to grow. True, there was also disagreement between Sears and Rosenwald; but their differences seem to have hinged less on personalities than on attitudes toward various specific aspects of company operations. It is perhaps not too farfetched to say that Sears and Rosenwald found it hard to get along with Nusbaum even when all three were in agreement on any given question.

Roebuck states that Sears told him often in those years that he was about ready to leave the firm which bore their names and establish another business of his own.[28] He asked Roebuck to join him if such a venture should come to fruition, and Roebuck consented. But the differences of opinion and personality clashes which had led Sears to that unhappy frame of mind were apparently either temporarily solved or at least sufficiently alleviated to dissuade him.

Early in 1901, however, Sears had pretty much returned to the same point of view. He walked into Rosenwald's office and said, in effect, "Someone's got to go. Either you and Nusbaum buy me out, or you and I buy him out." Sears then closed his desk and repaired to Roebuck's office to await Rosenwald's decision.[29]

It was a hard decision for Rosenwald to make—even assuming that Nusbaum might be willing to sell his interest. Rosenwald's whole family was very closely knit, and his wife was Nusbaum's sister. Julius Rosenwald was often tough and autocratic in his business relationships, but he intensely disliked any family friction. The friction between Sears and Nusbaum, and Rosenwald's own differences with his brother-in-law, had already exerted their frictional effect on Rosenwald's family life.[30] Furthermore, he felt a deep sense of obligation to Nusbaum for having brought him into the business. Too, he had some trepidation about continuing with Sears, whose audacity worried him and whose lack of interest in administration irritated him. At the same time, however, he recognized the truly great contribution Sears had to make, provided Rosenwald could canalize that eternal drive and ceaseless energy.

There was still another factor which, though difficult to evaluate now with any exactness, must have carried some weight with Rosenwald: neither he nor Nusbaum had much firsthand knowledge of farmers. Rosenwald had traveled little in the United States, and even that travel was largely from one urban center to another. Nusbaum knew even less about farmers. And specialized knowledge of the element which constituted the overwhelming majority of the mail-order firm's business was a rather ob-

CAPITAL AND TRANSITION

vious essential of success in that business. Richard Sears possessed that knowledge in abundance.

It is impossible to know, at this date, whether business or emotional reasons tipped the scales. But it seems certain that Rosenwald felt himself ready for both business and emotional maturity. He resolved to break with his brother-in-law and cast his lot with Richard Sears. He and Sears then agreed to buy out Nusbaum for an even million dollars, to which figure Nusbaum consented after some backing and filling. A contract was duly drawn, presumably by Albert Loeb. The time for signing came. Nusbaum balked. He hiked his demand by exactly a quarter of a million dollars.

Sears and Rosenwald were shocked and outraged. The argument that followed was personal and bitter.[31] The two partners had felt that they were already mortgaging their future in offering Nusbaum a million dollars. A million and a quarter was at least a quarter too much. But, finally, Nusbaum won, and the other two reluctantly agreed on May 7 to pay the higher sum.[32] It took them less than three years to pay off the entire amount from their expanding business. Payment of a dividend of $2,482,396.73 at a special board meeting on December 31, 1903, indicates the full amount must have been paid Nusbaum by this time. At this meeting Sears and Rosenwald purchased for $1,349,752.46 the five hundred shares Nusbaum had sold to the company.[33]

When Nusbaum tendered his resignation as secretary and treasurer on February 14, 1901, Albert Loeb was elected secretary (his salary was voted on March 22 to be $1,600 per annum), and Rosenwald became treasurer as well as vice-president.[34] Nusbaum's resignation as director was noted in the minutes of the special meeting of the board of directors held May 7 to accept Nusbaum's terms of sale. The succeeding paragraph of the minutes states that Loeb was elected to fill the unexpired term.[35] The stockholdings were further revised on March 1, 1903, when Loeb purchased seventy-five shares of Sears, Roebuck capital stock.

The special dividend of $2,482,396.73 declared on December 31, 1903, was followed soon by many others. On June 30 of the following year, at another special meeting of the board, a dividend of $922,101.07 was declared and ordered paid. Still another special meeting was held December 12, 1904, at which one dividend of $2,850,000 to be paid at once was declared and an additional dividend of $1,200,000 was also declared.[36]

The company's earnings and profits mounted so rapidly that also on December 12, 1904, at the same meeting which declared the aforementioned two dividends, the certified stock of the company was increased from $150,000 to $5,000,000. The additional capital was to be divided into 48,500 shares of par value of $100 each. "Sears, Rosenwald and Loeb offered to purchase said additional capital stock at par value in proportion to their respective holdings, therefore it was resolved that whereas the capital stock has this day been increased from $150,000 to $5,000,000, the offer be and hereby is accepted and the Secretary is authorized to issue said stock."[37] December 31, 1904, saw a dividend of $154,770.17 declared at a special board meeting.[38]

The very success of the company exerted a heavy pressure on its capital resources. Nevertheless, to accommodate the ever growing volume of orders, and to mitigate the chaos attending operations in many scattered locations, Sears, Roebuck committed itself to build a large new plant west of Garfield Park in Chicago.

The pressure on the company's space had grown steadily greater ever since 1896. On March 17 of that year the company moved from its Adams Street headquarters six blocks north to the Enterprise Building at Fulton and Desplaines streets, where it occupied a six-story-and-basement, L-shaped building, 170 by 171 feet. This gave the firm nearly two and a quarter acres of floor space—roughly 98,000 square feet. In addition, the Adams Street building was retained as a warehouse. In 1898 the Fulton and Desplaines building was increased in size to approximately 4.8 acres —or 211,000 square feet—by filling in the court and alley. In 1901 the space was again increased by construction of a new building 152 by 180 feet, eight stories and basement, adjoining the structure at Fulton and Desplaines streets. This move brought the total space to about 431,244 square feet.

Following the addition to the Enterprise Building, considerable space was rented and occupied within a radius of several blocks. Among these acquisitions were a large part of the Bradley Building, five stories and basement, 150 feet in depth; a large building on the corner of Union Street and Washington Boulevard; part of another near-by building; and many more. This was the period when Albert Loeb professed to be spending nearly all his time negotiating leases for space. Construction of the company's forty-acre plant at Homan Avenue and Arthington Street late in 1905 was to solve most of its space requirements for years to come, but prior to that the company was expending considerable sums of money for leased space. In 1903 total expenditures for real estate, buildings, and equipment were $80,012.85. The following year saw an increase to $335,-946.60, almost $249,000 of which was for property needed in connection with the new construction. The completion of the new Homan Avenue building late in 1905 involved a cash outlay in that year of $5,120,771.21.

Thus the concentrated and heavy expenditures for the new plant, aggravated by the necessity of financing large increases in sales, seriously depleted available working capital. In 1904 net working capital stood at $4,062,357. The end of 1905 testified to the drastic decline—the year-end statement showed net working capital to be but $694,738. Not since 1897 had the firm operated on such a tight margin. The need for additional capital became urgent.[39]

Rosenwald turned for help to his boyhood friend, Henry Goldman, in the spring of 1906. Sears and Rosenwald went to New York and requested a loan of $5,000,000 from Goldman, Sachs and Company. "Goldman suggested instead that they make their business a public company and issue preferred stock, based on the net assets of the company; and common stock, based on good-will and future prospects of the business."[40] Accordingly, arrangements were made, and Goldman, Sachs with Lehman Brothers organized a syndicate to underwrite the new issue. As of December 31, 1905, the net worth of the company was $7,292,645. Net working capital was $694,738. The statement for July 1, 1906, shows a net worth of $40,000,000, three-quarters of which was embalmed in the asset "good will." Working capital had increased to $1,247,193.

TABLE 3*

STOCKS OF COMPANIES OWNED, 1906

Company	Number of Shares	Value†
American Separator Co., New York	400	$ 50,000
Conley Camera Co., Minnesota	260	18,000
Hartford Plow Works, Wisconsin	375	40,000
Hercules Buggy Co., Indiana	423‡ / 846§	125,000
Meriden Fire Arms Co., Illinois	1,600	175,000
Napierville Lounge Co., Illinois	50	100,000
Rundle Manufacturing Co., Wisconsin (plumbing equipment)	500	50,000
Wehrle Co., Ohio (stoves)	500‡ / 1,500§	325,000
Wilson Saw and Manufacturing Co., Michigan	5,000	75,000
Total		$958,000

* Source: Statement submitted to Goldman, Sachs and Company prior to the 1906 public stock offering.
† The values are based approximately on the values of the stocks as shown by the books of the respective companies.
‡ Preferred. § Common.

On June 12, 1906, a special meeting of the stockholders of the company was held to pass upon recommendations made by the board of directors:

... inasmuch as the charter of this Company does not permit ownership of the stock of other corporations, and that officers and stockholders of Sears, Roebuck and Co. have financed nine corporations for the purpose of manufacturing goods especially for Sears, Roebuck and Co., and that a closer relationship between the manufacturing companies and Sears, Roebuck and Co. would be desirable, [the directors had passed a resolution authorizing the officers of the company] to cause to be promptly formed a new corporation having the same name as that of this company to be organized under the laws of New York, and that its capital stock shall consist of $40,000,000.00 of which $10,000,000.00 is to be 7% cumulative preferred stock and $30,000,000.00 of common stock.[41]

The nine companies financed by the officers and stockholders of the company are shown in Table 3. The certificate of incorporation and copy of the bylaws of the New York corporation were filed with the secretary of state of New York on June 16, 1906.[42] The amount of capital with which the new corporation was to begin business was $1,000. To comply with provisions of the Business Corporations Law of the State of New York, a resident of that state was added to the board of directors: Robert P. Sniffen, of 2394 Seventh Avenue, borough of Manhattan, resident manager of the company's buying office, who held one share of common stock of $100 par value. Sears, Rosenwald, and Loeb each held three shares of common; thus were the ten shares providing the $1,000 initial capitalization divided.

The first meeting of the directors of the new corporation was held in New York, at 27 William Street, in the financial district, June 19, 1906.[43] It was determined that the principal business office was to be in New York. And the Illinois corporation at the same meeting transferred to the New York corporation all its assets together with the capital stock of the nine manufacturing concerns financed by the officers and stockholders of the company. The voting at a special meeting of the stockholders on June 26, 1906, showed the distribution of the 50,000 shares of stock of the Illinois corporation as follows: Sears, 24,485 shares; Rosenwald, 24,365; Loeb 300; ten employees of the company, 740; "relatives of Rosenwald" (apparently five in number), 110 shares.[44]

On July 2 a special meeting of the directors voted salaries of $9,600 per annum for Sears, Rosenwald, and Loeb, and elected four new directors: W. O. Lewis, John Higgins, Henry Goldman, and Philip Lehman. On the same day, Sears, Rosenwald, and Loeb signed an agreement to devote their time and attention solely to the business of the company and not to engage in or become associated or connected with any other business of a similar character unless the same were owned or controlled by the company.[45]

An offerings circular was distributed by a syndicate headed by the New York banking houses, Lehman Brothers and Goldman, Sachs, for $9,000,000 of the preferred stock, some time after August 28, 1906—probably early in September.[46] The circular quoted the officers of Sears, Roebuck as saying that the firm sold

practically the whole of its enormous output, "cash before delivery"; that the business is distributed among upwards of six million customers, in all parts of the United States, whose orders for merchandise are received by mail; that the incoming letters averaged for the past year about seventy-five thousand letters per day; that the newly completed buildings for handling the merchandise and for administrative purposes cover a large part of thirty-seven acres of land, in the City of Chicago, and that the foregoing does not include any of the various manufacturing concerns in which the New York corporation of Sears, Roebuck & Company owns a controlling interest.

Underwriting charges for flotation of the stock issue amounted to $500,000 cash and $5,000,000 worth of common stock.[47] Sears and Rosenwald each received $4,500,000 in cash for his previous stockholdings.[48] The preferred stock, with a par value of $100, was placed on the market at $97.50 a share; $100 par common, at $50 a share. It was provided that the preferred stock could be redeemed by the company at its own option at any time,[49] but it was not until November 15, 1924, that all the preferred was called for redemption.[50]

Werner says that "the public bought the stock with avidity" and that on January 1, 1907, Rosenwald advanced about $90,000 to permit some of the older employees to purchase the new stock of the company.[51] The group was small, however, consisting primarily of the founders, employees, and friends, and numbering only 263 in 1907.[52]

Circumstances had precipitated the company's recapitalization at an opportune time. The capital market was buoyant with the prosperity that culminated in 1906. A year later the Sears, Roebuck recapitalization would not have been so readily managed, for the autumn of 1907 brought chaos to the money markets with the now famous panic of that year precipitated by a series of New York bank failures.[53] Professor Mitchell states that

> the panic of 1907 was followed by what the *Financial Review* declared to be the worst industrial paralysis in the country's history. During the first half of 1908 the production of pig-iron was barely more than 50 per cent of the production in the first half of 1907.... from January to August railway gross earnings showed losses of from 12 to 20 per cent each month, and clearings outside New York losses of from 12 to 17 per cent in comparison with the corresponding months of the preceding year. Unemployment assumed extraordinary proportions in the industrial centers and emigration ran far behind immigration.[54]

In 1906 Sears, Roebuck and Company had achieved its greatest success with gross sales of $50,861,763 during the calendar year,[55] an increase of 33 per cent over the remarkable achievements of 1905. At the close of the fiscal year on June 30, 1907, *net* sales had reached $50,722,840. It was evident that the record-breaking increases of the preceding years would not be matched. But sales were at least holding up—and there was still the seasonal increase to be expected in the fall of 1907 from the Christmas trade and the harvest.

On Tuesday, October 22, 1907, the Knickerbocker Trust Company opened its doors in New York to a run which so drained its resources that it was forced to suspend payments after three hours.[56] Panic spread. There followed the most extraordinary demand to hold money.

The expectation that Sears, Roebuck would witness a fall season impressive enough to maintain (or increase) annual sales was frustrated. The latter half of 1907 and the first six months of 1908 resulted in sales of but $40,843,866—a decline of nearly $10,000,000 in the twelve months ending June 30, 1908. Profits declined by more than 37 per cent—from $3,238,502 to $2,034,796.

That the company should suffer such marked contraction in sales is remarkable in view of the healthy condition of agriculture in these years. Of 1907 the Secretary of Agriculture said:

> No general crop failure afflicts the farmer this year, not even within small areas. The production of the farms . . . is well up to the average of the previous five years in quantity, while its value to the farmer . . . reached a figure much above that of 1906, which by far exceeded any previous year's wealth production on farms.
>
> Out of the farming operations of 1907 . . . the farmer will have more to spend and more to invest than he ever before had out of his year's work.[57]

Agricultural prosperity, contrary to the developments in industry, was even greater in 1908. "Billions upon billions the farmer has again piled his wealth . . . the total value of all farm products of 1908 . . . the most extraordinary amount in the world's history, $7,778,000,000."[58] But, despite his heralded prosperity, the farmer was evidently prey to the same craving for liquidity that characterized his "foes," the "denizens" of the eastern financial marts. So strenuous was the demand for lawful money that it generated widespread use of substitutes for cash. This was current in the smaller towns as well as in the great cities. Mitchell quotes one authority as estimating the total substitutes for cash as reaching more than $500,000,000.[59]

Although the company executives had not been exposed to the as yet uncoined terminology—"liquidity preference"—they sensed something of the nature of the problem. Richard Sears saw that a form letter went out urging people to send the firm notes, checks, or scrip in lieu of cash if necessary.[60] Despite such exhortations the prosperous farm market failed to sustain the company's sales in 1907–8. That short depression hit Sears, Roebuck hard. For the first time executives faced financial statements that failed to better those of the previous year.

CHAPTER V

Sales Pressure and Promotion

THE years following 1895 saw Richard Sears's talents and inclinations as a merchandiser sustain an effective procession of promotional schemes. The reorganization of Sears, Roebuck and Company in 1895, in addition to bringing more capital into the firm, had also brought for the first time top-flight assistance to Richard Sears in the management of the business. Rosenwald and Nusbaum (and, after 1901, Albert Loeb) were available to handle many details which Sears had theretofore had to grapple with himself, intrust to sometimes inadequate subordinates, or simply ignore. For the first time the cofounder was free (from the standpoint of time and responsibility) and equipped (from the standpoint of solid experience and sufficient capital) to pursue his natural bent and his determination to advertise on an unprecedented scale.

Just as promotable merchandise at low prices widely advertised throughout the land was all one package in Sears's mind, all a logical entity rather than merely the sum total of different components, so was his advertising all of a piece to him. The catalogue, issued on a more regularized basis after 1895, was the solid base of Richard Sears's advertising, for he could shape it to his will, he could make it as large or as small as he wished, and he could in great measure place it where he wished. All his other advertising was to a considerable extent adjunctive to his catalogue; it called attention to the greater galaxy of bargains to be found in his big book, it announced schemes which would be revealed in more profuse detail in his general catalogue, and it urged readers to send forthwith for the "great wish book" billed as "The Consumer's Guide."

Since the hostility of independent retail merchants made it difficult for Sears to employ many newspapers as an advertising medium after his business had become large enough to attract such opposition, he was encouraged further to rely heavily for a few years upon a class of magazines designed almost entirely for rural consumption. These periodicals were known generically as "mail-order magazines," from the fact that their columns were filled largely with advertisements of the many individuals and companies selling by mail. Their era of greatest affluence and influence coincided almost exactly with the period when Richard Sears keenly felt the need—and had secured the means—of advertising his company and his wares on a vast scale, as a part of his determined effort to intrench his firm's name, to consolidate Sears, Roebuck's merchandising position. Again, it was a classic confluence of a man and a situation, and it is a measure of Sears's particular talent that he capitalized upon that confluence.

It was the mail-order publications upon which Richard Sears now relied primarily to persuade people to request his catalogues. The bulk of the selling or "closing" had to be done by the catalogue; the "external" advertisements could feature only a few leaders from the company's merchandise line (though some sold in sensational volume). The use of these leaders, dramatized with strikingly low prices, was to a great extent a device to put Sears, Roebuck's name on every farmer's tongue and to persuade those farmers to write for the big general catalogue. Yet Sears never issued more than two general catalogues in a year, whereas most of the mail-order magazines were published monthly or semimonthly and thus offered a vehicle for blanketing much of the country quickly when Sears was eager to spread some sensational message within a short span of time. Also, Sears, Roebuck's great rival, Montgomery Ward, likewise issued general (and special) catalogues—another inducement to Richard Sears to advertise heavily and sensationally in the mail-order magazines, which Ward's was using on a less ambitious scale.

Those mail-order magazines reached millions of farm readers with their advertisements of goods for sale by mail and their fiction stories of virtue triumphant at the bitter end.[1] Jack was always there to lift the mortgage in their stories; and Richard Sears, after a while, was always there with an astounding offer to sell merchandise at what appeared to be less than manufacturing cost.

Subscription rates to these publications ran from around fifteen to fifty cents a year.[2] They were heavily subsidized by the public treasury in that postal authorities classified them as aids in disseminating knowledge, which entitled the magazines to a postal rate of one cent a pound. Hower points out:

> Magazines ... continued to advance by great strides. Between 1880 and 1890 their number increased 93 per cent, while their average circulation increased 50 per cent. Here was an important new means of reaching the public, an advertising medium considerably less ephemeral than the newspaper, in short, an opportunity which the observant advertiser could not fail to note. Moreover, the enterprising J. Walter Thompson agency had early begun to specialize in magazine work and dinned its virtues into the ears of business men. By the middle 'nineties, the growth of such periodicals as *McClure's, Munsey's,* and the *Cosmopolitan* could no longer be ignored; and in 1896 N. W. Ayer & Son announced that it would handle magazine as well as newspaper advertising.[3]

Among the magazines advancing by "great strides" were the religious "newspapers," which were actually in most instances weekly magazines of a popular nature. These religious weeklies made up one of the most popular advertising mediums in the last half of the nineteenth century. In many

Demerest's Family Magazine, June, 1894

Youth's Companion, July 15, 1897

Youth's Companion, November 11, 1897

SOME SEARS, ROEBUCK AND COMPANY ADVERTISEMENTS
IN PERIODICALS, 1894–98

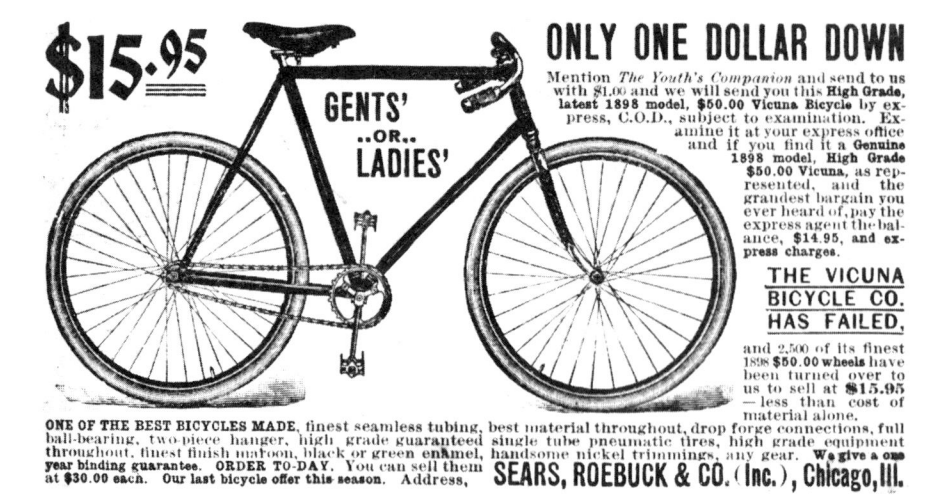

$15.95

GENTS' ..OR.. LADIES'

ONLY ONE DOLLAR DOWN

Mention *The Youth's Companion* and send to us with $1.00 and we will send you this **High Grade, latest 1898 model, $50.00 Vicuna Bicycle** by express, C.O.D., subject to examination. Examine it at your express office and if you find it a **Genuine 1898 model, High Grade $50.00 Vicuna**, as represented, and the grandest bargain you ever heard of, pay the express agent the balance, **$14.95**, and express charges.

THE VICUNA BICYCLE CO. HAS FAILED,

and 2,500 of its finest 1898 **$50.00 wheels** have been turned over to us to sell at **$15.95** — less than cost of material alone.

ONE OF THE BEST BICYCLES MADE, finest seamless tubing, best material throughout, drop forge connections, full ball-bearing, two-piece hanger, high grade guaranteed single tube pneumatic tires, high grade equipment throughout, finest finish maroon, black or green enamel, handsome nickel trimmings, any gear. **We give a one year binding guarantee. ORDER TO-DAY.** You can sell them at $30.00 each. Our last bicycle offer this season. Address, **SEARS, ROEBUCK & CO. (Inc.), Chicago, Ill.**

Youth's Companion, September 29, 1898

$4.95 FOR A Seal Plush Cape

SEAL PLUSH

$4.95 BUYS A $10.00 SEAL PLUSH CAPE. This circular cape is made of the finest quality seal plush; it is 20-in. long and extra full sweep, very elaborately embroidered in the latest vermicelli style, with soutache braid and beads, large storm collar also embroidered; collar front and bottom edged all around with Black Thibet Fur, making cape look 23 in. long. It is heavily interlined to make it warm and shapely, lined throughout with fine imported Italian metallic cloth.

OUR OFFER. Send to us mentioning *Youth's Companion*. **Send No Money.** State your weight and height, number of inches around body at bust and around neck, and we will send you this handsome Tailor-Made Seal Plush Cape by express C.O.D., subject to examination. You can examine it at your nearest express office, and if found perfectly satisfactory, exactly as represented, better value than any other house can give, and such a cape as was never seen in your town at within $4.00 or $5.00 of our price, pay the express agent **OUR SPECIAL PRICE, $4.95,** and express charges.
Write for Free Cloak Catalogue of everything in Women's and Children's Wearing Apparel. Address,
SEARS, ROEBUCK & CO. (Inc.), CHICAGO, ILL.

Harper's Weekly, October 6, 1898

$1.95 BUYS A $3.50 SUIT

3,000 CELEBRATED "KANTWEAROUT" double seat and double knee. Regular $3.50 Boys' 2-Piece Knee-Pant Suits going at $1.95.
A NEW SUIT FREE for any of these suits which don't give satisfactory wear.
Send No Money. Send to us mentioning *The Youth's Companion*, state age of boy and say whether large or small for age, and we will send you the suit by express, C.O.D., subject to examination. You can examine it at your express office and if found perfectly satisfactory and equal to suits sold in your town for $3.50, pay your express agent **our special offer price, $1.95,** and express charges.
THESE KNEE-PANT SUITS are for boys from 4 to 15 years of age, and are retailed everywhere at $3.50. Made with double seat and knees, latest 1899 style as illustrated, made from a special wear-resisting, heavy-weight, ALL-WOOL Oakwell cassimere, neat, handsome pattern, fine serge lining, Clayton patent interlining, padding, staying and reinforcing, silk and linen sewing, fine tailor-made throughout, a suit any boy or parent would be proud of. FOR FREE CLOTH SAMPLES of Boys' Clothing (suits, overcoats or ulsters), for boys **4 to 19 YEARS**, write for Sample Book, No. 90 C, contains fashion plates, tape measure and full instructions how to order.
Men's Suits and Overcoats made to order from $5.00 up. Samples sent free on application. Address,
SEARS, ROEBUCK & CO. (Inc.), Chicago, Ill.

Youth's Companion, October 27, 1898

SOME SEARS, ROEBUCK AND COMPANY ADVERTISEMENTS IN PERIODICALS, 1894–98

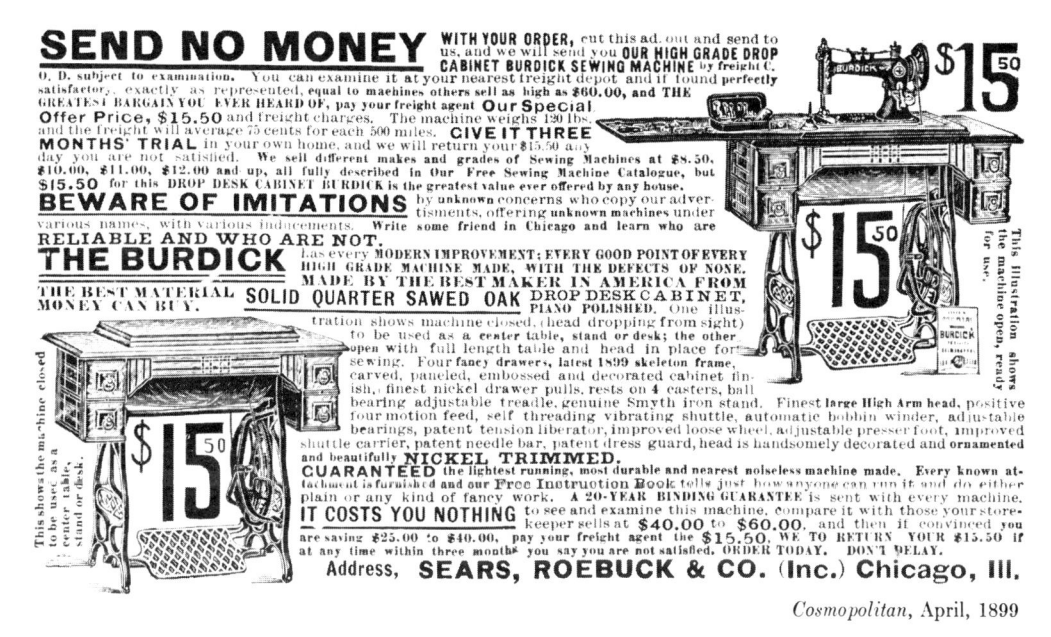

Cosmopolitan, April, 1899

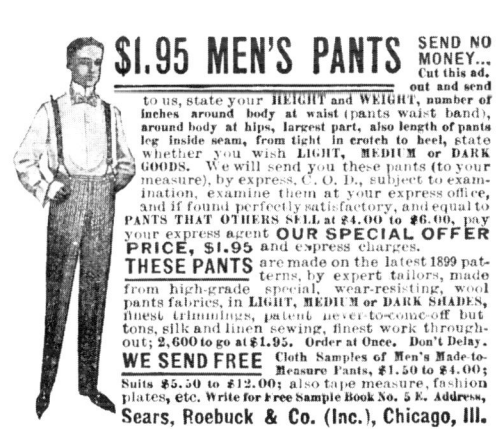

Munsey's, March, 1800

SOME SEARS, ROEBUCK AND COMPANY ADVERTISEMENTS
IN PERIODICALS, 1899–1906

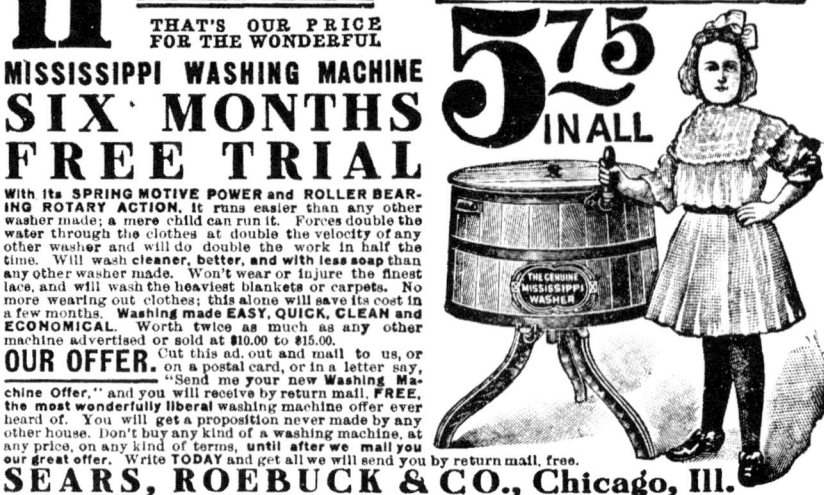

11 Cents a Week OR 48 Cents a Month
FOR ONE YEAR   FOR 12 MONTHS

5.75 IN ALL

THAT'S OUR PRICE FOR THE WONDERFUL

MISSISSIPPI WASHING MACHINE
SIX MONTHS FREE TRIAL

With its **SPRING MOTIVE POWER** and **ROLLER BEARING ROTARY ACTION**, it runs easier than any other washer made; a mere child can run it. Forces double the water through the clothes at double the velocity of any other washer and will do double the work in half the time. Will wash **cleaner, better, and with less soap** than any other washer made. Won't wear or injure the finest lace, and will wash the heaviest blankets or carpets. No more wearing out clothes; this alone will save its cost in a few months. **Washing made EASY, QUICK, CLEAN and ECONOMICAL.** Worth twice as much as any other machine advertised or sold at $10.00 to $15.00.

OUR OFFER. Cut this ad. out and mail to us, or on a postal card, or in a letter say, "Send me your new Washing Machine Offer," and you will receive by return mail, **FREE**, the most wonderfully liberal washing machine offer ever heard of. You will get a proposition never made by any other house. Don't buy any kind of a washing machine, at any price, on any kind of terms, **until after we mail you** our great offer. Write **TODAY** and get all we will send you by return mail, free.

SEARS, ROEBUCK & CO., Chicago, Ill.

Woman's Magazine, February, 1906

$19.90 — CREAM SEPARATOR.

For $19.90 we sell this high grade Dundee Cream Separator; capacity, 175 pounds per hour. Guaranteed the equal of cream separators offered by others at $40.00. Our Economy Cream Separator, guaranteed the very best cream separator made in the world is sold by us at one-third the price asked for any other high grade machine, and on it **we make A WONDERFUL FREE OFFER.** We will place the Economy in your home for a sixty-day free trial and test, and if you don't find it the closest skimming, easiest running, easiest cleaning, greatest capacity separator, in every way the very best separator made, the trial won't cost you one cent. This great free trial offer is shown in our Free Cream Separator Catalogue. Write us a letter or a postal today and say, "Send me your **Free Cream Separator Catalogue**," and the complete book, showing large illustrations and descriptions of our entire line of cream separators, our astonishingly low prices, our sixty days' free trial offer, liberal terms of payment, our $1,000.00 challenge to all other separator manufacturers, wonderful information on the advantages of a cream separator, everything will go to you by return mail, free and postpaid. You will also get our MARVELOUS OFFER of **THIS COUCH FREE.** If you buy from us you can get this full size 6-foot upholstered couch free, or your choice of hundreds of other valuable articles. Write now, sure, and get all our wonderful cream separator offers, prices, information, and this big free couch offer, the greatest propositions ever heard of. Address,

SEARS, ROEBUCK & CO., CHICAGO.

Woman's Magazine, April, 1906

SOME SEARS, ROEBUCK AND COMPANY ADVERTISEMENTS IN PERIODICALS, 1899–1906

homes they constituted the principal reading matter and, in the absence of livelier printed attractions, were read from cover to cover. "The advertiser, moreover, could assume that such a paper went mainly into the homes of hardworking, substantial citizens, who spent no money on frivolity or drink, and therefore could afford to buy comforts and luxuries."[4]

In the 1890's Sears became one of the largest buyers of space in the mail-order publications, religious and other. He had no set advertising budget; he simply bought space wherever and whenever he felt it would pay.[5] The sky was the limit as far as his total advertising expense was concerned, but with each publication he drove a hard bargain. He usually demanded a rate of one-quarter of a cent per agate line per 1,000 of circulation,[6] and by contracting for huge amounts of space he sometimes bought space for as little as a tenth of a cent per agate line per 1,000 of circulation. The publishers met the objections of their other clients by offering the same rates to anyone else who would contract for equal amounts of space. There were no takers. By the mid-nineties many such magazines were carrying as much as three pages of Sears, Roebuck advertising in each monthly issue, broken up between full page spreads and smaller amounts of space scattered throughout the publication. The name of the firm was fast becoming a byword in rural homes throughout the country.

The *Mail Order Journal*, published in Chicago, reported in January, 1901: "Sears, Roebuck and Company of Chicago are at present the largest mail order advertisers.... the January issue of *Comfort* contained 70 different ads of Sears, Roebuck and Company. More than 75% of the ads were therefore from Sears, Roebuck and Company.... In other mail order publications, Sears, Roebuck and Company are using even larger space."

Sears, Roebuck was represented in the February, 1901, issue of *Comfort* by sixty-seven ads. Of the two other merchandise advertisements in that issue, one was a prosaic statement by Montgomery Ward: "The Catalogue and Buyer's Guide for fall and winter will be sent on receipt of 15 cents to pay half postage." Sears's sixty-seventh ad, on the contrary, not only asked fifteen cents for his catalogue but also told the reader of the one thousand pages of illustrations in that book and of the volume of business done by the company and reprinted testimonials to the firm from five publications and one individual.[7] And in one issue of the *Home Monthly* the company had twenty-five double-page and single-column advertisements.[8]

It was in this period that Sears utilized another device for building confidence. Near the bottom of his ads he would insert a line reading: "Sears, Roebuck and Company are thoroughly reliable.—*Editor*." This line would be embellished in some of Sears's ads by such variations as "SEARS, ROEBUCK & CO. are thoroughly reliable and for $19.75 this is surely a wonder Bicycle. —*Editor*" and by such all-out efforts as "TO OUR READERS:—You can save $1.00 to $2.00 by ordering a pair of these shoes and besides get a more stylish shoe than you can likely get in your market at any price, and we would advise you to order at once. Sears, Roebuck & Co. are thoroughly reliable.—*Editor*."[9]

A good sampling of Sears's advertisements is available in, among scores of other magazines, Vickery's *Fireside Visitor* ("Devoted to Literature and the Entertainment of Its Readers") for April 1, 1894. The *Visitor* was a semimonthly published in Augusta, Maine. The back cover of that issue was solidly occupied by a Sears, Roebuck advertisement, featuring illustrations of the company's Minneapolis and Chicago offices and a huge globe encircled with the caption "Cheapest Supply House on Earth—Our Trade Reaches around the World." The text blocks flanking the globe proclaimed the firm's reliability and plugged its "big catalogue of 3000 engravings which we send free to anyone on application. . . . The Grandest Book of Information to BUYERS Ever Printed. IT COSTS NOTHING!"

There followed testimonials to the company from Publisher Vickery ("They give the most value for the money every time"), "a city official," and "a railroad man." That indorsement by the "city official" must have been considered important, for, in addition to his statement near the top of the page that "they give better values for the money than any other concern in the world," the advertisement printed this testimonial in a box in the lower right-hand corner:

> ENDORSEMENT AND ABSOLUTE GUARANTEE
> OF A CITY OFFICIAL!
>
> I, P. W. McAllister, member of the City Council of Minneapolis, Minn., do certify that I am personally acquainted with the firm of Sears, Roebuck & Co., their officers, directors and many of their employees. I take pleasure in recommending them to the entire confidence of the readers of this paper, and further, to make everyone feel absolutely safe, I do hereby personally guarantee every statement made in this advertisement, and will become personally responsible for any failure on their part to carry out any promise to the word and letter.
>
> P. W. McALLISTER, Alderman, 10th Ward

Readers were further invited to "ask any express agent in the U.S. about us, they most all know us and will gladly tell you who we are and what we do." Then came the something-for-nothing offer, the "Hurry-hurry-hurry" of the barker. An illustration of a hand, with finger imperatively outstretched, called attention to the jolting command, "Read This." The "Grand Offer to Readers" went on to offer prizes "to all who send in an order, no matter how small." These premiums ranged from an unspecified "nice present" to a $500 grand piano. Sears believed devoutly in belaboring even the obvious, in emphasis through repetition and paraphrase; the one paragraph offering a present with each order repeated the theme over and over and over.

Ordering was made easy: "Select what you want on this page, cut out the advertisement and send to us. If you send cash in full your present will be sent at once." Then, the preliminaries disposed of, the advertisement proceeded to list twenty-five separate items, with illustrations of each, and glowing messages proclaiming each item to be worth far more than Sears's asking price. And in each separate block there recurred a reminder of the "Grand Prize Offer"; customers were exhorted to rush their orders in to become eligible for the $500 grand piano. Watches were priced from $1.00 to $5.90; revolvers, from $1.68 for Smith and Wesson double-action .32 or .38 caliber. A "$10 baby carriage" was offered at $2.00. The ads contained such phrases as "Costs You Nothing To See and Examine" and variations on the phrase, "$8.95 buys a $15.00 road cart."

The inside back cover and its facing page of this issue of the *Fireside Visitor* were devoted entirely to Publisher Vickery's own offers of premiums to be sent in return for subscriptions obtained to the *Visitor*: harmonicas, ladies' shopping bag, *Leatherstocking Tales* by James Fenimore Cooper, a buttonhole worker, a horseshoe magnet, lace remnants, a "perfect fitting corset," and others. Most of the remainder of the magazine was devoted to other mail-order advertisements—ample evidence that, in addition to Montgomery Ward, Sears, Roebuck had competition, even if on a small scale. These ads offered a remedy for sexual weakness in males, cures for the narcotic and tobacco habits as well as piles, a sure cure for consumption and another for indigestion, literature (*Indian Horrors: Or Massacres by the Red Men, A Sin and Its Punishment, How Could He Help It, A Possible Tragedy, He Loved and Rode Away, Lucy's Lovers, A Woman's Plot*, and many others), and a wealth of kindred offerings.

Two conclusions emerge from even a casual glance at this publication, which was a typical one of that period. First, Richard Sears's huckstering was on no lower ethical or aesthetic plane than that of his contemporaries and competitors. Second, he beat them on prices in almost every instance; competing items such as revolvers and sewing machines were priced far higher than Sears's offerings.

As was frequently done, Sears followed up that "Grand Offer" so belabored in the *Fireside Visitor* advertisement with letters to potential customers, possibly directing the communications to those who had at some previous time purchased from the company. Those letters appear to have been imitation handwriting, of a high order, for the salutation, "Kind Friend," is not one Richard Sears would normally have used if he could have employed the prospect's name. The letter which follows was datelined Chicago, May 29, 1894, although the letterhead shows both the Chicago and the Minneapolis offices:

We believe if we can induce you to read this circular you will favor us with an order at once. True, you may not get the $500.00 piano or even a $50.00 gold watch, yet considering the small number of these offers we are sending out, you ought at least be in time for a gold watch if you answer at once. But, in case you do not get the piano, or a watch, you are sure to get some nice present. And the shoes we send you at $2.75 are worth nearly three times the price asked. If you will fill out the enclosed order blank and send to us at once, with $2.75, for a pair of shoes described, we will see that you get a nice present, and, if first, the piano; if not first of all, but first from your state, a $50.00 gold watch. As an *extra inducement,* if your order is received any time within 30 days, we will see that you get an extra nice present. But please answer at once and try to be first.

Vickery and Hill had several other magazines in this field, all similar to the *Fireside Visitor: Good Stories, Happy Hours, Hearth and Home,* and the *American Woman.* Vickery had a total circulation for its five magazines of around 2,500,000 a year.[10] There were other chains—Comfort, Ellis, Lane, and more—as well as specialized journals of religious, fraternal, agricultural, and trade-union nature. In addition, there were the regular periodicals, for example, *Harper's Weekly, Cosmopolitan,* and *Youth's Companion.* Sears advertised in nearly all of them at one time or another. He reputedly became the first man to use a full-page advertisement to feature a single item and soon became one of the largest advertisers in America.[11]

That was high station for a man who knew nothing of formalized advertising procedure. He violated every rule in the books. He never "lightened up" his copy with white space; he crammed every inch with tightly packed agate type, and he mortised in his illustrations to conserve every drop of space. He determined to counterbalance his lack of technical knowledge by writing messages so compelling that farmers would read through to the last line—and apparently they did. While professional advertising men would now stand aghast at the jolting, uncouth nature of Sears's ads, Sears himself basked in the reflection of the golden harvest of orders he was reaping.

Those orders increased in numbers almost every month and every year. Some of the more spectacular promotions brought in an unmanageable flood of orders for which the company was never quite prepared and with which it could not easily cope. That was Richard Sears's answer to every criticism of his advertising methods. Others had the techniques; he got the business.

Almost all his advertisements stood on the first draft; editing was slight indeed. He thought out every piece of copy thoroughly before he put a line on paper. And after the ads were in print, he held his own post mortems on them to discover how they could be improved.[12]

The emotional satisfaction of seeing orders pour in was at least as important to R. W. Sears as the money he was making. Even when business boomed so that all orders under $2.00 were returned to customers so the firm could concentrate on large and more profitable orders;[13] even when Rosenwald and others pleaded with him to hold his fire until the business could be stabilized; even when orders were so profuse that buyers were rushing out to secure whatever goods they could to meet the insatiable demand; even when all these things happened, Sears refused to retrench.[14]

And Asher tells of the time (apparently late in 1897 or early in 1898)

Sears's great sewing-machine promotion brought orders in such volume that the source of supply fell three weeks behind. Rosenwald and others sought to cancel or postpone a three-month advertising campaign on sewing machines worked out by Sears. Sears refused to hold his fire, insisting that delays were of no real consequence, since his rural customers would finally be so pleased with their sewing machines that they would forgive the delay. The advertisements ran, and supply lagged farther behind demand, but orders continued to pour in.[15] Sears was determined to keep that hot fire under the mail-order pot to maintain a bubbling caldron. He was convinced that to stand still, even for a moment, was to go backward; to him a lull was a retreat, and he believed devoutly in the attack.

A good analysis of the fundamentals of Sears, Roebuck's advertising is contained in a talk by Louis Asher to the company's correspondents, reprinted in a magazine called *White's Class Advertising*, in Chicago in January, 1905. Asher's points seem relevant to this whole general period:

> Our advertising problem has always been and is today simply the problem of getting to our customers and into the hands of the people at large in the country our descriptions and prices; to put before them in the plainest, easiest understood, and most matter of fact way the merchandise we have to offer, and the prices and terms at which we offer it, to enable them to order as easily as possible and to do business with us in the easiest manner. . . . Advertising to most people represents "Uneeda Biscuit," "Say Zu-Zu to the grocery man," or "See that Hump?" and this is advertising of one class, but a class with which we have simply nothing to do, not so much from choice as from necessity. Our advertising is another class, an entirely different proposition, a simple proposition, the simplest and plainest in the world, and that is to get our announcements regarding merchandise read by the people, to put into their hands our catalogues and price lists, to study our ways and means by which we can make it easiest for the farmer, the laborer, or mechanic to buy his goods from us, save money and feel that the transaction has been satisfactory, so that the second order comes to us too.
>
> We are a supply house. We deal in necessities. Our constant effort is to furnish these necessities at the lowest possible prices, so that the farmer at a distance can get his goods from us, and get a selection from the proper variety, and the right quality he deserves, and save money through the transaction. . . . our advertising is devoid of any fancy frills and is the simple proposition of getting up material so the people can order. . . .
>
> Even in our newspaper advertising where a circus stunt would be possible, if such is permissible anywhere, we hold close to the same policy. It is an announcement of this stove for so much money; this sewing machine for $——; an illustration of the article, the description and the price as plain as the English language will allow us to make it. Of course we try to get attention. . . . every advertiser must do his best to have his announcement attract attention, and we have found again that the best method of getting this attention is to name the article and the price which the advertisement refers to, to tell the story simply and directly. That is to say, the price is usually so low that the price in connection with the illustration arrests and commands attention from any one at all interested. . . .
>
> For Sears, Roebuck & Co. there is not much selling power in a joke in one of

our newspaper announcements at say $6.00 a line, or it may be a $300 joke. It does not help much to say something witty to Mr. Serious-Minded Farmer, or Sober Mechanic, who only wants to buy his clothing at the lowest prices, or save money on the next month's supply of groceries. . . . When space in our catalogue costs us $1000 per page for a season it behooves us strongly to use that page every inch and line and hair's breadth to the illustrating and describing plainly and clearly the merchandise we have to sell and crowd on the page as much as we can to do it justice.

Sears's passion for the attack led in 1895 to the great promotion of men's suits. It seemed great at the time, and—for the time—it was. Sears advertised men's suits at $4.98, C.O.D., with no deposit required. The copy surrounding the illustration was captioned, "COSTS NOTHING—to see and examine," and asserted that the company would sell two thousand of "these regular $10.00 suits at $4.98, made from FINE BLACK OR DARK BLUE OR LIGHT CHECKED WOOL SERGE CHEVIOT, heavyweight, nice soft finish, fast color, will wear like iron. . . . STYLE very latest, a neat dressy suit." The advertisement gave instructions on how to measure one's self and went on to offer a thousand "$20.00 suits" at $8.90 ("made for fine city trade"), samples of cloth free, and a silk handkerchief as a gift when cash in full accompanied the order.

Another ad asserted, "We are the largest handlers of Clothing in America." That was certainly drawing the long bow, but the claim was quickly to become much less fantastic, for the response to the offer was literally overwhelming. Clerks staggered under the mass of orders which came in. The shipping department found it impossible even to try to fill the orders with any great degree of accuracy; colors and sizes were hopelessly jumbled and haphazardly shipped. This, of course, led many customers to return the goods in high dudgeon. Buyers scoured the market to obtain suits to fill the orders, but they met with limited success, even though they bought out most of the stock of Rosenwald and Weil and Rosenwald and Company in Chicago.[16]

Richard Sears loved every minute of it. The orders lying in vast confusion were mute testimony to the power of his advertising, even though, in Roebuck's words, "the policy of shipping men's clothing for examination C.O.D. without any deposit came near destroying the business because of the large number of returns. This was largely because of lack of care in fitting, although there were some other important features responsible for it."[17]

By 1897 the company had built up a respectable trade in sewing machines, one of the items in greatest demand throughout the country and especially in the rural areas which were the company's bailiwick. Sears's machines were priced at $15.55, $16.55, and $17.55; the company was not without competition on this line, but it is difficult to establish the exact nature of that competition. Louis Asher, given to occasional generalizations, asserts that such leading machines as the Singer, the Domestic, and

"OUR $4.98 LEADER" FROM THE 1895 CATALOGUE

$24.⁹⁵ BUYS THE ECONOMY
THE BEST CREAM SEPARATOR MADE IN THE WORLD.

$24.95 BUYS THE IMPROVED ECONOMY CREAM SEPARATOR, the machine exactly as illustrated and described, with a capacity of 250 to 300 pounds or 120 to 140 quarts per hour. Suitable for a dairy of three to eight cows, and guaranteed to be a better separator in every way than has heretofore been sold exclusively through agents and dealers at $70.00 to $75.00.

At $24.95 to $33.95, according to capacity, we offer the genuine Improved Economy Cream Separators as the very best and highest grade and most improved cream separators on the market. Guaranteed the closest skimming, the easiest running, strongest, most convenient, easiest cleaned, and most satisfactory hand cream separators manufactured today, the superior of any separator on the market, regardless of name, make or price. **We are proud of our Improved Economy Cream Separator, and we have a right to be.**

It is today the ideal farm cream separator and a real marvel of simplicity and effectiveness. It is the result of many years of continual and exhaustive experimenting by a practical man who has been directly connected with the centrifugal cream separator business since its infancy and whose sole aim in life has been to produce a cream separator so simple that any farmer's boy could run it; so durable that if given the ordinary care required by any piece of machinery there could be no wear out to it; so effective that it would get all the cream from the milk in any form, thick or thin, for its owner with the smallest possible effort under all dairying conditions. The Improved Economy is the closest skimmer in the world, under all conditions, and we can prove it. There is no other just as good.

HERE ARE PLAIN SEPARATOR FACTS

PROVEN BY COUNTLESS TEST under all conceivable conditions: Of the dozen or fifteen different makes of separators sold in the United States, there are six or seven that do fairly good work at a temperature of 75 degrees or over. Of these there are four that will skim approximately as close as the IMPROVED ECONOMY, that is to say, will leave in the neighborhood of one one-hundredth of one per cent of butter fat in the skim milk under favorable conditions and at a temperature of 75 or 90 degrees Fahrenheit. Below a temperature of 75 degrees we part company; at 70 degrees there are but two other machines that will do work that even approaches that of the ECONOMY; at 60 degrees but one, and

AT 50 DEGREES WE STAND ALONE

The next best machine (one of the oldest and most widely sold) will on an average of a series of tests leave not less than three times the butter fat in the skim milk that the ECONOMY will at 50 degrees temperature. Skimming at temperatures of 50, 60, 70, 80 and 90 degrees, the next best machine will lose an average of twice the butter fat that is lost with the Improved Economy. The other machines lose from three to ten times as much

WE WILL GIVE...... $1,000.00 IN GOLD

to the separator manufacturer who can produce a machine that will outskim the Improved Economy at temperatures of 50, 60, 70, 80 and 90 degrees. We make this offer to the makers of the De Laval, the Sharples, the Empire, the United States and every other machine sold in the United States. We have tested them all and we know what we are talking about.

THE IMPROVED ECONOMY RANKS FIRST. THE BEST OF THE OTHERS IS A POOR SECOND.

There is no guess work about this. These are plain, proven facts. If they were not, we could not afford to make the offer that appears above.

$100.00 IN GOLD TO ANY SEPARATOR AGENT

who can outskim the Improved Economy with any other machine made by any other maker at 50, 60, 70, 80 and 90 degrees. We make this offer to all agents regardless of the machine they sell. If you are a separator agent and think the machine you sell will outskim the Economy, come to Chicago and try it. If you succeed we will give you $100.00 in gold. If you fail you lose nothing but your traveling expenses and time.

OUR GREAT SIXTY-DAY FREE TRIAL OFFER.

AS A GUARANTEE that the Improved Economy is the best and most satisfactory separator on the market today, as a proof of the truth of every claim we make we accept your order for a separator on these plain, simple terms, and with the understanding and agreement: You are to have 60 days trial on the Improved Economy Separator. Sixty days to set it up and test it on your own farm. Compare it with the best high priced separator that is offered you. We are perfectly willing that the expert agent run the other machine and you run the Economy, which you can easily do by following the simple directions send with each machine. If the Economy does not run easier, skim closer, skim colder milk and skim a heavier cream than the best machine in the hands of the expert; if the Improved Economy is not much the easiest to handle, to clean and care for, if the Improved Economy, after 60 days' use on your own farm, does not satisfy you that it is the best machine you ever saw or heard of and the one machine you would care to use, you are at perfect liberty to box it up and return it to us and we will promptly return all the money you have paid, including freight charges both ways.

THE IMPROVED ECONOMY CREAM SEPARATOR PRICE LIST.

No. 23F9173	Capacity, 250 to 300 pounds of milk per hour.	Shipping weight, 180 pounds.	Price, $24.95
No. 23F9174	Capacity, 350 to 400 pounds of milk per hour.	Shipping weight, 190 pounds.	Price, 29.95
No. 23F9176	Capacity, 750 pounds of milk per hour.	Shipping weight, 250 pounds.	Price, 33.95

CATALOGUE COPY ON THE "ECONOMY" SEPARATOR, FALL, 1906

the Wheeler and Wilson, all sold through agents on time payments, were priced at from $75 to $125.[18] Frank and Werner settle upon lower figures, declaring that most other firms were selling sewing machines for $35 to $55 and up (which would still have left Sears, Roebuck's prices considerably lower).[19]

Roebuck, however, advances what may have been a more cogent reason for the company to reduce its already low prices on sewing machines. He indicates that, while Sears, Roebuck may indeed have been underselling such standard makes as Singer and others, the company's more immediate competition had brought prices on nonstandard makes, such as Sears itself was selling, in line with Sears's:

> Even though there was a wide difference between our selling prices on the other mail order specialties and the standard prices on those commodities, especially sewing machines, a large number of competitors had come into the business the prices of all of which, including the oldest house in the general mail order business [obviously Montgomery Ward] were approximately the same [as Sears, Roebuck's]. The prices of non-standard sewing machines had become well known. . . .[20]

The company's price differential in relation to standard makes of sewing machines and its generally demonstrated ability to meet its competition were bringing in a pleasing enough number of orders on this line, and it seemed unlikely that any additional price reduction would bring orders in a volume sufficient to justify promotion costs. Nevertheless, says Roebuck,

> many times during 1894 and the early part of 1895 Mr. Sears and I discussed what the possibilities might be if there was a radical cut made in the sale prices. The possibility, however, of doing this successfully depended entirely upon the volume of business that might be obtained in excess of what we were already receiving. Our margin of net profit at that time would not permit a radical reduction, and such reduction would be practical only in case the volume of business could be very largely increased.[21]

In the two years since 1895 Richard Sears had accumulated additional experience in increasing volume through reducing prices, and in 1897 the company's top management felt the occasion was auspicious for a huge promotion effort to capture a larger portion of the sewing-machine market. Accordingly, in September of that year, the company slashed the price of the $16.55 machine to $13.50.

Orders deluged the company; thousands poured in within a month. Sears was intoxicated. He persuaded the manufacturer to lower his price to the company by one dollar per machine, down to $9.50. Then Sears, Roebuck likewise dropped its price—to $12.50. In October 19,000 orders made their way to the company; even after cost of advertising and order-handling this represented a profit of $19,000.[22] The master-promoter continued to advertise the great bargain throughout the land, and the public continued to buy the "Minnesota" five-drawer, drop-leaf model.

Roebuck appends an interesting footnote on the competitive effects of the company's sewing-machine promotion:

When the special price reduction campaign of Sears, Roebuck & Company was well under way, it resulted, as you will remember, in some of the formerly very successful mail order specialty houses, one of which was the Cash Buyers Union, having to eventually try a general line of merchandise, and finally go out of business.[23]

Sears maintained a steady barrage until he had so nearly saturated the market that the cost of obtaining orders through mediums other than the catalogue, which would "produce" an order for about 38 cents, became prohibitive. Louis Asher declared that from full-page advertisements in mail-order publications such as those of Vickery and Hill the company secured sewing-machine orders at a cost of 25 cents per order in the first burst of advertising on this promotion. But, he adds, the company spread its story so rapidly and "burnt over the field" so well that within two years most of the harvest had been reaped, and the cost of obtaining an order for a sewing machine through a mail-order magazine rose greatly. The cost made use of the catalogue preferable to external publications in selling sewing machines.[24]

A record of sewing-machine advertisements in thirty-odd magazines in August, September, and October of 1900 reveals that the cost of obtaining an order through this medium was far higher than the cost of obtaining one through the catalogue, if Asher's figure of 38 cents is correct for the latter. The record also reveals wide disparity in the costs of securing orders through magazines. An advertisement in the Kansas City *Journal* for the $12.75 "Edgemere" model sewing machine brought 102 orders at a cost of 33⅓ cents each. But an insertion in the *National Tribune* yielded only 33 orders, at an average cost of $4.04. Most of the magazines, however, showed an average advertising cost of less than $1.00 per sewing-machine order, an apparently satisfactory ratio. It is probable that advertising in the *National Tribune,* and in two other publications in which it cost from $2.00 to $3.00 to obtain an order, was quickly discontinued on this line.

Even after some of the bloom had faded from sewing-machine promotion after the turn of the century, Sears continued to exploit this item in the form of "inquiry-getters." He would advertise a sewing machine at a ridiculously low price but would give few details and no instructions on how to order; instead, he urged the reader to write for the special catalogue listing all the firm's sewing machines. True enough, that booklet would contain the inexpensive machine featured in the advertisements; but the emphasis was on "trading up" to higher-priced models, whose virtues were described in minute and glowing detail.[25]

"Inquiry-getters" were still being utilized in Sears, Roebuck advertising as late as 1905. Company records on a great deal of this type of advertising from 1902 on reveal both that a large number of magazines were being employed for this purpose and that there was as wide a disparity among them in the costs of securing inquiries as shown earlier for the costs of securing actual orders. An advertisement in *Homefolks* in December, 1902, brought twenty-five inquiries at an average cost of 44 cents; at the other extreme, the five inquiries obtained through *Harper's Bazaar* cost $6.34 each.

In October, 1904, advertisements on a $5.00 sewing machine appeared in sixteen monthly publications and forty weeklies and semiweeklies. The latter group, weeklies and semiweeklies, provided the greatest disparity: 6 cents per inquiry through the Atlanta *Semi-weekly Journal*, $12.58 in the New York *Tribune Farmer*. The monthlies as a whole showed a lower average cost and brought a proportionately greater number of inquiries.

The same kind of an advertisement, appearing in January, 1905, in fifty-four monthlies and ten weeklies and semiweeklies, brought several thousand inquiries, the majority of them for less than fifty cents each and most of the remainder for less than a dollar. By about this time the cost of obtaining inquiries, which was merely the first step in securing an order, had increased enough that the company ceased to utilize external advertising to any great extent for this purpose.

An illustration of Richard Sears's approach to advertising and selling is recounted by a former catalogue editor from one of his own experiences:

> As a young man whose training was based on a firm belief that "Honesty is the best policy," the Sears style of advertising struck me as being very misleading, and I determined to make bold some day to have a talk with him about it. One day I saw one of his ads soliciting requests for our stove catalogue. He used an illustration of one of our best cooking ranges; superimposed over the illustration, he had a display price of $4.38, with the main stem of the figure four extended down over the stove illustration to almost the full length of the ad. The copy started out something like this: "Why stoves can be sold for ridiculously low prices, Why we can undersell all others in stoves." Then there followed several other "why" phrases, and finally he said, "Is all told in our new 100-page stove catalogue." He then made a bid for their request for the catalogue which was "FREE" for the asking. The language of the ad throughout was glowing and exaggerated. I took the ad into Sears's office and asked him if it would not be better to tone down the statements in our ads to avoid overselling our customers. I figured they would be sure in many cases to believe they had been duped. Sears received me graciously, saying he was glad to tell me of the plan behind his style of copy.
>
> "Now," he said, "who would answer that ad?"
>
> I said it would be someone who wanted a stove.
>
> "Right," said he. "A man who wanted a saddle wouldn't answer the ad, would he?" I agreed.
>
> Then he argued that he made the language strong purposely because he wanted to get every living soul who had the faintest notion of buying a stove wrought up sufficiently to write for his catalogue. He said that just because of the big statements he made he was getting a tremendous response and that, when the prospects received the catalogue, they would find that we really were selling stoves below all competition, and they would forget all about the strong language

of the ad and the apparent deception of putting the $4.38 price over the illustration of a stove that sold for several times the price displayed. Of course there had been no statement in the ad that that particular stove sold for $4.38. It could only be inferred from the way the price was connected with the stove illustration. He then went on to say that if he wrote his ads as I suggested without using the exaggerated style, he would not get more than 10 per cent of the requests he was getting and consequently would not have the opportunity to get the catalogue into the hands of such a great number of prospects, and our sales would be far below what they are. Knowing that we were selling an enormous number of stoves at that time, my protest fell flat.

Sears's ability to foresee a great market in a product already developed, and his flair for moving in and capturing a large segment of that market, were well illustrated in his bicycle promotion. Bicycles were in at least as great demand as sewing machines in the nineties; their popularity was almost unbelievable. Schlesinger asserts:

The introduction in 1884 of the "safety" bicycle—possessing two medium-sized wheels of equal height—and the later substitution of pneumatic tires for solid rubber ones produced a cycling craze that ramified to every part of the nation. By 1893 a million bicycles were in use.... For untold thousands cycling renewed the forgotten pleasures of open road and countryside.... "It is safe to say," declared an expert of the Census Bureau in 1900, "that few articles ever used by man have created so great a revolution in social conditions as the bicycle."[26]

Sears visualized this situation as a great bonanza and moved in accordingly with his now customary technique of contracting for huge volume, slashing the price, and advertising profusely. His success was indicated by an article in a magazine called the *American Woman*, which editorialized thus in its April, 1898, issue, under the caption, "Big Drop in Bicycles":

Last year retailers succeeded in reducing the price of all $100 bicycles to $75, and then they held the trade at home; but what are they going to do now when a new 1898 bicycle is offered at only $5.00, on easy conditions?—other latest models outright at $13.95 and $19.75, on free trial. It appears the monopoly on the finest grade seamless bicycle tubing has been broken, and where the best tubing alone for a bicycle formerly cost about $18 it is now reduced to less than $4, and SEARS, ROEBUCK & CO., of Chicago, at these special prices, are waging war on all bicycle dealers. They send a Bicycle Catalogue free to anyone who asks for it, and, we are told, shipping several hundred bicycles every day to every state, direct to the riders at $5 to $19.75, on free trial before paying. If SEARS, ROEBUCK & CO. continue to wage their bicycle war throughout the season it will be a boon to all those who want bicycles, but a sad blow to bicycle dealers and manufacturers.

That same issue of the *American Woman* carried a large advertisement for Sears's bicycles ("Only One Dollar Down"), but none was shown at the price of $5.00 mentioned in the editorial; the cheapest referred to in the advertisement was $13.95. The copy chronicled in detail the superlative features of every part of the bicycles. A smaller item tucked away elsewhere—it is impossible to determine whether it was an advertisement or an editorial—does state that "bicycles are now being sold on easy conditions as low as $5.00." This figure apparently represented only the down payment. That issue also contained an editorial entitled "Farmers Break the Buggy Monopoly":

It is claimed that for years buggy manufacturers have secured exorbitant prices for their goods, but recently, through the combined assistance of the farmers of Iowa, Illinois, and other states, SEARS, ROEBUCK & CO., of Chicago, have got the price of open buggies down to $16.50.... and they are shipping them in immense numbers direct to farmers in every state.... This certainly is a big victory for the farmer, but a severe blow to the carriage manufacturers and dealers.

It is almost impossible not to discern Sears's own hand in these two editorials. Whether he wrote them himself and either placed them in bought space or cajoled the editor into using them, no one can tell now. But the victory for the consumer which each of them hails, and the blow to the manufacturers and dealers, is straight out of Sears's own soft-soap department. The purposeful confusion of advertising and editorial matter in "reading notices" was not at all uncommon even in the religious papers.[27]

Sears continued to "wage war" on bicycle manufacturers and retailers. In one year he sold 100,000 bicycles.[28] One of his devices in the campaign was the use of circulars containing catalogue proofs of the bicycle ad with a blank panel in the corner of the circular. He sent these out to names on his mailing list, with the information that for two dollars the addressee could purchase 1,000 of the circulars, with a rubber stamp for imprinting the addressee's name in the blank panel. He exhorted the addressee to distribute the circulars broadcast, after stamping his own name thereon. The circular was so phrased that it could be sent in as an order; when ten such orders were received bearing the stamp of any one addressee, he received a bicycle free. The circulars cost Sears about seventy cents per thousand to print, and he kept the presses rolling on them for weeks, around the clock. His real profits came, of course, from selling the bicycles, not the circulars. This promotion stunt reputedly brought in around half a million dollars' worth of business.

Another bicycle-promotion effort tried about the same time was, however, considerably less successful. A free-lance advertising agent named Harry Arney approached Sears with a scheme for advertising in weekly newspapers. Arney, on his own, had obtained signed contracts from some two thousand papers, each agreeing to furnish him 416 inches of advertising space in return for a bicycle. The space was to be utilized within a year's time; the bicycle was to be shipped to the paper after the first advertisement had appeared. When Arney's verbal agreement with another advertiser fell through, Sears accepted the arrangement, being in a position to supply the bicycles at small expense.[29]

Using Arney's letterheads, Sears, Roebuck sent out the advertising orders and electros, and, after receiving tear sheets showing insertion of the initial ad, shipped the bicycles. According to Asher, it promised to be a happy arrangement; the company would obtain an average of about eight inches of space a week for one year in the two thousand papers at a small cost. As a matter of fact, Sears was so impressed with the possibilities that, even before any returns were in, he began to cast about for another item to use in a similar arrangement. He decided tentatively upon typewriters. But it soon became clear that the Arney promotion scheme was hardly bringing in enough orders to cover the cost of the electros and the express charges. Sears carried out his part of the contract, but quickly ceased even to check the papers. There may have been some salvage value in Asher's discovery that some of the weeklies continued to run the ads long after expiration of the contract.

Sears's heavy advertising of bicycles must have been a not inconsiderable factor in influencing Presbrey's estimate that in 1898 advertising of that one line made up 10 per cent of all national advertising.[30] In fact, says Presbrey,

to the bicycle manufacturers of the 1880's and '90's advertising owes that which all owe a trail-blazing pioneer. Especially is the development of magazine advertising indebted to the bicycle, for the bicycle gave the magazine a measure of recognition as a medium which encouraged the use of large space and more frequent insertions by advertisers in general. . . . Twelve pages of bicycle copy in a magazine with sixty pages for all other classes of advertising combined was a common proportion in the middle 1890's.

It was bicycle manufacturers who first proved that an article of luxury costing $100 could be sold to the mass.[31]

Richard Sears may not have been the first to prove that that article could be sold for far less than $100, but it is clear from the foregoing that his determination to sell bicycles to America was in line with the objectives of many other advertisers of the period.

Early in 1897 the company unearthed a new stratagem for promoting men's suits. Circulars were distributed promoting four different men's suits featured in the spring catalogue for that year and ranging in price from $11.95 to $14.95. Accompanying the circular was a "credit voucher" good for $6.00 on the purchase of any of the four suits featured; the voucher also urged readers to send for the big catalogue, remitting 15 cents to help cover postage, and for the free clothing catalogue. The business was so large on this one effort that it was necessary to put on a night force in an attempt to fill the orders.[32]

Around 1898 the great electric-belt promotion was launched. In its basic nature, this sort of item was far dearer to Richard Sears's heart than an item so prosaic as a sewing machine. The public had long demonstrated its deep and abiding faith in nostrums of all sorts, even for the most improbable.[33] Patent medicines and drugs, while not a huge volume line, had shown a very high profit to Sears, Roebuck. Nostrums guaranteed to cure what ailed one were naturals for Sears's particular genre of exaggerated claims, enthusiastic descriptions, and sky-high promotions. Sears pulled the switch and loosed the full voltage of his advertising activities behind the belt. Catalogue illustrations showed the gleaming belts, in several price ranges, glittering with electric sparks—a relief in every spark, a cure in every volt.

"Heidelberg" alternating-current belts were advertised at $4.00 to $18 with the statement: "We, too, could get $20 to $50 for our belts because we have them in 20- to 80-gauge electric current, the only belt to reach the nerve centers." The belt was particularly recommended for nervous diseases, headaches, and backaches: "Are you tired of drugs? Are you sick, weak and discouraged?" Actually the belt at best merely generated a pleasant tingling sensation; at worst, it might—and sometimes did—short-circuit and cauterize the user.[34]

TABLE 4*

ELECTRIC-BELT SALES, 1901-5

YEAR	GROSS SALES	GROSS PROFIT		NET PROFIT	
		Amount	Per Cent	Amount	Per Cent
1901	$113,190				
1902	111,857	$76,702	68.6	$35,539	31.8
1903	97,704	63,977	65.5	36,501	37.4
1904	74,198	34,043	45.9	21,326	28.7
1905	15,144	†	†	†	†

* Source: Company records. † Discontinued.

But the American public was an unsophisticated group with a reverent respect for the scientific. They knew little about electricity except that it was in some way distantly connected with the name of Benjamin Franklin. After reading one of Sears's advertisements, a farmer might well have wondered how he had ever managed to grow to manhood without the rejuvenating effects of the electric belt. Sales of the belt are said to have brought profits of as much as $1,000 a day at one time.[35] If true, this must have been in the first two or three years of the promotion campaign, since data for later years contained in Table 4, while showing a high net and gross profit, do not indicate any such staggering dollar profits.

Further evidence of the popularity of the electric belt is found in advertisements of that item by "competitors" of Sears, Roebuck. The May 5, 1900, issue of *Leslie's Weekly*, for example, contains ads by a Dr. Sanden of New York City and a Professor A. Chrystal, each touting the electric belt. But they showed no prices, and their illustrations had but a fraction of the sparkle and appeal of Sears, Roebuck's.

Richard Sears never stopped searching for the best possible phrasing in his advertisements, for the "Open, Sesame" which would unlock the country's riches for him. In the full-page advertisement in the 1894 *Fireside Visitor* referred to earlier, there occurred such phrases as "COSTS NOTHING to see and examine this"—with the emphasis on the first two words—and "FREE to see and examine." By 1900 Sears came up with the phrase he had been searching for: "Send No Money." He had what he wanted, and he knew it.

He trumpeted the phrase from coast to coast. He led newspaper and mail-order magazine ads with that terse staccato: "Send No Money." He repeated it incessantly. Sears had discovered how, in the simplest possible way, to get across to the farmer that he could see and touch the goods without risking his money; that Sears, Roebuck and Company of Chicago assumed all responsibility for the merchandise until the customer had seen, handled, discussed, and approved.

"Send No Money" was the alarm in the night. It was C.O.D. at its pinnacle. It was the voice from afar offering special dispensation to the financially hard-pressed, to the unconvinced who hesitated to order even on a C.O.D. basis. The farmer knew now that he had a real friend, a corporation which trusted him all the way.

By 1902 Sears, Roebuck was enjoying a tremendous volume of business, had outdistanced Montgomery Ward, and was generally in a highly favorable position. There was, however, one disquieting note. Between $800,000 and $900,000 worth of refused merchandise had piled up in express stations, all ordered on that blithe confidence engendered by "Send No Money."[36] Drastic action was required to avoid heavy losses. The spring catalogue in 1902 interred Sears's wonderful phrase with one curt sentence: "Our only terms are cash with order."

It is interesting that it should have been the catalogue which ended "Send No Money," without even specifically mentioning that phrase, for the magic phrase never appeared in one of the company's catalogues, as far as can be determined. It was utilized in "external" advertising, and many of the advertisements which were surmounted by the phrase urged the reader to send for the big catalogue. "Send No Money" may thus have been used to a great extent to increase catalogue circulation, but it is noteworthy that some of the "Send No Money" ads did not even refer to the big book.

In 1901 Sears turned his efforts toward stimulating sales in the grocery department. He offered, "free as a present," a thirty-six-piece set of glassware. "Free" was, as so often in Sears's terminology, not strictly accurate; the ad went on to state that if the customer would send in $16.50, he would receive the company's $30.21 set of staple groceries, with the glassware set added gratis. If the customer ordered within fifteen days, he would also be given a free cookbook. Almost every night was "bank night."

In 1902 the catalogue offered special low prices on quantity purchases of drugs and medicines, urging customers to resell at a profit. The company must have concluded that the offer did not justify the space it consumed, for this plan was dropped within two years.

In the spring catalogue for 1901 there was a statement on "Our Banking Department," in which customers were invited to deposit money (not less than $5.00; not more than $1,000).[37] They would be allowed to draw against their deposits for purchases; meanwhile their money would be drawing interest at 5 per cent. Apparently there was some conflict with state banking laws; at any rate, the scheme was discontinued after one year. Sears had found something else which would not work.

The next year, however, saw him recoup with a vengeance in a smashing *coup de théâtre*. While on a hunting trip in North Dakota with Albert Loeb and J. F. Skinner, Sears saw a farmer using a centrifugal cream separator. He pressed the farmer for details. The machine had cost well over a hundred dollars. Sears decided on the spot that the separator could be sold at less than a third of what it had cost the farmer.[38] The hunting trip was forthwith abandoned; Sears had found what he was *always* hunting for, a "sure-fire, lead-pipe cinch" for a promotion campaign. He sought out a manufacturer, finally found one willing to operate his way, and placed a huge order based on anticipated volume sales.[39] Three sizes were to be offered, at three different prices: $27.00, $35.00, and $39.50, to allow Sears to advertise the cheapest one far and wide and to trade up to the most expensive.[40]

The separators went like the proverbial house afire. With other manufacturers selling them at from $60 to $125, Sears had the low-priced field almost to himself.[41] Capturing a considerable segment of the separator market in a short time was no mean feat, for, in the words of one former employee,

previous to that time the cream-separator business was handled entirely by local dealers and agents, who made a practice of installing the separator and teaching its use in much the same way as is done with milking machines today. It was, in fact, generally believed by buyers that this was absolutely necessary. Few understood the theory of centrifugal separation or the reasons for the variations in results obtained from time to time, and the agent was often believed to have an expert inside knowledge beyond the ken of ordinary men. This idea, fostered in many instances by the agents themselves, served to prevent all but the boldest from ordering by mail, even though by doing so they could save the agent's profit and expense.

The Sears, Roebuck catalogue met this competition head-on. The company offered $1,000 in gold to any separator manufacturer who could produce a machine that would outskim Sears's "Economy" separator at temperatures of 50°, 60°, 70°, 80°, and 90°. "We make this offer to the makers of the De Laval, the Sharples, the Empire, the United States and every other machine sold in the United States. . . . The improved Economy ranks first. The best of the others is a poor second." The catalogue then paid its respects to separator agents by offering to pay $100 in gold to any one of them who could outskim the Economy with any other make. The company hammered home the simplicity of its separator and struck at the very base of the agents' appeal: "We are perfectly willing that the expert agent run the other machine and you run the Economy, which you can easily do by following the simple directions we send with each machine." The Economy, even operated by an amateur, was guaranteed to outperform any other make, operated by an "expert agent."

Readers were urged to send for the special cream-separator catalogue, and records kept on the number and cost of inquiries obtained through nearly thirty magazines and newspapers show that the separator was widely advertised in external mediums. The inquiries listed in the records now available were secured at an average cost of from one to two dollars in 1903 and 1904. In view of the greater gross margin carried by the separators, this cost would appear to compare favorably with the cost of securing sewing-machine inquiries.

In 1904 the company initiated a chain of three or four retail food stores in Illinois.[42] Pontiac and Watseka, in the area south of Kankakee, were two of the locations; Joliet, a third, and the fourth was either in Elgin or Rockford.[43] The butter and eggs and similar produce sold by these stores were themselves interestingly come by; the stores accepted such commodities from farmers as payment for goods ordered from the catalogue by the farmers. This opened up two possibilities: first, that people who came to order from the catalogue (there was a catalogue desk in the rear of the store, with someone to help people make out orders) might buy some of the farm produce and other groceries, if they did not themselves bring in such produce to tender as payment; and, second, that people who came simply to buy groceries might also order something from the catalogue. Goods ordered from the catalogue were delivered to the stores, where customers called to pick them up.

As far as volume was concerned, the experiment was highly successful—the stores did the proverbial land-office business. There was, however, no staff with the necessary experience and know-how for such an operation; this resulted in a rather hopeless tangle, as Rosenwald himself discovered when he decided to "ride circuit" and visit the stores. According to Werner, the grocery stores were discontinued because they required special attention and handling which the company was not prepared to devote to them.[44] A Sears, Roebuck old-timer asserts, however, that opposition from independent merchants in the towns had something to do with the decision to close the stores. In any event, the grocery-store venture was short lived. It had never been promoted vigorously, and there is no indication that it represented an effort to launch any large chain of retail stores.

That same year of 1904 saw Sears step into water which in three years' time was to become neck-deep and too hot for comfort. The spring cata-

YOUR SEARS, ROEBUCK & CO.
CERTIFICATES HAVE DOUBLED IN VALUE

6 CHAIRS FREE

6 CHAIRS FREE

For Profit Sharing Certificates Amounting to $50.00.

F. JR. VALUABLE ARTICLES GIVEN FREE FOR $50.00 IN PROFIT SHARING CERTIFICATES.

$50.00 In our Profit Sharing Certificates will now be accepted by us in exchange in full, without further cost, for SIX HANDSOME DINING ROOM CHAIRS, as illustrated, or any of the articles illustrated in this advertisement, or you can now exchange $50.00 in Profit Sharing Certificates for your choice of many other equally valuable articles, shown in our new PROFIT SHARING BOOKLET (mailed free.)

$50.00 IN PROFIT SHARING CERTIFICATES now entitles you to any profit sharing article of merchandise, shown in our catalogues, issued during 1904 or 1905, in which heretofore required $100.00, and which are shown in the Profit Sharing Department of these catalogues at $100.00 each. LOOK AT OUR BIG CATALOGUE. If you haven't one, your neighbor has; borrow it; look at the last 16 pages, see the many articles we formerly furnished for $100.00 in certificates and which are now furnished for $50.00. Stoves, Sewing Machines, Clocks, Watches, Couches, Beds and many other beautiful things in furniture. Every article you see marked for $100.00 in certificates, we will now furnish for $50.00 in certificates.

OUR TOTAL SALES FOR THE YEAR 1905 EXCEED FORTY MILLION DOLLARS ($40,000,000.), and now we give back voluntarily (unsolicited) a big part of all our year's profit by accepting every outstanding profit sharing certificate in full on our new, liberal $50.00 reward basis; vastly more valuable articles throughout.

OUR PRICES ARE LOWER THAN EVER BEFORE,

but little more than one-half the prices charged by retail dealers, very much lower than any other catalogue house. We are now located in our new 40-acre plant, more than three times the room, three times the stock, three times the volume of sales, three times the facilities of any other catalogue house in the United States, therefore, we can give you much lower prices, much better variety, and ship much quicker than any other catalogue house. Big as our profit, for, when all your orders, past and present and future, have amounted to $50.00 or more, you get free such valuable articles as you may choose to select from the Profit Sharing Department in our old catalogues or our new catalogues, or our free Profit Sharing Booklet.

MORE THAN FOUR MILLION PEOPLE have received profit sharing certificates from us in return for goods sent us during the last 18 months. ARE YOU ONE OF THEM? Have you one or more of our profit sharing certificates? If you have, and they amount to $50.00 or more, you can exchange them now, or whenever you like, for many valuable articles. If you have certificates and they amount to less than $50.00, send your orders to us until your total certificates amount to $50.00 or more, and then select the valuable article you want as your share of the profit.

IF YOU HAVEN'T A PROFIT SHARING CERTIFICATE it is because you have not sent us an order in 18 months, in which case start now. Order your goods from us, and every time you send us an order, we will send you a profit sharing certificate for the full amount of your order, and when your profit sharing certificates have amounted to $50.00 or more, you can exchange them for your choice of any number of valuable articles, besides being guaranteed our prices much, very much lower than can be had elsewhere.

ORDER FROM OUR BIG CATALOGUE, No. 114 or No. 115. If you haven't a big catalogue of ours, borrow your neighbor's (you will find our big book in every neighborhood), or, if there is not one handy, on receipt of your request, we will mail our latest big catalogue to you by return mail, postpaid, free. Remember, if you order from a very old catalogue of ours, and the prices have been reduced in our latest catalogue on the goods you order, we will always give you the benefit of the lowest prices and return the difference to you in cash at once.

YOUR CERTIFICATES ARE GOOD.

If you have bought anything from us during the past one and a half years, a profit sharing certificate was sent you for the full amount of every purchase you made. All the profit sharing certificates you have received from us can be used on the $50.00 basis, whereas heretofore $100.00 in certificates was required for any of the valuable articles illustrated in this advertisement, or for your choice of the many valuable articles shown in our new, free, Profit Sharing Booklet, or for any of the articles shown in the Profit Sharing Department, in any of our big catalogues (sent out during 1904–5), which are listed therein for $100.00 in certificates. If you are now holding less than $50.00 in our profit sharing certificates, send us enough more orders to make your profit sharing certificates amount to $50.00, and you can then exchange them for your choice of the many valuable articles we offer.

OUR CUSTOMERS SHARE IN THE PROFITS OF OUR BUSINESS.

Any customer of ours, anyone buying goods from us, shares in our profit by receiving free of any cost any of the valuable articles we give free when your purchases amount to $50.00 or more. Whenever you buy goods from us, we send you a profit sharing certificate showing the full amount of your order, and when your orders have amounted to $50.00 in profit sharing certificates, you can then get your share of the profit immediately. Our profit sharing plan has enabled us to still further reduce our selling prices by reason of the increased sales it has made. You share in our profit and we can guarantee to you a big saving on every order you send us. We guarantee our prices are very much lower than retail prices, much lower than the prices asked by other dealers or catalogue houses, and we will send you the big catalogue free of charge if you haven't one. Look at the big book free; if you haven't one, borrow one from your neighbor, or, if there isn't one of our big catalogues handy in your neighborhood, drop us a postal card or in a letter simply say: "Send me your big catalogue free," and it will go to you by return mail, postpaid, free.

ORDER FROM ONE OF OUR BIG CATALOGUES wherever you may find it, your own, your neighbor's, or one you send for, and when your orders, past and present, have amounted to $50.00 or more in certificates, you can have your choice of any number of valuable articles offered, your own selection. Select from any big catalogue of ours in your neighborhood any article in the Profit Sharing Department that we heretofore gave for $100.00 in certificates, or any of the valuable articles shown in our new, free, Profit Sharing Booklet, which we give for $50.00, send us your certificates, old or new, or any you may get from your neighbors — there are THOUSANDS OF DOLLARS in valuable merchandise — a big share of all our profits — goes back to our customers at once. Nearly double the amount we originally promised.

GET YOUR CERTIFICATES UP TO $50.00 AT ONCE.

Get hold of one of our big books in your neighborhood, and order everything you need from us until your orders have amounted to $50.00 or more; when you will have $50.00 in certificates, then exchange the certificates for your choice of the many valuable profit sharing articles we give.

YOUR SEARS, ROEBUCK & CO.
6 CHAIRS FREE
CERTIFICATES HAVE DOUBLED IN VALUE

P.–H. VALUABLE ARTICLES GIVEN FREE FOR $50.00 IN PROFIT SHARING CERTIFICATES.

6 CHAIRS FREE — For Profit Sharing Certificates Amounting to $50.00.

$50.00

In our Profit Sharing Certificates will now be accepted by us in exchange in full, without further cost, for **SIX HANDSOME DINING ROOM CHAIRS**, as illustrated, or any of the articles illustrated in this advertisement, or you can now exchange $50.00 in Profit Sharing Certificates for your choice of many other equally valuable articles, shown in our new **PROFIT SHARING BOOKLET** (mailed free.)

$50.00 IN PROFIT SHARING CERTIFICATES now entitles you to any profit sharing article of merchandise, shown in our new Profit Sharing Booklet, for which $100 is heretofore required. $100.00, and which are shown in the Profit Sharing Department of these catalogues issued during 1904 or 1905. With the exception of our neighbor to borrow one, your neighbor has; borrow it, look at the late 16 pages, see the many articles we formerly furnished for $100.00 each **LOOK AT OUR BIG CATALOGUE**. If you haven't one, your neighbor has; borrow it, look at the late 16 pages, see the many articles we formerly furnished for $100.00 in certificates and which we now furnish for $50.00, Chairs, Tables, Men's Suits, Couches, Watches, Clocks, Guns, Beds and many other beautiful things in furniture. Every article is marked for $100.00 in certificates, we will now furnish for $50.00 in certificates.

YOUR CERTIFICATES ARE GOOD.

If you have bought anything from us during the past one and a half years, a profit sharing certificate was sent you for the full amount of every purchase you made, and if the profit sharing certificates you are now holding amount to so much as $50.00 you can exchange them now for any of the valuable articles shown in our new, free, Profit Sharing Booklet, or for any of the articles shown in the Profit Sharing Department, in any of our big catalogues (sent out during 1904-5), which are listed therein for $100.00 in certificates. If you are now holding less than $50.00 in our profit sharing certificates, send us enough more orders to make your profit sharing certificates amount to $50.00, and you can then exchange them for your choice of our most valuable articles we offer.

OUR CUSTOMERS SHARE IN THE PROFITS OF OUR BUSINESS.

Any customer or neighbor who buys goods from us amounting to $50.00 or more, will free of any cost, any of the valuable articles we give free when your purchases amount to $50.00 or more. Whenever you buy goods from us, we send you a profit sharing certificate showing the full amount of your order, and when you have received certificates amounting to $50.00 or more, you can get your share of our profit immediately. Our profit sharing plan has enabled us to still further reduce our selling prices. Our prices are very much lower than retail prices, much lower than the prices asked by other dealers or catalogue houses. **If you have never sent us orders**, order goods from us from time to time, as needed, and when your orders have amounted to $50.00 you will then have received a profit sharing certificate for which you can exchange our $50.00 valuable articles. **If you haven't a big catalogue No. 114 or No. 115**, use the big catalogue you have. If you haven't a catalogue handy in your neighborhood, then write for the big book. It is free for the asking. To get it, on a postal card or in a letter simply say: "Send me your big catalogue free," and it will go to you by return mail, postpaid.

ORDER FROM ONE OF OUR BIG CATALOGUES may find it, wherever you your own, your neighbor's, or one you send for, any number of valuable articles, past and future, have amounted to $50.00 or more, you can take your choice of many valuable articles offered, your own taking, Select from any big catalogue of ours, any article you want, or both of them. That is our Profit Sharing Department. We heretofore gave for $100.00 in certificates, or any of the valuable articles shown in our new, free, Profit Sharing Booklet, which we give for $50.00, send us your certificates, old or new, or both—they are all equally good—and the article you select will be sent to you free of any cost. **THOUSANDS OF DOLLARS** in valuable merchandise—a big share of our profits—goes back to our customers at once. Nearly double the amount we originally promised.

OUR TOTAL SALES FOR THE YEAR 1905 EXCEED FORTY MILLION DOLLARS ($40,000,000.),

and now we give back volume of all our year's profit by accepting every outstanding, unsolicited a big part of our new, liberal $50.00 reward basis: vastly more valuable articles throughout.

OUR PRICES ARE LOWER THAN EVER BEFORE,

but little more than one-half the prices charged by retail dealers, very much lower than any other catalogue house. We are now located in our new 40-acre plant, more than three times the room, three times the stock, three times the volume of business, three times the facilities of any other catalogue house in the United States, therefore, we can give you much lower prices, much better variety, and ship much quicker than any other catalogue house in the United States. You get back a big part of all our profit, for when all your orders, past, present and future, have amounted to $50.00 or more, you get free such valuable articles as you may choose to select from the Profit Sharing Department in our old catalogues of our new catalogues, or our free Profit Sharing Booklet.

MORE THAN FOUR MILLION PEOPLE have received profit sharing certificates from us in return for orders sent us during the past 18 months. **ARE YOU ONE OF THEM?** Have you $50.00 or more of our profit sharing certificates? If you have, and they amount to $50.00 or more, send them to us at once, tell us which valuable article you want from our Profit Sharing Booklet, or the articles listed for $100.00 on the profit sharing certificate pages of any of our big catalogues, and the article will be sent to you at once, all charges prepaid, as a free gift from us, as your share of our profit. If you have certificates and they amount to less than $50.00 send your orders to us until your total certificates amount to $50.00 or more, and then select the valuable article you want as your share of the profit.

IF YOU HAVEN'T A PROFIT SHARING CERTIFICATE

it is because you have not sent us an order in 18 months, in which case start now. To get your goods from us, and every time you send us an order, we will send you a profit sharing certificate for the full amount of your order, and when your orders for profit sharing certificates have amounted to $50.00 or more, you can exchange them for your choice of any number of valuable articles, besides, we guarantee all our prices on everything we sell to be very much lower than you can buy elsewhere.

ORDER FROM OUR BIG CATALOGUE, any one you may have, our haven't a big catalogue of ours, borrow your neighbor's (you will find our big book in every neighborhood), or, if there is not one handy in your immediate neighborhood, write for the big book. It will go to you by return mail, postpaid, free. Remember, if you order from a very old catalogue of ours, and the prices have been reduced in our latest issue, you will get the benefit of all reductions, we will write you the benefit of the lowest prices and return the difference to you in cash at once.

GET YOUR CERTIFICATES UP TO $50.00 AT ONCE.

Get hold of one of our big books in your neighborhood, and order everything you need from us, until your orders have amounted to $50.00 or more; when you will have $50.00 in certificates, then exchange the certificates for your choice of the many valuable profit sharing articles we give.

PROFIT SHARING BOOKLET MAILED FREE.

We have just issued a new Special Profit Sharing Booklet, illustrating and describing the many valuable articles which we give in exchange for $50.00, $75.00, $100.00 and upwards of our profit sharing certificates we give in exchange for certificates amounting to $60.00, $75.00, $100.00 and upwards. This new booklet will be sent to any address, by mail, postpaid, on application. Whether you hold certificates of ours or not, if you would like to see our latest and most complete list of articles we give in exchange for profit sharing certificates, just drop us a letter or postal card simply saying "Send me your new Profit Sharing Booklet, postpaid," and the booklet will go to you by return mail, postpaid, free, with our compliments.

OUR BIG, NEW, 1906 1200-PAGE GENERAL CATALOGUE, BOOK NO. 115, FREE FOR THE ASKING.

While our latest big general catalogue will be sent to any address by mail, postpaid, free, on application, and to get it, it is only necessary to put on a postal card or in a letter to say: "Send me your big catalogue," and the big book will go to you by return mail, postpaid, free, with our compliments, as a matter of fact, you have probably received one very recently within the last year, that you use the big book you have for sending us orders, or, if it is convenient for you to use your neighbor's big catalogue use your neighbor's; otherwise write for the latest big book, and it will go to you free. If you have profit sharing certificates amounting to $50.00 or more, we especially urge that you select one of the articles shown in the catalogue you have, which we hereafter furnish for $100.00 in certificates. We will hereafter give you anyone of these articles in exchange for $50.00 in certificates.

AMONG THE MORE VALUABLE ARTICLES

we give a fine UPRIGHT PIANO for certificates amounting to $695.00, a handsome organ for $295.00, a fine top buggy for $490.00, and a great variety of rich furniture, parlor suites, bedroom suites, chairs, couches, commodes, dressers, sideboards, bookcases, richly carved special dining room sets, chiffoniers, wardrobes, etc., for profit sharing certificates amounting to from $50.00 to $100.00 and upwards. By selecting one of the articles shown in this advertisement, or select one of the $100.00 articles shown in our profit Sharing Booklet, and make your selection from our latest book of profit sharing articles.

START YOUR ORDERS TO US AT ONCE.

Do not delay. If you already have a few dollars in our profit sharing certificates, $5.00, $10.00, more or less, get hold of one of our big catalogues in your neighborhood, start your orders to us, your choice of the valuable articles we give in exchange, and entitle you to any of our liberal profit sharing articles, consider the amount of certificates you already have before you buy anything anywhere, either in groceries, clothing, dry goods, hardware, anything that you need in the home, on the farm, in the shop, store or elsewhere. Buy everything of us, let us send you one of our big books, see how much money we can save you (we guarantee to save you a big part of the cost), and then see how quickly your certificates will amount to $50.00 or more, the very soon you will get your share of the profit by selecting the articles you want.

DOUBLING THE VALUE

BY THIS LIBERAL OFFER, OF MOST OF OUR PROFIT SHARING CERTIFICATES, making every outstanding certificate as good as the best, accepting every certificate we have issued in exchange for any article, with any $50.00 or more, we hope, and expect within a very short time, to receive orders from every one in nearly every big catalogue we have sent out during the last twelve or eighteen months. Do not delay to first write for a big catalogue. Dig up your old catalogue. You will find the amount of your neighbor's. We now double the value of your certificates. Remember, if our prices have been reduced, we will return the difference to you at once. Dig up one of our big catalogues, and send us an order and increase the amount of your certificates. We want you to start in the profits of our business. We want your trade, we want it all, but if we cannot, have every dollar of your business, we will be thankful for any that you will send us, and you can now share in our profits in proportion to the amount of your purchases twofold.

A FEW OF THE MANY OTHER VALUABLE ARTICLES WE NOW GIVE FREE IN EXCHANGE FOR $50.00 IN PROFIT SHARING CERTIFICATES, ARTICLES THAT HERETOFORE REQUIRED $100.00 IN CERTIFICATES.

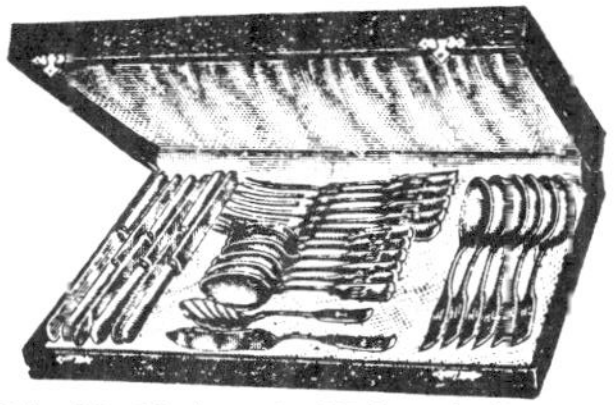

This handsome mantel clock given FREE for $50.00 in profit sharing certificates.

This handsome 12-gauge, automatic shell ejecting breech loading shotgun, given FREE for $50.00 in PROFIT SHARING CERTIFICATES.

This rich, 26-piece set of high grade silverware in a beautiful case, given FREE in exchange for $50.00 in profit sharing certificates.

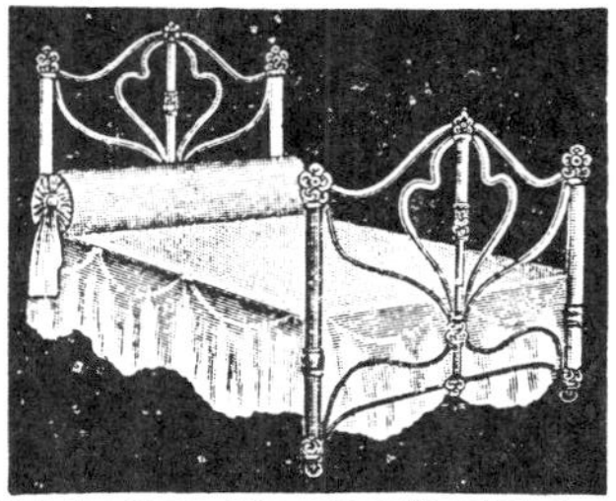

This handsome white enameled iron bed given FREE in exchange for $50.00 in profit sharing certificates.

This handsome overstuffed, full spring, fringe trimmed couch given FREE in exchange for $50.00 in profit sharing certificates.

This large, handsome art square or floor rug given FREE in exchange for $50.00 in profit sharing certificates.

This handsome, overstuffed, big, massive Morris chair given FREE in exchange for $50.00 in profit sharing certificates.

This beautiful solid oak cobbler seat rocker given FREE for $50.00 in profit sharing certificates.

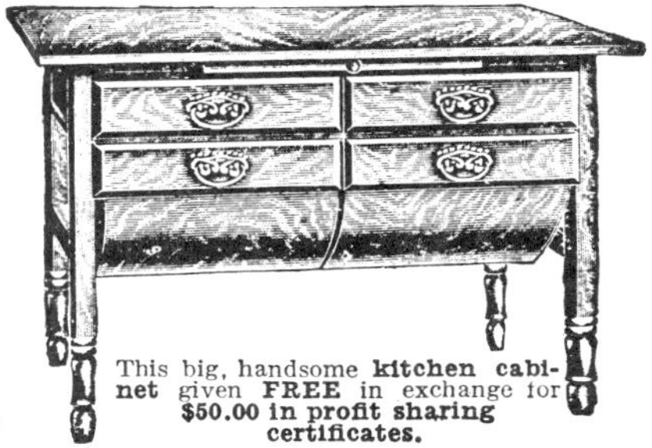

This big, handsome kitchen cabinet given FREE in exchange for $50.00 in profit sharing certificates.

This handsome big, elaborately finished banquet lamp given Free in exchange for $50.00 in profit sharing certificates.

WE ALSO GIVE FOR $50.00 IN CERTIFICATES YOUR CHOICE OF ANY ARTICLES HERETOFORE GIVEN FOR $100.00, BESIDES MANY MORE NEW AND VALUABLE ARTICLES SHOWN IN OUR NEW PROFIT SHARING BOOKLET.

PLEASE TELL ALL YOUR NEIGHBORS ABOUT THIS.

Tell them to dig up their old catalogues, tell them to hunt up their neighbors' catalogues. With this liberal offer extended we hope every catalogue out will do service. If you haven't a catalogue, if you cannot get a neighbor's catalogue, write for the big book, it is free for the asking. If you have an old book, and want to see all our profit sharing articles, write for the Free Profit Sharing Booklet. It is also free for the asking.

ADDRESS, SEARS, ROEBUCK & CO., Chicago, Ill.

Woman's Magazine, January, 1906

CUSTOMERS' PROFIT-SHARING

logue of 1904 announced the "Customers' Profit-sharing Premium Plan." With each purchase, the customer received a certificate lithographed in black and green, crediting him with the amount of that purchase. When the certificates in his possession amounted to $100, he was eligible for one of a number of prizes offered in a special (and sometimes in the general) catalogue—beds, raincoats, cameras, suits, stoves, shotguns, watches, and scores of others. A few premiums (organs, for example) ranged up to $500 in certificates; buggies up to $600; a piano to $1,000; and other prizes were pegged at $250. But the run-of-the-mill figure was $100.

The spring 1904 book, which launched Customers' Profit-sharing, devoted sixteen solid pages—as only Richard Sears could make a page solid—to explaining every detail of the plan and to illustrating and describing ninety-three separate premiums. The catalogue blandly asserted that the scheme had been devised solely as a means of allowing "any customer of ours . . . to share in the profits of this business." The statement declared that the company's profits were "no doubt much smaller than any other house in the world selling merchandise to the consumer"—so small, in fact, that "it would be dangerous to the interests of our business and the customers we serve to reduce our net profit even a fraction of one per cent." Still, the volume of business produced by the company's prices, "lower than any other house in the world," had made Sears, Roebuck so prosperous that its officers wished to share their good fortune with the customers who had made it all possible. Hence, Customers' Profit-sharing.

After reminding customers of how much money they could save, even exclusive of profit-sharing, just by ordering their goods from Sears, Roebuck, the catalogue went on to tell in some detail just how each customer could obtain *additional* profit-sharing certificates. Readers were urged to solicit their friends and neighbors for orders and to send those orders in their own names. "They will be glad to assist you by letting you send for their goods in your name" because such pooling of orders would reduce freight charges and thus bring an immediate saving to each person ordering goods. Every customer a salesman.

The catalogue also asserted that the increased volume of business which the profit-sharing scheme was going to bring in would in time enable Sears, Roebuck to lower its prices still further and also to liberalize its premiums—"There is no telling to what extent we may be able to go in the way of large, handsome and valuable articles of merchandise to be given to our customers in exchange for profit sharing certificates." The fourteen pages showing the articles available as premiums reiterated these themes endlessly: You, our customers, can win for yourselves all manner of fine articles by helping to increase our volume of business; as that volume continues to mount, there is no foreseeable limit to the benefits for you, through lower catalogue prices on all Sears, Roebuck goods and through progressively more lavish premiums.

The minimal amount was dropped from $100 in certificates to $50 by 1906, then to $25. Premiums varied, of course, in accordance with the amount of certificates accumulated; with customary gusto, Sears refused initially to place an expiration date on the certificates[45]—"these certificates are not limited as to time, and you may be months or years in accumulating certificates of a sufficient amount to entitle you to the article or articles you want, and they will be accepted by us when presented." Apparently the only restrictions, at first, were that the certificates would be issued for no purchases under one dollar and would be nontransferable. The customer, incidentally, paid transportation charges on premiums, just as on other goods.

Whereas Montgomery Ward, when it followed suit, gave no really prominent play to its "Customer Dividend Certificates," Sears cried his offer from the housetops—more specifically, from the catalogue's covers and in all his advertisements. In addition to the sixteen pages of material announcing the introduction of the plan and listing and illustrating premiums in the spring of 1904, Sears's catalogues for the next three years contained references throughout to Customers' Profit-sharing.

In 1905 the cost of premiums was more than 10 per cent of the total cost of advertising for that year, including catalogue expense; in two years the cost of premiums zoomed to more than $2,250,000—over 40 per cent of the total advertising cost.[46] The entire operations of the company became almost hopelessly enmeshed in the scheme; the correspondence department sagged under the volume of work engendered by Customers' Profit-sharing.[47] And, even so, there was no way of computing closely the size of the unknown obligation accruing to the company under this scheme.

A report to the New York banking houses of Lehman Brothers and Goldman, Sachs on June 28, 1906, attempted an analysis of the company's position as a result of the Customers' Profit-sharing Plan.[48] The report paid its respects to the sales-promotion virtues of the scheme with the words, "One of the factors which led to the increase in the sales of years 1904 and 1905 was doubtless the Profit-sharing Plan which was adopted on or about July 1st, 1904." The report then went on to describe in brief the principle of issuing with all goods purchased certificates redeemable for premiums, and added:

> There exists no accurate record of the amount of these Profit-sharing Certificates or Premium Coupons issued, but we are informed that the cost of the redemption of those which have been presented, averaged about 3½% of the amount of the sales they represent.
> The expense of redeeming these coupons has been only charged against the Profits when the coupons were presented, and no reserve has been created in respect of the liability to redeem those outstanding in the hands of the public, and we are very strongly of the opinion that provision should be made therefor. . . .

The report stated the opinion of various Sears, Roebuck executives that only about 43 per cent of the certificates issued would ever be redeemed and that the cost of such redemption would be equivalent to 3½ per cent of the sales represented by the redeemed certificates; this meant the redemption charge would be 1½ per cent of sales in the years in which Customers' Profit-sharing was in effect. The auditors projected this figure against sales for 1905 and concluded that, whereas only $260,563.65 worth of certificates had actually been redeemed in that year, there remained a further charge of $309,436.35 against 1905's profits. This figure was in addition to a charge of $231,396.44 still to be levied against earnings for 1904. For the year 1906 the auditors estimated that the cost of redeeming the certificates would reach $490,000; they concluded that, even though sales for the first four months of 1906 were nearly 50 per cent higher than for the corresponding period of the preceding year, profits for that portion of 1906 were by no means as great as in the first four months of 1905.

By the summer of 1907 even Sears himself was persuaded to give up the scheme; in early August of that year, Customers' Profit-sharing was abruptly scuttled. The company's customers were circularized to that effect.

Sears, characteristically, then turned to other schemes. Writing from Paris on September 30, 1908, to Asher, he declared:

> ... I am strongly of the opinion we will drift into the installment business on *Big Things*—and when we do, even if we confine ourselves to only our Best (highest price) Sepr. [sic] Buggy organ Piano Steel Range, Furniture, Sew Machine etc etc—I question if our factories can make enough of these goods for us. We want to approach the matter with *"Great Caution"* ... there is an I D E A and a way for us in it and *Theres Millions In It*. On Septs properly handled I believe we can sell 1000 a day as easily as we ever sold 250—and not 3% less and leave De Laval and others *No Place*....[49]

Sears's prescience was not confined to his prevision of the possibilities of instalment selling. He wrote from Berlin on December 29, 1906: "We do comparatively *very little* business in cities, and we like 'Wards' assume the cities are not at all our field—maybe they are not—but I think it is our duty to prove they are not our field." This was some nineteen years before the company seriously entered the retail field in the cities; and, while Sears wrote primarily with catalogue distribution in mind, to secure mail orders from urbanites, it was a closer and longer look at cities generally which led the company into the retail business in 1925.

And even before Sears, Roebuck or Montgomery Ward opened branch mail-order houses (the latter initially branching out into Kansas City in 1905), Richard Sears's teeming mind and restless letters sketched the possibilities—and, to him, the necessity—of expansion along that line.

It was in 1906 that the company decided to open a branch mail-order plant. More properly speaking, Richard Sears decided to open it; Rosenwald bitterly opposed this venture at the outset and for some time thereafter. Dallas represented a merchandising promotion, a psychological appeal to Texas chauvinism, since no goods were originally stocked there. All orders were sent to Chicago to be filled; Dallas was office space and letterheads and local pride.

Dallas did, of course, offer advantages, even though the company was slow to realize many of them fully: lower freight charges, faster delivery, and reduced damage to merchandise. The possible freight saving, for example, was considerable on a less-than-carload-lot basis, especially on fairly heavy goods, such as sewing machines, cream separators, and buggies, in which the company did a vast volume of business, and in stoves, pianos, organs, and other lines in which they did a sizable business.

There was another reason for opening the Dallas branch. Elmer Scott, as general manager of Sears, Roebuck, had incurred the disapproval of his superiors with his "frills"—his insistence on abolition of night and Sunday overtime work, his interest in employee welfare, and similar activities which it was felt had no place in business. Richard Sears was fond of Scott and wanted to ease him out by "kicking him upstairs."

All these factors applied to Dallas specifically. But Sears had great faith in mail-order branches *generally;* he felt that an expansion along that line not only was desirable but would eventually become necessary, according to some of his letters to Asher during that time:

> In our Texas experiment we are handicapped in many ways that I cannot here go into detail to explain and yet I am willing to stand or fall on the results of this experiment, but if we do get substantial encouragement in this experiment just set it *Right* and then there will be no telling what we can do . . . [Paris, November 10, 1906].

> If with this trial effort we can get any success, the next place will get the kind of preparation that will insure success and encourage us to cover the United States rapidly with 10 or more branches . . . [Nice, November 24, 1906].

> . . . We will have many advantages when we open branches at points nearer base of supply. For example, suppose we open in Boston for New England. We have an 80c first class, 45c 4th class rate of freight from Chgo, less from points east of Chgo to all points in N.E. . . . [Nice, November 25, 1906].

> . . . I fear to increase the business in Chicago very much. . . . We must put in branch houses to take care of increase. We will later be compelled to put in branches to meet our competitors for they will soon have more branches . . . [Vienna, December 11, 1906].

> . . . I would be the last to branch out and invest a million dollars in such a branch before we were in prime financial condition to do so, but I predict this will ultimately be our move, in fact I believe in time we will have to do it to hold our trade, whether we want or not. I believe too the more deeply we study into present conditions, the more clearly our course will point in the direction indicated . . . [London, January 20, 1907].

It should be noted, however, that those letters were written from Europe. Sears had had the grand conception of Dallas as a mail-order branch, had sent Elmer Scott there to operate it in accordance with Sears's conception, and then had gone to Europe. Scott was left to face the actualities in Dallas and the bitter-end hostility of Rosenwald in Chicago. Sears's operating conception had been, in simplest terms, that the Dallas "branch" should be little more than a correspondence office, routing to Chicago all orders it received. All shipments were to be made from Chicago.

The "home-industry" angle was to be played hard. The word "Texas" appeared six times on the cover of the first Dallas catalogue, issued in the fall of 1906, and nowhere was it abbreviated: "Texas Catalogue No. 1" . . . "Sears, Roebuck & Co. of Dallas, Texas" . . . "Address us at Dallas, Texas" . . . "Sears, Roebuck & Co. Chicago, Ill. and Dallas, Texas" . . . "Reference by Special Permission: American Exchange National Bank, Dallas, Texas" . . . "This Catalogue is for the State of Texas only." The inside pages of the catalogue repeated over and over: Texas, Texas, Texas. It contained everything except a picture of the Alamo and testimonials from Davy Crockett and Sam Houston. Its 307 pages—essentially reprints from the Chicago general catalogue, as the text and illustrations did not mention Texas—featured stoves, sewing machines, furniture, pianos, organs, buggies, saddles (of course), cream separators, safes, and farm implements—all heavy goods representing a chance to save on freight charges.

The most significant difference between the Chicago and Dallas catalogues was the line recurring constantly in the latter: "We prepay the freight." The company could well afford to pay the freight in view of the price differential between Chicago and Dallas. A check of Dallas and Chicago catalogue prices for 1906, 1907, and 1908 shows that the prices quoted in the Texas book were, on the average, 10–20 per cent higher than Chicago's. The chief exception noted was cream separators, which in 1906 were priced lower in Dallas than in Chicago, but this reduction disappeared by the spring of 1907, and from that time on the separator prices in Dallas were the higher.

In 1907 Scott began, surreptitiously, to stock buggies, on which he says that there was an extremely high freight rate. He followed this by stocking sewing machines and stoves to effect further economies in merchandising. In Scott's own words: "After the Rosenwald furore over this unwarranted action died down, it was permitted to issue the catalog of the Spring of 1908 which actually advertised shipments from Dallas."[50]

Prompted by his growing faith in the advisability of a real development of the branch plant, sometime in 1907 Scott took out an option on some land in Dallas. To quote him again:

As soon as I took the option on the Dallas property, I wrote to J. R., reciting my belief in the wisdom of establishing branches and the favorable outlook in Dallas, and reporting the option I had taken, wholly in behalf of the future. J. R. wrote at once, reflecting on my judgment, suggesting that there was no sense in my "going into the real estate business," intimating the doubt that the branch would continue, which, of course, would make the need of property out of the question. Then he suggested I give up the option and take a personal loss if necessary....

When Dallas finally became such a solid success that the company took up the option, it simply refunded to Scott the exact amount he had paid for the option. The company itself "went into the real estate business," opening its own plant in Dallas in 1912, the first unit having been built in 1908 after Rosenwald "finally gave grudging approval."[51]

By the time the spring 1908 Dallas catalogue was issued, the company was not only advertising shipments from there; it was featuring photographs of "Our Dallas Warehouses" and quoting shipping time from Dallas to fifteen Texas cities. It claimed, for example, that it took only three days for goods to reach Fort Worth; seven days to reach Brownsville: "We are prepared to ship to you your order from Dallas on the same day that we receive it. We will not ship from factory. We will not ship from Chicago." The fall catalogue that year listed on its cover "Offices and Sample Rooms" in Dallas and warehouses in Dallas, Fort Worth, Houston, and San Antonio. The book also proclaimed, "We prepay all freight to your station."

No figures are available on Dallas catalogue circulation prior to 1909, but in the spring of that year 72,314 books were distributed in Texas. In the fall of 1909 it was 98,792. The size of the catalogue in 1909 and 1910 is also unknown, but in 1911 the Texas fall book contained 1,366 pages, the same number as the one issued in Chicago (where, of course, all of them were made up and printed). By 1912, however, and for a few years thereafter, Dallas catalogues became progressively smaller.

At the end of 1908 Dallas was fast becoming the success Richard Sears had expected it to be, in the way Elmer Scott insisted it had to be. Thus what began as a grand promotion laid the groundwork for what would eventuate into a well-established pattern of branch mail-order plants covering all sections of the country.

Dallas and Elmer Scott may also have sown the seeds of "Sears International." In 1909 Scott experimented with extending operations to Mexico City as a means of implanting the Sears name early to take advantage of that country's development. He sent a carload of sewing machines to an agent in Mexico City. The goods were disposed of at a slight profit, but political developments in Mexico and the attendant instability dictated abandonment of the venture.

Richard Sears's fame was to rest primarily upon his talents as a master salesman and promoter. Henry Goldman, the New York banker, summed it up: "I think he could sell a breath of air."[52] Whatever his talent for selling air, Sears did indeed have a talent for selling himself and, through himself, his company and his goods. He linked that talent to what must surely have been one of the largest advertising "budgets" in the country. In letting his advertising expense run to $392,755 in 1898—13 per cent of sales and almost half the total expense in that year—he expressed in concrete terms his determination to establish the company's name and merchandising position, even if at tremendous cost. He was profoundly convinced that the cost would eventually be repaid many times over.

In 1900 the advertising expenditure rose to $606,786, or 9.44 per cent of sales (which had more than doubled in two years). Total advertising expense for 1902 is not available, but for the last six months of that year the bill ran to $854,615, or 9.25 per cent of sales. Advertising expense for the first half of 1906 was $2,239,319, or 9.62 per cent of sales. For the last half of that year, this item of expense dropped to $1,544,764, or 4.41 per cent of sales for that six-month period. Advertising expense for the whole of 1906 totaled $3,784,082, or 7.69 per cent of sales.

Advertising expenditures rose in the last half of 1907 to carry that item to a total of $5,195,857, or 11.07 per cent of sales for the year. In 1908 the retrenchment associated with the short depression culminating in that year saw advertising expense drop to $3,605,188, or 8.93 per cent of sales.

These data on advertising expense applied only to the Chicago mail order plant, but since all external advertising and most of the general and special catalogue expense were chargeable only to Chicago, the data presented account for the overwhelming proportion of total advertising cost. Dallas was the only branch plant operating in this period, and there is no indication that Dallas spent sums of any consequence on advertising, even though the cost of its catalogues (a small part of the whole) may not be included in the foregoing figures. And Dallas, of course, was not opened until 1906.

Evidence of at least partial success of Sears's whirlwind campaign to intrench his business rapidly is afforded in a statement by a man who was born in a small midwestern farming community shortly before the turn of the century (and who prefers to remain anonymous):

> The Montgomery Ward catalogue was one of the first things I can remember reading. It happens, I do not know why, that until a little after 1900 our farm community was so predominantly a Montgomery Ward one that I did not know about Sears, Roebuck. I can still remember being startled when I heard someone say that Sears, Roebuck was both a bigger and better mail-order firm than Montgomery Ward. That conviction spread rapidly, however, and long before I left home in 1913 the community had shifted over preponderantly to Sears, Roebuck. The opinion seemed general that on the whole the service was better and the lines of merchandise were more adequate in variety or better in quality or both.

Richard Sears would have been just about willing to let that statement stand as his answer to his critics; it was all the epitaph he would have wanted.

Sears's advertising bent was so much a part of his being that it carried over into his contacts with customers of the company. Stories of how far out of his way he was willing to go in services to his customers are legion and possibly, in large measure, apocryphal; but the following three told by one former employee shed some light on Richard Sears's determination to win over potential customers in every possible way.

An Ohio customer once complained that his son ran into a tree and broke his leg when the brake of the Sears bicycle he was riding failed to work. The boy's father wrote that the local doctor set the lad's broken bone improperly, with the result that the boy was apparently going to be lame for life. Richard Sears asked no questions. He had the man bring his son to Chicago, where a well-known surgeon reset the bone of the boy's leg—all, of course, at the company's expense.

On another occasion Sears, strolling through the plant, saw one of his guides showing a man and wife and their two children around. The guide was waving his lantern about in search of something. Upon questioning, the man told Sears that he thought he had lost a five-dollar bill in his tour of the plant. Sears forthwith handed the man five dollars from his own pocket with the assurance that he did not want any of his friends losing money in Sears, Roebuck's plant. The man was finally persuaded to accept the money over his own protestations that Sears should not feel responsible for someone else's carelessness.

Finally, the story which has circulated so widely in so many varying versions. A conductor helping a lady off a streetcar on which Sears was riding dropped his watch on the pavement, where it was badly smashed. Seeing the man's chagrin, Sears asked where he had purchased the watch. The answer was: "Sears, Roebuck." Sears had the conductor come to the plant, where he was given a new watch free. Sears reportedly told him: "We guarantee our watches not to fall out of people's pockets and break." Veterans of the company insist to this day that the incident was worth thousands of dollars to Sears, Roebuck in free advertising and good will. Stories of this kind are so numerous that, even if only a few of them are true, they still provide high residual evidence of good will and customer satisfaction.

The polarization of most of the lore and legend of the company in this early period around the characteristics and startling promotions of Richard Sears simply underscored the fact that his own dynamic personality and promotional talents were so magnetic that he completely overshadowed all his associates. The quiet, unspectacular contributions of Julius Rosenwald in husbanding and augmenting the company's working capital could never command the public notice which attached to Richard Sears's capacity for "ballyhoo." The efforts of Rosenwald and Loeb and lesser executives to bring administrative order out of chaos in those years could not possibly have seized the spotlight playing upon the man whose extraordinary promotions brought in the flood of orders which created that chaos. When Richard Warren Sears bestrode the stage, the remainder of the cast had perforce to bask in his reflected glory.

CHAPTER VI

Catalogue Appeals and Policies

THE period up to 1908 saw Sears, Roebuck's catalogue reflect every changing aspect of the company's approach as outlined earlier—the evolution of the guaranty and Richard Sears's pressure and schemes. It also saw the crystallization of the catalogue's role as the company's mouthpiece, as the most direct and intimate contact with its legions of unseen customers. At the same time the big book hurdled a host of obstacles of its own: internal problems of which the readers were only vaguely aware, such as format, size, method of distribution, allocation of space, physical production, makeup, and editorial policy over and above presentation of individual items of merchandise.

From 1887 until 1895 the catalogue, like the company itself, reflected the personality of Richard Sears, with all his flamboyance, his almost intuitive feeling for the farmer's idiom, his knowledge of what items would sell and what would not, his generalized exaggerations, and, of course, his conviction that mail order could survive only so long as a hot fire kept the pot boiling.

From 1895 until 1908 the book showed increasingly the new-found corporate stature of the company and its steadily expanding size, the trend toward "truth in advertising" with somewhat more accurate and more detailed descriptions of merchandise, and a great systematization of the entire business of producing the book.

Most of Sears's advertisements in mail-order magazines and in the limited number of newspapers whose columns were open to him sought in one way or another to interest readers in the company's general and special catalogues. His external advertising usually paralleled and supported his determination to present the company's full merchandise line and its editorial policy to customers, actual and potential. It was from the catalogues that the company hoped to make most of its sales. And the business of making sales involved initially not merely the presentation of goods priced low and backed by a guaranty of satisfaction but also the persuasion that ordering by mail was easy, convenient, and pleasant.

The catalogue therefore seldom rushed in to overwhelm a prospect with its full list of offerings before first showing the reader just how easy it was to order by mail from Sears, Roebuck—however illegibly scrawled or crudely phrased—"in any language." Richard Sears knew that winning the farmer's confidence in his mail-order company was not enough; he had also to build the farmer's confidence in himself and to make it as easy as humanly possible for the farmer to send in an order. Sears had to stand over the farmer's shoulder, pat him on the back, and persuade him that he could write as good a letter as the next man, that no one away off in Sears's Chicago company would ever laugh or even snicker at the painful scrawl and labored syntax of the farmer's letter. Sears knew full well from his own background how many farmers never wrote any kind of letter and how many more contented themselves with epistles of the barest simplicity.

On the first page of his catalogue, Sears's friendly messages sought to win the farmer over: "Don't be afraid that you will make a mistake. We receive hundreds of orders every day from young and old who never before sent away for goods. We are accustomed to handling all kinds of orders. Tell us what you want in your own way, written in any language, no matter whether good or poor writing, and the goods will promptly be sent to you." As for the details of sending that order: "Use our order blank if you have one. If you haven't, use any plain paper. Tell us in your own way what you want." And, finally: "If you live on a rural mail route, just give the letter and money to the mail carrier and he will get the money order at the post office and mail it in the letter for you."

The orders poured in, many in nearly illegible scrawl, many in languages other than English, many couched in such vague terms that the order-fillers had to make decisions on just what to send in return. But there was one great common denominator in numerous letters bringing orders: a note of friendly warmth, a ring of trust and faith, an unwavering assurance that Sears, Roebuck would somehow manage to make everything all right. This can probably be attributed primarily to the friendliness and camaraderie of Sears's own soothing catalogue messages and the bargains he offered in all his advertisements.

The keynote of the catalogues, particularly in the early years, was friendliness beyond the call of business duty. Customers were invited to visit the plant when in Chicago, to check parcels and write letters there. A man who hesitated to invite friends to his home in that period would have been suspect; Sears, Roebuck kept open house all the time.[1]

The catalogue indeed figuratively took the reader—that potential customer—by the hand and practically turned the pages of the book for him as the reader went from one item to another. The catalogue, before starting the reader on this journey, almost put a pencil in his hand to write out his order. One wonders in looking back how it happened that the company did *not* give away a pencil free with each catalogue.

One thing it did give away, in great procession, was bank references and testimonials. For years the catalogues cited the company's banking houses as gilt-edged references; the book even offered to let the customer send his money direct to the bank, to be held there until the customer expressed his complete satisfaction with the goods.[2] Testimonials from individuals were apparently easy to obtain, on everything from sewing machines to

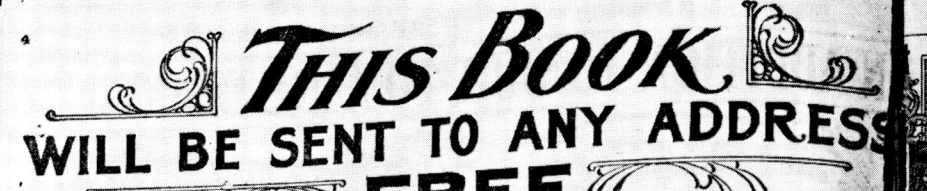

THIS BOOK WILL BE SENT TO ANY ADDRESS FREE BY MAIL POSTPAID ON APPLICATION

WRITE A LETTER OR A POSTAL CARD AND SAY **SEND ME YOUR BIG CATALOGUE** and it will be sent to you immediately free by mail, postpaid.

WRITE A LETTER OR A POSTAL CARD AND SAY **SEND ME YOUR BIG CATALOGUE** and it will be sent to you immediately free by mail, postpaid.

SIMPLE RULES FOR ORDERING.

USE OUR ORDER BLANK IF YOU HAVE ONE. If you haven't one, use any plain paper.

TELL US IN YOUR OWN WAY WHAT YOU WANT, always giving the CATALOGUE NUMBER of each article. Enclose in the letter the amount of money, either a postoffice money order, which you get at the postoffice, an express money order, which you get at the express office, or a draft, which you get at any bank; or put the money in the letter, take it to the postoffice and tell the postmaster you want it registered.

IF YOU LIVE ON A RURAL MAIL ROUTE, just give the letter and the money to the mail carrier and he will get the money order at the postoffice and mail it in the letter for you.

DON'T BE AFRAID YOU WILL MAKE A MISTAKE. We receive hundreds of orders every day from young and old who never before sent away for goods. We are accustomed to handling all kinds of orders.

TELL US WHAT YOU WANT IN YOUR OWN WAY, written in any language, no matter whether good or bad writing, and the goods will be promptly sent to you.

WE HAVE TRANSLATORS TO READ AND WRITE ALL LANGUAGES.

DON'T BE AFRAID OF THE FREIGHT OR EXPRESS CHARGES. You must pay them when you get the goods at the station, but they never amount to much compared with what we save you in cost.

IF YOU FIND IT NECESSARY TO HAVE SOME SPECIAL INFORMATION you can undoubtedly obtain it by referring to the matter contained within the first nineteen pages of this catalogue.

ENKLA REGLER ATT IAKTTAGA VID BESTÄLLNING.

Begagna vår beställningsblankett, om ni har en sådan. Om icke, begagna vanligt vent papper.

Säg oss på edert eget sätt hvad ni önskar, alltid uppgifvande katalognumret på hvarje sak. Inneslut beloppet i brefvet antingen i postoffice money order, hvilken köpes å postkontoret; express money order, hvilken köpes å expresskontoret, eller en vexel, hvilken kan köpas å hvilken bank som helst, eller också inneslut kontanta penningar i brefvet, tag det till postkontoret och säg postmästaren att ni önskar få det registrerat.

Var icke rädd för att ni gör ett misstag. Vi erhålla hundratals beställningar dagligen från unga och gamla hvilka aldrig förr sändt efter varor. Vi äro vana vid att expediera alla slags beställningar.

Säg oss på edert eget sätt hvad ni önskar. Skrif på hvilket språk som helst, bra eller dålig stafning, bra eller dålig handstil, och varorna skola blifva eder prompt tillsända.

Vi ha öfversättare som läsa och skrifva alla språk.

Det är icke nödvändigt för eder att genomläsa de första tio sidorna i denna katalog, såvida ni icke önskar någon speciell upplysning. Dessa tio sidor innehålla detaljerad upplysning, så att de som i alla delar önska göra sig förtrogna med sättet att beställa och sända varor, fraktkostnader o. s. v., o. s. v., icke behöfva skrifva till oss, utan helt enkelt kunna slå upp dessa sidor och finna den upplysning de önska.

Einfache Regeln zum Bestellen.

Gebraucht unsere Bestellungszettel wenn Sie welche haben, nicht nehmen Sie gewöhnliches Papier.

Im Bestellen erwähnen Sie die Catalog Numero an Sachen. Die Bestellung soll das Geld enthalten, entweder „Postoffice Money Order," (welche man gewöhnlich an der Postoffice bekommen kann), eine „Expreß Money Order," ein Bank Certificat, das man an jeder Bank bekommen kann, oder legen Sie das Geld in den Brief mit der Bestellung, in welchem Falle Sie den Eingeschrieben schicken sollten. Der Brief wird in der Eingeschrieben (Registered.)

Wir erhalten jeden Tag eine große Anzahl von Bestellungen von allen Leuten (Jung und Alt).

Sie brauchen nicht furchtsam zu sein Sachen zu bestellen, wir können Ihr Bestellung schon verstehen.

Schreiben Sie uns in Ihrem eigener Weise, und in Ihrer Sprache, was Sie wollen, einerlei ob gut oder schlecht geschrieben, und die Waare wird Ihnen sofort zugeschickt.

Wir haben Leute die alle Sprachen schreiben und übersetzen.

Die ersten zehn Seiten in diesem Catalog beziehen sich hauptsächlich an die Frachtbeträge der verschiedenen Waare und hat eine Wichtigkeit für Sie im Falle Sie in diesen Einzelheiten interessiert sind.

DO NOT FAIL TO GIVE SIZE, COLOR, WEIGHT, ETC., IF REQUIRED WHEN WRITING YOUR ORDER

"SIMPLE RULES FOR ORDERING" FROM THE SPRING 1900 CATALOGUE

patent medicines; perhaps the lure of seeing one's name spread broadcast over the land through the catalogue was irresistible. And those testimonials must have showed some effectiveness; Sears, Roebuck was not a company to waste space for long on anything which did not appear profitable.

Even testimonials, however, could not get across the whole story which Richard Sears wanted to tell his readers, so he frequently included in the catalogue various indexes of the scope of the firm's operations. The 1896 book, for example, pointed out that the mail-order house was selling nine thousand suits of clothing daily or four suits every minute (which may have been true, since this was the time of a great promotion of men's suits), a buggy every ten minutes, and a watch every minute.

And always the catalogue stressed the company's guaranty throughout. Guaranties on specific items naturally varied in accordance with the nature of the item; a farm wagon obviously could not be guaranteed to last as long as, say, a diamond ring. Sewing machines at one point carried a ten-year guaranty. Wagons and bicycles were warranted for one year. But always there was the general guaranty applying to merchandise upon arrival. In 1901 this read: "We Guarantee Satisfaction and Safe Delivery on Everything You Order." Five years later it was: "Your Money Back if You Are Not Satisfied." Finally, it was to become what it is today: "Satisfaction guaranteed or your money back."

The liberal guaranty was essential to both Ward's and Sears in their early years, not only to win public confidence in them as fair traders but, at least in Sears's case, because of the interminable delays in shipment, mistakes in sending the wrong goods, casual substitution of goods in place of those ordered, and mistaken addresses (such as Augusta, Georgia, for Augusta, Maine). The often haphazard, inefficient, disorganized operations of the early Sears, Roebuck and Company would probably have dictated such a guaranty even if it had not existed prior to that time.

By way of further enlivening its catalogue presentations, the company used many illustrations for such items as men's clothing, on which the heads of celebrities of the period appeared: actors, politicians, and others. In the 1899 catalogue, for example, the head of Colonel Theodore Roosevelt of the Rough Riders surmounts the illustration of a suit style for portly men.

The matter of helping the customer send in an order faced one great roadblock: freight rates. The buyer had to pay freight on the goods he ordered; everything over four pounds had to go by freight (or by more expensive express) until the advent of the parcel post in 1913. The catalogue always sought to allay the customer's fears as much as possible by assuring him that the freight charges would be less than he thought. Even though the charges might be reasonable, however, ordering by mail posed the problem of computing those rates closely enough to add the correct sum to the amount of his order.

In 1903 an advertisement for buggies listed the points from the nearest of which a buggy would be shipped to the buyer. When the great "Iowa-izing" campaign of forced-draft catalogue distribution got under way, catalogues designed for specific states included a wealth of information to show exactly what the freight charges would be on any given item of merchandise to any county in that state. Freight charges on best-selling items were indicated in tabular form by giving the exact weight of each item; from this the customer could compute precisely what the cost of shipment would be.[3]

The catalogue index apparently concerned the company far less than did freight rates, for this ready-reference listing of the firm's offerings received almost no attention until 1898. The index was expanded in that year, printed on pink paper to attract attention, and placed in the middle of the catalogue. And in the subsequent years several experiments were made with the position of the index, typography, illustrations, departmentalization of merchandise, and pricing. Departmentalization failed because it destroyed the otherwise alphabetical nature of the index. Listing of prices in the index also had to be abandoned; when last-minute price changes in the catalogue proper failed of inclusion in the index, the company was left with two prices shown for an item of merchandise.[4]

Richard Sears himself wrote virtually all the catalogue copy and supervised its makeup for several years. Even after such able assistants as Elmer Scott, Louis Asher, and William Pettigrew came to relieve him of the growing mountain of detail work, Sears still kept the reins tightly in hand. These subordinates had to meet the master's own conception of perfection, and some of them came to write in a style indistinguishable from his own.

Space was allocated even past the turn of the century largely on a rule-of-thumb basis; except for special promotion pages on items such as sewing machines or cream separators or some other best seller of the moment, the book was made up largely by "intuition." Advance allocation of space by departments on a tightly budgeted basis did not really become effective until after Sears had left the organization.[5]

In addition to issuing new catalogues at irregular intervals, special catalogues or booklets were published to push particular lines of goods. By 1907 the list of special catalogues numbered sixty-five and included booklets on such lines as farm implements, baby carriages, bicycles, cream separators, engines, farm wagons, fencing, furniture, millwork, pianos, refrigerators, sewing machines, shoes, stoves, tombstones, washing machines, windmills, and others. Some of the special catalogues were sample books, containing swatches of material for boys' and men's clothing (made to order and ready-made), wallpaper, carpets, baseball suits, building and roofing paper, dress goods, and house and barn paint.

But whatever the nature of any given catalogue, large or small, it always remained the company's one great medium of contact with its public. Readers might not see Sears's advertisements in the mail-order and other magazines of the day; opposition of local merchants might—and very often did—make it impossible for Sears, Roebuck to buy space in local newspapers; one great national magazine, the *Ladies' Home Journal,* refused even to accept Sears's advertising because its publisher, Cyrus Curtis, abhorred the crude makeup and the garish exaggerations of those ads.[6] But over the catalogue Sears, Roebuck held complete suzerainty; it was the company's to have and to hold, to alter with the times, to shape to its will, and to use as an avenue of direct contact with its customers.

This naturally produced a habit on the company's part of editorializing in the big book to offset the bitter criticism of the mail-order business by small independent merchants and a constant effort to place the catalogue in as many hands as possible. The potentialities of the first were realized long before the second was thoroughly exploited.

The whole tone and orientation of the book's editorial policy were set by Richard Sears, who dominated that sphere of operations until after the turn of the century and whose influence persisted for many years thereafter, through the men he had trained. Catalogue circulation, too, was determined in large measure by Sears himself; it was inseparably linked to his great promotions.

Getting that catalogue into every potential customer's hand preoccupied Richard Sears for years—a preoccupation which distressed some of the executives concerned with the cost involved. Even so, systematic, planned catalogue distribution shaped up but slowly, on a trial-and-error basis. In retrospect it seems almost astonishing that any charge was ever attached to the catalogue, in view of the company's eagerness (and most particularly Richard Sears's eagerness) to saturate its market with the book.

Further, the constant variations in the charge made for the big book offer an interesting field for speculation. The changes in "price" from year to year may have represented an effort to recapture a certain proportion of the cost of the catalogue, which itself varied with the times. Or it may have indicated the use of some arbitrary rule of thumb to keep out of the market those who would request a book without sending orders. Asher, one-time advertising manager, observed:

At first Sears, Roebuck & Company asked for five cents to help cover postage for the catalogue. As the catalogue increased in size, the amount was raised to 8 cents, 10 cents, and finally 15 cents. The request for 15 cents was, supposedly, a safeguard against waste. The theory was that if an applicant sent 15 cents, he was a legitimate inquirer.[7]

The company demanded five cents for the catalogue in 1893, while the 1894 book was free. The 1897 catalogue listed a charge of fifteen cents, and this same price obtained in 1898.[8] In 1899 the charge dropped to ten cents, owing possibly to the fact that the offerings of several departments were omitted from that book. The first page stated: "We have omitted from this our No. 108 issue for the Spring and Summer season our hardware, implement, dry goods, harness, grocery and furniture departments, lest the demand for these goods would grow beyond our ability to fill all the orders." But, the statement carefully pointed out, orders for goods from the departments omitted could be sent in from the previous catalogue; if that earlier catalogue was not available, the company would gladly send upon request a special cataogue listing goods from any department omitted from the 1899 book.

The 1900 catalogue stated the price as fifteen cents and announced that next year's catalogue would cost the same amount. The 1900 catalogue also announced a departure from the practice of issuing catalogues twice yearly; thenceforth there was to be only one annual book. This new practice, the catalogue itself asserted, was designed to save customers money and the bother of sending for a new book; the statement to customers declared that "we will save thousands of dollars that will go direct to our customers in the way of lower prices and better values."

But 1901 found Sears charging fifty cents, not fifteen, for its catalogue (the actual cost of printing and distributing it ran from fifty to eighty-five cents).[9] A select group of some 300,000 or more received the book free; the company had indexed its best ("A") customers for special handling, on the basis of the dollar volume of the orders they sent in.

The year 1902 saw another variation. While the paper-bound catalogue remained priced at fifty cents, listed in bold letters on the cover, a version of the book printed on slightly better stock and cloth-bound in brilliant red was priced at one dollar to the general public and sent free to all "A" customers.[10] Or at least virtually free; when an order was shipped to an "A" customer, it was accompanied by a fancy, embossed certificate "worth fifty cents." The customer was informed that if he would inclose that certificate in his next order, it would be redeemed for one of the finer catalogues. The plan of binding the catalogue in two quality levels was, however, abandoned after one year, even though the preferred customers continued to receive free the catalogue for which others were charged.

The company may have encountered some resistance to its price of fifty cents for the catalogue, if a sales-promotion letter dated March 15, 1902, is any indication. That circular is interesting for several reasons:

Willie Arbuckle
Gillstrap, Ky.

DEAR SIR:—

R. S. Arbuckle, a neighbor of yours who is a customer of ours, has just received from us our new, big, four-pound, 50-cent catalogue.

Why we are compelled to (and why we can) get 50 cents for this wonderful book, is fully explained in the enclosed pamphlet [no copy available]. Your neighbor writes us that you are welcome to use the big catalogue he has, whenever you like, and we are anxious for you to see and examine this big book, whether you wish to order anything or not, for the book is a revelation in price

CATALOGUE APPEALS AND POLICIES 91

making from beginning to end.... We enclose an order blank and return envelope that you can use at any time in case you wish to send us an order.

As your neighbor will be glad for you to use his catalogue, there is really no necessity for your going to the expense of sending us 50 cents for a catalogue, for you can use your neighbor's. . . .

Whether the company meant it or not, that surely must have been one of the few times it ever suggested that anyone could get along without its catalogue. And while there is no way of knowing how many copies of this circular were sent out, or what system was used for obtaining names of the addressee and the obliging neighbor, the fact that everything but the salutation and the name of the neighbor was mechanically reproduced indicates that the circular was intended at least for fairly wide distribution.

Further evidence of possible resistance to the relatively high charge for the catalogue appeared in the fall 1902 book, which devoted the better part of a two-page letter to customers to trying to justify the practice of "selling" the general catalogues. The letter also contained a good deal of hokum, particularly in regard to omission of certain facts. The message opened on this note:

This big catalogue has been made so thoroughly complete in every department that it is intended to be used for ordering goods and for reference, season after season.

This one book, if preserved, can be used for sending us orders and for reference for several years. . . . [Possibly true, but there was no indication of the fact that the company planned to continue issuing two general catalogues yearly.] If you should order from this book two or three years hence, and there should be any reduction in price on the goods ordered by you, we will give you the benefit of the lower price and return the difference to you in cash. [This promise was repeated in almost the same words in the succeeding paragraph. Nowhere was there mentioned that if prices should rise, the customer would have to pay the price prevailing at the time he ordered.]

The statement to customers went on to recount the expense, "so large, so colossal," involved in distributing catalogues free and the "enormous waste" just in postage alone entailed in sending catalogues to people who never submitted an order. "All this expense, all this wasted advertising that goes to people who do not buy, is paid for by the people who do buy. ... When you buy an article from a catalogue or mail order house that supplies catalogues free or for a fraction of their cost, you will pay an extra price to cover a number of catalogues that have been mailed to people who never buy."

The effort to justify the cost of the catalogue concluded on this note: "We do not compete with other houses on the price of catalogues, no more do other houses attempt to compete with us on the prices we make on merchandise."

Somewhere around this time the company apparently experimented with a return to the earlier practice of accompanying every shipment of goods with a catalogue, as indicated in a letter from Richard Sears to Louis Asher, dated January 23, 1904:

> Referring again to the distribution of our large catalogue at the rate of 7 to 8000 per day until March 1st, you know as soon as we have books sufficient we want to inaugurate our *already tested plan* to enclose a catalogue with every freight shipment that goes out of the house or from any factory, and you will remember the postal cards on which the receipt of these catalogues are acknowledged. . . .[11]

By 1904 it became apparent to one or both of the biggest mail-order firms that *any* charge for a catalogue defeated the book's purpose. Whether Sears or Montgomery Ward initiated the move is today uncertain; the step may have been taken simultaneously, although Asher takes credit for selling Sears on the plan and says Ward's followed suit,[12] while Werner maintains Ward's acted first and forced Sears to fall in line.[13] In any event, 1904 saw both the mail-order giants proclaim that their catalogues were thenceforth free for the asking.[14] Sears, Roebuck advertised the fact in magazines, in its catalogue, on all labels and shipping tickets, and through all other available mediums; the company pleaded for people to request its catalogue, with all the urgency which had earlier characterized Richard Sears's battle cry, "Send No Money."[15] The public responded; 1,557,376 more catalogues were issued in 1904 than in the preceding year.[16]

Circulation figures are unavailable for any year before 1897, when 318,000 general catalogues were sent out. This figure rose steadily to reach 853,000 at the turn of the century. The next year saw a drop of 3,000, but in 1908 the circulation was almost twice that of the preceding year. It jumped in 1904, when it became free (again) and spurted to 3,800,724 in 1905, the year "Iowaizing" began. Table 5 shows in detail the trend of catalogue circulation for the years 1902–7. All figures refer to the general catalogue.

The so-called "Iowaization" scheme represented Richard Sears's tactic for exploiting to the limit the fact that the charge had been removed from the book. Great circulation could have been achieved by placing one in every mailbox, but Sears wanted them in the hands of people likely to act upon them and send orders. The state of Iowa had from the outset been one of the states in which the company had done the greatest business and had the most friends.

A simple but highly effective scheme was devised. The company circularized its best customers in that state, asking each of them to distribute two dozen catalogues to his neighbors on a *quid pro quo* basis. When acceptances were received, the plan moved ahead: twenty-four catalogues were sent by freight to each person agreeing to serve as a "distributor." Each distributor in turn passed them out to twenty-four neighbors and sent Sears, Roebuck a list of those to whom he had given the books. The com-

CATALOGUE APPEALS AND POLICIES 93

pany, on its part, carefully listed those new names, mailed them promotional literature, and kept a record of all orders sent in by such new customers within thirty days.

Customers who had distributed the catalogues for the firm received premiums based on the aggregate volume of the orders sent in by those to whom they had given catalogues. If, for example, one group of twenty-four such new customers ordered goods in the amount of $100, the "distributor" had his choice of a bicycle, a sewing machine, a stove, or a variety of other goods. If the orders reached only $50, the premiums offered included a man's suit, a lady's silk dress, a desk, a set of silverware, and similar items. If the orders totaled only $25, there were lesser awards. And even if no orders eventuated, the distributor nevertheless received a small prize of some sort.

TABLE 5*

GENERAL CATALOGUE CIRCULATION, 1902-8

Season	Catalogue Distribution
1902 Spring	604,756
Fall	986,971
1903 Spring	402,347
Fall	541,076
1904 Spring	1,105,511
Fall	1,395,288
1905 Spring	2,079,699
Fall	1,721,025
1906 Spring	2,220,010
Fall	1,654,345
1907 Spring	2,092,433
Fall	3,034,260
1908 Spring	2,942,622
Fall	3,639,920

* Source: Company records.

The premiums were so arranged as to encourage each distributor not only to give the catalogues to the best prospects but also to follow up those prospects to induce them to order. The distributors were, obviously, already persuaded of the advantages of trading with Sears, Roebuck; and they transmitted their faith to the new communicants. This word-of-mouth advertising excelled all the company's own efforts. The net result was that the presentation of the firm's offerings was placed before the eyes and pocketbooks of more people than ever before, while those who did the placing for the company reinforced their own value as customers through their efforts to stimulate new sales.[17]

The managerial staff at Sears, Roebuck noted that Iowa skyrocketed to top position among the states in volume of business sent to the company. There could be no mistaking the success of this experiment in catalogue distribution.[18] Richard Sears was delighted—and determined to "Iowaize" the nation.[19] He did. The plan was extended throughout the country, with local variations of course.

A twenty-page booklet titled *$10.00 Cash for a Very Little Work* was used to interest customers of the company in becoming catalogue distributors. It was apparently issued early in the "Iowaization" campaign, for, while it does not appear to have been directed to any particular state, twenty-seven of the twenty-eight successful distributors whose pictures appeared in it were from Iowa (the twenty-eighth was an Ohioan). The booklet went into almost incredible detail on how anyone could succeed as a distributor. And the changes in the "ground rules" for success indicated a departure from the original requirements of dollar volume of orders sent in by the twenty-four people to whom the general catalogues were distributed.

The "pep talk" to prospective distributors on where and how to pass out the catalogues was a primer in mail-order selling:

Do not place one of our catalogues with anyone who already has one of our Big Catalogues, received within the last six months. . . .
Do not place more than one catalogue in one household, office, factory, or business institution. . . .
Do not give a catalogue to children; boys and girls under 18 years of age. . . .
Delivery among good reliable farmers preferred. . . .
. . . we recommend that you place a catalogue with every reliable **carpenter**, builder, factory owner, blacksmith, physician, photographer, one **catalogue in** each hotel, real estate office, printing office, sawmill, or other mill. . . .
. . . You may own or be employed in a sawmill, foundry, stove factory, implement factory, furniture or other factory, or employed in some enterprise where twenty-four or more men (heads of families) are employed. . . . We will be almost sure to receive twenty or more orders from these people. . . .

The booklet went on to stress the fact that the catalogues were free and to remind distributors of the savings offered both through Sears, Roebuck's low prices and through Customers' Profit-sharing. And the booklet further rehashed all Richard Sears's time-tested tactics of reassuring people how easy, convenient, and safe it was to buy from the company.

The cost of "Iowaizing" the state of Indiana in 1906 is shown in Table 6. The items for freight and postage (eighty cents and twenty cents, respectively, per "shipment") are based upon shipments of catalogues in bundles of twenty-five. The fact that both freight and postage are shown indicates that by 1906 the company employed distribution to strategically cited freight centers prior to distribution by mail. Cheaper freight rates were thus utilized to carry the catalogues as near final destination as possible before more expensive postage was employed.

The cost of "rewards" in "Iowaizing" apparently refers to actual cost of the premiums to the company, hence the odd cents shown. The cost of a little less than thirteen cents per catalogue delivered in this particular campaign would appear to be satisfactorily low for such large-scale, forced-draft circulation.

Figures on the cost of "Iowaizing" Michigan, closely comparable in many respects, reveal that 207,800 catalogues were distributed in that state at an average cost of twelve cents per book. The cost of rewards for the Michigan effort was considerably lower than for Indiana ($6,655.50 as against $9,073.29), but the greater distance brought freight costs almost up to the Indiana figures, and postage was almost identical.

TABLE 6*

INDIANA FREIGHT CATALOGUE DISTRIBUTION, 1906

No. shipments	9,994	No. catalogues delivered	217,300
No. catalogues	249,850		

Freight	$7,795.20	@ 80¢
Postage	1,998.80	@ 20¢
Rewards	9,073.29	
Pay roll	1,462.35	
Packing expense	1,270.70	
Boxing	2,798.32	@ 28¢
A 7376 Lay-out	1,423.20	
A 7096 Coupons	205.00	
A 7320 Report Blanks	107.50	
A 7605 Circular	39.30	
Cartons	1,375.00	
#12 Manila Env.	19.50	
A 7429 Notice of Shipment	14.50	
3 Punch-up letters	13.50	
Freight receipts	10.00	
Index cards	5.00	
Freight on return catalogues	494.40	
	$28,128.56	

Cost on no. catalogues shipped—11.2 cents
Cost on no. catalogues actually delivered—12.9 cents

*Source: Louis Asher's file (apparently from company records). A handwritten note on the itemized statement dates it November 27, 1906.

Sears's letters from abroad to Asher show an unflagging interest in "Iowaization" well into 1908. On May 21 of that year Sears wrote from Cork, Ireland:

... I am giving no thought to business, unless it be to the question—viz—the outcome of our Iowaizing.

Even though the returns on this may seem very slow I do hope none of you will get cold feet, but on the contrary will push it as hard as you can—for with a new and better book coming out in July I am confident when you have the best states mostly covered and *well punched*—you will find a big improvement, in fact I have great hopes for July '08 beating July '07 in sales.

By the way in spite of the high freight rates to western states and territories which makes the freight-plus the 10c about the same as postage, I believe so far as the towns can be reached by rail all the far west states and territories should be Iowaized. . . .[20]

Writing from London on May 26, Sears continued to stress the theme of "Iowaization":

> ... I feel our general success now lies in seeing how many catalogues we can put out by the freight method. There surely is a certain point when we will reach and pass any corresponding figure of sales and from there go on as of yore, showing weekly an increase over any corresponding record and all this at a very low percentage of cost if we confine our efforts strictly to this one method, practically eliminating every other item of advertising expense.[21]

Nine days later, on June 4, 1908, Sears wrote from Paris:

> Make the premiums as big and attractive as you dare—and then to protect yourself you may have to fix a minimum amount as well as number of orders. This whole idea with me being to get your 30M agents who are now done working—by an offer *more* attractive far than ever before, induced to see each of the 24, again giving each a new coupon—of course (print) fix up a nice & proper talk for the distributors to give to each catalogue holder.... the experiment might show it is the thing to do for all time....[22]

The summer and fall of 1908 found the company still "Iowaizing" and making the premiums as "big and attractive," apparently, as it dared. Distributors were urged virtually to hound their prospects into ordering from the company.

In addition to the "Iowaization" campaign, the company continued to send free catalogues to those requesting them and to add a book to each freight shipment leaving the factory unless the records, now better kept, showed that the customer already had been sent a catalogue. By 1907, the year of depression, catalogue circulation reached 5,127,000.

Unpublished notes of Louis Asher report Rosenwald and other executives as being disturbed by Sears's large distribution of catalogues in the era of "Iowaization." Analysis and statistics prepared by the general merchandise manager showed an excessively heavy distribution of books in some areas, which meant waste. Sears's answer to this, according to Asher, was that "advertising is accumulative" and that "if you analyze your advertising too closely, you will analyze yourself out of business." Asher estimates the waste involved in the forced-draft catalogue distribution at 10 per cent—admittedly an arbitrary figure—but insists that Richard Sears was prepared and willing to undergo such waste in his effort to bridge time and pre-empt various geographic areas for his company.

By 1907 Sears, Roebuck could claim—as it assuredly did, on the back cover of the catalogue—that "WE WILL FORFEIT TEN THOUSAND DOLLARS ($10,000.00) IN CASH TO ANY WORTHY CHARITY if anyone can prove that any other FIVE (5) catalogue houses in the United States, selling general merchandise exclusively to the consumer, the same as we do, can show combined sales for the twelve months ending July 30, 1907, aggregating as much as $53,188,901.00." That was $10,000 that even the ebullient Richard Sears could not spend.

Catalogue production in the watch-selling days was, of course, entirely the personal product of Richard Sears. Within a very few years the size of the catalogue and the number of copies printed combined to convert production of the book into a major project. Sears, however, continued for several years to write virtually all the copy himself and to select the artwork, which for years consisted solely of woodcuts. He did not delegate authority for any considerable part of copywriting until Scott, Asher, and, later, Pettigrew joined him after his return to Chicago in 1895. In the next five years more and more copy came to be written by the various merchandise men who headed up the several departments, but final editing remained in the hands of Sears, Asher, and Scott, Asher himself becoming catalogue editor prior to his appointment as acting general manager in 1906.[23]

The various department heads were merchandise men, not advertising men; they tended generally to describe their goods factually and to overlook the seduction of the reader which had always been a cardinal factor in Sears's copy. In view of Sears's philosophy, the editor's job perforce became one of embellishing the copy, of breathing life into the stillborn words submitted by the department heads. It was therefore only to be expected that when the company began more and more to alter its catalogue presentation, it was necessary to re-educate the editors themselves.

The move toward more restrained catalogue copy started well before William Pettigrew became catalogue editor in 1908, even though actual production techniques of the catalogue were still crude and fumbling. Among the various merchandise heads were capable men whose merchandising point of view was close to Rosenwald's: J. Fletcher Skinner (later to become general merchandise manager and, before his death in 1917, to establish the Sears laboratories), Frank Case, G. F. Fowler, "Bill" Williams, J. R. Scott, Fred Keene, and others whose names are forgotten but who made genuine contributions to the growth of the company.

Prior to 1908 there was no "lineup" of catalogue preparation, no plan whereby one could see at a glance the entire framework of the catalogue even before a line of copy was submitted. There was no real plan for advance submission of layouts, artwork, copy; no clear-cut allocation of space and position by departments; no prior determination of the different stocks to be used in printing, of the type faces and sizes to be employed; no rack-up of target dates from submission of first copy to putting the catalogue to bed.[24]

Nor, in fact, was there any concise compilation of policies on style, ethics, mandatory usages, taboo phrases, and everything else that makes up the *Advertising Guide* in use by the firm today. But when Pettigrew became catalogue editor in 1908, one of his first acts was to issue a booklet, *How To Prepare Catalogue Copy*, for the guidance of his copywriters.

It was a small primer of only a dozen pages, printed on stiff manila paper in coat-pocket size.

In 1903, apparently at the expiration of the printing contract with Conkey and Spangler, the company established its own printing plant, called the Metropolitan Press Syndicate; it was located in Chicago, and its equipment consisted largely of a number of old presses and a binder bought from Conkey. Further, Sears, Roebuck added insult to injury by hiring Conkey's superintendent to run its plant.

The fall 1905 catalogue devoted four pages to describing "Our New Forty-Acre Home," into which the company was then planning to move. Under the caption, "Our Printing Plant," the announcement stated:

> This building, constructed especially for our purpose, is ... intended to make for us the most modern and model printing plant possible. With ... railroad tracks to carry the paper leading direct to the printing presses, we look for greater economy. This building is built to contain twenty special Cottrell rotary perfecting catalogue printing presses, each made to our order, made especially to make our big catalogues. Add to this a large number of large, medium and small flat bed, rotary, and other printing presses, plate making machines, binding, covering, gathering, trimming and other machinery and equipment.... All the printing done in this building will be exclusively for our own requirements. Our own printing plant is another economy that makes for lower prices.

The next paragraph, titled "Building To Handle Our Advertising Matter," revealed that this structure "will be devoted in its entirety to the compiling, composition (typesetting) and mailing of our catalogues, circulars, and price lists of all kinds. In this building we will have a large photographic department for the making of cuts and engravings of all descriptions."

The company's new printing establishment was moved to new quarters on Chicago's West Side in 1906, when the company moved into its new building. To replace their Cottrell rotary presses, which delivered thirty-two-page sections ("signatures") in multiples of eight, Metropolitan acquired new and larger presses able to deliver ninety-six-page sections in multiples of twenty-four pages. A new binding machine was also acquired at the same time.

Sometime between 1903 and 1908 Sears, Roebuck also purchased several linotype machines on a tentative basis. Linotypes had been used since 1888, but Sears had never utilized them for type-casting catalogue copy. It was agreed that if the linotypes did not work out satisfactorily, in one year, the firm could return them to the Mergenthaler Company at no expense. Before the probation period ended, Sears, Roebuck ordered more such machines. They speeded catalogue production immensely.

The next technical improvement came with the purchase of presses for turning out four-color printing. These presses posed a greater problem in inks, which in turn created further paper difficulties.[25] It was necessary to evolve inks which would dry rapidly enough and well enough so that one color could be printed on top of another without skidding, smearing, or pricking the paper. A special research activity, attached to the advertising department, developed satisfactory inks and went on to find paper which would accommodate the inks properly.

The paper problem, however, went far beyond the mere difficulty posed by the inks. Paper represented weight, and weight represented catalogue mailing cost; a reduction of even a few ounces in the weight of each book spelled annual savings in postage amounting to thousands of dollars. Early efforts had been made to reduce the weight, chiefly by close trimming; this had reached the *reductio ad absurdum* stage when, after 1900, the trimming was frequently so close that the type near the margins was shaved off. Economy was proving too expensive until the company's researchers came up with paper light enough to cut mailing costs while still being sufficiently sturdy for high-speed printing.

In addition to pioneering in the realm of ink and paper—in which advances were made that were subsequently adopted by most of the rest of the industry—the special research department also made improvements in type metals, electroplating, illustrating, presswork, and related fields. Most of these improvements came after 1908; but the groundwork had been laid by that time.

By 1905 woodcuts still furnished about 60 per cent of all catalogue illustrations.[26] Halftones were used for practically all the wearing apparel, clothing, shoes, and haberdashery, and to a large extent for other goods where detail was an important factor in sales appeal. Black-and-white wash drawings were first employed for making halftones, but these gave way in time to photographs.

Sometime shortly after 1906 an electroplating foundry was established to take care of advertisements, with an initial appropriation of $10,000. Its uses burgeoned until by 1910 it had become the largest in Chicago. Sears, Roebuck was, however, already finding out that there were great difficulties inherent in operating a printing plant devoted almost solely to such a seasonal project as catalogues. As a catalogue deadline neared, the plant was badly overloaded; this period was followed by a slack time in which it was impossible to keep the plant busy. Meanwhile, though, problems or no, catalogues continued to roll by the millions every year. And they reaped a harvest of orders.

CHAPTER VII

Mail-Order Merchandise

ITEMS which readily lent themselves to great promotions, such as bicycles, sewing machines, and cream separators, tended inevitably to overshadow more prosaic lines of merchandise which sold in less spectacular quantities and often carried smaller gross margins but which nevertheless constituted the backbone of a general mail-order merchandise house that was fast becoming a complete store. Since a sewing machine might last its purchaser for many years and a cream separator might see a decade or two of service, lower unit-price goods of less durable nature had to serve as the nucleus of the company's merchandise line. This was necessary both in order to be able to satisfy all a customer's needs and thus pre-empt his patronage and in order to provide the solid point of departure for Richard Sears's dazzling tangential take-offs.

By 1895 Sears, Roebuck and Company had clearly begun to expand its merchandise line in many directions, even though a letterhead as late as March, 1894, saw fit to mention only that the firm dealt in "Watches, Jewelry and Silverware." After the influx of new blood and additional capital in 1895, the merchandise line expanded with greater rapidity and achieved a momentum which was to carry it for many years.

The 1895 catalogue proclaimed, "The following departments are now complete in every respect," and the order in which they were listed is interesting: crockery, bicycles, guns, revolvers, fishing tackle, sporting goods, baby carriages, furniture, agricultural implements, buggies, harness, saddlery, sewing machines, boots, shoes, clothing, pianos, organs, musical instruments, optical goods, watches, jewelry, diamonds, silverware, and clocks. There is ample evidence that many of these departments—most conspicuously, perhaps, clothing—were far from complete. But the listing of so many departments ahead of the old standbys—watches, jewelry, and silverware—may have indicated a desire on the company's part to be known as more than merely a purveyor of those three lines.

Watches did, however, open the catalogue's merchandise presentation; one model was featured at 98 cents, another at $1.68. ("How Good, How Cheap, That's the Question.") Others ranged up to $65 for a seventeen-jewel movement. The watches shown in 1895 were still of the open-face and hunting-case variety of pocket models for men and pendant or chatelaine watches for women. Wrist watches were still to come. The shoes were all high topped. The opening price for men's suits, "Our Leader," was

$4.98; women's (outer) clothing had not yet made its appearance. Gold-headed canes ranged in price from $2.75 to $8.95. The cheapest sewing machine, "Our Success Machine," listed at $8.50 (the great sewing-machine promotion was not to come for two more years). "While we do not care to recommend this machine too highly, we do not hesitate to say, it is fully equal to machines generally advertised at $18 to $25 and retailed at $25 to $35." This machine contained only one drawer and no cover, whereas the $13.90 machine had seven drawers and a cover.

The fanciest buggy, with full extension top and two seats, sold for $75, but cheaper models were available. A draped couch was priced at $5.45, while a "genuine full Turkish couch, finest quality leather"—and a monumental monstrosity it was—listed for $49.50. Bicycles were offered for $39.90; the great bicycle promotion, too, was yet to come. The last page of the 1895 catalogue featured an "$8.00 brass banquet lamp for $2.30."

These offerings were augmented two years later by talking machines, records, magic lanterns, arc lamps, lantern slides, motion-picture machines, films, and similar items. Interestingly enough, these items were produced by a separate company which Roebuck financed and managed; among his customers, other than Sears, Roebuck and Company, was Montgomery Ward.[1]

One interesting aspect of the development of the merchandise line is to be found in the grocery department, established during the first six months of 1895.[2] Groceries made their first catalogue appearance in 1896, occupying ten pages that spring. The logic behind this addition was twofold: first, the minimum freight charge (there was no parcel post) was based on a weight of one hundred pounds. Since it cost the customer, who paid the freight, as much for ten pounds as for one hundred, the company exhorted him to run the weight of his order to the full one hundred pounds by filling it out with groceries. The second factor was the conviction that groceries, while not really profitable in themselves, helped to secure orders for other merchandise; it was felt that some customers might not go to the trouble of ordering groceries from a competitor and then sending a separate order to Sears, Roebuck for, say, clothing. Farmers, particulaly in isolated areas, ordered groceries by mail in large quantities to last through the winter, when they were unable or unwilling to make trips to the general store for such purchases. The grocery department was, if not a "loss leader," at least primarily a "come-on."[3]

The limited data available on grocery-department operations show for the first six months of 1907 a loss of $16,991, or 1.91 per cent of sales. The situation worsened during the last six months of that year, which resulted in a further loss of $29,164.96, or 4.13 per cent of sales. While the grocery department succeeded in climbing into the black for the season ending June 30, 1908, it contributed only $7,045.29 of net profit—only a little more than 1 per cent on sales of nearly $620,000.

While any direct profit contributions of the grocery department were hard to discern, at least company employees benefited substantially by buying all their groceries from Sears, Roebuck at a noticeable saving. The earliest groceries included sugar, flour, canned goods, jellies, jams, preserves, hard candies, hams, bacon, and coffee. The quality of all these goods was apparently better than that of almost any other merchandise in Sears's listings.[4] Initially, this department occupied more space than any other and, for a while, led the parade in dollar volume.[5]

The ten pages of catalogue space allocated to groceries in the spring of 1896 dropped in the fall of that year to one page, which announced a monthly grocery bulletin. The company had decided that the rapid price fluctuations in this department dictated periodic bulletins rather than listing in the catalogue, where prices had to remain fixed for months. Succeeding years witnessed an alternation between these two approaches to groceries in the general catalogue—either lavish allocation of space to the grocery department, or just a page or so extolling the quality of the goods and urging readers to write for the periodic bulletins. There appears to have been so little rhyme or reason in the over-all approach that it is difficult to establish any clear pattern.

In 1896 Sears, Roebuck began selling patent medicines. A considerable variety of nostrums was described but only briefly and without illustrations. The following year saw this understatement remedied; illustrations appeared. In 1898 patent medicines occupied eight catalogue pages; in 1899 they were up to nine pages. The importance attached to patent medicines is illustrated by the fact that in 1900, when these nostrums still occupied nine pages in the general catalogue, they replaced watches and jewelry as the catalogue's initial offering. Patent medicines were again the lead-off line in the catalogue of 1901. "Dr. Echols' Australian Auriclo, a newly discovered cure for heart trouble," sold for 50 cents ("Retail price, $1.00.") —"Dropped Dead! Attention! Every fourth person has a weak or diseased heart." There were also "cures" for asthma, catarrh, indigestion, dyspepsia, and countless other ailments.

Drugs and patent medicines reached their apogee in the fall of 1905, when they held eighteen pages; specific "cures" included those for catarrh, consumption, headaches, the tobacco habit, and "female weaknesses." Even more interesting than these offerings, however, was a statement of "Our Position on the Patent Medicine Question":

> We sell nearly all of the advertised or so called patent medicines without adding our recommendation to any particular preparation. We simply furnish our customers such advertised patent medicines as they may want, and which they would buy anyway.... It must be understood, however, that we know nothing about the formulae or ingredients and we can, therefore, say nothing for or against the merits of such patent medicines.

The statement went on to claim that the company *did* know and guarantee the ingredients of all "household remedies" prepared in "our own laboratory." After that the statement asserted, "In all cases of acute sickness it is usually necessary, and in many cases of chronic diseases it is advisable, to employ the services of a skilled physician." The text continued: "We do not claim that any one of our household remedies is a 'Cure All.'"

The following page contained advertisements of "Dr. Wilden's Quick Cure for Indigestion and Dyspepsia" and "Brown's Vegetable Cure for Female Weakness." The next page advertised the "Wonder Heart Cure." Two pages later came the "Seroco Cure for the Tobacco Habit" and "Dr. Hammond's Internal Catarrh Cure." Additional "cures" followed. Sears, Roebuck was troubled with no problems of semantics.

In the prominent treatment it accorded patent medicines, the company was, as throughout most of its history, simply moving in concert with the times. As Presbrey points out:

Previous to 1865 proprietary-medicine advertising had reached a volume which constituted more than half the lineage in many papers. While the patent-medicine industry was large before 1860, it became tremendous after the Civil War. Patent medicines made up a very large percentage of the advertising in the several hundred religious papers in the '70's and later. The cures for "lost manhood" and alleged remedies for venereal disease ran riot in nearly all classes of media in the last half of the nineteenth century and were responsible for most of the disrepute which surrounded the industry. Great fortunes were built on patent medicines....

The patent-medicine proprietors, with individual expenditures running up to $700,000 a year, still were [in 1898] the most important group of general advertisers from the standpoint of expenditure....[6]

Presbrey also quotes the *Press and Printer* of Boston on its 1898 tabulation of advertisers regularly using periodicals of general circulation, excluding those who used only a few lines and the occasional advertiser. The total thus found was 2,583. Those in some of the various leading classes included: medicines, remedies, and articles sold in drugstores, 425; household articles, furniture, etc., 216; wearing apparel, 193; and bicycles, 133.[7]

In connection with the widespread popularity of patent medicines in this period—a popularity which has not even yet completely evaporated—it is well to remember Professor Hower's comments:

Bearing in mind the state of the medical profession at the time, we are not surprised that Americans were easily tempted to self-medication. As late as 1870 the head of the Harvard Medical School declared that written examinations could not be given because most of the students could not write well enough. In addition to their deficiencies of talent and training, the doctors were too few to serve the whole nation. A large portion of the population, moreover, lived miles from the nearest physician, good or bad. And few Americans... could have paid for proper medical attention had it been available. The situation provided a golden opportunity for the quack, and he made the most of it.[8]

By 1908 these nostrums still held five pages in the catalogue, but the tide had begun to turn. In the great muckraking period the *Ladies' Home*

Journal and *Collier's Weekly* crusaded against patent medicines. The muckraking which was instrumental in passage of the Pure Food and Drug Act of 1906 also helped to turn many people against patent medicines by educating them to the dangers of many of the potions and the uselessness of most of them. After the 1908 catalogue, Sears, Roebuck dropped a number of the more flagrant nostrums, but the highly profitable patent medicines clung to their place in the company's merchandise structure.

The "electric belt" made its first appearance in the catalogue in 1898, possibly as successor to an "electric ring," guaranteed to cure rheumatism. The ring had first appeared in 1896 but had been discontinued two years later. The belt occupied two full pages in 1899 and 1900, when the "Giant Power Heidelberg Electric Belt" was billed at $18—"In a month you will be a new man." The belt reached its heydey in 1901, when it held three pages in the catalogue. In two years this space dropped to one page, and in 1905 the belt bowed out. Sears, Roebuck's penchant for electricity also reflected itself in an electric insole for shoes ("A boon to those troubled with poor circulation and cold feet") and a battery plaster, but these soon went the way of the electric belt and ring. The electric-battery plasters offered positive relief to women from "the common and distressing backache incident to the sex at periods" and for "rheumatic kidney and muscular pain in the back."

By 1899 the company had twenty-four merchandise departments, according to the January 21 issue of the company's own *Seroco Topics*: music, buggies, stoves, carriage hardware, drugs, vehicles, shoes, notions, sewing machines, cloaks, sporting goods, dry goods, hardware, groceries, furniture and baby carriages, jewelry, optical goods, books, stereopticons, men's clothing, men's furnishings, bicycles, gramophones, harness.

The 1899 catalogue's splurge on color was a significant indication that Sears, Roebuck's offerings had come to include many lines to which black-and-white illustrations could not do full justice. Color treatment was accorded to shoes, carpets, rugs, "Oriental curtains," sewing machines, furniture, china, organs and other musical instruments, and baby buggies. It was not the company's first venture into the use of color, but it was its most extensive.

Still further additions were made to the merchandise offerings in 1900. The new century was ushered in with listings of paint, stationery, window shades, fancy goods and trimmings, infants' wear, plumbing supplies, and other additions to the standard lines. Sears, Roebuck was still far from being the complete store, but it was on the way. Every year saw new products added as the public acceptance of, and demand for, them became crystal clear.

Though displaced by patent medicines as the catalogue's initial offering in 1900, watches and allied lines nevertheless held 103 pages, exceeded only by the 140 pages devoted to hardware. Guns and sporting goods were responsible for 63 pages. Thirty-seven pages went to books and another 15 to stationery. Clothing—men's, women's, children's, boys'—reflected an expansion in the number of items offered and indicated the company was becoming a real mail-order haberdashery. The dry-goods department burgeoned to 22 pages, while curtains and floor coverings were good for 9 pages.

Watches were displayed in a greater variety of models than ever before. "Our Best Stereoscope" sold for $1.98, and the views included Spanish-American War scenes, comic views, religious subjects, scenes from Yellowstone National Park and Yosemite, and others. Zithers were featured, as was the "violin-guitar-zither, three instruments combined at the price of one"; the illustration might well have inspired a Rube Goldberg cartoon—or even have been one. Bicycles were down to $12.75, and men's silk ties sold as low as 19 cents. Ladies' hats were heavily befeathered and attained an almost incredible vertical projection; $2.35 would bring one of the least unbearable ones. The "Mackintosh" was still the raincoat of the period, and the "gingerbread" design of the stoves guaranteed a vast amount of work for housewives in cleaning and polishing. Buggies received prominent treatment, and couches and lounges showed little if any change since 1895.

The 1905 catalogue also shows the company's response to the yearning for "culture" at the opening of this century. In that year, when a house was not a home without a piano or an organ, the big book offered four different pianos. They ranged from the "Beckwith Home Favorite" ("a wonderful bargain at $89.00, weight: 750 pounds") to the "Beckwith Acme Grand Concert Piano" at $165. To "trade up" to the $165 instrument, the catalogue indirectly deprecated the $89 Home Favorite on a relative basis even while singing its absolute praises: "To enable us to offer a piano at this price, it is necessary to save wherever possible, hence the sounding board, while very strong, is not as large as in some of our other instruments; its metal plate is smaller, the strings are not so long, but nevertheless it is equal to pianos sold by music dealers for about $200.00."

In sharp contrast to the mere four pianos, the catalogue listed fifteen organs, covering 13 pages. In violins, Sears's advertising copy touted "Our Stradivarius" for only $1.95. As "The World's Largest Music Dealer," the company offered guitars, "singing" mandolins, and the "Autoharp"—"the musical wonder of the ages," the instrument which played itself with little assistance from the musician. Every man a king, every customer his own musician. The 60 pages of musical instruments featured in 1905 dropped to 27 in ten years, to 12 in another decade. By 1935 the catalogue was to contain only 8 pages of instruments.

The 1905 merchandise offerings also reveal that pocket and pendant watches were still the only types listed. Fancy engraved designs of animals, flowers, and initials were typical. The "Minnesota" seven-drawer, drop-head style sewing machine listed at $10.95, and buggies still held an important place in the catalogue. The sporting-goods department consisted largely of guns, revolvers, pistols, and ammunition. An engraved, specially finished, hammerless, double-barrel shotgun sold for $13.30 (that page contained also a picture of the company's own gun and revolver factory at Meriden, Connecticut).

"Harvard" disk talking machines (phonographs) ranged in price from $10.50 to $17.40, for "an extra large 30-inch black and gold horn, improved Harvard sound box and 100 needles." There was also the "Imperial Automatic Morris Chair." Men's and women's shoes were still high topped; ladies' hats were outstanding; and ladies' velvet and silk shirtwaist suits, up to as high $13.75, filled a stunning page of illustrations. Men's overcoats started at $7.00. There were, in addition, crockery and glassware, baby carriages, farm wagons, bobsleds, harness, saddles, currying supplies, lap robes, horse blankets, wallpaper and paint, cream separators, farm implements—these and a thousand and one other offerings. All this for the living; tombstones were advertised in a section entitled "Department of Memorial Art."

From 1905 to 1908 the company's merchandise line continued to grow with few really significant changes. Cream separators, sewing machines, watches and jewelry, and other tried-and-true lines were prominently featured. The host of more recent additions—hardware, plumbing supplies, building materials, clothing, etc.—followed the longer-established lines.

The most marked innovation came in the spring 1908 catalogue when the "2-4-6-8-cent" department appeared. Representing Sears, Roebuck's earliest clear attempt to move into the field of the five-and-ten-cent stores, the first appearance of this new department occupied eight pages in the back of the catalogue—two pages for each of the four price ranges. The number of items included in the "2-4-6-8" department was almost limitless: paring knives, socks, spoons, fans, hinges, tea balls, coat hangers, blotters, writing ink, doorknobs, trowels, hatchet handles, kitchen graters, handkerchiefs, pokers, garters, files, shovels, saw handles, flowerpot brackets, envelopes, collar buttons, mincing knives, steak-beaters, bridle bits, dress shields, mixing bowls, toothbrushes, and countless others.

The "2-4-6-8" items were priced practically at cost to serve as "order-starters"; they sold in such huge quantities that manufacturers' unit costs were reduced, which made even lower pricing possible. At the outset of this experiment, the goods were drawn from the merchandise departments in which they were normally stocked. But the demand for the inexpensive items became so great that a separate department was established to handle them. Clothespins, toothpicks, buttons, and wooden chopping bowls, for example, soon had to be ordered by the carload. Most of the items were genuine bargains and proved virtually irresistible to readers thumbing through the catalogue; and, since the minimal order accepted by the firm was fifty cents, they functioned well as bait for larger orders.

A 1918 memorandum to Julius Rosenwald from L. J. Brennan, who headed the "2-4-6-8" department in that year, gives further background on the success of this venture:

> In the Fall of 1907, Mr. Skinner conceived the idea of grouping merchandise to sell under 10 cents. . . .
>
> We had no idea how this arrangement would take with our customers and our entire stock of this merchandise to start this sale was not over $20,000.
>
> Our Catalogues were mailed shortly after January 1st, 1908 and the flood of orders fairly swamped us within two weeks. We had neither the merchandise nor the organization to handle this volume, and called on all Departments for help. . . . In less than a month the Dept. was enlarged by clearing out two entire rooms and by building two complete sets of bins covering almost one room. . . . In the first six months our sales amounted to $308,000.00 or something over 6,000,000 articles. Our buyers were put to a test in securing this quantity. In many cases Factories from whom we bought the goods returned our orders or wrote telling us they felt sure we had made a mistake in placing the order as we had specified so many gross when they felt sure we had intended to order dozens instead of grosses.
>
> The sales from this Dept. for the year 1908 amounted to $503,000.00 and has increased each year so that in the year 1917 it amounted to nearly $1,000,000.00.

The "2-4-6-8" double-page spreads moved to the forefront of the catalogue in 1909 and remained a catalogue feature until discontinued around 1918.

Scattered throughout such thundering successes as the "2-4-6-8" department, sewing-machine, and cream-separator schemes were the inevitable thud-and-blunder episodes. One of the greatest of such failures, and a fair exhibit in this category, was the stock-food promotion—"stock" being, in this case, livestock.

Richard Sears was never one to insult another man's creation by refusing to copy it. He had heard stories, possibly exaggerated, of the fortune accumulated by a man named Savage in Minneapolis, who had built a near monopoly in the sale of such stock foods aimed to produce more eggs, better milk, and happier days for farmers.[9] In 1906 the Sears, Roebuck catalogue spent twelve pages to introduce the "H. O. Davis Stock Foods." (Just where Davis came into the picture is not quite clear, even today.) Davis' name appeared on promotional literature, including a weighty tome, *One Thousand Pointers for Stock Raisers*. An order for the stock food brought the customer the book free.

Even Sears's magic copy, which had hitherto induced the farmer to buy almost anything, failed to move the readers.[10] Richard Sears responded to this marked lack of interest with further promotional activities including even more hortatory messages, more diversified "packaging," and his conviction that anything which failed did so because of insufficient pushing. He developed grandiose schemes for merchandising stock food,[11] but the farmers who bought that line apparently sent their trade to Mr. Savage. After two years, the line was dropped. Sears was in the position in which

Thomas Alva Edison was later to be, when he said he was making great progress in an invention since he had found a hundred ideas which would not work.

A department which had its ups and downs (whereas stock foods had only the latter) was "Modern Homes." The activity from which "Modern Homes" developed came into existence between 1895 and 1900 when a department was established to handle such building materials as composition roofing, gutters, downspouts, doors, windows, moldings, stair materials, porch work, wood mantels, etc. The first millwork catalogue was issued in 1902. Sales were satisfactory, but operating expenses were high and, with the exception of roofing, service was unsatisfactory and resulted in complaints, cancellations, and allowances. As a result, the department suffered consistent losses. In 1906, for example, sales were $1,194,000, but the department sustained a net loss of $35,000.

It was decided that the "Modern Homes" department should be closed out, and the liquidation process was assigned to one F. W. Kushel. After several months of studying how best to discontinue the department, Kushel became convinced that the department could be made efficient and profitable. He obtained authorization to reorganize the department and continue it. Sales were stimulated, service improved, and expenses brought under control. In 1908 the first "Modern Homes" catalogue was issued. By 1912 departmental losses had been wiped out, and the net profit for the preceding seven years totaled $630,000.[12]

It was not until 1909 that the company felt the automobile had firmly established itself, over the incredulity of the public, the skepticism even of some of its pioneers, the feverish exhortations of ministers of the gospel, and the advice of physicians. In 1901 the *Automobile Magazine* had quoted Dr. Winslow Forbes, a brain specialist:

> When these racing motor cars reach a speed of 80 miles per hour, they must drive themselves, for no human brain is capable of dealing with all the emergencies that may arise should that be maintained for any period worth thinking of. The human animal is not designed to travel 80 miles an hour; neither the human brain nor the human eye can keep pace with it.[13]

In 1909 the big catalogue listed motor buggies guaranteed to run as well as any others—dependent, of course, upon the care and handling given them by their owners, geographic conditions, and acts of Providence. Cognizant no doubt of the criticism of the still new automobile but likewise confident of a future market for it, the company named its first automobile "The Sears Buggy." It even had them designed with a hood resembling as much as possible the old-fashioned buggy, to which the farmer particularly was still devoted and which had been one of the company's best-selling lines for years. The models ranged in price from $370 to $525.

The automobile's invasion of the catalogue is indicative of the general growth of the merchandise line of the company, for the first appearance of any new item in a Sears catalogue had seldom marked the date when that item first became popular. It had simply marked the date when the item had established beyond peradventure that it was here to stay and the date when Sears, Roebuck was able to make satisfactory arrangements with sources for mass delivery of the item. Up to 1908 it frequently marked the date at which Richard Sears was able to profit by the trial-and-error of the innovators and finally to copy their product with improvements of his own and put it into mass production.

Yet, with due allowance for this time lag, the catalogue offerings of the company have remained one of the best yardsticks in most respects of the needs and wants of the people of this country during the period of Sears, Roebuck's existence. No item could long be in great demand without cropping up in the big book; and, by the same token, few items could hang on in the catalogue for any length of time after the public ceased to fancy them. As that public fancy expanded in scope, as America came of age, as its people accepted new products and lost their taste for some of the old, the Sears catalogue kept pace, albeit a cautious pace indeed. That, in its essence, is the story of the steady expansion of the company's merchandise line in this and other periods.

Richard Sears had a deep interest in the company's whole merchandise line. It would be easy to assume that the man interested himself only in a few items susceptible to his great promotions; but the truth seems to be that, while he did indeed care almost nothing for administrative details or organization, he had from the first an unflagging interest in the company's merchandise structure. Witness, for example, excerpts from a letter Sears wrote Louis Asher from London on January 4, 1907:

> There is hardly a manager in our house who cannot, in my humble opinion, and with a great benefit to himself, devote every spare moment he can get to the finding of ways and means of improving his line and the method of presenting the line, and to this end I believe that several managers would profit if they would carry the pages of their division or parts of their division with them so that in the spare moments of the evening, Sunday, or to and from the office, they might have ready reference to these most interesting subjects, which, while they will never be fully solved, for they will never be done so well but that ways will be found to improve, still we are right now so weak in many spots, many things have grown so stale, that we have need for very marked improvement in the near future, and it ought to manifest itself ... in our next fall's catalogue.... Mr. Skinner I know is very much awake to our needs along this line, but he will say, and rightfully, before we consider the catalogue, is our line right? That is a most important question which we have learned from experience. For example, for years we pushed made-to-measure clothing and our line there was not right until we got on to ready-made; for years we failed to bring ingrain carpets to the front and instead emphasized the more expensive tapestries. Our line was not right. This, I will agree with Mr. Skinner, is the first great question to be solved, and we are likely to err here, taking the fact that we are making big money or effecting the big sales as a proof that our line is right. ... I do hope Mr. Skinner will be able to awaken a wonderful interest along these lines, for I

fear our mercantile instincts are likely to become seriously dull by general results when they show a good profit....[14]

A study of the sales volume in each of the four major classifications into which the merchandise can be fitted—wearing apparel, domestics, hard lines, and miscellaneous—in 1902 and 1907 shows the trend in sales by *types* of goods. Wearing apparel, for instance, accounted for 20.28 per cent of the company's total net profit in 1902, as shown in Table 7. By 1907 this proportion had grown to 35.26 per cent, as illustrated in Table 8. As soft goods thus accounted for an increasing proportion of gross sales and of net profit in that five-year span, the proportion of hard lines in those categories declined within the same period—from 62.88 of total net profit in 1902, for example, to 58.23 per cent in 1907. Marked sales increases occurred in all merchandise categories, but the lesser rate of increase in hard lines made the mail order increasingly a soft-lines business.

As used in Tables 7 and 8, "Wearing apparel" includes such obvious lines as clothing (boys', men's, and women's), shoes, coats, infants' wear, work clothing, millinery, lingerie, and hosiery. "Domestics" includes such household articles as curtains, drapes, shades, piece goods, and similar lines. "Hard lines" embraces automobile supplies, bicycles, cutlery, hardware, harness, millwork, paints, plumbing and roofing supplies, tools, cream separators, furniture, baby carriages, pianos, stoves, washing machines, vehicles, and other durables. "Miscellaneous" refers to books, jewelry, groceries, lumber, optical merchandise, seeds, silverware, wallpaper, poultry food, and other items.

In the category of individual merchandise lines, cream separators furnish an interesting record of one outstanding "big ticket" (to adopt a term not formally used by the company until later). Table 9 chronicles the merchandise history of separators and makes it clear that in 1903, after the separator's potentialities were dramatized to Richard Sears, the previous year's net loss in this department was converted into a profit, even though a small one. From that date on, separators showed a generally higher and higher net profit, reaching a high point of nearly 29 per cent in 1908.

The whole story of the quality level of Sears, Roebuck merchandise, of the company's business ethics, of the degree of honesty represented in all its advertising, of the slow development from schemes and sharp practices to a mature philosophy of rigorously honest business—all this story is shot through with contradictions, with backing and filling, with cross-currents, with inconsistencies. For this story is in large part the story of the men who made and who were the company in this early phase; they were not static in their philosophy, in their approach to business. Nor was the public point of view toward business ethics a static quantity, even though in the 1880's the people seemed resigned to a cavalier business attitude which, by today's standards, would be bluntly termed dishonesty.

TABLE 7*
SALES AND PROFITS BY MAJOR MERCHANDISE DIVISIONS, 1902

Division	Gross Sales	Gross Profit	Gross Profit as Percentage of Gross Sales	Net Profit	Net Profit as Percentage of Gross Sales	Departmental Gross Sales as Percentage of Total Gross Sales	Departmental Net Profit as Percentage of Total Gross Sales	Departmental Net Profit as Percentage of Total Net Profit
Wearing apparel	$ 3,752,327	$ 811,404	21.62	$ 230,988	6.15	22.88	1.41	20.28
Domestics	249,910	68,967	27.60	20,335	8.14	1.52	0.12	1.79
Hard lines	10,425,519	2,452,322	23.52	716,073	6.87	63.58	4.37	62.88
Miscellaneous	1,970,572	628,541	31.90	171,418	8.70	12.02	1.04	15.05
Total	$16,398,328	$3,961,234	24.16	$1,138,814	6.94	100.00	6.94	100.00

*Source: Company records.

TABLE 8*
SALES AND PROFITS BY MAJOR MERCHANDISE DIVISIONS, 1907

Division	Gross Sales	Gross Profit	Gross Profit as Percentage of Gross Sales	Net Profit	Net Profit as Percentage of Gross Sales	Departmental Gross Sales as Percentage of Total Gross Sales	Departmental Net Profit as Percentage of Total Gross Sales	Departmental Net Profit as Percentage of Total Net Profit
Wearing apparel	$15,843,658	$ 4,310,420	27.21	$ 622,270	3.93	32.82	1.29	35.26
Domestics	1,139,658	263,977	23.16	26,448	2.32	2.36	0.05	1.50
Hard lines	25,151,407	6,195,123	24.63	1,027,865	4.09	52.10	2.13	58.23
Miscellaneous	6,142,067	1,905,090	31.01	88,412	1.44	12.72	0.18	5.01
Total	$48,276,790	$12,674,610	26.25	$1,764,995	3.66	100.00	3.65	100.00

*Source: Company records.

Sears, Roebuck and Company grew to young corporate manhood in an era when America was still to a very considerable extent a pioneer country. And Sears's customers were, for many years, drawn almost entirely from farmers and residents of small rural communities.[15] "Quality" was a word and a concept with connotations peculiar to rural residents. Quality meant serviceability and value; a piece of merchandise had to be good enough to perform the functions the catalogue said it would perform, and the price had to be low enough for them to afford it. That meant really low, and low prices often enabled them to buy goods which, even though perhaps shoddy, could not otherwise have been bought at all. It apparently meant little or nothing to the farmer that the ghastly, standardized furniture sold by Sears, Roebuck was almost utterly devoid of aesthetic

TABLE 9*

Cream-Separator Sales, 1902-8

Year	Gross Sales	Amount Gross Profit	Gross Profit as Percentage of Gross Sales	Net Profit	Net Profit as Percentage of Net Sales
1902	$ 272,300	$ 76,975	28.27	$ 17,039†	6.26†
1903	474,600	120,314	25.35	5,497	1.16
1904	696,000	177,174	25.46	18,811	2.70
1905	1,533,100	387,758	25.29	103,259	6.74
1906	1,865,400	670,342	35.94	244,086	13.09
1907	1,582,900	506,233	31.98	192,885	12.19
1908	1,316,200	594,445	45.15	375,221	28.51

* Source: Company records.
† Loss.

quality. Witness the experience of another merchant, even as late as the turn of the century:

[J. C.] Penney did not have to do too much fretting over the fickleness of styles. His customers did not thumb through the fashion magazines, and the names of Paris dressmakers were not household words in the small Western towns. Cotton dresses, shirtwaists, and suits in light, medium, and dark blue, black, white, and brown, with an occasional plaid, were for purposes of dressing up; kimonos and wrappers were sufficient the rest of the time.[16]

As far as the customers of Sears, Roebuck's (and, in fact, most rural customers) were concerned, if a dresser held clothes and if a bed offered a relatively comfortable night's sleep to a man who had plowed all day, that was sufficient—provided the price was low enough. Richard Sears saw to it that the price was "right."

The best gold watch sold by Sears in his early mail-order days contained just twenty-seven cents worth of gold, according to an analysis made later by the Sears laboratories. But that watch kept time, and some of them continued to keep time even for decades after the "gold" wore off.[17]

Sears offered men's suits at $4.98, when the general market price was often twice that figure. True, they were made of shoddy wool (and frequently contained a high percentage of cotton); they were ill-fitting; and they did not wear long in every case.[18] But where else could the farmer buy a Sunday suit for $4.98? When one talks of the quality of Sears, Roebuck's early merchandise—and most of the talk in that period rated Sears's quality pretty low[19]—one must never forget the relationship between quality and price. Sears's bedroom suite, three pieces for $8.50 at one point, was of inexpensive, hard birch. Birch has utility; beauty is to be found in oak and mahogany and other woods, but the Sears customers could not afford—and to a great extent probably did not want—anything better.

Sears guaranteed his $11.96 cookstove to cook. It cooked. And it cooked for years and years. Sears's plows would plow, and Sears's washing machines would wash. That was what farm families wanted; and that was what they got from Sears, Roebuck.

It would be absurd, of course, to claim that customers were always satisfied with the quality of the goods. They were not. And under Sears's merchandising policy[20] they knew they could return the merchandise, which was just what they often did in staggering quantities. There were times when returned merchandise occupied almost as much space as new goods ready for first shipment.[21] Returns sometimes threatened to bankrupt the company, as in the "Send No Money" promotion. But Sears, Roebuck always somehow muddled through, because there were always more happy than dissatisfied customers—or at least enough satisfied customers to keep the company in business.

Many of the shortcomings in quality of Sears's merchandise before and around the turn of the century can be laid to Richard Sears's sometimes indulged habit of promoting thousands of orders for goods without having any semblance of adequate stock. When orders flooded in, buyers procured whatever they could. This led to countless substitutions. But, by and large, the customers' own standards were low, and the substituted articles were often accepted cheerfuly. What the purchaser wanted, in many cases, was that bargain Sears was advertising. If, for example, the item was a suit, he could learn to like the color, and the fit was relatively unimportant.[22]

Yet even the great clothing promotion of the 1890's, which brought so much proximate chaos in filling orders, was in itself to contribute to some improvement within the company, for the very success of the venture indicated such profitable potentialities for the clothing department that that line was shortly thereafter rationalized and put on a sounder basis. In the words of an employee who joined Sears, Roebuck about the time Richard Sears launched that promotion:

After this sale a somewhat greater variety of goods was obtained, and I believe that before the first year was over, we probably handled about twenty styles. We also commenced to add a few single trousers and a few boys' suits.

After doing business for a few years in a slipshod manner, it became evident that clothing could be sold by mail, and practically a new policy was adopted. Orders were filled carefully, various kinds of garments, such as shorts, stouts, longs, etc. were provided and alterations on garments were made carefully.[23]

Obviously, one cannot safely take merely a "static" look at the quality of Sears's merchandise. Like every other aspect of the business, it was a changing, growing thing, never quite the same from month to month. Organization and systematization crept into the business, mothered by stark necessity. With it came a greater emphasis on quality of merchandise.

By the turn of the century the public was demanding higher quality, more nearly inflexible honesty in advertising and selling, and it was beginning to dawn on more and more businessmen that the customer, if not always right, could not at any rate always be wrong. The open season on customers was beginning to be hedged in. That this was an evolution not confined to the mail-order business is clear from Professor Nystrom's comments:

In the earlier stages of the use of retail advertising, both exaggeration and dishonesty were frequent. By degrees it became clear to established advertisers that permitting continued dishonesty in advertising would result in the loss of public faith in advertising and in business suicide for concerns depending upon advertising. . . .

Probably department stores as a group have been guilty of as much dishonest advertising in the past as any other institution. In view of the fact that department stores have been greater users of advertising than others, it is probable that their responsibility is also greater. Reforms in advertising came about in a very gradual way, although some of the earliest efforts to curb dishonest statements began in the middle of the nineteenth century. It was many years before the rank and file, even of department stores, accepted and began to practice advertising principles prohibiting overstatements and misstatements promulgated years before by the leaders. In fact, though much progress has been made toward cleaner advertising, actual practice still lags far behind the present accepted ethical standards of publicity.[24]

Thus there enters the problem of the business ethic of the times. That ethic was a deeply intrenched one; *caveat emptor*, like any human institution which has outgrown whatever usefulness it may ever have had, gave ground only under continued and relentless pressure. As improved manufacturing techniques, competition for public favor, and an increasing public demand for higher-quality goods exerted their inexorable influence, however, *caveat emptor* died a victim of attrition.

The pioneer country which demanded only crude utility grew to be a more sophisticated nation insistent upon higher-quality goods with some aesthetic appeal. As the United States so developed—and only so fast—sellers like Sears, Roebuck acceded to this growing demand. The country whose isolated farmers had been heavily dependent upon the great mail-order houses for essential goods became a country linked by highways and served by thousands of retail stores stocking increasingly better goods in ever greater variety. This change coincided with a considerable growth in purchasing power; and manufacturing processes, which had contributed to these changes, were in turn spurred on to greater achievements to feed the gaping maw of the lusty country with choicer merchandise.

Louis Asher says that the improvement in quality of the company's goods is attributable more to J. Fletcher Skinner, general merchandise manager, than to any other man. And Asher asserts that it was "about 1905" when Skinner began actively to seek better-quality goods, "hoping to accomplish this without too great advance in prices." But Asher also points out that, even before this arbitrary date of 1905, Skinner "stood for accurate descriptions in the catalogue and was a stickler for quality in merchandise."[25] Asher adds that Sears "seized avidly on Skinner's idea about improving the quality of the merchandise, and pushed it hard."

Lessing J. Rosenwald, who succeeded his father as chairman of the board in 1932, in a talk at a Sears forum on April 16, 1935, declared:

> Mr. Skinner was a splendid merchant and obtained the best in men by reason of his marvelous personality. I think to Mr. Skinner goes the credit for the insistence on minimum standards of quality. In other words, just any piece of merchandise was not enough. It had to be a serviceable, useful article before Mr. Skinner would consent to its use, and to him, I think, we owe this standard quality, at least the minimum standard that has grown up in our Company. I think he was the one who started the stock control systems and laid the basis for our present inventory controls.

Just as various attempts to polarize the whole story of improvement in quality around the conflict between Rosenwald and Richard Sears seem specious, so must it appear that neither did Skinner alone carry the battle for higher quality. The truth of the matter appears to be that most of the higher executives as well as the department managers were in general agreement on the policy of improving the quality of the company's merchandise.

The "inventory policy" of the company in its earliest days was just about what one could expect from the general haphazard nature of its operation: sometimes there was inventory, but seldom was there policy. In the first phase of his watch-selling career, Sears usually procured the goods and then proceeded to sell them through station agents and others. As his business began to expand and as he began to advertise widely, he still had nothing like a well-defined policy in regard to inventory. When his advertisements pulled well, he went out and bought the watches and items of jewelry with which to fill the orders. When on another occasion he might make large purchases, he simply stepped up his advertising and promotional schemes in order to move the goods for which he had contracted.

One such large purchase—for sixty thousand watches—so overinventoried Sears that it was a big factor in his selling out his first watch company.

The merchandise line steadily expanded, but policy did not keep pace unless operational anarchy can be called policy. In the first period in which such items as buggies and sewing machines were added to the merchandise line, Sears himself continued to do much of the firm's buying, by mail and by personal trips around the country. Operations had not been sufficiently organized to project anticipated sales with even a fair degree of accuracy for any given period. Sears simply bought what he could get hold of, in the amounts he thought he could sell; under the influence of his advertisements, he usually found he could sell several times the amount he had on hand and on order. This situation led to frantic appeals to sources for increased quantities and to searches for additional sources.

Until systematization began to take hold and order to emerge from chaos, the company seldom knew in any detail just what goods it had on hand. Returned goods often piled up and competed for floor space with new goods awaiting shipment. Correspondence and shipping were so disorganized that, when a customer did not receive his order within a reasonable time and wrote to lodge a complaint, he might soon find on his doorstep or at the railroad station a dozen of the items he had ordered. Since these items were eventually to be returned to the company (at its expense), they were part of its inventory. But just where they were, and in what quantity, no one knew.

Still another factor contributing to the confusion was the inadequate records system for the many items shipped to the customer direct from the factory. Orders sent by the customer to the company in Chicago were routed on to the factory, which was not always prompt in making shipments. This also helped pile up a profusion of goods which sometimes preempted a station agent's storage space. Roebuck quotes from a letter from William Pettigrew citing information Pettigrew had obtained from a Mr. Hoch, at one time a correspondent with the American Woolen Mills Department:

> Many of the shipments... originated at factories that were shipping goods direct to customers for our Company. For example, our sewing machine orders were very heavy at the time, and were shipped from the factory. The factories were slow in forwarding the shipping records to our Chicago office, and records were not entered promptly after receipt by us. The consequence was that when a customer complained of delay in shipment and the correspondent did not find a record of shipment on our Chicago books, he would mark the correspondence for shipment. As a result letters from customers were sometimes like the following: "For heaven's sake, quit sending me sewing machines. Every time I go to the station I find another one there. You have shipped me five already." I believe the period was the Fall of 1898 or Spring of 1899.[26]

Roebuck, speaking of 1895 and the expansion of the merchandise line around that time, quotes Sears as expressing the belief that the new departments could be conducted successfully "with very little stock on hand."[27] Inventory figures are available only for the years from 1896 on. In that year according to company records, Sears, Roebuck's inventory amounted to $254,045, while its volume of business was $1,741,040.[28] Data for inventory and volume of business by years are shown in Table 10.

Contributory to the disorder attending inventory was the sprawling character of the firm's warehousing. By the time the huge new plant was erected in 1906, Sears, Roebuck had spread out into a multitude of buildings scattered over Chicago. It was well-nigh impossible to keep accurate records of what goods were where, when Albert Loeb, who negotiated leases for storage space, was almost the only official who really knew in

TABLE 10*

INVENTORY DATA 1897–1908

Year	Inventory	Net Sales	Inventory as Percentage of Net Sales
1897	$ 489,387	$ 2,800,858	17.5
1898	853,357	5,394,100	15.8
1899	965,446	7,928,387	12.2
1900	†	10,637,367	....
1901	2,034,928	14,656,568‡	13.9
1902	2,853,980	15,945,397	17.9
1903	3,459,348	23,252,642	14.9
1904	3,264,915	27,602,721	11.8
1905	5,908,112	37,879,422	15.6
1906–7	6,011,426	50,722,840	13.6
1907–8	5,912,530	40,843,866	14.5

* Source: 1897–1901, A. C. Roebuck, "Some Early and Later History of Sears, Roebuck and Co." (2 vols.), *passim*; 1902–7, annual reports of Sears, Roebuck and Company. The inventory figures shown are as of December 31 of the year given or as of January 1 of the year immediately following, except 1907 and 1908, when the fiscal year ended June 30. It should be noted that all figures given are for total inventory. No data are available on inventory by departments.

† Unavailable.
‡ Gross sales.

just what buildings the company was operating. The crying need for additional space was a constant quantity.

Rosenwald, J. Fletcher Skinner, and others concerned with the day-to-day problems of the company must have suffered some unhappiness over an article written by Sears for the first issue of the *Publisher and Advertiser*, issued by the Agate Club, composed of Chicago advertising men, in 1905. Its title was: "Have the Goods; Then Advertise." The unctuous platitudes of the article were a play-by-play account of how Sears, Roebuck and Company did *not* operate. In spectacular instances, Richard Sears advertised; then it was up to the other executives to get the goods.[29]

"Sources" are the manufacturers from whom the company "gets the goods." Today they form one of the most interesting aspects of the Sears organization and operations. But fifty years ago sources presented one of the firm's biggest problems. Even in an economy as productive as America's had become by the 1890's, it was difficult for Sears, Roebuck to obtain the goods it wanted at the prices it was willing to pay. Under optimal conditions it would have been difficult, and conditions were far from the optimum and often not even tolerably good. The retail merchants' opposition to the growing mail-order giant was bitter and unyielding. Many manufacturers feared to sell to Sears, and others flatly refused, on the ground that other outlets would boycott them if they were found dealing with Sears. Even when a manufacturer was willing and eager to sell to Sears, his output was often so small that his contribution was of dubious advantage.

Too, some manufacturers feared to commit their whole output to one firm—particularly to Sears, Roebuck—with the possibility that such a step would give the company a life-and-death hold on the manufacturer. The firm had a habit of sometimes placing initial orders for a volume far in excess of a manufacturer's output. When Sears would order 50,000 bicycles, the incredulous source would ask, "Don't you mean 5,000? Nobody could sell 50,000 bicycles."[30]

Richard Sears early discovered that his best hope for obtaining what he needed was to seek out manufacturers who wanted to do business with him and, if necessary, provide capital to enable the manufacturer to expand his plant in order to make the goods. Two illustrations will suffice to point up this operation. The company was buying shotguns made by one Andrew Fryberg, in Worcester, Massachusetts. Sears sought him out and asked how much capital would be required to increase his output from around 15 guns a day to 200 daily. Fryberg figured a while and came up with his estimate. Sears lent him the money. Fryberg incorporated, gave Sears a part interest, and proceeded to step up production to around 300 single-barrel shotguns daily, as well as 50 double-barrel guns and 300 revolvers. The entire output went, of course, to Sears, Roebuck.[31]

For bicycles, Sears approached a manufacturer named Arnold Schwinn. The negotiations took roughly the same course as had those with Fryberg. Schwinn was able to expand his business enormously, and Sears in turn got the bicycles he needed to meet the demand created by his highly effective sales promotion.[32]

Generally speaking, Sears's policy was to buy no more than a half-interest in a plant and, where possible, not even to buy the entire output. He was determined that the plants should remain on a competitive basis, so that he might be enabled to buy at lower prices.

The demands of the company and the opposition to dealing with Sears, Roebuck were, however, sometimes so strong that the company was compelled to organize its own factories for particular goods. The nine companies into which the officers and stockholders of Sears, Roebuck had bought by 1906—cited in the directors' resolution authorizing formation of a corporation under the laws of New York State to replace the Illinois corporation—included factories producing stoves, vehicles, firearms, furniture, saws, agricultural implements, cream separators, plumbing equipment and supplies, and cameras.

The 1906 catalogue contained pictures and descriptions of sixteen manufacturing plants owned wholly or partly by the company, giving the cities in which they were located and the line of merchandise they produced. Even this list, however, reflected a sensitivity to the manufacturers' position in view of the possible boycotts to which they were subjecting themselves by selling to Sears. A company producing saws was located only in "southeastern Michigan." Reference was also made to factories producing a variety of items from clothing to hardware, but "lack of space" prevented a listing of such sources.

The 1910 catalogue repeated this theme. It carried illustrations of the "Famous David Bradley" farm-implement factory at Bradley, Illinois; a paint factory and a wallpaper mill in Chicago; a gun factory in Meriden, Connecticut, and a camera factory at Rochester, Minnesota; a vehicle factory in Evansville, Indiana, and two shoe factories in Littleton, New Hampshire; a safe factory and a stove foundry in Newark, Ohio ("the very largest stove foundry in all the world"); an organ factory in Louisville, Kentucky; a wire-fence factory in Knightstown, Indiana; and furniture factories in Chicago and in Binghamton, New York. Also pictured, but more vaguely located, were a saw factory in Michigan (the same vague phrasing as in the 1906 catalogue), a plumbing-goods factory in Wisconsin, and a cream-separator plant in Iowa.

The 1910 book was inexact as to just which of those factories the company owned outright, which it owned partially, and of just which it "controlled the output." The text asserted that factories supplying the company numbered "into the thousands."

One practice which did not make things any easier for the company was Sears's tactic in "bootlegging" nationally advertised merchandise. When manufacturers would not sell to him, he would somehow obtain some of their products, cut the price on the goods—and then mark his own brands lower[33] and feature the items together to develop acceptance for Sears's brands.

One of the company's greatest assets in locating adequate sources was, of course, its buyers. Many of these men, recruited from industrial firms, knew not only the product itself but also the suppliers. They knew where to seek out the goods; they knew reliable sources; they knew something about production costs. The buyers were given wide latitude amounting to sweeping authority as soon as they established themselves firmly.

The 1908 catalogue devoted considerable space to extol the skills of its buyers and to explain their methods of operating and their findings which on occasion projected the company into its own manufacture of some particular line. The four pages of space allocated to such institutional advertising opened on the theme of "Price and Quality" and pointed out that "we are being attacked by the hundreds of thousands of retail dealers, wholesale dealers, manufacturers, salesmen, etc., in all lines of merchandise in all parts of the United States on this one great question of quality." Therefore "we must furnish a quality of merchandise that will effectively disprove every argument of every kind raised against us." Warming to its subject, the catalogue went on to explain how it maintained what it claimed was its high quality of goods:

> Our buyers are instructed and reinstructed in private audience repeatedly and gathered in assembly are instructed to buy nothing, accept nothing . . . that will not pass the most rigid inspection. . . . A department of inspection such as we doubt exists in any other institution is maintained for the most exacting scrutiny of all goods made or purchased. . . .
> Millions of dollars have been expended by us in the development of sources of supply, that we might thoroughly control the quality of raw materials used, the iron, the steel, the lumber, the hides, the leather, the wool, the cloth, the metals. . . .
> As we sell more goods to the consumer than any other concern in the world, we feel it only reasonable that we should be able to buy our goods lower, on the whole, than any other concern in the world.

The catalogue then declared that each of the buyers, "necessarily knowing as much about the goods he is about to buy, how they should be made up and what they should cost to make as the manufacturer could possibly know," always analyzed each component of quality and cost of the merchandise under consideration. Sometimes, according to the company, buyers found a manufacturer making too great a profit; at other times, it found the manufacturer's costs too high because his factory was run with "too much overhead expense or waste." Often, the catalogue said, Sears, Roebuck was able to help a manufacturer reduce his production costs. By judicious placing of orders the company could make it possible for a source to operate at full, instead of half, capacity, thus reducing his unit costs and his selling price to Sears. Sometimes, however, it was not possible to obtain the quality the company sought at a price it was willing to pay; in such instances the company was driven to establish its own manufacturing facilities. The company's buying organization was "enormous":

> It's divided into a great many units. It reaches out into every part or resource in the United States and, in fact, over the civilized world. It begins with the most thorough research into the proper time, place and way of buying staple raw materials. . . . Our buying organization is a great college of commercial economies. Through this organization we study the methods of nearly all the manufacturers, wholesalers and retailers of the world. We bring together for comparison, selection and for study those things that are made in shops, big and small, all over the world. We devise ways and means of bettering, improving and perfecting styles.

The statement continued to the effect that, when the company found a man "with the peculiar experience and knowledge" necessary to make a certain product, it often had to "grub-stake him, as it were; that is, supply him with the necessary capital, and then we have had to nurse him along by seeing that he bought his raw material right." Further, the company asserted it also had to send its "statisticians, costs accountants, master mechanics, and inspectors" to oversee production.

What of the men who made up the company's corps of buyers? What were their qualifications, and how did they operate?

Comparatively few things, and on one class of merchandise in a limited variety, do we entrust to the care of one buyer, but this buyer must be a professional expert in the particular few things we entrust him to purchase for us.... One man cannot possibly buy a great variety of merchandise.... He must needs be a specialist in his limited line, and in this limited line he is not permitted to make any mistakes.

The company professed to have about a hundred such "professional buyers," each buying no more than one line; buying of hardware and furniture was even further subdivided for greater specialization. It was claimed that each buyer knew just where to find the required manufacturing facilities and just how to write out his specifications for the merchandise. The catalogue maintained that its buyer of dress goods used a magnifying glass to check the weave and "chemical analysis" to check the materials.

Reportedly the buyers were "more or less always on the road, visiting almost every exhibition, every fair, every center where merchandise is gathered together for the purpose of exhibition and comparison." To assist those buyers in covering all the United States and "every civilized part of the world," the company employed "missionaries." The missionaries were said to travel constantly, inspecting the stocks of virtually all retail establishments in the country, conversing with the public at large to discover their needs and desires, and buying goods "of all kinds and descriptions" to be sent to Chicago for comparison and study. Stoves, for example, were reputedly purchased in great numbers; upon arrival in Chicago, they were taken completely apart for intensive study to determine whether Sears, Roebuck could learn how to improve its own product in any way.

So said the catalogue. If all the foregoing were accepted as accurate, it would be easy to conclude that, even by 1910, Sears, Roebuck had pretty well mastered a program of basic buying (actually a recent development even today and one still in process). One could also conclude that the testing laboratories, not even in existence in 1910, would be but a gratuitous appurtenance when they did appear. It would further have to be concluded that the quality of the company's merchandise had reached a high point which left nothing to be desired. But the likeliest conclusion of all is simply that a highly competent copywriter, possibly trained by Richard

Sears himself, turned himself loose under a free rein to compose what could be taken for a posthumous tribute to the old master himself.

Despite the work of his buyers, Sears himself had long scouted the country for sources. In April, 1902, for example, this advertisement appeared several times in the *Atlanta Constitution* and about a dozen other leading southern newspapers:

> WANTED: to buy entire output or part of output of southern factories manufacturing furniture, woodenware, agricultural implements, machinery, blacksmith's tools, vehicles, team harness, stoves, and other heavy goods, such as are shown in our general catalog. Manufacturers are requested to address us in confidence marking your communication personal to R. W. Sears, Pres. of Sears, Roebuck & Co., Chicago. Mailing catalogs or illustrations and prices and naming the largest quantity of goods you could possibly turn out per year.[34]

Sears personally took many trips through the South to line up sources and was instrumental in establishing several companies to manufacture goods he needed. Mrs. Sears used to tell of how her husband would leave home in the morning for his office; in the early hours of the following morning she would hear from him, still at his office; the next word would be a telegram sent from a factory hundreds of miles away or from a train en route to the factory town.[35]

CHAPTER VIII

Management and Methods: Order Out of Chaos

EXECUTIVES of Sears, Roebuck and Company and of its various corporate forebears such as the R. W. Sears Watch Company had to make many major decisions—decisions which shaped in large measure the course and nature of the company's development. Up to 1895 such decisions were made by Richard Sears; Roebuck appears to have been willing, from the time he joined the firm, to accede to virtually all of Sears's plans. It was Sears who determined to move his business to Minneapolis, thence to Chicago, back to Minneapolis, and again in turn to Chicago. No matter how logical these changes may have seemed at the time, no matter how natural the move to different locations, they appear in retrospect as major decisions, which affected the character and scope of the business considerably.

The most important decision—the one which surely most affected the character and scope of operations—was Richard Sears's adoption of a policy of low prices coupled with aggressive promotion. This policy preceded Roebuck's affiliation with the business and continued even more vigorously in succeeding years.

It is possible, and even probable, that the decision to expand the merchandise line beyond watches and jewelry did not appear to Richard Sears to be one to ponder at length. New lines were added rather cautiously as they appeared profitable and as Sears sought additional business.

Certainly Richard Sears's decision to sell his watch company in 1889 was an important one, if only for one reason: if he had found banking in Iowa or some similar occupation both pleasant and remunerative, he might never have re-entered the general mail-order business. By the same token, his decision to return to that field of endeavor was equally important. And even when Richard Sears assumed an interest in A. C. Roebuck's company, the decision was almost totally the former's; Roebuck's assent seems to have been almost automatic.

These constituted the major decisions involving the company up to 1895, over and above the day-to-day decisions of a minor nature. In that year Sears made what was probably his most momentous decision to that point: to admit Nusbaum and Rosenwald as partners, each holding a quarter-interest in the company. The evidence makes it clear that Sears alone made that decision, as witness his correspondence with Nusbaum cited earlier. The year 1895 was significant for another reason: Roebuck made his first, if not only, decision which had a major bearing upon the company. He decided to sell his interest and retire as an officer and stockholder of record.

The departure of Roebuck and the entry of Nusbaum and Rosenwald wrought an important change in the structure of the company and the allocation of responsibility within it. The business was still of such size that it remained possible to vest all major policy decisions in the three partners; each of the three, in his sphere of jurisdiction, could still keep his finger on the entire business. The significant point was that for the first time Richard Sears had top-level associates to share the burden of the work. Sears himself assumed primary responsibility for advertising and sales promotion. Rosenwald was responsible for the merchandise line and much of the administrative work, while Nusbaum handled finances and some administration. The lines of authority were, of course, not clear cut or stratified; the allocation of responsibilities was not as the laws of the Medes and the Persians.

In determining *what* to advertise and promote, for example, Sears overlapped Rosenwald's sphere of merchandise selection; indeed, to judge from the preoccupation with the merchandise line manifested in most of Sears's letters, there was a recognition among the partners that Sears's special knowledge of the market and his uncanny merchandise sense were to be given adequate scope for expression. It also appears that, even before Nusbaum's departure in 1901, Rosenwald was interesting himself in the difficult problem of working capital; after Nusbaum left, Rosenwald handled this phase of the business almost singlehandedly. Nor did Nusbaum restrict himself solely to financial matters; R. P. Sniffen, former manager of the New York office, asserts that Nusbaum took an active interest in merchandising and was particularly interested and helpful in improving the quality of the company's goods.

There began to emerge in the period immediately after 1895 the increasingly important role of Albert Loeb. The law firm of Loeb and Adler, as previously pointed out, handled all details of reorganization of the company which attended the entry of the two new partners. From then on, Loeb handled the firm's legal work and began to negotiate leases for space for the expanding business. While he did not become an officer until Nusbaum left, it appears that he was often called on for advice.

An important decision was that regarding the events which led to Nusbaum's selling his interest. Here it was Rosenwald who ultimately had to make the choice; Sears had made it clear that he would not continue in business with Nusbaum. Rosenwald then had to decide whether to join with Sears in purchasing the interest of the third partner or to align himself with Nusbaum in buying Sears out.

After Nusbaum's departure Rosenwald and Sears dominated the scene, by virtue both of their offices and of their stockholdings. Loeb was elected to succeed Nusbaum as secretary and as a member of the board of directors, and he continued to handle legal matters. Rosenwald assumed the position of treasurer and with it most of Nusbaum's financial responsibilities, while additional administrative authority was delegated to Loeb. Albert Loeb was to achieve a remarkably strong position in company counsels even before he came to hold any considerable amount of stock.

R. W. Sears was traveling much of the time between 1901 and 1908, especially from 1906 to 1908. While he continued to propound schemes for merchandise promotion, catalogue circulation, and magazine and newspaper advertising, he also spent considerable time searching out dependable sources of supply. At the same time his very absence from Chicago almost automatically meant that more and more of the day-to-day decisions had to be made by Rosenwald. And since Rosenwald was steadily more engrossed in financial affairs, as well as in overseeing the expansion of the merchandise line and the improvement in its quality, an ever greater amount of administrative routine fell to Loeb.

Since Rosenwald and Sears experienced many personality clashes, Loeb's role was an important one to the company. He was often the go-between for the two and apparently was instrumental in reconciling differences before they erupted in open hostility. Rosenwald came more and more to rely heavily upon Loeb's talents (when the former entered public service during World War I, he left the business almost entirely in Loeb's hands as unofficial acting president). Richard Sears's high regard and warm affection for Loeb was manifested in what was the ultimate camaraderie for Sears: he called Loeb "Albert," a first-name accolade reserved for an infinitesimal few.

There were other factors which called for Loeb's ability to pour oil on troubled waters. Rosenwald, according to interviews with many veterans who worked under him in this and later periods, was often unapproachable to the point of rudeness. Some former employees, who held high positions, call him "The Great Objector" and insist that he took a negative approach to every idea or plan presented to him. There are, of course, two schools of thought on *why* he did so. One school holds he wanted always to be in position, if a scheme failed, to say, "I told you so"; if it succeeded, to say, "I let you go ahead with it." The other point of view, kinder to Rosenwald, maintains he simply wanted to compel everyone to present his case in the most forceful, best-thought-out manner possible. In any event, one thing is clear: many employees hesitated to approach him and preferred to talk with Loeb instead.

Loeb was admirably suited for his role. Certain former executives who idolized Sears and disliked Rosenwald, and some who admired Rosenwald and had little regard for Sears, unite in praising Loeb. His unquestioned high legal abilities appear to have been overshadowed by his kindly nature, his ability to send anyone out of his office cheered, encouraged, and convinced he had had a sympathetic hearing. Loeb was the pipeline that funneled to Rosenwald and Sears many suggestions and complaints which the lesser executives hesitated themselves to take to the top. Being a "prince among men" is not always sufficient in itself for success in business; but, coupled with the ability and integrity of Albert Loeb, it made for a force of incalculable value to the company in this period and until Loeb's death in 1924.

Possibly the next major decision facing the company after Nusbaum's departure in 1901 was the construction of its new forty-acre plant. In 1904 the company purchased a site of land on Chicago's West Side, and on December 22 of that year signed a contract with the Thompson-Starrett Company for construction of the buildings. The company began to occupy some of the buildings as early as October, 1905, and took over the entire plant on January 22, 1906. The plant and its equipment cost $5,600,000.[1]

It appears reasonable to assume that Sears, Rosenwald, and Loeb, as well probably as the next layer of executives, all recognized the urgent need for consolidating the space occupied by the company and for consolidating it in a structure built to their own specifications. But even though there was probably unanimity of opinion on building the new plant, the drain on working capital which the venture entailed must surely have placed it in the category of major decisions. Working capital was a considerable problem even before this outlay, a problem to which Rosenwald's efforts were almost constantly directed.

This very problem was, in fact, to lead to another major decision: to make their business a public company and to issue preferred and common stock. This meant, of course, that Sears and Rosenwald would have to surrender at least in some degree their nearly total possession of the company's stock. It further involved whatever uncertainty attached to the fact that the flotation of stock of mercantile organizations was a new enterprise in 1906, only a few general merchandising concerns having issued securities.[2] The stock flotation was engineered and handled for the company largely by Rosenwald, with the advice of his boyhood friend, Henry Goldman, of Goldman, Sachs.

The opening of the Dallas branch surely represented a major decision. It meant the introduction of a new element into the company's organization, even though it was conceived by Richard Sears primarily as a sales-promotion device. Correspondence between Sears and Asher, Sears and Rosenwald, and Elmer Scott and Asher, as well as interviews with Scott, indicate clearly that Rosenwald was bitterly opposed to the project; so much so that he very nearly liquidated it before it was able to prove itself. Sears, though he differed on details of operation with Scott, who was sent to open the branch, nevertheless championed the concept of branch plants and continued to support the idea over Rosenwald's objections.

The split decision over opening Dallas left wounds which were never healed and which were to be torn open afresh only a year later. Louis Asher dates the really great rift between Sears and Rosenwald at 1906 and asserts it focused largely on the Dallas decision.[3] It may be a dangerous oversimplification to set any one such date or event as the beginning of the final and complete rupture, since the two partners had often held strong differences of opinion since conjoining in 1895. But it *is* clear from the correspondence of that period and later recollections of Scott, Asher, and others that the split between Sears and Rosenwald over Dallas became personal and bitter.

These men—first Richard Sears, then the three partners, and finally just Sears and Rosenwald and, to a lesser but not unimportant extent, Loeb—constituted the fountainhead of decision in the company at any given time in this period, even though influenced as they must have been on many occasions by counsel of their subordinates. The decisions they made, however different at first glance, were bent in almost every instance toward improving the company's merchandising position and its merchandising techniques.

Richard Sears occupied himself with merchandising problems night and day. Rosenwald assumed responsibility for the general merchandising program despite his partner's almost obsessive interest in it. The company at first had no departments concerned with customer service, public relations, or similar later developments. The business of the company was to purchase, stock, sell, and ship merchandise, and occasionally to sell before purchasing and stocking.

The general merchandise manager, J. Fletcher Skinner, was a farm boy like Richard Sears and, according to many who knew him in that time, a great merchandiser. Skinner's place in the hierarchy fell immediately below Rosenwald's. Skinner enjoyed a wide degree of autonomy, however. He was one of Sears's earliest protégés and one of the few men in the company invited to Sears's home with any frequency. His insistence upon a steady improvement in the quality of merchandise and his generally sound merchandise sense appear to have created a great respect for him in Rosenwald.

Under Skinner came the buyers, who were actually department heads enjoying a wide degree of latitude in their respective bailiwicks. Each merchandise department was a separate dynasty, and the buyer was in complete charge.[4] They did the actual purchasing and decided usually what to stock (always, of course, subject to advice from higher authority), what to pay for it, and how to price it. In addition, each department had its own correspondence section to handle complaints and all other correspondence relating to that department. Each department also had its own returns division to handle merchandise sent back by dissatisfied customers. Finally, each buyer or department head very largely set the wage scales for his department and disciplined his employees. Company officers were unlikely to interfere so long as the department prospered.

Most of the buyers seem, if testimony of retired executives is accepted, to have been well qualified in many respects. Many of them were former salesmen or had been otherwise connected with the manufacture or sale of the very lines they later handled for the company. At least, they knew thoroughly in many instances the goods they were buying and selling; they had a good idea of what it cost to produce the goods and of what was required to increase production when that became necessary; and they knew something about quality.

Sears himself felt that a man who could merchandise one line successfully could also merchandise any other line with equal success. Louis Asher, for example, tells of the time Sears appointed Max Asher head of the stove department. When Asher asserted he knew nothing about stoves, Sears replied: "Well, my boy, you're a merchant, and a good man can merchandise one line as well as another." But Asher also points out there were times when Sears's belief in this respect led to less fortunate results. One thing Sears did do was to back his buyers to the hilt. Once they established themselves as capable, they were allowed to operate with much freedom.[5]

In 1902 the company opened a New York buying office to execute orders from Chicago. Robert P. Sniffen, later to become a member of the board of directors, was placed in charge. Sniffen declares that J. F. Skinner allowed him an increasing degree of autonomy in his work.

The first and final link in the merchandising organization's transmission belt was the company's "operating organization," which was responsible for the receipt of all incoming shipments, storage of goods, filling of all orders, and shipment of all merchandise and catalogues. In view of the haphazard nature of much of the company's operations in this phase, of Richard Sears's capacity to reap countless orders even when adequate space was not available for shipping operations, of the fact that until the company entered its new building in 1906 it occupied widely scattered space—in view of all this, the operating organization faced a gigantic task.

Goods had to be shipped in some kind of order. They had to be properly packed, else broken goods would be returned by the customer. Merchandise was shipped variously by freight, express, and mail. Shipments had to be routed to reach customers—who paid transportation costs—as cheaply and quickly as possible. An order for a heavy item like a stove or an organ might also include orders for dress goods, boys' shoes, farm tools, and groceries, for example; those "mixed" orders involving more than one department had to be correlated for shipment. Some heavy goods, like buggies, for instance, were shipped directly from factories to customers. Shipments were sometimes damaged by negligence on the part of the railroads or express companies, and some were lost; claims had to be filed and prosecuted against the carriers involved. Goods shipped from sources to the Chicago office had to be routed expeditiously to save time and money.

The operating organization was a hydra-headed monster, calling for driving, tough, capable direction. It had just that in the person of Otto C. Doering, long-time chief of operations. The company's functional structure, which vested great power in its buyers as department heads, naturally relieved the operating organization of some tasks. Goods were stored in the various merchandise departments; returned goods also went into the several departments, which were responsible as well for all correspondence and other details in connection therewith. But, even stripped of these responsibilities, the operating organization faced a truly formidable task. It is no exaggeration to say that the job might well have broken a lesser man than Doering.

Before the company moved into its forty-acre plant, incoming and outgoing shipments had to be carted by horse-drawn wagons to and from the railheads, the express companies, and the post office. The spur tracks entering the new plant solved much of that problem. But, prior to that time, according to recollections of former employees, the wagons piled up outside the company's various rented buildings in such congestion that the police frequently had to untangle the traffic jam.

The congestion at the loading platforms was paralleled by the log jams that arose in clearing claims against the express companies. The settlement of such claims, another facet of operations, was one which threatened at times to disrupt the business. These claims reached such volume that around 1904 the express companies in Chicago threatened to refuse to accept Sears, Roebuck business, large as it was, on the ground that the company's chaotic operations led it to make claims against the express companies for goods never actually shipped. This appears to have been a fair commentary on the firm's procedure at that point, and the confusion reigning in 1904 was no sudden development.

Veteran employees, many of them long since retired, all develop the thesis that the firm's procedure almost up to the completion of the new building in 1906 was simply confusion worse confounded. In the earliest days when the staff consisted of Richard Sears, A. C. Roebuck, and a few clerical workers, there was actually relatively little opportunity for confusion or much necessity for systematization. As the business expanded, however, the opportunity for chaos became unlimited, and the need for organization and systematization grew proportionately.

The business was floundering in such great confusion in 1895 that the obvious and pressing need for better administration may well have been a factor, along with the urgent need for additional capital, in persuading Richard Sears to sell a half-interest to Rosenwald and Nusbaum. Here is how Florence Kiper Frank describes what Rosenwald encountered when he joined the company:

"Chaos held eternal anarchy . . . and by confusion stood." Kitchen chairs were the seats, dry-goods boxes the tables; chickenwire netting the partitions between compartments. There was no suggestion of the mechanical aids to efficiency for which Sears, Roebuck and Company was one day to be famous. Only two telephones were available; no electric lights, no pneumatic tubes, no clever gadgets for opening mail, no robots for performing the tasks of driven, harassed men. Above all, there was no system. The growing business, that soon overflowed the two floors at first sufficient for its needs and threatened to burst the very building with its exuberant demands, outgrew systems faster than they could be invented.

When Rosenwald came to work in the morning he would find Sears, absorbedly writing at his desk in the large room that bulged with scattered heaps of merchandise. Boxes of watches, piles of clothing, samples of groceries in corners, files of correspondence, grimy with dust, on the floor. And in the midst of it all, that obsessed fiction writer, spinning more fancies to bring in more orders, more merchandise, more confusion. . . .

He found a harassed correspondence department doing its poor best with all manner of inquiries and complaints. . . . Still the orders poured in. Faster than the factories could supply the goods, faster than they could be cleared through warehouses and shipping rooms. Departments fell behind—thirty days, sixty days, sometimes three and four months. The panting executives were outstripped, and the order they sought to impose seemed an unattainable dream. The most pressing problem was the problem of space. Month after month the firm would add to its offices and shipping rooms, but the Mad Hatter's cry of "No room! No room!" became a chronic plaint. Now established as the attorney of the Company, Albert Loeb was saying that nearly all of his legal duties consisted of passing on new leases and building contracts. . . .

. . . crowded quarters and crude service continued. Reviewing this period from the eminence of calmer days, Rosenwald once said:

"With a business on our hands that was growing so fast that we were fairly dizzy, without any previously developed system for handling such quantities, you can imagine the confusion. Our shipping rooms were in a state of chronic congestion; every warehouse in Chicago was choked with our goods; every shipping point in the country and almost every station was running over with Sears, Roebuck and Company's merchandise. I recall a letter from one little station agent who said that his freight house was full of sewing machines, and that he had some of our sewing machines in the cellar of his home; and please, for heaven's sake, would we stop shipping sewing machines to his station until the farmers who had ordered them had a chance to come and get them."[6]

That was how the company looked even from "the top." A closer view emerges from an employee who writes from his own experiences of twenty-one years in the correspondence department, calling also upon recollections of employees with longer service:

With the expansion of the business in the late 90's, and early in 1900, the complaints increased tremendously and the number of trained people to handle these complaints was so small that the complaints accumulated until they had baskets upon baskets of them stacked up to be answered. Mr. C. D. Palmer, who was the Manager of the Department, realized that it was an impossible task to ever get caught up, so he took the very drastic action and made up a form similar to a hand-bill on which he placed several squares indicating the type of complaint. This form was sent to all customers from whom complaints had been

MANAGEMENT AND METHODS 131

received. After detaching the money from the complaints that they were holding, they burned all the complaints.

This method was resorted to on two different occasions prior to 1909. About 1907 the Company recognized the correspondence problem and hired a Mr. P. V. Bunn to come in and make a study of their correspondence problem. Mr. Bunn wrote a Manual of information for correspondents, and letter inspectors, which he published in August of 1907; but because of the rapid expansion of business, this Manual was obsolete before it was ever off the press.

After the Company moved into the present plant, and had enlarged quarters and added facilities, the correspondence and return problem did not become acute until after the inception of the parcel post business in 1914 [sic].

The C. D. Palmer referred to in the foregoing quotation came to the company in 1898 as a bicycle correspondent (and retired in 1928 as office manager). He had been a bicycle manufacturer until the depression of 1893–94 forced him out of business; his knowledge of that merchandise line merited a higher salary and greater authority than usually accorded a new correspondent. Palmer stated that, soon after he arrived at Sears, Roebuck, he discovered that by the time he could work his way through a mountain of correspondence, an equally great or even greater amount of correspondence would pile up. Concluding that many letters were so similar that they could be answered in identical terms, he developed several form paragraphs and numbered them. On each letter he would simply designate the applicable numbered form paragraph which the stenographer was to type as the reply. Even with this work-simplification device, however, Palmer still had often to dictate as many as three hundred letters daily on dictaphones using wax cylinder records. Around 1903 or 1904 correspondence reached such a chaotic condition that he was compelled to carry the "form paragraph" technique further. He printed a form letter containing twelve paragraphs referring to different subjects. Customers' letters were answered by sending them this form, with a large check mark by the applicable paragraph(s).

The chaos of the company's correspondence and the inadequacy of its space at any given time was attributable to the almost phenomenal expansion of the volume of business. In 1896 sales were more than double the 1895 record of $745,595. The first year of the new century saw Sears pass the $10,000,000 mark, and within five more years sales were almost quadrupled, reaching $37,879,422 for the year 1905.

In retrospect it is easy enough to see that the volume of business increased at a rate which could hardly have been foreseen. Each new plan evolved for systematizing the operations in hope of eliminating the backlogs became obsolete by the time it could be put into effect. New space leased to growing departments proved inadequate by the time it could be occupied. The business almost literally burst at the seams as its volume grew by leaps and bounds and thousands and millions of dollars.

Even before the "schedule system" was first tried, sometime between

1906 and 1908, Doering had made some progress toward systematization of order-filling and had passed the point where orders lay around often from two to six weeks before being filled. The scheme of weighing the mail bags each morning and calculating how many orders were coming in that day was refined to a point which allowed of little error. This foreknowledge of how much work lay ahead for the day made possible a more intelligent allocation of help in the shipping department, thus serving to speed up shipments.

Once an order was received, it was the operating organization's responsibility to handle all details incident to getting the merchandise into the customer's hands. If the order was for a heavy item shipped from a factory, it had to be forwarded to that factory for handling. Theoretically, the factory was to ship the goods immediately and simultaneously to notify the company. In practice, however, even when immedate or early shipment was made by the factory, the operating organization was not always soon so informed.

The result was inevitable and, for a time apparently, invariable. The customer would write the company that he had not received his goods. The factory would be ordered to send the customer the item in question; the factory might well do so, even though shipment had been made earlier and even though the customer might have received his merchandise a day or two after writing to complain. When stoves, pianos, or whatever piled up in express offices and customers' homes, operating personnel had to recapture the "surplus" merchandise and return it to stock.

When Richard Sears launched his "Iowaizing" method of forced-draft catalogue distribution, circulation of the book climbed immediately. In the campaign to saturate specific areas with the catalogue, the operating organization was Sears's striking arm. No figures are available on just what percentage of all catalogues circulated in the period of "Iowaization" went out as a part of that sales-promotion scheme, but Doering's department had to cope with all of them as well as with all the single requests from customers for the big book and with the copies automatically sent to preferred "A" customers.

Not long after the company moved into its new buildings Doering and his aides inaugurated the "schedule system" for making shipment on all merchandise usually within twenty-four to forty-eight hours after the order was received. The large plant was equipped with a vast variety of mechanical devices to speed the flow of merchandise in and out of the building. The 1905 catalogue, heralding the plant then nearing completion, declared:

> Miles of railroad tracks run lengthwise through, in and around this building for the receiving, moving and forwarding of merchandise; elevators, mechanical conveyors, endless chains, moving sidewalks, gravity chutes, apparatus and conveyors, pneumatic tubes and every known mechanical appliance for reducing

labor, for the working out of economy and dispatch is to be utilized here in our great Works.

Those mechanical aids were to be a chief accessory of the schedule system, and the ultimate refinement of that system was to await installation of more such devices. Provision had been made in the new building for holding merchandise in designated places preparatory to shipment. The problem of co-ordinating the movement of merchandise on outgoing orders was particularly serious in the case of heavy items. Such goods had to be shipped from the out-freight division; before being readied for shipment, they had to await the arrival of all packing materials necessary, as these materials had to precede the merchandise into the out-freight department.

It was extremely difficult to co-ordinate the movement of goods on "mixed tickets"—that is, orders on which the merchandise had to come from different departments. Faulty co-ordination led to serious bottlenecks and thus placed severe limitations on the amount of business which could be maintained in the available space. In short, the improper co-ordination of movements of mixed merchandise created a pressure on space which, in addition to delaying receipt of goods by the customers, imposed a ceiling on the volume of business which could be handled.

The heart of the schedule system involved a rearrangement in the organization of work so that a particular operation could be fitted into a predetermined timetable, for the system was in essence simply a timetable, predetermined on an admittedly stringent basis, and rigidly enforced. When an order came in, it was assigned to a given hour, or a fifteen-minute period of an hour, usually within a forty-eight-hour period. The period so assigned was stamped on the order; if a mixed order, on every component ticket going to the various departments concerned for filling. In more specific terms, a "single" order received at, say, 9:00 A.M. might be assigned the first quartile of the hour 10:00–11:00 A.M. This meant that merchandise in that order had to be delivered by the appropriate department to an appropriate bin in the shipping division within the specified fifteen-minute period, and that shipment had to be made by 11:15 A.M. A mixed order might be assigned to a time segment of the *next* day.

At the end of the specified quarter-hour the order was shipped, whether complete or not. Whenever any department failed for any reason to meet the deadline, that merchandise was sent to the customer under separate cover, express prepaid. The department concerned was penalized by having the express cost plus an additional flat penalty (initially fifty cents) charged against it, thereby impairing the department's profit showing. Since advancement depended heavily on their departmental showings, this penalty system drove into line some managers who had opposed the schedule system.

In Doering's estimate, the schedule system eventually made it possible to increase business within the space limitations by perhaps as much as ten times. J. F. Skinner, writing to one Albert Johnson on October 3, 1908, declared:

> The quantity of mail we receive in a day, of course varies in different seasons of the year. During October and November and the first two weeks in December, we will average about 100,000 pieces of mail a day. Of course, the very large mail is received Monday morning. We often get as many as 100,000 pieces of mail in the first delivery Monday morning. All of this mail has to be handled on schedule; in fact, all of the work connected with the house is supposed to be done on schedule.
>
> This is all done on schedule. . . . There are 27 different handlings on one order before it goes out of the house; and on a new schedule we have just adopted, all orders for single items received in Monday morning's mail are supposed to go through these 27 different handlings and be shipped the same day. All mixed orders, that is an order for different departments, we are supposed to ship inside two days.[7]

Even the officers responsible for instituting and refining the system are vague as to just when it actually started. Louis Asher maintains the schedule system took hold in 1906,[8] while Otto Doering said in an interview that it was either 1907 or 1908. Other former executives variously recall the date as sometime around 1906–8. A "Notice to Merchandise Departments" signed by Elmer L. Scott, general manager, and O. C. Doering, operations superintendent, and dated April 14, 1906, indicates that introduction of the schedule system was imminent at that time. The memorandum is captioned "Proposed New Schedule":

> On account of the very far reaching effects of the proposed new system of applying schedule on tickets, Mr. E. L. Scott and myself would like to feel thoroughly satisfied that the matter has been considered by the departments in all its various phases, and that we put nothing into actual operation until the departments are quite sure that they will be prepared to meet the various conditions that this new system will make obligatory.

The memorandum went on to call a meeting of all merchandise department managers and heads of the shipping-rooms for further discussion of the proposed schedule system, which "we believe . . . will be a very good thing for all departments."

A copy of "Instructions to Recheckers," dated March 30, 1908, shows clearly that the schedule system was then in force. It is less clear, however, just how effectively the system functioned at that time. The instructions warned, "No order must be held longer than 24 hours for any reason." But Lessing J. Rosenwald, who went to work in the shipping department in 1912, asserts that the schedule system was only then really becoming highly effective. It is his belief that, while the concept and some of the mechanics were adopted around 1906–8, it was five or six years before the "bugs" were ironed out and the mechanical equipment installed that experience had proved necessary to full functioning of the system.[9]

Asher gives credit jointly to Doering and his assistant, John Meier;[10] other former executives attribute the schedule system variously to Doering, to Meier, and to another, unidentified assistant. It is always difficult in such an organization, and at such a distance as the present time, to determine just when a department head was acting on his own inspiration and when he was adopting practical suggestions advanced by his subordinates.

But there is evidence to support the belief that Doering himself conceived the method, since it followed a pattern he had established while the company's new plant was under construction in 1905. In that year Doering evolved a system which provided enough bricks at the proper time for the army of bricklayers working on the structure and also co-ordinated the general flow of materials. In addition to overcoming delays in construction, Doering's plan provided a daily progress report. The schedule system adopted later bore a strong resemblance to this organization of the flow of materials. The exact identity of the innovator is far less important than the fact that the system speeded operations considerably.

The system was urgently needed at the time and was to prove an even greater boon in the period ahead as it became refined. Experience had showed there were usually forty orders per pound of mail. The letters were opened, at a rate of about 27,000 per hour, by automatic mail-openers developed by the company. Each letter containing an order (some letters contained, for instance, manufacturers' invoices or complaints from customers) was given a number. The time the merchandise was due in the shipping-room was stamped on the order; a bin in the shipping-room was simultaneously reserved for that order for the specified fifteen-minute period.

Orders were then checked to ascertain whether the catalogue number cited tallied with the description of the goods ordered and to find whether the remittance inclosed was correct. Notation was made of the manner of remittance; whether by cash, check, or money order. Labels were made out, and tickets for each item in the order were sent to the departments concerned.

All this was accomplished by workers on the early shift before the main body of employees arrived at 8:00 A.M. By that hour, the earlier shift could estimate for each department manager the number of orders he would probably have to handle that day. Clerks then selected the specified items of merchandise on any given order from shelves numbered to correspond with the catalogue numbers. Gravity chutes and conveyor belts carried the merchandise to assembly points, where it was dropped through chutes into the shipping-rooms. There mechanical conveyors carried the packed orders to loading platforms; precanceled stamps were attached, and the goods were ready to load on the adjacent railhead. Heavy goods shipped from factories owned wholly or partially by the company were, in many instances, shipped on the same or on a similar schedule system. The new assembly-line technique aroused great interest. Among those who came to inspect it, according to Doering, was Henry Ford.

One marvels at the success of Sears, Roebuck in the face of the turmoil that characterized operations for nearly two decades. It often appears that the company succeeded in spite of itself. That the myriad activities of "operating" achieved any order and that eventually the business developed systems that were the envy of all its competitors was due more to Otto Doering than to any other man. Even Richard Sears, constantly preoccupied with strategies of merchandising (and with the traditional merchant's disdain for operating details), paid high tribute to Doering. In a letter from Vienna on December 19, 1906, Sears wrote: "Please remember me to Mr. Doering and tell him for me, truly—'Distance makes the heart grow fonder' —there must be some sentiment in business, for you can't pay for the kind of work he is doing with money alone...."[11]

CHAPTER IX

Working Conditions, Welfare, and Wages

"SEND No Money," "Satisfaction Guaranteed or Your Money Back," "We Pay the Freight (Dallas)," and the colloquial catalogue chats of Richard Sears, reassuring and cajoling his reader-customers—all these evidenced an inspired and dramatized expression of concern for the convenience and satisfaction of the company's customers. Mounting sales and profits attested to the success of such market strategy. But what of the company's relations with another group upon whom the executives needed to rely for continuing success—Sears's employees?

When, in 1893, Richard Sears opened an office and shipping depot in Chicago, the number of employees was small, consisting of women for clerical work and occasionally a man in charge of a specific "scheme." The burden of planning, merchandising, and advertising (and much routine order-filling and correspondence) was carried by Richard Sears, aided by his partner, A. C. Roebuck.

In January, 1895, both the Minneapolis and the Chicago offices were moved to a five-story building on West Adams Street in Chicago. At that time the company had about eighty employees. The sales volume for the year was close to $750,000. Richard Sears was a tireless executive, working long hours and aggressively reaching out to capture more and more business. He did not spare himself, and employees worked as long as required.

The personnel policy of that day was certainly not formalized. Hours were long and the wage rates no higher than necessary to acquire and maintain a relatively small staff. A firsthand impression of the length of the working day has been given by Roebuck: "A great deal of overtime was put in and during 1894 and 1895 it was the custom to work from one to several nights a week, the quitting time usually being 11 o'clock. During the early part of 1895 there was seldom a night outside of Sunday that one or more departments did not work overtime."[1] Conversations with several retired Sears's employees demonstrate that a sixty-hour work week was expected, and, when the volume of orders warranted it, overtime at no additional pay was the rule. Of those days Louis Asher wrote:

The matter of labor turnover and absentees was a serious problem in the early days of the company. Departments were demoralized when employees walked out on their jobs. The work was shot with errors through the carelessness of apathetic workers who stayed at their desks long after closing time the night before, rewarded only by the 35¢ supper money the company provided.[2]

The business was increasing at such a rapid rate during these early years that space was always at a premium. In 1898 a newly hired correspondent for the bicycle department was introduced to his work place. Basket after basket of unanswered correspondence awaiting attention rested on improvised tables. A packing case served as a desk in this "office"—a room on the middle floor of a building housing a steam laundry on the lower level and a carpenter's shop above. Steam permeated the place and sawdust regularly showered down over the room. While free access was afforded the steam and sawdust, little light came through the dirty windows. Amid these surroundings the new correspondent attacked with ingenuity and dictaphone the work of explaining and cajoling dissatisfied buyers of bicycles.

Louis Asher has characterized the "personnel policy" of this early period as follows:

> This was a period when frills in the business did not come under the heading of either industrial codes or the law. Wages and hours were a matter of the survival of the fittest. Health was in the hands of the family doctor. Rallying round the banner was left to patriotic leagues and religions. . . . Richard Sears worked from eight in the morning until eleven or twelve at night and was far too absorbed in the work of advertising and merchandising to consider the evils of overtime. Rosenwald was curiously insensitive to the conditions around him.[3]

In the late nineties, when the business had been moved to larger quarters at Fulton and Desplaines streets in Chicago, Elmer Scott was made general manager. The early employee welfare aspects of company policy were pretty clearly the results of Scott's personal interest in employee relations. After two years of formal education at a Methodist college, Scott in 1895 had come to work as Richard Sears's office boy at nine dollars a week. His active interest in employee welfare seems to have been the result of his introduction to Jane Addams, founder of Chicago's Hull House, whom he met a year or so after going to Sears. Miss Addams stimulated Scott to apprehend working conditions that he had previously ignored or taken for granted—especially since he personally was receiving ten dollars a week, which he felt was a good wage. With the occasional stimulation of Jane Addams' upbraidings, Scott became sensitive to the working conditions in the "house," which, he reports, prior to 1906 were too often characterized by overcrowding and low standards of cleanliness and sanitation.

Scott's progress in the company was rapid, and, when he assumed responsibility for managing groups of workers, he was impressed with the high rate of turnover. While no records were kept, Scott reports that it was obvious that there was a great waste of manpower due to indiscriminate hiring and discharge by department managers. An employment office, established in the early days of the West Adams Street location, served as an agency to recruit workers as requested by department managers. On occasion, Aaron Nusbaum hired help in the streets, "barking" from a soap box.[4] Applicants were more generally attracted by newspaper advertisements. When more responsible jobs were open, blind ads were inserted in trade journals. Until Scott became interested in more efficient methods, there was no well-defined policy of upgrading employees into better positions—it was easier to hire them ready-made from the outside.

Under Scott's administration several innovations were made in the area of employee relations. The Seroco Club was inaugurated in January, 1899, as a device for improving the understanding of the various department managers. The membership was confined to that level of management, and the annual publication of *Seroco Topics* was a casual and amusing collection of comments directed to those men. The editorial appearing in the first issue of the *Topics* characterized the objectives of the association:

> There should exist between all heads of departments, and all employes as well, a firm bond of personal friendship, mutual interest and good fellowship. For this an organization of some kind is needed, and while it has been deemed wisest to start the ball a-rolling with a strictly social affair, it is intended to organize, this very evening, an association of permanency which will bring us together regularly. While each meeting will tend to develop personal contact between us as men, the first and principal feature will be a frequent interchange of thoughts and ideas bearing upon our business activity.[5]

The editorial went on to urge the managers to take full advantage of the opportunity to learn something of all the activities of "a house that may very truthfully be said to be the largest, most enterprising, most liberal and most progressive of its kind in the civilized world."[6]

Except for the lengthy editorial, the *Topics* was devoted to anecdotes and caricatures of the members and to the menu and program for the evening. Whatever merit the educational and morale aspects of that first meeting may have had, certainly the menu must have been a distinguished success:

CANAPE À LA RUSSE
BLUE POINTS   SHERRY
CREAM OF TERRAPIN, TRENTON
HORS D'OEUVRES VARIES
PLANKED WHITE FISH, MAÎTRE D'HÔTEL
                     SAUTERNE
DRESSED CUCUMBERS
POMMES SARAH
TENDERLOIN OF BEEF LARDED WITH MUSHROOMS
                     CLARET
FRENCH PEAS EN CAISSE   POTATOES DUCHESSE
FROZEN EGGNOG
  o o o   CIGARETTES
ROAST QUAIL EN CRESSON
LETTUCE AND TOMATO MAYONNAISE
FRUIT
ROQUEFORT OR CAMEMBERT CHEESE
TOASTED CRACKERS
CAFÉ NOIR   CIGARS

Such sumptuous feasting was to characterize only the annual Seroco meetings. The regular diet served up in speeches at the monthly forums was heavier fare, obviously designed to enhance the efficiency of operations in the "house." The minutes (1900–1905) of these meetings reveal the following typical titles: "Buying in Right Quantities and Caring for Stock," "What Constitutes an Assistant Manager and Wherein Do His Duties Become of Supreme Importance to the Department?" "Inventory Methods," "Economy of Floor Space," "Expediting Orders in the Busy Season."

Many Seroco meetings, usually those at which Elmer Scott was the speaker, were forums on employee relations and training. Of Scott's address, "The Training of the Young Help of the House," the secretary noted, "a very earnest talk." Among other kindred discussions were: "The Education and Training of Our People," "What Can or Should We Do To Elevate the Moral Standards of Our People?" "By What Measure Shall We Determine the True Value of Our Employees and in What Way Can They Best Be Taught What Our Standards Are?" And of another meeting the club secretary commented: "E. L. Scott gave a splendid talk on 'The Responsibility of Department Heads To Make Better Men and Women.'"

Less welfare-minded and of greater utility to Sears, Roebuck was the plan for employee-training that Scott unfolded at the Seroco Club's meeting of August 4, 1904, of which the secretary noted in the minutes:

> In the fifteen minutes allotted for short talks Mr. E. L. Scott outlined a plan that will be put into effect by which a school for employes will be maintained to train and teach them in the various branches of the mail order business, such as ticket pricing, order picking, correspondence, etc., etc., and from the enthusiastic reception that the club accorded this idea, it would appear to be an ideal and practical proposition that will go far towards solving the difficulties of a proper and efficient organization.

It was Scott's implementation of that plan that produced the first manual for the indoctrination of new employees as well as a manual for correspondents, in addition to some elementary job-training for order-fillers, pricers, and clerical workers. Further, Scott made arrangements with Chicago's Board of Education for Sears's people to take vocational training courses and imported YMCA speakers to provide "character training."

Seroco, designed to inspire and integrate the department managers, was not addressed to the vast body of employees. Of more immediate interest to rank-and-file employees were several clubs, some of them departmental in character, others dedicated to various special interests of the members. The earliest issues of the employee publication, *The Skylight,* carried brief stories of the various club activities and notices of meetings.

Unlike Seroco, heavily tinged with training objectives, the several employee clubs appear to have been essentially social in character. The earliest such clubs at Sears apparently were started prior to 1900; the first factory club in the United States of which there is any record was started at

Western Electric in Chicago in the winter of 1893–94 through the efforts of Hull House's Jane Addams.[7] The Western Electric club (The Occidental) was, however, essentially a means of providing low-cost feeding and developed later in many other directions, including a library activity. The Sears clubs, on the other hand, were primarily social and met at the homes of employees.

The Skylight appeared in 1901 as Sears, Roebuck's first employee magazine. Although there had been limited use of house organs published for distribution to customers, very few companies had employee magazines prior to World War I. In 1921 there were 334 such company magazines published in the United States, and, of these, 91 per cent had been initiated between 1917 and 1920.[8] Sears, Roebuck was in the vanguard of companies using this particular technique to build employee morale. *The Skylight* was first published twice monthly, but by 1904 the publication appeared only twelve times a year. While the earliest issues were one-page newsprint sheets, when the paper changed to a monthly it was expanded to two and sometimes four pages, which contained notices of the activities of employees, transfers, and promotions. In the earlier issues, at least, the greater portion of space was given to inspirational articles on such topics as thrift, ambition, and attention to duty and to educational notes on clerical routines of the company. Although the regular content of the publication was confined to company matters, the paragraph quoted below is illustrative of both the style of the editorials and the fact that *The Skylight* editorial content ranged on occasion beyond narrow company confines. Mourning the death of President McKinley, the fourth issue of *The Skylight* observed:

> For the third time has the vile reptile, anarchy, darted its poison against Government, this time striking down the world's best beloved—the wise ruler, the loving husband, the inspired statesman, the plain man of the people, the potentate of all earthly potentates, the simple citizen, the quintessence of all Americanism, the purest of all that represents righteous government.

Of further interest to rank-and-file employees, in May, 1902, the Seroco Mutual Benefit Association was organized to provide an insurance system to pay benefits to employees who lost time through sickness and accidents, as well as death benefits. The early program involved employee contributions of twenty to sixty cents per month graduated according to wages. The fund was entirely financed by the member-contributions. Benefits ranged from $4.50 to $12.00 per week (i.e., three-fourths of the employee's weekly salary). By 1906 the SMBA had over three thousand members. The earliest organization of the SMBA was apparently the work of the manager-members of Seroco, who, like several other industrial groups, applied the principles of mutual insurance to the problem of illness.

In the same year that the SMBA was organized, Sears, Roebuck ventured into the field of preventive medicine when employee services were expanded in 1902 to include a limited health service. A woman physician was employed to prescribe first-aid treatment in the plant and to work on general health education. "Physical equipment was bare and little home visiting could be attempted by the meager staff. Later [1906] when the Company moved into the new 40-acre plant, a well-equipped hospital and rest rooms were provided."[9] The medical service of the company was perhaps the outstanding aspect of this first period of employee welfare.

Few industrial companies maintained medical facilities prior to 1910, and still fewer had any program of health education. The tremendous post–Civil War railroad expansion had called company medical facilities into being in the undeveloped territories of the Northwest, and certain mining enterprises had established departments for similar reasons. Not until shortly after 1910, and the passage of workmen's compensation legislation, however, was industrial health service widely adopted even by the more progressive companies. Of the many possible explanations for the relatively late development of industrial health service, considerable weight must be given to ignorance. Lange points out:

Printed material was comparatively rare. Though various reports of investigations and articles of a general nature had appeared in print, no outstanding document covering the entire field was available up to 1910. Furthermore, the medical profession provided no leadership in the field and medical schools did not offer specialized training in industrial health and hygiene.[10]

The year 1902 saw, in addition to health service, the introduction of certain other employee-welfare activities, including free coffee served in the various departments at a reported cost of $4,500 a year. The company also made arrangements for employees to purchase coal at wholesale prices. The membership of Seroco was broadened to include assistant department managers and division heads. By arrangement with the Chicago Public Library the company provided facilities for circulating library books among employees.

One of the notable installations of these early years was the Employees' Savings Department. The savings bank was established by the company apparently at the suggestion of an employee whose letter appeared in the October 2, 1902, issue of *The Skylight:* "The idea of a house savings bank was first suggested by seeing the really wonderful success which has attended the SMBA from the start." The unsigned letter continued: "The management have purposely not been consulted. It seems better for a proposition of this kind to be suggested and discussed among the employees themselves and thus avoid any suspicion of self interest on the part of the house." Both the lack of a signature and the tone of the letter suggest that no ordinary employee wrote it.

The ensuing issues of *The Skylight* for 1902 contained numerous signed letters from employees enthusiastically supporting the notion of the bank. By December, 1902, the management committed itself to supporting the bank; and in January of the following year arrangements were made and the bank opened. Depositors received 5 per cent interest on their balances.

Thus was provided a machinery to encourage the practice of thrift, the virtues of which provided endless editorial chaff for *The Skylight*.

The emphasis of the early period of personnel policy was everywhere on self-improvement and individual initiative. The assumption of limitless opportunity was fortified by the recitation of numerous examples drawn from within and without the company. The employee publication was heavily larded with editorial ruminations on the personal requirements for success and the necessity of cultivating the habits that were commonly believed to mark the highroad to business leadership.

Under Scott's leadership as general manager night work was "eliminated" in 1902, when the following regulation was published:

> From a careful observation of causes and effects, leading up to and resulting from night work and Sunday work, it has been decided by the management that both are, while apparently necessary at times, entirely avoidable and injurious. ... Therefore ... night work and Sunday work in the house of Sears, Roebuck & Company are forbidden. It remains for each individual department therefore, to exercise ingenuity instead of the midnight oil in the operation of the department.

According to Scott the elimination of night work was necessary to efficient operation. Asher quotes him as saying:

> In my judgment it saved the business from collapse in its operation. The pyramiding of bad handling of our orders and correspondence by devitalized employees with its subsequent demands for adjustments (which were themselves badly handled) was creating a chaos in which no business could survive.... The immense increase of business in December 1903, was carried on with greater speed, greater accuracy, and with infinitely better results without night or Sunday work than the smaller business of December, 1902.[11]

It should be noted that the better handling of the seasonal peak volume was considerably influenced by returning to customers all orders below a specified minimum. Scott does not recall whether the minimum was one or two dollars.

Despite Scott's claims and despite the regulation in 1903 that no payment was to be made for the overtime that had supposedly been eliminated, managers continued to find it convenient, if not necessary, to work their departments overtime. In 1906 Richard Sears signed a bulletin strongly denouncing the practice. The letter seems to reflect more a concern over operating expenses than personnel policy:

THE QUESTION OF OVERTIME

> Overtime of any description at any time except under extremely abnormal conditions, such as the removal of a big business institution, is looked upon with disfavor.
>
> While it is not always so, even an infrequent request for permission to work to any extent overtime may usually be charged to some lack of management; in other words, it is the lack of ingenuity and thoughtful organization, which must be made up by the exercise of brute force in the form of overtime.
>
> While the last few months have brought with them peculiarly abnormal con-

ditions, and led to the permission of night and Sunday work, it must not be presumed that night and Sunday work is not looked upon with thorough disapproval, except in rare and peculiar conditions.

Overtime becomes sort of a mania sometimes, and is likewise exceedingly expensive. Managers of various departments must remember that a great many people are so willing to work overtime that they will soldier during the day in order to get extra pay at night or Sunday work.

Should, however, there arise an extremely unusual condition which would call for an evening's work or a Sunday's work, no additional pay will be given to the employe for this extra time, since the privilege of shorter hours at certain seasons of the year is extended freely to employes. A continuation of former methods is urged whereby a department shall, if they find it necessary, put in an extra hour or half-hour for some days, for which no extra pay will be given.

This accomplishes two results—one is that it very greatly discourages the desire for overtime, and the extra time that is put in is usually made up by the shorter hours given during the duller seasons of the year.

Very truly yours,
R. W. SEARS

Feb. 25, 1906.

If department managers could not avoid working their forces overtime, at least the company did not intend to subsidize such "inefficiency." Sears, Roebuck, like most every other management, intended to keep expenses as low as possible. In line with that objective the company paid wages only as high as necessary to maintain its work force.

According to Louis Asher, Scott introduced piece work into the business with salutary results—better and greater output with increased earnings for employees and lower labor expense for the company.[12] That method of payment evidently never became general in the mail-order plant, for every indication is that most of the force were paid on either a weekly or an hourly rate.

The earliest wage data available indicate that average earnings for employees beginning work at Sears in 1902 were $6.25 per week.[13] There was a substantial differential between earnings of male and female employees, men in that year receiving $7.00, and women $4.00. Although the weighted average of employee weekly earnings for 1907 increased to $7.82, earnings for those employed in 1902 and still employed by the company in 1907 increased from $6.25 to $12.67. Average earnings for those first coming to work for Sears in 1907 were $6.50 per week.

Salaries of officers were limited to $6,000 a year in accordance with a resolution passed at a stockholders' meeting in 1898. In 1900 only Richard Sears, Julius Rosenwald, and Aaron Nusbaum received this amount. When Albert Loeb was appointed secretary in 1901, he received an annual salary of $1,600. No employee might receive a salary in excess of $3,000 without the agreement of holders of 80 per cent of the stock. This last regulation expired with the Illinois corporation in 1906, and at the same time the annual salaries of the three senior officers were increased to $9,600.

Long before the advent of wage and salary administration plans, the company claimed a stated policy for salary increases—the merit of the individual. In the September 5, 1905, issue of *The Skylight* Scott wrote:

> The well-known method of Sears, Roebuck & Co. for advancing salaries is based solely on the merit of the individual; in other words, the earning capacity of a young man or young woman is not determined by the income of the one sitting at the next desk, but is purely a question of his own personal effort.
>
> The result is that not once a year or twice a year but 365 times a year is each individual employe considered from a productive standpoint, with a view to determining his own personal worth to himself and to the institution with which he is engaged.
>
> The natural result of this system is that every department manager and division head is expected to recommend for salary advance those who are actually worthy at the time they have proved their worthiness, and at no specified time is the wholesale advance of a number of employes undertaken with the natural result that in the lot a number will receive advances who have actually not deserved them.

Thus were the forms provided the department managers to assume the initiative in evaluating employees and recommending salary advances. That the ideal was followed in any systematic fashion is not so clear.

When the company's new plant opened in 1906, instead of the eighty employees of 1895, it was staffed by nearly eight thousand workers. The responsibility for the acquisition and maintenance of this large work force was assumed by the general manager of the plant. While there is no evidence that employment and welfare activities were administered as a major division of the company organization, the general manager in the person of Elmer Scott recognized the responsibility and established definite policies by which the department managers were presumably to be guided.

In 1907 a personnel manual was published under the title of *Sears, Roebuck and Company and Their Employees*,[14] meant to be oriented primarily to the needs of the new employee. The employees were warned of the evil of drink, the futility of smoking, the necessity of morality, and the virtue of diligence and thrift. Of the sixty-two pages in the book, the first twenty-eight were filled with what now appear as rather pompous and stultified homilies on what a young man or woman should know. Diagnosing the case, the manual stated:

> The trouble with a great many of us is that our ideas are wrong; our best judgment is warped, and we look for pleasure only in places where it must be paid for with money, and with this thought we therefore seek more money that we may buy more pleasure. This is not meant to imply that we should not seek more money, but that the seeking of it should be, not for the sake of spending it for more pleasure, but for ameliorating our actual physical condition more than ever before, and toward laying aside a greater sum in savings.

The personnel role of the department manager was outlined as that of supervisor and confidant:

It is to the department manager that the individual looks for recognition. Our employes should look upon the department manager not simply as their superior officer but as their instructor and their friend; it is to be hoped that they will look to him not only for personal recognition, but that they shall confide in him, shall seek his counsel in their various conditions of life. In their trouble they will find him a friend. In their pleasure they will find him a confidant. In the various relations of life they will find in him a counselor, and looking to your department manager as a counselor and friend, it is to be hoped that many of the conditions which frequently arise with employes through ignorance of legal and financial affairs, may be avoided and that the department manager will go even beyond his apparent present duties in the management of his department, that he may be the trusted confidant who will reach out beyond the every day business life and may serve his employes in their outside affairs.

This idealistic program rested heavily on the department managers, and the spirit of the policy undoubtedly found very uneven expression. The department managers were occupied with buying and selling and related duties, and the merchandising problems resulting from the mushrooming sales volume must have absorbed most of their interest.

From the 1907 manual the employee services and policies of that time can be summarized:

1. House physician and hospital for first aid.
2. Seroco Mutual Benefit Association supported by employee contributions to pay benefits for illness, disability, and death.
3. A branch of the public library located in the building.
4. The Savings Department—a company savings bank for employees, paying 5 per cent interest compounded quarterly on employee deposits. Interest paid on deposits in multiples of one dollar.
5. *The Skylight*—employee house organ published monthly.
6. Educational talks under the auspices of the YMCA given at the plant during the noon hours.
7. Night school arranged with the Board of Education. Employees paid $1.50 fee for twenty weeks' instruction in vocational courses.
8. Employees' restaurants—five restaurants located at the plant to serve employees at cost. A full meal was offered in the lunch room for fifteen to twenty cents. The cafeteria offered food at lower prices.
9. Employee discounts—10 per cent on purchases.
10. Vacations—after three years' service, employees received one week's paid vacation, and, upon completing five years, two weeks.
11. Night work had been eliminated in principle since 1902, but exceptions were undoubtedly the rule.
12. Hours of work—from 8:00 A.M. to 5:30 P.M. During certain summer months the plant closed at noon on Saturdays. "Employees are supposed to be at their post of duty by 8 o'clock at least. Most of the departments require that their employes shall be in the department at five minutes before eight. This precaution is taken so that the department may not be annoyed by employes who may be chronic latecomers."[15]

In the manual the general manager enunciated certain policies that department heads were to follow. Salary advances were to be based on the effectiveness of the employees' work and the profit or loss status of the department. Promotions were to be based not only on the candidate's technical qualifications but also on management's "faith in his character":

> Men are not advanced to positions of greater trust until their daily life in our house has been watched with painstaking care.... Realizing that the standing of an employe is measured in a large degree by what he knows and then by his ability to apply that knowledge, the various departments of the house are adapting more complete measures from time to time to determine the actual worth of individual employes. These measures are usually in the form of written examinations, and so successful have they become that this feature is of extreme interest to the management and of material benefit to the employe.[16]

On stability of employment the manual had this to say:

> It is our desire to so adjust our affairs that notwithstanding the fact that there are two especially busy seasons in the year we may retain during the duller seasons all of our desirable people—those who show evidence of interest in their work and anxiety to perform their duties with the greatest possible success. Hence while it is the policy of very many institutions to lay off a large percentage of employes on Christmas Eve, or in the early summer, Sears, Roebuck & Co. have stood for the permanency of employment and if employes are dismissed in these seasons of the year it is from the fact that after being weighed in the balance, they have been found absolutely wanting.... The only exception lies in certain instances where a number of people may be employed temporarily and are so advised at the time.[17]

That the company was aware of the problem of physical conditions of work by this time is indicated on page 57 of the manual:

> Every possible means is undertaken to create and continue the most sanitary conditions, and to add to the perfect safety of our people. Heat, light and ventilation are given the greatest possible attention, and every endeavor is made that all of this shall be the best that we can possibly give.

While Sears, Roebuck merits inclusion in any list of large-scale operators even before 1900, the nature of the business was such that power mechanization played a relatively minor role compared with manufacturing and extractive industries. The case would appear to be little different, however, whether the pace of operation is the proximate result of mechanical power or the routine of system. The expeditious processing and filling of orders representing millions of dollars of sales necessitates the co-ordination and control of hundreds of operations and tens of hundreds of employees. By 1908, when sales exceeded $40,000,000, orders were filled on the basis of a tight schedule, and the new plant was notable for some use of conveyor-belt systems. The pace was fast, and the routine exacting if the schedule was to be met. Thus discipline had to be maintained, and the vagaries of individuals' actions minimized.

Some idea of the behavior expected from employees may be gained from the "Rules and Regulations" posted in the express billing departments in 1898 and not changed in any material aspect for many years.

1. Talking to your neighbor is unnecessary and will not be tolerated.
2. Make all inquiries at the desk of the department manager or assistant manager.
3. Your work must be absolutely correct and errors as the result of carelessness will be charged to the guilty party in every instance.
4. Always be on time. When the first bell rings, be at your desk, ready to begin work at the sound of the second bell.
5. Only one employee at one time is permitted to leave the department during working hours.
6. Commencing on Monday, February 11th, each employee will keep a daily record of the amount of work performed and hand the same to the assistant manager every night before leaving the department.
7. For the benefit of all parties concerned, it will be absolutely necessary to strictly observe these rules. Any violation will be the cause of instant dismissal.

Discipline, if not machines, imposed routine on the workers.

In terms of today's standards at Sears and the current practices of many large, well-managed companies, the personnel program and the working conditions at Sears around 1906 do not seem remarkable. In terms of contemporary standards, however, Sears, Roebuck policies were, in many respects, advanced. For example, Sears employees generally worked 57 hours per week, exclusive of overtime. The long hours were characteristic of retailing history. Indeed, according to Douglas, standard hours per week in nonunionized manufacturing industry in 1905 were 61.1.[18]

There was no legislation restricting hours of work in Illinois at this time, the 1893 eight-hour law (which did not cover mercantile establishments) having been declared unconstitutional by the Illinois Supreme Court in 1895.[19] When Pennsylvania passed its hours limitation law in 1897, hours were limited to twelve hours per day and sixty hours per week. This was the first continuing legislation of this sort to cover mercantile establishments,[20] and regulation of hours of work was not on firm ground until the Oregon ten-hour law was upheld by the United States Supreme Court in 1908.[21] Thus while the usual hours of Sears's employees appear long, they were not worse than in industry generally. The whole tenor of Sears, Roebuck's personnel manual of 1907 and nearly everything included in its program were typical of the "welfare management" that characterized whatever formal industrial personnel programs existed at the time—and there were not many. It has been estimated that, of the eighteen million wage-earners in the United States, in 1908, probably one and a half million came within the scope of welfare management.[22]

What differences existed between Sears and the firm's welfare-minded contemporaries were primarily differences in timing. The company appears to have instituted medical department activities somewhat earlier than the others. Medical treatment, for example, was rarely included in the early welfare programs. Only two of more than a hundred such programs in the state of New York in 1903 boasted first-aid equipment and care under the supervision of medically trained personnel. It had been estimated that not more than a dozen other firms provided resident doctors and nurses.[23] Further, there is little evidence that many firms anticipated the company's adoption of a general vacation policy. For some other welfare activities Sears, Roebuck had to wait upon the completion of a new mail-order plant and offices. When those buildings opened in 1906, the welfare program was embellished and completed. In that year the company provided the sunken gardens, athletic playing fields, and low-cost lunchrooms that were really standard equipment for the welfare age.

The Sears program is a particular case in a whole management movement. In terms of general American experience it would appear that, while Sears was part of the advance guard, it shared that leadership with other large-scale employers, notable among them such firms as the National Cash Register Company, Eastman Kodak, Proctor and Gamble, and International Harvester. These and certain other companies which early in the century became employers of large numbers faced and sought solutions for the problems associated with the weakening of the personal bond between employer and employee. The significance of size and rationalization was indicated in the following remarks from a Labor Department bulletin of 1919:

Establishments were visited . . . in whose small works a complete absence of formality is accompanied by conditions of light, heat, ventilation, etc. which would be intolerable in a larger place with thousands of employees, but which are as cheerfully endured here as if the workers were in their own shops, the fewer employees, the lax discipline, the accessibility of the boss, rendering conditions not unlike those of the earlier days.[24]

The welfare movement in industry was undoubtedly also in some instances a response to the increasing numbers of workers joining unions, for the American Federation of Labor met with its first great successes in the years from 1897 to 1904. In those years membership in American trade-unions increased from 500,000 to 2,000,000, a rate of growth that was truly phenomenal.

At Sears, Roebuck, however, everything happening elsewhere was mainly important only as a source of suggestion to Elmer Scott. While the existence of new problems and the discovery of welfare programs were necessary, they were not sufficient conditions to justify the numerous activities that were generally considered "frills" among businessmen of the period. The prosperity of the business was such that the small expenses of the welfare program hardly constituted a burden, but welfare management was certainly not inevitable at Sears. Rather, it was the shadow of Elmer Scott, sensitive as he was to possibilities of increasing efficiency through improved morale and captivated as he was by the whole social and civic service movement in which he was later to find a career.

CHAPTER X

Opposition and Competition

THE development of Sears, Roebuck and Company from a business founded on the proverbial shoestring in 1886 to a solidly established organization whose volume of business exceeded $40,000,000 in 1908 might easily convey an impression of smooth sailing and of normal business growth in an expanding economy. The truth of the matter is, however, that Sears, Roebuck reached its commanding position only in the face of bitter, sustained, vigorous hostility on the part of retail merchants throughout most of the country.

That hatred of the local merchants for the great mail-order colossi was persistent and virulent. It was directed against the mail-order business in general, but primarily against Montgomery Ward and Sears, Roebuck for the simple reason that these two were the largest mail-order concerns. When Sears outstripped Ward in volume of sales, shortly after 1900, Sears naturally became the target of the most desperate and anguished opposition of those who felt the tentacles of the octopus reaching out to strangle them.

The expressed opposition to the mail-order houses increased from year to year in almost direct proportion to the prosperity enjoyed by such houses. From the perspective of a present-day vantage point, one can feel that the inadequate system of retail distribution would sooner or later have cracked under its own dead weight even without the mail-order companies. It is easy enough to see, in retrospect, that better roads, motion pictures, improved communications, the automobile—in short, the whole march of technological progress—would have had, as indeed it did, a profound effect on the operating techniques of retail merchants.

But all this is hindsight; many retail merchants saw their position deteriorating and found themselves forced to change their merchandising operations. Opposing change, and fearing its consequences, they fixed upon the mail-order houses as the root of most of their troubles. And as folkways tend to become mores and thus to become endowed with strong moral sanction, the retail merchants tended in the evolution of their "dialectic" to endow their own system of distribution with the virtues of morality and patriotism, while associating mail order with various evils.

As opposition to mail order assumed steadily more tangible form, as the fears and frustrations of local merchants became canalized into better-patterned hostility, as the whole concept of "independents" versus "chains" emerged (and the catalogue system of purchasing in some respects made "chains" even of mail-order businesses which had only one central location), the opposition to mail order became more highly organized and standardized.

As early as 1897 the story was widely circulated that Richard Sears or A. C. Roebuck or both were Negroes. Racism was a potent weapon then— as now—and especially in the South, where the whites were still seeking somehow to rationalize their coexistence with a race but recently emancipated from slavery. Roebuck reports encountering these stories himself as late as 1935; it is his belief that local merchants started them against Sears, Roebuck (as also against Woolworth, Kresge, and other chains) and gave them wider circulation through traveling salesmen who passed the rumors on.[1] The fact that Rosenwald was a Jew was also to furnish additional ammunition for the opposition to mail-order houses on the part of retail merchants. And Rosenwald's interest in, and financial support of, Negro education simply added fuel to the flames. (When the company began to build retail stores in the South many years later, it still had to face the "color rumor" and anti-Semitism.)

The hostility took many forms. In some small towns merchants were able to exert sufficient community pressure to compel townfolk to burn their mail-order catalogues in the public square in a grand but ineffective auto-da-fé.[2] In some instances local storekeepers offered prizes to those bringing in the greatest number of catalogues for destruction; in others, a straight ten cents per book was paid to provide fuel for the bonfire. Another device was to admit free to a moving-picture theater every child who brought a mail-order catalogue for destruction.[3] A candidate for mayor of Warsaw, Iowa, declared he would discharge any city employee found purchasing from a mail-order company.[4]

Local merchants also often insisted that their hometown newspapers refuse to accept Sears, Roebuck (or Montgomery Ward) advertising. The merchants also had access to the news and editorial columns of their local papers. Asher says:

The attack of the retail merchants in hundreds of little towns was more than a troubled undercurrent. It was outspoken and frequently libelous. The editorial columns of every town paper were open to the accusations of the small town dealers who joined in a concerted war against the mail order firms by building up the bugaboos of high freight rates, delays and damage in transit.[5]

As early as November 8, 1873, when Montgomery Ward and Company was only about a year old, the *Chicago Tribune* had delivered itself of this harangue: "Grangers Beware! Don't Patronize 'Montgomery Ward & Co.' —they are Dead-Beats. Another attempt at swindling has come to light." Going on to describe Ward's methods of operation and to quote some of its prices as obviously suspiciously low, the *Tribune* called those who patronized the new mail-order company "gulls," "credulous fools," and "dupes." The *Tribune* retracted *in toto* on December 24, but the tone had been set for many of the subsequent attacks on mail order.[6]

Typical of the charges leveled at mail-order selling was an article which appeared in the *Kingston* (N.Y.) *Leader* early in 1906, entitled:

PERTINENT QUESTIONS
To Those Who Are Buying of the Order Houses

A writer in one of the Leader's exchanges asks some pertinent questions of the man or woman who is sending to the mail order houses their cash in advance. His questions will thoroughly repay careful reading:

Did they ever do your home town any good?
Did you ever get a day's work from them?
Did they ever help you to a job of any kind?
Did you ever go to them for a favor or accommodation?
Did they ever pay any taxes to help maintain your schools?
Is their trade worth as much to you as ours and our employees?
Did they ever give any donation, large or small, to help support your favorite church?
Did you ever get any satisfaction when you wished to return or exchange goods?
Did they ever lend you any assistance to support to [sic] any cause whatever to help build up your town or community?
Did they ever sell you any goods for less money than the merchant in your home town did or can? If you think so, take the article to the store where you trade and make an earnest comparison.

In addition to strong editorial attacks and slanted articles in news columns—not that those two departments were rigidly separated in many rural newspapers of the period—some of the publications made frequent point of printing poems and jokes about (usually, i.e., against) the mail-order houses. Those firms were referred to by such appellations as "Shears and Rawbuck," "Monkey Ward," and others. Harking back to one such instance, Garfield V. Cox, dean of the University of Chicago's School of Business, writes:

I recall most vividly the bitterness of the local merchants toward both the mail-order houses. One of our small-town merchants was also a wag who supplied the local paper with a column of wit and humor. Sears, Roebuck was the butt of many of his jokes. He always referred to it as Rears and Soreback. I still remember, for example, one of his jokes. He said that Bill Jones had recently bought a great bargain from Rears and Soreback. It was a watch. Not only had he got it for half price, but also it ran twice as fast as any watch in town purchased from the local jeweler.[7]

It was, in fact, largely press attacks which persuaded Sears, Roebuck to continue the grocery department after it had reached a decision to abandon that line. The question of whether to drop groceries because of their unprofitability had been bruited about in company counsel for years until, late in 1906, the verdict was finally sealed in favor of discontinuation.

The news leaked out. The timing could hardly have been worse, for the Pure Food and Drug Act was passed in 1906, to become effective January 1, 1907. Discontinuation of a department most prominently affected by that legislation, just as such legislation was taking force, was a coincidence which the hostile rural press could not have been expected to overlook. The *Carlisle* (Ark.) *Tribune* did not. In the *Tribune's* eyes—or, at any rate, in its news columns—it was not coincidence; it was sheer cause and effect. Blared the *Tribune*:

FORCED TO SUSPEND
Suspension of the Grocery Department of the Great Sears Roebuck Mail Order Concern

In its issue of a few days ago The Tribune published an exclusive news dispatch from Chicago that is of the utmost importance to the mercantile interests of the country.

The dispatch in question announced the suspension of the grocery department of the great Sears-Roebuck mail order concern "because its maintenance has been made impractical by the national pure food law just passed."

What a confession it is! If you had to interpret the news item, would you conclude it is true that, compelled by law to sell pure food, the mail order house is driven out of business! Can it be that in the past, and in the absence of a law forbidding under heavy penalties the sale of impure or adulterated food, the mail order houses have made a practice of selling impure food? Is that the reason they have been able to undersell local competitors?

Good people, that is the case with every article sold by the average mail order house. Grocery adulteration is forbidden, and so the grocery business of the mail order houses is abandoned. Were laws to be enacted making the sale of "phony" jewelry unlawful, their jewelry departments would go out of business. Were it made a crime to sell furniture cheaply constructed out of poor material their furniture departments would go out of business.

You see, in order to undersell, they must underbuy. What does it mean to underbuy? It means to purchase undermade goods.

The unintentional good that is being accomplished by the pure food law in limiting the possibilities of mail order improprieties points a way for the final elimination of the mail order nuisance. Mail order traffic is peddling by mail. Cannot we have a national mail peddler ordinance in which it shall be required that a license in form of a tax be enacted from mail order houses, the volume of business done fixing the amount of the tax? This would operate as a protective tariff for the fostering of the home merchant. Something of this sort must one day be done.

A clipping of that story was sent to Albert Loeb, secretary of Sears, Roebuck, by D. Lewis, a Carlisle banker. Lewis' covering letter, dated February 12, 1907, also indicated that the "color rumor" was still being kept alive in Arkansas: "This article would make it appear that you were about to 'bust up,' like the Cash Buyers Union did, and so people might be afraid to send you orders. It is all just as silly as to say Mr. Sears is a 'nigger.'"

It may have all seemed silly to Lewis, but to the company's executives it was a grim business. Louis E. Asher, acting general manager, wrote Sears, who was then in Europe, on December 12, 1906 (nineteen days before the new law was to become effective):

> We will continue the Grocery Department; rather we have come to the conclusion that it would not be wise at this time to discontinue the grocery department and notify our customers to this effect, and I am sure Mr. Sears, if you were here on the ground, you would thoroughly agree with us and endorse this step. Up to this time we have not given out any statement to our customers that we would discontinue the sale of groceries; therefore it was not too late to change our plan. It happens that the National Pure Food Law, on which there has been so much comment throughout the country, goes into effect on January 1, 1907, and for us to give the papers and the press in general any further opportunity of attacking us, I believe would be a serious mistake, and they would be quick to seize an opportunity and point out the fact that we are compelled to go out of the grocery business because our cheap goods could not conform to the standards required by the law; and in fact some articles in the trade papers to this effect have already appeared ... getting out of the grocery business at this time would be about the best opening for attacks that the country papers and the trade papers have had in years. This business, it is true, is growing, is very prosperous, and if trade, say in half a dozen sections, is laid low by panic stricken reports, we perhaps would never feel it, and yet I believe it is our business to be watchful in these matters. The bigger the business grows and the higher rank it takes as an institution among the enterprises of the land, the more important, I think it is, that we hold ourselves clear and free from as much criticism as possible.[8]

The remainder of Asher's letter makes it clear that the newspaper attacks covered a far wider range than merely the company's alleged inability to meet the standards of the Pure Food and Drug Act.

J. F. Skinner took cognizance of the unfavorable publicity in a letter to Richard Sears in Berlin, on December 12, 1906. Skinner aligned himself with Asher in favoring continuation of the grocery department, his letter and Asher's apparently being written in concert, and went on to say:

> Personally I may be a little timid when it comes to newspaper notoriety, we of course, have had plenty of it; but really, the avalanche of criticism that has been going on in the commercial and country newspapers can't help but make us take notice. Heretofore, we could throw these criticisms in the waste basket because they had no foundation. I really believe that the criticism we would receive on account of dropping the grocery business at this time would have a strong tendency to upset the confidence of our customers. . . .[9]

The company reluctantly decided to continue the grocery department rather than to risk a serious loss in good will and reputation.

The January–February, 1907, edition of the grocery catalogue sang out in a ringing defense of its groceries. Page 1 was captioned, in large, boldface, capital letters: "The Pure Food Law and Our Groceries." Under "Our Attitude" the statement declared:

> We are glad indeed that now the consumer has some protection, and we are glad that at last every purchaser of a food product offered by any firm or indi-

vidual can know what he buys. We are glad that it is no longer possible for unscrupulous manufacturers and dealers to deceive the consumer by taking his money for articles unfit for consumption. . . . WE WERE THE FIRST TO COME OUT STRONGLY in favor of pure food legislation, and when last May it seemed somewhat doubtful that the people's representatives at Washington would carry out the will of the people, we said in the pages of this Grocery List that the agitation in favor of a pure food law "is justified by the frightful conditions which have prevailed for years in the grocery and drug trades. . . . Many manufacturers and producers . . . have been selling adulterated and impure food products. . . ."

The statement went on to quote more from the previous May's grocery-list statement on the need for pure-food legislation; most of that quotation simply extolled the careful methods Sears claimed to employ in obtaining the finest quality of unadulterated, pure foods. The statement further pointed out, in boldface type, that the grocery catalogue was still—even after the Pure Food and Drug Act had become effective—listing exactly the same brands of groceries. The grocery catalogue almost took credit for passage of that legislation.

The *Carlisle Tribune* provided a fair sampling of the role of small-town newspapers at that time in the independent merchants' fight against mail order. The same issue of the *Tribune* which had run the story on Sears's groceries carried a three-column spread under the caption "Home-Trade Clubs." The remainder of the headline read: "They Should Be Organized and Active in Every Community . . . Patronize Home Merchants . . . The Great Danger to Local Interests That Are Found in the Mail-Order Systems—Educate the Public." The diatribe against mail order was copyrighted, 1906, by Alfred C. Clark. It opened with the question, "Why should we trade at home?" and went on: "The greatest menace to the country merchants today is the mail order business, and with the decline of the country merchant comes inevitable loss to the citizens of both town and country. What at first was considered a great convenience and an exhibition of commendable enterprise has grown to be one of the crying commercial evils." The article added, with grudging admiration, a tribute to the mail-order companies which was conspicuously rare in most such attacks:

The success of the mail order house is the result of constant, extensive, and intelligent advertising. It is not by persistent swindling as some tell us, for no business was ever built up in that way. The home merchant can do no better than to adopt the same method, the judicious use of printer's ink. The merchants . . . could do much toward checking and correcting this growing evil, by liberal advertising and publishing prices. . . .

Tribute, indeed; for the local newspapers may well have decided, to judge from this article, that if they were to open their news columns to local merchants to fight the mail-order colossus, then they might also well levy tribute against those merchants in their own advertising columns.

The argument went on to this general effect: Newspapers should (and many do) decline to accept "foreign" advertising for goods competing with the home merchant. "Trade at Home" clubs should be organized. . . . Suppose you do save money through mail-order buying; even if you pay more at home, you get much of it back through contributions and taxes of local merchants. Then—almost in the next breath—you actually *don't* save money through mail order: "The home merchant can, and generally does, undersell the catalogue house." The two-column cartoon accompanying the article showed a bloated mail-order magnate sparkling with diamonds, siphoning off a community's wealth, while a local merchant stands sadly by.

Articles of this kind, which blossomed in the press simultaneously all over the country, were usually provided through the "patent-insides" industry, which was supported by local merchants and small-town newspapers. In an effort to saturate the country papers with material denouncing mail-order houses, Thomas J. Sullivan of Chicago, a choleric opponent of mail order, furnished such editorial service through the American Press Association in towns where businessmen wanted such articles. Sullivan later incorporated his articles in a volume titled *Merchants and Manufacturers on Trial*, "A complete survey of the illegitimate methods employed by the Retail Catalogue House System, with suggestions of modern means for preventing its further practice and growth. A logical and sane defense of local communities, local Retail Merchants and the Middleman."[10]

One of those "patent-insides" which blanketed much of the country appeared in July, 1907, under the caption, "Small Merchants Fight for Lives." Its date line was "Chicago, July 18," and the *Carlisle Tribune* carried it on July 30. It opened on this communique note:

War has been declared on the great catalogue houses of Chicago and other cities by the 500,000 retail merchants of the West. In one of the most striking economic movements this country has ever known, the small dealers are fighting, as they say, for their lives.

The mammoth institutions, which employ thousands of workers, doing their business entirely through the medium of their bulky catalogues, spending no money in the community whence they derive annually millions of dollars of patronage are forcing increasing numbers of home merchants to the wall and, so their opponents claim, are "making commercial graveyards of once prosperous towns."

In this life or death struggle, jobbers and manufacturers also are involved with the retail merchants. . . .

The story went on to say that an organized attack would be made against mail-order houses by the Home Trade League of America, composed largely of commercial associations, national, state, and local in character, in Illinois, Wisconsin, Iowa, Michigan, Kansas, and Minnesota. The manager of the league was listed as Alfred C. Clark. The long story on "Home-Trade Clubs" in the *Carlisle Tribune* of February 12, 1907, was copyrighted by Alfred C. Clark.

On December 7, 1907, D. Lewis, of Carlisle, sent Albert Loeb a clipping "from one of our county papers." The type face does not appear to be among those used by the *Tribune*, but the tenor was the same:

> The Interstate Grocer, published at St. Louis, Mo., gave an account last week of the famous case of R. H. Mills, of Des Moines, Ia., vs. Sears, Roebuck & Co., the big mail order institution of Chicago. The company misrepresented three different articles in their catalogue and through circulars to Mills, who reported them to Uncle Sam, and the Federal jury at Des Moines last week returned three separate bills against them for $500 each.

The story erred in referring to "three separate bills" of "$500 each," since grand juries do not—and did not—return bills in any specific amounts. The grand jury did, however, return a true bill or indictment against Sears, Roebuck. The company took the matter seriously enough to send the following circular to its customers in January, 1908 (it is not known just how many customers, and in what areas, were circularized):

> Referring to the charge brought against us in Des Moines, Iowa—this attack is instigated by the proprietor of a Retail Merchants' Trade Paper published in the interests of local dealers who are very antagonistic against us. We had no opportunity to answer the charges, make any explanation or present our side of the case; the first we know of the indictment was the item published in the paper. As soon as we get the opportunity to be heard we know we will be fully vindicated.
>
> Our business has been built up to its present size as a result of the fairest and most liberal policy known to the Mercantile World. Our millions of customers can testify to our fair, square and honest dealing. We have sold good goods at very low prices, saved money for thousands upon thousands of people, and in the process of doing this a few merchants have been compelled to ask smaller profits than they otherwise would ask, in order to try to meet our competition. Had we asked high prices and big profits these merchants would not cherish such bitter feeling against us and resort to such methods to annoy and harass us. The merchants have brought this case; not the people. The People are our Friends; we have saved them money and treated them right, and thanks to our strong financial resources, our impregnable position in the mercantile and manufacturing world, and our fair dealing policy, we will always continue to do so.
>
> Send us your orders as in the past, and we pledge you our word and our resources to serve you as well, as faithfully and as honestly as we know how and as we have always done.

Full-length novels could be written about the opposition to, and attacks upon, mail-order selling. But the foregoing samples will give some idea of the type and intensity of that hostility harbored by local merchants. It started early, and it still persists, as witness recent legislative activity at state and federal levels.

These attacks on mail order were to reach their zenith after 1910. The hearings of committees of the United States Senate and House of Representatives as early as 1910 on proposed bills to extend the parcel post, crystallized the opposition to mail order, or, at any rate, the articulation of that opposition. The hearings drew a sharp line of cleavage between "consumers" and distributors. Petitions from granges of the patrons of Husbandry, farmers' co-operative unions, farmers' institutes, farmers' clubs, and labor unions prayed for the passage of any kind of bill extending the parcel-post service. And almost without exception the petitions from businessmen and firms, groups of merchants, commercial clubs, chambers of commerce, boards of trade, retail merchants' associations, travelers' protective associations, and the like in towns and villages in nearly every state from coast to coast and border to border remonstrated against any extension of the parcel post.[11]

The protracted hearings of the Senate and House committees revealed that arguments against the proposed parcel post were in almost every detail the same arguments which had been used for years against mail-order selling. Opponents of the legislation stated bluntly that it would work to the advantage of mail-order companies and would completely wreck local merchants and all those whose livelihood was closely connected with those merchants: jobbers, traveling salesmen, middlemen.

The parcel-post hearings were, in short, a general review of all the opposition to mail order, expressed and latent, in the preceding twenty to thirty years. And just as farm and labor groups petitioned the Congress between 1910 and 1912 in favor of the bill, so had the same groups supported the mail-order houses against attacks in previous years. Sometimes their defense of mail order may have been vocal and articulate in their neighborhoods and in their organizations; but always it was effective in the form of orders dispatched to Sears, Roebuck and to Montgomery Ward. Many customers and friends of the mail-order giants, like the ubiquitous D. Lewis of Carlisle, Arkansas, wrote—to Sears or Ward's, as the case might be—to state that they were standing fast in their support of mail-order buying.[12]

Too, the mail-order houses found some support in magazines and newspapers such as the *Abilene* (Texas) *Farmers Journal*, which editorialized thus on August 14, 1907:

THE STAR WANTS TO KNOW, YOU KNOW

What we want to know of the Farmers Journal man of Abilene is, does Sears, Roebuck & Co. pay you a fixed salary, or just a commission on the business you send them?—San Saba Star.

Well, sir, if it will relieve your distress any to have the truth announced to you, we will say that Sears & Roebuck don't know there is such an individual in the wide, wide world as the Farmers Journal man of Abilene. They don't know there is such a paper in the world as the Farmers Journal unless, perchance, they have seen reference to it in some such flings as you flung out in your paper last week. Of course you don't understand how an editor can talk to his readers without having the welfare of the local merchants before his eyes all the time, day and night, but it can be done. The man who does it, however, must be disingrafted from the stem of commercialism, and must have before his eyes all the time, day and night, the welfare of that large class who produce the raw materials and buy and consume the manufactured products and he must live mighty hard. The local merchants are interested in exploiting this large class through the prevailing system of distributing these manufactured products for profit, and you,

Mr. Star Man, are interested with the merchants because the revenue of your paper comes from the merchants, and is a part of the profits which the merchants have made off the farmers. Hence you are as blind as a bat to any proposition made to the farmers that would ignore the scheme through which you rake in your revenue, and you will continue to misinform them and try to keep them blind as to what is their real interest. You can't do otherwise as long as you are a part of the scheme.

But what's this we notice in your paper, on the same page with your reference to the Journal man and Sears & Roebuck? It is an announcement which a San Saba merchant pays you to print, and it leads off thus: "I will leave the latter part of this week for St. Louis to purchase a large line of fall clothing and ladies' dress goods."

What! St. Louis? That's nearly as far north as Sears & Roebuck's city. Going to take money out of San Saba county and carry it to St. Louis to enrich the big concerns up there? Thought you believed in keeping San Saba money in San Saba? ... So far as any principle is involved ... does it make any difference whether your San Saba merchant stops in St. Louis and buys his stock from those big northern concerns, or goes on to Chicago and buys from Sears & Roebuck? ... It's the advertising that the Star is interested about and right here the Journal wants to say to the farmers and the public generally as consumers, that the plain, unvarnished reason why the newspapers make war on Mail Order houses is because, under that system of distributing merchandise, they would be cut off from their accustomed slices of pie in the shape of advertisements from the local distributors. Only that and nothing more. If all local mercantile advertising were abolished, the newspapers wouldn't care a continental how nor where you bought your merchandise.

But mail-order supporters like the *Farmers Journal* were too few and too far between for the great mail-order houses to rely upon in meeting the opposition of local merchants. Sears, Roebuck sought to offset the "color rumor" in the nineties by sending out, in catalogues and with shipments of goods, color pictures of Richard Sears. For a while, stereopticon views of Sears were similarly sent out, around 1906 or 1907, but the practice was eventually discontinued as being too costly.[13]

Too, the company made a point of answering all letters from its customers or, in fact, from anyone who wrote for information. Many such letters requested confirmation or denial of specific charges against the company which had appeared in the writer's local press or rumors the correspondent had heard. But the company realized, apparently, that for each person who went to the trouble of writing, there were probably more who had been exposed to the same rumors and slanders *without* taking the trouble to write and inquire. The catalogue remained, therefore, the one unfailing avenue of contact with the company's customers. The warm, friendly tone of the catalogue through the nineties derived in some measure from the necessity of showing the company as a friend instead of the ogre it was painted by the opposition. The homely camaraderie of the catalogue was an integral part of the determined campaign to meet attacks by indirection as far as might be possible.

By 1899, however, Sears's campaign was more or less out in the open—

though still all sweetness and light on the surface. The spring catalogue that year carried on its cover this statement: "This book tells you just what your storekeeper at home pays for everything he buys—and will prevent him from overcharging you on anything you buy from him." Long before this, the Sears, Roebuck catalogues had maintained that the company's huge purchases made possible such low costs that it could sell direct to the consumer at prices lower than local merchants had to pay at wholesale. But the foregoing quotation was rather obviously an attempt to smite the local merchant by indicating not only that the company's retail price was the local storekeeper's wholesale price but also that many merchants in fact purchased their goods from Sears, Roebuck.

The company's 1900 and 1901 catalogues featured on the inside-front-cover pages a "Notice to Dealers," outlining in full-page detail just how the firm would sell to merchants in quantity at the same unit price at which it sold to individual customers. One former employee says that this was "an attempt to allay the opposition of merchants throughout the country" and adds the belief that very little business was ever done by the company with dealers. It appears more realistic to assume Sears was knifing the merchants by indirection, for the moral was obvious: the statement, like that of 1899, made it appear that merchants *were* buying from the company (and, of course, necessarily adding their own profit to the price) and that the customers could therefore always buy directly from the company at lower prices than from their home-town merchants.

By 1902 the merchants' opposition to mail order had grown louder. Montgomery Ward seemingly concluded that its best defense lay in a frontal assault against such opposition. Ward's catalogue that year gave prominent space to a reprint of an article from a publication called the *Northwestern Agriculturist*, captioned: "The Tyranny of Villages." It was an all-out attack on local retail merchants and a ringing paean of praise for mail order:

> We believe the farmers of today are tyrannized over by the country merchants to a far worse extent than they realize. . . . Mail-order business has solved the problem for the farmer and released him from serfdom. He can now buy his supplies as cheaply as can the country merchants, and by the mail can annihilate the distance between himself and the great centers of trade. . . .[14]

Sic semper tyrannis!

Richard Sears evidently agreed with his principal competitor, and with Thomas Jefferson, that rebellion to tyrants was obedience to God. But Sears's approach was more suave and urbane. His approach was made clear in an editorial which appeared in the 1902 catalogue, "Our Compliments to the Retail Merchant." It was a masterpiece which showed Richard Sears with tongue in cheek, the brotherhood of man in his eyes, and calculated assassination in his heart:

[The retail merchant] fills an important place in commerce, in that he is a necessary agent for the distributing of all kinds of merchandise to the convenience of the customer everywhere. Very rarely the country merchant who sells you dry goods, shoes, hardware, and other merchandise overcharges you. As a rule, the merchant from whom you buy, adds as little profit to the cost of the goods as he can possibly afford to add, for example: if a certain article in our catalogue is quoted at $1.00 and your hardware merchant asks you $1.50 for the same article, we wish to say in behalf of your hardware dealer that this difference of 50 cents does not represent an excessive profit he is charging you; for by reason of his being compelled to buy from wholesale houses in small quantities, he is compelled to pay more for this article than we would pay, for we buy in very large quantities direct from the manufacturers; his sales are necessarily small, his expenses necessarily large in proportion to the amount of business he does, and he must get his cost, his expenses and a fair profit out of the goods he sells....

We number thousands of our very best customers among the merchants in all lines in every state; thousands of merchants in all lines are constantly buying from us. We feel there is ample room in this big, rich, growing country for all the country merchants who are engaged in honest merchandising, and there is also room for us.

It is not our desire to build up our business (now already very large) by attempting to tear down any retail business already in existence....

The country merchant who undertakes to antagonize the catalogue house really antagonizes his own customers, he really questions the right of his customers to spend their money where they like.... Instead of injuring the catalogue house he is injuring his own business and building up the business of the catalogue house.

In the following year's catalogue the company came nearer than ever to taking overt cognizance of the retail merchants' campaign against mail-order buying. Characteristically, while offering security to the individual customer against retaliation in his local community, the editorial also managed to slip the stiletto into the retail merchants again. It was titled "How We Make Every Transaction with Us Strictly Confidential" and read in part:

As many people, especially merchants, business houses, townspeople and others, do not care to have others know where or from whom they buy their goods, as many people object to having the name of the shipper spread across every box or package, so that when it is unloaded at the station or express office everyone can see what they are getting and where they buy it, to protect all those who care for this protection and make it possible for you to order your goods from us with no fear of anyone learning at the railroad station, express office or elsewhere what you bought or where you bought it, our name and address will not appear on any box, package tag, envelope or article of merchandise....

From this nonstop marathon sentence, the editorial went on to administer the coup de grâce to the local merchants whom Sears loved so excruciatingly:

For example: If you are a merchant and wish to buy goods to sell again, your customers will be unable to learn from any marks inside or outside where you bought the goods or what you paid for them.

If you are a professional man, or even in the employ of some merchant who for personal reasons might object to your sending to us for goods, you need have no fear, our name will not appear on any goods or packages you get.

While we would be glad to have our name appear on every article of merchandise and on every box and package, as a valuable means of advertising, we have learned that thousands of our customers need the protection that the omitting of our name affords. This applies especially to townspeople.

The persuasive "one-world" approach reached its apogee in the spring of 1906. A long editorial in the catalogue—reflecting Sears's own style, possibly through the pens of Asher and others, and much of Rosenwald's philosophy—told of the company's new $5,600,000 building (a not-so-mute witness to booming business and a harbinger of even greater service). The editorial went on to project the coming era of greater service in more specific terms, opening on this Lincolnian note:

With malice towards none and charity for all, we extend to all mankind our sincere wishes for greater prosperity and happiness.

. . . We are all entering an era of modern merchandising, better values . . . greater economies . . . many new and more modern methods in the selling of merchandise will surely develop. Retail dealers . . . will . . . be able to give better and better values. Many manufacturers selling to jobbers only will begin selling to the retail dealer direct, saving him a good portion of the jobber's profit. . . . Retail dealers . . . growing constantly keener and keener in their buying . . . with a few exceptions all sellers of goods regardless of place or method will give honest goods . . . and an evergrowing equivalent for the dollar. . . . The consumer today is buying from many catalogue houses . . . as well as from many thousands of retail dealers. He has a right to buy where he likes and every seller has the same equal right to solicit his trade. Let us all believe as we do, that every successful dealer, retailer, catalogue house or otherwise, is reliable. Let us rise above the jealousies and differences that so often grow out of competition so that in the evening of the day's work your competitor will be as welcome to break bread at your table as would be your doctor or your banker. We have a high regard for every honorable and reliable dealer and even though we may at times differ in our opinions, we bear no ill will against any maker or seller in our land.

He who sits atop the heap can afford to banish ill-will and to harbor only magnanimity; but the retail merchants continued to fight to remove that magnanimous boot from their neck, for they felt it pressing hard. Yet, the louder they inveighed, the greater became the pressure of that sweet-natured, hob-nailed boot of the great mail-order house.

In 1908 the catalogue openly admitted the hostility the company had aroused among local merchants. In a full-page statement of "Our Policy," the company asserted:

Covering a short period of about twelve years [obviously the company was here dating its real beginning from the arrival of Rosenwald in 1896] we have grown, from a very small beginning, to a position where our volume of sales is larger than any other house in the world selling general merchandise, a position where we probably sell more merchandise direct to the user than all other mail

OPPOSITION AND COMPETITION 163

order catalogue houses in the world. In making these rapid strides we have had much to do in bringing about a great change in the system of merchandising, in the economies of manufacturing, wholesaling, retailing, etc., much to do with lessening cost from everyone to everyone, much to do with bettering qualities, and while this great work of manufacturing, assembling, controlling, bringing together and distributing in a single year over Fifty Million Dollars' worth of merchandise to users all over the United States has made us millions of friends (for our customers are our friends), unfortunately for us, and not that we would have it so, nor because we bear any ill will toward any of our competitors, great or small, this wonderfully rapid growth and development has created for us a good many enemies, especially among the smaller retail dealers, storekeepers in country towns, and among manufacturers, especially from those manufacturers from whom we decline to buy goods, either because they cannot furnish us satisfactorily high qualities or satisfactorily low prices.

If our prices were not so much lower than people can buy elsewhere, if our qualities were not uniformly high . . . if the retail dealers and storekeepers of the country . . . did not know all this to be true, there would be no jealousy on their part, there would be no occasion for them to attack us with their thousand and one misrepresentations. . . .

The catalogue went on to declare that, while the company abhorred misrepresentations, it welcomed—aye, it thirsted for—kindly suggestions for improvement: "We Do Most Earnestly Solicit Honest Criticism. We Solicit Criticism More Than Orders." This orgy of soul-searching continued:

If you have reason to criticise and you don't criticise us, we therefore never learn that you are not entirely satisfied with a transaction with us, it means an awful loss to us. It may mean the loss of your good will, your trade and your influence with us. A mistake on one order on our part left uncorrected may cost us dozens, yes hundreds of orders; therefore we tell you honestly, anxious as we are for orders, if you have an honest criticism to make and an order to send, and we can't have both, we beg of you to send us the criticism, and don't send the order. . . .

As many tales and numerous protests in a nearly ubiquitous rural press testify, the company's most dramatic competition was focused in the retail centers for rural trade—crossroad stores and small-town emporiums. But the most respected (and recognized) competition came from Montgomery Ward. And while it is easy enough to point out that by 1908 Ward's was the chief competitor of Sears, Roebuck and Company, the situation during the early nineties was just the opposite, for not until 1900 did Sears's net sales exceed those of Montgomery Ward.[15] Ever since, Sears has been the leader and Ward's the chief competitor.

But regardless of which of the two big mail-order companies held the lead in any given year, or by how wide a margin, each of the two always acted as a competitive spur upon the other. Each had to make sure its prices were, at worst, not appreciably higher than its competitor's. Each had to live up to its guaranty of satisfaction or money back just as rigorously as it expected its competitor might. Each had to attempt to reduce expenses and improve operating efficiency to stay (or get) ahead of the other.

In short, both Sears, Roebuck and Montgomery Ward knew, after the former had established itself as a going concern, that competition was in truth their lifeblood—not simply because ineptitude on the part of one might give the greater volume of business to the other but also because it was always at least theoretically possible in this period for one of the two to capture such a large segment of the business as to drive the other out. By 1908 it was, of course, Ward's which had to contemplate that dreary possibility.

While Sears, Roebuck and Montgomery Ward dominated the mail-order field, they did not completely lack for competition even there. Advertisements in mail-order magazines throughout the eighties and nineties and after the opening of this century show clearly that numbers of firms or individuals were selling by mail. A scanning of *Leslie's Weekly* in January, 1895, for instance, reveals advertisements by small mail-order enterprises for patent medicines, revolvers, shotguns, bicycles, shoes, sewing machines, watches, clothing, and other items. Most of the vendors, however, sold one item or, at most, one line of merchandise. And in almost every instance their prices were higher than those of Sears, Roebuck (though it is impossible to know just what relationship existed between prices and quality).

Sears (like Ward's) also had to face some competition from other quarters. One quarter was the large department stores such as Macy's in New York, John Wanamaker's in Philadelphia and New York, Filene's in Boston, and similar institutions in other parts of the country. These did not present really serious competition with Sears, since the mail-order company was not seekng to exploit sizable cities to any extent. But Macy's and Wanamaker's did a considerable mail-order business for years, Macy's entering mail order twelve years before Richard Sears sold his first watches.

By 1891 Macy's catalogue had grown to 311 pages. In addition to the lines previously carried, Macy's now offered furniture, hardware, stoves, baby carriages, mattresses, lamps, several pages of artists' materials, tennis goods, harness and saddles. By 1903 its catalogue had shrunk to 41 pages, 4 by 6 inches. Offerings included buggies, bicycles, watches, shotguns, golf supplies, tents, refrigerators, washing machines, sewing machines, lawnmowers, and the aforementioned lines. Space compression allowed fewer illustrations and less descriptive text. Watches opened with two pages of illustrations; no prices were shown, however, until the third page. The book varied throughout from relatively much copy and little art to some artwork and almost no copy. In the actual presentation of goods, the catalogue seemed to serve more as a listing device than as a selling mechanism. That 1903 book also asserted, "We can and do undersell our competitors (no matter where located)." Customers were invited to deposit as much money as they wished in Macy's credit department.

OPPOSITION AND COMPETITION

Macy's 1903–4 fall and winter catalogue opened with three pages of freight-rate tabulations to selected cities throughout the United States or its continental territories. Whether Macy's was actually selling by mail to all states in the Union, it is impossible to say. Even as late as this 1903–4 catalogue, Macy's was still hewing to the line, "We do not send goods upon approval." That catalogue listed several pages of drugs and cosmetics, with a few illustrations. No patent medicines were illustrated, but several "specifics" were listed. One page boosted Macy's special grocery catalogue, sent free upon request; four additional pages listed groceries, without illustrations.

The 1905 Macy catalogue asserted: "All our goods are sold with an absolute guarantee that they are exactly as represented, and, if not entirely satisfactory, we will cheerfully refund your money. This has always been our rule." Possibly it had, but the note of cheerfulness now attaching to refunds was infinitely stronger than a few years earlier. With but slight disguise the Macy fall and winter book of 1905–6 took a slap at Sears, Roebuck and Montgomery Ward. After inviting comparison with "any other catalogue issued," Macy's declared:

> In buying from us your orders are filled from exactly the same stock shown over our counters, to the most discriminating shopping public in the world. . . . How different from buying from the exclusive mail-order houses, particularly those of Chicago. They display no goods to the public, have no competition in examination of quality, and fill your orders from a stock of goods which never sees the light of day. . . . The economy we offer is the . . . real economy of Satisfactory Goods. Many houses buy shoddy goods. . . .

A year later the inside front cover of the catalogue said:

> Make a comparison of our prices with the prices of those houses which do a mail order business only. You will find our prices invariably lower, and our goods always of a higher grade. You will get from us up-to-date New York merchandise, the kind New York shoppers SEE before they purchase, not goods bought to sell to the rural trade only. . . .
>
> We will prepay freight or express charges on all paid purchases—with the exception of furniture, pianos, refrigerators, sewing machines, boats, china, groceries and such goods as may be classed as heavy or bulky.

The explanation went on to point out that purchases of five dollars or more would bring free delivery as far north as New Hampshire and as far south as the District of Columbia. As the value of the purchase rose, so did the radius in which free delivery was promised. Purchases of seventy-five dollars or more would merit free delivery anywhere in the United States. This offer was shored up with the defensive statement: "Houses which offer more than we do in the way of free deliveries make up for the freight charges twice and three times over in the prices of the merchandise."

That 1906–7 catalogue also stated the guaranty in more nearly unequivocal terms than ever before: "You can have your money back without question or quibble." Then came the usual joust at the competition:

Do you know that the big "Catalogue Houses" do not welcome buyers to their stores; that their goods are not on display; and moreover that ninety-nine per cent of their stock is made up for the country trade on the principle that "the farmer does not know the difference" and "anything is good enough for a buckwheat."

In mid-1907, under the heading, "How To Order by Mail," Macy's took a page from Richard W. Sears's book—just about literally, too:

> Tell us in your own way what you want. Don't be afraid you will make a mistake. Every day we get orders from people who had never before ordered by mail. Just tell us what you want in your own way, in any language, no difference whether your writing is good or bad, we will understand and ship you the goods promptly.

(The same tortured syntax, the rushing wave of confidence, the innate friendliness of Sears's earlier writing—almost the same words in the same sequence, in fact.)

On page 7 of the 1907–8 fall and winter catalogue, Macy's lashed out in perhaps its strongest and most direct attack on Sears, Roebuck and Montgomery Ward. Sears had that year discontinued its Customers' Profit-sharing Premium Plan, which it had launched in 1904 (Ward's had followed in 1904 with a similar plan). Under a large, boldface caption, "The 'Something for Nothing' Plan Fails," Macy's trumpeted:

> We congratulate the American people. Once again they have justified Lincoln's estimate of them by refusing to be fooled continuously. Certain retailers and Catalogue Houses, in a spirit of deepest generosity, have been "sharing their profits" with the public by "giving" them various knick-knacks, pieces of furniture, etc., "for nothing."
>
> But the good common sense of the American people reasserts itself, and these dealers announce that they have discontinued the "profit sharing" plans. . . .
>
> It is interesting to note the announced reasons for the change; to enable "still lower prices to be quoted." So it seems that the cost of those "Free Gifts" was included in the prices after all. . . . We sell you goods cheaper than you can buy them anywhere else, but we don't give anything away. The free gift allurement is a snare and a delusion, a temptation only to the ignorant and unthinking. . . . Beware of the profit sharing articles and the free gift enterprises.

By 1911 Macy's was to cease paying transportation charges on any goods, no matter how large the purchase. And the following year was to see the company abandon the field—on the very threshold of the truly golden age of mail order.

All in all, Macy's seems to have been eternally conscious—even plaintively envious—of the success Sears, Roebuck and Montgomery Ward were enjoying in mail order; but Sears, Roebuck certainly appears never to have considered Macy's as a real competitor in any sense. No reference occurs in company records, correspondence, or interviews to any competitor but Ward's.

As already pointed out, Macy's claimed to sell goods of higher quality at lower prices than any other mail-order business in the country. A comparison of its prices with Sears, Roebuck's is extremely difficult for many reasons. Without the actual goods at hand, it is impossible to evaluate the relative quality, but it appears from their respective catalogues that Macy's goods were at least on a higher aesthetic plane. And since Macy's were selling in New York, where tastes were more refined and demands for quality possibly more insistent than in rural areas, Macy's quality may well have been somewhat higher at that time.

In 1903, for example, Macy's listed bicycles at $14.98 and up. Sears, Roebuck's lowest priced bicycle cost $10.95, and its offerings ranged through a large variety of models up to $16.75. That $10.95 bicycle was not, however, highly recommended; the catalogue traded up, posthaste, to its $13.75 and $15.75 models. In that same year Macy's shotguns started at $23.98. Sears's least expensive featured shotgun was $14.92, its costliest $77.72; tucked inconspicuously away in its offerings was an "imported" double-barrel shotgun for $6.75. While it is impossible to assess the relative quality of Macy's $23.98 gun with the Sears piece closest to that price, it is interesting to note that, whereas Macy's described only a very few models, Sears devoted eighteen pages to its shotguns, with heavy emphasis on cutaway and action illustrations. It was characteristic that Sears almost invariably offered a far wider variety of items in each merchandise line than did Macy's and usually started with a lower price and often ended up with more expensive models than Macy's.

When Macy's sewing machines ranged from $17.94 to $21.24, Sears's machines ran a gamut from $8.25 to $20.80. Macy's listed its lowest-priced buggy at $39.58, f.o.b. factory, while Sears started buggies at $27.95 (for an open model) and ranged up to $78.00 for a very fancy one. On watches, Sears probably dominated in both price and quality, because of Richard Sears's own intimate knowledge of that line. Whereas Macy's cheapest watch was $5.98, Sears's started at 84 cents and went through scores of choices to a far higher figure than Macy's. On lawn-mowers, Macy's started at $2.29; Sears began at $2.25 for what appears from the respective illustrations to have been a comparable mower.

Mail-order selling apparently was never greatly profitable for Macy's, except perhaps in helping to spread the firm's name. While the volume grew, the expense connected with it grew even faster. No data have survived on the amount of business done by mail, but the money expended in printing and mailing catalogues may give some indication; that expense reached $400,000 in 1911, and even that did not of course cover the whole cost of operating the mail-order division. That $400,000 amounted to 2.4 per cent of the total net sales of the whole store for that year and was obviously too high. The Macy catalogue by then numbered 460 pages, and some of its illustrations were in color.

In addition, mail order called for handling staple merchandise changing little in price or style durng the life of any given catalogue, while the department-store stock (from which mail orders had to be filled) consisted to a great extent of a more rapidly changing assortment of offerings. Finally, Macy's mail order, operating in its department store, used high-rent property, expensive fixtures, etc. After a real effort in 1911 to expand mail order and make it profitable, Macy's gave up its efforts to rival Sears, Roebuck and Company.[16]

John Wanamaker advertised heavily in *Leslie's Weekly* in the late 1890's. That firm's March 31, 1898, advertisement in *Leslie's* offered to send samples of any item stocked by Wanamaker's and concluded: "We think we have the fastest and most satisfactory Mail Order Service in the country."

Actually, of course, Sears, Roebuck's chief competition did not come from Macy's or Wanamaker's or even from Ward's; it came, as did Ward's, from local merchants throughout the country. These merchants' stores were institutions with their roots in local soil. These merchants were the men geographically closest to the people Sears was seeking as customers. These were the merchandisers with whom Sears really had to come to grips. And, the longer the battle continued, the more the local merchants came to improve their merchandising techniques in their fight to survive.

When one remembers that Sears, Roebuck was listing approximately a hundred thousand items of merchandise by 1908, one gets some idea of just how heavily engaged in competition the company was. It competed, for example, with virtually every shoe store in smaller communities. It even competed with grocery stores. It competed with farm-implement salesmen. It competed with clothing stores, bookstores, and distributors of thousands of other items. In short, there were few communities of any size, few stores even at country crossroads, where the mail-order firm did not find itself competing. All this naturally made it easy and logical for retail merchants in every line to band together to fight Sears, Roebuck. No mail-order house dealing in one, or even a very few, lines of merchandise could ever have aroused the concerted opposition and hostility which the retailers turned on Sears. The very measure and nature of that opposition was simply the other side of the coin in showing the competition the company faced.

CHAPTER XI

End of an Era

BY ANY standards, Sears, Roebuck and Company was an impressive organization by 1908. Its volume of business reached $40,843,866 in net sales by the close of the fiscal period, June 30, in the depression year 1908. Invested capital at the end of that year stood at $45,295,403, and merchandise inventory amounted to $5,055,896. Working capital at the close of that year was $5,646,236, and the company's total assets were $48,246,966. Despite the depression, the last six months of 1908 showed a net profit of $1,991,457 on sales of $21,813,592. The company's own plant, built to its specifications, occupied a forty-acre tract easily accessible by rail and motor. It was thought to be more than adequate to house the business as it stood and to provide ample room for expansion. The firm's employees were numbered in the thousands.

President Richard Sears, though absent from Chicago (and the United States) during most of 1907 and 1908, remained the restless entrepreneur bombarding his associates with suggestions and schemes. Vice-President Julius Rosenwald had assumed responsibility for finances, merchandise, and for most of the administrative detail, and Secretary Albert Loeb handled legal and some financial matters, much administrative routine, and a large share of personality clashes and differences of opinion within the company.

The second rung in the hierarchy was occupied largely by men with several years' experience in the company: Operations Chief O. C. Doering, General Manager Louis Asher, Merchandise Manager J. Fletcher Skinner, and a staff of competent merchandise department heads. Under Skinner a New York buying office had been opened in 1902 and had brought about significant improvements in textile-goods buying.

A mail-order branch had been opened in Dallas in 1906 and, though its function had not been fully determined or its possibilities yet realized, it was to succeed as the first of eleven such mail-order branches.

The organization of merchandise procurement had been developed to the point where sources were not the problem they had been; the company owned sixteen factories, wholly or partially, by 1906, according to the catalogue of that year. The merchandise line had expanded enormously, as Sears, Roebuck became more and more a general merchandise house after 1895.

Richard Sears's heavy advertising and the large circulation of catalogues in this period had made the firm's name a family byword throughout the nation. The production of the catalogue had by now become better organized, and the stage was set for introduction of the "lineup" and the entire process of building the book from cover to cover before setting any type or making a single engraving.

The "schedule system" of filling all orders and making shipment within twenty-four to forty-eight hours after receipt of an order had already been conceived and was already functioning; delays and mixups were still not uncommon, but they were at least no longer the standard practice of a decade earlier.

Clearly, Sears, Roebuck and Company had solidly intrenched its position as a going concern by the end of 1908. It had weathered depressions and opposition from merchants and newspapers. It had evolved, by trial and error, a policy of free catalogue distribution which was keeping its wares before millions of Americans. It had exhausted the mail-order magazines and newspapers as profitable advertising mediums and was ready to rely almost solely upon the catalogue for years to come. It had found out much about what goods people would buy, at what prices, and under what conditions.

The company had also, incidentally, amassed fortunes for Richard Sears and Julius Rosenwald—fortunes which could be and were used to plow additional capital back into the business. A handwritten note appended by Julius Rosenwald to a "Financial Statement showing the condition of our company on December 31, 1904" read:

Mr. R. W. Sears—President is worth outside of any interest in this business One Million Five Hundred Thousand Dollars—and Julius Rosenwald Vice-Pres.-Treas. is worth Five Hundred Thousand Dollars outside of any interest in this business. We are the owners of practically 95% of the stock of this Company.

JULIUS ROSENWALD

It is significant that after 1895 all additional capital needed to stoke the mail-order fire of Sears, Roebuck up to the time of its recapitalization in 1906 was provided out of earnings. Working capital was often supplemented by loans from Richard Sears and Julius Rosenwald. The 1904 financial statement listed under liabilities, "Personal Accounts of Officers—$33,511.15." Less than three years later the balance sheet contained the item, "Due to Officials of the Company for Loans, $2,226,989.94."

The extent to which profits were accumulated in the business in the years 1895–1906 is clear from the accompanying statement submitted by Rosenwald to Goldman, Sachs and Company prior to the 1906 recapitalization.

PROFITS OF SEARS, ROEBUCK & COMPANY
SINCE ORGANIZATION, [1895] AND
DISPOSITION THEREOF

Added to Capital	$ 4,850,000.00
Paid in Dividends	3,706,017.96
Surplus January 1, 1906	2,368,061.31
TOTAL PROFITS	$10,924,079.27

SEARS, ROEBUCK AND COMPANY HEADQUARTERS, CHICAGO (ADMINISTRATION AND TOWER BUILDINGS OPENED 1906)

Of nearly $11,000,000 in profits over the ten-year period, almost three-fourths remained in the business. The dividends accrued almost entirely to Sears and Rosenwald as owners of more than 90 per cent of the stock at that time. The remarkable profits of that decade appear more dramatic when one realizes that annual net worth over the same period averaged less than $2,500,000.

Although annual profit data are not available for the years prior to 1895, Roebuck provides a record of net worth for the years 1889–95. The profitability of Richard Sears's aggressive promotions is clear from the increase in net worth from $2,950 in 1889 to $79,149 in 1894. When it is recalled that no new capital was brought into the business and that Sears took out sums adequate to set him well on the road to his first million, it is plain that this earliest phase was marked by success.

In the span of little more than two decades the general mail-order business had made multimillionaires of the two men: Richard Sears, who had started with little more than $50 in 1886; and Julius Rosenwald, who had joined the firm with a borrowed $37,500, and even that not cash. Their fortunes were to grow even greater. Sears was to sell his interest in the business for $10,000,000 late in 1908, and that amount did not include any of his other personal holdings. At his death in 1914 Sears's fortune was estimated at $17,500,000.[1] Rosenwald's fortune was to reach great heights even after his philanthropies had disposed of some $63,000,000.

Table 11 provides a picture of the development of various indexes of the company's position up to 1908. Even by the most cursory examination, these figures testify to successful market exploitation. A healthy market, while essential, provided merely a culture. Growth depended upon proper cultivation; the same market was available to many. Montgomery Ward had the advantage of an earlier start, and the National Cloak and Suit Company (later National Bellas Hess Company) followed Sears's entry into the mail-order business by only two years. Besides these, whose names survive, in the first decade after the Civil War hundreds of other mail-order firms entered the market—not to mention the mail-order aspirations of department stores.[2] The most successful of these direct competitors was Montgomery Ward; and Sears, Roebuck and Company sales by 1908 exceeded Ward's by many millions.

In addition to tangible assets, the company had another, less easily weighed, though chronicled in the balance sheet at a value of $30,000,000. Sears, Roebuck had built a vast reservoir of good will along with the enemies it had made. Its customers felt a bond with the Company which was certainly remarkable in commercial history; they wrote Sears, Roebuck to ask for advice on family matters, to report on crop and weather conditions in their respective areas, or just to let the firm know they were getting along all right ("and recovered from the accident when the mule kicked me and broke my right arm, so I couldn't write sooner"). They sent

TABLE 11*

SALES, CAPITAL, ASSETS, AND PROFITS, 1889–1908

Year	Net Sales	Net Working Capital	Net Worth	Total Assets	Net Profits
1889			$ 2,950		
1890			10,452		
1891	$ 137,743		14,615		
1892	276,980		35,624		$ 30,293
1893	388,464		69,115	$ 89,020	
1894	393,323		79,149	119,515	
1895	745,595		54,571	132,735	49,108
1896	1,751,646†	$ 226,989	237,797	373,397	67,890
1897	2,800,858	352,553	369,457	628,118	141,204
1898	5,394,100	725,886	742,328	1,292,658	365,152
1899	7,928,387	1,044,224	1,044,224	1,506,536	574,597
1900	10,637,367				870,225
1901	14,656,568†	1,881,182	2,347,457	3,167,054	775,656
1902	15,945,397	2,489,276	3,713,798	5,324,146	1,215,825
1903	23,252,642	2,286,546	3,000,000	5,530,649	1,768,599
1904	27,692,721	4,062,357	5,135,776	8,183,615	2,276,871
1905	37,789,422	694,738	7,292,645	14,709,112	2,868,061
1907‡	50,722,840	2,948,434	42,292,899	49,707,376	3,238,502
1908‡	40,843,866	3,756,093	43,645,196	49,373,396	2,034,796

*Source: 1889–95, A. C. Roebuck, "Some Early and Later History of Sears, Roebuck and Co." (2 vols.), passim; 1896–1901, confidential reports of Sears, Roebuck and Company to Goldman, Sachs and Company; 1902–5, reports of Deloitte, Plender and Griffiths, auditors to Goldman, Sachs and Company; 1906 and 1907 fiscal years, annual reports of Sears, Roebuck and Company.

† Gross sales.
‡ June 30.

TABLE 12*

MEASURES OF SUCCESS, 1889–1908

Year	Percentage Change in Sales from Previous Year	Sales per Dollar Working Capital	Sales per Dollar Net Worth	Sales per Dollar Assets	Net Profits per Dollar Sales	Net Profits per Dollar Net Worth
1889						
1890						
1891			$ 9.43			
1892	101.08		7.78		$0.092	$0.851
1893	40.25		5.62	$4.36		
1894	1.25		4.97	3.29		
1895	89.56		13.48	5.62	0.066	0.900
1896	134.93	$ 7.72	7.37	4.69	0.039	0.286
1897	59.89	7.95	7.58	4.46	0.050	0.383
1898	92.59	7.43	7.27	4.17	0.068	0.492
1899	46.98	7.59	7.59	5.26	0.072	0.550
1900	34.16				0.082	
1901	37.78	7.79	6.25	4.63	0.053	0.331
1902	8.79	6.41	4.29	2.99	0.076	0.328
1903	45.83	10.17	7.75	4.20	0.076	0.589
1904	19.10	6.82	5.39	3.38	0.082	0.444
1905	36.79	54.52	5.19	2.58	0.076	0.394
1907†	33.91	17.20	1.20	1.02	0.064	0.076
1908†	−19.48	10.87	0.94	0.83	0.050	0.047

*Source: Calculated from data in Table 11.   † June 30.

in gold dust and currency notes to be kept for them. They showed their trust and even their affection in many ways.

Every sign points to the astuteness with which Sears cultivated the fertile rural market. A complete explanation of how the company outdistanced competition is perhaps too ambitious a task to assay. But it is worth while to review the conditions and policies that Sears pursued in the mail-order race. Underlying the sales of this whole industry was, of course, the expanding income and population on farms. There was further an opportunity for some distributive agency which would supply to the rural market something of what the department stores offered to urban residents. The country general stores were ill prepared to make available to customers a vast variety of merchandise. The local character of the store's market prohibited extensive stocks from which the farmer-buyer might choose, and limited sales, as well as other circumstances, dictated relatively high prices.

Thus, in brief outline, was the arena prepared for the mail-order invasion. Richard Sears's early and unqualified successes in watches and jewelry led him to exercise his faculties in the general mail-order business. One of his outstanding talents was his sense of merchandise selection. He sensed what the farmer wanted and at what price he was likely to buy. Residence, travel, and desultory conversation provided Richard Sears with a fund of information on his customers' motivations, grievances, and wishes, as well as their income. The merchandise he selected, the copy he wrote, and the prices he listed in his big "wish book" reflected his sophistication.

In a real sense the cornerstone of the business was a low-price policy. Sears would exercise great ingenuity in pushing down his buying price so that he might advertise lower selling prices on items whose potentialities he thought great. Long before Nourse, Richard Sears banked on demand elasticity. Though experience must have taught him that his low prices would be followed, he depended on "getting there first." He held firm convictions about the virtues of enjoying the initial advantage. Always he relied, and with justification, on his ability to start a new entry before the old was exhausted.

To depend upon radical price reduction without risking inferences of inferior quality, Sears early adopted the guaranty and a liberal returned-goods policy, which served to indorse the quality of the merchandise as well as to coax customers into experimenting with a not thoroughly familiar method of buying.

But surely all these policies were not too remote from those pursued by Montgomery Ward. Indeed, was not Ward's introduction a compact with the Grange to sell at lower prices? It was not alone the policies so far discussed that set Sears apart, for the potentials implicit in these stratagems were realized only through aggressive promotion, the capstone of Richard Sears's methods, and the hallmark of his strategy.[3]

Especially in the initial stages of his entry into the general mail-order business, Sears relied on heavy advertising expenditures. Hardly a periodical finding its way to farm homes in the nineties appeared without some message from Sears, Roebuck. But Sears was not only a buyer of prodigious quantities of space; he was also adept at filling the space with copy that captivated readers. More than anything else the farm market was captured by Richard Sears's imagination—his ability to dramatize the policies and merchandise that characterized his business. He never thought simply of merchandise selection, price policy, and promotion as separate and distinct operations. He thought in terms of *promotable* merchandise and prices as a package. The item and the price formed a part of each great scheme. Periodical, circular, and catalogue advertising—all carried carefully conceived copy proclaiming the superiority of Sears, Roebuck values with a conviction that was often transferred to the reader.

The overwhelming success of Richard Sears's strategy was achieved through constant application to his task. However many other men are described by Arnold Bennett's characterization of the American businessman, surely the founder of Sears, Roebuck and Company might have inspired Bennett's lines:

> The rough, broad difference between the American and the European business man is that the latter is anxious to leave his work, while the former is anxious to get to it. The attitude of the American business man toward his business is pre-eminently the attitude of an artist. . . . He loves his business. It is not his toil, but his hobby, passion, vice, monomania—any vituperative epithet you like to bestow on it![4]

Richard Sears was constantly preoccupied with his schemes. His workday started early and often lasted until late at night, and he appears never really to have been away from his business—even in the few hours away from the plant or on the trips abroad necessitated by his wife's ill-health. Primarily he was concerned with sales promotion, and he believed so strongly in constant promotion that he spent staggering sums to intrench the name of the house throughout rural America.

The earliest available data indicate that advertising expenditures in 1898 totaled nearly $400,000, or 13 per cent of net sales for that year. In 1902 Sears, Roebuck's advertising bill was almost $1,500,000—9 per cent of net sales. It is interesting to note that in the same year Macy's Department Store spent but 2.1 per cent of sales volume for advertising.[5] The mail-order firm spent more than $3,500,000 to advertise its wares in 1908. In none of the years for which data are available (1902–5) did the wage bill equal the advertising bill, which during most of the period under consideration constituted the largest single item of operating expense. Available data on operating expenses are summarized in Table 13.

The evidence available indicates that Sears's operating expenses were lower than department stores for the same period. Whereas the mail-order firm's total expenses ranged from 16.4 per cent to 18.4 per cent for these years, Macy's in New York was consistently higher, as Table 14 makes clear.

But if Sears, Roebuck's operating expenses were lower than Macy's, the same tendency is not so clear when one examines the gross margins of the two establishments, where there is a greater tendency to uniformity.[6] The result is a marked advantage in operating profit for the mail-order company.

TABLE 13*

OPERATING EXPENSES AS PERCENTAGE OF NET SALES, 1902–5

Expense Classification	Percentage of Net Sales			
	1902	1903	1904	1905
Advertising	08.88	07.28	07.35	06.69
Wages	05.31	05.17	05.52	05.66
Rent	00.54	00.47	00.46	00.41
Packing and shipping	01.10	00.92	00.81	01.09
Postage	00.44	00.52	00.51	00.55
General expenses	00.09	00.13	00.28	00.32
Carriage	00.69	00.77	00.79	00.90
Taxes	00.04	00.05	00.06	00.05
All other	01.30	01.09	00.17	00.97
Total operating expense	19.39	16.40	16.95	16.64

* Source: Calculated from statements of Deloitte, Plender and Griffiths.

TABLE 14*

COMPARISON OF R. H. MACY AND COMPANY AND SEARS, ROEBUCK AND COMPANY
OPERATING EXPENSE, GROSS MARGIN, AND OPERATING INCOME, 1902–5

Year	Operating Expense		Gross Margin		Operating Profit	
	Sears	Macy's	Sears	Macy's	Sears	Macy's
1902	18.39	19.06	25.68	23.17	7.29	4.11
1903	16.40	21.10	23.87	24.58	7.47	3.48
1904	16.95	20.89	25.02	25.23	8.07	4.34
1905	16.64	19.96	23.95	26.08	7.31	6.12

* Source: Sears's data, calculated from statements of Deloitte, Plender and Griffiths; Macy's data, from Ralph M. Hower, *The History of Macy's* (Cambridge: Harvard University Press, 1940), pp. 390, 394.

The emphasis given to advertising here should not blind one to the interest taken by the executives in controlling expense. This was an interest shared even by promotion-minded Richard Sears. He wrote from London on January 25, 1907:

> Referring to our 12% general expense, exclusive of advertising, it presents many points for study and research, even if but few opportunities for betterment.
> It strikes me as a *Great Example* of the loss of power in transmission for the handling of such a commercial problem as ours. . . .

Our general expense charged against the sale of a buggy, couch, harness, bicycle, or almost innumerable other items that I might add, is almost as much as the actual factory labour expense to make the same item. I feel that at least 60% of this general expense of ours is lost power in transmission. . . . I agree with you and Mr. Doering that you are on the right track in letting this great question absorb as much of your time as you can give it.[7]

Thus by 1908 progress had been made on many fronts. Appealing in an effective way to an ill-served rural market had produced dizzily mounting sales. Growing control over operating expenses contributed to highly profitable operations. Flanking these developments was a gradual if spotty improvement in merchandise quality and advertising practice.

Competition was, of course, an important factor in raising the quality of merchandise in this period. There were other factors as well: the steady improvement in quality of manufactured products, resulting both from technological improvements and from an increasing public demand for better goods.

It is certainly true that in the company's early days, often the sole criterion for any promotion scheme was its immediate success in bringing in business. But it should be equally obvious that Sears, Roebuck and Company did not attain the volume of $745,595 of business it reached in 1895 by sheer chicanery, by clever schemes; the public must have felt that, in the overwhelming percentage of cases, it received a fair enough *quid pro quo*. And lastly it should be observed that none of the company's executives entered the mail-order business bent upon redressing wrongs and athirst to start a merchandising revolution. The sober truth of the matter appears to be that the ethics of the company showed a gradual improvement, if halting and stumbling, for most of its life and that eventually there crystallized a general policy which placed greater stress on conservative merchandising techniques and on better-quality merchandise.

Witness, for example, the experience of William Pettigrew, who joined Sears, Roebuck in 1895, immediately after the company moved to Chicago, and remained with the firm for forty years. In 1905 he was assigned to prepare patent-medicine advertising copy for the catalogue, with the previous year's pages for his guide, and with a sheaf of testimonials. Pettigrew was, in his own words, "shocked." He completed the assignment and informed the general manager that he would not again accept such an assignment. The amazed manager asked him why. Pettigrew answered that the whole patent-medicine business was a fake and thoroughly dishonest. His superior commented that, if Pettigrew's evaluation of patent medicine were accurate, the whole medical profession would tumble.

Julius Rosenwald, it is true, had more faith than did Richard Sears in the permanency of the mail-order business without dependence upon advertising pyrotechnics. But it should also be remembered that Rosenwald was in no sense a promoter; he was a cautious merchandiser. He had never been a sensational salesman in his clothing businesses; he was, instead, a merchant seeking only to sell goods at a fair price and a reasonable profit. As a wholesaler of men's clothing, Rosenwald had maintained a close and personal relationship with his customers. The distant impersonality of the mail-order business, which sold to invisible customers, was new to him. Convinced that Sears, Roebuck had a real future and needed less, not more, audacious promotion schemes, he sought to place the business on what might almost literally be termed a calmer basis.[8]

When the Pure Food and Drug Act was before the Congress in 1906 and was being discussed in print all over the country, "truth in advertising" was very much in the public's mind. Rosenwald saw the handwriting on the wall and moved to anticipate it. Most of all, perhaps, he felt that Sears, Roebuck had attained a maturity in which the pranks of childhood were no longer in good taste—nor were they good business tactics or any longer necessary.

From his conviction that a customer was entitled to a dollar's worth of merchandise for his dollar (with which Sears certainly seems to have agreed), he proceeded naturally to the conviction that the customer should likewise know to the fullest degree of just what the dollar's worth was to consist. And this last point probably accounted for many of his clashes with Richard Sears. In the instances where the two partners clashed on such matters of policy, it seems probable that the clash was not so much on any broad philosophical basis of "truth in advertising" as on differences over discontinuing any highly profitable item and on differences in editing generalized, well-turned (and exaggerated) phrases in catalogue copy which promised to bring large sales.

Another source of conflict was Rosenwald's chief complaint against Sears's advertisements: simply that they were too effective. They brought orders by the thousands and the tens of thousands—while the company was still trying to fill the flood of orders resulting from the previous campaign. Rosenwald, the cautious merchant, wanted to pause to consolidate, to systematize the business, to eliminate thousands of complaints and unfilled orders, before pulling in new business. To speak in hypothetical terms, Rosenwald wanted to get 100 orders and fill all 100 of them promptly and efficiently so as to eliminate returns and complaints. Sears, on the other hand, wanted to get 1,000 such orders, fill 900 of them satisfactorily, manage to fill another 50 somehow after weeks of correspondence and headaches, and just ignore the dissatisfaction of the remaining 50 customers.[9]

Rosenwald was convinced that the public's opinion of the quality of Sears, Roebuck merchandise would be based largely upon the relationship between promise and performance. While seeking to better the performance of the goods he sold, he moved even more aggressively to bring promises in line with what could be expected in performance. He began to blue-pencil exaggerations and generalizations in catalogue copy; more conservative copy began to replace the fanciful verbiage which had graced the pages of the big book.

It was inevitable that Rosenwald and Sears should look differently on such matters. Sears knew he had established himself as a merchandising success. He was permeated with an affinity for the spectacular, especially as represented in incoming orders; Rosenwald was temperamentally at the opposite pole.

It is significant that opposition to many of Rosenwald's efforts to alter catalogue copy came not only from Richard Sears but from a host of other executives as well who felt that it was suicidal to launch a "reform" campaign without any assurance that the competition would follow suit. And some department managers felt that their own departments should not be "cleaned up"—with a possible immediate drop in sales—until and unless all departments were subjected to the same reform.

By 1908 the "new philosophy" was clearly in evidence. This steady reformation—for it was far more that than revolution—had laid the groundwork for really sweeping changes which were to come in steady procession in the next few years.

It is worth pointing out that Richard Sears came to align himself with the changing approach to merchandising. Witness some of his letters from abroad to Louis Asher. Sears wrote on August 22, 1908:

> The methods of merchandising especially in certain avenues have been undergoing changes about as great and rapid as has the problem of urban and interurban transportation, and to anyone whose ear has been at all close to the ground, reflecting over the past 10 years ... or better still go back further—can not help but see a great change—Things and ways that matched the times and brought most satisfactory results would be a great mismatch today.
>
> I believe we must evaluate with the times....

From Strasbourg Sears wrote one week later:

> There has been a great evolution working, things are different than they were—new ways must take the place of old ones *worn out*. That the old was not *bad for the time* we have the proof in at least a fairly successful career to date.... I believe the fewer discounts, impossible premiums etc we offer, even and perhaps *most of all*, what we offer to distributors of our catalogs, might better (if possible) be avoided.... We can't be too careful as to the kind of mdse, you know my views on this—the necessary ethicacy of our descriptions ... is pretty plainly set forth in the page in our present catalog—under the heading *Policy*, the subject much discussed by us.
>
> No doubt we *can and should* go much farther in carrying out (*in the letter*) what this page sets forth.... Our future will rest largely *on the Kind of goods, and service we give*.[10]

In the lore of the company, and elsewhere as well, most of the story of the steady improvement of the quality of Sears, Roebuck's goods and the nature of its advertising and promotion has been polarized around the conflict between Julius Rosenwald and Richard Sears. Elmer Scott, in an interview, stated, however, that the gradual improvement resulted from the day-to-day operations of the functioning management staff rather than from any top-executive decree. Sears, Roebuck's success had been such that growing size prevented detailed guidance of the hundreds of merchandise lines.

In the face of a constant barrage of criticism and opposition, in an atmosphere of hostility on the part of local merchants and newspapers, Sears, Roebuck and Company prospered and improved. Its catalogue wonderland of merchandise offered a seemingly endless array of effectively presented goods (as well as a highly convenient method of shopping). Its customers read the catalogue avidly. It was more to them than merely "The Consumer's Guide." It was literature, in a time when literature was not easily come by and seldom was free (as was the catalogue after 1904). It was recreation, in a period when recreational facilities were limited and, in some areas, almost nonexistent. Through all that has been written about the catalogue as "the great wish book," one fact shines out: Countryfolk looked forward eagerly to the catalogue; they embraced it when it came; and they frequently read it from cover to cover with interest, pleasure, and often awe. And, up to about mid-1907, they sent orders each year in ever increasing volume.

In every year since there had been a Sears, Roebuck and Company, the firm had seen its net sales and profits mount to a higher level than in the previous year. Net sales of $37,879,422 in 1905 had been eclipsed by a volume of $49,229,613 in 1906. The year 1907 opened just as auspiciously; sales in the first six months exceeded by more than $1,350,000 the volume for the corresponding period of 1906. But the onset of the financial panic in the fall of 1907 quickly exerted a depressing effect upon the company's sales. It soon became clear that sales for the last half of 1907 would be considerably less than for the last half of 1906—so much less, in fact, that total sales in 1907 would be lower than in the preceding year. The volume for the six months ending December 31, 1907, showed a decline of $3,664,233 from the record achieved in the last half of 1906 and brought total sales for 1907 to only $46,923,410—$2,376,203 less than the 1906 total.

The depression was on, and its bite had been felt sharply. The company still operated at a net profit, of $2,107,781, in 1907—down $483,380 from that of 1906. The shock of experiencing *any* drop in sales volume and net profits was new and great.

The first clear indications of a decline in the volume of business in the fall of 1907 caused company officials to worry over the large amount of merchandise they had on order, much of which was represented by cream separators. It was decided to use a variation of the "Iowaizing" scheme.[11] Farmers who had purchased cream separators were asked to send the company a list of others in their community who could use one. The company then circularized these prospects, and the farmer who had supplied their names received premiums based on the number of orders placed by the prospects during a specified three-month period.[12]

The premiums were tempting enough to persuade the farmer to turn salesman for Sears as well as being just a source of prospects. The sales reached such heights that Sears, Roebuck sold not only all the machines on order when the scheme was conceived but also every separator the factory could produce that spring. And even then supply fell well behind demand. There was so much gross profit on this item that even the cost of premiums could not bite heavily into it.

An itemized record of one phase of the cream-separator promotion, a special contest which ran to April 15, 1908, showed that a total of 396,454 special separator catalogues were mailed to names on lists supplied the company by solicitors. The over-all cost of that promotion campaign amounted to $64,527.01 and brought orders at an average cost of $9.77. The gross margin of the separator (estimated by Asher at around 40 per cent at that time)[13] was ample to cover this ratio. The value of the rewards, many of them in cash, totaled $20,612.16, including the item, "Tailor-made suits, $5,265.00." Records of a subsequent promotion (apparently on a much smaller scale) show a total expense of only $4,278.81. The cost per order was far higher than in the earlier campaign: $28.15.

The separator promotion, coming as it did at a time when the company's customer-solicitors were themselves eager to pick up additional cash and merchandise rewards, led many farmers to become active salesmen for Sears, Roebuck. Some of them even loaded their own separators on their wagons and hauled them around to demonstrate the machines to their neighbors.[14]

Roughly, $1,000,000 worth of cream separators were sold in the first half of 1908, returning a net profit of some $300,000—about one-quarter of the entire profits of Sears, Roebuck in that period.[15] Richard Sears, writing from abroad, was convinced that the new technique of separator promotion was a large part of the solution to the drop in business. He pleaded with Asher to extend the scheme to stoves, clothing, guns. Richard Sears wanted to ship a stove to the home of each of a selected group of local and interested customers and set it up there to help the customer (turned salesman) secure orders for stoves.

Richard Sears was convinced that only by overwhelming sales promotion could the company survive the crisis. Absent from Chicago accompanying his ailing wife to European medical centers, he was distressed at the "business as usual" attitudes he believed were dominating the Chicago scene. He wrote his general manager, Louis Asher, almost daily. On February 21, 1908, he wrote: "*We need Orders* . . . to learn that we had reached the grand total of 100 M per day would pls me *immensely* let the applications pile up mountain high and we be behind for a time *No Matter.*"[16]

From Strasbourg Sears wrote on August 8, 1908:

In my humble opinion We Must Have Volume—whether it be Easy in the Boat or not. Our very life *Demands Volume*—and if one hot fire doesn't get it I would build more fires—Iowaizing may bring it later (I believe it will) but with no better signs for the minute than you have right now, You Can't afford to Wait—later on if the Iowaizing does it you can let your emergency fires go out. . . .

. . . Were I at the wheel with power to act—before this, [in the] red as you are, I might be foolish but I would be burning lots of powder. Advertising is accumulative—therefore hard to measure. Whether you do 15, 18 or 25 or 28 million dollars this fall—with the same net dollars profit for the season may mean millions to the future of S. R. & Co.—in short the former may be a process of liquidation. . . .

. . . Let me suggest (my view only) if you can get 15 millions at 7% advertising—Good Take It—then take 10 or 12 millions more at 17% advertising if you can get it. It will keep S. R. & Co. alive and ready for another and better season. . . .[17]

His numerous letters attest further to his doubt that the sales reversal was temporary. He was profoundly convinced that the time was at hand for drastic and dramatic action. But here the sharply divergent personalities of Richard Sears and Julius Rosenwald again came into conflict.

Rosenwald was diametrically opposed to any additional advertising or other expense. He favored a very conservative course of action to ride out the storm and insisted that no amount or type of advertising could bring in a sufficient amount of orders to justify the cost when there just was not the money available in the country to buy more goods at the time. His solution was to reduce staff and other expenses to a level commensurate with anticipated sales and await better times. Rosenwald battled to keep his partner from rocking the boat.[18]

There lies in this situation the sharply etched Janus-like cameo of the company's top executives, Sears looking to offensive, aggressive tactics to expand sales, Rosenwald looking to defensive policy to conserve assets. A decision had to be made; time was short, and some clear course of action cried for adoption.

Ironically enough, with Sears and Rosenwald so strongly opposing each other as to achieve an almost dead balance, it was Sears's own lieutenants who tipped the scales—in Rosenwald's favor. Asher and Skinner, great and good friends of Richard Sears, his own disciples, trained by him, reluctantly wrote Sears in Europe that his promotion schemes were not applicable at the time; that schemes which had been highly effective a few years before had lost their validity. Asher himself took a strong stand against premiums. On August 16, 1908, he wrote Sears:

I have been giving lots of study to the analysis of the different Coupon or Agent's schemes we have tried out the past year and I find that they don't pay. (This does not refer to the Iowaizing which is a Catalog Distribution Plan—but to the various merchandise selling schemes based on or similar to the Separator Scheme.) The advertising cost in almost every instance equals the gross profit; therefore direct profit is hard to find.

As to indirect profit, I don't believe there is any; on the contrary, I believe in the spreading of these schemes we are *Cheapening our Merchandise Proposition* and *Dissipating our Goodwill* faster than we have realized and perhaps to a dangerous extent.

The Cream Separator Scheme, true, was successful, it offered unique and exceptional opportunities for just such exploitation. But in no other line do the Separator *Conditions* maintain.

Reviewing our order getting experience, watching the different methods rise up and fade away, I believe we are (or should be) done with all these schemes. They are expensive. Besides, the people have now seen all the Side Shows. *They Won't Buy Any More Tickets.*

I believe we must depend upon simple, straight-forward merchandising; . . .[19]

Richard Sears's reply showed that he was not persuaded:

While I can sympathize with practically every idea advanced in your letter of the 16th and in a general way endorse your views, there are points in my judgment quite debatable. . . . I am by no means sure that something sensational other than our big catalogue can carry will not be necessary from time to time. *I think it will.*[20]

Sears wrote again from Paris, shortly before sailing for home:

There are so many angles to every subject of order getting that I feel it best to wait until I see you to attempt to answer your letter on the subject. I believe it will require something to focus our customers' minds to the point of buying away from home—something more than just the mailing of our big catalogue flat—there is a certain kind of mental excitement that must be aroused—to get action. . . .[21]

But the die had been cast. Asher's letter to Sears deprecating the value of schemes and special promotions—a remarkably strong letter, in view of the fact that Asher had been Sears's right arm for years, had even been trained by Sears—had merely codified the policy the company was pursuing, for Rosenwald had triumphed earlier in his insistence upon conserving the profit margin in the face of declining sales. The firm had acted to pare expenses drastically. On November 20, 1907, there had gone out a terse memorandum from General Manager Asher to all department heads:

With pay-roll expense representing one-third of our entire total expense (including advertising), and with a business dropping off to 25% less than a year ago, it is most important now, at this time, for every manager to practice every economy possible that makes for a reduction of pay-roll expense. . . .

It is impossible to foretell how long this business depression may last. It may be months before our business is back to normal. Our cash receipts are much less than last year—much less than we expected or planned for—and we must AT ONCE RECONSTRUCT OUR ORGANIZATION ON THE BASIS OF WHAT WE ARE GETTING. We must shape our pay-roll to meet our sales. . . .

We must rebuild, simplify and economize. Nor can we overlook the fact that the labor market has suffered the same decline that the merchandise market has suffered. $50.00 a week men can be bought for $40.00, $25.00 a week men are asking for $15.00 positions, and so on down the line. . . .[22]

The defensive moves of this depression period continued through 1908 and met with positive results, as evidenced by Albert Loeb's letter to Henry Goldman, in which he said:

Our organization is watching the question of expense very carefully, and are still showing very good results. . . . For the week ending Aug. 8 the ratio of payroll to sales was 8.302 as against 9.751 a year ago. . . . If this same effort will continue so successfully for the remainder of the year, it means practically 1 per cent saved in payroll expense alone.[23]

The measure of success is to be seen in the statement for the six-month period ending December 31, 1908. On net sales of $21,813,592 the company realized net profits of 8.7 per cent, whereas for the fiscal year ended June 30, 1908, net profit had run slightly under 5 per cent of sales.

But the salutary outcome of economy measures was more impressive to Rosenwald and other executives than it was to Richard Sears. Sales were nearly stationary—slightly below the same period of the previous year (1907); and, of course, the 1907 figures had been below those for 1906. The company's cofounder had clearly lost the contest for strategy in these years. Declining sales were not within his experience. During the depression of 1893–94, Sears had still managed to increase volume. Certain of his contemporaries believe that Sears, if unrestrained, might well have wrecked the company in 1907–8 with his grandiose promotion schemes. The Rosenwald strategy merited the encomium that "it worked." This was not enough. Richard Sears feared that his fellow-executives were too insistent on banking the fire under the mail-order pot.

When Richard Sears returned from Europe in the fall of 1908, he had reached a psychological impasse. Rosenwald, as well as the lower-ranking executives trained by Sears himself, was opposing most of Sears's grandiose promotion schemes. For the first time, Sears was estopped; he had lost the momentum of initiative he had held in the firm ever since there had been a Sears, Roebuck and Company. Business had always been his chief pleasure and joy; with the excitement going out of it, little remained for him. He was so wealthy by then that money could hardly have been of the first order of importance in his decisions. In addition, his wife was in ill-health, as she had been for years, and was making a slow recovery from a leg amputation. Richard Sears's devotion to his wife was, and always had been, profound and unflagging. The need and desire to spend as much time with her as possible was strong.

Finally, there was the matter of his own health. He had burned the midnight oil, literally, ever since he had started in business. Roebuck's memoirs, Sears's own letters, and recollections of men who knew the cofounders are all filled with stories of the blistering pace Richard Sears set for himself and his subordinates. His business was such an obsession with him that daily he wrote voluminous letters from abroad, even on Christmas Day, and from almost every point he visited in this country; the letters were uniformly concerned with details of his great mail-order business. This closely confined sphere of interest inevitably took its toll. Roebuck says, "Although very robust during our early association, Mr. Sears' health began to fail about 1904 at the age of 41."[24]

On November 21, 1908, Richard Sears formally resigned as president of Sears, Roebuck and Company at an adjourned meeting of the board of directors. The ground was "ill health the preceding five years." The decision was apparently reached sometime before the board meeting. Louis Asher asserted, "There never had been a decisive quarrel [between Richard

Sears and Rosenwald]; apparently there was none now." The two men were closeted together for two hours in Rosenwald's office. At the end of the conversation, Sears strolled out and informed Asher that he and Rosenwald had reached an "understanding."[25] *Printers' Ink* some six years afterward quoted from a letter Sears had written to that magazine, dated August 22, 1909, explaining his reasons for retiring:

> I have been selfish enough to feel that a good part of a life's work devoted to the effort of helping, perhaps in a feeble way, to bring about the conditions of the present [in seventeen years Mr. Sears had built the annual sales from nothing to over $50,000,000], and the promise for the future in this line has earned for me something besides money, namely a little relaxation and a little time for my family; and perhaps some of the time that would otherwise go to merchandising will go to my dear old mother in her last years.[26]

At the time his resignation as president was accepted, Sears was elected chairman of the board of directors. Rosenwald became president of the company; Loeb, vice-president and treasurer; and John Higgins, secretary. Sears's new title apparently meant little to him. He never attended a meeting of the board during his chairmanship, which he soon resigned. Nor did he attend any meetings as a director. He formally resigned his directorship on November 26, 1913, thus finally severing his last connection with the company.[27]

In the years following 1908 Sears dabbled halfheartedly in various enterprises, but none of those ventures attained any stature. He was apparently more interested merely in occupying his time than in building another huge business.[28]

On September 28, 1914, Sears died. *Printers' Ink* summed up his career in these words:

> While Mr. Sears did not originate the mail-order idea, he was without question the originator in entirety of what may be called the mail-order business. To him is due entire credit for the mail-order style of advertisements, of form letters, of minute descriptions of goods, and of guarantees—in fact, the whole run of successful mail-order practice.[29]

And nearly four years later *Printers' Ink*, the magazine of advertisers, again paid tribute to Sears:

> R. W. Sears was a mail-order man, had the mail-order viewpoint, knew how to use advertising space, knew the value of copy, knew the conditions surrounding mail-order publications, and he succeeded in a big way because he possessed those qualities to a greater degree than any other mail-order man who ever lived.[30]

To all practical purposes, Richard Sears left his organization on November 21, 1908. An era had ended, and a new one was about to begin. One of the greatest hucksters of all had abdicated. The age of bold, aggressive promotion was giving way to that of more cautious, systematized merchandising.

JULIUS ROSENWALD

President, 1908–24; Chairman of the Board of Directors, 1924–32

The Maturity of Mail Order, 1908–25

CHAPTER XII

The Mail-Order Market

OVER the anguished and vociferous cries of complaining independent merchants, and of their auxiliary forces, the parcel-post system was enacted into law. "By 1910 modern life had developed a demand for a universal, low-rate, postal service which made inevitable the enactment by Congress in 1912 of the law establishing our modern Parcel Post."[1]

The extension of the parcel post may indeed have been inevitable, but opponents of the move were numerous, articulate, and well organized. They fought a protracted and skilful holding action. In that fight their heavy artillery was trained on the great mail-order houses—a euphemism, by that time, for Sears, Roebuck and Montgomery Ward—which, they claimed, would be the direct beneficiaries of such legislation. And this they surely were. The parcel post became one of the two firm underpinnings which provided the strong market that saw the "golden age" of mail order emerge within the period 1908–25. Hard upon the passage of parcel-post legislation followed another strong sustaining force, the tremendous rise in farm income accompanying the years of World War I.

The congressional hearings from 1910 to 1912 on proposed bills for extension of the parcel post served to bring to a peak the opposition of independent merchants, department stores, jobbers, traveling salesmen, and individuals generally fighting the catalogue houses. The hearings, in fact, marked a major engagement in the running battle between the catalogue houses and the small retailers. Witness after witness, directly representing or closely allied to the independent retailers, denounced the pending bills as class legislation designed to subsidize the mail-order houses at the expense of local merchants and thus to kill off the latter group.

Witnesses *for* the legislation came largely from farm organizations and consumer groups, representing in general the customers of the mail-order houses. The fight was bitter. Seemingly almost the only people who took no overt part in it were the executives of Sears, Roebuck and Montgomery Ward. With respect to Sears, Roebuck, there were at least two reasons for silence on this issue: first, the apparent belief of many top executives that parcel post offered the mail-order business almost none of the fancied benefits charged by opponents of the legislation; and, second, the fact that, if the mail-order business actually were going to benefit by the legislation, it would be impolitic to express any open interest in the bills in view of the already nearly frenetic nature of the opposition.[2]

Julius Rosenwald, in an interview, declined to support the parcel post, saying his company was well satisfied with existing conditions under which Sears, Roebuck and Company had prospered. He insisted that only a negligible amount of the company's sales went by mail and that what did was unprofitable, since it cost as much to handle such small sales as to handle much larger ones; jewelry was the only exception, he added, and the company advised using express even for that.[3]

The catalogue itself tended to substantiate the fear of the possible adverse effects of parcel post felt by some of Sears's executives. Every inducement had long been offered to persuade customers to order in large amounts and to have the goods sent by freight. And while goods sent by mail had to be paid for in full in advance—some deterrent perhaps to ordering goods sent by mail—goods sent by express or freight could be dispatched C.O.D. Express was recommended only for shipments totaling less than 20 pounds; above that weight, freight was preferable. Since the freight charge for 100 pounds was no greater than for 10 pounds, the company had long urged customers to "add enough to run your order to 100 pounds" (this sales promotion had been used particularly in connection with groceries). Customers were even urged to pool their orders or to form clubs in order that all goods could go in one 100-pound shipment.

As for Ward's, one of their executives, William Thorne (son of the cofounder), testified before the Senate committee that on the basis of value only 8 per cent of his firm's shipments went by mail, nearly all the rest going by freight (10 per cent by express). Thorne added that a parcel-post service would exert no appreciable effect on the major portion of Ward's business, since a preponderance of their shipments would continue to be made by freight and express. Finally, Thorne declared, Montgomery Ward had not supported the parcel post because it had not yet decided whether it would benefit therefrom.[4]

As for economy in shipping the catalogues themselves, they were classified as third-class matter, while the legislation under consideration dealt only with a fourth-class parcel post. In addition to this, catalogues were mailed at the time at a lower rate per pound than the proposed general parcels rate.[5]

A former employee states:

> There actually was skepticism on the part of some officials of the company as to its benefits because they saw their bulk orders formerly shipped by freight now were going to be split up into small parcels, and were concerned over the effect this would have on the costs of doing business. It looks odd, perhaps, from this side of the event but from the other side the cost question was formidable. Some even argued that it would make a mail-order concern out of all local dealers, too, and, as they were nearer to their customers than we were, they would have the jump on us.

The informant adds, however, a note which buttresses what may well have been the majority opinion within the company: "It was so patent to all those involved in the controversy at the time that the mail-order houses would benefit that it behooved them to let the matter alone lest their coming out for it would cause further opposition." Whatever the reasons, it seems clear that the mail-order companies remained as much in the background as possible and gave no overt support to the bills before the Congress.

The great battle was concluded in 1912, and the bill was signed by President Taft on August 24, to become effective on January 1, 1913. It was a popular success immediately, as rural free delivery had been some seventeen years earlier. The Post Office Department declared in 1938:

> In the 25 years since 1913, Parcel Post has leaped to *second place* in U.S. Postal Revenues; and in number of pieces handled annually it exceeds the *total* mail of *all* classes of certain foreign countries; proof of the service it renders, and the public's growing demand for this service. Parcel Post is the greatest extension of Postal facilities in world Postal history. . . .
> Parcel Post opened a hundred new avenues to commerce, hitherto closed, for rural communities, towns, and cities. It is safe to say that no other new development in the Postal Service has had the dynamic effect of Parcel Post on the economic and industrial life of the nation in the past one hundred years; this, despite the fact that it is only 25 years old this year.[6]

Before this service was initiated, the rate for fourth-class mail matter was one cent per ounce—sixteen cents per pound—virtually prohibitive rates for the mailing of much mail-order merchandise. Further, mailable matter was restricted as to kinds of items, and a maximum weight of four pounds was enforced. The relevant provisions of the 1913 Act were summarized for customers in the Sears catalogue issued in the spring of 1913:

> All merchandise mail takes the new parcel post rates. Packages up to 4 ounces in weight will continue to be carried at the old rate of 1 cent an ounce, regardless of distance. Packages over 4 ounces will be charged for by the pound. Rate per pound will vary according to the distance, and the Government has established a zone system, each zone covering a certain number of miles from point of shipment. . . . Packages up to 11 pounds in weight will be carried by parcel post and will be handled just like any other mail matter. They will be delivered to your box by your rural mail carrier if you live on a rural route, or delivered to your door if you live in a city where there is carrier service, or delivered to your local post-office if you live in a town where there is no carrier service.

The catalogue copy continued with a table of rates for various weights and zones. It did not include the fact that packages were limited in size to 72 inches in combined length and girth—in addition to the weight limit of eleven pounds.

Within the defined limits of bulk and weight, the mail-order houses were thus provided with an effective and convenient means for delivery of merchandise to their customers. Indeed, as Roper says, the firms were provided with an express service at low rates direct to the door of every rural-mail or city-dweller patron of the post offices. Small wonder that the large mail-order companies gained the first important use of parcel post for commercial purposes. Roper asserts, "With their organizations trained and waiting through months of anticipation these [mail-order] companies were ready and willing to put the parcel post to the most effective use."[7]

The postal services, always of importance in the growth of the mail-order method of trade, continued to improve, and limitations of the organic act of 1912 which had created the parcel post were reduced. In July, 1913, the weight limit on parcel post was increased to twenty pounds, and on January 1, 1914, it was raised again—to fifty pounds in the first and second zones; from eleven to twenty pounds for greater distances. The size limit was simultaneously increased from 72 inches to 89 inches combined length and girth of measurement.[8]

As originally enacted, the legislation excluded printed matter from the advantageous parcel-post rates, and the catalogues continued to be mailed at the relatively high third-class rate of one and one-half cents for each two ounces or fraction thereof. An amendment to the law in 1917 provided further sustenance for the growing mail-order business by making fourth-class rates applicable to printed matter weighing more than eight ounces. Homer Buckley, veteran advertising man, said of this:

> With this amendment to the parcel-post law has come the greatest development of mail-order history.... It has made possible the two-pound, three-pound, four-pound, and large-weight catalogue distributed by zones throughout the United States and its territorial possessions, making it practical to mail a four-pound catalogue in the first zone at the reasonable rate of ten cents parcel post as compared to thirty-two cents by third-class mail.[9]

It requires little imagination to appreciate the substantial benefits conferred upon the mail-order houses by the postal legislation of these years. By providing their customers with superior delivery facilities at low costs, the catalogue salesmen were permitted to overcome a substantial barrier to further growth. The new service reached more places than any other form of transportation. It delivered packages direct to the buyer's door—no longer the delays of freight shipments and the special trip to the railway station for a vast range of items. How easy now to order single items without waiting to accumulate quantities that fitted the unyielding schedules of freight classifications! Parcel post was perhaps even more beneficial to mail order than the inauguration of rural free delivery had been.[10] And shortly these facilities were augmented with the C.O.D. service and arrangements for insured mailings.

An institution of such obvious merit as the parcel post might have been expected to increase the number and total value of orders flowing to the

"Chicago houses." Statements of Sears's employees attest to marked increases in business following the inauguration of the new delivery facilities. But, while it is clear that the postal legislation was of immense benefit, it is not easy to separate its effects from those due to the rising income of the farmer—the mail-order customer—for the advent of parcel post coincided with the onset of an era of great agricultural prosperity following upon the generally good years which marked the turn of the century.

The economic status of the farmer at the beginning of the period may be noted from the enthusiastically punctuated statement of the Secretary of Agriculture in 1909:

Eleven years of agriculture, beginning [in 1899] with a production of $4,417,-000,000 and ending with $8,760,000,000! A sum of $70,000,000,000 for the period!
It has paid off mortgages, it has established banks, it has made better homes, it has helped to make the farmer a citizen of the world, it has provided him with means for improving his soil and making it more productive.[11]

The farmer was indeed in a strong position in these years to support the gaudiest dreams of the mail-order men. Sustained demand and the large crops induced by favorable weather, and increased acreage made possible by liberalization of the land acts (exemplified by the three-year Homestead Act of 1912), combined to lift farm income ever higher. There were the further aids following the interest of the federal government in land conservation and reclamation.

Even prior to the beginning of hostilities abroad, the American farmer had advanced far along the road to prosperity, mirrored in the increased value of farm land and buildings. Whereas the per acre average value of farm realty in 1850 had been about $11, by 1900 it had advanced to nearly $20. In the next ten years value doubled, and by 1920 the figure was near $70.[12] Faulkner has made an excellent statement of the farm situation at the close of the first decade of the new century:

The farmer, who had lived since the Panic of 1893 on the ragged edge of financial insolvency, looked forward with renewed hope; between 1900 and 1910 the prices of agricultural products increased by nearly half while the value of farm property doubled. Occasional sod houses were still to be seen on the prairies of Nebraska or the Dakotas, but the typical farm now had its frame house and commodious barns, and the agricultural West, which for three decades had seethed with unrest, showed by its well-kept buildings, its new equipment and improved roads that a new era had come.
There were few well-established farmers who could not afford spring buggies, upholstered furniture, a telephone and even a piano.[13]

These were the buggies, the furniture, and the pianos extolled in the Sears catalogue. Already comparatively prosperous in 1914, farmers were to realize further marked, if temporary, increases in material wealth as the crops of Europe were stunted by war. "In the days of Napoleon . . . English farmers used to pray for a long war and good prices."[14] American farmers realized at least the latter. The index of the wholesale price of farm products more than doubled in the five-year period 1915–19, which, combined with good harvests (and increased acreage), raised the farmers' cash receipts to unprecedented levels. In the peak year 1919, farmers received more than fourteen billion dollars for their products, and the prices for agricultural produce had risen faster and higher than for all commodities.

Land values in the grain states rose rapidly between 1910 and 1920, so that in the latter year the average money value of a farm was more

TABLE 15*

FARM INCOME AND PRICES

YEAR	CASH RECEIPTS FROM MARKETINGS (MILLIONS)	WHOLESALE PRICE INDEX NUMBERS (1926 = 100)	
		Farm Products	All Commodities
1910	$ 5,793	74.3	70.4
1911	5,596	66.8	64.9
1912	6,017	72.6	69.1
1913	6,248	71.5	69.8
1914	6,050	71.2	68.1
1915	6,403	71.5	69.5
1916	7,750	84.4	85.5
1917	10,746	129.0	117.5
1918	13,461	148.0	131.3
1919	14,602	157.6	138.6
1920	12,608	150.7	154.4
1921	8,150	88.4	97.6
1922	8,594	93.8	96.7
1923	9,563	98.6	100.6
1924	10,221	100.0	98.1
1925	10,995	109.8	103.5

* Source: *Statistical Abstract of the United States, 1946*, pp. 624 and 284.

than $12,000, virtually double what was indicated in the previous census. Improvement was even more marked in the West. The average Iowa farm was worth nearly $40,000.[15] The swift and staggering climb of farm income made possible the satisfaction of many wants formerly satisfied only in reverie. So strong became the market base that the facilities of Sears, Roebuck were hard put to meet their customers' demands.

The glorious prosperity continued but briefly into the postwar period. The agricultural price index that had climbed from 71.5 in 1915 to 157.6 in 1919 dropped slightly in 1920—and crashed in the following year. Farm prices fell more than 40 per cent between 1920 and 1921. While industrial prosperity was seriously interrupted also, the decline there was not so precipitous as in agriculture. As Table 15 shows, farm income fell from the

THE MAIL-ORDER MARKET

high mark of $14,602,000,000 in 1919 to little more than $8,000,000,000 in 1921, a decline of more than 43 per cent.

The precipitous decline in prices and income left a trail of wreckage. The preceding prosperity had been such that its sudden reversal was peculiarly vicious, as remarked in the following paragraph from Slosson's *The Great Crusade*:

> The high land values that had once been such an asset became an added handicap. A cornbelt farmer who had bought his holdings at the boom prices of the war and armistice period, perhaps borrowing heavily to do so, found a very costly white elephant on his hands. At the crest of the wave of prosperity American farmers were carrying a mortgage debt of more than four billion dollars, besides a great deal of unsecured or otherwise secured personal indebtedness. These mortgages were often assumed not to meet a pressing need but as a calculated business investment in the hope that the land purchased with the borrowed money would yield more than the six-per-cent interest demanded by the lender; so they signified prosperity rather than want. But now the banks, chary of making new loans and themselves hard pressed to find paying investments in a time of falling prices, had to be very exacting in demanding payment from their debtors. In the period 1920–1925 more than two-thirds of all bank failures took place in ten agricultural states of the South and West. The number of farm bankruptcies increased, the proportion of failures averaging nine times as much for the three years ending in 1926 as for the prewar decade. But the greatest number of farm bankruptcies took place two or three years after the big slump because the farmers, not wishing to abandon their homes at the first bad year, took their losses, hung on to their holdings, and stretched their credit until they could neither borrow again nor repay what they owed. Farms still solvent staggered under a burden of debt. The ratio of indebtedness to farm values increased from twenty-nine per cent in 1920 to nearly forty-two per cent in 1925. Continued high freight rates and local taxes also handicapped the farmer. From 1913 to 1922 the burden of direct taxes on farm property had grown from $315,000,000 to $861,000,000. And the farmer, whose wealth is frozen into land and buildings visible to all, was least able of any taxpayer to escape a property tax.[16]

To the bank failures and farm bankruptcies mentioned by Slosson were added the failure of many mail-order concerns,[17] among which Sears, Roebuck and Company came uncomfortably close to being included.

Throughout the period of Sears, Roebuck and Company's development, its fortunes had been closely tied to the circumstances of the rural population dependent almost entirely on the course of crops and prices. Nurtured by the farm discontent of the Reconstruction years and shortly buoyed up by the agricultural prosperity that characterized the years from 1897, the mail-order firm had waxed strong and prosperous. The calamitous agricultural decline following 1919 laid bare the tragic possibilities of the dependence of the mail-order "industry" on a single host.

While the rural population had been increasing throughout the years, it had progressively lost ground relative to the growth of the cities. In 1920, the year witnessing the onslaught of the depression, the census showed the scales finally tipped in favor of urban dwellers, as illustrated in Table 16. For the first time the United States was statistically urban, although the trend had been clear with every successive census since the first in 1790. While an ever widening domestic market is indicated in the population statistics, the relative losses of the rural sections are plain to see, although the shifts were never uniform throughout the land, as Table 17 shows.

TABLE 16*

POPULATION OF THE UNITED STATES
URBAN AND RURAL, 1880–1930

Census Year	Total Population	Urban Population Number	Urban Percentage of Total	Rural Population Number	Rural Percentage of Total
1880	50,155,783	14,129,735	28.2	36,026,048	71.8
1890	62,947,714	22,106,265	35.1	40,841,449	64.9
1900	75,994,575	30,159,921	39.7	45,834,654	60.3
1910	91,972,266	41,998,932	45.7	49,973,334	54.3
1920	105,710,620	54,157,973	51.2	51,552,647	48.8
1930	122,775,046	68,954,823	56.2	53,820,223	43.8

* Source: Bureau of the Census, *Urban Population in the United States from the First Census (1790) to the Fifteenth Census (1930)* (Washington, D.C., October 31, 1939), p. 1.

TABLE 17*

PERCENTAGE OF URBAN TO TOTAL UNITED STATES POPULATION BY
GEOGRAPHIC DIVISIONS, 1880–1930

Geographic Division	1930	1920	1910	1900	1890	1880
United States	56.2	51.2	45.7	39.7	35.1	28.2
New England	77.3	75.9	73.3	68.6	61.6	52.4
Middle Atlantic	77.7	75.4	71.2	65.2	58.0	50.2
East North Central	66.4	60.8	52.7	45.2	37.9	27.5
West North Central	41.8	37.7	33.2	28.5	25.8	18.2
South Atlantic	36.1	31.0	25.4	21.4	19.5	14.9
East South Central	28.1	22.4	18.7	15.0	12.7	8.4
West South Central	36.4	29.0	22.3	16.2	15.1	12.5
Mountain	39.4	36.5	35.9	32.3	29.3	21.6
Pacific	67.5	62.2	56.8	46.4	42.6	36.2

* Source: Bureau of the Census, *op. cit.*, pp. 6–7.

Adding to the population shift to undermine the prospects of a continued expansion of mail-order companies was the new mobility of the farmer. On April 19, 1892, the first gasoline automobile in the United States was operated by its inventor, C. E. Duryea.[18] The machine had a rapid success despite predictions of its transient character and fulminations against its dangers. It was to wreak perhaps a greater transformation in American life than any other invention; it was to change the face of the land, the way of life, and the shopping habits of a nation. Within eight years after Duryea first operated his automobile, many other manufacturers had entered the field. By 1900, 8,000 of the horseless buggies were registered, and the great industry was still in swaddling clothes. In another decade registrations jumped to 459,000, and by 1920 the figure stood at 8,226,000.

With the rise of the automobile, powered by a gasoline combustion engine, there also came gasoline-engine-powered farm machinery—threshers, combines, tractors. Without this mechanization it is extremely doubtful that the American farmer could have produced the immense crops which, coupled with unprecedented demand, so greatly improved his economic position from 1910 to 1920.[19]

The automobile, with its agricultural counterparts, was of course not the only invention which helped revolutionize the farmer's life in this period. Telephone service was considerably extended until by 1930 a third of all farms had telephone connections.[20] (The Rural Electrification Administration of the New Deal was to raise this figure.) The electricity which made the farmer's telephone possible also powered many of his farm implements, such as cream separators and milking devices. And as radio began to come of age, and further diminished rural isolation, the farmer gained new access not only to entertainment and educational programs but also to weather reports and crop intelligence which were of material assistance to him.

The secular trends of population shifts and technological development were bound to sap the strength of the foundations upon which the mail-order business depended for growth. To take advantage of the new conditions, and thereby further to "threaten" the catalogue companies, there developed by 1925 healthy retail competition in the form of chain stores. These distributors, notably J. C. Penney, locating in "county-seat" towns, brought improved store facilities to farmers and small-town folk. Opening his first store in 1902, J. C. Penney increased his chain to 676 stores by 1925, with total sales of more than $91,000,000.[21]

The mail-order market in the years from 1908 to 1925 was thus filled with shifts and contrasts. These years both unfolded a "golden age" and laid bare the elements that were to limit the growth of a kind of business operation that had depended for its fullest expression largely on the isolation of its customers and the attendant inferior retailing facilities available to them. Temporarily disguised by booming incomes, strong secular tendencies could not be overlooked when the artificial stimulus was dissipated. The strains were bound to show, and, while there were still possibilities for servicing a market that was large in an absolute sense, the conclusion was inescapable that this was unfavorable terrain for the battle of competitive achievement, which tends always to be cast in comparative terms.

CHAPTER XIII

The Debacle of 1921

THE golden age of mail order found Sears, Roebuck operating with the true Midas touch. As farm income mounted from year to year, so, of course, did the company's sales volume. Between 1908 and 1913 the annual volume of business more than doubled—from $40,843,866 to $91,357,276. The volume almost doubled again by 1918, when it reached $181,896,427. From this figure the net sales jumped to $234,242,337 in 1919 and to $245,373,418 in 1920. The volume of business in 1920 was roughly six times that of 1908.

Net income moved up likewise, from $6,192,361 in 1909 to well more than twice that amount in 1916, when it totaled $16,488,622. In 1919 net profits reached the unprecedented figure of $18,890,125. Net income after taxes in 1919 was more than three times that of 1909. At the end of 1919 there was a surplus of $33,574,919. In addition, the company had set up reserves of about $5,000,000 for income and excess profits taxes. During the war years the common stock was paying dividends of $8.00 per share per annum, and in 1920 the company declared a stock dividend of 40 per cent, which brought the outstanding shares of common stock to 1,050,000, carried on the balance sheet at $105,000,000.[1] There had been three common-stock dividends prior to that time. In 1911 a stock dividend of 33⅓ per cent was declared; in 1915 a dividend of 50 per cent; and in 1917 a third stock dividend of 25 per cent. Cash dividends of never less than 7 per cent (actually 8 per cent during 1918 and 1919) were paid on the par value of common stock through 1920.

Much of the foregoing took place, however, in the absence of President Julius Rosenwald. For most of the period from 1916 through 1919, he divided his time between Washington and Europe. The attention of the nation then was focused more on government than on business.

In 1916 Congress created a Council of National Defense. In October of that year President Wilson appointed the members of that body, which held its first meeting on December 6, 1916. The group met to prepare for war at the conclusion of a political campaign which had elected a candidate on a platform of peace. Among those who met as members of the Council in that anomalous atmosphere was Julius Rosenwald. A month later—on January 23, 1917—Count Bernstorff, the German ambassador to the United States, handed to the American Secretary of State a note announcing unrestricted submarine warfare. The atmosphere was cleared

THE DEBACLE OF 1921 197

considerably, and the Council was ready to organize as working committees. The chairmanship of the committee on such supplies as food, clothing, etc., went to Commissioner Rosenwald. Sears, Roebuck and Company was to see little of its president for the next few years.

Actually Rosenwald had even earlier been absenting himself from the company through his travels to Europe and other parts of the world. In addition, his increasing philanthropic interests had been taking more and more of his time. Rosenwald's philanthropies were to continue throughout his war service and were to assume an even more dramatic scale.

After the United States entered World War I, Rosenwald's supply committee swung into action. He recruited procurement experts from throughout the country, utilizing his own knowledge of sources acquired from his long experience in merchandising. Rosenwald helped persuade the Secretary of War to issue an order prescribing that the impending huge governmental purchases would no longer be made on open bids but instead negotiated directly with manufacturers and producers of commodities by representatives of the government. This order enhanced the value of Rosenwald's knowledge of sources and made the task of procurement of supplies (of a noncombat nature) similar to, but a vast enlargement of, Sears, Roebuck's operations.

While he was head of the Committee on Supplies, Rosenwald refused to permit his mail order company to sell any goods to the armed forces. On a few occasions when the services urgently needed articles available only from Sears, Roebuck, Rosenwald took elaborate precautions to see that the services obtained the goods at cost, with no profit to his company.[2] The Sears, Roebuck laboratories tested many articles for the government without charge. Rosenwald also had his company discontinue his salary while he was serving the government as a dollar-a-year man.

The Council of National Defense proved inadequate and unworkable as the scope of the procurement task grew ever greater. Its functions were gradually absorbed by the War Industries Board, the War Department, and other agencies. Rosenwald's job, like that of other Council members, eroded away until it became merely a hollow title.

While he was marking time in mid-1918, Rosenwald was asked to go to France as a representative of the YMCA, which was sending representatives of American industry to France "who shall carry to the soldier the story of American ingenuity, the romance of business in all its fascinating ramifications."[3] Rosenwald accepted the offer and prepared to go overseas as an "entertainer" under the auspices of the YMCA, but Secretary of War Baker requested Rosenwald to go as his official representative. He offered Rosenwald a commission with high army rank, but Rosenwald declined; it was finally agreed that he should wear a military uniform without insignia of rank. He took across with him a number of packing cases of Sears, Roebuck catalogues (by special dispensation of the Secretary of War), insisting he was not seeking to promote business for his company; he maintained the catalogues would be a welcome sight to men in hospitals. According to Secretary Baker, they were.[4]

In the fall of 1918, Rosenwald developed a mild case of pneumonia, accompanied by a pain in his left foot which made walking difficult. These ailments, added to the general strain of his trip to France, compelled him to remain inactive for some months after his return to Chicago. His doctors ordered complete rest. From October, 1916, then, until late 1919 or early 1920, Rosenwald had not been in direct touch with his business.[5]

During this extended hiatus, the reins of Sears, Roebuck were in the hands of Albert Loeb as *de facto* president (and also vice-president and general manager). As unofficial head, Loeb had a free rein. He set policies and ran the business in the fullest sense. Rosenwald gave Loeb authority commensurate with his responsibility. Functionally, Loeb *was* the president.

Sustained by a steadily increasing farm income during the war years, the company prospered under Loeb's regime as it never had before. Sales volume jumped year after year; the 1919 sales of more than $234,000,000 represented an increase of more than $52,000,000 over the previous year. This increase alone exceeded the total volume of sales transacted in any year prior to 1910.

The sharp increase in net sales of 1919 over the previous year was attributable in large measure to the pent-up demand for goods not available during the war. During 1919 the pressure of Sears's customers was such that the company was unable to meet their demands for merchandise. Tens of millions of dollars were refunded to customers because the goods they ordered were not in stock. As a matter of fact, heavy refunds arising from omissions had been noticeable even as early as 1917. Refund scrip issued by the company during those years ran as shown in the accompanying tabulation. It should be noted that the total refund for the fall 1919 and spring

Year	Spring	Fall	Total for Year
1917	$ 8,683,533.83	$ 8,104,061.40	$ 16,787,595.23
1918	9,676,582.25	14,020,264.73	23,696,846.98
1919	9,428,770.34	25,476,880.23	34,905,650.57
1920	20,981,894.63	8,222,688.53	29,204,583.16
Total	$48,770,781.05	$55,823,894.89	$104,594,675.94

1920 seasons amounted to $46,458,774.86 for those twelve months prior to July 1, 1920.

The tremendous quantity of these omissions, representing lost business, was naturally of great concern to the management. The high rate of omissions was apparently due not to any failure to anticipate increasing sales volume but rather to sheer inability to procure merchandise in the desired quantities in the seller's market which characterized that immediate postwar period. Sears, Roebuck had increased considerably its ownership in and of factories in an effort to guarantee delivery of goods, but even this tactic could not assure the Niagara flow of goods the company could have sold.

Rosenwald, meanwhile, returned to active management of the business and found, to his great annoyance, that the prosperity of the times had begotten a general laxity among the firm's executives. Many of them, according to a man who was himself an executive at the time, spent a good deal of time playing golf, since "business was so good that things pretty well ran themselves." This absenteeism was "especially irritating to Rosenwald, who felt that people were not earning their money unless they were at their desks." He forthwith proceeded to "raise all kinds of hell" in the process of tightening up administration.

To reduce omissions and to capitalize upon what appeared to be a steadily rising market, many departments doubled, trebled, and even quadrupled their orders to manufacturers. According to men who were in the executive group at the time, there was a general feeling throughout the company that there need be little concern with the actual size of purchase orders, since sources would probably be unable to fill all the orders anyway. Ordinary procurement procedures seem to have been scrapped or ignored to a great extent in this period. There were instances in which employees not authorized to issue purchase orders did so—frequently in pencil on odd bits of scrap paper, sometimes just by verbal commitments. As a result of this preoccupation with omissions and the determination to avoid them, and also of the general belief that prosperous times would continue indefinitely, the company's inventory of merchandise on hand rose steadily in 1920. In addition, merchandise on order likewise continued to increase through a good part of the year.

The general rise in business activity continued at a feverish pitch throughout 1919 and well into 1920. Each succeeding month saw commodity prices increase at an unprecedented rate. Purchasers everywhere were increasing orders tremendously in an effort to obtain delivery of normal quantities. Sellers boosted prices and increased their inventories. Prices and production rose to a maximum in the spring of 1920 in an atmosphere of maximum unfilled orders, cries of "underproduction," and exorbitant price levels.[6]

The spring of that year witnessed the beginning of a months-long period of puzzling cross-currents, of contradictions, of a welter of conflicting counsel sufficient to confuse most businessmen. Price cuts alternated with price rises; predictions of a general price decline were offset by predictions of sharp rises, all from highly reputable sources. In addition, the United States Department of Justice was prosecuting "profiteers" in food, fuel, fertilizer, and wearing apparel and was seeking "fair prices" for those commodities.[7]

Possibly in response to the Justice Department's drive, two Brooklyn department stores in late April announced price reductions on necessities, but the extent of the decreases was not specified. In that same month, corn, cotton, sugar, and wheat prices turned downward, belatedly joining the trend of cattle, hides, cottonseed oil, and pork, whose prices had culminated in the autumn of 1919.[8] On April 29, however, the Federal Reserve Board reported a marked tendency of prices to resume their upward movement but professed at the same time to discern elements which forecast a slowing-down in the skyrocketing of prices.

On May 3 John Wanamaker's proclaimed a flat price reduction of 20 per cent on virtually all its merchandise. And, to discourage speculation by manufacturers, Wanamaker's announced that it would purchase for cash a million dollars of merchandise weekly to be sold at the same 20 per cent price reduction.

Still there continued a spontaneous, unorganized "buyer's strike," the pressure of which was making itself felt all along the line, according to the *New York Times* of May 9, 1920. The succeeding two weeks saw a nation-wide wave of price-cutting as merchants sought to lure the reluctant consumers into their emporiums—and to reduce their swollen inventories before any real panic set in. To add to the general downward trend, the price of Australian wool broke sharply on May 20; only 30 per cent of the amount offered at Boston found purchasers, and the prices for that amount were down 10–20 per cent.

Even so, there was no unanimity of opinion. On May 27 J. I. Strauss of R. H. Macy and Company declared that "this price-slashing wave will cause increased prices by fall, and lines that have shown most spectacular tumbles may be higher than at present." And as late as June 18 the Federal Reserve Board held out "little hope for a reduction of prices," though qualifying that statement by adding that recent price changes might furnish the basis for a "more far-reaching alteration in the price structure." The Board did, however, observe that changes in May had "borne witness of many disturbing factors whose importance and persistence are as yet uncertain."

The importance and persistence of many of those factors became increasingly certain in the months that followed, however, and events proved the Federal Reserve Board prediction wrong. Price reductions continued. In September, 1920, Sears, Roebuck and Company and Montgomery Ward announced "substantial reductions" in many lines of merchandise. That list (issued as a catalogue supplement) included men's and women's clothing, shoes, furniture, and a few staple foodstuffs. In more specific terms, the mail-order houses cut prices by 10–20 per cent on "several lines," with reductions of 25–50 per cent in some cotton goods. A Sears official stated the supplements showing reductions from July catalogue prices did little to arrest declining sales volume.[9]

On September 25 Julius Rosenwald was quoted by the *Times* as stating prices had to be cut to stimulate buying in order to avoid widespread unemployment. He asserted that Sears, Roebuck had reduced prices on almost everything except hardware. The *Times* also reported that day that Marshall Field and Company had reduced prices by 30 per cent on some cotton goods.

By the time it announced its price reductions in September, Sears, Roebuck faced a serious, even if not yet critical, situation. Its balance sheet at the close of 1919 had showed merchandise inventories of $42,685,776, or 18.2 per cent of the sales for the year. By June, 1920, however, inventories had advanced to $98,264,471;[10] and, as a result of the casual and haphazard procurement procedures in effect, even this figure was not final, for it was impossible to make an exact estimate of the amount of goods on order. It became apparent early in the latter half of 1920 that sales volume probably would not show a sufficient increase over 1919 to preserve a satisfactory relationship between sales and inventory.

By the fall of 1920 the situation had become more serious for Sears, Roebuck. According to Donald Nelson, Rosenwald formed an advisory committee which met with him every morning to take up each phase of the business and to set policies on the spot. These men decided that the company needed an additional $50,000,000. In October, Sears, Roebuck issued serial gold notes in that amount bearing 7 per cent interest, through a banking syndicate headed by Goldman, Sachs and Company and including Lehman Brothers and four Chicago banks: First Trust and Savings Bank, A. G. Becker and Company, Continental and Commercial Trust and Savings Bank, and Illinois Trust and Savings Bank.

An offerings circular dated October 15, 1920, reveals the notes were all to be redeemed within three years, in three nearly equal instalments. The gold notes, the proceeds of which were to be applied entirely to reduction of current liabilities, were to constitute the only funded debt of the company. Its capital stock, representing an equity of about $130,000,000 at current quotations, ranked junior to the notes. The trust agreement covering issuance of the notes required maintenance of quick assets equal to at least one and one-half times all liabilities including the notes. The agreement further provided that no mortgage or other lien, except purchase money mortgages, might be placed upon any assets of the company.

By the end of 1920 the company's outlook had become even more depressing, as indeed had the general prospect. There was severe unemployment late in the year, and money became extremely tight in autumn.[11] Sears, Roebuck's sales volume for 1920 showed an increase over that of the preceding year, but the increase amounted to only about $11,000,000. Merchandise inventories, on the other hand, had mounted to $105,071,-

243;[12] the relationship of inventory to sales was clearly out of line. Further, there remained the incalculable factor of just how much merchandise was on order without adequate records of it in the company. Net profits for 1920 were $11,746,671, a decline of over $7,000,000 from the previous year even with an increase in volume of more than $11,000,000. The margin was obviously being whittled dangerously, and the merchandise on the shelves and on order had been purchased at high prices. In the words of one former employee:

> During the latter part of this boom in business, we were searching frantically for sources of supply, and manufacturers were very independent. There was scarcely any haggling about price, for the manufacturer would say, "Take it or leave it." If he couldn't sell it to us, he could sell it to others.

In 1921 general economic conditions became even worse. The price of wheat declined from $3.45 a bushel to $1.42; corn fell from $2.17 to 59 cents. The gross value of all farm production dropped from $24,025,000,000 in 1919–20 to $12,894,000,000 in 1921–22, a startling decline of nearly 50 per cent.[13] Persons wrote:

> The decline in general commodity prices during the thirteen months ending with June, 1921, was sharpened beyond all precedent.... The index of the Bureau of Labor Statistics fell from 272 to 148, or 46 per cent; Bradstreet's fell from $20.87 to $10.62, or 49 per cent; while the index based upon ten leading commodities, chosen because they are varied in nature, important in industry, and usually sensitive in price, fell from 277 to 107, or 61 per cent.... Although there was no breakdown in credit, the drastic fall of commodity prices caused the failure of a large number of business concerns and forced others into the hands of their bankers.[14]

In February, 1921, the company's regular quarterly dividend on common stock was due. Scrip was issued instead of cash, the paper bearing 6 per cent interest and being payable before August 15, 1922. (Rosenwald offered to purchase at par the scrip of all stockholders holding fifty shares or less of the company's stock, so that the small holders would not be forced to sell their scrip to traders at a discount in order to raise ready cash.) The company asserted that its surplus as of the end of 1920 was about $7,500,000 (a net addition for the year of some $4,000,000) and that normal prudence in conserving cash resources dictated issuance of scrip. Interestingly, the company also declared that its stock of merchandise was "safely adjusted" and that "outstanding contracts for goods to be delivered are almost nil."

A meeting of the board of directors of Sears, Roebuck on March 28, 1921, issued this statement to the press:

> The passing of the March dividend on Sears, Roebuck and Company's common stock has been definitely determined by its directors who authorize the following statement:
> The beginning of this year found the company with a large stock of merchan-

dise and an accumulation of indebtedness caused by the general slump in business and the greatly reduced demand for winter goods due to lack of cold weather.

Expenses have been curtailed and sales are showing substantial increases. March sales will be approximately $19,500,000, which is 16 per cent more than March, 1919, and only 29 per cent less than March, 1920. The condition of the company has greatly improved since January 1, and liabilities are being materially reduced.

The Company has no commitments, direct or indirect, other than those necessary for the current conduct of the business, upon the present volume of sales, and all of the company's commitments are based on the present level of prices.

Despite this tone of cautious and qualified optimism, Sears, Roebuck stock continued a downward trend on the stock exchange. From a high of $243 per share in 1920, it skidded to a low of $54½ in the following year.

In less than a year the company's position had become extremely hazardous. While the dollar value of inventories was lower by June 30, 1921, than at the end of 1920, the $80,453,265 figure was nearly equal to the net sales of $80,925,226 for the same period.[15]

On the company's consolidated balance sheet for June 30, 1921, "Accounts payable" showed only $4,490,951, some indication that orders for goods had been deeply cut. Also under "Liabilities" was shown, for the 7 per cent serial gold notes, $47,766,000 plus $798,744 accrued interest on these notes. The common dividend scrip, payable August 15, 1922, was listed as a liability of $2,080,944. The net loss on operations for the first six months of 1921 was $3,543,151. This loss alone reduced surplus to a little more than $4,000,000. The amounts deducted to allow for a 7 per cent preferred-stock dividend and a common-stock dividend reduced the balance to $1,642,158.

Just how astute company management had been in cutting back orders and seeking cancellations, it is difficult to determine. Werner asserts that Rosenwald declined to join the "unscrupulous rush on the part of merchants to cancel orders for goods as soon as the great break in prices had occurred."[16] A somewhat fuller and less moralistic explanation is advanced by Donald M. Nelson, former executive vice-president of Sears, Roebuck, who asserts it was a fixed policy of the company not to cancel orders until and unless such action seemed imperatively urgent. This policy, according to Nelson, was designed both to preserve good relationships with sources and to avoid giving encouragement to any general panicky stampede. Finally, of course, cancellations and cutbacks became obviously necessary; but, when the company moved to cancel wherever it could, the action apparently was too little and too late. Many of the cancellations, according to Nelson, represented a drain upon the company's working capital, because of the method employed, which required that the company negotiate a cash settlement for all or part of the manufacturer's anticipated profit on the order in question, thus actually buying off the contract.

By July, 1921, the number of unemployed reached about six million;

wages for those who could find work dropped sharply. In the first four months of that year, more than six thousand businesses failed, and the next eight months saw an additional eleven thousand go under.[17] Mail-order companies were hit with peculiar force. Table 18 traces the course of sales for three leading firms through the years preceding, during, and following the depression. All three firms followed roughly the same course, although Bellas Hess—with its concentration of soft goods—did not realize the pre-1920 expansion that came to Sears and Ward's. But the wearing-apparel firm experienced a less serious sales decline and a quicker recovery after 1921.

It is interesting to note that department stores fared much better than the mail-order houses, as is clear from a glance at the trend of sales for the

TABLE 18*

YEARLY SALES OF LEADING MAIL-ORDER CONCERNS, 1913-25

Year	Sears	Ward's	National Bellas Hess
1913	$ 91,357,276	$ 39,725,713	$13,276,259
1914	96,024,754	41,042,486	15,164,727
1915	106,228,421	49,308,587	17,371,650
1916	137,200,803	62,044,336	21,554,230
1917	165,807,608	73,512,645	27,649,537
1918	181,655,830	76,166,848	33,485,015
1919	233,982,584	99,336,053	39,449,985
1920	245,373,418	101,745,271	47,704,428
1921	164,039,720	68,523,244	37,481,210
1922	166,514,110	84,738,826	45,357,566
1923	198,482,946	123,702,043	52,399,783
1924	206,430,527	150,045,065	49,225,804
1925	243,798,351	170,592,642	46,685,376

* Source: Montgomery Ward and Company and Sears, Roebuck and Company sales from companies' annual reports; Bellas Hess Company from Paul H. Nystrom, *The Economics of Retailing* (3d ed.; New York: Ronald Press Co., 1939), I, 271.

two types of retail distributors shown in Table 19. Despite efforts to maintain current prices on a competitive basis by distributing notices of price changes, the mail-order houses were at a marked disadvantage in the struggle to maintain prices competitive with retail stores in a period characterized by rapidly falling prices. The stores invariably had the advantage. So desperate was Sears that it is reported the company sold job lots on occasion to dealers in the attempt to beat the downward race of prices.[18]

Although mail-order and department stores reached both their sales peaks and troughs in the same years, the sales decline of department stores was moderate—a fall of but eight points in the index—whereas mail order dropped thirty-one points. For these companies the sales declines were transmitted into actual losses in 1921—Sears's losses were 10 per cent of sales and Ward's 14.4 per cent of sales. Department stores, on the other hand, actually showed profits of 1.3 per cent of sales in that year.[19] Ny-

THE DEBACLE OF 1921

strom asserts: "Most mail order businesses suffered severe reverses not only in sales volume but profits as well during the business depression of 1920 and 1921. Many passed out of existence."[20]

Rumors were rife that Sears, Roebuck might any day be joining those concerns passing out of existence. Rosenwald was cutting personnel as sharply as possible and attempting to lower all operating expenses to the irreducible minimum. The average number of the company's employees dropped from 25,492 in 1919 to 21,652 in 1920, and to 18,144 in 1921. One former executive asserts that operating expenses were slashed by twenty million dollars in 1921.[21]

Despite these economies, however, it was clear to all the company's top executives by December, 1921, that the net loss for that year was going

TABLE 19*

RETAIL SALES INDEX NUMBERS
(1919 = 100)

Year	Department Store	Mail Order
1919	100	100
1920	120	103
1921	112	72
1922	113	78
1923	125	99
1924	127	105
1925	132	118
1926	136	123
1927	136	129
1928	138	147

*Source: Nystrom, *op. cit.*, p. 229, quoting Federal Reserve Board figures.

to be staggering (the final figure proved to be $16,435,469). Whereas twenty-nine of the company's fifty-odd merchandise departments had managed in 1920 to increase their dollar volume of business over the preceding year—though in one department the increase was in only three figures—exactly two departments did more business in 1921 than in 1920, and the increase in one of them amounted to less than $1,400. It was a uniformly bad and very nearly disastrous year. Tables 20, 21, and 22 show the sales by various departments in 1919, 1920, 1921, and 1922, with increases or decreases over the previous year from 1920 on. The departments represented in these tables accounted for an overwhelming majority of the total volume of business in those years.

A detailed examination of these departmental sales figures shows how importantly the emphasis on durable goods contributed to sales losses. These durable-goods items[22] accounted for 36.82 per cent of the company's net sales for 1919. While the decline in company sales between 1919 and

TABLE 20*
COMPARISON OF SALES, YEAR ENDING DECEMBER 31, 1920

Dept.	Commodity	1919	1920	Percentage Increase or *Decrease*
1	Furniture	$ 9,601,999	$ 8,622,638	*10.20*
3	Books and stationery	982,562	1,004,872	2.27
4	Jewelry	3,889,868	3,647,636	*6.23*
5	Silverware	1,491,103	1,406,122	*5.70*
6	Sporting goods	4,517,270	4,751,614	5.19
7	Groceries	8,776,568	8,800,171	0.27
8	Drugs and toys	3,232,754	4,821,202	49.14
9	Hardware	6,332,996	6,460,446	2.01
10	Harness and trunks	2,424,779	1,887,868	*22.14*
11	Vehicles	903,432	516,435	*42.84*
12	Musical instruments	1,337,623	1,578,114	17.98
14	Dress goods	4,480,250	5,191,660	15.88
15	Shoes	18,280,840	14,174,126	*22.47*
16	Underwear and hose	9,067,025	8,539,091	*5.82*
17	Ladies' coats, waists, etc.	13,180,158	8,014,072	*39.20*
18	Millinery	5,730,797	6,532,323	13.99
20	Phonographs	12,217,307	14,467,483	18.42
22	Stoves	3,922,404	4,839,630	23.38
23	Cream separators	1,826,404	1,369,445	*25.02*
24	Curtains and blankets	5,569,091	5,534,637	*0.62*
25	Ribbons and laces	2,942,242	2,969,194	0.02
26	Sewing machines	1,240,183	1,103,605	*11.01*
28	Bikes—automobile supply	7,483,518	7,909,569	5.69
30	Paints	2,724,685	3,739,481	37.24
32	Farm implements	4,000,295	4,621,434	15.53
33	Men's furnishings	7,889,993	6,563,228	*16.82*
34	Lighting fixtures	550,445	645,879	17.33
35	Crockery	1,267,738	907,864	*28.39*
36	Domestics	14,088,121	18,907,515	34.21
37	Carpets	6,413,954	6,065,927	*5.43*
38	Children's and women's wear	4,057,256	3,820,563	*5.83*
39	Paper patterns	72,912	89,064	22.15
40	Boys' clothing	4,504,598	3,452,630	*23.35*
42	Plumbing	3,154,678	3,599,461	14.10
44	Washing machines	492,850	957,485	94.28
45	Men's clothing	3,369,114	3,346,641	*0.67*
46	Pianos	4,093,797	3,708,991	*9.40*
47	Gas engines	1,865,925	1,866,752	0.04
48	Roofing	2,139,158	2,495,475	16.66
53	Wallpaper	2,404,094	3,153,542	31.17
56	Houses, lumber, etc.	1,543,604	1,448,228	*6.18*
57	Lighting plants		2,733	
58	Typewriters	185,670	508,037	173.62
60	*Encyclopaedia Britannica*	1,376,285	2,685,812	95.15
63	Millwork	1,375,134	1,537,406	11.80

* Source: Company records.

206

TABLE 21*

Comparison of Sales, Year Ending December 31, 1921

Dept.	Commodity	1920	1921	Percentage Increase or *Decrease*
1	Furniture	$ 8,622,638	$4,720,612	45.25
3	Books and stationery	1,004,872	673,383	32.97
4	Jewelry	3,647,636	1,838,361	49.60
5	Silverware	1,406,122	738,886	47.45
6	Sporting goods	4,751,614	2,820,617	40.64
7	Groceries	8,800,171	6,915,445	21.42
8	Drugs and toys	4,821,202	3,219,985	33.21
9	Hardware	6,460,446	3,158,040	51.12
10	Harness and trunks	1,887,808	859,640	54.47
11	Vehicles	516,435	161,446	68.74
12	Musical instruments	1,578,114	1,096,452	30.52
14	Dress goods	5,191,660	3,360,762	35.27
15	Shoes	14,174,126	8,797,242	37.93
16	Underwear and hose	8,539,091	5,348,900	37.36
17	Ladies' coats, waists, etc.	8,014,079	4,699,332	41.36
18	Millinery	6,532,323	4,862,795	25.56
20	Phonographs	14,467,483	4,422,051	69.44
22	Stoves	4,839,630	1,761,263	63.61
23	Cream separators	1,369,445	573,783	58.10
24	Curtains and blankets	5,534,637	3,221,600	41.79
25	Ribbons and laces	2,969,194	2,004,312	32.50
26	Sewing machines	1,103,605	592,282	46.33
28	Bikes—automobile supply	7,909,509	4,904,428	37.99
30	Paints	3,739,481	1,955,630	47.70
32	Farm implements	4,621,434	1,768,856	61.73
33	Men's furnishings	6,563,228	4,423,889	32.60
34	Lighting fixtures	645,879	328,558	49.13
35	Crockery	907,864	171,686	20.95
36	Domestics	18,907,515	9,114,292	51.80
37	Carpets	6,065,927	2,599,564	57.15
38	Children's and women's wear	3,820,563	1,989,348	47.93
39	Paper patterns	89,064	70,736	20.58
40	Boy's clothing	3,452,631	2,092,184	39.40
42	Plumbing	3,599,461	1,868,172	48.10
44	Washing machines	957,485	360,836	62.31
45	Men's clothing	3,346,641	1,852,895	44.63
46	Pianos	3,708,991	1,343,003	63.79
47	Gas engines	1,866,752	417,976	77.61
48	Roofing	2,495,475	742,284	70.26
53	Wallpaper	3,153,542	3,154,936	0.044
56	Houses, lumber, etc.	1,118,228	643,931	55.54
57	Lighting plants	2,733	94,501	3,356.72
58	Typewriters	508,037	123,997	75.59
60	*Encyclopaedia Britannica*	2,685,812	1,312,435	51.14
63	Millwork	1,537,406	651,098	57.65

* Source: Company records.

TABLE 22*

COMPARISON OF SALES, YEAR ENDING DECEMBER 31, 1922

Dept.	Commodity	1921	1922	Percentage Increase or *Decrease*
1	Furniture	$4,720,612	$ 4,863,628	3.03
3	Books and stationery	672,383	710,046	5.45
4	Jewelry	1,838,361	1,748,875	*4.87*
5	Silverware	738,886	764,466	3.46
6	Sporting goods	2,820,617	3,092,389	9.64
7	Groceries	6,915,445	5,314,356	*23.15*
8	Drugs and toys	3,219,985	3,250,314	.94
9	Hardware	3,158,040	3,487,498	10.43
10	Harness and trunks	859,640	1,216,100	41.47
11	Vehicles	161,446	156,130	*3.29*
12	Musical instruments	1,096,452	1,102,576	.56
14	Dress goods	3,360,762	3,342,884	*.53*
15	Shoes	8,797,242	9,822,329	11.65
16	Underwear and hose	5,348,900	5,918,049	10.64
17	Ladies' coats, waists, etc.	8,429,873	13,087,207	55.25
18	Millinery	4,862,795	4,972,742	2.26
20	Phonographs	4,422,051	2,152,705	*51.32*
22	Stoves	1,761,263	1,463,922	*16.88*
23	Cream separators	573,783	583,007	1.61
24	Curtains and blankets	3,221,600	3,454,733	7.24
25	Ribbons and laces	2,004,312	1,960,083	*2.21*
26	Sewing machines	592,282	482,391	*18.55*
28	Bikes—automobile supply	4,904,428	3,803,742	*22.44*
30	Paints	1,955,630	1,645,373	*15.86*
32	Farm implements	1,768,856	1,904,359	7.66
33	Men's furnishings	4,423,889	4,792,443	8.33
34	Lighting fixtures	328,558	251,770	*23.37*
35	Crockery	717,686	918,513	27.99
36	Domestics	9,114,292	8,614,859	*5.48*
37	Carpets	2,599,564	3,008,314	15.72
38	Children's and women's wear	3,437,823	3,734,345	8.63
39	Paper patterns	70,736	73,632	4.09
40	Boys' clothing	2,092,184	2,985,017	42.67
42	Plumbing	1,868,172	1,507,691	*19.30*
44	Washing machines	360,836	178,295	*50.59*
45	Men's clothing	4,585,986	4,787,507	4.39
46	Pianos	1,343,003	846,572	*36.96*
47	Gas engines	417,976	274,294	*34.38*
48	Roofing	742,284	709,525	*4.41*
53	Wallpaper	3,154,936	2,110,651	*33.10*
56	Houses, lumber, etc.	883,464	892,883	1.07
57	Lighting plants	94,501	114,230	20.88
58	Typewriters	123,997	37,705	*69.59*
60	*Encyclopaedia Britannica*	1,312,435	666,687	*49.20*
63	Millwork	651,098	657,367	0.96

* Source: Company records.

THE DEBACLE OF 1921

1921 amounted to 29.97 per cent, the fall in durable goods was substantially greater—50.89 per cent. A further indication of the critical role of durable goods in contributing to Sears, Roebuck's unhappy condition is the fact that, of a total decline of $70,202,617 in net sales between 1919 and 1921, 62.53 per cent ($43,895,221) was attributable to the shrinkage of sales in durable items.

One tremendously important factor in those dreary showings of the several departments in 1920, 1921, and 1922 was the drop in prices at which the company was selling goods—goods purchased at high prices in 1919 and 1920. Table 23 shows the successive price drops of various items taken from twenty-six merchandise departments for which comparable data are available. In addition to, and underlying, the drops in prices in those years there was a steady decline in the number of orders received weekly at the Chicago mail-order plant. The year 1920 opened on a higher level of activity than 1919 and held that lead, generally, until June. In that month, for the first time in 1920, orders dropped substantially below those for the comparable month in the preceding year. The number of orders continued a generally steady decline, with a few exceptional weeks, until the spring of 1922, as indicated in Table 24.

To return now to December, 1921, there was another element to accent further an already precarious situation: dividends on preferred stock were due to the amount of $559,188. To pass them would seriously impair the company's credit. And, perhaps most important, under the terms of the trust agreement governing the flotation of the serial gold notes the previous year, the firm had to maintain quick assets at least one and one-half times all liabilities. This provision of the trust agreement contained the real crux of the problem. Stripped of all verbiage, that portion of the agreement meant simply that, if the company failed to maintain the required proportion of quick assets, the banking houses would assume control of the company. Some means had to be found to improve the company's cash position. Time was short and very much of the essence.

Albert Loeb devised an arrangement whereby Julius Rosenwald would advance the firm $4,000,000 in cash or liquid assets and would assume additional commitments of some $12,000,000, in order to improve the firm's cash position immediately. Loeb further wanted Rosenwald to give the company $5,000,000 of his stock, with an option to repurchase that amount of stock at par when conditions improved; this gift was designed to reduce the over-all liability position of Sears, Roebuck. The total assistance Loeb was urging upon the president of the company amounted to some $20,000,000. It was pointed out to Rosenwald that practically all the other executives were willing to turn in their stock but that he was the only individual holding a sufficient amount to stem the tide.

The pleading at first fell upon deaf ears. It is said that this was one of the few times Albert Loeb failed to persuade his superior on a major point.

TABLE 23*

CHANGES IN SELLING PRICES OF CERTAIN COMMODITIES, 1920, 1921, AND 1922

Item	1920	1921	1922
Davenport and chair	$ 91.50	$ 68.30	$ 68.45
Three-piece bedroom suite	245.35	171.00	115.45
Remington shotgun	60.92	60.92	47.10
"Elgin" bicycle	53.45	35.95	25.95
26-in. hand saw—8 pt	3.35	3.35	2.70
9-in. smooth plane	4.40	3.45	2.70
No. 1½ hammer	2.40	1.70	1.50
Ironing board	4.95	3.95	3.60
Carpet sweeper	4.95	4.90	3.95
6-cup percolator	5.35	4.25	3.15
Men's shoes	9.00	4.98	4.60
Men's hi-cuts	14.00	7.95	6.95
Cotton union suit (boy's)	1.95	1.18	1.18
Cotton union suit (women's)	1.80	1.12	1.10
Lace-back corset	4.79	3.35	2.98
Elastic girdle	4.69	3.69	3.69
Sewing machine	45.95	37.65	32.75
Toaster	6.90	7.95	6.90
Coal and wood range	101.50	76.50	72.75
Gas range	49.85	42.60	39.60
72×84 wool blanket	22.50	14.75	14.35
Comforter	17.98	10.50	8.45
Battery (1920 Ford)	26.95	19.95	12.95
Ford seat covers	9.30	6.25	4.75
27×27 diaper (per doz.)	3.58	1.68	1.59
Sleeper	1.59	.75	.59
"Seroco" house paint (gal.)	2.85	1.85	2.25
Barn paint	1.75	1.15	1.45
4-in. paint brush	2.24	1.86	1.62
"Oakburn" harness	79.97	62.95	49.85
600-lb. separator	97.80	81.90	62.75
14-in. plow	102.60	85.50	66.95
White dress shirt	3.65	1.85	1.79
Men's hat	6.00	3.39	2.95
Cotton print (per yd.)	.54	.25	.27
Apron gingham (per yd.)	.39	.17	.19
9×12 rug	57.50	33.95	29.85
9×12 fiber rug	21.25	14.95	9.95
Women's sweater	12.75	7.48	4.65
Women's nightgown	1.69	.85	.79
30×3½ Cord tire	26.15	17.45	10.95
30×3½ Gray tube	2.30	1.60	1.37
81×99-in. sheets	2.79	1.37	1.49
81-in. sheeting (per yd.)	.99	.45	.49
Men's overalls	3.39	1.59	1.59
Work shirt	1.98	.95	.98
30-gal. range boiler	16.80	13.30	9.15
24-in. furnace	142.20	99.90	103.40
4½-ft. bathtub	58.35	43.50	41.95
Phonograph	215.00	215.00	180.00
Phonograph needles (pkg. of 12)	.95	.95	.75
Slate roofing (per roll)	3.95	3.15	2.50
6-ft. corrugated roofing	1.34	.76	.65
Men's cotton socks (per pr.)	.50	.26	.25
Pure silk hose (per pr.)	4.50	2.50	2.40

* Source: Company records.

Rosenwald simply did not agree. Since Rosenwald's own lawyer had advised against the arrangement, an outside lawyer highly respected by Rosenwald was brought in. This attorney admitted that Rosenwald was under no legal or moral compulsion to make the grand gesture but insisted also that it was a sound investment for the president of the company to take such a step in order to insure the value of the Rosenwald family's tremendous holdings of company stock. (Werner asserts the family was reputed to own 40 per cent of the stock listed at a par value of $105,000,-000.)[23] Doering pointed out to Rosenwald that there was really no question about the ultimate solvency of the business if this financial crisis could be weathered and control of the company retained. He had found on investigation that the company's customers were staying with the house, but,

TABLE 24*

NUMBER OF ORDERS RECEIVED IN CHICAGO MAIL-ORDER PLANT, 1919–22

Month†	1919	1920	1921	1922
January	374,381	393,223	308,418	312,043
February	444,306	571,311	327,686	291,284
March	455,572	422,348	321,516	316,189
April	433,005	461,246	303,354	336,015
May	451,663	461,032	284,745	321,590
June	355,625	255,178	255,048	250,593
July	341,420	319,172	243,321	307,518
August	440,703	276,686	237,167	251,576
September	334,528	287,838	263,927	298,472
October	465,288	273,832	291,766	302,091
November	544,544	467,008	284,927	313,929
December	829,835	420,762	365,204	379,462

* Source: Company records.
† Month cited represents in each case the first week of that month.

because of the sharp decline in business, were simply buying less. He sought to point out to Rosenwald that the company's prospects were bright as long as it was holding its customers. But, it is reported, this argument did not win Rosenwald to Loeb's plan; it was the consulting attorney's approach to the suggested arrangement, which emphasized the soundness of the investment, that is said to have swayed the president of the company. Finally convinced, Rosenwald consented to the arrangement, which was made public on December 29, 1921.

It proved to be the shot heard round the commercial world. The *New York Times* on its front page the following morning heralded the action in this wise:

CHICAGO, Dec. 29—Julius Rosenwald, President of Sears, Roebuck & Co., the big Chicago mail order house, pledged approximately $20,000,000 of his personal fortune today to see the company through the period of business depression and readjustment.

Mr. Rosenwald purchased certain of the company's Chicago real estate for

$16,000,000, making a first payment of $4,000,000 in cash and liberty bonds, and making a trust deed without personal liability for the balance of the purchase price.

In addition, Mr. Rosenwald made a gift to the company of 50,000 shares of its common stock having a par value of $5,000,000. It is stipulated that this stock is not to be sold for less than par and that Mr. Rosenwald shall have an option for three years to repurchase the stock for cash at par.

The purchase of the property provides that the company may continue to occupy it under a long term lease. Both the lease and the deferred payment of $12,000,000, which Mr. Rosenwald is to make, run on a 7 per cent. annual interest basis. In effect, this means that, aside from payment of interest on $4,000,000, the company will be enabled to use the property without charge.

The *Times* went on to assert that while the 50,000 shares of common stock represented a market value of $3,000,000, they would represent a $5,000,000 donation if sold at par. In any event, the gift would allow the company to reduce its capital liabilities by $5,000,000, while the down payment on the Chicago real estate increased the company's cash assets by $4,000,000. The *Times* added that the larger effect of Rosenwald's action would be that Sears, Roebuck would be enabled to work out its financial readjustment without impairing its capital stock and that the action would "bring appreciably nearer the time when the company will be able to resume the payment of dividends on the common stock, which were discontinued early this year."

The afternoon press, financial and general, accorded the story prominent treatment, along with comment. A financial wire service of December 30 carried this item:

Harry Sachs, of Goldman, Sachs & Co., when asked regarding Sears, Roebuck & Co.'s statement, made the following comment: "The action of the president, Julius Rosenwald, is one of the most generous acts of an individual that has ever come under my notice in the commercial world, illustrating, as it does, his remarkable attitude towards the company's stockholders. In my opinion it is also an indication of his confidence in the stability and future of the business, a view that I of course thoroughly share."

On December 31 C. W. Barron's *Boston News Bureau* carried a long front-page editorial captioned "A Pledge of Faith." It praised Rosenwald's act as an "unselfish offering" and paid glowing tribute to him as a man. It referred to his "commercial genius" and termed his gesture "a chivalric answer" to the popular conception of men of wealth as utterly selfish. C. W. Barron himself wrote to Rosenwald: "I do not know of anybody in the United States in the mercantile line who today is held in higher esteem or sounder regard than you and your great enterprise."[24]

Stockholders wrote to Rosenwald expressing their gratitude, and John D. Rockefeller, Jr., wired his praise. Over and above the favorable publicity for the company and himself which his gesture had brought, Rosenwald had retained control of the company by himself and the other executives. His gift and purchases rendered the firm's condition sufficiently liquid to meet the terms of the agreement under which the serial notes had been issued.

The effects of the move were felt in other ways. Sears, Roebuck stock rallied on the Stock Exchange on December 30 as a result, according to the *New York Times,* of Rosenwald's financial assistance to the company. It gained eight points to 67 and closed at 64⅞ for a net gain of 4¼ points for the day. That same story in the *Times* went on to state that sales of the company in December totaled $17,080,880 as compared with $16,186,495 in November and with $19,167,458 in December of 1920. The story continued with this Pollyanna touch: "This decrease of 10.89% as compared with last year was the smallest in amount and percent of any month this year except September." Total sales for the year 1921 showed a decrease of 30.08 per cent from 1920.

As part of the arrangement by which Rosenwald came to the rescue of his business, it was agreed that Sears, Roebuck and Company would continue to occupy the property at an annual rental of $280,000, based upon a return of 7 per cent on Rosenwald's equity of $4,000,000. The balance of $12,000,000 was evidenced by Rosenwald's notes, secured only by a trust deed on the real estate, the notes containing the provision that Rosenwald and his heirs and personal representatives be not personally liable upon the notes.[25] This meant, in effect, that Rosenwald was not legally liable for the remaining $12,000,000 due on purchase of the company's plant and real estate; that he was to receive 7 per cent interest on his $4,000,000 down payment for the property; and that the $5,000,000 of stock he donated to the company treasury would be both gift to the business and insurance of his own far greater holdings in that business.

On January 11, 1922, in what was both a review and a forecast, the *Wall Street Journal* wrote:

> ... the sale of real estate and President Rosenwald's gift would appear to have been necessitous. The $4,000,000 cash was undoubtedly needed, partially at least, for bank loans payable around January 1. Preferred dividend of 1¾%, amounting to $140,000, also was payable January 1, 1922. If company's surplus had been eliminated and capital impaired on December 31, payment of this dividend would have incurred personal liability on directors. . . .
>
> Sears, Roebuck's present situation calls to mind the 40% stock dividend paid in July, 1920. This increased common capital by $30,000,000 and, consequently, reduced surplus account by that amount. Thus, surplus of $33,574,919 at end of 1919, allowing for nearly $4,000,000 carried to surplus in 1920, was reduced to $7,564,374 at close of 1920. Obviously, had this stock dividend not been declared company's surplus account would have been ample to carry it through the readjustment period.
>
> Official figures of company's borrowings have not been available since showing on June 30, last, when bank loans were $30,000,000. While loans are understood to have been reduced in December, they are said to have been about $41,000,000 around November 1. The increase from June 30 figure was occasioned by borrowing to meet the $16,500,000 note maturity October 15, last. About $10,000,000 or more bank loans were made to meet this maturity. Sears, Roebuck has to pay

out approximately $20,000,000 in interest charges and maturing serial notes this year. This is without allowing for any reduction which may be made in bank loans.

On April 15 semi-annual interest on $33,500,000 serial notes, amounting to $1,160,000, is due. Interest on bank loans is not known, but it should at least equal that on the notes. On October 15, next, $16,500,000 serial notes mature and there will be another semi-annual interest payment due on the $17,000,000 notes maturing in 1923.

Vice President Loeb, in announcing the sale of real estate and gift of stock, stated the company was operating at a profit. On this basis it should have substantial earnings this year, if it sells anything like $178,000,000 of goods moved in 1921. Profits, of course, will be needed for maturities and interest payments.

The *Chicago Journal of Commerce* appraised the company's annual report for the disastrous year of 1921 in an article appearing January 25, 1922, under the headline, "Sears, Roebuck on Firm Basis for 1922 Trade." The story reported that inventory value had dropped from $105,071,248 in 1920 to $46,445,830, with working capital down from $108,000,000 to something over $86,000,000. The company was able to show a book value of $78.19 a share as compared to $81.89 a year earlier. Cash on hand in the amount of $10,867,859, greater by $3,000,000 than ever before reported, was augmented by Liberty bond holdings to give the company "a virtual cash account of approximately $20,000,000." The ratio of working capital to gross sales at the end of the year was 42.76 per cent, the highest ever recorded by the company.

Compared with 1921, the year 1922 proved a good one for the company. True, dividends on common stock were passed in both 1922 and 1923, finally to be resumed again in 1924. But by December 20, 1922, Rosenwald was able to write to his old friend and former business associate, Moses Newborg:

I am happy to be able to tell you that our company received more orders during the last two weeks than in any two weeks in its history and I know of no season when we did less to force business than we did this fall as we have been more watchful than ever of our expenditures in every direction, particularly in advertising. We are therefore very happy over this fresh assurance that our good will has not been impaired and that the prospects for the future are as bright as they were in our "pre-slump days." The only money indebtedness we have now is our Serial Note Issue and we have enough cash on hand today to care for the larger part of that.[26]

Net sales for 1922 rose only some $2,500,000—from $164,039,720 in 1921 to $166,514,110 in 1922—but as a result of improved margins the previous year's loss of $16,435,469 was converted into a net profit after taxes of $5,435,168. The year 1922 was generally one of revival and prosperity. Farm income rose by nearly half a billion dollars. Stock prices rose, there was a rapid improvement in employment, commodity prices were higher, and money was easier.[27]

The nightmare of 1921 seemed definitely over. Farm income rose from $8,594,000,000 in 1922 to $9,563,000,000 in 1923 and in the following two years to $10,221,000,000 and $10,995,000,000. Index numbers of wholesale prices for farm products and for all commodities continued to rise. For the first time since 1919, the index numbers for farm products were appreciably higher in 1924 than those for all commodities.[28]

Sears, Roebuck's annual net sales rose steadily: to $198,482,945 in 1923, to $206,430,527 in 1924, and to $243,798,351 in 1925. Net income after taxes followed a similar line upward, from $11,512,618 in 1923 to $14,354,397 in 1924 and $20,975,303 in 1925. But the cautious executives of the company kept inventories down to less than $50,000,000 through the remainder of this period. Not, in fact, until 1925 did inventory value equal or exceed that of 1921.

Those years after 1921 were good enough to allow the company to move rapidly to retire its preferred stock. Also, before the end of 1926, Rosenwald was able to repurchase the five million shares of common stock he had given the company in December, 1921.[29]

On March 12, 1931, nearly ten years after Rosenwald's gift to the company, an agreement was made whereby the company agreed to purchase its Chicago plant and real estate within thirty days after the death of Rosenwald, or on December 31, 1936, whichever date occurred later. The total price was fixed at $16,000,000, of which $4,000,000 was to be paid in cash and the balance by cancellation of the purchase money obligations of Rosenwald held by Sears, Roebuck. After Julius Rosenwald's death on January 6, 1932, the company and the estate entered into a final agreement including these terms, among others: (1) the estate to release the company from payment of the $4,000,000 in cash; (2) the estate to reconvey the Chicago real estate and plants to Sears, Roebuck upon cancellation of the $12,000,000 purchase money mortgage notes, the reconveyance to be made when designated by the company on or before the end of 1951.[30]

The company's annual report which chronicled those arrangements concluded its summary of the working-out of the 1921 arrangement in these paragraphs:

Thus the Treasury of the Company has received from Mr. [Julius] Rosenwald a total of $9,000,000, consisting of $5,000,000 cash paid by him to repurchase his stock previously donated to the Company, and $4,000,000 in Liberty bonds paid by him toward the purchase price of the Chicago property, from the repayment of which sum the Company has now been released by the Estate.

In consideration of the above, the Company has paid to the Julius Rosenwald Estate $750,000 in cash and has purchased from the Julius Rosenwald Estate 188,235 shares of stock of the Company at $21.25 each (which was the market price on the date of the agreement) with an option to the Estate to repurchase such stock on or before December 31, 1936, at the same basic price, with minor adjustments.

As a part of this transaction, the Company agreed to lend to the Julius Rosenwald Estate $1,000,000 if and when requested and to assume a portion of the loss that the Julius Rosenwald Estate might suffer by virtue of a guaranty of certain employes' accounts which Mr. Rosenwald assumed during the year 1929, such loss, however, to be limited to 50% of his loss and not to exceed $1,000,000 payment by the company.[31]

CHAPTER XIV

Reorientation of Merchandising

IN BROAD terms the company's merchandising organization represented in this period an island in a changing sea. While many changes were being made in the operating organization, in correspondence methods, in the relationship between the Chicago office and the branch plants, the merchandising organization seems generally to have resisted change. Sears remained throughout this period largely a "federation of merchants," in the terminology of certain employees of the company.

True, there were changes in the merchandise line, in relations with sources, in many of the merchandising techniques. But the merchandising organization itself appears to have withstood modifications of major character. Many of the functions earlier vested in the several merchandise department heads were allocated elsewhere; department heads no longer had to concern themselves with endless details of correspondence and returns, for example. But the buyers' wide autonomy in buying, pricing, and catalogue presentation was only slowly whittled down.

Even J. F. Skinner, a strong personality and an excellent merchant, dealt with his buyers largely on a basis of moral suasion. As long as buyers produced profits—which they did, in staggering amounts, up to the debacle of 1920—they were seldom interfered with. As a result, there was no over-all company merchandise pattern. One buyer might attempt to sell shoes priced extremely high by the firm's standards, while another would carry the cheapest line of socks and ties priced as low as fifteen cents. The very fact of the wide and, from this hindsight vantage point, occasionally rash experimentation in merchandise lines during this period furnishes evidence of the lack of any real general merchandise pattern. And that lack stemmed in large degree from the company's concept of its buyers as a "federation of merchants."

A former employee's account of his experiences as inspector of merchandise from 1917 to 1922 is filled with reports of clashes with merchandise department heads. Some of those buyers, the account says, not only refused to accede to some of Skinner's plans for improving the quality of the goods and the accuracy of their presentation in the catalogue but also bluntly threatened to join together, go to Rosenwald, and have the merchandise inspector ousted from his job. The inspector sought to utilize the findings of the company's laboratories to check catalogue copy submitted by the buyers and also to check the quality of the goods. He found that some, though not all, of the buyers gave the laboratories findings short shrift—further evidence of their confidence in their own power.

Donald M. Nelson, who started as a chemist in the Sears laboratories in 1912 and became head of merchandising in 1928, tells of his own work in checking merchandise against catalogue descriptions of it. Nelson asserts that he was given no authority by the general merchandise manager; he was simply to do his work "without fighting with anybody." The power of the several merchandise department heads was also illustrated in the development of instalment selling by the company.

To name only three instances, the heads of the departments handling "Modern Homes," phonographs, and the *Encyclopaedia Britannica* were able to thrust uncertain credit risks upon the credit committee. Liberal extension of credit was often deemed essential to increasing sales in various departments. Interviews with company executives who were present in those days make it clear that the merchants frequently threw their full weight against the credit committee, sometimes with unhappy results.

Illustrative of the importance of the merchandising executives was the fact that, where the company found it advantageous to own factories, the management of these factories was directly responsible to the merchandise manager whose goods they produced. Indeed, not until 1930 were Sears, Roebuck's wholly owned factories all brought under the control of a specially appointed top-management official. Further, in the years after 1915 the departmental merchants in Chicago captured functions that had formerly been shared (if sometimes by default) with managers of the company's mail-order branch plants, which became more numerous as the Dallas house prospered, as business boomed, and as the postal zones defined in the parcel-post legislation placed a premium on decentralized operation.

After the success of the Dallas experiment had become manifest, another branch was opened in Seattle in the spring of 1910. Just as Dallas' operating methods had not been clearly defined and had led to bitter differences of opinion within the organization, so did both Dallas and Seattle continue for some years to operate without a clear-cut articulation of their relations with the parent-organization in Chicago. Both branch plants were ostensibly just far-flung appendages of Chicago, with all authority for command decisions residing there. Actually, both branches moved toward a semi-independent status; their autonomy, fuzzy though it was and far from clearly defined, arose from the very nature of the operations involved.

Distance alone tended to allow them a freer rein than originally intended, because department heads and other executives in the parent-house simply could not "worry" about branches so far away. There was no system under which the head of, say, the clothing department in Chicago received any credit for the performance of the clothing departments in Dallas or Seattle. Some efforts were made to synchronize procurement, but no steps were taken to make the synchronization really effective. There was no incentive for a department head in Chicago to allocate any considerable part of his stocks to the corresponding departments in the branches. This led inevitably to some mixups and competition in procurement of merchandise. It also led to confusion on the part of sources, who were unable to distinguish between Sears, Roebuck in Chicago and Sears, Roebuck in Seattle or Dallas. Correlation of the three catalogues—for Chicago, Dallas, and Seattle—became increasingly difficult; instances in which lineups of merchandise, prices, and descriptions went wrong were frequent.[1]

It may well be asked why steps were not taken sooner to clarify and remedy this situation. The answer appears to be that, despite the confusion inherent in the plan of operations, these years (1909–20) were lush ones for the company. As farm income mounted to its dizziest and most exhilarating heights, the business showed handsome profits. As in the earlier years, business continued to expand rapidly—so rapidly, that refinements in the company's relations with its branches were relegated to the shelf and held in indefinite abeyance so that attention could be concentrated on more immediate problems.

By 1919 the company seems to have adopted Richard Sears's belief that further expansion would have to take the form of additional branch plants. In that year plans for opening a branch at Philadelphia crystallized. The head of the new plant was to be Lessing J. Rosenwald, son of the president and a former shipping-department employee who had worked his way up through the organization. Discussion of how Philadelphia would operate exploded the whole question of the relationship of branches to the Chicago plant and led to a re-evaluation of the situation. The two Rosenwalds, it is said, were determined to organize the new branch on the Dallas-Seattle plan—if that could really be called a plan. General Merchandise Manager Crawford presented a seven-page memorandum outlining the aforementioned difficulties adversely affecting operations of Chicago and its branches and pleading for a central control system to replace the "plan" then in force.

Under the central control system one general head for each line of merchandise (located in Chicago) would be responsible for that line in the Chicago plant and in all branches, even though he might have some of his buyers stationed in certain branches. The general head of a merchandise department (the supervisor) would govern development of sources of supply, the buying, and the general merchandising policy for his line in all plants of the company. Merchandise would be allocated equitably and rationally. Likewise, the catalogue editor in Chicago would feel coequal responsibility for all catalogues—Chicago's as well as those of the various branch mail-order plants. In short, the central control system would be just that; it would seek to knit all operations into one effective operating entity. An unbroken front would be presented to sources.

As so often happened, Albert Loeb served as the bridge between the Rosenwalds and those who favored central control. Loeb's belief in the advantages of centralization and his persuasiveness saw the central control system adopted, even though some fair degree of autonomy was left to heads of branch plants. It was, of course, inherent in the situation that the younger Rosenwald's position would allow him fairly great autonomy under any system. (Later, when ordered by a superior officer in Chicago to fire a man named Carney, Lessing refused point-blank; Thomas J. Carney later became president of the company.) And the advent of retail stores in later years, with the inevitable decentralization of authority (of which General Robert E. Wood was and is a vociferous exponent), led to still greater latitude for branch mail-order plants.

Thus throughout the years the merchants continued to exercise enormous and nearly independent control over the conduct of their various departments. On the whole the results of conferring such great discretion on the department managers were far from unhappy, even though they were uneven in certain instances.

The highly profitable years of World War I and the period immediately following, until the 1920–21 depression, brought forth some manifestations which have characterized nearly all of the company's really prosperous periods: a great general expansion in the merchandise line, studded by some failures as the firm sought to determine pretty much by trial and error the particulars of its true "mission" in the field of distribution.

The general expansion of the merchandise line reached at the height of the war boom a point which, according to one former executive, has never since been approached. This was the era in which Sears, Roebuck was indeed the "complete" store—complete even beyond its true logical function. It was almost impossible to lose money even on over-all operations during those lush years, and the company was willing to gamble on almost anything in the knowledge that if one line should fail, even disastrously, other lines would still keep the firm solidly in the black.

These various failures were, however, only the dramatic exceptions to the more prosaic general rule. The over-all expansion of the merchandise line between 1908 and 1925 may be characterized by the same generalization as applies to the preceding and following periods: the company, by and large, simply kept pace with the times. It was no innovator in merchandise types; generally speaking, no item was listed in the catalogue until it had pretty clearly established its popularity with the buying public, and no item remained in the list of offerings for long after the public had ceased to want to buy it. The few exceptions to this latter generalization are less paradoxical than might appear; Sears, Roebuck even today does a very large business in harness and saddles and in "old-fashioned" underwear. But this is attributable to the fact that competitors forsook these lines as the public demand for them began to shrink, while Sears continued to handle such lines and thus became the "natural residual legatee" of such business as did remain. And the failures lay in the introduction of lines which had gained popular acceptance—but not with the people who constituted Sears's market, under the conditions on which Sears sold.

Given the market which Sears, Roebuck sought to exploit, and given a knowledge of the tastes, aesthetics, and economic position of that market at any given time, the company's catalogue offerings can be projected with reasonable accuracy. And, conversely, proceeding from this assumption, one can estimate from the catalogue's offerings just what were the tastes and purchasing power of its market. By 1908 the company certainly had a clearer conception than ever before of just about what lines it should handle; later clarification of doubtful spheres came through trial and error. Addition of new items followed technological advances and public acceptance of the products stemming from those advances, and the size of the general merchandise line grew with the prosperity of Sears's customers.

The Chicago general catalogue (which will be cited in these comparisons as being generally typical of the Dallas, Seattle, and, later, the Philadelphia branch catalogues) in the fall of 1910 devoted to furniture the largest space allocation of any one merchandise line. Women's, misses', and girls' wearing apparel came next, followed by hardware (this department was beginning to lose space to others, notably soft lines), watches and jewelry, and men's and boys' clothing.

The position held in the catalogue by these various lines differed sharply, however, from the amounts of space they occupied. The first department listed, after the "2-4-6-8-12 cent" articles (more order-starters than a merchandise line), was dry goods, followed by wool and silk dress goods. Then came fancy goods and trimmings, corsets, millinery, ladies', misses', and children's wearing apparel, muslin underwear, infants' and small children's wear, and so on through men's and boys' clothing, for a grand total of nearly 450 pages. Next came carpets and rugs, curtains, blankets, draperies, and window shades, crockery, china, and glassware, wallpaper, paint, and, finally, furniture. After this came sewing machines, followed by musical instruments, photographic supplies, electrical goods, watches and jewelry, drugs, bicycles, guns and sporting goods, books and stationery, stoves, washing machines, kitchenware, builders' hardware, farm implements and supplies, plumbing, vehicles, and harness.

The merchandise lines added since 1900 numbered twenty and included gas and electric fixtures, school furniture, telephones and line material, flashlights, motorcycles, motorboats, heating plants, portable houses, concrete-block machines, automobiles, and others. Automobiles, which had first appeared in the catalogue in 1909, received special treatment in the 1910 book. Illustrations of this vehicle filled the back cover, while copy on automobiles occupied the inside back cover.

In their first appearance in Sears, Roebuck's merchandise line, the still new vehicle had been called the "Sears Motor Buggy," but the 1910 book termed them simply "Sears Automobiles." Six models were referred to, though only three were illustrated on the back cover. These three were priced at $395, $475, and $495, but the text mentioned another listing at $370; except for this reference to "Six Popular Models $370.00 and Up" and "See Inside Page of This Cover," that one-page layout contained only two other statements: "Strength and Economy" and "Simplicity and Reliability." The inside page referred to asserted that Sears's automobiles were blazing a trail from the Gulf to the Great Lakes, from the Atlantic to the Pacific, and were being driven by doctors, farmers, ranchmen, bankers, and businessmen:

> This automobile has marked a new epoch in the motor car industry—Sears, the embodiment of strength, endurance, reliability and economy. Since the summer of 1908 we have built, tested and sold hundreds of Sears cars and every one is doing the work it was designed to do and doing it well. Quality rather than quantity has been our aim. . . .
> A Sears by any other name would cost you double, because we save you the agent's commission. We build the Sears in our own automobile factory in Chicago. . . .
> Our Model "G" at $370.00 is safe, sound and smooth running, weighs 1,000 pounds and is doing some wonderful work.
> SPECIFICATIONS—Motor, two-cylinder, 14-horse power, nearly 1½-horse power for each 100 pounds of automobile. Speed, from 1 to 25 miles an hour; 1 gallon of gasoline will carry you 25 miles. Control located on left side; your right hand guides the automobile, your left controls the speed. Four full elliptic springs, together with resilient hard rubber tires, insure easy and comfortable riding; two mufflers deaden the exhaust. . . .
> Remember that you do not require a mechanical training in order to operate the Sears Automobile; our Book of Instruction tells you how in thirty minutes.

The statement went on to urge readers to send for a special automobile catalogue and for a booklet, *What Sears Owners Say* ("contains many real human documents—letters right from the people who drive and enjoy the Sears"). Despite this fanfare, however, automobiles were dropped from the general catalogue after some three years.

Their unprofitability had been soundly demonstrated. Gross sales of automobiles were $74,331 in the spring of 1909; the gross profit was $3,916. But the net loss was $9,135. In the succeeding two seasons gross sales totaled more than $165,000, but the total net profit was only $7,465. In the fall of 1910, automobile sales brought a net loss of $6,897; in 1911, automobile sales of nearly $400,000 resulted in a net loss of almost $42,000; 1912 sales of around $211,000 yielded a net loss of $21,000. The unprofitability of automobile sales was summed up in the story of "Jack" Westrich, a former buyer of the company, who purchased one of the Sears automobiles. He asked to be allowed to buy it at cost. Julius Rosenwald consented—and the cost proved to exceed the selling price at which the vehicle was listed.

The 1910 catalogue also listed a motorcycle at $189. It was called the "Sears Auto-Cycle," but the full page of copy which followed referred to it only as a motorcycle. Readers were urged several times to send for the free motorcycle catalogue, and an automobile-supply catalogue was announced on the same page. There were other evidences of mechanical progress: electric lamps ($1.48 and up) and electric irons, indicating perhaps not only that these items had come to popularity but also that electricity had come to more farms.

Pajamas had reappeared, after having made two earlier entrances and two exits from the catalogue, but they only shared two-thirds of a page with men's nightshirts. Oils and greases had been added to the paint department, possibly evidence of the increasing use of automobiles and other similarly powered equipment. Both disk and cylinder phonograph records were listed, with the former type predominating. Moving-picture machines and films held one page. Electrical goods included telephones as well as electric railroad toys. Dolls and Christmas tree ornaments had been added to the drug department. Hand-operated washing machines occupied four pages. Wood- and metal-working tools were electrically powered.

Women's hats were listed as low as $2.25, and an all-wool dress (this was before there was a laboratory to ponder the phrase "all wool") at $13.25. "Imported silk embroidered black lisle ladies hose" started at 42 cents a pair, and a wide variety of women's shoes was available at $2.95. Men's shoes were priced higher ($3.45), and men's suits ranged from $7.50 to $22.50. Ten-inch disk records sold for $3.50 per dozen or 30 cents each ("Why pay 60 cents each?"); the listings included a great variety, from selections from Lehar's *The Merry Widow* to "delectable rags," "brilliant, lively two-steps," marches, "ragtime two-steps," a Harry Lauder medley, and solos for accordion, violin, banjo, bell, chimes, clarinet, flute, and xylophone, as well as others. Among clocks, the cuckoo model appears to have predominated. Cosmetics included "Mrs. Gervaise Graham's Well Known Beauty Products" and "Dr. Charles' Celebrated Toilet Preparations." Twin auto-seat surreys were priced as high as $89.35.

The catalogue, which had grown from 1,100 pages in 1905 to 1,348 pages in 1910, increased in 1915 to 1,636 pages, a fact in itself amply indicative of a general extension of the lines and items offered. In 1915 there were 86 pages in color, as compared to the total of 32 color pages in 1910. There were other changes, more significant in relation to merchandising. Furniture had yielded the major space allocation to women's, misses', and girls' apparel. Men's and boys' clothing was in third place, in respect to space allocation, followed by drugs and toys and watches and jewelry.

An automobile-supply department had been established and given 14 pages. A gasoline-engine department likewise held 14 pages. The arrangement of lines within the book was roughly the same as in 1910, opening with soft lines, which filled about one-third of the catalogue, and following with hard lines. Building materials included a wider variety of offerings, as the "Modern Homes" department expanded steadily.

The 1915 catalogue reflected no appreciable price increases as a result of the outbreak of war in Europe; the real advance in prices was to come in 1917 with the entry of the United States into the war. There had, however, been a run on the company's groceries in 1914, when war was declared, that led to discontinuation of the grocery catalogue for several months until the backlog of orders could be filled. Some three million dollars of grocery orders was reportedly received within three weeks in 1914.

The forerunner of wrist watches for women ("bracelet" watches) was shown, but pocket watches were the only type for men. "Franklin" replaced "Minnesota" as the brand name for sewing machines, and electric lamps gained in the space allotment. Buggies were still in good demand and were given a double-page spread. "Built-in" bathtubs made a timid beginning that year. Men's and women's fashion had made few improvements, although oxford-type shoes were beginning to vie with the high type. Blue serge and other dark colors were still the most popular in men's suits. The furniture was still unspeakably monstrous, but kitchen stoves were beginning to show traces of modern design.

A résumé prepared in 1917 by an executive of the merchandising organization listed lines which had been added since 1910 and which were then still offered, as well as a group of lines which had been tried and discontinued in the decade up to 1917. The lines which had proved their profitability included church and theater furniture, electric household appliances, electric lighting plants, automobile accessories, marine supplies, stock foods (apparently revived after Richard Sears's earlier fiasco with this line), raw phosphate rock fertilizer, paper dress patterns, gymnasium and playground apparatus, building plans, dairy barn equipment, and machine-made houses.

Merchandise lines which had been attempted by the company and dropped because they did not lend themselves to mail-order sale (at least by Sears, Roebuck) included seed, bulbs, and nursery stock, automobiles, motorcycles, uniforms (such as railwaymen's, mail-carriers', and bandsmen's), self-binder reapers, silos, binder twine, moving-picture machines, stereopticon lanterns, and surgical instruments. That same résumé also pointed to some items which "we do not handle from a policy viewpoint; lines that do not represent real value, or from which customers do not receive real service, or which possesses a considerable element of danger." In addition to such obvious lines as whiskey and gunpowder, that list included patent medicines, rheumatic rings, and electric belts.

The increase in sales volume in certain lines was illustrated in a report from the head of the sporting goods department to Julius Rosenwald in 1918 on various random items. As many as 1,210 baseball clubs in a single season had been outfitted with uniforms and related equipment by Sears,

Roebuck. Roller-skate sales had reached as high as 22,000 pairs in one year. In 1917 the company sold 47,273 straight razors (as against only 12,954 safety razors) and 158,277 pocketknives. Tents sold in quantities as high as 10,000 in a year. In round figures, 540,000 sweater coats were sold in 1917 as compared with a volume in this item of 8,160 in 1905.

Possibly the outstanding feature of the merchandise offered in the 1920 catalogue was the price level. A rapid inflation had followed the entry of the United States into World War I, and its peak point was reflected in the book (men's suits were priced as high as $47.50). Soft lines still led off in the catalogue, which ran to 1,492 pages. Women's skirts were shorter, and men's suits showed style lines closer to those of today. Men's wrist watches—called "strap watches"—were prominent. Player pianos were popular, as were phonographs. A two-page spread on "Silvertone" phonographs contained the offer, "No Money Down," with the entire layout in color. Cooking stoves were neatly trimmed in white enamel, and bathtubs had made great strides in five years toward the built-in design. Complete bathroom sets were featured. In addition to guns long obtained from its own sources and carrying its own brand names, the company had added Winchester and Remington guns. "Justice" automobile tires were shown in 6,000- and 10,000-mile models, the latter ranging in price from $24.85 to $69.75. "Elgin" bicycles sold for $52.45. And buggies, which Richard Sears had striven for years to sell at three for $100, were selling for as much as $99.65 each.

Electric vacuum cleaners and electric- and gasoline-engine-powered washing machines were offered, and buggies still clung to their place in the book. There were other signs of the times: the automobile-supply department had grown to 26 pages by 1920. The best-selling items in the spring of that year were the 50-foot, four-ply garden hose at $4.50 and the 16-inch, four-blade lawn-mower at $7.00. Best sellers in the fall included a ladies seven-jeweled wrist watch at $12.80, a fifteen-jeweled Swiss pocket watch at $12.77, a Queen Anne period bedroom set (consisting of bed, dresser, and chifforette) for $137.95, a gasoline-engine-powered washing machine for $107.50, and an electric washer for $85.00.

By 1925, prices had returned to a level more commensurate with the Sears, Roebuck tradition. Elgin bicycles had dropped from $52.45 in 1920 to $29.95, with some models as low as $26.95, and the design was considerably improved. Men's suits had fallen comparably in price, and so in fact had virtually everything else. Low shoes had just about completed their triumph over high-top models, and pajamas had now attained a favorable ratio of five to three over nightgowns in the catalogue listings. Wrist watches had become predominant over pocket models. Radio had come to stay, and prices in this line ranged from $65 to $150. The built-in bathtub had finally clinched its place in the home, while electric milking machines had made a place for themselves on the farm. Automobile tires still carried the "Justice" label, though priced far lower than five years before, but this tire was soon to be replaced by another. The buggy still held one page in the big book, even though there were 9,232,000 automobiles registered in the United States by then.[2]

It is reasonable to assume from what is known of Sears, Roebuck's general merchandising philosophy, that, with the rare exceptions like groceries, those items which held sway in the catalogue for any length of time met with reasonably satisfactory public response—sufficient, at least, to pay their way in space consumed. There were, however, several ventures in this period which met with less fortunate results—and did not long remain in the catalogue. One of these, launched in 1916, was the "Lady Duff-Gordon" line of women's style clothing. Lady Duff-Gordon, one of the best-known fashion stylists in America, was engaged by Sears, Roebuck to design fairly expensive clothes for women. One magazine reported the arrangement in these terms:

> Lucile, the trade-name of Lady Duff-Gordon, has become a name to conjure with. She has designed frocks for the queens of Europe and the wives of America's finance kings, for millionaire weddings, for stage stars and grand opera prima donnas, for coronation fetes and the like. Her name has been tied up inseparably ... with smartness and elegance. And now comes a great mail-order house, Sears, Roebuck & Company, of Chicago, hires Lucile to design clothes for its patrons at prices ranging from $20 to $45, and sells the same in huge quantities. Romance and a sense of surpassing smartness are thus brought into the remotest homes that the Sears-Roebuck catalog reaches. ... The great mail order house stimulates its movement of women's wear to a degree that could probably never have been attained in any other way. Sears-Roebuck puts on the "dog" and multitudes of women put on Sears-Roebuck clothes.[3]

Fuessle's reference to Sears, Roebuck's selling those exotic creations "in huge quantities" could hardly have been farther off the mark. The venture into Continental fashions for the farm wives of the Plains was a resounding failure. Lady Duff-Gordon christened each of her creations with a name. One gown was titled "I'll Come Back to You." Company records, according to former employees, bore the name out in cold statistical terms; two were sold, and both came back. Departmental sales records told an even drearier story, as the accompanying tabulation shows.

Season	Gross Sales	(Final) Gross Profit or *Loss*	Net Profit or *Loss*
Fall 1916	$40,781	$ 7,363	*$ 74,783*
Spring 1917	49,428	*18,732*	*186,841*

The linen department furnished the staging area for the next move. In 1918, when wartime prosperity was booming all sales, the company decided to try high-style merchandise again and brought in an outside advertising agency to promote linens. Special catalogues were issued, and buyers were instructed to obtain the finest linens available. The linen promotion was just enough of a success in the flush year of 1919 to evoke plans for other, similar efforts.

The shoe department began offering shoes priced as high as $18.50, even though the firm's best-selling shoe was listed at $5.95. The $18.50 shoes did not sell; whereas the linen promotion had been a qualified success, the shoe enterprise proved an unqualified failure. Undaunted, the company then determined to promote an expensive line of men's clothing and hired a man from Marshall Field and Company to supervise the line. He immediately stocked up on high-priced goods and built a factory to produce the fine new clothing. Nearly $500,000 was spent on the factory before the company decided to write off the entire effort as a mistake. According to Elmer J. Voorhis, former manager of Sears's New York office, the department heads who launched these ill-fated ventures into high-style goods were prodded to do so by Crawford, the general merchandise manager, who was himself a fashion plate and apparently desired to dress the people of the country in his own image.

According to former company executives, these various failures pointed up two conclusions, one of which has already been touched upon: (1) such ventures are usually attempted only in times of great prosperity, and, conversely, times of prosperity usually beget such ventures; and (2) these failures always underscore Sears, Roebuck's true function as a distributor of merchandise that can be priced well within the budget of the farming, working, and lower-middle classes.

One venture which was later to be a failure but which attained a fairly high degree of success in the years up to 1925 was Sears, Roebuck's "Modern Homes" department. As recounted earlier, the "Modern Homes" department came into existence between 1895 and 1900 when a department was established to merchandise building materials, although the name "Modern Homes" department apparently was not adopted until 1911.[4] Its continued unprofitability led to serious consideration of discontinuing the department, but it was instead reorganized and put on a profitable basis, so that by 1912 the earlier losses had been wiped out. Net profit for the seven years up to and including 1912 totaled $630,000 on total sales of $10,967,000. The first deparmental catalogue had been brought out in 1908, and the department prepared to expand under its reorganization.[5]

In 1909 a lumber mill in Mansfield, Ohio, was purchased as part of the campaign to improve service and stimulate sales. In 1911 a lumber yard was built at Cairo, Illinois, and in the following year a millwork plant was purchased in Norwood, Ohio. Paralleling these moves, the first bill of materials for a complete "Modern Home" was sold in 1909, and two years later the first mortgage loan was made. By the end of 1912 an annual sales volume of $2,595,000 was reached, with a departmental net profit of $176,-

000 (in 1906, a sales volume of $1,194,000 had returned a net loss of $35,000).

Also by the end of 1912, $649,000 in mortgage loans had been written, of which $225,000 was cash and $423,000 represented materials. While a start had been made toward the sale and financing of complete house units, the great bulk of the business in those years lay in assorted building materials handled on a straight mail-order basis. This pattern was to continue largely intact through 1920, despite the growing emphasis on homes as such instead of solely on building materials.

The acquisition of the Norwood millwork plant and the lumber mill and yard put the company in position to furnish a complete line of building materials from its own sources. "Modern Homes" catalogues were enlarged to include a greater variety of houses, and their circulation was multiplied many times. The practice of mortgage financing of complete house purchases gradually increased. The eagerness of the "Modern Homes" department to increase sales apparently led, however, to an abuse of the handling of mortgage loan applications, with resultant losses. This function was transferred in 1913 to the credit committee, but later that same year Rosenwald ordered discontinuation of mortgage financing (which was revived in 1916 and by 1920 became an important factor in sales).

Ready-cut production of lumber for "Modern Homes" was instituted in 1916. This made possible three savings: (1) the company bought lumber in the most economical lengths rather than longer lengths selling at higher rates per 1,000 board feet; (2) the company was also thus able to use second-grade lumber, converting it into first-grade by cutting out the knotted parts and using the lengths thus obtained in appropriate parts of the houses; (3) with the wastage of timber so removed, freight charges were considerably reduced.

Also in 1916 the first applied roofing office was opened in Dayton, Ohio. Three years later the first "Modern Homes" sales office was opened, at Akron, to take advantage of the building boom which followed the rapid expansion of the rubber industry (and the end of wartime restrictions on building). This was the first step in a program which eventually largely removed the sale of "Modern Homes" from the catalogue and vested it instead in sales offices. By 1920 the combined annual sales of the building materials departments reached $6,000,000, with total net profits of $900,000. Total sales for the eight-year period since 1912 amounted to $29,160,000; total profits were $3,377,000. In the same period a total of $3,876,000 in mortgage loans was written, consisting of $310,000 in cash and $3,566,000 (or some 12 per cent of the total sales) in materials.

The opening of the Philadelphia branch plant provided an eastern base for "Modern Homes" operations and served as an entering wedge into that fertile market. The shrinkage in farm income resulting from the 1920–21 depression slowed the rural market, while the population movement from farm to city accentuated the postwar urban housing shortage, and both coincided with and accentuated the building boom which prevailed in almost all centers of population for the following years almost up to the "crash" of 1929. The "Modern Homes" department embarked upon a large-scale program of mass production and direct selling in which the "eastern" volume gradually overtook the "western" volume and became predominant.

In general terms, the period from 1921 to 1926 was one in which "Modern Homes" as such replaced building materials as the principal sales line, and during which the operation changed from that of a regular mail-order department to a separate administrative unit conducting a chain of sales offices and factories. It was also a period in which the expense increased to nearly 20 per cent, and the profits dropped from 15 to 10 per cent of sales.

In more specific terms, a complete "Modern Homes" department was organized at the Philadelphia branch plant in 1921, and sales offices were opened in Pittsburgh, Cleveland, Cincinnati, and Dayton. In the following year additional sales offices were established in Chicago, Philadelphia, and Washington; in 1924, in Columbus, Ohio; in 1925, in Detroit to further exploit the possibilities laid bare by the housing shortage. Wright says of these years:

> The shortage of housing produced by the war resulted in an upward movement of rents that continued till 1924, despite the fact that most other items in the cost of living had undergone a drastic price cut in 1920–21. Though building material costs and wage rates in this industry had fallen less than most, interest rates were relatively low. Moreover, the rapid growth of building and loan associations and the remarkable development and expansion of the market for real-estate mortgage bonds during this decade were a great aid in providing for the financing of new construction in the form of workers' homes, enormous apartment buildings, and skyscraper office structures.[6]

The steady expansion of the "Modern Homes" department was generally countered by a comparable decline in the company's grocery department. The establishment of the parcel post had virtually destroyed the usefulness of groceries in persuading farmers to "run their orders to 100 pounds" in order to save on freight charges. And the booming prosperity which was to lead "Modern Homes" into ever deeper water was characterized also by the rapid spread of grocery chains with which Sears's grocery department could not compete.

Groceries had never been counted upon to yield more than a very small profit, if any. Figures available for the years from the spring of 1916 through the spring of 1926 show that, for the twenty-one seasons represented, this department realized a net profit in eleven seasons and a net loss in ten seasons. But, whereas the highest net profit in any one season was 4.55 per cent (and ranged as low as 0.70 per cent), the greatest net loss in any season amounted to 27.42 per cent (in the fall of 1920, when the department lost $1,200,427). The net loss for the twenty-one seasons represented came to $1,287,621.

In the three years after 1926, grocery sales volume fell off steadily, dropping to $3,107,000 in 1927, to $2,673,000 the succeeding year, and to $1,208,000 in 1929. The latter year saw the discontinuation of the grocery department. It was no longer able even to seek to meet the competition of such food chains as A&P, and, in addition, the company had its own retail store chain by 1929 to engross its attention.

The abortive effort to discontinue the grocery department in 1906 had led indirectly to the establishment of one of the company's most interesting adjuncts, one which was to have a great influence upon the quality of its general line of merchandise. Quality of merchandise had, in fact, been the element upon which continuation of the grocery department after 1906 had hinged. The company had refused to subject itself to additional attack by its critics, which, while possibly focused primarily on the quality of the company's groceries and its alleged inability to meet the standards of the Pure Food and Drug Act, might also further have inflamed popular feeling against the quality level of the company's entire merchandise line. All available evidence indicates that, as a matter of fact, this was the one merchandise line of the company best able to withstand any searching examination. The quality of the groceries had always been high; higher, apparently, than that of any other department. The company had in fact advertised this high quality, with reliable weights and measures, as the real appeal of the grocery department.

General Merchandise Manager J. F. Skinner determined to improve and maintain the quality of groceries, as part of his general effort to raise the standards of the company's merchandise, and to comport fully with the spirit as well as the letter of the Pure Food and Drug Act. Skinner conferred early in 1911 with J. R. Scott, manager of the grocery department and himself a stickler for quality; Albert Loeb, by then vice-president and treasurer; and Lucien I. Yeomans, an engineer employed by the company as a trouble-shooter to iron out "bugs" in mechanical merchandise. Yeomans persuaded Skinner to approach a former associate of his, A. V. H. Mory, in regard to establishing a food-testing laboratory. Mory, an experienced chemist, had been employed by Armour and Company in Chicago as assistant chemist in the food laboratory up to 1901 and by the Armour Packing Company of Kansas City as chief food chemist until 1907. He had left Armour in that year to take charge of the United States Laboratory of Food and Drug Inspection in Kansas City, being deeply interested in the operation of the Pure Food and Drug Act.

When Skinner approached him, Mory had little interest in running a food laboratory for a commercial organization again, and he particularly had no desire to be connected with any mail-order house, of whose merchandising practices he had formed an unsavory opinion. He went to

Chicago largely at Yeoman's insistence. There he was interviewed by Loeb, Skinner, and Scott and was conducted through the plant and told everything he wanted to know about the operation of the grocery department.[7]

Mory was pleasantly surprised by what he discovered of the standards and merchandising methods of the grocery department. After several days in Chicago he informed Skinner that Sears, Roebuck had no need for a food-testing laboratory: its own standards of quality were extremely high; excellent sources were being utilized; and the Pure Food and Drug Act guaranteed source responsibility. He also reported that his own work in the enforcement of that legislation had revealed that nearly all infractions of that law with deliberate intent to defraud hinged on deception as to quantity or quality, there being very few instances in which adulterations constituted a menace to health. The chemist further told Skinner that what Sears, Roebuck really needed was a testing laboratory dedicated to bringing the company's entire merchandise line into harmony with the spirit of the Pure Food and Drug Act. This would involve a general chemical analytical division and a textile division. Skinner accepted his suggestion on the spot, according to Mory, and asked the latter to establish such a laboratory. Mory agreed.

Fireproofed quarters were soon established on the tenth floor of the tower in the merchandise building. Mory proceeded to employ additional personnel. He persuaded a young graduate in chemistry from the University of Missouri to work for Sears a couple of years in order to save money with which to obtain his doctorate from an eastern university; on April 1, 1912, Donald M. Nelson came to work for the laboratory. Nelson's first assignment was testing foods to insure compliance with federal legislation; his next was working on catalogue descriptions of the drugs the company was then carrying.

Skinner was also concerned at the time with the firm's textile offerings. A former clothing man, he knew woolens fairly well but was frank to admit, according to Nelson, that the company simply did not know just what it was getting when it bought woolen goods. Many, if not most, manufacturers mixed virgin wool with cotton and shoddy wool. It was virtually impossible to determine the actual content of textiles without having within the company someone who knew at least as much about textiles as almost anyone else in the country. Accordingly, Skinner arranged to send Nelson out to study the textile business, for as long as two years if necessary.

Nelson took the full course at the Lowell Textile School, then secured an apprenticeship in the Sterling Mills in Lowell, where, he says,

I worked for three months at every basic job in the woolen mill. My next job was as an apprentice in the American Woolen Co. I went to work at a quarter after six in the morning and worked until six o'clock at night, and as an apprentice operated every machine in the mill. In the Globe Mills at Utica, New York, I learned the dyeing, sorting, carding, and weaving of wool. I then wound up in the design room and designed a suit of clothes for myself; I was then sent to the Weybosset Mills up in Rhode Island, where they made a lower grade of woolen goods than did the Globe. My training having been completed, I returned to Sears, Roebuck & Co.[8]

Nelson was responsible to Mory. And Mory, as laboratory head, reported directly to Skinner and Loeb. He was given a great deal of authority and was soon termed the "watchdog of the catalogue." The policy of making the head of the laboratory responsible for keeping undesirable merchandise and descriptions out of the catalogue was developed to the point, Mory says, that, when an error was made, it was Mory and not the buyer who was held culpable.

Upon Nelson's return from his "postgraduate" course in textiles, the company started one of the first textile laboratories in the country, devising its own process for analyzing woolen fabrics to determine the proportions of cotton and shoddy wool. The laboratory technicians then began sampling woolen goods in every merchandise department to find how they comported with catalogue claims. Some products described as "all wool" proved to be as much as three-quarters cotton. Nelson was then instructed to insure the accuracy of catalogue descriptions of all textile goods, wool, silk, and cotton. Mere organization of that task consumed a month, but Loeb had assured Nelson of his and Rosenwald's complete co-operation.

Two particular departments, while the worst from the standpoint of quality and the attitudes of their heads, were not too atypical, Nelson declares. The merchant in the boys' clothing department asked, "What difference does it make? They are a good value. What difference does it make, if the customer doesn't care what the catalogue says?" And the head of the harness department, speaking of horse blankets, inquired, "What difference does it make to the horse? He doesn't know what the catalogue says." But when Nelson's analysis proved that the costliest horse blanket was the worst value and that the one in the medium-price range actually offered most warmth to the horse, the harness merchant was convinced. Similar analyses, presented in Nelson's diplomatic approach, won over other department heads. Some of them even requested him to sit in with them and their buyers when they were placing orders for merchandise.

Laboratory analyses disclosed wide differences in fabrics used by various departments. Percale cloth, for example, included such varied counts as 68 by 72, 64 by 60, 60 by 56, and others. The laboratory then advanced what was a radical suggestion for the time: that the company should adopt certain minimal standards for merchandise below which it would not go. For percale, a minimum count of 64 by 60 was established for all departments. Then standards were set for sheets and sheeting and, subsequently, other items.

Next on the list of laboratory inquiry came the hardness of cutting tools. Lawn-mowers, for example, contained knives of poor-quality steel, since they were not being purchased on any definite specification. A testing system was set up to enable the laboratory to determine quickly the quality of the steel used in all cutting tools.

The establishment of a merchandise comparison office in the laboratories to compare goods purchased from other mail-order houses with Sears, Roebuck merchandise facilitated comparison of quality on a competitive basis. One such venture in comparative shopping involved boys' clothing; the results convinced Nelson that "we were way behind the field" in that department. After testing thousands of samples of fabrics, Nelson concluded that the company should sell no boys' clothing made of a fabric testing less than 30 pounds to the inch on a standard textile testing machine. This standard was adopted. About the same time, Nelson was made merchandise manager of the boys' clothing department, which needed complete revamping. In Nelson's words:

> We had a terrible handicap in the tremendous inventories of merchandise which had been bought in '18, '19 and '20, and which we couldn't sell. I had the job of getting rid of that and at the same time building a new department. We didn't even know what we had in the warehouse. I had to bring in the cases and go all through them. There was an inventory in boys' clothing, when I took it over, of more than $400,000 worth of dead stock.

Julius Rosenwald informed Nelson one day around this time that a rival mail-order concern was outmerchandising Sears, Roebuck on boys' clothing, generally doing a better job with a better line. Nelson, feeling he had made considerable progress in overhauling his department, disputed Rosenwald's assertion and asked to be allowed to order everything the rival firm was selling in that line for a close comparison, item by item. Rosenwald consented ("gruffly," says Nelson). Then, Nelson reports:

> I ordered in a sample of everything they had, and I compared it with our own. I called up Mr. Rosenwald and took the lot over to him. The first thing I showed him was a pair of boy's knee pants, in which ours was marked size 12 and theirs was marked size 12. I also took one of our size 8's and showed it to him. Their size 12 was no bigger than our size 8. (And, by the way, that was another thing we did in conjunction with some of the departments—to try to standardize on sizes—to try to get sizes so that they really meant something, because that affected our returns. It was a straight thing to me—dollar basis—that it was no use sending out a size 12 in pants if it was only a size 8 and you got it returned.) When I got through, I showed him the boy's blouse. I showed him a suit. I showed him everything we had. He didn't say a word through the whole showing. It took the better part of an hour and a half to show him all this merchandise, bcause he looked at every piece of it thoroughly. We turned it inside out. I showed him the quality of linings. Again, we had adopted a standard of lining and didn't use cheese-cloth. We used again 64/60 percale as a lining. It cost only a cent or two more than the other, but it made a much better looking garment. When we got through, Mr. Rosenwald looked up at me, smiled, and said, "Don, I have complete confidence in you. You have standard merchandise and I like it very much."[9]

Rosenwald apparently did not, however, care a great deal for the laboratories in general; according to one former executive, he took no interest at all for several years because, as he once stated, he was "not interested in intangibles." It is said that Rosenwald considered the laboratories nonessential to a merchandising organization. The informant adds that he sought on one occasion to have the company arrange a dinner for some government officials and Sears's executives to show the former the company's good intentions and to create good will for the mail-order house. Rosenwald abruptly dismissed the suggestion as one of the intangibles in which he was not interested. It was apparently the influence of Skinner and Loeb that kept the laboratories in business at first; as time went on, these two were supported by various of the buyers to whom Nelson, Mory, and other laboratory employees had "sold" themselves.

How well Mory in particular had sold himself was illustrated even more clearly perhaps at the time of his retirement. Writing to the general merchandise manager to express a "great deal of regret" that Mory was leaving the company at the end of 1919, the head of the drug department with whom Mory had done battle some seven or eight years earlier asserted:

> Personally, to start with I was not very much in accord with Mr. Mory's work, especially inasmuch as it hit me so heavy, but I soon learned he was on the right side and I on the wrong, and today have the highest appreciation of Mr. Mory's service and the information he gives us.
>
> The Drug and Food Laws are nothing to fool with; and we surely want to be right with the Government and with the people on these two important lines of merchandise.

The writer of that letter went on to express the belief that Mory's wide acquaintance with "experts" in government, industry, and education was one of his "best assets" to the company. The drug-department head mentioned many instances in which Mory had obviated the need for expensive and time-consuming tests by telephoning a friend here and there, "headquarters on this particular information," and obtaining the desired information quickly at no cost to Sears, Roebuck. That testimonial was echoed by the grocery-department manager.

While this high regard for Mory and his work was widespread in Sears, Roebuck by (and probably well before) 1919, there had long been far less unanimity of opinion throughout the early years of the laboratories as to exact functions. One school of thought held that the laboratories should train merchandise managers by first teaching them thoroughly the characteristics of the goods they were to handle. The opposing school held that the laboratories should be a career; that they should achieve stability and continuity by retaining qualified personnel; and that their role was so important that they should be considered more than a mere training ground.

The "training ground" opinion appears to have prevailed for a good while; no women were employed until 1919, simply because there was no merchandising position to which they could graduate. The first woman to break that taboo was Elizabeth Weirick, who was summoned from Pratt Institute in Brooklyn, where she was teaching textile and dye chemistry. She was placed in charge of the textile division of the laboratories at Sears (Nelson had moved into merchandising) and eventually became director of the laboratories.

Mory's report on laboratory operations in 1918 listed more than six hundred materials which had been under examination by the laboratories in their eleven years, ranging from "Acid, Muriatric," to "Zinc, Oxide, Ointment of, U.S.P." Speaking in broader terms, Mory wrote:

> Since ... 1911 the demand for more exacting control of quality in commodities generally, and for more painstaking accuracy in the statement of that quality, has grown rapidly within and without. The facilities for going beneath the surface in this matter are more and more becoming a necessity, and the day appears not far off when the distributor who would entirely safeguard his reputation as well as hold the confidence of the consuming public will make free use of such facilities in order that his statements concerning identity of materials and character of performance may always be proved statements of fact.

Mory may have been speaking with professional optimism of the future nation-wide spread of testing laboratories (R. H. Macy and Company did not establish its laboratory until 1927), but Sears, Roebuck heralded its own laboratories loudly in the catalogues of 1919, 1920, and 1921. And the status of the laboratories is shown by the rapid increase in the pay-roll expense of that department, which was $23,230 in 1918 and $44,225 in the following year, and advanced to $50,400 in the peak year of 1920.

In his economy moves during and after the 1920–21 depression, however, Rosenwald appointed a new general merchandise manager, Max Adler, who was strongly antipathetic to the laboratories and discouraged buyers and others from making use of them. The chief of operations, Otto Doering, was also opposed to laboratory control. The laboratory personnel was sharply reduced. The staff dropped from 26 in 1920 to 16 the next year, and to 9 in 1922. The pay roll declined from $50,400 in 1920 to $31,200 in 1921 and to $17,810 the following year.[10]

The next years were dark ones for the laboratories. How much of its woe was due to opposition from above to testing as such, and how much to opposition to the way Dr. Hobbs wished to operate the laboratories, it is impossible at this date to determine. Hobbs had become director in 1920 when Mory resigned, and he insisted that some of his staff must periodically be granted time and facilities for pure research to avoid growing "stale" and losing interest in the more practical phases of their work. Certainly, in his 1922 report on the laboratories, Hobbs firmly advocated the wisdom of such a course. (He also stressed the need for establishment of a home economics department, expansion of physical equipment, and development of mechanical engineering lines, all of which came into being in later years.) In any event, top-level management appears to have been either hostile or indifferent to the laboratories at that time.

One indication of how little the laboratories had to do in the middle twenties may be found in the activities of Elizabeth Weirick, who, after planning to resign, had finally been persuaded by Donald Nelson to continue, with one assistant, in the textile division. She helped plan and decorate the studio of radio station WLS, set up by the company in 1924, and later wrote some programs for the station, a far cry from testing of merchandise.

The economy wave following the 1920–21 depression had swept away the merchandise inspection division in the same fell swoop that decimated the laboratories. Before these two divisions went into eclipse, however, they had, jointly and separately, done much to improve the quality of Sears, Roebuck's merchandise.

One of the many problems engaging the attention of the merchandise inspection division, both in Chicago and in the company's New York office, was that of clothing sizes. There was little assurance in the company's early years that, say, a size 12 from one manufacturer would be of the same size as a product of another source also labeled size 12. Customers buying over the counter in department stores and specialty shops could always hold the garment up to determine size; in the last analysis, it mattered less whether a garment was called size 8 or size 12 so long as the customer could be sure it fitted. Obviously, this buying technique was in no way applicable to mail order; Sears (like, of course, Ward's) had to know that any given size would be correctly labeled and that it would always be the same size, regardless of the source. In this connection the anguished recollections of Robert P. Sniffen, manager of the New York office from its establishment in 1902, are appropriate:

> In the beginning we had no end of trouble with sizes and quality of workmanship. There was no standard of dimension, and every manufacturer had his own ideas of how large or small a size 36, say, should be. . . . We persuaded them to have patterns made for all sizes instead of trying to grade with a single pattern, moving this over and marking their lays accordingly.
>
> It is astonishing to reflect how many manufacturers had but a single pattern, size 36, and guessed at the other sizes by moving the pattern over. Some marked buttonholes by a marker pattern; others simply guessed at where the buttonholes should be. One large-sized buttonhole was used for any sized garment, from a woman's heavy ulster-like coat to a child's coat of but two years. Day after day and season after season we kept after it until we had finally lined up quite a number of manufacturers who were trying to carry out our instructions.[11]

According to Elmer Voorhis, connected with Sears's New York office for forty years, better sizing became available around 1910, even though the decade after that saw a steady improvement as Sears continued to emphasize the theme. In this decade the company measured thousands of school children throughout the country in order to arrive at "average" sizes, and also used army and navy records and findings of hospitals and medical schools to determine accurate sizing. Voorhis asserts that the New York office hired its own pattern-maker to make patterns for sources; even where a source submitted a pattern, the company often had to make corrections upon a live model.

Voorhis says that Sears's insistence on quality merchandise in this period —especially with reference to soft goods procured through New York—led to some talk in the garment trade that the company was too exacting in this respect. That insistence on better quality seems to have stemmed primarily from Chicago, and it made itself felt throughout nearly every merchandise line. A letter written by the head of the clothing department in Chicago in 1918 refers to the emphasis on quality in such a matter-of-fact, casual way as to indicate that the emphasis was widespread in the company and no longer deserving of any comment. The last paragraph of that letter contains the statement, "Everybody is undoubtedly striving to get the very best merchandise obtainable."

The laboratories' tests for quality came less and less to be directed at potentially harmful or dangerous products, after the elimination of patent medicines in 1913, and more and more toward determining the accuracy of buyers' and manufacturers' claims. The laboratories' work in this field— impinging perforce upon that of the merchandise development division —resulted in considerable improvement in the quality of many of the items tested. For example, a machine was developed for testing mantles such as are used on gasoline lamps and lanterns; the objective was primarily to determine whether the mantles the company was selling were of a minimal acceptable quality. The findings of the laboratories enabled manufacturers to improve the mantles by as much as 900 per cent. Similar tests to ascertain the life and quality of wire scratch brushes resulted in an improvement of 600 per cent in that item.[12]

As time went on, the laboratories came to test much of the company's merchandise. New items were often tested before acceptance. Items delivered by manufacturers were spot-checked and tested, a few from each lot. A system was devised whereby the laboratories were able to order goods from the various mail-order plants incognito for further spot-testing. The questions asked by laboratory technicians of items already being carried dealt mainly with whether the goods were as presented in the catalogue, and whether the manufacturer was meeting the specifications established for the item. Questions asked of a new item under consideration included these:

> Is it practical?
> What is the extent of its usefulness?
> Are the claims made for it accurate?
> Will it give satisfaction or grief?

Is it in any way dangerous? If so, what are its limits of safety?
Are the directions to be issued with it clear and adequate?
Is it well constructed?
Can it be improved?

Simply the articulation of such questions represented an advance over earlier purchasing techniques, in which buyers "tested" the merchandise by sight, feel, or performance in the virtually complete absence of controlled conditions, and in which the closest approach to spot-testing after delivery consisted of the volume of goods returned by dissatisfied customers.

It would, however, be erroneous to conclude that there was any dramatic, significant, uniform improvement in quality in every merchandise department in the middle period. Not even the top executives and the zealots in the laboratories could wreak a revolution overnight. Pettigrew declares that during his tenure as inspector of merchandise (with the title of "Assistant to the General Merchandise Manager") from 1917 through 1922 he continued to unearth examples of poor-quality goods in various departments.

His first findings—as late as 1917—confirmed his belief, acquired as catalogue editor, that many errors of fact in descriptions of merchandise were slipping into the catalogue. He found himself compelled to select one or two merchandise departments each season for analysis. Supplied by the advertising department with first proofs of the catalogue pages of those departments, he "ordered" from those departments the goods advertised on the pages involved. Pettigrew and his assistants read the descriptions aloud while the staff and laboratory personnel examined the goods. All questions raised in the inspection were taken up with the appropriate department heads, and corrections made as needed. Pettigrew found the furniture department's quality so poor that he felt forced to agree with some other department heads who maintained that that department was actually a detriment to all others. That inspection system accomplished at least one thing, Pettigrew asserts: "We were assured that at least the copy of the departments we thus treated was as correct as it was possible to make it."

While that general merchandise inspection went on in Chicago, the New York office continued its own extensive inspection of clothing and other soft lines purchased there. One paragraph from Sniffen's previously cited memorandum of 1918 sheds some light on this operation.

> We have inspected in the past two years very nearly six million women's and children's garments at the New York Office. At the same time probably an equal number in the various lines were examined and inspected in Chicago. And a very large number of garments had to be rejected because of inferior workmanship or failure to comply with sample. Manufacturers, however, seem to have little difficulty in disposing of our returned goods.

What is perhaps most important is the fact that up to 1922—and again after 1928 when the inspection division, along with the laboratories, was revived—there was a system of inspection and an effort to obtain better merchandise as well as more accurate catalogue presentation thereof. Final judgments cannot, of course, be made solely upon the basis of effort or intention; but it is significant, in any evaluation of the quality of Sears, Roebuck's merchandise during this period, that both the effort and the intention were strongly present most of the time.

Since goods were seldom bought upon the basis of predetermined specifications, excepting, of course, some of the soft lines purchased through the New York office, quality was determined largely at the point of manufacture and was inseparably linked with price. The comments of the head of the company's men's clothing department in this connection are relevant. Speaking of men's work shirts, he wrote, in 1918:

> One of the most difficult things the buyers in this department had to contend with was the lining up of manufacturers who could get our viewpoint and were willing to make for us furnishing goods such as we wanted. As a rule, merchandise of this kind was bought at a price. To illustrate: there is what is known as the twenty-five-cent seller, the fifty-cent seller, the dollar seller, the dollar and a half seller, etc. To have articles to sell at the commonly accepted prices of the retail store, it is necessary that the buyer purchase at a certain figure, the jobber who sells to him must have an article at a certain figure, and the manufacturer has to make his goods to fit the price and still make his profit, so that the basis of the quality was decided by the ultimate retail selling price.

It must also be remembered that the low-price policy upon which Richard Sears had built his business persisted well into, if not throughout, this period. Sears's preoccupation with low prices, with quality of the goods a secondary consideration, was adequately illustrated by the remark his contemporaries have quoted him as making repeatedly: "If the price is low enough, you can print it on toilet paper, and people will still buy." And since many of the company's buyers had been trained by Sears himself, it is not unreasonable to conclude that, even after his departure from the company, price remained the dominant factor in deciding whether the company would purchase from any given source. This emphasis on low prices, coupled with the facts pointed up in the foregoing quotation from the men's clothing department manager, sometimes drove quality back to a fairly low level.

Just as there was no over-all merchandise pattern in this period, there was likewise no over-all pattern of relations with sources, no well-developed philosophy toward the "outside" manufacturers who supplied the company with merchandise. All the evidence at hand indicates that the buyers in the middle period simply lined up their own sources and exerted pressure to get invoice prices down to the lowest possible level. Most of them appeared to strive to measure up to the definition of a good buyer laid

REORIENTATION OF MERCHANDISING   239

down by Richard Sears in a letter to Asher, dated December 22, 1906, from Vienna:

> Mr. Adler [Max Adler, later general merchandise manager] is the ideal buyer—i.e., nver satisfied he has struck bottom. Skinner must get the managers (all) into the frame of mind—in their manner of merchandising—they can never strike bottom.[13]

The marked emphasis on price led in some cases to rather frequent changes in sources. The company came to deal with thousands of manufacturers. The policy of its buyers generally was simply to find what goods were on the market and to purchase them on a "trading basis" as low as possible. It was inherent in the nature of the system that continuity of sources was sacrificed if need be, and orders transferred from one source to another quoting lower prices.

Some factors tended to work in the opposite direction, however, and to lead toward greater continuity of relations with sources. The problem of clothing sizes, for example, harassed the company for years. Testimony by various executives and buyers in the New York office, which purchased most of the clothing, indicates that, whenever a source was found which could be relied upon to meet the company's specifications on sizes (and on minimal quality, as determined by the laboratories and the merchandise managers), the company sought to establish a close relationship. The manufacturer was rewarded with large orders and was given greater leeway in the rigorousness of inspection accorded his goods. Robert Sniffen indicates the tangible rewards accruing to some manufacturers who went along with the company's demands: "Many of the manufacturers who started to do business with us on a small scale grew very fast, and many of them also grew rich on a modest profit per garment."

By 1920 the New York office was insisting that before a manufacturer could proceed on production of a full order, he first had to submit three garments for inspection. After making any necessary suggestions or changes, the New York buying organization gave the source authority to manufacture the remainder of the order—subject, always, to rejection *in toto* upon inspection following delivery. Voorhis declares there was seldom any real shortage of sources, although on some occasions when a seller's market ruled, as in 1919, the New York office was forced to advertise for sources. Generally, however, manufacturers sought out Sears, Roebuck and submitted samples. The New York office did virtually no designing in the middle period; rather, it simply picked and chose from offerings submitted to it, making alterations as necessary, and sometimes making its own patterns.

The men's clothing department in Chicago, however, participated in design to a greater extent, at least on some selected items. The manager of that department became convinced that a work shirt "quite a little larger in dimensions than that used by the regular trade" would sell in sufficient quantities to justify the cost of the extra material. That larger shirt required from three to three and three-quarters yards more of cloth per dozen shirts than did the "regular" shirts of that kind. In terms of cost, this meant the company was paying around 19 to 30 cents more per dozen shirts. (The price of the cloth at the time ran around 6½ cents per yard.)

The manufacturer's claim that Sears, Roebuck was merely wasting cloth and costing itself money was refuted only when the company polled 100 men who had purchased the shirt in question. Of the 87 replying, 84 specifically pointed to the fuller dimensions as the reason for preferring Sears, Roebuck's work shirt to others. There was apparently substantial agreement with this group; in 1917 the company sold 86,000 dozen such shirts.

Even so it was sometimes necessary for the company to utilize a combination of specification buying (albeit elementary) and materials procurement to get the goods it wanted. "In a great many instances," according to the head of the men's clothing department in this period, the company purchased piece goods from mills, contracted with manufacturers for the cutting, making, and finishing, and specified the exact dimensions for each size garment.

Procurement of merchandise of satisfactory quality at satisfactorily low prices was, obviously, a difficult problem for the company. Sometimes it proved to be impossible. The result of such a situation was often the entrance of Sears, Roebuck into factory ownership, wholly or partially, in the merchandise lines in question. This had been the case in Richard Sears's day; it was also the case during the "Rosenwald era."

The inability to obtain satisfactory merchandise at an agreeable price sometimes arose from the determination of some manufacturers to sell only through normal distribution channels, involving jobbers, on the ground that Sears, Roebuck was a retailer and must purchase through normal retail channels instead of directly from the manufacturer. Addition of the profit margins of the various echelons in that normal scheme of retailing would have raised the price to the company to too high a level.

The determination of some merchants to sell only through jobbers was especially harassing to the New York office, but Robert P. Sniffen pretty well managed by about 1908 to overcome that obstacle. And even Sniffen was compelled for a while to purchase through an Ohio jobber—who happened to be his uncle and was willing to act merely as "agent" for nephew Robert. In areas where this determination of manufacturers could not be overcome, the company was driven to make other arrangements by buying into factories or establishing its own. And some manufacturers, even though not insisting upon doing business through "normal" channels, nevertheless refused to sell to Sears, Roebuck for fear of being boycotted by independent merchants as well as by wholesalers and other enemies of mail-order houses. Even the company's offer of anonymity failed to move some of these manufacturers.

Still another obstacle in the path of the company's purchasing was the existence of certain combines which maintained prices at a higher level than the company was willing to pay—higher, perhaps, than the company *could* have paid without pricing itself out of its market.

The farm-implement manufacturing "combine" was the largest single factor in persuading the company to buy the David Bradley factory to produce its own farm implements (which still carry that trade-mark), according to a speech made by Rosenwald to American troops in France in 1918. In addition to seeking to maintain prices, the farm-implement manufacturers were also apparently insisting upon operating through "normal" distribution channels.[14] Rosenwald asserted in that speech:

> We soon discovered that sources of supply for reliable, high grade farm implements were closed to us. The implement factories of the time were being very rapidly consolidated under the management of a few principal concerns. These concerns were operating through the old channels of business and were our natural competitors. We had either to content ourselves with the inferior merchandise of such small factories, as were too poor to attract the attention, or jump into the game with both feet and manufacture our own goods. Of course we chose the latter. We bought a million dollar implement factory. We chose the longest established and one of the best equipped factories in the United States. Today we are manufacturing perhaps a greater variety of farm implements than any other one factory in the country. Whenever the sales in any department called for more goods than we could buy in the open market or when some special conditions threatened our source of supply, or when we could see ways of making a considerable saving to our customers, we have gone directly into the manufacturing as well as the selling end. . . .
>
> By conducting these factories and controlling our sources of supply, we are in a position not only to assure our customers of more steady service in the face of unsteady market conditions, but also to guarantee uniform high quality of merchandise. And by making one profit cover both manufacture and distribution we save our customers a considerable amount.

The difficulties of procurement through normal channels had led the company to establish its own pants factory in New York around 1907 or 1908, but this was soon disposed of as merchandise from outside sources became more readily available on better terms. And in a report to the president and board of directors of Sears, Roebuck dated June 30, 1908, Secretary Albert Loeb reported that as an officer of the company he was holding in trust securities representing investments of the firm in the following factories which were making goods for the company:

500 shares of American Separator Company, New York
299 shares of Conley Camera Company, Minnesota
375 shares of Hartford Plow Company, Wisconsin
455 preferred and 909 common shares of Hercules Buggy Company, Indiana
1,215 shares of Meriden Fire Arms Company, Illinois

50 shares of Naperville Lounge Company, Illinois
500 shares of Rundle Manufacturing Company, Wisconsin
500 preferred and 1,500 common shares of Wehrle Company, Ohio
7,499 shares of Wilson Saw and Manufacturing Company, Michigan
100 shares of Employer's Teaming Company, West Virginia
375 shares of Binghamton Lounge Company, New York
2,500 shares of Independent Leather and Manufacturing Company, Iowa
910 shares of Parrish-Alford Fence and Machine Company, Indiana
1,000 preferred and 333 common shares of Belding-Hall Company, Michigan
100 shares of Nathan Herzog and Company, Illinois
100 shares of Davis Martin Company, Illinois
100 shares of Davis Stock Food Company, Illinois
200 shares of Crandall Typewriter Company, Illinois

That list apparently included only factories in which the company owned merely a partial interest; it omits, for example, the wholly owned David Bradley farm-implement factory.

In 1909, when Sears, Roebuck began selling automobiles, it owned its own automobile factory, at Harrison and Loomis streets in Chicago. In addition to manufacturing the Sears Motor Buggy (rechristened "The Sears Automobile" in 1910), that plant also produced automobiles for the trade under the name "Lincoln Motor Car Works." After the company discontinued selling automobiles through its catalogue in 1911, the factory manufactured a line of Lincoln trucks for a while in order to consume the parts on hand. The venture was unsuccessful, according to a memorandum by W. M. Tippett, former manager of the vehicle department (it lost some $27,000 in the five years ending 1917), and the factory was sold. As far as is known, the name had no connection with the Lincoln motorcars being produced today.

The 1910 catalogue's full page showing pictures of fifteen of "Our Factories" ("Some of Them We Own Outright, Some of Them We Own in Part and of Others We Control the Product") asserted:

> Our object in controlling these factories is to give our customers the benefit of the lowest possible manufacturing cost with one profit added instead of the usual three or four.
>
> The enormous investments we have made in manufacturing have but one object—to accomplish ECONOMY and QUALITY for our customers on all items where such things can be accomplished to better advantage by ourselves.

It is interesting to note that price preceded quality in the list of the reasons which impelled the company to make investments in manufacturing.

By 1917 Sears, Roebuck had acquired additional factories. In addition to those listed in the 1910 catalogue, it owned, for instance, plants for the production of trunks, tents, gasoline engines, buggies, lumber, and millwork (the latter two being part of the "Modern Homes" department), and a total of ten factories making shoes. It is probable that some of these additional factories were acquired before 1917, even though not necessarily featured in the catalogue earlier.[15] The increased factory ownership at that time was largely a consequence of growing merchandise shortages arising from World War I, according to Donald Nelson. The company was compelled to acquire additional factories in some lines in order to have any assurance of delivery of goods. Rosenwald further stated in his 1918 speech, mentioned earlier:

> Today we either own or operate or take the entire output of a large variety of factories located all over the United States. Among the lines we manufacture

TABLE 25*

FACTORIES WHOLLY AND PARTLY OWNED, 1918

Item	Location
Pianos, organs, talking machines	Louisville, New York City, Chicago
Agricultural implements	Bradley, Illinois
Men's and boys' clothing	Coal City, Illinois
Cameras and phonograph accessories	Rochester, Minnesota
Oil stoves	Kankakee, Illinois
Saws, buggy tops, hardware	Chicago
Ready-cut houses, lumber yard	Cairo, Illinois
Sewing machines, cream separators, bicycle parts	Buffalo, New York
Sash, door, other building materials	Norwood, Ohio
Planing mill	Mansfield, Louisiana
Wire fencing	Knightstown, Indiana
Shoe factories	Littleton, New Hampshire; Springvale, Freeport, and Saco, Maine; Holbrook, Cambridge, Marlboro and Newburyport, Massachusetts
School furniture	Muskegon, Michigan
Chairs	Sheboygan, Wisconsin
Music cabinets, piano benches, stools	Noblesville, Indiana
Buggies	Evansville, Indiana
Gasoline engines	Evansville, Indiana
Library furniture	Rockford, Illinois
General line of furniture	Eau Claire, Wisconsin; Bloomington, Indiana
Pumps, windmills, cider presses	Bluffton, Indiana
Vises, hardware specialties	Rock Island, Illinois
Bathtubs and lavatories	Milwaukee, Wisconsin
Stoves	Newark, Ohio
Musical instruments	Chicago
Paints, varnish, wallpaper	Chicago

* Source: Company records.

are pianos, organs and all kinds of musical instruments, talking machines, cameras, clothing, agricultural implements, stoves and furnaces, tools and hardware supplies, sewing machines, cream separators, wire fencing, all kinds of furniture, gasoline engines, bathtubs and plumbing supplies, harness and saddles, pumps and windmills, paints, varnishes and wallpaper. We have a large factory for making traveling bags and suit cases. Another for making tents and awnings. Another for making wooden packing cases for our shipping department. We have a large printing plant for manufacturing our own catalogs.... We not only own ten shoe factories, but we can tan our own leather. We also tan the leather we use in our harness and saddle factory. We conduct extensive logging camps to get the raw timber from which we make lumber for our ready cut houses and farm buildings. And of course we conduct planing mills and sash and door factories.

A memorandum for President Rosenwald prepared in July, 1918, by a Sears, Roebuck cost accountant listed thirty-three factories "owned and associated" (referring, apparently, to wholly and partially owned) as of that date. This list, the most nearly comprehensive one available, appears in Table 25.

In 1923 the company owned and controlled twenty-six factories and mills, according to an address delivered the following year by a company executive. Since, however, the company had reduced factory ownership when a buyers' market returned in the 1920–21 depression, it is highly probable that the figure of twenty-six mills and factories may have represented a fairly sharp cutback from an earlier and higher point. Articles manufactured in company-owned or company-controlled plants in 1923 included pianos, cameras and talking-machine accessories, sewing machines, cream separators, building material, shoes, varnish, paints, and wallpaper, furniture, agricultural implements, oil and gas stoves, ranges, tools (carpenters, mechanics, and blacksmiths), musical instruments, horse buggies, woodworking machines, wire fencing, safes, gasoline engines, carriage and wagon wheels, automobile bodies and plumbing goods, bathtubs, sinks, laundry tubs, and other items. Between 1913 and 1923 these factories supplied Sears, Roebuck with some $150,000,000 worth of merchandise,[16] or 8.8 per cent of net sales for the decade (assuming $150,000,000 represented the retail value).

In its participation in factory ownership, the company continued to hew closely to the line laid down by Richard Sears: to enter factory ownership only when compelled to and also to restrict its interest to 50 per cent or less wherever feasible. The firm was eager to do as little of its own manufacturing as reasonably possible. It sought instead to "get its foot in the door" in order to insure a supply sufficient for its own needs and to control quality (apparently a secondary consideration for many years) but preferred that the factory sell some of its output to other concerns in order to insure that it would operate on a competitive, economical basis. This was not, however, always possible. Sometimes the company needed the entire output of a factory it owned in whole or in part; and sometimes it had to own factories outright even though it might in turn sell some of the output to others.

CHAPTER XV

Changes in Catalogue Selling

"THE Modern Way" spelled out by Sears's copywriters for Sears's customers opened the 1915 fall catalogue in an appeal less blatant than the copy of a decade earlier but no less eager to exalt the company's virtues:

You may drive to town to get the price of wheat, or use the telephone—the MODERN way.

You may write a letter to accept a price for a hundred acres of land and find the offer withdrawn before your letter arrives, or wire your acceptance and clinch the sale at once—the MODERN way.

You may depend on hand power and find the day too short to do your work, or get a gasoline engine, do your work better and have time to spare—the MODERN way.

You may GO to an average store, spend valuable time and select from a limited stock at retail prices, or have our Big Store of World Wide Stocks at Economy Prices COME to you in this catalog the Modern Way.

No matter where you live, rain or shine, you can with this catalog do your shopping from your easy chair. Consult its pages as your needs arise and you will experience the comfort and economy in buying that have made this Big Store the supply house of so many million homes—Buy the MODERN way.

That was a change from the days of the Customers' Profit-sharing Premium Plan and from editorials denouncing combines and trusts and skilfully knifing independent merchants with dulcet, double-edged words.

The cover of the 1915 big book reflected a similar change. The globe, with the screaming caption, "The Largest Supply House on Earth—Our Trade Reaches around the World," had given way to the Goddess of Justice holding a pair of scales in her hand and surmounting a picture of the Sears, Roebuck plant. The only copy on the cover, outside the company's name, appears at the top: "Originators of the guarantee that stands the test in the scales of justice."

Those two changes—the cover and the message to the company's patrons—were fairly typical of the steady change in sales-promotion techniques between 1908 and 1925. The emphasis in this period, aided from 1911 on by the laboratories' findings, was generally on "respectability" in regard to goods stocked and to sales promotion and on more factual advertising in the catalogues and other mediums employed. Advertising copy was falling in line with rising standards of quality throughout the country. It was reflecting the company's emerging status as a solid merchandising organization instead of a spectacular promotion scheme, and it was going even beyond such standards as those imposed by the Pure Food and Drug Act. Sales promotion in this period centered largely on "truth in advertising," increased catalogue circulation (including, of course, the addition of special catalogues and circulars but without any such promotions as "Iowa-ization"), and the inauguration and extension of instalment selling. (One of the few sales-promotion devices which persisted well into the middle period was the "2-4-6-8-cent" department. Augmented by the addition of a line priced at 12 cents, this order-starting section continued for several years to hold the opening position in the general catalogue.)[1]

Up to around 1908, catalogue copy often ran the risk of impairing the company's reputation and good will, even in that age of *caveat emptor*. Flamboyant exaggerations such as "the best in the world," "lasts forever," and similar exuberances sometimes oversold the goods, with subsequent returns and customer dissatisfaction. Phrases like "all wool" meant almost literally nothing. Catalogue descriptions had dealt largely in generalities; an item would be "guaranteed," in whole and then by each component part.

One of the first major steps in the "cleanup" of Sears, Roebuck's advertising came in connection with catalogue descriptions of furs. J. F. Skinner issued instructions that catalogue copy on this line was thenceforth to contain not only the usual trade-names (such euphemisms as "Baltic Seal" and "Electric Seal") but also the fact that most furs marketed under such various glamorous names were dyed rabbit or something similar. Many of the merchandise managers, buyers, and other executives protested that such brutally honest nomenclature would bite drastically into fur sales and might even have adverse effects upon sales in other departments. Those Cassandras were confounded. Sales mounted, and, whether or not the point was soundly based, Skinner and Rosenwald were in position to claim that the public was showing its appreciation of this honest presentation in advertising.

How much appreciation the public might have displayed for such "reform" is of course moot, but the public at large, the advertising business itself, and many newspapers and magazines were clamoring for more truthful advertising. This widespread clamor for truth in advertising had been a factor in the passage of the Pure Food and Drug Act of 1906, and the outcry continued even after that legislative victory. In 1911 the advertising magazine *Printers' Ink* promulgated a "model statute," making it a misdemeanor for any advertisement to contain "any assertion, representation or statement of fact which is untrue, deceptive or misleading." The next year saw the slogan, "Truth in Advertising," widely adopted and approved by local advertising clubs and similar groups. Prosecutions were few and far between even in the twenty-four states which passed *Printers' Ink*'s model statute and in the fourteen states enacting similar measures, but the very passage of such legislation indicated some quickening of the public consciousness and conscience in this sphere.[2]

I. S. Rosenfels, then advertising manager of Sears, Roebuck, summed up the company's advance along this line in a memorandum to Rosenwald in 1918. Speaking of the time he joined the company in 1906, Rosenfels wrote:

> Old ideas of mail order advertising were getting into bad company. The spectacular and sensational business-getting methods of [Richard] Sears were being copied by a horde of fakers who had heard of his quick success. Needless to say, this class of competitors had no vision of future business, but merely looked for a quick profit and a quicker getaway. It was time to change, and change we did, though some of the details resembled surgical operations. Telling the truth both in picture and description became the hobby of the advertising department, and the pursuit of truth, it may be remarked, has all the earmarks of the ideal hobby.... It is a job that can never be complete, and we are still at it.

It is, of course, necessary to discount to some extent the natural ebullience of a man who headed Sears, Roebuck's advertising department; his enthusiasm may have led him to overemphasize the degree of improvement manifested by 1918. Even so, Rosenfels' statement would indicate a conviction that Rosenwald himself felt strongly about the subject. Rosenfels went on to say, not strictly accurately:

> It is worth mentioning that the integrity of the mail order catalog was established some years before any organized efforts had been made for better and more truthful advertising. When the catalog started out to reform itself, there was no National Vigilance Committee, no State laws against fraudulent advertising, no National or International Advertising Clubs. We adopted new methods designed not merely to get business, but to keep business, and to build up the reputation of the House with the customer....

One of the earliest and most dramatic episodes in Sears, Roebuck's march toward eminent respectability centered on patent medicines. The episode was in many respects indicative of the whole trend toward "respectability." This department had been one of the most profitable since its inauguration in 1896, and its abuses in catalogue presentation had likewise been perhaps the most flagrant.

Patent medicines of course sold very widely throughout the country around 1900 and for some time thereafter. Sears's chief competitor, Montgomery Ward, was also selling patent medicines but with a difference. Ward's fall and winter 1909–10 catalogue devoted nine pages to drugs and patent medicines, yet the presentation was considerably more restrained than that in the Sears, Roebuck catalogue. Most of the nostrums in Ward's big book were termed "remedies" instead of "cures," and the first sentence in its drug presentation stated, "You get PURE drugs, as they are guaranteed by us under the Food and Drugs Act, June 30, 1906." What followed, however, tended to indicate to some extent the contrary, in spirit if not in letter. "Blood purifiers" were offered as well as an internal catarrh remedy, iron tonic, stomach and dyspepsia remedy, and perhaps the grossest offering, "Pilgrim's Vegetable Prescription—Always Relieves Female Weakness—Falling of the Womb, Inflammation of the Parts, Nervous Depression, Painful Menstruation."

Yet, all in all, Ward's patent medicine presentation appears to have been a cut above Sears, Roebuck's—but not a very considerable cut. Much of the effect of the restraint in Ward's book was achieved by using nearly all text and few illustrations.

A. V. H. Mory, first director of the Sears laboratories, reports that the head of Sears's drug department—"one of the best merchants" he ever knew—presented obstacles to any reform of his department or of its catalogue presentation. Mory was, however, soon able to obtain discontinuance of some of the "worst of the patent medicines." That initial reform was reflected in the 1911 catalogue's presentation of this line. Many of the more flagrant "cures" of a few years earlier had disappeared, and descriptions of those that remained in 1911 were qualified in a way previously unknown. The emphasis was almost invariably less on the curative or healing powers of the medicines than on the mere fact that they had always enjoyed a wide popularity. The introductory page to the patent medicines was captioned: "Our Policy in Regard to Drugs and Remedies," and the text below that heading read, in part:

> We have ... selected from the great array of preparations found on the market a list of proprietary remedies, which from their popularity would appear to be reliable, and which we believe may also be depended on to do as much as is reasonable to expect of such remedies.
> The reputation we have built up for selling good goods and telling the truth about them, together with our desire to protect our customers against the possibility of being disappointed as to the results likely to be obtained has led us to be very conservative in our claims for all of these products. If we have understated the value of certain remedies, our customers will find it out; we would rather have it this way....
> The continued popularity of certain of these remedies, however, gives us sufficient confidence in them to keep them on our list.

That was in the fall of 1911, when the Sears laboratories were only a few months old. It represented a triumph of sorts for the laboratories, but it appeared in the following season to have been a Pyrrhic victory. For in the spring of 1912, patent medicines occupied even more space than in the previous catalogue. The statement of policy was, however, identical with that in the fall 1911 book. The list of drugs included blood purifiers, "pink pills for pale people," countless laxatives, liver and kidney remedies, pile remedies, remedies for stomach complaints, worm-killers, obesity remedies, and aspirin tablets ("The new popular and beneficial remedy for rheumatic and uric acid conditions").

But the fall 1912 catalogue marked the beginning of the end for patent medicines. They occupied one page less than in the previous season, and the offerings were preceded by "A Word concerning the Value of Medicines." The gist of that statement was summed up in its last sentence: "The modern tendency is to put less faith in drugs and more in correct living as the best means of helping nature to resist disease."

Donald Nelson had arrived at the Sears laboratories by that time and had joined forces with Mory. The two worked with a representative of the American Medical Association on a program to drop still more of the patent medicines. Nelson soon concluded that "one of the things we couldn't do in the catalogue was properly to describe the proprietary medicines." The two chemists then suggested to Skinner and Loeb that *all* proprietary medicines be dropped from the merchandise line and that nothing should be carried except those drugs which were in the *United States Pharmacopoeia* or the *National Formulary* or that were approved by the American Medical Association. Skinner and Loeb concurred in that recommendation.

The new policy was announced in the spring 1913 catalogue under the banner line: "Why We Have Discontinued Patent Medicines." That statement opened with a long attack on the evils of patent medicines and charges that most of them contained dangerous drugs likely to injure anyone taking the preparations—an interesting commentary on the company's own previous merchandising policies from 1896 through 1912. The editorial continued:

> Therefore we have decided to restrict our line of drugs and medicines to those officially approved by the leading drug and medical associations of the country as given in three well known publications: namely, the United States Pharmacopoeia, published by authority of the United States Pharmacopoeial Convention; the National Formulary, issued by the American Pharmaceutical Association; and the "New and Non-Official Remedies," accepted by the Council of Pharmacy and Chemistry of the American Medical Association. . . .
> We believe that the publications named above contain practically all that is of value in the field of medicine. From among the preparations that experience shows are of most value, we have selected a few simple remedies that we believe may be of use in the household. In presenting this list we wish to be understood as not urging the purchase of any medicine that is not needed. Again, if any of our customers have need of more than a few simple home remedies, such as those listed, we are frankly of the opinion that they should consult their family physicians rather than waste either time or money experimenting with drugs, whether patent medicines or any other.

The campaign was carried to a slight extreme, according to Nelson. "Vaseline," for example, was discontinued in favor of "petrolatum," the U.S.P. term for the same item ("Vaseline" being a trade-name). People simply did not buy petrolatum in the quantities in which they had bought "Vaseline"; the latter term went back in the big book.

A study of Ward's spring and summer 1914 catalogue, a year after Sears dropped patent medicines, reveals that Ward still listed "Lydia Pinkham" and similar nostrums. The space devoted to this line had, however, shrunk from nine pages in 1909–10 to only six, and Ward's general presentation was on the conservative side. Ward's, unlike Sears, did not seem to have any aversion to the term "patent medicine." Even as late as the fall and winter catalog of 1921–22, one section of its drug department was frankly labeled "Patent Medicines," but the offerings therein were of the reputable variety such as "Lysol," "Sal Hepatica," "Mentholatum," etc.

Dramatic though it was, and therefore somewhat atypical, Sears's discontinuance of patent medicines was nevertheless the hallmark of the intermeshing of its campaign for better-quality goods and the trend toward more conservative sales-promotion methods. That cautious basis and conservative approach were reflected more clearly in the catalogue presentation of merchandise than anywhere else.

The year that witnessed the discontinuation of patent medicines also ushered in a new era in promotion of men's clothing. In 1913 that department adopted the policy of stating in its catalogue descriptions the exact percentage of wool, worsted, or cotton in every garment. In the words of the man who headed the department at the time, "We found that this apparently was a very successful way because our sales immediately began to grow on these garments."

The mounting intensity of the campaign to enhance the accuracy of descriptions of merchandise passed a milestone in 1917. L. H. Crawford, after succeeding Skinner as general merchandise manager upon the latter's death in that year, directed that no statement concerning material of construction or character of service of any merchandise would be approved for catalogue copy unless accompanied by a laboratory report supporting the statement.

In the spring 1919 catalogue a double-page spread captioned "What Our Guarantee Stands On" proclaimed: "Descriptions of Merchandise Must Have the Approval of Our Testing Laboratories" and "Standards of Size, Capacity, Weight and Quality Must Be Fixed and Maintained." The text which followed declared:

> No statement that ordinary inspection cannot verify is made in our catalog until the facts are learned by scientific examination in our laboratories.... Our descriptions, therefore, are not based on guesswork but on the definite and accurate knowledge gained through laboratory test. If our catalog tells you, for instance, that a fabric is all wool, or nearly half wool, or about three-quarters wool, the statement is based on absolute knowledge gained by chemical test....
>
> We have certain standards of quality for mechandise below which we will not go.... We will not handle percales of a lower grade than 68-56, meaning 68 threads to the inch in the warp and 56 threads to the inch in the filling of the finished fabric.... Another example is offered in our boys' clothing.... A sample of every fabric used is tested on a standard breaking strength machine before the clothing is offered in our catalog.

The fall 1919 catalogue contained virtually the same text and layout, except that the guaranty had been moved up to page 1A. In the spring and fall catalogues of 1920 the presentation shrank to one page in each issue. The spring caption remained "What Our Guarantee Stands On," which changed by fall to "Descriptions Based on Laboratory Tests." By 1921, when the sharp bite of the business depression had been felt, the laboratories still received a page in the spring and the same space in the fall, but the text was confined to generalities. That was the laboratories' last catalogue appearance in that form for several years.

Roughly paralleling the rise of the Sears laboratories in point of time was the Federal Trade Commission, established in 1914. The Commission proceeded under Section 5 of the act creating it ("unfair methods of competition are hereby declared unlawful") to determine through its trade-practice conferences and other means just what *was* unfair and built up a long list of what it considered unfair competitive practices. The effect of such rulings on Sears, Roebuck's advertising (pre-eminently its catalogue presentation) has been twofold in nature: first, by publishing such lists of unfair practices, to enable and encourage the company to avoid them; and, second, to compel the company to cease and desist from such practices whenever indulged in. One clinching reason for adherence to FTC regulations was the fact that the company's mail-order business was (as it still is) almost entirely dependent upon the United States mail. Federal Trade Commission's rulings through the years became incorporated into the company's advertising guide, its best hope for avoiding mistakes.

While much of the Trade Commission's work in this field has been done since 1925 (and thus falls into a later section of this study), its inauguration of trade-practice conferences in 1919 did lead in the years immediately following to considerable clarification of what practices were deemed unfair. In the first of some twenty stipulations and affidavits signed with the Trade Commission in the thirty years beginning in 1918, Sears, Roebuck agreed in that year to cease and desist selling staple goods (such as sugar) below cost "conditional on purchase of other goods above costs and mis-statements of competitors' goods."

The search for accuracy in descriptions led to a closer relationship among catalogue executives, merchandise department heads, and laboratory officials. This, in turn, led gradually to a codification of descriptions allowable. This codification crystallized in the advertising guide, although that set of rules and regulations was long aborning by that particular name.

As early as 1908 Catalogue Editor William Pettigrew compiled a ten- or twelve-page booklet called *How To Prepare Catalogue Copy*. It was almost entirely a technical treatise, touching upon how to measure copy, proofreading symbols, some company rules on capitalization, etc. The next eight years saw little change in content or format of the booklet. In the 1916 edition the caption was the same, the contents were almost identical except for greater detail, and the format was still 3¼ × 6¼ inches. The booklet had grown to thirty-two pages. There was then no annual edition of the booklet; interim changes were handled through inserts, and their contents were included in the printed booklet whenever a new edition happened to be issued.

Through the years, however, decisions were made almost daily on particular cases that arose in cataloguing. Definitions and descriptive terms were worked out, and copywriters were instructed to adhere to the decisions, which gradually came to be incorporated in the advertising guide. To take just one example, the 1926 advertising guide discussed the much-abused phrase, "Factory to user." The term, with its connotations of elimination of other middlemen and rapid shipment to the customer, had grown up in the earlier period; by the middle twenties it had become imperative to circumscribe its use and to clarify the areas of its applicability.

Other editions listed the company's own trade-marks, as well as other marks which were not to be used. It also dawned on the catalogue-makers that everything appearing in the catalogue was nationally advertised in the fullest sense of the term; that phrase, theretofore applied to products bearing "outside" manufacturers' trade-names, was ordered dropped from the catalogue, since there was no such easy line distinguishing Sears's own nationally advertised trade-names from those of others. The phrase "nationally advertised" gave way to "other well known brands."

As the national vocabulary tended toward simplification, so did the catalogue. Copywriters were instructed, for example, to say "sweat," not "perspiration"; "go to bed," not "retire"; "food," not "nutrition"; "tears," not "lachrimal secretions"; and "men and women" instead of "ladies and gents." Also taboo became phrases such as "lowest prices in America," "world's largest dealer in lawn-mowers," "America's strongest work pants," unless justified by actual fact. The term "our one profit" became permissible only where the company owned the plant which made the item. The word "free" could be employed only when the item in question was, in fact, given without charge and with no tie-in purchase required; this has virtually driven "free" from the catalogue. "Knocking" competitors, even indirectly, has long been eschewed.

Merely "staying out of trouble" and simply seeking never to alienate customers or to impair the good will of the company were, obviously, only the "negative" requirements of catalogue copy. ("Copy," in the lexicon of the company, includes text and illustrations.) The positive requirement, upon which the company's continued profitability rested, was effective selling, for in mail order, advertising and selling were (and are) synonymous. Newspaper and magazine advertisements might serve their purpose if they brought customers into a store. Mail-order catalogues had to do far more; they had to persuade the reader to send an order for goods shown therein.

Low prices and outstanding bargains may have been the primary factors in Sears, Roebuck's selling by mail, but it was the catalogue copy which had to serve as the forceful selling instrument to dramatize those prices and to persuade the readers that they did indeed represent bargains. Copy, layout, and artwork were effective or ineffective in themselves. They could not depend upon the blandishments of dealers, distributors, or salespersons to "close." Catalogue advertisements simply sold goods or they did not; the carefully keyed book provided a strict accounting of success or failure. And that success or failure was almost immediately evident after the appearance of the catalogue. The initial response was usually sufficient to tell the merchandise heads whether to cut back commitments or to secure greater quantities of any given item.

Obviously, then, highly skilled presentation of goods was required in order to sell those goods in satisfactorily large quantities without at the same time running afoul the Federal Trade Commission or in some wise alienating customers. Trial and error through the years gave the catalogue-makers a rich fund of experience in determining what approaches would yield the desired results within the framework of the company's policies.

Catalogue presentation had to be simple and orderly. It had to make buying easy and pleasant. All pertinent information about merchandise—colors, sizes, composition, performance, characteristics, etc.—had to be "spoon fed" to readers in painless but concentrated fashion. Every distracting element had to be removed to focus full attention upon illustrations and text. Type faces had to be compatible and highly legible. Illustrations had to flash their meanings instantly and compellingly. "Trick" layouts were taboo, and short, simple sentences were mandatory. Artwork had, wherever possible, to show the item of merchandise in use; and the user had to make it clear to the reader that the article was both easy and pleasant to use.

Copy had to be keyed to art, even if separated from it. That copy had also to emphasize the strongest selling features of the item—economy, pleasure, fashion, or what-not. In short, catalogue copy had to do everything advertising copy is ever expected to do—and more, for the company ran a risk, as it were, of overwhelming a reader with such an immense array of goods portrayed between the covers of one book. Catalogue copy had to be able to arrest the attention of every reader—or, at any rate, most of them—who might be interested in any given item, to stop the reader as he thumbed through the book, and to rivet his attention on that item.

All that represented, of course, an objective toward which the company is even yet striving. The progress toward that goal was uneven in the middle period, but the direction of the drive seems to have been fairly clear. And, as the cost of space in the catalogue increased with steadily rising circulation and ever higher production costs, the drive gained in momentum.

Space in the big book came in this period to be "sold" rather than merely allocated. Each merchandise department had to "make money" by realizing sufficient margin to cover the cost of the catalogue space it occupied as well as merchandise cost and other expenses of the department. Previous sales records and anticipated sales based upon experience became the chief barometers in this "buying" and "selling" of catalogue space. That space had long since become too valuable to allocate by intuition.

Examples both of the value of space and of the skill the company's catalogue-makers had attained in using it as a selling instrument are abundant. One page of the fall and winter 1918 catalogue, for instance, brought sales of $754,000 of junior coats. And three-quarters of another page in that same book resulted in sales of $525,000 of children's garments. These instances are admittedly atypical; the results were staggering, for 1918 was a boom year. But such results are the stuff merchandising dreams are made on. They serve as a constant spur to emulation.

And even over and above its dramatic merchandise presentations—or, more properly perhaps, as an integral part of such presentations—the Sears catalogue created an enviable status for the company as "the people's friend."

The late Eugene Talmadge, former governor of Georgia, used to tell rural voters that they had only three friends: "God Almighty, Sears, Roebuck, and Eugene Talmadge." The smash-hit musical, *Finian's Rainbow*, which opened in New York in 1947, portrayed the mail-order house of "Shears and Robust" as the fountainhead of all material things good and desirable. Thousands of rural customers have written the company to request, among other things, that Sears, Roebuck select a wife (or husband) for them, that the mail-order house hold their Alaskan gold dust in trust, that the company help pick a name for their newborn child, and that the company advise on manners and morals.

Sears, Roebuck and Company long since intrenched itself in the American mind, idiom, humor, and folklore to an extent certainly unequaled since Paul Bunyan and probably unsurpassed in the commercial history of the nation. Up until 1925—and, for many thousands of customers, even to this day—the company achieved this near-miracle almost solely through its great catalogue. That catalogue, the total distribution of which in the last sixty-odd years numbers many millions, is the only contact many Americans have ever had with Sears, Roebuck. A catalogue usually served a whole family, and frequently several families.

What manner of book is it that wrought this mercantile alchemy? How did any such publication attain such acceptance? What is its status as historian and silent salesman? Just what *is* this catalogue? The answers to these questions are many and various. Many writers have tried their hand at answering. David L. Cohn wrote:

> This is the one fact indispensable to an understanding of this book: the catalog is based not upon hope but upon experience. There is no room in it for

CHANGES IN CATALOGUE SELLING   255

guessing, wishing, or, save occasionally and conservatively, experimenting. It does not attempt to cram down the throats of the public its own ideas of taste or merchandise. The catalog never leads; never crusades. It is based purely upon public acceptance of the goods it offers, and not until the public has clearly signified that it wants a thing does that thing appear in its pages. We know, therefore, that the catalog's pictures of American life are drawn not from the imagination but from the living model. The catalog occupies a unique place in American life. It is more than an instrument of business, although it was designed and is maintained solely as an instrument of business. It has become the best-known book in the United States, a part of American folklore, and, passing strange for a tool of business, it has also become the object of widespread affection. Wherever the traveler goes in the United States, he will find the catalog ... wherever it is found, a curious affection surrounds it, an expression that arises perhaps out of a subconscious longing for an America which is vanishing but which still continues to be exemplified by the catalog.[3]

That is what the catalogue has come to be in its lifetime; that is the totting-up of its accomplishments, the assessment of it as a social phenomenon. But some of what Cohn says might have fallen strangely upon the ears of the men who put that big book together, who allocated every precious inch of its space, who determined how many pages the catalogue would contain, what items would fill those pages, and what words would describe them, for those men had a job to do—a job simple in conception even if staggering in the details of its execution. Their task was to use page space to sell merchandise. Every decision on whether to use an illustration and, if so, of what size, revolved around the book's function as a salesman. Every decision on what text to employ was made on the basis of the effect in pulling orders. Improving ethics of catalogue presentation, improving aesthetic standards, fine-spun institutional homilies to readers—all these hinged on that pivotal and crucial aspect of the catalogue's nature, its very *raison d'être;* to sell goods. If the men who performed all those tasks made history, or recorded it, in the process, that was incidental to their main purpose.

By 1917 the company was annually producing seven main printing jobs: the Chicago, Dallas, and Seattle general catalogues each in the spring and fall editions; the flyers in two editions—January–February and July–August; bargain bulletins running sporadically throughout the year; a grocery catalogue issued bimonthly; approximately a hundred special catalogues mostly composed of bound sections of the general catalogue covering individual lines of merchandise; and a number of special catalogues printed on the better grades of paper for merchandise requiring a type of salesmanship beyond that of the general catalogue style of presentation.

The flyers were launched in 1909 by J. F. Skinner to cover slack periods when the general catalogue was being distributed but had not yet taken effect. The January–February flyer was designed to offset the recurrent slump in sales after the Christmas season, before the spring catalogue was circulated in force. The July–August flyer sought to stimulate sales after the first fine blush faded from the spring book. Skinner called his first such flyer, a midwinter edition, "The White Goods Sale." According to the catalogue editor at that time, it "created a sensation among competitors and boosted business materially."

The bargain bulletins were inaugurated in 1914 as a medium to market clearance merchandise. They listed left-over stocks from mail-order departments, occasional special bargains procured to "sweeten" the offering, and experimental offerings to test sales from new merchandise. The bargain bulletins were included in shipments leaving the Chicago plant (thus reaching the "livest" customers); eventually the bulletins were distributed in the shipments of all branch plants as well.

This group of printing jobs continued substantially unchanged until 1920, when the Philadelphia mail-order plant was opened, which added two more general catalogues annually as well as the lesser productions. From then on the circulation of the general catalogues increased and reached a new peak in 1926 when catalogues were circulated for the new Kansas City and Atlanta plants. (Between 1926 and 1929 the Memphis, Los Angeles, Minneapolis, and Boston plants were opened, which added that many more printing jobs to the roster.)

The necessity for producing catalogues in great quantity within a short time span had led Sears, Roebuck in 1903 to terminate its contract with W. B. Conkey and to set up its own printing plant in Chicago. This company-owned plant followed the firm in its move to the new, forty-acre home in 1906. That arrangement continued until after World War I, when the company decided to make a change in its printing arrangements.

Julius Rosenwald, struggling with the problems that developed out of the 1920–21 depression, was casting about to cut expenses at every opportunity. The possibility of eliminating the overhead expenses of the firm's own printing establishment was appealing. Despite the growth in catalogue circulation and the number of special books produced each year, there were inevitably slack periods for a press catering only to Sears, Roebuck's demands. Accordingly, the company abandoned manufacturing its own catalogues in 1923 when a contract was negotiated with John F. Cuneo of Chicago's "Cuneo Press."

Cuneo manufactured the bulk of Sears's catalogues for the next few years, although the W. F. Hall Printing Company also produced a substantial part of the mail-order firm's catalogue volume. Since 1928 the catalogues have been printed and bound mainly by the R. R. Donnelley and Sons Company. Hall continues to share the task. Donnelley's facilities proved adequate to handle not only Sears, Roebuck's "big book," but Montgomery Ward's as well.

Wherever the printing contract happened to reside at any given time, however, the company encountered an endless series of technical difficulties in the mammoth task of turning out millions of catalogues at a necessarily tremendous rate of speed. Most of these difficulties plagued other large contractors, and printers in general, and the solutions to some of them are not even yet in sight. But the progress made toward solving many of them is attributable in considerable measure to the research activities of Sears, Roebuck, the amount of time and money the company was willing and able to spend in this connection, and its general willingness to pass its findings on to all comers.

One reason for the problems was the simple fact that the company's own standards of quality improved greatly during this period. As the company demanded ever higher quality in printing of its big book and as it began to use increasingly complicated methods of printing and color reproduction, conditions which had earlier been acceptable took on the proportions of serious problems.

In the first years of its existence, the company needed catalogues so urgently that it would take almost anything the printers delivered—just as its customers would take anything they were sent in the nature of catalogues. But the cheap paper, easily smeared ink, blurred engravings, skipped pages, and similar shortcomings of the earlier era connoted a "cheapness" and a fly-by-night nature which the company was determined to slough off. During the years of great expansion the big book made the transition from the "penny dreadful" appearance to a much more "respectable" production.

Paper always presented a problem. In Richard Sears's day the problem was simply that increased weight of the paper due to humidity or any other reason might throw the book into a higher postal rate classification and thus add many thousands of dollars to the firm's mailing bill. Weighing rolls of paper at the mills proved of no value, as the moisture content could change greatly by the time a roll was put on the press. In addition to the weight aspect, breakage of paper under tension of high-speed presses was another difficulty. Breaks had to be analyzed, classified, and reported to the mills.[4] Opacity of paper was another quality which concerned the company's catalogue men. Other characteristics of paper which came to engage the firm's attention included glare, "take-off," ink and oil receptivity, brightness, machine speed, and others. The introduction of color printing on a large scale presented problems of its own with particular reference to paper. Ink presented comparable problems, as did engravings and binding. Sears, Roebuck's research men tackled them all; in the process of overcoming these obstacles, they made some solid contributions to development of the graphic arts.

The company's relations with its paper sources became one of give and take. The firm would submit suggestions to sources on how to overcome particular difficulties, or the source might come up with a new development of its own. In either event Sears, Roebuck was apparently always willing to spend time and money in testing the new product. Its critique which followed the testing was always, in the words of one of the research directors, "cold-blooded" but helpful. Interestingly enough, the results of many of the experiments were useful and profitable to outsiders even though of little or no value to the company. In connection with its research on paper, Sears, Roebuck joined the Institute of Paper Chemistry in order to get the Institute's aid in developing lightweight papers. The company also sent its research men to many sources to work with manufacturers on improvements. One policy which emerged from all its work on and with paper was that governing writing of specifications. In the company's words:

> We endeavor to write specifications giving each paper mill exact knowledge as to how the paper mill will be used and what its requirements are. These specifications cover as many as two dozen different requirements; however, they are usually simplified to take care of those qualities which are related to trouble in printing and catalog manufacture. We make certain that every specification is thoroughly understood by the paper manufacturer, going to the mill when necessary.

The men's and women's wearing apparel, shoes, and corsets, even prior to 1910, began to lead the procession in the use of the better and heavier grades of paper for a better presentation of those lines, usually calendered paper of chemical wood stock in a 45-pound weight. Some of the shoes in 1910 were shown in four-color printing on 60-pound enamel paper; in the same catalogue the carpets were shown in four colors on 70-pound enamel stock. (In the late 1920's it became possible to use the lighter-weight, supercalendered papers even for color work by improved printing methods.) In the early 1920's one-color rotogravure printing was used in the catalogue and developed into extensive use. (By 1929 two-color rotogravure pages appeared; the fall catalogue of that year had a number of stove pages printed on one side in two-color rotogravure and in three colors on the other side.)

There was also a gradual improvement in the methods of reproducing merchandise in the catalogue by means of illustrations. Woodcuts were used exclusively in the early catalogues in the 1890's, but by the fall of 1900 about 25 per cent of the illustrations were in halftones and zinc etchings made from pen-and-ink drawings. Watches and jewelry lines used woodcuts exclusively up until recent years. They were practical for all types of mechanical merchandise and many types of wearing apparel, dry goods, and furniture. The pen-and-ink drawings were used on merchandise with open spacing or where detail was unessential, as in shirts, work clothing, and harness items. The halftones, naturally, were used almost entirely at first by the wearing-apparel lines.

In the fall 1905 catalogue the woodcuts constituted about 60 per cent of the catalogue illustrations; halftones were used for practically all the wearing apparel, clothing, shoes, and haberdashery. A few items even in these lines were, however, reproduced from pen-and-ink sketches, these being items where detail was not so important in sales appeal. While the fall 1910 catalogues had a still lower percentage of woodcuts, it was not so much different from the 1905 book. But in the fall 1915 catalogue the percentage of woodcuts was less than 50. By that time some of the silverware was being shown in halftones, as was practically all the wearing apparel. The fall 1920 catalogue revealed a further swing to halftones, but still the mechanical lines, along with the watches and jewelry, utilized woodcuts. (By 1929 the woodcuts had dropped to a slim 25 per cent, all the furniture and even the guns being shown in halftones.)

The reason for the long reign of woodcuts for catalogue illustrations and the consequent postponement of the halftone era for many of the merchandise departments was the fact that the early black-and-white halftones were often too flat unless printed on high-grade enamel paper with heavy-bodied proofing ink. The web press printing resulted in smear and offset. Improvements in photographing technique, plates, and presswork, however, along with the use of rotogravure printing, eventually overcame these objections.

Presbrey's summary of some of the contributions of mail-order techniques to advertising in general apply forcefully to Sears, Roebuck and Company:

> Included in the benefits that have accrued from the mail-order business are several of importance in the development of advertising technique. In the need for illustrations that picture the fine-line detail of a product and present a true idea of it, the mail-order houses developed art methods that were adopted by advertisers in general, to the great advantage of advertising as a whole. It was in the mail-order catalogs also that color work was first done with success. The discovery that four pages in color would sell as much of the same goods as twelve pages in black and white was made by the mail-order houses. The relative attention value of different colors was determined by them in a series of experiments. They were the first to make a success of process color work, and in this and other phases of printing did laborious and expensive experimenting valuable to all periodical publications. In type and in economical arrangement catalog houses made further important contributions to advertising technique, their activities extending even to type designing. Altogether, in the mechanics of advertising the mail-order catalog has been a toiler whose step-by-step improvement in technique has been a constant guide for other advertisers.[5]

When Sears, Roebuck took up the subject of inks in 1916, it found almost nothing published which was of any material help. The company's research staff learned inks largely by making its own. One of those men asserts, "The printing ink industry was the last group in the Graphic Arts to reveal their 'secrets' and to see the need for technical development and pure research."

The campaign to develop better inks suitable for particular uses faced two chief difficulties. First, as already pointed out, ink manufacturers were playing their cards very close to their chests. And, second, many pressroom foremen reputedly had been given stock in an ink company or were receiving a "commission" with or without the knowledge of their employers. The company had to break the power of the foremen to specify inks; that power was broken, partly through the use of inks developed by the company. Even after that, however, officers of Sears, Roebuck were approached from time to time (presumably by ink manufacturers and/or printers) with the suggestion that pressure be brought on the research staff to specify some particular make of ink. The company refused to exert such pressure, however, and the catalogue production men continued to specify quality and price rather than make. To quote from a report by the research group:

It pays to use good ink, but there is one best quality for any given job. We have made a standing offer to printers, who occasionally feel we have specified too low a price, to pay more if they can show us an improvement in advertising appeal or in coverage equal to the additional expenditure. We welcome these tests.

Difficulties with binding dated from the earliest Sears catalogues. This problem continued even during the period when the company ran its own printing plant. Many catalogues were found to be so poorly bound that the pages would drop out. A sampling of every barrel of glue and glycerine on one occasion disclosed that some sources were supplying bone glue instead of the hide glue specified. Others were diluting the glycerine. The company began to experiment with a considerable number of binding mixes and developed a sticky mixture of resin and mineral oil to shorten the setting time of the binding glue mixture. A machine was developed to test binding quality by measuring the force required to pull pages out of the catalogue.

Another aspect of binding which was a source of continual unhappiness was the insertion of color inserts in the catalogue. They were placed by hand between or within black-and-white sections. The errors in insertion were so great, even after the company abandoned its own printing, that the company had to set up a binding inspection system; it was discovered at one time that only 25 per cent of the catalogues contained no serious defects. Missing and misplaced pages were the most serious errors, but in the course of years the number of missing pages was gradually reduced to a fraction of 1 per cent. The company's ambition remained (as it still does) "to streamline binding operations—gathering, binding, trimming, and wrapping in a continuous process."

Sears, Roebuck also experimented with plastic printing plates molded from patterns and type forms, thinking the time-saving might make the plastic plates preferable to electros. This venture did not prove successful.

Four "instruments" were forged within the company to keep pace with the many technical developments in catalogue production: (1) the "lineup" of the catalogue, to lay out and allocate all space before any copy was written or engravings made; (2) the logical corollary of the lineup, the Service Division, responsible for routing of all catalogue pages in every stage of production, for maintaining a running picture of the whereabouts of each page at every moment, and for maintaining schedules; (3) the organization charged with over-all execution of all the foregoing and all other details incident to catalogue production—the office of the advertising manager; and (4) the advertising guide, listing all the "do's" and "don'ts" of catalogue copy, as well as the various "how to's." All four instruments were organic in nature; the catalogue could not develop far without any one of them, and each of them in its turn was a growing, developing entity.

The lineup was mothered by necessity. Catalogue production was ill-planned, somewhat haphazard, and invariably frenzied during the period up to around 1908. Actual makeup of each page was accomplished pretty much at the last minute by a series of operations and maneuvers embracing cutting and pasting proofs, mortising of cuts, and "making do." Around 1908, however, the advertising manager created the lineup, which was possibly the greatest boon to catalogue production up to that time. Under the lineup the entire framework of the catalogue was shown in charts before any copy was submitted. The lineup determined, before submission of any layouts, artwork, or copy, the exact number of each department's pages, the location or position of those pages in the book, the location of special kinds of paper and of color printing, and the schedule dates for the layouts, artwork, copy, finished plates, and presswork.

The Service Division, initiated by a former railroad man skilled in routing, was to catalogue production what the schedule system was to shipping. The Service Division not only kept tab on just where every page of the catalogue was, hour by hour; it also saw that each page was where it *should* have been at the appointed hour. It utilized an elaborate control board with a multitude of oblong holes to hold cardboard tickets recording each specific operation on each page of the catalogue. The layout of each catalogue page, in all its many stages, was routed from point to point by the Service Division; different colored cards were flashed in the appropriate niche to record progress. And, just as a "Monday-colored" shipping label would stand out in the shipping department on Tuesday like a sore thumb, so would the "wrong" colored card instantly indicate that a catalogue page was behind schedule. It was the Service Division's responsibility to see that pages did not get behind schedule and to take fast remedial action when one did. A telephone call to the Service Division could ascertain in a moment the exact location of any page.

The third instrument—the organization responsible for production of the big book—grew also out of necessity and logical efforts toward systematization, but it is essentially a development of a later period. The advertising department manager, as he was then called, had charge of general copy preparation and editing, but most of the copywriting was done in the merchandise departments by copywriters on the pay rolls of such departments. The advertising manager supervised the artwork, editing, and typography, paper and printing-supply buying, and the production of the catalogue. But he was only a consultant on sales. The sales managers were the merchandise department heads.

Since advertising in mail order was (and is) equivalent to selling in retail stores, it represented in Sears a multimillion dollar investment to be handled with economy. Before any advertising money was spent, therefore, budgets were prepared in line with estimated sales. Such budgets were prepared seasonally, and sanction of the budget was secured well in advance of the season. The volume of mail-order advertising was determined by a review of past experience together with analysis of sales potentialities of the season under consideration. Expense was thus keyed to planned results.

Total mail-order advertising costs could be lowered in two ways: (1) lower unit cost per book and (2) reduced circulation. If the choice was (1), then the number of pages and quality of printing, that is, rotogravure, four-color, etc., offered an opportunity to reduce cost; if (2) were the preference, then classes of customers, that is, "first preferred," "second preferred," "previously preferred," would furnish the answer. (The customer classification was based on volume and recency of purchases.) Obviously, advertising costs could be increased through the same two means. No mail-order advertising budget could be formulated, therefore, without first determining the type of printing and breadth of circulation.

Circulation figures of the general catalogue, so laboriously produced, rose from a shade less than three million in the spring of 1908 to more than seven million in 1925, by which time four branch mail-order plants had been opened. The growth was relatively steady and usually showed a slight increase from year to year, with several instances of "backsliding," as indicated in Table 26.

These figures applied, as indicated, only to the general catalogue(s). To distribute this vast number of catalogues as rapidly as possible after they rolled from the presses, a complex system was evolved. Strategically sited shipping points throughout the country were utilized. They were selected on the basis of their accessibility by freight from Chicago, passenger-depot facilities, mail service to each of the post offices to be served from them, and economy in distribution cost, which included the freight from Chicago and the rate of postage from the distribution point.

The shortest and fastest routings were selected. Each shipment was traced and was expedited from the printers' docks to the distributing points, to avoid delay en route. A letter of instructions, including a list showing the number of catalogues for each post office, was sent to distributing-point postmasters and Railway Mail Service officials several days prior to shipment from Chicago. Also, telegrams were sent to them when the catalogues were actually shipped, giving the forwarding date, scheduled arrival time, and the car number. To avoid delays in unloading the books and dispatching them through the mail, field inspectors from the control stores visited the distributing points while distribution was going on.

Tests were made on each general catalogue distribution to determine the speed of mailing. The post offices included in these tests were picked at random. The customers involved represented about 2 per cent of the pre-

TABLE 26*

GENERAL CATALOGUE CIRCULATION, 1908-25

Season	Total Circulation	Season	Total Circulation
1908 Spring	2,942,622	1917 Spring	4,792,186
Fall	3,639,920	Fall	4,799,315
1909 Spring	1,928,872	1918 Spring	4,823,112
Fall	2,486,405	Fall	4,646,671
1910 Spring	2,246,773	1919 Spring	4,924,743
Fall	2,387,328	Fall	4,837,172
1911 Spring	2,609,265	1920 Spring	4,838,939
Fall	2,768,594	Fall	5,088,464
1912 Spring	2,814,003	1921 Spring	5,284,787
Fall	2,770,283	Fall	5,365,262
1913 Spring	3,346,048	1922 Spring	5,033,992
Fall	2,767,078	Fall	4,707,716
1914 Spring	4,080,530	1923 Spring	6,393,396
Fall	4,052,068	Fall	6,190,518
1915 Spring	4,484,036	1924 Spring	6,429,834
Fall	4,250,844	Fall	6,194,204
1916 Spring	4,786,504	1925 Spring	7,209,976
Fall	4,686,739	Fall	6,091,002

* Source: Company records.

ferred list. There is ample evidence that this system was in existence by 1917. Sears's general advertising manager, I. S. Rosenfels, wrote in that year:

Under the improved system of distribution made possible by the parcel post, these catalogues are shipped by freight to about seventy-five warehouses favorably located throughout the country. Each day typewritten address labels, representing the day's requirements from customers, properly assembled by districts, are sent by first-class mail to each distributing center. The warehouseman affixes the labels with the proper postage stamps for first, second, or third zone. Rarely does a catalog travel by mail a greater distance than 300 miles, and generally not more than 150 miles. The label may travel across the continent before being pasted on the wrapper, but it travels by first-class mail on the fastest trains. This rapid and efficient delivery of catalogues is cited merely as an instance of the economy possible in large operations.[6]

CHAPTER XVI

Selling on Instalments

WHILE the catalogue became progressively more conservative (and more accurate) in promoting sales for the great mail-order house, the company became involved in experiments with what was to prove a powerful "new" promotional instrument—instalment selling. Richard Sears had early experimented with various methods of payment ranging from fixed amounts or percentages of cash with orders (and the remainder C.O.D.) to "Send No Money." The catalogue often pointed out that the company had no credit terms; in 1899 it asserted: "We sell for cash, having no bad debts ... no expense for collections, we can sell at a far lower margin of profit than any other dealer and when you buy from us you are not helping to pay for all such useless expense." The "Send No Money" promotion actually represented no great change in the company's selling terms; rather, it was just a more effective phrasing of the offer to ship goods C.O.D. After this promotion was discontinued in 1902, the company's only terms for many years were cash in full with the order. In fact, subsequent catalogues went out of their way to claim that those who purchased on credit paid from 25 to 50 per cent more than when they bought for cash. Credit purchases were denounced, and the company's policy of selling for cash was extolled as a great money-saver for the public.

The years from 1902, with the exception of 1908, were highly prosperous ones for the firm, and there seemed little need for employing any system of selling on credit. The huge amount of returned merchandise engendered by the "Send No Money" campaign was still fresh enough in the minds of the company's executives to militate against any revival of a plan of that nature. It was obvious that the additional expense involved in selling on credit terms would either have to be absorbed in cash sales or else paid for by the credit customers. The company had no desire to absorb such costs and feared that the addition of any extra charge for credit would create sales resistance.

Despite the company's efforts to discourage credit transactions, requests to purchase goods on credit continued to come in. Sears, Roebuck halfheartedly sought to by-pass such requests by offering durable goods (such as pianos, organs, and cream separators) on thirty-day free trial. Customers were invited to deposit the price of the merchandise with a responsible bank and mail the company the certificate of deposit with their orders. If no objection were registered by the customer within thirty days, the company would draw on the bank for the amount deposited. Obviously, this was not quite what customers requesting credit had in mind. Grain farmers continued to ask to be allowed to pay for their goods in one lump sum after the harvest, while dairy and poultry and other farmers with more nearly steady monthly incomes wanted to pay by the month.[1]

What the company's customers were requesting represented no recent innovation in selling. Furniture had been sold on instalment terms since shortly after 1800, as had clocks (especially in New England).[2] Reavis Cox writes:

> Pianos and organs seem to have reached a considerable volume of sales on instalments by 1845. . . . By 1850 the Singer Sewing Machine Company . . . had begun to sell its machines to consumers through agents on instalments. Its competitors soon followed suit. When factory-made clothing developed after the Civil War, instalment selling soon came in to help customers take the product. . . . Book publishers broke into the field with house-to-house canvassers as early as 1871, and they may have sold on instalments to some extent before the Civil War. In the early 1880's instalment sales of watches and jewelry had become common.
> As the population spread westward, instalment buying went with it.[3]

Household goods came rapidly to be sold upon instalment terms, and by 1900 instalment selling was being used for a wide variety of goods; and it had been drafted into lines of trade with consumers of relatively low income. Instalment selling of automobiles began around 1910, and advertisements to this effect appeared in New York newspapers as early as 1914.[4]

Late in 1910 the company decided that, in view of the customers' demands for credit, and the prevalence of instalment selling throughout the country, it would be unwise to refuse terms any longer. Credit terms were therefore granted on certain heavy lines to customers of "unquestionable responsibility." A three-man committee (consisting of Max Adler, Otto Doering, and John Higgins) was named to decide on the terms to be offered. During 1910 the company added to a beginning balance of $154,957[5] debits amounting to $1,684,942. The statement of accounts, taken from a 1911 yearbook, is shown in the accompanying tabulation.

Accounts	Opened	Closed
C.O.D.	$ 661,056	$ 667,578
Deferred payment	310,090	272,466
Credit	319,577	318,855
Short remittances	237,556	227,371
Even exchange	156,663	143,340
Total	$1,684,942	$1,629,610

The 1911 catalogues made no mention of credit. Instead the company merely offered a thirty-day trial period on pianos provided the order was accompanied by a bank letter recommending that the company extend credit. During that same year it was found that many of the company's instalment accounts, the result of unsolicited requests for credit, were not paying out as agreed. A merchants' legal service was then engaged to handle bad accounts up to the time they were advanced to attorney cases.

Early in 1912 the company discovered that some individuals and agencies were buying cream separators and similar durable goods for cash and reselling them on exorbitant credit terms. In an effort to discourage this practice, and to promote Sears's separators, the company stated in its catalogue that year:

> If offered time or easy payment terms by an agent, do not accept his offer no matter how liberal it may seem without first writing us. We can prove to you that it is to your interest to buy and use our Economy Cream Separator. No agent can make better prices or more liberal terms than we can. We want your cream separator order and will meet or beat any and all competition.

The response to that statement was an increased demand for credit on the separator as well as on other items. The company acceded to this pressure in its spring 1913 catalogue. The piano pages of that book proclaimed, "If you do not wish to pay cash for your piano, write us for special terms. . . . Quality pianos sold on Easy Monthly Payments." Similar terms were advertised on farm implements, cream separators, gas engines, vehicles, and encyclopedias in special catalogues and circulars. The fall catalogue of that year advertised a $5.00 monthly payment on pianos, regardless of price. No deposit was required, no carrying charge was levied, and from three to five years was allowed to complete payment. The effect was immediately noticeable. Piano sales increased from $340,000 in 1912 to $846,000 in 1913 and to $1,089,000 in 1914.

In the latter year the company began receiving requests from mercantile establishments for terms on typewriters; these orders were accepted on a thirty-day payment basis. No definite changes were made in the credit policy in 1915 and 1916, but there appears to have been laxity ("promiscuity" in the company's own word) in granting credit terms. The farm-implement accounts accepted in 1915, for instance, proved of very poor quality. This was due at least in part to the use of "outside" address lists to solicit business, because the firm planned for a large increase in sales. The general merchandise office had felt the increased volume would tend to reduce uncollectible losses. The special catalogues and circulars which mentioned deferred and monthly payments brought in many inquiries for terms on buggies, cream separators, engines, sewing machines, the *Encyclopaedia Britannica*, school furniture, and miscellaneous farm equipment.

The company's collection experience on credit accounts for the years 1911–16 showed that on $12,719,000 of sales, 83.9 per cent was received in cash, while returned merchandise accounted for 12.7 per cent of the credit sales. Uncollectibles totaled 2.9 per cent of the total volume, and policy allowances (representing amounts the company felt it cheaper to give away than to haggle over) ran to 0.5 per cent.[6] Pianos, implements, cream separators, engines, and vehicles accounted for most of the credit sales. Pianos also accounted for most of the returns in that period, as Table 27 shows. It is also interesting to note from this table that returns and uncollectibles were higher for fall-term accounts (designed to allow farmers to pay after harvest) than for the shorter terms of contract.

While Sears, Roebuck was selling significant amounts of merchandise on terms, it is interesting that Montgomery Ward's 1914 spring and summer

TABLE 27*

SALES ON CREDIT, 1911–16

Commodity	Total Credit Sales	Average Percentage of Returned Merchandise	Average Percentage of Uncollectibles
Pianos	$5,202,157	11.8	1.0
Implements	1,635,505	5.8	5.3
Cream separators (fall-term accounts)	634,769	6.7	5.2
Cream separators (monthly payments)	623,577	4.6	0.8

* Source: Company records.

catalogue contained no reference to instalment selling and, on the contrary, even sought to discourage C.O.D. shipments in these words:

Our complete guarantee of satisfaction, which in every way protects you, seems to us to make C.O.D. shipments unnecessary....

If, however, you have some reason for wanting an article shipped C.O.D., we will ship merchandise to you in receipt of a certain sum—usually about one-fourth the value of the article.

Remember that this is an expensive method, because you have to pay the charges for the collection of the money as well as transportation charges.

Goods shipped C.O.D. by express are subject to examination in the express office, if requested in your order. If you are satisfied, you pay the agent the balance of the purchase price.

You can only inspect merchandise sent C.O.D. by freight after all freight charges have been paid.

There are certain expensive articles that we will ship to you without deposit of any kind, if your order bears the indorsement of your postmaster, express agent, banker, or a merchant that has a commercial rating. We reserve the right to ship these articles to ourselves and send the bill of lading with draft attached, to your bank for collection.[7]

The Ward fall and winter catalogue of 1916–17 made no mention of instalment terms. The fall and winter book for 1921–22 mentioned, almost surreptitiously, that Ward's "Pipeless Furnace" could be purchased on easy payments—$7.49 a month for the $99.90 model, $15.63 per month for the

$181.25 model. But the catalogue clearly pointed out that the model which sold for $99.90 on terms could be bought for $89.90 cash, while the model listed at $181.25 on terms was available for $159.75 cash. The Ward catalogue for 1921–22 listed on instalment terms, in addition to the pipeless furnace, phonographs, pianos, and cream separators. These were offered in that and the succeeding three books at, variously, as little as $5.00 down and as much as a thirty-day free trial. But, except on pianos and phonographs, credit terms were made generally inconspicuous.

At Sears, on the other hand, the period 1917–21 was known as the "No Money Down" era. Credit was extended liberally, with a minimum of investigation; this was true not only of the aforementioned lines offered on instalment terms but on "Modern Homes" as well. Of the liberality of the company's policy to would-be homeowners, J. J. O'Connor stated in a 1918 memorandum to Rosenwald:

> Under our plan we supply practically all the material on credit and, if necessary, advance a portion of the cash required to pay the workmen for putting up the house....
>
> Sears, Roebuck and Co. is probably the only institution which negotiates building loans without meeting the borrowers and making a personal appraisal of the land on which the dwelling is to be erected and the locality where the property is situated....
>
> Besides the material furnished in connection with building loans, we sell large quantities on straight credit terms. The transactions work out with a minimum of loss. Out of sales aggregating eleven hundred thousand dollars, comprised in one class of accounts we opened during 1917, the uncollectibles figured two hundredths of one per cent.

Much of the credit on lines other than "Modern Homes" was offered through agents and newspaper advertising, and this attracted a considerable amount of undesirable credit business which later gave the company some difficulty in liquidating a tremendous outstanding balance. No special order form had been used up to this time for credit sales, but in 1917 credit order blanks of a simple nature were inserted in all catalogues containing a credit offer. Only three items of information were asked for: (1) length of time at present location; (2) occupation; and (3) two references. The sales agreement to be signed by the customer read:

> You may ship me the [piano] above described, freight charges paid, for 30 days' trial, without any obligation on my part to buy unless I am satisfied. If, after 30 days' trial, I should decide to keep and use the piano, I will send you a first payment of $——— and the freight charges which you paid for me, and will pay the balance at the rate of $——— monthly on the ——— day of each month starting the first month after 30 days' trial, until I have paid in full; then the piano becomes my property. If after 30 days' trial, I should decide that the piano is not satisfactory, you are to give me freight receipts so that I may return it to you at your expense. I have always been faithful in paying my obligations, and I am making this statement for the purpose of inducing you to grant me these terms and to assure you that you may feel safe in trusting me to pay as agreed.

This system enabled the firm to handle volume with greater dispatch and less expense, principally because the average order was of a high quality. This influence was attributed in large part to the fact that patronage was secured from a type of customer who had not hitherto bought from Sears, Roebuck. The previous absence of a credit blank had naturally led many potential customers to assume the sales would have to be secured by chattel mortgage in the customary way, which would have been unacceptable to many. After the introduction of this form in 1917, company records showed many orders from bank cashiers and others in comparable brackets of income and "respectability" for pianos, phonographs, and similar goods. The firm's credit men claimed the new system brought marked improvement. A memorandum from J. J. O'Connor of the credit "department" to Julius Rosenwald, written July 20, 1918, attests to the firm's satisfaction:

> Nothing is left undone to see that our offers make no promises, direct or implied, that we could not strictly live up to. The order blank contains no legal or technical language, nor conditions which might offend. At the same time, the scheme is sufficiently restricted to stave off the unworthy or tricky from ordering. As we do not require a chattel mortgage, or similar form of security, our plan appeals strongly to the average person, especially the type of customers who are sensitive about their credit.
>
> It will be noted that all the pre-arranging is directed toward securing orders from people who would be considered good credit risks, not particularly the ones possessing money and property, for they are not always the best payers, but the HONEST individuals, earning livable incomes, who are prudent and buy within their means. That we have been remarkably successful in attracting this desirable class of patronage is evidenced by the fact that our loss for the year 1917, chargeable to uncollectible accounts, was, you might say, nominal, being only fifty-eight hundredths of one per cent, or a trifle more than one-half cent out of each dollar's worth sold.

The "No Money Down" period also saw credit terms extended on new items. Phonographs were added in 1917, with a two-week free trial, maximum monthly payments of $5.00, and a contract life extended over a period of twenty-eight months. No deposit was required, and no carrying charge added. Customers were also requested to write for the "Easy Payment Building Offer," and in 1918 they were allowed to add records to their easy-payment orders for phonographs. Typewriters were offered with a ten-day trial period and a $1.50 deposit, with eighteen months to pay and no carrying charge.

In 1919 the catalogue began to advertise credit terms for lines other than pianos, phonographs, and typewriters. And, for the first time, separate prices were quoted for cash and easy terms. On cream separators, for example, a $2.00 discount for cash was allowed on $47.50 and $74.75 models. For credit terms a lengthier questionnaire than that used earlier was employed, with seven questions asked:

1. How long at present address?
2. How many cows do you milk?
3. How large is your farm?
4. Do you own your farm or rent?
5. Were last year's crops good or bad?
6. What is your net worth?
7. Do you have any delinquent debts?

During this period credit terms on various items were advertised as shown in Table 28.

As a fund of experience was accumulated toward the end of the period 1917–21, the original credit terms (more or less arbitrarily set) were altered occasionally, either restricting or lengthening the contract life. The general trend was toward greater uniformity. Table 29 illustrates the credit expe-

TABLE 28*

CREDIT TERMS, 1919–21

Year	Commodity	Deposit	Months To Pay	Carrying Charge
1919	Organs	None	24	None
	Furnaces	None	10	6%
	Stoves	$5.00	20	10% discount for cash
	Washers	$5.00	10	5%
	Farm engines	$5.00	10	6%
	Encyclopaedia Britannica	$1.00	"Write for terms"	
	Plumbing supplies	Approx. 10%	10	5%
1920	Bible lovers' books	$1.85	10	None
	Electric-light plants	"Send as much as possible"		6%
	Vacuum cleaners	None	18	6%
	Garages	"Special terms in special catalogs"		
1921	"Modern Homes"	"Up to six years to pay"		

* Source: Company records.

rience of the company on various items from 1917 through 1921 (the figures include the Philadelphia branch plant from its opening in 1920, but no figures are available for the Dallas and Seattle branches). The company's collection experience on credit accounts by years is portrayed in Table 30.

The collection experience for the years 1917–21 was obviously unsatisfactory, especially in the depression years of 1920 and 1921, when returns soared to record peaks. Many customers requested extensions of time on the credit accounts. These petitions showed that the most important reason for such requests was crop failures, which accounted for 33.8 per cent (169) of the cases analyzed. Of the 500 accounts investigated, 135 who requested an extension of thirty to ninety days gave no reason, and were classified under "will pay soon." "Flu" accounted for 77 of the delinquents, military service was listed by 22 others; and nearly 20 per cent (97 cases) gave other reasons classified as "miscellaneous." This catch-all covered vicissitudes such as:

> ... cannot get threshing done, unable to haul to market, temporarily embarrassed due to investments in liberty bonds or other war activities, banks refuse to loan money, compelled to leave farm and go to work in city, lack of help in harvest time, and has requested Federal Farm Loan, but cannot say when it will be available.

TABLE 29*

CREDIT EXPERIENCE BY MERCHANDISE ITEMS, 1917-21

Commodity	Sales	Per Cent Returned Merchandise	Per Cent Uncollectible
Pianos	$15,280,318	20.8	2.1
Implements	3,583,280	7.7	11.8
Cream separators	3,647,261	8.1	3.4
Vehicles	364,049	4.5	8.5
Engines	1,380,703	10.0	6.4
Typewriters	941,257	24.1	5.8
Encyclopaedia Britannica	7,770,050	20.4	4.1
Phonographs	35,281,644	16.8	6.7
Organs	435,558	8.7	3.5
Plumbing and heating supplies	1,961,682	5.7	2.3
Stoves	3,804,470	4.8	5.0
Washers	1,291,917	15.2	4.0
Bible lovers' books	102,544	18.7	10.5
Electric-light plants	77,730	9.6	4.6
Vacuum cleaners	106,003	15.3	2.4
Garages	108,452	3.4	3.0
School furniture	1,056,341	0.8	0.6
Sewing machines	1,138,109	8.9	5.2
Kitchen cabinets	632,399	1.9	6.2

* Source: Company records.

TABLE 30*

COLLECTION EXPERIENCE ON INSTALMENT SALES, 1917-24

Year	Sales	Per Cent Cash	Per Cent Returned Merchandise	Per Cent Policy Allowance	Per Cent Uncollectible Allowance
1917	$ 10,476,000	82.5	13.7	0.8	3.0
1918	9,491,000	82.9	11.8	1.0	4.3
1919	19,397,000	81.4	11.8	1.1	5.7
1920	26,377,000	75.4	17.0	1.2	6.4
1921	14,837,000	70.1	23.9	1.0	5.0
1922	4,173,000	86.5	11.4	0.7	1.4
1923	3,097,000	92.9	5.7	0.7	0.7
1924	3,361,000	92.4	6.5	0.5	0.6
1911-24	103,928,000	79.7	14.8	0.9	4.6

* Source: Company records.

The unsalutary experience of the sharp decline in cash recoveries in credit accounts in 1920-21 demonstrated that falling prices were of substantial importance, although no such category was included in the "reasons" for "extension requests."

As a result of the generally unsatisfactory collection record of the previous five years, the company determined to adopt a stricter credit policy. The change began in the latter part of 1921, when credit purchases were limited to orders for not less than twenty-five dollars. Several items were removed from the authorized credit list: farm engines, plumbing supplies, and vacuum cleaners. In 1922 more items were removed from that list: cream separators, stoves, washers, furnaces, electric-light plants, and water-supply systems. This left only five items on which credit was advertised: pianos, phonographs, typewriters, organs, and encyclopedias.

In 1923 the general restriction of credit terms continued. Phonographs were taken off the "No Money Down" plan, and the contract life on pianos was reduced. Washers and stoves were returned to the authorized credit list that year, but with a shortened contract life and a deposit double the former amount. Furnaces were also reinstated, but on more stringent terms illustrative of the change in policy. Instead of the 6 per cent interest charge, approximately 15 per cent was added to the cash price. Finally, the order blank for credit items was made much more inclusive in the 1923 catalogue, when the following information was requested:

1. Where customer was located.
2. Where formerly located if less than five years at present address.
3. Whether owned property, rented, or boarded.
4. Age.
5. Marital status.
6. Occupation.
7. Employment status.
8. Length of employment.
9. Weekly earnings.
10. Name and address of employer.
11. Method of shipping goods.
12. Size of farm.
13. Owner of farm.
14. Means of income.
15. Total monthly earnings.
16. Distance from depot.
17. Two references.

In 1924 the contract was strengthened by including a judgment clause, and three references instead of two were required. With improving business, the credit plan was broadened that year, but a conservative policy was continued in approving credit orders. Vacuum cleaners were again placed on the list of items authorized to be sold on credit, radios were added, and the contract life slightly lengthened on stoves and washers. Total sales, returned merchandise, and uncollectibles by commodity from 1913 through 1924, according to sequence of approval for credit sales, are outlined in Table 31.

In 1925 business continued to improve. Radio-phonographs were added to the items approved for credit. The contract life was six months, and the down payment 25 per cent of the purchase price. A carrying charge of 10 per cent was added. An intracompany report stated:

By 1926, business had improved to such an extent that we lengthened the contract life on washers, vacuum cleaners, and radios. The continued improvement of business was also reflected in the fact that in 1927 typewriters were reinstated with a contract life of nine months instead of six.

In the three years 1925–27 the new items approved for credit sale included radio-phonographs, sewing machines, harness, furniture, kitchen

TABLE 31*

CREDIT WORKOUT, 1913, 1917–20, AND 1924

Year Approved	Commodity	Sales	Per Cent Returned Merchandise	Per Cent Uncollectible
1913.....	Pianos	$23,414,079	17.1	1.6
1917.....	Phonographs	38,765,057	15.9	6.2
1918.....	Typewriters	1,083,436	22.4	5.2
1919	Cream separators	5,664,294	7.5	3.0
	Organs	521,317	8.3	3.2
	Encyclopaedia Britannica	14,999,752	19.1	3.5
	Stoves	4,346,620	4.7	4.5
	Washers	1,651,290	13.7	3.2
	Farm engines	1,619,940	9.5	6.2
	Plumbing and heating supplies	2,865,844	4.6	2.0
	Electric-light plants	88,970	9.4	4.0
	Vacuum cleaners	294,119	8.3	1.0
1920.....	Garages	240,827	2.8	2.3
1924.....	Radios	425,431	20.1	0.2
Items not formally approved for credit purchases:				
	Implements	$ 5,456,420	7.1	9.5
	Vehicles	684,593	2.9	6.7
	School furniture	1,490,708	0.9	0.4
	Sewing machines	1,145,053	8.9	5.2
	Furniture and kitchen cabinets	651,172	1.9	6.1
	Harness	7,431	0.9	3.9
	Electric ironers	4,106	16.0	....

* Source: Company records.
† These include items not advertised on credit terms in the catalogue. Credit was apparently advanced on them in the response to requests from customers despite the company's desire not to publicize such terms in its catalogue.

cabinets, ironers, and baby carriages. The contract life ranged from four months on baby carriages to twelve months on sewing machines and harness. The down payment was $5.00 for all these items except radio-phonographs (25 per cent) and for furniture and kitchen cabinets (12 per cent). The carrying charge was 10 per cent, except for ironers, for which 12 per cent was assessed.

While credit policy became more conservative as to terms and selection of risks after the latter part of 1921, the catalogues gave increased emphasis and prominence to the "Easy Payment Plan" beginning in 1925. By 1927 pages exhibited "Easy Payments" in boldface type, and frequently the amount of the monthly payment was given more prominence than any other feature of the copy.

The revision in credit policy resulted in a decided improvement in collection experience. Of the years from 1917 to 1921, the best year from the standpoint of uncollectibles was 1917, when that category showed a ratio of only 3 per cent of credit sales. The worst was the depression year of 1920, when uncollectibles ran to 6.4 per cent. The inauguration of more stringent terms lowered the figure to 1.4 per cent in 1922. By the end of 1927, of $9,539,000 of credit sales, 93 per cent eventuated in cash payments; 5.8 per cent was repossessed; 0.4 per cent was "allowed"; and only 0.8 per cent was completely lost—a striking improvement over the period 1917–21.

Throughout the years to 1927 credit policy was determined by a committee of executives, all of whom had other important responsibilities. In the fall of that year a credit manager having authority and responsibility for credit operations was at last appointed to work under the general supervision of the vice-president in charge of operating. By the end of 1927 further progress had been made in creating greater uniformity of credit terms; on practically all authorized lines a carrying charge of 10 per cent had been established. An effective organization of credit operations was becoming increasingly apparent; by 1928 credit sales accounted for nearly 5 per cent of all sales.[8]

In the initiation and use of instalment selling in this period, Sears, Roebuck was generally acting in line with a well-established trend. Montgomery Ward sold on instalment terms, and another Chicago mail-order concern—Spiegel's—specialized entirely in instalment selling by mail. Many department stores, however, and so-called "quality" retailers held back on instalment selling until the 1930's. Macy's for instance, waited until 1939 to inaugurate instalment selling and thus to reverse its "cash-only" policy.[9] But throughout the country "easy-payment" plans were promoted vigorously. So great was the growth of instalment selling that by 1927 some 15 per cent of all goods was sold on the instalment plan, at retail prices about six billion dollars' worth, while at any given moment between two and three billions of outstanding debt could be accounted for by instalment purchase. Over 85 per cent of furniture, 80 per cent of phonographs, 75 per cent of washing machines, and the greater part of all vacuum cleaners, sewing machines, radios, and electric refrigerators were bought in this way.[10] Slosson writes of this period:

> Thrift in the sense of just not spending, as distinguished from investment, was indeed at a discount in all classes. The best proof of this was the great increase in consumer credits, the purchase of goods on so much down and so much a month.[11]

Most of the industries in which instalment buying was the rule were new industries based on recent mechanical inventions producing goods to retail at high unit prices. As home radios, refrigerators, electric washers, and the like represented a considerable investment, many a housewife would have hesitated at so much expense for a novel luxury but for the seductive argument of easy payments.[12] Reavis Cox considers those mechanical inventions as one of the five most important factors aiding the rise of instalment selling. The other factors he cites include the steady expansion of consumer incomes; the increasing urbanization of the country; the organizing of financial facilities to carry a load of several billion dollars; and—with some qualifications—a change in the social attitude toward instalment buying, which to many people had been synonymous with going into debt.[13]

Manufacturers, particularly of durables, also stimulated and guided the growth of instalment selling in many ways from its beginnings. They urged an increase in instalment selling in order to increase their own volume, and they aided their dealers in carrying the financial burden involved.[14] So did Sears's volume-minded merchandisers embrace the opportunity to stimulate sales of high-unit-price items through "easy payments." The years of mail-order maturity provided a laboratory in which credit policies were made through trial and error—in preparation for the vast expansion of "easy-payment" sales that was to follow in the wake of the retail stores.

CHAPTER XVII

Operating Methods and Employee Welfare

BUYING and selling depended for their most effective prosecution on a servicing organization that became more and more elaborate (and essential) as the business developed. Such servicing activities were the responsibility of the operating department, presided over by Otto C. Doering (first as general superintendent and later as vice-president) from 1906 to his resignation in 1928. Doering's preoccupation with methods and systems marked him as a singularly successful example of the type of executive contemplated by Frederick Taylor's "scientific management"—a movement that emerged during the same era that witnessed the perfecting of Sears's mail-order procedures.

Doering and his aides brought the schedule system of filling orders to a high state of refinement. Every effort was bent, first, to making the schedule system foolproof and to diminishing steadily the time limit within which each incoming order could be shipped and, second, to extending applicable characteristics of the schedule system to other operations, such as correspondence and returns. A post office—now one of the largest in volume of any in America outside New York or Chicago—was established in the company plant. Express companies also established offices on company premises; as fast as express packages were delivered from chutes, they were received by express-company clerks and placed upon their own trucks.[1]

The use of color for scheduling was developed to a fine point. Address labels of different colored borders were used for each day of the week to facilitate recognition at a glance; a red label sticking out on, say, a "green" day was an immediate danger signal calling for expediting. Special colored envelopes furnished with order blanks were supplied to customers; these could be distinguished from all other incoming mail immediately. And cash registers provided an automatic accounting of the money received from each state, furnishing valuable information for making seasonal comparisons of business by states and of the regional pulling power of the catalogue(s).

By 1923 Sears's own fleet of fifty-one trucks was engaged in almost continuous hauling to and from the main post office for eighteen hours each working day, making one trip (often involving, however, more than one truck) every hour on the hour. When the trucks disgorged their bags, the mail-opening department opened the sacks and assorted the contents by classifications. Mail-opening machines opened four hundred letters a minute, simultaneously printing on each communication the day of receipt. Another division of workers promptly attached to the contents of each envelope a colored slip in accordance with the color schedule.

Remittances were checked for accuracy. After further processing, the order reached the index department, where millions of names were filed according to post offices. The index cards contained a complete record of each customer's previous purchases from the company with the dates and, of course, provided the mailing list for catalogues and other matter. Each index card contained a stencil for addressing the customer's name on stickers and pasters for parcel-post and express shipments.

When the orders—now "tickets"—arrived in the schedule and distribution department, they were sorted into four classes: mixed parcel post ("mixed" referring, of course, to an order calling for items from more than a single department), mixed express, mixed freight, and single orders. The "singles" were then further broken down according to the means of shipment to be employed. After this and subsequent operations, the separate tickets were dispatched to the various merchandise departments for filling of the order. All postage stamps used for the company's shipments were precanceled by arrangement with the post office before being affixed to shipments. (On December 21, 1923, $22,000 worth of stamps were thus consumed in one day.) Stamps affixed, the packages then went by conveyor belt to a department of the Railway Mail Service of the Post Office Department, which was a complete parcel-post terminal.

A vital link in operations was the traffic department. The subdivisions within this department convey some idea of its functions: rates, settlement, over-short-damage, in-bound freight tracing, and city freight tracing.

As the company's volume of business increased in succeeding years, the number of shipments increased enormously, especially after the inauguration of parcel post in 1913. As operations became better organized and systematized, claims against carriers for lost shipments apparently diminished somewhat despite the greater volume of shipments. The very fact of the constant increase in the volume of business increased the work of the traffic department more or less proportionately and dictated constant efforts to improve procedures.

Tacit evidence of this steady increase in the volume of work—as well, of course, as the logic of geography—is found in the fact that a regional traffic department was established in Dallas in 1906, coincident with the opening of that first branch plant. In 1910 a regional traffic department was set up in the Seattle branch opened that year. Similar regional traffic departments were opened in the remainder of the several branch plants as each went into operation.

While the original schedule system of shipping demanded that orders be filled within twenty-four to forty-eight hours after receipt, the improvements during this period reduced the usual shipping time. By 1918 bundles of orders were being dispatched at ten-minute intervals throughout the day. These orders had to be filled, packed, and delivered to the transportation agency within four hours after their distribution for order-filling. Although the system had originally been introduced over the opposition and skepticism of many executives, it was made increasingly clear that the top management intended to make the system work; it became a creed, with fanatic devotees. Its status as a creed was further enhanced by its extension to other operations.

Refunds, for example, were soon "streamlined." Refunds arose from two sources: remittance of too much money by the customer or the company's desire not to delay a customer when it could not fill an order immediately. Three methods of refunds in such instances were evolved: by credit voucher postal card, for amounts from 2 to 49 cents; credit vouchers, for amounts to 99 cents; and checks, for all amounts of $1.00 and over. The vouchers and postal cards were, of course, good only in exchange for Sears, Roebuck merchandise.

Correspondence, frequently mounting to huge backlogs, had been the company's bête noire from the day Richard Sears began to pull mountains of orders, frequently leading to complaints because they could not be filled. After Doering had established the success of the schedule system in shipping merchandise promptly, steps were taken to schedule correspondence. The typist-correspondent was developed to replace the two-man team of dictating correspondent and stenographer.

As had happened earlier in the company's history, assistance from the Post Office Department played a role in improving the handling of the company's correspondence. The postal ruling allowing letters carrying first-class postage to be affixed to packages meant that correspondence concerning returns could be attached to the packages bearing the goods being returned. Another boon was the Post Office's authorization of the inclosure of invoices with shipments. Some light is shed on the handling of correspondence by this résumé compiled in 1946 by A. L. Starkey, in charge of correspondence for the parent-organization in Chicago:

> When I entered the Company in 1915, we were then receiving such a volume of business, especially grocery orders made up primarily of sugar and flour, which were the hard-to-get items then during the war period, that our Correspondence Division was swamped with complaints due to the way this increase in volume was handled. By the spring of 1917 the correspondence volume dropped off to such an extent that Mr. Beal, then the Manager of the Correspondence Department, took a picture of the racks in which we kept our complaints to show that we were up-to-date. In order to do this, however, he had to have several baskets of mail pushed under the table to make it a good picture. In those days we considered we were up-to-date if we were handling complaints within a week after they were received, whereas today we endeavor to handle all complaints within 24 hours—and do so the greater part of the year.

METHODS AND EMPLOYEE WELFARE

During 1915, 1916 and the early part of 1917, all customers' papers concerning their orders were kept, and the entire East section of the fifth floor of the Administration Building was used exclusively for filing purposes. The correspondent receiving a complaint would have to draw the papers from the file, and if he could not get all of them would have to try and try again before handling the complaint. In 1917, after a test was made, it was decided to return all bills to customers, requesting the return of them in case of complaint. This system has been followed ever since with very little difficulty.

The extension of the schedule system concept to other phases of operations was indicative of the general improvement in the company's mail-order service. Sears, Roebuck's methods of operations responded avidly to "the golden age of mail order." Not all operations, however, were adaptable to quite such a system. One of the biggest problems the company had to solve in this period was that of addressing millions of catalogues and flyers. Up to World War I this was done by hand—a slow and costly process. The addressing was done from heavy, bulky index cards. C. D. Palmer had previously interested himself in operations as one of Otto Doering's assistants and around 1914 had helped develop the conveyor-line method whereby order tickets were dropped off automatically at the appropriate desk, increasing the efficiency of indexing and order-filling.

During World War I, Palmer developed a lighter, more flexible index card (which minimized demands on filing space) and cut a stencil of the name and address into one end of the card. The other end of the card could then be folded back against the stencil and, by inking, the name and address transferred to the lower end of the card to facilitate filing. After obtaining executive approval, he worked with the Elliot Machinery Company to design a machine for this type of mechanical addressing. The patent was assigned to the company, and the invention made it possible to get out a mailing of 25,000,000 addresses within sixty days.

The mechanization of addressing operations was characteristic of the progress made in applying labor-saving methods to Sears's problems. Doering's penchant for efficiency was everywhere manifest, and the mail-order house became distinguished for its use of conveyor-belt systems and orderly mechanized operations. But however relentless the search for economy, and however numerous the labor-saving techniques became, the nature and volume of Sears's business demanded increasing numbers of employees. The employment and welfare of this work force was another responsibility of the operations officer.

The aggressive promotion of welfare and social activities for employees that characterized the "personnel program" in the years to 1906 appears to have been essentially an extension of Elmer Scott's personal convictions. The encouragement of employee clubs, Seroco, *The Skylight*, the library, and "educational talks" were products of Scott's reign as general manager. During the years following 1906 many of these activities (e.g., various departmental clubs) survived, but without the nourishment and encouragement of an active sponsor.

According to Asher's account, Seroco was allowed to "drift into painless dissolution" when Scott went to Dallas.[2] Scott's program had the objectives both of "improving" workers and of building *esprit de corps*. The numerous activities sponsored by Scott were not viewed with enthusiasm by top management. Richard Sears wrote to his general manager, Louis Asher: "Mighty glad to see your Seroco action and to learn that after December 26 all frills will be cut out. I know you want practice and not theory. Me too."[3]

Julius Rosenwald did not demur against Sears's viewpoint on this matter. In operations, a dedication to efficiency and low-cost performance and the accompanying interest in systems and procedure implied that employees were expected to conform to the system as a condition of continued employment.

But if the absence of Scott resulted in minimizing the role of company-sponsored social activities among employees (although annual "field days" were held for many years), the years of the greatest growth of the mail-order business brought extensions of personnel policy in some other directions. Early in 1909 Operating Superintendent Doering announced that the company would introduce a noncontributory plan for disability benefits. Employees absent on account of illness were to be reimbursed so that the combined benefits of the Sears Mutual Benefit Association (established in 1902) and the company allowance equaled full salary. Eligibility for such allowances was limited to employees of at least five years' service.

It was assumed that all employees were members of the mutual benefit association, "because not to do so would be to discriminate unfairly against the SMBA members, who pay their dues not only for their own protection but for the protection of their fellow employees."[4]

In 1912 the illness allowance policy was liberalized so that employees who had completed six months' service were eligible for benefits. Longer service was recognized by exempting five-year employees from the prevailing two-day waiting-period provisions. Further, the company now committed itself to pay full salary to workers who had applied for benefit association membership and had been rejected (for failure to pass a physical examination).

Whereas formerly no time limit on benefit payments was specified, Doering's memorandum (House Policy 164) of April 17, 1912, specified a maximum period of ten weeks' allowance. Some exceptions were, however, provided in cases where "there is no other income in the family; [and where] home conditions are poor, try to keep our employees from being a case for the public charities."

In the same memorandum the company declared that the policy for compensation for accidents occurring "in the house" required that the employee be paid in full for all time off and for all hospital bills incurred. In the case of accidents occurring off the premises, employees received the same allowance as medical cases, except that, where the person might receive payment (damages) from a source other than Sears, the company did not pay the regular illness allowance.

While the mutual benefit association still functioned under the 1912 policy, the company had taken a long step toward assuming the full burden of illness allowance. The acceptance of a full-scale noncontributory illness allowance plan came in 1919. The motivation and the thinking which led to this early adoption of a noncontributory plan is not known. Possibly it was a reflection of some of the interest in personnel management that was evident in American industry about the time of World War I. It is equally possible that it simply reflected a serious concern for the employees' risks of income loss due to illness. There is little doubt that the company-financed benefits plan was adopted in advance of American industry generally. Indeed, as late as 1939 the National Industrial Conference Board found only a few companies had such a program:

> In 1926 the United States Bureau of Labor Statistics discovered that in only 14 out of 430 establishments were such policies in force, while in connection with the present survey.... Information was obtained from 48 companies with genuine plans of this character.[5]

The same consideration that prompted a more liberal illness allowance for employees with substantial accumulation of company service led to the inauguration in 1912 of another program which was designed specifically to stimulate (and reward) such constancy. In that year the system of anniversary checks was inaugurated. Upon completion of five years' service, employees would receive on their anniversary date a check for 5 per cent of the past year's salary. The "bonus" increased by 1 per cent for each additional year of service until the limit of 10 per cent was reached. Anniversary checks were at first limited to employees receiving not more than $1,500 per year, but in 1920 the limit was raised to $2,000. In 1923, when employee service classes were established in the profit-sharing program, the anniversary checks were discontinued. Table 32 indicates the number of employees participating and the amounts distributed in anniversary checks during the twelve years the plan was in effect.

The more than $2,500,000 distributed in anniversary checks in twelve years was to pale into insignificance as the company's contributions to profit-sharing reached larger and larger sums, until in the single year 1924 more than $3,000,000 was contributed to the profit-sharing fund. This, the best known and most spectacular of the company's welfare activities, was inaugurated in 1916.[6]

As launched in 1916, the profit-sharing fund was characterized by these objectives:

> ... that employees may share in the profits of this business, and to encourage the habit of saving ... [to] furnish to those who remain in the employ of the

Company until they reach the age when they retire from active service, a sum sufficient to provide for them thereafter, and that even those who achieve a long service record, but who may not remain with the Company all of their business life, will have accumulated a substantial sum.

The plan provided that employees who wished to become members would deposit 5 per cent of their earnings up to a certain maximum amount. In 1916 the maximum employee deposit allowed was $150 per year, which was revised in 1924 so that no limit was stated. In 1925 a $300 limit was established, which was maintained until 1934, when the present ceiling of $250 was established. The purpose of defining such a limit was, of course, to prevent the higher-salaried employees from gaining at the

TABLE 32*

ANNIVERSARY CHECKS, 1912–23

Year	No. of Employees Participating	Amount Distributed
1912	1,895	$101,957.39
1913	1,923	115,421.01
1914	2,258	136,070.35
1915	2,843	169,397.30
1916	3,158	196,108.80
1917	3,679	244,253.05
1918	†	†
1919	3,836	297,221.25
1920	3,596	327,494.75
1921	3,447	354,510.95
1922	3,228	302,180.80
1923	3,081	284,450.30

* Source: Company records.
† No figures available.

expense of the great majority of workers. To the fund created by employee deposits, the company committed itself to contribute 5 per cent of net income before taxes and dividends. The combined company and employee contributions were invested in the common stock of Sears, Roebuck, which was allocated to the profit-sharing members' accounts and allowed to accumulate for the primary purpose of providing retirement security. The growth in the profit-sharing program for the years 1916–28 is shown in Table 33.

Employees who were working for Sears at the time state that there was considerable skepticism among the rank and file when the program was announced. Not until they saw at the end of the first year that the participants received three times as much from the company as they had deposited were they very enthusiastic over the program. It is reported that the experience of the first year brought large numbers into the plan. By

1918 more than 90 per cent of the employees eligible to participate had elected to become fund members.[7]

Profit-sharing at no time was to be considered a substitute for wages. Writing to Julius Rosenwald in 1923, Albert Loeb stated:

Profit sharing should never be made a substitute in part for wages or a palliative for long hours or poor working conditions. True profit sharing gives the employees a share in the prosperity of the business *in addition* to a good compensation. It avails nothing, however, and is doomed to disaster unless these three elements precede any profit sharing:

1. A fairly liberal salary at least as good or better than the competitive scale of wages.

TABLE 33*

PROFIT SHARING FUND PROGRAM, 1916-28

Year	Number of Members	Employee Deposits	Company Contributions	Value of Stock Held by Fund
1916	6,064	$136,311.63	$ 412,215.55	$ 545,893.77
1917	6,712	324,162.12	905,484.04	1,751,984.40
1918	6,056	349,145.30	1,077,883.19	3,298,407.20
1919	7,528	441,929.01	1,191,942.06	4,636,344.22
1920	7,875	580,853.51	587,333.30	6,956,206.93
1921	6,392	501,333.12	....	6,260,674.33
1922	5,748	408,921.56	271,758.41	5,911,475.32
1923	5,502	394,169.18	575,630.90	5,941,775.73
1924	10,016	661,259.10	3,172,196.45	8,356,671.64
1925	10,330	708,402.27	2,194,612.29	10,444,953.82
1926	11,450	740,228.93	2,181,593.43	13,220,766.28
1927	12,404	808,891.01	2,333,046.34	15,975,580.13
1928	15,318	927,644.42	2,209,666.75	17,830,554.63

* Source: Fund records.

2. The right number of working hours, also based on what your neighbors are doing.

3. The right kind of working conditions. (In this division may be included so-called welfare work, paid vacations, pay for sickness, accidents, etc.)[8]

It is possible to gain some idea of the wages paid for the years prior to 1920 from the hearings of the Chicago Vice Commission in 1910 and from those of the Illinois Senate Committee's *Report on Vice*, published in 1916, which give some evidence of the prevailing rates in retailing in the Chicago area prior to World War I. When Julius Rosenwald testified before the Illinois Senate Vice Committee, he offered the following figures in evidence of the rates of pay at Sears. The figures are for the pay-roll week ending March 8, 1913. The company had 4,732 female employees, who received an average weekly salary of $9.12. The wage policy, that is, the minimum rates paid by the firm, established $5.00 as the lower limit for girls under sixteen years of age and $6.00 for girls between the years of sixteen and eighteen. The range for girls over eighteen was from $8.00 to $21.00 a week.

These figures did not include salaries to female department heads. The highest salary paid any woman department head was $35.00 per week. G. H. Miller, of Sears, testified that "there are only twenty-three women whose average is $26 a week."[9]

The committee was of the opinion that $8.00 was the minimal weekly salary on which a working girl could be expected to support herself in the city. The average weekly wage for Sears's women employees at this time was shown to be $9.12. The testimony indicated that Sears made a cost-of-living study in 1911 and on that basis established an $8.00 minimum for girls not living at home. The average weekly salary for men over twenty-one at Sears was $18.82, compared with $18.97 for "selling men" at Carson, Pirie, Scott and Company and $15.36 for "non-selling men." The average for males of all ages at Sears was $15.41 (minimum wage for boys under twenty-one was $5.00). In summarizing the evidence, one of the committee members commented, "Mr. Rosenwald gave $15.41 as the average male wage at Sears, Roebuck and Company. This is a much higher average than obtained in many other establishments."[10]

Despite the evidence offered at the various Commission hearings, there was a feeling in certain areas that women at Sears were "low paid" and worked under undesirable conditions. Undoubtedly there were isolated cases of inept supervision which were interpreted as general company policy.

Mr. Rosenwald saw nothing abhorrent in paying the wage rate ruling in the market. He was proud of company employee policy and invited the committee to the plant.

> I would like to state for the benefit of the committee that Sears, Roebuck and Co. would welcome a visit from the committee, and the questioning of any employees in connection with the institution. I would also like them to have this information, that all of our employees who have been in our employ five years or more receive on the anniversary of their engagement . . . an additional compensation of from 5 per cent to 10 per cent of their yearly earnings. I would also like to state for the benefit of the committee that over one thousand of our women employees have savings accounts, and a goodly number are stockholders in the company.[11]

The general trend of earnings for Sears's employees is indicated by figures from personnel records believed to be reasonably representative of the trend during the period. The figures are not substantially at variance with the testimony presented to the Vice Committee, and they are in general agreement with information supplied by former employees (Table 34).

In terms of these data, the period shows a considerable increase in earnings. In the case of men there was a fourfold increase over 1907, and for women just slightly less. Unfortunately no data are available for wages in retailing generally. A comparison of the fragmentary data in Table 34 with Douglas' figures for manufacturing industries (Table 35), however, reveals much less of a differential than is commonly believed to have existed. The comparison also indicates that in terms of a relative increase Sears's employees did much better than did workers in the "pay-roll" manufacturing industries. Undoubtedly part of the increase in the retail trades was the result of the competitive pull on labor exerted by the higher absolute wages in manufacturing. That increased earnings in the distribu-

TABLE 34*

EMPLOYEES' AVERAGE WEEKLY EARNINGS, 1907-27

Year	Male	Female	All Employees
1907	$ 8.11	$ 7.30	$ 7.82
1912	11.33	9.31	10.48
1917	16.76	12.28	14.10
1922	21.97	17.17	19.24
1927	34.85	25.27	29.77

* Source: Company records.

TABLE 35*

UNITED STATES AND SEARS, ROEBUCK AND COMPANY
EMPLOYEES' AVERAGE WEEKLY EARNINGS, 1907-22

Year	Sears	Manufacturing Industries
1907	$ 7.82	$11.27
1912	10.48	11.86
1917	14.10	17.31
1922	19.24	23.66

* Source: Table 34 and Paul H. Douglas, *Real Wages in the United States* (Boston: Houghton Mifflin Co., 1930), p. 124.

tive trades was characteristic is evident from Hower's study of Macy's, which it is useful to compare with Sears. Hower says:

In 1914 ... the minimum rate of pay for selling-employees was $6.00 per week, and the store was in the process of increasing it to $7.00, in addition to which the store had long paid a premium on sales over quotas. In 1915 the average weekly earnings per Macy employee were just under $10, as compared with less than $5.00 in 1870-73.... The average wage paid by Macy's more than doubled between 1915 and 1919.[12]

Table 36 gives some idea of the hiring rates for various classifications of jobs in 1920 and 1929 at the Philadelphia mail-order plant, which helps to give a more detailed picture than is possible in the general averages previously cited. It reinforces the impression of the drift to higher wages which characterized the expansion of the 1920's. It also indicates the advent of the policy of giving special consideration to the financial responsibilities of married men, which was introduced about 1920.

Elmer Scott had introduced piece work for certain jobs prior to 1906, but it remained for operating superintendents at a later date to develop more elaborate incentive methods in the tradition of the "scientific" managers that followed in the wake of the publication of F. W. Taylor's *Shop Management* in 1911. Within the decade Sears, Roebuck had installed a plan whereby the standard performance set was tied to unit labor cost, and a premium paid for every increase in production above the standard

TABLE 36*

PHILADELPHIA MAIL-ORDER HIRING RATES, 1920 AND 1929

Activity	1920	1929
	Male	
Messenger	$10.00	$12.00–$14.00
Order-filler	10.00	14.00– 21.00
Packer	12.00	16.00– 21.00
Stockman:		
Interage (18–20 yr.)	†	18.00– 21.00
Adult—single	21.00	21.00– 26.00
Adult—married	23.00	23.00– 28.00
Laborer	20.00	21.00– 23.00
	Female	
Inexperienced clerical	$ 9.00	$12.00–promotional
Experienced clerical	10.00	14.00– 19.00
Typist	14.00	15.00– 18.00
Typist-correspondent	†	16.00– 28.00
Stenographer	18.00	18.00– 25.00

* Source: Company records.
† Did not employ.

that lowered the unit labor cost. Old employees recall individual (exceptional?) cases in which persons on jobs where the "going rate" was $15 per week regularly had weekly earnings of $25 to $28.

Work customarily began at eight o'clock. Official closing time was five-thirty. Testimony presented at the Vice Committee hearings in 1913 indicates that "girls under sixteen work eight hours a day . . . and that those over sixteen work eight and three-quarters hours or over."[13] The maximum was said to be 9¼ hours. The legal maximum for women was 10 hours per day. There was no legal maximum for men, and reports of employees indicate that at least up to 1920 the sixty-hour week was common.

Although 8:00 A.M. was the usual starting time, departmental managers did not hesitate to call workers in an hour earlier. Sunday work, especially for men, was not infrequent, and no overtime was paid. Until 1912 people working nights received a thirty-five-cent meal ticket for supper. In that year dissatisfaction among men in the shipping-room caused the supper money to be paid in cash.

Although night work had been "abolished" in 1903, department managers frequently did not recognize the fact. The experience of a veteran employee of more than thirty years at Sears testifies to what was probably a fairly representative case. He earned $12 a week working in the shipping-room in 1913–14 from eight in the morning to six in the evening. During the fall and winter seasons he worked three nights a week for thirty-five cents supper money. While he worked all day every Saturday, he had every second Sunday off. Sunday work was rewarded by fifty cents for dinner. Three years of such diligence brought an increase in salary to $14 per week.[14]

Department managers were better paid, of course. The manager of the billing department in 1913 received $100 per month for managing the departmental routines and the 150 girls working in the department.[15] Managers, especially merchandise supervisors, had virtually feudal authority within their own domains, extending even to such petty details as to whether employees working overtime would receive cash or restaurant checks for supper money. As late as 1919 some departments received such cash payments while others did not.

Reduction in working hours had made considerable headway in manufacturing in the period 1910–20.[16] The decade 1920–30 saw a somewhat parallel reduction in Sears, Roebuck and Company. The official work-week in the twenties was reduced to 46½ hours in winter and 42½ hours in summer. Three weeks of the year (pre-Christmas) were on a 48-hour base. By the middle of the decade, the 5½-day week was typical. This, at any rate, was the defined policy; but undoubtedly there were not infrequent departmental exceptions.

Although it appears that the shorter work-week came to Sears (and retailing establishments in general) rather later than to employees in manufacturing, the vacation policy was well established in the company long before it became a common feature in American industry. Until 1912 employees received one week's paid vacation after five years' service. In 1912 the eligibility requirement was reduced to three years.

The most dramatic world event of the middle years was, of course, World War I. It is interesting to note the attitude of the company toward the problems of employees eligible for military duty, if simply for the background of the policies adopted in the similar case arising twenty-five years later. As far back as records are available (1910) the company policy encouraged National Guard duty, as indicated in the following statement issued in May, 1916, which was evidently a formal announcement of a policy that had been followed for some time:

Realizing the distinct moral and physical value of the training acquired in the service of the Illinois National Guard and Illinois Naval Reserve, we have always tried to recognize this in our policy toward employees who are members of these organizations. So that our attitude may be generally known, we wish to state that any employee who is absent on duty of the Illinois National Guard or Illinois Naval Reserve will be entitled to full pay, and this time will not be considered as part of any vacation that may be due.[17]

Although there was no formal system of subsidy payments to all employees called for military service during World War I, the following statement was issued in March, 1917:

All employees who were members of the Illinois National Guard or the Illinois Naval Reserve prior to January 1, 1917, and who were in our employ prior to that date, will, when they respond to the Government call for service, be paid their regular wages from the time of call until the end of 1917.[18]

In the first World War employees who had been absent from company service received credit for time lost to apply on their employment records, so that military service was included in company service for purposes of computing eligibility for vacations or any benefits that might have specified service requirements. Upon entering military service, employees withdrew from the profit-sharing fund. The fund regulations generally provided that employees who had withdrawn were not eligible for reinstatement. Returning veterans were, however, reinstated in the fund at their option, and military service was counted as applying toward the three-year waiting period then in force prior to membership in profit-sharing.

While it is apparent that the company was in many ways carrying on various activities now common among the personnel departments of corporations, there is no evidence that personnel management as such was recognized as a major function of management. In the industrial sector of the American economy, personnel management experienced its first notable growth in the post–World War I period—the prosperous twenties.

In so far as Sears had any designated person exclusively concerned with personnel problems, the job appeared not at the level of top management in the parent-organization but as one of the responsibilities of the operating superintendent in the mail-order house. The organization pattern, in the Philadelphia house at least, designated an employment manager who reported to a special assistant to the operating superintendent. The employment manager co-ordinated medical services, personal services, and employment activities.

Medical services included the dispensary, which by 1925 boasted a fully equipped emergency hospital and the availability of several doctors and nurses. It became the practice to require physical examinations of all job applicants; medical advice was offered to all employees without charge. Cases of long illness, accidents, and the host of activities associated with the personal difficulties of workers were handled by an employees' service division. In connection with such personal services, it appears that Lessing Rosenwald was an important influence in the introduction of policies to ameliorate the financial burdens of employee illness. According to the testimony of older employees, the younger Rosenwald, as manager of the Philadelphia operation, felt a deep concern for the well-being of Sears's employees. He made a conscientious effort to know all his employees by name, and it is reported that on his daily tours through the plant he would make it a point to talk with workers of all ranks, usually addressing these people by first names.

The major task of the employment manager was that of providing workers on requisition to the various departments. By 1920 Sears's employees numbered about twenty thousand. Considering the relatively high turnover characteristic of workers in distributive trades, and the seasonal swings in sales volume with its demand for additional workers, it is clear that any approximate efficiency required some specialization of the employment function.

In recruiting employees, the employment manager acted upon instructions from the operating superintendent's office. When heads of departments wanted to expand their work force, they submitted requisitions which were then cleared and acted upon by the employment office. Whenever it was necessary to hire large numbers of employees for seasonal requirements, newspaper "help-wanted" ads were often utilized.

While the employment office was thus largely responsible for procuring an adequate work force, the selection of applicants was on a "commonsense" basis. There were interviewers to interrogate applicants. The interviewing procedure was unstandardized, and no testing was done except for rudimentary and unstandardized proficiency "tests" for certain jobs, such as typing and stenography. When carpenters and other skilled tradesmen were hired, they were sent to the master-craftsmen to be interviewed so that some idea could be gained of their competence.

There appears to have been no systematic employee-training program. With the exception of a "vestibule-type" indoctrination in "house" policies and procedures to which new correspondents and stenographers were briefly exposed, newly hired applicants were assigned directly to operating departments under the supervision of more experienced workers—essentially a process of training by total immersion. New employees were expected to become acquainted with the plant, and the relation of their own job to the whole operation, by trips through the plant and by verbal instruction whenever convenient. The entire process of induction and training was on a haphazard basis, dependent primarily on the interests and abilities of the department managers and the demands of the work schedules.

While the employment office did not control promotions, all such recommendations by department managers were cleared through the employment office. This process of clearing expanded the possibilities for employees in any single department. Promotions were based entirely on the estimates of employees' job performance by department managers. There was no company policy of periodic rating reports in the early 1920's. Evidently certain departments in the Philadelphia plant went through the ritual of merit rating not long after the branch opened in 1920. The functional importance of these ratings is doubtful, since dusty accumulations of such reports from the billing department were unearthed in 1924 on the occasion of a change in Philadelphia plant superintendents.

The years from 1909 to 1925 witnessed an expansion of large proportions in the company. Sales increased from $51,000,000 to $244,000,000. Sears's

TABLE 37*

AVERAGE NUMBER OF EMPLOYEES, 1909–25

Year	Number of Employees	Year	Number of Employees
1909	6,160	1918	13,683
1910	7,651	1919	25,492
1911	7,800	1920	21,652
1912	8,074	1921	18,144
1913	9,469	1922	18,938
1914	9,868	1923	19,946
1915	10,447	1924	18,784
1916	12,616	1925	23,193
1917	15,113		

* Source: Company records. For the years 1909–17, inclusive, 1923, and 1925 the figures are the average number on pay roll for the twelve months of the year. For 1918 the figure is the average for the six months, January through June. For the years 1919–22, inclusive, the figure is the number on the pay roll in October for the years indicated. For 1924 the figure is an average for the eleven months, January through November.

NOTE.—It is not clear whether the data for 1907–18 refer only to the Chicago plant or to all the mail-order plants. The marked increase in 1919 indicates that earlier figures may refer only to Chicago.

employees numbered more than 6,000 in 1909 and had increased to more than 23,000 in 1925. Except for the 1920–21 depression, nearly every year brought more workers to Sears's mail-order business. As Table 37 shows, the depression of 1920–21 resulted in a marked curtailment of Sears's personnel.

The following passages are quoted from a manuscript used by Julius Rosenwald for addresses to troops made when he toured Europe with Secretary of War Newton D. Baker in 1918. The lengthy excerpt reproduced here is useful for indicating the dominant note of "welfarism" in company policy as well as for the summary of the firm's activities which Rosenwald conceived as being personnel policy:

With the Profit Sharing Fund and the Anniversary Checks combined, the company is giving away to its employes, entirely aside from all salary obligations, between four and five thousand dollars a day.

These are just two of the many means that we employ to humanize the relationship between the firm and the employes. With the first development of business on a large scale, the employment of a large number of workers developed a more or less mechanical relationship between employer and employee. Whatever we may think of it, big business is the order of the day. And wherever business is done on a large scale, helpers must be employed in enormous numbers. It is impossible that the head of the firm know each one personally, and yet it is necessary that in this new order of things, the employe shall not be reduced to the status of a mechanism. Although we may not know each of our employes personally, we do have very real interest in their welfare, and these voluntary contributions that we make entirely in addition to salaries are a tangible and a rather sizeable proof of that interest. . . .

Realizing that the right kind of outdoor exercise is essential to health, we have provided extensive athletic grounds. We have two large baseball diamonds and two leagues organized among the employes. We have fifteen tennis courts. We have a running track and a large field for all kinds of miscellaneous events. We conduct a yearly track meet which creates a tremendous amount of interest and promotes keen competition. We have had as high as twenty-five thousand spectators at this event.

Directly in front of the Administration Building is a large open space filled with flower gardens and ponds for lilies and gold fish. Shade trees and a pergola offer attractive lounging places to employes during the noon hour. Every Friday afternoon we also have a band concert here, given by our own band organized among the employes. We have a choral organization of about one hundred mixed voices.

We have the largest private restaurant in the world. By private I mean, of course, a restaurant operated for the employes of any single institution. This restaurant is divided into several sections, providing lunch counters, cafeteria for men and women, a large general dining room and a grill room. We feed daily between six and seven thousand of our employes. Wholesome, well cooked food is served here at less than cost, the deficit being made up by the firm.

We maintain a library for the use of our employes. Here in addition to seven thousand books of our own, any employe can get any book from the Chicago Public Library.

Convenient to the large offices in which most of our girls are employed, we have a large rest room, which is used for lounging during the noon hour and during the rest periods that are given morning and afternoon. This room is also used for concerts, dances and Red Cross work. . . .

Close to our plant is what is known as the S.R. branch of the Y.M.C.A. The company gave the ground for the building and also $100,000 towards its construction. This makes an ideal home for several hundred of our young men.

Despite the increasing scale of operations and the ever larger number of employees, the period from 1908 to 1925 saw no real development of personnel management. Wages and hours were improved over the earlier period. Employee restaurants were continued, and the "sunken gardens" at Homan and Arthington in Chicago were planted each season. The most striking welfare policy was, of course, the profit-sharing plan; and of more immediate benefit to ailing employees was the really liberal illness allowance policy. But except for the annual "field days"—picnics and games— the emphasis on group social affairs earlier sponsored by Elmer Scott was gone. The department managers continued to dominate employee relations, and, while over-all average earnings were improved, great disparities among departments were common.

In American industry personnel management as a special function was largely the proximate result of World War I.[19] While there were more fundamental forces operating through time, for example, the humanism of the nineteenth century, scientific management, and the shift in immigration, it was apparently the tight labor market of the war years that brought about the first important trend to personnel management.[20]

While Sears had not during these middle years paralleled the course of certain large firms with respect to functionalized labor management, the company had been progressive in terms of illness allowances and profit-sharing. This apparent inconsistency may be explained in terms of the psychology of Julius Rosenwald, who, while he was not "progressive" in a class sense, was likely to be sympathetic to individual cases of hardship. While Rosenwald as chief executive had to approve major policies, the evidence appears to support the view that his lieutenant, Albert Loeb, had a singularly important part in developing the profit-sharing plan. It is remarkable that old employees are unanimous in attributing whatever "soul" the company had in these years to Albert Loeb—and later to T. J. Carney and Lessing Rosenwald.

There seems to have been an absence of internal pressures in the company which might have given rise to a felt necessity for a better-integrated program of personnel management. The development of systems proceeded apace under the leadership of Otto Doering. The effect of rigorous systematization was that in the mail-order plants relatively unskilled labor could be used with a minimum of training on the job. In most jobs effective performance did not make serious demands on the higher faculties of employees.

One has no idea how high turnover may have been, but, at least for many jobs, replacements appear not to have been a serious problem. Probably the strongest factor serving to hold the more able and ambitious employees was the possibilities for promotions. The business was expanding at a prodigious rate; sales multiplied sixfold from 1908 to 1925; branch plants were opened in Dallas, Seattle, Philadelphia, and Kansas City; merchandise lines were broadened. The atmosphere throughout the period was one of expansion, except for the near-tragic decline of 1921. As the company grew, opportunities for promotion multiplied, and these promotions were made largely from within the company. It is difficult to estimate the powerful influence that such mobility must have contributed to the level of employee morale and stability, especially among the more talented workers.

CHAPTER XVIII

The Period in Review

SEARS, ROEBUCK had by 1908 established itself firmly as a going concern, clearly indicating not only that the mail-order business was here to stay for a long time but also that the company was pre-eminently the leader in that field. But whereas the company closed its first period with an annual volume of net sales of some $40,000,000 after a peak of $50,000,000 in 1907, it ended the middle period in 1925 with a resounding annual volume of $243,798,351 in net sales, only $1,575,067 below the peak of 1920. Since 1908 it had multiplied its annual volume some sixfold. In the process the company had seen its business rise to unprecedented heights during the great upsurge of farm income in the years of World War I; it had weathered a short but severe depression which had taxed its resources almost to the breaking point and had very nearly cost Rosenwald and the other top executives control of the business.

The years following 1908 proved to be highly profitable for Sears, Roebuck and Company. The sharp decline in sales and profits that frightened the company's leaders in 1907–8 proved not to be indicative of the fortunes that lay ahead. Indeed, the "crisis" of 1907–8 was illusory in that there was simply a temporary reversal of trend in sales and profits. Whereas the company had become accustomed to annual increases in sales and profits, sales declined in 1908 by about one-fifth, and profits one-third; but substantial profits were still realized in the amount of $2,034,796—5 per cent of sales.

Beginning in 1909 sales became substantially more productive of profits, as data in Table 38 clearly show. Whereas profits in the years *preceding* 1909 cluster about an average of approximately 7 per cent of sales, profits in the eleven years *following* 1909 never dropped below that figure, and in most years the profit ratio was well above this minimum of 7 per cent. In two years it was 12 per cent or more; in six years it was at least 10 per cent; and in ten of these eleven years prior to 1920 it was more than 8 per cent. Sears's acknowledged principal competitor, Montgomery Ward, failed to match the company's enviable record. Data on Ward's are available beginning with 1913. Table 39 shows a comparison of the profit ratio for the two mail-order firms.

From 1913 through 1919 Sears outstripped Ward's by wide margins, as shown in the relative position of the two companies in Table 40. Only in one year (1922) of the thirteen years from 1913 to 1925 did Ward's

TABLE 38*

SALES AND PROFITS, 1908-25

Year	Percentage Change in Sales from Previous Year	Sales per Dollar Working Capital	Sales per Dollar Net Worth	Sales per Dollar Assets	Net Profits per Dollar Sales	Rate of Return on Invested Capital
1908	−19.48	$10.87	$0.94	$0.83	$0.050	....
1909	26.92	5.85	1.05	0.96	.121	12.80
1910	20.23	6.23	1.17	1.06	.110	13.02
1911	4.54	5.13	1.15	1.06	.109	11.51
1912	20.28	3.75	1.28	1.17	.108	13.95
1913	18.47	2.99	1.39	1.20	.099	13.98
1914	5.11	3.03	1.34	1.24	.095	12.92
1915	10.63	2.41	1.36	1.27	.104	14.41
1916	29.16	2.22	1.53	1.34	.120	19.09
1917	20.85	1.86	1.70	1.27	.085	14.63
1918	9.56	1.67	1.75	1.21	.070	12.24
1919	28.81	2.07	2.01	1.51	.081	16.49
1920	4.87	4.21	2.03	1.06	.048	9.37
1921	−33.15	3.11	1.47	0.89	− .100	−13.64
1922	1.51	3.09	1.45	1.09	.033	4.57
1923	19.20	3.01	1.58	1.34	.058	9.18
1924	4.00	2.95	1.63	1.43	.070	10.81
1925	18.01	3.57	1.72	1.45	0.086	14.90

* Source: Calculated from data in the company's annual reports.

TABLE 39*

NET PROFIT AS PERCENTAGE OF SALES, SEARS, ROEBUCK AND COMPANY, MONTGOMERY WARD AND COMPANY, AND R. H. MACY AND COMPANY, 1909-25

Year	Sears	Ward's	Macy's
1909	12.1	....	5.82
1910	11.0	....	5.08
1911	10.9	....	3.76
1912	10.8	....	5.81
1913	9.9	4.2	4.54
1914	9.5	4.9	7.40
1915	10.4	5.0	9.19
1916	12.0	7.3	11.27
1917	8.5	5.6	7.99
1918	7.0	5.8	8.45
1919	8.1	4.2	9.96
1920	4.8	− 7.7	....
1921	−10.0	−14.4	....
1922	3.3	5.4	....
1923	5.8	5.8	....
1924	7.0	6.2	....
1925	8.6	6.7	....

* Source: Sears, Roebuck and Company and Montgomery Ward and Company data calculated from the companies' annual reports; R. H. Macy and Company data from Ralph M. Hower, *The History of Macy's* (Cambridge: Harvard University Press, 1946), p. 390.

exceed Sears in the profitability of its sales, although following the depression of 1921 the gap tended to narrow. Ward's did, however, succeed in increasing its share of the combined sales of the two houses from 29.5 per cent in 1921 to 41.2 per cent in 1925. While Sears had substantial losses in 1921, Montgomery Ward suffered more severely, and at greater length, for it had losses in two years of the period. Sears also excelled in profitability the fabulous New York department store, R. H. Macy and Company, although the last two years for which data on Macy's are available show a significant advantage for that firm.

TABLE 40*

RELATIVE POSITION OF SEARS, ROEBUCK AND COMPANY AND MONTGOMERY WARD AND COMPANY SALES, 1913-25
(In Thousands)

YEAR	NET SALES			PERCENTAGE OF TOTAL	
	Sears	Ward's	Total	Sears	Ward's
1913	$ 91,357	$ 39,726	$131,083	69.7	30.3
1914	96,025	41,042	137,067	70.0	30.0
1915	106,228	49,309	155,537	68.3	31.7
1916	137,201	62,044	199,245	68.9	31.1
1917	165,808	73,513	239,321	69.3	30.7
1918	181,656	76,167	257,823	70.5	29.5
1919	233,983	99,336	333,319	70.2	29.8
1920	245,373	101,745	347,118	70.7	29.3
1921	164,040	68,523	232,563	70.5	29.5
1922	166,514	84,739	251,253	66.3	33.7
1923	198,483	123,702	322,185	61.6	38.4
1924	206,431	150,045	356,476	57.9	42.1
1925	243,798	170,593	414,391	58.8	41.2

* Source: Sales figures from the companies' annual reports.

Some indication of the efficiency of merchandise management at Ward's and Sears is evident in a comparison of the inventory figures of the two competitors. As Table 41 makes clear, Sears had consistently lower inventory ratios (and thus greater turnover) than Ward's through 1919.[1] The determined effort to eliminate omissions in 1920 led to the sharp increase in Sears's inventories in that year, from which the firm did not fully recover for several years. Except for these latter years there seem to be no substantial or consistent differences in Sears's inventory ratios in the years preceding 1908 and those which followed.

Contributing to the profitability of the company's sales was the ability to maintain the sales ratio in terms of employees. If the data in Table 42 can be accepted as accurately reflecting employee productivity, there is no tendency evident for the sales ratio to decline in the face of heroic increases in the scale of operations. Rather the record shows a surprising tendency to uniformity except when the average is lifted by very large increases in dollar sales in a relatively short time as occurred from 1915 to 1919.

The company's management remained pretty nearly intact during this middle period, with Julius Rosenwald as clearly dominant in leadership as Richard Sears had been earlier. The differences in points of view between Rosenwald and Richard Sears were resolved with the departure of

TABLE 41*

MERCHANDISE INVENTORIES, SEARS, ROEBUCK AND COMPANY AND MONTGOMERY WARD AND COMPANY, 1909–25

Year	Sears's Inventory	Ward's Inventory	Inventory as Percentage of Sales	
			Sears	Ward's
1909	$ 8,362,780		16.4	
1910	9,309,338		15.2	
1911	9,381,021		14.6	
1912	11,332,224		14.7	
1913	13,176,911	$ 7,691,916	14.4	19.4
1914	13,273,927	6,780,823	13.8	16.5
1915	14,837,661	8,010,392	14.0	16.2
1916	25,370,055	13,797,462	18.5	22.2
1917	36,873,214	17,171,113	22.2	23.4
1918	47,531,097	27,101,516	26.2	35.6
1919	42,685,776	28,136,166	18.2	28.3
1920	105,071,243	30,282,672	42.8	29.8
1921	46,445,830	16,767,593	28.3	24.5
1922	34,737,519	18,718,024	20.9	22.1
1923	40,272,512	24,451,485	20.3	19.8
1924	35,021,821	26,322,434	17.2	17.5
1925	49,724,060	34,699,569	20.4	18.7

* Source: Calculated from data in the companies' annual reports.

TABLE 42*

EMPLOYEE PRODUCTIVITY, 1908–25

Year	Net Sales per Employee	Year	Net Sales per Employee
1908	$ 7,474	1917	$10,971
1909	8,281	1918	13,276
1910	8,016	1919	9,179
1911	8,219	1920	11,333
1912	9,551	1921	9,041
1913	9,648	1922	8,793
1914	10,828	1923	9,951
1915	10,168	1924	10,990
1916	10,875	1925	10,512

* Source: Calculated from data in the company's annual reports.

the latter from the firm. Divided responsibility was replaced by unified command.

Rosenwald's absence from the company from 1916 to 1920, while he was engaged in public service, shattered the continuity of top management less than might appear, for Albert Loeb moved up easily and logically to unofficial acting president. The one really significant change in the next layer of executives came in 1917, when General Merchandise Manager J. F. Skinner died; this change constituted a real loss. L. H. Crawford succeeded Skinner and was in turn succeeded, after the 1920–21 depression, by Max Adler. But Otto Doering continued throughout as operating chief, and

TABLE 43*

MERCHANDISE RETURNS—MAIL ORDER,† 1912–25

Year	Percentage Merchandise Returns to Sales	
	All Departments	All Departments Less Groceries
1912	3.6	3.8
1913	4.0	4.3
1914	3.9	4.3
1915	4.3	4.7
1916	4.9	5.4
1917	5.8	6.3
1918	6.3	6.5
1919	6.6	6.9
1920	7.4	7.7
1921	9.2	9.7
1922	9.6	10.1
1923	9.3	9.7
1924	8.6	8.9
1925	8.3	8.6

* Source: Company records.
† Refers to Chicago store.

most of the other executives remained in their positions. Rosenwald, even *in absentia*, surrendered the reins to Albert Loeb only for day-to-day decisions; ultimate control remained firmly in the hands of the former. The very favorable showing in the company's profit ratio is in itself convincing testimony of generally able management. Indeed, the problem of expense control must have been one of significant proportions in the face of the increasing merchandise returns.

Table 43 shows a marked tendency for returns to grow. Excluding groceries, which produced large sales volume with virtually no returns, returned goods increased steadily from 3.8 per cent of sales in 1912 to 10.1 per cent in 1922, after which the ratio fell to 8.6 in 1925. Including the grocery department the figure of 4.0 for 1913 is comparable to Macy's experience for that year, when Macy's returns ran to 3.92 per cent of sales.

Thereafter, the mail-order house had markedly worse return ratios than did the New York department store. For the eight years 1913–20 Macy's highest ratio was reached in 1917, when returns amounted to 4.38 per cent of net sales. In that year Sears recorded 5.8 per cent for all departments, and 6.3 per cent when groceries were eliminated. While Sears's returns mounted to more than 7 per cent in 1920, Macy's fell to 3.36 per cent.[2] Unquestionably the advent of parcel post contributed heavily to the worsening mail-order experience in this regard. While this postal service made it more attractive to order goods from the mail-order companies, it also made it easier to return merchandise—and Sears paid the postage both ways on returns.

In addition, the sudden rise in the number of orders which parcel post induced compelled the company both to improve and to alter rather sharply its schedule system of shipping. The average value of orders received in 1912 was $7.91; in 1913, the first year of parcel post, the average value dropped to $6.84, a decline of $1.07—yet the total volume of business rose from $77,116,859 in net sales in 1912 to $91,357,276. In more specific terms, the year of parcel post's inauguration witnessed a fivefold increase in the *number* of orders received.

According to testimony of retired Sears's employees, the company was far more willing than ready when the new legislation took effect, for the tremendous increase in the number of orders wreaked something close to havoc in Sears, Roebuck's shipping department. Customers apparently found it more convenient to send small orders frequently instead of accumulating their needs and sending one large order. The company sought to reverse, or at least to stem, this trend by advertising the fact that even parcel post had its gradations in the cost per pound and that it therefore still paid to send larger orders. (The parcel-post rate for the second pound in a package, for example, was less than for the first pound, and one ten-pound package cost much less to ship than three packages totaling ten pounds in weight.)

Sears, Roebuck was compelled to make an extensive rearrangement of the physical facilities of its shipping department. Prior to 1913 the shipping facilities were arranged on the basis of freight centers; the destination of a shipment determined its location on the platform to make it accessible to the proper spur line. After the advent of parcel post, however, more and more shipments had to go through the post office, necessitating considerable rearrangement on the company's part. Within fifteen months after the inauguration of parcel post, the company was sending out an average of 20,000 parcels a day through the mails and paying postage of $6,000 per day. It was soon the largest single user of parcel post.[3] According to one Sears employee, the Chicago Post Office was as unprepared for the increased shipping arising from parcel post as was Sears, Roebuck and Company. He says that the post-office facilities were so limited that postal officials there were "humiliated" in the holiday seasons of 1915 and 1916.

The steady improvement in the company's schedule system of shipping, and the extension of that principle to other phases of operations, must surely have been of great assistance in enabling the company to secure and handle its steadily growing volume of business. By 1926 the company claimed "actual tests show that 99 out of every 100 mail orders are shipped within 24 hours after we receive them. In fact, about half the orders are shipped within 10 hours after they are received, because the orders received up to noon are shipped the same day and those received in the afternoon are shipped by noon the next day."[4]

Parcel post, in addition to compelling further improvements in the shipping system, also exerted its effect on the company's merchandise offerings. Whereas up to 1913 the emphasis had been primarily on hard lines and heavy goods for shipment by freight or express, the emphasis was to switch more toward soft lines with "eye appeal" to encourage customers ordering by parcel post to order more often. The greater emphasis on soft-goods items in the sales records, with the increase in numbers of styles and patterns, also contributed to higher returns.

The responsibility for this expansion of the merchandise line and, concomitantly, of the number of sources supplying the company, lay almost entirely in the hands of the department heads or buyers; as pointed out earlier, there was no over-all merchandise pattern in those years, nor was there any clearly articulated pattern of relationships with sources. The company continued to add to the list of its own wholly or partially owned factories and to the list of "outside" suppliers. Yet despite the lack of any real over-all merchandise pattern, trial and error during those years tended to define Sears, Roebuck's merchandise program. The enormous successes of some lines and the resounding failures of expensively priced, "high-style" lines helped to point up the particulars of the company's true mission in distribution. The losses on the Lady Duff-Gordon women's wear and the expensive men's wearing apparel sharply underscored the nature of Sears's market and clarified hitherto nebulous spheres of operations.

At the same time the point of departure for those unfortunate ventures—a desire to improve the quality of its goods—yielded happier results in other respects, for the general quality of the goods offered by the company did improve considerably during the years after 1908. Not only were such dubious lines as patent medicines discontinued, but the lines which did remain were subjected to closer scrutiny not only to ascertain whether they were of a quality high enough to merit the prices asked for them but also whether they were even of the best quality available at the price being paid for them. The laboratories were of great assistance in determining the quality of merchandise, and it was not until after their inauguration that the company's buyers discovered how at times the lowest-priced item might prove also to be of better quality. In short, the laboratories helped destroy stereotypes of thinking about relationships between price and quality.

Just as the laboratories helped ascertain the quality of merchandise, so did they also unearth additional factual information about each item of merchandise they examined—its tensile and compressive strength, its resistance to fading, washing, sunlight, its tendency to rust, to shrink, to wrinkle, or whatever. In short, the laboratories made possible for the first time really accurate and detailed descriptions of goods. Those descriptions enabled the catalogue to present goods not only more accurately but also in more detailed terms than ever before. Those who sought most diligently to "reform" catalogue presentation now had for the first time a positive alternative to loose generalizations.

The beginnings of a new emphasis on correct and conservatively phrased descriptions in the big book made itself felt also in the sales-promotion approach. It would have been too glaringly inconsistent to describe merchandise in detail on one catalogue page, giving perhaps the exact count of broadcloth and rate of shrinkage, and then on the facing (or any other) page to scream the glad tidings of a great promotion scheme offering much of something for very nearly nothing. More conservative catalogue presentation found itself almost perforce the handmaiden of similarly more cautious sales-promotion devices.

The company's sales promotion in this period was highlighted by two activities which were in one way greatly similar and in another sharply dissimilar. The "Modern Homes" venture and the sale of a variety of goods on the instalment plan were alike in that each offered easy-payment arrangements which enabled many customers to purchase high-unit-price durable goods when they might otherwise have been unable to do so. The great dissimilarity between the two lay in the fact that, while "Modern Homes" came to be predicated upon an ever more unsound basis of overly generous nature, which culminated eventually in near-disaster and led the company to abandon that field perhaps permanently, instalment selling came to operate upon an ever sounder structure, especially after the advent of the retail stores, and to become one of the firm's most potent selling instruments. Even in this period, instalment selling added materially to the firm's sales volume so productive of profit.

The profitability of the Sears operation in this period is truly impressive, especially when one realizes that, while the profit ratio was high, it was not gained at the sacrifice of sales volume. Table 44 chronicles the bare relief outlines of the company's growth during these years. From 1909 to 1925 net sales increased nearly five times; net profits more than three times. If one uses the 1925 "net income before federal income taxes" figure ($25,453,165), profits had increased approximately 400 per cent over 1909.

An analysis of changes in sales and profits by decades further emphasizes the very successful record achieved by Sears in the twenty years following 1906. Table 45 charts the company's experience in ten-year periods. Even a cursory examination impresses one with the ability of the firm to expand sales greatly with no material sacrifice of profit margins. Indeed, for the decade 1906–15 the profits increased more than 500 per cent with a sales increase of less than 400 per cent. The decade 1916–25 brought further notable increases (despite the 1921 depression), although, of course,

TABLE 44*

INDEXES OF GROWTH, 1908–25

Calendar Year	Net Sales	Working Capital	Net Worth†	Total Assets	Net Profit‡ or Loss
1908§	$ 40,843,866				$ 2,034,796
1909	51,011,536	$ 8,720,480	$ 48,560,476	$ 53,257,173	6,192,361
1910	61,329,792	9,846,506	52,344,691	57,805,712	6,759,876
1911	64,112,194	12,497,042	55,743,760	60,768,949	6,984,967
1912	77,110,859	20,556,660	60,059,286	65,883,832	8,322,611
1913	91,357,276	30,598,452	65,727,638	75,954,037	9,027,670
1914	96,024,754	31,878,314	71,449,990	77,725,078	9,081,521
1915	106,228,421	44,087,673	78,141,429	83,866,578	11,100,388
1916	137,200,803	61,685,790	89,458,773	102,734,992	16,488,622
1917	165,807,608	89,140,078	97,470,505	130,468,809	14,119,928
1918	181,655,830	108,619,356	103,616,135	150,555,314	12,704,064
1919	233,982,584	113,019,747	116,574,919	154,834,632	18,890,125
1920	245,373,418	58,338,877	120,564,734	230,668,197	11,746,670
1921	164,039,720	52,814,443	111,935,760	184,818,815	16,435,469
1922	166,514,110	53,917,975	114,621,587	152,867,921	5,435,168
1923	198,482,946	65,967,681	125,575,017	147,573,414	11,512,618
1924	206,430,527	69,974,876	126,440,452	144,403,108	14,354,397
1925	243,798,351	68,328,777	141,908,667	167,982,622	20,975,304

* Source: Calculated from data in the company's annual reports.
† Capital plus surplus.
‡ All profit figures are after federal taxes and contributions to profit-sharing.
§ Fiscal year ending June 30, 1908.

the rate of increase was noticeably less. The table also points up the significance of the "new" tax legislation after 1916.

The very successful sales results of the company appear to have necessitated progressively larger amounts of working capital. It must be here noted, however, that conclusions on this score may be subject to significant error for two reasons: first, prior to 1920 the company's annual reports were not truly consolidated statements, and the method of reporting was such that it is impossible to get very accurate estimates of working capital;[5] second, the only figures available for calculating working capital are provided by end-of-year statements. In terms of what information is available, the middle years (1909–25) show marked increases over the first period (1886–1908). Sales per dollar of working capital (Table 38) in 1908 were $10.87. In certain previous years working capital had been even further economized, the sales per dollar of working capital having been $54.52 in 1905 and $17.20 in 1907. In only two years from 1896 to 1908 did the figure fall below $7.00. Certainly the very high efficiency of working capital in 1905 may be attributed largely to the fact that only the year-end figure is available. It was in that year that liquid resources had been drained by construction of the new plant.

The years after 1908 show a definite increase in working capital needs. In no year, except 1910, did the ratio of sales to working capital exceed 6.0;

TABLE 45*

SALES AND PROFITS BY DECADES, 1896–1925

Decade	Net Sales	Profits after Income Taxes Amount	Percentage of Sales	Profits before Income Taxes Amount	Percentage of Sales
1896–1905..	$ 147,939,108	$ 10,924,080	7.38	$ 10,924,080	7.38
1906–15...	684,298,942	65,589,840	9.58	65,589,840	9.58
1916–25†...	1,944,306,205	109,791,427	5.65	135,836,540	6.99
1916–25‡...	1,780,266,485	126,226,896	7.09	152,272,009	8.55

Decade	Sales Increase over Previous Decade Amount	Per Cent	Increase in Profits after Income Taxes over Previous Decade Amount	Per Cent	Increase in Profits before Income Taxes over Previous Decade Amount	Per Cent
1906–15...	$ 536,359,834	362.55	$54,665,760	500.42	$54,665,760	500.42
1916–25†...	1,260,007,263	184.13	44,201,587	67.39	70,246,700	107.10
1916–25‡...	1,095,967,543	160.16	60,637,056	92.45	86,682,169	132.16

* Source: Calculated from data in the company's annual reports.
† Including 1921 sales volume and losses.
‡ Excluding 1921 sales volume and losses.

and in most years sales per dollar of working capital were nearer $3.00. The years of the great sales boom, 1915–19, reflect clearly the tendency of working capital needs to outrun sales increases. In general, it is probably true that in these years of maturity the company could better afford advances in working capital than it could in the earlier phase when its resources were not so ample.

Sales per dollar of assets and/or net worth do not reveal the same tendency as has been shown in connection with working capital, although, in general, the years preceding 1908 showed much greater exploitation of assets than the years following 1908. The inclusion of $30,000,000 "good will" in the total assets and capital figures after 1906, however, is largely responsible for the difference observed between the two periods.

The ultimate economic test of relative efficiency in the utilization of capital is to be discerned, of course, in the rate of return on invested capital. Calculations of this nature are extremely uncertain.[6] Throughout the period 1909–25 the rate of return on invested capital appears to decline—in contrast to the fivefold increase in sales and the expansion of plant measured by any other standard. As compared with the years prior to 1907 the middle period shows a marked decline. One could hardly expect to continue indefinitely at the level achieved in 1895—a return of 90 per cent on net worth; or the 85 per cent of 1892. A clue to the lower rates of return in the ensuing

TABLE 46*

RATE OF RETURN ON INVESTMENT, SEARS, ROEBUCK
AND COMPANY AND MONTGOMERY WARD
AND COMPANY, 1909–15

Year	Ward's	Sears Excluding Good Will†	Sears Including Good Will
1909	. . . .	34.4	12.8
1910	. . . .	31.0	13.0
1911	. . . .	27.2	11.5
1912	. . . .	28.1	13.95
1913	. . . .	26.1	13.98
1914	13.3	22.6	12.92
1915	14.9	23.6	14.41
1916	24.1	29.4	19.09
1917	18.9	21.2	14.63
1918	17.1	17.2	12.24
1919	10.0	22.6	16.49
1920	−15.9	12.7	9.37
1921	−26.4	−19.0	−13.64
1922	13.9	6.6	4.57
1923	18.8	12.7	9.18
1924	20.0	14.5	10.81
1925	21.1	19.6	14.90

* Source: Calculated from data in the companies' annual reports.
† These figures indicate rate of return when "good will" has been excluded from the capital investment base. In 1906 common stock was issued against $30,000,000 "good will" as well as tangible assets. In 1926 the company began to write down "good-will" valuation by charges against surplus until the original $30,000,000 was reduced to $1.00 in 1934.

years is found in the abrupt decline from 1905, when the rate of return on invested capital was 39.4 per cent, to 1907, when the figure stood at 7.6 per cent. Between these two years the capital base was increased by the $30,000,000 good-will valuation at which common stock was evaluated. The return on invested capital for Sears and the company's largest competitor is compared in Table 46, which also shows the rates of return with alternative treatments of good will.

When Sears and Ward's are compared in this regard, the advantage seems to lie with the former enterprise until the onset of the 1920–21 depression. For the predepression years, Sears was clearly superior when good will is excluded from the capital base. Conclusions on this point, however, are not clear, since the capital base for Sears tends to be larger due to certain reserves having been included in the capital base when they were believed to be surplus reserves. In the absence of any special knowledge the figure for Ward's, on the other hand, was derived simply from the capital and surplus figures indicated on the financial statements.

The years 1922–25 show a clear advantage for Ward's—as does the relative gain in sales for these years (Table 40). That company's recovery from the 1920–21 cataclysm was noticeably more rapid than was Sears, Roebuck's. In this connection it is interesting to recall the comment in the January 13, 1928, *Wall Street Journal:* "As vice president of Montgomery Ward & Co. it was generally understood that General Wood contributed largely to the comeback of that company following the struggle of 1920 and 1921."

The solid quality of the "golden age" has been evident in the foregoing review of the company's growth and prosperity. As the volume of business and profits mounted, Sears's stockholders reaped rich rewards. In this period, in addition to dividends, holders of equity shares saw all prior claimants of profits eliminated. Until the end of 1920 Sears's capital structure contained no bonded indebtedness. In that year recourse was made to the issue of $50,000,000 in 7 per cent serial gold notes. These notes were entirely paid off by the end of 1923. It will be remembered that at the time of the reincorporation in 1906, preferred stock was issued in the amount of $10,000,000. The retirement (out of surplus) of the preferred stock began in 1909 and was virtually completed in 1924. Dividends of 7 per cent had been paid each year on the preferred stock outstanding.

Thus by 1925 the firm's capital structure consisted simply of 1,005,000 shares of $100 par value common stock. In 1926 these shares were exchanged for no-par stock in the ratio of four shares of the new stock for one of the old. But the shareholders did not have to await the elimination of prior claimants to realize income from their holdings of common stock. Information on outstanding stock and dividends is summarized in Table 47.

The first dividend to holders of common was paid in 1909—4½ per cent in cash. This was increased to 7 per cent in 1910. The dividend of $7.00 per share continued until 1917, when $7.75 was paid. The following year the dividend rate on the par value of shares was raised to 8 per cent, where it remained through 1920. The depression which fully materialized in 1921 brought dividends down to $2.00 per share—paid in scrip. The full burden of the depression, the pressure of interest charges, and the 7 per cent payable on preferred stock dictated that dividends on common be passed in 1922 and 1923. More prophetic voices would have dictated a similar course in 1921, but dividends had been declared before the catastrophe was fully appreciated.

In the decade 1911–20 outstanding stock was increased from 300,000 shares (common) to 1,050,000 shares by the declaration of generous stock dividends of 33⅓ per cent in 1911; 50 per cent in 1915; 25 per cent in 1917; and 40 per cent in 1920. In February, 1926, equity shares were converted from the original $100 par value basis to no-par stock in the ratio of four to one. Despite the great expansion of the business, no new equity capital was brought into the company. Instead, the capital necessary to finance expansion was derived from surplus by converting it into capital through the issuance of stock dividends. As Table 48 makes clear, in only two years of

TABLE 47*

STOCK AND DIVIDEND RECORD, 1907–25

Year	Number of Stockholders	Shares of Common Outstanding	Shares of Preferred Outstanding	Amount Distributed in Cash Dividends	Cash Dividend per Share Common	Stock Dividend (Per Cent)
1907	263	300,000	97,500	$ 682,500†		
1908	283	300,000	97,500	682,500†		
1909	870	300,000	90,000	2,019,375	$4.50	
1910	1,014	300,000	88,000	2,717,750	7.00	
1911	1,412	400,000	85,000	3,223,628	7.00	33⅓
1912	1,487	400,000	80,000	3,385,617	7.00	
1913	1,866	400,000	80,000	3,359,318	7.00	
1914	1,897	400,000	80,000	3,359,169	7.00	
1915	2,773	600,000	80,000	4,408,948	7.00	50
1916	2,763	600,000	80,000	4,759,062	7.00	
1917	3,902	750,000	80,000	6,108,197	7.75	25
1918	1,550	750,000	80,000	6,558,434	8.00	
1919	4,436	750,000	80,000	6,558,712	8.00	
1920	6,684	1,050,000	80,000	7,757,216	8.00	40
1921	8,041	1,000,000	80,000	2,658,658	2.00‡	
1922	8,656	1,000,000	80,000	559,188†		
1923	9,271	1,000,000	80,000	559,188†		
1924	8,411	1,000,000	§	3,488,982	3.00	
1925	5,965	1,005,000	§	6,007,089	6.00	

* Source: Calculated from data in the company's annual reports and from company records.
† Dividends paid only on preferred stock (7 per cent).
‡ Paid in 6 per cent scrip redeemed August 15, 1922.
§ All preferred capital stock was called for redemption on November 15, 1924. The balance sheets show "Preferred Capital Stock Not Presented for Redemption" in 1924, $154,071; in 1925, $51,231.07.

the span from 1908 to 1925 was as much as 50 per cent of net income paid out in cash dividends, and in most years the proportion was appreciably less.

The effect of stock dividends combined with a "constant" dollar dividend rate was to increase the percentage return (and dollar income) of stockholders who held shares purchased at the time of the company's initial issue in 1906. The results of the company's dividend policy for investors are visible in Table 49. A purchaser of one share of Sears's common stock in September, 1906, would have held the equivalent of 3.5 shares by the end of 1925; by the end of February, 1926, the same stockholder would have held 14 shares, and would have received a total of $239.08 in cash divi-

TABLE 48*

PROPORTION OF NET INCOME PAID IN CASH DIVIDENDS, 1908–25

Year	Percentage Net Income Paid in Cash	Year	Percentage Net Income Paid in Cash
1908	33.54	1917	43.26
1909	32.61	1918	51.62
1910	40.20	1919	34.72
1911	46.15	1920	66.04
1912	40.68	1921	†
1913	37.21	1922	10.29
1914	36.99	1923	4.88
1915	39.72	1924	24.31
1916	28.86	1925	28.64

* Calculated from data in the company's annual reports.
† Dividend, $2,658,658; net loss, $16,435,469.

TABLE 49*

DIVIDEND RECORD AND STOCK INCREASES, 1906–26

Year	Stock Dividends	Original Share Would Equal	Cash Dividends Per Share	Cash Dividends Total
1906		1		
1907		1		
1908		1		
1909		1	$4.50	$ 4.50
1910		1	7.00	7.00
1911		1	1.75	13.25
	4/1 33⅓%	1.33⅓	5.25	6.998
1912		1.33⅓	7.00	9.333
1913		1.33⅓	7.00	9.333
1914		1.33⅓	7.00	9.333
1915		1.33⅓	1.75	2.333
	4/1 50%	2.00	5.25	10.50
1916		2.00	7.00	14.00
1917		2.00	1.75	3.50
	4/1 25%	2.50	6.00	15.00
1918		2.50	8.00	20.00
1919		2.50	8.00	20.00
1920		2.50	4.00	10.00
	7/15 40%	3.50	4.00	14.00
1921		3.50	2.00†	7.00
1922		3.50		
1923		3.50		
1924		3.50	3.00	10.50
1925		3.50	6.00	21.00
1926		3.50	1.50	5.25
	2/23 4 for 1	14.00	1.875	26.25

* Source: Goldman, Sachs and Company.
† In scrip.

dends, nearly five times more than the $50 paid for the original share in 1906.

Too, the capital value of his holdings would have shown an impressive growth. Even at the very low stock-market prices of 1921 an original share of Sears, Roebuck and Company would have brought $62.65. Such a sale in 1925 would have returned $163.59. If this hypothetical trader had held his share until 1926 before selling, he would have realized $736.12—a capital gain of 1,470 per cent on his $50 investment of twenty years earlier![7]

As capital values climbed and cash dividends supplemented the stock dividends, increasing amounts of outstanding stock came to be more broadly held. Whereas in the years prior to the New York incorporation in 1906 nearly all the stock was controlled by Richard Sears and Julius Rosenwald, the following decades saw substantial increases in the number of stock holders until more than nine thousand persons were registered as shareholders, as shown in Table 44. By the end of 1925 greater concentration appeared and the number of stockholders declined to 5,965—still a very much broader distribution than in 1908, when 283 stockholders held all the outstanding stock of the company.

That steady growth in the number of stockholders was paralleled by a great expansion in catalogue circulation, which rose from 6,582,542 in 1908 to 13,310,978 in 1925. The lineup system and other devices worked out before 1925 made physical production of the book so systematic that more attention could be devoted to every word and phrase in it, making for improvement in its presentation. An important part of the increase in catalogue circulation was certainly attributable to the addition of more mail-order branches. Following the success of the Dallas branch, opened in 1906, came branches in Seattle in 1910, at Philadelphia in 1920, and at Kansas City in 1925. By the end of 1925 Richard Sears's dream of a chain of branch plants covering the country was on the way to coming true.

The greatly increased catalogue circulation and the blanketing of much of the country with branch mail-order plants were important factors in enabling the company to increase steadily the percentage of farm cash income represented by its mail-order sales. That percentage rose from 1.12 in 1910 to a peak of 2.26 in 1923; after reaching 2.02 in 1920, it did not again in this period drop below 2 per cent, as Table 50 clearly shows. Thus Sears's sales were not simply the result of riding the crest of farm income. The effectiveness of management policy is plain in the successful efforts to increase the portion of farm income which the company captured.

This and all the other impressive accomplishments had not, however, been achieved without opposition of the character which had fought the mail-order houses in the earlier period, for the enactment of a parcel post, which served to crystallize and polarize that opposition, did not mark its end. The character of the opposition by many independent retailers did not change; its intensity simply diminished during the lush years leading up to the debacle of 1920. That same undercurrent of opposition continued at a somewhat abated pitch throughout the 1920's (abated at least as compared with its earlier stridence), only to flare up higher in the great depression beginning in 1929.

Much of the local merchants' opposition in this period was directed at chain stores of various kinds, which enjoyed a greater increase in business after the first World War than any other class of retail trade.

But the independent local dealer generally felt the mail-order house an even deadlier enemy than the chain store, for it even more directly "took money out of the town." Often a politician did not dare buy beyond his city limits lest it be construed as a reflection on the local merchants. New slogans appeared on trolley car and bus signs, "Patronize your NABORHOOD druggist" and "NABORHOODS loyal to their stores have the best stores," boldly challenging at once the old-fashioned spelling and the new-fangled mercantile centralization.[8]

TABLE 50*

PERCENTAGE OF FARM CASH INCOME REPRESENTED
BY COMPANY MAIL-ORDER SALES, 1910–25

Year	Percentage	Year	Percentage
1910	1.12	1918	1.48
1911	1.23	1919	1.77
1912	1.38	1920	2.02
1913	1.54	1921	2.18
1914	1.67	1922	2.12
1915	1.76	1923	2.26
1916	1.90	1924	2.18
1917	1.66	1925	2.24

* Source: Company records.

The local merchants' opposition to mail-order houses had stemmed in large part from the fact that mail order's natural market lay largely in farm trade. And mail order's ability to hold its own—and more—in a time when the essence of its earliest appeal was manifestly being eroded away was a constant irritant to independent retailers, for mail order throve despite the fact that the bitter isolation of life on the farm, which had helped initially to make mail-order buying attractive, was diminished to a rather considerable degree in this period, through the telephone, radio, improved roads, and other advances. Accompanying the diminution of the physical isolation was a notable improvement in retailing facilities available to the people, as great chain stores spread across the land. And, of course, the novelty of buying by mail and the "surprise" and pleasure of opening packages from distant cities must have worn off long before 1925.

Yet the great mail-order houses experienced their most profitable years during this period, ample indication that they still had something vital to offer their customers. The mail-order houses surely had several things remaining in their favor despite all the great changes going on in the living and buying habits of a nation. Their guaranty remained rock-ribbed: satisfaction or your money back. The guaranty by Sears, Roebuck (and, of course, Montgomery Ward) was at least as scrupulously observed in the middle as in the early period. All considerations of price and quality aside, that service to the consumer must have been of incalculable value to the company, assuring the customer as it did that he could not lose.

Actually, however, considerations of price and quality were never laid aside; the company saw to that. It continued to stress price, even if in terms less dramatic than those employed earlier by Richard Sears. The buying public seemed to feel that the mail-order houses did sell for less. *Fortune* magazine later mirrored the prevailing view that Sears, Roebuck's (and, by implication, Montgomery Ward's) prices were lower in this period:

> The solid worth of the original mail-order Sears in the economy may be taken for granted; 5,000,000 farm families on the catalogue list testify to that. Over the past half-century mail-order buying has saved them countless millions in the cost of goods, and performed a service function that the crossroads general store could not match....[9]

Yet it should be kept in mind that the quality of the goods sold received almost coequal "billing" with price. The catalogues of both large mail-order houses stressed quality at every conceivable opportunity, partly perhaps to escape the inference that lower prices connoted lower quality and to escape the connotation of "cheapness" with which both had earlier had to cope. Ward's led the way in *documentation* of quality in at least one respect, for its 1908 catalogue pointed out that Ward's groceries bore the seal of approval of an analytical chemist. But Sears leap-frogged this claim, and landed far on the other side, when it established its own testing laboratories in 1911. Sears's emphasis on laboratory-determined quality reached its peak in the 1919 catalogue with the two-page layout describing the functions of its laboratories in pin-pointing quality in all its merchandise.

Sears held still another attraction for consumers in the breadth of its merchandise line. Customers apparently came to feel that they could secure virtually any goods of any kind they might need—including homes and even, for a few years, automobiles—from the company. Sears became pretty much the "complete" store. And coincident with the growth in the variety of its offerings was an increasing emphasis on style and fashion. Even before, and certainly after, the fiasco of the Lady Duff-Gordon clothing venture, Sears emphasized that it stood ready to make fashion plates of all its customers—at price offerings not usually associated with the height of style. Ward's catalogues in this period devoted considerable space to picturing their New York buying office (apparently quite similar to Sears's) and asserting that their location in that metropolis kept them fully abreast of every change in fashion, no matter how slight, and that the farm wife in Montana could grace an Easter Parade with all the éclat one could hope to find on Fifth Avenue. Sears's catalogues likewise stressed fashion—and punched the argument home with what appeared to be convincingly low prices.

Those goods were in actuality only a portion—albeit a considerable portion—of the goods which helped to increase the physical comforts of farm life and thus to alleviate its isolation and discomfort. In Slosson's words, "The multiplication and usual cheapening of such luxuries as the automobile, telephone service, phonograph, radio, central heating, plumbing fixtures and the like transformed the farmhouse radically."[10] But since the mail-order houses offered most of those goods, and a host of others, frequently on instalments and always at what the farmers felt were lower prices, their catalogues continued to find a warm reception.

The expansion of the company's merchandise line and the introduction of a new sales-promotion device in the form of instalment selling were undoubtedly more important in maintaining the catalogue's "prestige" than any magic art of the makers of that book. One writer pointed out in 1946:

> The catalogue has been a power in making primitive standards of living obsolescent. Outdoor plumbing, for example, is today regarded, even in the most remote areas, as being the mark of poverty or extreme backwardness. Year after year the catalogue has presented indoor plumbing systems, with an eloquence that only the most backward farmer or villager could resist.
>
> Much has been said about the profound influence motion pictures have had on American life in creating a national standard of dress, making people conscious of personal appearance, and forming desires for new luxuries and physical comforts. Actually the mail-order catalogue was having all these effects two generations before motion pictures became popular.[11]

But the mail-order houses were by no means the only outlets for indoor-plumbing fixtures; what is significant is how much of such merchandise they—and, for our purposes, especially Sears, Roebuck—sold in the face of what became almost ubiquitous competition. And as for the motion pictures, it is significant that mail-order houses not only helped "nationalize" American dress and habits before the advent of the "flickers" but that the mail-order catalogues were able to continue pulling such a great volume of business in the face of all the new competition and the old opposition. It does not appear too far-fetched, from the records at hand, to conclude that the company's vast array of merchandise offerings, presented at dramatically low prices in its well-made catalogue, still put it in a position where it was supplementing rather than competing with the brave new world so clearly evident in the celluloid glamour of Valentino, Pola Negri, and Pearl White and all the rest of the storied stage which unfolded before Hollywood's still-silent cameras.

Development of Retail Stores, 1925–48

CHAPTER XIX

Urban America

WITH some misgiving, in 1925 Sears, Roebuck and Company turned to accommodate itself to the unrelenting trend toward urbanization that had become increasingly evident with each successive census. Although there had been clear signs of migration to the cities for a very long time, this became the characteristic feature of population movement as the great westward expansion of the nineteenth century came to a close about 1890.[1]

Of a total United States population of 3,929,214 in 1790, all but 5.1 per cent lived in rural areas. The first post–Civil War enumeration found the urban population had increased to 25.7 per cent of the total. The census of 1890, four years after Richard Sears began selling watches, disclosed that more than one-third of the people were urban residents. The population had been increasing at such a rate, however, that at the turn of the century the number of rural residents had more than doubled in number since 1850. Thus in 1900 the rural population still outnumbered the urban group by more than 15,000,000 despite the fact that over the fifty-year period the relative population status of rural residents had worsened until they accounted for but 60.3 per cent of the total population compared to the earlier 84.7 per cent.

Two decades later, however, the balance tipped in favor of urban America; 1920 saw the United States population concentrated in urban areas. Of 105,710,620 persons, 54,157,973, or 51.2 per cent, were classified by the census as living in "urban places." Ten years later the Bureau of the Census enumerators reported that 68,954,823 persons were urban dwellers—56.2 per cent of the United States population. The 1920's registered great gains for the cities, whereas the absolute increase in rural communities was little more than 2 million persons (from 51,552,647 to 53,820,223) the cities gained more than 14 millions over the 1920 figure of 54,157,973.

The urban population increased more than 63 per cent between 1910 and 1930 in contrast to an increase of but 8 per cent in the rural population. Over the forty years from 1890 to 1930 the impressive character of Americans' preference for town and city life is evident in the 209 per cent increase in urban population. Over the same years rural population gained but 32 per cent.[2]

"Farm" population showed an even more marked loss in position than

313

did "rural" population. In 1910 the farm population numbered 32,076,960. By 1920 that figure had declined to 31,614,269, and in 1925 it stood at 27,853,000.[3] Among those persons classified by the census as "rural," there was an increasing tendency to cluster in villages—both agricultural and industrial. By 1930, when the census first presented the subclassifications, 43 per cent of the total rural population was in the nonfarm category.[4]

The early years of the 1930's saw the short-lived "back-to-the-farm" movement, but by 1940 the urban figure had risen to 74,423,702—56.5 per cent of the population.[5]

The movement from farm to city was especially pronounced during the 1920's, but it was not evenly distributed throughout the country, nor had it been since 1900. Indeed, the loss of rural population appeared to be most important where agriculture was most prosperous. It was in those areas that mechanization proceeded fastest, and in an effort to maximize the gains from such mechanization there was some tendency to effect a consolidation of smaller farms to realize what economies might accrue from large-scale production. Thus it was that several prosperous agricultural states in the Midwest experienced absolute declines in rural population after 1900.[6]

Especially in the years after the close of World War I, the urban population was showing signs of centrifugal movement, and a shadowland was developing between town and country, posing new opportunities—and new problems—to retailers of many types. The suburban movement was well advanced as Sears, Roebuck turned to the opening of retail stores and attendant problems of location.

Already in the decade prior to 1930 the population within the core cities of ninety-six metropolitan districts had grown only a fifth, while their fringes increased almost two fifths. This trend continued through the thirties, the number of metropolitan districts advancing from a hundred and thirty-three in 1930 to a hundred and forty ten years later, at which time they comprised forty-two million people in the central areas and twenty million on the periphery. Thus, while Americans showed their incorrigible attraction to metropolitan civilization, they revealed an increasing desire to escape from its nuclear tyranny.[7]

The traditional mail-order market was not only failing to increase in terms of population, but ground lost in the severe decline in prices and income in 1920 and 1921 was never regained in agriculture until the country was at war again in 1942. And the farmers labored long under the heavy volume of debt contracted in the expanding market of the earlier war. Table 51 contrasts the course of farmers' cash income and national income from 1919 to 1929. As Morris Copeland notes, "The growth of national income has been in spite of the depression in agriculture."[8]

From the high of over fourteen billions in 1919 the cash receipts of farmers fell to barely eight billions in 1921; from this figure cash income slowly climbed to $11,303,000,000 in 1929 only to collapse once more and recede to a low of $4,747,000,000 in 1932. In 1940 farmers' cash receipts had still not regained the losses of the past decade, and, in fact, were below the figure for 1923. Throughout the decade of the 1920's the farmers' share of the national income continued to decline, and the early years of the following decade brought farm production even lower until in 1933 it represented but 7 per cent of the national income.

Contributing further to the problems the farmer faced were the introduction of new products and the output from competitive areas and the shifting preferences of consumers. Dixon Wecter has commented:

[The farmer] had to face the bewildering problem of changing consumer tastes. The cotton farmer sadly pondered not only the cheaper production of new

TABLE 51*

FARM INCOME AND NATIONAL INCOME, 1919-29
(In Millions)

Year	Farm Income	National Income
1919	$14,602	$68,200
1920	12,608	69,500
1921	8,150	51,700
1922	8,594	59,500
1923	9,563	68,300
1924	10,221	68,800
1925	10,995	73,700
1926	10,564	76,600
1927	10,756	75,900
1928	11,072	78,700
1929	11,303	87,355

* Source: farm income (cash receipts from marketings and government payments), Statistical Abstract of the United States, 1946, p. 624; national income, J. F. Dewhurst and Associates, America's Needs and Resources (New York: Twentieth Century Fund, 1947), p. 696. These data are unpublished estimates of the Bureau of Foreign and Domestic Commerce of the United States Department of Commerce.

regions like Arizona and California, the Orient and South America, but also the rise of synthetic fabrics. As for dietary habits, it was clear that cereals, potatoes and meat were slipping in popularity with a generation which eschewed the epic meals of its ancestors.[9]

While the fortunes of agriculture languished after 1920, the industrial economy of the nation recovered more quickly, and, in contrast to farm income, national income reached new highs by 1929; and as Table 52 indicates, farm income since 1929 has generally accounted for less than 10 per cent of national income.

The trend of population and income pointed unmistakably the lesson that the mail-order business was in danger of becoming a residual legatee. Significant expansion of the order to which the large catalogue houses were accustomed could not be hoped for in view of the condition of their traditional markets, for by 1919 manufacturing had noticeably outstripped agriculture as the most significant area of economic activity in the United

States. The high place of agriculture in nineteenth-century America could not be maintained as the resources of the continent came more and more to be organized and exploited with the rise of the generation of the renowned industrialists. Wright observed that "agriculture, so preeminent until the close of the nineteenth century, has been relegated to an inferior place."[10]

The prosperity that emerged after 1921 did not (and could not in the nature of the case) lift agriculture to the same levels as other sectors of the

TABLE 52*

FARM INCOME AS PERCENTAGE OF NATIONAL INCOME, 1929-47
(In Millions)

Year	National Income	National Income Originating on Farms	Per Cent Originating on Farms
1929	$ 87,355	$ 8,002	9.2
1930	75,003	6,022	8.0
1931	58,873	4,625	7.9
1932	41,690	3,080	7.4
1933	39,584	4,521	8.9
1934	48,613	3,568	7.3
1935	56,789	6,231	11.0
1936	64,719	5,327	8.2
1937	73,627	7,249	9.8
1938	67,375	6,003	8.9
1939	72,532	6,120	8.4
1940	81,347	6,599	8.1
1941	103,834	8,880	8.6
1942	136,486	12,937	9.5
1943	168,262	14,524	8.6
1944	182,407	14,805	8.1
1945	181,731	15,255	8.4
1946	179,289	17,972	10.0
1947	202,500	19,287	9.5

*Source: 1929-43, *National Income Supplement to Survey of Current Business*, July, 1947; 1944-47, *Survey of Current Business*, July, 1948.

economy. The "new prosperity" was forged out of the accretions of a rapidly expanding technology imposed upon the wealth of natural resources of the new world. The great increase in material wealth was largely associated with the overwhelming expansion of certain strategic industries, especially capital goods production. Dulles summarized the situation in these terms:

The underlying factors responsible for the general prosperity of the nineteen-twenties . . . were the efficient exploitation of natural resources, improved methods of industrial production, and the intensive development of both domestic and foreign markets. Good times were perhaps even more directly due to the spectacularly rapid expansion of a number of key industries. Some of them were entirely new; others were undergoing their period of greatest growth. Together they gave a tremendous impetus to economic development all along the line. Their need for raw materials and for machines stimulated production and employment in the country's mines, steel works, and durable goods industries. Their own operations provided jobs for additional millions of industrial workers, thereby even more directly increasing mass purchasing power from which other manufacturers as well as themselves could profit.

The automobile industry was the most important of them all, and both at home and abroad it became a token of American prosperity. . . .[11]

And the increasing popularity of the automobile further eroded the soil in which the mail-order business had flourished—compounding the effects of the declining relative importance of agriculture in the industrial economy of the United States.

In 1900 there had been but 8,000 passenger cars registered in the United States; twenty years later more than 8,000,000 cars were registered. By 1929 the figure had virtually tripled, and thereafter registrations slowly and with slight reverses through the 1930's climbed to a high of 29,602,000 in 1941, as shown in Table 53. By 1929 the automobile had claimed America, and there was one car to about every five persons.

The increase in automobile registrations was paralleled by a similar rise in highway and rural road mileage. Up to 1891 the construction and maintenance of highways had been intrusted almost entirely to counties or even smaller governmental subdivisions. This system became increasingly inadequate as the number of automobiles in use grew rapidly, and both federal and state support was enlisted. Extensive federal grants to further construction of interstate routes began in 1916, and by 1917 every state had created its own highway department.[12] Of the estimated 2,151,379 miles of rural roads (i.e., excluding streets of municipalities) existing in 1904, only 153,645 miles were surfaced, and only 144 miles had "high type surface" or some form of paving.[13] By 1921 the total mileage of rural roads increased to 2,925,000, of which 387,000 miles were classified as "surfaced," including both "high" and "low" types of surfacing. The total rural road mileage grew only to 3,005,000 by 1944, but the proportion of surfaced roads grew enormously, to 1,430,000. The mileage included in state highway systems rose to 324,496 in 1930 and to 573,234 in 1945.[14]

The snowballing auto-registration figures (and the lengthening ribbon of paved roads) attest to the strong affinity of the average American for his "car." As Wecter so aptly remarks, "Americans tend to cling almost wistfully to their automobiles through all vicissitudes."[15] The automobile has become the symbol of American production "genius," and the assembly-line technique of the Detroit plants has been adopted in countless other industries. The motor vehicle has had profound effects on the social pattern of a nation, contributing as it has to a much greater mobility of persons and to changes in the working and recreation patterns of the population. It has both destroyed and created industries and has revamped the communities of twentieth-century America. And with the growing popularity of the automobile the isolated character of life on the farm became less and less marked.[16]

With the automobile contributing to increased mobility and the industrialization of a continent having its natural magnetic attractions thus reinforced, it is not surprising to find that great shifts occurred in the functional patterns of American communities. For if the rural element was becoming urbanized, there is evidence that to no little degree the city reached toward ruralization. And the effect was to lessen the differences between residents of city and country. The tendency of an era toward the "metropolitan com-

TABLE 53*

AUTOMOBILE REGISTRATIONS IN THE UNITED STATES, 1900–1942
(In Thousands)

Year	Registrations	Year	Registrations
1900	8	1927	20,219
1905	77	1928	21,379
1910	459	1929	23,122
1914	1,626	1930	23,059
1915	2,310	1931	22,348
1916	3,298	1932	20,884
1917	4,657	1933	20,644
1918	5,622	1934	21,532
1919	6,771	1935	22,583
1920	8,226	1936	25,178
1921	9,483	1937	24,450
1922	10,960	1938	25,262
1923	13,540	1939	26,201
1924	15,461	1940	27,435
1925	17,496	1941	29,602
1926	19,237	1942	27,974

* Source: *Statistical Abstract of the United States, 1946*, p. 488. Figures shown are for registrations of passenger cars, busses, and taxis.

munity" is marked in the following passages from R. D. McKenzie's monograph published as part of *Recent Social Trends in the United States:*

With the increasing ease and rapidity of travel, particularly by motor car, the large city has not only brought under its sway much territory that was formerly rural, but has extended its influence far out into territory that is still classified as rural. Smaller communities within a wide radius of every urban center have lost much of their former isolation, provincialism and independence. Even beyond the commuting area, the city reaches out with its newspapers, radio broadcasts, amusements and shopping facilities. In this process the character of the city itself is somewhat altered. If the suburban and country districts are urbanized the city is in a degree ruralized. Its people more and more go outside the corporate limits to live, to spend their vacations and find recreation. . . .

Two outstanding factors in the changing character of the local community are: (1) the increase in the aggregate population of the community and the extension of the area within which local activities are carried on in common; (2) the increased mobility of products and people, resulting in a wider range of individual choice, more specialization of local services and a more closely-knit community structure.[17]

The near-disastrous depression which celebrated the opening of the 1920's had (with cause) terrified mail-order executives. As the decade unfolded, it was plain that more permanent engines of destruction whirred to threaten the position of a business that had thrived very largely by virtue of rural isolation. The automobile and paved roads, both cause and effect, one of the other, were strong influences breaking down that isolation, as was the improved service of interurban carriers. Strong pressures to link and "standardize" the shopping habits of the nation came as well from other sources.

Menaced thus by the increased contacts of their former customers, the mail-order firms might turn to another horizon in search of clearer skies but only to encounter there the growing legions of the invading chain stores hastening to pre-empt favorable positions in the trading centers of outlying communities. Indeed, on every side the rural customers were greeted by a broadening range of shopping alternatives. It is reported that for the average village the total number of retail outlets, exclusive of chain stores, increased from 27.7 in 1910 to 39.6 in 1930, and with that 40 per cent increase went increasing specialization. This proceeded furthest in the larger villages, of course, as illustrated by the fact that in 1930 large villages averaged 6.5 apparel stores in contrast to 1.5 for villages of smaller size.[18]

Virtually concurrently with increased availability of merchandise through village stores, the big-city department stores were extending their influence along expanding radii from their central locations, thus manifesting another sign of the country's growing metropolitan regionalism and the progressive destruction of rural isolation. As McKenzie noted:

> The retail shopping areas of the larger cities, as measured by the daily free delivery service of central stores, have expanded greatly in recent years. It has become common practice for the larger stores throughout the nation to deliver their merchandise regularly within a radius of 30 to 50 miles. City department stores report not only an extension of their delivery systems since 1920 but also an increasing volume of trade from outlying territory. Some stores provide free telephone service . . . and some rebate fares, depending on distance traveled and volume of purchases.[19]

In all the changing patterns of retail-trade relations perhaps the greatest threat to the continued prosperity of the old mail-order business was the emergence of strong chain-store systems. It was estimated that in 1914 there were about 2,030 parent-companies operating chains controlling some 23,893 store units doing a business of not more than one billion dollars. Fifteen years later the chains had grown to include 7,046 organizations composed of 159,826 stores with sales of nearly eleven billion dollars in 1929.[20] Thus in the postwar decade it is said the chain-store movement showed signs of becoming a latter-day echo of the heroic combinations in some of the older industries.[21]

Modern chain-store organizations began in the grocery field. The Great Atlantic and Pacific Tea Company appeared in 1858 and is, so far as is known, the oldest chain-store organization now in existence in the United States. The F. W. Woolworth Company, the oldest of the five-and-ten-cent stores, was established in 1879, when the first store was opened in Utica, New York. There had been earlier efforts in the five-and-ten-cent-store business, but the Woolworth business was the first to succeed and remain on the scene to the present time.[22]

Among the best known of the concerns established early in this century are the United Cigar Stores Company, founded in 1901; the J. C. Penney Company, established the following year; and the W. T. Grant Company, founded in 1906. The success of the various chain-store organizations moved Nystrom to say in 1930:

> Chain stores are showing a much greater gain in retail sales volume than any other type of retail institution at the present time. Since 1914, it appears that the retail volume passing through chains has considerably more than quadrupled, while department store and mail order house sales have only doubled. Unlike the department store and mail order house sales trends, the largest part of the chain store gain has been made since 1920.[23]

The chains, as Nystrom pointed out, pyramided their volume of business enormously—and chains of one type or another came to compete with Sears, Roebuck in almost every line of merchandise. The country became almost literally dotted with chains selling shoes, shirts, clothing, toilet goods, automobile supplies, and a thousand and one other items. If any tribute be needed to the success of chain-store organizations as a retail type, it can be found in the opposition of independent merchants, for the plethora of anti-chain-store legislation which followed the rise of the chains was but a latter-day manifestation of the same opposition which had fought mail order so bitterly in its early days.[24]

The general merchandise chains especially, and most notably J. C. Penney, located in towns tributary to agricultural (and mining) areas where they grew strong by virtue largely of an astute combination of chain- and department-store methods adapted to the smaller communities. Sears, Roebuck saw a dangerous competitor who tempted Sears's customers into the stores stocked with "live" merchandise that might distract attention from, and dilute the old loyalty to, the catalogue.[25]

The growing competition presented by the multiplication and improvements in shopping facilities was tangible, as were the improved agencies of transportation and communication. But there existed other and more subtle influences also working to undermine the market position of the mail-order houses by changing the buying habits of their customers, who more and more became targets for the hammer strokes of advertising, branding, and styling.

National advertising, the sibling of the brand, increased tremendously so that an estimate of advertising expenditures in 1929 placed that figure at $1,782,000,000, leading Lynd and Hanson to remark: "In current advertising we are therefore viewing commercial consumer stimulation on the

TABLE 54*

PROGRESS OF CERTAIN CHAIN-STORE ORGANIZATIONS, 1902-28

Year	J. C. Penney No. of Stores	J. C. Penney Sales (In 000's)	W. T. Grant No. of Stores	W. T. Grant Sales (In 000's)	F. & W. Grand No. of Stores	F. & W. Grand Sales (In 000's)	Neisner Brothers, Inc. No. of Stores	Neisner Brothers, Inc. Sales (In 000's)
1902	1	$ 28						
1907	2	166	1	$ 99				
1908	4	218	2	169				
1909	6	310	4	398				
1910	14	662	6	752				
1911	22	1,183	9	1,083				
1912	34	2,051	12	1,361				
1913	48	2,636	16	2,000				
1914	71	3,560	20	2,565				
1915	86	4,825	23	3,061				
1916	127	8,415	25	3,659				
1917	177	14,880	30	4,510	18	$ 1,628		
1918	197	21,336	32	6,029	19	2,328		
1919	197	28,778	33	7,941	19	2,642		
1920	297	42,822	38	10,192	19	2,941		
1921	312	46,641	45	12,728	19	3,657		
1922	371	49,035	54	15,382	22	4,321		
1923	475	62,188	60	20,625	23	5,416	8	$ 1,695
1924	571	74,261	73	25,316	28	6,576	11	1,907
1925	676	91,062	77	30,411	37	8,536	13	2,695
1926	745	115,683	109	36,074	41	10,500	17	4,497
1927	892	151,959	158	43,743	55	12,882	22	6,477
1928	1,026	176,698	221	55,690	81	17,259	35	10,292

* Source: Paul H. Nystrom, *The Economics of Retailing* (3d ed.; New York: Ronald Press Co., 1930), p. 231.

greatest scale yet attempted, totaling in 1929 about 2 per cent of the national income or nearly $15 per capita."[26] The major significance to the mail order industry of the expansion in advertising and branding was that it was "educating" consumers in all parts of the country to new products and new preferences, often to products much more easily sold by stores than by the silent catalogue, whose most titillating persuasion was inevitably limited to the printed page in four colors in one dimension. And many of the new products which first came into mass consumption in the 1920's were those that demanded servicing facilities convenient to consumers. And this was, of course, much more easily provided through stores than by the highly centralized mail-order operation.

The barrage of advertising worked also to create new preferences (as well as to divert preference from one purveyor to another). And one feels that a scrutiny of advertising copy would reveal that appeals were increasingly cast in terms of product virtues less measurable than "performance." Encouraged by the aggressive efforts of sellers, and supported by growing wealth and greater leisure, customers came to demand merchandise that satisfied the accepted (if sometimes synthetic) canons of taste. Whimsical shifts of "the vogue" were increasingly evident, most prominently in women's apparel but not absent in automobiles—or even hardware. The influence of fashion was extended through virtually all levels of income groups and to numerous product types. Styles changed more frequently, and the vogue of particular styles ceased to follow traditional patterns of diffusion in terms of either geography or income. Evidence abounds that testifies to the overweaning importance which fashion assumed in the American culture, but one of the best statements on the trend has been provided by Lynd and Hanson in their monograph, "The People as Consumers":

> A speeding up of the tempo of style change as well as a broadening in the scope of fashion influence to new commodities and through new sections of the population occurred during the 1920's as an accompaniment of increasing prosperity and wide diffusion of wealth. On the consumer's side it was apparently stimulated by war time mobility, by a philosophy of youth bred of post-war emotional exuberance stressing change and resiliency in living, and by increased leisure. Mechanical changes increasing speed of transmission of ideas and of goods were likewise facilitating factors. To merchants style and fashion offered an opportunity to extricate merchandising from the profit-wasting traditional emphasis upon competitive prices, and to this end entire industries pooled their attack to make the consumer "style-conscious.". . .
>
> This increased emphasis on style was encouraged by advertising and editorial content in periodicals and newspapers. The *Ladies' Home Journal,* for example, after devoting but 16 percent of its non-fiction editorial content to fashion in 1918 and 1920, raised this to 28 percent in 1921 and to 30 in 1922–1923, while popular magazines have increasingly taken over high style artists formerly used only by exclusive style journals such as *Vogue* and *Harper's Bazaar.* During the 1920's the style expert began to be supplemented by the style forecaster as exemplified in the great increase up to 1927 in trade research bureaus, forecasting and coordination agencies and other devices for finding out quickly in advance what the public will accept.[27]

Perhaps no more signal testimony exists to the triumph of taste over utility than Henry Ford's capitulation to the rapidly spiraling trend. In 1927 America's unregenerate individualist abandoned his insistence on producing the efficient, long-lived, and cheap "black tin lizzie" in favor of the several colors of the new "model A."

The mail-order business, bound to its catalogue method of selling, was ill equipped to capitalize handsomely on the new interest in fashion merchandise. Catalogue customers were ever more exposed to changing designs, patterns, and colors. Access to the displays of the city, or even the county seat, stores resulted often in comparisons unfavorable to catalogue wares. Nor were the catalogue houses in a position to pursue the opportunism incumbent on the successful fashion merchandiser—frequent changes of display and merchandise clearances through necessitous price reductions at strategic times to clear stocks for fresh merchandise.

The impact of fashion on the farm (coupled with the greater mobility of the farm population and better trading facilities) was evident in the distance traveled by farm families to purchase women's clothing. A study of 1,328 midwestern farm families in 1930 showed that the average distance traveled for such purchases was 19.5 miles. Similar studies made in 1929 and 1930 attest to the tendency for farm families to gravitate to larger centers for many types of goods. "Local" trading facilities were coming to be relied on mainly for services and everyday purchases. The "faraway places" lured shoppers for items of less frequent purchase and for goods of high unit price or marked style influence.[28]

The years since 1925 brought a sequence of important environmental shifts for Sears, Roebuck and Company. The latter part of the decade that saw Sears's and Ward's first stores opened witnessed the highest peaks of prosperity thus far achieved in American economic history. But this achievement was simply prelude to a most severe and prolonged depression which was hardly vanquished before another great war was at hand.

The bitter experience of the depression which began in the fall of 1929 spawned innovations in governmental policy which changed the character of the business environment in many respects and posed new kinds of problems for business managers. Another child of the depression with peculiar significance to Sears was the renaissance of bitter opposition to mass distributors. This attained such political importance that the opponents of the chains sought and received the protection of the legislatures.

Despite the near-cosmic significance of depression and war, Sears's path after the midtwenties was cut more nearly in terms of developments that had been long aborning by that date. Of all the social attributes upon which the old mail-order business had thrived, perhaps the isolation of rural folk had been predominant, and isolation was no more.

Faced with the new mobility and increasing sophistication of buyers in what had proved a highly volatile market during the depression of 1920–21, viewing the mounting ascendancy of manufactures as against agriculture, and confronted by the spectacle of new trading facilities as well as a nation of urban residents, the mail-order industry faced the necessity of selecting a planned strategy that offered the prospect of continuing an expansion that had been so seriously interrupted by the postwar collapse in 1920.

CHAPTER XX

The New Management: Ascendancy of Robert E. Wood

JULIUS ROSENWALD proclaimed in the early 1890's that his goal in life was to earn $15,000 per year, of which one-third should be laid aside, one-third should go to charity, and the remaining third should be used for his own family's support.[1] His income within a few years after that exceeded even his gaudiest dreams; as early as 1904, he was able to write that he was worth $500,000 outside any interest in Sears, Roebuck. And he and Richard Sears between them owned 95 per cent of the stock of the company, in roughly equal proportions. By 1920 Rosenwald and his family were reputed to own about 40 per cent of the $105,000,000 par value of common stock of the mail-order house.[2]

Rosenwald had further been enriched year after year through the succession of dividends chronicled earlier. While he may not have hewed strictly to his original ambition, he had indeed become internationally famous for his philanthropies even before the first World War. He had interested himself in a wide range of activities, extending from civic work in Chicago (which in itself included a wide variety of activities from widening of streets to reform of politics) to improvement of the lot of Negroes, particularly in the South. His donations were constant and generous to the point of being breath-taking in their size.[3] In all such activities Rosenwald had the complete support and intelligent understanding of his wife. As Werner puts it:

During the first decade of the twentieth century ... philanthropy became a social design. Men with large fortunes, far too great for their personal needs and far beyond the needs of their descendants, were looking for means of disbursing their surplus. . . .
. . . Leadership in charity gradually passed from the church and state to the business man, who preferred individual initiative to governmental action.[4]

This is not the place for an intensive exploration of the motivations and *modus operandi* of the "first-generation philanthropists." Nor is it the place for a detailed discussion of Rosenwald's own philanthropies and his philosophy of using his own gifts to stimulate even greater contributions from other wealthy men and/or from a community. It is sufficient to point out that during his thirty-two years of life in the twentieth century, Julius Rosenwald gave away some $63,000,000, while the fulfilment by his estate of commitments for which his heirs felt a moral obligation increased the total to some $75,000,000.[5]

Perhaps the most significant aspect of this interest, from Sears, Roebuck's point of view—outside the warm arc light of favorable publicity which Rosenwald's philanthropies perforce turned upon the company—was that it came to engross Rosenwald more and more after the company's recovery from the depression of 1920–21. His philanthropies had consumed much of his time, as indicated earlier, even before he entered government service in the first World War. But when he felt compelled to regrasp the reins of management after the debacle of 1920–21 and to devote almost his full time to it, he proceeded also to abolish his own salary (which had been $100,000) entirely until 1924, when it was reinstated, at $60,000 per year. At the same time he reduced his philanthropic contributions, which had averaged about $500,000 yearly since 1912; they dropped in 1921 to $218,555 and in 1922 to $145,893. By 1923, however, the company's prospects were so bright that his donations rose to $482,081.[6] But the task of brightening those prospects had tired Rosenwald considerably. Also, with his own great fortune again made secure by the brightened outlook for the company, he was eager to devote more time to philanthropies.

He began an intensive search to bring new blood into Sears, Roebuck and Company. His first task was to find a replacement for the ailing vice-president, Albert Loeb, who had been suffering from heart disease since 1922. While Loeb was not to retire formally until October, 1924, he had been inactive in the company's affairs for months before that time, living quietly with his wife in close seclusion until his death, on October 27, 1924. On July 28, 1924, Rosenwald wrote to his son Lessing in Philadelphia requesting the following information from employment agencies specializing in placing top executives: (1) the names of ten outstanding railroad vice-presidents under fifty years of age; (2) the age of each, with a comprehensive report of his experience; and (3) the charge to be made by any such agency if an executive recommended by it were employed by the company. Rosenwald's obsession with securing a railroad man was believed to date from his public service during the first World War, when he developed a tremendous respect for the efficiency of railroad administration through his association with Daniel Willard, president of the Baltimore and Ohio Railroad.[7]

Rosenwald was to find both a president and a vice-president in the fall of 1924, and the latter was to prove a particularly colorful man. Robert Elkington Wood, born in Kansas City, Missouri, June 13, 1879, was a graduate of the United States Military Academy in the class of 1900. After a tour of duty as lieutenant of cavalry in the Philippines from 1900 to 1902, he served as an instructor at West Point for a year before being assigned to the Canal Service in Panama. In his ten-year hitch with the forces constructing the "big ditch," Wood was variously superintendent, assistant chief quartermaster, and chief of the building department. Wood apparently thrived on the insalubrious climate, which saddled yellow fever on many less hardy, and under the tough command of Goethals, who proverbially drove men until he broke them or promoted them. He promoted Wood —to captain, in 1913, with the title of chief quartermaster. Wood assumed responsibility for recruiting, housing, and distribution of labor and later was chief of requisition, purchase, and distribution of all supplies for the Panama Canal and the Panama Railroad. Throughout part of this time, he was the good right arm of Goethals, who was to become quartermaster general in the first World War.

Wood was director of the Panama Railroad and Steamship Line in 1913 and 1914 and was chairman of the board to pass on all railroad construction in the Republic of Panama. In May, 1915, Wood was promoted to major and allowed to retire. He then became assistant to the vice-president of the E. I. Dupont de Nemours Company. In October of that year, he left Dupont to become assistant to the president of the General Asphalt Company, in charge of production mines, manufacturing plants, refineries, and railroads in the United States, Trinidad, and Venezuela.

When America entered the first World War, Wood returned to active duty in the grade of major. He first organized the purchasing department of the Emergency Fleet Corporation, after which he went to France with the Forty-second Infantry ("Rainbow") Division as a colonel. Upon arrival there he was assigned to the general staff, in charge of transportation. Later Wood became assistant to the director of the Army Transport Service, in charge of all ports, water terminals, and shipping in France and England. In April, 1918, he was ordered back to the States and promoted to brigadier general as acting quartermaster general. He then became director of purchase and storing in charge of all army supplies except ordnance and aircraft. In March, 1919, Wood returned to civilian life as general merchandise manager of Montgomery Ward and Company, soon becoming vice-president in charge of merchandising.

Wood proceeded to build Ward's tire business from 100,000 casings a year to over 1,000,000.[8] (The impetus of this drive was such that in 1925 Ward's tire sales reached a volume of $1,969,000 as compared with Sears's tire sales of only $700,916.) And, as pointed out earlier, Wood was also considered to have contributed substantially to the comeback staged by Ward's after the 1920–21 depression. But Wood clashed with Ward's President Theodore Merseles on bases both of personality and of policies. (For one thing, Wood continued to insist that Ward should expand into retail stores, on a large scale.) Whether Wood was discharged or whether he got his resignation in under the wire while Merseles was lowering the boom is a moot point and an academic one. The important point is that Wood, a man with experience in transportation, construction, organization, administration, the mail-order business, and some retailing, and with a determined belief in the future of retail stores operated by mail-order businesses, left Montgomery Ward in 1924.

Rosenwald had met Wood in Washington during the war, when the former had been chairman of the civilian committee in charge of procurement on noncombat supplies. They met again shortly after Wood had left Ward's, when, according to a former Sears executive, a mutual friend of Rosenwald and Wood suggested that a meeting of the two men be arranged. According to this version, Rosenwald, despite his eagerness for new talent in his company, was not particularly eager to employ Wood; after some consideration, however, Rosenwald offered Wood a place in Sears. Wood reportedly declined, on the ground that he had another business connection in prospect. In the course of the subsequent conversations, Wood is reported to have asserted that Ward's had achieved some success in its still experimental retail-store venture. This statement of his competitor's success in what was still a new field for mail-order houses aroused Rosenwald's interest. (Rosenwald himself had so far been restrained from entering retail both by the determined opposition of some of his subordinates and by his own uncertain evaluation of its potentialities.)

Rosenwald was at this same time closing his search for a successor to himself. Two chief qualifications still were demanded: first, that the man chosen be a railroad man, since, as indicated earlier, Rosenwald had a vast respect for the administrative abilities of railroad executives and felt that the company sorely needed such executives to avoid a recurrence of the debacle of 1921; and, second, that the man be reasonably young and not yet wealthy, since Rosenwald felt that men who had won their riches had little incentive left.

Rosenwald finally settled upon Charles M. Kittle, executive vice-president of the Illinois Central Railroad. And, apparently at almost exactly the same time, he persuaded Wood to accept a vice-presidency; Wood's consent came after Rosenwald told him that a forthcoming split of profits for officers of the firm would represent a most substantial windfall for Wood, too. On October 28, 1924, Kittle was elected president, and Wood was made vice-president in charge of factories and retail stores. The two new executives assumed their duties on November 1.

Kittle faced sizable obstacles from the outset. The company was, in the verdict of many who were there at the time, torn by several conflicting factions. The general merchandise manager and the chief of operating, both vice-presidents, were veteran employees and forceful, driving personalities. It is said that each had apparently expected that one of the two would surely be chosen to succeed Rosenwald. In addition to their understandable chagrin over the appointment of an "outsider" as president, they (and, it should be added, others) opposed the practice of bringing in as president a person with no previous mail-order or even merchandising experience.

In briefing Kittle for his new duties, Rosenwald apparently stressed the necessity of developing strong top administrative discipline. Kittle seems to have been admirably suited for that task. According to testimony from retired executives of the company, he was frequently rude even to Julius Rosenwald. Werner says, "Kittle was a man of outstanding ability, but he was brusque and ruthless. He treated Rosenwald and the other executives of the company with little respect."[9]

Lessing J. Rosenwald recalls one particular incident which he says prejudiced him strongly against both Kittle and retail stores; it took place while he was traveling outside the United States. Kittle abruptly ordered Thomas Carney, operating manager of the Philadelphia branch plant which young Rosenwald headed, to rip out the first floor of that mail-order plant to instal a retail store. The younger Rosenwald was neither consulted nor even advised of this *fait accompli;* he learned of the act only upon his return to this country. Lessing was furious, and his relations with Kittle remained strained throughout the latter's tenure.

During his three years as president, Kittle apparently had perforce to content himself with two primary approaches to the business: first, trying to learn, from the ground up, how business operated; and, second, making broad policy decisions of a general executive nature. The evidence indicates that he accomplished the latter surprisingly well in view of his lack of intimate knowledge of the former. For example, he supported the construction of additional mail-order plants (in Kansas City, Atlanta, Memphis, and Los Angeles during his tenure). This may have been attributable at least in part to the fact that his five-year contract included a percentage of the company's sales, a natural inducement to stimulate sales even if at some risk of increased operating costs and lower profits.

Kittle also supported the expansion of Sears's retail stores, twenty-seven of which were established during his presidency. His railroad experience in absorbing masses of figures enabled him to study reports, balance one set of figures against another, and dig out discrepancies with an ability which the *Wall Street Journal* termed "uncanny." He utilized this ability to wring an ever greater measure of efficiency and discipline from the organization, even though his tactics in improving efficiency apparently did not win many friends for him in the company.

Kittle also believed firmly that the company should be owned by the common stockholders and that no holders of bonds or preferred stock should come between those common stockholders and earnings available for distribution. That belief was translated into action in two ways. First, the preferred stock was steadily retired; and, second, the expansion of fixed assets in the form of four new mail-order plants and twenty-seven retail stores was paid for out of surplus. When the four-for-one stock split occurred early in 1926, Kittle placed the new stock on an annual basis of $2.50, roughly half the $4.99 a share earnings of 1925, his first full year as president. In keeping the dividends relatively low, and thus financing expansion from surplus, Kittle avoided issuance of any bonds or incurrence of any bank loans which might have imperiled control of the business.

His tenure marked a prosperous period for the company; no matter how much of that prosperity was attributable to Kittle's own policies and administration, and how much to the prosperity of the nation as a whole, the volume of business and the net profits after taxes continued to climb from year to year. The volume rose from $243,798,351 in 1925 (the first full year of Kittle's presidency) to $258,212,750 in 1926, and to $277,502,387 the following year. Net profits after taxes increased from $20,975,303 in 1925 to $21,908,121 in 1926 and to $25,025,553 in 1927.

Kittle's regime was short, for he died on January 2, 1928, only a little more than three years after assuming the presidency. Whether those three years were happy ones for his associates and subordinates, most of whom outranked him considerably in point of service, they were at any rate lucrative ones for the company. The *Wall Street Journal* of February 15, 1928, headlined its summary of the deceased president's accomplishments: "Kittle's Regime Prosperous One—Under Leadership of Late President, Sears, Roebuck & Co. Attained New Industrial Heights." Even with due allowance for its long-distance analysis and summary of Kittle's accomplishments and its *de mortui nil nisi bonum*, the *Journal's* story racks up an impressive record of achievement:

> Progressive merchandising, efficient and economical operation, and conservative financing marked C. M. Kittle's tenure of office as president of Sears, Roebuck & Co. . . .
>
> He sought to build up customer goodwill, holding it Sears' greatest asset. . . . An outstanding innovation during his regime was the development of retail department stores. . . .
>
> Well over a year ago he remarked: "I propose to build this business—and build it—and build it." His death did not occur until much of his program was completed or well under way. As it is, he leaves Sears-Roebuck with an enhanced customer goodwill, greatly expanded facilities for service, an efficient, smooth-running organization, mounting sales and earnings, and an almost impregnable balance sheet position.

On January 11, 1928, nine days after Kittle's death, General Wood was elected president. Two of the vice-presidents—Max Adler and Otto Doering, in charge, respectively, of merchandise and operating—resigned forthwith.

There are two versions of that episode. Donald M. Nelson reports (and he is not alone in his version) that both Doering and Adler confidently expected that one of them would succeed Kittle; they felt that Julius Rosenwald could hardly again by-pass both of those senior executives. Nelson declares that Adler told him, a few days after Kittle's death, that in the event he (Adler) became president, he would want Nelson as his merchandise vice-president. This version, articulated by Nelson and held by others, maintains that Adler and Doering, close friends for years, had agreed that, no matter which of the two should become president, the other would remain to assist him.

Lessing Rosenwald has an entirely different explanation. He says that Max Adler definitely wanted to retire from the firm, had no desire to become president, and felt no bitterness at being passed over in favor of Wood. Doering, according to the younger Rosenwald's version, had in the fall of 1927 asked Kittle for permission to retire. Kittle requested Doering to remain for another year, and the latter assented. When Kittle died, Doering felt that he was relieved of his commitment to remain until the fall of 1928, and accordingly again requested to be allowed to retire. Lessing Rosenwald thinks that if matters had been left at this, Doering would have felt no resentment; but matters were not so left. The elder Rosenwald felt that he had to choose between Doering and Wood. He sent his son Lessing to sound Doering out to find whether, in view of his requests for retirement, he would remain if elected president.

According to Lessing Rosenwald, his father merely wanted to determine whether he had indeed to choose between Wood and Doering or whether the latter had eliminated himself from consideration and thus left the field clear for Wood. Doering informed Lessing Rosenwald that he would reconsider his request for retirement and would remain if made president. When Wood was subsequently chosen instead, Doering resigned.

The story of how the presidential race was narrowed to Wood and Doering is an interesting instance of the working of the human equation in corporate operations. Lessing Rosenwald asserts that he resolved, upon Kittle's death, to succeed to the presidency of the company. He had been a director for eleven years and a vice-president for about four years; he felt that he had worked hard, through nearly every phase of the company, and had earned the right to the presidency. He informed his father that if he were not chosen for that position, he would resign from the company. The elder Rosenwald replied that he was not opposed to considering Lessing for the presidency; when he visited his wife, ill in a hospital, he informed her of their son's desire.

It was Mrs. Julius Rosenwald who swung the pendulum. She told Lessing that she fully understood his desire for the presidency and agreed that he deserved the opportunity. Then, says Lessing, came the masterful dissuasion. His mother pointed out that the position could be nothing more than a sop to his pride—and a sop with many drawbacks. She declared that, as long as Lessing was in Chicago and Julius was alive, the son would receive little credit for his accomplishments; he would always live in his father's shadow, and people would attribute his accomplishments to being "the boss's son."

While Lessing Rosenwald remained in Philadelphia, his mother pointed out, he would retain his own individual status, which he had moved there

THE NEW MANAGEMENT

to achieve. He and his family were rooted in that city; a return to Chicago would mean a fresh start. Lessing's zeal evaporated under his mother's persuasion. He informed his father that he no longer wished to be considered for the presidency. With Adler voluntarily out of the race (according to Lessing's version), the field was narrowed to Wood and Doering.

It is difficult, if not impossible, to determine just what factors led to the selection of Wood instead of Doering as president, although several reasonable conjectures present themselves. Lessing Rosenwald, while not professing to have the "inside story," points out two factors which were consistent with his father's convictions. First, Doering was already wealthy, while Wood was still to make his fortune; and the elder Rosenwald felt that wealthy men had little incentive. He preferred men whose circumstances would spur them to great efforts to secure wealth. Wood fitted perfectly into that approach. Second, Wood was younger than Doering and therefore promised several more years of active leadership than Doering might have been expected to provide. Kittle's early death had been a blow to Julius Rosenwald's desire for management continuity; in the twenty-nine years from the time Rosenwald joined Sears, Roebuck until 1924, the company had had but two presidents.

It is doubtful that Wood's evangelistic devotion to retail stores was a very important factor in his elevation to the presidency. Julius Rosenwald, the chief factor in that appointment, was not a real retail enthusiast at the time. Nor was Lessing Rosenwald (who admits he was prejudiced by Kittle's peremptory method of opening the first Philadelphia retail store). Wood's support in the establishment of the early retail stores had come almost entirely from Kittle (and from some of the directors), and Kittle was obviously gone.

Whatever actually tipped the scales, Rosenwald decided after little more than a week of deliberation to recommend Wood to the board of directors as the next president. Immediately upon his election, Wood proceeded to complete his lineup for the great expansion in retail which was to follow. Lessing Rosenwald succeeded Doering as vice-president in charge of operating, and Donald Nelson replaced Adler in charge of merchandising, although he was not to receive the rank of vice-president until 1930. E. J. Pollock became comptroller.

Within some two years after his accession to the presidency, Wood saw the country plunge into what was to become a full-fledged depression, much more severe than that of a decade earlier. But the company was far better prepared to meet the emergency beginning in 1929 than it had been in 1920–21. For one thing, it had by 1929 a large enough chain of retail stores to enable it to effect rapid price reductions easily and to dispose of merchandise in a falling market with less loss than would have been incurred if Sears, Roebuck had still been solely a mail-order concern.

Another great factor in the company's favor in the more recent depression was its merchandise inventory position. At the end of 1920 Sears had been caught with an inventory of more than $105,000,000 on its shelves and with an incalculable amount (estimated as high as $67,000,000) on order. But the lesson of that debacle had been learned well. At the end of 1928 the company's inventory was only $67,269,306. Despite the booming prosperity and the rather widespread conviction that it might well last indefinitely, the inventory rose only to $77,937,239 at the end of 1929. The bubble had burst before the end of that year, and in the two succeeding years the company was able gradually to drop its inventory to $60,090,365 and then to $52,028,455. Even by the end of 1931 the company had not felt the bite of the depression nearly as sharply as in 1920. True, the net income after taxes dropped by about half between 1929 and 1930—from $30,057,652 to $14,308,897—but the company was still in the black. And in 1931 the record was comparatively even better; net income after taxes dropped by only a little more than $2,000,000, to $12,169,672. By 1932, however, when the country reached what appeared to be the terminal trough of the depression, the company found itself in the red, to the extent of $2,543,651.

That dark year of 1932 saw the severance of a link of nearly thirty-seven years' standing. On January 6, 1932, Julius Rosenwald died. He had been in poor health ever since the death of his wife in May, 1929, and he had gone to Honolulu in December, 1930, for rest and recuperation. After his return from Hawaii, he had been confined almost continuously to his home. Rosenwald's passing brought great sorrowing not only within Sears, Roebuck but throughout this country and in other lands where his philanthropies had helped to relieve human suffering. The newspapers of this and other countries were filled with praise; Rosenwald was universally acclaimed as one of the greatest benefactors to humanity of his time.[10]

Yet Rosenwald's death was not the blow to management continuity in the company which it might have been years earlier, for he had some time before ceased to take any really active part in business affairs. Wood was firmly in command as president, and the Rosenwald family had continued to be represented in the company's councils by Lessing's election as a director on January 24, 1917, as a vice-president on December 14, 1923, and as senior vice-president and vice-chairman of the board on March 4, 1930. On January 9, 1932, three days after his father's death, Lessing J. Rosenwald became chairman of the board.

The new board chairman had been employed by Sears, Roebuck on September 11, 1911, after he returned from college, as a worker in the shipping department. He had worked his way up through various echelons of the company, to become the first manager of the Philadelphia branch mail-order plant. There his interest in their well-being had made him a prime favorite with the employees. The younger Rosenwald apparently had in abundance a quality which his father lacked and greatly longed for: the faculty of charming people, of communicating his own basic warmth. Julius Rosenwald was respected and admired; Lessing Rosenwald was, and is, warmly admired, respected, *and* liked within the company.

The younger Rosenwald's second year as chairman of the board brought a sharp improvement in business. The end of the "red" year 1932 had seen the company's merchandise inventory stand at $49,084,895, the lowest point since 1926. With inventory reduced to that point, Sears was able to rebuild its inventories while prices were at rock bottom. As a result, 1933 saw Sears reap a net income after taxes of $11,249,295 and to finish that year with an inventory of $72,296,877. Salary and wage cuts of 20 per cent across the board in 1932, and a reduction of an additional 10 per cent in 1933, plus a general slash in operating costs, enabled the company to attain that net profit of more than $11,000,000 in 1933 even with a volume of net sales almost $1,500,000 less than in 1932. As far as Sears, Roebuck was concerned, the depression was over. Sales and profits were to rise steadily in the succeeding years; by 1936 net sales were some $80,000,000 higher than the previous peak year of 1929.

Another factor in mitigating the effects of the depression on the company was apparently of less importance than the two already mentioned but admittedly far more difficult to assess accurately—government spending. Heavy outlays to farmers and to unemployed urbanites by the federal government (and, to a lesser extent, by state and municipal governments) obviously benefited directly those people who constituted the bulk of Sears's market. As far as the urbanites were concerned, however, it must be remembered that most of their income from various governmental public works projects was, at least at the outset, essentially marginal. Most of that income went to such prime necessities as rent and food, with little left over for the goods Sears was offering. Aid to the farmers was of more direct benefit to the company. Not only did government spending in cities enable the residents of those cities to purchase farm produce, but a considerable share of the governmental outlays went directly to the farmers. Farm cash receipts had dropped from $11,296,000,000 in 1929 to $4,743,000,000 in 1932—the lowest point since before 1910. In 1933 this figure rallied to $5,445,000,000; government payments to farmers amounted to $131,000,000 that year. By 1934 farm cash receipts rose to $6,780,000,000, with government payments accounting for $446,000,000 of it. From then on the climb was steady except for a recession in 1938, but the march upward was quickly resumed the next year. Government payments to farmers climbed to $573,000,000 in 1935, and farm cash receipts in that year went to $7,659,-000,000, the highest point since 1930. Government payments were at a lower level in the following three years but increased again in 1939 to $807,000,000.[11] Always, of course, in addition to direct government payments, farmers were receiving assistance of many sorts from a variety of government activities. (Loans, for example, are not included in payments shown above.)

But perhaps the most interesting aspect of government spending and New Deal policy in general for Sears was General Wood's profound conviction that the New Deal was helping the country, particularly the farmer, and that it was therefore helping Sears, Roebuck. The company "New Dealed" in its catalogue and elsewhere.

The year that had seen the inauguration of the New Deal and the upturn in Sears's fortunes was notable for still another reason: it marked the return to the company of cofounder Alvah Curtis Roebuck, after an absence of more than thirty years. In 1925 Roebuck had sold his small manufacturing interests and moved to Florida to enter the booming real estate business. After that bubble burst, Roebuck returned to Chicago in 1929. In 1933 he joined Sears, Roebuck and devoted himself largely to compiling for the company the "Early and Some Later History of Sears, Roebuck and Co." cited frequently herein. In September, 1934, a store manager asked Roebuck to appear at his store for a sales promotion, to meet customers of the store and let them see what the cofounder looked like. The device apparently met with some success, for in the remainder of that year Roebuck made ten personal appearances and in 1935 a total of forty-five such appearances. The "act" was refined and polished, and the "tour" extended for several more years to include over a hundred stores and several fairs and other expositions. The retail store would advertise the forthcoming appearance of the cofounder, and radio interviews and appearances before service clubs would be arranged. Roebuck would sit at a table in the retail store, and clerks would ask all customers if they would like to meet one of the two men who had established Sears, Roebuck and Company. It turned out that most of them would. Customers came in from as far as a hundred miles away to shake the hand of the man whose name had been a byword in their families as long as thirty to forty years.[12] (After several years of "touring," Roebuck returned to the work of adding to his unpublished history of the company and to other tasks until his death, on June 18, 1948.)

In January, 1939, when Roebuck's store-visiting program was still in full swing, Lessing Rosenwald retired as chairman of the company's board of directors. General Wood was elected to succeed him, and Thomas J. Carney became president. D. M. Nelson was made executive vice-president, and T. V. Houser succeeded Nelson as vice-president in charge of merchandise. Carney had gone to work for Sears, Roebuck in 1902 as a temporary employee in the shipping department during the Christmas rush. He was head of the billing department at the time Lessing Rosenwald came to that department in 1911. In 1912 Carney was sent to Dallas to head up the billing, shipping, and receiving departments of that mail-order plant, and the younger Rosenwald took over Carney's job in the billing department in Chicago. When Lessing Rosenwald became general manager of the Philadelphia mail-order plant upon its opening in 1920, Carney, then operating manager in Dallas, became his operating manager. When Rosenwald became operating vice-president in 1928, after Doering's resignation, Carney was named general manager of the Philadelphia plant. Then in 1930, when young Rosenwald became senior vice-president and vice-chairman of the board of directors, Carney again replaced him, as vice-president in charge of operations. Carney was simultaneously elected a member of the board of directors. When he was elevated to the presidency of the company in 1939, there was little that Thomas Carney did not know about the company (he had served under every president it had ever had) and virtually nothing that Lessing Rosenwald did not know about Carney.

Carney assumed the presidency in a year in which war was to break out in Europe; before his regime ended, America was in the struggle. As an operating man for much of his career at Sears, Carney proceeded to emphasize service to customers, although not to the extent of neglecting merchandising. In his first year as president, he saw the company's volume of net sales reach a record high of $617,414,266, an increase of nearly $116,000,000 over 1938. That 23 per cent increase in sales volume was in itself obviously encouraging, but it was completely dwarfed by the jump in net income after taxes, which rose from $23,354,364 in 1938 to $37,255,274 the following year—a rise of a little more than 59 per cent. Carney's second year in office saw the sales volume rise to $704,301,014, an increase of $86,886,748 over 1939. But in that same year net income after heavy taxes *decreased* by $1,168,606. The year 1941 represented a variation on the same theme; net income after taxes in that year rose slightly while the volume of sales was increasing enormously. In more specific terms, the net income after taxes rose by $624,836, while the volume of sales grew by $210,756,614 to reach $915,057,628. Sears was crowding the billion-dollar mark for the first time, even though wartime taxes were eating heavily into its earnings.

Government restrictions on use of materials and manpower, conversion of factories (including Sears's factories) to war production, drafting of personnel into the armed services, and the campaigns for increased purchases of war bonds, all combined in 1942 to turn the company back from its billion-dollar goal. The net volume of sales for that year dropped to $867,834,052 (though that figure still represented the greatest sales in the company's history with the one exception of 1941). Net income after taxes dropped by $2,764,515, although net income *before* taxes increased by nearly $2,300,000 despite the drop in sales volume.

President Carney did not, however, live to see those final returns. He died on June 29, 1942, at the age of fifty-six. His active direction of the business had virtually ceased even earlier, as he had been in the hospital since February 2. Carney, at the time of his death, had been in the employ of the company longer than almost any other employee.[13] He had lived to see the company's string of retail stores increase to 645 (counting 28 agencies) in 1941 and account in that year for 68.4 per cent of the company's total volume of sales.

Nearly two months elapsed after Carney's death before a successor was chosen, on August 24. The new president was Arthur S. Barrows, who had joined the company in 1926 after eight years as a merchandising executive with Montgomery Ward and nearly two years in the wholesale hardware business. He had become a member of Sears's board of directors in 1935 and, in 1941, vice-president in charge of the Pacific Coast territory, from which point he directed all mail-order and retail operations in that area.

In 1943 the company's volume of sales dropped again, falling a little more than $15,000,000 below the volume for 1942, as merchandise became increasingly difficult to procure. The net income after taxes, however, showed a decrease of only $80,902. And in the following year the company's net sales volume came closer than ever to the billion-dollar mark, reaching a total of $988,770,171, an all-time high. But excess profits taxes stepped in to hold down net earnings after taxes, for while net income *before* taxes climbed to a record $103,608,644 (crossing the $100,000,000 mark for the first time), net income *after* taxes rose only to $34,176,111—an increase of but $310,024.

The year 1945 was the banner one, the year for which Sears's management had been straining. Net sales shot over the billion-dollar mark to reach $1,045,258,832. And one trend was reversed, with pleasing results for the company; while net income before taxes dropped by nearly $7,000,000, net income *after* taxes rose by $1,658,725 to reach $35,834,836 (still well below the more than $37,250,000 net after taxes in 1939, when the volume of sales had been only slightly more than $600,000,000). But if 1945 was the year Sears's men had been hoping and working for, it was 1946 that exceeded all their wildest dreams. Net sales in 1946 skyrocketed by nearly 60 per cent to $1,612,569,050. Net income before taxes jumped from less than $97,000,000 to more than $168,000,000—and those taxes, in that first full year of peace since 1940, dropped to leave the net income *after* taxes at a record $100,098,516. Earnings per share in that millenium year were $4.24.

By the time that record of more than a billion and a half dollars in sales volume had been made, Arthur Barrows had returned to the equable climate of California. He had resigned as president on March 27, 1946, to become vice-chairman of the board of directors, with headquarters in California. Shortly thereafter he retired from the company.

Barrows' successor was another company veteran, Fowler B. McConnell, who had put in thirty years with Sears, Roebuck by the time he became its seventh president. He had joined the firm in 1916 as a stockman. After rotating through a variety of jobs in the company, McConnell had become one of Wood's top lieutenants in the inauguration of Sears's retail stores. In 1930 he had returned to mail order, to manage the Philadelphia branch plant (after Carney had left that position to go to Chicago), but in 1931 he was back in retail, as territorial officer in the South. In 1932 McConnell was transferred to Chicago to become assistant to the vice-president in charge of retail administration. Three years later he was named assistant to the president and secretary of the company. In 1939 he became vice-president in charge of retail administration. When Barrows stepped out, McConnell stood groomed and ready.

While presidents came and presidents went in those years following 1939, Board Chairman R. E. Wood went right on. Wood provided management continuity which would otherwise have been sorely lacking in view of the rapid presidential turnover.

The momentum of 1946 carried over into the following year, and net sales rose to $1,981,535,749. The business which three years earlier had been knocking at the billion-dollar portal stood now on the two-billion-dollar threshold. During the period from 1925 through 1947, Sears, Roebuck maintained a steady lead over its closest competitor, Montgomery Ward. In 1925 Sears's volume of net sales accounted for 58.6 per cent of the combined Sears-Ward's sales, and in 1947 Sears's share of the combined sales stood at 63.1 per cent, the highest point at any time in this period. The sharpest jump in any comparable time span came between 1942 and 1947, when Sears's share of the combined sales of the two houses rose from 57.7 to 63.1 per cent. Sears, Roebuck's margin of superiority in that respect showed a percentage increase in each of those six years.

CHAPTER XXI

Learning Anew: The Retail Stores

WHILE Richard W. Sears sold watches and jewelry over the counter in his early mail-order days, he did so only as a minor adjunct of the mail-order business he was seeking to build. Nor did the short-lived grocery-store-*cum*-catalogue venture indicate any real effort on the company's part to build a retail business; that appears to have been primarily a sales-promotion device, never actively prosecuted. By 1921, however, when the company was seeking ways to lift itself out of the financial morass into which it had fallen, top-level executives seriously debated entering the retail field on a planned and determined basis. In that year the company sought to stimulate sales by giving exhibitions of merchandise in public rooms. The exhibitions attracted large crowds, and many persons sought to purchase on the spot the goods which were available only for display.

But the frequent and prolonged conferences on the question of branching out into retail resulted in a protracted stalemate. One former executive reports that as late as 1924 he witnessed great crowds thronging one of Ward's retail stores in a mail-order plant and reported that fact to Rosenwald. The operating vice-president sent a representative to make a detailed report on Ward's initial retail operation; the resultant report constituted a lengthy list of reasons the retail store could not succeed and why Sears should not attempt to follow suit. One of the most often-repeated arguments against Sears's entering retail was the contention that the company would, at best, only take business away from itself. This argument apparently rested upon the assumption that retail stores could only divert, not stimulate, business and that, in view of this, there was no sound reason for establishing a whole dual system of distribution, with attendant higher costs, especially in a field in which department stores had already amassed a fund of knowledge and experience.

The argument that expansion would only bring diversion had been made by some company executives in the early 1900's, when establishment of additional mail-order plants outside Chicago was under consideration. (Experience subsequently indicated that some diversion from the Chicago plant to branch plants did indeed take place at first but that the entire volume of business soon became larger with the addition of branch plants.)

While the Sears executives were debating the question, Ward's was taking tentative steps along that line. Actually Ward's, like Sears, had much earlier "dabbled" in retail—but, also like Sears, in a desultory fashion.

In 1880 Montgomery Ward opened what it called a "branch store" in Milwaukee, carrying "large stocks of such goods as are usually kept in strictly first class dry goods establishments." In the spring of 1882, however, that effort was declared a failure, and the store was closed. Meanwhile, Ward's mail-order sales had risen from $409,688 in 1880 to $702,728 in 1882. Beginning about 1916, Ward's provided facilities whereby citizens of Chicago and Kansas City could come to the firm's mail-order plants in those two cities and place orders to be claimed and paid for when their names were called.

In 1921 Ward's began experimenting with "outlet stores" located in the basements of mail-order plants. These represented an outgrowth of the 1920–21 depression and were makeshift affairs designed to dispose of overstocks and discontinued lines. General R. E. Wood, who became vice-president and general merchandise manager of Ward's late in 1920, originated the outlet stores. When Theodore Merseles, former vice-president of the National Cloak and Suit Company, became president of Ward's on January 4, 1921, it is said he found so much distress merchandise to be disposed of that he established additional outlet stores not located in mail-order plants—one in Aurora, and one in Springfield, Illinois. Those two stores operated under the name "George Lane Stores," and all identifying markings which would connect Montgomery Ward with them were removed from the merchandise, in the hope that prices higher than those of mail order could be realized. The stores were a complete failure and were closed within a few months with sacrifice sales to jobbers. The outlet stores *within* the mail-order plants were, however, sufficiently profitable, or at least potentially so, to invoke the following statements from Vice-President Wood in a report to the officers of Ward's on October 28, 1921, entitled "The Past, Present, and Future of Ward's":

> I originally tried to extend the house sales as an aid to our mail order business. I think in itself it can be developed to a very large and profitable business without interfering with our mail order business and aiding it in many ways. With the assistance of house sales I think we can make progress in the turnover of our mail order business that we have not dreamed of. Moreover the business will be in itself profitable—on an inventory of around $18,000,000 at the close of every season there will be at least 5% of seasonable merchandise on hand, which, under the catalog system, we have got to carry on our shelves until the next season. Five percent of $18,000,000 means $900,000 and that can be distributed over the counter through our four stores [Ward's then had mail-order plants in Chicago, Kansas City, Fort Worth, and Portland; the St. Paul branch was to open later in 1921] inside of eight weeks. Our money will be realized and interest charges lessened!
> ... The keenest competition of all that we have to face is the chain store competition.... There are two weak spots in connection with the chain stores, the first being that with the exception of the old established grocery chains like the

A&P they have no distributing warehouse system. For a multitude of small stores they must at some place and some time perform the function of jobbers for themselves, that is, assemble goods in carload lots and distribute them. Many of these chains have not had the foresight to so group their stores as to work out a good system of warehouse distribution.

I feel that if we are so inclined, we can beat the chain stores at their own game—that we have certain advantages which they do not possess and that we can easily and profitably engage in the chain store business ourselves with a relatively small amount of capital. We have four splendid distributing points; we have an organized purchasing system; we have a wonderful name, if we choose to take advantage of it, and we ought to be able to build up our organization as good or better than the chain stores themselves and without harming our mail order business.

... We should experiment carefully and just as soon as we feel sure enough of our ground to go ahead, we should go ahead as rapidly as possible.

Wood's recommendations (a revealing testament to his sympathies for retail expansion) apparently received scant consideration from Ward's management, which was convinced that any attempt to operate retail stores selling at catalogue prices was impractical. Three years to the day after his report was submitted—during which time he continued to pressure President Merseles to enter retail on a large scale—Wood was appointed vice-president in charge of factories and retail at Sears, Roebuck. From the time he assumed his new duties, he held forth constantly on the advantages and necessities of the mail-order firm's entry into retail.

Perhaps his largest single battering ram in breaching the wall of opposition within Sears, Roebuck was the knowledge he had brought to the company from Ward's. He had facts and figures to show that Ward's was making a good profit from its retail venture. But Wood's arsenal of factual information was not limited to his knowledge of Ward's operations. He had early developed a passionate fondness for the *Statistical Abstract of the United States,* and he spent endless hours poring over its statistics. He had a remarkable capacity for grasping reams of figures and relating them to his problem at hand.[1] He expounded to others in the company on the significance of the population trend which had in 1920, for the first time, made the United States a predominantly urban country, and he projected that trend into the years ahead to show that much of Sears's market was literally moving away from it and into cities, where those former customers would probably buy from department stores and other retail outlets.

Wood held forth on the significance to the mail-order business of the great increase in automobile registrations and in other means of transportation. He pointed out the rising income of industrial workers in the cities and the fact that farmers were not sharing in the "Coolidge prosperity" to anywhere near the same extent to which they had prospered in the decade ending in 1919. Finally, to the argument that entering retail would only mean losing mail-order business by diverting part of it into retail channels,

Wood replied: "Better to lose that business to one's self than to someone else." The "someone else" was, of course, Montgomery Ward.

Wood received some support from the company's directors. But it was clearly Wood who carried the main brunt of crystallizing the latent sentiment and overcoming the bitter-end opposition of his management associates. He found a sympathetic audience for his passion for retail in the person of C. M. Kittle, who became president of Sears on the same day Wood was chosen to head up the company's factories and the still nonexistent retail effort. Wood's activities along that line in the following year and a half were to explode the time bomb he had left in Montgomery Ward's pigeonhole. Within weeks after the two men joined Sears, Kittle gave Wood authority to launch the venture into retail. The foremost disciple of mail-order houses' selling over the counter was at last able to act.

Wood's green light from Kittle represented merely the authority to open one retail store, in the Chicago mail-order plant at Homan and Arthington streets, although it seems certain that the two men planned to open such stores in all branch plants as rapidly as feasible; and it is highly possible that Kittle had already been persuaded by Wood's eagerness to blanket the country with retail units. The most remarkable thing about the authority to establish that first store and, in fact, the most remarkable thing about Sears's whole retail venture was the fact that the company even went into retail at that time. Only two men in the top layer of executives—Wood and Kittle—favored the retail plan, and only one of these approached the mission with evangelical zeal. The two Rosenwalds, while not opposed to the plan, were at best only open to persuasion based upon returns still to come. Other executives flatly opposed entering retail.

Wood moved rapidly, after permission was secured, to organize and stock the first store. Yet caution remained the watchword, and the selection of the Chicago plant for the venture bespoke a desire to hedge against any considerable loss, in money or prestige, if it should fail. The retail store opened for business on February 2, 1925. It was followed in the remainder of that year by seven more retail stores, all of the "A" class, with four of them located in mail-order plants. The Seattle retail store followed Chicago within three months, after which came Dallas and Kansas City in August (the Kansas City store opened simultaneously with the new mail-order plant in which it was housed). The retail system was extended to the Philadelphia branch plant in October, and in November two more retail stores were opened in Chicago (one on the North Side, the other on the South Side), in addition to the store located in the mail-order plant in that city.

The first retail store to be established outside a city containing a mail-order plant was the one in Evansville, Indiana, opened in October. The eight retail stores reached a combined sales volume of $11,819,000 in 1925,

4.5 per cent of the combined mail-order and retail sales of $258,318,000 in that year. The year 1926 saw only one additional retail store established (in the mail-order plant opened in Atlanta that year), but 1926 testified to improved promotion and merchandising operations, for the sales volume of the retail "chain" almost doubled, to reach a figure of $23,046,000. Mail-order volume in 1926 dropped to 91.5 per cent of the total mail-order-plus-retail volume. The next fifteen years were to witness a steady decrease in mail order's proportion of total sales volume, unbroken in its downward trend except for the one year 1935, when it rallied by almost two percentage points.

Montgomery Ward, meanwhile, had in the spring of 1926 established "mail-order agencies" in small towns as a stimulant for its mail-order business. The system was somewhat analogous to the present-day catalogue order offices; a fairly large line of merchandise items was displayed, but only automobile tires could be purchased on the spot. Ward's for some time had exhibited merchandise in special displays at county fairs and expositions of various kinds. The firm discovered that people were extremely eager to buy its goods both at the fairs and in its mail-order agencies. One reason for this, outside the immediate accessibility of the goods, was (according to a Ward employee) that local independent merchants assured the public that the goods Ward's was displaying were of much higher quality than the people would obtain if they ordered from Ward's by mail. The merchants were insisting that Ward's had purchased the goods being shown solely for display and that this merchandise was not a part of regular stock.

Ward's had found in the course of many state-fair exhibits that the goods displayed became worn and soiled from handling in the course of time, which impaired their later salability. In order to avoid having to unload the goods at a loss at the end of their usefulness for display purposes, Ward's display representative evolved an astute plan. He would sell the goods to local people eager to buy, at full catalogue prices—with the proviso that such customers could not obtain possession of the goods until they were removed from the display. The local merchants' opposition had apparently backfired; people were so convinced that the Ward goods being shown were of far superior quality to the merchandise quoted in the catalogue that they were willing to pay full price, have the goods handled and soiled by "lookers," and ultimately take delivery of the display-worn goods. Ward's management thoroughly approved of this selling arrangement, since it removed an appreciable portion of the cost of displays in expositions.

The next step in local selling came when a Ward employee was accosted at the mail-order agency in Plymouth, Indiana, by a would-be customer who literally would not take "No" for an answer. This person was determined to buy a certain saw on display in the agency. Reiterated assertions that the saw was not for sale left him unmoved; he wanted to buy it at catalogue price, he intended to buy it, and he refused to depart until he *had* bought it. His nuisance value paid off, and he was finally allowed to buy the saw. The news of that transaction circulated rapidly by word of mouth, with the result that scores of people poured into the agency demanding to buy the goods on display. With the dam already breached, the agency personnel gave in; everything in the agency was sold forthwith. The agency promptly reordered a full stock from Ward's mail-order plant— and just as promptly sold all the goods over the counter at catalogue prices, then reordered from its service of supply again.

By this time the extraordinary movement of goods to the Plymouth agency came to the attention of President Merseles. When he discovered the agency was selling merchandise directly, he was outraged. Ward's, he cried, had always claimed that the mail-order business' efficiency in handling orders and its elmination of "overhead" enabled the firm to undersell all over-the-counter merchants. The practice of selling at retail for catalogue prices, he maintained, negated the whole basis upon which the business rested. It was pointed out to Merseles that because of the rapid turnover the agency outlets could sell fast-moving items at a higher net profit than mail order's average and that the Plymouth agency was dealing in just such fast-moving merchandise. The agency further claimed that it was netting 20 per cent profit. Special audits were made. The evidence was unassailable. Merseles authorized two other mail-order agencies—at Little Falls, Minnesota, and at Maryville, Kansas—to sell over the counter. The resultant profits were equally encouraging. Merseles was completely convinced, and Ward's board of directors was collectively enthusiastic (they may also have discovered by that time that Sears's retail stores up to that point had proved profitable).

Sears, meantime, was continuing its own retail expansion. In 1927 it opened more "A" stores, two of them in the new mail-order plants in Memphis and Los Angeles and five others in Camden, New Jersey, Milwaukee, Philadelphia (that city's second), and Chicago (for a total of four in that city). The first stores of two new types made their appearance that year: eight of the "B" class and three of the "C" class. By the end of 1927 there was a total of twenty-seven stores in operation, three times the total number operating at the end of the previous year.

Ward's took steps in 1927 to whittle down Sears's retail lead. Ward's opened stores at Woodstock, Illinois, on January 15; Monroe, Wisconsin, February 5; and Clinton, Illinois, February 26. A brief lull followed, but on April 9 Ward's established a retail unit at Fostoria, Ohio. Then Crawfordsville, Indiana, was opened on May 7; Kankakee, Illinois, on June 25; Fairbault, Minnesota, on July 30; and Evansville, Indiana, on August 8. This gave Ward's ten retail stores (the Little Falls, Minnesota, store had been closed) in addition to the outlet stores in each of its branch mail-order plants. Those mail-order plants numbered seven by 1927—Chicago, Kansas City, Fort Worth, Portland, St. Paul, Oakland, and Baltimore. Branches at Denver and at Albany, New York, were to follow in 1929.

In late summer of 1927 Ward's issued instructions to its retail staff to step up the rate of expansion sharply and to get into "choice" towns before Sears did, even at the realized prospect of many costly errors. One mistake Ward's sought *not* to make was that of being too slow. Ward's generally favored entering towns with populations between 4,000 and 75,000 (it is interesting to note that Ward's had already started entering towns much smaller than those in which Sears first located its stores) on a breath-taking scale, seeking to have fifteen hundred retail stores in operation by the end of 1929. They compromised on a more practicable target figure of five hundred stores by that date; but even that number appeared difficult of attainment, since Ward's had only thirty-seven retail stores in operation as of January 1, 1928, exclusive of the stores in seven mail-order plants—a total of forty-four.

Sears, Roebuck was driving ahead with equal force to spread its chain of retail stores over the country and to beat Ward's to the best locations in the best cities. Sears's greatest expansion to that point came in 1928, when more than six times as many new stores were established as in the preceding three years combined. The "A" stores more than doubled in number that year, growing from 16 to 37, but the really great expansion came in the "B" stores—from 8 to 150. Only 2 "C" stores were added, bringing that class to a total of 5. Two of the "A" stores added in 1928 were located in new mail-order plants, at Minneapolis and Boston, with another opened in Boston outside the branch plant. These 192 retail stores turned in a sales volume of $107,179,000 for a resounding 30.9 per cent of total company sales.

Ward's assumed the lead in total number of stores in 1928, with 244 retail units in operation by the end of that year, exclusive of the 7 outlet stores located in mail-order branches. But these 244 stores handled net sales of only $48,000,000, less than half the $107,179,000 reached by Sears's 192 stores. Ward's realized a profit of $4,452,055 on its retail sales that year, and retail accounted for 22.4 per cent of its total sales.

An interesting example of the keen competition between the two mail-order firms occurs in a report made to General Wood on May 31, 1928, by T. J. Carney (soon to be parent operating vice-president), on the simultaneous opening of the Sears and the Ward retail stores in Huntington, West Virginia. Carney's résumé covered everything from the space occupied by the two stores to their advance publicity for the openings. All in all, Ward's appears to have had a sizable lead over Sears in almost every respect, at least in the Huntington effort. In addition to buying more newspaper space to advertise the opening, Ward's also sent letters to all its mail-order customers in the Huntington area telling them of the coming of the retail store. Both stores carried an assortment of hard and soft lines, with

Ward's giving more emphasis than Sears to the latter. Ward's aisles were wider, their signs better, their displays more attractive, and their fixtures superior, and the store generally made a better impression than Sears, according to Carney, who added:

> Our store was one of the best of our Eastern stores in appearance, but seemed flat after a visit to Ward's. . . . It is of interest to note that several of our men heard reference to Sears "hardware" store—Ward's store attracted women without seemingly affecting the number of men customers. . . . Ward's advanced the opening date of their store and sent a number of additional men in training for store managers to handle opening. They made statement—"It was their best effort." A remark was credited to Patton [manager of Ward's Huntington store] that they had seen most of our stores and the Huntington store was the best looking one we had.

By the end of 1929 Ward's had opened five hundred stores—one-third of the number earlier hoped for. To reach even that figure of five hundred, Ward's had frequently opened as many as twenty-five stores a week during 1929.

In that same year Sears's expansion drive also continued apace, though not at the same rate of increase, to reach a total of 324 stores. Again it was the "B" stores which led the race; that class grew from 150 to 237, while only 11 "A" stores were added for a total of 48, and 29 more "C" stores for a total of 34 of that type. The retail stores' volume of sales increased from $107,179,000 in 1928 to $174,625,000—an increase of a little more than 61 per cent. And retail-store sales in 1929 accounted for 39.6 per cent of total sales.

The year 1930 saw a net addition of 27 Sears's retail stores. Aided by the additional stores, retail sales volume increased by some $6,207,000 over 1929—but mail-order sales *decreased* by $56,490,000 from a high of $266,043,000, with the result that retail sales that year constituted 46.3 per cent of total volume. The company apparently concluded that, with mail-order sales dropping and retail volume rising, it should put its chips on the latter. In 1931 it added 40 retail stores, all of the "C" class, and saw the pattern of 1930 repeated in large measure: total mail-order sales decreased, while retail sales showed a gain over the previous year. The net decrease in mail order amounted to $47,683,000, dropping mail-order net sales volume to $161,870,000—its lowest point since 1917. Retail sales, on the other hand, showed a gain of $4,509,000 over 1930 to account for 53.4 per cent of total sales—the first time retail had exceeded mail order in sales volume.

The year 1932 saw retail further increase its share of the total sales, to 57.7 per cent. Mail-order sales in that black year skidded to $116,729,000 (the lowest in dollar volume since 1915), a decrease of $45,141,000 from 1931, while retail sales dropped by $26,313,000. The year 1932 marked the bottom of the pit for Sears, Roebuck, and the only year of that depression in which it actually operated at a net loss, for the following years witnessed a steady rise in sales volume and profits. And whereas the debacle of 1921 had accounted for a net loss of $16,453,469, the year 1932 saw a net loss of only $2,543,651. Even the sharp drops in sales volume in 1930 and 1931 had left a profit at the end of each year, even if a steadily decreasing one. And the latter depression was of far greater duration than the former and carried the country through a far bitterer and more damaging experience. By 1929, however, Sears had its own chain of retail outlets and thus could match all competition on price reductions, from day to day and, if necessary, from hour to hour.

The years which marked a cataclysm for the nation at large represented in Sears's progress simply a time for consolidation and reorganization, for the trough of the depression in 1932 marked the end of the first phase of the company's retail organization.

The doldrums of 1932 carried Sears, Roebuck stock to a record low of 9⅞ on the New York Stock Exchange. It should be noted in this connection that farm cash receipts had dropped from $11,296,000,000 in 1929 to $4,743,000,000 in 1932—and the farm market was mail order's chief bailiwick. The drop in factory wages—lifeblood of the retail stores—almost exactly paralleled the decrease in farm income.[2] In the annual report for 1932 General Wood noted that the "A" stores had in that year shown a loss for the first time, "though a small one."

Yet even in the depressing year of 1932, the company continued to demonstrate its faith in retail stores. In March it opened its State Street store in Chicago, the first operation it had sited in a downtown metropolitan business district. In the same month it announced a $4,500,000 store-building campaign for Brooklyn, New York, and Hackensack and Union City, New Jersey—the "New York group." Hackensack opened with fanfare on October 27, with New Jersey's Governor Harry A. Moore heading the welcoming committee and making the first purchase. The salesman handling that transaction was Board Chairman Lessing J. Rosenwald. When the Brooklyn store opened on November 5, the welcome was extended by Mrs. Franklin D. Roosevelt, in her last public appearance before her husband's election to President. For the Union City opening, on November 10, the wife of New Jersey's governor and a group of mayors formed the welcoming committee.

The cost of closing some "B" stores—this type had experienced the sharpest decline in sales with resultant losses—was placed in the annual report at $710,000, including lease settlement, inventory losses, and fixtures. Wood states: "We believe that the closing of these stores has eliminated for the most part the unsatisfactory units." The 94 "C" stores showed a profit in 1932. And the annual report further mentioned that all salaries and wages in the company had been reduced by 20 per cent during that bleak year.

In general terms, 1932 marked a period of consolidation of the retail effort by both Ward's and Sears. Each of these firms proceeded to eliminate their most unprofitable retail units. And since salvation did not appear to lie in opening an ever greater number of stores, as it had up through most of 1929 and even after that, a thorough reappraisal of the entire effort was in order. For the first time it apparently became urgent to re-examine the whole plan of operations of the retail units, of the personnel who managed and staffed them, of the merchandise structures for the various types of stores, and of related aspects of the operation. All these problems had actually been involved from the outset of the retail venture; booming prosperity and mounting sales had simply tended to obscure and to some extent to alleviate the necessity for reappraisal.

Sears, Roebuck's (and, for that matter, Ward's) chief asset in its invasion of the retail field in 1925 was the reputation for integrity, quality of merchandise, low prices, and good service it had achieved in mail order. But that vast reservoir of mail-order experience threatened at the same time to be Sears's greatest drawback to successful and profitable retail operation, for the mail-order reputation which helped induce customers to trade in the company's retail stores was, perhaps unavoidably, accompanied by a "mail-order" concept of merchandising not appropriate to the retail stores. Even before the first store was opened, for example, the question arose whether to peg retail prices at a slightly higher level than mail-order prices. The very fact that this should have been a question for argument is in itself ample evidence of how firmly most of the executives were wedded to mail-order concepts. General Wood, however, was strongly of the opinion that retail prices had to be somewhat higher to compensate for the greater expense of selling over the counter—for salaries of clerks and managers, for rents on buildings, for increased service costs, and so on. Most of the other executives insisted this would be bad public relations, that customers would not understand being unable to purchase over the counter at catalogue prices, and, moreover, that higher retail prices were not necessary. For a short while after Sears entered retail, mail order and retail prices were the same, but Wood's insistence, Julius Rosenwald's approval, and the slow accumulation of experience soon turned the tide to a differential pegging retail prices some 6–7 per cent higher than those of mail order. The reasons for the differential were explained to each retail customer who raised the question. In due time those who were dissatisfied with the explanation were offered the opportunity of ordering goods from the catalogue through the stores. (This was eventually refined into the system of catalogue desks now prominent features of all retail stores.)

It is an interesting fact that most employees of the company in position to know agree that a clear conception of retail operations did not finally emerge within Sears until some ten years after it entered retail (even though, of course, the stores had become profitable long before then). It appears in retrospect that almost the only thing Sears, Roebuck knew about retail in the first years after 1925 was that it had entered that field.

The first period (even the first decade) of Sears in retail constituted a time of what might be termed profitable confusion.

Several basic problems confronted Sears's executives when the long-bruited decision to establish retail outlets finally crystallized: the location of the stores (in regard to the cities selected and the sites and buildings within those cities), merchandise structures for the stores (there came to be five basic types of stores—"A," "B-1," "B-2," "B-3," and "C"), type of personnel to staff the stores at the local level and to organize and direct the stores at the parent-level in Chicago, the procurement of merchandise and the utilization of the already existing service of supply (the mail-order plants), and, of course, other problems of lesser nature. Decisions on all these fundamental questions were made initially on literally a mail-order basis, for mail-order plants housed the first retail stores, thus "solving" the problem of location.

It should, however, be pointed out that Wood doubtless planned, even before the first retail store opened, to extend the chain to a wide geographical area, possibly to embrace the entire country. The use of mail-order plants then in existence (and subsequent branches as fast as they were opened) as retail-store locations was sound strategy. At relatively little cost in rent, fixtures, etc., the company would be able to obtain some valuable experience for a few months before branching out into cities and towns relatively remote from the branch plants. This plan further allowed the company to exercise the closest possible supervision over the fledgling stores and to staff them with experienced mail-order employees. There is ample evidence at hand to indicate that this and other decisions were reached after careful analysis of the situation late in 1924 and early in 1925.

Before the first year of Sears's retail experience was over, it appeared desirable to forsake the safety and refuge of mail-order plants as locations for stores. Two stores were opened in Chicago in 1925 in addition to the one already operating in the mail-order plant, and one was established in Evansville, Indiana. In less than a year, then, store location—in broad terms, that is, as a matter of policy—had become an issue which had to be decided. The decision appears to have been perhaps the wisest of all decisions made in the formative period of retail. Wood insisted that Sears's primary field, at least for "A" stores, was not the downtown shopping districts of high-rent areas and traffic congestion but rather outlying districts where ample free parking space could be provided at relatively low rentals. This plan, Wood held, was essential to maintaining the company's competitive position in the low-price field and to making shopping easier. The decision to locate retail units of the "A" type in outlying districts is one of the few earliest policies still rigorously followed with few exceptions; some of the other policy decisions of that time, as will be shown, had to be altered or scrapped. "B" stores were always located "in town" and only much later came to be sited in outlying districts. The "C" stores were originally (and still) located in or near the shopping center of town.

The company built most of its "A" stores. For the smaller stores, Sears early adopted a policy of negotiating rental agreements on a sliding scale, based on a minimum guaranty and assuring the landlord a percentage of the store's sales above the minimum covered by the guaranty. The generally profitable nature of the retail operation meant satisfactory rentals for landlords and at the same time helped the company to hedge against such sharp declines in sales as occurred in 1932. As it gained experience in retailing, the company bought several "A" stores outright, including the stock. These generally proved unsatisfactory; the customers apparently preferred Sears's merchandise in Sears's surroundings. As late as 1932, however, the vast majority of the structures occupied by the company's retail stores were rented. The annual report for 1932 stated that the firm in that year occupied 345 of its 385 stores on leases, which ran as follows: 135 were to expire in 1933 and 1934; 92 to expire between 1935 and 1937; 82 to expire between 1938 and 1942; 25 to expire between 1943 and 1952; and 11 to expire after 1952. That annual report went on to say:

> Due to the decline in sales volume, our rentals in 1932 were higher in percentage than any previous year, but were less than 4% on sales. Our total rental on leased stores for the calendar year 1932 was $3,277,397. On the basis of the present rental market, it is estimated that our excess rental charged on leased stores in 1932 amounted to about ½ of 1% on their sales.

At the end of 1926 only one of Sears's nine retail stores (all "A's") was sited in a city where it had no mail-order plant. The decision on merchandise lines for the stores had not yet become a pressing matter. Wood had, however, insisted from the beginning that the stores should stress hard lines over soft goods, in contradistinction to most department stores; whereas most of the latter were essentially "women's stores," the Sears stores were to be more in the nature of "men's stores," with heavy emphasis on hard lines and no "frills" in buildings, fixtures, or displays. Yet the Sears "A" stores, as indicated, were by no means to confine themselves to hard lines; they were pretty much to run the gamut of the catalogue in their merchandise line. *Fortune* summarizes Wood's concept of his retail chain in these terms:

> General Wood's great idea was to supplement the existing services. The department store was a woman's place and the chains were doing a good job distributing food, clothes, and novelties. But the chains had overlooked hardware, sporting goods, farm implements, household furnishings, plumbing—the hard lines that were basic in Sears' catalogue business. So the Sears' store would be fundamentally a man's store. Whatever the department stores were doing, General Wood proposed to do the opposite. Whereas they had crowded like sheep for central locations, he proposed to settle in the outlying places, near a highway, with plenty of free parking space. That way, he'd catch the new phenom-

enon, the motoring shopper. That way, too, he'd cut overhead. And mindful of the city wage earner who also had to think of price, he proposed to take a leaf from the catalogue whose price structure was based partly on *lack of service*. The Sears store would do business on cash, offer no free delivery. As for competing with the catalogue, Wood said no. The Sears stores would be confined to cities of 100,000 population or more. Such cities did not contribute more than a fraction of 1 per cent of the Company's gross.[3]

It appears, however, that Wood did not fully communicate his concepts to all his associates. Lessing Rosenwald says that there was a "lack of understanding" among Sears's officers about what the retail stores would really be; Wood was "probably the only man" who saw clearly what those stores might become. It is Rosenwald's belief that if Wood had properly "sold" the other officers at the time the company entered retail, he would not only have been able perhaps to make them see the stores in terms of what they actually became but might also have minimized the officers' fears of competition with department stores and thus have eased the task of persuading his associates.

When it came to translating Wood's conception of the merchandise structure of the retail stores into concrete terms, the initial solution was naïvely simply. The retail units were stocked by pulling some of almost everything off the mail-order shelves. The earliest retail stores were not accorded even that much respect in regard to their merchandise offerings. A memorandum from Sears's general merchandise office, dated September 30, 1925, to all department heads, read:

As of October 1st, please report to this office your surplus merchandise . . . and also your discontinued merchandise. . . .
We want to make every effort to clean up our surplus and discontinued merchandise through the retail stores.

As for the service of supply for goods (through the mail-order plants), the retail stores were at most only a few hundred yards away from their "warehouses," and mail order could simply increase its total purchases of goods if the retail stores increased the total volume of sales. Retail then seemed to be to some extent merely an adjunct of mail order, almost nothing more than a new sales-promotional device for the old, established system under which Richard Sears and Julius Rosenwald had prospered so greatly.

The opening of seven more "A" stores in 1927 presented no question as to the lines to be stocked, nor did the three "C" stores opened the same year, since the latter type was to deal almost solely in automobile supplies, paints, hardware, radios, batteries, and a few other, similar hard lines. But the eight "B" stores opened in 1927 *did* present a problem in the assortment of lines, for their mission was far from clarified. They were expected to have as a rule about 10,000–12,000 square feet of selling space (as against only 3,000–4,000 for "C" stores) and to carry a fairly complete selection of lines, with only a few items within each line. The result of this situation was that, while both the "A" and "C" type stores had a fairly well-defined merchandise character, the "B" stores did not. Those "B" stores were spreading themselves too thin in attempting to carry too many classifications of merchandise. The "B" stores therefore had incomplete departments of odds and ends, with constant changes in merchandise content—the proverbial "rag, tag, and bobtail" effect.

The "A" stores were in the vast majority of instances profitable from the start. The "C" stores were also generally profitable from the outset, largely because the "Allstate" automobile tires they sold were priced about 20–25 per cent below other tires of comparable quality. But the "B" stores floundered, in the main, until the mid-1930's. Their potentialities for profitability were sorely impaired by their incomplete and spotty stocks; with no assurance that a customer could find what he wanted at a Sears "B" store, a shopper was quite likely to go instead to a department store—or to a Ward retail store.

Even when the merchandise structure for any given store had been determined in the early days of retail, great problems still remained. Mail-order buyers continued to buy for all retail as well as for mail order. Mail order had never been compelled to "pin point" its operations to a particular city or even to a particular state; what did not sell in one city or state might sell very well elsewhere in the same region served by a given mail-order plant. What mattered to a mail-order plant was how any given item sold within its whole region; but what mattered vitally to a store manager was how an item sold in his own particular store. As a result of mail order's inexperience in this pin-pointing, some retail stores found their shelves bulging with slow-moving items, while other stores were unable to obtain that same item in anything like the quantity they wanted. Proper localizing of inventories came slowly as experience was gained in retailing. Before any considerable fund of such experience was accumulated, however, stores in the South had skis and other winter sports equipment to sell—as well as Decoration Day displays. Some retail units in ice-locked Maine and snowbound Minnesota found tropical sportswear items in their midwinter inventories. San Diego, California, was shipped some earmuffs.

Because of the relatively low style quality of mail-order goods, mail-order buying and retail buying turned out to be sharply dissimilar operations in some respects. Retail customers frequently wanted to see the types of merchandise shown in competing stores in the community, not merely the goods listed in the mail-order catalogue. And mail-order goods were unacceptable to many retail customers. Fashion, color, and design were of secondary importance to most mail-order buyers—so much so, in the opinion of one former executive who made a series of departmental studies of buying, that sources sometimes appeared to be "dumping" poorly styled merchandise on the company. As a result there developed some sentiment in favor of having two separate buying organizations, one for mail order, another for retail. But, aside from the fact that such a procedure would have weakened the power of the company's mass purchasing, there was the fact that the company's only buyers were mail-order buyers. It was therefore decided that the mail-order organization was to continue buying for both mail order and retail and was to concentrate upon raising mail-order merchandise to the quality level of retail. But during the slow accomplishment of that task, unbalanced retail inventories continued. The process of cleaning store stocks which followed cost the company millions in markdowns and more millions in lost sales.

The losses in markdowns arose from the fact that goods which had languished for months on the shelves of retail stores had to be repacked and retransported to the mail-order plants. In addition to this cost, the goods themselves had become soiled and worn from handling and exposure and often the seasonal demand for them had passed. The goods therefore had to be marked down, and stores were credited with only a fraction of the initial cost charged to them by the mail-order plants, thus sustaining serious merchandise losses. The cost in lost sales stemmed from the fact that many stores could have sold much more of various items had those items been on their shelves instead of in the stocks of stores which could not move them.

One of the greatest difficulties in operating the retail stores was that of obtaining proper personnel to staff and manage them. The company bestowed formal recognition of a sort on the fact that it was in the retail business when, on May 27, 1925, Wood issued an executive notice to department heads: "Effective at once, Mr. W. H. Alexander is appointed Acting Manager of Retail Stores, and Mr. J. Goldsmith is appointed Acting Manager of the Chicago Retail Store." In an executive notice dated August 12 of the same year, General Merchandise Manager Max Adler revealed that merchandise of the retail stores was to receive some particular attention: "Mr. B. F. Watson and Mr. C. N. Austin have been appointed as assistants to Mr. W. H. Alexander in the merchandising of our Retail Stores." But three men do not an organization make, and personnel continued a major problem. It was to a large extent from this difficulty that many other problems arose.

Most of the mail-order employees assigned to retail in the years immediately following 1925 proved woefully out of place in that sharply different type of selling operation. They were accustomed to operating strictly according to manuals, and they assumed that the retail units could be made to operate successfully under the same, or at least a closely similar, system. As a result, retail stores were the subject for a barrage of bulletins and instructions from a central headquarters which attempted to manage the stores without the knowledge or appreciation of the technique of local retail-store operations. Parent-executives harassed the stores by an endless procession of bulletins, memorandums, operating procedures, and other instructions. Not only was the volume of this material so great that few managers could find time to read all of it; in addition, the instructions often contradicted each other, and some mandates were rescinded soon after issuance. In the words of one former retail executive, "The smart managers just didn't read the stuff at all."

Selling from the catalogue was such a unique practice that the mail-order people were oblivious to the principles of store layout. Space in a store often seemed then to be allocated on two bases: (1) the most influential merchandise supervisor got his goods near the door and (2) the supervisor most recently in a store had his goods moved to the location nearest the front door. Proximity to the door appeared to be the greatest desideratum, regardless of the type of merchandise involved.

As the inadequacy of most mail-order personnel and procedures for the expanding retail operation became increasingly evident, and in fact all too painfully clear, the pendulum began to swing in the opposite direction, and with a vengeance. The belief arose that the proper place for the company to recruit its retail-store personnel was from department stores and other types of retail establishments and chain stores. This became increasingly easy to do in 1930 and 1931, for Sears was still expanding retail in those years, while department stores particularly had felt the first sharp lash of the depression and were already retrenching. (It was the concern over competent managers for the stores that prompted Sears's management to consider seriously a merger with the J. C. Penney Company.) The energetic recruiting campaign, which, incidentally, was to lead to establishment of the company's personnel department, brought a vast number of "outsiders" into the Sears retail organization. But an interesting fact soon became apparent: while mail-order personnel had not generally proved capable of manning the retail operation, the fact still remained that retail, in the Sears scheme, depended to some extent upon mail order. The two operations could not be divorced. And just as the Sears mail-order people had revealed an insufficient knowledge of retail practices, the countless retailers brought into the company from the outside proved to be equally inadequate for the job.

Mail order continued, to a considerable extent, to be the source of supply for the retail stores; mail order was retail's "jobber." Inept as mail order may have been in grasping the merchandise needs of retail, it was still the base of operations. The "outsiders" simply did not understand the whole mail-order structure, its procurement procedures, its relationships with thousands of sources all over the country, its highly refined and codified operating techniques. Nor had many of them had extensive experience in stores which stocked the kind of goods the Sears stores handled. Most of the outsiders recruited as store managers had had experience in groceries, drugs, soft lines, hardware, five-and-ten-cent stores, and similar fields, but few had been connected with the diversity of goods they were required to stock in the Sears stores.

Most store managers lacked the necessary intimate knowledge of Sears as an organization. Mail order, on the other hand, while it had not proved adequate to the task of managing or (at first) even supplying the retail stores, was at the same time endowed with a wealth of knowledge about the character of Sears. Mail order had been refined to a high point by 1925. It was later to develop interesting and profitable new techniques, but it had also already developed a general orderliness. In contrast to the wide variations from retail store to store, mail order was standardized; its general catalogues might vary somewhat from region to region, in the merchandise offered and the position and space accorded it, but the over-all treatment was standardized—a reader would find no grinding contrasts between the catalogues of, say, the Seattle and Boston regions. Each catalogue was consistent within itself; the treatment accorded different lines of merchandise might vary considerably, but the total effect was generally harmonious.

Moreover, the catalogue was neat. It represented good housekeeping practices. Its space was allocated, to a considerable degree, on the basis of previous sales records, of planned promotions, of each item's carefully calculated potentialities. Mail order always knew just what volume in each line and each item was being sold. And mail order's display problem was limited almost entirely to the catalogue.

Retail presented pretty much the opposite side of the coin. Its early display fixtures were of the orthodox variety, bought in the same market which served other (and frequently dissimilar) retailers, or built for Sears along traditional lines. Even these fixtures varied greatly from store to store, and the individual store manager's utilization of the fixtures varied even more. In the words of L. S. Janes, Sears's director of store planning and display, display soon showed up as "the weakest link in the entire Sears operation."

Many of the managers of smaller stores apparently took seriously Wood's early dictum that their units were to be essentially men's stores. In the words of one company executive, some managers seemed almost to say to their customers, "If you spit on the floor at home, you go right ahead and spit on the floor in this store." The "men's stores" apparently proceeded on the assumption that men are notoriously poor housekeepers and therefore would not object to trading in a store whose housekeeping was equally poor.

In addition to the general sloppiness, there was poor utilization of space, especially of vertical space. Display efforts tended to spread merchandise laterally across the store, wasting vertical space and often either overspacing or underspacing specific lines. Relatively little attention was given to the types of display called for by different types of merchandise; some managers seemed to feel that skis or ladies' slips or automobile tires could all be displayed to customers in pretty much the same way and in juxtaposition. Even after the company's Store Planning and Display Department began to develop fixtures designed better to display goods, there remained the fact that each store manager was charged for such fixtures; he had therefore to weigh the relative advantages of installing new fixtures to replace the often inadequate ones he already had. The general appearance and character of each store came soon to represent to a great extent the character and convictions of its manager, adapted to the physical characteristics of the store building and to its location (which in many instances was poor).

On top of all this, there were problems of supply—problems of getting the right goods for a particular store in a city with particular needs and of getting them at the right time and in the right quantity. In reviewing the operation from this point of hindsight, one feels that many of the sins of the store managers were silently accepted as satisfactory practices for a good while. It was really remarkable that stores could operate so profitably in view of the vast confusion and the steady changes going on within the organization as a whole.

Many stores which had been set up on an anticipated annual sales volume of, say, two million dollars, within a few years doubled that volume. Space shortage became chronic in almost all stores, leading to incomplete and inadequate stocks, slow turnovers, and subsequent markdowns. At the same time, Sears's competition was more and more utilizing newer display techniques and fixtures, while many of the Sears stores continued to cling to the austere, frill-less character of "men's stores"—when their customers were predominantly women. The company was engaging in some reorientation of its merchandise structure, but the changes were not fully reflected in the presentation of goods in the retail stores, which showed little real change.

One former executive asserts that the chaos and bungling inherent in the whole retail organization in its infancy was summed up for him in what he discovered in one store. The store was obviously a hard-goods outlet, but the first display inside the door was of bedroom slippers. In explanation, the store manager pointed out that the girls from the brothels in the area depended upon Sears for their bedroom slippers. The parent-executive remained undecided as to whether the prime error lay in the display or in the store location.

Despite all these glaring shortcomings, retail became the favorite child of top management at Sears within a very few years. With a love traditionally reserved for the firstborn, the top executives showered the lion's share of honors and rewards upon the newest phase of the business. And in that attitude lay the seeds of dissension, for, anthropomorphically, retail assumed the mannerisms of the spoiled child, while mail order became the jealous sibling.

Many of the developments of the early years of retail served to sharpen the antagonisms and to bring relations to a bitterness approaching the "fighting" point. When retail managers had to return to mail-order stocks goods they felt should never have been shipped to their stores, and then saw mail-order plants mark down those goods with retail bearing the loss, store managers screamed in anguish that they were being victimized. Many of the store managers, new to the Sears organization, had only a hazy knowledge of mail-order operations, even though mail order remained an important support element for retail; mail-order personnel resented seeing their side of the business dismissed as being of subordinate, if not negligible, importance.

The sharpening antagonisms led to an increasing lack of co-operation between mail order and retail, and each instance of lack of co-operation increased the hostility. The circle was a vicious one. Retail constantly resented its dependence upon mail-order buying and upon mail-order accounting. The parent auditing-control department, the mail-order instrument which organized and established the retail accounting system, was a focal spot of tension. Retail-store managers frequently tended to attribute losses to the accounting methods employed. Auditing-control responded, understandably, with an attitude of unfriendliness, stiffness, and suspicion, which reached its apogee at one point when auditing-control personnel refused to eat with retail personnel. In its relations to auditing-control, retail saw another form of mail-order "domination," for that parent-department was in truth the kingpin of mail order—what it said went without argument. But what it said regarding retail went usually *with* argument, sometimes bitter.

A similarly unsatisfactory relationship developed between retail-store personnel and the central buying organization which purchased goods for both retail and mail order. Many store managers openly considered the buyers incapable of buying for the fast-moving retail operation. This situation was further aggravated by a belief, frequently enunciated by some top executives, that retail had no real obligation to "buy" goods purchased for the stores but could instead accept or reject the merchandise at will. Actually, of course, retail *did* have to accept the merchandise, by and large; stores were not allowed to perform their own buying, in addition to which the store managers were equipped to sell, not to buy. The central buyers responded to retail's hostility—bordering at times upon contempt—with a chilly relationship and a concentration upon buying for mail order, which "appreciated" them. Too, buying for mail order was an old habit for most of the buyers, and it came easier; the retail store was not their natural habitat.

Up to the early 1930's the company's top executives were relatively little concerned with these shortcomings of the retail stores; they were not unaware of the problem, but their eyes were properly fixed on broader questions and more important, immediate problems. The paramount job was, of course, to blanket the country with a chain of stores, to get the stores into operation first and to worry over details later.

By 1932 the chain of retail outlets was fairly well scattered across the country, and the time had come to pause and consolidate. That was the year in which retail administration was reorganized to centralize direction of the retail effort in a vice-president in charge of retail administration in Chicago. It was also the year in which the Store Planning and Display Department was established, with a name which pretty clearly indicated its functions. The year 1932 marked a time of planning and thinking, a time of outlining broad general policies and of setting the course for years ahead. Much of the thinking and planning which affected the retail selling operation emanated from the Store Planning and Display Department; its publications and pronouncements in the succeeding years shed much light on the problems and malpractices of the retail operation as well as the techniques devised to improve it.

In the course of time, as was probably inevitable, each of the Sears "belligerents"—in broad terms, retail and mail order—came increasingly to understand the position, the responsibilities, and the potentialities of the other. The increase in understanding, born of the hard facts of the situation (hammered home from the highest level in a long educational campaign), led in time to a far more harmonious relationship among the various disputants. Once retail and mail order both realized they were complementary to each other, concessions came more easily. Retail realized that it was receiving an important jobbing service from mail order, for which the older branch of the business was entitled to a reasonable profit instead of having to subsidize retail by performing services without compensation. Retail also came to concede that it derived a substantial boon from the mail-order catalogues, which helped to keep the company's name before millions of people. And, as the buying organization developed a better understanding of retail's needs, the criticism advanced by retail became less harassing and more constructive. Even so, most of the tangible rewards in the form of salaries and bonuses continued for some while to go to retail personnel. This was one of the last adjustments to be made in paving the way for better relations between retail and mail order by providing more equitable compensation for the latter.

CHAPTER XXII

New Patterns of Organization

AT THE time of Sears's entry into the retail field in 1925, the company's organization was a highly centralized structure on a functional basis, which had arisen and been refined as a consequence of the peculiarly centralized nature of the whole mail-order operation. In addition to the president (operating under a board of directors and its chairman), there were three vice-presidents. The vice-president in charge of merchandise was responsible for all buying and selling and also for some share of branch-house supervision. The vice-president in charge of operating was responsible for receipt, storage, and shipment of merchandise at all the mail-order plants, as well as for such obviously operational functions as maintenance and traffic. The vice-president serving as comptroller directed auditing control and finance. The mail-order plant general managers executed instructions from Chicago, where the president and all three vice-presidents were located.

The entire plan of operations was largely susceptible to regimentation. The Chicago office issued detailed instructions to the mail-order plants on virtually every phase of activity. The general manager of a mail-order plant had to maintain proper stocks of the goods procured by the vice-president in charge of merchandise, to handle customer orders originating from Chicago-made catalogues in general accordance with operating policy acceptable to the operations vice-president, and to remit moneys to the comptroller in Chicago.

Sears's entry into the retail field brought numerous problems which could not easily be solved through the established organization pattern. The thoroughly intrenched and generally inflexible mail-order business had been operated effectively through the tightest control from "the top," but retail operations posed the problems of localized management in many communities, localized inventories, localized competition, localized customer and community relations—in short, a situation in which the answers varied from day to day and from store to store. Yet the retail stores initially were responsible for all administration to branch mail-order plant managers who, in turn, had to cleave largely to essentially rigid instructions from Chicago. The situation was somewhat eased by the personal factor: when Wood became president, and Adler and Doering resigned as vice-presidents in charge of merchandise and operating, respectively, Wood appointed his own "team" in charge of operating, merchandising, and auditing control. Those executives worked well with one another and with mail-order and retail executives in the field, but the structure still creaked from the strains put upon it by the expanding retail system. When Wood assumed the presidency, the company had only 27 retail stores; his first year in office saw 165 more added, and by the end of 1929 Sears was operating 324 stores in addition to 10 mail-order plants. Each retail-store manager reported to the general manager of the mail-order plant serving his region. Authority, like merchandise, stemmed from the mail-order plants, which were managed by men possessing virtually no experience in retail operations. The arrangement was not a happy one.

In 1929 General Wood appointed a committee of company executives (E. J. Pollock, J. M. Barker, and T. V. Houser) to work with an outside firm of consulting engineers and accountants in Chicago, in order to evolve a new organization structure which would assist in the attainment of three objectives: (1) to develop the mail-order business and to operate it more efficiently; (2) to organize the "jobbing" end of the business, i.e., the development of a service of supply for the retail stores through the mail-order plants; and (3), most important of all, to organize and develop a more satisfactory system for retail-store operations. A new organization plan was recommended formally by the committee on January 6, 1930.

A senior vice-presidency (to which Lessing Rosenwald was appointed) was established, as was an eastern vice-presidency (filled by J. M. Barker). The three functional vice-presidents retained pretty much the same scope of authority they had carried before. The plan of organization was designed to provide immediate and constant direct communication between the parent-head of each function in Chicago and the subordinate officers wherever located in the field. To co-ordinate this functional organization, there was created an Officers Board consisting of the senior vice-president as chairman and including the vice-presidents in charge of merchandise and operating, the eastern vice-president, and the vice-president serving as assistant to the president and factory manager. The secretary of the company was the secretary of the Officers Board.

In addition, committees consisting of members of the Officers Board were set up on factories, advertising, credit policies, merchandise budgets, operating, and retail personnel and procedure. One of the principal functions of these committees was to make recommendations which might further be considered by the Officers Board and which might result in a more thorough co-ordination of all the activities of the company.

One of the most important aspects of the new organization was the appointment of four territorial officers, located in Philadelphia, Atlanta, Chicago, and Los Angeles. Each was the "representative of the president," in his territory, which included all mail-order plants and retail stores in that territory. Each territorial officer had a small staff: a general mail-order manager, with functional assistants in charge of auditing, merchandise, and operating, and a district manager for retail stores, with assistants handling auditing and sales. The several territorial officers reported directly to the president or the senior vice-president of the company. Orders issued by a territorial officer were issued with the authority of the president and/or the senior vice-president and were senior in the territory to any orders issued by any of the three functional vice-presidents in Chicago. The principal duties of the territorial officers were to be the selection and training of retail-store managers and the co-ordination of service of supply between the retail stores and the mail-order plants.

Of the four territorial officers—J. M. Barker in Philadelphia, F. B. McConnell in Atlanta, C. B. Roberts in Chicago, and H. W. Kingsley in Los Angeles—only Barker had the rank of vice-president. And Sears, Roebuck in those days was notoriously "rank conscious"; the saying went that little weight was attached to any document signed by an official of lower rank than vice-president.

The plan was illustrative of Wood's determination to decentralize authority as far as possible in order to localize decisions on the local problems of the local retail stores. From the beginning Wood contended that there should be as little supervision from Chicago as possible (he bluntly referred to it as "interference") and that the successful managers should generally be let alone and only the less successful ones prodded. His fear that the territorial offices would become "little Chicago's" led him to dilute their authority considerably; the nature of that dilution was such that the essence of authority continued to reside in the three functional vice-presidents in Chicago. It was clearly specified that each functional officer in the parent-office was authorized to communicate directly with the various mail-order plants and retail stores "as circumstance required," and each responsible employee in the mail-order plants and retail stores was authorized to communicate directly with his functional superior in the Chicago office. The only restriction was that copies of "all important communications" were to be sent to the territorial officer involved; that officer had the power to suspend such regulations as might be involved in the communications—but in all such cases was immediately to notify the president, senior vice-president, and the functional vice-presidents of such action.

The district managers operating under each territorial officer were to report directly to the president and senior vice-president as well as to the territorial officer and were also allowed direct communication with the functional vice-presidents. And the scope of authority of those district managers was confined to the same functions as delimited the territorial officers: to make recommendations of personnel and to supervise requisitions on the mail-order plants for goods for the retail stores. A district manager could be (and usually was) also the manager of one of the "A" stores in that district and was empowered to draw such assistance as he needed from the various stores in his district. The district sales manager, operating under the district manager, further illustrated the "direct communication" aspect; he reported not only to the district manager and to the territorial officer but even also to the retail-sales manager in the office of the vice-president in charge of merchandise in Chicago. Each retail-store manager was expected to carry out the operating instructions of the vice-president in charge of operating and auditing procedures of the comptroller without deviation.

Possibly the chief virtue of the complex system of territorial officers was that it removed retail administration from the supervision of the general managers of the mail-order plants and vested responsibility for it in a chain of authority running from the three functional vice-presidents down through the territorial officers, thence to the district managers. To assist them in the prosecution of their two chief functions—selection and training of retail-store personnel and co-ordination of the service of supply from mail order to retail—the territorial officers were, as has been pointed out, given full responsibility for the mail-order plants and retail stores in their respective territories, that responsibility being, however, limited to the two primary functions. To see to it that each territorial officer did not become a bottleneck for all transactions in his territory, the company conspicuously refrained from providing such officers with a staff of assistants of any considerable size. The territorial officers were under no circumstances to perform functional work or the work of the stores. Where functional work was required in the mail-order plant or in a retail store, the territorial officer was to report that fact to the appropriate functional vice-president in the parent-office in Chicago, following up the matter only to the extent of seeing that the orders and recommendations which then came from that functional vice-president were carried out.

The retail district managers were expected to draw what staff they needed—various merchandise assistants, for example—from the "A" stores in their districts, such personnel to perform dual functions by serving an "A" store and the district manager's office at the same time. The district manager was likewise expected to utilize the merchandise supervisors at the mail-order plants as fully as possible, in order to strengthen the supervisors at both levels (mail order and retail), while avoiding amassing an expensive staff of his own.

Viewed from the perspective of developments since 1930, the organization plan's principal weakness appears to have been its sharp separation of functions into merchandise, operating, and control, which compelled retail-store managers to report to too many different individuals. In pleasing the vice-president in charge of merchandise, a manager might well find himself at the same time in the bad graces of the operating vice-president, since those two spheres of influence often overlapped. A retail-store manager might also find himself reporting to the wrong functional vice-president on any given matter, since most of the managers were new to the Sears organization and could hardly have been expected to grasp all the fine shadings between various functions. By and large, however, the new structure was welcomed by the mail-order people, for two chief reasons: mail order had always operated under a system not radically different from the new one, and three of the four territorial officers (Barker excepted) were former mail-order men. The retail personnel responded less warmly to the 1930 structure, even though they did welcome being removed from direct supervision of mail-order management.

By the beginning of 1932 the problems of the retail service of supply had been reasonably well met, and retail personnel had in general been better adjusted to the requirements of the stores, although the emergence of an adequate retail personnel program was still ahead and though the merchandise structures for the types of stores remained to be clarified fully. By that time, too, the bite of the depression had become far sharper, and Sears was entering what would prove the only year of that depression in which it operated at a net loss. The company decided that it was time to consolidate the retail effort by unifying its character country-wide and by providing a more intimate contact between the retail stores and the financial, operating, and merchandising executives of the parent-organization than was possible with the territorial officer system. The urgent necessity for economy of operation, and the determination to utilize the retail stores fully as an instrument with which to combat the depression, led to a drive for the closest possible supervision over the retail stores. The territorial offices were abolished, and Barker was brought to Chicago as vice-president in charge of retail administration in May, 1932. Under him, in the new setup came some thirty-odd district managers holding a tight rein over their stores in traditional chain-store fashion. The stated objective of the reorganization was "intensification of the retail administrative effort with a view to welding the retail organization into a more homogeneous and ordered whole." Centralization of authority had returned with force. In the phrase of Sears's employees of that time, "Chicago praised and Chicago damned." The company's problem at that time was not precisely how much profit a store could be made to yield and should be expected to yield but rather how to avoid losses wherever possible and stay "in the black." The exigencies of the situation demanded assurance that every directive from Chicago would be executed promptly and fully in the field. To co-ordinate the efforts of the parent-organization to cope with the emergency, a retail committee was established, composed of the three functional vice-presidents under the chairmanship of Barker.

Retail functional responsibility was sharply delineated from retail administrative responsibility, only the latter centering in Barker, with the former divided, appropriately, among the three functional vice-presidents in parent. Barker's three chief administrative problems were to be the selection, training, promotion, and compensation of retail personnel, interpretation of operating results and executive action on them, and indirectly control of the lines carried in the stores.

As the nation slowly emerged from the worst of the depression, and as the company began to show profits again, the tightness of supervision was gradually relaxed even within the framework of the centralized setup. The "good" managers—those who made a profit close enough to what could be expected of them—were given greater freedom to operate their stores; the "bad" ones (everything was black and white in the early thirties) still operated under close supervision. The individual most closely associated with the actual tightening and loosening of the reins, outside of Wood, was Barker. He had joined the company late in 1928 after having been an assistant professor of civil engineering at Massachusetts Institute of Technology, his alma mater, and later a banker in New England and Argentina. Like Doering, he was a "strong" man, with force and drive; he was also a man with much intellectual curiosity. He insisted upon "store discipline" because he felt that the company had to be able to count upon immediate compliance with all instructions. But he insisted at the same time that the prime function of administration was to convince the district and store managers of the soundness of company policies, to obtain compliance through explanation and understanding. Barker spent much time in the field, spot-checking stores and district managers; spot-checking became almost an obsession with him. He worked, as far as possible, with men and not merely with intructions issued from the top, even though he expected the former to obey the latter.

Barker's administrative technique was such that he or his assistants could spot-check a store very quickly, in a manner so simple that local store management could easily see the importance of the procedure. In the retail branch of Sears's business, Barker was the first really good administrator. In a sense he did for Sears's retail what Otto Doering did for mail order in the days when it was devoid of organization.

Barker felt that a good profit-and-loss statement did not necessarily represent good management but that good management invariably produced good sales and good profits. To him a good profit-and-loss statement could not hide a poor store. If a store was repeatedly out of stock, if its inventory was unbalanced, if it had too much old merchandise, that store was no good in Barker's eyes, even though it showed a high net profit percentage.

Under Barker's regime the earlier insistence that "A" stores not be separated from smaller stores in the district administration, lest the help available from the stronger "A" store staffs be lost to the "weaker," smaller stores, gave way to a trend toward separation. From the first it had been apparent that the "A" store and "B" store problems were so different that few men had the experience to handle both, and, as the managers of the individual "A" stores became seasoned, the advisability of separating "A" stores from districts became increasingly evident. Where there were two or more "A" stores in the same city, they could be set up as a group under a single experienced manager. The smaller stores required specialized administration different from that needed by "A" stores, and Barker proceeded to develop that type of administration.

The removal of "A" stores from the districts left each district manager freer to concentrate on the "B" stores and, when a certain degree of perfection had been attained, to take on more stores. As a result, it was possible by early 1933 to combine some of the districts. A number of "B" stores had reached a point where they depended comparatively little on the district office. As it had been the policy so far as practicable to pass responsibility to the field, the company experimented in early 1933 with the separation of twelve "B" stores from district management. This produced good results, indicative of its possibilities.

The removal of some of the "A" stores from district management was known in the company as "reporting direct to Chicago." The determination not to allow district managers to "interfere" with "A" stores, most of which by then were "good" (i.e., relatively efficient and profitable), led gradually to a determination not to allow the district managers to interfere too greatly with the smaller stores. The system of district management was gradually eliminated through the creation of the so-called "zone officers," who were given the supervision of large numbers of small stores, but only a small staff to visit and inspect those stores. Even so, the equivalent of the district-manager supervision for small groups of stores persisted, though the title had been abolished. The zone officers under various pretexts "pirated" the stores and developed a group of assistants who visited stores and assisted in planning sales promotion and in operating. This "surreptitious" building-up of staffs by the zone officers apparently arose from their conviction that the training and development of local store managers was still an essential function despite the injunctions and exhortations to the contrary.

By the late 1930's the gradual extension of greater and greater autonomy to local store managers had exceeded even that contemplated in the short-lived reorganization of 1930. The one function which had in no way been decentralized was buying; it remained the job of the vice-president in charge of merchandise to utilize the company's mass buying power to procure goods in sufficient volume and at the right price to meet the needs of the mail-order plants and retail stores.

But the decentralization in all other phases of the business had reached a point by around 1940 where it awaited only *de jure* recognition. This process was put in motion in 1941 with the appointment of A. S. Barrows as vice-president in charge of the Pacific Coast territory. The war halted further decentralization, but the process was resumed in 1946. In a speech delivered in Atlanta on January 15 of that year, General Wood foreshadowed that resumption:

> I have been in an unusual position to observe the problems that "bigness" brings to a business. In many ways these problems are identical on a smaller scale with those connected with the growth of our government in Washington. In a corporation, as in government, it means the growth of staffs, a hierarchy of officials, a multiplicity of reports, delays in decisions, removal on the part of executives from the feel of the communities in which they do business. In other words, very great size in business creates what we describe in government as bureaucracy and red tape. Some five years ago we determined to see how we could cope with this problem, and we set up the Pacific Coast as a separate administrative unit.... As a result of that experiment, we found that every function of the company except the buying function, could be entirely decentralized, and that it was unnecessary except in the very rarest cases to refer anything to the Company's headquarters in Chicago. The results have been gratifying beyond our hopes.

On January 15, 1946, J. F. Moore was appointed vice-president in charge of the southern territory, and G. B. Hattersley vice-president in charge of the eastern territory. The organization was completed on April 26, 1948, when H. F. Murphy was made vice-president in charge of the midwestern territory, and C. B. Roberts vice president in charge of the southwestern territory. Chart I shows the top-management organization of Sears as of the end of 1948.

In broad terms the chairman of the board formulates general policies and exercises supervision over top personnel. The president operates and administers the company; in his direction of the vice-presidents, he is assisted by a small staff of specialists in personnel, operating, and public relations; four vice-presidents (one the comptroller and secretary, the others in charge of merchandising, factories, and the New York office); and the treasurer. Superior to the officers, of course, is the board of directors, which numbered twenty members at the end of 1948. Fifteen of these were executive employees of the company with an average length of service of over twenty years. Four of the five nonemployee directors had been on the board for fifteen to twenty years.

As Chart I indicates, the parent-organization was designed to function as a staff organization with the one exception of the vice-president in charge of merchandise. It represents the company's "superplanning" group at the highest level and includes many specialists and a few very powerful executives. While this organization promulgates clearly defined policies in such fields as merchandising, operating, personnel, and public relations, the territorial officers are very nearly autonomous—with one great exception. Buying remains fully centralized in the general merchandise office, and it seems improbable that the company will ever voluntarily sacrifice the vast buying power of its mass purchasing. With this one exception,

CHART I
Top Management Organization

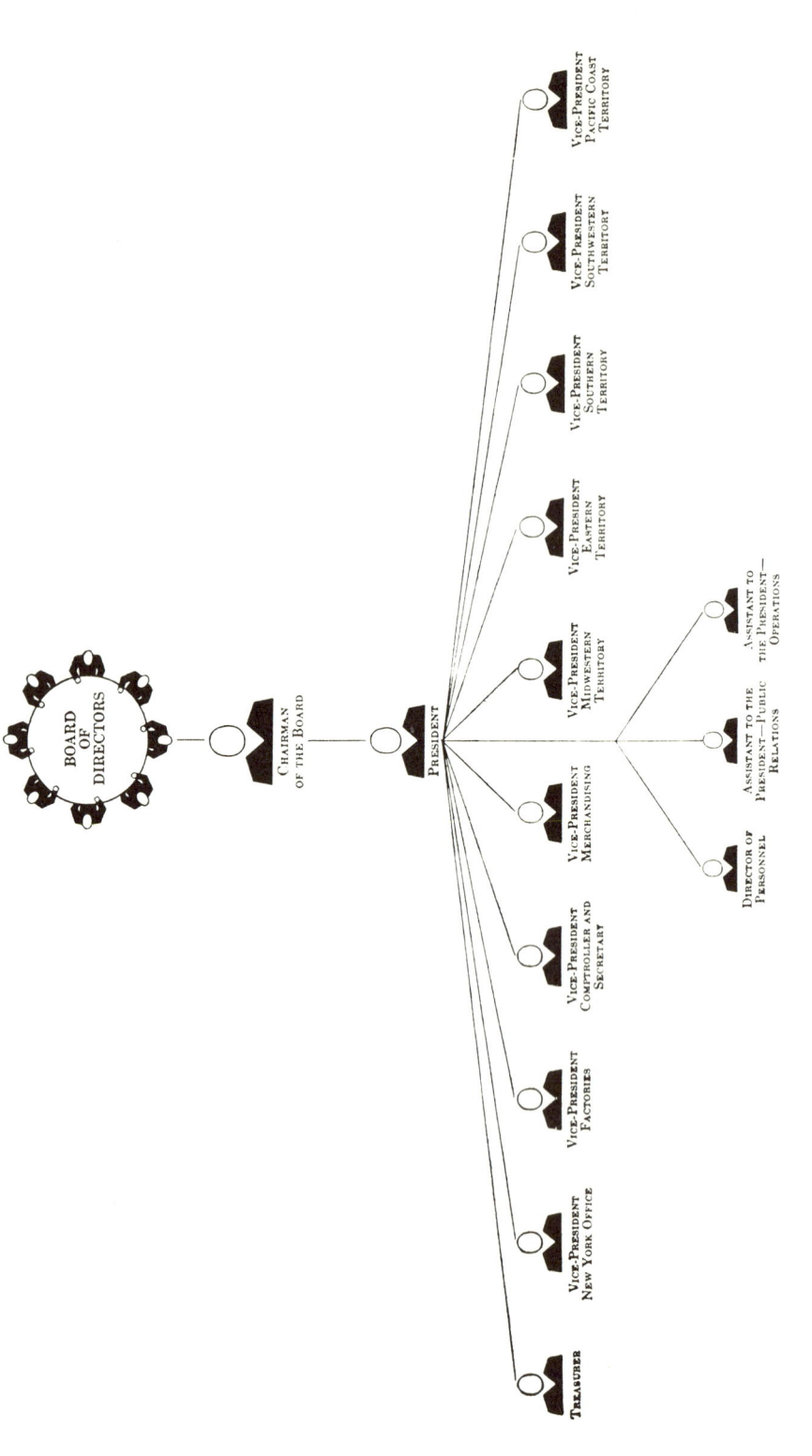

functional organization has largely been replaced by direct-line administration.

Each territorial vice-president has complete supervision over all mail-order plants, retail stores, pool stocks, warehouses, order offices, and telephone units in his geographical area. Each territorial head has a staff including, among others, individuals handling personnel, public relations, store planning and display, operating, merchandise, credit, traffic, auditing, legal, real estate, and construction. On the surface, the present administrative organization is closely akin to that put into effect around 1930; actually, the great difference is that the present territorial vice-presidents have real and sweeping authority and are expected to use it. Lower echelons do not by-pass the channels of communication. From an administrative standpoint the territorial officers report only to the president of the company; from the standpoint of merchandising, however, they report to the vice-president in charge of merchandising.

Several factors account for the company's willingness to vest such great authority in its territorial officers and for the efficiency with which this plan of organization appears to have operated. All five territorial officers are Sears's veterans, with an average of around twenty years' service in the organization, and most have had experience in both mail order and retail, rising from relatively low positions to their present eminence. Each is thoroughly familiar with all phases of the company's operations and thus naturally tends to make haste slowly. Each territorial officer as a member of the board of directors participates in the formulation of top-level policy, which in Sears is hammered out slowly by a process of continuous compromise which may not fully satisfy anyone but which seldom deeply dissatisfies anyone. The five territorial officers, along with the vice-president in charge of merchandise as chairman, constitute the Merchandise Policies Committee. The other co-ordinating committee on which the five territorial heads sit is the Committee on Organization Problems; this body also includes the president and the vice-president and comptroller.

As shown in Chart II of the midwestern territory (which does the largest volume of all the territories), the vice-president in charge is provided with a staff large enough to handle problems which cannot easily be delegated to a lower level but not sufficiently large to "police" the entire territory and thus exercise too great supervision over lower echelons. The groups shown in this chart include stores which are geographically so closely bunched (in this territory, within the same city) that uniformity in pricing, promotion, and related operations is essential. The group manager, sometimes also the manager of one of the "A" stores in that group, represents the company's best retail talent. As shown in Chart III, his staff includes a merchandise and sales-promotion manager, under whom come an advertising manager and several merchandise managers; and pool stock, operating, personnel, display, and credit managers and a group auditor.

CHART III
Group Organization

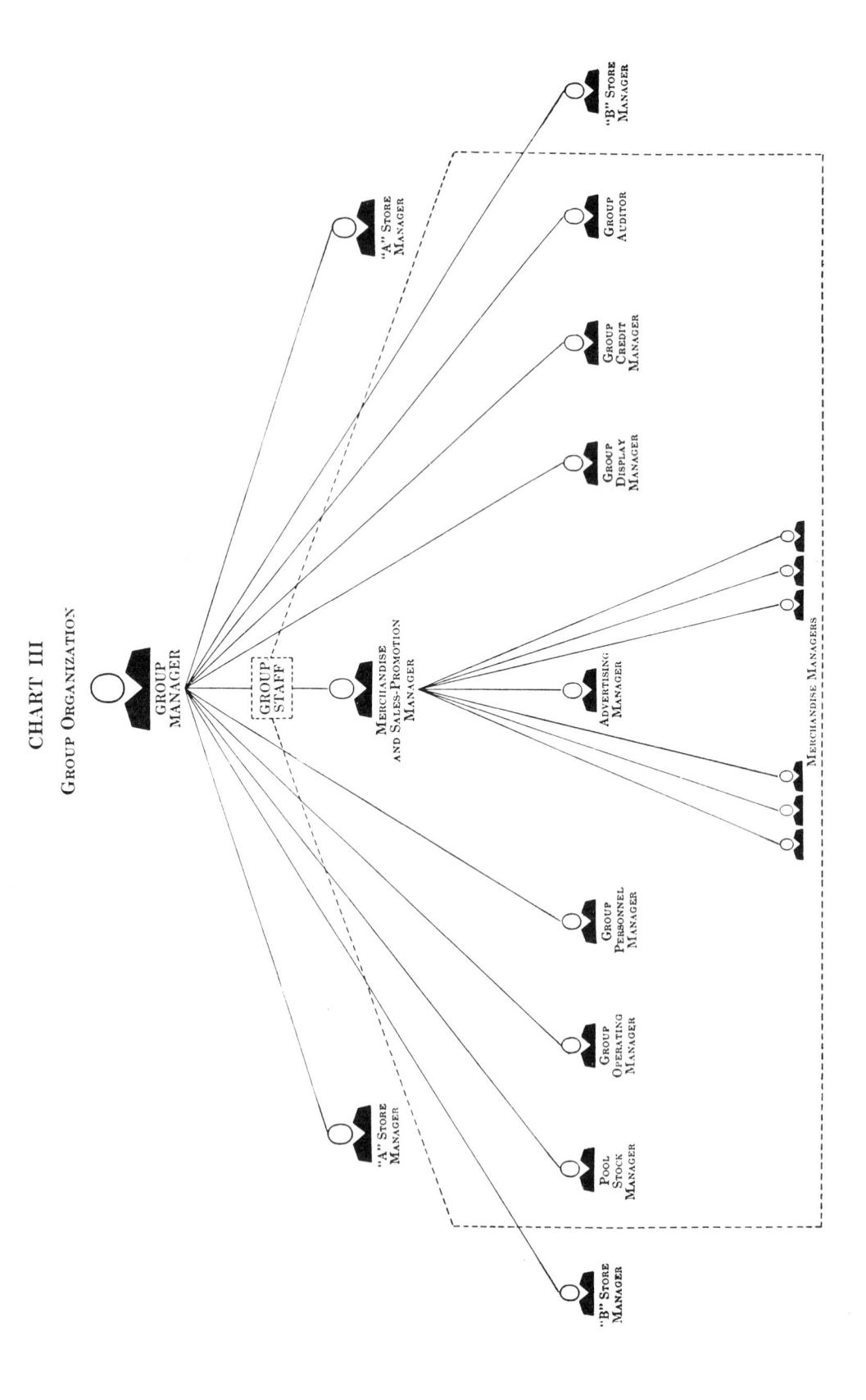

- Group Manager
  - "A" Store Manager
  - "B" Store Manager
  - Group Auditor
  - Group Credit Manager
  - Group Display Manager
  - Merchandise and Sales-Promotion Manager
    - Advertising Manager
    - Merchandise Managers
  - Group Personnel Manager
  - Group Operating Manager
  - Pool Stock Manager
  - "A" Store Manager
  - "B" Store Manager
  - Group Staff

The key executives reporting to the group manager include the managers of the stores under his jurisdiction, as well, of course, as the staff executives in the group office. The merchandise and sales-promotion manager is the group manager's key assistant. He directs the activities of the advertising manager and the various group merchandise managers. Those group merchandise managers perform for the stores in the group the same general merchandising functions performed by the merchandise managers in an "Independent A" store. They work directly with the division managers in the stores in carrying out group merchandising activities. While they do not have the store manager's supervisory authority over division managers, they work closely with them and supplement the activities of the sales superintendent in each group store. The advertising manager handles advertising for all stores in the group, thus centralizing this function in the group office.

What the chart of the midwestern territory refers to as the " 'B' Store Organization" is better known in the company as the zone system (shown in greater detail in Chart IV), a latter-day version of the old district management setup. Whereas groups embrace stores which are placed under unified control because of factors arising from physical proximity, the zones include stores which may be and usually are more or less widely separated but of which none is large enough to maintain its own sales-promotion and advertising staff or personnel for various other specialized functions. The zone officer has a relatively small staff of specialists to perform these functions for all the stores within his zone. This staff usually includes an assistant, a group of merchandise field men, and managers of inventory control, sales promotion, advertising, and display.

The key assistant to the zone officer is the assistant zone officer. His activities may include any phase of zone operations, and his assignments for working with the stores are determined by the zone officer. Reporting directly to the zone officer, and working closely with the assistant officer, are the inventory-control manager, sales-promotion manager, advertising manager, and display manager. These men work with the stores in carrying out their particular activities. Also reporting to the zone officer are the various merchandise field men who travel the stores and who act as "contact men" for their particular lines of merchandise between the parent-organization, the zone office, and the stores within the zone.

Each general manager of a mail-order plant, of which there are three in the midwestern territory, is responsible not only for the operation of his plant and sales promotion through special catalogues and circulars but also for the operation of the order offices, telephone offices, and agencies as well, of course, as serving as a source of supply for the smaller retail stores within that mail-order region. Each general manager of a mail-order plant has five chief aides: a personnel manager, a regional auditor, and superintendents of sales, merchandise, and operating. Each of these men

CHART IV
ZONE OFFICE STAFF

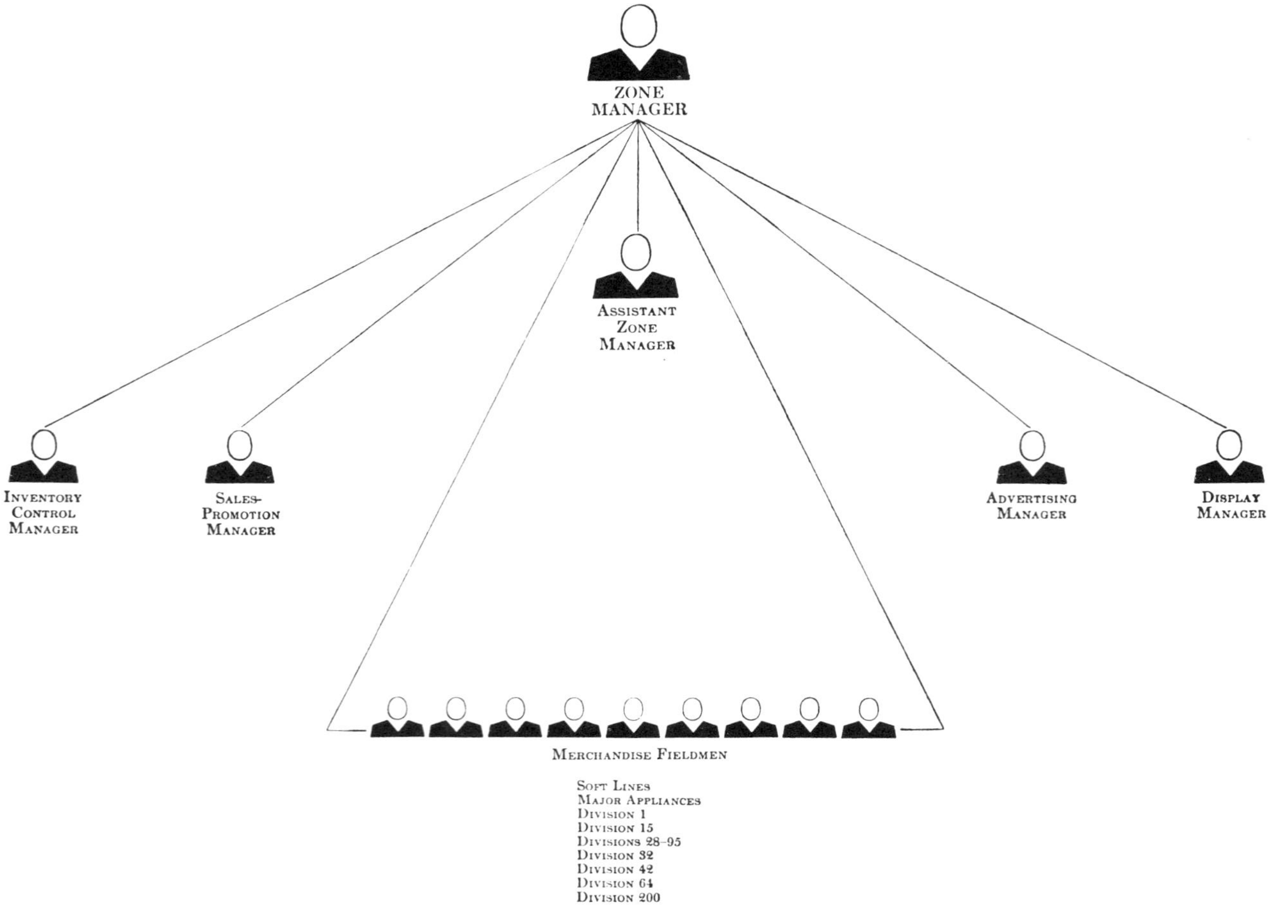

- ZONE MANAGER
  - DISPLAY MANAGER
  - ADVERTISING MANAGER
  - ASSISTANT ZONE MANAGER
  - SALES-PROMOTION MANAGER
  - INVENTORY CONTROL MANAGER
  - MERCHANDISE FIELDMEN
    - SOFT LINES
    - MAJOR APPLIANCES
    - DIVISION 1
    - DIVISION 15
    - DIVISIONS 28-95
    - DIVISION 32
    - DIVISION 42
    - DIVISION 64
    - DIVISION 200

has, of course, a staff to perform the various specialized activities associated with each function.

The development of Sear's administrative system was guided largely by a policy expressed in the early thirties by President Wood:

> While systems are important, our main reliance must always be put on men rather than on systems. If we devise too elaborate a system of checks and balances, it will only be a matter of time before the self-reliance and initiative of our managers will be destroyed and our organization will be gradually converted into a huge bureaucracy.

The essence of that statement was summed up in Wood's frequent reiteration, "If you have the right man and he is properly trained, all your problems will take care of themselves."[1] This emphasis on men as against systems is basically what the company executives have in mind in their constant references to "decentralization," expressed in the latest organization structure of Sears.

In a letter dated October 14, 1948, Wood outlined to his officers what he termed the "official policy of the Company, to be translated into action all through the Company in all layers of authority":

> We complain about government in business, we stress the advantages of the free enterprise system, we complain about the totalitarian state, but in our industrial organizations, in our striving for efficiency we have created more or less of a totalitarian organization in industry, particularly in large industry. The problem of retaining our efficiency and discipline in these large organizations and yet allowing our people to express themselves, to exercise initiative and to have some voice in the affairs of the organization is the greatest problem for large industrial organizations to solve.

That problem of "letting people express themselves and exercise initiative," while at the same time retaining "efficiency and discipline," has been approached by Sears in a manner which seems distinctively Wood's. The emphasis on individual initiative could not become so exaggerated as to imperil the very heart of a business as big as Sears—good administration.

There must be kept in mind two basic factors which make the company's type of organization practicable. First is the fact that the store managers need to perform no buying function—central purchasing guarantees the procurement of goods, their delivery to the stores, a satisfactory gross margin, and an established merchandise pattern for each type of store. In addition, central purchasing creates the general sales-promotion plans, including store planning and methods of display. Second in importance is the fact that the company's principal administrative, operating, and control procedures have been formalized and are therefore an integral part of company policy from which no local deviations are permitted.

The Sears principle of decentralized retail administration is now the cornerstone of organization policy, responsible to a great extent for the company's retail success, as well as for some difficulties which occur now and then, such as local overpricing of goods, poor service, out-of-stock conditions, and excessive and unbalanced inventories. But company officers believe strongly that the advantages of decentralization far outweigh its disadvantages.

Under the Sears system of decentralized management, the local retail unit has sufficient autonomy to provide for itself and its employees most of the advantages of an independent operation. The local manager has authority and responsibility to make all or nearly all important day-to-day decisions. He is limited by the general framework of company policies, but within that framework he has adequate leeway for handling on the spot practically all questions which arise. Because of his own intimate knowledge of the immediate situation and of the people involved, his decisions can carry a far larger measure of effectiveness than would be possible if the decision-making authority were reserved to a functionary in a central office.

Sears has been careful to strengthen and preserve the integrity of the line organization because it feels that only on the basis of a strong, independent line can autonomous local management ever be a reality. In Sears the staff has therefore deliberately been kept small, and there is a clear understanding that its functions are advisory and not authoritative. Those who have gravitated into staff work have had to develop a high order of skill in operating on this basis to accomplish their responsibilities. In other words, in the Sears organization the staff operates to *strengthen* the line, not to undermine it.

Basic to the principle of decentralized management is a tendency to rely on individual initiative and confidence in the capacity and judgment of the people in the organization. This is clear, of course, so far as store managers and other key executives are concerned, but it is also substantially true of people at all levels in the organization, particularly in the retail stores.

Superficially, it might appear that the roots of the company's present policy and philosophy lie far back in its history, for Sears apparently developed, during its first twenty-five or thirty years, on a loose, informal basis where there was ample leeway for individual growth and for the display of individual judgment and initiative. Most business organizations pass through a similar stage of vigor and informality during their earlier years; but this earlier stage is often followed by a gradual solidifying of the structure, a tightening of controls, and a growth of administrative hierarchies and of staff bureaucracies.

This process of maturing was already far advanced in Sears by the middle 1920's. But Wood, on his accession to power, did two things which restored the vigor and youth of the company. He launched the retail program and thereby, in a very real sense, created a new organization engaged in a new enterprise. Of equal immediate importance but greater long-range significance, he developed a type of administrative structure and provided a caliber of executive leadership calculated to preserve and strengthen the dynamic characteristics usually associated with young organizations, so that those characteristics might not be lost as the rejuvenated organization itself began to move into its own period of maturity.

The success of that effort may perhaps be evident in the extent to which Sears, particularly in its parent and retail branches, is still characterized, after a quarter of a century, by the vigor, flexibility, drive, and enthusiasm of a young organization. It is significant that the only branch of the company for which this statement is not wholly true is mail order, which had already reached maturity when General Wood came on the scene.

A higher order of administrative skill is required to manage effectively an informal, loosely knit organization such as Sears than to manage one of the more conventional pattern. It was Sears's good fortune to find in Wood a man who had that order of skill to an unusual degree and who was able to communicate that skill to his close associates and key executives with whom he surrounded himself. If Sears, Roebuck can be considered an example of the dictum that an "organization is the lengthened shadow of a man," it were wise to keep in mind the weakness of most such organizations—that the shadow seldom long survives the man. This fate is unlikely in the case of Sears because of the extent to which Wood has been able to develop, among his officers and executive staff, a comparable degree of skill for administering the type of organization which Sears has become. This is certainly true of F. B. McConnell, who had not only acquired Wood's philosophy even before becoming president but over the years had also been one of the instrumentalities through which Wood's business philosophy was put into practice.

McConnell's advancement to the presidency of the company was a fact of considerable significance. On the one hand, it reflected the degree to which his own administrative skill and competence developed under the influence of the system of decentralized management under which he operated and which he epitomized as retail administrator. On the other hand, it apparently represented a conviction on the part of Wood that the great task of management in an organization as huge as Sears was (and is) not so much merchandising or operating or control or finance as it was the building and maintenance of a sound organization, without which these and other functions could not properly be carried on.

CHAPTER XXIII

Some Aspects of Central Buying

ALL buying in Sears is completely centralized in the office of the vice-president in charge of merchandise, known within the company as the general merchandise office. This relatively small organization, which includes some one thousand to twelve hundred employees, sets all general policies governing buying and selling; studies sources from the point of view of reliability, quality, productive potentialities, cost, location, and related factors and handles relations with sources; and, through its buying commitments, determines the over-all merchandise inventory investment. This office is in actuality the very hub of the entire Sears operation; policies set here determine the whole merchandise structure, the selling prices to a great extent, and in large measure the company's potential profits. In a study of this office and its operations lies one of the keys to understanding the Sears operation and the company's position in the distribution field.

The general merchandise office "suggests" retail-store selling prices and insists upon maintaining minimum profit margins and, through its buying, necessarily determines what the retail stores and mail-order plants shall sell and in what quantities and at what times the goods shall be available. To this extent it of course influences selling, for the vice-president in charge of merchandise is also responsible, generally, for the broad pattern of selling. For this purpose he has two principal assistants: a mail-order merchandise manager, who directs catalogue selling, and a retail merchandise manager, who supervises (sometimes directly, usually indirectly) selling in the retail stores.

Since the overwhelming majority of mail-order sales comes through catalogues (even if utilized at desks in retail stores or order offices or by telephone), the control of the general merchandise office over centrally prepared catalogue copy enables it to "dominate" mail-order selling at the point of origin. As a matter of fact, the buying organization largely dominates all the company's selling through its control of buying, through its staff services such as the preparation of advertising materials for system-wide distribution, and through the constant research on various aspects of the selling operation.

The general merchandise office shapes the broad outlines of the various successive monthly spheres of emphasis, beginning February 1, which is the opening of the company's fiscal year. For retail that month is devoted, on a nation-wide basis, to promotion of furniture, rugs, and home furnishings. March is the month of the "March Value Demonstration," while Easter goods and house and garden needs are stressed in April. In the next month comes the "May Economy Festival," followed in June and July by clearances, since inventory is taken at the end of June. Special promotions are resumed in August, when furniture, rugs, and home furnishings are emphasized. The annual "Anniversary Sale" comes in September. October is a relatively quiet month, as far as national promotion is concerned. November includes the "Leadership Sale" to stimulate Thanksgiving and Christmas shopping. The Christmas season carries December, and in January come more clearances. That, in broad outline, is the year-round promotion for the retail organization.

Mail order's year-round promotion is based primarily upon seven recurrent catalogues, issued at more or less regular dates year in and year out. These seven include two general catalogues (spring and summer and winter and fall) for each region, plus a total of five flyers and bargain bulletins. These seven are augmented by special catalogues promoting individual departments (such as power tools, wallpaper, etc.), circulars, and other promotional material, as will be developed later. The important fact here is that mail order, like retail, operates upon a promotional attack planned over a period of an entire year. The general merchandise office must support the projected, year-round mail-order and retail-selling operation. It must obtain proper amounts of goods, properly priced to maintain the company's required gross margin, timed for proper delivery to the appropriate points.

Every item offered for sale through mail order is photographed or otherwise illustrated in the catalogues. And for almost every item to be sold through the retail stores, prepared illustrations in mat form are made available to the retail units. Descriptive material accompanies the mats, and both are used in local display advertising. But the actual selling operation is performed through the more than six hundred retail stores and eleven mail-order plants; unlike in other types of distributors, especially conventional department stores, buying and selling are performed by different corps of personnel.

The actual supervision of selling and, more directly, of buying falls to some thirty-five to forty supervisors, or directors of buying, generally one supervisor for each major merchandise department. It is each supervisor's function to direct and train his buyers and their corps of assistants in what goods to purchase, in what quantities, from what sources, at what times, at what prices, and in what manner. To aid him in reaching these basic decisions, each supervisor has a controller to supply him figures of past sales volume, potential sales, planned sales, planned inventories, commitments, and kindred data. Just as the vice-president in charge of merchandise has, among others, a mail-order merchandise manager and a retail merchandise manager to advise him, so do merchandise supervisors' staffs usually include mail-order and retail-sales managers. Chart V (facing p. 380) outlines the organization of the entire general merchandise office.

Under the regime of T. V. Houser, vice-president in charge of merchandise since 1939, the company relies more heavily upon a statistical approach to merchandising than ever before. Yet the statisticians themselves represent something of an anomaly in the highly centralized buying organization, for Sears has no centralized statistical department. While the general merchandise office does have a few statisticians (and economists) on its "general staff," most of the statistical and analytical work is performed within each merchandise department by personnel assigned to the various supervisors. The total number of statisticians runs into the hundreds.

The company feels that its merchandise statistics are reliable for two reasons: first, the statistics are prepared by men who know the merchandise as well as knowing statistical analysis; second, the fact that Sears is truly a national distributor makes its averages reliable for all practical purposes, despite regional and local variations.

The merchandise vice-president exercises over-all inventory control, which includes not only merchandise on hand but also that on order. Once the total figure is arrived at, it is budgeted to the field—the mail-order plants, retail stores, and retail pool stocks. Control of the quantity of purchases to be made by the buyers is facilitated by the fact that most members of the buying staff are stationed in Chicago. The control of retail inventories, however, is extremely difficult and a constant subject of concern to those responsible for the total inventory investment of the company.

The decentralization of retail administration and the fact that each store enjoys a wide degree of independence in ordering merchandise makes it difficult to control company inventories efficiently. The difficulty of making such control really tight, as is necessary at times, arises largely from the fact that goods for the stores are ordered by several thousand local division managers in the stores who, to obtain the goods, have merely to sign a requisition. Unlike an independent merchant, a division manager in a Sears store does not run out of funds, nor does he have to resort to borrowing to buy merchandise; a signature on an official form brings the requested merchandise.

Within the stores, inventories are controlled on the basis of unit store control records which show for each item (by style, color, and size) the number on hand, actual sales, and the number ordered. From these data estimates are made of orders to be placed to maintain sales for a period long enough to replenish stocks. Properly utilized stock-control books are therefore the essence of inventory control in Sears. In handling inventory problems, Sears retail managers have been taught the importance of not being out of stock and the urgency of moving slow-selling items. It has been

Sears's policy for many years to have as little "old" merchandise (goods in stock over one year) as possible. Careful record-keeping has in recent years held old merchandise to a minuscule percentage.

The supervisors, who direct the buying, averaged slightly more than forty-six years of age in a survey made in 1945. Thirteen per cent of them reached their positions as supervisors before the age of thirty-five; 72 per cent, before forty-five. Their average length of service with the company at that time was about twenty years. Thirty-one per cent of the group came from the parent (i.e., either by working their way up through the buying organization or through transfer from another department, or both), about 20 per cent from retail, 42 per cent from mail order, and 7 per cent from some other branch of the company (including factories and the laboratories).[1] The buying organization, in which those supervisors are a key factor, is supported by three staff services: the technical laboratories, the merchandise development department, and the merchandise comparison and inspection department.

TABLE 55*
PAY ROLL FOR LABORATORIES, 1929–44

Year	Total Pay Roll	Year	Total Pay Roll
1929	$ 30,702	1937	$247,358
1930	35,107	1938	267,841
1931	57,665	1939	323,677
1932	65,972	1940	367,999
1933	69,680	1941	375,856
1934	106,721	1942	268,575
1935	154,142	1943	270,166
1936	193,825	1944	335,591

* Source: Company records.

When D. M. Nelson entered the general merchandise office in 1926, he sought to return the laboratories to the relatively prominent position they had occupied before going into eclipse after the 1920–21 depression. When Nelson became general merchandise manager in 1928, the laboratories experienced their renaissance. The textile division was expanded, the chemical division reactivated, mechanical, electrical, and home economics divisions established, and a scientific library set up and staffed by personnel with scientific training.

In 1929 General W. I. Westervelt joined the company as director of technical service, with jurisdiction over the laboratories. Westervelt soon merged that activity with the merchandise development division. He was also instrumental in obtaining the interest and co-operation of General Wood in the laboratories and, through Wood, enlarged funds for further expansion. The steady increase in the funds allocated to laboratory work from the time Westervelt came is illustrated in Table 55. The figures shown in that table represent only pay-roll costs of personnel charged directly to the laboratories and do not include such costs as machinery, equipment, rent, heat, light, etc. Nor do the figures include the salaries of many buyers working with the laboratories but not on that pay roll. In addition, the company spends thousands of dollars annually in contracting for outside agencies to conduct research projects and testing.

The work of the laboratories came, in time, to fall generally into three chief classifications:

1. Check-testing to verify a manufacturer's or buyer's claims. Information thus obtained could be used for catalogue copy and other promotional material and for ascertaining whether an item being purchased was meeting the quality specified by the manufacturer.

2. Comparative testing, generally performed before an item was purchased, to compare it with similar items available on the market, similar items previously tested in the laboratory, and merchandise being sold by competitors.

3. Fact-find testing, which covered the determination of a wide variety of information such as: Of what does an item consist? Will it serve the purpose for which it is intended? How will it stand up under certain conditions of service? The cause of complaints concerning merchandise—is the complaint really justified or has abuse by the purchaser been the chief factor?

Five major divisions execute the functions of testing and development:

1. The chemical laboratory, staffed by trained chemists, some of whom have specialized in pharmaceutical, paint, leather, rubber, and metallurgical chemistry. These employees are equipped to make chemical analyses and to perform many physical tests in which a knowledge of chemistry is important in the interpretation and evaluation of results.

2. The textile laboratories, staffed by textile chemists, equipped to determine the chemical and physical properties of textile fibers and fabrics, such as color fastness, strength, waterproofness, and resistance to aging, and to identify fibers and to make fiber composition determinations.

3. The electrical laboratory, staffed by electrical and radio engineers, qualified to make tests essential in evaluating the performance of all electrical appliances from vacuum cleaners to electric brooders.

4. The home economics laboratory, staffed of course by home economists. This division includes two test kitchens in which home equipment can be used under home conditions; it offers facilities for determining the practicability of new designs and trying new designs in improving work methods. The home economists' testing runs the gamut from coffee-makers to stoves and home freezers.

5. The mechanical, combustion, refrigeration, air-conditioning, and automotive laboratory, embracing combustion engineers and machinists, runs physical tests on hard-line merchandise. This laboratory tests plumbing and air-conditioning equipment. A combustion laboratory permits the evaluation and improvement of stokers, furnaces, stoves, and heaters.

In addition to the scientists working within any of the five categories mentioned, by 1948 there were specialists in wood, glass, ceramic, and plastic products and in manufacturing techniques and production processes. Such a staff, with such a scope of work, took shape gradually through the years. So did the physical equipment with which they worked.

Testing devices fell into two general categories: (1) the standard devices found in almost any modern testing laboratory, such as variable temperature rooms and wind tunnels, dynamometers, Fade-o-meters, Launder-o-meters, and breaking-strength and abrasion machines, for example—devices all thoroughly familiar to the American Society for Testing Materials and the Underwriters Laboratory—and (2) "special purpose machines" built by the company to conduct certain types of tests; they were not standard equipment and could not therefore be purchased from commercial producers of testing equipment.

The special purpose equipment, now extensive, arose gradually as problems were presented which did not lend themselves to solution through available testing devices. Laboratory scientists, working with machinists and carpenters, proceeded by trial and error and intuition to fashion devices which would permit the evaluation desired. Frequently, of course, it was necessary to test the testing devices to insure that they would render the required performance. Given competent personnel and adequate physical equipment, the next requirement—and possibly the most important—was a determination of the type of tests necessary to a proper evaluation of the product to be tested. Formulation of standard testing procedures became a major task. A survey covering thousands of items tested in the mechanical division of the Sears laboratories between 1942 and 1946 revealed that standard testing procedures (formulated by such organizations as the American Society of Refrigerating Engineers, the American Gas Association, and the American Society of Heating and Ventilating Engineers) were applicable to only about 15 per cent of the tests. In formulating satisfactory evaluation methods covering consumer merchandise, the first step was to determine what factors had real significance in ascertaining the suitability of merchandise for ultimate use. The second step was to find adequate, quantitative means for measuring the significant factors.[2]

The expansion of the laboratories following their renascence in 1928 led in October of that year to the appointment of the first full-time librarian and the formal organization of the technical library. While the primary function of the library was and is to render an information service to laboratory personnel, its resources are available to anyone in the company. The major holdings of the library came to cover textiles, applied chemistry, electrical engineering, home economics, and mechanical engineering and to include, in addition to general works (encyclopedias, almanacs, dictionaries, texts, and directories), an extensive pamphlet collection. The pamphlets furnish access to the work of such government bureaus as the National Bureau of Standards, the Bureau of Entomology and Plant Quarantine, the Bureau of Mines, and other federal agencies; state extension divisions and agricultural and engineering experiment stations; trade and technical associations, such as the American Society for Testing Materials, the National Electrical Manufacturers Association, and others; and specifications of the armed forces. The library subscribes to about two hundred and fifty scientific journals and trade papers, and these, like the pamphlets, are catalogued in some detail. All documents and publications are scanned for articles of special interest to particular employees.

Tasks of library personnel range from finding the answer to a specific question to preparing extensive bibliographies on various topics and even to abstracting all pertinent literature to save reading time for executives. The librarians also collect and summarize the various state laws covering sale of particular types of merchandise, make preliminary patent searches, extract items from current periodicals covering particular merchandise lines for Sears's merchandisers, and gather statistical information to assist buyers in predicting the market for their merchandise.

Typical of many such libraries founded by industrial organizations in the last fifteen to twenty years, the fundamental purpose of Sears's library is not to house outstanding collections of books but rather to train its staff to understand the informational needs of the company and to supply those needs by utilizing *all* library resources. Most of those needs center, of course, in the laboratories.

In addition to the laboratories, the merchandise comparison and inspection department also supports the operations of the general merchandise office. The comparison and inspection department embraces four chief subdivisions: shopping, merchandise review, inspection, and trade practice. The shopping division handles requests from supervisors, buyers, and others concerned for full information on competitive merchandise in both mail order and retail. The comparative shopping is performed in such varied places as stores in the Chicago Loop and department stores in outlying districts of that city; Penney's, Ward's, and other stores in near-by cities; department and specialty stores in Milwaukee, Aurora (Illinois), St. Louis, Detroit, and more; and, through the New York buying office (a subsidiary of the parent merchandise organization), in New York and outlying districts of that metropolis. When a nation-wide survey is required, the comparative shoppers utilize the various division managers in Sears's retail stores.

In addition to these specific shopping missions, the division is expected to remain constantly alert for new trends, new items, new developments that appear on the market, and to pass this information on to the proper members of the merchandise organization. A newspaper clipping service brings in competitors' advertisements twice each week.

The merchandise review division handles requests from supervisors for complete studies of merchandise lines in Sears's mail order and retail in relation to similar lines among all competitors in both fields. Among the features studied in a merchandise review are the ingredients of the item, price ranges, color and pattern assortments, style, types of fabrics, design, labeling and packaging, display, etc. Sears's volume of sales in the line under study is usually projected against the national volume to afford a clear picture of the company's position with reference to nation-wide sales. Staff personnel of the merchandise review division work closely in such reviews with personnel from the technical laboratories and from the merchandise development department, since the conclusions reached in these intricate reviews frequently dictate development of new products or changes and improvements in others.

A typical study of the merchandise review division was one made on men's dress shirts in the mid-1940's. The problem was to study Sears's and competitive merchandise from the standpoint of fabrics, colors, patterns, and construction for the purpose of developing specifications for good values at each price point and to develop sources to manufacture them. The study included the offerings of scores of stores and haberdashers; it included Macy's and Gimbel's in New York, Marshall Field's, Carson, Pirie, Scott and Company, and The Fair in Chicago; Penney's, Ward's, and Grant's stores in several different cities; and many more. Purchases were made of samples of every dress shirt shown in each store at each price point up to and including $7.50. A complete line of each of four nationally known brands was reviewed. Everything from buttons to collar styles, from prices to fabrics, was studied. The operation was a costly one, but at its conclusion Sears had a clear and complete picture of the shirt situation.

The inspection division makes continuing spot checks to determine whether Sears's merchandise fulfils every claim made for it by the company and whether its quality measures up to that for which the buyer originally contracted. Orders for mail-order merchandise to be inspected are put through on regular tickets so that the departments never know they are filling test orders. Retail merchandise is simply drawn from the stores directly. The inspectors seek to analyze the merchandise from the customers' point of view and to base their opinions on what they would expect from the catalogue presentation of any given item. Any shortcomings which appear serious from this point of view are reviewed with the buyers and supervisors, who in turn sometimes bring in manufacturers or their representatives to discuss the problem of maintaining quality. In 1944, a typical year, some six thousand items of merchandise were inspected by this division, which works its way through the whole merchandise line by inspecting different lines and items each year.

The whole matter of inspection had itself been evolutionary. As pointed out earlier, this activity after 1922 lapsed for years. Its re-emergence in anything like its present comprehensive form dates from 1930; in June of that year, Vice-Presidents Carney and Nelson developed and enunciated a detailed program of inspection of merchandise, not only through the division in the parent-office just touched upon, but also on the part of mail-order plants and retail stores receiving goods from manufacturers.

The trade-practice section has the responsibility of seeing that all catalogue presentation, retail-store advertising, circulars, and, in fact, all company advertising matter comports fully with regulations of the Federal Trade Commission (compliance with which is, of course, mandatory) and also with groups to whose standards the company voluntarily subscribes, such as Better Business Bureaus, the American Medical Association, the National Underwriters, etc.

That, in brief outline, was the shape of the general merchandise office as of the end of 1948. But before the general merchandise office as a whole reached that stage of development, an overhauling of the company's entire merchandise structure and of the organization responsible for purchasing that merchandise had to be effected.

Richard Sears had based his merchandising operation not alone upon a policy of low prices widely advertised and upon durable goods dramatically priced; he had also relied heavily upon his buyers. He sought to obtain men with knowledge of the goods they were to sell for him, even though he felt this factor less important than a man's demonstrated ability to sell any given line. Those buyers were department heads and, as such, were general executives completely responsible for the operation of their respective departments—their own wage scales, handling of returned goods, correspondence, and, of course, satisfactory profits. Buyers who had proved themselves enjoyed wide autonomy within the framework of general company policy.

Julius Rosenwald, after succeeding Richard Sears as president, made no fundamental change in the merchandise organization. Items like patent medicines were discontinued, the quality of the merchandise line as a whole showed noticeable improvement, general merchandise managers came and went, and the merchandise department heads were relieved of some peripheral functions such as correspondence and handling of returned goods. But the fundamental power of the buyers remained intact. The merchandise organization in the years of Rosenwald's presidency continued to be a "federation of merchants." Each buyer represented a small dynasty akin to a princely domain; each was secure against attack as long as his department showed a satisfactory profit. Rosenwald himself feared the emergence of any too closely regimented bureaucracy and therefore supported the "federation" concept.

A statement made in 1918 by one of the company executives indicates that the "federation" type of organization was not merely tolerated but actively championed, at least by some within the firm:

Another feature is the confidence we place in the leaders of our departments.... Each department manager is given a large measure of responsibility in developing his department work according to his ability. The business is his business. He is not hedged with limitations, such as dull the initiative. The result is that these men have responded with their best.... We have applied the principles of democracy to a commercial enterprise.[3]

The wide scope of authority vested in the merchandise department heads extended even to factory operations; each factory was under the direct line control of the manager of the department stocking the goods made by that factory. Even the procurement of raw materials for the factories was equally decentralized, being handled independently at each factory. William Norman Mitchell summed up what was probably the prevailing viewpoint in the company when, writing in 1924, he commented:

As long as profits are large and the sailing is clear, seemingly little interest can be aroused on the part of management in questions of internal organization. If the results being obtained are satisfactory, there is an inclination to feel that the existing organization is the best possible, and managers are inclined to feel that the study of organization is more or less academic.[4]

The large profits and satisfactory results mentioned by Mitchell certainly characterized the company's experience up to the 1920–21 depression (for even the panic of 1907–8 had merely *reduced* profits), and the company recovered from that debacle well before 1925. At the same time, however, the far-reaching effects of the "federation of merchants" type of organization had led to the emergence of several factors which were to prove incompatible with the company's retail experience which began in the mid-twenties, for that experience created a demand not only for a far greater volume of merchandise but frequently also for goods of higher quality and even of a different type. These demands were in time to circumscribe considerably the autonomy of the merchandise department managers, as there became more clearly visible the necessity for a tighter merchandise organization to cope with new problems and to implement the organization with new techniques.

The so-called "federation of merchants" had created a very spotty level of quality in the company's merchandise. While Sears, Roebuck had considerably improved the general quality of its goods by 1920, aided by the findings of the laboratories and the effective persuasion of Merchandise Manager J. F. Skinner, the picture was still uneven. There was a wide discrepancy in the quality of various lines, ranging from the very good to the very poor; this was inherent in a system which allowed one department head to sell relatively expensive clothing, for instance, while another manager sold ten-cent socks and fifteen-cent neckties. Since each department manager was responsible for making his own arrangements with sources, some naturally sought sources of the best quality, while others sought manufacturers quoting the lowest prices. Each buyer did his own "trading," some of it so sharp as to impair the company's reputation with sources.

Yet even the level of quality attained by 1920 suffered from the retrenchment following that depression. The laboratories went into eclipse, not to emerge as a strong factor again until after 1928. And the unyielding opposition of certain influential executives to the whole concept of laboratory testing as a function of merchandising dictated a return in large measure to earlier practices and policies. In this connection, Lessing Rosenwald's recollections of the furniture department, which Max Adler continued to supervise even after becoming general merchandise manager, are apropos. That department, according to the younger Rosenwald, was almost the only one which as late as 1928 had showed no improvement in quality in years. "The stuff was so awful that we used to wonder where Uncle Max managed to find it; nothing could have been quite that bad accidentally."

Sears, Roebuck was somewhat slow to develop a real concept of its merchandise structure if by "concept" one means "clear concept," and if by "structure" one means a structure conceived, planned, and executed in terms of close analysis and directed concentration of effort. Richard Sears was remarkably adept at concentration of effort upon whatever item he had decided to promote at any given time, but neither he nor his associates appear to have undertaken any close analysis of the over-all merchandise offerings or even of the assortment of items within any one line. And even Richard Sears's concentration of effort upon, say, sewing machines or cream separators was largely intuitive in origin; no long-range series of promotions seems to have evolved. The depression of 1920–21 forced closer analysis of the company's operations in general, but the net result manifested itself largely in reduction of operating expenses.

As a result, the company's merchandise line grew steadily. Items which had demonstrated popular appeal were added to the company's offerings and remained in the catalogue as long as they demonstrated their profitability (or, as in the case of groceries and the "2-4-6-8-cent" line, indicated potency as "order-starters"). Consequently, there was a great mushrooming of assortments—both of lines and within lines. It is true that Richard Sears's greatest promotions were hard-line items—what later came to be known as "big tickets." But this seems to have been due largely to the fact that these items, with their heavy dollar gross margins, were already showing widespread popular acceptance (as with sewing machines or bicycles) or seemed to Sears to have potentialities for such acceptance (as with cream separators).

In the years following Richard Sears's departure from the business, General Merchandise Manager J. F. Skinner sought to bring order of a sort out of the near-chaos surrounding the merchandise structure. Under Skinner's regime (he died in 1917) there was a notable improvement in the quality of the company's merchandise, but the over-all structure at the same time became ever larger. Sears, Roebuck came more and more to carry literally everything. Certainly this did not prove unprofitable, and whether at the time another policy would have been *more* profitable, one can hardly say at this date. The immense variety of items did not pose too serious a problem as long as a nation-wide mail-order business only was involved, since large inventories carried in relatively low-rent warehouses could better afford to stock slow-moving items which were distributed over the nation, or at least over several states. With the coming of the retail stores, however, and the premium thus placed on space, there was a new emphasis to build certain lines that were (and still are) dominant lines for Sears. This meant sacrificing at least a part of the "complete-store" concept, but not a willy-nilly elimination of all less profitable lines—or even of all unprofitable lines.

Donald M. Nelson became general merchandise manager in 1928 and directed the company's merchandise effort until his elevation to executive vice-president in 1939 (except for some eighteen months during the depression when he was on loan to the government to assist the NRA). When he assumed the merchandise reins, that phase of the company's operation reflected a wide dispersion of effort; the merchandise program lacked a directed concentration along lines of a well-conceived grand strategy. Sears's mail order was generally averse to change in its offerings, especially to elimination of any given item which yielded a net profit. The retail stores were, however, a horse of a spectacularly different color. Though still floundering to a great extent in 1928 (and for some years following), they at least wanted to flounder in merchandise which would meet the competition of specialty shops, department stores, chains, and Ward's retail stores in their various cities.

Merchandise structures for the various types of retail stores had not moved far toward clarification, but the question of buying for mail order versus buying for retail had already become a live one, posing the possibility of establishing separate buying organizations to serve the two types of selling. (Some latter-day statistics point up graphically the over-all merchandise variations as between mail order and retail: whereas retail business is dominated in Sears by hard lines and especially "big-ticket" items, mail order does more than half its business in soft lines and shoes. As late as 1941 soft lines accounted for 56 per cent of the total mail-order volume; big tickets, 20 per cent; hard lines, 17 per cent; and miscellaneous, 7 per cent.) The company's merchandise organization had to plan ahead to evolve a merchandise structure adequate for the company's over-all needs and malleable enough to accommodate itself to the various types of retail stores on which the company had decided.

Wood had cut his eyeteeth at Ward's on automobile supplies and hard lines generally, especially hardware, paints, and sporting goods. His concern with Ward's textile lines had been negligible. But the hard lines he had pushed at Ward's were generally the lines which carried heavy gross margins and which were proving to be the goods most in demand for sale on instalment terms. Wood's early emphasis on tires, which manifested itself in the new "Allstate," was symptomatic of what would prove an increasing stress on hard lines and big-ticket items as predominant features of the merchandise structure.

The company's merchandise offerings began to show fairly substantial changes shortly after the retail stores began to spread in force and as the managers of those stores began to exert their effect. Even so, the changes resulted mainly in additions to the line, increasing its size and variety. Once the decision had finally been made that instead of establishing separate buying organizations for mail order and retail, the central buying organization would seek rather to broaden its approach so as to meet the special needs of both, steps were taken toward establishing a definite merchandise structure for each type of retail store.

As that structure developed, it brought an improvement in the quality, variety, and balance of all merchandise, both mail order and retail, while at the same time forcing concentration on lines which generated large volume (or at any rate could reasonably be expected to). It was decided early that the merchandise structure of the "C" stores should embrace a few hard lines, to the total exclusion of soft lines. It was likewise decided early that "A" stores should be complete department stores, with the addition of hardware and other lines which most department stores considered a necessary evil, if indeed they carried such lines at all. The "A" stores, in other words, carried pretty much some of everything listed in the mail-order catalogues, plus (as time went on) items procured especially for the retail stores. In between the "A" and "C" types came the "B" stores: these were a merchandise "no-man's land." Their weird assortments included smatterings of many things and full offerings of few lines.

The "B" stores were seeking to be small "A" stores without adequate space to accomplish that. The problem posed by the efforts of the "B" stores to carry such large assortments in limited space was, to some extent, also applicable to the "A" stores. That space problem, as much as anything else, led to a clarification and consolidation of Sears's merchandise structure.

It became increasingly clear that the thing to do was to reduce the assortments wherever possible by eliminating classifications and price lines which brought little volume, to concentrate on the items which showed the greatest sales potentialities, and to promote these selected items as strenuously as possible. The active prosecution of this policy resulted in making it possible for each type of retail store to stock representative selections in each merchandise line included in its merchandise structure; to display such goods in less space than theretofore, leaving more space for more attractive displays, wider aisles, demonstration areas; etc. In reducing the total number of items offered through the catalogue, the policy allowed greater space in the book for better presentation of lines and items. And in both mail order and retail, the reduction of assortments and concentration on the "best sellers" facilitated trading up through the "Good–Better–Best" technique for designating distinct quality levels in any line.

Not least of the benefits derived from the concentration upon fewer lines was that the buying organization was then able to concentrate its efforts on a narrower field instead of scattering its fire over a vast, sprawling, unwieldy assortment of merchandise. This not only made possible a more thorough approach by each merchandise department but also enhanced the company's mass buying power.

This whole refinement and reorientation of the merchandise structure also offered an opportunity to make the countless Sears brand names employed up to then really mean something; to make a given merchandise line stand out distinctively; to identify the "Good—Better—Best" in sharper focus. The profitable lines and items, fewer in number, were to be (and, experience proved, could be) promoted vigorously enough to more than offset the loss in volume arising from a diminution of the multitude of very slow sellers.

This program of reducing the number of assortments and of according greater emphasis to big-ticket items was keyed to the over-all company program and was at the same time responsive to external pressure. General Wood from the first insisted that the retail stores should be primarily "men's stores" as distinguished from the conventional department stores; stress on hard lines as against soft lines was an integral part of his concept of what the character of Sears's retail units should be.[5] At the same time, instalment selling throughout the country was reaching unprecedented heights; Sears, Roebuck itself was liberalizing its own credit policies by adding more and more durable goods to its approved list; and these durable and semidurable goods were those which led the list of goods sold on instalment terms throughout the United States.

Sears needed to drive a competitive wedge into the urban shopping "door." In offering low prices (as well as instalment terms) on high-unit-price items, the company was making a virtue of the necessity of appealing strongly to customers in a way in which conventional department stores had not made a strong appeal. As the proportion of goods sold on instalment terms became steadily greater at Sears, the proportion of instalment sales accounted for by big-ticket items likewise became greater. It may well be that Sears's competitive stratagem of low prices on high-unit-price items, plus the steady increase in instalment sales (largely on such items), exerted as much influence on the reorientation of the company's merchandise structure as did the space limitations of the retail stores and the tastes and needs of urban shoppers as contrasted with catalogue customers.

In the course of clarifying its merchandise structure, the buying organization came to divide its concept of merchandise into three principal categories: hard lines, soft lines, and big tickets. The terms "hard" and "soft" lines were probably at least as old as the company, but the process of reconstituting the whole task of procuring and selling those lines was a latter-day phenomenon. And as the merchandise program was reoriented, with a concomitant effort to promote more vigorously the hard lines with higher gross margins, the term "big ticket" was added to company jargon. It applies to furniture, rugs, "Coldspot" refrigerators, "Kenmore" stoves, washing machines, and similar major appliances. Hard lines include, of course, a wide variety of durables and semidurables, while soft lines run the gamut from diapers and sheets to men's and women's wearing apparel.

The increasingly rationalistic approach to the merchandise structure was paralleled by increasing efforts within the company to localize the real control of production and merchandise design within its own organization. These efforts represented an attempt to reverse a historical pattern; or, more properly perhaps, to formalize and refine the company's intent to reverse this pattern by establishing a new pattern.

In the Reconstruction period following the Civil War, the control of sales often rested with the wholesaler, who came to dominate the scene by his strategic position as financier to the producer, on the one hand, and to the ultimate seller, on the other. By the nature of his whole operation, however, Richard Sears was led to by-pass the wholesaler and go direct to the manufacturer and, in some cases, even to enter the manufacturing phase himself. In addition to the fact that manufacturers often insisted that Sears, Roebuck was a retailer and therefore should be compelled to purchase from wholesalers and jobbers like any other retailer, there was the fact that the company's operation emphasized skirting all intermediate distribution levels and establishing a relation in which the only participants were the manufacturer, the company, and the ultimate consumer. Richard Sears therefore began early to deal with sources on a basis which was in some ways characteristic of the phase of the present-day situation in which Sears, Roebuck exercises the dominant voice in determining what goods shall be manufactured.

When Richard Sears would decide upon a great promotion of such an item as a cream separator, for instance, he would have to negotiate with a manufacturer in order to arrive at a cost to Sears which would allow him to sell to the consumer at a predetermined low price and still maintain his likewise predetermined gross margin. If Richard Sears decided, for example, that he wanted to sell a cream separator at $26.50, with a gross margin of profit of, say, 30 per cent, he might well have to look far and wide to locate a source who would agree to produce the number of units Sears was willing to buy. In the course of the negotiations, the manufacturer might well say he could meet Sears's demands only by eliminating certain "gadgets" or other features from the product or by substituting cheaper materials for costlier ones. But it appears that, in this phase of negotiations, it was the manufacturer who was primarily responsible for suggesting alterations and for evolving the final design.

While the great promotions of cream separators, bicycles, sewing machines, and other hard lines were of course the most spectacular merchandising operations, these items did not dominate the over-all merchandise structure; that structure was heavy with countless lines purchased on the prevailing "trading" basis. Men's socks, children's shoes, babies' diapers, and similar goods neither demanded nor lent themselves to any such extensive negotiations with sources. The negotiations in connection with this merchandise centered almost entirely on prices, amounts, and delivery dates. The company did not decide in advance to sell, say, a certain selection of socks or handkerchiefs, have those goods made even to rough specifications, and then advertise them in its catalogue. Rather, the buyers went out, found an item reasonably similar to what they had been selling and wanted to continue selling, drove the price down as low as possible, and then prepared catalogue copy to present whatever goods they had been able to obtain. Price was so important that it was often the determining factor in what goods were bought; the particular clothespin carried by the company might (and likely would) depend on what source offered them for five cents less per thousand.

As the laboratories began to develop after 1911, they began to exert some influence on merchandise procurement in relation to quality. When, for instance, minimum specifications for percale were adopted by the company, that step at least restricted the sources from which percale could be purchased to those meeting minimal specifications. In examining various items of merchandise submitted by buyers or manufacturers prior to approval for purchase by the company, the laboratories often discovered flaws and shortcomings in merchandise which a change in the design of the product or in some of its materials might remedy. Fundamentally, however, the task of the laboratories was to improve quality, to eliminate harmful or dangerous items, to help procure the best possible goods available within a given price range, to assure that merchandise comported with the claims made for it by buyers or manufacturers, and to assure that catalogue presentation accorded with facts established through laboratory analysis. It was not until 1929 that the testing laboratories absorbed the merchandise development department and thus integrated the elements which were to be instrumental in the intensified program of developing the company's own products and designs.

Possibly the first really important example of merchandise development came in automobile tires. As pointed out earlier, Montgomery Ward was far ahead of Sears, Roebuck in automobile tire sales in 1925; Ward's annual sales volume in this department ran to $1,909,000 in 1925, as contrasted with Sears's volume of $700,916 in that year. Wood naturally carried his interest in tires to Sears when he joined that firm; there he found the company selling a tire trade-named "Justice." It was, according to all accounts, a tire of grossly inferior quality. Two or three small manufacturers were supplying this item, working entirely without specifications; price was the only basis of purchase. Sears then proceeded to design its own tire and to evolve detailed specifications for its manufacture. The contract was awarded to Goodyear, already a famous manufacturer of tires, and production of the new tire began in May, 1926. Here sales promotion dovetailed with merchandise development. A contest with cash prizes aggregating $25,000 was held to select a name for the new tire, which, the public was assured, would be vastly superior to the old "Justice." Considerable promotion was placed behind the contest, through advertising in the catalogues and through other mediums. Some 937,886 people submitted a total of 2,253,746 names. The entries came from every state in the Union and in twenty-five languages. "Allstate," submitted by Hans Simonson, then working as a draftsman in Bismarck, North Dakota, to save money to enter art school, was selected as the winning name; $5,000 went to the winner as first prize.

The tire was as successful as the contest which named it. Allstate tires were priced at about 25 per cent under the prevailing market price for casings of comparable quality. The item quickly became a best seller and was a large factor in the early success of the retail stores. Meanwhile, the same merchandise development program which had created Allstate continued experimenting in efforts to build better tires. A test-car operation was started in 1926, in which four automobiles (one equipped with Allstate tires, the others with tires made by Sears's leading competitors) were driven at sixty miles an hour for 975 miles a day, five days a week, to test the wearing capacities of the various makes of tires. (The operation continues to this day.)

By 1928 the merchandise development program was ready with another tire: the "Super Allstate," guaranteed for 25,000 miles. It was reportedly the first tire of its kind ever produced by the tire industry; it marked a distinct advance, and it was completely a Sears product. At that time few tires were guaranteed for more than 12,000–15,000 miles. The company received testimonials from some customers who claimed to have driven the Super Allstates for as much as 60,000 miles. In 1935 the company introduced a new Allstate tire, broader and flatter and involving new principles of tread design. This development was the product of research conducted right through the depression years. The program of development in this one item has been and is costly, for in addition to the expense of constant research there is the fact that a switch-over to a new tire has meant completely scrapping the old. But the rewards of such expenditures outweigh the costs. In the year after the first Allstate tire appeared, Sears's sales volume in this department rose from only a little more than a third of Ward's to a figure only about $44,000 under Ward's. And in 1928 Sears's tire sales jumped to $3,247,463, while Ward's amounted to $2,046,000.

Even more dramatic than the development of the Allstate tire was the Coldspot electric home refrigerator in 1931. Electric refrigerators were at that time still a relatively recent innovation; there seemed to be a large market for them, and Sears's merchandise executives believed that market would be far larger if the high prices of the electric refrigerators could be brought down. The company had itself had an unhappy, if minor, experience with electric refrigerators. General Wood had earlier insisted upon buying five hundred of them; according to an authoritative source, "he succeeded in losing money on them." This loss simply spurred the efforts of Nelson and General Westervelt, head of the merchandise development division, to develop a Sears refrigerator.

Whether consciously or not, the company's merchandisers were proceeding on something very close to Richard Sears's intuitive grasp and guess of the measure of demand elasticity. The refrigerator they had in mind may not have represented a deadly parallel to the cream separator of earlier vintage, but the similarity was strong. The only greatly *dis*similar aspect lay in the fact that this time the company planned to design its own product almost from the ground up.

D. M. Nelson, his assistants, and Westervelt decided the Sears refrigerator should be of a "sandwich" type, to minimize the service problem; the freezing unit should be easily removable by the customer. Nelson brought into his organization Herman Price, who was known to be a good refrigerator man. And Westervelt, meantime, found what he thought would be a satisfactory refrigerator; Sears paid the owner of the patents, a man named Tippett, about $2,000 for his patents. An Evansville, Indiana, manufacturer named Carson received the initial order for one hundred of the boxes. Carson had been making locomotive headlights of a special type, and the cylinder used in his lights was a basic principle of the electric refrigerator. Carson contributed further developments to Tippett's design; the original Sears refrigerator, as it first appeared, was developed by Carson.

It was at this point, according to Nelson, that the Coldspot refrigerator business was really sparked by Supervisor Herman Price's plan to sell a six-cubic-foot box for the price others were getting for a four-cubic-foot refrigerator. When the company had first begun to investigate the entire electric-refrigerator field, it had discovered that manufacturers were promoting four-foot boxes, in a wide variety of types. Boxes of this size were then accounting for about 60 per cent of all sales, but Sears's merchandisers were convinced that most families really preferred a six-foot box—provided they could afford one that size. Sears determined to confine its refrigerator to only three sizes—of four, six, and eight feet—to hold production costs down, and to promote most actively the six-foot box at the price customarily asked for a four-foot refrigerator. Once Price's stratagem was adopted—and Nelson insists it was the most important single element in putting the company in the refrigerator business—Raymond Loewy, a well-known industrial designer, was employed to develop the design of the box.

Sears's engineers meantime redesigned the box's electrical unit and produced one which any customer could easily separate from the box. Up to that time, a refrigeration mechanic's services had been required even for "access" to the freezing unit. Sears's approach allowed the customer to remove the unit and insert and connect one sent him by the company. Sears's detailed analyses of its competitors' electric refrigerators indicated that one of the weakest spots was their shelving. This had first been made of steel dipped in lead, but these shelves usually rusted; they were replaced by some manufacturers with stainless-steel shelves, which proved very expensive. Sears developed an entirely different kind of shelving of aluminum, which cost only about a third as much as stainless steel. The refrigerator which emerged from all this development activity as the Coldspot proved one of the company's greatest merchandising successes since the great promotions of Richard Sears. Sears, Roebuck was enabled to sell for $149.50 a refrigerator of quality equal to those selling for as much as from $40 to $50 higher; expressed in other terms, Sears could sell a six-cubic-foot box for what competitors were charging for a four-foot box. Within less than ten years the Sears Coldspot became one of the three or four best-selling electric refrigerators in the country.

Allstate and Coldspot stand out as dramatic examples of merchandise development, each producing annual sales volume of many millions. Their success has tended to overshadow less dramatic but nevertheless important successes of lesser scope and generally contemporary with them in point of time. The depression years particularly marked a period of merchandise development, partly perhaps because of the importance of discovering profitable new items in popular demand, but also partly because the steadily expanding retail stores (which grew in number in every year except 1932, when the reduction was negligible) demanded such development. *Business Week* magazine wrote of the program:

> Manufacturers who are alert and eager, both to lower costs and improve quality, find Sears, Roebuck eager and willing to give them active cooperation, share the benefit of the research department's services. The efforts of this department during the depression period have met with marked success. One of the outstanding developments of the year enabled the company to reduce the price of a gasoline-engine driven washing machine from $125 to $89.50. Since only a small fraction of farm homes can use electric machines this item has wide potential sales....
>
> Another product of the ingenuity of the research engineers is a guaranteed "non-shrinkable" workshirt at 79¢ to 89¢, offered this spring for the first time. This is one result of the company's extensive experimental work with textiles predating the research department....
>
> Among other significant research developments are new processes that will affect many products. Non-inflammable window curtains, Christmas tree ornaments, insulation board are in the offing; a process of lithographing on wood, metal and asbestos is in the works; so is a new type of pressed wood, durable and inexpensive, with possibilities of wide adaptation for decoration on furniture and numerous other uses for a solid pressed out of a plastic.
>
> A large staff of field agents supplement the work done in offices and laboratories. A study is being made to determine what sizes, styles, types, colors, and prices of floor lamps are most in demand. This survey was made through actual

shopping trips in more than 300 cities and examination of hundreds of newspaper advertisements. The general result of such studies is to simplify the lines in both catalogues and stores, reduce the number of units offered, and increase the sales of each.

A recent study of neckties included not only a comprehensive survey to discover the average man's taste . . . but also laboratory experiments to find out which of 11 principal methods of manufacture produces the best tie. The company will concentrate on what it considers the best type and forget the rest.

These developments will have a distinct effect on the market. Mail order houses were pioneers in forcing down prices on tires, stoves, washing machines, batteries, and phonographs. Today they sell in excess of 10% of the entire national output of these products. Sears, Roebuck and Montgomery Ward sales combined represent 10% of the national volume of other goods—bicycles, lawnmowers, sporting goods, children's wagons, farm engines, milk separators, harness.[6]

The depression of the 1930's had hit the country's automobile-makers even harder than most groups. Manufacturers of automobile bodies were therefore highly receptive to a development worked out by the company: to build kitchen sinks and cabinets of a pressed-steel base instead of the heavy cast iron then being used. Sears's merchandise development department had been seeking a method of reducing the 350-pound weight of the ordinary sink. The researchers concluded that the really important thing about a sink's wearing quality was its enamel surface; if the enamel coating could be preserved, the base of the material would not be of any great importance. A base of pressed steel would lower the weight of a sink from 350 to 60 pounds. The Briggs Auto Company agreed with Sears's engineers that the scheme was feasible. The pressed-steel sink with enamel coating went into production.

The sharp reduction in the weight of this item had several effects. It made a great difference in the cost of material, cost of transportation, and cost of handling in warehouses and retail stores. The lighter weight of the new sink also made it possible to eliminate the legs from the design, since the new product could be supported securely by wall brackets. This left more space for sink cabinets, but such cabinets up to this time had usually been custom built and were costly. Sears was able to develop a standardized steel cabinet which sold for about one-half the customary price; as a matter of fact, the sink and cabinet sold for less than sinks alone had cost in the cast-iron days.

Merchandise development turned from sinks to roller skates, which were then selling for around $2.00. Sears's engineers had an idea which they believed would make it possible to produce a good roller skate to sell at a profit for $1.00 (the company was then paying $1.15 per pair for skates). Skate manufacturers vetoed the scheme and refused to deal on the proposed design. The company found a battery manufacturer who had formerly made radios and had much idle equipment on hand. His battery business was confined largely to the fall season. The skates were made, and Sears was able to sell them for $1.00 and realize as much profit as it had previously obtained on the skates for which it had *paid* $1.15. The battery manufacturer became one of the largest producers of roller skates in the country.

Paints had always been a large sales producer for Sears, Roebuck, and paint factories were among the earliest acquired by the company. At the time the company entered the paint business, paint and similar materials were packaged in wooden kegs, which often leaked, were difficult to open, and were nearly impossible to close once they had been opened. Their weight made them expensive to transport, and their shape made them inconvenient to handle. William Hoch, head of the paint department at Sears, was finally able, after being scoffed at and turned away by many sheet-steel manufacturers, to find one who would make all-steel containers for paint. The first of the all-steel containers were crude and unsightly, but they were an improvement in every way over the wooden kegs, and in time steel completely replaced wood for packaging paints and similar goods.

Even so, the Post Office Department insisted almost to the end of the 1920's that paint to be shipped by mail must be packed in a stout container with sufficient absorbent packing material to absorb the entire contents of the container in the event of breakage or leakage. Sawdust was used by Sears for this purpose; when a gallon of paint was mailed to a customer, he had also to pay the freight on approximately a gallon of sawdust. In the depression, when Sears began prepayment of postage, it was brought home with a vengeance what a postage bill the company had been saddling on its customers for years. To circumvent this expense the company developed a simple closing device which locked the lid or plug in an ordinary friction can, yet at the same time permitted it to be easily removed and replaced by the customers. Tests conducted by Sears, outside testing laboratories, and the Bureau of Standards in Washington showed that a can of paint sealed with the locking device and packed in a simple corrugated carton would stand rougher treatment than an ordinary can packed in sawdust. The Post Office Department studied the findings, examined the locking device, and permitted paint packed in cans so sealed to be shipped without the absorbent material. The locking device is now in general use throughout the country.

One incident which spurred the company's merchandise development program in the mid-1930's was the Federal Trade Commission's ruling in the Goodyear case, which will later be referred to at greater length. When the Trade Commission ordered Goodyear to cease and desist from making Allstate tires for Sears at discounts even below those given to Goodyear dealers (who, of course, sold Goodyear tires, not Allstate), it struck a blow at a widespread industry practice. Firestone was reputedly the only tiremaker not producing tires under someone else's brand name; in other fields of manufacture it was also a widespread practice for a brand-name manufacturer to produce goods under other brand names of the distributors for whom they were made. The Goodyear decision underscored what had already become a strong feeling in Sears—that it would be advisable for the company not only to develop more and more of its own products but also to purchase that merchandise from manufacturers not producing goods under other brand names. The Goodyear decision and the effects growing out of it helped further the trend then already evident and referred to by Houser seven years after the Goodyear decision, when he said:

Just as the small dealer needs a powerful ally, which he finds in the large manufacturer . . . so the small manufacturer needs an ally who can furnish what he lacks—acceptance by the public, expert product leadership, and assured volume. He finds this in the development of the large distributor. So, as I see it, we are developing two parallel systems, each having its place in the total economy of the country. On the one hand the dominant, large manufacturers with their own branded lines, distributing their products through thousands of independent dealers—on the other hand, the mass distributor with his many and various branded lines, buying each of these lines from smaller manufacturers. You can see that in each case the production of goods is in the factory and in the retail sale to the public is in a store, but in one case the manufacturer determines the character of product, i.e., its design, quality, prices, and production schedules; while in the other case, these functions are assumed by the mass distributor.[7]

Sears, Roebuck's power-tool business represented a good example of one of the two "parallel systems" of which Houser spoke. Sales in this line were built to an eminent position in the company through its development of its own saws, lathes, drill presses, and similar tools, with the result that by 1936 the company was said to be the world's largest distributor of power tools. Hand tools were likewise developed, and Sears became one of the largest distributors of this line. As the retail stores, with their parking lots and automobile service stations, spread across the country, the company moved aggressively to expand and improve all its automobile-supply line. Allstate tires had proved within a very short time to be a vast asset. The efforts to improve the rest of its merchandise led the company to develop a battery of its own. Wood, while at Montgomery Ward's, had been able to slice in half the price of automobile batteries, which had been selling for above $20.[8] Some while after he moved to Sears, the company had its engineers bring into the laboratories samples of all the outstanding makes of batteries in the United States for extensive testing and analysis. As a result of the test Sears developed substantially lower-priced batteries which it claimed were of a superior quality, with improved grids and separators. The company first guaranteed its batteries for eighteen months, but the performance was good enough to lead them soon to extend the guaranty to two years.

Sears's Drug and Sundries Department (a catch-all which also includes sickroom and hospital supplies, cosmetics, and candy and foods) decided in 1939 to enter the booming vitamins market, which reflected at that time a penchant for self-medication reminiscent of the electric-belt era.[9] Sears's first major effort at merchandise development in this line was "Dr. Walters Cod Liver Oil Concentrate Tablets." ("Doc" Walters was the pharmacist who headed this department.) This item soon became the best seller in the whole department. Within two years the department developed a product containing eight vitamins plus minerals and liver concentrate. The product was named "Super-Kaps," and it became another best seller. The spring 1946 general catalogue sold approximately ten times as many vitamins as did the spring 1941 book in which they were first listed; by 1946 the Sears Super-Kaps were, according to the head of this department, in second place in dollar volume of all brands being sold in the country.

By 1946 the merchandise development division was working on nearly fifty major projects, including such items as steel kitchen cabinets, vacuum cleaners, sewing machines, fountain pens, outboard motors, children's shoes, pressure cookers, radios, wheelchairs, stoves, batteries, water heaters, washing machines, ironers, electric welders, wrenches, electric tools, power saws, refrigerators, and many more. In addition to the efforts to redesign and improve established products, the engineers were working on such relatively new items as a wire recorder (which was introduced in 1947), a dairy-barn ventilator, and a hay-drier. The development work on most of the established items dealt with such elements as improvements in quality, more economical production techniques, better geographical distribution of heavy-goods sources to save on high transportation costs, or establishment of specifications for items not already on a basic buying basis.

By 1946, when scarce materials were again becoming available, the spring and summer catalogue announced the production of Sears's home and farm freezers. The newspaper story describing this item, which was a latter-day merchandise development in the Coldspot line, said:

> The outstanding thing about the Sears unit will be their price, which is believed to be considerably below the level at which home freezers have sold. A spokesman for a firm here which handles several makes of home freezers said, "The Sears competition will be pretty rough." He said Sears' prices are about half those for the best known line of home freezers his firm carries, and much less than any other makes handled. The Sears units probably will have the effect of reducing prices throughout the field, he said.[10]

Following its now-established policy of concentrating its efforts on a manageable assortment of items within any given line, Sears brought out the home freezers in four models, in 6, 9, 12, and 18 cubic feet. Prices ran from around $167 for the smallest to $297 for the largest.

By 1948 the general plan of merchandise development led to a complete overhauling of the color scheme in Sears's home furnishings. Harmonizing colors had long been a problem to the company. Rose-colored draperies, for example, made by one source, might clash with a rose rug produced by another manufacturer. Each factory was using its own colors, and the clashes which resulted were impeding the company's sales of home furnishings. The fall and winter 1948 catalogue announced the institution of "Harmony House Colors." Sears's buyers and supervisors selected eighteen basic colors which they considered the most attractive to the company's customers. Each of these eighteen basic colors came in light, medium, and dark shades, and occasionally in in-between shades. Manufacturers were briefed and equipped to conform to the newly established color pattern.

As in nearly everything else it does, the company is convinced that its work in merchandise development pays its way in dollars-and-cents terms. Even allowing an ample margin of error for occasional wasted effort, a few resounding successes like Allstate and Coldspot have gone a long way toward justifying the whole program and toward offsetting the cost of less successful efforts. It seems apparent, too, that the company embarked upon its program of merchandise development out of the conviction that Sears must grow or find itself relegated to a subordinate position. Expressed in other and more concrete terms, with the launching of its retail chain the company found it had to make its own brand names mean at least as much to customers as any other brand names in the country; to do this, it had to develop distinctive products in order that a Sears brand name would have intrinsic importance; and it had always to improve even those items which it had not itself developed.

A considerable number of suggestions for merchandise development come to the company unsolicited from "inventors." From one hundred to two hundred letters a month bring requests that the company add such-and-such a product to its offerings; the letters also often bring samples of the invention. Around 1936 such communications numbered nearly two hundred each month, but dropped to around a hundred monthly by 1948. The drop may have been symptomatic more of better times, with consequent easing of the urge to supplement incomes, than of any drying-up of inventive talent. In 1936 the policy was to refer such letters to the general merchandise office or the research division of the laboratory, both of which generally replied with polite letters declining with thanks.

The policy in effect today leans more toward urging the inventor to secure a patent immediately; the company has no desire to see his product before it is patented, else it might face litigation for alleged "piracy." Once an item is so patented, the company makes a reasonable effort to direct the inventor to a manufacturer or to someone else who could conceivably assist the inventor in exploiting his products. The inventions run from new toys to calf-weaners, from home dry-cleaning machines to novel hairpins. Few of the inventions, even when samples are submitted, are of any value to the company, however; its own merchandise development department and the engineers of its sources are usually ahead of the amateur field.

The emergence of Sears's "basic buying" program, of which signs first appeared during the 1930's, was essentially a gradual codification, formalization, and extension of the whole program of merchandise development to capitalize to the fullest upon the economies offered by that program. Basic buying, during its first few years, operated sporadically, manifesting itself largely in isolated instances of rather dramatic and highly profitable development of big-ticket items. Around 1935, however—if an arbitrary date has any validity in this connection—the company's merchandise structure had generally attained its redefinition and consequent overhauling. And by that time the buying organization was in position to prosecute the basic buying program more vigorously. When T. V. Houser succeeded Nelson as vice-president in charge of merchandise in 1939, basic buying was intensified and extended to more and more lines.

"Basic buying" is often loosely referred to as "specification buying"; the latter term is, however, an incomplete definition, for basic buying as it operates in Sears goes beyond what is usually meant by "specification buying." An organization buying to specifications usually specifies little more than the ingredients and design; if the organization has in mind a predetermined selling price which will in turn fix its maximum purchasing price, negotiations between buyer and manufacturer may be necessary. But specification buying does not necessarily involve complete product design or calculation of costs in terms of such specific components as materials, labor, overhead, and profit to the manufacturer.

Under Sears's basic buying policy the company's central buying organization develops its own product in close conjunction with the merchandise development division of the technical laboratories and engineering representatives of a manufacturer. Before the manufacturer enters the picture, the company has determined (in instances in which this is possible) where the manufacturer is to be located. Distribution cost is a consideration in all phases of basic buying; an effort is made to locate sources close to the points where the goods will ultimately be sold, although this factor must also be correlated with location in respect to raw materials.

Here Sears (like, of course, Ward's and Penney's) enjoys an advantage over many department stores in the type of buyers it has. These buyers are trained to search for sources—in trade jargon, to "pound the pavements." Many department-store buyers confine their purchases largely to primary sources, well known and usually conveniently located, mainly because such buyers lack the knowledge, time, or willingness to look elsewhere. Sears's buyers, on the contrary, when they find primary sources unsatisfactory, examine secondary sources which, though less well known and perhaps located off the beaten path, produce quality merchandise often available at lower prices than that of primary sources. And, of course, where an item is very important from the standpoint of potential volume, Sears's buyers sometimes develop sources to produce it.

Once the source has been selected, Sears expects that source to provide primarily a fabrication function, with all worries about selling removed

SOME ASPECTS OF CENTRAL BUYING

from the manufacturer. The company's basic buying policy involves purchasing goods on the basis of known production (or platform) costs. Sears initiates the production process and assumes the selling risks and builds its price on the basis of which it buys from sources in terms of the following known item costs: material, direct labor, overhead, and profit. In a sense, Sears is buying not so much finished products but simply the components of those products, such as material, direct labor, etc.

When the company assumes the design function, it necessarily undertakes certain responsibilities. One of the most important of these is that of bearing the tool-and-die expense, which in refrigerators, it is estimated, amounted after the war to about two million dollars. It is clear therefore that the company must have the possibilities of developing heavy volume if it is to support its basic buying plan. The company insists the plan has advantages to a manufacturer, over and above the obvious fact that it brings him an order for merchandise. In line with all Sears's buying, demand is projected in terms of a year or, at the least, of a season. This means that buyers generally do not go out and buy ten thousand units and then return in a few weeks to purchase an additional five thousand units. Instead they buy on a rate of production basis determined by their earlier projection, which is based on records of previous sales, with additions or cutbacks based on developing market trends. A source usually knows pretty well at the outset what the size of his order will be. Further, Sears likes to point out, that "outset" is so timed that the manufacturer is enabled to schedule the part of his production that is to go to Sears at times when he would otherwise experience a slack season. The source is thereby helped to achieve steady, year-round production instead of slack periods alternating with rushes of peak activity. As one example, Houser asserts, Sears's lawnmower production is almost complete by December, whereas jobbers hardly begin to buy before January, in the South, and March, in the North.

Under Houser's regime Sears has come to concern itself just as vitally with production as with distribution. The job of the Sears buying organization is so to conceive and execute its operation that sources can make reasonable profits on Sears's business and thus survive to guarantee the company continuity of supply, and at the same time so to help sources reduce their own production and distribution costs that Sears can buy cheaply enough to maintain its low prices and a satisfactory gross margin. After that it is, of course, solely up to Sears to hold its operating costs to the maximum allowable in distribution of the merchandise; but it is the "before" rather than the "after" which has become the essence of Sears's buying. Distribution is one factor which operates in both the "before" and the "after" spheres, in the production and sale of goods by the manufacturer as well as in Sears's own distribution cost. Every cent the company can shave off a manufacturer's distribution cost can either increase the manufacturer's profit or reduce the cost of the goods to Sears, or both.

Distribution costs, especially those of manufacturers, are almost an obsession with Houser. In virtually every speech he stresses over and over the necessity of reducing all distribution costs in order to provide the public with increasingly better quality merchandise at progressively lower prices. In Houser's words, "If the justification for private enterprise is its ability to provide more goods and at lower prices, then the various units going to make up the sum total of private enterprise in this country must see that their operation stands this test."[11]

In an effort to minimize its own distribution costs, the company in the middle 1930's established what it called "pool stocks"—actually warehouses to handle heavy and bulky items (initially plumbing and heating equipment) destined for retail stores. Because of the weight involved in big-ticket and hard-line items and because of the fact that most of its retail stores had to obtain less-than-carload deliveries of merchandise, economical transportation assumed the utmost importance in Sears shortly after its retail chain was established, for the final net profit realized by a store was obviously affected to a considerable degree by the cost of delivery of goods to the point of sale.

The company soon began to utilize the experience acquired in the construction of its own specifications to meet its own peculiar needs, siting the pool stocks with consideration of the location both of the source and of the ultimate consumer. Freight cars could be unloaded on one side of the platform and the merchandise conveyed through the warehouse to the waiting trucks; all necessary servicing could be done during conveyance through the building. The use of pool stocks not only enabled the retail stores merely to stock sample items in their stores and make deliveries direct from the pool stocks, thus saving space; it also reduced transportation costs by eliminating cross-hauling and multiple handling.

The manufacturer who takes a reasonably long view must concern himself with the ultimate selling price of his product, not merely with the short-range view of the price he receives from the wholesaler, jobber, distributor, or whoever buys his product. Houser emphasizes the necessity for the manufacturer to go back beyond even that point and concern himself with all the elements which combine to determine his selling cost.

Sears has come to deal with its sources in some of the following ways. First, the production cost of an article is known in advance under Sears's basic buying system, since the company, in effect, buys not the product, but the components of that product, such as raw materials landed in the plant, direct labor, overhead, and profit to the source. This means that the source is not confronted with the danger of finding he has quoted a price so low that he will lose money on the order, nor will the source find that he had lost the order because he had to quote such a high price to assure any profit that someone else underbid him. Second, on Sears's orders all cost of advertising, promotion, and selling is eliminated for the source; his market for a specified number of units is assured when the contract is signed with Sears. Third, the source can plan well ahead both on his procurement of raw materials (and the company's buying organization often advises him even on this) and on his scheduling of production. Sears aims to place its orders well enough ahead to allow sources to produce the goods in what would otherwise be a slack period.

Each of those three factors is intended to reduce the producer's costs; the source is guaranteed what Sears considers a "reasonable" profit, which he

TABLE 56*

DISTRIBUTION COSTS OF MANUFACTURERS IN SELECTED INDUSTRIES EXPRESSED AS PERCENTAGE OF MANUFACTURERS' NET SALES, 1939

Sales and Distribution Costs	Paints and Varnishes	Pneumatic Tires and Tubes	Household Electrical Appliances	Agricultural Implements and Machinery†
Net sales	100.00	100.00	100.00	100.00
Cost of merchandise sales	66.60	70.59	74.18	....
Gross margin	33.40	29.41	25.82	....
Distribution expense:				
Salesmen's salaries	4.68	2.59	1.67 ⎫	
Salaries and wages of other distribution personnel	6.09	5.67	3.16 ⎬	10.70
Salesmen's commissions and bonuses	1.71	0.33	1.41 ⎭	
Social security and pension-fund payments	0.59	0.33	0.24	0.33
Commissions to brokers, factors, etc.	0.43	1.00	0.05	....
Advertising and sales-promotion expense	2.94	4.10	5.58	1.31
Transportation outward	2.49	3.83	1.51	....
All other distribution expense	6.30	7.34	4.92	2.68
Total distribution expense	25.23	25.19	18.54	15.02
Provision for bad debts	0.47	0.32	0.23	0.81
Total including provision for bad debts	25.70	25.51	18.77	15.83

* Source: Developed from data published in *Report of the Federal Trade Commission*, Parts III and IV (Washington: Government Printing Office, 1944).
† Data are for 1940.

can calculate pretty accurately in advance. Still other elements in the basic buying policy allegedly aid sources. Sears will not only take receipt of the goods throughout the period of their production, often obviating the storage problem for the source (which could tie up a considerable amount of working capital), but will also advance a source money when that appears desirable and necessary. Table 56 offers some idea of just how much of a manufacturer's margin may be eliminated through obviating his uncertainty by guaranteeing him a market for a certain proportion of his output.

Sears can help a manufacturer avoid a not inconsiderable portion of his distribution costs (at least on the part of the output taken by the company) as shown in Table 56, as expressed in terms of salesmen's salaries, commissions and bonuses, commissions to brokers and factors, advertising and sales-promotion expense, and provision for bad debts. This operation is somewhat akin to the shibboleth of "eliminating" the middleman, since Sears simply assumes the function of selling from the manufacturer. Still, it may represent a substantial saving, since the company has guaranteed outlets and heavy volume of many types of goods to carry its selling expenses.

The force of the company's argument, in this respect, depends largely upon the proportion of any given manufacturer's output it purchases. Its soundness diminishes in proportion as the percentage of his output taken by Sears diminishes and as the manufacturer is accordingly compelled to sell a higher proportion of his production through jobbers or through his own selling and sales-promotion organization. In such instances the manufacturer naturally hesitates to discontinue his established selling organization.

It should be apparent that sources, to produce according to Sears's standards and basic buying policy, must have modern, well-equipped plants and must have both the facilities and the inclination to conduct adequate research and development programs. Plants can be modernized and kept modern, and research and development can be conducted, only by plants which are profitable. The days in which Sears could cavalierly discard a source in favor of another quoting a slightly lower price, thus sacrificing established quality and continuity of supply while taking little reck of a source's capacity to modernize or to conduct research, seem to be gone. The very nature of the basic buying policy, which has been extended to about half the company's total merchandise purchases (soft goods are less susceptible to the policy, and textiles still present a nearly insuperable obstacle), dictates that sources shall be reasonably profitable, content, and interested in the company's program. But, in Houser's words:

> Our concern is not with "How much does a manufacturer make on his production for us?" but "What does he do with those profits?" We feel that adequate sums should be plowed back into the business for the purposes indicated and into expanded facilities....
>
> As a matter of fact, in all our important lines we require such a research program, with an agreed sum of money appropriated, the character of the research problems agreed upon, and the program paid out of a definite apportionment of the unit price.[12]

Sears's whole program of basic buying is predicated to a considerable extent upon the assumption of continuity of sources of supply. Continuity becomes particularly important in cases (such as refrigerators) where the company must make a large outlay for tools and dies which can be recovered only over a period of several years of production by the source or sources involved. The 1940 annual report touched upon this theme when it asserted:

If it costs $500,000 to tool up a line of refrigerator cabinets, this is but $1 per cabinet if the subsequent volume is 500,000 units. But it is $10 per cabinet if the volume is only 50,000. The same principle holds true through the whole range of general merchandise, hard lines as well as textiles, small articles as well as big.

With the recognition of the fact that continuity of sources was important and that only profitable sources could offer that continuity, particularly since the mid-1930's, the company laid increasing stress upon building close personal relations with as many of its sources as possible. Buyers came more and more to appreciate and study the manufacturer's problems and the contributions a source had to offer and less and less to seek simply to knock prices down to a point which might spell little or no profit for the supplier but, on the contrary, might reap a harvest of ill will for Sears.

The three men in the company who have perhaps devoted the greatest effort to build sound relationships with sources are Donald Nelson, R. E. Wood, and T. V. Houser. Nelson began to apply himself to the problem while still in the laboratories, where his analyses and tests gave him considerable insight into manufacturers' problems and into what the manufacturers had to offer to the company. When he entered the general merchandise office in 1926, he was able to work more directly along this line; and when, in 1928, he became general merchandise manager, Nelson made better source relations a major project. His elevation to a vice-presidency in 1930 simply strengthened his position within the company and with the sources supplying Sears. Both as a merchandiser interested in continuity of supply and in forging an integrated team and as a genial personality extremely adept in human relations and moral suasion, Nelson was well equipped for his task.

Nelson sought to make it clear to sources that Sears, Roebuck was not interested in becoming a manufacturing colossus and in swallowing up independent manufacturers. He also sought to persuade sources that Sears was interested in their problems and in their continued profitability; in this realm, of course, some reversal of company policy was necessary to make the deeds comport with the words. Nelson insisted that sources had to be considered by the company as a vital part of its structure, to be assisted in every way possible, to be given greater leeway when they had established their reliability, to be tided over in times of crisis rather than thrown overboard. He maintained that continuing relations with a source over a long period of time meant not only continuity of supply of given items of consistent quality but also a feeling of security which would allow the source to concentrate its full efforts on whatever production it was selling to Sears. And Nelson also proclaimed that sources had a mighty contribution to make to Sears if their full enthusiasm could be aroused and unleashed on the problems at hand.

In 1932, for example, a large manufacturer of enamelware, used in plumbing equipment, who had been supplying Sears, informed the company that there was a combination in the industry to ruin him by cutting prices below his cost. He stated frankly that the company could, in these circumstances, buy products of quality equal to his for less money elsewhere than he could afford to sell for. The source faced a loss which threatened to amount to several thousands of dollars. Sears, Roebuck agreed to stand by the source and to guarantee any loss he might sustain by being compelled to sell below his cost until the crisis passed. The company increased the size of its order in 1933, and the supplier's loss was held to only $25,000, which the company made good.

Nelson relates other instances in which the company advanced cash to sources to purchase raw materials or to modernize their plants, and cases in which the company has taken goods off the manufacturer's hands before required to do so, when sources could not afford to hold the inventory. Nelson attempted to bring the buyers to work on the premise that, when Sears asked a source to allocate a greater proportion of its output to the company, Sears automatically assumed a moral obligation not to discontinue that source capriciously or, in fact, for any but the most cogent reasons.

When Wood came to Sears in 1924, he envisioned a great expansion in the company's volume of business through the addition of retail stores. By the time he assumed the presidency in 1928, the retail outlets had shown signs of profitability, actual and potential, and Wood was prepared to drive ahead in a far greater expansion program. The company was also adding mail-order plants during the late 1920's, which further increased its demand for merchandise. Wood realized that procuring the mountains of goods he expected the company to need was not going to be easy; that it would require the best efforts not only of the Sears executives and the buying organization but also the full co-operation and if possible the spontaneous enthusiasm of the sources as well; and that, if this was to be accomplished, Nelson's philosophy as outlined above would have to be translated into actual operating practices. It seems clear that the two men moved in concert.

Wood's own feelings were spelled out time and again in his statements in the company's annual reports, in which he frequently has written of the company's responsibilities under five headings: to its customers, to the public, to employees, to sources of merchandise supply, and to the stockholders. In the report for 1936 Wood said of the company's responsibilities to sources:

> The best test of your Company's fairness to its merchandise sources is shown by the length of their association with it. This Company is dealing with 6,461 manufacturers. Of this number, 294 manufacturers have been selling to the Company for 25 years or more; 1,292 have been selling to the Company for more than 15 years; 3,045 for more than 10 years; 4,460 for more than 5 years.
> Business relations like this with companies not financially connected with Sears, Roebuck & Co. do not endure in this way unless the relationship is a mutually satisfactory one.

In the 1937 annual report Wood said:

> In a year of fluctuating prices such as 1937, I cannot overemphasize the importance to both parties of that enduring community of interest of the company and its sources, to which I made reference last year. It has made possible the solution of complicated problems and the continuance of these outstanding relationships.

Houser shared the feelings of Wood and Nelson toward source relationships. He, too, repeatedly pointed out that sources must be assured reasonable profits and a reasonable degree of security in dealing with the company. In his development of basic buying, Houser carried the details and techniques of source relationships further than any of his predecessors. In point of time, he is the "last" (i.e., the latest) in this triumvirate; but from the standpoint of the size and complexity of his task, both of which factors have been increased by the drive toward decentralization of sources

TABLE 57*

LENGTH OF SERVICE OF SOURCES, 1946

Number of Years	Number of Sources	Per Cent
Less than 5	3,637	45.5
5– 9	1,699	21.2
10–14	967	12.1
15–19	669	8.4
20–24	1,034	12.9
Total	8,006	100.0

* Source: Company records.

and by intensification of the basic buying program, he is perhaps first, for proper merchandise development and proper factory production need a high degree of co-operation and enthusiasm from sources. Houser's entire buying operation would have necessitated close effective working relations with sources even if he had not begun, as he did, with that point of view. And Houser's success in safeguarding the company's position as a great merchandising organization through a world war which necessarily denied Sears access to many of its staple items and which disrupted all source relationships greatly would not have been possible in the absence of the generally satisfactory source relationships he had been instrumental in forging.

By 1946 Sears's merchandise organization was purchasing from more than eight thousand sources located in forty-five states. Roughly, one-third of those sources had been supplying Sears, Roebuck for longer than ten years, as Table 57 shows.

Table 58 breaks the length of service of those sources down in even finer terms. Of the 697 sources shown in Table 58 as having supplied the company for 24 or more years, approximately 150 had served Sears for as long as 30 years; 82 for 35 years; 35 for 40 years; 14 for 45 years; and 45 for 50 years. The hardware and cutlery department boasted 23 sources with continuity of as much as 50 years, while 11 sources had been supplying floor coverings to the company for half a century or more. These were the outstanding instances of long-term suppliers, but some 11 other sources supplying various other departments also fell in the 50-year category.

By 1938 Sears's purchases of merchandise averaged almost $3.00 per capita per year for the country as a whole. Except for the West South Central and the Mountain States (as defined by the United States Census), the company was buying from $1.09 to $6.41 per capita in all other census groups in the country. And since the West South Central and Mountain

TABLE 58*

LENGTH-OF-SERVICE BREAKDOWN OF SOURCES, 1946

Number of Years	Number of Sources	Per Cent	Number of Years	Number of Sources	Per Cent
1	772	9.6	14	146	1.8
2	1,293	16.2	15	167	2.1
3	855	10.7	16	116	1.5
4	717	9.0	17	121	1.5
5	436	5.4	18	140	1.7
6	370	4.6	19	125	1.6
7	337	4.2	20	106	1.3
8	290	3.6	21	77	1.0
9	266	3.3	22	68	0.9
10	186	2.3	23	86	1.1
11	194	2.4	24	697	8.7
12	299	3.7			
13	142	1.8	Total	8,006	100.0

* Source: Company records.

States produced fundamental raw materials such as wool, hides, and cotton, the company was indirectly a large buyer of their basic products.[13] Table 59 illustrates just where and in what amounts the company purchased its merchandise in various years from 1929 to 1943 and shows graphically how the company has sought to stimulate manufacturers in various states and regions—not primarily, of course, to build up the purchasing power of those regions and achieve a better balance between industry and agriculture but largely to reduce transportation costs and also to build local good will—by scattering its buying more and more. For example, the number of sources located in the South and West has increased steadily, just as has the volume of dollar purchases from manufacturers in those regions. The tendency toward broader geographic distribution serves also to mitigate the frequently voiced objections that "chain stores take money out of the community." Buying across the nation, as Sears does, "puts money into many communities." And, in terms of regions, the distri-

TABLE 59*

MERCHANDISE PURCHASES, 1929–43

STATES (By U.S. Census Divisions)	1929 Number of Sources	1929 Purchases	1935 Number of Sources	1935 Purchases	1939 Number of Sources	1939 Purchases	1943 Number of Sources	1943 Purchases	Increase or Decrease 1943 over 1929 Number of Sources	Increase or Decrease 1943 over 1929 Purchases	Percentage Increase or Decrease 1943 over 1929 Number of Sources	Percentage Increase or Decrease 1943 over 1929 Purchases
New England:												
Maine	21	$ 3,272,292	27	$ 1,177,111	28	$ 2,489,371	37	$ 3,250,019	16	$ 22,273	76	1
New Hampshire	16	1,245,579	25	1,800,074	28	845,701	33	2,939,144	17	1,693,565	106	136
Vermont		565,003			18	543,451	15	827,343	1	262,340	7	46
Massachusetts	263	13,099,943	423	12,075,297	404	22,356,009	380	28,217,503	117	15,117,560	44	115
Rhode Island	85	1,735,848	83	3,205,910	55	3,915,162	51	5,446,695	34	3,710,847	40	214
Connecticut	114	5,350,487	193	4,618,116	180	11,812,481	157	14,318,142	43	8,958,655	38	167
Total	515	$ 25,278,152	751	$ 22,871,508	718	$ 41,912,175	673	$ 54,998,846	160	$ 29,720,694	31	118
Middle Atlantic:												
New York	1,394	$ 72,983,872	2,014	$ 35,956,407	1,658	$ 63,981,346	1,692	$101,925,537	298	$28,941,665	21	40
New Jersey	80	4,470,561	273	7,041,594	311	15,167,308	265	16,253,228	185	11,782,667	231	264
Pennsylvania	400	14,541,535	611	18,885,771	575	33,459,963	518	44,360,386	118	29,818,851	30	205
Total	1,874	$ 91,995,968	2,888	$ 61,883,772	2,544	$113,609,217	2,475	$162,539,151	601	$ 70,543,183	32	77
East North Central:												
Ohio	295	$ 45,137,691	408	$ 15,091,137	458	$ 32,029,264	423	$ 21,050,748	128	$24,186,943	43	53
Indiana	165	10,735,073	246	13,172,203	245	24,581,303	227	17,438,297	62	6,703,224	38	62
Illinois	1,206	59,915,951	1,303	49,210,141	1,316	64,899,397	1,364	81,343,476	158	21,427,525	13	36
Michigan	133	7,518,894	238	6,445,560	251	14,710,748	210	8,893,657	77	1,299,763	58	17
Wisconsin	140	10,536,944	197	11,034,802	192	17,031,725	202	19,346,846	62	8,759,902	44	83
Total	1,939	$134,019,553	2,392	$ 94,953,843	2,462	$153,240,737	2,426	$148,073,024	487	$ 14,053,471	25	10
West North Central:												
Minnesota	57	$ 2,135,358	123	$ 7,082,449	118	$ 13,134,767	131	$ 6,977,358	74	$ 4,842,000	130	227
Iowa	45	932,736	53	600,068	72	5,137,222	83	5,938,263	40	4,945,527	93	408
Missouri	170	3,514,238	206	4,963,784	213	3,161,055	205	10,801,294	35	7,287,056	26	207
North Dakota			2	270								
South Dakota			2	3,297	1	15,889						
Nebraska	6	36,944	21	198,585	21	281,423	22	504,299	16	407,355	267	420
Kansas	5	20,104	12	55,076	12	46,184	12	235,922	7	215,818	140	1,074
Total	281	$ 6,759,380	419	$ 12,905,529	437	$ 25,774,540	453	$ 24,457,136	172	$ 17,697,756	61	262
South Atlantic:												
Delaware	3	$ 37,107	13	$ 47,402	15	$ 561,712	15	$ 3,154,925	13	$ 3,117,818	650	8,402
Maryland	32	1,279,444	63	2,026,306	70	2,514,614	61	2,611,993	29	1,332,549	91	104
District of Columbia			7	16,620	8	54,666	6	22,069	6	22,069		
Virginia	17	755,956	45	1,887,041	55	3,689,627	59	6,309,339	42	5,553,383	247	735

* Source: Company records.

TABLE 59*—Continued

STATES (By U.S. Census Divisions)	1929 Number of Sources	1929 Purchases	1935 Number of Sources	1935 Purchases	1939 Number of Sources	1939 Purchases	1943 Number of Sources	1943 Purchases	Increase or Decrease 1943 over 1929 Number of Sources	Increase or Decrease 1943 over 1929 Purchases	Percentage Increase or Decrease 1943 over 1929 Number of Sources	Percentage Increase or Decrease 1943 over 1929 Purchases
South Atlantic (continued):												
West Virginia	25	$ 547,011	38	$ 644,294	34	$ 2,146,014	33	$ 1,891,629	8	$ 1,344,618	32	% 246
North Carolina	22	640,542	77	2,854,289	103	6,562,467	128	16,696,129	106	16,055,587	482	2,507
South Carolina	3	12,051	19	1,587,412	33	3,980,125	33	6,420,728	30	6,408,677	1,000	53,180
Georgia	77	2,323,441	90	3,689,303	132	7,937,681	134	10,388,976	57	8,065,535	74	347
Florida	3	13,185	18	35,591	25	261,081	28	410,170	25	396,985	833	3,011
Total	181	$ 5,608,737	370	$12,688,258	475	$27,704,937	497	$47,905,958	316	$42,297,221	175	% 754
East South Central:												
Kentucky	31	$ 1,094,644	43	$ 1,258,276	43	$ 3,412,022	43	$ 3,527,541	12	$ 2,432,897	39	% 222
Tennessee	64	1,842,094	85	4,789,073	110	8,694,866	128	17,766,402	64	15,924,308	100	865
Alabama	7	82,999	20	3,833,399	41	2,681,405	50	6,383,304	43	6,305,305	614	7,597
Mississippi	3	259,345	11	1,294,614	22	5,805,769	24	11,852,348	21	11,593,003	700	4,470
Total	105	$ 3,279,082	159	$11,125,362	216	$20,594,062	245	$39,534,595	140	$36,255,513	133	$ 1,106
West South Central:												
Arkansas	7	$ 62,096	12	$ 188,447	12	$ 560,063	14	$ 1,512,735	7	$ 1,450,639	100	$ 2,334
Louisiana	4	61,668	23	225,928	28	478,486	32	1,048,927	28	987,259	700	1,601
Oklahoma	2	1,314	14	283,612	10	564,443	14	1,170,101	12	1,168,787	600	88,949
Texas	69	763,235	106	641,179	127	2,557,464	125	5,917,001	56	5,153,766	81	675
Total	82	$ 888,313	155	$ 1,339,166	177	$ 4,160,456	185	$ 9,648,764	103	$ 8,760,451	126	% 986
Mountain:												
Montana												
Idaho												
Wyoming												
Colorado	4	$ 39,463	14	$ 47,779	18	$ 160,319	19	$ 310,777	15	$ 271,314	375	% 688
New Mexico												
Arizona	1	1,616	3	2,875	1	10,755	1	64,819		63,203		3,911
Utah			3	7,742	7	138,906	8	294,807	8	294,807		
Nevada	1	1,156							1	1,156	100	100
Total	6	$ 42,235	20	$ 58,396	26	$ 309,980	28	$ 260,403	22	$ 628,168	367	$ 1,487
Pacific:												
Washington	138	$ 1,009,969	148	$ 1,019,437	143	$ 2,259,105	114	$ 4,191,996	24	$ 3,182,027	17	% 314
Oregon	18	320,610	23	511,158	48	1,249,324	45	1,422,258	27	1,101,648	150	344
California	149	2,041,741	383	5,148,836	513	10,979,121	514	18,195,512	365	16,153,771	245	791
Total	305	$ 3,372,320	554	$ 6,679,431	704	$14,487,550	673	$23,809,766	368	$20,437,446	121	% 606
GRAND TOTAL	5,286	$271,243,740	7,718	$224,505,265	7,754	$407,793,654	7,655	$511,637,643	2,369	$240,393,903	45	% 89

bution of Sears's purchases tends more and more to parallel the distribution of Sears's sales. A speech delivered by T. V. Houser in Boston early in 1943 sheds some light on how the company has effected this gradual geographical shift in its buying:

> I suppose it is only natural that your [New England] manufacturing plant which was developed on the premise of supplying manufactured goods to a large part of the country should lose ground.... The census shows some 23 per cent loss in the ten years from 1929 to 1939. I thought a comparison of the six New England States with the Southeastern States would be interesting in emphasizing this trend. These six states show a total gain during this time of some 2 per cent. As national distributors Sears has attempted to decentralize buying so as to purchase as much as we can in the territory where it is sold. Despite this policy, we did not contribute to this loss of volume here, since our purchases in 1941 in New England were 50 per cent greater than in 1929. This amounted to over $100,000,000 at selling in 1941. However, we have here a good measure of this movement to smaller plants in smaller towns, nearer raw materials and foodstuffs, as evidenced by the fact that Sears purchased in 1929, 2.6 times the volume of sales made in the New England States, while in 1941, even though increased in amount by 50 per cent, it represented only 1.6 times the sales.
>
> Since I mentioned the Southeastern States, a comparison here again emphasizes this point. In 1929 we sold three times as much goods as we purchased in these six states, whereas by 1941 we were purchasing just as much as we were selling in these states, and we were selling 2½ times as much as in 1929.[14]

Sears's annual report for the year 1940 had earlier touched upon the same theme, when it asserted that "the Company ... has sometimes told manufacturers not only what to make and how to make it but where it should be made. And in the *where* of this counsel lies the firm's obsession with the decentralization of industry, a major plank in the platform of the Company." That report went on to nail this plank down with more specific documentation:

> For several years Sears has had no reticence about advising its sources to move closer to their necessary raw materials, to locate away from the artificial costs of operation in big cities, to gauge the point where small factories may be more efficient than large factories. It has gone further. To speed up such healthful moves, it has given financial support to manufacturers who were willing, but not able, to accept this advice: $700,000 to build a stove factory in Tennessee, $600,000 to erect a tire-factory in Mississippi. These examples, however startling, are only a few among many; if the Sears city fathers have their way these are only the birth pangs of a giant trend.

What of the sources? What do they think of this "giant trend"? How have they responded to the efforts of Wood, Nelson, and Houser to cement better source relationships? How amicably have they adapted themselves to the techniques of basic buying and to the gargantuan task of supplying more than two billion dollars' worth of goods, at selling price, to the gaping maw that is Sears? Two statements appearing ten years apart in *Fortune* magazine imply a considerable improvement in source relationships within the decade. In 1938 *Fortune* danced delicately around the subject in this oblique fashion, with "hinting darkly" overtones:

> Sears buys upwards of $400,000,000 worth of goods a year. The antimonopolists contend that by bringing this massive buying power to bear against small manufacturers and threatening to whisk it away once they have been ensnared, Sears can force them to submit to prices on which a living profit is often impossible. That Sears drives a hard bargain, that it deals mostly with small manufacturers, and that it roves the country for new sources, is indisputable; but that it makes a practice of high-pressure buying Sears denies....
>
> Sears' apologia for tight-margin contracts is a familiar one: that mass buying makes for savings in advertising, overhead, and other costs, in which the buyer is entitled to share. A manufacturer's life with Sears may be a hard one; but the company points out that of the 6,000 firms with which it does business, about 250 have been selling to Sears for twenty-five years, nearly 1,300 for over fifteen years, some 3,000 for over ten years, and nearly 4,500 for over five years.[15]

Ten years later, in 1948, *Fortune* made no mention of the "antimonopolists'" position; in a statement shorn of most of the qualification earlier evident, the magazine wrote of Sears:

> Its relations with some 8,000 suppliers are generally conceded to be among the best in industry, and in recent years this rapport has paid handsome dividends. Sears' suppliers have tried to take care of their monolithic customer and have generally shown that they approve its buying philosophy.[16]

As the two foregoing quotations indicate, the company has to a considerable extent overcome much of the hostility engendered in some manufacturers in the days when some buyers tended to court and discard them on the basis of momentary needs, but a residue of the dislike and distrust inevitably remains. Present sources run the gamut from those who are enthusiastic over their relationship to the Sears operation and feel themselves integral parts of the organization, to those understandably concerned over dealing with a large, impersonal corporation and determined never to commit a very considerable portion of their output to the company (or to any other one company).

Many sources feel some insecurity in dealing with Sears or any other very large-scale buyer because they fear that a sudden change in Sears's buyers or top officials might simply leave them out in the cold. Some manufacturers feel that the company's standards of quality are too high and that its inspections are unduly strict. Others feel that there is still too great a discrepancy between the procedures and operating practices of buyers and the over-all policies enunciated by the company.

By and large, however, most sources seem generally content with their relations with the company. Most of all, perhaps, sources like and respect the fact that Sears's buyers do not welsh on a commitment; no matter what happens to the market or business conditions generally, even a verbal "go-ahead" commitment from a Sears buyer is usually considered good. Sources also appear to like the fact that there is relatively little haggling involved in dealing with Sears's buyers. If the goods, the quality, and the price are "right"—and the Sears buyer usually knows whether they are—the company orders the goods. If any or all of those factors are not right, sources know by now not to attempt to sell Sears. This favorable attitude toward its buyers is possibly one of the firm's greatest assets and doubtless goes a long way to counteract such objections from sources as the fear and insecurity of "putting too many eggs into one basket."

One factor which makes supplying Sears attractive to many sources is the assistance in research and development extended under the basic buying program. Improvements in technique evolved in one plant working on such an order for Sears are made available to other plants. Technological advances and "short cuts" thus made available are frequently helpful to a source in his work on contracts for firms other than Sears. Also, the company is sometimes able, by applying its massive buying power, to procure materials which a single source would find it costlier to obtain. And even in instances where Sears is not furnishing material or even securing it for the manufacturer, the company's merchandise organization can offer advice, gleaned from a knowledge of nation-wide production, on where the source can obtain the materials he needs.

Yet relatively few sources are willing to commit all or the major part of their output to the company for two principal reasons. First, there is the element of insecurity already referred to, the fear of too great a degree of dependence upon an outlet which might at any time switch to another source. Second, there is the fact that the heads or top executives of many manufacturing companies have been salesmen and still remain salesmen at heart. They patiently explain to Sears's representatives that selling the goods they produce affords the greatest pleasure they have and that having a guaranteed taker for all their output would remove their greatest joy in business. This seems particularly true of sources supplying wearing apparel, intimate apparel, children's clothes, and other textile goods.

The company is itself in no position to argue cogently that any given source should commit its entire output to the mail-order house, for Sears refuses in most cases to commit itself to purchase the entire output even of its own wholly or partly owned factories. The emphasis in regard to its own factories is on trying to keep them competitive by compelling them to sell varying proportions of their product in the open market. As has been pointed out much earlier, the company's policy toward factory ownership has always been that it should be a product only of necessity; that the company should buy all or part interest in a manufacturing plant only when it was otherwise impossible to obtain the merchandise in question at what the firm considered a fair price, or when plant ownership was necessary to maintain uniform quality.

The company's "philosophy" toward factory ownership was summed up in the 1938 annual report in these words:

The company for many years has followed the policy of not increasing the number of its wholly owned factories. In cases where the volume of a particular sort of merchandise is large and the sources so limited that dependence on them might be hazardous from point of view of continuity of supply, the company has from time to time acquired partial stock ownership in such sources, which strengthens its merchandising policies.

The number of factories which Sears owns outright, or in which it owns an interest ranging from partial to controlling, has waxed and waned through the years, generally tending toward expansion in times of prosperity (when it is more difficult to obtain goods) and toward retrenchment in less happy times (when supply exceeds demand). In 1935 the company owned eighteen factories completely and owned a 50 per cent interest or less in eleven others. The total output of those factories in that year was valued at $37,272,183, of which $23,012,458 of goods was sold to Sears, the remainder to outsiders. Seven per cent of the firm's total sales in 1935 came in goods made in company-owned factories.

The company's 1940 annual report outlined the extent of its ownership of factories and at the same time hinted at reasons for not increasing such ownership: "In 1940 Sears owned 14 factories and had a minority interest in quite a few others. The pain and melancholy which occasionally descend on those who undertake the manufacture of goods are by no means unknown to Sears." Five years later the company's factory investment stood at $10,640,000, and in 1946 it climbed to $14,390,024. In the latter year thirteen wholly owned plants and some twenty-five partly owned factories shipped Sears some $205,000,000 of goods, 12 per cent of total sales. The thirteen wholly owned plants provided Sears with $36,135,000 of goods, 70 per cent of their total production. By 1947 Sears's investment in wholly owned factories alone was $29,300,000, and those factories produced $62,900,000 of goods; of this output, Sears took $44,000,000. And the output of partially owned factories swelled this $44,000,000 to $334,000,000, or 16 per cent of total sales that year.

Total annual profits (before bonuses, taxes, and profit-sharing) from Sears wholly owned factories increased from $840,721 in 1935 to $1,821,886 in 1937 but declined sharply to $406,193 in 1938. Factory profits recovered in 1939, amounting to $2,403,303. In 1940 there was a moderate increase to $2,939,929, and 1941 brought the figure to its high point of $4,111,173.

Sears wholly owned factories in 1940 (eleven in number) manufactured such items as radio cabinets, farm implements, sashes, doors, and other building materials, paints and varnishes, and furniture. The thirty-one wholly and partly owned (or "affiliated") plants produced such goods as rock wool, automobile and truck tires, vacuum cleaners, hardware, stoves, roofing, batteries and spark plugs, insulators, radios, washing machines, cast-iron enamelware, bathtubs, refrigerators, pottery, automobile seat covers, bedsprings, mattresses, and other items.

When Germany invaded Poland in 1939, the company surveyed all its wholly owned and affiliated factories with a view to eventual conversion to war production. The contents of each such factory survey included such factors as geographical location, transportation facilities, plant capacity, products being made, products to which the plant could be adapted, manufacturing equipment, labor pool, and related details. This information was submitted in the form of brochures to the various branches of the armed services and, as they were established, to the defense agencies in Washington. The government was thus furnished early with a rather complete picture of the status and capacities of the Sears factories, and by 1940 some of the affiliated factories were working on "defense" orders.

Conversion of the Sears factories to war production proved literally to be a matter of beating plowshares into swords; the David Bradley farm-implement plant was among the earliest to convert. The general pattern of conversion followed the familiar outlines: from stoves to antiaircraft shells, from refrigerators to cartridge cases. The total volume of war production by the Sears factories was not immense; its significance lay more in the fact that conversion of the plants to a war footing inevitably operated to reduce (and, in many cases, to eliminate entirely) the production of civilian goods which were the backbone of Sears's merchandise structure. Actually, of course, the plants would have been lost to civilian production anyway through prohibitions on the use of scarce materials and the tightness of the manpower pool.

As prohibitions on the use of various critical materials were decreed by war-production agencies, and as other materials became progressively in shorter supply, the company's merchandise development department revealed extraordinary ingenuity in evolving substitutes, adapting to synthetic materials, and even redesigning some products. For months Sears's engineers stayed one jump ahead of priorities. For example, when stainless steel went on the priority list, Sears switched to chrome-plated steel. When chrome was added to the list of critical materials, the company utilized painted steel. When steel was made unavailable for nonessential goods, Sears adopted butyrate plastic and, when this was ruled out, wood. Throughout the war the company placed increasingly greater emphasis on the use of wood, glass, and ceramics.

"Substitute" material goods were an important enough factor as early as late 1942 to lead the company to identify all such items in all its inventories (mail order, retail stores, and pool stocks) with the designation "XX." Monthly records showed the exact dollar value of all such items on hand. As the end of the war loomed in sight in 1944, instructions were issued for clearance of all "XX" merchandise with little regard to markdowns and losses. By the end of that year most of the "XX" goods were sold or donated to charitable organizations.

Possibly the least successful of the company's war-born innovations was its "convertible" Coldspot electric refrigerator. This box, made of non-critical materials, was designed to use ice for the duration of the war; when relaxation of controls made it possible to resume production of freezing units, the customer who had bought a "convertible" could simply purchase the freezing unit and convert from ice to electric refrigeration. Customers failed to respond in any great numbers to this innovation.

The end of the war and a return to more or less normal conditions permitted the merchandise organization to turn its efforts from substitute materials and products to peacetime quality, "regular" goods and to give closer attention to its selling functions. The company had realized, even if not clearly, that its use of its own brand names was an important element in selling, but its progress in the most effective use of brand names had been halting and lacking in direction and cohesion. Even Richard Sears, promoter that he was, was slow to realize the full importance of the utilization of brand names.

Curiously, even the watches which were the base on which Richard Sears had built his mail-order business never carried strenuously promoted trade-names. Sears apparently made no effort to coin his own names and to market his watches and jewelry under them. Even as late as 1893, for instance, the catalogue devoted half a page to a "Stem-Wind Watch for $1.68," with glowing tribute to its value—but without any name. And in the following year, when the leader in this department was priced at $1.15, that watch was only incidentally referred to in small type as "our Victoria Patent Wind, Nickel Watch," made by the New Haven Clock Company. In 1895, when $38.95 bought "A $100.00 Organ," one had to read far down the column to find it was named "Our Peerless." In that same catalogue men's suits, ladies' boots and shoes, sewing machines, buggies, furniture, and other items appeared without any identifying brand names. The stoves and bicycles did have brand names—very unimaginative ones such as "Sunshine" for the stoves ("Sunshine Square," "Merry Sunshine," "Box Sunshine," "Bright Sunshine") and "Electric" for the bicycles ("Electric No. 4" and "Electric No. 5").

All that period was, of course, prior to Richard Sears's great promotions. It is significant that, when sewing-machine sales reached great heights, that item carried its brand name in huge letters: "Minnesota" (which later gave way to "Franklin"). Sears's stoves, bicycles, buggies, stock foods, and many other items were identified by some trade-name, and those names were shouted to the skies in all the company's advertising—the "Minnesota," five-drawer, drop-leaf sewing machine—"Beckwith" pianos and organs, "Elgin" bicycles, "Acme" stoves, and others. The electric belt was promoted under the name "Heidelberg." All patent medicines, of course, carried prominent brand names, possibly because Sears was discovering the importance of promoting such names and also perhaps because so many of the specifics were labeled "Dr. So-and-so's Wonder Remedy." The cream separator which was so widely promoted was named, aptly, the "Economy." Stock foods, which failed so disastrously, bore the "H. O. Davis" label. In these same years the first great efforts of national advertisers were bent to the promotion of trade names.[17]

The 1907 Dallas catalogue was replete with such names as "Our Texas Special Double Driving Harness," the "Denison" plow harness, the "Pasco" saddle (as well as "San Antonio," "El Paso," "Pan Handle," and other saddles), the "Texas Queen" buggy, etc. Nearly every item in that book not already named and promoted prior to the opening of the Dallas branch was given a Texas place name or bore the word "Southwest." Stoves, organs and pianos, cream separators, sewing machines, and a few other items with already established brand names escaped the "Texas" touch. Even so, it appears that in this instance Richard Sears was less interested in promoting brand names as such than in appealing to local pride in every possible way. Items in the grocery department were always profusely labeled, and the brand names were exploited, but the names relied upon connotations of bucolic swank rather than of description: "Montclair," "Rivera," "Kingston."

Among the earliest trade-names still extant is the "David Bradley" line of farm equipment. Sears, Roebuck bought this factory early, when satisfactory sources for plows and allied equipment could not be found. Another early name, "Pilgrim" (for men's shirts, ties, underwear, and other accessories), still survives; possibly to help establish it, the front cover of a general catalogue depicted the landing of the Pilgrims. One of the early attempts to tie in the company's name with one of its merchandise lines was the use of "Seroco" for paints. "Lo-cost" was another name applied to paints. Both these brand names were followed by "Master White" (for outside white house paint) and finally by "Master-Mixed," which today identifies most Sears outside paints even though some types still carry the "Seroco" label. The "J. C. Higgins" trade-name (taken from the name of a company executive) was coined early for application to many sporting-goods items and later extended to the complete line including bicycles.

The large sales of "Silvertone" phonographs and, after World War I, radios helped make the company "name-conscious," but still there was no over-all program for brand-naming, which remained for many years a hit-or-miss business. Little effort was expended to plan and systematize the application or exploitation of brand names on an intelligently directed basis. Almost any buyer, assistant buyer, copywriter, or anyone in similar position could coin a brand name pretty much on the spur of the moment and apply it to any given item or merchandise line.

For a while it was the policy in some departments to add a new name for each new line. Thus overalls were sold under the name "Hercules," with "Double Duty" representing the second grade and "Sturdy Oak" the third. Substantial confusion was added when a fourth line was christened

"Drum Major." Following the success of various substitutes for linoleum, there developed an eagerness in the trade to sell "hard surface" floor coverings; Sears branded its line "Floor-O-Leum." (These names were, however, eventually discarded because of the plan to establish "Harmony House" as the one over-all brand name for home furnishings.)

The expansion of the repertoire of brand names paralleled the great and finally unwieldy merchandise expansion. The subsequent reduction of redundant assortments and greater concentration on the assortments retained were ultimately to lead to a similar overhauling of the company's brand names and to the institution of a carefully conceived policy in this respect. Vice-President Houser asserts that the policy of permitting "anyone who thought up a brand name to put it on the product" had resulted in the company's having "hundreds if not thousands of trade-names used on Sears's products." Another executive, in a memorandum prepared in 1936, put the number of brand names at around four hundred at the time, of which some three hundred were in general use. There were also many unregistered trade-names in use in Sears, registration having been refused by the Patent Office.

Despite this increasing abundance of brand names, which meant that the company's promotional efforts were being scattered over a wide field, there were forces at work leading to a change. For one thing, Sears had been developing many of its own products, at considerable expense. The company's merchandisers felt that, with Sears's extensive and continuing contact with customers, it had a great advantage if it could marshal all its talent to capitalize upon its knowledge of what customers wanted and needed in the way of products designed for them. Product design was also induced by the desire to avoid comparison and unpleasant and embarrassing issues in another respect. According to one executive, Sears's price-cutting had grown to be tolerated by manufacturers, who could take a certain amount of it when the price-cutting was confined to the catalogues. But this price-cutting was more hazardous, from the manufacturers' point of view, when a Sears retail store engaged in it; a store located on the same street with competition selling the same item brought the problem closer to home than did the catalogue. And merely putting a Sears brand name on the identical product did not alleviate the situation; the Sears brand name had to mean more than simply a change of stencil or name of a product.

Retailing thus inspired a change of policy in regard both to product development and to brand names. And the increasingly severe shortage of space in retail stores, with resultant emphasis on better space utilization through better display, also in time prompted a reduction in the number of brand names in order that each of fewer names could be given more intensive promotion. The 1930's were attended, if not by a reduction of the total number of brand names, then at least by somewhat more thoughtful selection and exploitation of them by the company. One of its most successful efforts in brand-naming—the Allstate tire—came even earlier, in 1926, but that name was the fruit of a prize contest designed largely as an instrument of sales promotion. "Allstate" was later extended to automobile supplies, accessories, and insurance.

The development of its own new electric refrigerator in the early 1930's, however, led the company's merchandisers to careful thinking and planning. Discarding several variations of "Polar," "Icy," and "Frigid," Sears finally settled upon "Coldspot." How much of that refrigerator's subsequent great success was attributable to its happy brand-naming is, of course, a rather moot point.

But the Coldspot did touch off more activity in brand names for other lines. The hardware department was among the first to begin concentrating on its most profitable items to the subordination or exclusion of those which accounted for a smaller percentage of the sales volume and profits. Hand in hand with that trend went increasing stress on evolving better brand names for hardware, names which would lend themselves to better promotion. Working around its power-tool line, the hardware department first tried such brand names as "Master Craftsman" and "Master Craft" before settling on the simpler "Craftsman." Even so, the policy in that one department was not yet refined very highly, for "Dunlap" (named for the head buyer in the hardware department at the time) was used to denote the "Better" line, and "Fulton" for the "Good" line, thus still leaving three brand names to be exploited in connection with one department.

Other departments similarly overhauled their own brand names, though apparently not in conformity with any established policy. The drug and cosmetics department, after some fifteen years of trying such names as "Lady Janis" and others, finally decided upon "Ann Barton" for its cosmetics line. "Sears Approved" replaced "Dr. Walters" and "Challenge" on drugs. Shoes were sold under a variety of names for years, including "Dr. Case," "Dr. Johnson," "Good Luck," "Shod Rite," "Civil Service," "Green Grip," and, for men's work shoes, "Construction Boss." "Gold Bond" was ultimately chosen as the brand name for men's shoes; women's shoes were labeled "Kerrybrooke," which term also applied to all women's outer wearing apparel. "Kerrybrooke" had replaced a welter of names including "Desirables," "Adorables," and "Junior Miss." For a while the difference in mail-order and retail prices led the company to sell some items under two brand names, one for mail order and one for retail. "Water Witch" mail-order washing machines, for example, were sold in retail stores under the "Kenmore" name.

As mentioned earlier, manufacturers' objections to Sears's price-cutting on some items had been one of the factors inducing the company to undertake development of its own products. Even so, the company could still indulge in a considerable amount of price-cutting—until the passage of the "fair-trade" legislation. That legislation not only spurred on the company's product development but also underscored the importance of keying such developments to its own brand names in order to be able to continue selling goods at the prices it wished to set on them.

In 1945 the company at last decided that major surgery was called for to thin out its growth of brand names and to rationalize the whole structure. In that year a committee appointed for the purpose attempted to reduce the list of Sears's own brand names to less than fifty (shown in

TABLE 60*
BRAND NAMES PROPOSED IN 1945

ALLSTATE—Automobile and truck tires and accessories
BILTWELL—Children's shoes
BOYVILLE—Boys' clothing
CHARMODE—Women's intimate apparel
COLDSPOT—Electric household refrigerators and home freezers
CRAFTSMAN and DUNLAP—Tools
DAVID BRADLEY—Farm implements
ELGIN—Boats and outboard motors
FAIRLOOM—Piece goods
FARM-MASTER—Farm supplies
FASHION TAILORED—Men's clothing
FRATERNITY PREP—Older boys' clothing
GALE—"Support" corsets
GARDEN MASTER—Garden supplies
GOLD BOND—Men's and youths' shoes
HAPPI-TIME—Toys
HARMONY HOUSE—Home furnishings
HEARTHSIDE—Notions
HERCULES—Work clothing
HERITAGE—Memorials
HOMART—Plumbing, heating, and builders' supplies
HONEYLANE—Girls' clothing
HONEYSUCKLE—Small girls' clothing, furniture, and accessories

J. C. HIGGINS—Sporting goods
KENMORE—Washing machines, stoves, vacuum cleaners, and small electrical appliances
KERRYBROOKE—Women's outer wear and accessories
MAID OF HONOR—Housewares and cleaning supplies
MASTER-MIXED—Paints
PILGRIM—Men's furnishings
RANGER—Cameras and photo supplies
ROYAL PURPLE—Women's hosiery
SEARS "APPROVED"—Drugs
SILVERTONE—Musical instruments and radios
TOWER—Office equipment, school supplies, watches
TRADITION—Diamond rings
WEARMASTER—Men's and youths' work shoes
WEBSTER—Fountain pens
WORKMASTER—Painters' and paperhangers' supplies
YORKSHIRE—Smokers' articles

* Source: Company records and catalogues.

Table 60) and enunciated a policy for the peripheral area around the use of brand names. That subsequent practice did not entirely conform to the committee's recommendation is evident from a perusal of post-1945 catalogues, which list a number of brand names not included in the 1945 listing. There are, however, markedly fewer brand names than prevailed before the committee studied the problem.

A company publication titled *Revitalizing a National Selling Machine* appeared in 1946 and contained a summary of trade-name policy. Items were thenceforth to bear only one name, to apply in both retail and mail order. Subnames were not to be used to identify single items or to denote quality difference; instead of selling "Challenge," "Merit," and "Bestmade Fre-zee-zee's," Sears would sell "Maid of Honor" ice-cream freezers in several quality levels. In lieu of "Wondervalue," "Launderite," "Super Launderite," or "Guest Chamber" muslin sheets, Sears would offer "Harmony House" muslin sheets "woven to give 3, 5, or 7 years of wear." Wherever possible, this type of description would be used to express trade-ups; e.g., "2-ply, 3-ply, 5-ply"; "5 h-p., 10 h-p."; "light, medium, heavy"; "guaranteed for 12 months, 18 months, 21 months"; etc. "One-time" and special-buy merchandise would, however, be allowed to carry a name other than that governing the particular line, in order to indicate its special and transient nature.

The *common* name under which any item was to be advertised, displayed, or sold, under the *over-all* name, had to be the name by which it would be most probably identified anywhere. That is, Sears was to offer a pressure cooker, not a "Kook Kwick"; an electric rotary tool, not a "Crafty Jack-of-all-Trades." "Synthetic" words were to be eschewed, even in denoting quality differences; "distorted" words like "Fit Mor" for socket wrenches were to be taboo. When the trade-up involved an accumulation of merchandise factors impossible to express in a simple phrase or sentence, more extensive descriptive copy was to be employed, as well as the company's system of three colors—green, red, and blue, with the trade-up from green to red to blue (the highest quality).

Items requiring identification by pattern—such as silverware, china, and glassware—were allowed to continue using pattern names, although pattern numbers were considered preferable (as in yard goods). Merchandise of nationally known materials (nylon, for example) or processed by nationally advertised methods (Sanforized shrunk) could be so denoted. Style terms used throughout the fashion industry and generally understood by the consumer were also acceptable: "Chesterfield" for coats, "snap-brimmed" for hats, etc. Brand names which had been discarded in the overhauling could be utilized for "a limited period of time" provided they had gained real consumer acceptance and provided they were subordinated to the new over-all name. "Kenmore" electric irons, for instance, could carry "Formerly Heatmaster" in small type.

The fall and winter 1946–47 general catalogue was the first book to reflect the new policy on brand names. In the books issued since that one, there appears a steady falling-off in the keying of abandoned names to those on the approved list, possibly an indication that the company senses consumer acceptance of the approved names. But as for the edict that "distorted" and "synthetic" words were not to be employed, the results have fallen short. Many such banned terms appeared even as late as the fall 1948 book.

While the postwar rationalization of the company's brand names did thus reduce the number of such names it used, it had little effect on the amount of the company's merchandise carrying "outside" brand names, for Sears had much earlier ceased to stock more than a very few items bearing other brands. Most of those few were found in the drug and cosmetics line or in watches, cigarette lighters, cameras, typewriters, and a negligibly few others. Several reasons underlie Sears, Roebuck's policy of promoting its own brands. Selling others' brands does not, for instance, help build Sears's own reputation; further, the company has refused to risk dependence upon an "outside" branded source, from which it might conceivably be cut off at any time. Sears further feels that its own quality is at least as reliable as that of the most widely advertised other brands and that the tremendous amount of advertising it puts behind its own brands (through the general catalogues and retail-store newspaper advertisements, for example) is equal to, or greater than, that of most other national advertisers. Also, since the company unconditionally guarantees its own goods, it feels that it must have its own standards of quality and be able at all times to control that quality. Finally, of course, there is the fact that Sears's whole merchandising operation is posited primarily upon the goods it procures through basic or specification buying, and in this respect it has invested too much money in merchandise development to fail to capitalize upon it through the exploitation of its own brands.

Sears's use of its own brand names was also a considerable factor in the reorientation of its merchandise structure, which centered largely upon reducing the number of price lines and definitions of levels of quality. In most merchandise lines the number is now limited to three—"Good," "Better," and "Best"—with the company's own brand name symbolizing the whole line.

The best-selling items are incorporated, by intent and design, in the "Better" category. This price level contains the widest variety of assortments as well as the best gross margin. Inventory investment concentration on those best-selling items also makes for less frequent "out-of-stocks," the bane of any store, and for an easier and more effective control of gross margin. For if the gross margin on the best sellers is adequate—not only for itself, but also to cover possible loss on beginning, or promotional, numbers—the whole gross-margin problem nears solution.

The relatively limited number of price lines carried by Sears is, of course, no innovation in mass merchandising; most successful chains adopted the practice even before Sears. The idea was advocated for department stores as early as 1930 by the Boston merchant, Edward A. Filene.[18] He proceeded upon the truism that "every producer, every distributor, and every buyer is faced with this problem—how to have the right goods, in quantities neither too great nor too small, at the times when they will be desired most, and at prices which will sell best." Sears's pursuance of price-lining coupled with exploitation of its own brand names contributed much to inventory control, for the avoidance of national brands obviated the necessity for carrying products of similar quality and price points of a number of "nationally known" manufacturers.

CHAPTER XXIV

Merchandising Influences and Adventures

THE company's annual report for 1940, twenty-four large pages in color plus a twelve-page folded insert using illustrations to amplify the balance-sheet figures, reviewed the history of Sears, Roebuck and Company in broad outline from the day Richard W. Sears sold his first watch. That report stated:

The course and direction of Sears' merchandising since the birth of the retail system has not changed but the river-bed has broadened and the stream feeds a market which has been multiplied by four.

For example, retail stores provided access to an incomparably bigger buying public for electrical and mechanical equipment than the company had ever known. The stronger demand in these lines stimulated the development of a better product. Some of the company's noteworthy triumphs in merchandise development were hastened by the opportunities which retail presented for the sale of such items as electric refrigerators, electric washing machines and vacuum cleaners, heating plants, plumbing installations, radios and gas and electric stoves. The rapid climb of the firm to leadership as a distributor of automobile tires and accessories was due largely (apart from the fact that in the middle twenties a superlative product was developed) to the selling avenues opened by the new retail market.

The growth of retail patronage induced greater emphasis upon the style consideration in all categories of merchandise although this movement was in progress during many years when the company was exclusively mail order. Style consultants were hired for the ready-to-wear, piece goods, and various home furnishings departments, among others, and outside experts were occasionally called in. But this was the continuation, not the inception of a policy, for the rural market has not been insensitive to the style factor in its appraisal of merchandise. (Sears merchants are aware that farm folk are not so different from city folk as most of the learned authorities seem to believe. They have an unusually high level of taste and intelligence. They are well informed and yield nothing to their city cousins in their desire to live in attractive homes and wear fetching clothes. Except that they perhaps do not react quite so quickly or violently to new style trends, they have, within the same income groupings, about the same appreciation for fashion and eye appeal in the things they buy.)

As the foregoing indicates, the company's entry into the retail field constituted one of the two greatest single influences upon its merchandise line. The other of those great influences, still to come when the 1940 annual report was written, was World War II. The former influence was the greatest and, obviously, the first; its effects had been registered in very nearly complete terms before the influence of the war, with its many shortages and enforced substitutions, made itself felt. And retail has been an effective influence ever since 1925, while the effects of the war were transient and lasted but four to five years.

The embarkation upon the retail sea had coincided with, and been accompanied by, many powerful forces at work in the period following 1925. These forces strongly influenced the character of the merchandise line. Engineers, within and without the company, were developing a galaxy of new mechanical and electrical appliances and were improving and redesigning established products. New synthetic products came on the market—rayon, nylon, synthetic resins, plastics. Concurrently with these developments—arising from them and, in turn, contributing to them—came changes in public taste: a trend toward a greater *joie de vivre*, a desire for lighter and prettier house furnishings to supplant the somber items of an earlier generation. There also came a greater participation in outdoor activities, ranging from canoeing and hiking to baseball, tennis, golf, and similar sports. A general rise in factory wages, coupled with progressively shorter hours, also spurred the movement to the out of doors. Coincident with these changes in working conditions came an improvement in shop cleanliness, which was reflected in heavier purchases of matched work shirts and trousers. And America was "streamlined" during this period; automobiles underwent radical changes in design, for example, and the result was a steady change in the type and character of automotive supplies.

All these influences made themselves felt, sooner or later, in Sears's merchandise offerings. Sears, as always, catered to the mass market, and the foregoing changes influenced the mass market more directly than, say, increases in taxes affected the "carriage trade" by making villas on the Riviera prohibitive. The company responded, perforce, to those influences. In the early years of retail there was, as has been demonstrated, some divergence between retail and mail-order merchandise offerings. The efforts to support the retail venture fully by providing the lines and items demanded by over-the-counter customers exerted a great effect upon mail-order merchandise, until gradually the two became very nearly as one. The quality and variety of mail-order merchandise were brought up to the level demanded by retail, and this improvement in catalogue offerings was (as has been pointed out) accompanied by a complete overhauling of the merchandise structure, by elimination of fringe price lines and emphasizing complete assortments in most popular price lines. By the middle or late thirties, mail-order and retail merchandise had pretty well been integrated; mail order still carried some "rated number" items which retail did not stock, but the quantity of items carrying "basic numbers" had been so increased as to cover most of both mail-order and retail goods and to guarantee that items constituting the backbone of the whole merchandise structure would appear in both outlets.

Therefore the catalogue merchandise came to be increasingly representative of both mail-order and retail merchandise. And since catalogue space is an accurate barometer, by and large, of what is selling in what volume, a survey of the catalogues since 1925 affords a satisfactory running picture of the general nature of Sears's merchandise line in this period.

Venetian blinds first appeared in the catalogue in the spring of 1934, when one-sixth of a page was taken to list them, in three widths and in six-foot lengths, in wood only. By 1941 this item filled three pages, in rotogravure, and was listed in wood, steel, and fiber. The war removed the blinds from the catalogue in 1944, but they reappeared in the spring of 1947, in wood, steel, and aluminum. A therapeutic lamp was offered for the first time in 1927, with one listing of a hand type at $2.98. By the fall of 1930, there were seven such items, occupying a full page and running a price gamut from $2.60 to $14.50. A "sun-ray" lamp, at $42.50, was added in 1931. The 1941 book included nine listings under this item, with the "sun lamp" priced at $26.95 and a violet-ray one at $10.50, but all such lamps soon joined the list of wartime casualties. The spring 1938 catalogue accorded half a page to electric razors, of three types, but the fall book of that year saw them hold a full page, with the ten choices running from $6.95 to $15.00. In three years' time the space allocation had shrunk by exactly half, but the least expensive of the five razors offered was priced at only $4.95. After a wartime blackout, electric razors reappeared in the spring of 1947; selections were down to three, all of the Schick brand, but prices up ($7.95–$18.00).

The oil lamp managed to survive this era of great electrification and still occupied half a page in 1947, even though some of the models had by then been designed to resemble closely electric table lamps. Radios (first listed, in 1919, under "telegraphic instruments") rose to fill twenty-four pages, fifteen of them in rotogravure, by 1941. In that year battery sets still outnumbered electric models in the catalogue, but by 1947 electric models strongly predominated, and frequency modulation sets were offered as well.

Wearing apparel reflected an increasing trend toward casualness, brighter colors, and more "daring" effects. From a 1935 low near the ankles, skirts rose almost to the knee by 1940 and managed to remain near there until 1948's "new look" drove them down again. Higher waist lines showed up for the first time in the catalogue in 1932, and the spring of 1936 saw the first listing of women's slacks and shorts. Jodhpurs first appeared in 1931, but a decade elapsed before the bra-top playsuit with bare midriff showed up. Women's open-toed shoes arrived in 1937; zippers entered women's dresses the following year; and both open backs and cuban heels appeared in 1939. This latter year also witnessed the arrival of platform shoes, which was ushered in as a play shoe but rapidly became a "dress" item. Throughout these years, too, scarves and kerchiefs tended to replace hats in women's wear.

Boned corsets, extremely popular during the fad of the boyish figure, lost ground during the depression years, but elastic corsets gradually attained popularity in the middle and late thirties. The sweater girl was born (more properly, perhaps, unveiled) in the thirties, and brassières featuring the uplift and "contour molding" became popular. On the more intimate side—if such there be—heavy-weight underwear and lingerie gave way to garments which emphasized warmth without weight, and even men's and boys' underwear reflected this trend. At the same time, however, Sears became pretty much the "residual legatee" of the "old-fashioned" underwear business, as it continued to cater to those of its customers who refused to bow to newer trends. Most of the catalogue trade in underwear continued to be in cotton garments, but rayon and then silk came to hold a more prominent place. By 1948 about 80 per cent of women's underwear listed by the company was of rayon.

Women's hosiery furnishes a good example of the development and impact of new synthetic products. Virtually all stockings sold through the catalogue up to 1940 were of silk; rayon did not sell well, and cotton hose sales were rapidly declining, possibly because Sears was able to offer full-fashioned silk stockings for as little as 39 cents per pair. Nylon hosiery was introduced in 1940 and, despite its higher price, soon began to edge out silk. When the government "froze" silk in 1941, nylon sales zoomed, but nylon also joined the prohibited list in 1942. Only rayon was left, and large numbers of women preferred to paint their legs rather than revert to rayon stockings. Sears's summer 1944 catalogue listed five such leg paints under names ranging from "Harriet Hubbard Ayer Stocking Lotion" to the more prosaic "Duration Leg-Do." The reappearance of nylon hosiery in 1946 gave the kiss of death to the "leg-do's."

Men's clothing moved after 1925 away from formal, close-fitting, blue and oxford-gray serge to more comfortable, colorful, loose-fitting sportswear. Bright-hued "loafer" coats, worn with contrasting slacks, became more and more popular. These same years witnessed a near revolution in the American kitchen. Cooking, laundry, and house-cleaning materials were redesigned for better performance and better appearance and adorned in bright colors, as were all other kitchen accessories from curtains to "step-on" garbage cans. Pressure cookers reduced the time spent in the kitchen, while also better preserving the vitamin and mineral content of foods. Home canning was likewise made easier and faster.

The catalogue's bedroom furniture in 1932 was in elaborate two-tone finish or colored enamels; by 1939 the styles were more varied and included Eighteenth-Century English, Modern, and Colonial. The 1932 living-room designs were all heavily overstuffed and in matching suites with floral, reversible cushions. By 1939 Duncan Phyfe, Lawson, Chippendale, and Modern were in vogue, and sofas and other pieces could be purchased separately. The same years saw large kitchen cabinets give way to ensembles and built-in types, with complete units sold as "packages." Wooden lawn furniture was steadily replaced by all-steel items, with chaise longues and lawn umbrellas becoming more popular. Tubular aluminum has, since the war, become the leading item in this line.

The ingrain and granite carpets listed in the 1932 catalogue long since ceased to sell or even to be manufactured. In that year Sears offered a plain-color, seamless broadloom carpet in velvet weave, 9 × 12 feet, for $28.95 (by 1947, that rug, even though in brighter colors, cost $69.00). Curtains, drapes, bedspreads, and slip covers likewise blossomed out in a riot of color after 1925 and in fact became essentially more decorative than protective in nature. While such items as damask hangings lost ground, the old chenille bedspreads firmly held their own.

The general home decoration scheme promoted by Sears under the name of "Harmony House" not only brightened and standardized the colors of all such home furnishings as those just mentioned but also brought together under one grouping various merchandise lines previously scattered among several departments: lamps, mirrors, pictures, dinnerware, glassware, and giftware. Each of these items changed considerably in design after the mid-1920's, but all continued to sell briskly. Lamps, for example, reflected the trend toward indirect lighting, and fluorescent fixtures became more and more popular. Venetian (unframed) mirrors now sell in twice the volume as the framed models, and even the frames of the latter type have been modernized. The Harmony House department also came to include crystal glass tableware designed and made solely for Sears. Stemware assortments increased, and monogrammed glassware was added about 1932. Heat-treated tumblers are now featured in the big book. All the glassware, as well as dinnerware, became more graceful as the "gingerbread" of an earlier period was sloughed off. Patterns in dinnerware design were extended through kitchenware and accessories, offering an opportunity for harmony of color and design on a wider scale.

In the toy department, even dolls were indicative of the period. Dolls with rubber arms and legs were introduced in 1932, followed in the succeeding year by all rubber dolls. "Mickey Mouse" watches were introduced in 1934 and were highly successful, an indication of Walt Disney's impact upon children. The real banner year for toys, however, was 1935, when the "Shirley Temple" doll made its debut (replicas of the Dionne quintuplets in dolls, brought out in 1936, were not nearly so popular). The wetting doll, that dubious blessing, also came out in 1935, as did streamlined wagons, trains, and automobiles in toy form. The personalized trend continued, with "Charley McCarthy" and "Sonja Henie" dolls in 1939. In 1937 rubber toys in the form of farm implements were extremely popular; in four years' time the vogue switched to tanks and machine guns and dive-bombers.

From 1932 to 1936, 95 per cent of the fiction books sold from the catalogue consisted of reprints priced from 63 to 87 cents. The most popular authors in that period were Gene Stratton Porter, Edgar Rice Burroughs,

Harold Bell Wright, Peter B. Kyne, Zane Grey, and Ethel M. Dell (of these, only Grey's works are still featured, along with those of Grace Livingston Hill), while best sellers included *Anthony Adverse, Magnificent Obsession, It Can't Happen Here,* and *North to the Orient.* The 1948 catalogue included such authors as James M. Cain and Dashiell Hammett. Emily Post's *Etiquette,* a best seller in 1932, was selling at an even brisker rate in 1948, and Hoyle's *Book of Games* also retained its popularity. Present best sellers in the fiction list are offered through the Peoples Book Club.

The hardware line featured such items as electric drills, acetylene and electric welders, power saws, and similar items, as there was a lessening of demand for blacksmiths' drills, blow torches, and hand-turned grindstones. Lawn-mowers acquired rubber tires in the last fifteen years, and use of the molding process for garden hose made it possible to produce that item in lengths up to 500 feet as against the standard 50-foot lengths of earlier days. All vacuum cleaners in the 1937 catalogue were of the rotary brush type, with the best seller priced at less than $24, but by 1941 the newer tank models predominated even at a price $15 higher. Changes in design of automobiles wreaked similar change in Sears's automotive supplies. Floor mats moved away from the flat type as the center of gravity in cars was dropped lower and lower, so that the mats had to fit the new contours of the floors and to accommodate the drive shaft and transmission. Radiator hose was produced in semiuniversal sections from which hose could be cut in various ways to fit different makes of cars.

Automobile tops, side curtains, and similar accessories were prominently listed in 1932 but finally disappeared in 1942. Clocks and rear-view mirrors enjoyed a heyday, but the market for them shrank when automobile manufacturers began to include them as standard equipment on many models. When fancier grillwork appeared on the front of automobiles, however, it created a large market for replacement grills and for bumper guards to protect the grills. When temperature gauges were installed in the dashboards of cars, this eliminated a market for Sears, but this was later offset by the market created for metal and plastic rims to simulate white side-walls on tires when those items became a war casualty.

In 1939 automobile-makers began equipping cars with sealed-beam headlights, in which the filament, lens, and reflector were sealed in a self-contained unit. Sears developed a sealed-beam conversion kit in 1940 to enable owners of older cars to equip them with the sealed-beam headlights. By 1946, when the peak of sales of conversion kits was reached, several million sets had been sold out of an estimated market of about ten million. Another development since 1932 was the change from replacement of individual parts to replacement of entire units. Instead of replacing, say, one part of a carburetor, a customer could order a rebuilt carburetor and receive a trade-in allowance on his own carburetor. So with fuel pumps, distributors, generators, and so on, even including engines.

Bicycles also underwent some changes in design and improvements. Two chief factors emerged in connection with this item. First, women now buy some 40 per cent of the bicycles the company sells, whereas in 1931 only one woman's model was listed. Second, the public wants no major changes in the appearance of bicycles. During the late thirties, Sears spent substantial amounts in an ambitious effort to redesign completely its bicycles, both in line and in color schemes. In the words of one of the former key executives closely associated with this fiasco, "they didn't even look like bicycles when we got through." The ultra-streamlined lines and the rainbow color pattern, including pastels in all colors, did not appeal to customers. As that same executive puts it, "We learned two things: the Sears public wants its bicycles to look just like bicycles always looked; and, second, boys want red bicycles, girls blue. No other colors will sell in any degree worth bothering about."

Farm implements underwent a slower and far more successful process of change than did bicycles. Farm work was greatly speeded up in the 1930's—cultivation up to six miles an hour, plowing speeds of four to six miles an hour, harrowing up to twelve miles an hour. Flat-bed wagons of all-steel construction, mounted on rubber tires and roller bearings, can be drawn by horse or tractor, and milking machines have been made lighter and faster. Most other farm tools and equipment have been redesigned to give greater strength with less weight, better performance at relatively lower cost. One boon to farmers was the company's used-tire program. All "David Bradley" implements were designed to take the same wheels and roll on rubber; farmers could use on them tires which were no longer safe for use on automobiles. Few tires were needed, since even the wheels were interchangeable.

Sears, Roebuck's merchandise line during the years since 1925 has generally been typical of its line in all other periods in one basic respect: the company has almost never been an innovator in products. It has generally been content to let others pioneer. As *Fortune* magazine has pointed out:

Sears, Roebuck, growing up in an age that produces some new mechanical marvel, such as a radio, an electric icebox, a washing machine, every year, has wisely waited until the popularity of the icebox, the radio or whatnot has grown, through the pioneering efforts of other manufacturers, substantial roots in American buying soil before trying to sell it on a large scale to its own customers. . . .
. . . the Catalogue walks very warily or not at all into untried fields. An important household article breaks into those pages only some time after it has made a dent in the nation's consciousness.[1]

What was true in 1932—as that statement surely was—has remained generally true ever since, with a few exceptions. One such exception occurred in 1947, when the company's merchandise development department released a home wire-recorder—an instrument which had *not* yet demonstrated widespread popular acceptance or, indeed, any popular acceptance at all. The development of wire-recorders had been largely a war phenomenon, and the civilian market for them remained substantially unknown. The wire-recorder marked the company's first such venture into unexplored territory. As such, it could conceivably be the harbinger of a new pattern which would mark a sharp reversal of policy. Or it could be just a "sport," not to be repeated for a long while—and a "sport" it turned out to be.

Even if this be just the exception which proves the rule, other facets of that truism quoted from *Fortune* remain similarly true. Sears, Roebuck's 1948 furniture offerings, for example, were manifestly far superior to those of 1925; but, by sophisticated standards of taste, they still left much to be desired. The simple truth, and the important one, is that the taste and style level of Sears's merchandise, whether in furniture or misses' dresses, is on a par with the taste of the bulk of its customers. That way lie profits and long life, if not the furtherance of the arts.

The most awesome event of this century, which threatened not only profits and the arts but even life itself, was of course World War II. The effects of that struggle upon Sears, Roebuck's merchandise structure were profound even if, in the long view, fleeting. Transient though those effects were and of brief duration, they nevertheless could well have upset Sears's merchandise apple cart. The very materials which were critical in the war effort and which were proscribed for civilian use early in the conflict were essential components of the durable items which accounted for so important a part of the company's sales.

There was, as with almost every other business, a great drain on manpower resources as thousands of employees—many of them holding key positions—entered military service. But whereas many "essential" industries, such as shipyards and munitions plants, were able to augment their work forces through manpower priorities and high wages, Sears was obviously "nonessential" and actually lost employees to such essential industries. Manufacturers producing civilian goods were often able to convert their plants to war production and thus to survive the crisis; but their continued operation and profitability were, on the whole, of little immediate benefit to a distributor deprived of the staple goods it had previously obtained from them. In short, distributors such as Sears were smote hip and thigh by the war. The fact that the company met the crisis as well as it did and emerged from it with flying colors was attributable to several factors.

The company's top management anticipated America's entry into the war (as, of course, did many other business leaders). As pointed out earlier, Sears even surveyed its own factories late in 1939 with a view to conversion to a war footing. Sears's buying organization sought even before America went to war to place large orders for hard-line and big-ticket merchandise, and also laid the groundwork for emphasizing "availables" whenever the dominant lines should become scarce or unobtainable. But a considerable difficulty arose from the fact that the "defense" program with its attendant priorities took hold well before Pearl Harbor. And the fact that the company was ordering its goods months ahead, as always, gave no assurance against government pre-emption of such goods at any time. A *New York Times* story of July 22, 1941, sheds considerable light on several phases of the company's dilemma and its efforts to cope with the problem:

Chicago's mail order houses are facing their most perplexing merchandising problems since the last war in contracting for materials for their 1942 Spring and Summer catalogues. The outcome probably will be increasing emphasis on the sale of soft goods lines to make up for the inability to acquire from manufacturers such items as washing machines, electric refrigerators, ironers, power tools, in anything like normal quantities.

Responsible sources pointed out that the Fall and Winter catalogues which recently went into the mails were "normal" in so far as merchandise listings were concerned.

The *Times* went on to declare that, aside from special inserts of "hedge clauses" to protect them from the effects of special taxes and other defense by-products, neither Sears nor Ward's showed any major changes in space allotments or color-photograph emphasis from the previous catalogue. The article continued:

Virtues of washing machines, refrigerators, and other "hard line" merchandise are extolled with equal prominence and aluminum ware is on sale in fairly complete array, just as it was in the Fall of 1940.

The reason for this ability to offer adequate stocks of such merchandise at a time when smaller stores are worrying over deliveries from wholesalers and manufacturers is the timing of the mail order buying program. The retail outlets operated by both Sears and Ward may be able to shift their displays and inventories according to the emergencies of the moment but the mail order divisions must lay in stocks and plan their sales appeal a good six months ahead.

The goods back of the latest catalogues were contracted for earlier this year, and as both houses pointed out, do not fully reflect recent price advances in the wholesale markets for that reason. Neither do they reflect the full extent of the growing grasp of government priorities orders on defense materials which have long been considered vital in the consumer goods industries.

Contracts are one thing and deliveries another, however, and this accounts for the anxiety of both Sears and Ward to take deliveries as soon as finished products are ready. This is a marked departure from the system in normal times which called for a certain percentage of factory deliveries each month, based on anticipated sales to consumers.

The *Times* also quoted a salesman for a concern which supplied "fill-ins" when catalogue items outsold their anticipated quotas as saying, "Never have I seen mail order warehouses so jammed with goods to the very ceilings as at present." The article also referred to a government order calling for a sharp reduction in the output of washing machines and electric refrigerators and concluded with this obvious truism:

> It is too early yet to decide what the final reaction will be but, in the words of a well-posted source: "As a matter of long range planning, the emphasis will be more on soft goods lines until the emergency passes."

It was true that the emphasis was to be on soft lines, but the *Times* failed to point out that many of these would also soon be in short supply; even such staples as sheets and pillow cases, for example, became difficult to procure. And the emergency was not to pass, officially, until late in 1945, while the scramble for materials which followed the easing of government controls after the war would see a tight market continue for some while in hard-line and big-ticket items.

The trend to soft lines became fully apparent in Sears's 1942 fall and winter catalogue, issued in July of that first full year of war for the United States. That book contained 196 fewer pages than the catalogue of one year earlier, but the specific omissions were far more significant than the mere space reduction. And the book contained other features which set it off sharply from its predecessors of the previous twenty-odd years, and which made it starkly clear that America's industrial plant was rapidly attaining a war footing. The catalogue listed 103 omitted items, all hard goods with the exception of a few items such as burlap, nylon hosiery, and tennis shoes. The omitted items constituted the very nucleus of Sears's merchandise line—aluminum cookware, copper boilers, corn-shellers, disk harrows, and almost the whole gamut of electrical appliances: radios, washing machines, refrigerators, sandwich toasters, heaters, irons, stoves, and more; washtubs, tractors, gas ranges, even gasoline washing machines, kerosene stoves and refrigerators, shotguns, rubber-tired farm equipment, stainless-steel cookware and tableware, wheelbarrows, vacuum cleaners, and virtually all the rest of the hard lines and big tickets.

Fortune sketched Sears's dependence upon big-ticket and other hard-line staples in these terms:

> For all its diversity, Sears in the past has been overbalanced on the side of hard lines. At Montgomery Ward & Co., Inc., the only comparable company, hard lines normally account for some 40 per cent of sales. Their share at Sears was nearer 60 per cent. Among 618 Sears retail stores, more than half were shy on soft goods, and 63 carried none at all. With its Coldspot brand, Sears has been the third biggest merchandiser of electric refrigerators, with 1939 sales of 280,000 units worth $37 million. Same year Sears sold 160,000 Kenmore washing machines ($16 million), hundreds of thousands of Silvertone radios, Allstate tires, stoves, vacuum cleaners, *et al.* This emphasis was profitable, since hardline markups are high, but it was bound to have a wicked backlash as soon as priorities took effect. ... Normally tires, electric refrigerators, washers, stoves, and plumbing and heating equipment can be counted on to supply a total of 25 per cent of Sears's summer business. As the period began, Sears expected a 30 per cent decrease in its plumbing and heating sales, 65 per cent in stoves, 85 per cent in tires, 98 per cent in washers, and 100 per cent in refrigerators.

In the "normal" year of 1939 Sears did $210 million worth of business—41 per cent of total net sales—in lines now eliminated or restricted by priorities. Add the apparent general decline in consumer demand for available goods, and Sears's position looks grim.[2]

The "grimness" of the company's position is illustrated by the variations during the war period of the proportion of its net sales accounted for by durable goods. With 1939 equated at 100, the index number for 1940 rose to 102, and in 1941 again leveled off at 100, a point not to be reached thereafter until 1947. For 1942 saw the index number drop to 84; and 1943, to 70. In 1944 it stood at 72. In 1945 the index number climbed to 85, in 1946 it

TABLE 61*

Sales Trends in Dollar Volume, 1932–45
(1932 = 100)

Year	Soft Lines Mail Order	Soft Lines Retail	Soft Lines Total	Hard Lines Mail Order	Hard Lines Retail	Hard Lines Total	Big Tickets Mail Order	Big Tickets Retail	Big Tickets Total	Miscellaneous Mail Order	Miscellaneous Retail	Miscellaneous Total
1932	100	100	100	100	100	100	100	100	100	100	100	100
1933	116	112	114	92	102	99	99	108	106	99	107	100
1934	124	125	125	110	115	114	120	138	133	115	283	203
1935	155	135	146	145	132	135	177	185	183	143	343	247
1936	175	165	171	188	161	167	234	273	264	191	182	186
1937	173	175	174	203	188	192	241	307	291	196	249	223
1938	169	168	168	205	192	195	212	267	254	188	279	235
1939	195	202	198	232	234	234	252	338	317	216	475	351
1940	207	234	219	228	261	251	266	409	374	235	607	429
1941	266	312	286	324	337	334	390	520	488	302	739	530
1942	297	439	358	264	292	286	310	383	365	325	404	366
1943	312	545	413	259	267	265	272	262	264	341	461	404
1944	336	661	477	323	304	308	322	303	307	388	502	447
1945	262	648	429	435	387	398	397	376	381	480	598	541

* Source: Company records.

reached 95, and in 1947, it moved up to 108. Table 61 shows the sales trend, in dollar volume, of soft lines, hard lines, and big tickets over a fourteen-year period spanning the war.

Still speaking of Sears in America's first full year of war, *Fortune* said:

Scarcely a ruling by WPB and OPA fails to touch it in some way. Indeed, by observing how government regulations have affected Sears, one can gain a good insight into their effect on the civilian economy as a whole. In a sense Sears has already become an auxiliary of the government: it is a rationer of goods, a vehicle for getting needed things to critical places, a mighty spigot wherefrom flow low-priced consumer goods to quench the appetite of the newly prosperous low-income groups.

Finally Sears at war is an example of how a smart American business can not only survive but thrive in the face of high taxes, severe government controls, lost sources and materials, and enough other obstacles to make Adam Smith's restless ghost wail.[3]

Fortune was optimistic about "thriving" in the year 1942, for the company's sales volume dropped from $915,057,628 in 1941 to $867,834,052 the following year (and to $852,596,706 in 1943). The upturn was, however, to come in 1944, when sales mounted to $988,770,171, an all-time record to that point. And 1945, still a full war year as far as merchandise procurement was concerned, would see sales zoom over the billion-dollar mark. The *Fortune* article cited above also quoted General Wood's observation, "If you can't sell refrigerators, you can sell baby chicks," but Sears's survival (and, eventually, its thriving) during the war years was due to more than mere promotion of available goods. The *New York Times* of July 18, 1942, quoted the company as saying:

> The circulation [of the catalogue] now takes into account the movement of people to defense areas and a probable stimulation of catalogue business in cities, due to gasoline rationing and the tire situation. These factors have resulted in increasing the number of 1942 Fall and Winter catalogues going into urban centers.

TABLE 62*

CIRCULATION OF THE GENERAL CATALOGUE, 1942–45

Issue	No.	Issue	No.
1940 Spring	6,834,712	1943 Spring	6,506,501
Fall	7,047,064	Fall	7,443,344
1941 Spring	7,147,847	1944 Spring	7,111,182
Fall	7,424,472	Fall	7,202,463
1942 Spring	6,689,785	1945 Spring	6,620,591
Fall	7,226,789	Fall	7,324,712

* Source: Company records.

It was true that circulation of the 1942 fall and winter catalogue was greater than that of the spring and summer book of that year (the fall book is, as a matter of fact, always circulated in greater quantity than the spring issue), but the 1942 fall circulation was smaller than the 1941 fall circulation. Circulation figures for the general catalogue during the war period are shown in Table 62.

In addition to the tactic of routing a greater proportion of its catalogues to urban areas (where the geographical distribution of retail stores, particularly of the "A" type, enabled the company to cater to the well-paid war workers), another factor which proved of assistance to Sears was its buyers' knowledge of materials and of production. They were able to devise substitute materials for a wide variety of goods; and, by roaming the country to purchase scrap materials and industrial cast-offs of all types, they obtained much material which could be used in their products.

While many items, as has been pointed out, became unobtainable, a large number of items was made obtainable by customers (and by Sears) under certain restrictions. Such goods could be sold to customers having priority certificates and could be replaced by Sears through the process of turning such executed certificates over to manufacturers. Sears's sources had some of these goods and were eager to sell them, but the sources had not the facilities for seeking out priority-holding customers. The company therefore established a unit ("Division 400") to serve as the link between the sources and the customers. Those customers came increasingly to include the armed services and other government agencies (including Lend-Lease), as well as war industries and their workers. Again Sears's knowledge of manufacturers throughout the country came into play, for Division 400's scope quickly exceeded the catalogue offerings of the company. To quote from *Fortune* again:

> A typical "400" sale was made not long ago to the Army Signal Corps, which was in the market for a big number of tool kits. Each kit contained 250 items, ranging from plumbing tools through electrical and radio tools. The Signal Corps wanted fast delivery, and only at a place such as Sears could it hope to get it.... "400" found that 90 per cent of the items were in Sears's own or its sources' inventories, leaving only twenty-five pieces to round up. Tools have been among "400's" most active lines, selling well to both defense workers (in many trades the workman traditionally supplies his own tools) and defense plants. One day Packard Motor called to say that the delivery dates promised by its sources on socket wrenches were impossibly late: if Sears could find enough wrenches, Packard would double the order it had tried to fill. From its own and its manufacturers' stocks, Sears collected enough—$300,000 worth....
>
> While selling restricted standard goods is its main purpose, "400" is concerned also with developing new lines tailored to the needs of war. Sears now stocks special steel-tip work shoes, and big, factory-size mops and brooms. Some U.S. Army commando troops are equipped with sleeping bags from Sears. Many female defense workers wear Sears's coveralls, designed by a personnel worker at Allis-Chalmers.... Sears has developed another uniform, without pockets or metal closures, for workers in powder and shell-loading factories....
>
> Through "400," Sears perforce operates in ways it had piously avoided in the days of peace. Sears had never sold anything it couldn't lay hands on within minutes [*Fortune* was apparently not thoroughly conversant with the merchandise techniques of Richard Sears]; it now must employ a special search party to help buyers hunt for goods. Sears, moreover, heretofore has rarely deviated from the price it figures will give it an honest minimum markup. Although the catalogue price is "400's" nominal guide and applies to small orders, a big order will set the division to bidding until it may bid away all profit. Generally, having assumed a jobber's function when it takes a big order, Sears expects no more than a service charge or a jobber's margin. Sales, like profits, are unpredictable.[4]

Sales were indeed unpredictable, and, as one of the Sears merchandising executives observed, "The war will be over some day. Our main object is to ride it out—take a beating if we have to, but be in the right position to get going again afterward."[5] Part of the job of riding out the war included further consolidation of the merchandise line with further reductions of the number of assortments offered in many lines. While it is difficult to determine to what extent shortages accounted for the reduction in the total number of offerings, it is interesting to note that the 122,000 items listed in the fall and winter book of 1941 dropped to 95,000 in the succeeding general catalogue, and dropped by another 3,000 in the 1942 spring and summer book.

The conversion of many of Sears's factories to war production obviously deprived the company of a fairly considerable portion of goods of the types those plants had been producing. By 1944 the war's needs had cut a wide swath through Sears's merchandise offerings and through Ward's. In the spring and summer catalogues mailed in January, 1944, Ward's showed a sharp drop of 356 pages from its corresponding book of the previous year, falling to 814 pages. Sears's book dropped by 170 pages to 1,062. Both companies attributed the smaller books partially to the companies' desire to co-operate with the government's paper-saving program; Sears's book, for example, weighed eight ounces less in the spring and summer of 1944, which represented a total saving on seven million copies of over three million pounds of paper.

Both great mail-order companies' books showed a severe shrinkage in the availability of home furnishings items, but a great expansion in the space allocated to diamonds, watches, jewelry, greeting cards, mirrors, bric-a-brac, seeds, bulbs, and garden supplies. Each company went in to some extent for its own rationing program, restricting any one customer to specified amounts of various items. The scarcity of toys may have been responsible for the remarkable increase in sales of children's books, which virtually doubled between 1934 and 1944 and reached their peak in 1945 at a point 123.4 per cent over 1943. This record dropped by only 4 per cent in 1946, and sales of children's books in the ensuing two years remained at a high level. What was true of children's books during the war was likewise true of all books offered by Sears. Bible sales in 1944 were 274.6 per cent over those of 1937 and 154.9 per cent over 1940's sales. Reprint fiction sales from the catalogue in 1944 were 197.7 per cent higher than in 1937 and 127 per cent greater than in 1940. Technical books jumped in 1944 sales 400 per cent over 1937 but showed sharp drops amounting to nearly 50 per cent in the years 1945–46.

By mid-1944 merchandise shortages were acute. Sears's fall and winter catalogue, issued in June of that year, dropped to 904 pages. Inserts printed *after* the catalogue had gone to press contained notices that certain merchandise was not available; these inserts were particularly prominent in the textile section. Sheets and sheeting were not even listed. By way of promoting availables, Sears offered color reproductions of a dozen oil paintings, ranging in price from $4.79 to $19.50 (each complete with a free information pamphlet giving the history of the painting and of the artist). Books received sixteen solid pages, and a plastic bugle was offered for $6.75.

By late 1945, shortages had reached their worst point. The fall 1945 catalogue contained no rugs except a few cotton scatter rugs. Linoleum was featured, for wall as well as floor covering.

The percentage of unavailable items denoted in the catalogue index by asterisks had reached 4.7 by the spring 1943 book, and 8.9 in the fall of that year. In the spring of 1944 the figure stood at 11.5; in the fall, it reached its wartime peak of 12.6 per cent. The spring of 1945 saw the unavailables drop to 4.5 per cent of total index listings, but in the fall of that year they were back up to 8.1. Those percentage figures applied simply to items not available in *any* quantity and did not take into consideration shortages in countless lines. The spring 1946 catalogue dropped the asterisks, apparently on the assumption that industrial conversion to civilian needs would be rapid enough to supply most essentials before the end of 1946.

That book was the largest spring and summer edition in twenty-five years, numbering 1,380 pages—432 pages more than the spring and summer book of 1945. It contained a greatly increased offering of "back-again" items which had made their first postwar appearance in the Christmas flyer of 1945: electrical appliances, heating supplies, innerspring mattresses, aluminum cooking ware, automobile seat covers, electric alarm clocks, radio, steel furniture, and other goods which had been unobtainable. Vacuum cleaners and steel kitchen cabinets were also offered again in the spring 1946 book, although with the notation that they would not be available for a few weeks. Still missing in this book were washing machines, electric refrigerators and stoves, nylon stockings, and some other staple items. The company stated that, while the availability of merchandise had not shown the expected improvement during the time that the catalogue was being prepared, it was hopeful of being able to supply most of the mail-order demand during the six months the book would be in circulation. That assumption proved erroneous; in 1946 Sears had to refund $250,000,000 to customers, representing orders it could not fill—over four times the dollar value of refunds in 1919 which had led to excessive inventories in 1920. The *Wall Street Journal,* in its story announcing the issuance of the 1946 fall and winter catalogue on July 1, 1946, reported:

> Refunds ran about $1 million a day last spring when Sears put radios, vacuum cleaners, home freezers and other war casualty items into its catalogs. Some of the goods never came through at all; other wanted articles came through in dribbles. Meanwhile, the company received as many mail orders in one day for some items as it would normally have received in six months.

Despite a more extensive offering of women's apparel, the fall 1946 catalogue was considerably smaller than the spring and summer book of the same year; it omitted entirely such items as electric refrigerators and mixers, radios, sewing machines, stoves, hot-water and steam heating plants, oil burners, bed sheets, window screens, some farm tools, pillow cases, men's pajamas, and other items. Apparently still hopeful, however, that much merchandise would come through before 1946 was out, the company listed many items as being available by mid-September. The spring 1947 catalogue continued to omit many items in short supply, such as electric refrigerators, heating plants, stoves, sewing machines, additional big-ticket items, and even some soft lines.

Yet despite the worsening of the supply situation in respect to the company's staple lines, Sears had come within hailing distance of the one-billion-dollar mark in sales volume in 1944. And in 1945 it crossed that mark with sales of $1,045,258,832. Before the end of the latter year, the conclusion of hostilities had brought demobilization of men under arms to a rapid rate. Factories were reconverting to peace, and controls on materials were slipping away. The year 1946 was to be industry's banner year, as it strove to meet the long pent-up demand for consumer goods. It was, to an even greater degree, a banner year for Sears, Roebuck; sales volume rose by nearly 60 per cent to reach $1,612,596,050. The war was over for Sears, even though supply of many of its big-ticket items would run below demand for some time.

The second and possibly more dramatic of the two great influences on the company's merchandise line during the period had therefore been, if not taken in stride, at least weathered. The company, freed from the stresses of war, was again subject to the effects stemming from that other great influence upon its merchandise structure, the entry into the retail field. Meanwhile, some of the company's merchandising "sports" had also weathered (and some had even been birthed during) the war.

Despite all the overwhelming evidence of Sears's close accouplement to its times and milieu, the company did branch out in the years following 1925 into some new ventures in merchandising, some of them off the beaten path for a mail-order-and-retail business. One of these in particular not only represented a merchandising byway but was also initiated in what must have seemed an inauspicious time, when the depression was leading Sears to what would be its first year "in the red" since 1921.

Early in 1931 General Wood was approached by a Chicago insurance broker named Carl Odell, who had handled some of Wood's personal insurance, with the proposition that Sears, Roebuck sell insurance by mail. Odell's chief talking point was one which must have had a peculiarly strong appeal to Wood and others in the company; he maintained that too great a part of the public's insurance dollar was represented by distribution costs, which could be reduced considerably through selling by mail to reduce sales expense and thus reduce costs to the insured. Automobile insurance appeared to Odell to offer the greatest opportunity. He presented his plan to Sears's board of directors, which approved, and the Allstate Insurance Company was formed on April 17, 1931 (its name was taken from the company's automobile tire, a logical extension of that brand name and a euphonious name for an automobile insurance company).

Some of the company's executives were less than enthusiastic about the insurance venture, especially in a year of depression which was worsening by the month. Insurance was admittedly far removed from Sears's traditional bailiwick of goods customers could see, touch, and use daily, for insurance is peculiarly intangible. Nothing is sold in such a transaction except the promise of protection and of the performance of an accompanying service if and when needed; the customer simply buys that protection and, through it, perhaps peace of mind.

Some outside the company were also apparently concerned about the venture, perhaps because of the possibly great success it might attain under the strong Sears organization and the effects of such success upon the agency system of selling insurance. The *Wall Street Journal* of March 16, 1931 (a month before the Allstate company was to start operations), asserted, in a story significantly datelined "Hartford":

> Sears, Roebuck & Co.'s plan to organize the All State [sic] Insurance Co. to write automobile risks by mail will be watched closely. Insurance may be written without state license anywhere, but registration and license is [sic] necessary to "do business" in a state. Sending an agent to solicit business or an adjuster to settle claims into a state constitutes doing business. Underwriting experience on business obtained without personal contact will be watched by insurance executives, who will also be interested in the experience in settling claims.
>
> The experience of new companies engaging in business is that large sums are necessary to set up unearned premium reserves in proportion to the volume of business written. These reserves are proportionate according to one, two, three or more years of coverage. First year percentages are large. These reserves are drawn from surplus in newly organized companies, hence a large premium on the par value of stock is necessary.
>
> A policyholder having a legal action against a company not licensed in the state where he lives has to go to the domicile of the company to get into court.

Sears invested $700,000 in Allstate, of which $350,000 was set up as capital and $350,000 as surplus. All operations except claim settlements were to be by mail. A quotation and application form would be mailed to the prospect (solicited through the catalogue); if the form was returned with the premium, a policy would be mailed to the customer. The company was licensed in only a few states at the outset, and only about twenty people were employed to handle the work.

Allstate was conceived pretty much as another merchandise department. It was expected to make profits for the stockholders by offering a good value to the customer. Most of its personnel came from the Sears organization. Lessing J. Rosenwald was the first chairman of the board of Allstate. G. E. Humphrey, a Sears officer, was appointed president. Odell was listed as vice-president-secretary and acted as general manager, and W. N. Lowe (a methods man and trouble-shooter for T. J. Carney, Sears's vice-president in charge of operating) was assigned to Allstate to make sure the mechanics of its operations conformed to Sears's principles and utilized fully the company's fund of experience in operating economies.

The new insurance company handled a premium volume of $118,323 in the eight months of 1931 in which it was in operation, and, true to the usual pattern of new companies, failed to show a profit. Unlike most new insurance companies, however, Allstate operated at a profit in its second year; in 1932 its premium volume rose to $539,950, an increase of 314 per cent over 1931. That great increase—interesting and significant in view of the fact that 1932 marked the trough of the depression, and the company as a whole operated at a loss—was due at least in part to the establishment of a companion insurance firm: the Allstate Fire Insurance Company.

The Allstate Insurance Company could legally operate nation-wide with a license only from the state of Illinois. But, as the *Wall Street Journal* had pointed out in the article previously cited, Allstate could not "do business"—that is, settle a claim or send an agent to solicit business—in any state in which it was not licensed. The fact that an Allstate policy-holder in, say, California, would theoretically have had to go to Illinois to institute court action for a claim was a road block on the company's line of march. It therefore became apparent even before the end of 1931 that Allstate would have to be licensed in many states, in order to increase its premium volume and expedite customer service. The insurance laws of many states forbade the underwriting of casualty and fire insurance under the same company charter. Hence the establishment on January 5, 1932, of the Allstate Fire Insurance Company, launched with capital of $200,000 and surplus of $75,000.

The fire company limited its writing to fire insurance on automobiles in connection with the casualty and public liability lines underwritten by the casualty company. Allstate Fire Insurance absorbed the fire insurance already written on automobiles in states which demanded a separation of the two types of protection. It was also chartered to write the standard lines of fire insurance such as on dwellings, tornado, riot and civil commotion, windstorm, and related lines. Its officers were the same as those of the slightly older Allstate Insurance Company, which took the new organization firmly under its wing.

The combined premium volume of the two companies reached $673,000 in 1933, all of it written by mail. The limitations inherent in operating solely by mail were, however, even then apparent. In 1934 the first agent was employed by Allstate. But that year was more significantly marked by expansion in a different direction. The depression years which had proved profitable for Allstate had been the undoing of many life insurance companies, whose investments in some cases had proved unsound. Two of the leading life insurance companies in Illinois were placed in state receivership in 1934, and bids were called for to reinsure the business of the two firms.

Allstate bid for and obtained the right to reinsure the business of the National Life Insurance Company of the United States of America, which, despite the impairment of the value of its investments, had a backlog of sound insurance in force. The management of Allstate became the management of National, which was promptly rechristened "Hercules," a brand name drawn from Sear's work clothing. One of the provisions of the court order awarding Allstate the National business was that contracts between the bankrupt National and its general agents be maintained by the new Hercules Company. Hercules required some time to establish its own policies, rates, and general plan of operation, but the agents wanted and needed something to sell. They were given, as a stop-gap device, contracts to sell Allstate policies.

The agents were located largely in metropolitan areas, whereas the method of selling by mail had brought sales primarily from the rural areas and smaller communities. Sears by then had retail stores operating in most of the cities in which the agents were located; the latter gradually gravitated to the former, to establish the present pattern of Allstate agents located in the larger retail stores to write insurance "over the counter."

The Sears annual report for 1934 listed Hercules' assets and liabilities separately from those of the remainder of the company (as it did Allstate's). Under that listing came a statement which was to appear in subsequent annual reports as long as Sears held Hercules:

NOTE: The Hercules Life Insurance Company on February 8, 1934, entered into a reinsurance agreement with the Receiver for the National Life Insurance Company of the United States of America.

The assets of the National Life Fund shown above [$26,954,486.91 in 1934, and $32,081,879.32 at the end of 1937] are held and administered solely for the benefit of the former National Life Policyholders, who have no claim on any other assets of the Hercules Life Insurance Company.

Allstate, meanwhile, continued to flourish, paying a dividend of $157,500 on January 24, 1936 (out of a surplus of more than $1,000,000), and another dividend, of $56,000, on January 22, 1937. Premium volume reached $2,619,000 in 1937 and $3,025,000 in 1938. By that time the automobile insurance venture had moved four times within Sears's administration building, had taken over two floors of the former printing building, and, when the parent-organization could spare no more space, had taken an entire floor in Chicago's Civic Opera Building. The Hercules Life Insurance Company, however, was having a sharply different experience, as the company found that selling life insurance by mail was quite different from selling automobile insurance through that medium (and through retail stores).

Between 1934 and the end of 1936, the amount of Hercules insurance in force dropped from $148,000,000 to $133,000,000, while premium receipts in the same span decreased from $3,699,480 to $2,821,298. Hercules' assets at the end of 1936 totaled more than $33,000,000 as against a total of $3,475,000 for the two Allstate companies. But the Allstate companies were operating at a profit, and Hercules was not; Sears suffered a net loss of $176,390 in 1937 in the operation of the three insurance companies, including adjustment of about $300,000 in market value of securities and an increase in reserves of about $150,000.[6]

In March, 1938, Sears concluded that life insurance was not within its merchandise purview, and sold the Hercules company to the Washington National Life Insurance Company of Evanston, Illinois. General Wood explained the company's reason for the sale in one succinct sentence: "We can't sell life insurance from a catalogue."[7] The annual report for 1938 mentioned that Sears, Roebuck had in that year acquired the "small amounts" of Allstate Insurance Company and Allstate Fire Insurance Company stock which had been in the hands of "others," with the result that Sears now owned 100 per cent of the capital stock of the Allstate companies. (The annual report for 1937 had showed Sears, Roebuck as owner of 92.5 per cent of the stock of each of the two Allstate companies.)

Allstate meanwhile grew rapidly. Its premium volume of $1,794,108 in 1936 led the company to institute a new system of handling claims. Up to that year Allstate had been "farming out" its claims settlement business to an independent company which in turn farmed them out to other independents. Allstate resolved to eliminate one link in this chain of subcontracting and in 1936 began farming out claims directly to independents who would make the adjustments.

In 1939, when the combined premium volume of the two companies totaled $3,704,335, the first of a series of branch offices was opened in Chicago. In the succeeding year, additional branches were established in Los Angeles, Kansas City, and New York; Detroit, Seattle, Newark, and Philadelphia were added in 1941. Others followed, until by the end of 1947 Allstate was operating twelve branches in addition to its home office in Chicago. Management changes followed in the wake of the expansion. Odell, the first vice-president and general manager, who had succeeded to the presidency in 1936, resigned in 1939. Gilbert Alexander, a retired Sears merchandise supervisor and an Allstate director for several years, followed Odell. Alexander's executive vice-president, Calvin Fentress, Jr., was an Allstate "sport"—he had come directly to the company from the investment field in 1932 without Sears experience, had become treasurer of the Allstate companies, and in 1938 a vice-president. When Alexander died during World War II and Fentress succeeded to the presidency, a longtime Sears director and former executive became chairman of Allstate's board of directors: J. M. Barker, who had headed up the retail effort in the early 1930's.

During World War II gasoline rationing and the consequent sharp reduction in automobile insurance rates failed to halt Allstate's climb. Its premium volume mounted to $7,200,000 in 1941, to $8,902,000 in 1944. In that latter year many states adopted stricter financial liability laws under which a motorist forfeited his right to drive if unable to pay, through insurance or other means, for any injuries, deaths, or property damage he might inflict. This legislation, of course, heightened the demand for automobile insurance, and Allstate received its share of the additional business; its premium volume soared to $12,029,798 in 1945, the largest increase it had ever experienced in one year. (As a matter of fact, Allstate had never in any year since its inception failed to show an increase in volume, even though the automobile insurance business as a whole showed a marked drop in 1942 and 1943.) Allstate's premium volume in 1946 exceeded $16,000,000, and in 1947 the volume of business exceeded $22,000,000. Table 63 portrays several aspects of Allstate's rise to this position.

TABLE 63*

PREMIUMS WRITTEN AND ADMITTED ASSETS OF THE ALLSTATE INSURANCE COMPANY AND THE ALLSTATE FIRE INSURANCE COMPANY, 1931–45

YEAR	PREMIUMS WRITTEN (AFTER REINSURANCE)			NUMBER OF POLICIES	ADMITTED ASSETS		
	Casualty Co.	Fire Co.	Total		Casualty Co.	Fire Co.	Total
1931	$ 118,323		$ 118,323	4,217	$ 710,296		$ 710,296
1932	432,920	$ 107,029	539,949	18,796	1,001,012	$ 317,356	1,318,368
1933	657,816	14,695	672,511	22,065	1,219,264	318,831	1,538,095
1934	829,920	52,438	882,358	29,518	1,760,583	387,219	2,147,802
1935	1,168,365	190,437	1,358,802	49,097	2,273,726	529,212	2,802,938
1936	1,456,859	337,248	1,794,107	59,997	2,796,926	697,909	3,494,835
1937	2,167,359	451,977	2,619,336	80,271	3,283,336	812,235	4,095,571
1938	2,471,315	554,047	3,025,362	91,180	4,056,666	977,208	5,033,874
1939	2,905,868	798,466	3,704,334	113,472	4,685,687	1,180,772	5,866,459
1940	3,570,984	1,109,796	4,680,780	137,864	5,504,410	1,501,358	7,005,768
1941	5,111,266	1,725,934	6,837,200	189,162	8,157,297	1,844,414	10,001,711
1942	5,494,064	1,706,416	7,200,480	189,970	9,831,783	2,265,571	12,097,354
1943	5,214,416	2,133,752	7,348,168	231,166	10,560,522	2,685,273	13,245,795
1944	6,368,157	2,534,458	8,902,615	248,433	12,438,165	2,911,481	15,349,646
1945	8,448,562	3,581,235	12,029,797	327,430	16,217,684	2,877,936†	19,095,620
Total	$46,416,194	$15,297,928	$61,714,122				

* Source: Company records.
† Collision coverage insured in the Casualty Company as of September 30, 1945.

All in all, Allstate represents one of Sears's most successful ventures down the byways of merchandising. It has operated generally on the company's long-established guaranty of "satisfaction or your money back." It has also pioneered cautiously in several directions, most of the innovations being in line with over-all company policy. Instalment selling, for example, was early extended to include the insurance line. The graphic presentation of the mail-order catalogue found its counterpart in Allstate's "Illustrator Policy," containing sketches which show in easily understood form just what the text is saying at greater length. And the captions for the illustrations implement the policy of simplification. The text contains such hallowed verbiage as: "To pay for loss or damage to the automobile, hereinafter called loss, caused by collision of the automobile with another object, or by upset of the automobile, but only for the amount of each such loss in excess of the deductible amount, if any, stated in the declarations as applicable hereto." In the caption under an illustration, that tortuous sentence comes out: "When your own car is bumped or smashed-up."[8] The innovations and the underwriting policy appear to have been eminently sound. By the end of 1947 the original investment of $700,000 in Allstate had grown to total admitted assets for the two companies of more than $31,000,000.

Business Week magazine described Allstate's "cut-rate auto-liability insurance" at some length in an article which asserted: "A young auto insurance company is challenging the conventional methods of automobile insurance. . . . Allstate offers low rates, made possible by direct-mail sales through the Sears catalog and sales at booths in Sears stores." The magazine quoted the company as saying that its new method of rating cars for insurance (utilizing twelve classes instead of the customary four) lowered costs uniformly: some 15 per cent for auto-liability rates, about 12 per cent for collision insurance, and about 10 per cent for comprehensive coverage against fire and theft.[9]

The year of Allstate's establishment, 1931, also saw Sears, Roebuck re-enter the banking business. As pointed out earlier, Richard Sears had put the company in the "banking business" briefly around 1901, when a "Banking Department" was established to receive deposits of $5.00 to $1,000, against which customers could draw for purchases. That scheme was discontinued after one year, but some thirty years later the company returned to the banking business on a more serious, even if small-scale basis, and not as a sales-promotion device, by taking over the Community State Bank in Chicago.

The Sears–Community State Bank opened on July 6, 1931, with an "inheritance" of 7,550 depositors and deposits of $1,120,344. The bank was capitalized at 8,000 shares of $25 each (doubled in 1939 to 16,000 shares at $25, and doubled again on a one-for-one basis in 1947). The number of depositors grew in five years to 17,901, and, by the end of 1946, to 27,010. Resources of the bank totaled almost $50,000,000 at the end of 1945, during which year profits after all charges and reserves amounted to $198,643, equivalent to $8.27 per share on the 24,000 shares of $25 par then outstanding. Four quarterly dividends of 50 cents each were declared and paid in 1945. At the end of 1948 the resources of the bank were over $63,000,000.

The Sears–Community State Bank is a cross between a company-owned and operated merchandise venture and a typical small-town bank seeking to grow. Annual reports urge the stockholders to bring their friends into the fold to "help build your bank," and all depositors are urged to take advantage of all facilities of the institution, including loans. Sears's employees and their families (mostly executives) hold most of the stock; in 1946 this group owned 14,894 shares, or 62.06 per cent of the shares out-

MERCHANDISING INFLUENCES

standing, according to a calculation of the auditor of the bank. The bank, incidentally, is a member of the Federal Reserve System and of the Federal Deposit Insurance Corporation. The chairman of its board of directors at the end of 1948 was E. J. Pollock, retired vice-president and comptroller of Sears, and six of the eight directors were company executives.

The years since 1925, which saw Sears enter the insurance field and wet its feet in banking, also witnessed Sears's greatest activity in connection with the *Encyclopaedia Britannica,* which, after 1920, the company bought, sold, rebought, and ultimately gave away. In its unusual history under the Sears aegis, the *Britannica* promised at times to become a highly profitable experiment and at other (and far more frequent) times to be a small-scale "Modern Homes" fiasco.

The famous publication, initiated in 1768, was brought to America in 1899 by Horace Everett Hooper and Walter Jackson, who had purchased control of the *Britannica* and brought the plates to this country. The eleventh edition was published in the United States. World War I brought the *Britannica* to a financial crisis; people were loath to invest $100 in the book while a great conflict was in progress. The London office was closed, the New York office greatly reduced, and $630,000 of new capital raised. A "Handy Volume" issue was prepared, identical with the Cambridge edition except for narrower margins and smaller type. Arrangements were made with Sears to father the sale of the "Handy Volume" issue, which the company offered on instalment terms of as low as one dollar down. Fifty-five thousand sets of the "Handy Volume" issue were sold between the fall of 1915 and June, 1916. In October of the latter year an intensified advertising campaign was launched and the price of the *Encyclopaedia* raised slightly. The second phase was a pronounced success for several months, with each month showing a considerable increase over the corresponding month of the previous year.

But after America entered the first World War, sales of the *Britannica* dropped almost to the vanishing point. The financial position of the *Britannica* became so critical that it was compelled to curtail its business sharply and turn its management over to a committee of bankers, who made the necessary collections on accounts outstanding (not, of course, the Sears, Roebuck accounts) and handled the *Britannica*'s debts. On February 4, 1920, the *Encyclopaedia Britannica* was sold completely to Sears, Roebuck, largely because of the personal interest of Julius Rosenwald, a golfing partner of Hooper.

The *Britannica* organization, with its trained personnel, was still largely intact, and there was still a considerable amount of money outstanding to be collected. Ten years had passed since publication of the eleventh edition, and during that decade a great war had been fought and changes of world-wide importance had taken place. The officers of the Britannica Corporation and of Sears, Roebuck agreed that new volumes of the *En-*

cyclopaedia should be prepared. On April 23, 1920, Hooper made an arrangement with Sears whereby the company agreed to advance to him $325,000 to prepare a three-volume supplement to the *Britannica*. Hooper received the right to sell the Cambridge issue of the *Britannica* and the three new volumes in Cambridge form throughout the world, and to sell the "Handy Volume" issue and the three new volumes in the "Handy Volume" form everywhere except in the United States. Sears reserved to itself only the right to sell the "Handy Volume" issue and the three new volumes in that form in the United States. A certificate of dissolution of the old Encyclopaedia Britannica Corporation was filed on April 27, 1920. A new company, the Encyclopaedia Britannica, Inc., was chartered on October 14, 1920; to it was transferred the aforementioned contract cover-

TABLE 64*

ENCYCLOPAEDIA BRITANNICA, INC., GROSS SALES
AND NET PROFIT ANALYSIS, 1933–42

Year	Gross Sales	Net Profit or Loss
1933	$ 863,068.00	$ *309,438.00*
1934	873,975.73	*426,784.07*
1935	1,095,954.19	*294,053.20*
1936	2,151,476.01	*184,997.41*
1937	2,986,776.70	53,212.59
1938	2,750,096.67	71,771.56
1939	2,081,598.86	33,404.83
1940	2,518,912.11	33,288.69
1941	3,164,397.58	112,152.07
1942	4,840,858.52	283,610.00
Total	$23,327,114.37	*$1,301,773.96*

* Source: Company records.

ing the $325,000 advance and the sale rights (actually two separate contracts). The new corporation had 3,500 shares of stock of no par value.

The new arrangement coincided pretty closely with the onset of the 1920–21 depression. Heavy instalment sales of the *Britannica* "Handy Volume" in the period of the boom leading to the crash left Sears with large accounts outstanding and heavy returns. In the years immediately following that depression, when Julius Rosenwald took drastic action to reduce expenses and to curtail ownership of factories and other subsidiaries, the *Britannica* was sold—back to Hooper. Sears had taken a loss of some $1,848,000 on its venture.

After General Wood became president of Sears in 1928, the company purchased $500,000 of preferred stock of the *Encyclopaedia* and thus was again in full control of the *Britannica*. Gross sales of the *Britannica* mounted higher and higher, but in the decade from 1934 to 1943 the company sustained a net loss, as Table 64 indicates.

In 1932 Sears assigned its secretary and treasurer, E. H. Powell, to the task of putting the *Britannica* on a sound financial basis, if indeed that were possible. After surveying the situation, Powell resolved upon two lines of action. The first was to substitute revised printings of the *Encyclopaedia*, bringing various subjects up to date, on a continuing basis in place of the plan of bringing out complete new editions at long intervals. This proved feasible, since the overwhelming bulk of the material in the *Britannica* was "pat" and not subject to revisions in light of further research and discoveries. Powell's second approach was to build up a force of outside salesmen for direct selling instead of relying almost solely upon mail order. At the time the *Britannica* was employing only about half-a-dozen such outside salesmen. Powell proceeded to establish branch sales offices in key cities, and by the time World War II came he had blanketed the country with thirty-five such offices. Also during Powell's campaign to "save" the *Britannica*, the *Britannica Junior* was launched in 1934. In 1938 came the *Britannica Book of the Year*.

By 1938, when Franklin H. Hooper, brother of the original co-proprietor, H. E. Hooper, retired as editor to be succeeded by Walter Yust, Sears concluded that it had strayed far afield again in reacquiring the *Britannica* and initiated attempts to dispose of the publication. Disposal proved a difficult problem. The company felt that to sell the *Britannica* to a "commercial" institution would detract from the great prestige of the *Encyclopaedia* and sought therefore to sell it to a university or institution of learning which would protect the prestige of the publication. No university could afford to buy it, however, as none had the necessary funds to exploit and to develop the *Britannica*; in fact, no university would accept it free of charge unless the donor furnished an endowment.

In January, 1943, arrangements were concluded whereby Sears donated the *Britannica* outright to the University of Chicago. President Arthur S. Barrows of Sears gave as the reason for the gift the explanation that the enterprise "is now foreign to our business." He added: "As one of the great universities of the world, the University of Chicago is best equipped to conduct an enterprise of such educational importance as the Britannica." President Hutchins declared: "Financially, the gift should be an important one to the university. We are grateful for it."[10]

What Hutchins and the *Times* neglected to point out was the problem of "endowment" of the publication. While negotiations between the company and the university were in progress, it became clear that the latter could not accept the gift without the investment of working capital. The required funds were made available by William Benton, then a vice-president of the university. Benton in turn received the common stock of the *Britannica*, with the university retaining the preferred (and, through escrow arrangements, the right to resume control of the common at Benton's death).

President Hutchins became a director of the *Britannica,* chairman of its executive committee, and chairman of its board of editors; but he announced at the time of the gift that the university would not actively operate the publication. Sears's officials refused to estimate the value of the *Britannica* but pointed to the company's annual consolidated statement, which since 1937 had listed the *Encyclopaedia's* value at $1.00. The university participated in the income of the *Britannica* through dividends on the preferred stock and through occasional fees paid for the advice of its professors. These payments were estimated to have exceeded a million dollars in the first four years of the university's connection with the publication.

On January 31, 1943, when the *Britannica* was formally deeded away, Sears had an *Encyclopaedia* balance of $2,960,639 on its books. By January 31, 1946, this figure had been reduced to $10,509. Operating costs and charge-offs were kept well within the $580,224 in reserve at the time of the donation. More than $260,000 of that amount was transferred to surplus, and an additional $41,929 credited as interest. The remaining reserve was equal to 100 per cent of open accounts: $10,509. Accounts owned by the *Encyclopaedia* and serviced by Sears (which agreed to handle such accounts for a period of five years from the date of transfer of ownership) stood at $3,819,533 at the end of 1944, and at $4,769,197 at the end of 1945. Sears advanced $1,048,256 to the *Encyclopaedia* on the 1945 balance. The year 1945 also saw new *Britannica* credit sales mount to $7,030,580, an increase of 18.8 per cent over the previous year. Under the agreement by which Sears was to handle the *Encyclopaedia's* accounts through January 31, 1948, operating expense was charged to the *Britannica* on an actual cost basis, and interest on the amount advanced was figured at 3 per cent.

About the time it was giving the *Encyclopaedia Britannica* to the University of Chicago, Sears initiated planning on another and different encyclopedia. The results of that planning, which became visible in 1948, indicated that the swing from one type of encyclopedia to another was analogous to a return from the Lady Duff-Gordon "high-style" apparel to some more suitable for the less sophisticated. For the half-decade of preparation (under the direction of Walter Dill Scott, president emeritus of Northwestern University, and Franklin J. Meine, encyclopedist and specialist in American literature) brought forth the *American Peoples Encyclopedia,* with a treatment as simple and as well keyed to Sears's mass market as the defiantly democratic title suggests. In the words of one magazine:

Designed for use by every member of the average family, the 20-volume set will lean heavily on visual-education techniques. Its simple, nontechnical writing should appeal to families who find the venerable Encyclopedia Britannica, and other existing reference sets, too high-brow. It has over 15,000 photographs, diagrams, maps, graphs, charts, drawings and paintings.[11]

The first volume was ready in January, 1948, three more volumes in April, and the remaining sixteen by the end of the year. The spring and summer 1948 general catalogue screamed the tidings on a double-truck spread, with one page in four colors, with a phrase straight from Richard Sears's vocabulary: "Send No Money." Readers were invited to take one volume for "FREE" examination; or to take all four volumes forthwith and receive the other sixteen at the rate of one a month as they were issued; and in either case to feel free to utilize the easy-payment plan, with $7.50 down and $6.00 a month. The special prepublication price (good only until July 31, 1948) was cut from $79.50 to $71.55. The display featured photographs of eight Nobel prize-winners who had contributed to the encyclopedia and a testimonial from Walter Blair, professor of English at the University of Chicago.

Ownership of the *American Peoples Encyclopedia* entitled one to a ten-year research consultation service, *à la Britannica* (good for a hundred research reports prepared in answer to an owner's questions); and the opportunity to purchase at half-price up-to-date supplements for ten years. The promotion went on to offer three special booklets free with the purchase of the set or even with just one volume sent for "FREE" examination: "How to get the most out of an Encyclopedia"; "How a great Encyclopedia is created"; and "What leading educators say about the *American Peoples Encyclopedia*." The very fact that Sears, Roebuck re-entered the encyclopedia field after its costly experience with the *Britannica* is evidence that the company felt that it had discovered, even if at great expense, something about encyclopedias and, even more important, something about what its customers wanted in such a publication. Sears, as so often throughout its history, advanced by trial and error and utilized its previous mistakes to establish what it believed would be a profitable item.

The years between disposal of the *Britannica* and launching of the *American Peoples Encyclopedia* found Sears entering still another field of mail-order merchandising of literature. In 1943, when war-born shortages had eliminated many Sears staple items from its catalogue and when the company was promoting "availables," a book club was launched. Several other book-a-month clubs had prospered for some time; during World War II book sales in this country reached record heights; and Sears had to compensate for its inability to procure its famous big-ticket items and many of its soft lines. In July, 1943, the Peoples Book Club was announced.

The pattern differed little from the usual book clubs (one new book a month offered to members, who were committed to purchase four books annually, receiving one book as a dividend for each four bought), but the "orientation" was distinctively Sears's: the Peoples Book Club was to provide "good, clean, wholesome reading." None of its books would be "objectionable"; rather, they would constitute "*family* reading," for people who "like to read without blushing." The Peoples Book Club was to rise in four years to include some 250,000 blushless members. As early as October 19, 1946, *Business Week* termed the club "outstandingly successful."

The club was actually a three-way venture in which Sears handled only the sales and distribution. Simon and Schuster, New York publishers, assumed responsibility for editorial and publishing phases, with actual physical production in the hands of the Consolidated Book Publishing Company, of Chicago (an affiliate of the Cuneo Press). The books were designed to sell for a uniform $1.66, plus postage. Selections have included such wholesome titles as *The Miracle of the Bells, Hope of Earth, The Robe,* and *The Green Grass of Wyoming.* A "People's Jury" (unostentatiously assisted by George Gallup's American Institute of Public Opinion) selected the books to be distributed by the club.

If the object of the club was primarily to sell books at a profit, it became successful. And if the primary goal was to make clean, wholesome reading available to the American people, the great success in that respect was witnessed by the statement in the spring and summer 1948 general catalogue by Daniel Poling, editor of the *Christian Herald:* "I have yet to receive a Peoples Book Club selection that violated good taste or failed to be good literature."

The success of the Peoples Book Club spread the "something-a-month" mania to another Sears's merchandise item: phonograph recordings. The 1946 Christmas catalogue announced formation of the "Silvertone" records-of-the-month club. Eight new records were issued monthly, but members were required to purchase only eight or twelve records annually (depending upon whether they joined Plan A or Plan B). As with books, there were "bonus" records in proportion to the volume of a member's purchases. A monthly publication, the *Silvertone Voice* ("Silvertone" being Sears's brand name for radios and phonographs), informed members of new recordings available. These ran the gamut from Tchaikovsky's "Romeo and Juliet Overture," recorded by Erich Leinsdorf and "the 76-piece Silvertone Symphony Orchestra," to "Bunky the Monkey Who Startled Yellowstone Park." The venture was, however, short lived.

Some eight years before the company finally gave the *Britannica* away and embarked upon an encyclopedia of its own to utilize the lessons of painful and costly experience, Sears was doing roughly the same thing in another field. By 1935 Sears had just about bailed itself out of the "Modern Homes" fiasco; it promptly re-entered the housing business, in a way designed to prevent a repetition of the earlier experience in which mortgage financing had cost it millions of dollars. In August, 1935, Sears announced its plan to sell prefabricated homes—only one step removed from its "ready-cut" "Modern Homes"—but this time it was *not* to erect or finance purchases of the homes. The structures, to sell from $2,900 to $4,200 (plus, of course, cost of erection by a local contractor), were designed by General

Houses, Inc., of Chicago, which also handled construction and financing. The chief difference between the homes to be sold by Sears and General Houses' regular product was that the Sears line was to have a plywood exterior. The thirty-odd different models were marketed as "Sears Houses."

The customer's down payment included an unencumbered lot and a small cash payment. Monthly instalments were spread over a fifteen-year period. Sears supplied the fixtures included in the homes as standard equipment covered by the purchase price. In addition, fixtures of all kinds were sold through mail order and retail to any customer, whether or not he purchased a prefabricated home, and building materials continued to be sold, even if not as actively pushed as before. Sales of these lines ran to $2,000,000 in 1936; $3,500,000 in 1937; and $2,750,000 in 1938. By 1939 the old catalogues were outdated, and a new "Book of Modern Homes" was issued by the company. Before that date, however, the connection with General Houses had petered out; in the words of one magazine, "Sears 1936 tie-up with General Houses, Inc., ended unhappily, with dissatisfaction over too close a relation between exterior and interior temperatures in the prefabricated structures."[12]

CHAPTER XXV

New Techniques of Mail-Order Selling

SEARS'S mail-order selling program up to 1925 was relatively simple in nature even if large in size and complicated in the details of its execution. That program relied almost completely upon the general catalogue, auxiliary catalogues such as the flyers and bargain bulletins, and special catalogues for individual departments such as wallpaper and, up to 1929, groceries. The printed word, illustrated and shipped to unseen customers, was relied upon to bring in business. By and large—at least up to the depression of 1920–21—that approach was eminently successful. But the many changes in the fabric of American life, which combined to induce the company to enter retail, also induced changes in mail-order methods.

In 1925 the annual agenda of mail-order selling mediums comprised the following: two large general catalogues, spring and fall, for each of the four mail-order plants then existing; two interim flyers to stimulate business in the slack seasons, January–February and July–August; bargain bulletins listing chiefly surplus stock quoted at close-out prices, the bulletins being circulated in the Chicago and Philadelphia regions by inclusion in shipments of merchandise to customers, with only an occasional edition being mailed separately; some sixty special catalogues elaborating on lines which could not be developed fully, without great cost, in the general catalogues; and (until its discontinuation in 1929) a bimonthly edition of the mail-order grocery catalogue, which was circulated from the Chicago plant only. These various publications were extended to the additional mail-order plants opened in succeeding years, although the period saw the elimination of many of the special catalogues developing particular lines of merchandise. The necessity of developing new techniques for the mail-order business, while not clearly apparent by 1925, was slowly beginning to be visible. But the booming prosperity of the late 1920's was running at a sufficiently high level to keep mail order prosperous and, in the Sears operation, ahead of retail in sales volume and profits. The depression which was to begin in the last year of that decade was to see retail forge ahead in sales and attain a lead never since lost; it was also to witness mail order's response to the changed situation through development of new sales techniques of its own.

One of the first of those new techniques was short lived, while some of the others became permanent fixtures; and this first effort, interestingly, was launched at the height of the boom as a sales-promotion device for a time of plenty and continued in the years immediately following as an essential device in times of depression. In the spring of 1929, following the most successful year in its history, Sears announced on the cover of its general catalogue, "We Pay the Postage!" repeated three times in the cover text block. The message added:

> Sears, Roebuck and Co. announce with the issuance of this catalog the greatest single forward step in mail order merchandising since the establishment of the Parcel Post. . . . Every article in this catalog which can be conveniently sent by parcel post will be shipped to you POSTAGE PREPAID. . . . Remember *that* fact when comparing our prices with others. Think of the convenience—NO ADDITIONAL POSTAGE TO FIGURE.

The convenience was stressed as much as the money-saving feature of the plan in the development of the postage prepayment theme which filled the first four pages of that catalogue. In one respect this policy harked back to the time of the founder, for, as Louis Asher related, Richard Sears had often worried over the fact that the necessity of computing transportation costs was probably costing the mail-order industry a considerable volume of business.

The first inside page of the spring 1929 book asserted that the company had worked for years to make possible prepayment of parcel-post charges and had been estopped only by not having enough mail-order plants to blanket the nation. The editorial declared that establishment of ten mail-order branch plants had increased total sales and made possible operating economies which would allow Sears to absorb "a large part of the parcel post charges." The catalogue asserted, opposite a map of the United States showing the ten mail-order plants and additional warehouses, "Our prices are the lowest in America!" A letter signed by General Wood ("My PLEDGE to our customers") stressed over and over the theme of "Service—Quality—Savings." Each of these three points was still further developed on the facing page; under "Service" on that page was the assertion that 99 out of 100 orders received at all mail-order plants were shipped in less than twenty-four hours.

Montgomery Ward apparently realized that Sears's prepayment of postage might well entice Ward customers and promptly retaliated with an offer to prepay freight as well as postage. The race was on, and Sears's 1929 fall catalogue met Ward's full offer by prepaying both postage and freight; that catalogue, like its immediate predecessor, devoted its entire cover to that sales-promotion plan. It also featured more institutional advertising, even promoting the retail stores and proclaiming, "This is our GREATEST CATALOG." Shortly after that catalogue was put into the mails, the great depression set in. Prepayment of postage and freight was continued through the spring of 1930; as in the fall of 1929, express was *not* paid, but customers wishing their orders shipped by express were credited with what the cost of freight would have been. In the fall of 1930, prepayment of freight was abandoned, but postage continued to be prepaid. The fall of 1931 saw an alteration in even that plan; postage was then prepaid only on orders of $2.00 or more.

On December 24, 1932, the *Wall Street Journal* announced that, "as an experiment," Sears and Ward's would shortly discontinue prepayment of postage on orders received in their Minneapolis and St. Paul branch plants, respectively. (Those regions were selected because their geographical boundaries happened to coincide exactly in the case of both companies.) What had happened was that postage rates were, of course, based on weight, not value; and whereas both companies' sales prices had declined steadily since 1929, postal rates had actually increased somewhat, with the result that the postage cost on the same physical volume of goods had increased considerably in proportion to dollar sales receipts. Dollar sales receipts had declined sharply; it was clear by the time that newspaper story appeared, in the last week of 1932, that Sears had operated at a net loss in that year. The experimental discontinuation of prepaid postage by the two companies apparently worked out satisfactorily, for on April 29, 1933, the *Wall Street Journal* announced that postage prepayment was being discontinued everywhere. The Sears and the Ward fall 1933 catalogues confirmed this; the former by a magnificent piece of indirection, through merely reminding customers how to compute parcel-post charges.

The over-all effects of that promotion scheme are difficult to assess. The *Wall Street Journal* stated of Sears:

Under then existing conditions this move brought it a large and profitable volume of additional business. Ward at first decided not to follow suit, but declining mail order sales finally led it to do so in its next general catalog. . . .

Payment of freight proved unprofitable to both houses, and was discontinued. . . .

It was found also that payment of postage on all orders resulted in customers' sending in more frequent orders for small individual items instead of waiting until they had accumulated sufficient orders to make a package which would be carried at maximum economy under parcel post rates.[1]

Specifically, Sears found that the value of the average sale dropped, after prepayment of postage was announced, from $5.51 to $4.55 in 1929. After that, it was difficult to determine just to what extent the worsening of the depression was responsible for the diminution in the average value of orders and the extent to which postage prepayment was responsible. But the company did feel that it was being hit in two ways: prepayment of postage (and, for a short while, of freight) *plus* the increased operating cost arising from handling a greater volume of paper work for the same volume of business, for those were years of serious price declines, as well, of course, as of marked losses in the volume of business. On July 10, 1930, Sears and Ward's both announced what the *New York Times* called "drastic" reductions in prices. Ward's, according to the *Times,* initiated the reductions in a letter mailed to ten million customers, making the price cuts effective immediately. Sears's reductions took effect with its fall catalogue issued shortly afterward. General Wood claimed the prices shown in that book were the lowest Sears had quoted in ten years, amounting to as much as 25 per cent reductions on some items.[2]

The midwinter flyers of both companies, mailed in December, 1930, showed still further cuts in prices and other inducements to persuade customers to buy. *Business Week* analyzed the flyers of Sears and Ward's in these terms:

> General style of presenting offerings, methods of attack rather new to the mail order field but time-tested in retailing circles, indicate greater diffusion of experience gained by both companies in their retail stores. For instance, Ward's offers thrift specials—certain items sold regularly at stated prices but offered during specified 2-week periods at reductions ranging up to 30%.[3]

Ward's also liberalized its instalment terms, offering radios, refrigerators, bicycles, cream separators, and similar durables for as little as one dollar down, the offer to expire on February 28, 1931. In fact, Ward's offered almost everything but groceries on instalment terms. (Sears had discontinued its grocery department in 1929.) Ward's flyer was the largest mid winter edition that firm had ever issued, and so also was Sears's. Sears guaranteed its prices only through February, 1931. To quote *Business Week* again:

> In the Sears, Roebuck book, many prices now quoted are less than half of the peak levels of 1920, others are even lower than 1917 prices, although now the company pays parcel post charges on such items.
>
> Price reductions on important groups show copper boilers down 21.4%, domestic cotton goods 18.6% . . . electrical appliances 9.2%, . . . silk goods 27.5%, woollens 16%. . . .
>
> Significant is the fact that prices on automobile tires, heavy volume builders, take one of the heavy cuts. They are reduced 14.5%, with a further cut approximating 4% if tires are bought in pairs.[4]

The *Journal of Commerce* of July 14, 1932, under the heading, "Sears, Roebuck & Co. Again Cuts Prices," asserted that the fall and winter book of that year showed reductions of from 17 to 34 per cent on "a selected line of items." The *Journal* pointed out that household necessities had been especially reduced. And the *Wall Street Journal* of December 28, 1932, greeted the company's midwinter flyer with the statement that average prices in it were off "only" 9.2 per cent.

Sears, Roebuck sought to capitalize fully upon the price reductions which followed the worsening of the depression. The inside front cover of the 1932 spring catalogue was filled with pictures dramatically illustrating the lower prices of that depression year. Twelve items of merchandise were pictured; on each illustration there appeared a date and a price. A lady's dress, for example, was shown in the style of an earlier period, with the caption, "1905: $11.50." Next to it was a lady's dress of the then current style, with the caption, "1932: $3.98." The earlier year for the various comparisons in price of the several items ranged from 1895, for the bicycle, to as late as 1921, for a washing machine. The merchandise so pictured included, in addition to the items already mentioned, automobile tires, men's shoes, girls' dresses, radios, men's suits, ladies' bathing suits and hats, and others. The facing page contained a letter over General Wood's signature, further stressing low prices (and high quality), plus the usual guaranty, as well as this additional warranty:

> We guarantee the low prices quoted in this book for the Spring and Summer season, 1932, unless otherwise stated. . . . Even though our costs advance, all orders will be filled at these low prices. As in the past, in the event of a decline in our costs, you will be given the benefit of the reduction immediately.

The spring 1932 catalogue devoted still another page to the theme of price reductions. The 1931 and 1932 prices, with the percentage decrease reflected in the latter, were shown on sixty-two items listed under the headings of wearing apparel, dry goods, automobile and sporting needs, home modernization, home furnishings, and farm needs and hardware.

The fall 1932 catalogue continued to play variations on the same theme of lower prices. The keynote was set in Wood's letter to customers:

> These are not ordinary times nor is this an ordinary catalog. . . .
> Of greatest importance today are the costs of the necessities of life. This we have realized. We have planned for it. We have sacrificed our own profits so that those most affected may still be able to secure the needs of their families at the lowest prices at which satisfactory, dependable goods can be sold. I cannot emphasize this broad Sears policy too strongly.
> We realize that men and women who work, and their children who go to school, must be warmly clad this fall and winter. So arctics and shoes, flannel shirts and work gloves, overalls and warm clothing, have been drastically repriced.
> We realize economy dictates that more women must sew this year. . . . And we at Sears meet this emergency with radical price reductions on all sewing needs. . . .
> Repairing, rather than replacing, will be the order in many families. In this book there is welcome news in the low prices on shoe repairs, automobile repairs, harness parts and many, many others.
> We recognize the struggle that is taking place everywhere to make ends meet.

Following that letter was a two-page spread of institutional advertising. The first page was headed "Sears, Roebuck and Co. Mail Order Prices Are the Lowest . . . Quality Considered." The facing page bore the caption, "Sears, Roebuck and Co. Retail Store Prices Are the Lowest . . . Quality Considered." That layout represented the catalogue's first attempt to explain, and to make palatable, the higher prices of retail as against mail order. The low prices of Sears's retail stores were extolled, but the still lower prices of mail order were not only extolled but explained as well. The book asserted that "the mail order method of selling is the most economical ever devised, particularly for rural districts and small towns," and went on to point out some of the costs of retailing, such as customer service on some items, sales personnel, fixtures, rent, etc.

The differential between mail-order and retail prices was again touched upon in the spring 1933 catalogue, which also contained this statement:

> In the event the United States or any state should increase by taxes or otherwise the cost or selling price of any of the merchandise described in this catalog, we reserve the right to add any such taxes and increase of cost or of selling price to the prices shown in this catalog.

And, like its predecessor, the spring 1933 book promoted Allstate automobile insurance, "sold on easy terms at no extra charge." The warranty quoted above was not repeated in the fall 1933 catalogue, at which time there came a general upward movement in prices; one phase of that upturn gave a fair illustration of what happens when costs advance after distribution of the catalogue. In the fall of 1933, price changes occasioned by the NRA and the cotton-processing tax permitted Sears to reprice cotton-goods items in wearing apparel and yard goods. A test was made by the company to determine customer reaction to this move. As orders were received, the new prices were written on the bills and a form letter of explanation sent. Some increases were as low as 3 per cent and could simply be added on to the bill, when the goods were shipped, without much risk of alienating customer good will. Some increases, however, were as great as 47 per cent; in these instances, customers were queried on whether they still wished to purchase the goods at the increased prices. Out of a test group including 5,691 price advances, only 10 complaints were received.

The fall 1933 book indicated, as a matter of fact, a somewhat paradoxical approach to prices. The opening three pages emblazoned the belief that the country's economic situation was already on the way up, yet subsequent pages listed many items priced lower than in 1932. The two-page layout introducing the price theme opened with a picture of General Wood ordering some of his buyers to "GET BUSY! AND HELP THE HOME. IT'S UP TO SEARS to offer the lowest home furnishing prices in America."

In the spring 1934 book the same topic of low prices was again hammered at, in a manner almost reminiscent of Richard Sears's earlier keynote, even though the latter-day presentation was more restrained. Wood's letter to the customers, by that time an integral part of the general catalogue, asserted that almost a year earlier he had ordered his buyers to purchase "literally many, many millions of dollars worth of merchandise. Our great warehouses were crowded to their very roofs with goods bought *before* prices approached their present levels." Wood went on to declare that all such goods were being offered "*on the basis of what they cost us—* not what we might be able to *get* for them." Under a picture of NRA's blue eagle there again appeared the statement reserving the right to increase prices if that were necessitated by any state or federal action.

That same page announced a contest "to secure new and original ideas suitable for front-cover designs on Sears General Catalogs." Cash prizes aggregated $2,500, the first prize being $1,000. Possibly as a result of the contest, which closed April 30, 1934, the fall 1934 catalogue featured a poem by Edgar A. Guest, titled, not surprisingly, "The Catalog" ("Written especially for Sears, Roebuck and Co. by America's best loved poet"). The catalogue itself again stressed the theme of low prices. Wood's letter declared:

> When it came to setting prices in this Fall 1934 Catalog, we felt that it was only fair and right, under the circumstances, for us to think first of our customers' present ability to buy, to disregard wholesale costs and to make, if need be, a real sacrifice of our profit.
> This has been done.
> You will note that prices in this book, despite advances in raw materials, wage rates and increased expense in practically every direction, are in most cases below those of our Spring Catalog and in many cases lower than a year ago.
> ... we have priced articles of real need—underwear, hosiery, shoes, utility apparel, textiles—close to actual cost of production. ...
> The mission of Sears, Roebuck and Co. is to sell merchandise at the lowest prices consistent with honest quality. That mission, we feel, has been excellently performed this season, as prices in this catalog prove.

There followed a long listing of items priced lower that fall than in the preceding spring.

In 1936 the company celebrated its fiftieth birthday (fifty years from the time Richard Sears sold his first watch, but actually only forty-three years from the incorporation of Sears, Roebuck and Company) with a "Golden Jubilee" catalogue, which went all-out on institutional advertising in reviewing the history of the firm and asserting its guaranty was "Still as Good as New." The celebrate its half-century in business, the company sponsored an elaborate and expensive program on a national radio network. Listener response was unsatisfactory, possibly because the effort to satisfy both rural and urban tastes resulted in pleasing neither group, and the program was soon abandoned.

By spring 1937 the big book was still splurging on institutional advertising. The line, "— things really are better!" surmounted by a picture of a grinning, prosperous-looking farmer, introduced Wood's regular letter. The General asserted, among other things, that "we have kept the price of goods to our customers on an even keel since 1933," and added that the spring 1937 book was offering merchandise at "practically the same levels as a year ago."

On the following page the banner line, "America looks forward," was illustrated with a photograph of a young man and a young woman apparently preparing to walk hand in hand together down the lane of life. The text asserted, "America doesn't need any rear-view mirror—our eyes are on the road ahead. We confidently believe that this country, right now, is making the greatest leap forward in its whole history." That catalogue also contained another implicit tribute to Richard Sears in the form of an almost verbatim repetition of one of his stratagems: "Please Lend This Catalog to Your Neighbors." The copy which followed bears repeating:

> After all, that neighbor of yours who hasn't got a Sears catalog probably doesn't know how much it could save him. Why not lend him yours! He'll appreciate it. So will we. And here's a tip . . . you'll save on shipping charges if you get together with some of your neighbors and make up a big order to be sent to one address.

The spring 1937 book also devoted a page to advertise the company's "Consumer Shopping Guide," consisting of 40 cards, "on which are mounted 115 actual samples of typical fabrics . . . goods that you use every day of your life. With these fabric samples comes a magnifying glass and definite instructions on just what to look for." The outfit, which also included a forty-page *Book of Facts,* sold for a dollar.

Well before 1937, however, mail order had developed new techniques of selling in addition to the catalogues; or, more properly, new means for better utilizing the catalogue as a selling instrument. As has been mentioned earlier, the company determined shortly after entering retail that prices in its stores had to be pegged some 6–8 per cent over mail-order prices to compensate for the increased expense in over-the-counter selling. Some customers demurred at having to pay more for any article in any Sears outlet than shown in the catalogue prices. Retail sales personnel were instructed not only to explain the price differential to such customers but also to remind them that they could examine goods in the retail stores and then return home to order that merchandise from the mail-order plant if they desired.

The next step in this line of reasoning was simple: Why turn away a customer after spending money on advertising to lure him into the store? Why not, instead, offer him a chance to place his catalogue order in the store? Accordingly, catalogues were stocked in the stores; customers were referred to them, and sales clerks occasionally helped the customers make out their catalogue orders. At first the arrangement was makeshift; the clerks were generally too busy serving their retail trade to assist anyone who turned out to be a "mail-order customer." Retail-store managers were usually less than enthusiastic about the system, since it demanded space in the store and some minimum of clerical assistance. Furthermore, mail order items competed quite often with identical retail-store items at higher prices.

Too, there was strongly present, as has been pointed out earlier, a poor working relationship between mail-order and retail personnel. Retail in general tended to scorn mail order and showed no desire to assist the older, "rival" side of the business. Retail was offered a division of the profits on mail-order sales filed through retail stores, which helped inaugurate the plan in 1930, but retail's profit was not sufficient to induce it to promote the arrangement with any vigor. An increased share of profits and some knocking-together of heads by the company's top executives finally persuaded retail to push catalogue sales. A "customers' service desk" was devised, manned by clerks trained in mail-order technique and supplied with all current catalogues. Mail-order sample books of clothing, wallpaper, and certain house furnishings were added to the equipment. Customers' mail-order service desks were eventually installed in all retail stores. Customers patronizing them received the full run of mail-order services; special circulars and booklets listing limited stocks of mail-order goods were distributed through the catalogue order desks.

In short, the company's full merchandise line was offered to the customer in one form or another: either physically present in the store or available by mail through the general or other catalogues. This was particularly important in building sales—largely, that is, to avoid *losing* sales—in the smaller retail stores, which, because of insufficient space, were inadequately stocked. The catalogue order desks in the retail stores languished after 1930, however, and the system was ineffective until about 1935, when the company determined to make a success of it. Store managers were made to see that a lost mail-order sale, through poor operation of the catalogue order desk, was actually a lost *company* sale and that it was to the advantage of the stores to offer every customer the full gamut of Sears's facilities for buying. This campaign was successful; by 1946, Division 200, which operates the catalogue order desks, was reporting an annual sales volume in excess of $75,000,000.

Much of the business done through these catalogue desks in retail stores was the result of referrals by sales clerks unable to furnish the item a customer wanted. But the company found an increasing number of mail-order customers who visited the retail stores only to order through the catalogue desks, possibly an indication of the convenience of not having to execute one's own order unaided or to have to compute postage. Customers ordering through this service had the choice of calling for their orders in the retail stores or of having the goods delivered direct to their homes. The former was cheaper for the customer, of course, since it allowed the company to capitalize upon bulk shipments with consequently lower transportation charges.

While the system of catalogue order desks in retail stores was still young, Sears began to experiment with still another new technique for securing mail-order business—the "Telethrift" shopping service. Under this device, a customer had only to pick up his phone and place his order. Goods were delivered to his door within two days. It was almost magically simple. But Ward's had been ahead of Sears on it. *Business Week* reported in November, 1934, that after several months of experimenting with the service in Chicago by both companies, Ward's had already issued full-page newspaper advertisements promoting its telephone service in five cities in which it had mail-order plants—Chicago, Baltimore, Albany, St. Paul, and Kansas

City. (Sears was still experimenting with the new technique in Chicago but planned to extend it soon to Los Angeles.) In the words of *Business Week:*

> The move marks Ward's first direct invasion of the larger cities. Its mail-order and retail stores have heretofore confined their operations exclusively to the smaller centers. Thus the new step does not enter into competition with existing units. Sears, with department stores in larger cities, has a greater problem on its hands. In Chicago it has confined telephone solicitation to regular mail-order customers....
>
> Department stores—with important exceptions—have fought shy of telephone orders, preferring to have the customer come into the store. Such service requires considerable description on the part of the customer. Ordering from mail-order catalogues is simplified as the articles are numbered.
>
> Stickers attached to several thousand small catalogues which went out 2 months ago marked the beginning of the tryout. The resultant telephone orders which came into both firms were beyond expectations. Repeat orders were numerous. The plan does away with letter writing or making a long trip to a store, eases the way to obeying impulses stirred by the catalogue lures.[5]

Ward's phone service units were installed in its mail-order plants, as Sears's were also to be shortly. Ward's charged fifteen cents on packages up to fifty pounds, and a small additional charge for heavier parcels, for delivery within a radius of about twenty miles from Chicago's Loop. Sears used a somewhat different method: no C.O.D. charge on orders of $2.00 or more, but a ten-cent charge on smaller orders; charges for truck delivery service on orders weighing less than twenty pounds were the same as postage on a parcel-post shipment. There was some relative saving on heavier packages which could be shipped by freight or express.[6]

The experiment succeeded well enough to lead the company to extend the plan in 1935 to several other mail-order plants. Throughout the late 1930's and the early 1940's the company established Telethrift in the larger towns of many of the mail-order regions. By early 1947, eleven such additional units had been set up in the Chicago mail-order region, fourteen in the area served by the Philadelphia plant, five in the Boston region, two in the Dallas region, and one each in Kansas City and Seattle—all in addition to Telethrift units in the mail-order plants in those cities. Telethrift was advertised by inserts in catalogues circulating in the area involved. These inserts gave the telephone numbers for the nearest Telethrift service and emphasized the simplicity of that method of buying—Telethrift even handled C.O.D. orders and time-payment orders. Truck drivers of the local package delivery service collected the C.O.D. payments; they also collected down payments on instalment purchases, as well as obtaining the customer's signature on the contract. Telethrift was organized also to handle exchanges or refunds when merchandise was unsatisfactory. A phone call from the dissatisfied customer brought the delivery service's driver to pick up the merchandise, prepared to issue a check to the customer who wanted his money back.

The company's experience shows that a large majority of the Telethrift service orders represents new business, not merely business diverted from the normal and less expensive channels. Analyses of orders from old customers also indicate that Telethrift has encouraged many of them to order more frequently through that system than they had in the traditional way of mailing in their orders. Telethrift, in many ways, represents a marked simplification in mail-order buying.

By late summer of 1939 Sears—and, inevitably, Ward's—revealed still another system for augmenting mail-order business. In communities too small to justify the opening of even the smallest retail store, Sears established catalogue order offices. The equipment was almost exactly the same as in the order desks in the retail stores: clerks trained in mail-order techniques, full collections of all the most recent catalogues, and even a small display of some representative merchandise. The customer was given the choice of having the goods shipped direct to his home or to the order office, where he would pick them up. Instalment payment accounts could be approved in the order offices, and payments on such accounts made there. Goods could be returned, and adjustments (refunds or substitutions) made.

The average order office's sixteen hundred square feet of space was divided about equally between selling space and space for receipt and storage of orders to be picked up. The mail-order plants supervising and serving the various order offices early made arrangements to give special handling to orders received through that channel, just as had earlier been done for the catalogue order desks in the retail stores and for the Telethrift service, in order to assist in promoting these techniques. By the end of 1939 a total of 66 order offices had been established and, by the end of 1940, 181. The annual report for 1940 asserted that in that year the 181 order offices accounted for "somewhat more" than 3 per cent of the mail-order sales. The number of such offices was steadily increased, crossing the 300 mark in 1945 and totaling 338 by the end of 1947.

These new techniques of mail order—the catalogue order desks in the stores, the order offices, and Telethrift—all obviously represented new ways of stimulating the volume of business derived from catalogues once the books were distributed. Before books were actually distributed, however, many questions demanded answering. How was the number of catalogues to be printed determined? Would a customer who received, say, the general catalogue automatically receive any or all of the other catalogues? How many catalogues should be printed? Should there be more or less in any given editions? Would a larger press run automatically bring in a proportionately larger volume of business? What was the optimum circulation point, and how was it found? These questions were fundamental, even before 1925.

Answers to them—as far as answers have been found—reside in the company's catalogue research section, which has spent literally hundreds of thousands of dollars conducting hundreds of tests in an effort to determine as closely as possible just how many books should be printed, just who should get them, what the most effective distribution is, how use of books that are distributed can be increased, how the customer list (or "index") can be developed and new customers recruited to replace those who disappear from the rolls, and other factors bearings vitally upon the company's mail-order business. The findings of the catalogue research section are summarized in its report, *A Quarter Century of Sears Mail Order Advertising Tests and Studies.*

For an understanding of what follows—taken almost *in toto* from the aforecited publication—some definitions are necessary. The "index" is the customer list, made up of "index cards," one for each customer, bearing the customer's name and address cut into a stencil used for addressing packages and labels. The date and dollar value of each of the customer's orders are indexed on these cards, of which there are several millions, filed alphabetically by post office(s). A "preferred" customer is one whose volume and recency of purchase(s) entitle him automatically to receive a general catalogue without request. By the same token, a "nonpreferred" customer is one whose purchases do not *entitle* him to automatic receipt of the catalogue.

Voluntary requests for the catalogue fall into two categories: (1) "indexed" requests, from nonpreferred customers whose names are on file, and (2) "not-indexed" requests, from people for whom there are no index cards. "Stimulated" requests are those developed by direct mail or some other means of promotion. The master-index also notes the difference between two-or-more-order cards (on customers who have, at no matter how widely separated intervals, bought more than once from the company) and one-order cards. "New" customers are so indicated, "new" referring only to one particular season; some of these will become preferred customers, buying relatively heavily year after year, while others will never order again and will thus in another season or so join the "one-order" ranks. The "test index" is a sample of the general index used for testing purposes. It contains cards of all the customers in several hundreds of towns, and their number totals several tens of thousands.

Finally, the words "profitable" and "unprofitable." "Profitable," to the catalogue research section, refers only to a promotion which is profitable in immediate dollar sales; the promotion must represent less outlay than the profit on the business it stimulates. When promotions are necessary to find more volume at high cost to hold the organization together in a trying period, or when protection of the customer list or some similarly desirable step is involved, and when these promotions appear to warrant the cost, they are termed "advantageous," "expedient," or "advisable." "Profitability" simply connotes more money in the till, after all expenses. "Unprofitability" means just that. There are, of course, wide variations in the "profitability" even of preferred customers.

The customer classification system for separating preferred from nonpreferred is a flexible approach and has varied widely through the years in its requirements of activity (recency of purchase) and dollar volume within the customer's life-span in the index. In the spring of 1911, for example, the requirement was an order of any amount within the previous six months and a total previous record of $5.00 or more business. In the fall of that year the requirement was an order in the previous twelve months and $20 or more on the card. In succeeding years the activity period was, variously, six, eight, nine, ten, and twelve months, and the minimum dollar volume of orders ranged from $5.00 in multiples of $5.00 up to $25. Studies of the files show that these requirements were settled by rule of thumb. The number of preferred books was predetermined; tests were made to see how many names would be developed on a tentative basis, which was then altered as necessary to address the desired number. This frequently involved errors of some magnitude.

No serious attempt was made before 1922 to study the firm's customers more closely (by means of the test index) to work out a system which would *first* select the best classes, thereby providing information on how many books could be distributed profitably. The first studies showed that the really determining factor in how much a customer would probably buy in the coming months was the amount of business from him in recent months. Neither recency of a purchase nor the total volume of purchases over a period of years was by itself an adequate weathervane.

Combining the factors of recency of last order, value of recent business, and the customer's complete record in various ways gave the testers several hundred classifications of customers. About thirty such classes have come to be used by the testers, who thus visualize the index as being composed of some thirty layers or strata. If the top layers are considered the best, then the value of any catalogue mailing or other promotion declines rapidly as it is extended down this series of layers. The crux of the whole problem is to determine in any given promotional effort at about what layer profit ends and waste begins. A total of several hundred tests has been directed at one or another of those various layers. The top layers constitute the "cream"; some 10 per cent of the preferred customers provide about one-half the company's mail-order business.

In somewhat oversimplified terms, the task is to keep this top 10 per cent buying (heavily), to induce the layers below this one to buy more heavily, to persuade the nonpreferred customers to move up at least into the lower rank or outside fringe of the preferred, and to keep "new blood" flowing into the index in the hope that a reasonable percentage of these additions can be made profitable through fairly large purchases over a relatively short period of time or through smaller purchases over a longer time span.

Each phase of that task poses problems of its own. How can the "cream," that top 10 per cent, be persuaded to buy even more or, at any rate, to keep on buying at all? What special services and handling will help retain their demonstrated allegiance? How can buyers in the lower strata of the preferred group be induced to buy enough to become "super-preferred"? How can people who have not bought from the company in a long while be returned to the active fold? And how can people who have never purchased from Sears, Roebuck be led to make their first purchase? The continued existence of the company's mail-order business depends upon finding reasonably good answers to a reasonable percentage of these questions; for, while few mail-order executives even hope for all the answers or for "perfect" solutions, they proceed on the hypothesis that mail order must grow or die.

Certain facts emerge clearly from a study of the findings of the catalogue research section: (1) Sears, Roebuck has been willing to spend large sums of money for experimentation in the ceaseless search for bigger and better mail-order business. (2) The testers have conducted tests on countless possible approaches to increasing the mail-order business and in their work have apparently had strong support from top executives in the company, as indicated by the fact that many tests involved "disruption" of operations by printing special catalogues and by printing special pages or sections in selected test samples of large numbers of catalogues. And (3) the testers retain a candid and cautious skepticism about their findings, so many of which are negative (though that, of course, does not necessarily lessen their importance), and constantly reiterate the necessity of conducting many tests again under better-controlled conditions.

The problems of making use of customer classifications of thirty (or one hundred, or any other number of) layers is and always has been greatly complicated by the fact that it has had to rest upon a simple system of visual application and selection, even though vastly more complex systems may have been thought by the research section to be far preferable. In the absence of mechanization to make selection automatic—possibly the most urgently sought mechanization within the company—systems of classification and selection well below the optimum have of necessity continued in force. This fact has influenced and colored all tests of the research section, which has asserted that the coming of a "machine age" in customer classification and selection will require a recheck or revision of most existing practices and may well serve to enhance the utility of many experiments thus far found to be of little or no value. In short, stubbornly inadequate means of mechanization have circumscribed and hampered all the activities of the thinkers. In fact, the testers' conclusions in their report lists mechanization of the customer index as one of the three hopes for the company to increase its mail-order business in the future.

In 1922, following the testers' initial findings in connection with customer classification (which led to revision of thinking on what constituted preferred customers), steps were taken to extend the circulation of the general catalogue—the first really serious efforts since Richard Sears's "Iowaization." Some three hundred thousand catalogues were distributed in the Chicago area alone in the fall of that year on requests stimulated by letter from the better classes of nonpreferred customers—which the new customer classification system had but recently learned to identify. This effort was so successful that the stimulation of requests was immediately adopted in other territories (Dallas, Seattle, and Philadelphia) and extended to the complete nonpreferred list. The circulation of the general catalogue jumped by over a million books, and the addition was highly profitable (the company's annual volume of business rose from $164,039,720 in 1921 to $166,514,110 in 1922 and to $198,482,945 in 1923, aided of course by improving business conditions).

While pondering the prospects of increased catalogue circulation, Sears started in 1923 to advertise heavily in papers with a rural circulation. From 1923 to 1926 over a million dollars was spent for space—the first such campaign since Richard Sears's earlier effort. After 1926 advertising for general catalogue requests was limited to territories where new mail-order plants were opened, except that a national program was again tried in 1930 and 1931. However fruitful the rural press had been for the founder, it seemed to yield a less bountiful harvest to his successors. As a consequence, mail order abandoned such advertising after its 1931 effort.

Continued efforts at stimulation of nonpreferred customers finally revealed roughly where profitability ended and unprofitability began. The program steadied to a preferred list of some three million and the stimulation of an additional two million requests from about half the nonpreferred list. The only circulation to the "lower" half of the nonpreferred list was made in answer to unsolicited requests for catalogues. This system, which continued through 1930, seemed to establish five million (about half the size of the index) as the maximum number of catalogues which could profitably be forced into the customer list, though of course this number varied with the size of the index.

A serious defect in that circulation plan was the fact that four million nonpreferred customers had to be stimulated each season to secure two million requests for catalogues, at a cost of roughly $250,000 annually. The decision was reached to make preferred the "top" two million of the names formerly classified as nonpreferred. This worked out to the complete satisfaction of the company. In one way, it was a return to the policy in effect in 1911: predetermining the "right" number of books and then seeing how far down the strata of the index to go in distributing them. The difference, however, was that in the later stage that predetermined number, instead of being "pulled out of the air," was set by a definite relationship among the customer list, sales volume, and the sales trend at the time of each catalogue printing.

Studies concerned with possible deviations by control stores (branch mail-order plants) from the one preferred basis decided upon revealed that the optimum arrangement was to use one classification applied across the nation. Likewise, distance of the customer from the control store proved to make no significant difference. It had been felt that perhaps the customers geographically closest to the branch plants might buy more because of better service, faster delivery, etc., but tests showed that the nearest customers were no better than the most distant ones. Nor were any real seasonal deviations among the several control stores discovered.

In the process of experimenting with bases for catalogue circulation, the company made some important discoveries as to the most effective types of order-stimulators. Experiments were made with first- and third-class letters, post cards, "trick" pieces, circulars, and small catalogues patched up of leaders from the general catalogue. Several types of inclosures were used. Experiments were made with various colors, with varying numbers of inclosures, with different type faces, even with the size of catalogues, letters, and other material. Similar tests were made to determine optimum circulation of flyers, bargain bulletins, supplements, special catalogues, and other mailing pieces. By way of summary, it may be said that it was decided that the problem was not how to distribute more books but rather how to make the number presently distributed produce more business, as well as how better to distribute the same number of books.

The approach to a policy of mailing fewer books, to eliminate waste, centered largely around stricter bases of culling the index, efforts to prevent duplication, and revisions of address lists according to information supplied by postmasters on customers dead or departed. In general terms, the task of eliminating various classes of customers from various mailings (for the big book, flyers, etc.) promised to be more expensive in many cases than duplication would be. One great saving was, however, made in 1942, when the unusual movement of customers during wartime and the company's own personnel shortages had placed the index in admittedly bad condition. All but one of the control stores revised their indexes, largely on information supplied by postmasters, to eliminate duplicates and "dead" names (customers whose addresses were unknown). More than 500,000 duplicates and still more dead names were dropped. The cost of that culling operation was $182,000. It brought an immediate net saving of over $250,000, with, of course, additional savings in subsequent seasons.

In studying better distribution of the same number of books, the mailing time came up in several different ways. When the stimulation of catalogue requests from the nonpreferred customers was abandoned in favor of mailing to a single, broader, preferred distribution, the company continued to address and release first all those catalogues going to those in the former preferred classes (called "first-preferred"), and then to the "second-preferred" group which had replaced the stimulated requests. The prevailing opinion was that any delay in the release of books resulted in a loss of business and that, since the loss was on a percentage basis, it would obviously represent a smaller dollar loss when applied to the poorer section of the list. Two factors conspired to change this system. It was felt by some of the company's executives that it was important to saturate a community at one time with all the catalogues which were to be mailed to it. And, second, the system of two mailings complicated the addressing problem, increased the work at the printers, and added to distribution costs because of double shipments. It was abandoned in favor of one mailing to all classes qualifying automatically.

Another aspect of the time element arose in connection with the actual release date of any given general catalogue. It was found that every day was important in rushing the book to customers: each two-week delay appeared to represent a loss of 2 per cent in total seasonal business, which gave promise even of reaching as much as 5 per cent. Sears did, however, come to favor certain of its regions over others in certain seasons: the South now receives the first spring catalogues, since the season comes sooner there, while Kansas City and Minneapolis are favored in the fall. As always, similar tests to determine the best timing for release were made in connection with flyers and other books.

Since there appeared to be little or nothing to be gained by increasing or decreasing the total circulation of the general catalogue and the other catalogues, the research section turned its attention to promoting greater use of books already in circulation. This activity represented some of the most comprehensive and most expensive testing, largely because it necessitated abnormal expenditures for printing, direct-mail promotion, press and radio advertising, and establishment of special service units within the company.

In addition to these efforts, preferred customers who had never purchased on credit were urged to do so; certain lines (musical instruments, books, etc.) were promoted by post cards sent to individuals shown on the index as purchasers of these or allied lines. Special circulars were used at one point in the 1930's in an effort to capitalize upon government payment of bonuses to farmers for cotton and wheat acreage reduction.

Special catalogues were printed at one time in three separate test editions, in which the key letter, price, and postage copy were changed from the regular edition for every item in the book. The postage was quoted in exact amounts on every item and even, in some of the books, prepaid by the company, in an effort to determine whether the old bugaboo of computing postage was costing the company business. (As late as 1942, a check of 12,000 Chicago orders showed that on only 30 per cent had the postage been figured correctly; 20 per cent underestimated, and 50 per cent allowed too much.)

Special handling of inquiries and complaints on selected index layers was tried. Miscellaneous advertising devices such as samples, calendars (with an order form printed on the back of each leaf), gift certificates, business reply envelopes, stamped three-cent government envelopes, special money-order application blanks (the company's name and address were imprinted on money-order blanks furnished by the Post Office Department, which was seeking to boost sales of money orders), a special company pictorial consumer's magazine called *The American Fireside,* stuffers, and other devices—all were used variously in controlled tests applied to owners of the general catalogue, the flyers, etc.

Changes in the general catalogue itself and other catalogues were tried: improvements in binding, alterations in layout and copy, makeup, use of swatches of material in books, special binders for the catalogue, specially priced leader items to serve as "order-starters," psychological pricing (68 cents instead of 70 cents, etc.), the size of the book, the catalogue's index—all these topics and more occupied the testers.

Development and protection of the customer list, through all the devices previously indicated, were followed by an intensive study of customer buying habits. In this project the research section sought to ascertain almost everything ascertainable about the company's customers which might shed any light on the over-all objective: to obtain more customers and to promote heavier buying by those customers.

In the conclusion to the summary of their twenty-five years of testing, the researchers listed three great hopes for continuing to extract a profitable volume of business from the company's customers with a minimum of wasted advertising expense: (1) the mechanization of the index, previously mentioned; (2) several successful direct-mail ideas tested shortly before 1945; and (3) the local circular program. The report on a quarter-century of looking at Sears, Roebuck's customers closed on this note:

> We do not believe, however, that efforts should be relaxed in the attempt to sell more goods by improvements in our service, merchandise, pricing and catalog make-up. Facts shown in the closing section of this paper have demonstrated that great numbers of the catalogs we circulate on the best system yet devised do a very poor job—either producing no order at all or only one or two. Something seems to be needed which will make mail order more attractive to such poor prospects, something apart from catalog circulation, or promotional follow-up. If these efforts are successful, then the quantity of catalogs needed will rise automatically since more customers will come within the profit range; and our direct mail programs will work more surely since the better the customer, the better his response to any advertising material. And, if one or more of our "hopes" for the future fail to do the anticipated job, our business will rest solidly on the fundamentals responsible for its original growth.

The foregoing account of Sears's testing of catalogue circulation and sales-promotion policies makes it clear that catalogue circulation, customer classification, and sales promotion have long ceased to operate by happenstance. The company has capitalized upon the peculiar advantage possessed by the mail-order business for market research—the knowledge of exactly who the customers are. Present policies rest upon what appears to the company to be the wisdom of demonstrated experience in cultivating its market.

Sears's mail-order market is made up of several geographic segments, and sales records through the years have registered the differences that characterize each of these submarkets. The regional catalogues of the company have come to represent more than merely localized cover treatment or variations in merchandise offered to accord with the more obvious variations in climate and geography, for the company's merchandisers have long since found regional preference and eccentricities in habits and modes of living growing out of climatic and geographical differences. In the words of one writer, "America, to Sears, Roebuck, has become ten Americas, each revolving around a key city.... Their boundaries may be as indistinct as a bald man's hairline, but the catalogue cartographers have outlined their respective preferences in clear distinct lines of merchandise."[7]

This is not to say that the majority of Sears's merchandise is not listed in every general catalogue; the overwhelming majority certainly is, but the company has learned which goods will not pay their way in catalogue space in any given regional book. Corsets, for example, appear in all general catalogues; ample evidence, perhaps, that the eternal battle of the bulge is fought pretty much on the same terrain throughout the land. But velvet hats, evening gowns, slips, and accessory-shop novelties did not appear in the 1940 catalogues for Seattle and Los Angeles. Woolen union suits for women, fur coats, fur jackets, and rayon bathrobes at $18 were omitted from the Dallas, Memphis, and Atlanta books (the climate could account for that); also omitted, surprisingly, were cotton-, tobacco-, and sugar-raising implements in those three regions. The breadbasket of the nation registered its effect through the fact that steel cribs, bins, and silos were advertised only in Chicago, Minneapolis, and Kansas City. Dallas, on the other hand, did not list automatic milkers, steel stalls, or stanchions for cows. Only in Chicago and Philadelphia was Swedish Modern furniture listed; only in Seattle and Los Angeles was cabana-style furniture offered. Only Chicago and Boston books offered broadloom rugs at $40, although innerspring mattresses were listed in all regions, except the three in the South. The eight-cubic-foot Coldspot refrigerator was offered only on the West Coast. Gas ranges were not available in the Seattle, Atlanta, and Memphis regions; cheap power through Bonneville and the TVA made electric ranges better offers.[8]

Analyses made in 1947 by the general managers of the company's mail-order plants shed even more light on regional variations in the demand for merchandise. The Dallas plant finds 62.66 per cent of its customers living in places of less than 2,500 population; another 15.15 per cent in places from 2,500 to 5,000 in population; and 15.23 per cent living in towns with population of 5,000–10,000. This predominantly rural and small-town populace enjoys a growing season ranging from 300 days in a year in the Rio

Grande Valley of Texas to 179 days in the northern portion of the Texas Panhandle. The mean annual temperature for the entire state of Texas is 66.3°, ranging from a mean of less than 56° in the northern part of the state to a mean of 74° in the Valley. Weather of 100°–110° throughout the state is not uncommon through the summer, while the Panhandle experiences subzero weather in the winter. The mean annual precipitation for the entire state is 30:54 inches, made up of extremes of as much as 55.14 inches on the Louisiana border to 7.89 inches at El Paso in the west.

Texas is not a highly industrialized state, but it is perhaps the most chauvinistic in the nation. Nor is it a wealthy state, despite its oil, cotton, and sulphur barons. That, in brief, is Texas, and Texas is a fair sample of the whole Dallas territory. The volume of business done by the Dallas branch plant is about comparable to that of Minneapolis or Boston, and Boston does usually 7 per cent of the company's total mail-order business. How do the various afore-mentioned characteristics of the Dallas region manifest themselves in what the people buy from Sears, Roebuck?

Diapers sell particularly well in Dallas, since they are often a baby's only item of wearing apparel from April to October. By the same token, Dallas sells 20 per cent of the electric-fan volume of all Sears's mail order. Brassières account for better than 10 per cent of the mail-order total, and panties for 9, but girdles in Dallas sell only 6 per cent of Sears's mail-order total. Unpainted furniture sells particularly well, since the rural customers prefer to do their own painting or even to use the furniture in its unfinished state. Modern bedroom suites receive better-than-average customer acceptance in this region, running 244 per cent ahead of the volume sold by the Chicago branch plant. Living-room suites, occasional chairs and rockers, and, in fact, nearly all other furniture in relatively low price ranges likewise sell in heavy volume. Dallas does a land-office business in lawn and garden tools, but mechanical tools sell poorly. Woodsmen's tools hardly sell at all, since three-quarters of the Dallas region is untimbered.

Wire and wiring devices sell particularly well, owing largely to the increase in rural electrification and to the fact that farmers in the Southwest prefer (or more properly, perhaps, find themselves compelled) to do their own wiring. Dallas' share of Sears's over-all sales of electrical appliances rose from 5 per cent in 1941 to 8 per cent five years later. Sewing machines excel; the company has found that a very large proportion of the women in the Southwest make their own clothes. For the same reason, piece goods also sell exceptionally well. Piece-good sales in drapery and curtain materials and upholstery goods have often been "sensational." Coat and coat sets for children sell poorly indeed in the Southwest, and suits, skirts, jumpers, blouses, and jackets are simply not in vogue there in the spring. Playsuits sell in far greater volume, as do sheer dresses. Snow suits are rarely profitable.

Lace-trimmed slips sell better in Dallas than in any other mail-order region, because sheer dresses have a longer wearing season there. Women's nightgowns outsell pajamas two to one, which is a direct reversal of the situation in the North and East. Sweaters sell very poorly in the spring, by comparison with the North and East, but satisfactorily in the fall. Matched uniform sets, acceptable both for work on the farm or in a garage and for wear to town on Saturday, sell particularly well in Dallas; they give a dressy effect at little more than the cost of overalls. In the fall of 1946 Dallas sold more commodes than any other Sears mail-order store, doing some 22 per cent of the company's total sales of this item. High-priced, sturdily built work shoes do not sell well in the Southwest (less industrialization means fewer workers compelled to stand for long periods on concrete floors), but cheap work shoes sell in vast quantities. Dallas stands in sixth place among the mail-order plants in its volume of shoes, and cowboy boots are held largely responsible. Texas is surely the only state in the Union, and possibly the only area in the world, where such boots are sometimes worn with evening clothes.

At the opposite pole from Dallas is the Boston branch plant. Whereas Dallas' market is largely agricultural, Boston's is largely industrial. Farming in New England consists mostly of dairy and poultry farming, plus some specialized agriculture like potatoes in Maine and tobacco in the Connecticut Valley. The Boston plant has benefited more from order offices, catalogue desks in retail stores, and Telethrift service than any other region; New England is literally a network of small cities. The region is also a land of craftsmen, and Boston tends to hard lines, ranking fourth in tool sales among the eleven branch plants. Cold weather calls for warm clothing, and phrases like "100 per cent virgin wool" pull business. Steady incomes and high average incomes enable customers to buy better-quality clothing, as well as other goods. Boston sells more heating equipment using oil for fuel than any other Sears plant. Small windows in most of the homes and bitter wintry blasts make storm windows and storm doors excellent sellers. Rubber footwear also sells well, but other shoes do not, as the region is filled with outlet stores of its many shoe manufacturers. The huge vacationing income from resorts makes itself felt in unusually heavy sales of sporting equipment. The large professional class offers good customers for such hobby items as power tools.

Hard by the Boston area lies the Philadelphia region, but it is a sharply different zone. Philadelphia serves one of the most concentrated and diversified markets in the country, reaching from central and northern New York State to North Carolina, from eastern Ohio to the Atlantic seaboard. When it is still late winter and cold in New York, it is early spring and warm in southern Virginia. The Philadelphia branch transacts one-fifth of the company's mail-order business. Philadelphia does excellently in women's fashion wearing apparel. But the chief factor which distinguishes that plant is its foreign and export business, which reached $5,000,000 in 1946, using port facilities and ocean freight as well as air-freight service to open up markets in Central and South America. In 1947 the Philadelphia plant flew catalogues to American troops in Germany for the opening of its catalogue shopping service in 137 Army service centers in that occupied country.

Immediately west of Philadelphia is the Chicago region, the most nearly "average" of all. While Atlanta and Dallas sell more automobile tires than Minneapolis because of their ruinously hot weather, Chicago strikes an average between them, as its climate includes very hot and very cold areas. Boston and Philadelphia sell coveralls in large sizes, as railroad and other workers wear them over their clothing; Kansas City sells this item in smaller sizes, as the farmers in its region wear them directly over their underwear, but Chicago, including railroad men and farmers, sell coveralls in both large and small sizes. Shoes generally run larger in the South than in the North; Chicago finds its shoe market runs to average sizes.

Atlanta has, on the other hand, deviated greatly from the average in some lines. That region in 1947 was doing approximately 11–12 per cent of the company's total mail-order volume. Yet in watches it accounted for nearly 17 per cent of Sears's mail-order watch sales. Atlanta's volume of the company's hardware sales has risen in the last six years from 7 to around 11 per cent; kitchen utensils have repeated the same pattern. The government-sponsored power and electrification projects helped boost Atlanta's sales of electrical appliances to 13 per cent of the company's national volume in appliances. Sales of piece goods for making curtains run particularly high, since many southern windows are too large to use the small curtains shown in the catalogue. Sewing machines and supplies also sell well. Atlanta even tops Dallas in diapers, selling 22 per cent of Sears's mail-order total. Baby chicks also sell better there than in any other region, but harness in the Atlanta area accounts for only 8 per cent of Sears's total harness sales. In work clothing Atlanta does 17 per cent of the company's volume, and it sells almost twice as many hats as Chicago. Toys sell poorly, even at Christmas, but Atlanta is responsible for 20 per cent of all company business in radios.

Cross-country from Atlanta is the Pacific Southwest, served by the Los Angeles branch plant. Within the six states of Arizona, California, Colorado, Nevada, New Mexico, and Utah are found the most extreme range of contrasts and the largest variety of major industries in any part of the world. California has a range of topography varying from the highest point in the United States (Mount Whitney, with an elevation of 14,996 feet) to the lowest (Death Valley, 276 feet below sea level). The climate ranges from frigid to torrid. Central Valley, larger in area than England, produces 220 different crops, including half the world's supply of dried fruits, and has over a thousand factories processing foods. Cash farm income in California is the largest in any state in the Union. California is the number-one automobile market of the United States.[9]

The Los Angeles mail-order plant does a little more than 5 per cent of all Sears's mail-order business (from 1942 through 1946 this region averaged 5.1 per cent of total mail-order sales). Yet in sporting goods and luggage Los Angeles does variously from 7.2 to 9 per cent of Sears's national mail-order volume, and in books and cameras (mostly the latter, in that scenic region) 7.6 per cent of the total. In hardware and cutlery the sales record of that region is even more impressive: 10.8 per cent of the total mail-order volume. Housewares, china, and glassware are also above Los Angeles' general average, with figures of 7 per cent each, and electrical appliances furnish the same percentage. In rugs and carpets Los Angeles does 8.4 per cent of Sears's mail-order total. But the same climatic advantages and high income which help account for high sales in those lines spell out an inverse picture in two other departments. In boys' clothing Los Angeles slips from its national proportion of 5 per cent of mail-order volume to a little less than 3 per cent, and men's suits and trousers generally sell even less well in that region. The trend to gay sports clothing induced by the equable climate is something the company is still unable to cope with.

So it goes, region by region, merchandise department by department, item by item. And what is really significant is not merely the regional variations but the evidence they offer of the company's continuing analysis of all its merchandise lines and items to find which are paying their way in each regional catalogue and which are not.

The similarities between regions are greater, of course, than the differences, and the great bulk of catalogue offerings are common to the whole market. The catalogues of all regions reflect any very fundamental changes of the terms on which Sears, Roebuck buys and sells. So did all the fall 1941 books mirror the uncertain conditions of that year by reserving the right to raise prices if there should be "any increase in our costs by reason of any federal, state, or local government regulations or taxes." As before, small price increases would simply be added on and the customer so notified when he received his merchandise; where large increases were involved, the customer would be queried to determine his wishes.

While that catalogue was reaping its initial harvest of Christmas orders, America went to war, and mail order's job thenceforth became not to sell the goods it had so much as to try to obtain the goods it knew it could sell. And the institutional and sales-promotional space came to be the vehicle for sale of war bonds and similar endeavors and for reiteration of the theme, "the wants of our government are supreme. In America today nothing is as important as America itself."

Prices throughout the 1942 fall book conformed to regulations prescribed

NEW TECHNIQUES OF SELLING

by the Office of Price Administration, but the company took twenty pages of appendix to list 18,535 items (out of the total offering of 92,300 items) priced below OPA ceilings. That appendix listed both the ceiling prices and the offering prices, and explained that the general OPA ceiling order was amended for mail-order catalogues to base mail-order prices on March retail prices minus the "normal differential" due to lower distribution costs by mail order. One newspaper said of the prices in that catalogue:

> Prices in the new catalogue average about 25 per cent above those in the company's last fall and winter book, released a year ago. The prices of only a few items, however, are higher than appeared in the last major Sears Catalogue, the spring and summer issue of last January.
>
> Although price comparisons between the new book and the January catalogue are difficult because of changes in merchandise, the average increase appears to be not more than 2 or 3 per cent. This price stability is the result not only of price control, but of the Sears policy of offering many items below ceiling prices.
>
> The prices of many standard or staple articles in the new catalogue are the same as in the January book, however. This illustrates the fact that Sears and other large mail order firms were in relatively favorable positions for price control because of the substantial price boosts made when the previous major catalogues were issued.[10]

Editorially, the catalogue also "went to war." The book devoted space to help sell war bonds and to urge support for collection of scrap and called for the public's co-operation in civilian defense work and in appeals being made by the Red Cross and the USO. The listing of omitted items under the heading, "This merchandise is not available in your Sears catalogue this fall," was preceded by this foreword:

> To make sure that the men who are fighting our battles have the guns and planes and tanks and ships they need we at home must do without many of the things we formerly enjoyed. Even if the list were many times this big, and it may well grow larger as our war needs increase, we should be glad to make the sacrifice, and we know that every American will.

On items which could be purchased only with priority orders or ration certificates, the pages listing them included forms to be executed and dispatched with the order. In addition, the book devoted eight pages to interpretations of restrictions on such goods as plumbing, heating, and building materials, tires, and electrical equipment, and additional space to instructions on how to preserve the life of washing machines, refrigerators, fabrics, and other goods.

The war years saw Sears's mail order concentrating steadily greater effort upon available goods to compensate for inability to procure even the staple soft lines which accounted for the majority of its sales volume. The widespread shortages, graphically illustrated in the growing lists of unavailable items in the catalogues, posed a problem in allocation of goods that *were* available. Goods in only limited supply could be readily disposed of through the retail stores. But, once goods were listed in a catalogue, it cost the company as much to process omissions for them as to fill an order. Allocations of available goods were made on a "fair," rule-of-thumb basis as between mail order and retail.

As the shortages began to ease after the end of the war, hard lines and major appliances made their first reappearance in the retail units; the catalogues (which took months to prepare, print, circulate, and run out their allotted time span) had never been a major factor in the sale of those lines, and any listing of scarce goods simply invited omissions. Items procured in driblets would better be sold through retail, where no listing or even advertising was necessary. Unavailability of an item in retail represented, of course, a lost sale, but it did not entail the cost of the processing and correspondence required in a mail-order omission.

Preoccupation with omissions gave way at the close of the war to other catalogue worries. High on the list was uncertainty over the course of prices and price controls. The spring 1947 catalogue was well under way in physical production in October, 1946; on November 9 President Truman issued a general decontrol order. Consequently, prices for most of the 100,000 or so items were those prevailing under OPA ceilings. Montgomery Ward was, of course, likewise caught short by the sudden end of controls. The 1946 general catalogues of both companies had contained hedges against having to absorb "burdensome increases" in prices due to unpredictable possibilities, reserving the right to pass such price increases on to customers. That same hedge clause, like earlier ones, also stressed the converse aspect: any lower costs to Sears or Ward's would be passed on to customers in the form of reduced prices, with cash refunds made along with the delivered orders. Inserts in the spring 1947 catalogues (distributed in January) prepared customers for some price jumps on catalogue goods which the companies expected to come early in 1947. The *Wall Street Journal* summed up the situation facing Sears and Ward's:

> If consumer buying falls off alarmingly, Sears and Ward can use their midseason "flyers" (small catalogs) to advertise goods on which prices have been slashed. This was a pre-war practice which was discontinued during the war when there was nothing to offer at bargain rates.
>
> Sears and Ward will pledge themselves to "hold the Line" against any inflation of prices as long as possible, and agree to notify customers of any higher price before making shipment....
>
> To date nearly all the manufacturers' price hikes on goods listed in (the Fall 1946) catalogs have been absorbed by the firms.
>
> "It is a good public relations gesture. We will do it as long as we can," one mail order executive declares....
>
> [One] mail order executive sums up the reluctance to ask customers to pay more money for an article than is specified in the catalog:
>
> "It is a hard job to ask customers to pay more for goods. It costs money and the time of our employees to request the extra remittance."
>
> Sears and Ward both say they could easily refuse to send out catalog goods on which profit margins have become too narrow or have evaporated entirely. They

merely would send customers "omission" slips, declaring the articles are not in stock.

Then such articles would be sold at a higher retail price through the more than 1,200 retail stores these two merchandisers operate.

But both companies had to do so much omitting on mail orders during the war period, they are anxious to satisfy millions of customers who patronize the "wish books."[11]

The shortages of the war years extended, of course, to paper and effected a reduction in the number of mail-order mediums. Most of the special catalogues were dropped; the survivors included those listing wallpaper samples, men's clothing samples, paint samples, and informative booklets required to help customers obtain the best possible service from certain types of merchandise. The war also made scarce or unobtainable the surplus stocks which had been listed in the bargain bulletins, and this medium was discontinued. At the same time, however, mail-order plants were given wide discretionary power in printing circulars to stimulate business; the circulars required relatively little paper, and, moreover, the paper required could often be obtained locally with little difficulty or, sometimes, diverted from retail-store paper quotas. Circulars were frequently used to list goods which were not available in sufficient amounts to permit listing in the general catalogue.

These circulars were, in fact, the first tangible result of an organization established in 1941 to assist regional mail-order sales promotion. A director of regional sales promotion was appointed in the office of the general mail-order sales and advertising manager in Chicago, to work with limited staffs of advertising personnel in each of the mail-order plants. By the time the war came, mail order was using seven annual catalogues, in addition to the bargain bulletins (soon to be discontinued) and circulars (just starting on a regional basis): the spring and summer general catalogue, the January–February flyer, the midseason fall flyer featuring back-to-school merchandise, and the Christmas flyer. In addition there were, of course, a few special catalogues (wallpaper, paints, etc.).

The total cost for these seven mediums for the year 1946 was $25,150,000, including distribution costs, as compared with a cost of only $9,700,000 for a slightly greater total circulation in 1932. In addition to higher production costs (the company estimated that 1946's production costs were practically twice those of 1932), the higher total cost was also accounted for by the greater numbers of pages in the 1946 books, as well as more pages involving costlier printing techniques. Of the $25,150,000 bill of 1946, 84 per cent was represented by production cost; 16 per cent by distribution cost. The costliest items of production were roll paper stock (24.9 per cent of the *total* cost), presswork (21.6 per cent of total cost), and artwork (8.1 per cent). The parent-organization expense accounted for only 5.4 per cent of the total expenditure. More than half the distribution cost—8.8 per cent, to be exact—was represented by postage. In 1932, however, postage accounted for 15.7 per cent of the total cost, even though distribution costs were 25 per cent of the total in that earlier year, production accounting for only three-quarters of the over-all expenditure.

The use of more and more color illustrations, with accompanying higher production costs per color page, led the company to some fairly sharp departures in layout from earlier years. Richard Sears had preached the gospel that descriptive text must abut on artwork, that copy had to go under or next to (or, occasionally, even over) the illustration of the item. He feared that any separation of text from illustration would lead to confusion in ordering and to errors by customers. This doctrine held sway for many years after Sears's departure. As the catalogue began to use more and more color pages, however, it became increasingly expensive and impractical to devote costly space on color pages to copy, when color space could be reserved for merchandise enhanced in presentation by the use of color, while copy could go on the facing page and be set in ordinary black type on white stock for far less money. In the first period of separation of text and artwork, Richard Sears's fears were partially borne out, but the editorial staff soon learned how properly to key the merchandise and the text, with the result that customers' errors were diminished. The kinks were ironed out, and separation of copy and art was extended more and more even to items to be printed in black and white or rotogravure, since much merchandise lent itself to overlapping "fan" displays with subsequent conservation of space.

By the end of the war Sears found that its mail-order selling had undergone about as great a revolution in some ways as the whole company had undergone after the entry into retail. When this latter period opened and, indeed, even up to 1930, all the company's mail-order business came directly from its various catalogues, and the great majority of it of course from the two annual general catalogues. In other words, the total volume of mail-order business was represented by orders which customers had made out from a catalogue and mailed to the company. In the postwar period a great change was visible. Of the 1945 net mail-order sales, about two-thirds came from "straight" mail order—that is, from orders mailed in by customers. Seventeen per cent of the mail-order volume came from the catalogue order desks in the retail stores—still mail-order business, but "assisted" instead of "straight" business—while some 10 per cent came through order offices. And about 5 per cent of the total mail-order volume was derived from Telethrift sales.

In some regions the changes since 1930 were even more apparent. The Philadelphia region in 1946 did only about half its mail-order business on a straight catalogue basis; the remainder came through the catalogue order desks, order offices, and Telethrift. (Possibly as a result of this, Philadelphia's Telethrift selling grew from 3 operators and $125,000 in business in

1934 to 15 offices, 186 operators, and several millions in sales in 1946.) The first order offices opened in 1939 did roughly $500,000 of business in that first year; and 47 such offices operating in 1946 did more than twenty times that volume.

In the Boston region, mail-order sales from the three auxiliary services accounted for more than half the sales volume in 1946. Total order-office sales in that region were greater in 1946 than in any other region, even though several control stores have more order offices operating than does Boston.

Changes in the company's selling instruments both reflected and encouraged changes in Sears's market. As late as 1925 the great preponderance of the company's business had come from rural areas, and most of that volume was derived from farmers' purchases. But a comprehensive national study made in 1941 revealed that only about 30 per cent of mail order's customers were farmers. The proportions of farmer customers were 58 per cent in the Memphis region, 54 per cent in Kansas City and in Minneapolis, and 43 per cent in Atlanta. But wherever the company's customers were, and important as the catalogue order desks, order offices, and Telethrift service were in reaching them, all those selling techniques continued to rest upon the same base as did "straight" mail-order selling: the catalogue.

The catalogue—and for purposes of present exposition that refers to the two annual general catalogues—continued in the years after 1925 to be basically what it had always been to Sears, Roebuck. The techniques changed in some respects, but the fundamentals did not. The big book still remained the vehicle for displaying attractively priced and illustrated merchandise, for "speaking" directly to the customers, for extolling the mail-order (and even Sears's retail) method of buying, for editorializing in the wake of the suppressive legislation which emerged from the great depression, for sales promotion and public relations—in short, for performing the same essential functions as in Richard Sears's day, through techniques adapted to the altered times.

The twenty-odd years since 1925 have seen the catalogue take on more polished overtones, but it has continued on a less sophisticated level than the Ward catalogue. The Sears catalogue continued to stress low prices, particularly during the depression years, but it never neglected to proclaim the high quality of its goods. It remained throughout in step with the changes in the company's merchandise structure. Most of the changes in the book, as in the whole company, came slowly. The *Advertising Guide*, still the bible of catalogue-makers, continued to be expanded and to be made more restrictive in allowable usages, but even this, as will be developed later, did not make the company immune to occasional attention from the Federal Trade Commission. The catalogue is simply too large a book, too big a production job employing too many different people, to be able always to hew to a specified line with no divergences.

The 1946 edition of the *Advertising Guide* said in its Foreword:

> Over the years, Sears, Roebuck & Co. has built and earned its reputation for honesty and fair dealing. The public's confidence in us, in our merchandise and in our presentation of our offerings is the result of carefully planned policies, which are the responsibilities of all agencies of the business and all our employees.
>
> We who approach the public through advertising have definite obligations, which must be zealously followed. We do not make the company's policies, but it does fall to us to interpret them and safeguard them. We do not set the regulations of the Federal Trade Commission, but we must, nevertheless, adhere to them. We do not originate the recommendations which come from organizations, such as the Better Business Bureaus; but, once accepted, these recommendations must be followed.
>
> But, above and beyond company policies and Federal Trade regulations, stands the Sears guarantee giving the word of the company that we will honestly describe and illustrate our merchandise; that every article we sell must give complete satisfaction.
>
> There is thus no alternative but to present our goods so that no criticism may be directed against Sears. For these reasons, we have assembled the policies, rules, and regulations which must guide us in preparing Sears advertising and will insure uniformity of understanding and compliance. Other helpful information is included in this book for your guidance.
>
> Remember, the slightest deviation from the stated rules and policies may result in embarrassment to the company and possible legal action.

In addition to the regulations of the Federal Trade Commission referred to in the foregoing, the company had, long before, evolved copywriting standards based upon its own laboratory findings and upon the standards of the American Medical Association, the Pure Food and Drug Act, and the Better Business Bureaus. The 1946 edition of the guide devoted 164 pages to definitions and rules governing descriptions of merchandise, bringing the firm's roster of advertising terms up to the most refined status ever. The company, nevertheless, occasionally found itself cited by the Federal Trade Commission for violation of various regulations dealing with "unfair trade practices" enunciated by the Commission. Between 1930 and 1948 the Trade Commission concluded three affidavits and sixteen stipulations with Sears, Roebuck. One of the earliest stipulations, approved December 18, 1934, dealt with one of the shining examples of the company's merchandise development: Allstate tires. Sears agreed to cease and desist from representing in its advertisements, which, of course, included the catalogues, (1) that its Allstate tires were used by about 12,000,000 families; (2) that nine out of ten motorists chose its Allstate tires; (3) that its Allstate tires had two breaker strips; (4) that the cord fabric was made in New England; and (5) that tests proved the Allstate tire equal to or better than any tire advertised as "six plies under the tread."

Later stipulations dealt with radios (erroneously termed "all-wave"), comforters (labeled as "hand-made" or "hand-stitched" when such was not the case), the stone monuments (which had "lasted forever" or been "eternally beautiful"; this stipulation, in 1940, indicated that Richard Sears's flamboyant descriptions sometimes still lingered). Other stipulations dealt with exaggerated claims for vitamin products. Of its nineteen brushes with the Trade Commission in the last twenty years, however, none of the stipulations or affidavits contained terms which materially affected the company's sales promotion. The chief effect appears to have been to restrain unduly enthusiastic copywriters.

In addition to the "ethics" and accuracy of catalogue descriptions, copywriters also had to concern themselves with other phases: good taste (based largely on a determination "never to embarrass") and effectiveness of presentation. The taboos listed under the good-taste approach include illustrations of women smoking or drinking (this same prohibition was ultimately extended to men as well), "too full" brassières, "sexy" legs in stocking advertisements, etc. The approach is usually chaste. In 1946, for example, company executives were debating whether glorification of the female anatomy should be more or less conservative in its corset section. The argument was clinched when *Esquire* magazine ran a cartoon in which two hillbilly characters sprawling under a tree watched a third chasing a girl, and one commented: "Si must have been looking at the corset pages of the Sears catalogue again." Conservatism won without further argument.

That same general policy led the company in 1946, after another mail-order seller had difficulties with the Post Office Department over its listing of certain sex books, to drop sex books from the Sears catalogue. Suggestive titles of recordings bearing such *double-entendres* as "She Went and Lost It at the Astor" and "Some Girls Do and Some Girls Don't" had been discontinued earlier. As always, however, there were contradictions in the pattern. The 1948 spring and summer catalogue, for example, listed six sex books, very plainly labeled as such and adequately, if cautiously, described.

The Peoples Book Club, which was given the back cover and two inside pages, stressed "wholesome, *family*" reading matter; the blurbs made it clear that nothing even remotely suggestive of passion or violence would be allowed to creep into any of the Peoples Book Club selections. Yet passion and violence abounded on page 619 of that book, which offered titles by Erskine Caldwell, J. T. Farrell, and James M. Cain, as well as listing *Forever Amber*. One way of summarizing the eternal drive toward eminent "respectability" might be to say that the most glaringly wholesome offerings received large displays, while items which might be offensive to various groups were buried inconspicuously.

The covers of the catalogue came themselves to be a powerful vehicle for attuning the book to the conservative tastes and morals of its predominantly rural customers. As mentioned earlier, Sears even conducted a $2,500 prize contest to enlist the interest of its readers in selecting catalogue covers. A poll conducted for the company revealed that the most popular cover ever run on the big book was a reproduction of a landscape painted by George Inness. In 1938 the company, in the words of the *Wall Street Journal,*

> radically modernized its catalogue layout to a greater extent than since 1896 when the page size was changed to the present 6½ by 9½ inches. Sears has attempted to bring the catalogue nearer home to customers by putting illustrations on the cover representative of the most dramatic activity of each major geographic region of the country. Merchandise treatment utilizes the department store idea of feature shops by grouping merchandise under fashions, sports, shop goods, etc.[12]

Another newspaper said of that fall 1938 book:

> It makes the greatest use of color printing and rotogravure in its history. Instead of one cover, used on books distributed in all of the firm's mail order regions, there

CHART VI

MAIL-ORDER EXECUTIVE ORGANIZATION

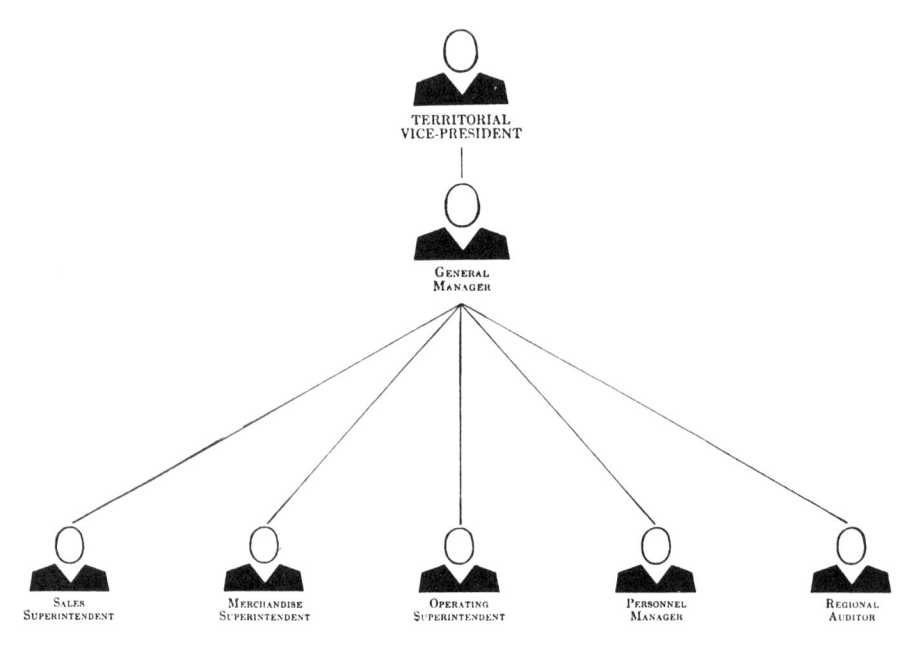

```
                    TERRITORIAL
                   VICE-PRESIDENT
                         |
                      GENERAL
                      MANAGER
     ┌──────────┬──────────┼──────────┬──────────┐
   SALES    MERCHANDISE  OPERATING  PERSONNEL  REGIONAL
SUPERINTENDENT SUPERINTENDENT SUPERINTENDENT MANAGER AUDITOR
```

is a different cover for each region in which the catalog is distributed. The cover pictures are huge photographs which bleed to the edges of the page and the subject matter typifies the industry, the scenery or the sentiment of the territory covered by the book.[13]

If all evidence of the last fifty-odd years were to be trusted, it seemed highly probable that the big book would continue always to change as America itself changes, and just as slowly. It appeared equally probable that the mail-order business, which had evolved three new techniques of selling since 1925, would continue seeking new auxiliary sales devices and might find some. L. S. Janes, director of Store Planning and Display, took perhaps the longest glance at the indiscernible future. He envisaged the possibility that some day catalogues might be transmitted in four colors to the customer's home by facsimile reproduction or television; orders might be dispatched to the company by teletype, and goods delivered by parachute drop or helicopter.

Pending that push-button age, Sears, Roebuck would in all probability just continue issuing millions of catalogues annually and exploiting them as fully as possible to reap the largest harvest of orders. Certainly it was clear that mail order, after shaking off its lethargy around 1930, had demonstrated new vitality. In addition to attracting and filling orders sent by customers through "straight" mail order as well as through the auxiliary devices developed in the last twenty years, the mail-order side of the Sears operation had also assumed an additional responsibility of secondary nature: to serve as a source of merchandise supply for the smaller Sears retail stores.

As of 1947, those two chief functions lay largely in the hands of a group of men who themselves demonstrated the new-found vitality of mail order, for the average age of Sears's mail-order executives in that year was 44.8 years, 85 per cent of them having been appointed to executive positions before the age of 45. Their average length of service with the company was 17.4 years. Nearly 29 per cent of the executives came to Sears with college degrees, while 23 per cent had "some college education." Almost half—specifically, a little more than 48 per cent—had not attended college. The executives also proved the truth of the maxim that a college education is not necessarily fatal to success; those with college degrees advanced to executive rank in 9 years, while those with no college background required 15.9 years to achieve that position.[14] The relative simplicity of the framework within which those men operate is indicated in the organizational structure of a mail-order plant shown in Chart VI.

CHAPTER XXVI

Expanding Over-the-Counter Sales

AT THE end of 1948 Sears, Roebuck and Company was operating 632 retail stores, of five different classifications, according to size and type: "A," "B-1," "B-2," "B-3," and "C." After several years of experimentation, each category has come to be identified with a characteristic merchandise structure.

The "A" stores, with selling areas usually of from 70,000 to 125,000 square feet, are full-fledged department stores carrying full assortments of hard lines, big tickets, soft lines, and miscellaneous goods. These stores account for more than 50 per cent of the company's total retail volume. The "A" stores are almost invariably located a goodly distance from a city's central shopping district, feature free parking lots large enough to accommodate customers' cars, and have auxiliary buildings for service stations and for farm implements.

"B-1" units, with selling space generally from 20,000 to 50,000 square feet, carry soft and hard lines as well as big tickets, but in none of these merchandise categories are assortments so large as in "A" stores. "B-2" stores, with selling square footage of between 15,000 and 25,000, carry only hard lines and big tickets, while outlets of the "B-3" and "C" type generally stock automobile supplies and accessories, hardware, paint, and sporting goods.

The Sears store which alone defies all classification by merchandise structure, even though technically of the "B-1" type, is the one in Temple, Oklahoma. Known as the "B & O," the name saddled on it by the previous owners, this store includes not only a service station but also an extensive livestock adjunct and a somewhat unique barter system of merchandising. In its livestock auction department as many as a thousand head of livestock are bought, slaughtered, and refrigerated weekly. As many as forty carloads of turkeys are moved each Christmas. The store also operates frozen-food lockers, and its creamery buys raw sour cream and converts it into butter. The Temple outlet also purchases eggs from farmers, candling, casing, and reselling them through commercial houses. The store quite often engages in barter trade in cream, milk, eggs, chickens, and turkeys; Sears offers farmers slightly higher prices for those products if the farmer is willing to accept merchandise in lieu of cash as payment.

The descriptions of the several types of store organization, as given later on in this chapter, are based upon organization charts prepared by the

CHART VII

Independent "A" Store Organization

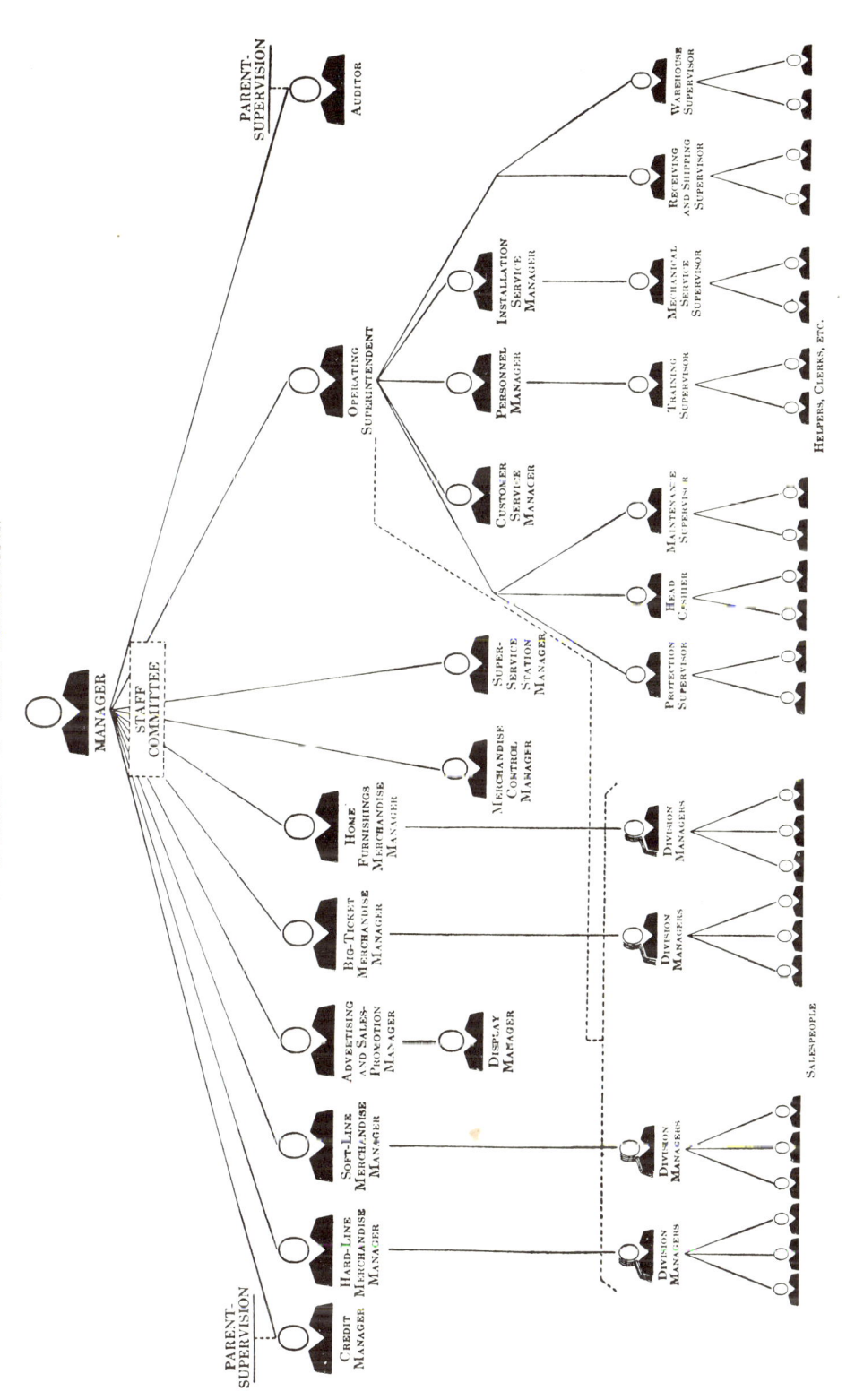

CHART VIII

Medium "B" Store Organization

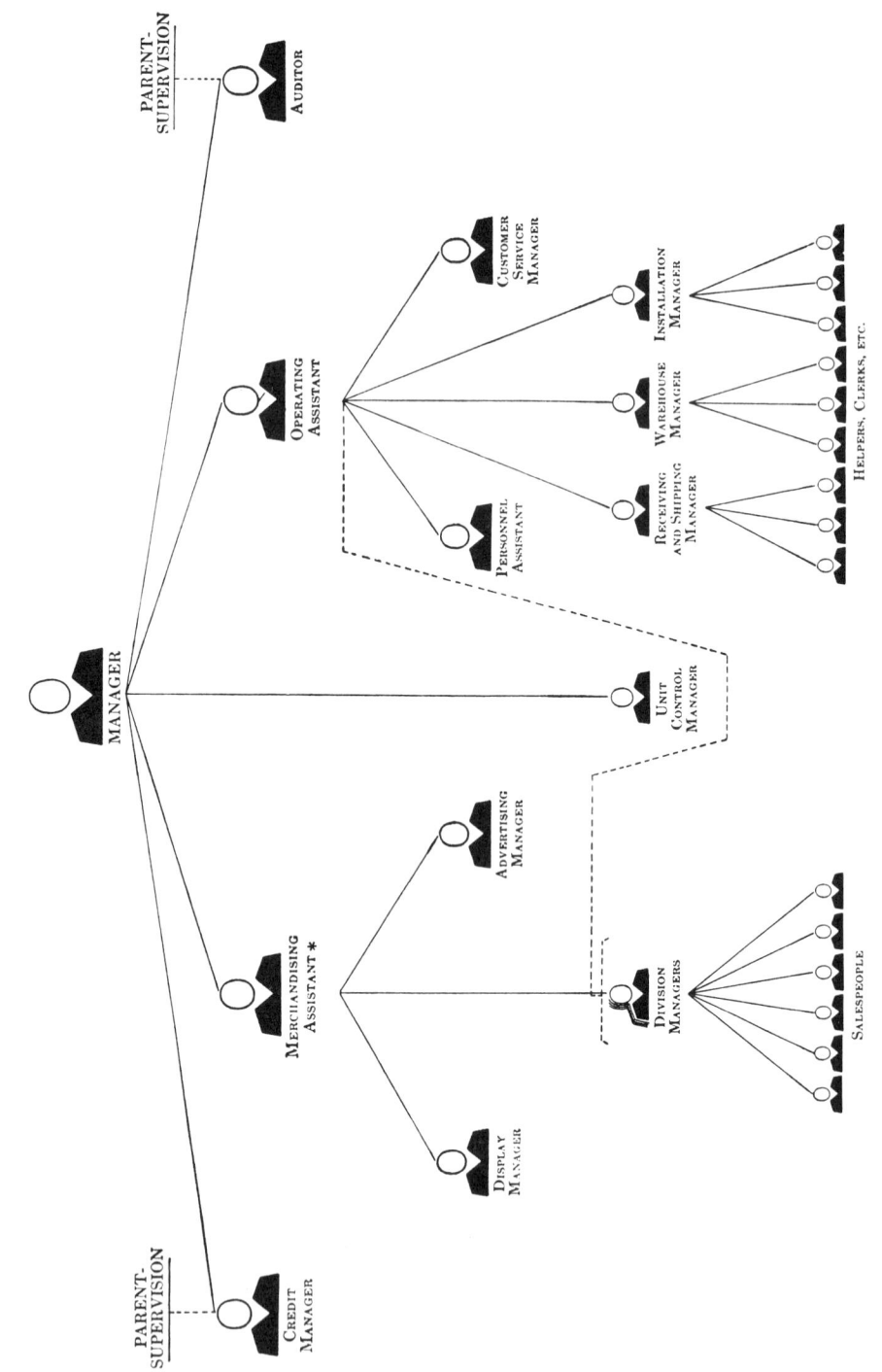

* In some of the larger "B" stores, instead of a merchandising assistant there are two merchandising managers, one in charge of soft lines, the other in charge of hard lines.

parent for the information and guidance of Sears's retail executives. They represent a cross-section of company thinking in regard to typical organization of stores of various types in varying volume brackets. Sears's experience has indicated that there is no single "right" way of organizing a retail store, though the general pattern is followed throughout the company. Delegation of responsibility and authority, from store manager to his key executive staff, normally varies with the key people themselves, their degree of training, and their capacity to assume and carry out responsibility, as well as with the merchandising and operating requirements of the individual store.

The primary objective in setting up a store organization is, of course, the creation of smoothly functioning teamwork. Sears operates on the belief that a well-knit supervisory group which works together harmoniously assures profitable store performance and public acceptance. In recommending organization structures to its field retail executives, several basic principles are kept in mind:

1. The supervisory organization should be simple enough to permit easy contact between store manager and store activities. Through his key people, the manager should be in a position to learn easily and quickly what is going on in his store.

2. The organization should insure easy and free communication, both up and down the line, between the manager and all store personnel. Organized methods of communication, which includes making management decisions a matter of group discussion, help build the supervisory staff into an effective team.

3. Each member of the store supervisory staff should understand clearly what his responsibilities are, and should be held accountable for performance in line with defined responsibility. Overlapping of responsibility must be avoided. Delegation of responsibility must always be based upon delegated authority.

4. Store executives should know about each other's duties to permit temporary interchange of assignments when abnormal workload, vacations, and other such conditions make periodic adjustments imperative.

Chart VII gives a clear outline of the organization of a Sears "A" store. These stores are of two types—a single "A" store in a locality, known as an independent "A" and reporting direct to the territorial vice-president, and "A" stores within groups, located in the same city. Since an independent "A" is self-sufficient all by itself, its organization is somewhat more elaborate. "A" stores within a group are usually under the direction of a group manager, who co-ordinates the sales promotions of a group within a city. A group "A" has therefore a somewhat simpler organization, since the group manager's staff assumes responsibility for sales promotion for the group as a whole. In such a setup the store manager reports to the group manager, who in turn reports directly to the territorial vice-president.

Charts VIII and IX show typical organization of "B" and "C" stores.

Table 65 outlines the company's principal merchandise departments. On a national basis big tickets in 1941 accounted for about 40 per cent of

CHART IX
"C" STORE ORGANIZATION

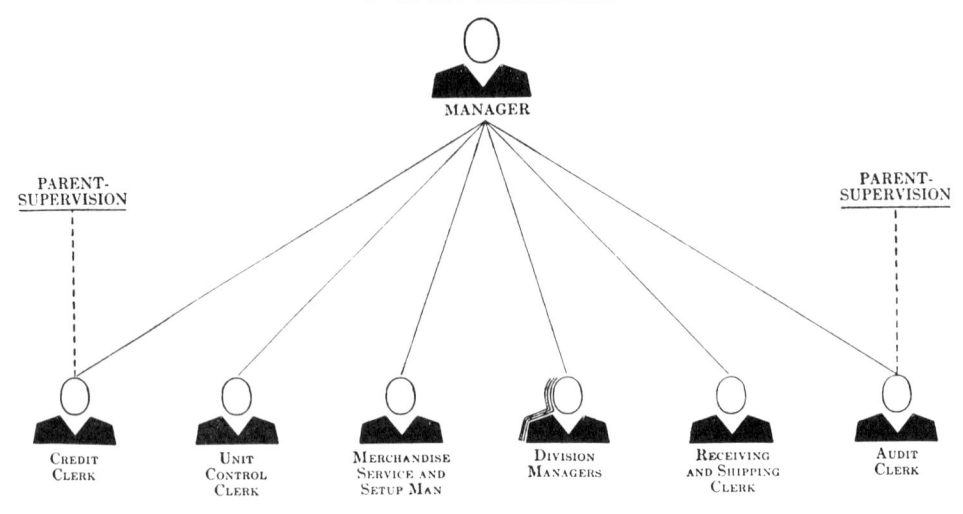

MANAGER

- PARENT-SUPERVISION
- CREDIT CLERK
- UNIT CONTROL CLERK
- MERCHANDISE SERVICE AND SETUP MAN
- DIVISION MANAGERS
- RECEIVING AND SHIPPING CLERK
- AUDIT CLERK
- PARENT-SUPERVISION

TABLE 65*
PRINCIPAL RETAIL MERCHANDISE DEPARTMENTS

HARD LINES:
  Sporting goods
  Hardware
  Miscellaneous house furnishings, pet shop
  Auto accessories, oil, grease, batteries
  Auto tires and tubes
  Paints and oils, varnishes, brushes
  Electrical lighting fixtures, appliances
  China, glassware
  Toys
  Building material
DOMESTICS:
  Linen, handkerchiefs
  Draperies, curtains
  Notions, umbrellas
  Cotton, silk, and woolen goods
  Patterns
  Bedding, toweling, blankets
SOFT LINES:
  Shoes—men's, women's, children's
  Women's ready-to-wear
  Girl's wear
  Men's furnishings—shirts, accessories, underwear, pajamas
  Intimate apparel for women
  Corsets
  Infants' wear

Boys' clothing
Millinery
Women's hosiery
Handbags and neckwear
Men's dress clothing
Men's work clothing
BIG TICKETS:
  Furniture, beds, bedding
  Vacuum cleaners, sewing machines
  Stoves
  Washing machines, ironers
  Farm equipment and supplies
  Floor coverings
  Plumbing, heating
  Electric refrigerators
  Home freezers
  Radios, phonographs, and accessories
MISCELLANEOUS:
  Stationery, books, cameras
  Jewelry, silverware, clocks
  Drugs, sundries, toilet articles
  Gifts, lamps, pictures
  Wallpaper
  Shrubbery, plants
  Employees' store
  Candy
  Gasoline
  Repair parts

* Source: Company records.

the company's total retail volume. Second place in major classifications went to hard lines, with 30 per cent. Soft lines represented roughly 21 per cent of the total, while miscellaneous accounted for some 8 per cent of all retail sales.

Table 66 traces the growth of the company's retail stores from 1925 through 1948, while Table 67 reflects the geographical distribution of those outlets as of the end of 1948.

The selling operation of the stores starts of course with the arrival of the merchandise, the responsibility for the procurement of which is vested in the general merchandise office in Chicago. The individual store does not "buy" its merchandise as much as it simply orders it from authorized merchandise lists. Such orders, or requisitions, go variously to one of three

TABLE 66*

NUMBER OF RETAIL STORES BY YEARS, 1925–48

Year	Number	Year	Number
1925	8	1937	473
1926	9	1938	182
1927	27	1939	520
1928	192	1940	595
1929	319	1941	617
1930	338	1942	599
1931	378	1943	596
1932	374	1944	606
1933	400	1945	604
1934	416	1946	610
1935	428	1947	625
1936	440	1948	632

* Source: Company records.

sources of supply: the mail-order branch warehouses; the pool stocks, which are special warehouses set up since the advent of retail to supply the stores particularly with major appliances and heavy items; or manufacturers authorized to ship direct to the stores.

The merchandise lists furnished the retail stores by the central buying organization contain the names of certain authorized sources producing for Sears from which the retail stores can order goods direct. Such direct shipments are of course preferable if the quantity ordered is substantial enough to provide economical or prepaid transportation. Instances in which a retail store procures any merchandise other than from control stores, pool stocks, or approved Sears's sources are rare indeed and are confined to real emergency situations.

The merchandise ordered from control stores is "sold" to the retail units at landed cost at the control stores plus a small percentage of cost to cover service and, of course, cost of transportation to the store. Retail stores serviced by any given pool stocks pay the landed costs at the pool, plus cost of

TABLE 67*
RETAIL STORES BY STATE AND TYPE, 1948

STATE	TOTAL STORES	TYPE "A"	"B-1"	"B-2"	"B-3"	"C"
Alabama	10	1	3	4	2	
Arizona	8	1	1		1	5
Arkansas	3		3			
California	38	12	13	5	8	
Colorado	3	1	2			
Connecticut	9			8	1	
Delaware	2			1		1
District of Columbia	3	2			1	
Florida	13	1	9	2	1	
Georgia	9	1	4	2	2	
Idaho						
Illinois	60	7	21	5	10	17
Indiana	34	4	8	7	2	13
Iowa	16		8	5		3
Kansas	7		5			2
Kentucky	8	1	4	2	1	
Louisiana	6	2	4			
Maine	6		4	1	1	
Maryland	6	1	1	2		2
Massachusetts	24	2	7	7	7	1
Michigan	22	6	10	2	2	2
Minnesota	12	1	4	1	1	5
Mississippi	8		4	4		
Missouri	12	4	2	1	1	4
Montana						
Nebraska	6	1	2	2		1
Nevada	2		2			
New Hampshire	4		1	2	1	
New Jersey	21	4	6	2	9	
New Mexico	2		2			
New York	46	4	6	11	22	3
North Carolina	10	1	5	3	1	
North Dakota	3		2	1		
Ohio	39	5	9	14	5	6
Oklahoma	6	2	4			
Oregon	5	1	3		1	
Pennsylvania	46	4	11	13	7	11
Rhode Island	3				3	
South Carolina	5		3	2		
South Dakota	5		4	1		
Tennessee	5	2	2	1		
Texas	36	6	23			7
Utah	4	1	1	2		
Vermont	2		1			1
Virginia	9	1	3	4	1	
Washington	15	3	10	1	1	
West Virginia	6		2	4		
Wisconsin	28	2	7	5	2	12
Wyoming						
Total United States stores	627	84	226	127	94	96
Foreign stores†	5	2	2			1
All stores	632	86	228	127	94	97

* Source: Company records.
† The larger stores were located in Havana, Honolulu, Mexico City, and São Paulo.

transportation to the stores, plus pro rata cost of operating the pool. On goods ordered direct from sources, the store pays the price agreed upon by the manufacturers and Sears's buying organization, plus transportation costs if shipment is not prepaid.

All merchandise coming into a retail store carries a "suggested" selling price, arrived at by the buying organization and designed to make it possible for the store to achieve the gross margin needed. Merchandise offerings are usually shown on three separate lists—large, medium, and small—and lists are dispatched to stores on the basis of their type and size (ranging from the large "A's" to the small "C's"). Each merchandise list contains both mandatory and optional items (or "basic" and "rated" items). The mandatory items are, obviously, those which the company determines every store of a particular class must carry; the optional items are those whose stocking is left to the discretion of the store manager.

One line of completely mandatory merchandise in all "A" stores (and most "B-1" stores) is ladies' ready-to-wear and millinery, handled by the Henry Rose organization, which has been the outstanding leased department in Sears's retail operation. Early in the company's retail history it became apparent that, of all failures of mail-order merchandise to satisfy the needs of retail stores, ladies' ready-to-wear was the most glaring. Mail-order buying methods necessitated buying "safe," conservative merchandise in large quantities on the basis of several months of selling. In respect to ladies' ready-to-wear this produced merchandise which, while perhaps of good quality and intrinsic value, was nevertheless lacking in the essential fashion touch and in rapid response to changes in styles. To divorce the fashion business from its conventional methods of buying and control, the company induced Henry Rose, a successful manufacturer of women's coats and suits and a large supplier of Sears for many years, to form the Henry Rose Stores, Inc., to merchandise all ladies' ready-to-wear and millinery in the retail stores. Sears purchased a quarter-interest in the Henry Rose Stores, which operated as a concession. That enterprise was furnished space, light, heat, and power in the Sears stores carrying the line, in return for a small percentage of sales; Sears, owning a quarter-interest in Henry Rose, naturally also received 25 per cent of the dividends.

Henry Rose Stores operate from New York, and all shipments of ready-to-wear and millinery are shipped from that city. Under the *modus operandi* of this concession, the individual store manager has little responsibility except to allocate space and to see that the concessionaire adheres to Sears's policies in dealing with employees and customers. Henry Rose personnel restock the stores on the basis of reported sales, being responsible not only for automatic replenishment but also for mandatory assortments, mandatory pricing, and mandatory markdowns.

On January 1, 1944, the Henry Rose Stores became a wholly owned Sears subsidiary, although continuing to operate as a separate specialized unit. The officers, buying staff, and personnel continued unchanged under Rose's direction. In the same year the merchandising of women's handbags was placed under the Rose operation. The merchandising of all mail-order ready-to-wear and millinery was subsequently also intrusted to Henry Rose. The Henry Rose operation (up to the time Sears became sole owner), while the outstanding concession in the retail stores, was not the only one. A well-known Chicago grocery company operates grocery and meat departments in some of the large "A" stores in Chicago. The company also farms out beauty-parlor, optical, barber-shop, shoe-repair, watch-repair, tobacco, and a few other concessions, such as soda fountains.

The success of the company in merchandising style goods, through the Rose subsidiary, is only relative; style merchandise has never been Sears's forte. The company has instead preferred to concentrate its efforts and its peculiar talents upon staple items (in textiles, rugs, furniture, and even staple items of men's, women's and children's furnishings, for example) which, even if they do not lend themselves readily to the basic buying program which has been so successful in hard lines and big tickets, are nevertheless adaptable in some degree to specification buying. Staple items of this nature can also be purchased in vast quantities, bringing Sears's mass buying power to bear, since they are not susceptible to rapid changes in fashion. This is certainly not applicable to women's ready-to-wear, in which fashion changes can be rapid and in which merchandise turnover must likewise be rapid. The result of these factors is that Sears does, at best, a mediocre job in style merchandise but an outstanding job in staples.

The retail selling operation is conceived in long-range terms, and promotional activities have to be co-ordinated with buying. At the top level these responsibilities center in the office of the retail merchandise manager (an assistant to the merchandise vice-president), who is assisted by retail sales managers in charge of various buying departments. Each such retail sales manager is in charge of the promotion of his department's merchandise and prepares the retail merchandise list for his department. All retail promotional activities are directed through the retail merchandise manager. On the promotional phase, all advertising layouts and store sales plans are prepared and released through this office. The retail advertising department periodically furnishes each store with promotional ideas and actual advertising layouts—all to be used largely at the discretion of the individual store managers.

The retail merchandise office also supervises and directs the work of the Store Planning and Display Department, which has been mentioned earlier and will be discussed in more detail later. This department plans suggested layouts for new (and even old) stores, diagramming all display sections and suggesting space allocations for the various lines of merchandise. To do this, Store Planning studies customers' habits, flow of traffic into and through stores, and sales records by stores and, on a national basis, by lines and departments; it also evolves special fixtures designed to give optimum display to the merchandise and thus to increase sales. These activities of the Store Planning and Display Department, and their translation into working terms on the store level, are of course of little avail unless customers can be induced to come to the store. One of the chief reliances of the stores in attracting customers has been newspaper advertising, circulars, and, to a minor extent, radio advertising. The annual report for 1940 asserted:

> At length, the company discovered, through trial and error and torment, that the best vehicle for retail promotion was the daily newspaper. Accordingly, the company became the largest direct buyer of newspaper column inches in the country and its bill for white space in 1940, for example, was more than $11,000,000.

Its bill for 1940 actually proved, when all returns were in, to have exceeded $12,000,000, marking five consecutive years in each of which the

TABLE 68*

NEWSPAPER ADVERTISING EXPENDITURES, 1930-47

Year	Advertising Expenditure†	Year	Advertising Expenditure†
1930	$ 5,621,674	1939	$11,409,649
1931	7,049,751	1940	12,219,824
1932	6,430,335	1941	13,087,780
1933	9,251,210	1942	‡
1934	7,494,360	1943	10,808,415
1935	8,753,280	1944	‡
1936	10,548,854	1945	11,130,000
1937	11,261,763	1946	15,069,000
1938	10,748,176	1947	19,134,400

* Source: Company records.
† For space only.
‡ Unavailable.

company had expended more than $10,000,000 for newspaper advertising. The $10,000,000 mark had actually been crossed, for the first time, in 1936; within eleven years that figure was almost to double, as Table 68 indicates.

The company insists that the use by retail stores of parent's mat service and basic descriptions of items tends generally to place advertising by its stores on a higher plane than that of some of the local competitors of the stores. The theory appears to be that, with so much of the carefully supervised work of description and illustration already done for him at the "top," the local Sears store manager is unlikely to create additional work for himself through writing much of his own descriptive copy or preparing his own artwork. Hence, his use of parent-supplied material makes for accuracy and honesty.

Through the use of this newspaper advertising, placed and purchased by the various store managers, and through the use of merchandise displays in display windows of the stores to attract the attention of passers-by, the company seeks to draw potential purchasers into its stores. From that point on, the merchandise itself (and the display thereof) and the sales personnel are depended upon to "close." The sales clerks are supported by every possible means of "automatic" or "mechanical" selling aids the company's Store Planning and Display Department can provide. The displays themselves seek to present the merchandise as dramatically and attractively as possible and to leave it "open" so customers can touch and examine the goods, which are generally grouped by color, size, and price for easy selection. Display tags state clearly the price, as well as something of the use or ingredients of the merchandise, and "Info" (information) tags on the goods itemize the ingredients, quality, instructions on use (and if applicable, on washing or cleaning, etc.), and other pertinent data—as much for the sales clerk's information as for the customer's. All prices shown on the display tags in the retail stores are the cash prices; additional charges are made for instalment terms.

With only a few exceptions the Sears stores have no charge accounts and offer no free home delivery. Items which do have to be delivered include the delivery charge in their prices. One thing the retail stores do have is the company guaranty: satisfaction or your money back. The guaranty is as rigidly observed in retail as in mail order.

Within a relatively short time after Sears entered the retail field it became apparent that the company had overshot its space limitations or else had underestimated its sales volume, or both; it was "bad news" with cheering balance-sheet overtones. Stores designed to achieve an annual sales volume of a given amount frequently soon doubled the projected volume, and space became inadequate. One of the solutions to the space shortage was the overhauling of the merchandise structure to reduce the number of departments with a resultant increase in emphasis on merchandise assortments in departments which were left. The shortage of space was particularly noticeable in the various "B"-type stores, especially in the "B-1's," which were overextending themselves in endeavoring to carry too wide a variety of departments and assortments in too great a number of price lines. The problem was alleviated, but not solved, through a redefinition of the merchandise structure of the "B" stores in accordance with the selling space available, accompanied of course by the general overhauling of the company's merchandise offerings to those stores.

In 1936 the Store Planning and Display Department fired a heavy broadside under the interrogative title, *More Room?* The keynote of the booklet was struck in the statement:

> Out of the recent sales and space analysis comes this sharply defined truth: Many of our "A" stores are not getting nearly what's coming to them out of the

space they have at their disposal. By tightening up layouts, revising stock and table arrangements and, in general, revitalizing all display activity, it is a safe bet that about 15% or 20% more selling space can be picked up in any "A" store. Taking the longer view and considering all of the factors involved (merchandising, ordering problems, etc.) it may be said that in certain stores we are not up to 50% of our possible efficiency. What most stores need is not more room, but more intensive merchandise presentation in the space they now have.

The publication admitted that some stores *did* need more space and that mistakes had been made in the construction of certain stores to handle projected volumes of sales which had long since been exceeded. But the Store Planning Department insisted that, in considering the possibilities of enlarging or remodeling a store as against maintaining the status quo, serious attention had to be focused upon factors over which the company could exercise control. First, there had to be a strict definition ("and limitation if necessary") of the departments and of the number of price lines a store was to carry in relation to sales. Second, there had to be a complete survey to show what divisions were profitable and why and what divisions were over- or underspaced. Third, a thorough examination of the merchandise presentation of each individual unit—tables, wall sections, etc.—was required, plus a traffic picture showing the number of transactions, the average transaction, and other data pertinent to the nature and density of the business. Finally, each store's "profit history" was to be studied to determine what percentage of profits could justifiably be put back into the store for remodeling or enlarging. After pleading for more functional store buildings, the booklet went on to add:

While it is apparent that the merchandise lists are being refined and improved every day it would still seem, in the light of some of the facts turned up in this review on sales and space, that the stores are given too much latitude in choosing the number of price lines and the extensiveness of the assortments they carry. Makeup of the lists should be revised to make a direct correlation between anticipated volume, square feet of selling space and the recommended inventories.

It is agreed that smaller low volume stores cannot afford large enough inventories to carry everything on the present *basic* merchandise lists. This same principle stands in terms of space: smaller area "A" stores of say 70,000 square feet or less can't afford to carry the same assortments as stores of 100,000 square feet. If they attempt it they are liable to let themselves in for trouble in the way of cluttered merchandise presentation, diminishing turnover and excessive markdowns which will eventually have to be taken.

It is recognized that 85% of the volume in our stores is done on one-third of the items carried. This is an important fact and must be remembered.... More merchandise doesn't necessarily mean more new business and brand new items should be added to the line very slowly—perhaps only after a careful testing in a group of representative stores so that their claims of "best seller" can be proven....

By regulating on a space basis, the size of the merchandise lists offered to certain stores we will be moving towards the minimizing of over buying, top-heavy assortments, too numerous price lines, out of stock conditions, slow turnover and many other storekeeping evils that result from a lack of appreciation of the value and limitations of the space at hand.

From there the Store Planning Department went on to strike a blow at what had been up to that time one of the outstanding "sacred cows" in the Sears retail operation: the conception and insistence on austerity of presentation, stripped of frills and furbelows generally associated with prestige department-store display. The planners wrote:

> A common comment on the general problems of storekeeping goes something like this:
> "After all a lot of our customers are laboring men and their families, farmers, small townsmen, people of little cultural background or pretensions. These people don't want a store that's too good-looking. Let us make them feel at home. Let's keep our stores homely and comfortable—like an old pair of shoes, etc. . . . etc."
> IN THE LIGHT OF COMMON EXPERIENCE and in view of what's going on in certain other branches of the organization this is a position that cannot be defended.

It was further declared that to show Silvertone radios, "the world's most beautiful refrigerator," or the largest-selling brand of hosiery in the country against a shoddy, lifeless background was as incongruous as dressing a pretty girl in a gunny sack or peddling diamonds from a battered felt hat. Further, the planning department called attention to the money the company had invested in "developing merchandise to new aesthetic heights," adding that stores must not lag behind in proper housing and presentation of that merchandise. The argument continued in terms of "the excitement, relaxation, news, and drama" that was shopping. Store Planning insisted it was not advocating ultra-elaborate displays but maintained at the same time that competition in this respect had to be met—specifically that of Ward's and Kress's.

In 1938 there was issued a booklet, *Profits Out of Space*, addressed to store and display managers throughout the company and to all store personnel, buyers, and sellers, "with the sincere hope that it will bring to all concerned the single fact: the importance of display." The Foreword asserted:

> If we are to maintain satisfactory profit levels we *must* obtain a larger volume of sales without adding proportionately to store expense—and it is shown here that good display can be the cheapest, yet most valuable form of store publicity you can have and that one way to more profit is through intensive improvement of merchandise presentation.
> We show here that in the Sears system there are millions of dollars spent before a single sale is made. The total investment we make for men, merchandise and a place to do business reaches staggering proportions before the cash register tinkles even slightly. The payoff in profits comes at the *point of sale*—where man meets merchandise and hands over cash for what he wants.

The booklet went on with illustrations and text to assert that some three hundred million dollars was being spent annually ("Millions for Merchandise . . . A Fortune for Rent . . . Hundreds of Thousands for Promotion . . . And for Man-Power . . . Still More Money") to interest the customer in

Sears's merchandise and get him inside a store. The central thesis was stated in these terms:

> Only recently, say in the last ten years, has display graduated from the role of the shabby, often neglected little step-sister of advertising. Comparatively speaking, only recently has it come to the serious and scientific attention of forward looking store executives. And out of this recent recognition comes a whole new concept of retailing tactics. Facts, not fancy, now dominate display and it has become as exact a science as intensive research and statistical work can make it....
>
> Especially in a Sears store is the importance of visual selling at its highest. We just can't afford a salesperson for every potential customer that comes in. In our stores it frequently happens that there are six customers to one salesperson. We're out-numbered and in the interest of economical operation and low selling prices we must approach the "self-service" setup as closely as possible. Display becomes doubly important—good display becomes doubly profitable.

The booklet went on to point up some facts recently unearthed. Surveys showed that 24 per cent of people entering certain of the Sears stores shortly before had stated that the window displays had brought them in; only 11 per cent of the customers were traceable to newspaper advertising —which form of advertising was estimated to cost at least 50 cents per 100 readers. Traffic counts made at "A" and "B" stores indicated that six million people passed the display windows of the Sears stores daily—and the display cost averaged 50 cents per 1,000 circulation, or one-tenth the cost of newspaper advertising per reader. The moral pointed was: Stores should concentrate more attention upon their window displays, which attracted potential customers at low cost.

Obviating what it called an "apparent need" for expansion in floor areas was the prime consideration of the Store Planning and Display Department throughout most of the thirties and remains so even today. Such expansion would indeed become necessary in Sears's great postwar drive, which will be discussed later, but Store Planning fought a protracted and skilful delaying action which materially improved the presentation of merchandise (and, presumably, the sales volume and profits) of the company's retail stores.

The year 1940 found Les Janes, director of store planning, crying an alarm, *There's Somebody at the Front Door!* That publication developed two themes: (1) the numbers of people who were walking out of Sears's stores without buying anything and (2) the important relation of the contingent (part-time) salesperson to the problem. The booklet asserted that, in 1939, 296,000,000 adult customers entered Sears's stores—of which number 129,000,000, or 44 per cent, walked out without making a purchase (the basis upon which the figures were arrived at was not given). Walkouts in "B" stores were 59 per cent of the total number entering, in "A" stores the percentage was over 23. And, of a total of 193,107,000 sales transactions in that year, 70,000,000, or 38 per cent, were completed by contingent personnel. The conclusions were that the company's advertising and display approach had brought it a vast amount of potential increase in volume upon which it had failed to capitalize; that one more sale per shopper would have doubled the store's profits; that, with better training and assistance, the contingent personnel might well have increased their sales; and, finally, that if the contingent personnel had failed to close on half their sales, total volume would have dropped by 19 per cent. The booklet added:

> The first step toward sound store layout and sensible stock arrangement is the proper evaluation and use of space in relation to sales. The formula of good store planning starts with the allotment of space department by department and the allotment of space within the departments table by table; and so on to the table itself where space must be portioned out to each item according to its present or potential worth in the sales column.

The quickest way to apply that formula, the booklet continued, was correct use of *The Space and Sales Guide*, a handbook which listed the items in each line in the order of their relative selling importance. It showed the percentage of the line to the total division and the sales by quarters. The entry titled "the largest unit sale item" showed the best-selling item of the line, and other data indicated results obtained by placing traffic items near a related high gross profit item or a new item, to attract customer attention to the item to which the company desired to trade up.

The *Guide* showed figures on a national basis and was intended to be used in conjunction with local store control books showing similar data for any one store, for purposes of comparison. The Store Planning Department felt that many stores were simply repeating and continuing their own merchandise errors by depending solely upon their own store records; thus an item selling fairly well might be given preferential display space and continue selling fairly well, whereas items which national experience had shown *could* sell exceptionally well might never be given an opportunity.

The company's enforced emphasis during the war on availables—which meant mostly soft lines—brought soft goods into many retail stores which had not previously stocked them and increased the attention accorded them even in stores, such as the "A's," which had always carried soft lines. This change in the merchandise structure, which became progressively more noticeable in each succeeding war year, wrought considerable change in the display arrangement of the retail stores. Prominent space formerly devoted to refrigerators, washing machines, radios, and other big tickets came to be filled with wearing apparel and other available goods. As for the impairment of the selling effort due to loss of personnel, inability to secure materials for new fixtures, and allied factors, the simple fact was that in the sellers' market of those years the primary task was to obtain the merchandise; the market was, generally speaking, waiting and willing to buy.

The company's volume of sales in that year (1942) dropped from the then all-time high recorded in 1941, and 1943 saw sales drop again although still remaining at a higher level than ever before up to 1941. In 1944 the sales volume shot up even over 1941's figure to set a new record and continued after 1944 to increase considerably in every succeeding year.

As early as 1943, however, the company was peering ahead toward the end of hostilities and was training its sights on the postwar market. On June 30 Board Chairman Wood and President Barrows issued a joint statement on selection of new store locations, asserting among other things that all "B-2" stores were eventually to be converted into "B-1's"; that "A" and "B-1" stores, as well as whatever "B-2" stores were continued, had to be provided with ample parking facilities and sufficient area for outside selling space and service stations. In November, 1943, the company appointed a Reconversion Committee of its top executives to lay detailed plans for the Sears postwar retail operation. The committee divided its work, and its findings, into two categories or phases: *pre*-postwar conversion, to begin immediately to capitalize upon the already evident "improvement in availability" of merchandise, and postwar conversion, to chart in specific terms the pattern to be striven for in the company's retail operation whenever peace should return.

The company was concerned not alone with the chronic space shortage which had for some while been hampering its retail operation but also with the fact that most of its stores, particularly those which had carried only hard lines before the war, had lost "character." The exodus of hard lines and big tickets and the influx of soft lines (mostly in motley assortments and odds and ends picked up wherever the buyers could find them) had created an unsatisfactory situation in such stores. Sears had learned by trial and error during the preceding two decades that a retail store, to be successful, had to have a definite character and had to render a definite service; it could not be a smattering of many lines, without doing a good job in any line. The committee therefore faced as its first task the immediate restoration of character in the company's 324 "B" and "C" stores, without waiting for the end of hostilities.

As previously mentioned, one reason the Reconversion Committee turned its attention first to pre-postwar conversion was the increasing availability of merchandise. Near the end of 1943 Sears estimated its sales for the coming spring on the basis of an increase of better than 11 per cent in all hard lines and of about 8 per cent in soft lines. In more specific terms regarding hard lines, hardware was expected to show a 10 per cent increase; household utensils, 11 per cent; automobile supplies, 1 per cent; crockery, 20 per cent; building materials, 20 per cent; and automobile tires and tubes, 45 per cent. This meant, in the words of the Reconversion Committee, that "these departments have to be reinstated to full size for spring '44—in display, in assortments, in division management, in sales personnel. . . . We feel that, as the spring season progresses, one or two other hard line departments may gather strength with the result that they, too, might have to be reinstated to full size before the fall."

Proceeding pursuant to the ensuing recommendations of the committee, the company established priority lists, by types of stores, for the restoration of prewar lines and elimination of lines added since the start of the war which had proved either unprofitable or out of character. Hand in hand with eliminations went more intensive study of space utilization in all stores. Simultaneously with this pre-postwar conversion, stores were directed to submit layouts showing position and exact space allocation then accorded each department, plus the position and space to be given each department in the postwar period. The dribs and drabs of merchandise, as well as "substitute" goods of inferior quality, were to be cleaned out of the stores without equivocation.

Elimination early in 1944 of shoes, curtains, boys' clothing, and a few other soft lines from certain traditional hard-line stores indicated a minuscule drop in sales—0.8 per cent of Sears's total volume in the six departments affected. Eliminations then proceeded more rapidly, pin-pointed store by store throughout the country. The committee listed each store in the country, by type, showing its exact selling space, departments to be eliminated, and the effective dates of elimination (the dates being usually in the late winter or early spring of 1944).

The Reconversion Committee then turned its attention to the postwar period and listed the company's problems under several headings:

1. Establishment of a policy controlling the selection of store locations.
2. The need for a survey, store by store, of all existing properties to determine the most logical first adjustments to meet postwar requirements.
3. Co-ordination of merchandise structures, sizes of assortments, stock arrangements, grouping and alignment in the store.
4. Planning the store structures:
    a) The possibility of standardization of stores by sales areas.
    b) The addition of outside selling space.
    c) Stockroom, receiving, and handling facilities to be handled as flexible units.
    d) Departmental location and space allocation.
    e) Continued simplification of architectural design.
    f) Increased emphasis on customer facilities and convenience.
    g) Provision for future expansion.
5. Development of color and design in store fixtures and interiors.
6. Packaging and labeling.
7. Simplified, "open" selling.
8. Finding the facts and figures to serve as the foundation of the planning.

The Reconversion Committee translated these problems into concrete recommendations by assigning preference ratings for the first-, second-, and third-year activities, together with the supporting data to justify the relative urgency of each step. The ratings reflected essentially (1) lease expirations, (2) inadequate facilities, and (3) unsatisfactory conditions requiring correction. All stores were to be reconverted immediately for big-ticket merchandise. Eight "A" stores were to be enlarged in the first year, five in the second, and three in the third. Two "A" stores were to be relocated in the first year, one in the second, and two more in the third. Five "B" stores were to be converted into "A's" in the first year, and four in the second. Three new "A" stores were to be built in the initial period, two in the second year, and one in the third year. Similar priorities were assigned to adding ten service stations to "A" stores and for air-conditioning four such stores and for adding fifteen farm stores to existing "A" stores.

When the war ended, that program was put into effect, as Sears launched its greatest expansion drive since the late 1920's. *Fortune* declared:

> In 1945 . . . General Wood took the biggest gamble of his career. He staked $300 million on the conviction that the postwar economy would warrant Sears's immediate expansion, and Sears is reaping a rich reward. In the first two years after the war its sales shot up from $1 billion to almost $2 billion, and Sears emerged as the sixth largest industrial enterprise in the U.S. Its fat net earnings of $107,700,000 in 1947 were the fifth largest in the country and represented the biggest take of any merchandising concern. Sears earned a whopping 22.7 per cent return on net worth, a demonstration of earning power unmatched by any company with a billion dollar volume. . . .
>
> . . . Sears's $1,981,535,749 of sales last year represented nearly twice as large a volume of merchandise as that handled by its biggest competitor, Montgomery Ward, and was roughly equal to 1 per cent of the highest U.S. national income in history. . . . Thanks to General Wood's adventurous optimism, Sears is not simply prospering in the biggest retail market ever, but is getting a bigger chunk of that market than ever before.
>
> In 1945 not everyone shared General Wood's sanguine outlook. The economic predictions emanating from Washington were mostly dismal, construction costs were soaring, and many business men thought any postwar boom would quickly collapse. Sewell Avery, of Montgomery Ward, for example, elected to sit tight, and did nothing about expansion. . . . The General put his staff to work and mapped out his campaign. There was a big element of risk to be considered, of course. If the boom should fail to materialize, Sears would be caught with heavy inventories and commitments, and overexpended store capacity. But if a seller's market prevailed for about two years, Wood estimated, Sears would at least break even; if it lasted from three to five years the firm would profit heavily.[1]

In 1946 no new "A" stores were opened, and the company ended the year with 5 fewer "B" stores and 11 more "C" stores, a net gain of 6 stores. And, in 1947, 9 "A" stores (including the one in Mexico City) and 22 "B" stores (including enlargement of the one in Havana, Cuba) were added—more than half the total arising from reclassifications—but the company closed that year with 16 fewer "C" stores. Yet that does not begin to tell the story, for, in addition to adding 21 stores between the end of 1945 and the end of 1947, the company relocated 32 others to relieve space limitations and made major additions to 18 more. A total of more than $23,000,000 was spent on opening the eleventh branch mail-order plant, at Greensboro, North Carolina, early in 1947, and in enlarging the warehouse area in other plants and in pool stocks. More millions were poured into Sears's factories. Of a total of more than $130,000,000 spent on new capital facilities, $97,000,000 was spent on retail stores—just about what had been spent on them between 1925 and 1941. Additional order offices and Telethrift services were established. A vast deal of the expansion funds were spent in the South, Southwest, and West. Further, the company entered 1946 with $300,000,000 of goods on order as compared with $179,000,000 on order a year earlier. The inventories rose from $181,595,547 at the end of 1945 to $351,002,299 at the end of 1947, an increase of nearly $170,000,000. (This, added to the outlay of $130,000,000 on fixed assets, yields *Fortune's* figure of $300,000,000.)

Coincident with that physical expansion went a great extension of a new retail selling technique inaugurated in March, 1944—telephone selling through Division 200 (which handles mail orders through the catalogue order desks in retail stores), almost identical with the Telethrift shopping service developed ten years earlier by mail order.

That was also the period which saw Sears attempt to invade foreign markets for the first time since Elmer Scott had tried to sell sewing machines in Mexico in the early 1900's. Sears International, Inc., was chartered December 12, 1934, for the purpose of "export trade of Sears merchandise and merchandise produced by Sears' wholly and partly owned factories to foreign countries." Sales were made in Europe, Africa, South America, and Asia and consisted largely of such items as batteries, refrigerators, electric vacuum cleaners, enamelware, and radios. The capitalization consisted of 2,350 shares of common stock with a total value of $11,750. Sears International operated through 1943, at a final net loss of some $300,000. The largest volume in any one year was $1,661,189.

Sears, Roebuck and Company, Ltd., was organized January 1, 1936, in London, and capitalized at 100,000 shares of one pound each, owned entirely by Sears. The English organization became the exclusive outlet of Sears International for Great Britain. It operated through 1941, by which time it too had lost some $300,000.

The unprofitable character of these two foreign operations did not deter the company from more ambitious plans to enter overseas markets, possibly because these other ventures outside the continental United States were to operate on a different basis. In 1942 the company opened a relatively small store in Havana, Cuba, which it later enlarged. In the fall of 1946 *Business Week* reported:

After months of rumor and trade speculation, Sears, Roebuck & Co. last week officially revealed its plans to invade the Latin American retail market. The company will risk a $7,000,000 total investment in three complete department stores, one in Mexico and two in Brazil.[2]

The magazine added that the Mexico City store would open early in 1947, and Rio de Janeiro later that same year, and continued: "General Wood frankly characterizes the venture as a gamble. But outsiders recall that similar skepticism greeted Sears' entry into the retail store field."[3]

The Mexico City store, like Havana before it, was highly successful. In the words of *Fortune* magazine:

When the Mexico City store was opened last year Sears had to issue passes to hold down the crowds. For although Sears charges more in Mexico than it does in the U.S., it has been underselling the local merchants sharply and has substituted fixed prices for the usual Latin haggling. . . . The store grossed $16 million the first year, and Sears, which has already invested more than $7 million in Latin America, is putting in $3 million more and will soon open shop in Rio, São Paulo, and Caracas. The entire project, needless to say, is the personal scheme of General Robert E. Wood.[4]

The first Sears's South (as distinguished from Central) American retail unit to open was that in São Paulo, Brazil, in March, 1949.

The company's 1948 annual report, listing a capital expenditure for the year of $45,627,008 on twenty-two new retail stores and on additions to twenty existing stores, put the figure of total investment in all foreign stores at $11,565,501 as of January 31, 1949. Adding that retail stores were still under construction in Rio de Janeiro and Caracas, the report said of two other overseas units, "The store in Mexico City, which has been in operation for two years, has more than met our expectations and our Havana store, which was opened in 1942, likewise has proved to be very satisfactory."

Most of the merchandise for the stores south of the border was being purchased locally. Original plans had envisaged importation (i.e., exportation from the United States) of the great majority of the goods, including most of the lines carrying the company's own well-known brand names. But the chronic dollar shortages in the various foreign countries forced a sharp reversal of policy, with the result that local buying organizations were established to procure merchandise locally for the overseas retail units. The buying proceeded, initially, at least, on the "trading" basis of haggling over prices which the company had long since sought to abandon in this country. While an eventual extension of the basic buying program to Central and South American countries was envisaged from the outset, it would probably be some while before that merchandise approach could be adapted in the Southern Hemisphere on anything like its scale in the United States.

Around the time the Mexico City store opened, Sears also expanded to the North, though on a small scale. To its catalogue order office in Newfoundland, Canada, the company added one in western Canada, at Vancouver, British Columbia. In opening the latter order office, Sears incorporated a Canadian subsidiary which General Wood termed a "very modest operation" consisting only of order offices. Customers of the Vancouver order office, and the Victoria office opened a month later, were supplied by the Seattle branch plant. All Canadian order offices were later closed because of the tightness of currency and Canadian government restrictions on the use of scarce dollar exchange.

TABLE 69*

YEARS OF SERVICE PRIOR TO APPOINTMENT TO STORE MANAGEMENT, 271 STORE MANAGERS REPORTING TO CHICAGO AS OF MAY, 1946

Years of Service	Number of Managers	Years of Service	Number of Managers
Less than 6	0	18	42
6	4	19	35
7	5	20	5
8	3	21	5
9	0	22	5
10	7	23	2
11	8	24–27	0
12	20	28	1
13	16	29–31	0
14	31	32	1
15	36	33	1
16	29		
17	15	Total	271

* Source: Company records.

These foreign ventures are, however, peripheral to the Sears retail operation, which continues to rest upon the more than six hundred retail stores in the continental United States. What of the men who manage those stores and thus execute the retail selling operation? What are the background, experience, and characteristics of the six-hundred-odd men to whom the company intrusts such great collective responsibility and who in turn accomplish sales in excess of two billion dollars? Considerable light is shed on these questions by an analysis made in 1947 of the length of service, age, educational background, and other characteristics of 271 Sears's store managers, located largely in the Midwest.

None of the 271 had been in Sears's service for less than five years, and more than 90 per cent of them had been in service ten years or longer. The actual distribution of the group by length of service is shown in Table 69. About 45 per cent—126 in actual number—were between 29 and 40 years of age, and exactly the same number were between 41 and 52 years old.

EXPANDING OVER-THE-COUNTER SALES 503

In more detailed terms, the various age-group classifications are revealed in the accompanying tabulation.

Years of Age	Number of Managers
29–32	10
33–36	33
37–40	83
41–44	62
45–48	35
49–52	29
53–56	15
57–60	4

The educational backgrounds of the managers, as detailed in Table 70, reveal a steady increase in the amount of formal education since the period prior to 1931. It is interesting to note that the number of managers with one to three years of high-school education was the same in the period 1941–45 as in the years 1931–35, while the number with four years of high

TABLE 70*

EDUCATIONAL BACKGROUND OF RETAIL-STORE MANAGERS BY PERIOD OF FIRST APPOINTMENT TO STORE MANAGEMENT, 271 STORES REPORTING TO CHICAGO AS OF MAY, 1946

Amount of Formal Education	Prior to 1931	1931–35	1936–40	1941–45	Total	Per Cent
Grade school only	2				2	0.7
1–3 years' high school	2	6	9	6	23	8.5
4 years' high school	7	23	29	52	111	40.9
1–3 years' college	5	12	32	32	81	30.0
4 or more years' college	3	14	14	23	54	19.9
Total	19	55	84	113	271	
Per cent	7.0	20.3	31.0	41.7	100	

* Source: Company records.

school and with varying amounts of college education has steadily increased. (The data on educational background gleaned from the survey of the 271 managers paralleled very closely a similar analysis of 525 store managers and may therefore be assumed to be illustrative of the entire group.) The constant increase in the amount of formal education of store managers at the time of their appointment is attributable largely to the personnel program's emphasis on recruiting the best talent it could secure.

A recent study of 240 store managers made for the company by Social Research, Inc., yielded further data on those executives. Most of them are from relatively small communities, at least as distinguished from large metropolises; 37 per cent of the group analyzed came from cities with populations under 5,000, and an additional 31 per cent from cities ranging in population from 5,000 to 100,000. The average age of those 240 managers at the time of their appointments to that position was 34.8 years, and their average age at the time the survey was made was only 42.1 years. Their educational backgrounds fell into roughly the same categories as indicated in the two studies previously mentioned. But it is interesting to note that possession of a college degree did not appear to speed the *advance* to executive positions. The managers holding college degrees spent an average of 8.2 years in service before appointment to that position; for those with no college, the average length of service was 8.1 years. The group with *some* college enjoyed the most rapid promotion; their average service at the time of appointment to store managerships was only 7.7 years.

As has been indicated, the Sears store managers enjoy an important degree of autonomy as long as they maintain good sales, good profits, and satisfactory community relations. They are also expected to exhibit common honesty, loyalty to Sears, and general respectability. There is a saying in the company that Sears's store managers are fired only for stealing money or for running away with their secretaries, which behavior, while infrequent, is not unknown.

These, then, are the men upon whom the company depends in great measure for its continued prosperity. Whatever changes in the Sears retail operation are wrought by shifts in technology, public taste, and an uncertain world, these store managers and their successors will be primarily responsible for making them effective. As a group they demonstrated their competence for their task in achieving a retail sales volume of some billion-and-a-half dollars in 1948. In its twenty-four years of existence at the end of 1948, retail could look back over a record which was more than good enough to justify Wood's insistence on entering that field in 1925.

CHAPTER XXVII

Easy Payments and "Modern Homes"

THE great growth of instalment selling in Sears, Roebuck and Company came with the equally great expansion of its retail stores. In 1928 the number of retail stores increased from 27 to 192. That year also marked a significant turning point in Sears's credit policy, and the period through 1931 set the stage for the tremendous increase of credit sales in later years.[1]

Prior to 1928 merchandise offered on credit had been priced individually for credit sale, but in that year two fairly comprehensive tables were devised to apply to *lines* instead of *items*. Those tables, designed to encourage combination purchases of various items within the two lines (furniture and light fixtures), adjusted the contract life of the instalment terms to the dollar value of the purchase. Purchases on easy payments from the furniture department ranged from a minimum of $25 to a maximum of $300, with the contract life ranging accordingly from six to eighteen months. The carrying charge was approximately 10 per cent, and the deposit approximately 15 per cent, on any purchase within those dollar limits. On light fixtures the minimum was also $25, but the maximum was held to $100. The carrying charge was likewise 10 per cent, but the deposit was only about 12 per cent. The balance was payable in six to twelve months, depending upon the size of the purchase. The use of tables for those two departments obviated the necessity of listing credit terms for each item.

Several additional items were also approved for instalment terms in 1928: portable phonographs, ice boxes, bathroom outfits, bicycles, and rugs. Deposits ran from 10 to 20 per cent, variously, while the contract life extended from four months to a year. The carrying charge was uniformly around 10 per cent. Credit sales for the year increased by 83.9 per cent over the previous year. (In this connection it should be remembered that 165 new retail stores and two more mail-order plants were opened in 1928.)

The following year saw the United States riding the crest of the greatest boom in its history, and Sears broadened its credit policy accordingly. More new items were approved for credit sale in 1929 than in any one previous year. They ran from clocks to concrete-mixers, from adding machines to transmissions. The tables on furniture and lighting fixtures which had first appeared in the catalogue in the preceding year had worked out so satisfactorily that two more were added, for plumbing and heating fixtures (including air compressors) and for roofing. On plumbing and heating items the terms were the same as on the 1928 furniture table, but terms on furniture were liberalized by increasing the maximum to $500, with other, minor concessions. The table for lighting fixtures remained unchanged, while that for roofing was almost identical except that the maximal amount was $150. Sears's liberalization of its installment terms in the late 1920's was certainly not out of tune with the times, for, as Wecter writes of that period:

> The common man knew more about overexpansion of credit in such homely shapes as installment buying. Intensive campaigns to break down "sales resistance"—often insufficient purchasing power among small citizens—led to new extensions of the time-payment plan for cars, clothes, electric washers, refrigerators, furniture, jewelry.... By 1929 felicity on the installment plan had lured its tens of millions.[2]

In February, 1930, a general credit office was organized to supervise credit policy and collection activities for all mail-order and retail stores, and a credit committee was appointed to govern that office's activities. (That is the committee hereinafter referred to.) That same year marked a greater recession in general business activity, which posed the question whether the company should retrench on its credit terms as it had in the 1920–21 depression. The committee decided that the company's whole system of instalment selling had by that time been placed on such a sound and conservative basis that retrenchment was not in order. Actually, credit terms were liberalized and were advertised more extensively that year.

The 1930 catalogues added tables for farm implements and diamonds to the four tables already being publicized, with terms generally similar. Shotguns and watches were added to the approved credit list, deferred payments on farm implements reinstated, applied roofing sales solicited even more vigorously, and piano terms extended to thirty months. All these steps were generally in line with those taken by Sears's competition. It was also decided to advertise terms on split coach trailers, which would be financed by an automobile financing company.

In the fall of 1930 Montgomery Ward made a special credit offer of everything in its catalogue on terms. Sears countered by authorizing its mail-order plants to extend credit on all lines of merchandise in response to inquiries from good customers, but Ward's move caused only a very small increase in the number of inquiries Sears received for credit on items not previously sold on instalments. In this connection it should be remembered that credit terms, being a component of a sale, are naturally competitive. The competitive situation in mail order is always clear, since it is readily apparent through the catalogues, and each of the two great mail-order firms usually quickly adjusts its terms to those of the other. In retail, however, Sears (and, of course, Ward's) has to compete in credit terms with the thousands of independent merchants and with other chains. In Sears, credit terms are set by the parent in Chicago, which seldom resorts to changes in those terms unless it feels an appreciable number of its retail units are simultaneously and similarly affected. Changes are generally reflected first in the catalogue and are extended to retail upon pressure from the latter.

To promote its credit plan further, Sears culled its general index in the fall of 1930 and sent letters to five hundred customers who had been consistent cash purchasers, offering them credit without any investigation. This promotion was followed by the use of "add-on" and "good-will" letters. The former urged credit customers who had paid 50 per cent (amounting to at least $50) on their accounts in regular instalments to buy "Easy Payment" merchandise in amounts of $20 or more and add it on to their accounts. As extra inducement, no deposit was required, nor was there any increase in monthly payments unless the amount of the add-on purchase exceeded the amount which had been paid on the account. The "good-will" letters were sent to reliable customers upon receipt of their last payment on their instalment accounts and urged them to order more merchandise on easy payments.

Three budget scales were also approved in 1931 for inclusion in the catalogue; they sought to encourage combination purchases to promote sales from several allied departments. The scales included home furnishings, home modernizing, and farm equipment, and each of these three categories included a wide variety of merchandise. In addition, the minimum for credit purchases was lowered from $25 to $20, with a carrying charge of $2.50, a deposit of $4.00, and monthly payments of $4.00. The 1931 catalogue listed terms on electric refrigerators: a carrying charge amounting to 10 per cent of the cash price, a deposit of $10 on units selling for up to $200 and of $25 on higher-priced refrigerators, a contract life of ten months, and a minimum payment of $10 per month. Also, for the first time, October 1 terms on furnaces were advertised in the flyer catalogues, to induce customers to instal furnaces in the summer and make the first payment at the beginning of October.

The next seven years ending in 1938 marked the full maturity and extension of the company's credit system. But the period began in the lowest point of the depression, and 1932 credit sales showed the first decrease from the preceding year since 1923. Even so, collection results continued to be satisfactory, an indication of careful screening of applications. The only new item added to the approved credit list in 1932 was automobile radios, as a result of requests from retail stores.

In 1933 Sears devised four basic plans to govern credit terms on various lines of merchandise in both mail order and retail:

Plan No. 1, to apply on home furnishings, modernizing materials, farm machinery, etc., with up to 18 months of contract life and a deposit of approximately 10 per cent of the sale.

Plan No. 2, to apply to stoves, washers, etc., allowing the same terms as the first plan, except with deposits of $5 on purchases from $60 to $100 instead of 10 per cent of the sale.

Plan No. 3, covering bicycles, watches, diamonds, musical instruments, etc., with a maximum of 10 months to pay and a deposit of around 20 per cent of the sale.

Plan No. 4, applying to automobile radios, boats, shotguns, paint sprayers, etc., with a maximum contract life of 4 months and a deposit of 20 per cent of the sale.

Pianos, electric refrigerators, and vacuum cleaners were excepted from those plans and were offered on more liberal terms. No new items were approved for instalment sales in 1933. Collection figures for the year mirrored the improved economic situation in the country, resulting in a higher percentage of cash and a reduction in the amount of returned merchandise and uncollectibles. The general improvement led the firm in 1934 to seek to promote more credit business; it was felt that many customers previously rejected for credit terms were now better risks and that accordingly a somewhat more liberal policy should be followed to avoid the loss of profitable business. Store managers were at the same time complaining to the parent-organization that Sears's carrying charges were higher than those offered by competing retailers, many of whom were charging only 6 per cent for twelve months. A survey conducted by the company reinforced its belief that Sears was losing little business because of its higher carrying charge (around 10 per cent) and that a reduction to 6 per cent would not increase the volume of credit sales enough to offset the loss in carrying charge.

In the fall of 1934 the company organized the Sears Finance Corporation to purchase notes resulting from Federal Housing Administration modernization loans made by Sears. FHA insured losses up to 20 per cent on sales of modernizing materials, which enabled the company to offer "No Money Down," "Three Years To Pay," "Lower Carrying Charges," and "Loans for Labor" on modernizing loans from $100 to $2,000. Under that plan, Sears's sales of modernizing materials amounted to $4,000,000, the majority of these accounts being sold to the Commercial Investment Trust Corporation with the Sears Finance Corporation as intermediary.

Also, in 1934, several new items were approved for credit sale: automobile tires and tubes and, under Plan No. 4 mentioned earlier, invalid chairs and Henry Rose wearing apparel, the Henry Rose line being offered on credit in only seventeen stores. Simultaneously deposits on electric refrigerators were reduced to $5.00 on units priced up to $150, and $10 for all higher-priced boxes, with the balance payable in not over eighteen months at minimum monthly payments of $5.00. Manufacturers' pricing policy on Elgin and Bulova watches pegged the company's minimum prices on those items, but a plan was devised which, in effect, cut the prices for credit sales: the watches were sold on credit terms with no carrying charge. To keep its records straight, the company simply deducted the usual carrying charge from the advertised price.

By 1935 the company was receiving an increasing number of requests for terms on "cash merchandise" (soft lines and miscellaneous goods). A survey the company made of the general trend of retail credit business in the country showed that department stores had in the past year greatly extended the selling on instalment terms of cash merchandise, including wearing apparel and soft lines, and that Sears's own stores were meeting an increasing consumer demand for terms on such goods. The study further showed that there was an increasing amount of agitation for lower finance charges on instalment accounts, which was somewhat influenced by government credit plans for financing consumer credit at low rates, and that there was also an increasing effort toward legislation for the control of credit rates. Despite these findings, the credit committee determined to make no immediate reduction in its carrying charges or in its policy—relating to the sale of soft-line merchandise. Several more lines were approved for credit in 1935, on varying terms: men's and boys' clothing, made-to-measure clothing, optical goods, movie cameras (offered under the afore-mentioned Plan 4), and, under Plan 1, draperies, shades, and venetian blinds. Terms on power tools, bicycles, watches, diamonds, and automobile radios were reduced to those prevailing in Plan 1. The volume of instalment sales for 1935 was $07,000,000, or 16.1 per cent of the company's total business that year, as compared with 13.3 per cent in 1934 and 10.7 per cent in 1933.

The mounting volume of instalment sales in the thirties was causing a heavy drain upon the company's working capital, tying up as it did large sums of money for relatively long periods of time. Relieving this strain was one of the first tasks taken on by J. M. Barker, after his appointment as financial vice-president in 1935, in conjunction with Comptroller E. J. Pollock. Barker had been a banker in New England and in Buenos Aires before joining Sears late in 1928. By the mid-1930's the company was faced with three choices: to increase its capital, to hold down instalment sales, or to secure outside financing for those instalment sales.

Barker and Pollock set themselves to the last-named task. Banks at that time were allowing finance companies to develop considerable importance; the banks generally did not believe in the advisability of themselves granting consumer credit. But they were at the same time willing to lend large sums to the finance companies, which in turn lent it to small borrowers either as direct loans or through the purchase of time-payment contracts for merchandise sold with the protection of what amounted to chattel mortgages. Banks were willing to purchase time-payment contracts from Sears provided the company would accept 100 per cent contingent liability for the sale. But the finance officers at Sears saw no virtue in that course, for its ratio of losses on credit sales was very small, in addition to which the company could borrow freely from banks at low rates without the complication of transferring a huge number of small individual loans to a bank and still ending up with contingent liability for the full amount.

The company therefore sought to sell to a bank a portfolio of time-payment contracts and to limit the recourse of the bank to Sears, in case of loss, to 10 per cent of the portfolio thus sold. The bank would become the owner of the time-payment contracts and thus would in effect be making an individual loan to each of the many Sears's credit customers. Sears would serve as the bank's agent in collecting the loans. Ten per cent of the portfolio balance owing to the bank would be established as a reserve, against which losses might be charged up to that amount. In other words, if Sears were to sell a bank contracts of a face value of $100,000, the bank would credit the company with $90,000. As Sears delivered additional contracts to the bank, the company would be credited with 90 per cent of the amount of such contracts. Sears would of course continue to collect from credit customers and to remit the proceeds to the bank. The company's reserve would remain at 10 per cent of the total amount of the portfolio sold to the bank, which would in turn charge a reasonable discount fee for the money credited to Sears.

After having its proposal rejected by one of its major banks, the company was able to interest the National City Bank of New York in its plan. After that bank agreed—and on a very substantial basis—other banks became interested, and the plan was extended all over the country, to include over a hundred banks. It has, of course, since been utilized by many other merchandisers selling on instalment terms.

In 1936 Sears's credit terms were further extended and liberalized. Electric food-choppers and stainless-steel cooking utensils were added to the approved list (under Plan 1 terms), portable power plants (under Plan 4), and automobile and camp trailers (one-third down and the balance in six months). Ladies' fur coats were offered, in mail order only, with a 20 per cent deposit, the balance payable in four months. Terms on tractor tires were extended to Plan 1. Terms on washers, ironers, and sewing machines were reduced to $5.00 down and $5.00 a month, with a maximum contract life of eighteen months.

Sears's spring 1937 flyer sent to selected customers in the Chicago, Boston, and Philadelphia territories announced that all those receiving that book (preferred customers) could buy anything from Sears on easy payments. This marked the first time that the company had extended credit terms to all soft lines for any such group of customers. The flyer announced that "responsible people with a regular income" (the indexed list of addressees for the flyer fell generally in that group) could disregard any reference in that flyer or even in the general catalogue which limited instalment terms to durable or semidurable goods. The flyer further announced a minimum purchase of $20 for soft goods, with a carrying charge of $2.50 on orders from $20 to $25, a deposit of $3.00 and monthly payments of $4.00.[3]

Early in 1937 Montgomery Ward's flyer announced a reduction of that firm's minimum for credit purchases from $20 to $10. Sears decided not to follow suit, but the company did decide to figure carrying charges thenceforth at a rate of approximately 10 per cent of the unpaid balance. That decision was withheld until the fall and winter general catalogue, to prevent Ward's from meeting its terms in Ward's own fall and winter 1937 book. In that same fall catalogue, Sears introduced three new plans for mail-order credit terms:

1. For the Chicago, Philadelphia, Boston, Atlanta, Memphis, Los Angeles, and Seattle plants, the carrying charges were reduced to apply on regularly authorized lines.
2. In Minneapolis the terms were the same as those outlined in the preceding paragraph except that everything in the catalogue was offered on credit.
3. In Kansas City and Dallas everything was offered on credit down to $10, but the carrying charge remained at 10 per cent of the full cash price.

Ward's promptly retaliated by offering a similar table of terms except that Ward's customers were instructed to figure carrying charges in *all* regions at 10 per cent of the unpaid balance. Ward had to move fast to accomplish this; many books had already been mailed, which necessitated mailing the new table with a special letter to all those who had received the book. In the books not already released, Ward's made appropriate changes. It was then Sears's turn to reply: terms for Kansas City and Dallas were changed to show a carrying charge of 10 per cent of the unpaid balance. To accomplish this late switch, Sears had to utilize bargain bulletins and other special promotion. At the same time, however, Sears retained the $20 minimum for credit purchases in all its retail stores even though applying the reduced carrying charge to all of them.

In 1937 Sears made a study to determine the effect of credit rejections on customer good will. Of a group of 2,749 customers whose applications for credit were approved, 89 per cent ordered on instalment terms. Of 2,248 who were rejected in applying for credit, 70 per cent ordered by mail within six months. The 70 per cent response from the rejected group was just about average for all customers. The company concluded that diplomatically handled rejections apparently engendered little ill will.

An analysis of the fall 1938 catalogues of the two great mail-order companies showed that Ward's was allowing twenty-four months to pay on electric refrigerators, as against Sears's eighteen months. And on washers, ironers, sewing machines, and stoves, Ward was offering $3.00 down and $4.00 monthly, whereas Sears was offering terms of $4.00 down and $5.00 monthly. In November, Sears moved to meet these terms of Ward's and ordered its retail stores to make the policy effective immediately. "B" and "C" stores competing locally with Ward's stores were instructed to advertise the new policy immediately and heavily, through newspapers, circulars, and posters. Stores of these two classes *not* in direct competition with

Ward's were to advertise the terms in the stores and in the windows. Some "A" stores were to utilize newspapers, circulars, and internal promotion to herald the plan; others were not to advertise the plan until January 1, 1939, but were to make the terms available to customers on request.

The January, 1939, flyer announced an extension to all mail-order regions of the general credit offer covering all items of merchandise which had first been tried, on a regional basis, in Kansas City, Dallas, and Minneapolis in 1937. The credit policy committee also agreed to extend the same general offer to retail, and stores were instructed to begin advertising that fact on January 1. For the first time in its history, the company was offering every item it stocked on easy-payment terms throughout the country in every one of its outlets. The minimal amount of such instalment purchases was $10 for new sales and $5.00 for add-ons. The percentage of instalment sales to total sales rose from 23.03 in 1938 to 28.15 in 1939 and to 30.72 in 1940. This percentage dropped to 28.4 in 1941, even though the actual dollar volume of instalment sales in 1941 increased by some $46,500,000 over 1940.

The extension of the general credit offer in 1939 to all Sears's mail-order regions and retail stores provides an interesting example of the power of changing circumstances and competitive pressure to cause a reversal of decisions reached after great deliberation. Referring evidently to Ward's early adopted policy of "everything on credit," *Fortune* declared in 1938:

> The wisdom of following Ward's action in offering credit on everything in the catalog was argued through a year's lunching, and finally the idea was dropped on the General's observation that "you can repossess a refrigerator without much loss, but when you get back a pair of pants with the seat worn through you haven't got a damned thing."[4]

In January, 1939, customers of Sears might take their choice of refrigerators or pants—on credit.

The years 1939 and 1940 saw few changes made in Sears's (or Ward's) instalment terms, except for slight liberalizations here and there. Sears's fall 1941 general catalogue continued to trumpet, "Anything in This Catalog on Sears Easy Payment Plan." A full page was devoted to answering obvious questions which might arise in a reader's mind, even to explaining why there was a carrying charge. A lengthy table showed the exact carrying charge, the down payment, and the amount payable monthly on every dollars-and-cents amount from $10 to $300. Readers were urged to write for terms on purchases of more than $300. That page even offered the company's assistance in securing FHA modernization loans "with no money down . . . as long as 3 years to pay." On August 8, 1941, after that catalogue had been printed and mailed, the Sears credit committee decided to increase the minimum credit order from $10 to $15 in both retail and mail order, to increase the minimum deposit from $2.00 to $3.00, and to increase monthly payments slightly.

On August 9 the board of governors of the Federal Reserve System issued Regulation "W," to be effective September 1, 1941. That regulation specified minimum down payments on a variety of items: 33⅓ per cent on outboard motors and power-driven boats; 20 per cent on a number of items including washers and ironers, refrigerators, sewing machines, stoves, musical instruments, and others; 15 per cent on a group including furnaces, stokers, water heaters, plumbing supplies, and more; and 10 per cent on furniture and lamps, ice boxes, portable fireplaces, bed springs and mattresses, and pianos. Amendment 2 to Regulation "W" allowed exemption from the deposit requirement on sales where the deposit was $2.00 or less but demanded that the consolidated balance on add-ons pay out in fifteen months. On March 23, 1942, came Amendment 3, which listed additional items, increased deposits on some previously regulated items, and reduced the contract life from eighteen to fifteen months on most of the regulated items.

TABLE 71*

"CASH MERCHANDISE" AS PERCENTAGE OF
TOTAL CREDIT SALES, 1937-41

Year	Retail	Mail Order
1937	4.2	29.3
1938	7.2	44.5
1939	10.9	57.4
1940	17.1	59.0
1941	17.5	55.2

* Source: Company records.

Regulation "W" and the amendments thereto abetted by the absence of Sears's big tickets, whittled the percentage of credit sales to total sales of the company steadily down through the war years. The percentage dropped from 28.36 in 1941 (down more than two points from 1940) to about 11 in 1944 (the lowest percentage since 1933). In 1945 and 1946 the percentage rose slightly; and in 1947 credit sales accounted for a little less than a quarter of the company's sales volume.

Only a shortage of durable and semidurable goods in 1946 and 1947 kept the percentage of instalment sales so low, for it had been largely the big-ticket lines, such as Coldspot refrigerators, stoves, washing machines, radios, plumbing and heating equipment and supplies, and similar items, which had spearheaded the instalment sales up to the war. The share of retail-store instalment sales accounted for by the refrigerators alone was impressive, amounting to 24 per cent in 1937, 18.7 per cent in 1938, 22.2 per cent in 1939, 19.7 per cent in 1940, and 15.4 per cent in 1941.

"Cash merchandise" accounted for a steadily increasing proportion of total credit sales in those same years, as is shown in Table 71. It is evident that, just as the hard lines and big-ticket items sold better on instalment terms in retail than in mail order, so did "cash merchandise" sell better in mail order than in retail. Company credit experience over the years is summarized in the data brought together in Table 72.

In a span of twenty years Sears's credit system advanced from an essentially cautious one, embracing relatively few lines and resulting in an annual volume of only $17,539,000 in credit sales, to a far more liberal and an all-inclusive policy which in 1947 resulted in credit sales of nearly $475,000,000. In dollar terms that volume increased more than twenty-seven times. Net sales in the same period increased only some 600 per cent.

TABLE 72*

INSTALMENT CREDIT EXPERIENCE, TOTAL INSTALMENT ACCOUNTS
ALL STORES (MAIL ORDER AND RETAIL), 1911–39
(In Thousands)

Year	Sales	Per Cent Cash	Per Cent Returned Merchandise	Per Cent Allowances	Per Cent Uncollectible
1911–16	$ 12,719	83.9	12.7	0.5	2.9
1917	10,476	82.5	13.7	0.8	3.0
1918	9,491	82.9	11.8	1.0	4.3
1919	19,397	81.4	11.8	1.1	5.7
1920	26,377	75.4	17.0	1.2	6.4
1921	14,837	70.1	23.9	1.0	5.0
1922	4,173	86.5	11.4	0.7	1.4
1923	3,097	92.9	5.7	0.7	0.7
1924	3,361	92.4	6.5	0.5	0.6
1925	4,665	93.4	5.5	0.5	0.6
1926	6,474	93.7	5.1	0.5	0.7
1927	9,539	93.0	5.8	0.4	0.8
1928	17,539	90.8	7.7	0.4	1.1
1929	32,063	85.5	12.7	0.4	1.4
1930	33,552	85.9	12.0	0.3	1.8
1931	37,140	86.0	12.1	0.2	1.7
1932	29,594	89.3	9.8	. . . .	0.9
1933	30,782	92.3	7.2	. . . .	0.5
1934	47,814	93.0	6.6	. . . .	0.4
1935	73,064	93.4	6.2	. . . .	0.4
1936	114,358	93.7	5.8	. . . .	0.5
1937	140,408	93.9	5.5	. . . .	0.6
1938	104,671	94.6	4.7	. . . .	0.6
1939	185,215	94.8	4.2	. . . .	0.7

* Source: Company records.

The breakdown of credit sales by retail and mail order from 1925 through most of the 1930's shows that, while the retail stores had a significantly higher percentage of returned merchandise than did mail order (as much as three times as high in the depression and pre-depression years), retail had at the same time a lower percentage of allowances and uncollectibles. Mail order, however, showed a consistently higher record of cash collections.

During the "war period," from 1941 through 1947, total instalment sales in one year crowded the half-billion-dollar mark. Returned merchandise in that period ranged from a low of 3.09 to a high of 3.91 per cent. Cash collections and uncollectibles showed no violent fluctuations. One of the most interesting phenomena in the war years was the high rate of recovery of charge-offs, made possible in large measure by swollen incomes. For the five-year period ending with 1945, almost 20 per cent of the charge-offs were subsequently collected; the average was substantially influenced by the experience of 1945, when 40 per cent of the charge-offs were collected.

Table 73 shows the percentage of instalment sales, broken into mail-order and retail sales, to total sales for the years 1928 through 1941. In this connection it should be remembered that total net sales grew from $328,760,314 in 1928 to $915,057,628 in 1941.

TABLE 73*

PERCENTAGE CREDIT SALES TO TOTAL SALES, 1928–41

Year	Mail Order	Retail	Total
1928	4.92	4.31	4.73
1929	5.34	9.79	7.10
1930	5.64	12.17	8.62
1931	5.58	15.38	10.68
1932	4.25	14.79	10.15
1933	3.49	15.00	10.20
1934	4.67	18.87	13.27
1935	6.39	22.94	16.09
1936	7.55	27.96	20.15
1937	10.60	31.10	24.46
1938	11.94	28.76	23.03
1939	19.27	32.53	28.15
1940	22.45	34.40	30.72
1941	19.12	32.61	28.36

* Source: Company records.

Throughout its history up to around 1940, the company's knowledge of its customers—their occupations, income, marital status, etc.—was sketchy. Richard Sears had a personal knowledge of farmers (who constituted the bulk of the company's customers up to 1925) and their wants and needs, and an almost intuitive knowledge of what they would buy in quantity. But even in Richard Sears's day and in the period that followed, most of the company's knowledge of its customers was deductive; if a certain item sold well, the inference was that that item met a need and desire on the part of the customers. Knowledge of what competitors were selling also enabled the company to make some sort of evaluation before adding a new line or a new service. In 1940 the company sought to obtain more specific and comprehensive data on some of its customers, in the form of compilation of data obtained from certain of its customers who were buying on instalments.

In that year the company surveyed 20,054 of its retail customers buying

516   CATALOGUES AND COUNTERS

on instalment terms, the number being almost equally divided between those taken from the records of ten stores in industrial areas and those from eleven stores in primarily agricultural areas. The average credit sale had a dollar value of $60.83, and the contract life averaged 8.7 months. The occupational breakdown revealed that the largest single group—45.3 per cent of the total—was classified as industrial workers. Government employees (local, state, and federal) made up the next largest group, with 10.8 per cent, even though the catch-all classification, "All Others," accounted for 25.3 per cent. Retail employees totaled 9.5 per cent and farmers only 3.3 per cent; Sears's employees and "Contractors" made up the remaining 5.8 per cent. In respect to income, the largest group (56.9 per cent) fell in the $1,001–$2,000 classification, with 23.2 per cent making between $2,001 and $3,000, and 16 per cent $1,000 or less. Only 3.9 per cent reported incomes in excess of $3,000. More than two-thirds of the credit customers had been employed in their present jobs over three years, and virtually the same number were under forty years of age. Nearly 85 per cent were married, but only 40 per cent of the 20,054 had telephones.

In 1941 Sears's general credit office conducted a survey designed to unearth and correlate more nearly complete information on some of its credit customers. The survey was based upon records of the mail-order plants, which had records of their own mail-order credit customers as well as of those of the smaller "B" stores; and of "A" stores, which maintained their own credit departments, through a selected sample covering stores in ten key cities across the country. The survey included 4,985 mail-order customers, 2,141 from "B" stores and 2,086 from "A" stores—a total of 9,212. The credit customers of the latter group proved to have the highest average income: $2,035 per year. The credit customers of the "B" stores were in second place with an annual average income of $1,688, while mail-order instalment buyers averaged $1,345. The "A" store credit customers also led the list in homeownership, with 48 per cent, followed by mail order with 40.7, and "B" stores with 37.4 per cent. The survey also showed that 85 per cent of the credit customers of the "A" stores were married, as against 79.5 per cent for mail order and 78.5 for the "B" stores. In respect to numbers having bank accounts, mail order led with 52 per cent, followed by the "A" stores with 46 per cent and the "B" stores with 34 per cent. The largest proportion of customers in all three categories fell in the 31–40-year-old age group. Other data brought to light by the survey are shown in Tables 74 and 75.

The 1941 survey also illustrated clearly that the bulk of the company's credit business was confined to relatively few departments. The ten departments reporting the greatest number of transactions and the greatest dollar volume in proportion to total dollar volume of credit business accounted for well over two-thirds of the instalment sales. The composition of the ten leading departments varied slightly from mail order to retail "B" to retail "A," but the lists for all three types included radios, furniture, "combination" (orders from two or more departments), Coldspot refrigerators, plumbing and heating, farm equipment, washers, and stoves. In mail order, for example, women's apparel, tires, curtains and drapes, and electrical appliances were included in the ten "best-selling" departments.

TABLE 74*

DISTRIBUTION OF INSTALMENT SALES
BY CUSTOMER'S OCCUPATION

Occupation	Per Cent of Total		
	Mail Order	Retail "B"	Retail "A"
Retail and individual business	8.4	13.1	15.6
Business management	6.1	8.4	14.6
Skilled labor	26.3	37.1	51.7
Unskilled labor	16.5	15.1	6.7
Professional	4.8	5.1	5.7
Local and federal government employment	3.3	3.9	3.3
Farmer	23.7	10.7	1.1
No occupation reported	10.9	6.6	1.3
Total	100.0	100.0	100.0

* Source: Company records.

TABLE 75*

AVERAGE INSTALMENT SALE BY CUSTOMER'S OCCUPATION

Occupation	Average Sale in Dollars		
	Mail Order	Retail "B"	Retail "A"
Retail and individual business	$37.50	$50.00	$73.00
Business management	32.20	44.40	65.95
Skilled labor	31.20	49.75	68.00
Unskilled labor	22.50	37.15	61.65
Professional	31.15	43.75	68.75
Local and federal government employment	36.07	51.80	73.35
Farmer	26.20	44.20	71.95
No occupation reported	28.30	39.40	60.80
Average for all occupations	$29.00	$46.00	$68.00

* Source: Company records.

Yet retail "B" included rugs, but not tires, and tools and hardware, but not electrical appliances. Retail "A," on the other hand, *did* include rugs and tires. Coldspot refrigerators, even when lumped together with stoves and washers, accounted for only 3.5 per cent of the total value of mail-order instalment purchases. In retail "B," however, Coldspots alone accounted

TABLE 76*

ANALYSIS OF EASY-PAYMENT CUSTOMERS BASED ON
CONTRACTS APPROVED IN TWENTY-ONE STORES
SPRING, 1944

Customer Characteristics	Per Cent		
	Industrial Areas (10 Stores)	Agricultural Areas (11 Stores)	Total (21 Stores)
Occupation:			
Industrial	73.3	44.3	58.2
Retail	5.9	6.7	6.3
Government	9.3	18.9	14.4
Sears	0.6	1.9	1.3
Farmer	0.9	15.2	8.3
Contractor	4.2	2.7	3.4
All others	5.8	10.3	8.1
Annual income:			
$1,000 and less	0.7	7.3	4.2
$1,001–$2,000	10.6	44.1	28.1
$2,001–$3,000	38.7	38.5	38.6
Over $3,000	50.0	10.1	29.1
Length of employment:			
Up to 1 year	26.4	31.8	29.1
1–2 years	19.5	16.3	17.9
2–3 years	9.2	7.0	8.1
Over 3 years	44.9	44.9	44.9
Age:			
Up to 30	26.6	29.8	28.3
31–40	35.0	33.2	34.1
41–50	24.7	24.3	24.5
Over 50	13.7	12.7	13.1
Marital status:			
Married	91.0	89.6	90.2
Single	6.7	7.8	7.3
Widowed	2.3	2.6	2.5
Tenancy status:			
Own	44.6	47.4	46.2
Rent	51.9	46.1	48.8
Board	3.5	6.5	5.0
Telephone:			
Yes	56.8	38.5	47.3
No	43.2	61.5	52.7
Bank account:			
Yes	53.4	39.0	45.8
No	46.6	61.0	54.2

*Source: Company records.

for 20.7 per cent (in value) of total credit sales, and in retail "A" this one item represented 32 per cent of the value of all credit sales.

In 1944 the company conducted a survey of 5,187 of its credit customers to bring up to date its 1940 and 1941 findings and to obtain more information on the effects exerted by wartime conditions upon its instalment purchasers. The 1944 study embraced 2,476 credit customers chosen from the records of ten stores in industrial areas and 2,711 credit customers from eleven stores in agricultural areas. The average sale was $48.45; the average contract life, 5.8 months. Some of the other findings, by the two types of areas and by the average of the two, are shown in Table 76.

Two conclusions were indicated by the findings of the foregoing survey, sketchy in coverage as it was. One was the nature of Sears's credit market: the characteristics of its customers in terms of income, occupation, marital status, etc. All those factors had a vital bearing on what merchandise the company's customers wanted and how much they were able and willing to pay for it. This, in the long run, determines Sears's merchandise structure. In terms of the period before World War II, it meant a best-selling men's dress shirt priced between $1.00 and $1.39; a washing machine at around $50; a radio-phonograph at around $79; a woman's slip for about $1.00 and a cotton dress at $1.98; a 600 × 16 automobile tire for less than $10; a baseball glove at $1.98 to $2.49—upward variations being possible and desirable in each case, provided such price points did not cost the item its mass appeal.

The second significant point of the data uncarthed in the surveys was that a relatively few departments, some ten in number, accounted for a preponderant majority of total sales volume sold on instalments. This fact may offer evidence of the wisdom and success of reorienting the merchandise structure in order to concentrate effort on the most profitable lines and items. It may also be evidence of the soundness of Sears's "basic buying" approach, of which the Coldspot refrigerator, with its high gross margin and tremendous sales volume, is the best-known example.

Both those conclusions are, however, necessarily tentative and are applicable only to the degree that the survey covered credit purchases only, thus completely omitting two-thirds of the company's sales volume from consideration; and even the number of credit customers so studied contributed only about two-tenths of 1 per cent of the company's total instalment sales in 1944.

The entry of Sears, Roebuck into the retail field, which led in time to this refinement and extension of its instalment selling, coincided also with a vast extension of credit in a venture posited upon a far less sound basis—"Modern Homes." As pointed out earlier, the "Modern Homes" department had nearly a dozen sales offices, most of them located in the Middle Atlantic region, by 1925. On January 1 of that year the Federal Reserve Bank of New York noted in its *Monthly Review:*

The index of building ... throughout the greater part of the period [1900–1924] increased at a rate approximately equal to that of population growth. Beginning about 1910, however, building tended to decline, and during the [first World] war fell far below the population trend, leaving an accumulated shortage from which the present activity appears to have been a normal consequence.

Sears did not intend to miss the opportunity, even if it meant an excursion into the mortgage banking field.

Except for a brief interlude between April, 1922, and February, 1923, when Julius Rosenwald limited the granting of mortgage loans, the company's loan policy responded steadily to sales pressure and continued to be liberalized. In 1926 a 65 per cent, five-year mortgage program was adopted.

The rapid increase in sales in the eastern territory created a demand for a building materials source which would offer greater advantages in delivery time and transportation expense. Port Newark, New Jersey, was selected as the site for this eastern source, and a plant was erected there in 1926. Arrangements were made with the city of Pork Newark whereby the municipality would lease Sears, Roebuck and Company a fifty-acre tract on tidewater at an annual rental of 2 per cent of the taxable valuation. The city was to hold the firm tax free and was to put in lights and streets and keep the streets cleaned at its own expense. The company in its turn was to employ a minimum of four hundred people.

The erection of this plant apparently helped hang an albatross around the "Modern Homes" department's neck. The original company appropriation for the structure was $480,000. At the last minute, however, the operating organization discovered that the president of the company considered the Newark plant an operations job and would hold operations responsible for it. The company's regular architects were then called in and the plans redrawn; one result of the last-minute switch was that the final cost was around $2,000,000.

Of perhaps more importance to the company's fortunes than this $2,000,000 investment, however, was the essence of a report on building activities in the *Monthly Review* of the Federal Reserve Bank of New York, dated December 1, 1925:

Building undertakings continued large in October, approximately 27 per cent above a year ago, according to the F. W. Dodge Corporation's figures of contracts let and the S. W. Straus Company's report of permits issued. In this district contracts, after falling below a year ago in the first half of this year, gained 63 per cent over 1924 in the months from July to October, while for the country as a whole, a gain of 15 per cent during the first six months was converted into a gain of 50 per cent from July to October. The following table compares the percentage increase for the entire ten months over last year with changes in previous years.

	1920	1921	1922	1923	1924	1925
Percentage change from preceding year	−0.6	−8.2	+42.0	+4.8	+12.3	+28.4

Residential building continues to be largely responsible for the maintenance of high building totals....

... While precise estimates of building surplus or shortage are impossible, owing to such factors as changing standards of living, changing character of cities through suburban development, longer use of old buildings, etc., it would now seem probable that recent construction has eliminated most of the shortage heretofore existing as a result of underbuilding during the war. This conclusion appears to be in keeping with the general consensus of estimates by competent authorities and with the moderate decline in rentals in many sections.

Arthur Burns's figures indicate rather clearly that the bank was correct in its cautious belief that "most of the shortage had been eliminated"— which was another way of saying that the peak of the building boom had passed, as shown by Table 77, which illustrates not only the high level of

TABLE 77*

CONSTRUCTION ACTIVITY IN THE UNITED STATES, 1910–29
(1913 = 100)

Year	Index	Year	Index
1910	115.1	1920	68.0
1911	114.2	1921	123.8
1912	120.9	1922	102.4
1913	100.0	1923	210.7
1914	98.1	1924	221.6
1915	111.4	1925	263.1
1916	116.5	1926	257.0
1917	54.0	1927	201.4
1918	25.1	1928	229.4
1919	84.4	1929	203.1

* Source: Arthur F. Burns, *Production Trends in the United States since 1870* (New York: National Bureau of Economic Research, 1934), pp. 302-3. Burns's table is based on building permits issued in seven cities, the figures of building permits being deflated by an index of changes in costs of construction. The Federal Reserve Bank of New York's *Monthly Review* of January 1, 1925, cited by Burns, identifies the cities as Boston, New York, Chicago, Minneapolis, Cleveland, Philadelphia, and San Francisco. For support of Burns's use of building permits for a long-period study of detailed variations see C. D. Long, *Building Cycles and the Theory of Investment* (Princeton: Princeton University Press, 1940), p. 98.

activity in the construction industry in the 1920's (note, for example, that its volume increased considerably even in the depression years of 1920 and 1921) but also the fact that the year (1926) in which Sears, Roebuck launched its biggest expansion in the housing field was to mark the first tapering-off from that peak of activity.

By 1926 the annual sales volume of the department had reached $8,438,-000, with a departmental net profit that year of $945,000. Rapidly mounting sales cost was, however, beginning to bite into the net profits. On an increased volume over 1921 of nearly $2,500,000 there was an increased net profit of only $45,000. The profit margin had declined from 15 to 11 per cent. Total sales for this six-year period amounted to $36,066,000, and net profits aggregated $3,655,000. During the same period the total mortgage loans written reached a sum of $22,259,000, of which $5,077,000 was cash and $17,181,000 was materials. Nearly half the sales in this period were on a mortgage basis. Owner-built houses had become the dominant factor in both sales and mortgage loans, and appraisals for loans were becoming more and more generous. According to a statement made by J. H. O'Connor of the company's credit department in the 1926 annual report on mortgage loans, this generosity had reached a point where loans frequently financed construction 100 per cent.

The 1926 "Modern Homes" catalogue, a book of 144 pages, provides a sample of "Modern Homes" promotion at its height. That book was printed almost entirely in color, from one-color rotogravure to four-color letterpress printing. The cover referred to the easy-payment plan, which was also mentioned thoughout the book; the text of the book promised the reader almost everything but a cash bonus if he would but allow the company to construct for him one of its "Honor Bilt Modern Homes." Every angle of the advantages of homeownership was cited, abetted by illustrations and tables. Tables compared monthly payments on "Modern Homes" with what purported to be typical rentals at various levels to show how low payments on Sears's homes were and sought to show that one could complete payment for a "Modern Home" in a few years, whereas he would otherwise continue paying rent as long as he occupied a rental dwelling.

The illustrations showed everything from "Give the Kiddies a Chance" (children romping joyously on their own grounds) to "Have Real Friends and Neighbors" (the friendly handshake). There was also a note addressed to employers, telling how Sears's "Modern Homes" for their employees would reduce absenteeism and labor turnover and mitigate "unrest." And there was reprinted a letter from the Standard Oil Company of Indiana expressing its entire satisfaction with two hundred homes built for it by Sears, which, Standard said, "we are able to offer... to our workmen at very low prices." (A check for $1,000,000 tendered by Standard Oil of Indiana for "Modern Homes" was reputedly the largest ever received by the company from any purchaser.) The catalogue listed seventy-three "Honor Bilt Modern Homes" by their several names, from "The Albany" to "The Woodland," eight "Standard Built" low-priced homes (from "The Estes" to "The Selby"), as well as sunrooms, garages, summer cottages, outhouses, and miscellaneous items.

The book repeated incessantly that "skyscrapers are ready cut—why not your home?" Cut-away illustrations showed how each piece of lumber was "ready cut" at the factory and numbered for easy construction. A 40 per cent saving in carpenter labor (backed by an affidavit) was claimed for the Sears homes. The homes sold by the company were complete with hardware, various interior items such as closets, etc., and three coats of exterior paint. Prices ranged from $474 for the Hudson (two bedrooms, livingroom, kitchen, bath, and porch) to $4,319 for the Lexington (an elaborate two-story structure). Garages started at $82.50.

EASY PAYMENTS AND "MODERN HOMES"

The solid page devoted to the easy-payment plan and containing an application blank stated:

If you own a good, well located building lot free and clear from debt, and have some cash on hand, you can buy from Sears, Roebuck and Co. an "Honor Bilt" Modern Home, consisting of Lumber, Lath, Millwork, Sash Weights, Hardware, Nails, Paint, Building Paper, Eaves Trough, Down Spout and Roofing Material, Plumbing Goods, Heating plant and lighting Fixtures, or a STANDARD BUILT Home, on easy payment terms, and in some instances we will advance part of the cash for labor and material, such as brick, lime and cement, which we do not furnish.

By 1927 the "Modern Homes" department had actually very nearly reached its maximum development. Sales offices scattered throughout the East were headed up in the Philadelphia headquarters; throughout the Midwest, in the Chicago headquarters. This organization sought an ever increasing sales volume. By this time, however, country-wide building activity had receded, and it became more difficult and more expensive to maintain, much less increase, volume in a declining market. In 1928, therefore, the 75 per cent fifteen-year mortgage plan was introduced, and in 1929 the company adopted the policy of construction of homes in addition to the sale of materials. More expensive dwellings and special designs constituted more and more of the volume, with resultant increases in architectural and service expense. The profit margin for the "Modern Homes" department dropped to less than 5 per cent in the years 1928, 1929, and 1930 from a high of 15 per cent in 1919 and 1920, and an average of more than 10 per cent for the period from 1921 to 1926.

A sales office had been opened in Kansas City in 1927 (and closed in 1928) and another opened in St. Louis in 1929. The peak point in sales came in 1929 with a volume of $12,050,000, $5,622,000 of which was on a mortgage-loan basis. Sales for the next year declined to $10,658,000, of which $6,854,000 was on a mortgage basis. The total mortgage loans for that year, including cash furnished in the amount of $4,160,000, was $11,014,000 and actually exceeded sales by over $350,000. For the four years from 1927 through 1930, sales amounted to $42,112,000, of which $24,702,000, or 59 per cent, was on a mortgage basis. Mortgage-loan accounts receivable had reached a total of $37,000,000, and increasing difficulty was encountered in collections. Foreclosure and resale of houses was to become a real problem.

Business Week, in its issue of March 26, 1930, used Sears's policy of constructing homes as a peg on which to hang a résumé of the home selling and building operations of both Sears and Montgomery Ward:

For several years mail order houses have been selling ready-cut houses delivered at the building site. Now both Sears, Roebuck & Co. and Montgomery Ward Co. have gone two steps farther. They not only sell and deliver the houses, with every stick and timber cut and numbered, but they also finance and supervise construction.

About all the customer has to do is to say, "Build me such-and-such a house on such-and-such a lot." The company does the rest and collects over an instalment period of 14 years, 8 months. The purchaser pays $8.56 a thousand a month, which is 6% interest and payment in full of principal in 15 years, including carrying charges amounting to 1% a year on the material, or about ½% on the entire loan. Savings over time-hallowed methods of building are said to be 18% in materials, 30% to 40% in labor costs.

The new plan of home building has been in operation only a few months, but both companies have found it exceedingly popular. Before its adoption, Sears, Roebuck & Co. sold about 3,000 houses a year; since the new system of finance and construction went into effect, this total has been greatly increased. . . .

The article went on to describe the "Wardway" homes offered in Montgomery Ward catalogues, among them "The Devonshire," with seven rooms and bath; payments on that structure averaged only $40 monthly. It was "an attractive house with high sloping roof, L-shaped floor plan, far different from the standardized structures sometimes seen in builders' rows." Other offerings included "The Cranford," at $35 a month; "The Dover," at $30 monthly; and others. The Ward catalogue was quoted as saying:

We supply materials without any down payment. We advance additional money to help you pay for labor. All you need is your building lot and a small amount of cash if you live in a town of 800 or more. We charge only 6% interest, and you need never worry about refinancing or paying exorbitant rates for a new loan after a few years' time.

The magazine asserted that the Sears "Honor Bilt Modern Homes" catalogue listed forty-eight sales offices, all east of the Mississippi and north of the Mason and Dixon Line. Ward's, on the other hand, listed only fifteen such sales offices, located "in five states around Chicago," according to *Business Week*, which added that five additional sales offices had been established since the Ward catalogue was issued. The magazine stated that Sears's salesmen numbered 350; no figures were given for the number of Ward's salesmen. The article concluded:

If the ground on which the house is to be built is 25% or more of the total value when improved, then no down payment is required. Otherwise, [the buyer] must make up the difference in cash. Monthly payments begin four months later. The mail order houses have connections with local real estate men, banks, and building and loan associations, through which reliable appraisals of vacant lots are secured. . . .

No attempt is made to interfere with the local contractor's established methods of hiring or using labor. If union labor is available it is likely to be used. Economies are sought, but not at the workingman's expense. They result from speed in building, which follows naturally when parts are supplied accurately cut to measure and numbered, each for its place, and when workmen move on from one job to another gaining in skill and experience as they go.

In an effort to offset the decline in business accompanying the depression, the company announced a new scheme in the fall of 1930: a fund of

$5,000,000 to enable owners of old residences to finance a home modernizing and remodeling campaign on a monthly part-payment basis. The program was to operate initially only within a radius of fifty miles of New York City; if successful there, it would be extended to other large cities. The *Wall Street Journal* of October 6, 1930, termed this "the first attempt within the construction industry to apply to the reconditioning of old residences the long-term financing which in the past has been available only for new home building or such specific items of remodeling as the major contracting jobs of modern heating, plumbing, reroofing and repainting."

Special offices for administration of the $5,000,000 fund were established in White Plains, New Rochelle, Mount Vernon, and Jamaica, New York, and in Newark, Paterson, and Hackensack, New Jersey, in addition to one in the New York City office of the building materials division. The minimum repair job accepted under the plan was $100, including materials and labor; down payments ran as low as 10 per cent, and monthly payments were stretched over as long a period as two years. Local labor was to be used exclusively. And Sears, Roebuck was to furnish the materials as well as the architectural and contracting service and the financing.

At the end of 1930 the "Modern Homes" department was again reorganized—paradoxically enough, by establishing it. Until this time there had actually been no one department handling the sale of all items represented in "Modern Homes." Various items connoted by that phrase had been stocked in a number of departments; while special "Modern Home" catalogues were widely distributed, the component items of the homes had been scattered throughout different merchandise departments. They were all brought together in 1931 under the Home Construction Division, which was to handle the sale and construction of modern homes, garages, summer cottages, applied roofing, and any other building sale for which special service was offered the customer. The organization was set up by districts, six in the East and six in the West, with complete sales, service, and construction office personnel in each.

In mid-July of 1931 the Home Construction Division opened a retail store and lumber yard for the sale of building materials and equipment at Keyport, New Jersey, on a frankly experimental basis. It was declared that if that venture succeeded, similar retail stores and lumber yards would be opened elsewhere. But the clouds of the great depression were lowering over those "if's" which accompanied each of the company's searches for new business in those years.

The January 22, 1932, issue of the *Wall Street Journal* carried a story on Sears's Home Construction Division which eloquently emphasized the constant efforts to find a new business and the failure which attended most such efforts. The first paragraph announced the extension to Chicago of the home-remodeling service first tried in New York in October, 1930; the minimum figure had dropped from $100 to $50, while the contract life had been lengthened from two to five years. The second paragraph announced that the Home Construction Division expected to build its one hundred thousandth home during 1932 and that Sears, Roebuck was taking on slum rehabilitation, on which it was reported "willing to spend several millions of dollars . . . on a return as low as 3%." The third paragraph sounded the muted overtones of an obituary note, flashing back to the 1906 reorganization of the company's building materials business. And the final paragraph added an even stronger obituary note, with a quotation from General Wood on some aspects of the company's business in the previous two years: "Between 1929 and 1931 it was necessary for us to let go about 5,000 people in our organization."

The Home Construction Division was feeling the pinch of the decrease in business activity even more sharply than the other departments of the company. That accentuated decrease was simply in the nature of the beast, for, as Long writes:

Altogether, the building industry manifests two features that cause it to be the focus of the problem of great depressions. The first feature is its huge size [building is, as Long points out elsewhere, the largest single investment goods industry], the fact that it is the nation's largest single industry next to agriculture, having a strategic position with regard to the production and employment of almost every other industry in the country. The second is . . . the severity of its fluctuations, the fact that swings in productive activity from valleys to peaks are the widest of any important industry.[5]

Despite reorganization of the "Modern Homes" department late in 1930, the liberal mortgage policy in force, and all the promotions listed earlier, it was impossible to maintain volume in the face of the deepening business depression. Sales continued to fall, from $8,442,000 in 1931 to $6,324,000 in 1932 and to $3,670,000 in 1933. Late in the latter year mortgage-loan financing was discontinued and complete construction abandoned except in the urban territory around New York City.

The *Wall Street Journal* of November 20, 1933, announcing that move, added that the company would continue to sell building materials for cash throughout the country and asserted: "For the fiscal period from December 31, 1931, to January 28, 1933, sales declined more than 40% from the previous period, and the division showed a net loss of $1,154,985." The *Journal* listed as one of the factors which had led to the decision to curtail construction operations the "shortage under present conditions of mortgage money available for rediscount of the mortgages taken by Sears from home buyers to cover a part of the purchase price." The newspaper also asserted that the restriction of construction to the urban New York area was expected to reduce the company's home construction activity by 60–75 per cent. The reduction actually amounted to 90 per cent or more of the volume and eventuated in the liquidation of the department. Contracts on hand were completed in 1934, when final liquidation took place; sales that year were a mere $357,000.

"Modern Homes" had enjoyed a history of profits from 1907, the year following its first reorganization, through 1930. The total profit from 1906 to 1930, inclusive, was $10,064,000; the losses from 1931 to 1934 inclusive (a total of $1,310,000) reduced the profit to $8,754,000 for the twenty-eight-year period, or 6.4 per cent on total sales of $137,000,000. From 1911 through 1934 a total of $80,945,000 of mortgage loans was written. Of this amount $25,129,000 (or 31 per cent) was cash, and the remaining $55,816,000, materials. Of the total sales of $137,000,000, about $73,000,000 was represented by complete homes and about $64,000,000 of sales of materials other than complete house units.

Mortgage loans, which had been inaugurated in 1911 and discontinued in 1913, were revived in 1916 and grew rapidly in the succeeding four years. In 1920 mortgage loans were written in the amount of $1,619,000, or 27 per cent of the total sales. In the period from 1916 to 1920 the cash involved in the mortgage loans amounted to only a little over 3 per cent, the remainder consisting of materials. In this period arrangements were made with the Prudential Life Insurance Company whereby Prudential would buy from Sears, Roebuck such of those mortgages as met with the former's approval. A similar arrangement was later entered into with the Metropolitan Life Insurance Company of New York. Thus capital for mortgage financing was replenished.

Since the mortgages sold to the insurance companies were covered by a repurchase agreement and therefore the ultimate responsibility rested with Sears, no distinction is made in the figures which follow on converted and unconverted mortgages. From 1921 to 1926 mortgage loans became the largest single factor in "Modern Homes" sales. In 1926 mortgage loans written amounted to $8,171,000 and represented 97 per cent of the total sales. The proportion represented by cash had risen from 3 to 28 per cent, and the balance outstanding had grown from $1,917,000 in 1920 to $15,564,000 in 1926. From 1927 to 1930 mortgage loans continued to increase. In the latter year the amount written was $11,014,000, over 100 per cent of the total sales, and in that year 38 per cent of the loans were in the form of cash. The balance outstanding had grown to $38,510,000 by the end of 1931 and reached its peak in 1932 with $45,075,000 and remained at about this level through 1933.

Sears, Roebuck's annual report for 1932 stated:

The ["Modern Homes"] department had a continuous record of profitable operation for nineteen years.

Since September, 1931, this department has operated at a loss. Its sales declined over 40% in our fiscal year, with resulting losses of $1,154,984 during the year. With the reorganization and the reduction of expense that have been effected, it is believed that in 1933 this branch of the business can be operated without loss, even if we should encounter a further reduction of 20% in volume of sales. . . .

Beginning with the summer of 1931, there has been a large increase in the number of properties reacquired. In the period September, 1931 to November,

1932, the number reacquired exceeded the total of the preceding ten years. Since November, this number has begun to decline.

On September 1, 1931, the number of properties reacquired or in process was .... 420 with an unpaid balance of $1,650,100
From September 1, 1931, to January 28, 1933, we reacquired additional properties .... 661 with an unpaid balance of 2,720,542
1,081 with an unpaid balance of 4,370,642
During the same period we resold ...... 219 with an unpaid balance of 830,921
Leaving on our books, as of January 28, 1933 .... 862 with an unpaid balance of $3,539,721

The above mentioned 219 properties, with a book value of $830,921 were sold for $695,151, or for 83.66% of their book value.

In November, 1931, we began renting some of the properties. As of January 28, 1933, there were rented 503 properties on an annual basis of $127,248.

The annual report for 1933 touched on the same theme:

Continuing our process of curtailing the importance of our Modern Homes Department, sales in 1930 were $12,033,069; in 1931, $12,731,054; in 1932, $7,516,835; in 1933, $3,575,878. It is planned to further curtail operations in 1934. The department operated at a small loss in 1933. Collections have improved and it seems probable that it will be necessary to re-acquire very few additional properties. Since September, the number of properties sold has exceeded the number re-acquired. Our books as of January 29th showed a total of 934 re-acquired properties, with an unpaid balance of $3,906,202. We anticipate that our mortgage receivables will show a very substantial decrease in 1934.

From 1934 on the company moved vigorously to reduce the value of its mortgage-loan accounts receivable. By far the largest single factor contributing to the reduction was the sale, at a loss of 17½ per cent, to the Home Owners Loan Corporation in 1934 and 1935 of 4,137 accounts whose ledger balances aggregated $15,902,000. Mortgage-loan accounts aggregating $5,000,000 were sold to the Metropolitan Life Insurance Company in 1935 on a nonrecourse basis. Further reduction (down to $28,133,000 by the sixth period of 1936) was accomplished through cash received and write-offs taken in the sale of repossessed property, mortgage loans refinanced by mortgagors, and, of course, regular instalment payments.

The company's annual reports spelled out the dreary details of the liquidation of the "Modern Homes" department. In 1934 this statement appeared:

About $11,000,000 in mortgages was liquidated during the year and the Modern Homes Department was discontinued. The losses, amounting to $1,637,000, incident to the liquidation of mortgages, closing of the department, and the reacquiring of properties, were charged to surplus even though the reserve available would probably have been ample to cover both this write-off and the future remaining liquidation losses.

EASY PAYMENTS AND "MODERN HOMES" 529

The annual report for 1935 declared:

On January 29, 1933, our total Mortgages Receivable Account was $41,544,-132, of which $29,465,483 was held by the Metropolitan Life Insurance Company, and there were $3,539,721 in Repossessed Properties. On January 29, 1936, our Mortgages Receivable Account stood at $16,135,634, of which $8,870,-977 is held by the Metropolitan Life Insurance Company under a repurchase contract, and our repossessed properties, amounting to $1,641,505, were charged to the Surplus Account. The less desirable properties have been repossessed and a large number of the delinquent mortgages have been taken over by the Home Owners Loan Corporation at a substantial discount, and the remaining mortgages are the better ones. Repossessed properties are selling freely and at prices very little below our book value.

During the year 1935, the Company sold to the Metropolitan Life Insurance Company mortgages amounting to $5,000,000, with the understanding that if there were any losses in the collection of these mortgages, our responsibility would be limited to the $500,000 now in reserve. As practically all of these mortgages have never defaulted on payment of interest or principal, even during the depression, it is anticipated that this particular reserve will not be needed for this purpose.

The annual report for the year 1939 revealed further reductions:

During 1939, "Mortgages Receivable" were reduced $1,541,510 and our investment in "Properties held for resale" (under the old contracts of the Modern Homes Department which have been systematically liquidated for several years) was reduced $246,126. The reserve for "Collections and Losses" is considered ample for the expenses and losses incident to the liquidation of these balances.

Prior to 1929 a financing fee of 2½ per cent had been charged and included in the mortgage loans written. The sum of these fees for all years amounted to about $1,000,000. The charge was presumably intended to cover collection expenses and losses, but the fees were included in revenue and were not set up as a reserve. Beginning in 1929, a markup of 15 per cent was included in the mortgages and was set up as a reserve; in six years' time $2,639,000 was so set up. Collection losses and expense, however, soon depleted this reserve, and by 1932 it was apparent that further provision was needed for these losses and expenses.

From 1932 through 1935 additional reserves of $5,912,000 were provided from earnings. The afore-mentioned loss of 17½ per cent on sales to the HOLC—amounting to $2,795,000—was the largest debit to the reserve from any single cause. Losses on the sale of repossessed houses from 1933 through the first six periods of 1936 totaled $996,000. The expense of foreclosing, reconditioning, maintaining, including interest and taxes, and selling was almost double the ledger balance loss.

In addition to the financial consequences of the "Modern Homes" adventure, there were other, more subtle, accompaniments to the whole campaign. The company's most valuable asset was the immense good will of its customers. The spectacle of the "farmer's friend"—the great mail-order distributor—foreclosing mortgages was an unlovely one. There were the further "contingent liabilities" of customer dissatisfaction with homes built by the poor workmanship of inexpert, green hands and conflicts with union labor in the building trades.

In recapitulation, it would appear that, so long as the promotion and sale of building material lines were the principle objectives of the "Modern Homes" department, its volume grew and its profits increased. As "Modern Homes" increased in importance and volume, it became necessary to set up an elaborate sales and service organization to handle the business and to assume the risks of mortgage banking. Such an organization was expensive to maintain and led to reaching for more and more volume for its own justification and support. In order to secure this volume, it was necessary to liberalize the mortgage terms, to accept business in undesirable locations, and to approve undesirable credit risks. The result of all this was to create an ever increasing and ever more unsound mortgage receivable structure. At any time subsequent to 1926, the onset of a business depression would probably have developed losses comparable to those which actually were incurred after 1929; the condition was inherent in the structure. Mortgage-loan losses might easily have been far greater than they were (if, for instance, the HOLC had not provided a market for nearly $16,000,000 of such loans).

From 1906 to 1934 the building material sales amounted to $69,255,000 and returned a profit of 8.9 per cent, or $6,142,000. For the same period sales of homes as such amounted to $87,052,000 and returned a profit of 4.9 per cent, or $4,295,000. After applying the subsequent mortgage-loan losses of $6,912,000, the profit was converted into a loss of $2,617,000 on "Modern Homes" (as homes). The entire "Modern Homes" operation (as apart from sale of building materials) was interred and summarized in Clark's report as follows: "Over a twenty-five year span, close to $90,000,000 of business was done, and a loss of over $2,500,000 was incurred in order that the building material factories might make a corresponding profit."[6]

Sears, Roebuck was to enter the prefabricated housing field in 1935 but not on the same basis upon which "Modern Homes" had collapsed. In the words of the *Wall Street Journal* of August 26, 1935: "Sears will not erect or directly finance purchases of prefabricated homes, but states that by the time the first home is completed this Fall, it expects to have financing arrangements worked out 'with an outside source' that will permit purchase of homes in the Chicago area on an easy payment plan."

CHAPTER XXVIII

Store Planning and Design[1]

FROM the time of the company's entry into the retail field in 1925, major decisions of a basic nature had to be made in several spheres of operation: personnel to staff and manage the new enterprises; physical location of retail stores both as to cities and as to specific sites within each selected city; and—one of the greatest problems as time went on—the actual physical organization and layout of the new retail stores.

Sears's entry into the retail field had, as pointed out earlier, been cautious and deliberate. The company proceeded on a plan of calculated risk, but it sought to pare that risk to the irreducible minimum. While the company built virtually all its "A" stores, it rented buildings for the smaller stores and arranged to guarantee the landlord in each case a minimum rent, to be revised upward in proportion to sales volume, above the minimum of sales covered by the rent guaranty.

The architecture of the early stores built by the company was almost totally devoid of imagination. The structures were more or less standardized for the entire country, with no concessions to regional influences. And, even within the framework of this standardization, the stores were not conceived in dynamic functional concepts; the basic purpose, the very *raison d'être*, of the buildings—easier selling—received scant consideration. Yet in this, as in most things it had done, Sears, Roebuck moved in the milieu of the times. Pioneering, innovations, audacity, came to be increasingly difficult to sell to a company which had, by and large, thrived handsomely on cautious orthodoxy, albeit punctuated by some truly daring innovations here and there (as, for example, Richard Sears's great advertising and promotion schemes). And pioneering in such a field as architecture must have seemed to the company's executives to offer less enticing possibilities in immediate sales volume and profits than innovations in dramatic merchandising schemes or dynamic sales-promotion devices.

Innovations and audacity were, however, only the inevitable by-products of the mission assigned to Store Planning and Display when Sears created that department in 1932: to increase the potentialities of easy and comfortable customer buying, to win profits out of space, and to create the buildings and equipment capable of such performance. Each innovation that has eventuated has been only what Store Planning, trying to shake off the fetters of conventional approach, felt to be the best solution to any given problem confronting it; there has been no single instance of pioneering for its own sake.

The planning and designing of a commercial structure such as a department store begins when planners and architects join in considering purpose rather than in seizing the problem at hand as an opportunity for an idea in architecture. This poses for the planner the problem of how to place effective equipment for the central function of a store and how to design the shell of the building around the whole. Given this objective and the facts supplied by merchandise research and experience, the building takes its shape from a space analysis which determines the area to be allotted each line. The equipment needed to display the various lines of merchandise determines how and in what shape each of these individual areas will be used. Recognizing the importance of traffic flow, the location of entrances and stairs and other means of vertical transportation is selected with a discerning eye to the flow and direction of the available traffic from the outside, which can be estimated with fair accuracy and influenced to a certain degree by the exterior planning of the building.

A general store tends to observe an equality of emphasis toward each of the thousands of items carried. No preference other than that of space or location can allow departure from this unity of design. No factors other than the necessities for complementary display should be permitted to disrupt the standard of the store in its entirety. Remembering always the amount of space to be given to a table, showcase, or other item of equipment is one of the yardsticks that measures the way to the final objective and its success.

The foregoing simply points up the necessary dependence of the architect upon the merchant. The planning of a retail structure becomes much like retailing itself: a series of separate units that must be concentrated and directed toward the final co-ordination for layout and design. The material which follows shows the gradual influence of this theory upon the buildings erected by Sears, Roebuck between 1930 and 1941. The planning and designing technique developed in that period represents a service of a more comprehensive nature than the mere drafting of a plan. It is rather an engagement in continuous research to establish the completely functional aspects of department-store needs and to find the uncompromising answer to its expression in architecture.

Prior to the 1920's, store planning was in its prolonged infancy. The average merchant who wanted to build a store selected the location on the basis of traffic possibilities, probable volume, and population trends. He did more thinking about the "right" location than about any other factor. He should *first* have considered the merchandising problem and *then* have secured a location for the proper type of store. Instead, since he reversed this logical order of priority, it was often necessary to construct a multistory building, on the location selected, to house his merchandise.

The merchant hired in almost every case an architect who worked without the help of a store designer, although there were store-designing firms available which made the purpose and efficiency of the store the basis of their planning. But even if an architect employed the services of store designers, he usually hired them only to plan the interior of a building the exterior of which was already established. The merchandise problems of the owner obviously had little effect upon the character of the building. The information given the architect was, at best, obscure. He was told, in effect, "Here's a location on which I want a store this big." The merchant went on to tell him what he would like in the way of appearance but felt only vaguely responsible for explaining his real merchandising problems.

The architect obviously wished to satisfy the merchant, who had little or no experience with construction. As a result the architect designed from his knowledge of other buildings, which were copies of generally practiced architecture and were no different for the housing of a store than for any other purpose. Activities in various fields—a bank, a newspaper, a hotel, and a department store, for example—were often housed in virtually identical structures.

There were some structures conceived and built as functional units: the Carson, Pirie, Scott and Company Building, the Tribune Tower, and the Palmolive Building in Chicago, the Daily News Building and Rockefeller Center in New York. Relatively few architects, however, continued to think in those terms; the performances required of a store had clarified independently of the services of their profession, and they were not in good position to keep abreast of such developments. The few good examples were entirely out of proportion to the immense building activity, which revolved at that time largely around decorations without regard for the purpose; effect was mistaken for cause. The overemphasis on decoration caused architects to lose sight of the fact that a merchandising job had to be done in planning buildings for specific purposes. In building stores, the architect failed to create genuine store buildings because he had an inadequate knowledge of the functions a store must perform; and the information given him concerning these functions was limited by the merchant's failure to realize and explain his merchandising problem.

To please his merchant-employer, the architect spent much of his effort on a façade; this technique resulted in a fancy front and an ugly appearance from the back and side. Since the design and location of entrances, exits, and show widows were merely an outgrowth of the originally approved front, little consideration was given to the practical influences affecting them. If the merchant already owned a store, some identifying mark was usually worked into the new store to indicate common ownership. Otherwise the façade reflected the personal style of the designer and not the specific needs of the store.

Where such a store was located in an outlying district, outside forces such as the increase in automobiles and changes in living and shopping habits created the need for parking facilities. Too often, however, the merchant failed to provide for parking or handled it as a separate problem indepedently from the store.

Until 1932, when it created its own Store Planning and Display Department, Sears, Roebuck operated in a similar manner. The new department came, however, to combine the planning and architectural designing with sound merchandising principles suitable to Sears's own particular problems. With gradually increasing emphasis, Store Planning pointed to the necessity for realistic appraisal before actually building and for advice to the architect concerning the company's store operations. The chief "pointer" was, of course, Les Janes, the first (and, as of late 1948, the only) head of the Store Planning and Display Department.

The new department became a clearing-house to which the merchandising department brought its decisions on assortments and price lines. Operating personnel presented evidence regarding freight handling, merchandise storage, delivery, shipping, employee facilities, office space, etc., and the maintenance department presented its problems. The display department itself furnished information on the sizes and kinds of display windows, and a general review was made of all these requirements before any final plans were developed. By co-ordinating the work of these specialists, a fund of knowledge was obtained from which to plan a practical store. By using this knowledge in planning a building as housing for these functions, a new concept of department-store architecture slowly emerged, just as in other fields factories, schools, and airplane hangars have more and more been evolved in terms of the functions to be performed.

One of the first problems encountered was the layout of merchandise lines. Its solution was based on merchandise information furnished by the various departments, translated into terms of space and location. The search for an optimum allocation of space involved a study of various lines: the range of assortments, the best-selling items, and the relative importance of locations for different lines. Closely related were decisions on entrances and exits which affected the flow of traffic in relation to the merchandise and the location of stairs and escalators to facilitate traffic to other floors. The study further covered the best methods of presenting various types of merchandise and an analysis of space conservation pertaining to each department and its relation to the store as a whole, as well as many varied considerations in other details of the building, down to the selection of colors which would best set off the merchandise.

Analysis of these factors led to studies of the many branches of decorating involved in interior lighting and floor coverings, directional and departmental sign studies, the creation of interior displays, and the standardization of their materials, which also played an important part in the development of show-window equipment and its service. Considerable experimentation was done in the development of selling equipment. By the use of steel for many types of tables and showcases, for instance, great savings were effected because the services of skilled cabinetmakers and painters were eliminated in favor of the less expensive manufacturing processes. Steel tables were assembled of interchangeable parts made in large quantities. A basic table was developed to which combinations of parts could be added to assemble different types of tables for various purposes. The 25 per cent reduction in the cost of steel equipment as against the wood it replaced began in 1936 and brought the company an estimated annual saving of a quarter of a million dollars. The switch-over also brought an additional saving of indefinite amount, since steel tables last longer and are easier to maintain.

The thinking of the Store Planning and Display Department also exerted a catalytic effect in stimulating other departments to greater efforts. Where merchandise departments had formerly selected mail-order or odd-lot merchandise for the stores, they began to make improvements in the merchandise itself when they found how effectively it was being displayed. In some instances even the merchandise design was influenced by this department in order to improve its appearance in keeping with the prominence given it in display. Another and further development in merchandising occurred when the parent buying departments analyzed the strong and weak points of their items and improved their purchasing by taking advantage of this analysis. Better packaging was a direct result of the stock arrangement and display policy advocated early in the history of the display department.

While some departments did not consciously realize these influences in Sears's stores, they did recognize the forward thinking shown in the planning of the World's Fair buildings, county fairs, community centers, exhibitions, and showrooms, the execution of which became more and more the responsibility of the Store Planning and Display Department. Its scope was widened to include such outside problems as the adaptability of building materials, the investigation of lighting improvements, the design of new and better fixtures for store purposes, and many other details of various consequence to better and more efficient selling.

These increasing responsibilities of store planning and the display department's activity have been widely recognized as compelling influences in recent architecture. Stories and photographs of Sears's buildings have appeared often in such publications as the *Architectural Forum*, the *Architectural Record*, *Chain Store Age*, and others.

The combined result of all the planning and designing was the creation of store buildings in which the function of merchandise selling could be best performed. Experiments along this line have never stopped. Planning of roadside and movable stores, roof parking and other ideas, detailed research on fixtures and equipment—all these, even when "futuristic" in nature, have had their effect on the stores actually built.

The building of those stores, as far as Store Planning and Display is concerned, goes back of course to the time when Sears was not building all its own stores. A case in point is the State Street store in Chicago, opened on March 3, 1932. Since the building Sears was entering had already been used as a store, the main problem was the remodeling of the interior and of its selling equipment, at a cost to the company of about a million dollars. The selling area was originally to consist of two floors, primarily because no previous Sears's store had utilized more than two floors for that purpose. As the planning progressed, however, the number of lines to be carried was increased to a point which dictated enlargement of the originally contemplated selling space. Floors were added until plans included the first five floors and all the basement.

The fixtures, while built to order in some cases, were mostly of stock design, picked from catalogues. As the merchandise came into the store, the display department took up the problem of how best to display each line, working from existing sales figures to determine which items and groups should be accorded the best selling areas in relation to traffic. This was the beginning of stock arrangement, working hand in hand with sales analysis. Some merchandise was grouped into specialty sections where the customer could find related items in close proximity; model rooms of furniture and model bathroom setups were installed.

The large number of display windows in the State Street store created a problem. To meet it, interchangeable standard properties were developed, so that a small quantity of materials could be adjusted and rearranged to obtain different effects. Sears's stores had long been content to show an item of merchandise in quantity and to give it a price and a name; now an attempt was made to create a desire for the merchandise in the customer's mind by showing the merchandise in use. Accompanying this was a copy message with illustrated material designed to arouse an interest in the results to be obtained from the use of the product rather than its mere glorification. In the corner window theatrical lighting was attempted for the first time in window display (show windows had formerly been confined to strip lighting). Banks of adjustable lights and tinted lenses were used to create various color effects and to spotlight specific merchandise.

Although the State Street store in Chicago was Sears's three hundred and eighty-first, it was the initial location in a downtown metropolitan section. Under the rental arrangement, the estate which owned the building received 1½ per cent of the store's net sales for five years, with a minimum guaranty of $75,000 per year above taxes after three years. The lease ran for twenty years and was subject to revision after five years.

Following the experience gained in the State Street store, there came the three buildings in the New York group (Brooklyn, Hackensack, and Union City), which also opened in 1932, in which the first attempts were made to escape from traditional store design. This time the size of the stores was determined from the merchandise lines and assortments to be carried. A new architect was employed in an effort to improve the design, but this brought only a slight simplification in the exterior treatment; there were superficial changes but, in the eyes of the display department, no real improvements. The display department was convinced that outside architects were unable to think creatively in terms of Sears's store functions and that any changes which would translate the experiences and ideas of the company into architectural terms would have to come from within the company; the changes would have to be worked out in the architect's office after being co-ordinated with all divisions responsible for the operation of the stores.

In the three stores in the New York group, the tower remained as an outstanding feature in the general design of all three and as a carry-over from the main Chicago plant (where it had first appeared, in 1905) and other company buildings. It was continued mainly, of course, as an identifying mark of Sears; it had been so widely and enthusiastically hailed on its initial appearance that it had become a very nearly sacrosanct "trade-mark" of the company. As a water-tank inclosure, it had lost its meaning, since, compared with store buildings erected before 1930, the use of city water obviated such necessity. Suggestions to eliminate the traditional fancy façade were, however, partly successful. Out of consideration for residents of adjoining properties, and because the first view of a customer approaching the building from a parking lot was likely to be from the back or side, an effort was made in each case to make the building attractive from all angles.

Planning for the appearance of these three stores and their maintenance in years to come resulted in consultations with the construction department for the selection of limestone facing, which improves with age. Agreement was reached on other exterior materials such as granite for the bases of the buildings on the street sides because of its natural and lasting beauty, and bronze frames for windows and doors. The cost of these materials exceeded that of those used for previous stores, such as Milwaukee, Miami, Rochester, and Evansville, but the expense was justified by the permanency and practicability involved.

To insure easier and less expensive maintenance, the interiors used terrazo floors, suspended ceilings (which covered ducts and pipes formerly detracting from the merchandise and disturbing the distribution of light), and paint textures of more durable types and colors for walls, dado, and staircases. Escalators were utilized to speed vertical traffic. These had been used in stores by others, but this was the first time Sears had obtained the best possible results from up-and-down traffic. The escalators were so sited that the customer always remained in the sales area and always had an unobstructed view of the merchandise, which is not possible in elevators. The use of mechanical ventilation was improved by operating through ducts concealed in suspended ceilings instead of direct radiation. This equipment was so designed that artificial cooling could be added later if desired.

The planning of the New York stores represented the beginning of the correlation of other parent-department activities by Store Planning and Display. When, for example, a study of natural traffic flow was made, and the importance of the parking-lot entrances was discovered, it was found that the entrance which would normally be the back door would in this instance be the main traffic entrance. Consequently, the first-floor departments were laid out with this in mind. From such studies in the arrangement of merchandise came the beginnings of a "scientific" approach to store layout. Quite logically, the objective became more and more to design a building to display merchandise to the customer effectively.

Further development in stock arrangement, begun at State Street in Chicago, was evident in these three stores; in the latter instance(s) it was a direct outgrowth of the display department's association with the actual planning of the buildings. The twelve specialty shops within each store were set off from one another by characteristic decorations, fixtures, and wall coloring, with all twelve, however, blended into a harmonious whole. An attempt was also made toward standardizing colors for various departments.

The next major step in store planning and construction occurred in 1934, when Sears initiated construction of a store on the Becker-Ryan site in Chicago, acquired for that purpose in 1929. Conditions differed sharply from those which had obtained in connection with the New York group. Adjoining parking space could not be procured for the Englewood store in Chicago, as it came to be called, and the size of the site located in a concentrated shopping district on a heavy traffic corner necessitated a multi-storied building.

Reanalyzing its previous experience, the display department came to the conclusion—a novel one for its time—that windows (not, in this sense, to be confused with display windows) had no place in a department store, which had to be a showplace for merchandise. Windows had been taken for granted by architects and were considered an integral part of almost any building. The display department held that windows were virtually useless as a source of light, since daylight affected a negligible percentage of the total floor space; the only possible value of such daylight was for the examination of textiles and style merchandise. As a matter of fact, windows were actually a hindrance even in lighting, since they served to mix daylight with artificial light. Further, they interfered with heating, air conditioning, and ventilating systems by setting up cross-currents. And, perhaps most important of all from a display viewpoint, windows broke up wall space to the point of mutilation. A windowless store would, for the first time, make possible air conditioning without the necessity of sealing the windows.

The concept of the windowless store was, however, so novel that the Chicago building code had no provisions for it; in fact, the code specified that some windows must be provided for fire protection. This ruling was met by the inclusion of some glass panels, but these were placed next to the stairs so as not to interfere with the wall sections which were to be placed against the outside wall.

Interior planning for the Englewood store included escalators in the sales area, but the planning department was overruled on its insistence upon more or larger facilities, with the result that a separate set of escalators had to be installed within a few years. Otherwise, the interior display was integrated with the building to a far greater extent than before, and particular attention was given to interior decoration. An attempt was made to hold the entire expanse of floors, walls, merchandise, and display together like one great stage setting. The color scheme was designed to attach individuality to each department while still achieving an over-all harmony.

The Englewood store, opened in 1934, was the first for which every fixture was specially designed. Departmental identification was developed in the form of photomurals located over each department above the fixture height. An institutional theme in the murals showed the merchandise in actual use or being tested in the laboratories. Also designed for this store were wood tables with extruded aluminum rims; standard fixtures were not yet available to meet the department's newly developed requirements. Experimental work had been carried on with tables which would create a second level on which merchandise could be displayed, and a chinaware table made of wood and masonite tile was developed for this store. This idea later developed into the steel tables; but the changes were made in each instance to achieve selling improvements and not simply to beautify the table.

The Englewood store won greater interest from store owners over the country than had those in the New York group. The innovations of Englewood crept into architects' plans for many stores of Sears's competitors. The *Architectural Forum* in a lengthy, illustrated article stated in part:

> The window dies hard. For fifteen hundred years it has been a fundamental unit of architectural design.... The nearest approach to a windowless structure for other than storage or manufacturing is Sears, Roebuck's new retail store in Chicago....
>
> The windowless store is not an advertising stunt. On the contrary it represents a definite advance in the technical planning of the retail department store. The original impetus came from Mr. L. S. Janes, Sears' director of display....
>
> Interesting by-product of the construction of a completely sealed building was discovered in a test of the air conditioning apparatus. This showed that the building retained its heat at night, even in the coldest weather, for a much longer than normal time. The natural corollary is that it will retain cool night temperatures much longer in hot weather. In either case savings are indicated in operating costs even greater than those expected.[2]

Architect and Engineer, under the caption "No Windows," hailed the Englewood store as a $1,500,000 experiment with every likelihood of success. This article went on to point out how fifty-eight-foot-high glass columns provided sufficient daylight for inspection of style goods and textiles, without creating problems to which windows could have given rise.[3]

The next important turning point in Sears's construction work came with its Glendale, California, store, even though the structure suffered to some extent from compromises. This time Store Planning and Display was called in to assist in the location of the building on the property, to suggest the general type of building and its number of stories, and to submit a sketch of its floor plan. The first chance to build a store from the inside out had arrived. Where earlier buildings had had definitely established physical properties to be filled with merchandise departments and their fixtures at a later stage in the process, the Glendale store had its inception in a first-floor merchandising plan of a size and variety established for expected acceptance in that neighborhood. The shell of the building was designed around this idea of the sales-assembly chart.

This concept was, however, so novel that it led to a compromise design which was to characterize the next series of stores to be built. The Glendale building, opened in 1935, was the first of a newly recommended monolithic concrete construction, of radically simplified design, and only two stories high. The traditional tower hung on, but this marked its final appearance. Because of its placement at the most prominent corner, the tower could not be used for the water tank at all; an additional penthouse had to be built over the back part of the structure to house the air conditioning and other machinery. The $80,000 additional cost thus involved made this tower possibly the most expensive background for a sign ever constructed.

Wall fixture heights established at Englewood were maintained. Systematically placed display cases were built into the wood paneling created between the curtain wall and the fixture itself. The full effect of savings and maintenance advantages of the steel table became apparent in the Glendale store. Steel showcases with bronze frames were designed. Standardization of wall equipment made of steel for the hard lines also effected a saving in time and money.

All these were important advances and stamped Glendale as Sears's best effort to that time. In the opinion of the display department, however, the most significant fact was that it had reached the point where it could expect to be consulted from the very beginning in discussions of store locations and sizes on to the completion and opening of the stores. Display was acquiring more and more of the answers to operating, display, stock arrangements, and general service to the customer; the authority delegated to this department was to increase steadily.

After Glendale came Highland Park, Michigan, in 1938, as the next important step forward. Highland Park received the best layout yet designed.

STORE PLANNING AND DESIGN 541

Sales, stock, and office space, sizes of individual divisions, relative locations of departments in respect to traffic flow, design of fixtures, and handling of receiving and shipping were worked out completely and efficiently. The parking-lot entrance was treated as the main entrance; show windows were installed on that side, and the departmental layout was oriented to that entrance. An outdoor sales area, in harmony with the main building, was provided for shrubbery, lawn furniture, etc., thus solving the problem of how to handle seasonal selling and the unsightly, temporary structures usually required for it.

The display of many soft-line items such as hosiery, gloves, bags, and millinery was improved in order to impart a department-store appearance. All in all, Highland Park came close to an ideal arrangement for a normal store with a standard basement and two-story operation. And as each improvement took shape, photographs and complete information were forwarded to the display department's field service to facilitate acceptance by stores already operating.

The Baltimore, Maryland, store, completed in 1938, taxed to the fullest Store Planning's flexibility in basic thinking and its willingness to apply past experience to new problems without becoming enslaved by that past. The primary difficulties arose from the unusual nature of the site, with its various elevations. Two conclusions were reached early: (1) the main traffic would come from the parking lot and (2) the parking lot would be one story higher than the street level. Further planning proceeded from these premises. The back of the store facing the lot was given the prominence usually accorded the street façade; show windows, entrance treatment, and signs received emphasis coequal with those on the street side. The interior of the building reflected the second conclusion; the "basement" merchandise was brought in line with the street, and the first floor in line with the parking lot (which was on the second-story level).

Even though hard lines were on the street level, this floor could not be treated as a basement, for obvious reasons. Accordingly the display department advocated distinct wall treatments to enhance the appearance of each floor. On the street floor, holding what was normally basement merchandise, these decorations were rather directly commercial in character; the second, or parking-lot, floor represented a strong public relations motif in the form of colorful murals. There had been some resentment in the community over the use of this particular site for a store, since events of great historical interest had taken place there during the Revolutionary War. The company therefore decided that the murals should depict the early history of Baltimore; intensive research was devoted to local history, with the result that a touch of chauvinism helped turn hostility into friendliness. The exterior likewise reflected a sensitivity to local feelings; a simple but monumental architectural design was chosen, with impressive corner treatment revolving around what was then considered the largest show window in the United States. Stage lighting was used for the window, with automatic controls, grids, catwalks, provision for properties and sets, and other paraphernalia reminiscent of a small theater.

Equal attention was given the interior to improve the appearance of escalators, lighting fixtures, electric signs, and store fixtures in general. The objective was to design an interior architecture so well that it seemed almost to disappear by the time the merchandise itself took over; merchandise was treated as the most valuable and impressive quantity to compete successfully with any possible architectural decoration such as the murals. This was perhaps the Baltimore store's greatest contribution to those yet to come.

The Irving Park store in Chicago was one that Store Planning and Display would prefer to forget, at least in regard to its exterior. Irving Park, completed in 1938, represented little progress except in a few interior innovations; the exterior was an unhappy compromise with the outside architects. Escalators placed in the center aisle instead of along the walls did, however, prove the best solution for easy access to each floor. Also, more emphasis was given to the general appearance of fixtures for the hard lines, which, because of space limitations on each floor of the four-story building (the basement went to a food concessionaire), had to be mixed with the first-floor equipment. The elaborate natural wood trim applied to the steel fixtures and carefully selected background materials helped to mitigate the abrupt change from soft lines to hard.

The display department was then ready for the Pico Boulevard Store in Los Angeles the following year, the first store placed entirely under this department's jurisdiction. The innovations which were to bring the company such high praise in this venture arose gradually and logically, as the display department planned literally from the ground up. That ground was similar in many ways to the terrain encountered in Baltimore; Pico went a step further in using the higher elevation to provide roof parking for the first time. And a balcony adaptable for an outdoor restaurant or sales area was featured on the long and prominent side of the building facing the parking lot. The monolithic type of construction was maintained, but this time a pattern was introduced into the concrete to obtain a more attractive texture and to help eliminate the showing of fine surface cracks unavoidable in this type of building.

On the street side, a second level of show windows was introduced to face the heavy motor traffic of Pico Boulevard. These windows were treated with special feature merchandise and were handled primarily in billboard fashion. The building itself consisted of two stories and basement; the large floor area on each floor permitted better location of stockrooms, which obviated the necessity of sales personnel leaving a floor to get merchandise. The store embraced 117,000 square feet. The large floor area permitted the location of all style and soft lines for men and women on the first floor,

AN EARLY RETAIL STORE, HOUSTON, TEXAS, 1929

A MODERN RETAIL STORE, HOUSTON, TEXAS, 1947

PICO BOULEVARD STORE, LOS ANGELES, CALIFORNIA, OPENED NOVEMBER 2, 1939

a radical departure from previous layouts where limitations of space had driven ready-to-wear to the second floor. That second floor was given over solely to home furnishings. Throughout, special emphasis was placed on merchandise presentation by means of simply designed equipment and backgrounds; all items of decoration were blended carefully with the merchandise.

Pico Boulevard marked the reaching of a firm understanding between Store Planning and the construction department: henceforth, the ideas and first studies for each new building were to be the bailiwick of Store Planning and Display. *Architectural Forum*, in an article which was both eulogy and analysis, replete with photographs, saluted the Pico Building. After referring to the use of roof parking as well as an additional parking lot on the more conventional plane, the magazine went on to say:

Emphasis has been laid on this elaborate provision for parking because it typifies the designers' approach throughout, with intense concentration on merchandising rather than "architecture." To judge from the distinguished example of commercial architecture which has resulted, the approach would seem a sound one....

The functional approach has been rigorously adhered to within the store, the column spacing and other features of construction being determined by merchandise requirements. In a similar fashion the architectural treatment has been subordinated. Display and storage cases have been reduced to a few standard types, again for the purpose of concentrating attention upon the merchandise. In this connection the architect has made the following comment: "The focusing of all efforts on merchandise and none on the building would seem to sacrifice many a possibility, but such disappearance of 'architecture,' or rather its shifting to plain performance is a sign of maturity in retailing." And one might add—in architecture.[4]

The tribute by retail business to Sears's work in store planning and building was expressed by J. W. Strauss of the May Company at the opening of the Pico Boulevard store in Los Angeles in 1939: "In my long experience in the retail field I have yet to witness a retail unit which equals Sears Pico store in practical efficiency, merchandise engineering, operation, layout and presentation of merchandise."

After Pico, Store Planning went into Houston. It also went deep into experimental design and came up with a suggestion for a huge, single-story store covering the entire property, with access to roof parking through unusual ramps. The plan was vetoed as too extreme a departure; the compromise was a three-story and-basement store, with many features adapted from Pico.

One new feature in Houston, completed in 1939 (another "A" store was to be built there in 1947), was an annex adjacent to the second-floor sales area; it was intended to be used both for fashion shows and seasonal selling as well as for gatherings of community organizations. Not only were murals portraying local history employed, as in Baltimore; special carpeting was designed and woven, with the state flower of Texas, the bluebonnet, as part of the pattern. Finally, the service station and the outdoor sales area were sited in the location most desirable in relation to the flow of traffic—the first time this had been fully achieved.

Architectural Record devoted eleven pages in text and photographs to a detailed roundup story on Sears's new stores in Baltimore, Detroit (Highland Park), Chicago (Englewood), Los Angeles (Glendale), and Houston. Speaking of the impact of the automobile upon the nation's shopping habits, the *Record* went on to say:

> For a time, increase in motor travel merely meant that it was easier for more people to get to the city for shopping. Soon, however, downtown sections frequently became hopelessly congested, and the ease of moving about was canceled out by the impossibility of finding a place to stop moving within a reasonable distance from the retail stores.... Certain stores have found it expedient to remove their locations from the congested downtown area altogether. The outlying site is large enough to include within it ample parking areas as well as the store itself....
>
> Noteworthy exponents of this type of development are the large branch stores of Sears, Roebuck and Company, which for several years has been a leader in providing more efficient retail-store units for a motoring public.[5]

The article went on to praise Sears's stores for "extraordinary" facilities for the comfort and convenience of on-the-move shoppers—services ranging from generous parking space to automobile service stations and community buildings:

> In the provision of services and facilities over and above those of the store proper, the Sears-Roebuck stores are unusually noteworthy. Each scheme is, of course, developed around the most efficient store unit possible. Almost as important is the convenient parking area of sufficient size.... Among the extraordinary services for the customers are departments set up to aid in such things as determining the proper-size pump needed for a water supply, recommend and lay out an efficient heating plant, and even to prepare for the construction of a complete house....
>
> Departmental layout and display technique in such large retail stores as Sears-Roebuck's are the direct result of mass-merchandising needs. Two basic factors in particular determine the basic arrangement—the fact that there will be large crowds of shoppers and the desire for the greatest convenience possible in getting customers and merchandise from the store to exits and waiting automobiles.... Display windows follow recent trends. Once it was thought that the larger these were made, the better. Modern selling technique, however, requires the arrangement of special windows for special purposes, and in these stores windows run the gamut of size from small ones for the display of small objects, such as jewelry, up to the main display window in the Baltimore store, which is substantially a stage in area height, and the lighting facilities provided.[6]

With the Honolulu store in Hawaii, the display department faced its first approach to an overseas locale. The department suggested a single-floor store of 42,000 square feet, larger than a regular "B-1" type store but smaller than the normal "A" type. As plans developed, the store took on more and more the nature of an "A" store in respect to merchandise lines and fixtures, even though the basic considerations and the budget were nearer those of a "B" type. The building was located in the rear of its property, with the main front facing the parking lot. The over-all layout permitted preservation of many old and rare palm trees, which added considerably to the final appearance. Expansion was also provided for; the properties for future escalator and stairwell framing were incorporated in the structural design. Honolulu, opened in 1939, was one of the happiest experiences of Store Planning and Display.

Birmingham, Alabama, marked the company's first single-floor "A" store. The Houston veto had not been entirely forgotten, but Store Planning was able to overcome the lingering reluctance to abandon three stories for one. The site was a large one in a downtown location, which led to the decision to have entrances on three streets. The one-story operation, as Honolulu had showed, effected a saving of 10 per cent of the total area, by eliminating vertical transportation and other utilities.

The length of the aisle forced the use of special type signs, but the length of the store also afforded a highly desirable flexibility. Since hard lines, style lines, and house furnishings abutted one on the other, each group could be expanded as seasonal selling required simply by taking space from one of the other groups. Stock was adjacent to selling space, which simplified the movement of merchandise within the building. The service station was attached to the building.

The exterior of the store was finished in brick, laid in simple design in two colors. Show windows were strategically spotted at the entrances and corners in relation to the amount of traffic expected. In the window planned for furniture display, the background was eliminated so that the customer received an unobstructed view of the furniture sales area, which became a huge showroom.

Honolulu and Birmingham (the latter opened in 1941) were signal accomplishments. *Architectural Forum* paid its respects in a feature article including photographs which pointed up sharply the distinguishing features of those stores.[7] Sears had scored again with the architectural world, even though its sole goal had been merchandising improvement.

The stores referred to herein were all "A" stores (except Honolulu, a hybrid of "B" and "A" features), of which type the company had 84 by 1948 (out of a total of 625 retail stores). Around the mid-1930's the company began constructing some of its "B" class stores. The reasons were much the same as those which had earlier dictated construction of "A" stores: rented buildings were too often incapable of serving as the selling machines the company sought, and the sliding-scale rental contracts based upon a percentage of sales were converted, by the highly successful sales records of the stores, into expensive dollar rents for buildings usually sited in out-of-the way locations. There was still another factor: the merchandise pattern of the "B"-class stores clarified later than that of the "A" stores, and this clarification had an obvious effect on the character of buildings required to house, display, and move the merchandise.

So much for the highlights of what was accomplished in the first sixteen years of the Store Planning and Display Department in the Sears organization. What of tomorrow? Here, in Janes's words, is how the department sees the future:

> Besides the continuation of its former profitable sales planning, a store must achieve the significance of being a community enterprise of definite characteristics as a clearing house for many functions and activities which can be anticipated.
>
> What these are can be explained by mentioning briefly the merchandising problems of the future. What type of industrial surprises through new inventions and production systems will this future bring we cannot know as yet, but we can safely assume that the entire process of supply and distribution will be on a very promising upward trend: The change from a planned scarcity and competitive production to one of abundance and increased consuming power is apt to revolutionize the entire concept of selling. Not through display or advertising alone will features of merchandise be advanced, but also through educational demonstrations and continuous propaganda. Consequently, a revision in economy and quality of merchandising will demand a new idea in presentation which we may call the service store.
>
> Even without the present emergency [World War II] which forces more and more soft line sales planning, we must realize that a similar reorganization in the general field of merchandising would have come anyway.

Janes's report was written in 1942, and he was admittedly looking far ahead. A pronouncement issued June 30, 1942, by Board Chairman Wood and President Barrows, titled "A Statement of Policy Governing the Selection of New Store Locations," sketched the immediate, postwar future in far more prosaic and conventional terms. The gist of the statement lay in these words:

> In the last analysis, the parking lot has been the largest single factor responsible for the success of our "A" stores.
>
> Our experience in the last ten years has proved that parking space and service facilities are more important to us than the so-called 100% location. In almost all cases, it is obvious that the land costs of locations in the so-called 100% districts will prohibit the selection of sites with sufficient parking space. We must reiterate the paramount importance of ample parking facilities for future stores because post-war cars probably will be cheaper to buy and to operate, and the parking problem—even in small towns—is due to increase enormously.

The chronological juxtaposition of the Janes and the Wood-Barrows statements was significant. Janes was looking into the misty reaches of the cloudy future, while Wood and Barrows were blueprinting the tremendous postwar expansion. When the distant future whose outlines Janes seeks to envisage comes nearer, the company's top executives will doubtless approach it in terms of specific problems. But in the years immediately following 1945 and V-J Day, the company's eyes were firmly fixed on the main chance.

CHAPTER XXIX

Personnel Management Matures

SEARS made its debut in chain-store retailing in 1925, opening eight stores in that first year. By the end of 1929 the company was well advanced in its first wave of the retail expansion with 324 stores open. In 1925, employees numbered 23,193, of whom 987 were classified as retail; by the end of 1929 the number of employees had increased to 41,751, of whom approximately 13,000 were classified as retail employees. The overwhelming increase in personnel came indeed in the retail expansion.

The rapid rate of expansion plus the marked differences in techniques associated with face-to-face consumer selling nowhere effected more significant changes than in the area of personnel policy and organization. Measured by any standards, Sears was a large-scale operation even prior to its invasion of the retail-store field. By 1925 more than 17,000 persons were employed in five mail-order plants. Almost 5,000 more employees worked in factories owned by the company. While the increasing size of the firm exerted certain pressures which led to some specialization in employment operation, such specialization was manifest only at the operating unit level. In the mail-order plants the personnel activity consisted essentially of routine employment clearance and maintenance of records; medical care; recreation program (the parking lots for customers and employees at the main plant in Chicago were formerly tennis courts for employees); and, finally, an undetermined volume of special individual case work. Even at the plant level these various activities were not brought together under one administrative head.

At the level of top management (in Chicago) there was no recognition of a specialized personnel function. At least a partial explanation for this lack is to be found in the following conditions.

While the number of employees was large, they were concentrated in relatively few operating units. Whatever co-ordination of personnel policy was believed to be desirable was facilitated by the small number of contacts necessary among the major executives. In addition, the largest number of employees was employed on routine operations in the mail-order plants. System was developed to a high point, and evidently it was not difficult to bring new employees to an acceptable level of efficiency. Thus the employment function, confined generally to recruiting and crude methods of selection, became specialized at the plant level. The problem of providing replacements and candidates for supervisory positions was met generally by casting about for "likely looking" men who had served long apprenticeships in the company.

The absence of a specialized personnel function as part of the technical apparatus of top management does not imply that the company executives were unaware of, or unsympathetic to, employee problems. The existence of a *fonctionnaire* in the mail-order plants whose special concern was akin to what would now be termed social case work would belie such an interpretation.

A central personnel department was a departure from the policy of Julius Rosenwald, who had looked upon the company largely as a federation of special merchandising departments, a point of view which carried with it the implication of considerable departmental autonomy in matters of compensation, employment, and promotion. Apparently Rosenwald was not unaware of the increasing recognition in American industry of the specialized personnel organization; but he distrusted it. He preferred a company built rather strictly as a line organization whose departments were free of staff interference. It is said he feared that a personnel department might become an autocratic agency exerting control over line departments as a result of the intimate relationship of the personnel department with employees.

Julius Rosenwald had joined Richard Sears in 1895, and after thirty-five years—most of them prosperous ones—the firm had ten mail-order plants. But within five years of the first tentative excursion into retail outlets, the company had more than three hundred new operating units. Thus the problem of co-ordination was vastly complicated, and the provision of competent managers for far-flung units precipitated personnel problems on a scale unknown in the mail-order business.

In 1928 Sears first attempted to develop a retail-store-manager training program and began work on a combination classroom and store-training project which never eventuated in anything very effective—if for no reason other than the crucial weakness that the "curriculum" depended so heavily on store managers who at that time were frequently ill prepared for the task. At about the same time Alvin Dodd, who had been brought to Sears to instil some "retail know-how" into the organization, was finding that building an effective retail organization was seriously handicapped by badly selected and improperly prepared personnel. According to Dodd's assistant at the time, Ira R. Andrews, Alvin Dodd had a real sense for the personnel problems faced by the retail organization and encouraged Andrews in his attempts to codify the principles of Sears's personnel policy for the retail business. Andrews had himself undertaken on his own initiative to compile a manual on company personnel policy, a tool he felt was urgently needed in view of the frequent inconsistencies in "policy" that were everywhere evident as a consequence of the very rapid retail expansion administered often by men of inadequate retail experience.

Andrews found little sympathy for his project manifested by any of his superiors except Alvin Dodd, who succeeded in bringing the draft of the proposed manual to the notice of Lessing Rosenwald, then senior vice-president. Rosenwald's reaction was enthusiastic, and he urged that the project be brought to the attention of T. J. Carney, who had succeeded to the vice-presidency in charge of operations.

Carney was very sensitive to the personnel needs of the business. Many years' experience and a rise through every phase of operating procedure had given him an intimate knowledge of the company's employees and a keen appreciation of their viewpoint. Having come to Sears in 1902, he had lived through the innovations of Elmer Scott and had been impressed by Scott's approach. Under the tutelage of Lessing Rosenwald during his years in the Philadelphia plant, Carney's interest in employees was nurtured and expanded. Out of this interest and experience Carney worked to gain Wood's approval for establishing a personnel function in the business, an object which was aided and abetted by Ira Andrews.

The obvious desirability of a personnel department was strengthened by the opinion of the consultants engaged by the firm in 1929 to study the retail organization. These harbingers, the unsatisfactory (though profitable) conditions of retail operations growing out of the confused organizational patterns and numerous conferences of senior executives, paved the way for approval of a retail personnel organization in 1931. On October 1, 1931, the following notice was sent out from the operating executive's office:

October 1, 1931.

PARENT SUPERVISORS:

It is desired to advise all executives in or connected with our Retail Stores that a Retail Personnel Organization has been created at the request of General Wood.

As a member of this office, Mr. I. R. Andrews will handle all policy and planning matters connected with retail personnel, such as employment standardization, training, progressive appraisal, compensation, providing for promotion from within, etc. This office will also act as a clearing house for desirable applicants, employe appeals, requests for men not locally available, etc. Methods and materials carefully adapted to our own personnel problems will be supplied to the field as rapidly as is practical.

Contact with the stores will be maintained through the Territorial Officers, each of whom will have a specially assigned assistant for such work.

T. J. CARNEY

The early organization as set up in late 1931 was to be concerned only with retail, and the department was designed to operate through the structure shown in Chart X.

One of the first concrete achievements of the new department (designated as Department 705) was to issue a personnel manual codifying principles and procedures "for confidential use of all retail store managers."

So quickly did the first edition become obsolete that on September 1, 1932, old manuals were recalled and replaced by a revised edition.

So many new problems appeared in the course of Sears's aggressive efforts to establish itself in the retail-store business that it is hard to single out any one as *the* crucial problem. But certainly the problem of staffing the stores was apparent to the executives. The selection and training of store personnel, especially store managers, came increasingly to be identified as the crucial problem of retail administration. It was soon made plain that the several territorial functionaries were saddled with too many other duties to perform effectively the role of selecting, training, and guiding store managers. The whole retail program had assumed great scope and complexity. Further, in an effort to effect economies throughout the company

CHART X

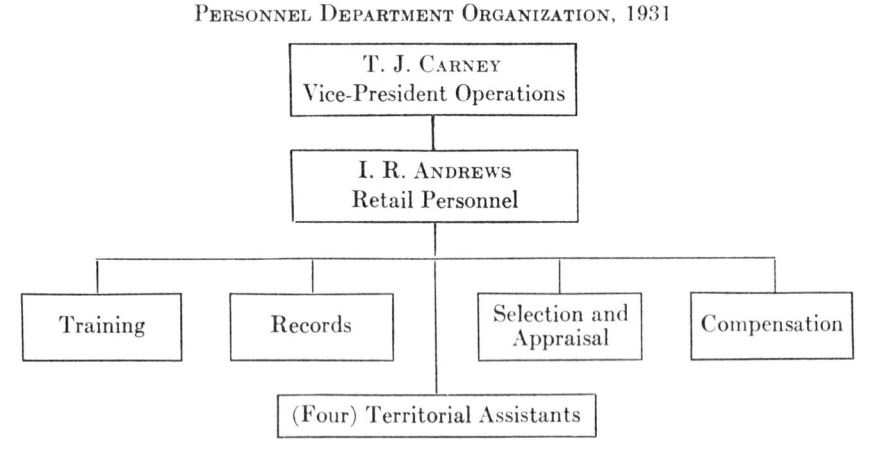

PERSONNEL DEPARTMENT ORGANIZATION, 1931

```
                    T. J. CARNEY
                Vice-President Operations
                          |
                    I. R. ANDREWS
                    Retail Personnel
                          |
   ┌──────────┬───────────┼────────────────┬──────────────┐
 Training   Records              Selection and      Compensation
                                  Appraisal
                          |
              (Four) Territorial Assistants
```

and to make the retail stores more quickly responsive to instructions from Chicago, the territorial offices were abolished in May, 1932. At the same time, General Wood appointed J. M. Barker as vice-president in charge of retail administration, which was made to include the personnel activity.

When Barker took over in 1932, personnel was removed from the aegis of the operating vice-president, T. J. Carney, under whom the department had come into being less than a year earlier. At that time Ira Andrews was succeeded by F. E. Burrows, whom Barker brought to headquarters from the field, where he had been one of the territorial assistants in the first field organization. Barker appreciated the heavy task he faced in reorganizing and refining the ill-defined, often confusing and unworkable retail design that had emerged by 1932 as the result of a series of particular decisions. In the face of the task before him it is not surprising that Barker preferred men reporting to him with whose general thinking and previous experience he was familiar.

C. B. Caldwell was brought to Chicago as retail assistant to Burrows in 1933 after establishing a successful record as a Sears store manager in Jackson, Michigan, and Lafayette, Indiana—the climax of some twelve years' experience at J. C. Penney and a shorter stint for National Bellas Hess. Less than ten years after Caldwell came to Chicago as an assistant to an assistant, he became personnel director of the company.

In October, 1933, a personnel conference was held in Chicago. Four days were devoted to meetings attended by operating superintendents and personnel assistants from stores throughout the country. President Wood's remarks at the opening meeting were indicative of the new interest in personnel development:

We have found out, in the last five years, that personnel is our big problem. Mr. Nelson buys goods at the right price at the right value; Mr. Pollock can put in a good auditing system; Mr. Carney can have a good operating system—but it all falls down if: (1) The managers are not right; (2) The men and women in the stores are not right. . . . No large business like our own, which is widely scattered, can succeed unless the manager of the store is right, and unless the men and women in that store feel that they are working for a company that is trying to treat them fairly and justly.

We have made a great many mistakes. . . . But we always have had the end in view of trying to have a contented, well treated force.[1]

As concrete evidence that the company intended to treat employees fairly, Wood personally decreed that employees having five years' service might not be discharged without the approval of the central personnel department in Chicago, which was charged with the responsibility for making a complete investigation prior to approving the discharge of such long-service personnel.

The entire 1933 conference was concerned only with retail problems, but there was clear evidence that the small personnel force contemplated in the initial organization but two years earlier had been considerably expanded. Indeed by 1933 there were personnel assistants in "A" stores whose primary concern was the implementation of personnel policy at the store level. As shown in Chart XI, the personnel assistant reported to the store's operating superintendent and was responsible for the various activities comprehended under the heads of "employment," "training," and "employee relations."

Before the end of 1935 a place was made for a mail-order personnel program when Ira Andrews returned to the Sears personnel organization and assumed responsibility for personnel activities in mail order, to which responsibility for parent-personnel was soon added. Thus by 1936 the personnel department, then less than five years old, was administered by a manager of parent and mail-order personnel and a manager of retail personnel, both of whom reported to the personnel manager, who was in turn responsible to F. B. McConnell, assistant to the president in charge of retail ad-

CHART XI
"A" Store Personnel Functional Chart

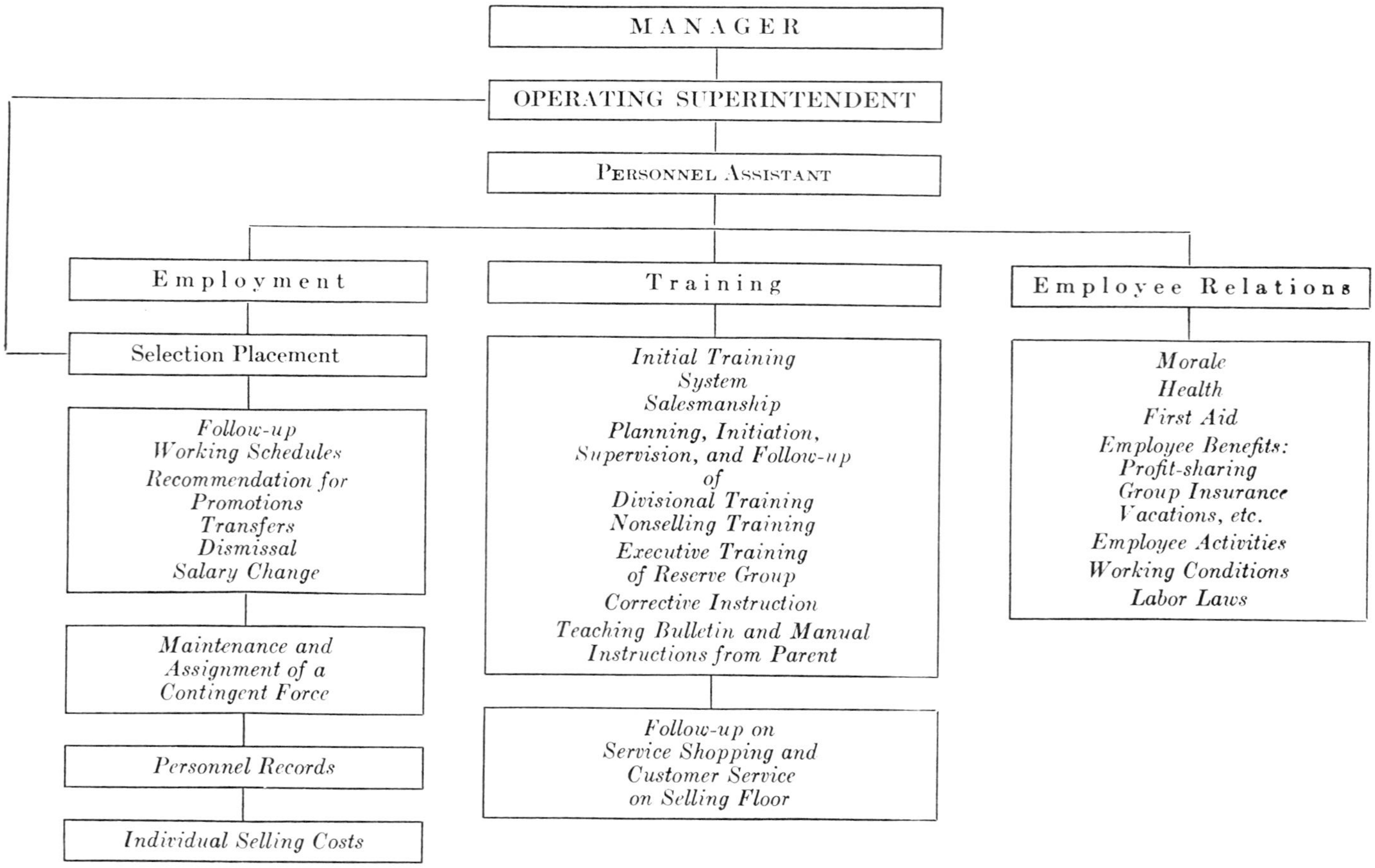

MANAGER

OPERATING SUPERINTENDENT

PERSONNEL ASSISTANT

Employment

- Selection Placement
  - Follow-up
  - Working Schedules
  - Recommendation for Promotions
  - Transfers
  - Dismissal
  - Salary Change
- Maintenance and Assignment of a Contingent Force
- Personnel Records
- Individual Selling Costs

Training

- Initial Training System
- Salesmanship
- Planning, Initiation, Supervision, and Follow-up of Divisional Training
- Nonselling Training
- Executive Training of Reserve Group
- Corrective Instruction
- Teaching Bulletin and Manual Instructions from Parent

Follow-up on Service Shopping and Customer Service on Selling Floor

Employee Relations

- Morale
- Health
- First Aid
- Employee Benefits: Profit-sharing Group Insurance Vacations, etc.
- Employee Activities
- Working Conditions
- Labor Laws

ministration and director of personnel. (The department's numerical designation was changed to Department 707.)

McConnell, later to be appointed president of Sears, Roebuck, had succeeded Barker when in 1935 the latter had turned his attention from retail administration to the financial affairs of the company. It is noteworthy that with McConnell's appointment the personnel function was for the first time given high executive status. When Barker had been made vice-president in charge of retail administration, he also had the responsibility for general supervision of personnel activities; when McConnell assumed Barker's responsibilities in 1935, he was specifically designated as senior executive for personnel as well as retail administration.

That arrangement was to be short lived, however, for by the early part of 1937 a reorganization resulted in eliminating the position of company personnel manager so that the personnel managers of mail order (and parent) and retail reported directly to McConnell, as did the manager of factory personnel after that position was created in 1938. The strong retail forces within the company contributed to the retail personnel officer (C. B. Caldwell) becoming in fact (if not in any organization chart) the dominating figure in the company's personnel organization. This was clearly the case as early as 1937.[2]

While it is evident that the personnel department had increased materially in scope, the task it assumed was one of immense proportion. Investigations carried on by personnel of the department in the mid-thirties laid bare the conditions that had developed through previous decades. In addition to the manifold problems of the "new" retail stores, there was found to be little standardization in personnel practices in other branches of the business, especially in buying departments. Each merchandise supervisor appeared as a rule unto himself. With respect to personnel each department was conducted as though it were a separate business. Between different departments there were widely varying rates of pay for comparable jobs; the compensation policy depended primarily on the generosity of the department manager. No systematic method was provided for co-ordinating varying employment levels between different departments; when the personnel needs of one department resulted in some curtailment of employment, it is said the individuals concerned had to "peddle" their services throughout the house largely on their own initiative and lacking information about the needs and qualifications required in other departments.

In its beginnings the personnel department was little more than a plan—and a plan of limited scope. Growth and progress toward maturity came with accretions of activities, and the conception grew as experience and events shaped the thinking of administrators. The development of the personnel department as substance was to be found largely in the evolution of particular activities. The first such activity—literally first, as far as the employee was concerned—was selection.

Throughout the mail-order development of the company, the selection of personnel never achieved a very formalized status. From the array of job-seekers, employees were chosen on the basis of "common sense." Applicants were "sized up," and the successful selection of personnel was a function of the interviewer's judgment, aided by whatever information unstandardized application blanks produced. Not until very recently have attempts at more nearly precise methods of selection been employed, and then only on a limited scale.

At the 1933 personnel conference there was no session devoted to selection and employment. Although the importance of capitalizing on individual differences among twenty thousand employees was noted, little more was said on the subject of selection and placement, except for a few brief remarks concerning the physical conditions and hours for interviewing applicants for rank-and-file positions.

In selecting managerial talent in the initial retail expansion, considerable reliance was placed on one of the executive placement agencies in New York. The mail-order plants were drawn upon, but the techniques of mail-order and retail-store management proved sufficiently different that this source was inadequate to the task. New store managers came to Sears from department stores of the traditional type, single-line stores (e.g., hardware dealers), and from chain-store organizations such as J. C. Penney, Schulte-United, and National Bellas Hess. Given the rapid rate of store expansion, there was little choice but to "import" managerial talent.

However, as early as 1928 it was realized that, if the company was to develop a successful and well-integrated retail organization, some provision had to be made for training managers within the organization. This conclusion was apparent from the great variation in the quality of store management, and it was consistent with the company's policy of "promoting from within." In 1928 Sears began its first recruitment of men from colleges. Previous to this time there had been some informal arrangements of a similar sort made upon the initiative of mail-order-plant executives in different territories. By 1934 the company was recruiting from the colleges on a systematic basis, and the "reserve group" was inaugurated to feed various operating units with "promotable" men.

At about the same time the reserve-group training program was getting under way in 1934 and 1935, the retail personnel assistant brought together material for a manual to be used by store managers in the selection of division managers for their stores. The new manual, which appeared in the fall of 1935, entitled *Aids for Selecting Division Managers,* gave to store managers an outline of the qualifications to be expected of all division managers and then proceeded to discuss the special qualifications necessary for managers of various merchandise lines. Questions and answers were suggested for use by store managers in interviewing prospective division heads to spot-check the applicant's qualifications and previous experience.

In 1937 another personnel conference was held, and one session was devoted to "Problems of Selection and Placement." The titles of the participants on the panel showed that the personnel department had developed some specialization of persons in employment work. The content of the discussion demonstrated that selection was still based solely on the judgment of the interviewer and that the bulk of actual employment work was that of "filling orders" for personnel. While there was no indication in the records that interviewing was conducted on any standard basis, the following paragraph indicates that the importance of selection was recognized and that some attention was being given to defining the attributes believed to be desirable in prospective employees:

> On the subject of selection, it might be well to mention that it is necessary that much more care be exercised in the hiring of people today than was used a decade ago. Society has come to view the responsibility of the employer in much more definite outline than in the past and so today, whether it is considered that the employe has a vested interest in his job or not, good and sufficient reasons must exist for severing an employment relationship of fairly long duration. Therefore, such factors as age, health, native intelligence and ability, and the influence of home environment are of surpassing importance in selecting applicants with whom to build a virile, progressive organization.[3]

Discussion of how interviewers might discover and evaluate "native intelligence and ability and the influence of home environment" does not appear to have been discussed prior to 1939,[4] when indications appeared that the problem of evaluating job applicants had been bothering the store managers. In commenting on this problem, one speaker said:

> Several managers have asked for a general discussion of the interview and a number have asked whether there is any recommended standard method of rating applicants. Of course, there are any number of tests which have been developed, and some companies are experimenting with so-called scientific aptitude testing of applicants. We are doing some of it ourselves for certain types of jobs. We are now conducting a study ... with an "Interview Guide and Rating Chart," but we cannot yet guarantee its value. It is generally agreed by those who have made a study of testing for employment that of all the vocational groups, it is most difficult to apply tests to salespeople, because a formula for testing salespeople has not been developed as successfully as tests for other groups.[5]

The use of testing in the selection of sales personnel has generally lagged behind the development in manufacturing industries and office management.[6] That Sears continued to rely on personal judgment in the selection of employees was at least partly the result of the narrow range of practicable alternatives.

There is every indication that the personnel department was increasingly preoccupied with the necessity for improved selection procedures. In 1940 a "Pre-employment Interview Guide and Rating Chart" was issued for the use of the large stores. The development of this interview guide had begun in 1938, and its validity had been checked in terms of the rating of fifteen hundred employees whose performance was known. It was found that about 73 per cent of those rated well on the basis of performance were correctly classified by their scores on the interview guide. It was clearly emphasized that "the chart cannot be considered so much a means of selection as a means of elimination." The interview guide constituted the first attempt at standardizing interviewing procedure, but it never received wide adoption in Sears.

The appearance of the interview rating form and remarks in the personnel department's 1940 report to top management foreshadowed the development of a testing program begun in 1942. The thinking of the personnel staff on the problem of improving employee selection and the stage of evolutionary development reached prior to World War II is illustrated by the following quotation:

> Improved techniques of selection to supplement (not replace) the method of personal interview have long been recognized as a pressing need in business and industry. The progress of a scientific approach to this problem through the use of tests and rating systems has been slow and to a degree disappointing; slow because of the magnitude and complexity of the problem, disappointing in that when initiated there is a tendency to over-estimate the reliability of test and ratings and to consider them panaceas to the problem of selection. Consequently, when imperfections appear, even in obviously exceptional cases, the tendency is to discredit and discard the technique entirely, thus interrupting the progressive development necessary to approach perfection in an undertaking so involved.
>
> Leading authorities in the field of tests and ratings are of the opinion that it may take a decade of consistent improvement to accomplish a degree of simplification and perfection which will be acceptable generally to business and industry. Nevertheless, the problem of improving employe selection is acute. However unreliable the present best known methods of testing and rating may be, they are worthy of experimental use and development.[7]

The increased emphasis on selection procedures was due in large part to the conviction that errors in the selection of employees were an important cause of higher personnel turnover as well as (1) loss of sales through poor customer service and ineffective selling; (2) indirect expense through increased cost of training, errors in handlings, damage to merchandise, and recruiting costs incurred for replacements; and (3) higher costs for employment insurance benefits for released employees.[8]

The preceding discussion has been concerned primarily with the selection of rank-and-file employees. The techniques of selecting executive personnel were not essentially different in kind. Until 1940 the selection of executives and potential executives was based on interviews and an examination of the experience of applicants. The essential difference between executive and rank-and-file selection was one of time involved and number of interviews rather than method. A more searching examination was made of the applicant's record, and more personal judgments were involved when executive selection was considered. When the development of a psychological testing program was inaugurated in 1942, it is interesting that the testing program was directed to executive selection only.

While psychological tests had been used with some success in industry for many years following the experience of the army in the first World War, testing had not been widely adopted in retailing; but by the beginning of World War II the testing achievements of several leading American industrial firms had been observed. Of some influence also was the knowledge of a successful use of tests for selection purposes in numerous categories of the armed services.

Important in explaining the experiments in psychological testing is the method by which Sears's executives operated. The nature of Sears's organization was such that changes in policy and method were generally induced through persuasion rather than imposed by authority. This was especially true of the personnel executive's methods. As the personnel department came more and more to influence important appointments, the staff became embroiled in argument and exchange of opinions about the merits of candidates for key positions. Such appointments demanded that many different executives be satisfied and were inevitably occasions for difficult attempts to reconcile the opinions of persons each of whom held tenaciously to his own estimate of a candidate's qualifications. The testing program was very largely an attempt to uncover more or less objective measures to minimize such subjective estimates and thereby lift the discussions above the realm of opinion and prejudice.

As an outgrowth of these events and a realization of the increasing need for more precise aids to improve the caliber of executive placements, a research program was inaugurated in 1942 under the direction of L. L. Thurstone of the University of Chicago. That project was directed to the development of a battery of tests of factors of intelligence and schedules of personality traits and vocational interests. The program involved the construction of tests custom built to the requirements of Sears's jobs, to be validated in the course of continuing experiments. The ultimate end, of course, was to improve selection by providing profiles of the personality traits and the aptitudes necessary for successful job performance.

The testing program was developed cautiously, but every sign pointed to Sears's growing faith in the method. Contrary to the practice of many firms, testing was initiated at Sears at the executive level, and not until 1948 were experiments extended to include the testing of rank-and-file employees.

In the course of the testing program 41,159 tests had been administered to 14,924 persons in the three-year period ending January 31, 1948.[9] In addition to Chicago, testing offices were established in New York, Boston, Philadelphia, and Atlanta. Consideration was being given in 1948 to opening offices in other mail-order plants through which both mail-order and retail units could be serviced.

The following excerpt from the *Postwar Personnel Report* indicates the way in which the personnel department looked upon the usefulness of testing:

It is not intended that exclusive reliance be placed on test results. The test report and the doctor's report are merely two items among the variety of factors which the interviewer weighs and considers in evaluating the individual's probable value to the company. There can be no substitute for good judgment as the basis for any personnel decisions. However, test results can be a valuable additional aid to sound personnel judgment.

The testing program is already proving its value. Frequently, latent sources of difficulty cannot be ascertained even by a skillful interviewer. An excellent personality may disguise a lack of native intellectual capacity, or a deep-seated temperamental maladjustment which might not become evident except in periods of stress. Conversely, outstanding mental qualifications are sometimes obscured by other factors not necessarily pertinent to the situation. Psychological tests fre-

TABLE 78*

LENGTH OF SERVICE OF PRESENT STORE MANAGERS AT TIME OF FIRST ASSIGNMENT TO MANAGEMENT

Time of First Assignment	Average Length of Service (Years)
1925–30	2
1931–34	3
1935–39	7
After 1939	8.5

*Source: *The Retail Personnel Program for 1940*, p. 2, and a special report, "Who Are Sears Executives?" (1948), p .5.

quently can suggest to the interviewer possible areas of weakness or strength in the applicant which might not otherwise be discovered, or discovered too late. With such possibilities brought to his attention, the interviewer can make special efforts to verify or refute the evidence of the tests, with consequent improvement in the soundness of his employment decision.

Tests, of course, need not be restricted to employment. They may also be used when employes are being considered for promotion. It is anticipated that tests will be an important aid in discovering latent promotional qualifications in many employes now working in minor positions. The tests can be a means of unearthing talents and channeling people into lines of work for which they are best fitted and on which they will make the greatest contribution to the company's welfare and their own job satisfaction.

While the testing program was a clear indication of the interest of the company in improving the effectiveness of personnel performance, the prospects of high-level performance were further enhanced by training. Whereas virtually all retail managers had been recruited from outside the company in 1929, ten years later two-thirds of all store managers were company trained. Some measure of the success of the company's efforts in this direction are indicated in Table 78.

The success in training executives for the retail stores was achieved largely through the reserve-group program, inaugurated in 1933. Candidates for that program were selected from colleges as well as from the ranks of employees. In terms of selection, the essential criterion was "promotability." Continuing effort has been made to identify the characteristics that distinguish persons with executive abilities from those possessing mere competence for routine performance.

Great stress was laid on "promotion from within." In an effort to implement that policy, major emphasis was placed on discovering employees having the qualifications for executive performance. Store managers were asked to review their organizations for promotable material, and territorial executives were charged with a similar responsibility. As the parent personnel department developed, field visits were made for the purpose of discovering talent for the reserve group. A consistent effort has been made to comb the stores as sources for promotable material. Caldwell recalls that, when he was retail personnel assistant between 1933 and 1935, virtually all his time was spent inspecting stores and appraising the quality of the personnel. In 1939, for example, representatives of the parent-department visited 234 stores.

In the course of these visits an effort was made to interview each regular employe personally and to appraise both his effectiveness in his present assignment and his qualifications for advancement. These visits were particularly effective not only in locating potential executive material not previously reported, but more particularly in impressing store managers with their responsibility in recruiting and developing executive personnel.[10]

The training aspect of the reserve-group program had the objective of developing men with a sufficiently broad experience to qualify them for executive responsibility after a period of four or five years. The basic technique was that of job rotation. The trainees were assigned to productive employment in the stores, with the responsibility for actual training placed on the store managers. However, the training program or schedule was provided by the company personnel department, and follow-up made by the territorial personnel offices. Some idea of the number and type of training schedules assigned in the reserve-group program is indicated in Table 79.

Since the need for developing managers was most acute in the retail expansion, little attention had been given to preparing men with retail experience for parent and mail-order departments. Beginning in 1940, however, training schedules were developed to help qualify executive trainees for positions on the parent staff and the mail-order departments after their initiation in the retail stores. This phase of executive training was begun by assigning twenty-five of the "apprentices" employed during 1939 from the colleges and universities.

Until 1939 the company subsidized the program of retail executive training in the stores by paying at least part of the trainees' salaries. In 1939 this policy was re-examined, and the officers concluded that "the development of executive personnel is primarily the responsibility of the retail stores themselves and that the subsidization of executive training is inconsistent with sound management principles."[11] Since 1939 subsidization of salaries for executive trainees has been confined to exceptional cases of intensive training schedules for high-level executive jobs. Not only was the actual training responsibility thus placed on store managers in the field but even the recruiting process was to rest primarily on the field units.

It is impossible, as well as undesirable, for Department 707 [the central personnel department] to recruit more than a small proportion of all potential executive

TABLE 79*

RETAIL EXECUTIVE TRAINING

Type of Schedule	Number Assigned		
	1937	1938	1939
Senior apprentice†	156	110	265
Operating superintendent	16	17	17
Merchandise and sales promotion	21	21	40
Advertising	2	3	16
Customer service	10	4	21
Personnel assistant	24	20	46
Junior apprentice	127	31	181
Special	17	26	81
Total	373	232	667

* Source: *The Retail Personnel Program for 1940*, p. 9.
† Intensive schedules for management and assistant management.

material. Primary reliance must continue to be placed on retail store executives, with Department 707 confining itself primarily to recruiting sufficient manpower to offset any deficiency in the number originating in the field.[12]

But the tendency appears to have been for busy store managers to leave the responsibility of recruiting executive trainees to the parent personnel department, which relied largely on college visitations, always supplemented by the continuing search for promotable talent to be found working in the stores. It is important to note that, while the actual training program was carried on in the stores, provision was increasingly made for supervision by representatives of the parent personnel department traveling in the field to check on the training progress of reserve-group members.

The general company thinking about executive training prior to World War II is well summarized in the following paragraph from the 1940 report, when, after discussing proposed training plans including revised correspondence courses for store managers, management clinics to be held in exceptionally well-managed stores, and the re-establishment of Chicago training classes for assistant managers, Caldwell said:

It should be emphasized that the above plans are intended to provide only the finishing touches. The most important training for managerial, as well as for other executive responsibilities, will continue as in the past to be actual productive assignments rotating progressively through all major phases of store operations.

Plans for postwar expansion necessitated, of course, the expansion of recruitment activity to provide promotable manpower. A parallel development was the provision of an adequate executive training program capable of providing the skills and knowledge required for successful management in the face of expected changes in postwar conditions—intensified retail competition, and the growing complexity of administrative tasks.

There is particular need for developing men who are not only fully informed as to their regular field of work, but who have a broad, company-wide viewpoint rather than the narrow interests and knowledge of the specialist.[13]

Sears's heavy reliance on planned job rotation for executive trainees was based on the assumption that there can be no substitute for experience and for the intimate knowledge of the organization to be gained through productive working assignments. To direct and enhance the learning process through job experience, all postwar training schedules and outlines were revised in the light of changed competitive conditions and the changed character of the trainees. Prior to the war the average age of men coming into the executive training program was about 22 years. After the war the average age of such men was 26.5 years. Because of increased maturity, and stronger motivation accompanying family responsibility, which is characteristic of the group, the training schedules became more intensive, and the average training time was cut almost in half.[14]

A postwar innovation in executive training was a plan of staff schools to supplement job-rotation training. This device proved useful not only as a means for accelerating training but also as a method for broadening the outlook and understanding of trainees by bringing them into more direct contact with key executives. The staff school progressively became a tool of management for getting things done—often very specific things such as effecting smoothly changes in store organization. The scope of these schools included by the end of 1948:

1. *Parent basic training.*—Two-week courses conducted regularly during nine months of the year, designed to acquaint check-list employees coming into the headquarters organization with the structure, functions, and interrelationships of the departments and activities. In the period 1945–47, 419 employees have participated.
2. *Merchandise manager school.*—A six-week program conducted during 1947 to provide intensive training in Chicago for "A" store merchandise manager

positions. "Students" received two weeks of classroom instruction by executives on the broader phases of merchandising and four weeks of individual training by retail sales managers on the specific problems of individual merchandise lines.

3. *Assistant manager school.*—A one-week training meeting for potential "B" store assistant managers covering important aspects of the job. Instruction was provided by experienced field executives as well as by key members of functional departments at headquarters.

4. *Customer service manager school.*—A five-week program of intensive training for prospective service managers.

5. *Personnel manager conferences.*—Two-day meetings conducted in the field by headquarters staff members for "A" store personnel managers, designed to acquaint them more directly with headquarters thinking and, through discussion and the exchange of ideas, to improve the quality of personnel management in the stores.

All the early staff schools were experimental and confined primarily to the midwestern territory over which (until early in 1948) the parent personnel department exercised direct control. An indication of the acceptance of the staff-school idea is apparent from the requests from other territories for guidance in setting up such programs. The subject matter of these schools was not at all fixed; the program depended on flexibility to meet the changing needs and specific objectives appropriate to circumstances. While job rotation remained the basic method for executive training, the staff schools represented a recognition that it is not the only method. These schools point to the adaptability in thinking and the experimental attitude of the management in seeking the optimum combination of methods and subject matter required to produce effective executives and to achieve recognized business objectives.

The immense size of the Sears operation as well as changing conditions in the economic and social environment make heavy demands on major company executives. The reserve-group program which has been discussed was directed to promotable talent which is promising, young, and usually inexperienced. The job objectives of these men were at the intermediate level of executive performance where their responsibilities were significant but where their activities were subject to a considerable degree of direction by more mature and experienced administrators. In the past these top-level positions were filled by people who "grew into them by virtue of proficiency in previous jobs and promise of further development. There is no sharp line of demarcation between executive levels; but there are grounds for broadly distinguishing such levels on the basis of breadth of action required. The senior executive positions involve responsibilities that transcend specal functions and/or areas of both merchandise and geography. Decisions involve a wide margin of discretion, and errors result in serious consequences extending beyond narrow boundaries.

An important postwar development at Sears was the recognition that something more than accidental preparation should be required for senior executive positions. Acting upon the suggestion of the president (F. B. McConnell) in 1946, the personnel department prepared an "organized plan for the development of back-ups for senior executive positions in retail, parent, and control stores." This plan ("senior reserve") followed the general principles of the regular reserve-group program, but the plan began where the regular reserve group left off—the level of store management or equivalent. In retail these positions included the group manager, independent "A" store manager, group "A" store manager, zone manager, and assistant zone manager. The senior-reserve-group positions in mail order comprehended the following jobs in each branch: general manager, operating superintendent, merchandise superintendent, sales superintendent, and personnel manager. The list was completed by the inclusion of "key staff assistants" in parent and the territories and the various merchandise supervisors in the former organization.

The most unique feature of the senior-reserve-group training plan involved training schedules which were custom-made to the individual's needs, based on the particular job objective in view. Detailed training programs of this sort were prepared for over one hundred persons during 1947. Of course, job-rotation training of some sort has almost inevitably been the case for business executives generally. Two aspects of the new Sears program were interesting, however. It represented an attempt to recognize and really plan rotation so that no important areas were overlooked and some breadth of experience assured. Further, an emphasis on training in human relations came to pervade the "senior courses"—as it did all levels of the training program. Indeed, many aspects of training were specifically directed toward improved morale.

While an executive training program was being evolved, the preparation of rank-and-file employees for better job performance also received attention. At the first personnel conference in 1933 every one of the officers who spoke emphasized the necessity of employee training; that subject received more discussion than did any other aspect of personnel management. According to D. M. Nelson, then vice-president in charge of merchandise, sales training was the most important problem the company had to solve at that time.

It was early realized that the training process itself must be carried on in the stores. Specialists in the home offices operated from the beginning entirely as advisers in methods of training and created materials of aid to the store managers, who were charged with responsibility for employee training. Such materials consisted very largely of merchandise manuals, and the mail-order catalogue was used as one of the major sources for merchandise training. The earliest manuals were prepared for lines requiring technical treatment and for high-unit-value items (big tickets). There have always been at least two important objectives in Sears's training activities: to raise the level of employees' merchandise knowledge and to aid salespeople to augment the company's efforts to achieve customer acceptance. The latter objective was particularly important in the early period of retail expansion.

In the course of time the personnel department provided the stores with more and better tools for training. Various techniques were used in presenting materials for store use, and subject-matter emphasis was adapted to changing needs. The use of slide films was begun in 1936, and the popularity of such training aids among store managers led eventually to considerable emphasis on visual methods.

As experience was gained in the solution of training problems, there developed better co-ordination between the merchandising, promotion, and training personnel. Prior to the outbreak of World War II a substantial degree of success was achieved in the distribution of training aids to stores to coincide with sales-promotion events. By 1941 the employee-training division was well established as a very active section of the personnel department. Materials were provided in three different areas: (1) merchandise training aids, which were concerned with facts and methods peculiar to particular merchandise divisions; (2) tools that met the needs of employees selling many different merchandise lines as exemplified by the "courses" in "Merchandising and Operating Fundamentals" and "Adventures in Salesmanship"; and (3) employee handbooks, calculated to inform the worker of his relation to the company and providing general information useful to him as an employee, as well as initial training (at store expense) not only to teach new employees the important facts about the selling system but also to provide a more effective orientation for the new employee. There was also apparent an increasing interest in the "how" of training, and efforts were made to develop a manual on training method.

In the continuing expansion of the training program, an attempt was made to avoid training for its own sake. It was early accepted as a guiding principle that "the test of training is performance." "Performance" was largely defined for practical purposes as the scores made on shopping reports submitted by the professional "shopping service" to which the company subscribed. Periodic analysis of such reports by stores served as a guide to the weak spots in the performance of sales personnel. In addition to these reports, field visits by staff representatives were used both as a guide to training needs and as an evaluation of previous training effort. Store managers and personnel managers in the field were active in expressing themselves as to training needs and the usefulness of the programs developed in the home office.

The period after V-J Day witnessed marked expansion in the scope and character of training at Sears. The magnitude of the task is dramatic. As indicated in Table 80, there was a staggering increase in the number of Sears's employees between 1939 and 1947.

The real task is more apparent, however, when one realizes that, to attain a net increase of 53,891 employees between 1945 and 1947, it has been estimated that over 400,000 new people were hired, most for part-time help, of course. While the problem of hiring on such a scale has been significant, the job of training such a large number of new people was even greater. That burden was greatly increased due to the abnormally high turnover which inevitably accompanied the war and early postwar period. The level of turnover by years assumed the pattern indicated in Table 81. While these

TABLE 80*

NUMBER OF EMPLOYEES, 1939–47

Year	Employees
1939	82,812
1940	103,728
1941	131,128
1942	123,029
1943	126,169
1944	129,673
1945	124,702
1946	152,318
1947	178,593

* Source: Company records. These figures are for December 3 of each year.

TABLE 81*

PERCENTAGE ANNUAL PERSONNEL TURNOVER, REGULAR RETAIL TIME-CARD EMPLOYEES, 1940–47

Year	Turnover
1940	26.3
1941	40.8
1942	68.5
1943	72.5
1944	47.7
1945	49.1
1946	47.4
1947	39.3

* Source: Company records.

figures are for retail employees, it is believed from the limited information available that there was a parallel movement for mail order as well. In view of the size of the task, considerable effort and ingenuity went into developing training materials and methods that it was hoped not only would be more efficient but would also contribute to employment stability by improving employee effectiveness on the job and to that extent increase the satisfaction to be derived from work experience.

The war and postwar training developments, unlike the introduction of testing in selection procedures, did not represent a marked change in the company's personnel program. Training had become well established soon after the retail expansion was under way. Certain developments in this area are, however, worth noting. Perhaps the most important influence working on Sears's policy was the advances made in training methods in the armed services and war industries. From the former much was gained by a study of the use of visual aids in training—motion pictures and sound slide films. The Training within Industry Division of the War Manpower Commission contributed the techniques of its now famous trilogy: job relations training (J.R.T.), job methods training (J.M.T.), and job instructor training (J.I.T.).

Perhaps more important than method, the widely advertised results of wartime training activities helped create a favorable climate for the extension of training activities in industry. That Sears's management was receptive to the personnel department's plans for increased emphasis on training is evident in the increased size of expenditures for training materials detailed in Table 82.

TABLE 82*

EXPENDITURES FOR TRAINING MATERIALS

Year	Amount
1940	$ 42,971
1941	70,790
1942	21,696
1943	7,433
1944	28,810
1945	52,720
1946	157,790
1947	262,936

* Source: Company records.

In the postwar years 1945–47 almost $500,000 was spent on training materials of all kinds. In this period 221 new items were added to an already extensive training library. The wide use of visual aids became a special feature of the Sears program. In the postwar period the company commissioned twenty-eight sound slide films and several sound motion pictures. In addition, recourse was frequently made to charts, slides, and related techniques. One overwhelming advantage which these techniques possess (besides the important impression made by visual mediums) is that of getting information across without distortion to thousands of people in widely dispersed locations. The production of sixty new manuals (largely devoted to sales training and division-manager training) further enhanced uniformity of presentation.

Especially for rank-and-file jobs, there was a growing tendency to take training nearer and nearer to the job itself in line with the experience of war industries. Wherever possible, materials came to be designed for use on an individual basis under the guidance of sponsors, carefully selected employees with successful job experience, appointed to instruct new employees in the stores in their job duties and assist them in various ways until they were well launched on their new jobs. The inauguration of the sponsor system in Sears's retail training was an outgrowth of the necessities of the war period, although this system had been used in the department-store field sometime before. Aside from method, the content of sales training was increasingly directed to merchandise knowledge on the assumption that, if the salesperson really knew the merchandise, he could make selling presentations which were more effective than any "pattern" sales talk. Further, a marked trend developed for the personnel department to serve as a co-ordinating agency, with the actual preparation of materials being done by the merchandise department concerned.

Indeed, in 1948 at Caldwell's suggestion merchandise and sales-training responsibilities (and the staff personnel therefor) were transferred out of the personnel department to the retail merchandise office. The move was made partly to achieve closer co-ordination between training and other phases of the merchandise program, including more expeditious handling of the distribution of training materials to the stores. But the most important reason leading to the shift was that it was believed that the retail merchandise office might achieve better application of training efforts in the field.[15]

The training efforts of the personnel department were not confined solely to the preparation of training materials. The department sponsored many training meetings and conferences with field personnel managers and assistant store managers to develop effective means of organizing training activities within field units. There was also a continuation of company-wide conferences held in Chicago in which territorial personnel officers and store executives came together for a week to discuss matters of common interest. There were also special courses developed for specific needs. Among these special courses, one of the most interesting was the vocational training course. That program offered an opportunity for employees to acquire higher clerical skills, thus providing the means to advancement in status and earnings as well as furnishing qualified personnel to the company when it was badly needed. The vocational course was made available in Chicago free of charge to all Sears's employees on the basis of recommendation by the employee's supervisor. The courses, staffed by instructors from private and public schools, were started in 1944 to help meet the wartime clerical personnel needs of the company. Between 1945 and 1947, 867 employees were "graduated," trained in such skills as typing, shorthand, comptometry, etc. While the plan was conceived as a device to meet the labor-market conditions which characterized the war and postwar periods, its contribution to employee morale was believed to be so significant that consideration was being given in 1948 to the possibility of extending the program to other units of the company.

While training activities transmit much of company lore and policy in the course of achieving their objectives, Sears adopted still another instrument to help interpret company policy to all employees. In 1936 a monthly picture tabloid, the *News-Graphic*, was established "to tell the story of Sears to its employees." The paper in 1948 had a distribution of over 100,-

000 copies. The *News-Graphic*, while depending for its organization and technique on a full-time staff in the headquarters organization, relies heavily for contributions on correspondents appointed in each mail-order unit and retail store and in the New York office.

Editorial content in 1948 was no longer marked by the heavily written "inspirationals" characteristic of *The Skylight* at the turn of the century. The *News-Graphic* has attempted to provide news of the varied activities of the company and works to promote better understanding between management and the employees. To further "local" interest, the *News-Graphic* in 1945 started publishing special sections for each mail-order plant. The decentralization of Sears's administrative organization in 1948 led to providing each territory with special first and last pages of particular interest and relevance to the respective territories, achieving an effect of special editions.

Another means of "mass communication" has been the Sears Forum, an annual meeting in Chicago for employees held at the close of the fiscal year when the firm's annual report is published to the stockholders. These forums have been held each year since the early 1930's. The chairman of the board of directors and the officers of the company appear and explain and comment on the record of the previous year, an important feature of which always is the review of the profit-sharing fund. Following the discussion of the financial reports of the company and the fund, employees are given an opportunity to submit (anonymously) any questions they would like to have answered by the officers. The questions submitted have been frank, sometimes embarrassing, and frequently humorous.

Of prime interest to employees is, of course, the subject of wages and hours, and, in view of the critical importance of the wage bill in retailing, the matter of compensation and hours of work has long been of great importance to Sears's management. The long-established policy of the company had been to pay "market rates or better"; it was the store manager's responsibility to keep his compensation plan adjusted to movements in the local labor market. The same general policy existed regarding hours.

The years from 1929 to 1937 were marked by an instability of standards, in the light of pressures from the general economic and social environment. The standard Sears work-week in 1929 was forty-eight hours with time and one-half paid for overtime. In June, 1930, payment for overtime was abolished and limitations on weekly hours eliminated. In 1932 provision was made for the payment of overtime after sixty hours.

Even that concession was lost early in 1933 in the face of the depression drive for stringent economies. In notifying employees of the suspension of overtime payments, J. M. Barker, vice-president in charge of retail administration, wrote:

> Other companies have found it necessary to effect extreme economies in order that they might continue their existence and provide employment in some

PERSONNEL MANAGEMENT MATURES 569

measure for deserving employes within their organizations. The officers of your company have suspended the overtime policy at this time only because they feel that such action is in the best interest of the company's employes.

In a parallel notice to store managers, Barker stated:

This suspension has been authorized to permit you to operate at a minimum expense, but it is not intended that any employe in your store shall be required to work an unreasonable amount of unpaid overtime.... I am depending on you, therefore, to schedule the working hours of your employes with careful regard for their interests.[16]

There is every indication that Sears was an enthusiastic supporter of NRA code provisions, and wages and hours were adapted to the demands of the codes. In addressing the members of the personnel conference in 1933, Barker explained the company's position:

There are severe penalties for infringement of the NRA rules ... but this is not the reason why we expect you to adhere to them. It is our wish that this organization live up to the *spirit* of the code.

This attitude is again indicated in President Wood's memorandum to all store managers in May, 1935, which declared: "The recent ruling of the Supreme Court, declaring NRA unconstitutional, should not, in our opinion, materially affect our basic wages or working hours."[17]

As shown elsewhere in this volume, Wood's acceptance of the New Deal measures was more than toleration. Indeed, the influence on Sears of NRA appears to have been significant. The Recovery Administration exercised a peculiarly strategic influence as a result of the requirements of the Retail Code that the company establish (a) employment standards; (b) a means for policing the observance of such standards; and (c) participation in a clearing-house arrangement for interpretation of standards. Thus the advancing retail flank of the firm was spurred to its first real attempt to standardize and *enforce* the many activities comprehended in "personnel policy."

Despite the demise of the codes when the Supreme Court effectively disposed of NRA in the Schechter case, elements of the retail code were maintained at Sears and became a spearhead for the elaboration of personnel policy. The company continued the basic forty-eight-hour week and enforced its own program of minimum wages enunciated in the now famous (in Sears) Bulletin 0-399 issued in April, 1936, and revised many times since.[18]

When the 1936 version of the bulletin was first disseminated to store managers, it was supplemented by a letter over the signature of President Carney that stated:

Sears was one of the first ... to accept the N.R.A. in its entirety. We were probably the first chain organization to do so. We were sold lock, stock and barrel on the idea. . . .

. . . When the Supreme Court held the N.R.A. unconstitutional, we did not permit deviation from the N.R.A. requirements as to wages and hours. Despite the action of competitors and the pressure from within our own organization, the Officers ... have refused to permit deviation from the N.R.A. minimum wage and maximum hour provisions.

After observing that Sears had found clear advantages followed the adoption of minimum-wage and maximum-hour requirements, Carney concluded:

Our experience has shown that the way to effect operating economies is to pay relatively high wages to a fewer number of high type, competent, experienced, and trained employes, rather than have a low rate of pay for a relatively large number of average or mediocre employes.
You know ... Sears policy. ... You are expected to adhere strictly to the policy.[19]

Bulletin 0-399 (1936) established a schedule of minimum wages for the forty-eight-hour week with regional differentials as shown in the accompanying tabulation. Higher minimums were established for married men.

Population of Cities or Towns	North	South
Over 500,000	$15.00	$14.00
100,000–500,000	14.00	13.00
25,000–100,000	13.00	12.00
2,500–25,000	11.00	10.00
Less than 2,500	10.00	9.00

For cities of 100,000 population the minimum in the North for married men was $19 per week; in the South, $18. For cities having less than 100,000 population, the comparable northern minimum was $17; the southern, $16.

In 1937 a revised bulletin raised the weekly minimums for northern cities by $1.00. More important, and in effect raising the entire structure of wages, was the 1937 change lowering the basic work-week from forty-eight to forty-four hours.[20] In later revisions of the bulletin the minimums were raised, and the classifications were refined to include job distinctions. In all such bulletins it was emphasized that the schedules were only minimums, and average wages were, of course, substantially higher.

Bulletin 0-399 represented a really significant mark in the development of employment standards at Sears. It is hard to appreciate now what a radical step was taken when a mandate of minimum-wage rates was imposed upon the hundreds of managers in the company. In some cases it meant substantial increases in the wage bill of the stores and brought a vision of increased operating costs to the managers who were striving zealously to make good profit showings for the company and good bonuses for themselves. The personnel department, charged with disseminating and policing the policy throughout the organization, met with determined opposition on the part of some executives in the field. The new concept of employment standards, sustained by the strong support of Wood, Carney, and McConnell, was made effective, however, and the recalcitrant managers learned to comply as a preferable alternative to severe disciplinary action at the hands of company officers.[21]

No detailed information is available to indicate the effect of reduced hours on operating costs, although at the 1937 personnel conference an operating executive reported:

> The shortening of hours from our standpoint is not a disturbing thing. Of course we have got religion in the last three or four years, not because we had to get religion but ... as we have gone along with the shortening of hours ... there have been some material gains rather than the losses that were anticipated....[22]

It should be noted that in making the necessary adjustment of employee hours in the face of store business hours that were longer than the employee work-week, store managers were faced with difficult problems of scheduling. The problem was further complicated by the official company policy that split shifts would not be tolerated. Complaints from the field were frequent in the initial period—not only from managers but occasionally from the employees as well, some of whom preferred split shifts.

In 1939 a policy was adopted to limit executive hours of work to a maximum of fifty-four hours per week, on the theory that executive activities involve a high degree of nervous strain which, unless compensated by adequate leisure and relaxation, was likely to involve serious impairment of health and personal effectiveness. The 1939 report added:

> Basic hours of non-executive employes correspond closely with the practices followed by local competitors and with what is considered fair and reasonable in various communities. In only three instances, each involving quite unusual circumstances, are basic employe hours in excess of 48 per week, and steps are being taken to bring these stores down to the 48 hour maximum. Slightly more than half of all retail timecard employes work on a 48 hour week while the remainder work on shorter hours. Average basic hours for all regular timecard employes in retail are about 46 per week.
>
> It is recognized that basic employe working hours may be subject to downward revision in the future to meet the requirements of state or federal legislation or for other reasons. Generally speaking, however, the schedules now in effect are equitable, and further reductions need not be made unless changes occur in objective social conditions.[23]

The effect of World War II was to interrupt the trend to shorter working hours, and the pressure from Washington was, if anything, necessarily to encourage a lengthening of the work-week rather than the reverse. The war over, Sears's work-week was appreciably shortened in line with the general trend in progressive retail practice, which was to parallel the pattern that had come to be typical of manufacturing. In January, 1946, the company officially adopted the following general policy:

The company recognizes the trend toward a shorter work week throughout industry and it is our policy to anticipate changes and to take the lead in the adoption of desirable working hours rather than follow along with or make changes after our competitors have done so.[24]

By 1948 all "A" stores were on a 40-hour basic work-week for all employees. Hours in "B" stores varied from 40 to 44, depending on local community practices, but the greater majority of "B" store employees were in stores on a 40-hour week, as indicated by the fact that during 1948 the average basic work-week for all "B" store employees was 41.9 hours. The average basic work-week for all regular Sears's employees in 1948 was 40.6 hours, reflecting the marked reduction in hours for retail personnel since 1939. The mail-order plants were all working on a 40-hour basic work-week and had been for almost ten years.

The personnel department has long been concerned with methods of compensation. At the 1933 personnel conference it was stated that three methods of compensation had been decided upon for employees in retail stores: (1) straight salary, (2) salary plus commission, and (3) drawing account against commission. The straight salary was believed best for most selling and nonselling employees and for those whose duties were divided between these categories. Salary plus commission was recommended for use as an incentive for division heads and supervisory sales personnel. The third plan was suggested as most appropriate for outside salesmen and salespeople in specialty divisions, but as having sufficient flexibility to serve as an incentive method for selling personnel in all major divisions.

Statements in the 1940 report indicate that the installation of the approved compensation methods outlined in 1933 had not been accomplished in any uniform manner:

A survey conducted during 1938 revealed a total lack of uniformity in the compensation arrangements used in the retail stores. As many as 18 different methods were in effect . . . for compensating division managers. Since many of these arrangements were essentially unsound, and since extreme diversity in method has an inevitable tendency to undermine employe morale, a consistent effort was made during 1939 to eliminate the more undesirable types of compensation arrangements. In establishing authorized methods of compensation, the following fundamental principles were kept in mind:

1. The actual earnings resulting from the method must be fair.
2. The system must be simple and readily understood by the employee.
3. From an accounting standpoint the system must be easily operated and inexpensively maintained.
4. No compensation plan can ever be substituted successfully for intelligent supervision on the part of the management.

By adherence to these principles, considerable progress has been made toward the simplication and standardization of compensation methods in force. This effort will be continued . . . and, when necessary, a stronger stand will be taken with store managers in order to insure conformity.[25]

To round out the company's wage policy a system of semiannual salary review and merit increases was inaugurated prior to 1937. During 1938 the program was temporarily suspended as a result of the decline in sales and profits. In the following year merit increases were resumed.

The most interesting feature of Sears's wage and employment policy occurred with the introduction in 1935 of the company's own version of guaranteed employment, when experiments with "constant income" plans were begun in the mail-order plants. The first installations occurred in the following year. The mail-order plants had long experienced extreme fluctuation from month to month, for example, 60 per cent more customer orders are received in December than are received in the summer months. Hours of work have depended directly upon the volume of orders received, so that weekly incomes of employees tended to be as unsteady as the volume of orders.

The new plan first tried in mail order was sponsored directly by T. J. Carney, who was then vice-president in charge of operations.[26] Essentially it provided for a flexible work-week with a guaranteed income for each week equivalent to earnings on a full-time (forty-hour) basis. If an employee worked less than forty hours, he was advanced the difference between his income for the hours actually worked and forty hours. Such advances were termed "debt hours." In any week when an employee worked longer than forty hours he received his hourly rate times forty. If he had no "debt hours," he also received payment (at time and one-half) for such overtime hours. If he had accumulated debt hours, an appropriate part of his overtime in that week was credited (at the time and one-half rate) to retire the debt hours. Thus the employee might be "indebted" to the company, but the company was never "indebted" to the employee.

The constant-income plan was started with several objectives:

1. To reduce the number of persons subject to the worry of layoff with each downward fluctuation of hours.
2. To stabilize the weekly income of employees and thus facilitate better personal budgeting practices by eliminating substantial variations in weekly incomes.
3. To benefit from the improved morale that it was believed should follow from accomplished objectives (1) and (2).
4. To achieve possible economies by avoiding the training and (retraining) costs associated with employment fluctuations.
5. To maximize savings on unemployment insurance costs under merit rating provisions. "It was very obvious that the extensive hiring and separating were bound to cost us a considerable amount in benefits. Therefore, it appeared that we could offset, to some extent by this tax saving, the additional expenses which it seemed we would certainly meet in inaugurating a 'Constant Income Plan.' "[27]

The experience with the plan was so successful that in 1938 variations of the mail-order plan were tried in some of the retail stores. There is no better way to outline the company thinking on this subject than to review selected paragraphs from a letter written by C. B. Caldwell to Lessing Rosenwald, then chairman of the board of directors, who was always intensely interested in employee welfare. The substance of the letter is further indicative of the serious interest of top management in the problem of employment stability and also of the degree to which interaction and imitation between various companies in different industries are effective in shaping policy and techniques:

Mr. Rosenwald:

This is with further reference to your recent conversation with me concerning the problem of employment and hours of work during peak periods of the year.

Retailing, generally, has long recognized the social problem created ... by following the trends of business in hiring and releasing employes. The Operating and Personnel Departments have made an effort for a number of years, to improve our performance in this respect by educating the managers to set up and retain in each retail store a basic organization which has full time employment throughout the year, irrespective of seasonal trends. Much benefit has been derived from application of this plan, both from the standpoint of the employe and the company.

The morale of the employe has been better, he has been more efficient and effective, and the company has benefited in that store appearance has been maintained, pre-seasonal merchandising preparations have been accomplished on schedule, and we have provided better customer service.

Sometime ago, Mr. Carney discussed with Mr. McConnell and me the possibility of application of some type of constant income plan to the retail business. Paul Mertz of this department was assigned to this project and has made a comprehensive field study of the several plans now being used in some industries. Mr. Mertz visited Nunn-Bush, Hormels [sic], and McCormick & Co., Baltimore, as well as several other concerns which are using this plan, or extracts of the plan in so far as it can be applied to their particular business.

Conclusions arrived at after an analysis of Mr. Mertz' survey, indicate that a constant income plan properly developed may be applied successfully to our retail stores.

Effective at the beginning of the ninth period, five retail stores began a test with two variations of the constant wage plan. [Three stores] will work on a *variable week plan* similar to the Mail Order store plan. [Two stores] will work on a *constant week plan*.

In the latter case the basic organization will be guaranteed employment, with out reduction of force of full weeks of work until mid-year inventory July, 1939, when the test will be concluded. This latter plan features job flexibility, permitting shifting of employes to other than their assigned duties ... and they will receive the compensation they have been receiving for their regularly assigned duties.

Under both plans, extra employes will not be used at any time when a regular employe can be trained and assigned to this work.

We hope this program can produce the following results:

a) Constant income weekly for a high percentage of all employes in these stores;
b) Possible reduction in unemployment insurance liabilities;
c) Better economic status for the employe through ability to budget family income and expenditures properly;

PERSONNEL MANAGEMENT MATURES

d) Reduce personnel turnover with consequent increased morale and efficiency;
e) Constantly improving morale as the result of relative job security in return for efficient work.

There are other desirable by-products that should materialize also. From the company's standpoint, our unemployment insurance costs should be materially reduced as a result of the application of this plan.

... If these plans show promise of success—and to date such is the case—definite extension to other stores will be recommended for consideration in advance of the test completion in the stores mentioned.

We are hopeful that the final development and application of a plan which specifically fits our retail operation will accomplish the results which you have outlined and which we agree are so vital to the continued progress Sears can accomplish for retailing generally in a partial or whole solution to this problem.[28]

Although the employment security plans had good acceptance on the part of managers and employees, the program was never extended to all units of the company. Undoubtedly the employment conditions created by World War II were of great importance in interrupting extensions of the plan, which at one time was installed in all but two of the mail-order plants and in ninety-six retail stores. Indications of the initial success of the plans in retail stores are evident in the department's report to top management in 1940:

The following results were achieved during the first year the plan was in operation:
1. Layoffs during slow seasons were appreciably reduced.
2. All time off of employes under the plan was with full pay.
3. The income of major appliance employes was more evenly distributed over the year.[29]
4. The amount of paid overtime was reduced.
5. Fewer extras were necessary.
6. Many employes received additional income at no greater cost to management and without working excessive hours.
7. There was no apparent increase in expense, as all stores had lower expense rates than for the previous year. However, other factors probably contributed to this result.

The reaction of the managers in the stores in which constant wage plans have been in operation may be summarized by their frequent comment, "Why didn't we do this long ago?" In view of the unqualifiedly enthusiastic reception of this program, arrangements are being made for its further extension during 1940. Within another year it is hoped that virtually all retail stores will be included under the constant wage program.[30]

As a result of the tight labor market and the high turnover associated with employee shifts to military and war work, the guaranteed employment arrangements proved unnecessary (and probably ineffective), and in October, 1942, it was decided to discontinue the program, at least until such time as conditions warranted the adoption of a plan to stabilize employment.

The fundamental basis of wage-earners' financial well-being depends, of course, more than anything else on earnings, a function of both hours worked and rates of pay. With the removal of wartime controls after V-J Day, industrial wage rates (and earnings) began to rise sharply under the influence of a tight labor market. The situation at Sears was similarly affected. Between 1941 and 1947 straight-time hourly earnings of time-card employees increased markedly—as did efforts to perfect and extend the program of wage and salary administration. Some idea of the extent to which average weekly earnings (exclusive of bonus) increased may be gained by noting that for employees hired in 1922 and still with the company in 1947 there was an increase of nearly 100 per cent in the decade 1937–47. Earnings rose from $30.78 per week in the former year to $39.35 in 1942 and advanced again to $58.33 in 1947. When nonexecutive employees in this group are considered separately, their earnings are seen to have increased from $23.88 in 1937 to $46.98 in 1947.

In addition to wages and salaries, employees received important additions to income through bonus payments, especially men in management. The bonuses have been particularly important as part of the retail-store managers' compensation. At first the bonus was largely confined to this group, but there has been a marked tendency to broaden the base. In 1945, for example, 28,044 retail employees participated in a bonus distribution of $7,790,769. In the other divisions of the company some 17,702 employees shared in a bonus distribution which totaled $4,731,438.[31]

An increasing number of policies have been adopted which enhance the income created by direct wage and salary payments to rank-and-file employees. The most significant of these is "The Savings and Profit Sharing Pension Fund of Sears, Roebuck and Co. Employes," a detailed study of which is to be found in Appendix A. As the company continued to grow and prosper in an environment of changing social standards, these benefits, intended neither to supplement nor to substitute for wages, became more and more prolific until during 1948 the cost of such benefits amounted to more than $52,000,000.

Employee discounts, profit-sharing, illness allowances, as well as vacations with pay were by 1925 all policies of long standing. Employee subscriptions for company stock developed during the latter part of the decade of the 1920's. In those years a number of large firms encouraged employee participation in stock ownership. The stock-market collapse in October, 1929, and the depression which followed braked the strong movement of the twenties. But the years from 1929 to 1933 constituted only a breathing spell in employee stock subscriptions at Sears. Between 1933 and 1940 Sears's stockholders approved four plans for offering Sears's stock to employees at prices lower than current market, to be paid for by them over a period of three to five years. Employees receiving such stock options were given the privilege of canceling them at any time prior to the expiration date; the options usually ran for a period of three years, the company retaining the shares in the treasury until paid for. The four offerings were fully subscribed and the stock taken by those who received options.[32]

Invented by underwriters to exploit a neglected field, group insurance has rapidly come to be standard equipment of industrial personnel programs. At Sears, group life insurance was first adopted in 1931. Under the plan life insurance is made available to employees in amounts related to employee earnings; the face value of policies varies from $1,000 to $10,000, and the cost of administering the group insurance program is borne by Sears. Employees leaving the company pay roll may, at their option, convert their insurance into any regular policy written by the insurance company; employees retiring at age sixty (or over) and satisfying certain service requirements are continued in the group insurance plan at the expense of the company.[33]

In 1935 the first credit unions were established by units of the company. The credit unions, chartered by the federal government, were not technically made a responsibility of the personnel department but added an important activity to the list of employee services. By 1940 there were fifty-nine Sears's credit unions having a total membership of 27,500 employees, and estimated deposits of $1,550,000.

One of the most serious financial problems faced by workers has been the unpredictable incidence and high cost of medical attention, especially hospitalization. Sears, for many years, provided some cushion for such expense through the illness allowance policy, which, while maintaining family income, did not provide for the extraordinary expenses of hospitalization. In response to increased public interest in group hospitalization, and with a view to employee welfare, the company in 1939 established the "Sears, Roebuck and Company Employes' Group Hospitalization Plan." Employees electing to join the plan paid $6.00 per year, and Sears assumed all administrative costs. Owing to certain legal technicalities, only employees were eligible for participation. In order to provide coverage for members of employees' families, employees could elect to come under the "Blue Cross Plan" for hospital care, thus receiving somewhat broader benefits and family coverage at higher contribution rates than Sears's own company plan.

The capstone of Sears's benefit program is the company's program to provide retirement security. Sears's retirement policy and auxiliary benefits may best be summarized in terms of a bulletin dated April 16, 1948, from the president to the managers of all units and regions:

> Under the present retirement policy, employes who earned less than $5,000 during the preceding year, or who earned more than $5,000 but hold non-executive positions, must work until age 65 before receiving retiree benefits. Many employes may be financially able to retire, or for other reasons wish to leave before the regular retirement date, but have been reluctant to do so because they did not want to leave without receiving retiree benefits.

Therefore, effective immediately our retirement policy is to be amended as follows:

Employes who have reached 60 years of age, have completed 30 or more years of service, and who would not normally be retired until age 65 may retire voluntarily with full retirement benefits at any time between the ages of 60 and 65.

The retirement benefits are:
1. Retirement allowance which amounts to one period's [four weeks'] salary ...
2. Continuation of Group Life Insurance at company expense (for those who belong to Sears Group Life Insurance Plan), and
3. Annual retiree discount card, as long as present policy is in effect.

The auxiliary or "fringe" benefits indicated above supplemented the two major features of the company's retirement policy: profit-sharing and the more conventionally financed "Supplemental Savings and Retirement Plan of Sears, Roebuck and Co. Employes" adopted in 1945.[34] The latter plan was in line with an increasing popularity of executive pension plans throughout the United States, a vogue undoubtedly encouraged by the peculiarities of federal tax regulations and sharply increased surtax rates in higher income brackets.

The reasons given for the adoption of the supplemental retirement plan were summarized in the following extracts from the company's 1944 annual report:

As Company contributions to the [profit-sharing] fund are credited to the members in proportion to their contributions, and compensation in excess of $5,000 is excluded in determining contributions, this has the effect of limiting the benefits of members whose annual compensation is more than $5,000 to the benefits of members receiving $5,000. Consequently the retirement security of employes whose annual compensation exceeds $5,000 is not on an equality with employes receiving up to $5,000.

The purpose of The Supplemental Savings and Retirement Plan of Sears, Roebuck and Co. Employes is to restore equality to those employes whose annual compensation exceeds $5,000 by providing retirement benefits proportionate to the income in excess of $5,000. This is in accord with the policy of the Company which has long recognized and observed that principle of retirement security that is only recently coming into general acceptance. In keeping with this trend, the plan strengthens the Company's position in industry by adding to the attractiveness of employment to those in the ranks who carry the greatest responsibilities. This group, the store managers, the buyers, and the other key employees of the merchandising, operating, financing and accounting forces will be strengthened by providing a plan of retirement which systematically will keep the force young and aggressive.

The supplementary retirement system was made similar in broad outline to traditional funded pension plans. Eligible employees electing to participate in the plan each year contribute 5 per cent of their annual compensation in excess of $5,000 for the year. The company's contribution for the four years ended January 31, 1948, totaled $6,000,000—$1,500,000 each year. The amount of pension received depends on both the employee's compensation and the length of time he has participated in the plan but may not exceed $10,000 per year. By the end of 1947, 3,695 employees were participants in the supplementary plan; 40 of them were retired and receiving retirement allowances.[35]

In addition to the pension plans and the other financial benefits, including the 10 per cent discount on employee purchases, Sears had adopted (evidently between 1925 and 1930) a plan of dismissal compensation, variously known as service or separation allowance. All regular employees released by the company for any reason other than proved dishonesty or immorality receive dismissal compensation based on length of service.

While employee morale is a function of many variables, employee benefits have become an increasingly important factor at Sears, as they have

TABLE 83*

Cost of Voluntary Employee Benefits, 1939–48

Year	Total Cost	Cost per Regular Employee	Cost as Percentage of Sales	Cost as Percentage of Pay Roll
1939	$ 8,928,623	$158	1.45	9.29
1940	10,971,995	169	1.56	9.91
1941	16,297,366	206	1.78	10.92
1942	17,226,949	237	1.99	11.81
1943	16,736,324	225	1.96	11.35
1944	21,016,073	333	2.13	12.76
1945	24,296,795	351	2.32	13.41
1946	34,639,926	389	2.15	12.72
1947	42,866,621	401	2.10	12.46
1948	52,493,600	442	2.33	13.29

* Source: Company records.

generally in progressive personnel practice. Nearly all the features of the benefit program were pre–World War II developments. Indeed, many of them were of long standing—some, such as vacations and hospital facilities, having originated just after the turn of the century; and profit sharing, which accounted in 1947 for more than 50 per cent of the cost of all benefits, was adopted by Sears in 1916. As the figures presented in Table 83 show, the total expenditures for employee benefits have increased markedly since before the war.

The total cost of benefits was more than six times as high in 1948 as it had been in 1939. This pronounced increase was a result of both more liberal benefits and a larger number of employees. The total benefit cost per employee more than doubled between 1939, when the figure stood at $158, and 1948, when $442 reflected the gains of a decade. The most important single item in the totals is the marked increase in the company's contribution to employees' profit-sharing, which in 1948 accounted for some $20,000,000. Even when this predominating factor is eliminated, however, increased liberality is reflected in a decided increase in cost per employee of 1948 benefits over the 1939 figures.[36] Company policy is kept constantly under review to stay abreast of competitive practice in this regard and to assure Sears's people of a program adapted to changing circumstances.

Company policy during World War II was notable for an extensive system of benefits for employees in the armed forces. A special division of the personnel department was established to maintain records and administer the military personnel policy. Records of all regular employees going into military service were transferred to that division (707-M); by 1944 over 14,000 employees were carried on its rolls (Table 84). During the five-year period 1941–45 a total of nearly $3,500,000 was paid out in "military benefits" for these employees.

TABLE 84*

REGULAR EMPLOYEES ON MILITARY LEAVE, 1940–46

Year	Employee Losses (Leaving for Military Service)	Military Discharges, Rejections, Death	Total No. on 707-M Roll End of Year
1940	244		244
1941	1,726		1,970
1942	7,695	284	9,381
1943	4,365	775	12,971
1944	2,074	730	14,315
1945	1,035	5,813	9,537
1946	335	7,806	2,066
Total	17,474	15,408	

* Source: Company records.

The most important financial benefit to employees on military leave was the maintenance of their profit-sharing contributions. Through 1942 the company assumed the burden of making contributions at the regular rate of 5 per cent of employees' salaries. Beginning with the first part of 1943, this was reduced to 2 per cent of the salary rate. The change in policy was dictated by the large number of men and women going into service and by the uncertainties faced by Sears on account of the war.[37] (For the same reasons company maintenance of group life insurance for military leave personnel was abandoned later in 1943.)

While it was found necessary to reduce the amount of subsidy for employees' contribution to their respective profit-sharing accounts, the company continued its contribution to the profit-sharing fund on the regular basis of 5 per cent of net profits before taxes and dividends. This amount (the "company contribution") was distributed to employee accounts as though the absent employees had made their regular (5 per cent of salary up to $5,000) payments. Thus personnel on military leave were building up their profit-sharing equities very nearly as much as if they were still Sears's full-time workers.

When the problem of military service first became really serious, the company sought some plan of mitigating the effects of the marked reduction of income that often accompanied the shift from civilian to military life. In 1941 a system of income-difference payments was initiated, whereby regular employees having five years' service with the company received the difference between their military pay and their Sears's salary rates if they had dependents. Employees meeting the service standards, but having no dependents, received one-half the difference. As the war continued, the necessity of the military services was such that more and more men having family responsibilities were required for service.

Sears's officers believed that perhaps the most serious and unsettling influence affecting married male employees was the prospect of greatly reduced income attendant upon military service. To combat this problem and to adjust to the changing demands of the situation, the income-difference payments plan was abandoned early in 1944 in favor of a program of "fathers' allowances," an attempt to meet the problem created by the drafting of "pre–Pearl Harbor" fathers. Under the plan the company paid up to 75 per cent of the Sears salary rate with an absolute ceiling of $5,000. This move to provide adequately for the families of men called into service involved payments of over $800,000 in the years 1944 and 1945.

In addition to the special plans designed to protect the family living standards of men going into military service, the company paid all employees one week's salary when they left the company for military duty; and each Christmas of the war Sears's employees in service received a ten-dollar gift certificate if they were in the United States or a money-order for that amount if they were abroad. The *News-Graphic* was sent to all employees overseas and featured letters from servicemen who wrote sometimes to the company and often to their fellow-employees who had organized letter-writing clubs. Catalogues were sent to all Sears's servicemen, and they received their regular discount on any merchandise they ordered.

The direct money outlays incurred by the company in its program for Sears's personnel in the armed forces are summarized in Table 85.[38]

It seems obvious that such policies as continued participation in profit-sharing and the special allowances for fathers must have done much to emphasize in the absent servicemen's minds a continued integral connection with the company. It is significant that 81 per cent of all Sears's absentees discharged from military service returned to the company, whereas the national average was said to be approximately 35 per cent.[39] Clearly the payment of military benefits was not the sole factor responsible for this excellent showing; but the program must have been a powerful influence working toward good employee relations.

During the years 1940–46, 17,550 Sears's employees entered military service, more than the total number of persons employed by the company during World War I. As in other large firms, the problem of reabsorbing these thousands of employees was one of serious proportions, since it involved the criteria of both fairness to the servicemen and minimum disturbance to the established organization. The problem was further complicated by the rapid rate at which United States forces were demobilized. The number of Sears's employees discharged from military service was 649 in 1944; 3,594 in 1945; 9,982 in 1946; and 1,142 the following year.[40] Despite the rate of discharge during 1945 and 1946, the task of reabsorption appears to have been achieved with a high degree of smoothness. Much of this adjustment was accomplished through the advance planning of the personnel department. It should be kept in mind, however, that a major

TABLE 85*

COSTS OF MILITARY BENEFITS, 1940-46

Year	Income-Difference Payments	Insurance†	One Week's Pay	Profit-sharing‡	Father's Allowance§	Christmas	Total
1940							$ 8,085
1941	$44,940	$ 10,187	$ 32,881	$ 53,612		$ 17,830	159,450
1942	12,825	61,578	231,977	314,456		87,543	708,379
1943	92	63,828	155,545	272,296		127,350	619,111
1944			72,821	337,805	$413,189	156,000	979,815
1945			39,906	302,310	445,846	131,828	919,890
1946					69,563		69,563
Total	$57,857	$135,130	$533,130	$1,280,479	$928,598	$520,551	$3,464,293

* Source: Company records.
† Discontinued May 1, 1943.
‡ On 5 per cent basis through 1942, 2 per cent basis from first period 1943 through 1945.
§ Plan in effect since February 1, 1944.

factor contributing to the relative ease of the transition from war to peacetime operations was Sears's expanding need for manpower in practically all classifications, which minimized the need for extensive personnel changes to accommodate returning veterans.

Advance preparations of the personnel department prior to the end of the war proceeded in several directions. Reflecting perhaps the widely held apprehensions concerning the "problem" of returning servicemen, the company commissioned the Committee on Human Relations of the University of Chicago to undertake a survey of the various problems likely to be encountered. Happily, all but a small minority of returning servicemen failed to fulfil the gloomy predictions that had filled the pages of so many popular magazines. The full employment that characterized the years following the war eased veterans back into the normal pattern of their work lives. Nonetheless, Sears's personnel men maintain that their survey was useful both for formulating general policies and procedures and for counseling store managers and other executives.

The management pursued a policy of extensive advance planning on an individual basis. Every unit of the company was directed to make specific plans for each of its military absentees. Each man's background and training were reviewed and his military service evaluated to the end of making the best possible use of his capacity and experience.

Because of the serious attention given to preparing for the transition to peace, and the happy economic climate that made company expansion possible, few problems appeared even during the months of most rapid demobilization. Evidence obtained through morale surveys discussed below indicates that Sears's veterans, as a group, exhibited favorable attitudes toward the company and its management.

Workers' attitude toward management is obviously a factor in labor turnover, which is probably the most widely used measure for evaluating the effectiveness of personnel policies. Prior to the middle of the 1930's no turnover data are available for the company, since not until then was there any specific provision for the administration and evaluation of personnel policies. Unfortunately, no data are available with which to compare Sears's turnover experience, since published turnover data are confined to manufacturing. Nonetheless, it seems useful to examine Sears's experience in this regard.

Between 1934 and 1939, inclusive, average annual turnover of store managers amounted to 7 per cent. More than half of all such separations were the result of unsatisfactory work. Whereas average annual turnover for store managers over the period 1934–39 was but 7 per cent, among retail time-card personnel average annual turnover amounted to 26.6 per cent for the period 1936–39.[41]

This turnover figure was roughly in line with what was generally believed "normal" among larger retail stores, although it was lower than some estimates for larger stores.[42] Sears's retail personnel turnover increased from 29.7 per cent in 1936 to 31.9 per cent in 1937. The following year brought the figure down to 20.3 per cent. Improving business conditions were reflected in the turnover increases in 1939 and 1940, when the figures rose to 25.2 and 26.3 per cent, respectively.[43]

When the United States entered the war in the closing days of 1941, Sears, Roebuck and Company had for the first time closed a year in which it employed over 100,000 men and women, who carried on a business of more than $915,000,000. One of the most serious management problems of the war period for Sears was the maintenance of manpower. The magnitude of the task is manifest in the loss of more than 151,023 employees from 1939 to 1945 inclusive, which implied a sizable task of replacing employees and a constant juggling of schedules and jobs to improvise solutions to problems created by the loss of skilled men in positions requiring supervision and planning. As shown in Table 86, Sears's personnel turnover rates increased markedly during the war period, although turnover was not so high as in some other industries.

Apart from the magnitude of the replacement task, the effects of such instability involve high costs—obvious money costs, and, probably more important though less apparent, the mounting costs of lower efficiency. Each separation from the pay roll meant the loss of a certain investment in the employee and some replacement cost. It is possible that there were further hidden costs due to lost sales and loss of customer good will, although the fact that all large retail stores were facing similar problems probably equalized such competitive disadvantages, and under these circumstances it is unlikely that the company suffered any important losses of this sort. It is clear that Sears's turnover fluctuated for the most part with turnover in other industries. The same factors operating throughout the labor market were bound to influence the company, although there were evidently many firms with more adverse experience.

TABLE 86*

PERSONNEL TURNOVER RATES, 1939–45

Year	Sears	Other Industries
1939	23.3	37.7
1940	24.8	40.3
1941	40.0	46.7
1942	65.2	77.7
1943	68.7	86.9
1944	48.3	81.8
1945	48.5	99.6

* Source: Company records. The turnover is calculated by dividing the number of separations by average number of retail and mail-order employees. The figures for "Other Industries" is the same as that which appears in the company's "Report on Personnel Turnover during the War," which cites the National Industrial Conference Board's *Management Record* as its source.

From 1940 through 1946 the company lost over 17,000 men (and women) to the military services. It is often assumed that high turnover was due primarily to loss of personnel to the Army and Navy. An analysis of separations for the years 1939–45 shows this not to be the case. While the total loss to military service over the entire period (17,000) was very large—representing about 40 per cent of the annual number of regular male employees—the separations in any year on this account were not nearly so important as some other reasons for personnel losses (Table 87).

In every year of the period 1939–45, the most important reason for leaving was "another position." In many cases this was not unrelated to the military service category. The classifications "Another Position" and "Unclassified" probably included cases of movement to defense industries for the purpose of postponing entry into the armed services. The "nonessential" industries would be expected to suffer heavier turnover than those classified as essential to the war effort. Higher wages were typical of the latter group of industries, of course, and, in addition, of considerable importance there was the patriotic attraction of war plants, and the strong pressure placed upon men and women to move into war work. As a consequence of these factors, Sears could not prevent movements of employees into war work, and it was difficult (and often impossible) to secure high-grade employees as replacements.

In addition to the military and "near-military" reasons for high turnover rates during the period, there was the further element of generally increased business activity. It is commonplace that turnover tends to fluctuate with general business conditions, since employment opportunities are improved and since workers have more alternatives from which to choose.

There is the further factor of the increase in the number of new employees hired by the company which causes the proportion of short-service workers to increase, and these are the least stable employees. For the three-year period 1938–40, of all employees leaving the company, 67 per cent

TABLE 87*

REASONS FOR LEAVING, RETAIL REGULAR
TIME-CARD EMPLOYEES, 1939–45

Reason for Leaving	1939	1940	1941	1942	1943	1944	1945
Another position	7.5	9.3	17.0	33.2	30.4	16.5	13.7
Military		0.8	3.9	10.4	6.6	2.1	1.3
Marriage (women only)	3.2	3.2	4.6	6.5	8.7	6.9	8.7
Unsatisfactory work	7.2	5.7	5.1	4.1	5.6	5.1	6.6
Misconduct							
Reduction of force	4.1	3.3	4.6	4.8	3.6	2.4	4.1
Ill-health, retirement	1.2	1.4	1.5	2.2	3.5	2.8	3.3
Unclassified	2.0	2.6	4.1	7.3	14.1	11.5	11.4
Total turnover	25.2	26.3	40.8	68.5	72.5	47.7	49.1

* Source: Company records.

had less than two years' service.[44] It is probable that most of the increase in turnover during the war years was due to the heavy proportion of these new, relatively unstable employees.[45] The necessity of frequently replacing men with women during the war was common, and women were repeatedly hired to replace men in jobs which had previously "demanded" male incumbents. Disturbing as it may be to the male ego, the female replacements did such creditable work that new job opportunities for women at Sears were considerably broadened. By 1944 the ratio of female to total employees had increased from a "normal" of 45 per cent to 75 per cent. It is interesting to note that this also tended to increase turnover as is clear from the separations due to marriage.[46]

While company-wide personnel turnover had declined substantially by 1947 over wartime experience, it remained above prewar figures. Whereas retail personnel turnover was a little more than 26 per cent in 1940, in 1947 it was nearly 39 per cent—slightly above the 37.9 per cent experienced in mail order.[47]

In addition to regular reports on turnover, the personnel organization has used other techniques to check on employee morale and on the level of workers' acceptance of company policies. In the larger stores the local personnel office early carried on continuous spot-checks among employees, but this technique was only as effective as the personnel assistant was skilful in carrying out the program. A second means of tapping employee sentiment was attempted in connection with the suggestion system. A "question-week program" invited the submission of questions on an anonymous basis. Like the spot-check, this technique suffered from inability to get a comprehensive and measurable index of morale, partly perhaps because Sears appears not to have cultivated the possibilities of its employee suggestion system so assiduously as certain other devices intended to promote morale. Extended to the retail stores in 1939 after some experience with a suggestion system in mail order, it seems to have had a prosaic development despite some $30,000 paid out for suggestion awards in 1947.[48]

An ambitious attempt to measure employee morale was begun in 1939 and continued in 1940 when the company engaged an independent research agency to conduct an opinion survey. Thousands of employees in 158 company units were covered at this time—all the mail-order units and approximately one-third of the retail stores. By the end of 1941 the opinion studies had been administered to more than 40,000 Sears's employees. Aware that executives, like most others, spend more time talking than listening and believing that personnel policies are important instruments in the manipulation of employee morale, Sears undertook to find out what employees thought about their employer and the business.

The survey of employee opinion was made by having questionnaires filled out anonymously during working hours. The subject matter covered both "general" and "specific" attitudes. One group of questions attempted to gauge how well employees liked the company and its management in general and how well they thought of Sears in comparison with other employers. The bulk of the questionnaire was concerned with more specific issues at the store, department, and job level. This section of the questionnaire covered numerous aspects of the employee's relations to his job; his supervision, his local store or department's standing on wages, hours, and working conditions; and his fellow-workers.[49]

No absolute standards existed to indicate what scores "should" be on such a survey; by scoring the questionnaires, however, it was possible to compare company units on the basis of their ranking. By this method management was provided with some quantitative index of employee attitudes and of the degree to which various policies and procedures were accepted among employees. Information generated in the survey was used as a guide to the formulation of policy and as an indicator leading to detailed investigation and remedy of situations where scores were deemed to be unsatisfactory. Some insight into the use made of the early survey results may be gained from the remarks of a Sears vice-president speaking at an American Management Association Conference in 1940:

In one department where the morale rating was unsatisfactory, the cause was found to be crowded working conditions. The problem had been previously recognized, but it was just one of those things which was not judged to be serious enough to warrant the expenditure that would be required to remedy the situation. It was "one of those things" only until the survey gave us something to think about.

In one store, this question was asked, "Are you told how you stand with your department manager?" In the best departments, more than 90 per cent of the employees said "Yes." In the poorest division, fewer than half had an affirmative answer. Undoubtedly, in the lower rated departments, the division heads or department managers need further training.[50]

In a very real sense virtually all activities of the personnel department are directed toward the improvement of employee morale—that complex of attitudes which prompts workers to co-operate in the achievement of the ends of the organization. There had long been a realization of the importance of morale in the industrial situation, but in the 1930's management in the United States became increasingly preoccupied with the problem, as workers, profoundly affected by the unemployment of the depression, turned more and more to organized labor. Aided by favorable legislation, the unions took the offensive, and the consequences of the organization drives, coupled with the depression-fathered psychology of American labor, reaped a bumper harvest of industrial unrest. Academic groups turned also to concentrate on industrial relations, and methods of the social sciences were applied in an effort to investigate and lay bare the determining factors in the problem of industrial morale.

A new direction was given to morale investigations as W. J. Dickson and others proceeded with experiments at the Hawthorne plant of Western Electric. Interpreted and abetted by Elton Mayo of the Harvard Graduate School of Business Administration, the Hawthorne experiments attracted much interest, as the investigators shifted from a preoccupation with physical conditions of work to the position that group or human relations is the key to productivity. The monographic reports of the Hawthorne investigators culminated in the publication in 1939 of the Harvard University Press's *Management and the Worker*, by F. J. Roethlisberger and W. J. Dickson. The students at Western Electric succeeded in casting considerable doubt on numerous oversimplifications and preconceptions about the nature of employee morale.

The Western Electric experiments not only developed a new direction to the study of employee morale but produced new techniques for studying the problem. In the methodology, largely built during the Hawthorne studies, Sears found a device it believed would overcome some of the limitations in the opinion questionnaires used in 1939 and 1940. The questionnaires used in the survey technique produced information on the general level of employee "feeling" in the unit surveyed; but the technique held only limited possibilities for discovering the reasons for the level of "feeling." It was to remedy this defect that a new program of "morale" or "organization surveys" was developed during the war in consultation with Burleigh B. Gardner of the University of Chicago, who had earlier been associated with the extensive experiments of the Harvard group at Western Electric Company.[51]

While Gardner's first job was the survey of a department associated with the mail-order division, most of the survey work has been done in retail units since that time. It may be noted here that this has been a characteristic of the personnel development of Sears—the designation of a formalized personnel function within the company was associated with the retail expansion, and by far the greatest attention has been given to retailing. While benefit policies have been company-wide in their application, the emphasis on recruitment, selection, and training have all been directed primarily to retail personnel, with secondary emphasis on the parent organization and, finally, mail order. Not until 1947 does it appear that really serious efforts were made to develop a more effective personnel program for the mail-order units and to integrate mail order more nearly into the program for the recruiting and training of executive talent.

The results of Gardner's first studies were considered so useful by management that the survey technique was incorporated as one of the more prominent aspects of Sears's personnel management. Initially, Gardner and his staff used a somewhat modified nondirective interview technique, which gives maximum opportunity for the employee to talk about the things he thinks important. At first the interview method was used exclusively, but, with the extension of the technique to more numerous situations, it became necessary to modify the method to achieve greater coverage.

By the latter part of 1947 the "experiment" with a combination of the questionnaire and the interview techniques became standard procedure; this made it possible by the beginning of 1948 to cover more than 10,000 employees in surveys conducted in thirty of the retail stores, three parent departments, and four other company units, including one factory. As the survey program developed, the conception of its devotees broadened well beyond the narrow limits which were contemporary with the prewar surveys as was clearly indicated in the remarks of a Sears personnel man to a conference of the American Management Association in 1947:

> The surveys have as their scope the functioning of the organization as a whole and the entire pattern of formal and informal relationships which comprise the organization. Our effort is not merely to determine the general level of employe morale, but to analyze strains and cleavages within the organization which may impede its proper functioning....
>
> In a very real sense, the function of the survey is to assist in "liberating" or "focussing" the creative resources of the executive and supervisory staff.... Various alternatives may be suggested, but in all instances the decisions are made by the responsible executives and not by the survey team.[52]

The survey technique is one of the most novel devices in the personnel program, and its continued use by Sears's management attests to the new emphasis on the human elements in organization. The results of individual surveys have been used as means not only for solving particular problems but also for instructing men in high executive positions on the problem of human relations in industry.

The surveys have shown that morale varied widely among different units of the organization but that, on the whole, Sears's employees were well disposed toward their employer. An analysis of the responses of some 12,000 employees to the 1940 questionnaire revealed that 72 per cent thought that Sears was either "better than average" or "one of the very best" places to work, and only 3 per cent thought Sears "poorer than average." Ninety-five per cent said that they would rather work for Sears than almost any other company of which they knew. Corroborative evidence is forthcoming from men who have been conducting the more recent organization surveys. In a position to judge Sears in terms of some perspective, these investigators have frequently commented on the generally favorable tone of most employee interviews and on the high regard most people seem to have for the company.

The morale surveys indicate that size of organization is an important influence contributing to differences in the level of employee morale. Viewed as a totality, Sears is immense, but operationally the company is an aggregation of units, many of them small by contemporary standards; and the relatively small scale of individual operating units may be counted as of fundamental importance contributing to good morale.

The "activities" of Sears, Roebuck cover a wide band on a "size scale." Whereas the "C" stores may employ fewer than ten workers, the largest mail-order plant employs thousands. Both the 1939–40 surveys and the more recent studies of employee attitudes have brought out clearly the fact that morale tends to decline with increasing size of the organization. Average "morale scores" (using the present scale of measurement) are highest for the "C" stores, which score 58.7. Stores of the "B" class rank somewhat lower, with a score of 53.4; and "A" stores, largest of the retail types, rank still lower, with a mark of 49.2. The morale scores of the mail-order plants are lower even than the largest retail-store types. A "small" mail-order plant has scored 46.2, while the largest unit of the company's eleven plants is characterized by the lowest morale rating, 36.5.

A statement ascribed to President McConnell placed the survey program in the perspective of company thinking on personnel policy and served as well to attest to the central place of that policy in the firm's strategy for achieving its over-all business objective.

In practical, business terms, the aim of all these projects has been to assist in developing a more effective organization. Implicit in this aim is the premise that an organization cannot be effective for business purposes unless it is also effective in meeting the needs and expectations of those who comprise the organization. The projects, therefore, are directed toward building a dynamic, cooperative organization which will maintain a high level of morale and enthusiasm, tap the human resources of men and women at all levels, stimulate the growth of individuals and achieve the purposes of the company because it meets the human requirements of its people.

The approach employed avoids the usual oversimplification of human motivations and behavior which have produced such sterile results over wide fields of business and industry. A far more adequate conceptual framework has been brought to bear on some of the thorniest problems confronting American management today. Thus, while the projects have been highly useful in helping the company deal effectively with a wide variety of specific situations, the greatest benefit has been an increase in the knowledge and understanding of key executives, and an improvement in their skill in dealing with the basic problems of the organization.[53]

The discussion of Sears's personnel policy has necessarily been confined to the course of events in the over-all policy-control department—Department 707 in Chicago, the head of which is the director of personnel. The perspective has consequently been a broad one. The administration of personnel policy in particular units is undoubtedly uneven. In line with the decentralization completed in 1948, Department 707 (Chicago) was left no formal administrative jurisdiction over the territories. The territorial personnel officers, reporting to the territorial vice-presidents, were made responsible for all personnel actions and decisions within their respective areas operating within the general policy formulated by the director of personnel and the officers of the company.

Both General Wood and F. B. McConnell have emphasized the importance of consistency of basic policies throughout all units of the company. Such matters as vacations, holidays, separation allowances, profit-sharing, group insurance, and other formal employee benefits must be the same for all employees, regardless of location. Responsibility for actual administration of these policies was decentralized, but the policies themselves must be uniform.

This uniformity is to be achieved, not by placing authority for policy-making in Chicago, but by more informal means. Department 707 (Chicago) is centrally located and in a favorable position to keep informed on important current trends in personnel problems and practices not only within Sears but in business generally. Furthermore, the head of the department is in almost daily contact with the chairman of the board, the president, and the other officers of the company and key assistants. He is thus able to gauge their thinking and to translate their wishes in terms of specific actions and policies. Not least important is the fact that Department 707 has an adequate and experienced staff of specialists devoting full time to the various aspects of personnel administration. The territorial offices, on the contrary, have only skeleton organizations whose members are so fully engaged in daily administrative responsibilities that they have little opportunity to perform the work that is necessary for any important change in basic personnel policies (see Chart XII).

While Department 707 plays a key role in initiating policy changes and in securing the formal approvals necessary for their adoption, the terri-

CHART XII
STAFF ORGANIZATION

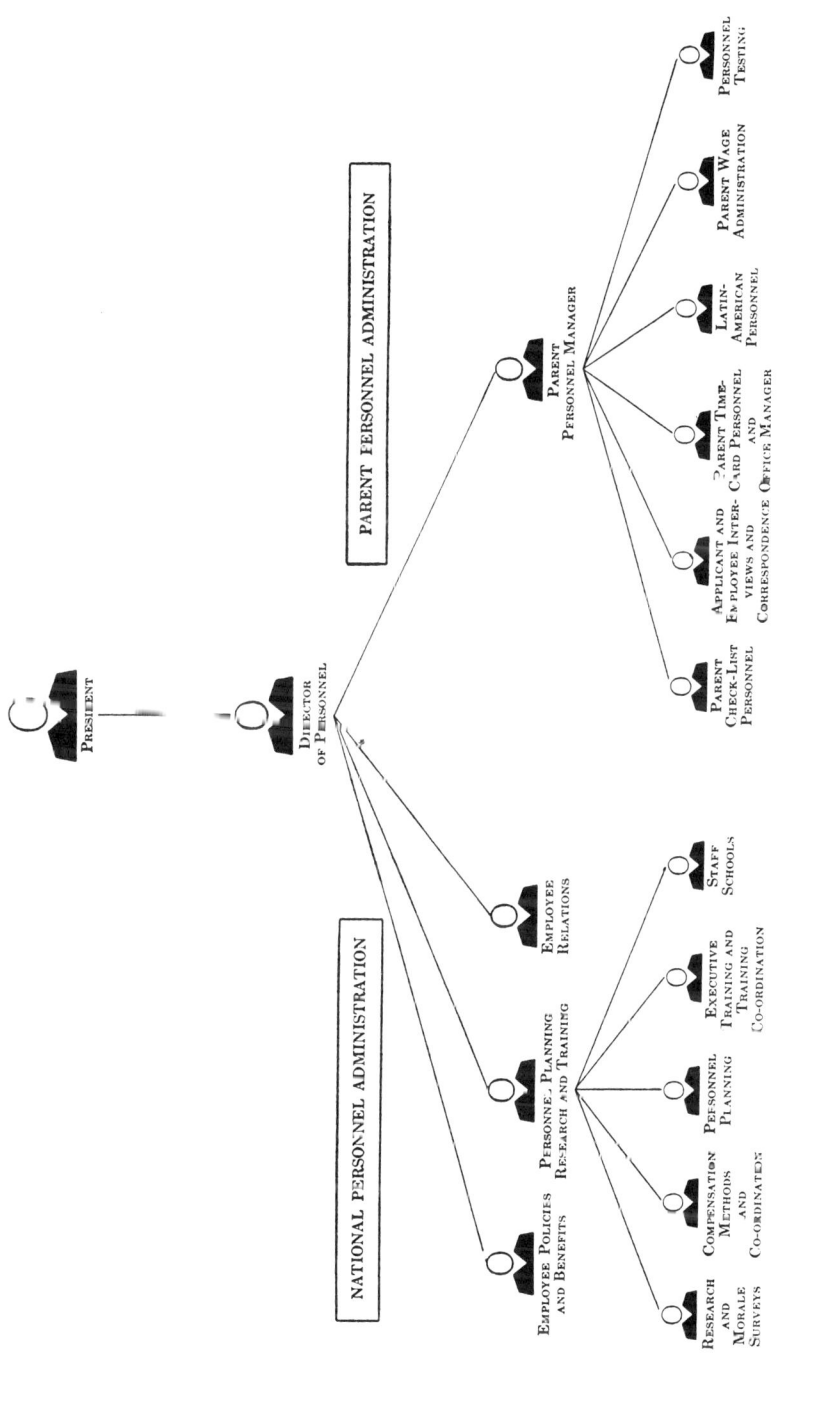

NATIONAL PERSONNEL DEPARTMENT

PRESIDENT

DIRECTOR OF PERSONNEL

NATIONAL PERSONNEL ADMINISTRATION

- EMPLOYEE POLICIES AND BENEFITS
- PERSONNEL PLANNING RESEARCH AND TRAINING
  - RESEARCH AND MORALE SURVEYS
  - COMPENSATION METHODS AND CO-ORDINATION
  - PERSONNEL PLANNING
  - EXECUTIVE TRAINING AND TRAINING CO-ORDINATION
  - STAFF SCHOOLS
- EMPLOYEE RELATIONS

PARENT PERSONNEL ADMINISTRATION

PARENT PERSONNEL MANAGER

- PARENT CHECK-LIST PERSONNEL
- APPLICANT AND EMPLOYEE INTERVIEWS AND CORRESPONDENCE
- PARENT TIME-CARD PERSONNEL AND OFFICE MANAGER
- LATIN-AMERICAN PERSONNEL
- PARENT WAGE ADMINISTRATION
- PERSONNEL TESTING

torial personnel officers meet in committee at least twice a year to discuss all proposed changes in company personnel policy. At these meetings differences of opinion are expressed in the attempt to reach common agreement on the proposals that should be presented to Sears's officers for adoption. Thus by the time new regulations are disseminated it is to be expected that they have already been agreed upon by the men responsible for administering the policy decisions.

In the field of training, the over-all responsibility of Department 707 remained somewhat more direct and explicit. Though responsibility for actual use and application was decentralized to the territories, the development of training plans and materials is an activity which can readily be centralized. Production of sound slide films, manuals, and other training materials is facilitated by the existence in Chicago of a skilled and experienced training staff to perform a service for the entire company.

Long-range personnel planning and research continued to be another field in which Chicago plays a leading role. Sears must give constant attention to the problems of maintaining effective organization and, as one means to that end, must be continually alert for ways and means of improving all aspects of its personnel activities. Here, again, proximity to the national headquarters of the company and the existence of a trained and specialized staff places Department 707 in a position of leadership.

Co-ordination between Chicago and the territories is maintained in a number of ways. There is frequent correspondence with personnel executives in the territories on specific questions. Likewise, the territories are kept advised of the results of various research activities and of other developments of broad and general significance. Another important means of co-ordination is the participation of Department 707 in the meetings of such groups as the Retail Committee, the Mail Order Committee, etc., where significant problems are discussed with key executives from all parts of the country.

Perhaps the most important means of co-ordination, however, has been through periodic conferences. A general personnel conference was held in Chicago in November, 1946, at which all phases of the company's personnel activities were reviewed in detail and a common understanding reached on all fundamental points. This meeting was followed by a training conference in February, 1947, and a personnel testing conference in March. In June, 1948, following the completion of the decentralization program, a national personnel conference was held in Chicago to discuss and clarify the division of functions and responsibilities between the national director of personnel and the territorial personnel officers. Strong reliance is placed on these periodic conferences with the aims both of pooling the thinking of territorial personnel executives and of maintaining a sound and consistent company point of view.

One outgrowth of these conferences has been a request from the territories that certain members of their staffs come to Chicago for training and experience in various specialized fields of personnel administration. Men responsible for training in the territories have themselves received intensive instruction for such work at the parent-office. A special three-week program was recently conducted to train men from the Pacific Coast in the current methods of conducting studies of employee attitudes and morale. A psychologist employed by the Southeastern Territory spent six months working with the Testing Division in parent before assuming her responsibilities in Atlanta.

With the progressive decentralization of administration, the relative roles of Chicago and the territories became more clearly defined. The personnel department assumed the character of a clearing-house to aid in maintaining uniformity on basic company policies, and a central unit to service the entire company on training and related matters. Department 707 continues to exercise an important leadership, the foundations of which are primarily (1) the department's location in Chicago and close relationship with the top officers of the company and their key assistants and (2) the existence of a staff experienced in the various phases of personnel activities and sufficiently free from daily administrative responsibilities to do a long-range planning and developmental job.

Speaking to the personnel officers of the company at the June, 1948, meeting, General Wood summarized his conception of the administrative arrangements for personnel under decentralized operation:

> In the type of organization we have, where so much is decentralized, the personnel department is one of the keystones of the company. I remember some fifteen years ago when we decided to "turn the stores loose," more or less. I said that this scheme would work if we had a strong personnel department, and would not work if we did not, and it *has* worked since. The freedom of action that I would like to see given to the retail stores, mail order plants, buying departments, or any other, will work only when you have good men and good women. It is my opinion that people work better when they are free to express themselves and to carry out their own ideas and then be judged by the results. But, to do things this way, it is essential that we have a strong personnel department. . . .
>
> . . . In broad terms, general personnel policies of the company will be set by the Director of Personnel in Chicago in consultation with the President of the company, Mr. McConnell, and myself. The execution of those policies rests with these territorial personnel officers. That means, so to speak, you will be operating officers. The general policies are laid down by Mr. Caldwell, and he will also take care of coordination that needs to be done. Generally speaking, that same distinction exists between the present Chairman of the Board, and the President of the Company. The president operates the company, and the chairman lays down general policies and exercises supervision over the top personnel.

As Wood indicated in his opening paragraph, the personnel department really emerged only within the last two decades. From a very modest and uncertain beginning the personnel management function at Sears evolved to one recognized as being of first importance.

To implement the over-all intention of recognizing the importance of employee relations, the company has relied on certain particular policies.

Thus it was recognized that the personnel department had to be an important adjunct to top management, and the personnel director was made directly responsible to the president. Further, it became widely accepted that definitions of policy had to be clear cut, and thoroughly understood and accepted by top management, if particular policies were to be successfully applied in the field. This does not mean that operating executives in the field did not have an opportunity to express themselves on personnel methods and procedures. On the contrary, it became accepted practice to "field-test" policies under consideration to get the benefit of the counsel of store and plant managers who can often visualize practical problems of application not anticipated at headquarters. It is believed that such "field-testing" immensely increases acceptance of policy in the field.

It has been felt by Sears's management that policies are more likely to be effective if they are in writing. In line with this, it came to be considered especially important that the reasons for specific policies be explained, where possible, in a personnel manual. To complement the limited possibilities of indicating the "why" of policies in the manual, national and local meetings as well as special bulletins were used. The serious attempt to explain the reasoning leading to specific policies was again an attempt to enhance the acceptance of a company-wide program at the local level.

The company thinking on these matters may be summarized in terms of one of the personnel department's special reports:

1. Management must visualize in broad terms its place in the community and its responsibilities to its employes and to the public.
2. Management must be sincere in the objectives toward which its personnel policies are directed.
3. Individual policies and their underlying principles must be mutually consistent.
4. Policies must be developed on a basis of sound planning and research.
5. Policies must be expressed in writing and carefully codified.
6. Line executives must be educated thoroughly in the spirit as well as in the letter of the policies.
7. The actual application of policy in day to day situations must be spot-checked and carefully controlled.
8. The reaction of employes must be gauged and modifications made in all cases necessary.
9. The importance of the personnel function itself must be recognized.[54]

Basic management thinking had pretty much crystallized on the role of personnel management by 1940. A rather elaborate administrative organization had evolved. These achievements were very largely the results of seven years' effort, since prior to 1933 there had been no company-wide personnel department. What influences led to the new emphasis on the personnel function? What happened both within the company and outside it that might explain the course of events?

Clearly, in terms of activities, the years since 1925—especially since 1933—witnessed a very substantial development of personnel management. The explicit recognition of the personnel function as a special area of management responsibility was the result of forces operating both outside and within the organization. One of the important forces operating within the company was the scale and rate of increase in the number of employees. As shown by Table 88, the number of employees increased more than fivefold from 1924 to 1945.

The overwhelming increase in numbers, more than 75 per cent, was in the retail classification. In so far as the specialization of the personnel

TABLE 88*

AVERAGE NUMBER OF EMPLOYEES, 1924-45

Year	Mail Order	Factories	Retail	Parent	Total
1924	15,153	3,630			18,784
1925	17,267	4,939	987		23,193
1926	17,674	5,555	1,586		24,815
1927	17,927	6,397	2,728		27,052
1928	19,946	5,865	5,973		31,784
1929	25,051	3,757	12,943		41,751
1930	20,680	2,335	13,549		36,564
1931	18,818	1,556	14,257		34,631
1932	15,942	1,543	15,035		32,520
1933	17,515	1,967	24,019	2,121	45,865
1934	16,110	1,981	23,151	2,339	43,581
1935	17,215	2,558	27,220	2,504	49,496
1936	18,724	2,935	34,997	2,911	59,117
1937	18,901	3,346	38,762	3,276	64,286
1938	17,500	2,760	37,781	3,225	61,269
1939	20,555	3,400	45,660	3,046	73,261
1940	22,233	3,213	52,864	4,210	82,520
1941	29,099	3,724	64,968	5,317	103,108
1942	25,401	2,781	60,024	4,745	92,951
1943	29,100	2,794	64,890	3,809	100,593
1944	31,053	2,851	63,898	3,350	101,152
1945	30,580	3,384	65,729	3,405	103,098

* Source: Company records.

function was a response to pressure indigenous to the company, it is important to keep in mind the preponderance of retail personnel. It can hardly be said that the growing personnel consciousness of Sears was a response to sheer size, since by 1925 the company employed almost 25,000 persons.

A study of the available evidence indicates that the successful invasion of the retail field brought with it personnel problems on a scale not previously experienced. More than anything else the necessities of training large numbers of people to operate Sears's stores located in areas physically remote from the parent-organization precipitated the institutionalized training program. Having experimented with the importation of store managers both from Sears's own mail-order plants and from other retail stores, management was convinced that the company must train its own managers if the best results were to be achieved.

The indoctrination of managers was believed to be essential, first, because of their physical separation from the control center. No matter how comprehensive standard procedures might be made, top management learned, after a few years, that the particular market in which each store operated was in some ways unique. Thus, even if the policy of Sears had not been to encourage decentralization, each store manager inevitably operated with an important measure of discretion. These circumstances emphasized also the importance of proper selection of personnel.

The emergence of personnel administration as a major function of Sears's management having waited upon the retail expansion, it is understandable that an ideal balance has not been consistently maintained between mail order and retail. There are probably many reasons for this, but perhaps the most important has been the prodigious expansion in the number of retail stores. For twenty years the mail-order organization was composed of ten plants. Not until 1947 was a new mail-order plant opened. In contrast to that stability, the number of retail stores showed yearly increases. Further, the difference in the character of the operations is such that a considerably higher ratio of key personnel to total employees characterizes retailing. As a result of these facts there have been both greater necessity and greater opportunity for providing qualified executive material in the retail operation.

Apart from the company-wide benefits policy, probably the most notable single aspect of the Sears personnel administration has been the recruitment and training of executives—a task most closely allied with the needs of retailing. Since the end of the war, however, there has been a marked effort to integrate mail-order personnel administration more closely into company-wide activities—a program begun prior to 1941 and interrupted by the war.

The size and rate at which the company grew, especially since 1925, resulted in a necessarily complex organization. The scope of Sears's operations by the end of 1947 included 11 mail-order plants and 625 retail stores (including some foreign affiliates) plus 338 order offices and 14 factories, scattered over a large area. The headquarters organization (parent-departments) operates from Chicago, the seat of major policy decision and control. To improve efficiency in the gigantic task of administering the organization, there has been an increasing tendency to decentralization. More and more discretion was delegated to units in the field.

The close relationship of personnel consciousness to retailing was indicated by the earliest title of the top personnel executive appointed in 1935: "vice-president in charge of retail administration and director of personnel." The vice-president had three personnel assistants who assumed responsibility for directing the personnel activities of the major structural divisions of the company—retail, mail order, and factories. Parent personnel was combined with mail order. The overwhelming importance of the retail organization is indicated by the fact that by 1937 the retail personnel

PERSONNEL MANAGEMENT MATURES

manager had fifteen responsible assistants, while the parent and mail-order manager had but five, and the factory manager only one. The strategic position of the retail section was further marked by including as it did whatever company-wide staff operations the personnel section carried on.

The number of operating units to be supervised and the fact that they were scattered throughout the United States help to explain the early preponderance of staff in the retail section, for an important part of the retail personnel manager's task was that of checking on the application of company personnel policy in the stores. A significant part of the manpower in the retail section was concerned with this kind of follow-up work, as well as counseling local store managers and scouting promising talent. The necessity for providing continuing follow-up to assure proper performance at the operating level was clearly indicated by the results of the morale surveys in 1939 and 1940. The most important shortcomings found by these surveys were said to be defects of policy application at the operating level rather than lack of an appropriate company policy. The decentralized character of Sears's operations thus gave rise to a development of what might loosely be described as personnel audits.

In addition to the problem posed by the inherent character of field operations, there was the further condition of the peculiarities of Sears's retailing as contrasted with other retail institutions. While the Sears stores may appear to customers as being not markedly different from other retail institutions, the internal structure is significantly dissimilar from other department and unit stores. Thus there was a need for providing an organized technique for transmitting information and techniques that were peculiar to the company and relevant to the management of company units.

In an attempt to remedy the inadequacies of store managers in the early days of the retail expansion, the necessity for training was apparent; and the decision to develop managers from within the company precipitated the training program. As experience increased, training was extended to rank-and-file employees. At this level, too, the retail store posed problems which had never been faced while Sears, Roebuck was a mail-order house. The retail salesperson who meets the customer is in a vastly more strategic position than is the order-filler of the mail-order unit, whose work can be more closely supervised and systematically checked.

It has not been possible to indicate very exactly either the timing of changes in personnel policy or the persons responsible for particular changes. But the scale of operations of the personnel department in 1941 was far advanced from that of a decade earlier. Obviously, policy changes are not spontaneous. They reflect the thinking and the decisions of particular men in positions exercising a controlling influence over company affairs. The growth of the personnel organization is evidence of a concern on the part of top management to develop a more effective utilization of human resources in operating the business. This was a function both of men and of events.

Prior to the retail expansion, no consistent attention appears to have been paid to personnel problems. At the turn of the century, a marked exception appeared in the person of Elmer Scott, who, on his own initiative (and under the influence of the distinguished social worker, Jane Addams), developed a (for then) elaborate program of the welfare type. Scott's transfer to Dallas in 1906, and the disintegration of his plan, is typical of the lack of interest in such matters on the part of both Richard Sears and Julius Rosenwald. The inauguration of profit-sharing in 1916 has long been construed as evidence that Julius Rosenwald was early concerned with employee welfare. Undoubtedly, both he and Richard Sears had evinced some sporadic interest in particular workers and their welfare; and promotion from within had long been a somewhat casually applied company policy. However, as a matter of over-all policy there is no indication that much thought was given to employee relations. The weight of verbal evidence indicates that even the profit-sharing plan was as much the child of Albert Loeb (then vice-president) as of Julius Rosenwald.

With the advent of World War I, Julius Rosenwald went to Washington, not to return until 1919. Then followed the 1920–21 depression, which almost engulfed the company. The heroic efforts to save the business did not include marked concern for matters of personnel relations. The chief operating executive of Sears from 1920 to 1928 was Otto Doering, who is remembered by his associates and employees as a man of forceful personality, constantly in pursuit of increased efficiency. Doering had great talents for developing systems and methods and achieved notable success in controlling operations and costs. He was, according to old-timers, less interested in the newer techniques of the personnel management movement, which was gathering momentum in American industry after the first World War.

Much of the credit for the beginning of organized personnel work in the company must go to the "new management" of Lessing Rosenwald, T. J. Carney, and R. E. Wood. When the Philadelphia plant was opened in 1920, Lessing Rosenwald became its head. He took Carney (who was to become president of Sears eighteen years later) with him as his first assistant. The Philadelphia team of Rosenwald and Carney, operating eight hundred miles from Chicago, went about matters in its own way, especially in employee relations. The procedures may have been rudimentary, but the departure was new and apparently not too popular with some of the reigning authorities in Chicago.

From these uncertain beginnings the personnel department was developed under the regime of R. E. Wood, and enthusiastically fought for by Carney (strongly supported by Lessing Rosenwald), who succeeded Wood as president, when the latter was elevated to the chairmanship of the board of directors. Both Wood and Carney held strong convictions that personnel was the limiting factor in the success of the organization—a conviction that may be summarized by the former's previously cited statement: "While system is important, our main reliance must always be put on men rather than on systems."[55] Carney's similarity in viewpoint is made clear in his statement: "In the final analysis the problem of getting a job done is finding the right man to do it."[56] Statements such as these are indicative of management's increased realization of the role of personnel in profitable operations.

These pronouncements point to the importance of persons in profitable operations as contrasted with the earlier preoccupation with things (merchandise and systems) as the determinants of profits. Such an underlying philosophy is consistent with specialization of the personnel function and the maintenance of an activity whose peculiar responsibility is to perform a staff function in the acquisition, training, and maintenance of the labor resources of the company.

However important internal pressures may have been, there were economic and social forces in motion outside the firm that must also have influenced company personnel policy. Every enterprise operates in an environment, some forces of which it cannot control, and is faced with the problem of adaptation. During the decade of the 1930's firms in the United States were exposed to a series of significant changes in public attitude and policy which represented marked departures from the business environment of an earlier day. Nowhere were these shifts of attitude more evident than in the field of labor relations.

The crippling depression following 1929 underlay many of the economic "reforms" of the 1930's. Never before in the history of the country had the economic organization experienced such a precipitous and prolonged depression. All economic groups suffered seriously—investors (and firms) frequently through very low profits or actual losses, farmers through low prices, and workers through lower wage rates but mainly through unemployment on an unprecedented scale. In the face of such circumstances, there developed large-scale shifts in attitude and policy which served at least to prompt a reorientation if not directly to modify management action.

In the area of government regulation of business there was the National Industrial Recovery Act and the industrial codes whose influence on Sears has been commented on previously. In addition to the wage-and-hour regulations of the codes, the desirability and legitimacy of collective bargaining were emphasized. Under Section 7(a) of NIRA, workers were given government protection to encourage membership in labor unions, and employers were enjoined from interfering with labor's right to organize. Following the Supreme Court's decision declaring NRA unconstitutional, the National Labor Relations Act of 1935 restated the right of employees to organize, specified certain employer practices as unfair, and established machinery to implement the provisions of the law. Largely as a consequence of such legislation, and the ravages of the depression, great strides were made in the organization of workers, and collective bargaining was extended to industries that had formerly been impervious to successful labor organization.[57]

Among the industries witnessing the "new unionism" was retailing. Although a retail clerk's union had been founded as early as 1890 (Retail Clerks' International Protective Association), labor organization in retail trade was never important until after the middle 1930's.[58] The retail union had a voting strength of only 10,000 at the American Federation of Labor conventions of the 1920's and but 5,000 at the 1933 convention. The RCIPA (later shortened to RCIA) did not even hold conventions during the fifteen-year period 1924–39.

Despite the fact that retailing employed more workers than any other industry, it was a field long considered ill adapted to stable labor organization. But in the face of favorable legislation, and the general increase in unionism, signs of life appeared in the retail union. In 1935 dissatisfaction in the RCIPA resulted in an aggressive group's establishing a rival organizing committee, which later became the Retail, Wholesale and Department Store Union and an international of the Congress of Industrial Organizations.

The latter group engaged in active organization work in eastern cities. At the same time new leadership and enthusiasm was developing in West Coast units of the American Federation of Labor's Retail Clerks Union. So successful were the organizing activities of both the AF of L and the CIO unions that at the outbreak of war in 1941 each was said to be approaching the 100,000 mark in membership. The strength of the AF of L Retail Clerks was in the West, while the CIO was intrenched in eastern cities, especially New York, Philadelphia, and Pittsburgh.

Organizing Sears, Roebuck was plainly an objective of the CIO union. The goal was to capture first the mail-order plants and to use this leverage to complete the job in the retail stores. The union's position was made clear in the 1942 report of the president of the URWDSEA, CIO, and in its *Proceedings* of that year: "Our organizing work must continue in full force. We should concentrate our resources where they will yield the greatest gains. Signing up Montgomery-Ward and Sears, Roebuck are key objectives."[59] That the promised drive on Sears failed really to get under way was due very largely to the crippling effects on the union treasury of their campaign to organize Montgomery Ward employees. Organizing funds appear to have been depleted in that prolonged drive, and internal political problems of the union further sapped its strength.

The number of organized Sears's employees in 1948 was rather small; an informed estimate placed the figure at less than 10 per cent, and most of the organized units were in Sears's factories and warehouses. A few of the retail stores were organized, however—units located in such highly unionized communities as Seattle, San Francisco, and Detroit. The earliest organization was in stores serving the coal fields of southern Illinois, where the locals were affiliates not of any retail clerks' international but of the United Mine Workers.

Officially the company has assumed an attitude toward unions that accorded with the prescriptions of legislation. But surely it would seem gratuitous to assume that retail unionism was not an important element to be considered in the grand strategy of management. While not the determining factor perhaps, certainly new vitality in the retail unions must be included as an external pressure influencing management policy.

The pressure of competition is always important in the markets for raw materials and labor as well as in the markets for finished goods. It is generally conceded that nonprice competition has been increasing in the markets for finished goods. But nonprice competition has also become of some significance in the hiring of productive services, especially in the labor market. Companies seek to attract workers not only by wages paid but by a whole complex of devices and policies which affect employees. An important part of the personnel department's job is that of developing and administering such policies. In this sense, competition was developing in retailing during the period which saw Sears's personnel department develop. Thus the raising of competitive standards of personnel service in retailing also acted to condition Sears's policy.

All these things reinforced the general social forces that resulted in the New Deal and the particular policies (e.g., social security, minimum wages, and maximum hours) which distinguished the national policy of the time. There was the further, and not unassociated, factor of the political vulnerability of "big business." These were the days of virulent castigation of the "economic royalists." All business was suspect, and big business stood accused. It would be only sensible to pursue policies in such a time that minimized the "guilt."

Employee welfare was surely an area which promised some remission of the sins of which large corporations stood indicted. Of course, the major response to this kind of pressure was through public relations work—but for companies having thousands of employees in hundreds of communities, there is a shadow zone in which the objectives of public relations and personnel relations cannot be clearly distinguished.

All these influences may be presumed to have influenced personnel policies, especially the increases in employee benefits—although the latter would have been impossible except for the profitability of Sears's business. But the role of the personnel department and its evolution at Sears seems in the main to have been the result of a recognized necessity to build executive personnel for the retail stores—and the increasing attention to integrating mail-order personnel activities was largely a response to the same kind of problem.

This primary concern with executive personnel has been especially marked at Sears, and the department derived from it a prestige in the company not enjoyed by personnel departments in many other firms. The emphasis on building executive personnel has further significance in that it greatly influenced the manner in which the department operated. Instead of a proliferation of devices involving direct action at the employee level, the Sears personnel department has worked essentially to influence the whole organization by working from the top down, most frequently by means of relatively informal personal contacts.

C. B. Caldwell, currently head of personnel, is first of all a merchant of demonstrated ability. His experience has prompted him to insist that members of the personnel staff acquire an appreciation of merchandising problems. Sears is first and last a merchandising organization, and the personnel director's well-known record as a successful store manager contributed substantially to the prestige of his department and the acceptance of his recommendations. It is this background, too, that helps explain the unique emphasis to be found in Sears's personnel department on improving the organization structure—as well as the men in it—of operating units.

The final objective of personnel policy is, of course, to improve the functioning of the organization to the end of building sales and profits. Of the company's achievement in this respect, the president of one of their larger competitors said:

It is a well known fact that Sears personnel is ... difficult to pry away.... Sears' personnel is trained from the ground up in company policies and in Sears' enthusiasm which, in turn, is translated to the consuming public, this gives consistency and continuity to the Sears operation.

That Sears has in the course of the last two decades achieved an effective system of personnel management seems clear. The fact that the program evolved out of attempts to meet particular problems rather than as the implementation of any grand plan is worth noting. It may in fact be just that kind of development that contributed to one of the signal improvements hammered out in the course of the company's history—the integration of personnel management with the merchandising and operating activities that are the heart of Sears's business. The company has succeeded in getting personnel work into the line management and has avoided the tendency to create an ancillary activity that in practice tends often to undermine the integrity of the line.

It is probably impossible to identify with real precision the reasons Sears has the good morale that appears to exist. While the techniques that characterize the morale survey program (which are more or less standard equipment of the "human relations approach" that has assumed some popularity in recent years) are intended both to measure and to explain the level of employee morale, it is by no means everywhere granted that these objectives are fully realized.

Sears became more and more personnel-minded, and, in the tack it took in executive training, the company found a potent means of inculcating that preoccupation in the line of executive authority and avoided an exclusive concentration on the "mechanical" aspects of supervisors' jobs. In improving the administration of executive tasks, the personnel department made a noteworthy contribution to improving employee morale. Executive training was itself called into being and sustained by the opportunities for promotion made possible by the continued growth and expansion of the business. The consistently applied policy of promotion from within at once demanded an organized executive training program to serve management's need for qualified manpower to fill the ever growing number of responsible positions and also helped satisfy the needs of those employees who were both ambitious and able to advance. That policy served as well to demonstrate to all employees that they were part of an organization in which demonstrated ability was recognized.

The whole program of executive training is an instance of the continuing process of differentiation that characterizes technically efficient organization, which demands a recognition of individual differences as well as the continuing study of division of work possibilities. The search for technical efficiency thus tends to place a premium on change, and in the process of differentiation evolves various levels of work arranged in some kind of hierarchy. In a sense, the pursuit of efficiency, through these pressures which are constantly emphasizing the differences among people and jobs, tends to disintegration of the organization. Out of that tendency arises the necessity to provide an integrating force that in turn makes it possible for management to strive for efficient organization. It is essential to take account of considerations over and beyond the view of labor as a commodity if management is to capitalize on the motivation that is unique to human resources and is to realize some degree of spontaneous collaboration, for the crucial aspect of management is the managing of persons, which involves some degree of acceptance by the "managed."

In achieving that collaboration, for which wages are of course the primary price, the importance of able executives can hardly be overemphasized; but the task may be facilitated by the use of certain devices among which welfare activities or employee benefits loom large, and which in Sears have been broadened and probably increased in effectiveness because they have been dramatized, a process to which the profit-sharing fund is especially well adapted. Here, again, one suspects the influence of employee benefits on employee morale is registered indirectly. Important as the economic benefits of the various plans may be, perhaps their chief significance is the fact that they are tangible evidence of management's interest in the personnel of the organization. This is not to minimize the economic aspects of the benefits, especially of profit-sharing; they are likely to be the more effective as symbols because they are substantial and serve the better to demonstrate the sincerity of management's concern for Sears's employees.

CHAPTER XXX

The New Opposition

IN THE fifteen years preceding 1929 the United States passed through a war boom into a very brief postwar relapse and thence to a boom of extraordinary proportions from the spring of 1919 to the middle of 1920, followed by a brief but severe depression lasting into 1922, after which came a period of unprecedented but spotty prosperity which waned in 1929, became a full-fledged depression, and reached its nadir in 1932.

Sears suffered far less damage from the protracted depression beginning in 1929 than from the shorter one of 1920–21. In specific terms the company's net sales volume declined from $415,379,987 in 1929 to $355,180,257 in 1930 and to $320,057,397 in 1931—a drop of some $95,300,000 in two years, or roughly 23 per cent. Net income after taxes dropped by more than 50 per cent in the same two-year period, yet the company operated at a sizable profit even in 1931. Net income after taxes dwindled from $30,057,-652 in 1929 to $14,308,897 in 1930 and to $12,169,672 in 1931. It was not until 1932, when net sales tumbled to $274,707,651, that Sears sustained a net loss—of $2,543,651. And the following year brought a profit of almost $11,250,000 on a volume of business almost $1,500,000 *less* than that of 1932. Table 89 illustrates the fortunes of other mail-order and chain-store businesses in the four years running into 1931.

Sears was also increasing its percentage of the total United States retail-trade volume in the depression years. Sears's total annual sales in 1929 were 0.91 per cent of total retail trade. In 1930 the company's percentage remained the same, but in 1931 it climbed to 0.98 per cent, and in 1932 to 1.09. In the following year the company's share of total retail sales rose to 1.14 per cent. (That upward climb was to continue unbroken until 1942, when it dropped from its high of 1.72 in the previous year to 1.59; and even in the lowest point of the war years the percentage never fell below that of 1937.)

Both in terms of its own general profitability and in terms of its competitive situation, then, the company suffered only moderately from the immediate economic effects of the depression. The net operating loss of some $2,500,000 in the one year 1932 was more or less compensated for, in the long view, by Sears's increasing share of the national retail-trade volume and by a cheering proportion of mail-order sales to farm cash income. And indeed even the net loss in that one "red" year was a signal accomplishment in view of the losses suffered by many other retailers.

But there remained one dark cloud upon the horizon, a cloud hardly larger than a man's hand at the time of the depression but a sizable mailed fist before the decade of the 1930's closed. That cloud was the threat of suppressive legislation, directed in the thirties primarily against food and drug outlets rather than mail-order "ogres" but potentially more dangerous to Sears, Roebuck than the earlier catalogue pyres. It was classic irony that a

TABLE 89*

PERCENTAGE CHANGE IN CHAIN-STORE SALES, 1927–31

| | Per Cent Change ||||
Type of Business and Firm	Year 1927–28	Year 1928–29	Year 1929–30	9 Months 1930–31
Mail order	+15.7	+24.2	−11.9	−11.5
Sears, Roebuck	+19.0	+26.2	−13.1	−7.4
Montgomery Ward	+14.8	+24.7	−6.8	−17.9
National Bellas Hess	0.0	+8.2	−30.0	−4.0
Food	+28.1	+20.1	+0.1	−3.6
Great Atlantic and Pacific	+27.8	+8.3	+1.1	−2.2
Safeway	+48.5	+106.7	+2.7	−5.4
Variety	+11.5	+10.8	−2.4	−1.7
J. C. Penney	+16.3	+18.7	−8.0	−9.5
S. H. Kress	+12.0	+5.3	+1.2	+1.2
F. W. Grand-Silver	+28.9	+27.7	+24.4	−1.2
W. T. Grant	+27.3	+18.3	+8.3	+8.3
J. J. Newberry	+36.8	+34.8	+8.6	+5.7
Drug	+47.2	+45.5	+10.0	+5.7
Walgreen	+50.2	+48.5	+10.8	+6.1
People's Drug	+39.5	+37.0	+7.8	+4.4
Melville Shoe	+26.7	+13.1	+12.3	−5.8
Western Auto Supply	+11.5	+27.5	−13.0	−9.4

* Source: Compiled by Merrill Lynch and Company and reprinted in various issues of the *Commercial and Financial Chronicle*; quoted from Edwin Gay and Leo Wolman, "Trends in Economic Organization," in *Recent Social Trends in the United States* (New York: Whittlesey House, 1934), p. 243. Data are for fiscal years.

company that had staved off frontal attacks for decades was to be so threatened by an incidental flanking action.

Sears, Roebuck had hardly turned to retail-store operation in 1925 when it encountered a wave of opposition reminiscent of the earlier attacks on mail-order business. But while the anti-mail-order movement had been vociferous and spectacular—involving the reported occasional great catalogue bonfires in the town squares—the protagonists of the movement had achieved little if anything of permanence. The new opposition originating in the 1920's was prompted by the same trade interests as had fostered the previous attacks. But with more effective organization, greater cohesion, and healthier treasuries, all brought to bear during a period of crippling depression and the resulting sharper competition, the new opposition spawned a formidable collection of legislation designed to maim (if not entirely destroy) the chain stores. Unlike in the earlier era of anti-mail-order propaganda, the fortunes of Sears were not directly responsible for the attacks against chains. The company was, in a sense, an innocent bystander. In its attempts to escape from the problems posed by increasing urbanization, Sears was precipitated into the midst of the fray that was of primary interest to druggists and grocers. Having espoused store operation, however, Sears, Roebuck stood to be as vulnerable to unfavorable legislation as the Great Atlantic and Pacific Tea Company. The opponents did not distinguish between chains selling vegetables and those selling general merchandise.

As mentioned earlier, the modern chain-store operation had its origins in mid-nineteenth-century America. Especially in groceries, but also in drugs, variety stores, and some other lines, chains developed vigorously through many years. It is generally agreed, however, that their period of greatest growth was from 1920 to 1929. It is said that chain sales volume tripled between 1920 and 1927 and that during the same period chain-store units increased from 27,000 to about 100,000.[1]

In 1929 the United States Census of Distribution reported that chain stores accounted for 20 per cent of the volume of retail trade. The activity of chains during that decade is manifest when one recalls that chain-store volume was estimated at but 4 per cent in 1920.[2] It is really not surprising then that, during the decade of great growth, unhappy cries were heard from many sources who saw themselves put in a vulnerable position as new and more efficient competitors emerged in force. Maurice Lee has commented on the appearance and source of the anti-chain-store sentiment:

> The early 1920's witnessed the development of a reaction against the corporate chains which grew increasingly hostile. This attitude originated in the ranks of the independent retailers and wholesalers, but for some considerable period of time was not evident in the public mind. Groups of independent businessmen, representing a militant minority, were able to impress legislators with the political value of their cause. It is, in reality, a mistake in terminology to call this early anti-chain movement a social-control program. It was instigated by any but social motives. Its sponsors were a group more interested in penalizing their rivals than in considering whether such penalization might have a beneficial or detrimental effect upon the public. The significant point, however, is the fact that in the middle 1920's a movement began to control and curb the expanding power of the corporate chain.[3]

The agitation begun shortly after 1920 was unusually effective; legislation was introduced in two state legislatures in 1925. In each year since 1925 at least one state legislature had been host to anti-chain statutes, as can be seen in Table 90, which shows the course of state legislation since 1925.

The first punitive tax bills to pass the legislatures appeared in 1927, when Georgia, Maryland, and North Carolina passed discriminatory chain-tax statutes. In that year thirteen bills were introduced, as compared to only two in the previous biennium. By 1929 the number of such bills increased to sixty-two, and that figure nearly tripled at the 1931 meetings of state legislatures. The anti-chain movement had quickly become a serious threat

TABLE 90*
STATE CHAIN-STORE LEGISLATION, 1925-48

Year	Bills Introduced	Laws Enacted
1925	2	None
1926	1	None
1927	13	3
1928	4	1
1929	62	3
1930	80	3
1931	175	3
1932	125	2
1933	225	13
1934	40	4
1935	163	9
1936	27	2
1937	97	8
1938	19	1
1939	99	4
1940	10	2
1941	45	2
1942	7	None
1943	20	None
1944	4	None
1945	10	None
1946	1	None
1947	12	None
1948	3	None

*Source: Institute of Distribution, *Retail Tax Manual, Supplement No. 2*, October 15, 1948; a total of 1,244 bills were introduced from 1925 to 1948 inclusive. Of these, 60 were enacted into law, and, as of October 15, 1948, 18 of these laws were in effect.

to operators of multiple stores. As Nichols said: "The anti-chain store movement, once started, developed quickly until in 1929 there were more than 400 cities and towns throughout the United States supporting active local organizations formed to fight the so-called 'chain store menace.'"[4]

The adverse legislation was concentrated in the 1930's, as is clear from Table 90. It was such legislation that threatened Sears (and other chain groups) much more seriously than did the depression. Several factors account for the increased "popularity" of the anti-chain statutes after 1930. Most important probably was the depression itself, adding as it did to the distress of retail merchants, wholesalers, and manufacturers. In a sense, the tax laws were make-work projects promised to restore jobs to millions, enactments reflecting simply another variation on the theme of restrictionism that flourished during the period. The chains were accused as fomenters of depression, and it was held that their elimination would introduce a new prosperity.

In monumental collections of economic irrelevancies and impressive affronts to economic logic, documents appeared reminiscent of (but inferior to) many of the mercantilist tracts of two centuries past. One of these stands unchallenged for economic naïveté—except perhaps for some of the testimony presented in the course of the 1940 congressional hearings on H.R. 1. But the author's remarks are useful to indicate the character of the arguments that supported the great wave of anti-chain legislation. He defined the "evil" in the following curious terms and emphasized a unique concept of the "middleman" when he stated:

> The real chainstore evil is not necessarily confined to chainstores. It is manifested in the elimination of opportunities for *middlemen* to participate in the profits in the distribution of merchandise by the so-called direct-to-the-consumer method of merchandising (the term "middlemen" including all people between the factory, or farm, and the consumer, such as lawyers, accountants, carpenters, barbers, stenographers and others who earn their livelihood by serving others engaged in the field of distribution) and in the constant depletion of the resources of our communities by the continuous removal from circulation in those communities of the profits on retail transactions in those communities.[5]

Having developed at undue length the "necessity" for something called the "Florida Recovery Act," the tract continued with the economic romanticism that characterized much of the anti-chain agitation:

> It [the "Florida Recovery Act"] calls for a return to the old American system of merchandising, our old American method of redistributing wealth and opportunity, and our old American manner of maintaining trade balances between the states. It is not only a constitutional measure, but also a taxless one. While it is sufficiently drastic to accomplish the eradication of the chainstore evil, it is no more drastic than is actually necessary to accomplish this purpose.[6]

Although that plan opposed the use of taxes to root out the chains, the wave of protest continued to rely on taxes. And the unhappy depression condition of state finances undoubtedly tended to encourage these measures which their highly articulate proponents made to appear politically popular.

Another factor encouraging the spread of that legislation was the Supreme Court's approval of the Indiana statute in 1931. At last a formula had been hit upon which the Court considered constitutional.[7] After the decision in the case of *State Board of Tax Commissioners of Indiana v. Jackson*,[8] the states multiplied these tax statutes, most of which graduated the tax as the number of a firm's stores in the state increased—the Indiana pattern. Certain variations were introduced by some states, of course, and in 1934 Louisiana ventured into a new combination. That state graduated the tax on the basis of the number of stores wherever located. The Supreme

Court in 1937 upheld the Louisiana statute,[9] which threatened the national chains even more seriously than had the earlier laws.

Of particular interest to Sears (and Ward's)—if the general direction of things were not unpleasant enough—were the laws of Georgia (1936) and Minnesota (1937) which imposed taxes on mail-order units as well. There has been no litigation under these acts, and it is presumed that the Georgia law is constitutional; the Minnesota act has since expired by limitation. In addition to the state legislation, the decade of the 1930's saw several municipalities pass punitive laws, but general acceptance was discouraged in the face of certain adverse court decisions.[10]

It is not surprising that opponents of the chains, finding success at the state level, were encouraged to advance to the federal jurisdiction. The Robinson-Patman Act (amending the Clayton Act), passed in 1936, represented their first successful federal statute. Referring to that statute, it has been authoritatively stated: "The present enactment of Congress, though it never mentions chain stores or their purely intrastate competition with local grocers and druggists is the climax of a long agitation against the chains."[11]

Thus encouraged, Representative Dies of Texas attempted unsuccessfully in 1937 to have federal legislation similar to state laws passed for the District of Columbia.[12] In February of the following year Wright Patman introduced H.R. 9464 in the lower house, but it failed to be reported out by the House Ways and Means Committee and was thus neglected as the Seventy-fifth Congress adjourned. Undismayed, Patman reintroduced his bill, as H.R. 1, at the first session of the Seventy-sixth Congress in 1939. In the spring of 1940 a House subcommittee of the Committee on Ways and Means held hearings on the so-called "death-sentence bill."

The Patman Bill as first presented has been conveniently summarized in Lee's monograph:

The proposed statute provided for a tax of $50 per store on chains having 9 to 15 units; a tax of $100 per store on chains having 16 to 25 units; $200 per store on 26 to 50 unit chains, and so on up to a maximum levy of $1,000 on each store of a chain having more than 500 units. In addition to the foregoing, the bill provided for the complete extermination of all large chains of national scope by an additional section which requires a chain operating in more than one state to multiply the applicable tax by the number of states in which the chain operates.

Chains whose gross annual sales amounted to less than $250,000 were to be exempt, as were those having fewer than nine stores [changed in H.R. 1 to ten]. During the first year of its operation the proposed bill would levy these taxes at rates amounting to 50 per cent of the full stated rates provided. In the second year the figure would move up to 75 per cent, and the full levy would be achieved in the third year after enactment. . . .

Mr. Patman has frankly stated that the intention of his proposal is to drive the large chains out of existence.[13]

The Patman Bill, as its sponsor never tired of repeating, was directed against the large interstate chains. Local chains were to be protected, wrapped as they were in the virtues of "home industry." Indeed, Patman, and the whole anti-chain movement, phrased their pleas in terms of the interests of the local community. Their high-minded activities emerged, they said, not from any selfish concern for the fate of the independent merchant. It was instead, they alleged, their interest in preserving the warp and woof of the American community fabric.

The hearings on H.R. 1 were a tedious display of the resurgence of protectionism and self-sufficiency, spiced by castigations of the "money masters"—the "denizens of gilded Wall Street retreats"—and occasional ghostly overtones of physiocratic doctrine. One cannot resist quoting Mr. Patman on one of his frequently recurring themes—a flight of fancy in the confusing corridors of monetary theory. As a result of chain stores and absentee ownership, dire consequences must follow, the Congressman predicted:

> The local reservoir of credit will be destroyed in the local bank, which will close the local bank. Net profits remaining in the community and deposited in the local bank circulate many times a year among local citizens. I do not care how much the absentee-owned chain apologists claim that they save the people on a purchase in a local community; regardless of that, if they take their net profits out of town, eventually the net profits taken from that town will be sufficient to completely wipe out the local reservoir of credit and drain out all the money and within a comparatively short period of time.[14]

The federal bill was strongly supported by adversaries of the chains, and the testimony of Theodore Christianson at the hearings echoed the sentiments of Patman, with an air of greater suavity, perhaps, but with no less conviction. Christianson's affiliations typified the proponents of the bill. According to his own statement, Christianson was "public relations counsel for the National Association of Retail Druggists; president of the Freedom of Opportunity Foundation, a coordinating group of officials and other representatives of trade associations representing independent manufacturers, wholesalers, and dealers."[15] The Freedom of Opportunity Foundation characterized in its title the battle cry of the wounded independents and in its effects stimulated many letters to Congress and pleas for the curtailment of chains in the interests of providing greater opportunity for American youth.

It must be remembered, too, that the Patman Bill was being considered seriously even after the thirty-five-volume report on chains completed by the Federal Trade Commission in 1934, the final report of which included the following statement:

> To tax out of existence the advantages of chain stores over competitors is to tax out of existence the advantages which the consuming public have found in patronizing them, with a consequent addition to the cost of living for that section of the public. That portion of the public which is able to pay cash and is willing to forego delivery service in return for the advantage of lower prices will be deprived of that privilege, generally speaking, although there are exceptions both ways. It will also tend toward an arbitrary frustration of whatever saving in

cost of production and distribution results from integration of the functions of producer, wholesaler, and retailer. So on the whole the number of people adversely affected by such a tax would constitute a very substantial percentage in comparison with the number adversely affected by present conditions. The graduated tax on chain stores cannot accomplish fully the social ends aimed at by such legislation without producing incidentally these results.[16]

Hearings on the Patman Bill (H.R. 1) were held from March 27 through May 16, 1940. The 2,257 pages of testimony and exhibits attest to the organization of both sides to the controversy. Testifying for the bill were, of course, certain independent retailers, trade associations of retailers, and representatives of wholesalers and jobbers selling to small retailers. In addition, there was a procession—albeit small—of congressmen. And, of course, the National Retail Druggists Association was, next to Patman, the most ardent champion of the "people's cause."

The testimony dedicated to defeating the proposed legislation loomed much bulkier than did that of the bill's proponents, although there was often not much to choose as between the level of economic literacy of one side or the other. The Patman adversaries found the real basis of their arguments in self-interest as often as did their opponents. And the specious arguments of "protecting home industry" were as often espoused by the one group as the other. But the interests of the people as consumers coincided with those who argued against the bill and won their arguments—at least for the time. But in the great array of witnesses for the chains few confined themselves to the basic issue or spoke with the intelligence of Caroline Ware, who stated:

> The end and aim of all economic activity is, of course, to produce and distribute the things which people need and want. This is so obvious that it seems absurd to repeat it, yet the truth of the matter is that it is one of the facts most frequently overlooked. Whereas the consumer interest should be paramount, we who speak for the consumer sometimes have to shout very loud in order to get enough attention even to be heard.[17]

And after referring to her own observation, the Federal Trade Commission Study, and the Twentieth Century Fund investigation, Dr. Ware summed up:

> The evidence seems conclusive that chain stores, along with such other modern methods of distribution as super markets and mail-order houses, have brought real advantages to American consumers, first, by savings in price, partly through allowing people to avoid paying for services they do not want or cannot afford and partly through economies in wholesale handling, standardized displays, advertising, and so forth; secondly, by bringing greater variety of merchandise and more sanitary and attractive stores, especially to remoter places; and, thirdly, by inducing better merchandising methods in nonchain stores and thus affecting the whole system of distribution with which consumers deal.[18]

The chains had indeed learned much since they first came under attack, and the obvious consequences of Patman's measure moved the chains to large-scale efforts to save themselves. In addition to the appearances of certain chain-store executives, their case was stated by "65 witnesses [who] appeared on behalf of agriculture, 46 on behalf of manufacturers and processors, 8 on behalf of labor, 6 on behalf of real estate, 7 on behalf of consumers, 4 outstanding economists and marketing experts, and 12 representing miscellaneous interests, all opposing and condemning H.R. 1."[19]

It is interesting that neither of the great mail-order houses appears to have sent company officials to the hearings, but Sears, Roebuck and Company sent a letter to the chairman of the subcommittee conducting the hearings. The letter briefly outlined the history of the business, pointed out the features of its employee relations and community relations, and concluded with the following paragraph, over the signature of D. M. Nelson, then executive vice-president:

> In conclusion, and without attempting to answer the accusations made against chain stores by the proponents of H.R. 1, or to enter into any discussion of the many different factors involved in the subject of mass distribution, we wish to go on record as being unalterably opposed to H.R. 1, and any form of legislation designed to prevent or interfere with the free intercourse of commerce between different States, on the ground that such action is a blow at the very democratic principles on which these United States were brought into being. It is also our belief that there are already a sufficient number of Federal laws to prevent the alleged abuses of organizations engaged in mass distribution, and that these laws should be used to correct evils which may exist, rather than the enactment of new laws which would seriously cripple and in many cases destroy such an important segment of our national economy.[20]

Needless to say, the chains, including Sears, Roebuck and Company, were seriously distressed about the adverse legislative enactments of the 1930's which culminated in the dismal prospects laid bare in the Patman Bill. The burden that bill would have imposed on Sears was indicated in a memorandum submitted to the Ways and Means Subcommittee. Based on 1938 data, H.R. 1 would have imposed a tax of $12,910,500 on the company.[21] The 1938 net income of Sears before federal taxes was slightly more than $29,000,000. Montgomery Ward, whose net before taxes was $19,600,000, would have borne a tax under H.R. 1 of $16,813,000.[22]

Fortunately for the chains (and consumers), the Patman Bill failed to become part of the federal statutes,[23] and state legislatures became less active on the anti-chain front. Although such bills were introduced in various states every year, no new statutes have been added since 1941. As of October 15, 1948, discriminatory tax legislation was effective in eighteen states.[24] Nonetheless, these chain-store taxes have become an increasing, if not unduly burdensome, part of the taxes paid by Sears, Roebuck, as shown in Table 91.

The discriminatory tax laws of the states, like the Patman Bill, were all clearly labeled anti-chain measures. But the 1930's brought forth also an impressive array of statutes whose objective was no less clear, even though the technique was designed to maim the corporate chains rather than clumsily to kill them off. Such legislation includes the enabling acts permitting price maintenance, euphemistically called "fair-trade" acts, and their companion euphemism—"unfair-trade" acts.

"Fair trading" in the United States had its origins in the statute first passed by the California legislature in 1931 and amended in 1933. In 1935 eight more states, including Illinois, enacted resale price maintenance legislation. The following year the United States Supreme Court held the California and Illinois statutes constitutional, and by the end of 1937 an additional thirty-three states had legalized fair-trade agreements. In that same year the United States Congress passed the Miller-Tydings Act countenancing those contracts in interstate commerce when the commodity affected was to be resold in a state where such contracts were lawful. The popularity

TABLE 91*

CHAIN-STORE TAXES PAID BY SEARS,
ROEBUCK AND COMPANY, 1932–47

Year	Amount	Year	Amount
1932	$ 940	1940	$32,448
1933	2,027	1941	57,975
1934	1,326	1942	61,286
1935	9,171	1943	45,534
1936	13,466	1944	56,455
1937	18,530	1945	67,257
1938	21,344	1946	69,103
1939	22,502	1947	98,542

* Source: Company records.

of this legislation (and the strength and organizing talent of the drug trade association) is evident in the fact that by the end of 1948 only Missouri, Texas, Vermont, and the District of Columbia were without resale price maintenance statutes.

The "fair-trade" laws enacted now in forty-five states permit resale price control by the producers (and proprietors) of trade-marked items. In 1937 the Miller-Tydings amendment to the Sherman Act and Federal Trade Commission Act destroyed the state boundaries as the limits of the price-control movement. As Grether has remarked: "The vigorous opposition of the President apparently had doomed the [Miller-Tydings] act; its final acceptance demonstrated the weight of the pressure behind it."[25]

The "unfair-trade" acts were efforts of the state legislatures to prevent retailers' sales below "cost"—diversely defined in the various acts. The objective was to eliminate the use of "loss leaders" that were undoubtedly used as features by many large-scale retailers. Some states passed "antidiscrimination" laws, but the nature of industrial arrangements limited the effectiveness of state legislation. The Congress passed the Robinson-Patman Act in 1936 prohibiting "discrimination" in prices, discounts, and allowances. The aim was deletion of the buying advantages of the large retailers—department stores and chains.

The whole battery of legislation represents the achievements of the new opposition both intensified and encouraged by the "Great Depression" and its consequence in government—the experiments in "orderly" trade agreements under NRA which had attempted to protect the margins of literally "everyone." Denied the protection of the "self-government" of the codes, it is plain that other remedies were sought. The romantic attachment of Americans to the "home town" and the vast number of independent retailers made the anti-chain legislation possible; and occasional and real indiscretions of the large-scale retailers made such legislation certain. The exercise in practical politics has been noted in Grether's work:

> At the base of the recent movement lie the economic and political pressures emanating from the interests and demands of the great mass of small, independent dealers whose means of gaining a livelihood and security have been removed or threatened by increasingly severe competition. . . . The Fair Trade Laws and the miscellaneous horizontal controls approved by the states, the Miller-Tydings Fair Trade Enabling Act, and the Robinson-Patman Act approved by the federal government are clear-cut evidences of the new-found political strength of small shopkeepers in the United States.[26]

What of Sears, Roebuck? What was the company doing during this period of development of the new-found political strength of the small shopkeepers? How did Sears move to meet the resurgence of opposition and the legislative threats to its very existence?

It is interesting that Sears, Roebuck and Company was almost as silent and circumspect in the legislative halls as it had been some three decades earlier during the parcel-post hearings. But that silence was deceptive, for this time the company belonged to certain trade associations which were alert and active in opposing H.R. 1. Further, Sears had in the depths of the depression responded actively to the new opposition manifesting itself in state anti-chain-store legislation and in the hearings on chain stores proceeding in Washington.

Sears's response took several definite channels. The catalogue was used as an editorial "mouthpiece," to an extent not seen since Richard Sears's heyday, to woo both the public and the national administration. Top company executives, such as Donald Nelson and General Westervelt, were lent to the federal government for special services (the former to the NRA, the latter to the AAA). The company moved to align itself even more closely with farm groups (which groups, interestingly, were later to record almost solid opposition to H.R. 1) and to integrate itself more closely into community life wherever it operated. Even the annual reports reflected the increased sensitivity of Sears's management; they became expository where up to 1931 they had been bare statements of operations, not even listing the names of officers and directors of the company. While much of the new hostility in the air remained largely a threat—even though the most serious such threat the company had ever known—there were sharp and specific repercussions from the Robinson-Patman Act and from the Miller-Tydings Act.

The catalogue's response to the new opposition took the form of seeking to strike a warmer, friendlier tone, to show readers that the great mail-order house had a deep and abiding interest in their welfare and a real knowledge of their problems in the depression years from 1931 on. The catalogue sought especially to impress farmers with the company's close identification with the welfare of that group, by emphasizing the belief that economic recovery could proceed only with a genuine improvement in agriculture and most particularly in commodity prices.

The Sears catalogue in the early years of the New Deal repeatedly pledged the company's co-operation in all recovery activities, particularly those bearing on agriculture. The spring 1933 catalogue, distributed before Roosevelt took office, contained an editorial signed by Wood and captioned "Industry and Labor Look to the Farmer":

> We at Sears, Roebuck and Co. believe that Americans—whatever their occupations or their businesses—must look to the farms for signs of returning prosperity. Agriculture is still our basic industry. Merchandise will be bought, factory wheels will turn, construction work will go forward, railroad traffic will increase, when farm products again command a fair return. . . .
>
> We pledge the support of this company, unreservedly and whole-heartedly, to further any sound plan that, in our judgment, offers agricultural relief—in our own interest, in the interest of the millions of farmers, and in the interest of all Americans.

The company's candid self-interest in agriculture was further illustrated by a chart appearing on the same page, showing the close correlation between Sears's sales and farm income.

The fall 1933 general catalogue carried a letter over Wood's signature repeating the last paragraph quoted above from the spring catalogue and adding:

> Today agriculture is on its way up. Farm prices have definitely risen. Hand in hand with this advance has come a corresponding recovery in industry and employment. . . .
>
> This company and its officers will continue to work for a return of farm prosperity because agriculture is still America's most important industry.

Next to Wood's letter was reproduced one to the General from the Secretary of Agriculture, hailing the company's pledge of co-operation as "a positive affirmation of the interests of business, and particularly your business, in the prosperity of farmers." It was signed by Henry A. Wallace. That exchange of bouquets was followed by a double-truck spread captioned "The New Deal":

We have seen since March 4th of this year, the greatest executive and legislative activity in the country's experience.

Designed primarily for the betterment of the farmer and the wage earner, the vast program of national recovery has gone steadily forward. . . .

Catalogues in those and succeeding years stressed repeatedly the company's concern with the plight of wage-earners and housewives compelled to budget every cent and to cut every possible corner of expense. The big book devoted a vast deal of valuable space to chronicling in detail the company's unflagging efforts to reduce the costs of necessities, particularly of household needs and clothing, and even maintained that Sears was selling many items virtually at cost in order to hold the line against high prices in times of reduced incomes. This editorial content was contained in letters to the customers appearing in each general catalogue over General Wood's signature. Of Wood's "New Dealing," *Fortune* wrote, more than five years after the inauguration of the New Deal:

Wood himself admits to having voted for Roosevelt in 1932 and again in 1936. (He is normally a Republican.) Wood admitted, as late as 1938, to having supported "every reform measure put in by the government" and added, "If the things they are doing in Washington are for the social good, as I believe many are, business must benefit in the end."[27]

The personal tone which Wood injected into the catalogue was also reflected in the annual reports beginning with the one for 1931. In that report there appeared over Wood's signature a letter to the stockholders which outlined the trend of the company's business, the rapid rise of its retail sales volume with some specific information on new stores established in specified cities, and prospects (and great hopes) for the future. Annual reports in ensuing years continued to inform stockholders in some detail of the company's operations, even to listing consolidated balance sheets of the Allstate insurance companies, locations of all retail stores, and even some of Sears's best-known brand names. By 1936 Wood was devoting considerable space to discoursing upon the company's responsibilities—to its customers, to the public at large (community service), to employees, to sources, and to stockholders. Wood stressed as much as anything else the company's obligations to the community and reiterated time after time, "Good citizenship, municipal, state, and national, is a fundamental principle in the operation of this company." That conviction was expressed in the 1936 annual report in these terms:

Your directors, executives and employes generally have been free, when called upon, to accept the responsibility of public service. In its many geographical subdivisions, both mail order and retail, employees have been not only allowed but expected to take part in the interests of the communities of which they form a part, by contributing both time and company money to worthy charitable and public enterprises. Your management considers its stores and mail order plants as an integral part of the business and community life of the cities and towns where it is represented.

Two years later Wood's tone had grown a little more trenchant:

> There has been much discussion in all circles as to the advantages and disadvantages of "Bigness in Business.". . . There is one argument against large corporations which I feel they have too often neglected, their failure to observe their social responsibilities. The impersonal large national corporation with branch factories, branch offices, stores scattered all over the nation, must do its part as a citizen and contribute its share in the upbuilding of each community in which it is located. . . .

In the 1939 annual report Wood stated his own succinct version of the social compact:

> Sears, Roebuck and Co. freely recognizes that you cannot have rights without responsibilities, or privileges without obligations. It recognizes that the rights and privileges of doing business in any community entail self-imposed responsibilities and obligations to that community. These responsibilities and obligations extend beyond the letter of the contract; there is no slide-rule formula for the determination of their limits. They lie within the definition of good and decent citizenship. Your Company has made a sincere effort to perceive and discharge the responsibilities of good citizenship in all of the cities and states where its stores are members of the various communities. . . .

Shortly after the company's delicately attuned ear responded to the temper of the times, with its threat of depression-nurtured suppressive legislation, there developed an episode which bore upon one of its best-selling items and one of its outstanding examples of merchandise development. In the unfolding of that episode, the effect of one piece of such legislation was to strike home hard. On October 19, 1933, by which time Sears had sold close to twenty million tires since development of the "Allstate" brand, the following article appeared in the *Journal of Commerce*:

> There appears to be the possibility that the Federal Trade Commission will be projected into a rather broad study of the question of so-called private brands.
>
> This fact is seen as the outgrowth of a complaint issued under Section 7 of the Clayton Act, against the sale of the product of a nationally advertised company for marketing, under the private brand of a large distributor, at prices allegedly discriminatory against other large distributors.
>
> This case is viewed as a kind of test, upon the success of which may depend the filing of additional complaints against other producers, who sell to chain stores, mail order houses and other large distributors, goods branded with the trademarks of the purchasers respectively, while these producers also are selling their own branded goods to other distributors for sale to the consumers.
>
> It is insisted in Federal Trade Commission circles that the case in question, that of the Goodyear Tire & Rubber Co., involving sales to Sears, Roebuck & Co., is an individual, independent issue.

The background to that story was a Federal Trade Commission charge, inspired by a large tire manufacturer, that the prices at which Goodyear was selling tires to Sears were so much lower than Goodyear quoted to others (including its own dealers) that the contract between the two companies tended to destroy competition and to create monopoly. In hearings spread over a period of two years and held in half-a-dozen cities, the FTC sought to establish that Goodyear's discounts to Sears were from 29 to 40 per cent greater than to independent dealers; that these discounts were not justified by differences in quality or quantity or the necessity of meeting competition; and that they had the effect of "substantially lessening competition and tending to create a monopoly" by making it impossible for independent tire dealers to compete with Sears and still make a reasonable profit.

Sears, Roebuck was in actuality not cited by the Commission; Goodyear was the defendant, but Sears's stake in the hearings was obviously great. Its outcome might well shape the company's policies in buying, product development, and brand-naming. Goodyear maintained that the discounts were not excessive and that the Commission grossly magnified their size; the tiremaker insisted that its normal advertising and sales-promotion expense should not be apportioned over that part of its output (some 18 per cent) which went to Sears, since no such selling expense figured in the contract with the mail-order house. Goodyear further pointed out that it had to pay transportation on tires to every purchaser except Sears, to whom the price of the tire was the f.o.b. price. As for a monopoly on its side of the trade fence, Goodyear insisted that, when its contract with Sears was renewed for ten years in 1931, such other tiremakers as Firestone, Goodrich, and United States Rubber sought the contract.

A factor in Goodyear's winning the contract was one which also helped confuse the question of the size of that firm's discount to the mail-order house. In obtaining the contract renewal in 1931, Goodyear paid Sears a premium in the form of 18,000 shares of Goodyear stock valued at $400,000 plus a cash consideration of $800,000 which was used by Sears to purchase an additional 32,000 shares of Goodyear stock. The bone of this contention between the FTC and Goodyear was whether the amount of the premium should have been charged off as an item of cost in the one year 1931, or pro-rated over the ten years of the contract, as Goodyear insisted. The Commission alleged a "gross discrimination" by Goodyear in the amount of $41,943,007 to Sears on tire sales in the eight years ending in 1933.

The hearings brought out some interesting facts and allegations. The witnesses were, not surprisingly, almost entirely independent merchants. A tire dealer from Joliet, Illinois, described his difficulties in endeavoring to get a higher price from his customers "for a tire of equal quality" to Allstate, the Sears tire. He said that at that time (early 1934) Firestone, Fisk, and Goodyear tires in Joliet were priced about 10 per cent above Allstate. A Chicago dealer asserted, "The whole trouble was caused by Sears being put in position to offer a high-grade tire that forced business their way." A Goodrich dealer declared that, while he needed about 25 per cent gross profit to conduct his business successfully, he had to cut his profit "maybe 10 per cent" in respect to Sears's competition. To meet that competition, the dealer had to stock Goodrich's third-line tire, which compared in price with Sears's second-line tire.[28]

The hearings also revealed that between 1925 and 1933, Sears, Roebuck sold 22,277,029 automobile tires, and about 80 per cent as many tubes. Table 92 (introduced as an exhibit) traces the growth in sales after introduction of the Allstate and the dominant role of the retail stores in the distribution of that tire. The hearing at which that exhibit was produced also heard testimony from a former manager of special accounts for Goodyear that Sears's gross profit on tires bought from that source ranged from 30 to 40 per cent, while the gross profit of Goodyear dealers ran around 25 per cent and on one line dropped to as low as 22½ per cent.

The hearings were concluded late in 1935, and the Trade Commission's ruling was issued March 5, 1936. It ordered Goodyear to cease granting

TABLE 92*

SEARS, ROEBUCK AND COMPANY TIRE SALES, 1925–33

Year	Total No. Tires Sold	Mail Order	Retail
1925	700,916		
1926	1,087,923		
1927	1,791,570	1,238,158	553,412
1928	3,247,463	1,221,933	2,025,530
1929	4,379,667	1,328,516	3,051,151
1930	3,462,858	801,414	2,661,444
1931	3,238,016	630,242	2,607,776
1932	2,525,892	506,158	2,019,734
1933	1,842,724	444,550	1,398,174

* Source: *Wall Street Journal*, February 2, 1934.

price favors to Sears, Roebuck, on the ground that the practice tended to destroy competition and create monopoly. The Commission found that, because of the alleged special prices, Sears had increased its volume of tire sales "more rapidly than any other retail distributor" and that Sears's competition was "a major factor in driving out of business a large number of retail tire dealers." The *New York Herald Tribune*'s story on the FTC ruling added, "The findings have broad implications in relation to special discounts granted by manufacturers to large buyers of goods."[29]

Goodyear announced immediately that it would appeal the decision to the courts.[30] Meanwhile, it negotiated a new contract with Sears, to run until 1942, under which it would make tires to Sears specifications on a cost-plus basis. On July 16, 1936, however, the contract was terminated; Goodyear announced on that date that terms of the Robinson-Patman Act, which had become effective on June 19, made it impossible to fulfil the requirements of its contracts with Sears. The mail-order company then turned to other sources which could make the same tire to the same specifications without violating the Robinson-Patman Act. As a matter of fact,

Goodyear had not made a tire for Sears after June 19. The *Wall Street Journal*'s story announcing the termination of the Goodyear tire contract asserted:

> Although no current figures are available, the special brand tires manufactured by Goodyear and sold by Sears, Roebuck by mail order and through its retail stores have from 1926 ranged between 2.8% and 9.6% of the total tire replacement market in individual years. . . .
>
> In addition to the impact on Goodyear's business, the significance of the termination rests in its possible repercussions on comparable contracts held by other companies in the tire industry and other fields. The Goodyear–Sears, Roebuck relationship . . . is believed to have figured prominently in the drafting of the Robinson-Patman measure as an outstanding example of practices against which the bill is directed. . . .
>
> . . . from the start of the contract in 1926 through 1932 the dollar volume of this Sears business was $122,000,000 as compared with Goodyear's total sales of $1,400,000,000 over this period. Goodyear's net profit from its Sears business during these years was placed at about $6,000,000 while the amount of fixed overhead expense absorbed was placed at $8,000,000 and the raw material inventory losses absorbed at $4,000,000. . . .
>
> It has been frequently predicted following the passage of the Robinson-Patman bill that it would tend to force manufacturers into two groups, one serving the large distributors of the country, with consequent real saving in various costs due to the fewer and more substantial accounts on the books, and the other serving numerous small distributors. Sears' new sources of tire supply are understood to number three or four instead of one as formerly, and presumably they belong to the manufacturing group which will serve large distributors.[31]

While Sears, Roebuck was still adjusting its tire purchasing to the new situation created by the Robinson-Patman Act, it found itself somewhat harassed by the type of state legislation which sought to vitiate its "low-price policy" on trade-marked items—the "fair-trade" laws. In April, 1937, the company abruptly announced it could no longer accept mail orders or orders from retail-store catalogue desks on nearly six hundred items listed in the catalogue. One newspaper reported that step in this fashion:

> Fair trade laws adopted by Illinois, Pennsylvania, California, Washington, and Tennessee permit manufacturers of trademarked merchandise to set minimum retail prices on such items within the boundaries of the State. Some of the articles in the catalog are priced below these minimums. Thus retail and mail order stores in these States cannot accept orders on these items for delivery at catalog prices. Therefore, in order to avoid complicated handlings, Sears have decided to discontinue selling such merchandise in Pennsylvania and the other four states until the issuance of the fall and winter general catalog—at which time price adjustments will be made or the numbers eliminated.[32]

When that fall and winter 1937 catalogue appeared, early in August, it contained a strong attack on price maintenance laws, then in effect in forty-one states. The chief effect of that legislation on Sears appears, of course, to have resided in its drug and cosmetics department—ample testimony of the source of the legislation. Items in that department included a large number of trade-marked products whose price was fixed by the manufacturers; under each such product appeared the notation, "Price fixed by state law. See page 819." The message on that page stated, in part:

> If you are interested in buying quality merchandise at money-saving prices (and who isn't?) ... we suggest and recommend that you ... buy Sears' own guaranteed products at prices not fixed under state laws.
>
> Recent laws enacted by most states now permit the manufacturer of trade-marked articles to fix the minimum retail price you must legally pay for his goods in intrastate transactions in such states.
>
> We have, therefore, no alternative in such cases but to quote the minimum price permitted by state law for intrastate shipments. . . .
>
> We can and do, however, offer articles of highest quality, laboratory tested and approved, under our own trade names at decided savings in cost.

Just about two weeks after that catalogue went into the mail, President Roosevelt reluctantly signed the Miller-Tydings Act, allowing similar control of resale prices on trade-marked articles in *interstate* commerce. Sears refused to surrender meekly to the advancing wave of price maintenance. Instead, in some subsequent catalogues, it utilized a combination of the "sour-grapes" and "sweet-lemon" approach, interlarded with overtones of the technique Richard Sears had once used when manufacturers refused to sell him their goods and thus compelled him to "bootleg" them. The catalogue made a point of listing price-fixed drugs and other goods in immediate juxtaposition to Sears's own product, to capitalize upon the company's lower prices. Sweet were the uses of adversity.

At the same time, however, the company's top management realized that a favorable climate of public opinion was of little avail to stem the onslaught of suppressive legislation, for an impressive array of public opinion had been insufficient to turn back the skilfully led and well-organized advocates of the price maintenance legislation. (President Roosevelt himself had in vain thrown the tremendous weight of his office and popularity against the Miller-Tydings Bill.) Sears seemingly concluded that its basic buying program, which would enable it to skirt much of the price maintenance legislation, had become as necessary as it had earlier been simply advisable. It is not surprising to find that that program was accordingly accelerated after 1937.

While, as reported earlier, the Patman Bill never became law, its failure of passage offered scant encouragement to Sears, for a survey by the Opinion Research Corporation, undertaken at the company's suggestion and released in November, 1939, had showed that 45 per cent of the public favored levying upon chains specific taxes not levied upon other distributors, even though "only" 6 per cent favored *elimination* of chain stores. Much of that public was in the cities, and the rest of course in towns and on the land. The company bestirred itself more vigorously than ever before to integrate itself, through its store managers and other representatives, into each community; to discharge its obligations of citizenship; to become everywhere "local" instead of "foreign"; to root itself in the country which had nurtured it so well.

CHAPTER XXXI

Public Relations: Scholarships and Special Services

LONG before the phrase "public relations" became intrenched in the American vocabulary as a description of an increasingly important phase of big business, Richard Sears was practicing the art with a skilled hand and on a large scale. The business he hoped to (and eventually did) build called for many customers, and he exerted himself to effect close and warm relations with those customers. His winning catalogue editorials, the unflinching execution of the guaranty on which his business rested, his "Send No Money" campaign, his Customers' Profit-sharing Premium Plan—none of these could completely be divorced from public relations, even though their primary function was that of sales promotion. And the overt, organized hostility of the independent retailers of the country compelled Richard Sears to go well out of his way to win as many friends as possible for his business.

Julius Rosenwald's philanthropies, beginning in earnest at about the time Sears resigned as president, also fulfilled one of the primary missions of any public relations program by reaping favorable publicity in which the name of the great mail-order house inevitably appeared. Rosenwald did not preoccupy himself in his philanthropies with assistance to farmers, as the company's formalized public relations program was later to do, nor did he seem often to take overt cognizance of the continuing hostility of local merchants to his business.

Yet one of his earlier gestures, made in the name of the company (which paid the bills involved), could certainly appear tailored to order both to win friends among farmers by bettering their lot and to allay (or at least to help overcome) the merchants' opposition. For in May, 1912—when the hearings on the parcel post had brought the opposition to mail-order houses before the powerful sounding board of congressional committees—Rosenwald announced an offer of $1,000 to each county in the United States which would raise enough additional money to employ a trained agricultural expert for that county.

Company records show a total of $110,000 expended for this project, under the heading "Crop Improvement": $19,000 in 1912 and $91,000 in 1913. The 110 participating counties were in Illinois, Wisconsin, Iowa,

Indiana, Ohio, and Michigan. There is no record of any company expenditure under this heading for the years after 1913; the Smith-Lever Act, passed by Congress in 1914 and providing federal grants to match state funds for the purpose of employing expert agricultural agents appeared to mitigate the need for Sears, Roebuck's program.

It cannot, however, be claimed that any of Richard Sears's or Julius Rosenwald's acts constituted anything even bordering upon an organized public relations program. Sears's approach was essentially to win friends by his warm approach and by proclaiming that he gave people "the biggest bunch for the dollar"; while Rosenwald's philosophy—certainly as it applied to business—was to sell goods, honestly and fully described, at fair prices. After the 1912 offer the company took no more dramatic steps having public relations overtones for a decade. The times were so prosperous for the company that its main concern came to be securing enough goods to fill all orders. And in that period of great prosperity the opposition of independent retailers subsided considerably, since they too found their lot improved.

By 1923, however, at least two things were certainly clear to the company: (1) the farmers had fallen on evil days indeed during the 1920–21 depression, and their income was reduced sharply; and (2) a great many of the countless independent merchants whose businesses had failed in that depression, as well as those who survived but with reduced profits, tended to hold the great mail-order houses responsible for the decline in their fortunes. The company itself was by 1923 pulling out of the seemingly bottomless pit into which it had fallen two years earlier, but the aftereffect of the fright was still present.

It was manifest that the precipitous decline in the prices of farm commodities in 1920 and 1921 had been a signal factor in the company's net loss of more than $16,000,000 in the latter year. It was obviously desirable to help increase the farmer's income and to do it in such a way that Sears, Roebuck would profit by receiving an increasingly larger percentage of farm cash income in its mail-order sales.

The Agricultural Foundation, operating under the general advertising manager, was chartered in 1923, with the avowed objective of helping the farmer "farm better, sell better, and live better." Its pledged purpose was "aid to farmers, and cooperation with all recognized agencies, Governmental, semi-official and private, which work toward that end." The Foundation was organized on a "for-profit" basis and represented an attempt to mobilize the company's contacts and resources for the educational, social, and financial advancement of rural people. In addition to various contests, through which the Foundation hoped to spotlight certain problems and to suggest solutions for them, the most extensive and ambitious activity in the organization's first years was its crop intelligence service. With the Department of Agriculture and the land-grant agricultural colleges, the Foundation's publicity division was another, though less extensive, influence for the education of the average farmer in the economics of his business.

Few things are more important to swine growers, for example, than the corn-hog ratio. A farmer raising both has to know whether it is more profitable to sell his corn outright as grain or to feed it instead to his pigs and eventually sell it in the form of pork. The question is simply one of how far the individual farmer should carry his "manufacturing" process toward the ultimate consumer. Statisticians have often come up with the answers—the famous corn-hog ratio—in statistical and graphic form not readily comprehensible to the average farmer. The Foundation, on the other hand, translated this information into "dirt farmer's language" and distributed it through the press of the nation. The Foundation's pictorial charts and accompanying text gave the farmer a clear, relatively complete, but succinct picture of the price trends of livestock and grains and the ratios between them.

The Foundation's Farm Service Division was designed to serve the individual farm family in an individual way. Counselors advised by mail on the best ways to cure a cow of milk fever, to destroy a bug which was itself destroying beans, to safeguard a child against rickets, to match colors for a hat, and just about anything else within reason that a member of a farm family needed to know. The Farm Service Division was abolished, some twenty years ago, when the expanded activities of the Extension Service of the United States Department of Agriculture took over the same type of work on a much larger scale.

One of the primary initial responsibilities of the Agricultural Foundation was to be the operation of the radio station the company was then building and, through that station, to assist the farmers with crop and weather intelligence, marketing information, education, and entertainment. The radio station opened on April 12, 1924, with the call letters "WLS"—the "World's Largest Store." The original 500 watts was increased to 5,000 in 1925. The station began sending on its new wattage on November 1, 1925. WLS was called, by its staff members and by many of its listeners, the "shirt-sleeve station." Informality was the keynote, and programming kept the farmer foremost in mind.

There was considerable opposition within the company to the venture into radio. Vice-Presidents Doering and Adler reputedly opposed the scheme. Rosenwald was reportedly lukewarm over the station, while C. M. Kittle supported it strongly. Yet, in view of Rosenwald's indifference and the opposition of Adler and Doering, it is rather difficult to understand how the station actually came into being, more than six months before Kittle joined the company. Whatever the answer, Kittle continued to support WLS, even after the cost of the operation reached sizable proportions.

The station refused to sell advertising time, since almost any potential advertiser would have been a competitor of the company. There was therefore no visible revenue from the station, as there was from the catalogue, even though, not surprisingly, the station management insisted that the radio operation was selling hundreds of thousands of dollars worth of merchandise.

In addition to the WLS operation, the Agricultural Foundation established a radio service on Station WSB, in Atlanta, Georgia, where it maintained a staff of its own to conduct the Sears part of the program and to answer all mail from listeners. This arrangement cost the company about $45,000 annually. Similar arrangements were made with stations in Kansas City, Dallas, Memphis, and St. Paul, with the cost running around $45,000 a year for each. Over and above this outlay of approximately $225,000 annually, the company was spending about $500,000 a year to operate WLS; a total outlay, in other words, of almost $750,000 a year on which it was impossible to estimate accurately any return in the way of increased sales volume. In the summer of 1928 after the death of the station's strongest supporter in high place, C. M. Kittle—the company decided to liquidate its radio operation entirely and to sell WLS.

The utilities magnate, Samuel Insull, then still building his empire, sought to purchase WLS. Insull owned a station (WENR) which operated on the same wave-length as WLS but had only two-sevenths of the allotted broadcasting time, with the other five-sevenths of the time allocated to WLS. Possession of WLS would have given Insull a clear wave length. Julius Rosenwald felt, however, that Insull did not have the facilities or the inclination to continue WLS as a radio station devoted to the interests of the farmer. It was further feared that Insull might use the station to further his very active stock-selling campaign for his various utilities, which might eventually backfire against the company as the former owner of the station.

After some negotiation, the station was finally sold to the *Prairie Farmer*, an Illinois state farm magazine which was long on farm talent but short on funds. The insistence by *Prairie Farmer* that it wanted to continue the station on the same plane and with the same orientation won the company over. Sears, Roebuck's actual investment in the station was at least $158,068.20, according to all records available, and the good will (in the opinion of many of its staff members) worth considerably more. It was agreed, however, to sell WLS for $225,000, which gave the *Prairie Farmer* 51 per cent of the stock of WLS, with an option to buy the remaining 49 per cent at the same price as the 51 per cent. The terms were $10,000 down and the balance to be paid over twenty years. The company then capped even these easy terms by agreeing to advance the *Prairie Farmer* $12,000 a month for six months to help the new owner get started.

The new management (actually the same management as far as personnel went, since most of the staff simply moved over to the *Prairie Farmer* building and continued the same duties) organized an advertising staff, and WLS became an almost immediate financial success. The new owner was able to pay off the remaining $215,000 owed for 51 per cent of the stock by the summer of 1934, and on October 1 of the same year to purchase the other 49 per cent in one lump sum. Men who worked at WLS while Sears, Roebuck owned it point to this financial accomplishment as evidence that the company itself could have operated WLS profitably on a commercial basis while still using it to make friends. Be that as it may, the company retired from the radiobroadcasting field, apparently for good.

During the period of its operation by Sears, WLS had served to promote a variety of efforts, ranging from general humanitarian projects to advertising special company activities. The station raised large sums of money (more than $200,000 in one instance) for disaster relief after storms and tornadoes, issued highly successful appeals for toys and money for needy children at Christmas, and performed many other functions now lumped together in the trade as "Pican" ("public information, convenience, and necessity," as outlined by the Federal Communications Commission).

In 1925 the company concluded that some of its customers and potential customers needed a service more specific in nature than that offered by the radio station. Some trappers had written the company to complain that they could not get fair grading of their pelts from their local raw-fur dealers, from traveling buyers who canvassed the country, or from consignment houses located in the larger cities. Whether the fur-buyers were actually giving the trappers a "fair deal," the fact remained that many trappers thought not. The company decided that it would be sound business to help all trappers increase their income from that source, since the company would reasonably expect a proportionate share of any increased purchases of merchandise. In 1925 Sears, Roebuck announced the establishment of its Raw Fur Marketing Service, which would dispose of trappers' pelts at the best possible prices at no charge to the trappers. At the outset only the good name and reputation of the company stood behind that new service. Grading is admittedly a somewhat arbitrary procedure, and market prices for furs not infrequently fluctuate sharply. The trapper would just have to take Sears, Roebuck's word that his furs had been graded honestly and marketed at the best possible price. Trappers took that word with alacrity and sent in their furs. Sears, Roebuck actually supplied only its name to the plan; all operations were performed by an outside organization. Even today, only three employees of the Fur Marketing Service are on Sears, Roebuck's pay roll. Yet all communications have been handled in the company's name, all drafts issued by (or at least on) the company, and no other organization's name has ever appeared in connection with the fur service.

The company soon began issuing booklets to teach trappers more about all phases of the fur business. *Tips to Trappers* (by "Johnny Muskrat") has been distributed by the millions (some seven million copies had been mailed by mid-1946). The booklet shows the right and wrong ways of almost every operation in trapping (Sears, Roebuck, of course, sells traps and related equipment) and pictures of prize pelts and prize-winning trappers.

In 1929 the company decided to dramatize the advantage of proper pelt preparation by staging a national fur show, which has since become an annual event. Cash awards now exceed $7,500 at each show, $2,000 cash going to the owner of the best-prepared pelt (chosen from among the daily award-winning pelts). To encourage large shipments throughout the trapping season, prizes are also given for the best-prepared shipments of five or more pelts (all awards being, of course, additional to the market value of the pelts concerned). By 1946 more than $100,000 had been distributed in awards.

Today the Raw Fur Marketing Service claims to receive more furs direct from trappers than is collected through any other source in the world. Enthusiastic patronage by trappers has long since shown their confidence in the company's handling. A survey has found that approximately 67 per cent of those who send furs to Sears are indexed mail-order customers, and it is believed that a reasonable percentage of the others are customers of the company's retail stores, although no figures are available. Fur shippers are encouraged to attach orders for merchandise with their furs, the cost of the order to be deducted from the value of the pelts. Some trappers even have their time payments deducted from the value of their fur shipments. And, finally, the company has found that many of the drafts it sends trappers for furs are cashed at Sears's retail stores.

By June, 1946, twenty-one years after its establishment, the Raw Fur Marketing Service had handled four million fur shipments from forty-eight states and had paid out Sears's drafts to trappers to the value of $45,000,000. This activity falls in a special and rather anomalous category: it is classified by the company as a straight sales-promotion plan under the advertising department, despite its strong overtones of special service (its profit-making features preclude its falling under the Sears, Roebuck Foundation). The fur marketing service is included in public relations here as a striking example of how good public relations policies can be and are applied to a straight sales-promotion device.

An adjunct to this activity is the Raw Wool Marketing Service, inaugurated in 1929 and operated through the same concessionaire and along lines identical with the fur service. Under the wool program, the company markets raw wool in the summer months at Chicago and Dallas. The wool service does not operate in all states, as does the fur service, nor does it operate on anything like the same scale. During the first sixteen years of the wool marketing service, the company handled about 50,000 shipments totaling about 13,000,000 pounds of wool, for which Sears's drafts of more than $3,000,000 were issued. Government controls on wool marketing beginning with World War II somewhat limited this activity of the company, but the wool service continues to operate.

In 1930 the Dressed Poultry Marketing Service was instituted for the benefit of poultry shippers in North and South Dakota and Montana. As with the fur and wool services, this one was inspired by growers who complained that they were at the mercy of commission houses and agents and had no recourse against low prices, improper grading, and similar practices. The company offered poultry raisers a guaranty of one-half cent per pound above the market price, with a handling charge of 4 per cent deducted from the shipper's return on his poultry. The charge is used to defray costs; Sears makes no profit on this activity.

In the first sixteen years of operation, 25,949 shipments were received, for which the raisers were paid $1,115,178.87. (In 1945–46 the program was extended to include all of Minnesota and a greater area in South Dakota.) The only advertising is an announcement folder sent each year to post-office and Star Route boxholders in the areas served. A 1943 survey of thirteen hundred poultry shippers showed that each received an average of $106 from Sears for poultry shipments that year. A separate survey by the Minneapolis mail-order plant in the same year revealed that 90 per cent of the poultry shippers were indexed as "preferred" customers.

A Foundation investigation in 1925 led to the belief that the seed corn of the nation was in poor condition, which meant resultant poor yields for corn planters. In order to dramatize that belief and to persuade farmers to test their seed corn before planting, the Foundation conducted a national seed-corn show. The best ear of corn from the 27,411 entries brought its owner a cash prize of $1,000, with lesser awards for runners-up. Every ear submitted was tested for vitality and for disease, with a report made to the grower. The vast amount of information so obtained was classified by states and by counties and was made available to the public.

During the fall of 1925 the Agricultural Foundation gathered a herd of baby beef cattle to attempt a dramatic demonstration of the return of beef cattle to a place of economical production on the average farm. The demonstration sought to show young people on farms how to produce 1,000 pounds of beef from one cow in one year.

By 1927 the company's retail expansion had begun to gather momentum, and plans had already been made for even more rapid expansion along this line in the forthcoming two years. The growing importance of the retail stores and the desire to exploit their openings for publicity purposes, as well as to orient the stores to their communities, led to the formal establishment in 1927 of a public relations department. The first director of public relations was the chief announcer of Station WLS. One former executive of the company attributes his appointment to the belief that "if he hadn't gotten the company in trouble in two years on the air, he probably had a fair chance of success."

In addition to his instructions to "keep the company out of trouble," the public relations director was further admonished to utilize no publicity which was not in "good taste." The director was active in promoting publicity for the new retail stores which began to spread across the country, the additional mail-order plants which were established, and various other activities of the company. But it was not until the mid-thirties that all public relations activities were centralized in one department, under E. J. Condon, who, as assistant to the president, is still director of public relations. Even before that consolidation, however, public relations was intermeshing its activities closely with those of the Agricultural Foundation.

In 1928 the Foundation executed an extension of its 1925 seed-corn show by sponsoring a national single-stalk cotton show in the South. Again the object was to increase the farmers' income by encouraging him to improve his product, in the certain knowledge that the company itself would eventually profit therefrom. Sears's farm experts were convinced that the single stalk was the basis of all successful cotton production and that no cotton acreage would yield a better return than the average of its fruited stalks. Working with the United States Department of Agriculture and the National Fertilizer Association, the company offered a prize list aggregating $10,000 in awards to farmers submitting the best single stalks of cotton. The show, open to every farmer in the country, resulted in the largest exhibition of cotton ever held, with more than 20,000 entries.

The cotton show was followed in 1929 by a national canning contest, which likewise included cash prizes and which brought some 43,000 entries from farm women. The succeeding years, with the exceptions of 1931–32 at the worst of the depression, saw a series of similar national contests. In 1930 it was the 4-H Club scenario-writing contest, which brought some 2,000 entries. In 1930 a "Home Beautiful" competition yielded a record 150,000 entries. The Century of Progress quilting contest in 1933 counted 17,000 entries, while 102,000 aspirants competed in the Century of Progress national baby contest the following year.

Both these latter competitions were held in connection with the Sears, Roebuck building and exhibit at the Chicago Century of Progress, which in itself represented an ambitious public relations campaign. The strikingly modernistic building housed a history of merchandising in ten dioramas, exhibits of prize-winning quilts and furs, photographs of thousands of babies entered in that contest, demonstrations of catalogue-making and merchandise testing, lectures on child care, restrooms, restaurants, lounging rooms, free checking facilities, telephones, telegraph offices, an information desk, a travel department, and other attractions and conveniences. Booklets recounting the history of the company in glowing terms were distributed broadside.

In 1935 the company's national "Make It Yourself" contest drew 46,000 entries. In that same year the company offered a 4-H clubhouse to the winner of a county progress competition. The motivation was twofold. First, the company was simply seeking, as always, to work as closely as possible with all such groups as the 4-H clubs and to enlist their warm friendship and support. And, second, General Wood and others in the business pointed out that in earlier days it had been the custom for successful merchants to "do something" for the community, such as donating a hospital, library, or similar structure. Wood and his associates felt that it was time the company took more active steps to overcome the "absentee-ownership" argument leveled at chain stores and to answer in specific terms the oft-repeated charge that mail-order houses "took everything out of a town and gave nothing in return."

The winner of that nation-wide contest was the 4-H Club in St. Louis County, Minnesota. Before actually initiating construction of the clubhouse, on which it was committed to spend as much as $17,000, the company sought to enlist as much local co-operation as possible, on the theory that citizens of that community should be glad to furnish at cost whatever they were able to provide for such a project. A local townswoman was easily persuaded to sell for a dollar a beautiful site on Lake Eshquagama. Another citizen offered to donate a stand of timber, but he could not afford the cost of logging and transporting it. The Forestry Service provided the necessary labor for those two functions. A utility company offered to pull in a telephone line if a strip of forest could be cleared; again the Forest Service volunteered. To make a long story short, the community received a building valued at $30,000–$35,000. The cost to Sears, Roebuck was $12,000.

The Minnesota experiment's success encouraged the company to urge its store managers actually to seek out such projects in order to intrench the company even more firmly in various communities. In November, 1935, the firm donated playground equipment valued at $3,000 to the city of Fond du Lac, Wisconsin. A year later it built a $10,000 amphitheater for Tyler, Texas, and in 1938 it spent $5,600 on a livestock arena in Abilene, Texas, which has since helped make Abilene a livestock center. In the fall of 1939 the company allocated $5,000 for playground equipment for Lafayette, Indiana.

The experience gained from these projects had convinced management of the soundness of the idea. Accordingly, the program was formalized to a greater degree in 1939, when fifty cities containing Sears's retail stores were surveyed, and ten of them selected for community projects. Two chief conditions governed the choices. First, the community had to be one in which Sears had enjoyed excellent business for a certain period, preferably at least five years, and in which the Sears manager had indicated his ability to extract the greatest amount of good for the project. Second, the project decided upon would have to fill a recognized need, attested to by a committee of community leaders; and preference would always be given to projects whose facilities would be available to low-income groups who would not otherwise have access to such facilities. It was understood, in all cases, that the community would be completely responsible for maintaining the project according to agreed standards and that the project would be turned over to the community in entirety when completed.

A public bathhouse at Waukegan, Illinois, was the first project approved and constructed under the "new" program in the summer of 1940. The community was naturally blessed with an excellent beach but had no facilities for bathers. The cost of the bathing pavilion was $9,500. A succession of projects followed.

The coming of war halted all such construction. The thirteen community projects up to that point had cost the company $113,720—an average, in even figures, of $8,747, well within the $8,000–$10,000 range agreed upon in 1939. Even as late as three years after the end of the war, the company still hesitated to resume construction activities in this program, while so many thousands of war veterans were still without adequate housing.

Everything up through 1935 was as nothing compared with two projects launched in 1936, for that year saw the birth of the college scholarship plan and the equally famous "cow-hog-hen" program.

The scholarship project began in August, 1936, when General Wood conferred with the deans of four Midwest land-grant colleges. Wood pointed out there was a need of "astonishing magnitude" for financial assistance to farm youths desiring to study agriculture (a survey by the Foundation had unearthed facts that depressed even Sears, Roebuck, which is not nominally considered an educational institution). He added that the number of scholarships of all kinds available to farm youth was "shockingly small" and "bore no reasonable relationship to the applicant's real qualifications."

The General's reaction to that situation was a proposal that Sears, Roebuck give scholarships to needy and deserving farm youth. The deans, if they were agreeable, would handle all operations of the program. Sears would merely pay the bill. The deans were not to consider athletic ability, fraternal connections, ancestry, religion, or other similar factors. Wood wanted only these strings attached to the offer: the youths selected must be sorely in need of financial assistance—must, in fact, be so poor that without such help they could hardly have had any chance at all ever to enter college; the youths must have shown scholastic ability in high school; they must be deeply interested in agriculture; and it was hoped they would plan to return to farming in some connection after completing their education.

Wood's offer was promptly accepted. The later addition of six other deans brought the total to ten educators, who were told that they would have 146 scholarships to grant that first year. The cost to the company was $22,500. The educators could select all winners themselves or have committees of their own choosing handle the selection. As a program developed, the participating schools came to require extensive information about each applicant from himself, his teachers, county agents, and other local leaders. Competition became progressively keener, as high-school youths in large number began to realize that many of them would for the first time have an opportunity to attend colleges of agriculture.

For the school year 1937–38 the original 146 grants grew in number to 385, embracing seventeen states, at a cost to the company of $49,375. In the following year 408 scholarships, in the same number of states, cost Sears, Roebuck $52,084. The year 1939–40 saw grants awarded to 584 farm boys in twenty-five states, with the bill standing at $67,875. By the end of 1941 the scholarship program had spread to all forty-eight states, Alaska, and Puerto Rico. In that year 1,132 students held Sears, Roebuck scholarships (the company had long since become the largest single donor of scholarships in the United States; it had granted more than 7,400 such awards by 1948). Of the more than 1,000 youths holding scholarships in 1948, 92 were Negroes, attending a dozen land-grant colleges in the South and in Missouri and Maryland. As an experiment the program had been extended to girls to study home economics, in Colorado, Kansas, Missouri, Nebraska, and Wyoming, and the cost of this one phase of the program to the company in 1946–47 was $12,000.

In the academic year 1942–43 an auxiliary program was inaugurated for high-school students in certain cities in the United States. These scholarships allowed the winners to pursue studies in any field of their own choice without being confined to agriculture; and such grants were approved in 1945, for example, for Atlanta, Dallas, Kansas City, Memphis, Minneapolis, Oklahoma City, Philadelphia, Seattle, and Boston. The winners are chosen by committees appointed by the school boards. As in the case of agricultural scholarships, the Foundation has nothing to do with choosing the winners. The exact handling of the program varies in different cities, depending on the wishes of local school authorities. Since the inception of this program, over 300 scholarships had been awarded by the end of 1948.

During the war years the number of agricultural scholarships dropped to around 250 a year. It was felt at that time that perhaps the "G.I. Bill" would eliminate or at least mitigate the need for the company's scholarships, but after the war the number of scholarships increased from the low of 246 to 490 in 1946, and in 1948 was back in full stride with more than 800 yearly.

The returns to the company from this activity are believed to be truly enormous, in many ways. The good will won from educators, from the recipients of the grants, and through word-of-mouth publicity in farm areas has been very nearly incalculable. And the company's original purpose—to improve agriculture by extending a "leg up" to potential farm leaders of the future—seems to have been met and exceeded. A survey taken just before the war showed that almost every youth who had received one of the grants had gone into (more properly had returned to) farming and that most had worked into positions of leadership. Many had become extension

PUBLIC RELATIONS

service workers, many were teaching vocational agriculture, and others were farming.

The program has received the unqualified indorsement of heads of agricultural colleges and farm leaders throughout the nation. The scholastic standing alone of the overwhelming majority of the farm youths so assisted would be enough to win the acclaim of educators. Dean Kildee of Iowa State College, at a luncheon given by the company in 1946 to deans of state land-grant colleges and directors of extension service, asserted that

> 284 superior but financially handicapped Iowa farm boys from 81 counties have been among Iowa State's best agricultural students. The percentage of these men graduating, although only financed during their freshman year, is double the normal graduation percentage. These men ranked very high in scholarship activities and leadership on the campus and as graduates. Usually 70 to 90 per cent of the high 10 per cent of scholastic attainment are Sears scholars. Some of the best recent graduates had been out of high school for two to three years and would not have entered college had not Sears scholarships been provided.[1]

That record itself is remarkable enough in view of the fact that the scholarships generally are for one year only, with the student on his own after that—frequently entirely on his own, since one big factor in his original selection was his family's inability to assist him. Equally good is the record of the scholarship holders in extra-curricular activities; it would be good even without the consideration that the students are almost entirely self-supporting. It should here be noted that the company's financial assistance does not in every case cease at the end of the scholar's freshman year. By 1941, 58 of the 2,564 boys who had held freshman-year scholarships had won additional $200 sophomore scholarships (plus a trip to Chicago at the company's expense). Of the 58, 3 had won $500 junior-senior year grants, in competition with the other 55 holding the second-year awards; 4 others had received $250 junior scholarships, and the remaining 51 were given $100 junior scholarships. That constant incentive, even through the fourth year of college, may help account in some measure for the high proportion of Sears's scholars graduating.

At the end of each scholastic year the company brings to Chicago for a week's "working holiday" the outstanding scholarship holder at each school and the dean of that school. The week's party includes sight-seeing, tours through the company, the Merchandise Mart, the Chicago Stock Exchange, and the great meat-packing plants like Swift and Armour—all designed to show the youths where the produce they make is handled and how it is processed. There are, of course, also luncheons, banquets, theater parties, and other pleasure rounds.

The comments of Dean Paul W. Chapman of the University of Georgia represent the sort of thing Sears likes to hear about its agricultural program:

> A vast amount of good has been done, and Sears, Roebuck is responsible for the training of some outstanding leaders in the field of agriculture, and for the

improvement of the agricultural program in the Southeast. In Georgia, the financing of livestock projects is bringing about a better balance in agriculture than we have ever had in the past and has already added untold millions to the total income of the state.[2]

An adjunct of the college scholarship program is the "Sears Adult Farmer's Short Course." County agent committees or some similar bodies pick one farmer from each county to attend a short course (four to five weeks) at the college of agriculture in each state where the program operates. Sears pays all the expenses of the farmer-students. The college faculties prepare special classroom and laboratory schedules to fit the farmers' needs and desires. The curriculum includes farm business problems, agronomy, animal husbandry, livestock sanitation, dairying, agricultural engineering, and similar fields. The schedule is a hard one; the day usually begins no later than 6:00 A.M. and frequently runs until well into the evening. The farmers attending the short courses are selected partly on the basis of leadership and are expected to pass along their recently acquired knowledge to their neighbors when they return home. The "short-course" plan started in Alabama and was extended to Georgia, North Dakota, Kansas, and Minnesota.

All these activities helped amass a store of information on farm problems. One problem which there seemed to be no way of overcoming easily was that created by the one-crop system in much of the South (if that can be said to be just one problem). Local, state, and federal agricultural agencies and agriculture colleges, among others, had long crusaded for crop diversification and for livestock improvement through the introduction of better bloodlines. Everyone seemed agreed that purebred cows, hogs, and hens were essential to a well-balanced farm program in the South. Literature had been distributed and lectures given, but this exhortation had come to nought.

Sears concluded that inertia and lack of funds were the two chief obstacles to the desired change and decided to replace exhortation with action. The cow-hog-hen program was born, and county agents came to be the chief instrument of its execution. The project was introduced in the Atlanta territory, on a contest basis, often operating through the school system.

Units made up of four adjacent counties were utilized. To each of the thirty-two boys or girls (eight from each county), from twelve to eighteen years old, submitting the best essays on "Advantage of the Cow-Hog-Hen Plan of Farming" was given a purebred registered gilt. Each winner agreed to feed and care for the gilt and to breed her, at the proper time, to a purebred, registered Hampshire boar furnished by the company. Each youth further agreed to return to the county agent, for similar distribution the following year, one choice gilt from the first litter, in order to perpetuate and extend the plan.

At the end of the year winners of the original gilts were judged on their care and development of the gilts as breeding stock. The winners of this competition in each county received 150 baby chicks, with awards to other contestants scaled down so that the eighth prize winner received 25 baby chicks. The boy or girl adjudged the winner in the four-county unit received, in addition to 150 baby chicks, a purebred, dairy-type heifer. In every instance the livestock winner promised to return to the county agent part of the first herd, litter, or brood for further distribution. Hence the company's description of the program as the "chain-litter" movement.

The program quickly spread to 608 counties representing about half the predominantly agricultural area of eleven southern states. By 1940 the plan was operating in counties in North and South Carolina, Georgia, Alabama, Mississippi, Arkansas, Louisiana, Texas, Oklahoma, and Kansas. In subsequent years it spread to such widely separated areas as Upper New York State; the "inland empire" of eastern Washington State; Lancaster County, Pennsylvania; Los Angeles; Nebraska, Ohio, Wisconsin, Colorado, Utah, Idaho, Oregon, and others.

The full value of the cow-hog-hen program is difficult to estimate with any close degree of accuracy. The company's last estimate, made in 1941, put the total progeny of all the livestock it had distributed at 692 cows, 2,645,000 hogs, and 18,650,000 chickens. The *Topeka* (Kan.) *State Journal* paid this tribute to the program in its editorial columns on May 26, 1944 (the entire lengthy editorial was devoted to Sears's various farm activities):

> The cow-hog-hen projects at Hutchinson, Wichita, Salina and Coffeyville were established similar to the project at Topeka, and while the Topeka project is the largest of them all, the other programs have been very effective as well in starting youngsters off in the livestock business and in improving the quality of swine. Claude King, 4-H club agent for Shawnee county, reported earlier this year that a total of somewhere around 10,440 head of purebred pigs had already resulted from the Topeka project [established in 1939]. Mr. King said, . . . "The Duroc hogs in this county, as a result of this project, are second in quality to none, even including those of breeders who have been in the business for years. These purebreds served a great purpose because before 1939 there were only two farms in the county raising good purebred hogs."

Certainly no program it has ever launched has been dearer to the hearts of the company's public relations department than the cow-hog-hen project. It can and does—point to statements from scores of livestock experts to support its claim that the project has done at least as much for American livestock improvement as any other one campaign of any kind. It has data to show that one youth attained a gross income of $59,896.38 from livestock in the nine years from the time he won his first Sears, Roebuck pig. In recent years the emphasis has shifted more to swine than to cattle, for two reasons. Some agricultural colleges are permitting students to specialize in swine, without diverting much of their time to poultry and cattle. The other reason is financial: the prewar price of from $50 to $75 per head for purebred heifers more than tripled by 1948, making gilts appreciably less expensive.

The company's interest in livestock improvement has not been confined to the cow-hog-hen program alone. After the great depression, followed by two years of killing drought in Utah, that previously great beef-producing state found that the quality of its beef cattle was steadily deteriorating. Vigorous measures for improvement of the stock seemed imperative. The president of Utah State College, discussing the problem with a Sears official, asserted that the bloodlines of one really fine animal could be spread to such an extent as to assist the whole cattle industry in that state within a comparatively short time. Sears consented to help and purchased a prize bull, "Advance Domino III," for $2,000. Before sending the animal to Salt Lake City, the purchasing committee entered the bull in the Denver livestock show, the nation's ranking Hereford competition. "Advance Domino III" won first prize in his own class and was also crowned grand champion of the entire exposition. In these few hours his value had more than tripled.

When "Advance Domino III" arrived at Salt Lake City, he was guest of honor (*in absentia*) at a banquet attended by four thousand educators and leaders in the state's livestock industry. The bull's services were subsequently made available without charge to all qualified 4-H Club and Future Farmers of America youth. By the end of 1946 "Advance Domino III" had fathered upward of two thousand purebred descendants, most of them products of artificial insemination. Louis L. Madsen, of Utah State College, estimated the bull's progeny's worth at around $600,000 and asserted that the direct and psychological benefit to cattlemen of the state was valued at at least $3,000,000.[3]

The company's next such livestock improvement program of the same general nature took place in the South, where the cow-hog-hen program had started. Through General Wood's friendship with LaFayette Hughes, one of the largest (if not the largest) Hereford cattle producers in the country, the company obtained fifty purebred, registered, yearling, Hereford bulls and distributed them to fifty Future Farmers in North Carolina. The bulls were to be the property of the various F.F.A. chapters and were to be utilized for breeding service in the fifty school communities. (The project was extended later to South Carolina and Georgia.) The company estimated that the bulls would provide from 2,000 to 3,000 breedings during the first two years of the program in each state. The original bulls would continue on that basis for five or six years and would, from about the third year on, be aided by their progeny.

The other special state or regional activities of the company are numerous and indicate rather clearly not only the recognition that one state may have problems and opportunities different from those of its neighbors but that there are variations even among counties in the same state. Sears,

Roebuck has, for example, sponsored garden contests and sheep-raising in the mountain counties of northern Georgia, forest preservation in Mississippi and Washington, a special poultry program in Florida, needlework in Tennessee, and many more. It is, for instance, supporting an effort to restore the grape industry in the Ozarks by providing funds for vines and equipment for the four-year period before the vineyards can yield any return. It has enabled rural folk in West Virginia to capitalize upon the lush growth of holly by caring for the trees, cutting judiciously, making the holly into wreaths, packaging it intelligently, and marketing it profitably. The holly project also included honey and walnuts as sources of farm income.

Probably the most spectacular of all such localized efforts was the farmers' market in Atlanta, adjacent to the huge retail store and mail-order plant. The market was apparently the idea of E. J. Condon and represented at least a partial solution to furnishing a short cut from producer of foodstuffs to consumer, akin to the company's own merchandising short cut. Condon picked C. H. Bishop, an outstanding Georgia agricultural leader, to organize the market. Support was immediately forthcoming from the state college of agriculture, the bureau of markets, vocational teachers, and other farm officials. As far as the company was concerned, it was to be a nonprofit activity based on recognition of the simple fact that Sears's income parallels that of the farmer. The immediate, operating objectives were fivefold:

1. To enable farm families to sell direct to the consumer
2. To offer a similar service to groups under direction of county agents, home demonstration agents, vocational teachers, women's clubs, etc.
3. To encourage farm families to grow, find, and make things which would furnish some income in every month of the year
4. To furnish the small farmer training and experience leading to the use of larger trade channels
5. To encourage farmers to try out new products

The farmer was allowed to sell at wholesale or retail and paid only fifty cents daily for an eight-foot table space or space to park a truck. Farmers were encouraged to sell only their best products, to grade those products, and to make grades and prices attractive. Participants were further encouraged to pool shipments with their neighbors to reduce transportation and selling costs. Special feature events were held from month to month, climaxed by midwinter and midsummer festivals. The company advertised the market, and particularly the special events, through leaflets dropped from a plane, radio and newspaper advertising, and other mediums.

These efforts were, however, as nothing compared with the outpouring of free publicity given by virtually every state agency and countless private organizations. The *Market Bulletin* of the State Department of Agriculture publicized the market, the governor of Georgia broadcast to the entire state about the market, and clubs of all kinds held "all-Georgia products" dinners. (The state was at that time importing most of its eggs from Tennessee.) A Sears, Roebuck Georgia Products Dinner in February, 1932, brought General Wood and Donald Nelson to Atlanta. Soon no course in vocational agriculture was complete without at least one day spent at the farmers' market, and youngsters from the backwoods (sometimes from as far as three hundred miles distant) poured in by bus to visit the famed market. College classes toured the market.

All in all, few activities ever received such a nearly smothering eruption of affection as did Sears's Atlanta farmers' market. The affection grew through the years. The company never claimed to be doing other than what it always sought to do: to help the farmer farm better, live better, and sell better—a philosophy summed up in its own statement:

> Everything attempted in this field has been grounded squarely on our acknowledged debt to the farmer—a debt which we don't believe we can ever repay. So we have no sense of holy satisfaction about any achievements, real or imagined. If they have tended to help American agriculture, we must admit that they haven't cost this company a dime.

The farmers' market was financially successful, maintaining itself and paying for the first building and the newer building erected after it outgrew the first. The market operated in the red only in the year it opened (1930), unless one includes 1936, when the cost of the new building was written off entirely. In addition to paying for its two buildings, the market spent some $25,000 on advertising and public relations, the latter including many activities not directly related to the market (e.g., as much as $2,000 for scholarships in some years). The market was reluctantly abolished, after World War II, when the retail store adjacent to it needed that space for a farm store.

Sears's activities in agricultural education go farther, however, than just scholarships, livestock programs, and a farmers' market. The company began to utilize the graphic arts more actively in the 1930's with a series of motion pictures. (It had been making movies as early as 1924, but only on a small scale.) Its approach to this medium was characteristically canny; it opened with a 4-H Club scenario-writing contest in 1930, which, as indicated earlier, brought in some 2,000 scenarios. The contest aspect not only provided the company with a wide selection of scripts from which to select; it also gave a good indication of the kind of motion pictures its audience wanted, since the 2,000 persons who submitted scenarios were, almost without exception, from among those who would constitute the audience for the pictures.

And in line with its impartial approach to both the 4-H clubs and the Future Farmers of America, the company soon made a film extolling the aims and achievements of the latter group. Among the many films produced and distributed by the company are such titles as *Under the 4-H*

Flag, The Green Hand (glorifying the ideals of the F.F.A.), *An Ounce of Prevention, Where the Road Turns Right, The Golden Egg,* and more. They range from eleven-minute shorts to full-length features, replete with plot, hero, heroine, and villain. Some are in black-and-white, some in color, all in sound. As in most of the projects in which it engages, the company makes most of its motion pictures in co-operation with established agencies to fit a particular purpose, often to meet a specific need. Co-operating agencies have included, in addition to the 4-H clubs and the F.F.A., the United States Department of Agriculture, the United States Soil Conservation Service, Purdue University, the National Livestock Loss Prevention Board, and others.

The motion pictures are made available without charge to farm groups and organizations of all kinds, to educational institutions, women's clubs, and just about any group which can establish any reasonably close "eligibility." The only cost to the groups showing the movies is that of transportation. In 1947 the Sears movies were shown to audiences aggregating 4,280,-163 people, at a distribution cost of less than four-fifths of a cent per person. Movies also accounted for about $85,000 (roughly 10 per cent) of the Foundation's total expenditures for 1947. Some of the movies are launched with premières involving a good deal of fanfare. *The Green Hand,* for example, had its première early in 1940 in Athens, Georgia, the locale of the state college of agriculture. The dean of that agriculture college, Paul W. Chapman, not only wrote the book on which the film was based but also played the role of himself in the movie. The première was attended by the governor of Georgia and hundreds of farm leaders from the state. In two years' time *The Green Hand* was seen by 190,792 people at 671 showings, and it is still on circuit.

In 1944 the Foundation produced *A Stitch in Time,* in co-operation with the National Safety Council. That film was directed toward preventing accidents on the farm. The Foundation had discovered, through its work with the National Safety Council, that farming was one of the most hazardous occupations in this country. Some 16,000 farm people a year were losing their lives through accidents. (A Foundation survey indicated that accident fatalities in farm work were 53 per 100,000 workers, as compared with 19 per 100,000 in manufacturing.) Further, in the critical war year 1944 the farmer was very nearly indispensable, and there was no one to step into the breach when a farmer was incapacitated or killed. Nor was there any financial protection for the average farmer—no workmen's compensation laws, no industrial insurance, no group hospitalization, no union to assist him.

To make its film on farm safety, the Foundation turned to Kansas State College, where it felt that the best work in the country had been done on farm accident prevention, and to the National Safety Council. *A Stitch in Time* won the National Safety Council Plaque for 1945 as the outstanding contribution to farm safety. Prints were bought by the Canadian government, which translated the film into French, and requests for the movie came from as far away as the Union of South Africa. By the end of 1945 the film had been viewed by 635,057 people, and all prints had been booked solidly through October, 1947. Even the American Medical Association asked to be allowed to circulate the film among its members.

An Ounce of Prevention was made in 1945, when the company was co-operating with the National Livestock Loss Prevention Board in care of livestock shipped to market, grub control, and the proper use of DDT and similar sprays in the war against flies and various parasites. The brochure advertising *An Ounce of Prevention* pretty well summarizes the film's contents. Two lambs of the same age are shown—one, well cared for, is a prize-winner; the other, neglected, is the very prototype of the agricultural "Sad Sack."

A more recent Foundation venture into vocational training involves supplying model retail selling units to high schools to be used in distributive education courses as part of the general vocational education program. High schools had been offering such distributive education courses for years on a dual approach: to train high-school students for retail employment and to provide upgrading training for employed salespeople. The former courses took place almost entirely in schools; the latter, in both (night) schools and in the stores themselves.

The chief weakness in the school program seemed to be the lack of realistic atmosphere found in stores. In 1943 the director of distributive education in the Seattle public schools persuaded the Foundation to supply a model retail selling unit. The first such unit was supplied in April of that year and furnished a replica of a display and selling unit in a modern retail store. The cost of the original unit was between $700 and $800, but postwar costs were considerably higher.

The experimental unit received favorable publicity from educators and educational journals, and the program soon grew to include school systems in Spokane, Yakima, and Tacoma, Washington, Portland, Oregon, and Salt Lake City. Wartime shortage of materials soon forced abandonment of the program, but the Foundation proceeded, with the co-operation of the United States Office of Education, to plan extension of the program to thirteen states in the central region surrounding Chicago. It was decided to construct one model unit for each city selected in each of the thirteen states. Two basic considerations governed selection of those cities. First, the educators sought to make sure that the town chosen would be one in which the distributive education program was functioning well. And, second, the company was determined that the unit should go to a community where the Sears store manager would grasp the possibilities of the program and would give it strong support.

In 1947 the Foundation spent $22,000 on model retail selling units, as compared with $4,071 spent on them in 1946. The company operates, as usual, through its local store managers on establishment of the units. Following the installation of a unit in the local school system, a dinner is is held. Those attending include the students taking the course, leading merchants, heads of merchants and trade associations, members of school boards, and others. Surveys indicate that enrolment in all classes provided with such units increases. The company's own interest and confidence in the program is shown by the fact that many young people who have completed the retailing course are now working in Sears's retail stores.

Another public relations activity is the company's Consumer Education Division, which prepares exhibits and pamphlets to instruct consumers in buying, to teach them how to judge the character and content of merchandise, how to appraise materials and construction. Its battle cry, "Hidden Values," appears on all its pamphlets and exhibits, which are distributed (free, of course) through home demonstration agents, agricultural and home economics leaders, schoolteachers, extension service workers, and others in similar capacities.

The pamphlets, 3½ by 6½ inches and usually containing six or eight pages of text and illustrations, cover such items as hosiery, slips, foundation garments, shoes, children's clothes, fabrics, bedding, better lighting, cooking utensils, home furnishings, etc. The booklets are jam-packed with information on what to look for when buying the item, what various trade terms actually mean, in what materials various items come, and how best to preserve the item for longest wear after the customer has once bought it. The name of the company appears only once, at the bottom of the last page.

Exhibits, which are sent on loan, are more ambitious and usually include actual samples of the item under discussion or swatches of material, or, if the item is fragile or too bulky (dinnerware or mattresses, for example), photographs. Promotional folders describing the consumer education service are sent periodically to state specialists, 3,000 home demonstration agents, and some 15,000 vocational home economics teachers. The promotional material includes request forms for the loan of exhibits and for the dispatch of the pamphlets. In 1945, 9,563 exhibits were lent to participating individuals and groups and were viewed by an estimated 1,273,000 people (almost all of them women).

The public relations program had grown by around 1941 to include a large variety of activities upon which considerable sums of money were being spent annually. Some of these activities were manifestly of a for profit, or sales-promotional, nature; others, just as obviously, could be classified as nonprofit, even though the company stood to gain in the long run from all its public relations efforts. Yet nearly all the various activities were conducted through the Agricultural Foundation, organized in 1923 on a for-profit basis. The company therefore resolved to liquidate the Foundation by dissolving its charter and replacing it with an organization which would be similar in most respects but which would be on a strictly nonprofit basis.

Accordingly, the Sears, Roebuck Foundation was chartered on May 8, 1941. The "corporation" was formed in the names of R. E. Wood, F. B. McConnell, and E. J. Condon. The charter clearly stated its objectives in the second paragraph:

> The object for which it is formed is for the following purposes to the extent that such purposes are exclusively charitable, scientific or educational; to promote and improve agriculture and the breeding of better livestock and poultry, to conduct and supervise farm contests and educational activities in various communities and states throughout the United States, to aid and contribute to community chests, public projects and philanthropic and eleemosynary institutions or organizations, to grant scholarships and funds to enable persons to study at schools and colleges, and to do or perform all or any of such objects either alone or in cooperation with colleges, societies and organizations operated exclusively for charitable, scientific or educational purposes; to receive gifts, legacies and donations from any sources whatsoever; to make gifts and appropriations from any or all of its resources from time to time to carry out the objects and purposes of the association; and to exercise all such power and authority as may be necessary to carry out the purposes and objects above specified, but it is expressly declared that no dividend shall ever be declared or paid to any of its members, and that none of its property, real or personal, shall ever be used or expended except in carrying into effect the legitimate ends and aims of its being.

All contributions to the Foundation have come from the company: $600,000 at the time of its incorporation in 1941, and a total of some $9,000,000 in the first seven years of its operation (in the form of both cash and stock). Disbursements in the first seven years totaled around $3,000,000.

Shortly after the rechristened Foundation started operations, food became one of the world's most precious commodities. The country rang with cries that food would "win the war and write the peace." Victory gardens, warmly encouraged at the highest levels of government, sprang up over the country. Sears offered tangible inducements to victory gardeners through its Foundation (for the nonprofit aspects) and through its retail stores (for the sales-promotion, or for-profit, aspects). The program operated through the National Committee on 4-H Clubs, in connection with the War Food Production Program. Cash prizes and war bonds were offered, and the response was enormous.

Company records indicate that the program was responsible for the planting and cultivation of 1,578,359 gardens. These were not the regular farm gardens renamed victory gardens, but, under the terms of the project, represented separate plots totaling 1,130,000 acres in addition to the regular gardens. The value of the yield from this additional acreage was estimated by the 4-H committee at $1,722,798,000. War Food Administrator Marvin Jones said that the Sears, Roebuck victory-garden program was the outstanding organized effort in the whole war food production program.[4]

The victory-garden program was obviously largely rural in character (even though it produced 52,838 gardens within the city limits of Los Angeles alone), but, like practically all other such rural programs, it was built around the retail stores in the communities served. Those store managers are in more than 90 per cent of the cases the individuals around whom the *entire* public relations program of the company revolves. While it is true that most of the firm's *organized* public relations activities operate in the rural field (the nonprofit ones through the Foundation), it is also true that the "urban" participation (in Community Funds and similar activities, Chambers of Commerce and various trade associations, etc.) costs more than twice the amount of money spent by the Foundation.

Sears, Roebuck is completely convinced that public relations, like charity, begins perforce at home. General Wood has insisted, from the time the company entered the retail field, that its stores must be an integral part of each community if they are to succeed financially and that there is and of necessity must be a direct ratio between the operating results of any retail store and the "social consciousness" of its manager. Company surveys have borne this thesis out; Sears's store managers selected for the best public relations work are invariably found, when the profit and loss statements are brought out, also to be the most successful merchants. The interrelationship of the two factors is incessantly highlighted. Energetic promotion of various public relations programs—whether scholarships, cow-hog-hen programs, victory gardens, community buildings, or what—has in almost every instance been accompanied by a corresponding increase in the volume of business of the local store whose manager handled the promotion.

It must not, of course, be inferred that a store manager's first task is to rush out distributing money or sending needy youths to college. His job is to do those things and more while selling an ever increasing volume of goods to realize increased net profits. Store managers are enjoined to align themselves with the local chamber of commerce and retail merchants' association, as well as service clubs such as Rotary, Kiwanis, Lions, etc. In addition, local store managers are encouraged (the company's faculties for encouragement are potent) to affiliate themselves with any or all other representative civic and commercial organizations. All this is, however, only the beginning. Store managers are further expected to give their time and effort in each of the above-cited organizations by serving as officers and committee members and by demonstrating in every possible way that they are solid citizens of their particular community. And they are expected to donate generously to the Red Cross, Community Fund, and similar "drives."

If his store happens to be the leading retail unit in its city, the store manager's contributions to worthy causes are expected to compare favorably with (and frequently to exceed) those of his competitors. While the company tries to avoid committing any store manager to contributing any specific percentage of his sales volume, since his contributions come out of his store's profits and thus affect his own bonus, it has nevertheless arrived at what is considered a fair working proportion. Store managers whose contributions appear too low are reminded of the importance the company attaches to community participation.

On top of their normal contributions to Community Funds and similar campaigns (and, where local sentiment happens to be strongly in favor, even to colleges, YMCA's, etc.), store managers have something bordering on carte blanche in disaster cases or mercy missions. Where floods or fires or similar catastrophes occur, store managers in the affected regions can lend or donate generators, hire vehicles, give food and clothing, etc. The prompt and sometimes lavish actions of various store managers in such cases has perhaps won the company as many friends as almost any other single activity. Year-by-year figures are not available, but, as a sample, the company gave $1,859,322 in contributions to the Red Cross, Community Chest, and similar causes in 1944.

A 1941 survey of 593 Sears's store managers revealed that every one was a member of his local chamber of commerce where such an organization existed. It was also found that 347, or 58 per cent, were members of retail merchants' associations; that 353 were not only contributors to but also active members of their Community Funds; 396 were members of the Red Cross; and 217 were on the working roster of the Salvation Army. The managers were also active in other organizations, to the numbers shown in parentheses: Boy Scouts (220), Girls Scouts and Camp Fire Girls (131), YMCA and YWCA (290), service clubs such as Rotary, Kiwanis, and Lions (407, or 69 per cent), and other organized activities (575).

As pointed out earlier, only the nonprofit activities among all the foregoing qualify under the Sears, Roebuck Foundation. All activities which have any "for-profit" connotations of sales promotion are carefully segregated from the Foundation activities, even though everything which can be termed public relations still comes under the supervision of that department. The strictly "not-for-profit" activities which do qualify under the terms of the Foundation's charter include community projects such as 4-H clubhouses; the entire scholarship program; the cow-hog-hen and related livestock projects; the motion-picture program; and general agricultural projects such as corn and cotton shows and efforts to improve pasture land and practices. All other aspects of the public relations program—membership in trade associations, and consumer education, for example—are excluded from the Foundation's auspices.

The apparatus which directs this whole vast enterprise is, of course, the public relations office in the parent-organization in Chicago. As shown in Chart XIII, the director of public relations carries the title "Assistant to the President."

CHART XIII
Public Relations Organization

- President
- Assistant to the President
  Director of Public Relations
  - "News-Graphic"
  - Publicity
  - Regional Representatives
  - Washington Representative
  - Assistant
  - Sears, Roebuck Foundation
  - Educational Division

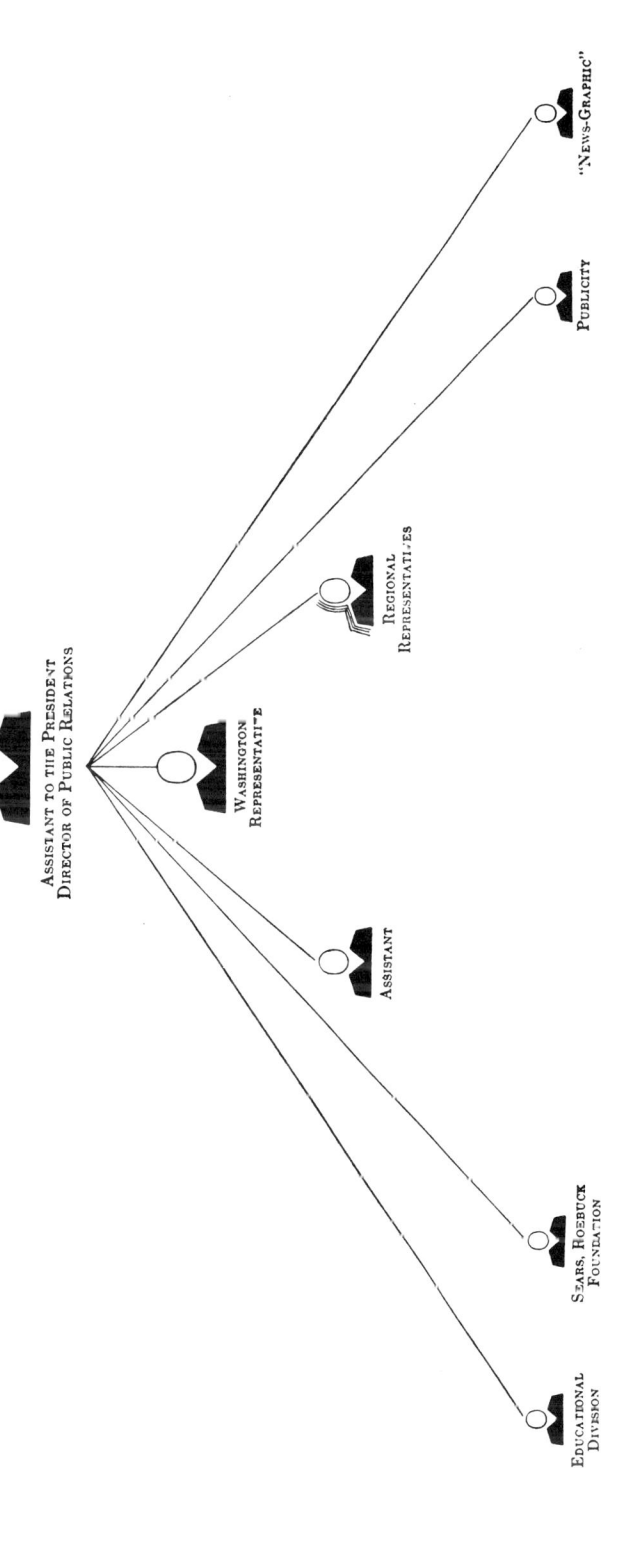

The *News-Graphic*, a house organ written for Sears's employees, is actually more an employee relations device than a public relations effort. The regional representatives shown on the chart are the public relations directors in each of the territorial offices. Their chief function is general supervision over the store and group managers intrusted with responsibility for purely localized press and radio material in their respective communities. The company's top management has long insisted on maintaining at its national headquarters a tight control over press relations. No public relations man in the field is permitted to deal with national publications of any kind.

At the same time the company also insists that local press relations are the direct responsibility of store and group managers, not to be delegated to any subordinate. Sears, Roebuck is extremely eager for its store managers and group managers to develop personal relationships with the editorial sides of the newspapers. One reason for this is the fact that advertising relationships *are* delegated to subordinate staff specialists—and Sears is determined to keep a clear line drawn between its status as one of the nation's largest advertisers and its status as a merchandising concern.

This desire not to overstep the thin line between a corporation understandably seeking favorable publicity and a corporation utilizing its weight as an advertiser has in fact led to a highly conservative attitude toward publicity. The company feels that any appearance of overstraining to get its name into the newspapers might well do more harm than good. Its public relations men insist that Sears's status as a tremendous advertiser is actually more handicap than help.

However that may be, one clear fact stands out to support this conservative policy toward publicity, which has led public relations to spend most of its time answering press inquiries rather than preparing "handouts." That is the fact that Sears receives about as much free publicity as any business institution in the world. It takes a variety of forms. Awarding of a scholarship or a hog to a "home-town boy" is obviously a newsworthy item for the local press. The issuance of a general catalogue brings forth "book reviews" analyzing the offerings therein, noting price changes and alterations in the merchandise line. Routine press interviews with high-level executives in their travels around the country keep the company's name in the public eye.

Word-of-mouth advertising of a gratis nature centers largely on anecdotes, burlesque skits, smoking-car jokes, and the "for men only" type of publication. Whether mildly risqué or downright lewd, as some of them are, such stories nevertheless serve to intrench the firm's name in the public consciousness. It is perhaps significant—and traceable possibly both to the company's active public relations efforts and the quiet work of the men directing them—that most of the anecdotes revolving around Sears, Roebuck are essentially good-natured in character. And references to Sears in the public press are almost uniformly favorable—at least in the sense of being seldom unfavorable, as some front-page stories about its chief competitor have been.

This is surely attributable in large part to General Wood's own almost intuitive "feel" for good public relations. Wood has generally seen to it that the company's actions comport with the philosophy behind the whole program. That philosophy, trenchantly enunciated by Wood from the time the company entered the retail field and subsequently hammered out in various annual reports, was summarized in the 1940 annual report:

Sears, Roebuck and Co. believes:

That neither it nor any other firm has a moral right to skim profits off a community which has been created by the struggle and labor of others and not plow some of those profits back into that community;

That it owes an eternal debt to the farmer and must be ceaseless in its efforts to repay that debt;

That taking as much as possible out of an economic system and giving in return as little as necessary is not just bad business morals; it is also bad business;

That the privileges of private enterprise under American democracy are unique in all history and that it is the duty of private enterprise to cherish and protect, up to the limits of its resources the system under which these privileges have been made possible.

CHAPTER XXXII

The Period in Review

SOME three-score years, virtually the life-span of a man, elapsed before Sears, Roebuck and Company achieved the eminence attaching to an annual net sales volume of one billion dollars. And within three years after that accomplishment the company was literally catapulted into the even more rarefied atmosphere of a two-billion-dollar record. In little more than two decades since Sears opened its first retail store in 1925, this merchant to America sold more than ten billion dollars worth of goods to customers across the land—and across the border.

The years since 1925 witnessed a great transformation in the company's business and in the way that business was done. From a highly centralized operation the old catalogue house evolved a new character highlighted by decentralized operations. Beset by new challenges of varying intensity, Sears found and developed men adequate to the moment—adequate, indeed, to effect a tenfold increase in sales since 1925.

The theme that dominated the whole sweep of Sears's experience after the recovery from the 1921 collapse was, of course, the retail expansion, for it was that shift in policy which was the grand strategy to which the company turned in its effort to cope with the rising tide of urbanization. But while the achievements of the period were virtually all tributary to the expansion into retailing, that decision itself and events generated outside the company presented many challenges, demanding tactics appropriate to the occasion lest the major strategy be engulfed and frustrated.

It was, of course, the shifting pattern of social and economic relationships that had precipitated Sears into the retail-store business: population movement, the decline of agriculture, the rise of new industries, and increased social mobility in the mail-order market accruing from advances in communication and transportation that reduced the degree of the farmer's isolation.

The momentum of the retail expansion served to carry Sears through the hectic years that followed hard upon October, 1929. Indeed, in only one year (1932) since 1922 did the company fail to show a profit on operations —and brought off a much better record in the severe depression of the thirties than it achieved in the shorter-lived debacle of 1921. This performance was achieved in spite of the sales losses suffered in each of the four years following 1929, shown in Table 93. The sales losses of the early thirties were paralleled by severe cuts in operating expenses, and in that orthodox manner was the experience of negative profits contained within the single year of 1932, when Wood stated in the annual report:

> Expenses have been greatly curtailed in the past four years. During this time, the catalog expense has been reduced over $6,000,000, and payrolls by approximately $17,000,000, both on an annual basis. All salaries and wages were cut 20% in the year 1932. Every effort has been made to exercise all possible economies, but the decline in volume has been in excess of the decline in expenses.

TABLE 93*

SOME INDEXES OF BUSINESS EFFICIENCY, 1925–47

Year	Percentage Change in Sales from Previous Year	Sales per Dollar Working Capital	Sales per Dollar Net Worth	Sales per Dollar Assets	Net Profits per Dollar Sales†	Rate of Return on Invested Capital†
1925	18.01	$3.57	$1.72	$1.45	$0.086	14.90
1926	5.91	3.33	1.71	1.49	0.085	13.78
1927	7.47	3.46	1.73	1.50	0.090	14.96
1928	18.47	4.20	1.91	1.57	0.082	15.21
1929	26.35	4.59	2.16	1.65	0.072	15.79
1930	−14.49	3.67	1.81	1.52	0.040	7.00
1931	− 9.89	3.25	1.62	1.40	0.038	5.85
1932	−14.17	5.83	1.63	1.30	−0.009	− 1.25
1933	− 0.45	4.46	1.52	1.18	0.041	6.29
1934	16.31	4.53	1.76	1.47	0.047	7.88
1935	23.28	4.55	2.03	1.68	0.055	11.14
1936	26.24	3.62	2.09	1.80	0.062	13.04
1937	8.54	3.89	2.25	1.89	0.057	12.12
1938	− 6.62	3.47	2.07	1.75	0.047	9.23
1939	23.07	3.71	2.35	1.91	0.060	14.01
1940	14.07	4.10	2.56	2.01	0.051	12.58
1941	29.92	4.98	3.23	2.37	0.040	12.25
1942	− 5.16	4.43	3.06	2.24	0.039	10.72
1943	− 1.76	3.91	2.88	2.10	0.040	10.65
1944	15.97	4.17	3.21	2.34	0.035	10.83
1945	5.71	4.05	3.26	2.24	0.034	10.95
1946	54.27	5.34	4.24	2.68	0.062	26.95
1947	22.88	5.99	4.43	2.79	0.054	24.79

* Source: Calculated from data in the company's annual reports.
† After taxes and profit-sharing.

Even the annual report mentioned here was a victim of the economy drive, appearing tardily as it did as a result of accounting reports being sent to Chicago only by regular mail and the prohibition of overtime work for the auditors.[1] The impressive recovery from the doldrums in which the decade of 1930 began is evident in the various indexes of the firm's progress shown in Table 94 (as in virtually all the other tables in this chapter).

General Wood's commentary on the course of business during 1932 was but the second such "discussion" in the firm's annual reports, and really the first appearance of much detail, for the 1931 report which marked the debut of textual material in those reports was very general, but it did carry at least the names of the company's officers and directors. Prior to 1931 Sears's annual statements (like those of most other corporations) were severe presentations in black and white providing a bare outline of assets, liabilities, and operating results. Neither the first World War nor its depressing aftermath was noted.

TABLE 94*

MEASURES OF GROWTH, 1925–47

Year	Net Sales	Net Working Capital	Net Worth	Total Assets	Net Profit
1925	$ 243,798,351	$ 68,328,777	$141,908,667	$167,982,622	$ 20,975,304
1926	258,212,751	77,501,787	150,867,190	173,766,257	21,908,120
1927	277,502,387	80,267,374	160,390,082	184,740,453	25,022,552
1928	328,760,314	77,241,171	171,772,074	209,282,236	26,907,902
1929	415,379,987	90,491,563	192,637,946	251,841,326	30,057,652
1930	355,180,257	96,889,690	196,064,333	233,965,566	14,308,897
1931	320,057,397	98,523,371	198,050,927	228,428,725	12,169,172
1932	274,707,651	47,153,703	169,028,688	210,845,756	2,543,651
1933	273,471,379	61,305,161	180,279,159	231,598,235	11,249,295
1934	318,060,563	70,247,911	180,643,852	217,090,981	15,020,551
1935	392,097,720	86,130,227	193,367,069	234,023,637	21,519,218
1936	494,968,022	136,813,316	236,709,866	275,291,947	30,660,199
1937	537,242,403	137,959,817	239,038,398	284,072,867	30,828,248
1938	501,676,644	144,373,083	242,920,904	286,084,551	23,354,364
1939	617,414,266	166,420,443	262,546,037	323,687,405	37,255,274
1940	704,301,014	171,888,244	274,972,950	350,430,159	36,086,668
1941	915,057,628	183,830,287	283,619,587	386,798,683	36,711,504
1942	867,834,052	196,020,050	283,781,137	386,586,781	33,946,989
1943	852,596,706	218,142,645	296,032,641	405,595,739	33,866,087
1944	988,770,171	239,696,991	308,472,733	423,037,908	34,176,111
1945	1,045,258,832	258,115,367	321,021,983	467,174,685	35,834,836
1946	1,612,596,050	301,741,060	380,501,867	601,681,660	100,098,516
1947	1,981,535,749	330,765,435	447,021,572	711,174,893	107,739,892

* Source: Calculated from data in the company's annual reports. 1932 data include thirteen months due to a shift from calendar year to a fiscal year ending January 31. Beginning in 1933 the fiscal year ends with the close of the thirteenth period late in January. In that year the company adopted a thirteen-period calendar.

Stockholders were not even informed in the annual reports when the company, a mail-order concern for thirty years, went into the retail business. Those statements were silent on the fact that Julius Rosenwald retired from the presidency in 1924; that Sears had a new guiding hand in Charles Kittle, a railroad man; that Kittle died and was succeeded by Robert E. Wood. The first report to carry even Julius Rosenwald's name was that issued for 1931, which contained his obituary.

The commentaries begun in the annual report for 1931 have become a regular feature of these statements and have grown more extended with the passage of time. Since those reports represented the chief means of communication between the stockholders and their corporation, one is prompted to wonder how well informed the shareholders were about their company's business. Perhaps the almost uninterrupted flow of dividends and the "scores" posted on the exchanges were sufficient indicators of Sears's health. And perhaps stockholders read in the press of the rumors of mergers.

Surely it is not surprising that Sears should have been touched by the spirit that marked the 1920's and which accompanied unprecedented numbers of consolidations.[2] Rumors of a Sears-Ward merger evidently circulated freely in financial circles beginning in the early 1920's, inspired perhaps by the urgent economy drives made by both companies in the 1921 depression. A consolidation of the two mail-order houses would have saved millions of dollars in catalogue costs alone. Banking interests, often the entrepreneurs of such consolidation, saw in a merger obvious and clear advantages to their own interests. Notices in the press almost invariably carried statements pointing to the "financial interests" encouraging a merger.

While mergers were reportedly contemplated prior to 1925, the real epidemic of rumors—and actual negotiations—followed the decisions of both firms to go into retail stores. The tenor of the rumors is typified by the head of an April 22, 1929, story in the *Chicago Journal of Commerce:*

<blockquote>
SEARS-WARD
MERGER RUMOR
NOW STRONGER

CONTINUED WHISPERING OF
CONSOLIDATION LIFT PRICES
OF STOCKS

STRAWN MAKES DENIAL

*But LaSalle Street Hears That
Morgan & Co. Have Taken
a Hand in Deal*
</blockquote>

The story went on for three columns to detail the resuscitation of the rumors, and the "understood" attitudes of Strawn (Ward's board chairman), the House of Morgan, and the Rosenwalds. Nor did it fail to note the uncertainty felt by the principals regarding the attitude of the attorney-general toward such a merger.

In 1930 newspaper reports of Sears-Ward negotiations again appeared to be confirmed, but then in 1931 they were dismissed when Wood issued the following statment: "Discussions that have recently been going on between directors of Sears, Roebuck & Co. and Montgomery Ward & Co., looking to the possibility of a merger of the two companies, have been definitely terminated, as the parties have been unable to agree on terms."[3]

While the merger of Sears, Roebuck and Montgomery Ward never did materialize, the fact that the rumors were not unfounded is clear both from Wood's statement and from Werner, who said:

As there was duplication between Sears, Roebuck and Montgomery Ward in the effort to obtain a large share of both the catalogue and retail store business, it was natural that bankers and mail-order executives should consider a merger between the two companies at a time when mergers were prevalent in financial circles. Rosenwald, hating waste and duplication, was anxious for the merger. He took the matter up with bankers and other interested people and developed data to show the advantages of a merger to stockholders and customers. Negotiations finally broke down, however, because an agreement could not be made on the matter of management for the combined companies and on the problem of the fair ratio of exchange of Sears, Roebuck and Montgomery Ward stock.[4]

But if a merger of the catalogue houses was frustrated, that did not deter the interested parties from considering consolidation with other firms, specifically J. C. Penney. In 1929 Ward's and Sears each considered combining with Penney's. While the mail-order companies were experienced in catalogue selling, they were both still novices in operating retail stores at that time. Penney's had been in the chain-store dry-goods field since 1902 and was operating 1,395 stores, which in 1929 had gross sales of nearly $210,000,000.[5]

Montgomery Ward and Penney's completed their mutual consideration of a merger and came to a negative decision apparently in the early autumn of 1929. Sears then embarked on similar investigations with Penney's. Beasley details the course of events:

Scarcely had negotiations between Montgomery Ward ended when Sams [Penney's president] received a letter from R. E. Wood. . . . Like Montgomery Ward, Sears saw advantages in a merger with Penney; and, as with Montgomery Ward, Penney executives gave serious consideration to the proposal.

After an exchange of correspondence between Sams and Wood, the latter wrote (October 29, 1929) telling Sams, "I had a talk with Mr. Julius Rosenwald . . . and I find him sympathetic to the idea, as he has a great admiration for your organization and its methods." . . . Closing his letter Wood stated, "Our position is that we are ready, if you are, on any fair basis."[6]

Both firms made serious investigations of the merits of combining. Executive committees appointed for the task inquired into the status, methods, and merchandise of each operation. The report submitted by the committee appointed at Penney's contained the following concluding paragraphs, of more than routine interest:

We can get into no argument with the Sears company. They have been quite as free to point out their problems and difficulties as we have been eager to find them. They know the hardships of having to start from "scratch" with no personnel. In spite of that, they point to a volume of business at retail that is little short of amazing. Sears will do this year approximately $195,000,000 of retail business.

They claim that their success in this direction lies fundamentally in the same state of facts that Mr. Penney and the earlier founders of our company found. Namely, that retailing is so poorly done and merchandise is at such a high price, especially in hard lines, that with inadequate personnel and plant, people come and take the merchandise out of the basement and from the counters.

Your committee recognizes that there are many difficulties to be met and many personal inconveniences in such a merger. These will come out of the discussions later. However, it is our conviction that when advantages and disadvantages to our organization over a period of years are carefully weighed, the tremendous economic advantages and possibilities which are apparent in this merger warrant favorable consideration for the proposed merger.[7]

Despite the favorable reaction of at least the Penney group, and after weeks of further intensive investigation and discussion, nothing came of the meetings, and the proposed merger was buried with other memorabilia. The J. C. Penney Company concluded the negotiations on E. C.

TABLE 95*
GROSS SALES, MAIL ORDER VERSUS RETAIL, 1925–41
(In Thousands)

Year	Mail-Order Sales	Retail Sales	Total	Percentage Mail Order	Percentage Retail
1925	$246,499	$ 11,819	$258,318	95.5	4.5
1926	249,294	23,046	272,340	91.5	8.5
1927	253,101	40,001	293,102	86.4	13.6
1928	240,086	107,179	347,265	69.1	30.9
1929	266,043	174,623	440,666	60.4	39.6
1930	209,553	180,830	390,383	53.7	46.3
1931	161,870	185,339	347,209	46.6	53.4
1932	116,729	159,026	275,755	42.3	57.7
1933	120,334	167,860	288,194	41.8	58.2
1934	133,136	204,075	337,211	39.5	60.5
1935	171,746	243,291	415,037	41.4	58.6
1936	200,828	324,604	525,432	38.2	61.8
1937	202,504	366,285	568,789	35.6	64.4
1938	187,436	344,800	532,236	35.2	64.8
1939	218,068	435,406	653,474	33.4	66.6
1940	229,119	515,322	744,441	30.8	69.2
1941	306,707	662,394	969,101	31.6	68.4

* Source: Company records.

Sams's note that Penney's "could not deliver to a new company the values we now enjoy."[8] As with Ward's earlier, Sears and Penney's went their separate ways—with profit to each.

Despite the handicaps of "green" personnel, Sears's retail venture proved to be a resounding success and gathered strength as it gained experience and as the country slowly pulled itself out of the depressed 1930's. As Table 95 shows, sales were greater through the stores by 1931 than they were through the catalogue and continued to be so as they climbed year by year until retail sales accounted in 1941 for more than two-thirds of the company's business and, after the postwar retail expansion, for about three-quarters of the total volume. Thus was demonstrated the superior wisdom of the early advocates of retail stores—none of whom was more insistent and effective than Wood—over the executives who had wished to cling to the tested method of an exclusively mail-order business.

Indeed mail-order sales did not again see their 1925 level until farm income was swept high in the years of World War II, which at once enriched farmers and imposed restrictions on the physical mobility of customers. The war years saw mail order gain somewhat, relative to retail. An important part of that gain may be accounted for by the character of merchandise sold through the two types of outlets. The company's retail sales were heavily weighted by durable and semidurable goods—items practically eliminated in the wartime shortages of metals and tools. The mail-order business, on the other hand, had come to be (and remains today) primarily a "soft lines" business in which major appliance sales were relatively much less important.

TABLE 96*

Capital Expenditures, 1925–47

Year	Amount	Year	Amount
1925	$15,708,366	1937	$13,994,845
1926	8,933,471	1938	7,596,402
1927	15,430,013	1939	11,671,361
1928	24,031,852	1940	14,233,893
1929	18,655,995	1941	16,856,477
1930	1,438,437	1942	9,917,386
1931	2,630,867	1943	2,053,042
1932	7,776,878	1944	6,079,265
1933	2,133,419	1945	9,406,392
1934	5,545,163	1946	60,417,955
1935	3,220,239	1947	70,237,360
1936	8,337,818		

* Source: 1925–37 and 1946–47, company records; 1938–45, company's annual reports.

It was not surprising that Sears's big-ticket sales were concentrated in the retail stores. One of the factors which, especially after World War I, was weakening the position of mail order was the appearance and increasing popularity of products (major appliances) that were most readily sold under conditions where the customer could see the merchandise, often witness a demonstration, and be assured of convenient facilities for installation and postpurchase servicing. For all these things retail stores in hundreds of localities were inherently better adapted than were the giant mail-order bastions confined to ten or eleven strategic locations.

To build and equip the hundreds of stores across a continent, the company spent hundreds of millions. A record of Sears's capital expenditures for the past twenty-two years is available in Table 96. During the five-year period ending 1929 the company invested nearly $93,000,000 in plant and equipment. By no means was all of this accounted for by the retail expansion, since six additional mail-order plants, each involving large expenditures, were opened between January, 1925, and December, 1929. It is doubtful, however, that investments in those additional plants would have been made on such a scale except for their intimate relationship as supply bases for many of the 324 retail stores (and for the 200 more yet to come) which Sears could count by the close of 1929. In a very real sense the expenditures for the control stores were tributary to the retail expansion.

A cyclical pattern is evident in the record of capital expenditures, although the $8,000,000 disbursed in 1932 was certainly not typical depression behavior. Despite sales decline and losses for Sears's "A" stores in 1932, the company opened four such new stores in that year, three of which were actually Sears-built ("the New York Group") and another (Chicago's State Street Store) that required substantial investments in alterations and fixtures. While there is a general tendency evident that Sears's expenditures have roughly followed the business cycle, there was not a single year since 1925 that the company failed to open some new stores, and it would seem from the figures in Table 96 that World War II interrupted what was to be a substantial expansion of facilities. It should be noted that no easy parallel can be drawn between the number of stores added and capital expenditures, for heavy investments in control stores, warehouses, and other agencies were necessary to support the 625 stores operating in the United States and Latin America by 1947.

The company had by then established outlets in the islands of Cuba and Hawaii and in Mexico City and was committed to sites in Rio de Janeiro and São Paulo, Brazil. Sears's foreign expansion was hitting its stride, and the capital expenditures in 1946–47—more than $130,000,000—registered a great fortissimo and belied any acceptance of the notions of a contracting economy. Contrary to many economists and less hardy businessmen—and the company's closely watched competition—Sears proceeded at Wood's insistence to improve and multiply the counters over which goods are sold. The 1947 annual report informed stockholders how their money had been spent and, in so doing, gave a serviceable profile of what "capital expenditures" are in Sears, Roebuck. The report said:

Major additions were completed in 18 existing retail stores and 53 new and relocated stores of various types were built and completed during the two years. New and modern fixtures were installed in a large number of other stores. Total capital expenditures for retail stores during the two years, including land, buildings, alterations, service stations, parking lot improvements and furniture and fixtures, amounted to $97,140,149.

A new store was built in Mexico City and the existing store was enlarged in Havana, Cuba. Stores are under construction in Rio de Janeiro and São Paulo, Brazil. Total investment thus far in foreign stores is $7,286,991.

The report went on to note that capital expenditures for additional warehouse space, and the Greensboro, North Carolina, mail-order plant were $23,365,767; and for wholly owned factories, $9,968,415. The review concluded:

Repair and maintenance expenses were $13,146,041 against $11,370,087 last year. These expenditures were large for the following reasons: increased costs;

large volume operation; and repairs of a nature that had to be deferred these past few years until materials and labor were available. Our effort is constantly directed towards keeping the properties and equipment in first class condition and replacing facilities, which are outdated and expensive to maintain and operate, with the latest developments in adaptable modern facilities.

On such capital expenditures Sears spent nearly $350,000,000 since 1925, an average of about $16,000,000 annually. The company had larger annual capital expenditures than most department stores had sales volume. Expansion on such a scale has obviously made heavy demands on company resources, and it is surprising that one fails to find Sears going to the capital markets for funds except in 1936. With that single exception—and that of only modest proportions—the entire expansion program since 1925 has been financed primarily out of earnings, supplemented more recently by the sale of real estate.

Since the end of 1924—when Sears had both paid off the principal of the $50,000,000, 7 per cent gold-note issue contracted in the distressing year of 1920, and also called in the preferred stock—the company had no outstanding bonds or shares except common, which carried a par value of $100 until changed in 1926 to no-par shares. In that year also the stock was split four for one, and at the end of the year there were, as Table 97 indicates, 4,200,000 shares outstanding. In 1928 the level of authorized stock was raised to 5,000,000, and that increase was used largely in the distribution of stock dividends between 1928 and 1931, a policy adopted as early as 1911 as a means of conserving the earnings for expansion needs.

For many years the capital employed in building additional facilities and increasing inventory investment had come from earnings. The proportion of net income paid out in cash dividends each year was less than 50 per cent in the period between 1908 and 1929 inclusive, with the exception of 1918 and 1920. The markedly higher cash distributions in 1930 and 1931 and the infinitely high figure in 1932 were due to the great decline in profits rather than to any premeditated increase in dividends. The distribution of virtually all net income in 1936 and 1937 represented a response to the New Deal undistributed profits tax of 1936, which was repealed two years later.

Under the stimulus of the 1936 tax legislation, the number of shares authorized was increased to 6,000,000 and 588,689 shares sold to stockholders and employees at $72 per share.[9] This had the twofold effect of increasing the capital base, desirable for tax reasons, and the not unwelcome result of bringing more than $42,000,000 cash into the business. The magnitude and utility to Sears of that issue was somewhat modified, however, as indicated by the following statement from the 1938 annual report:

In January, 1937, $42,382,608 was received from a new stock issue offered to shareholders and in which employees were allowed to participate, but $34,-584,323 was paid out in extra dividends on account of the tax on undistributed

TABLE 97*
STOCK AND DIVIDEND RECORD, 1925–47

Year	Number of Stockholders	Shares of Common Outstanding	Amount Distributed in Cash Dividends	Cash Dividend per Share Common	Percentage of Net Income Paid in Cash Dividends	Stock Dividend (Per Cent)
1925	5,965	1,005,000	$ 6,007,089	$6.00	28.64	
1926	7,468	4,200,000	9,449,597	3.37½	43.13	4-for-1 split
1927	9,206	4,200,000	10,499,661	2.50	41.96	
1928	12,919	4,284,418	10,525,911	2.50	39.12	2†
1929	18,222	4,537,654	10,924,902	2.50	36.35	4†
1930	25,657	4,747,973	11,528,960	2.50	80.57	4†
1931	30,251	4,920,530	12,104,704	2.50	99.47	2†
1932	35,002	4,780,064	6,147,463	1.25	‡	
1933	34,902	4,780,111			§	
1934	33,875	4,794,715			§	
1935	34,650	4,794,715	8,097,796	1.75	37.63	
1936	36,004	5,476,478	30,484,713	3.75	99.43	Warrants‖
1937	47,601	5,526,943	30,308,395	5.50	98.31	
1938	50,726	5,526,943	16,653,875	5.50	71.31	
1939	52,668	5,643,501	23,876,712	4.25	64.09	
1940	55,011	5,704,407	24,132,712	4.25	66.87	
1941	57,200	5,777,499	24,415,691	4.25	66.51	
1942	58,764	5,780,774	24,557,535	4.25	72.34	
1943	59,762	5,837,968	24,714,003	4.25	72.98	
1944	59,502	5,865,571	24,891,614	4.25	72.83	
1945	73,159	23,577,956	25,020,126	4.25	69.82	4-for-1 split
1946	89,664	23,625,304	41,328,777	1.75	41.31	
1947	92,682	23,634,205	41,353,702	1.75	38.42	

* Source: Annual reports and company records.
† Declared 1 per cent quarterly.
‡ Dividend, $6,147,463; net loss, $2,543,651.
§ No dividend.
‖ Warrants issued December 26, 1936, to purchase one share at $72.00 per share for every ten shares held.

TABLE 98*
DEPRECIATION RESERVE AND OTHER RESERVES, 1932–47

Year	Depreciation Reserve	Other Reserves
1932	$ 25,700,612	$15,492,585
1933	30,659,134	14,865,402
1934	36,050,084	12,110,572
1935	42,242,163	12,814,461
1936	49,412,573	18,198,495
1937	55,528,710	20,829,000
1938	61,331,730	22,065,096
1939	66,702,416	28,033,302
1940	70,000,240	27,338,235
1941	78,223,157	36,845,898
1942	83,278,602	44,289,264
1943	85,786,339	47,084,600
1944	92,902,149	44,931,525
1945	97,743,417	39,524,012
1946	93,505,272	45,839,278
1947	105,559,470	59,552,541

* Source: Calculated from data in the company's annual reports.

profits. The net addition to working capital resulting from the new stock issue less the extra dividends related to the undistributed profits tax was therefore only about $8,000,000.

Since 1936 the company relied primarily on earnings to provide capital, despite the fact that from two-thirds to three-fourths of annual net income was distributed in cash dividends from 1938 to 1945. The effect of the heavy postwar expansion is indicated in the decline in cash distributions in 1946 and 1947, when about 40 per cent of net income went to the stock-

TABLE 99*

SEARS, ROEBUCK AND COMPANY, MONTGOMERY WARD AND COMPANY, AND DEPARTMENT-STORE NET PROFITS (AFTER INCOME TAXES) AS PERCENTAGE OF SALES, 1925–47

Year	Sears	Ward's	Department Stores
1925	8.6	6.7	
1926	8.5	4.8	
1927	9.0	7.0	
1928	8.2	8.3	
1929	7.2	5.0	
1930	4.0	0.2	
1931	3.8	−4.4	
1932	−0.9	−3.2	
1933	4.1	1.2	
1934	4.7	3.7	
1935	5.5	4.6	2.95
1936	6.2	5.6	4.10
1937	5.7	4.6	3.25
1938	4.7	4.7	2.15
1939	6.0	5.7	3.35
1940	5.1	4.5	3.65
1941	4.0	4.3	4.10
1942	3.9	4.2	3.65
1943	4.0	3.5	3.70
1944	3.5	3.4	3.60
1945	3.4	3.5	3.60
1946	6.2	5.4	5.90
1947	5.4	5.1	4.55

* Source: Sears's and Ward's figures calculated from the companies' annual reports; department-store data, from Harvard Bureau of Business Research Bulletins 117 and 128.

holders in cash. In 1945 the stockholders had each received three additional shares in the four-for-one split approved in October, the effect of which was to broaden the stock's distribution. As shown in Table 97, the number of shareholders increased from about 60,000 in 1944 to more than 90,000 in 1947.

Really staggering capital expenditures of approximately $130,000,000 were made in 1946 and 1947. In addition, Sears financed a $169,000,000 increase in inventories. The great bulk of the necessary funds was financed from the company's own resources. Of notable assistance was the unloading of real estate and its conversion into cash. In the two years after February 1, 1946, nearly $69,000,000[10] was realized from the sale of store properties—primarily to such institutional investors as insurance companies, from which the company leased back the stores.

That Sears resorted to no additional equity financing or bank borrowing was facilitated by its previously discussed method of financing instalment sales through banks. Another source of financial strength was conservative

TABLE 100*

PERCENTAGE RATE OF RETURN ON CAPITAL INVESTMENT, SEARS ROEBUCK AND COMPANY AND MONTGOMERY WARD AND COMPANY, 1925–47

YEAR	WARD'S	SEARS Excluding Good Will[†]	SEARS Including Good Will
1925	21.1	19.6	14.9
1926	15.6	17.5	13.8
1927	21.4	18.1	15.0
1928	10.5	17.5	15.2
1929	9.0	17.2	15.7
1930	0.2	7.5	7.0
1931	− 5.7	6.3	5.9
1932	− 4.3	− 1.4	− 1.3
1933	1.7	6.8	6.3
1934	6.7	8.5	7.9
1935	9.3	11.1	
1936	11.7	13.0	
1937	10.3	12.1	
1938	10.1	9.2	
1939	13.0	14.0	
1940	10.4	12.6	
1941	11.6	12.3	
1942	10.5	10.7	
1943	7.8	10.7	
1944	7.7	10.8	
1945	7.8	11.0	
1946		27.0	
1947		24.8	

* Source: Calculated from data in the companies' annual reports.
† These figures indicate rate of return when "good will" has been excluded from the capital investment base. In 1906 common stock was issued against $30,000,000 "good will" as well as tangible assets. In 1920 the company began to write down good-will valuation by charges against surplus until the original $30,000,000 was reduced to $1.00 in 1934.

accounting practices, which resulted in understating earnings to the extent that, especially since 1932, heavy entries were made for reserves. In 1947, for example, as *Fortune* pointed out:

Sears reported net earnings of $189 million before taxes, but the most casual appraisal of its balance sheet shows that Sears actually earned much more. It paid federal income taxes ($81 million) on earnings of $213 million. The $24-million discrepancy represents part of the price General Wood and his stockholders pay to ensure their unfettered ownership. Sears used some $10 million of profits *after* taxes for excess depreciation, and increased its reserve accounts by $14 million.[11]

Ever since Wood brought the full force of his business acumen to bear at Sears, he insisted on heavy depreciation and generous reserves. Table 98 shows the increasing figures for depreciation and other reserves, attesting to the long-standing character of these policies.

The self-financed expansion that characterized Sears's retail development attests to the successful and profitable record that attended the com-

TABLE 101*

STATE, LOCAL, AND FEDERAL TAXES, 1925–47

Year	Net Income before Taxes	Net Income after Taxes	Difference between Net Income before and after Taxes	Taxes as Percentage of Net Income before Taxes	Taxes per $100 Sales	Taxes per Share
1925	$ 25,265,869	$ 20,975,304	$ 4,290,565	16.98	$1.76	$ 4.27
1926	26,558,511	21,908,120	4,650,391	17.51	1.80	1.11†
1927	29,973,426	25,022,552	4,950,874	16.52	1.78	1.18
1928	32,061,415	26,907,902	5,153,513	16.07	1.57	1.20
1929	35,496,475	30,057,652	5,438,823	15.32	1.31	1.20
1930	18,218,519	14,308,897	3,909,622	21.46	1.10	0.82
1931	16,358,059	12,169,172	4,188,887	25.61	1.31	0.85
1932	− 214,925	− 2,543,651	2,328,726	. . . .	0.85	0.49
1933	16,497,803	11,249,295	5,248,508	31.81	1.92	1.10
1934	19,997,131	15,020,551	4,976,580	24.89	1.56	1.04
1935	29,118,475	21,519,219	7,599,256	26.10	1.94	1.57
1936	43,611,237	30,660,199	12,951,038	29.70	2.62	2.36
1937	44,722,527	30,828,248	13,894,279	31.07	2.59	2.51
1938	36,412,619	23,354,364	13,058,255	35.86	2.60	2.34
1939	56,367,279	37,255,274	19,112,005	33.91	3.10	3.39
1940	69,085,907	36,086,668	32,999,239	47.77	4.69	5.78
1941	106,836,605	36,711,504	70,125,101	65.64	7.66	12.14
1942	101,778,872	33,946,989	67,831,883	66.65	7.82	11.73
1943	96,339,281	33,866,087	62,473,194	64.85	7.33	10.70
1944	115,246,399	34,176,111	81,070,288	70.35	8.20	13.82
1945	110,187,760	35,834,836	74,352,924	67.48	7.11	3.15†
1946	181,667,648	100,098,516	81,569,132	44.90	5.06	3.45
1947‡	209,778,090	107,739,992	102,038,098	48.64	5.15	4.32

* Source: Company records. "Net Income before Taxes" is obtained by adding to "net income" shown in published statements the total of state, local, and federal nonrecoverable taxes.
† Stock split four-for-one in these years.
‡ Estimated.

pany's activities. Table 99 indicates that, except for 1932, the firm did not since 1925 experience a profit (after taxes) lower than 3.4 per cent of net sales. Throughout these years Sears demonstrated a somewhat better record than did Montgomery Ward. But both "mail-order" houses established records superior to the achievements of department stores in most of the years for which comparable data are available.

Another index of achievement is found in a review of the figures in Table 100, which attempt to show year by year the return realized on the capital investment of Sears and its chief competitor. Whether gauged in terms of the profitability of sales or investment, one fact is clear. The later years of the period showed lower returns to the company per dollar of investment than did the period ending in 1929. Excepting years of depression Sears had been accustomed to profits of 8–10 (occasionally more) per cent of sales in the two decades ending in 1929. As a review of Table 93 will show, the latter-day decline in Sears's ratio of profit to sales occurred in spite of the increasing productivity of working capital and assets.

The most important single factor explaining the tendency of the profit ratio to decline is perhaps to be found in the marked increase in the

TABLE 102*

Tax Burden, 1925–48

Year	Nonrecoverable Federal Taxes	Nonrecoverable State and Local Taxes	Total
1925	$ 3,152,032	$ 1,138,533	$ 4,290,565
1926	3,269,043	1,381,348	4,650,391
1927	4,122,575	828,299	4,950,874
1928	3,983,315	1,173,198	5,153,513
1929	3,745,237	1,693,586	5,438,823
1930	2,257,110	1,652,512	3,909,622
1931	1,816,048	2,372,839	4,188,887
1932	254,911	2,073,815	2,328,726
1933	3,050,342	2,198,166	5,248,508
1934	2,615,507	2,361,073	4,976,580
1935	4,792,802	2,806,454	7,599,256
1936	9,242,902	3,708,136	12,951,038
1937	8,845,488	5,048,791	13,894,279
1938	7,294,527	5,763,728	13,058,255
1939	12,169,952	6,942,053	19,112,005
1940	25,361,200	7,638,039	32,999,239
1941	60,397,409	9,727,692	70,125,101
1942	58,620,677	9,211,206	67,831,883
1943	53,907,133	8,566,061	62,473,194
1944	71,615,948	9,454,340	81,070,288
1945	65,340,493	9,012,431	74,352,924
1946	69,688,242	11,880,890	81,569,132
1947†	86,512,166	15,526,032	102,038,198

* Source: Company records.
† Estimated.

company's tax bill. In 1925 that bill amounted to something more than $4,000,000; by 1947 the figure was more than $100,000,000, nearly half of Sears's net income before taxes. The mounting tax costs are delineated in Table 101. Whereas taxes accounted for 17 per cent of "net income before taxes" in 1925, the comparable figure in 1947 was 49 per cent. In 1925 it can be seen that taxes accounted for but 1.8 per cent of sales as against more than 5 per cent in 1947. The overwhelming increase in taxes came in the federal tax category (mainly in corporate income tax), although state and local taxes absorbed substantial revenues, as can be observed in Table 102.

Throughout the period from the inception of over-the-counter selling through the early returns on the postwar expansion, Sears multiplied net sales almost fivefold; and net profits (except for the depression and war years) followed a parallel course. Taxes, however, increased some twenty-five times over their 1925 base. Table 103 shows the changes in sales and profits by decades. The years 1926–35 showed a 65 per cent sales increase over its predecessor and an almost identical increase in profits before taxes. The ten years 1936–45, however, showed a sales increase of 184 per cent and a much greater increase in profits before taxes—248 per cent. But, after taxes were paid, the increase in profits was but half the increase in sales

TABLE 103*

SALES AND PROFITS BY DECADES, 1926–45

Decade	Net Sales	Profits after Income Taxes Amount	Profits after Income Taxes Per Cent of Sales	Profits before Income Taxes Amount	Profits before Income Taxes Per Cent of Sales
1926–35†...	$3,213,430,406	$175,619,709	5.46	$224,064,889	7.00
1926–35‡...	2,938,722,755	178,163,360	6.06	224,279,814	7.63
1936–45....	9,137,715,788	332,720,280	3.64	780,588,486	8.54

Decade	Sales Increase over Previous Decade Amount	Sales Increase over Previous Decade Per Cent	Increase in Profits after Income Taxes over Previous Decade Amount	Increase in Profits after Income Taxes over Previous Decade Per Cent	Increase in Profits before Income Taxes over Previous Decade Amount	Increase in Profits before Income Taxes over Previous Decade Per Cent
1926–35†...	$1,269,124,201	65.27	$ 65,828,282	59.97	$ 88,443,274	65.11
1926–35‡...	1,158,456,270	65.07	51,936,464	41.15	72,007,805	47.29
1936–45....	5,924,285,382	184.36	157,100,571	89.57	556,523,597	248.38

* Source: Calculated from data in the company's annual reports.
† Including 1932 sales volume and negative profit.
‡ Excluding 1932 sales volume and negative profit.

for the decade. One fails to find any inability to maintain profitability with marked sales increases—taxes excepted.

Despite increased taxes, a substantial part of which was associated with fiscal policies of World War II, the years since 1925 were rewarding ones for the company. And Sears's shareholders had little complaint to make in view of the record of dividends and stock splits. Table 104 continues the chronicling of dividend and stock increases begun in Table 49 of chapter xviii. The calculations are in terms of the dividends and (share) value of the 1906 issue. By the end of 1947 a person who had bought (and held) one share of Sears's common for $50 in 1906 would have held 60.1 shares and would have received more than $105 in cash dividends in 1947. A buyer of one share in 1925 would have seen his shares multiplied seventeen times

THE PERIOD IN REVIEW

in the twenty-two years since that time and would have received about $30 in cash in 1947, not to mention the market appreciation of his stock, which was pleasantly exhilarating even in the mercurial and "unhealthy" condition of the securities exchanges of 1946 and 1947.

Another indication of Sears's achievements may be found in a study of comparative performance. It has already been shown (Table 99) that the

TABLE 104*

DIVIDEND RECORD AND STOCK INCREASES, 1925–47

YEAR	STOCK DIVIDENDS Date	STOCK DIVIDENDS Amount	ORIGINAL (1906) SHARE WOULD EQUAL	CASH DIVIDENDS Per Share	CASH DIVIDENDS Total
1925			3.50	$6.00	$21.00
1926			3.50	1.50	5.25
	2/23	4 for 1	14.00	1.875	26.25
1927			14.00	2.50	35.00
1928			14.00	1.875	26.25
	9/1	1%	14.14		
	11/1	1%	14.281	0.625	8.925
1929	2/1	1%	14.424	0.625	9.015
	5/1	1%	14.568	0.625	9.105
	8/1	1%	14.714	0.625	9.196
	11/1	1%	14.861	0.625	9.288
1930	2/1	1%	15.009	0.625	9.38
	5/1	1%	15.159	0.625	9.474
	8/1	1%	15.311	0.625	9.569
	11/1	1%	15.464	0.625	9.665
1931	2/1	1%	15.619	0.625	9.761
	5/1	1%	15.775	0.625	9.859
			15.775	1.25	19.718
1932			15.775	1.25	19.718
1933			15.775		
1934			15.775		
1935			15.775	1.75	27.606
1936			15.775	3.75	59.156
1937			15.775	5.50	86.763
1938			15.775	5.50	86.763
1939			15.775	4.25	67.04
1940			15.775	4.25	67.04
1941			15.775	4.25	67.04
1942			15.775	4.25	67.04
1943			15.775	4.25	67.04
1944			15.775	4.25	67.04
1945			15.775	2.25	35.49
	10/1	4 for 1	60.100	0.50	30.05
1946			60.100	1.75	105.18
1947			60.100	1.75	105.18

* Source: 1925–37, Goldman, Sachs and Company; 1938–47, company records.

company surpassed conventional department stores in earnings. Corollary to that record is the increasingly favorable sales record of Sears compared to department stores. Table 105 compares the sales records of these two groups of outlets for certain years since 1929. Even a cursory examination indicates the strength inherent in the marriage of mail order and retail

TABLE 105*

SEARS, ROEBUCK AND COMPANY SALES AND
DEPARTMENT-STORE SALES, 1929–47

(In Millions)

Year	Sears's Net Sales	Department-Store Sales	Sears's Sales as Percentage of Department-Store Sales
1929	$ 415	$ 4,350	9.5
1933	273	2,538	10.8
1935	392	3,311	11.8
1939	617	3,975	15.5
1940	704	4,266	16.5
1941	915	5,027	18.2
1942	868	5,566	15.6
1943	853	6,132	13.9
1944	989	6,764	14.6
1945	1,045	7,428	14.1
1946	1,613	9,621	16.8
1947	1,982	10,534	18.8

*Source: Department-store sales, including mail order, 1929–45, *Statistical Abstract of the United States, 1946*, p. 952; 1946–47, *Survey of Current Business*, February, 1948, p. 16; Sears's sales, calculated from data in the company's annual reports.

TABLE 106*

RELATIVE POSITION OF SEARS, ROEBUCK AND COMPANY AND
MONTGOMERY WARD AND COMPANY SALES, 1925–47

(In Thousands)

YEAR	NET SALES Sears	NET SALES Ward's	NET SALES Total	PERCENTAGE OF TOTAL Sears	PERCENTAGE OF TOTAL Ward's
1925	$ 243,798	$ 170,593	$ 416,391	58.6	41.4
1926	258,213	183,801	442,014	58.4	41.6
1927	277,502	186,683	464,185	59.8	40.2
1928	328,760	214,350	543,110	60.5	39.5
1929	415,380	267,326	682,706	60.8	39.2
1930	355,180	249,097	604,277	58.8	41.2
1931	320,057	200,400	520,457	61.5	38.5
1932	274,708	176,489	451,197	60.9	39.1
1933	273,471	187,633	461,104	59.3	40.7
1934	318,061	249,806	567,867	56.0	44.0
1935	392,098	293,042	685,140	57.2	42.8
1936	494,968	361,297	856,265	57.8	42.2
1937	537,242	414,091	951,333	56.5	43.5
1938	501,677	413,961	915,638	54.8	45.2
1939	617,414	474,882	1,092,296	56.5	43.5
1940	704,301	515,911	1,220,212	57.7	42.3
1941	915,058	632,709	1,547,767	59.1	40.9
1942	867,834	635,007	1,502,841	57.7	42.3
1943	852,597	595,933	1,448,530	58.9	41.1
1944	988,770	620,969	1,609,739	61.4	38.6
1945	1,045,259	654,779	1,700,038	61.5	38.5
1946	1,612,596	974,257	2,586,853	62.3	37.7
1947	1,981,536	1,158,675	3,140,211	63.1	36.9

*Source: Companies' records and annual reports.

stores. Both Ward's and Sears made great sales advances during these years, but, as Table 106 shows, the latter maintained its position relative to Ward's, its principal competitor; although even as late as 1947 Sears had not climbed back to the place it once occupied—prior to 1921—when Ward's did only about 30 per cent of the combined volume of these two great houses.

It may be recalled that Sears had increased its share of the mail-order market in the years 1910–25. In 1910 the company's mail-order sales attracted 1.12 per cent of farm cash income. By 1925 customers were sending 2.24 per cent of that income to Sears, Roebuck and Company, and the years since 1925 have seen no diminution of Sears's share of farm income. Indeed, as Table 107 makes clear, the company actually improved its position in

TABLE 107*

MAIL-ORDER SALES RELATIVE TO FARM CASH INCOME, 1925–41

Year	Mail-Order Sales as Percentage of Farm Cash Income	Year	Mail-Order Sales as Percentage of Farm Cash Income
1925	2.24	1934	1.95
1926	2.36	1935	2.22
1927	2.35	1936	2.36
1928	2.17	1937	2.30
1929	2.35	1938	2.41
1930	2.33	1939	2.65
1931	2.54	1940	2.69
1932	2.51	1941	2.74
1933	2.17		

* Source: Company records.

that regard—except for the war years, when shortages took a heavy toll in the catalogue business and when each year saw Sears refund hundreds of millions to its customers because their orders could not be filled. It must be observed, however, that since the mid-thirties an increasing volume of what Sears classifies as mail-order business came from nonfarm customers —via the new techniques of mail order discussed earlier.

Perhaps the clearest indication of Sears's successful market exploitation is to be found in a study of how well the company did in capturing business for the kinds of products it sold, which Table 108 attempts to show. It is evident that Sears met with marked success in selling its products, for the company's share of national personal consumption expenditures for Sears-type products increased from something more than 2 per cent in 1929 to just under 5 per cent in 1947. Again the effect of the war is apparent in the lower ratios of 1942 through 1945, when shortages, especially in durable goods, bit hard into Sears's sales. The same general tendencies are evident in an analysis of Sears's sales in terms of national income and its various components.

It is difficult to summarize the factors that characterized Sears and were responsible for the company's success in the years since 1925. The effective adaptation to the changes in social and economic conditions of the period cannot be gainsaid, and the preceding chapters have chronicled the process of that adaptation. Certainly the dominating feature of these years—the

TABLE 108*

RATIO OF NET SALES TO NATIONAL PERSONAL CONSUMPTION
EXPENDITURES FOR SEARS-TYPE PRODUCTS, 1929–47

Year	Sears's Net Sales (In Thousands)	National Personal Consumption Expenditures for Sears-Type Products (In Millions)	Percentage Sears's Sales to National Personal Consumption for Sears-Type Products
1929	$ 415,380	$18,952	2.19
1930	355,180	16,174	2.20
1931	320,057	13,636	2.35
1932	274,708	9,959	2.76
1933	273,249	9,067	3.01
1934	318,061	10,873	2.93
1935	392,098	11,736	3.34
1936	494,468	13,307	3.72
1937	537,242	14,369	3.74
1938	501,677	13,782	3.64
1939	617,414	14,948	4.13
1940	704,301	16,021	4.40
1941	915,058	19,140	4.78
1942	867,834	21,104	4.11
1943	852,597	23,375	3.65
1944	988,770	25,280	3.91
1945	1,045,259	28,598	3.66
1946	1,612,596	37,233	4.33
1947	1,981,536	41,625	4.76

*Source: National personal consumption expenditures for Sears-type products have been developed from data in the National Income Supplement to the *Survey of Current Business*, published in July, 1947, by the United States Department of Commerce, Bureau of Foreign and Domestic Commerce.

theme that unifies a whole series of particular events and policies—was the determined expansion of the retail stores, which built upon the well-established reputation of the old mail-order business.

To more than any other single man the achievements of this period were a monument to R. E. Wood, who brought to Sears the force of new ideas and the strength to see them executed, often (especially initially) in the face of determined opposition. Wood assumed the burden—and meted out the penalties and rewards—of an often hard but effective schoolmaster, during the trying years that Sears learned a new business, for the retail stores proved to be essentially a different business from that of mail order, and it required a discerning hand to conserve the best in the latter and build the new business.

In his successful efforts to create the new pattern of "storekeeping" it was Wood who brought efficient management in the modern sense, and it was he who really built an organization competent to the tasks before it. Wood combined the strength of leadership with an appreciation of the necessity for antonomy once a man was assigned a task. A student of population trends, it was Wood who greatly influenced the geographical locations of the retail stores that he was convinced were Sears's only hope of growth, if not survival. And growth the company realized—profitable growth through more than twenty years marked by numerous important changes in the American community and public attitudes, and scarred by depression and war. In the face of obstacles that lay both within and without itself, Sears entered again upon determined expansion—an attitude that has characterized the business since its earliest days.

CHAPTER XXXIII

In Retrospect

IN THE more than five decades since its formal incorporation as Sears, Roebuck and Company in 1893, the company has survived business depressions, wars, hosts of competitors, suppressive legislation, and significant shifts in the population trends and buying habits of the United States. Sears, Roebuck has not merely survived; it has succeeded on a remarkable scale and has experienced a record of almost uninterrupted growth.

In general, there are two ways in which a business enterprise may grow while catering to the same market: (1) through feeding on an expanded income in the market the firm serves and (2) by capturing a larger share of that market. Sears, Roebuck has grown in both of these ways. But markets seldom remain stationary, and, since continuing success depends primarily upon the successful exploitation of market situations, the continued prosperity of a company requires that its management identify correctly the characteristics and potentials of its markets and that its products, policies, and methods be adapted to the ever changing environment.

The most outstanding example of a changing market in Sears's development was, of course, to be found in the declining relative importance of the farm market. To meet that shift, the company diversified the facilities of its selling organization by turning to retail stores and also expanded the geographic area and the population categories served. The geographic expansion had earlier been evident in the increased number of mail-order plants as a means not only of extending the market but of simplifying distribution problems as well. Continued diversification of selling facilities was resorted to in a later period of company growth by development of telephone sales and order offices to bolster the mail-order sales of the company.

And almost since its beginnings Sears, Roebuck expanded sales by increasing almost indiscriminately the number and value of the products it sold. This was especially the case through the years that saw the fullest development of the mail-order business. More recently, however, notably in retail, greater selectivity and sales effort have been exercised in merchandise lines—by forceful emphasis on full assortments in the best-selling price lines in place of an indefinite multiplication of "fringe" items.

The record of the company's accomplishments underlines the importance that management assumes in business progress. The pattern of growth that has characterized Sears, Roebuck's history was neither inevitable nor automatic. The markets which the company has exploited with such singular success for more than fifty years have, obviously, been precisely the markets open to its competitors. And the singularity of Sears's success is particularly manifest in the fact that within a year or two after the opening of this century Sears had surpassed the volume of its chief competitor, Montgomery Ward, which had been selling general merchandise by mail for fourteen years by the time Richard W. Sears sold his first watch in 1886.

In any evaluation of the wisdom and soundness of the policies pursued by Sears, Roebuck in accommodating itself to new conditions, two cardinal factors emerge: (1) the company has never been an innovator, on a scale large enough to merit serious note, in its merchandise items, although it has at every critical stage been something of an innovator in its techniques of buying and selling and related operating aspects; and (2) in each of the three broad periods into which the company's history most conveniently falls, its leadership has been not merely adequate but also particularly well fitted to the moment. Each of the company's three outstanding leaders—Richard Warren Sears, Julius Rosenwald, and Robert E. Wood—are conspicuously characterized by the foregoing generalizations.

In a way, the success of Sears, Roebuck was rooted in the policies of its earliest period—policies laid down and developed largely by Richard Sears and still discernible in broad shape even today. Alvah C. Roebuck, cofounder, withdrew in 1895, having contributed a watchmaker's skill and little else but his name. Richard Sears determined upon a low-price policy, and he advertised it on an unprecedented scale. The success of this tactic was sufficient to provide the profits which soon enabled him to expand his merchandise lines sufficiently to capture an even larger segment of his market by offering rural customers the opportunity to order most of their wants at one sitting. Thus did Richard Sears come to advertise goods to satisfy the majority of mankind's wants, in most instances at dramatically low prices—rendered even more dramatic at one point by his widely advertised sales slogan, "Send No Money" and again by his Customers' Profit-sharing Plan.

Richard Sears's own instinctive knowledge of the needs of rural folk, who for many years constituted his firm's natural market, equipped him with an unsurpassed ability to divine not only what goods his customers wanted but also what prices they were willing and able to pay. Those goods were the ones for which a demonstrable demand was clearly visible. While Sears's use of watches as his first merchandise line was fortuitous, it is important to note that a large demand for watches existed. The only barrier between most rural folk and a shiny, "gold," "city-type" pocket watch was the price.

Richard Sears's determination to advertise his wares on a truly vast scale represented both a desire to sell a large volume of goods in the short run and a lurking uncertainty that the mail-order method could not long survive without appropriate pyrotechnics of some sort. It resulted, nonetheless, in intrenching his business' position, and in making "Sears and Roebuck" a household byword. It helped pre-empt large areas of trade for his company. His truly lavish advertising at a time when working capital was at a low ebb was obviously a gamble; in Sears's own view, it was perhaps a calculated risk—not carefully calculated, since he was no business logician, but rather conceived as a risk he could not afford *not* to take.

By the time of the 1907–8 business depression Richard Sears had achieved virtually everything he had striven for, and possibly a great deal more. He had built a mail-order business stocking many thousands of items at low prices—at any rate, at prices which most of his customers and competitors appeared to feel were low. He had made the name of his firm synonymous with mail-order selling. He had exploited his merchandise guaranty—itself a stratagem the necessity of which he seems never to have questioned—throughout the land. His policy of "Satisfaction Guaranteed or Your Money Back" has stood to this day without alteration. And, perhaps most important to the long-range growth of the company, he had built a vast reservoir of good will. His unique advertising methods had created a bond with millions of unseen customers. A business which was becoming a giant corporation had also made a reputation as a friend of the people. It is surely almost impossible to overestimate the importance of this good will.

By virtue of the policies and techniques that were "inventions" of Richard Sears, the business was established and the market opened up. It was Sears's signal contribution that he "created the demand" for Sears, Roebuck's merchandise. In doing so, he left the firm an invaluable legacy which was conserved and husbanded by the officers who guided the firm's destinies under the general direction of Julius Rosenwald. Richard Sears's contribution was dramatic and readily apparent. Rosenwald's contribution, less dramatic, is therefore more difficult to assess. Edwin Embree, long associated with Julius Rosenwald's philanthropies, has characterized him in the following terms:

> It is difficult to assess Julius Rosenwald's contribution.... He was quick and astute, but never pretended to be a business genius. He had a gift for judging the worth of other men and putting them in responsible posts. He demanded efficiency and got it. He was hard working, energetic, resourceful. He held firmly to the policy of rigorously honest dealing. And he had an intuitive sense that continually astounded his associates. Frequently, at business conferences, after listening quietly to a proposal, he would shake his head and say with conviction, "I can't tell you what's wrong with it, but I don't like it." And he was equally quick to seize on what seemed to him a good idea. Almost invariably he was found to be right.[1]

Embree's characterization is confirmed by most of Rosenwald's close business associates. General Wood has indicated his general agreement

IN RETROSPECT 671

with that evaluation in his statement: "Julius Rosenwald could be wrong on small things, but he was usually right on larger things. And by his action in 1921 he saved the company."

Another of Rosenwald's actions, taken some five years before the 1921 fiasco, was later to be brought to spectacular fruition under Wood's regime. Sears, Roebuck's celebrated Employees' Profit-sharing Fund, inaugurated in 1916 with little more than $400,000, prospered so that by December 31, 1948, some 96,000 employees owned 19 per cent of the company's outstanding stock having a market value of $176,118,175, in addition to $44,586,802 in cash, bonds, and other securities.

It was, of course, ironic that Richard Sears's classic flair for promotion, which had built the company into a dramatically successful concern by 1907, was to serve as the proximate cause of his departure from the organization he had founded. Yet, while Julius Rosenwald and Richard Sears's own disciples felt compelled to restrain Sears from grandiose promotion schemes during the 1907–8 depression, the company was to find itself able for nearly twenty years after Richard Sears's departure to capitalize upon the momentum his earlier activities had supplied. For the subsequent period, which may loosely be called the "Rosenwald era" (1908–25), following the company's quick recovery from that short-lived business depression, was essentially one of great gains, consolidation, and conservation. Agricultural prosperity in that "golden age" of mail order was itself sufficient to have sustained the company's sales at progressively higher levels; but the company managed also to increase the percentage of farm cash income flowing to it in the form of orders for merchandise, thus compounding its own prosperity.

The company's primary tasks in its "middle" period included constant improvement in the quality of its goods and in customer service, a cautious stewardship of finances, and an adaptation to rising standards of business ethics and honesty in the country. Julius Rosenwald and his alter ego, Vice-President Albert Loeb, were admirably fitted for the requirements of this period. Under their leadership such dubious lines as patent medicines were discontinued, the testing laboratories were established to improve and exactly determine the quality of merchandise, sales promotion became more cautious and catalogue descriptions more nearly accurate; additional mail-order plants were established to provide better service to more customers at lower cost to the company.

Better control of operating costs—a prime essential in any phase of conservation—was reflected in the triumph over operating problems in the middle period. This triumph was so great that, by the end of that period, mail-order operating (meaning customer service) ceased to be a major problem. The schedule system of shipping, and its extension to other activities, had been refined under the capable leadership of Operating Vice-President Otto Doering. In subsequent years Operating Vice-President T. J.

Carney became Doering's counterpart, in solving operating problems for the retail stores. Under Carney's direction a code of operating techniques was developed which made it possible for the retail managers to concentrate their attention on buying (ordering) and intensified selling.

The "Rosenwald era," which saw the greatest prosperity the company had known to that time, also encompassed the very nearly disastrous debacle of 1921, largely a result of the company's inability to control its inventories, and came finally to a stark view of the waning mail-order market. The decreased share of agriculture in the general American prosperity, the rise of chain stores as potent competitors of the mail-order houses, the increase in automobile registrations and paved roads, population shifts trending toward greater urbanization that by 1920 relegated rural residents to a minority position—all these and other factors by 1925 called for new measures on the part of established mail-order firms.

To accommodate Sears, Roebuck to the changed situation, the company had a man more than adequate to the moment. Vice-President R. E. Wood, who succeeded Charles M. Kittle when the latter's three-year tenure as president ended in 1928, was an expansionist with a passionate conviction that Sears's destiny lay in immediate entry into the retail field. More than that, he envisaged the company's retail units as instruments far more flexible than mail order had proved in trying periods; he brought a new conception of the character of such retail stores and a correct visualization of the geographic population trends, as evidenced by Sears's great expansion into the South and West—even at what seems to have been a premeditated neglect of such large eastern markets as Boston and Philadelphia with their stationary population. Further, Wood was young and vigorous enough to face without flinching—even, in fact, with relish—the task of building a new business, of adapting the company's organization structure to the needs of the new business, of reorienting its merchandise structure the better to meet new demands and new opportunities.

In the wake of Sears, Roebuck's entry into what experienced department-store executives considered a lion's den, problems appeared which might well have swept away much that was good and usable in the company's history and structure; it was Wood, more than anyone else, who salvaged the best of the old and skilfully blended it with the essential components of the new, to forge a unified team adequate to meet the demands of both retail and mail-order selling.

Had a "new management" not assumed leadership after the company recovered from the 1921 depression, Sears, Roebuck's latter-day evolution might have been quite different. The guiding hands of the business were old hands by 1924, and it is not unlikely that the company might have continued to rest upon the comfortable, though not expanding, volume that a straight mail-order activity had achieved. Had such been the case, it is doubtful if even mail-order volume could have been sustained, for that achievement came to be realized only through the use of devices that were fostered by the infusion of new blood after Julius Rosenwald relinquished the presidency. In no small degree the survival of mail order has been associated with the "new blood" that created Sears's retail organization.

The excursion into retail stores in 1925 represented the most marked departure from established mail-order practice since the company's founding. The sales and profits that have so clearly vindicated Wood's judgment have resulted very largely from his concept of what kind of stores the company ought to have and what kind of men were to manage them.

While invidious comparisons are often made between the accomplishments of Sears and those of conventional department stores, the better record of the former is largely attributable to the fact that the Sears operation has really supplemented department stores. In its retail phase the company has supplemented department stores in the sphere of merchandise, by stressing hard lines and "big-ticket" items, which even to this day remain more or less "foreign" to most department stores, certainly from the point of view of net profits. For the latter, having had their genesis in dry goods, were basically of the soft-lines genre, and they lost by default in the later day of heightened consumer interest in hard lines. Sears, on the other hand, was able and determined to put its peculiar strength of development and procurement behind the hard lines which make up durable and semidurable goods. In a sense, Sears and Ward's are the only complete department stores, for they serve their customers from the cradle to the grave—from diapers and teething rings to shrouds and tombstones.

Another area in which Sears capitalized upon the inertia of conventional department stores was in its policy of store location. Sears's store location policy was such as to supplement the company's own mail-order business; as between areas dependent mainly upon agricultural income (the traditional mail-order market) and "industrial" areas, Sears chose the latter. But, more notably, Wood embraced the concept of "America on wheels." He held that most of the company's retail stores could be located in outlying districts which would offer the advantages of lower rentals yet would also, because of the great mobility of Americans, still be within reach of potential customers. It was clear to Wood as early as 1925 that automobile registrations had outstripped the parking space available in downtown metropolitan areas. The locations Wood envisaged for Sears's retail stores would be in uncongested areas where ample parking space was available free to customers.

Ultimately the success or failure of a business enterprise rests largely upon the degree of acceptance it finds among consumers. Throughout its history the fundamental appeal the company has had for buyers has been standard-quality goods at low prices. In its earliest years the dramatic message of the company's advertising was that of "low price." While it has not been possible to make detailed price comparisons of Sears's retail offerings versus "competitive" offerings, it does seem clear that the customers of Sears, Roebuck and Company were convinced that Sears sold for less. The opponents of the mail-order business and of chain stores have time and again conceded this and used it as a weapon of attack. There is hardly a modern department store that today does not carefully study Sears's, and Ward's goods and their mail-order and retail prices.

To the extent that Sears advertised comparable goods at lower prices, it may be essayed that Sears, Roebuck exerted still another effect on the cost of living. By setting prices for goods and publishing them in the catalogues, the company in effect influences prices throughout much of the United States. Local merchants are often compelled to bring their prices in line with Sears, Roebuck's.

The early mail-order business, dependent as it was on the catalogue, had to adopt a "one-price" policy at the outset, and undoubtedly facilitated the adoption of that system, especially in the West, where the bargaining "instinct" had survived after such merchants as Filene, Macy, and Wanamaker had established the one-price system in much of the East.

The low-price policy that has been a continuing characteristic of Sears's strategy for many years rested on the relatively lower operating cost that characterized mail-order methods, as evidenced by the differential between Sears's own retail and mail-order prices. In retail stores there remain, however, generally lower rentals than are typical of department stores, and further the economies that result from refusing to compete on the basis of a multiplication of "free" services characteristic of conventional department stores. Sears's retail stores generally have no free home delivery; items such as refrigerators and other "big tickets" obviously requiring home delivery include the cost of that delivery in their selling prices. Sears's stores generally have no charge accounts, thus eliminating bad debts. Further, the absence of charge accounts has a marked tendency to reduce costly returns.

In addition to the economies made possible by the policies just referred to, other economies derive from the whole nature of the Sears operation, as it has developed since 1925. As indicated previously, the company's cost of reductions is lower—markdowns are less of a problem, since Sears deals largely in staple and semistaple lines subject to much less depreciation and fewer style changes than fashion goods which are heavily emphasized in conventional department stores. And, finally, the company's buying organization and its mass purchasing power—augmented by, and increasingly attuned to, its distinctive buying methods—have made it possible to purchase goods usually at lower costs.

Relevant to both present and past company policy is the fact that Sears has avoided the great risks incident to pioneering really new products. An important reason that Sears, Roebuck has traditionally offered some truly dramatic "bargains" is that the company has never assumed the burden of building a market during the expensive stage of innovation. Rather it has performed the very useful service of broadening the market for products once a popular demand for the products has been created.

Currently, probably Sears's greatest strength lies in its technique of basic buying applied to lines for which a mass demand exists, and in which the company can realize substantial economies because of mass production. In attempts to maintain a competitive advantage in distribution, Sears, Roebuck has come more and more to be interested in production; its most notable achievements lie currently in the way it buys goods. In capitalizing upon existing demand and popular acceptance, and in implementing its basic buying program, the company has come to dominate the distribution sequence by assuming responsibility for the selection and design of products. For many of its sources Sears has assumed the initiative normally residing in the manufacturer and, in so doing, has assumed some of the manufacturer's normal selling costs. The company, with its more than six hundred retail outlets and eleven mail-order plants, is in a position to reduce risks and selling costs which manufacturers would otherwise have to bear in the costly competitive struggle for outlets.

Knitting the company's multiple activities together and providing for its continued prosperity is, of course, the task of top management. One of the most generally remarked dangers of large-scale operation is that of building a top-heavy bureaucracy. To avoid that hazard, Sears has adopted the policy of administrative decentralization, which strives to give executives in the field maximal scope for initiative—while maintaining a central buying organization to achieve maximal advantages in the procurement of merchandise.

In formulating and executing its organization pattern, the company not only has paid little heed but has actually run counter to one of the favorite tenets of modern management theory—the "span of control," which seeks to limit the number of subordinates reporting to a single individual in order that that individual may exercise the detailed direction and control generally believed essential. In flouting this concept and in building a "broad" or "flat" organization instead of a "vertical" or "tall" organization, Sears, Roebuck has deliberately given each key executive so many assistants that it is impossible for him to exercise very close supervision over their activities.

This means, of course, that each executive is thrown largely on his own, to sink or swim, since he cannot rely upon his superiors to more than a limited extent; and those superiors in turn cannot severely restrict, through detailed supervision and control, the growth and development of their subordinates. A corollary to this "broad" or "flat" type of organization structure is the severe limitation of staff authority and the preservation of line responsibility. The number and influence of staff specialists have been held to a minimum in Sears, for the company has been eager to preserve and strengthen the integrity of the line, without which decentralized administration can be neither real nor effective.

The decentralization program was not completed until after the company had acquired sufficient experience to codify its operating procedures and to train its own store managers in the ways to realize maximal benefits from the company's buying facilities. Aware that good administration is crucial to profitable operation on a large scale, Sears long ago decided that it must evolve a system which could be translated into action and kept in motion by personnel of what may, without disparagement, be described as "quality mediocrity." In other terms, the company concluded that, while business "geniuses" are rare, reasonably capable administrators are far more numerous and can be developed without great difficulty within the framework of a broad and far-reaching personnel program. Hence Sears evolved a system which demands not too much initiative—despite all the talk of that quality—but leans rather upon adaptability and the demonstrated ability to master simple and well worked-out procedures. For example, one reason Sears's store managers can safely be allowed what appears a wide degree of autonomy is the fact that all buying is centralized in Chicago; the local store manager cannot go far wrong on merchandise selection from parent-prepared merchandise lists. An individual store manager works within a relatively rigid framework of general personnel policies established by the parent. So with other aspects of the business—receiving, storage, credit and collections, etc. Despite the limitation of autonomy within the framework of apparently great autonomy, this general policy appears to have achieved considerable symbolic value; the very feeling of being "on one's own" may have helped to capitalize upon and exploit to a fuller degree the human resources that ultimately manage Sears, Roebuck and Company.

Appendixes

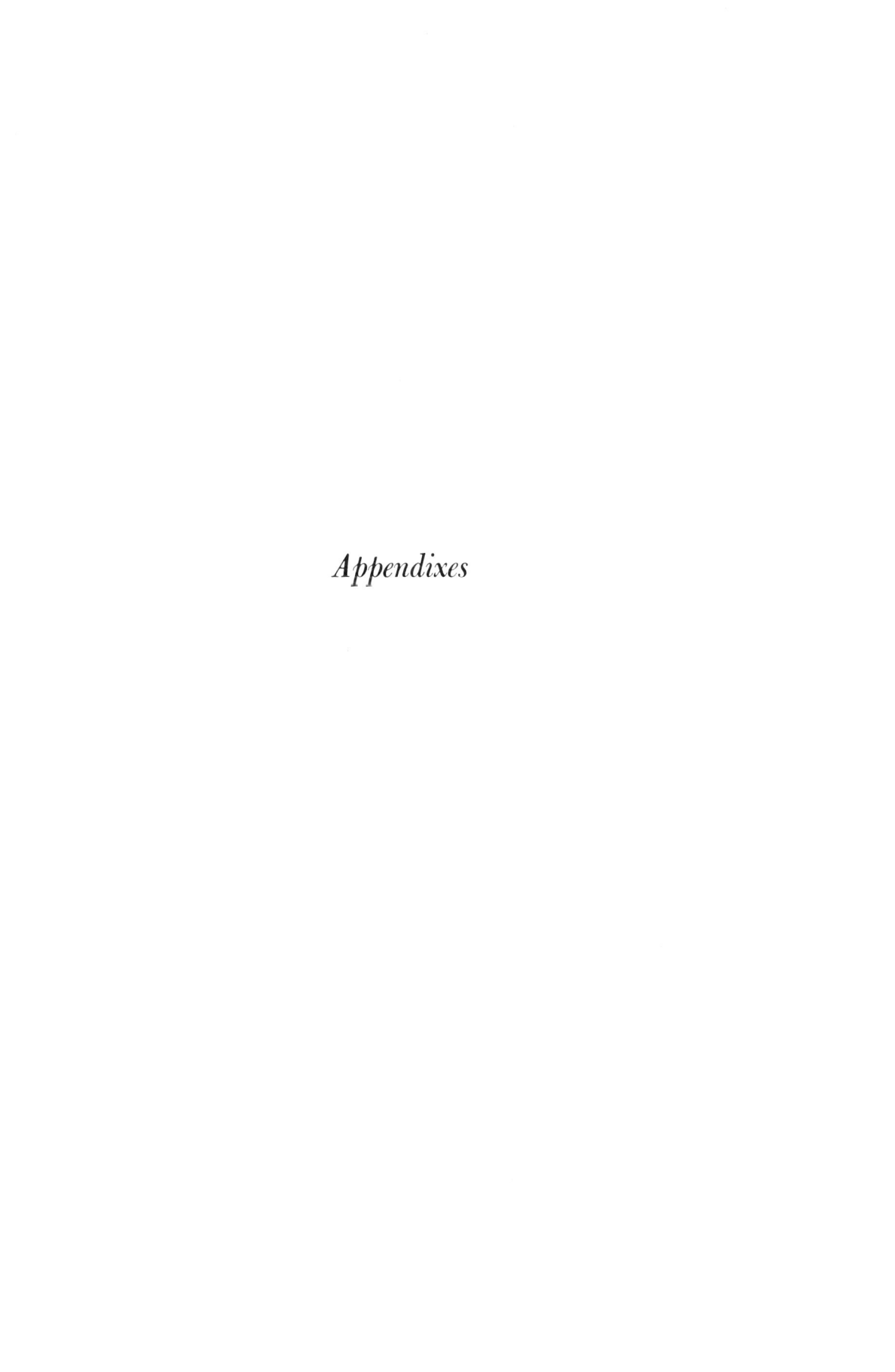

APPENDIX A

Sharing Profits with Employees

AT THE beginning of 1948 some 81,863 Sears's employees held claims to $131,765,659 of assets that appeared on the financial statements of "The Savings and Profit Sharing Pension Fund of Sears, Roebuck and Co. Employes."[1] Small wonder that profit-sharing is one of the most frequently discussed aspects of Sears's operations. Almost as unique as the present impressive financial status of the fund is the pension aspect of the plan, for profit-sharing is the principal instrument relied on to provide retirement security for Sears's personnel.

While profit-sharing is not a recent innovation at Sears, having antedated by nearly two decades the modern personnel department of the company, the profit-sharing idea is considerably older than the Sears plan. The existence of some sort of profit sharing arrangements has been indicated by various writers as early as 1794 in the United States, 1820 in France, and 1829 in England.[2]

Although the nineteenth century saw the development of a number of plans in England, not until early in the present century does there appear to have been much interest in profit-sharing in the United States. As late as 1916 Boris Emmet reported:

> Profit sharing, properly speaking, i.e., as confined to plans in which distributions of specified proportions of the net profits of the enterprise are made to at least one-third of the total employed, does not appear to have reached any considerable proportions in the United States. The number of such plans known to be in operation at the present time does not exceed 60.[3]

Even now profit-sharing is not generally accepted practice.

On July 1, 1916, the same year that the Bureau of Labor Statistics published Emmet's study, Sears, Roebuck inaugurated profit-sharing. Until recently the only available indication of the immediate source of the Sears plan was the following letter sent to Julius Rosenwald by Mrs. Joseph T. Bowen, a stockholder of the company, dated February 11, 1915:

> I had hoped to see you this past week to talk over with you a matter which had been troubling me, but as I have not been able to go anywhere I am writing although it is not half as satisfactory.
>
> As a stockholder in Sears, Roebuck and Company holding seven hundred shares, I am wondering if it would not be possible at the annual meeting of the stockholders on February 23rd to consider the question of appropriating a part—perhaps a small one—of the stock dividend, for the use of the employees of

the Company; either to be added to the Pension Fund or as a bonus to be divided between them.

As a stockholder I am, of course, glad that the Company has had such prosperous years that it can afford to pay me such a large return upon my investment, but I must also confess, to a feeling of responsibility as a stockholder—and perhaps some sense of guilt—that in these hard times so large a sum is to be distributed among the stockholders, and, that the employees are to have no share whatever in it.

While I have not talked with any of the other stockholders I believe that I am voicing the sentiment of many of them who feel the same responsibility, and who believe that some distribution of the profits would not only tend to better the feeling between employer and employed, but would redound to the interest of the Company in better service, as the employee would feel that he was not merely a cog in a machine but a participant in the profits of the business created by his work.

This is, in no sense, intended as a criticism; I presume that the question has already been discussed. But it is perhaps a kindly protest, addressed to you as a friend, against the distribution of so large a sum to the stockholders without some participation by the employees.

Rosenwald never answered this letter, nor did he discuss the matter with Mrs. Bowen.[4] It seems unlikely that Rosenwald would have failed to communicate with Mrs. Bowen if, in fact, she was responsible for planting the idea in his mind—since Rosenwald had occasion to meet frequently with her in connection with their mutual philanthropic interests.

It is possible that Rosenwald may have been indirectly influenced to consider favorably a profit-sharing plan by a suggestion introduced in the hearings before the Illinois Senate Vice Committee in 1913. The committee was interested in establishing a causal relation between low wages and immorality. To this end the committee took testimony on wages paid by various Illinois companies. Rosenwald appeared several times. In the course of the testimony, Lieutenant-Governor Barratt O'Hara examined Rosenwald as follows:

Examination of J. Rosenwald by Lt. Governor Barratt O'Hara, March 17, 1913:

Q. Then the total profits, or the net profits, of your corporation for the fiscal year of 1911, were approximately what according to this statement?

A. Something over $7,000,000.00.

Q. Could you apply a generous portion of these profits to increase the wages of employees and still pay your stockholders interest on the money invested? That is, could you take $2,000,000.00 from the total profit of $7,000,000.00 and apply it to the wages of employees and still pay interest on the money invested in your business?

A. The question of interest is hardly applicable because the value of the shares of the company are not entirely represented by interest on the capital invested, but I would say we could take $2,000,000.00 and still pay some dividend, some income to the shareholders of the company.

Q. What dividend are you paying now, Mr. Rosenwald?

A. We are paying now 7% on all of the preferred and common stock of the Company.

SHARING PROFITS WITH EMPLOYEES 681

Q. How much surplus have you after paying that dividend?
A. I would not want to state that off-hand. I am not just sure what that figures. I think our surplus, according to our books, was something in the neighborhood of $12,000,000.00 at the end of the year 1912.
Q. According to this statement your surplus for the year 1911, was $13,700,-000.00?
A. For that year, yes, sir.
Q. And you are paying 7% dividend. Then it would be possible for you to take $2,000,000.00 of this surplus and give it to your employees?
A. It would be entirely possible, yes.
Q. If after investigating the matter yourself you reach the conclusion that you can pay the girls enough money to live on decently you will take money from the surplus fund and give it to them in decent wages?
A. I wouldn't say we will take it from the surplus fund. We endeavor to pay all our employees what we feel is fair wages and will always continue to do so.[5]

Although the origin of the Sears plan is popularly attributed to the Bowen letter (even among present company executives), the fact seems to be that the Harris Trust and Savings Bank of Chicago was the immediate source of Rosenwald's inspiration. Executives at Sears had been studying pension plans for some time with the view of installing an employee pension program. According to a source who was close to policy-making at the time, Mr. Rosenwald returned one day from a visit to the Harris Bank with marked enthusiasm for the profit-sharing arrangement the bank installed January 1, 1916.[6]

Apart from the immediate and direct impetus to establishing the profit-sharing plan, the Sears policy seems to be part of a larger movement. Although profit-sharing has by no means had a general or widespread adoption in American (or European) industry, the decade 1911–20 saw the initiation of many such plans in both the United States and Great Britain. Of 193 plans in the United States, Balderston found in 1936 that 75 had been started between 1911 and 1920, more than three times as many as had been initiated in any decade prior to that time. He found that in that same decade 224 British plans had appeared, ranking the period well ahead of the years 1921–30, the next most active decade, with 160 plans started.[7]

Whatever the immediate stimulus to Sears's adventure in profit-sharing, there appears to have been a general trend supporting the practice. The historical development of pension systems attests to the fact of a rather widespread preoccupation with retirement security about the time Sears, Roebuck and Company established its plan. Latimer found that, of 421 plans established between 1874 and 1929, over half (221) first appeared between 1911 and 1920.[8]

It was really an interest in pensions that led Sears into profit-sharing—partly as a means of circumventing the objections of certain company officers to the abuses that had been associated with traditional plans in some other companies. In most retirement plans the pension was available only upon retirement and at the discretion of the employer. If workers were discharged for any reason, they lost their pension rights. Former Sears's executives report that they were aware of more than one firm where discharges were timed to avoid the pension liability. To remove the possibilities of such an occurrence, the earliest rules for the Sears's plan provided that at any time after ten years (for men, and less for women leaving the company to marry) the fund member might withdraw all sums credited to his account. Thus the employee was assured against loss of retirement credits whenever his employment terminated, for reasons of either voluntary or involuntary withdrawal. Further, the profit-sharing arrangement avoided the necessity of incurring a fixed financial obligation, a characteristic of traditional pension plans.

Although there is a widespread conviction among Sears's executives that company operations are more efficient and profits larger as a result of the profit-sharing program, this happy condition, if it is a fact, was evidently not important in the policy-makers' decision to adopt the program. All the evidence indicates that profit-sharing was originally viewed as a pension program. It has proved impossible to determine now with any degree of certainty whether Rosenwald and his contemporaries had any other purposes. One may well speculate whether the program was looked upon as a means of promoting satisfactory employee relations. Through the associations made in the pursuit of his philanthropic interests Julius Rosenwald was constantly in touch with persons interested in "improving" the lot of the workingman. And there seems no question that Albert Loeb was active in trying to make Sears a better place to work. Indeed, in numerous conversations with retired Sears's personnel, one encounters overtones that Loeb may have been more responsible than Rosenwald for bringing profit-sharing into being. There seems to be no doubt that he was primarily responsible for working out the details of the plan.

But profit-sharing could not have been adopted without at least acquiescence from Julius Rosenwald. One may speculate on the reasons that impelled him to embrace the profit-sharing and retirement plan. Rosenwald has been characterized by certain of his associates as "first of all a businessman." He firmly believed, for example, in paying no more than the market rate of wages. At the same time his philanthropies attest to his acute awareness of humanitarian objectives and of the desirability (if not necessity) of ameliorating some of the unsavory conditions that existed co-extensively with the rapidly developing American capitalism. A combination profit-sharing and pension plan offered the opportunity of giving his workers both a capitalistic stake in the business and the basis of retirement security.

The decision to use accumulating funds to invest in the common stock of the company is a reflection of Rosenwald's boundless faith in Sears's destiny. On every possible occasion he recommended the purchase of Sears's common stock to his friends and associates. (While he was a trustee

SHARING PROFITS WITH EMPLOYEES 683

of Chicago's famous Hull House, Rosenwald invested part of the endowment in his company's stock, so convinced was he of its possibilities.) Surely there could be no greater promise of old age security than a block of Sears's stock. The contributory character of the plan Sears adopted and the statement of the fund's objectives attest to the importance the founders attached to thrift, a much-admired virtue in that pre-Keynesian age.

The essential mechanics of the profit-sharing plan are simple and clear. The fund is, in a sense, an investment trust whose sources of capital are (a) the deposits of employee-members (depositors) and (b) the annual company contribution out of the firm's net profits. With these moneys, shares of Sears common stock are purchased and distributed to the members' accounts on the basis of their respective deposits. It is the accumulation of these shares and the reinvestment of the earnings thereon that are depended upon to provide each member's "pension." That the foregoing brief description is an oversimplification—but not a distortion—of the elements of Sears's profit-sharing will become clear in the detailed discussion which follows.

The profit-sharing fund is an employee trust and is so recognized for tax purposes under the Internal Revenue Act by the United States Treasury Department. Formal control of fund assets and determination of investment policy are legally and financially separate from company management. The direct relationship of the company to the fund is limited to the determination of the company contribution. The direct and immediate management of the fund has been vested in the trustees (six in number). Their control is absolute and complete, subject, of course, to Securities and Exchange Commission regulations, since fund investments are primarily in the company's common stock.

While at present the fund is governed by six trustees, the rules provide that there may be not less than five nor more than seven, all of whom are appointed by the board of directors of the company. The directors may, at their discretion, select one trustee not an officer, director, or employee of Sears. Currently, Robert M. La Follette, Jr. (former United States senator), is such a trustee. In respect to the three categories into one of which all the other trustees must fall—officer, director, or employee—a majority of the trustees must be either officers or directors of the company. In 1948 the Sears officers (and directors) serving as fund trustees were R. E. Wood (company board chairman), C. E. Humm (company vice-president), and R. J. De Motte (company treasurer). Employee trustees were Carl Kresl and W. W. Langeloh. It is clear that essentially the "managers" of the company manage the fund. They are at once company directors and officers and fund trustees.

The trustees now hold full authority with respect to management of the plan. As first introduced, the trustees were limited to the adoption of rules and amendments to effect the general purposes of the plan, but no substantial change could be made without a majority vote of the depositors. In 1924 a referendum vote was held to effect a change in the regulations to permit final and definitive interpretation and changes in all matters relating to the fund by the trustees. The depositors approved this omnibus change, and since 1925 the trustees have exercised complete over-all control and direction. Until recent years not only the major policies of the fund but, to a considerable extent, details of operation as well were relegated to one of the trustees, an officer of the company, and the trustees in a body considered problem cases on their individual merits in numerous instances.

The active management of the fund has now developed into a major full-time job involving the supervision of many employees concerned ex-

TABLE A*

VALUE OF SHARES IN PROFIT-SHARING FUND, 1916–47

Year	Value of Shares (Cost)	Year	Value of Shares (Cost)
1916	$ 545,893.77	1932	$20,296,549.75
1917	1,751,984.40	1933	19,740,078.79
1918	3,298,407.20	1934	20,699,339.49
1919	4,636,344.22	1935	21,369,489.60
1920	6,956,206.93	1936	25,813,944.52
1921	6,260,674.33	1937	29,898,498.79
1922	5,911,475.32	1938	32,423,686.65
1923	5,941,775.73	1939	37,719,528.29
1924	8,356,671.64	1940	43,737,404.33
1925	10,444,953.82	1941	46,557,341.55
1926	13,220,766.28	1942	47,482,592.03
1927	15,975,580.13	1943	49,599,434.14
1928	17,830,554.63	1944	56,264,931.39
1929	20,905,903.51	1945	60,164,497.07
1930	19,612,602.22	1946	76,113,100.08
1931	22,053,293.38	1947	95,064,755.06

* Source: Fund records. Value of shares here expressed in terms of average price per share paid by the fund, as of balance held at end of year.

clusively with fund operation. In 1939 the maturity of the plan was recognized, and the trustees provided for an executive director to be selected by them. The director assumed the duties of executive officer to administer the policies and to provide expert advice on fund problems. Since the institution of the office of executive director, the executive committee of the trustees has been eliminated, and the director not only has assumed responsibilities for administering the general policies but to some extent creates policy by his decisions.

The number of individual problem cases with which the trustees have to deal at their infrequent meetings is much reduced, and in general the plan has been vitalized and improved by the provision of an agency whose entire attention is devoted to management of the program, which has assumed significant proportions as indicated by the value of fund assets. It is apparent from Table A that the Sears profit-sharing fund is big business. The value of shares held in trust by the fund has increased from something more than $500,000 in 1916 to more than $95,000,000 in 1947, a figure greatly in excess of the invested capital of most United States corporations.

Aware of the developing sentiment in the community generally, and perhaps conscious of the apparent anomaly of the management control of a trust established for tens of thousands of employees, and eschewing the appearance of paternalism, the trustees in 1939 adopted the device of an advisory council "to consider and discuss with the Executive Director and with the Board of Trustees in respect of questions relating to administration, procedure, rights and obligations of the members of the Fund, total and partial withdrawals, and amendments to the Rules and Regulations of the Fund, and such other matters as the Board of Trustees shall indicate from time to time as being subject to consideration by the Council." The advisory council meets with the board of trustees semiannually for purposes of such discussion.

The seventeen members of the council are elected from among the company's employees for one-year terms. The number of the council and the frequent elections make possible a relatively broad base of participation. Obviously, the most important achievement of the council plan is the psychological sense of participation among employees. The elections serve to help keep the fund before the minds of members, and the regular association of the council members with other employees is a valuable contact point between the profit-sharing fund and its members.

The council has no power of legislation. It performs only an advisory function, as indicated by its name, and its proposals are considered by the trustees as a basis for policy. It should not be inferred because the council is not a legislative body that it is a "rubber-stamp" device. In fact, several changes in regulations and interpretations have originated in the council and been subsequently adopted by the trustees. The council is depended upon to reflect the attitudes and wishes of employees in regard to the fund; and their suggestions, which often arise out of complaints in the field, are taken seriously and adopted when the trustees consider them feasible and financially sound.

The council is ideally the agency of interpretation between the members and the trustees, and any such device is likely to be worthless unless real participation in policy-making is possible. The trustees neither desire nor can afford to ignore or treat lightly the suggestions of the council members. Although many such suggestions are rejected, they are not rejected without thorough consideration and explanation.

In view of the present distribution of policy-making power, the choice of the executive director is extremely important, not only from the point of view of efficient operation, but especially from an employee relations standpoint. The director must be a person well known and trusted by the employees as well as an effective administrator. His is a heavy responsibility, and he is a significant factor in the scheme of things far beyond what would be required in terms of the mechanics of the job. He is the continuing link between the members and the trustees, and he co-ordinates company management and the fund. His is the task of interpreting the plan and the action of the trustees to the members, and interpreting the sentiment of the members to the policy-makers. In a real sense he creates policy.

The director and his staff are the only persons whose full-time energies are devoted to the fund, including, for example, approval and supervision of all payments to withdrawing depositors, which were valued at $21,942,-443 in 1946 and $13,329,728 in 1947. In the course of administering the established policies as a matter of day-to-day routine, he becomes acutely conscious of the shortcomings of particular policies and develops a sense of the needs and wishes of the members. Thus he brings to the trustees the benefits of contacts and analyses interpreted in terms of relevant (human as well as legal and financial) data. The knowledge developed by the executive director and his staff is also of value to the company in establishing personnel policies.

Under the present arrangements it is important that the executive director be a person who is well qualified technically but, perhaps more important, well known and respected among numbers of employees. These qualifications are well met at present in the person of William Wallace. Wallace has been a Sears employee since 1913, when he went to work in the Chicago mail-order plant's shipping department. After experience in correspondence work, Wallace joined the group that organized and opened the Philadelphia branch in 1920. In 1935 he returned to Chicago, where he assumed responsibility for directing some sales-promotion activities. In 1941, after twenty-eight years of Sears's service, Wallace left the advertising department to become executive director of the fund at the age of fifty-one.

Wallace succeeded John Mullen, who retired in 1941 after serving two years as the first executive director of the fund, of which he had been a trustee since its inception, in 1916. Mullen had been with Sears since 1897 and, like Wallace, had worked up and through many parts of the organization.

Both Wallace and his predecessor were "old hands" at Sears when they were appointed to head the fund. But the "old timers" are increasingly retired, and the men who grew up with the company are becoming a thing of the past. The possibilities of finding men who are well qualified technically and have developed a wide acquaintance throughout the company become narrower with the growth of the business and the passage of time.

Until 1937 the trustees directly managed the investment operations of the trust. In that year they appointed an executive committee and granted to it the authority to make investments under the general supervision of the trustees. That, however, was a short-lived arrangement, for in 1939 at the same time the job of executive director was created, so was an investment committee, which has since made investments on behalf of the fund.[9]

The investment policy is essentially defined in the regulations in the following terms: "It is intended so far as practicable and advisable, the Fund will be invested in the capital stock of the Company, to the end that depositors may, in the largest measure possible, share in the earnings of the Company." Although the trustees have for long been given broad discretionary power in making investments, the policy had been always to invest solely in the common stock of the company. In 1945, however, almost one-

TABLE B*

PERCENTAGE OF TOTAL OUTSTANDING COMPANY COMMON STOCK HELD
BY THE PROFIT-SHARING FUND, 1916–47

Year	Percentage of Total Outstanding Common Stock of Company Held by Fund	Year	Percentage of Total Outstanding Common Stock of Company Held by Fund
1916	0.04	1932	8.63
1917	1.50	1933	8.62
1918	2.81	1934	9.21
1919	3.61	1935	9.51
1920	5.46	1936	9.17
1921	5.44	1937	9.88
1922	5.25	1938	10.50
1923	5.45	1939	11.33
1924	7.40	1940	12.32
1925	8.23	1941	12.87
1926	8.85	1942	13.58
1927	9.51	1943	13.51
1928	9.11	1944	14.25
1929	8.09	1945	14.28
1930	7.70	1946	15.02
1931	8.89	1947	16.83

* Source: Fund records.

half of the funds available for investment were retained in cash and government bonds; in 1946 almost 20 per cent, and in 1947 almost 30 per cent.

The policy of maintaining substantial amounts in highly liquid condition is dictated by the desirability of being always in position to return at least the employee's contribution plus interest. During the severe depression of the thirties, the market value of Sears, Roebuck's stock dropped so low that, unless the company had made special contributions to make up the difference, withdrawing employees would in many cases have received less than the contributions which they had made over a period of years. With the degree of uncertainty created by the late war, and the possibilities for error increased thereby, the investment committee has appeared to emphasize the necessity of liquidity.

The degree to which the trustees have followed th objective of investing in the common stock of the company is well indicated by the fact that, of the total outstanding common stock of the company, the fund held less than one-half of 1 per cent in 1916, while at the end of 1947 the fund held about 17 per cent of the outstanding common-stock issue. Table B shows the growing importance of the fund as a stockholder of company securities.

TABLE C*

PROFIT-SHARING FUND STOCK PURCHASES, 1916–47

Year	No. Shares Purchased on Market	No. Shares Purchased from Members	Total
1916	2,473	....	2,473
1917	8,052	161	8,213
1918	9,865	1,314	11,179
1919	5,953	1,242	7,195
1920	18,441	2,785	21,226
1921	....	6,664	6,664
1922	....	4,190	4,190
1923	4,900	5,570	10,470
1924	23,059	3,664	26,723
1925	10,258	4,182	14,440
1926	50,423	18,608	69,031
1927	40,670	22,392	63,062
1928	17,280	23,204	40,484
1929	40,699	5,035	45,734
1930	39,851	9,907	49,758
1931	91,444	9,598	101,042
1932	....	15,409	15,409
1933	9,290	16,898	26,188
1934	47,190	20,962	68,152
1935	43,674	16,220	59,894
1936	88,762	9,239	98,001
1937	82,901	8,809	91,710
1938	81,114	12,106	93,220
1939	93,110	12,919	106,019
1940	100,343	27,847	128,190
1941	76,896	35,203	112,099
1942	81,312	60,342	141,654
1943	45,419	51,827	97,246
1944	75,453	45,211	120,664
1945	132,723	156,437	289,160
1946	420,607	151,974	572,581
1947	567,021	106,845	673,866

* Source: Fund records.

The profit-sharing fund is now the largest holder of record of the company's outstanding securities.

In 1938 Sears, Roebuck and Company was classified as a "widely held" corporation by the Temporary National Economic Committee.[10] At the time (1938) the TNEC reported that the Rosenwald family held 13.95 per cent of the outstanding stock, and the fund held 9.52 per cent.[11] The fact that the fund now holds the greatest single block of stock raises interesting questions of corporate control. In effect, owing to the composition of the fund trusteeship, it gives management the greatest single block of voting stock, since the fund stock is voted by the trustees.

The fund (through the investment committee) is constantly acquiring stock whose primary source is the security market. Depending upon the amount available for investment, which is a function of the employee plus company contributions and the earnings of the stock already held, the in-

TABLE D*

ANNUAL AVERAGE PRICE OF SHARES, 1916–47

Year	Net Price Paid by Fund	Average Price on New York Market
1916	$ 55.19	$ 53.50
1917	37.43	43.27
1918	38.52	36.90
1919	50.53	10.76
1920	36.47	42.89
1921	19.66	17.90
1922	20.23	19.61
1923	21.38	20.23
1924	29.53	25.79
1925	42.25	46.74
1926	51.27	52.58
1927	62.30	65.08
1928	97.83	125.32
1929	138.68	146.23
1930	59.95	72.50
1931	50.52	48.97
1932	46.79	21.78
1933	38.00	31.37
1934	41.85	42.08
1935	46.69	47.49
1936	69.77	77.46
1937	69.54	81.87
1938	61.27	65.27
1939	73.75	75.53
1940	75.88	78.90
1941	65.48	70.21
1942	53.35	53.57
1943	78.61	76.45
1944	92.42	93.96
1945	115.90	131.12
1946	160.24	167.36
1947	143.44	146.84

* Source: Fund records. The figures for 1916–25 have been adjusted so that they are comparable with the quotations for the years after the four-for-one split in 1925. For 1945–47 the figures are on the 1944 basis before the four-for-one split in 1945.

vestment committee goes into the market and purchases stock for the members' accounts. In addition, the fund also acquires stock from withdrawing members. The market (New York Stock Exchange), however, determines the price paid in these cases, since the fund pays for the shares in terms of the closing New York stock-market quotation the day previous to that on which the application of the withdrawing member is received at the fund office in Chicago. The extent to which the fund buys shares on the market varies from year to year as indicated in Table C.

The primary cost of stock acquisition is the price paid for shares. Table D indicates the extent of the variation in the prices of shares to the fund. The difference between the price paid by the fund and the average price on the New York market is to be accounted for by the method used in calculating the "price paid by the fund." The fund price is the market

CHART A

COMPANY CONTRIBUTIONS, EMPLOYEE DEPOSITS, AND
COMPANY SALES, 1916–47

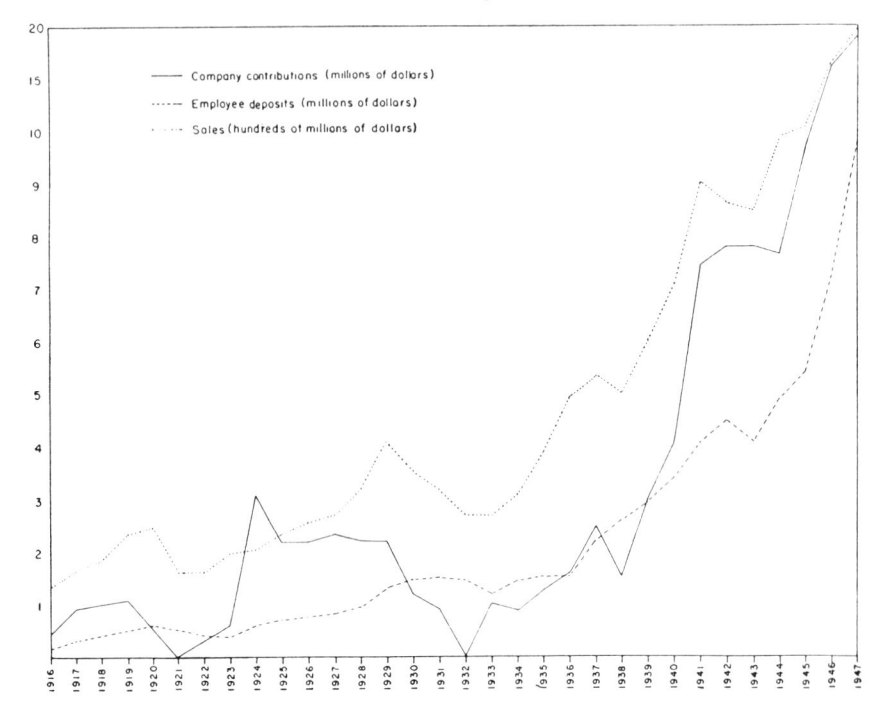

price plus brokerage fees, plus the capitalized expenses of administering the fund, *less* the dividends received on the stock purchased during the year in question. Dividends on stock purchased in previous years and distributed to members' accounts are credited directly to members' accounts. Final price to members (not shown in Table D) includes deduction for "lapse" credits.[12] The notable differences in market price and the fund price in the years 1917 and 1920 is probably to be explained in terms of the 25 per cent and 40 per cent stock dividends paid in the two years.

The profit-sharing arrangement has the advantage, from a financial management point of view, of avoiding a fixed expense which is laid upon the company regardless of earnings. Chart A indicates the large element of fluctuation in the company's contribution. In nine of the thirty years covered, employees' contributions exceeded company contributions. In 1921 and 1932 the company made no contributions, having experienced losses of $16,435,000 and $2,544,000, respectively, in these years. The chart indicates, too, something of the degree to which the company's contributions vary with sales and profits. This would be expected, certainly, because of the contingent character of the company subsidy.

TABLE E*

PROFIT-SHARING FUND EARNINGS, 1917–40

Year	Dividends	Lapses	Total
1917	$ 36,077.25	$ 29,483.98	$ 65,561.23
1918	105,778.00	111,190.00	216,968.00
1919	171,516.00	77,101.56	248,617.56
1920	288,584.00	137,372.30	425,956.30
1921	114,724.00	44,173.91	158,997.91
1922	10,325.16†	37,250.31	47,575.47
1923		32,603.60	32,603.60
1924	169,563.00	48,512.40	218,075.40
1925	465,838.50	366,902.43	832,740.93
1926	782,887.76	440,196.22	1,223,083.98
1927	954,095.01	309,231.78	1,263,326.79
1928	977,317.51	274,372.16	1,251,689.67
1929	908,607.51	373,123.53	1,281,731.04
1930	850,627.51	70,215.54	920,843.05
1931	972,360.34	69,524.41	1,041,884.75
1932	544,929.78		544,929.78
1933			
1934			
1935	790,544.75	118,031.19	908,575.94
1936	2,891,354.75	256,347.83	3,147,702.58
1937	2,874,780.75	224,253.63	3,099,034.38
1938	1,741,968.00	228,078.55	1,970,046.55
1939	2,578,249.25	229,040.73	2,807,289.98
1940	2,743,761.50	268,126.00	3,011,887.50

* Source: Fund records
† Interest on scrip dividend.

Since sales are largely a function of general economic activity, it is to be expected that the business cycle would prove important in conditioning the size of the fund. It is interesting that deposits (employee contributions) appear to fluctuate much less widely than either profits or sales. The chart indicates that annual deposits follow the trend of sales with only minor variation. This is perhaps evidence of a tendency to maintain employment during periods of declining sales. It is generally believed that personnel requirements do not fluctuate with the same intensity as do sales, or at least that "regular" personnel adjustments cannot be made as frequently, or to the same degree, that sales fluctuate. Of course, one must avoid the inference that complete employment stability is effectively achieved, since the "extra" system of hiring employees carries much of the variation in sales activity and since the deposits in profit-sharing reflect only employees who have qualified as "regulars."

Another way in which the fund is affected by the cyclical character of business is through the effect on fund earnings. In addition to the fluctua-

TABLE F*

DISTRIBUTION PRICE, DIVIDENDS, AND RETURN, 1916–47

Year	Profit-sharing Distribution Price	Dividends	Percentage Rate of Return†
1916	$220.75	$7.00	3.17
1917	149.70	7.75	5.17
1918	154.08	8.00	5.19
1919	202.12	8.00	3.95
1920	145.88	8.00	5.48
1921	78.65	2.00	2.54
1922	80.91		
1923	85.53		
1924	118.10	3.00	2.54
1925	168.98	6.00	3.55
1926	51.27	3.37	6.51
1927	62.30	2.50	4.01
1928	97.83	2.50	2.56
1929	138.68	2.50	1.80
1930	59.95	2.50	4.17
1931	50.52	2.50	4.95
1932	46.79	1.25	2.67
1933	38.00		
1934	41.85		
1935	46.69	1.75	3.75
1936	69.76	3.75	5.38
1937	69.54	5.50	7.91
1938	61.27	5.50	8.98
1939	73.75	4.25	5.76
1940	75.88	4.25	5.60
1941	65.48	4.25	6.49
1942	53.35	4.25	7.97
1943	78.61	4.25	5.40
1944	92.42	4.25	4.60
1945	28.40	1.06‡	3.73
1946	39.20	1.75	4.46
1947	35.00	1.75	5.00

* Source: Fund records.
† On basis of given year's per-share price and dividend.
‡ 1.06 on new basis of four-for-one split; 2.75 on basis prior to split.

tions in absolute earnings (shown in Table E) and stock value, the annual rate of return on investment varies widely as shown in Table F.

While the rate of return on Sears's stock purchased for the fund has fluctuated sharply, it has evidently held up better than declining bond yields. Income obtainable from high-grade bonds has been estimated by investment consultants in recent years as only half as large as it was at the low of the depression in the 1930's. While the character of fund investments does not provide the benefits of any diversification of management, alternative investment patterns are probably not so important for the Sears program as they might be for some other companies. The distribution of risk that is ordinarily achieved through diversification of security holdings is to some extent inherent in the company's business, which is national in character and comprehends both rural and urban groups. It is not dependent on any single industry but trades in a great variety of merchandise including both durable and nondurable consumer and (to a lesser degree) producer's goods. It is well known that retail sales do not suffer the degree of fluctuation characteristic of capital goods industries.

The purpose of the profit-sharing and retirement program is to provide employees with something in addition to their regular compensation. Fund membership has no bearing on promotion, compensation, or dismissal. From the beginning of the plan, and especially in recent years, it has been emphasized by frequent memorandums to executives (as well as in the official personnel manual) that profit-sharing is not and cannot be a substitute for adequate pay and good working conditions. It is to be considered something separate and apart. All salary and wage scales are established without consideration of profit-sharing, and in discussing wage adjustments with employees executives are forbidden to mention profit-sharing, lest their intent be misunderstood. Wallace has stated top management's position in the following terms:

> A true profit-sharing retirement plan cannot be successful if used as a substitute for something else. Wages paid must equal or better what employees are earning in related lines of industry. Paid vacations, sick allowances, and other employee benefits must equal or better what is offered by competition. Working conditions must at least equal those offered by competitors. Profit-sharing is something on the top of all these.

The purpose of the Sears fund was outlined in the first announcement which appeared in 1916: "... that employes may share in the profits of this business, and to encourage the habit of saving ... [to] furnish to those who remain in the employ of the Company until they reach the age when they retire from active service, a sum sufficient to provide for them thereafter, and that even those who achieve a long service record, but who may not remain with the Company all of their business life, will have accumulated a substantial sum." These were the purposes as outlined in 1916, and these are the purposes today. The pension aspect of the Sears plan has been its guiding feature. Decisions of policy with respect to investment and operation have been made predominantly in terms of the criterion of pension security and adequacy.

Starting with a membership of 6,064 employees in 1916, participation had swollen to include 81,863 members by the end of 1947, at which time the company's regular personnel numbered approximately 107,034 employees. Of this latter number not all were eligible to become profit-sharing members, since a regular employee must have one year of continuous service at Sears before he is invited to become a member of the fund. Of the 83,784 employees who satisfied that requirement as of March 1, 1948, 81,348 were participating in profit-sharing—97.7 per cent of those eligible for membership.[13]

TABLE G*

PROFIT-SHARING FUND MEMBERSHIP, 1916-47

Year	Membership	Percentage of Regular Employees
1916	6,064	
1917	6,712	
1918	6,056	
1919	7,528	
1920	7,875	
1921	6,392	
1922	5,748	
1923	5,502	
1924	10,046	
1925	10,330	
1926	11,450	
1927	12,404	
1928	15,318	
1929	20,951	
1930	22,551	
1931	22,284	65.5
1932	20,156	59.4
1933	21,477	57.8
1934	23,868	64.8
1935	21,090	50.0
1936	19,619	41.0
1937	35,772	66.9
1938	38,061	75.0
1939	40,364	70.4
1940	46,312	69.0
1941	50,598	63.3
1942	48,322	68.5
1943	47,450	76.35
1944	54,119	85.80
1945	56,973	83.71
1946	64,284	71.13
1947	81,863	76.48

* Source: Fund records.

Table G summarizes the growth of membership since the inception of the fund in 1916 and the percentage of regular employees belonging to the fund since 1931. The figures are those of total membership as of the end of each fiscal year. Thus, in thirty years there has been something more than a tenfold increase in membership. The most important element explaining this increase is, of course, the growth of Sears, Roebuck and Company in sales and personnel, but the timing of changes appears to be the result of (1) changes in the waiting period—the minimum period of employee serv-

SHARING PROFITS WITH EMPLOYEES 695

ice necessary for eligibility; (2) company expansion into the retail field; and (3) cyclical fluctuations affecting employment and profits.

The first large increase appeared in 1924. Membership then doubled over the previous year, which is accounted for by the reduction of the waiting period from three years to one year, beginning January 1, 1924. The more than 50 per cent increase of 1937 over 1936 is to be explained largely in the same way. The large 1937 increase, however, is also due to the special opportunity for re-entry allowed (from February 1 through May 15) for the benefit of employees who had found it necessary to leave the fund during the depression. The sudden increase from 15,000 members in 1928 to 20,000 in 1929 reflects the company's invasion of the retail-store field, which, starting in 1925, numbered 324 stores by the end of 1929. In 1928 alone, 165 stores were added; in 1929, 132 stores. Likewise, the gain of 17,579 members in 1937—27 per cent over 1936—reflects postwar retail expansion and sales increases.

With few exceptions membership has continued to increase each year. Significant declines in numbers of depositors (members) are concentrated at two periods: a loss of 2,373 members in the years 1921–23 inclusive and a similar decline between 1930 and 1932. Both of these periods were marked by severe business depression generally, and the repercussions appear in the profit-sharing group as a result of curtailed employment and of voluntary withdrawal by personnel remaining on the pay roll. In periods of contracting employee earnings, the accumulations of credits in the fund may be looked upon, to some extent, as a type of unemployment insurance, a reserve to be liquidated in periods of "below-normal" income.

In 1921 and 1932 the company suffered heavy losses, which resulted in a cessation of dividends to stockholders and failure to make the customary contributions to profit-sharing. Significant also is the possible effect of extreme declines in quoted stock prices on the attitudes of depositors. The market price of shares on the New York exchange fell from a high of $243 in April, 1920, to $51.50 in November, 1921. In June, 1932, Sears's stock was quoted on the "Big Board" at $9⅞, a drop of approximately $187 from its high of $197 in the autumn of 1929.[14] All these considerations may have inhibited the enthusiasm of some employees, especially short service employees, to become fund members. There is the further possibility that lower employee incomes of depression years resulted in their being unable to afford the 5 per cent withholding of earnings necessary to continue fund membership.

The more severe and prolonged depression of the 1930's was responsible for a net membership loss less than that experienced in the 1921 depression. This appears to be explicable only in terms of the difference in the position of the company in the two periods. The 1921 episode was potentially much more serious for Sears, Roebuck than the depression of the decade following. The company lost $16,435,000 in 1921, while its losses for 1932 amounted to only $2,544,000. Between 1919 and 1921 the number of employees was reduced by almost 29 per cent, whereas between 1929 and 1932 the work force was reduced by less than 15 per cent. Because of the retail expansion, retrenchment in the 1930 period was not nearly so drastic as in 1921, when the continued survival of the company was in serious jeopardy as a result of heavily unbalanced inventories.

It is interesting to note the variations in the required waiting period in the experience of the fund. When profit-sharing was first introduced in 1916, the required waiting period was three years. Since that time there have been three changes in the length of the waiting period. The history of eligibility in terms of waiting period may be summarized (all years inclusive):

```
1916-23..................... 3 years' service
1924-33..................... 1 year's service
1934-36..................... 3 years' service
1937-to date................ 1 year's service
```

In 1942 the trustees again considered lengthening the waiting period to three years, and the executive director of the fund headed a committee which made a study of the relation of fund membership to changes in the waiting period. The investigation disclosed that in the ten-year period 1931–41 the ratio of fund members to regular employees reached the low point of 41 per cent in 1936, the end of the three-year waiting period inaugurated in 1934. When one-year eligibility was re-established in 1937, the membership increased 82 per cent; this was interpreted as being indicative of interest of new employees in the fund. It was found, further, that members withdrawing from the fund did not appear to change proportionately with changes in membership and waiting period. The ratio of member withdrawals to regular employees averaged approximately 12 per cent for the 1931–41 decade. The conclusion and recommendation of the committee was as follows:

> These figures show the relation between the three year waiting period, also that the 1937 performance indicates short service employes on the payroll were anxious to join the Fund ... they also indicate that three year eligibility weakens the Company's opportunity to use the profit sharing as a morale appeal for a very large percent of Company employes, and the percent whose loyalty is in many respects hardest to hold.... It is the feeling of the Committee that since comparatively little work is involved in putting employes in the Fund and taking them out, also that those leaving with less than five years service receive deposits and interest, that it would be to the ultimate advantage of the Company and the Fund to continue permitting employes to enter after one year's service, even though they do not stay, rather than to debar them from the privilege.[15]

It is obvious, of course, that as the waiting period is greater (and consequently the number of fund members less) the return per dollar of employee deposits would be greater for a given company contribution to the fund. For firms which had not enjoyed large dollar-profit volume this would be a much more important consideration than it has been in the case of Sears, Roebuck and Company. Assuming that company contributions can be relatively generous, there appears little advantage in lengthening the waiting period. In so far as profit-sharing exerts any significant influence in the reduction of labor turnover, its strongest effect would probably be exerted upon short-time employees, since the greatest instability is likely to occur among employees with limited service. The one-year waiting period seems well adapted to giving the new employee a "stake" in the company at as early a date as can reasonably be expected and makes possible the inclusion of greater numbers, thereby emphasizing the interest of the company in the well-being of "all" its employees.

TABLE H*

PROFIT-SHARING FUND WITHDRAWALS, BY LENGTH OF SERVICE AND BY SEX, 1937

YEARS OF SERVICE	NUMBER WITHDRAWING			PERCENTAGE WITHDRAWING		
	Male	Female	Total	Male	Female	Total
Less than 2	846	558	1,404	32.15	25.39	29.07
2	404	311	715	15.36	14.14	14.81
3	369	283	652	14.02	12.88	13.50
4	233	150	392	8.86	7.23	8.12
Less than 5	1,852	1,311	3,163	70.39	59.64	65.50
5–9	588	666	1,254	22.35	30.30	25.97
10–14	134	178	312	5.09	8.10	6.46
15–19	24	27	51	0.91	1.23	1.06
20 and over	33	16	49	1.26	0.73	1.01
Total	2,631	2,198	4,829	100.00	100.00	100.00

* Source: Fund records.

An analysis of employees withdrawing from profit-sharing in 1937 indicates that, of 4,829 depositors leaving the fund, 3,163, or 65.5 per cent, were Class A members, that is, employees with less than five years' service. The proportion of depositors withdrawing declines noticeably with increasing length of service as shown in Table H.

It is apparent that the most "unstable" employees are people in Group A, which is made up of those having less than five years' service. Of the 3,163 in this class who left the fund in 1937, more than half were men. Table I covering the years 1940–47 confirms the concentration of withdrawals among short-service employees, but it indicates that during the war years 1942–45 women substantially outnumbered men in accounting for withdrawals. This reflects the fact that during the war years the company greatly expanded the number and proportion of female employees.

The overwhelming majority of employees leaving profit-sharing also leave Sears. An analysis of withdrawals by reasons (1940–47), summarized in Table J, shows that voluntary resignation from the company constitutes the chief reason for leaving the fund. Only a few persons choose to resign their fund memberships and continue to work for Sears.

The trustees have evidently been convinced that early membership in the fund is desirable in building a base for retirement security; that for

TABLE I*

PROFIT-SHARING FUND WITHDRAWALS, BY GROUPS AND BY SEX, 1940–47

YEAR	A No.	A Per Cent	B No.	B Per Cent	C No.	C Per Cent	D No.	D Per Cent	MALE	FEMALE	TOTAL
1940	4,823	70	1,252	18	814	12			3,463	3,426	6,889
1941	7,998	76	1,659	16	903	8			5,263	5,297	10,560
1942	14,773	73	3,904	19	1,555	8			9,615	10,680	20,295
1943	8,854	71	2,474	20	1,063	9	47		4,407	8,031	12,438
1944	6,621	75	1,359	15	803	9	65	1	2,418	6,430	8,848
1945	7,330	76	1,427	15	740	8	95	1	3,082	6,510	9,592
1946	7,785	65	3,029	25	1,013	8	226	2	5,177	6,876	12,053
1947	7,910	73	2,015	19	711	7	168	1	4,337	6,467	10,804

* Source: Fund records.

TABLE J*

PROFIT-SHARING FUND WITHDRAWALS, BY REASONS, 1940–47

REASON	1940	1941	1942	1943	1944	1945	1946	1947
Resignations—marriage	1,418	2,457	3,399	2,629	2,497	2,850	3,788	2,895
Other resignations and deaths:								
To work elsewhere				477	2,187	1,883	2,081	2,136
Dissatisfied	1,984	4,355	10,832	6,484	1,795	1,490	1,800	1,089
Leaving city	270	459	957					
Business for self	139	141	130	163	241	369	623	447
School	86	120	183	93	119	179	407	296
War-agency jobs			145	279	54	14		
Illness	311	426	613	490	578	632	674	582
Death	105	92	110	128	209	233	157	171
Military career	84	158	68	19	18	6	33	30
Unsatisfactory work	871	1,048	1,007	680	698	780	978	1,174
Layoff	1,313	842	2,110	407	152	834	816	1,375
Not leaving company	242	388	741	589	292	292	312	394
Retirement due to age	66	74			8	30	384	215
Total	6,889	10,560	20,295	12,438	8,848	9,592	12,053	10,804

* Source: Fund records.

those employees who actually do continue with Sears the remainder of their business life a three-year waiting period imposes an unmerited penalty. Furthermore, the morale value of profit-sharing must be largely a function of the breadth of the program, and, as indicated earlier, the one-year waiting period is desirable in that it significantly broadens the base of membership. It can be argued, too, that the one-year waiting period is more realistic in so far as it implies a realization of the high rate at which employees tend to discount the future. To the young worker the end of the third year hence is indeed remote in time and prospect, and immediate advantages are most desired. But for the group of workers whose ambition exceeds their ability, discouragement from lack of promotion to successively higher jobs is probably cumulative, and, to the degree that such frustration can be mitigated by higher pay, larger profit shares (a function both of net profits and of the number of members) might be expected to have a significant effect. The higher rate at which long-service employees participate in the company's contribution to the fund tends to offset, however, whatever dilution might result from the inclusion of larger numbers of participants induced by the shorter waiting period.

When an employee joins the profit-sharing fund, he becomes a depositor of 5 per cent of his earnings (through pay-roll deductions). The maximum annual deposit of an employee is limited to $250. The company's "contribution" is added to the employee deposits. The amount of that "contribution" is figured before dividends and corporate income taxes or contributions to any profit-sharing or pension plan and varies from 5 per cent to 9 per cent of the net profits, depending upon the amount of profits. In 1947 the company contributed $18,734,846, and employees made deposits of $9,828,762.

Each depositor has a separate account, and the annual "contribution" is distributed to the accounts on the basis of the employee's deposits in that year. However, the *rate* at which the employee participates in the amount contributed by the company is determined by his length of service. There are now four classes of depositors designated as A, B, C, and D. *Group A* consists of employees having less than five years' company service; *Group B*, having from five to ten years' service; *Group C*, having from ten to fifteen years' service; and *Group D*, having fifteen or more years' service *and* being over fifty years of age. *Group A* participates on the basis of the year's deposits; *Group B* on the basis of twice the deposits; *Group C* on the basis of three times; and *Group D* on the basis of four times the deposits.

The funds thus credited to the members' accounts are used primarily to buy no-par-value common stock of the company. It is the depositor's *stockholdings* which represent his retirement security. More recently some of the credits have been kept in cash, government bonds, and a mortgage note. At any given time an employee's equity in profit-sharing is represented by the balance in his account which is composed of cash, bonds, and mortgage notes (the "uninvested" part) and shares of stock (the "invested" portion).

In addition to his own deposits and his share of the company's contribution, the employee depositor's account is built up by the "lapses" credited to his account. These are the moneys and securities which Group A members leaving the fund are not entitled to withdraw. In general, members withdrawing prior to the completion of five years' continuous service are entitled to withdraw only the amounts they have deposited plus 5 per cent simple interest on each year's deposits computed from the end of the calendar year in which made, to the month of withdrawal. The remainder

TABLE K*

EMPLOYEE CONTRIBUTIONS (DEPOSITS), PROFIT-SHARING FUND, 1916–47

Year	Employee Deposits	Year	Employee Deposits
1916	$ 136,311.63	1933	$ 1,255,810.85
1917	324,162.12	1934	1,427,277.43
1918	349,145.30	1935	1,520,273.76
1919	441,929.01	1936	1,523,008.29
1920	580,853.51	1937	2,223,968.69
1921	501,333.12	1938	2,660,597.28
1922	408,921.56	1939	2,953,974.91
1923	394,169.18	1940	3,441,627.12
1924	661,259.10	1941	4,132,258.07
1925	708,402.27	1942	4,577,466.68
1926	740,228.93	1943	4,147,387.44
1927	808,891.01	1944	4,900,052.95
1928	927,644.42	1945	5,458,787.90
1929	1,307,231.93	1946	7,263,233.00
1930	1,480,778.33	1947	9,828,762.00
1931	1,539,784.64		
1932	1,458,816.16	Total	$70,084,348.59

* Source: Fund records. The figures indicated are the gross savings deposits according to the audit reports as at the end of each fund year. Net figures would be somewhat less as a result of the deduction of current-year withdrawals.

of these accounts is distributed annually to the then members, in proportion to the number of shares of capital stock of the company to the credit of their accounts at the beginning of the year in question and not withdrawn during that year.

The profit-sharing fund is built up basically from the contributions of employees and the company. Since the inception of the plan in 1916, employees upon becoming members have been required to contribute 5 per cent of their salaries. Since 1934 the maximum yearly contribution allowed per employee is $250.[16] The limit is established "so that the higher salaried employees may not too largely participate in the fund." The annual amounts of these deposits are shown in Table K. At the close of the thirty-one years ending in 1947, employees had deposited a total of more than seventy million dollars in profit-sharing.

To the deposits of employees is added the annual contribution of the company, which until 1946 was established as 5 per cent of the combined net profit of the company before taxes and dividends. The rules were revised early in 1946 so that the 5 per cent company contribution is augmented in 1 per cent increments for net income which exceeds $40,000,000. Currently the company's contribution is graduated on the basis of the schedule shown in the accompanying tabulation.

Consolidated Net Income	Contribution Rate (Per Cent)
Less than $40,000,000	5
$ 40,000,000 but less than $60,000,000	6
$ 60,000,000 but less than $80,000,000	7
$ 80,000,000 but less than $100,000,000	8
$100,000,000 or more	9

The 1946 revision of the regulations marks a change in three respects from the previous policy: (1) the scale of company contributions is adjusted to the level of company profits above a minimum of $40,000,000 per year; (2) the "escape clause," which gave the company the option of deducting Social Security contributions from net income prior to calculating the company's contribution to the fund, has been eliminated, the tax for Social Security by this time being recognized as pay-roll cost; and (3) the responsibility of subsidiaries as separate enterprises has been recognized. Formerly, the profit-sharing contribution was a deduction *from the consolidated income of all subsidiaries.* The new regulations provide for calculations of the company's contribution on the basis of the consolidated income but allocate to the constituent companies their share of this amount on the basis of credits to their employees. If the profits of a subsidiary company for a given year are not adequate to bear this burden, then the employees of that subsidiary do not participate in the company's contribution for said year.

While for many years the rate of company contribution specified in the regulations was 5 per cent of net profit, in practice the actual contributions often exceeded the various contract rates shown in Table L. The additional amounts were in part occasioned by company subsidy of the fund's administrative cost. In terms of dollars the company has contributed to the fund from 1916 to 1947, inclusive, a total of $113,588,288.82 in yearly contributions as shown in Table M, approximately $1.50 for each $1.00 of employee deposits.

When the fund was inaugurated, the company contribution was distributed to members' accounts annually on the basis of their deposits in that year. In this way the primary determinant of the degree to which a member shared in the company's contributions was the employee's earnings with the limitation on maximum contributions. In 1924 the basis for member participation in the profits was changed so that long-service employees were favored. Depositors were then classified in three groups:

GROUP A—Consisting of depositors who have been in the service of the company for less than five years

GROUP B—Consisting of depositors who have been in the service of the company for five years and less than ten years

GROUP C—Consisting of depositors who have been in the service of the company for ten years or more

TABLE L*

CONTRACT RATES OF COMPANY CONTRIBUTIONS

Period	Contract Rate of Contribution	Period	Contract Rate of Contribution
1916–23†	5.0	1940	5.0
1924‡	7.0	1941	5.0
1925–28	8.5	1942	5.0
1929–33§	7.5	1943	5.0
1934–36	5.0	1944	5.0
1937	5.0	1945	5.0
1938	5.0	1946	9.0
1939	5.0	1947	9.0

* Source: Fund records.

† In 1921, owing to the critical condition in which the company found itself, no contribution was made to the fund.

‡ An unusually high rate paid to the fund in 1924 was due largely to the change made in the basis of computing the company's contribution in that year, which provided a sum equal to one-third of the remainder of net earnings for the year, after deducting from net earnings for the year all dividends payable during such year on outstanding preferred stock, plus a sum equal to 10 per cent of the aggregate par value of outstanding common stock, but before deducting federal income taxes; provided, however, that the minimum amount to be contributed by the company to the fund should be equal to 7 per cent of net earnings for the year, without deduction for any dividends or for federal income taxes.

§ In 1932 the company made no contribution to the fund.

TABLE M*

COMPANY CONTRIBUTIONS, 1916–47

Year	Amount	Year	Amount
1916	$ 412,215.55	1933	$ 1,040,693.86
1917	905,484.04	1934	861,682.90
1918	1,077,883.19	1935	1,291,513.83
1919	1,191,942.06	1936	1,699,647.16
1920	587,333.30	1937	2,561,749.90
1921		1938	1,535,492.85
1922	271,758.41	1939	3,013,435.46
1923	575,630.90	1940	4,136,140.44
1924	3,172,196.45	1941	7,475,142.82
1925	2,194,612.29	1942	7,721,083.69
1926	2,181,593.43	1943	7,732,084.69
1927	2,333,046.34	1944	7,667,697.20
1928	2,209,666.75	1945	9,708,314.00
1929	2,211,477.86	1946	16,786,535.00
1930	1,267,478.47	1947	18,848,363.00
1931	916,393.98		
1932		Total	$113,588,289.82

* Source: Fund records.

Participation of depositors in Group B was based upon one-and-one-half times their respective deposits, and Group C upon twice their deposits.

In 1934 the premium in favor of long-term employees was further strengthened, so that the deposits of Group B were doubled, and those of Group C were tripled, for calculating the distribution of the firm's contribution. The basis to which the appropriate multiplier refers is the previous year's deposits, *not* the total deposits credited to the account of the fund member. In the revision of the regulations published in October, 1941, a fourth group was created—Group D. That classification was created in an attempt to further improve the position of members approaching retirement age at comparatively little cost to members in the other groups.[17]

The predominant character of the program is protective in the sense of building an equity for the purpose of retirement. The guiding principle of retirement security is further buttressed by special withdrawal privileges permitted Group D members; elective provisions for the purchase of single-premium annuities; or transfer of stock into cash to be held in the depositor's account, if desired by members of this group and approved by the trustees. That the fund is still thought of primarily as a pension plan is indicated by the following remarks of General Wood published in the annual report to stockholders for the fiscal year 1936:

> Your Company has for years endeavored to promote the well-being of its employes, not by any paternalistic influence over their private lives, but by paying adequate wages and salaries with provision for proper working conditions, vacations, group insurance, recognition of ability and *security for old age through its Profit Sharing Fund* [authors' italics]. . . . This Fund has been in existence in Sears since July, 1916 . . . twenty years before federal [Social Security] laws were enacted.

The definition of a "Group D" is essentially a recognition of the maturity of the company. The employees are growing up—and growing old. The rules of the fund have been adapted to meet better the needs of the increasingly large number of superannuated personnel. A moral obligation of the company to long-service employees has been realized. To prevent declining efficiency and accumulation of deadwood, the management has been provided a program which permits compulsory retirement.

In addition to the advantageous basis of participation, Group D members enjoy especially liberal withdrawal privileges for the purposes of purchasing annuities. Upon request of Group D depositors and with approval of the trustees (in fact, on approval of the executive director or his assistant, acting for the trustees), sufficient credits in the account of the depositor will be liquidated for the purchase of a single-premium annuity contract from an insurance company and through an agent *of the depositor's own choosing*.[18] From November 6, 1945, through December 31, 1947, $3,215,539 in annuities were bought.

The provision for annuity purchase is a recognition of the desirability of increased security for employees approaching retirement and of the inexperience (and inability) of many employees in handling large sums of money. Obviously, the sudden acquisition of control over several thousands of dollars is replete with possibilities for mismanagement and misadventure on the part of persons who have been for the greater part of their lives among the lower middle income groups. Although conversion of the entire profit-sharing fund into annuities has been more than once discussed by the trustees and recommended by the sellers of annuities, the program remains optional.

In 1946 the regulations were revised to permit the trustees, at their discretion, to allow withdrawals for single-premium annuity purchases *by Group B and C members or their beneficiaries.* This is clearly to be interpreted as applying only to Group B and C depositors approaching retirement age, who conceivably will not enter Group D while in company service.

Similarly, Group D members at any time within the five-year period preceding their normal retirement dates or after attaining normal or emergency retirement dates can request the trustees "to liquidate all or any of the securities" then to the credit of their accounts.[19] The present practice in such cases is to retain as cash at bank, or in the equivalent of cash, proceeds from the sale of stock credits under the foregoing provision. From January 1, 1942, through December 31, 1947, $3,607,919.48 was deposited in the so-called "Retirees' Pension Reserve"; and the balance remaining as of December 31, 1947, was $1,250,641.75 (the figures quoted do not include interest at the rate of 1 per cent per year credited to the deposit balances). The effect is to give Group D members approaching retirement an opportunity (at the discretion of the trustees and without liability to them) to liquidate a portion of stock standing to the credit of their accounts at what may be considered a favorable market price, thus removing possible loss through a future price decline.

Since 1941 the trustees have thus been given discretion to liquidate and hold in cash (or, at the option of the trustees, to reinvest) the share credits of Group D members *within five years* of their normal retirement dates. Although this involved the assumption of additional financial responsibility for the trustees, it was a means of mitigating somewhat the critical association of retirement security with the unpredictable behavior of the stock market. A comprehensive study of the profit-sharing program and variation in the value of Sears's shares indicated that at some time during a five-year period the stock value was favorable. Although the trustees have such discretion, and must have, to qualify the plan as a trust fund, they have not seen fit to exercise their prerogative except upon request of the prospective retiree.

The entire objective of these flexible regulations is the enhancement of retirement security; and the discretion that is permitted has been developed by the trustees with a view to obtaining the depositor's opinion concerning disposition of his own accumulating credits as he approaches the retirement threshold, with the final decision, as always, in the hands of the trustees.

Despite these recent modifications, as will be further discussed below, the relative retirement well-being of retirees is still intimately associated with a happy coincidence of retirement and high stock quotations. In general, for long-service employees who have not dissipated their account by too large previous withdrawals, it is believed that the fund has provided a relatively generous old age competence due not a little to the formula used in distributing the annual profit-sharing contribution of the company to the members' accounts.

The significance of the 1-2-3-4 method of distributing the company contribution to the fund members is clearly indicated by study of annual allocations to the various member classifications shown in Table N. Necessarily, it is the short-service employees who are at a relative disadvantage in any differential system of distribution such as this. Of course, the employees who graduate from the junior ranks, and remain with the company for considerable periods of time, in due course gain the advantage of the "new juniors," so that for this group the earlier losses are more than reclaimed.

Any plan looking to an accumulation of funds to provide retirement income must be protected against capricious withdrawals by members prior to their retirement date. The provisions of the plan in this respect are definite and strictly enforced. Depositors having less than five years' full and continuous company service may completely withdraw from the fund at their option, but by so doing they forfeit their interest in the company's contributions and the earnings in their accounts, except for 5 per cent simple interest.[20] Thus they receive their own accumulated savings, plus a rate of interest more than double that now paid by savings banks. Depositors who have completed the five years' service (prior to 1942 continuous service of ten years was specified) may withdraw from the fund all moneys and securities credited to their accounts. They receive the entire value of their interest in the fund, which includes the company contributions and the earnings on the invested sum. Withdrawal from the fund is in general irrevocable, except in the case of employees who leave the company and, if re-employed, again qualify as regular employees. Such employees may again join the fund after the required waiting period.

There have been five occasions on which the trustees have modified the irrevocability clause. Three of these instances were associated with business depressions which made it unduly burdensome for many employees to maintain membership in the fund. The other concessions were made to permit the return of employees who withdrew on account of military service during World Wars I and II. In the case of veterans of World

War I, the trustees simply provided for their re-entry into the fund. In the other instances there were specified time periods allowed during which former members might again become depositors.[21]

A similar modification was the suspension during 1932 of the regulation that a member "participating in the Fund shall withdraw upon failing to regularly make his deposit." This was in recognition of the problems created by the depressed economic conditions of the period and the demands made upon the reduced income of employees at that time.

Partial withdrawals, with the privilege of remaining in the fund, are not

TABLE N*

COMPANY CONTRIBUTIONS PER DOLLAR OF MEMBER DEPOSITS, 1916–47

YEAR	GROUP			
	A	B	C	D
1916	$3.09	$3.09	$3.09	
1917	3.02	3.02	3.02	
1918	3.26	3.26	3.26	
1919	2.81	2.81	2.81	
1920	1.07	1.07	1.07	
1921				
1922	0.72	0.72	0.72	
1923	1.58	1.58	1.58	
1924	3.47	5.20	6.94	
1925	2.43	3.66	4.86	
1926	2.26	3.39	4.52	
1927	2.21	3.32	4.42	
1928 (mail order)†	1.89	2.83	3.78	
1928 (retail)†	1.32	1.32	1.32	
1929	1.41	2.12	2.82	
1930	0.74	1.11	1.48	
1931	0.50	0.75	1.00	
1932				
1933	0.64	0.96	1.28	
1934	0.36	0.72	1.08	
1935	0.48	0.96	1.44	
1936	0.59	1.18	1.77	
1937‡	0.38	0.77	1.38	
1938	0.35	0.70	1.05	
1939‡	0.49	0.98	1.47	
1940‡	0.52	1.04	1.56	
1941‡	0.74	1.48	2.22	$2.96
1942‡	1.03	2.04	3.09	4.12
1943	0.97	1.94	2.91	3.88
1944	0.84	1.68	2.52	3.36
1945	0.94	1.88	2.82	3.76
1946	1.27	2.54	3.81	5.08
1947	1.15	2.30	3.45	4.60

* Source: Fund records.
† Company contributions made separately for mail-order and retail divisions on basis of respective profits.
‡ In these years the company made *special contributions* credited as follows: 1937, Groups A, B, C, 0.47; 1939, Groups A, B, C, 0.20; 1940, Groups A, B, C, 0.35; 1941, Groups, A, B, C, D, 0.64; in 1942 the special contribution was allocated on the 1-2-3-4 basis: A, 0.35; B, 0.70; C, 1.05; D, 1.40. From 1939 through 1941, the special contribution was applied only on the first $91 of deposits.

permitted until employees have been depositors for ten or more years' continuous service, except that, in case of death or serious illness in a depositor's immediate family, application for an unusual partial withdrawal may be considered. Employees having less than five years' continuous service may in no instance apply for withdrawal in excess of their own deposits.[22]

The rule for the trustees' action in approving or disapproving "regular" partial withdrawals is stated in terms of whether the desired partial withdrawal is to be used to further the depositor's retirement security. Further, depositors may make withdrawals which do not aggregate more than one-half of the credits in their accounts after fifteen years of being a depositor. In this case, however, petitions for withdrawal may be denied by the trustees, in their discretion, if the proposed withdrawal plus all previous withdrawals aggregate more than the total deposits of the depositor. The limitation here is in terms of deposits, not total credits. This is a significant proscription, since the total credits in a given account are characteristically most heavily weighted by the company contribution and the earnings on the account investment.

Although the withdrawal provisions are more generous now than they have been in the past, the trustees have been careful to avoid liberalizing the rules to the extent that partial withdrawals can frequently be made to meet purely temporary emergencies. While every effort has been made to protect the retirement security aspect of profit-sharing, the fund management has attempted on occasion to establish temporary regulations regarding withdrawals that are appropriate to changing circumstances. During World War II, for example, the rules were amended so that employees on military leave of absence could continue as fund members, with the accumulation of service deposits credited as regular employee desposits. It was further provided in that case that depositors on military-leave status could withdraw up to 95 per cent of the amounts credited to their accounts in case of financial emergencies arising out of absence on military leave. Later an extension (six months beyond the discharge period) of the 95 per cent military-leave withdrawal privilege was allowed. And currently, during the national housing shortage, members in Groups B and C may withdraw up to 60 per cent of the credits in their accounts (less prior withdrawals, if any) for the purchase of a home, if threatened with eviction from present quarters and unable to rent other living space. This latter privilege is circumscribed also by the discretion of the trustees.

The generally restrictive character of the withdrawal regulations has been facilitated by the company personnel program, which includes other devices, notably, in most company units, the credit union, to meet the vicissitudes that might otherwise require the absorption of the fund accumulating to provide old age security.

A most important aspect of Sears's profit-sharing is its connection with the variation in quotations for the company's shares on the securities exchange. The value of accounts is markedly affected by changes in the stock quotation. Table O clearly illustrates the general effect of such fluctuations. It should be noted that these figures include payments to all members withdrawing from the fund, few of whom were retirees.

Over the years 1916–24 and again in the interval 1931–35 there were substantial losses in *total investment*. The market loss in these cases was greater than the earnings for the respective periods. It must also be observed, however, that in all four periods withdrawing depositors realized worth-while returns on their own savings—as a result of the company's contributions and the fund earnings. Over the entire period 1916–40 fund members withdrawing received $4.27 per dollar saved. When it is considered that a very small proportion of this group had been members of the fund for the entire period, it is apparent that the profit-sharing plan, over the years, offered a greater return than could probably have been achieved in most other avenues of investment. The value of one dollar of savings at 5 per cent interest compounded annually for the twenty-four years is $3.23.

The plan has, in general, provided a generous return on savings, but the performance for particular periods is clearly uneven. If shorter periods were considered, the performance would vary even more. The negative character of market profits in the periods 1916–24 and 1931–35 reflect the sustained low values of the stock market associated with the depressions of 1921 and 1932.

Essentially the adequacy of the fund in providing retirement security is a function of the value of the employee's stockholdings at or about the time of his retirement. Since there are so many factors working to determine the value of these holdings, it may be helpful to consider the *possibilities* of profit-sharing by examining some type cases. These illustrations assume unbroken service, constant annual earnings of the employee, and his retention of his credits intact since the fund was established in 1916. If all these conditions were satisfied, the earnings experience of the fund would have produced by 1945 the results shown in Table P for the three hypothetical employees, X, Y, and Z, earning, respectively, $1,000, $2,000, and $3,000 per annum.

An employee whose annual earnings had remained at $1,000 over the twenty-nine year period, and had made no withdrawals from his profit-sharing account, would have accumulated 1,132 shares of Sears's stock in addition to the $3,300 in cash and bonds (Table P). The significance of stock-market fluctuations is illustrated in Table Q. If, in the case of Employee X, his shares were sold when Sears's stock was quoted on the exchanges at $48 a share, his holdings would bring him over $54,000. But

TABLE O*

SUMMARY OF CLOSED ACCOUNTS, PROFIT-SHARING FUND, BY PERIODS, 1916–40

Period	Employee Savings	Company Contribution	Total Original Investment	Fund Earnings	Total Investment	Paid to Depositors	Profit or Loss on Original Investment	Market Profit or Loss on Stock Investment	Increment on Savings	Number of Withdrawing Depositors
1916–24	$ 1,855,271	$ 3,022,137	$ 4,877,408	$ 633,750	$ 5,511,158	$ 4,068,018	$ 809,390	$ 1,443,140	$ 2,212,747	13,715
1925–30	3,310,901	7,963,140	11,274,041	2,761,121	14,035,162	28,690,254	17,416,213	14,655,092	25,379,353	23,702
1931–35	3,887,399	4,532,641	8,420,040	1,922,786	10,342,826	8,367,008	53,032	1,975,818	4,479,609	24,937
1936–40	5,652,590	5,896,300	11,548,890	4,957,443	16,506,333	21,735,402	10,186,512	5,229,069	16,082,812	26,386
Total	$14,706,161	$21,414,218	$36,120,379	$10,275,100	$46,395,479	$62,860,682	$26,740,303	$16,465,203	$48,154,521	88,740

Period	Contribution per $1.00 Savings	Original Investment per $1.00 Savings	Fund Earnings per $1.00 Savings	Total Investment per $1.00 Savings	Paid Depositors per $1.00 Savings	Percentage Market Profit or Loss on Total Investment	Market Profit or Loss per $1.00 Savings
1916–24	$1.63	$2.63	$0.34	$2.97	$2.19	26	0.78
1925–30	2.41	3.41	.83	4.24	8.67	104	4.43
1931–35	1.17	2.17	.49	2.66	2.15	19	0.51
1936–40	1.04	2.04	0.88	2.92	3.85	32	0.93
Total	$1.46	$2.46	$0.69	$3.15	$4.27	35	1.12

* Source: Fund records

if the market fell to $35, and he had to sell, his shares would be worth $14,716 less.

The hypothetical cases indicate clearly what might have been accumulated *if* no withdrawals were made prior to retirement. In these cases, even at a relatively low market valuation of shares, the fund would have offered retirement security of a high order. The actual statistics on value of withdrawals tend to underestimate the possibilities of the plan, since often the available statistics indicate only the value of the employees' accounts at the time they are closed. Particularly in the case of long-service employees, substantial amounts have often been withdrawn *prior to retirement*.

TABLE P

HYPOTHETICAL ACCOUNTS, 1945

Employee	Annual Income	Savings	Shares	Cash and Bonds
X	$1,000	$1,475.00	1,132	$3,326.97
Y	2,000	2,950.00	2,265	6,653.92
Z	3,000	4,425.00	3,397	9,980.90

TABLE Q

VALUE OF HOLDINGS AT VARIOUS MARKET PRICES

Employee	Market Quotation $48.00	Market Quotation $35.00	Difference
X	$ 54,336	$ 39,620	*$14,716*
Y	100,720	79,275	*21,445*
Z	163,056	118,895	*44,161*

The type cases serve also to indicate the crucial significance of the market value of stock at time of retirement. This, obviously, is the weakest element in the profit-sharing program as a pension plan. The value of common stock is correlated to a high degree with cyclical fluctuations in business. The depression of 1921 brought the first serious decline in Sears's stock value since the fund was started in 1916. From a high of $243 per share in April, 1920, the market price dropped to a low of $54.50[23] per share in January, 1921. The fund and the company were young at this time, and the retirement problem was nonexistent, so that no serious repercussions developed.

The depression of 1932 resulted in the company's subsidizing losses on closed accounts. While figures are not available on retirees as such, the data covering the first eight periods of 1932 indicate something of the serious condition that prevailed in the cases of those employees who may have found it necessary to withdraw when the market price had fallen to dangerously low levels. Accounts closed during the period involved 12,807,657 shares whose accumulated market value was $306,459.37. These accounts represented $439,213.35 in employees' savings and accrued interest on savings. The loss on these closed accounts was $132,753.98. This actual loss to members withdrawing at the time was met by the company so that, while withdrawing employees did not gain substantially from their participation in the fund, they did not lose any of their investment.

The results of profit-sharing as a retirement program may be further illustrated in terms of the following actual cases, characterized by the executive director as typical cases of how profit-sharing "pays off at retirement":

Mr. A went to work for Sears in 1912 and had never earned more than $2,291 a year. He began putting money into the Fund when it was established in 1916. He withdrew enough to pay for his home. Then he withdrew some more and built a summer home. He came to the office some time ago and said "I'm retiring." His credits were on that date $9,426 in cash and 400 shares of Sears stock worth approximately $47 a share. Not many people can retire at 65 like this fellow did—with two homes paid for and about $27,000 to be paid to him over a period of five years. (His total deposits amounted to $2,508.)

Mr. B was employed by the Company in 1913 and joined the Fund in 1916. He had to retire . . . at the age of fifty-five because of [ill-health]. Before retiring the Fund purchased for him from his credits, an annuity policy to pay him $200 a month for as long as he lives, with any unpaid balance at his death reverting to his wife and children. In addition to this, he had accumulated 1,027 shares, which, at the time he retired, had a market value of $44⅞ per share, or a total value of $46,100. (His total deposits amounted to $6,898.)

Miss C retired from the Company at regular retirement age. Her credits at the time of closing her account were 948 shares and $3,798 cash. Her total profit, including previous withdrawals, amounted to $72,697. (She had deposited in profit-sharing from her wages a total of $5,638.)

An examination of the records of profit-sharing members who retired and whose accounts were closed between January 1, 1946, and November 5, 1948, shows that one depositor realized a profit of more than $208,000 on his own investment of about $7,900. This was the most outstanding of the 426 records available. But the record includes several accounts of $100,000, and a large number of cases where profits exceeded $25,000. For the group as a whole the average deposit of the retiree was $2,134 and the amount of profit realized was, on the average, $20,117. As Table R makes clear, however, there was great dispersion about the average, with the highest returns going to those individuals who fell in the categories of thirty to forty-four years of service.

It is not surprising that great variation is found in the profits realized, since that amount is a function of so many variables including: how much the employee earns (although the annual employee deposit is limited to $250); the years in which the employee's deposits are at a maximum; the length of time the depositor is in the fund; the earnings of the company; the variation in stock-market values; and whether and when the depositor has made partial withdrawals prior to his retirement.

A serious difficulty in evaluating the plan as a pension program is the multi-purpose character of the fund. The program partakes at once of the several aspects of profit-sharing, unemployment insurance, stock ownership, a fund to care for extraordinary expenditures, and in some cases a means of accumulating capital to go into business. This "all-purpose" character of the Sears profit-sharing program is in many ways its strength. But in a retirement plan it may be at the same time a substantial limitation.

But profit-sharing at Sears is more than a pension plan. Throughout the company and at virtually all levels one encounters a strong faith in the

TABLE R*
PROFIT-SHARING RECORDS OF RETIRED EMPLOYEES
BY YEARS OF SERVICE

Years of Service	Number of Employees	Totals Deposits	Totals Profits	Average per Employee Deposits	Average per Employee Profits
10–14	127	$143,228.65	$ 675,973.62	$1,128	$ 5,323
15–19	124	211,839.73	1,341,003.71	1,709	10,815
20–24	45	89,448.02	683,534.86	1,988	15,190
25–29	34	99,558.06	1,078,748.55	2,928	31,728
30–34	31	120,366.19	1,464,628.48	3,883	47,246
35–39	39	125,668.01	1,691,723.99	3,222	43,378
40–44	18	82,287.89	1,116,228.82	4,572	62,013
45–49	17	34,597.78	495,186.09	2,035	29,129
Over 49	1	2,159.44	23,145.49	2,159	23,145
10–50	426	$909,153.77	$8,570,173.61	$2,134.16	$20,117.71

* Source: Fund records.

effectiveness of profit-sharing as a morale builder. In carrying on the employee morale surveys discussed in chapter xxix, interviewers have found profit-sharing an important element in employees' favorable reaction to the company.

The justification of profit-sharing from the management point of view must lie in the assumption, however vaguely realized or articulated, that it is an effective device to maintain and improve either employee behavior or "sound" public relations, or both. Since it is the habit of people to discount the future at a relatively high rate (and this is probably especially true among lower-income groups living among the dramatic exigencies of immediate responsibilities), the protective type of profit-sharing plan which Sears represents must keep the employee "sold" on the advantages of the plan, through personal contacts, house organs, and other mediums.

A former executive, who was in Sears's employ for fifteen years in sev-

SHARING PROFITS WITH EMPLOYEES

eral important capacities, both in the field and in the parent-organization, and who in conjunction with his work has come in contact with literally hundreds of employees within the ranks and without, is definitely of the opinion that

the most important single factor responsible for the company's good morale is the profit-sharing system. New employees are constantly exposed to the large holdings which the older employees have in the Fund because they talk about it constantly. Nonparticipating employees (in service less than one year) invariably keep on talking about the time when they will be eligible to participate. It is a common saying in the retail trade that nobody can take people away from Sears, and one of the reasons for that is, without doubt, the profit-sharing system. It seems certain, however, that the effectiveness of profit-sharing in building morale would have been less had Sears personnel policy been less comprehensive and liberal.

How some Sears's employees regard profit-sharing is indicated in the following statement of a young man, age twenty-two, who entered the company's service early in 1947 after graduating from college:

In the retail advertising department where I work there are twenty-two people, all but four of whom are men. The ages range from twenty-one to about forty-five. Most of the men between thirty-five and forty-five have been with Sears for seven or eight years and there is one who has been there about fifteen.

Everyone, without exception, thinks profit-sharing is a wonderful thing. However, the people who follow it most closely are the married men with families. Some of the younger men don't think they'll stay with Sears so they don't seem to worry too much about it. I feel differently. I can't wait for my year to be up so I can join.

Profit-sharing certainly is on everyone's mind. Often when we go for a cup of coffee, people tell "fables" about profit-sharing. The one I've heard most is about an elevator operator who had been at the store for years who, when she finally had to retire, had about $35,000 in profit-sharing.

From what I can gather, profit-sharing is the thing that most of the employees base their savings on. It is their mainstay for the future, and everyone takes it very seriously. There are some who at times get dissatisfied at Sears, but they wouldn't leave because of their profit-sharing. The remark is usually, "I can't afford to leave Sears—I have eight (or fifteen or whatever it is) years in profit-sharing."

There are some in the department who didn't go into profit-sharing when they originally could have, and they are still regretting it. One man, for instance, could have twelve years in it, but he didn't join until seven years ago. He is still kicking himself.

At the present time everyone in the department who is eligible is in profit-sharing and keeps informed about it. It is honestly their financial mainstay for the future and they know it.

It is difficult if not impossible to establish the value of profit-sharing to Sears's management in terms of dollars and cents. It cannot be established in quantitative terms that the moderate diversion of profits from stockholders to employees results in ultimately equal or greater dollar returns to Sears. But there is no question that a virtually unanimous opinion exists among company executives that profit-sharing is of the first order of importance in maintaining employee morale.

All employee benefit policies may be interpreted as tangible evidence of management's concern for the welfare of its employees. Profit-sharing, however, has gradually assumed a role at Sears which executives believe transcends that function. To these men working in the organization day after day and intimately observing Sears's personnel at work, profit-sharing is accepted as a doctrine of faith. Profit-sharing has become a "unifying principle"—a symbol around which the organization revolves; a means of integrating the activities of tens of thousands of individuals in pursuit of the common goal. And the work of William Wallace as fund director has greatly accelerated the development of Sears's profit-sharing as a "unifying principle" of the organization.

Profit-sharing has come to exemplify the common objective of all parties to carrying on Sears's business. As the fund acquires a greater and greater proportion of outstanding stock, potential conflict between the interests of stockholders and employees becomes less and less likely. The making of profits for absentee stockholders has never been a rallying point around which the enthusiastic support of employees could be organized. Where employees and stockholders tend more and more to become the same people, however, profitable operations—with all that implies—becomes a rallying point of greater and greater effectiveness. These are the articles of faith held by the reasonable men in Sears's management—and familiar sounds they make to those who are at all acquainted with such early exponents of profit-sharing as M. Leclaire in France and Gilman in the United States.

But whereas the exponents of profit-sharing have generally emphasized the purely economic advantages of their plans to employees and assumed that workers would make the direct connection between their efforts and the pecuniary benefits to be derived from profit-sharing—thus resulting in ultimately increased benefits to the firm—Sears tends to view the value of profit-sharing in somewhat different form. The morale surveys made among employees in recent years have indicated that the fund's influence on employee attitudes derives largely from the symbolism that profit-sharing has become. The actual holdings of individual employees appears to be not nearly so important as the fact that the huge holdings of the fund symbolizes to employees that they and the company are one.

It is difficult to avoid being impressed with the strong faith that Sears's executives have in the effectiveness of profit-sharing as a means of influencing employee behavior. One is inclined to accept the judgment of men who have more and more become statistical merchants and who place great store by precision and exactness when they are convinced of the value of profit-sharing *despite* the difficulty in measuring that value.

APPENDIX B

Method for Calculating the Capital Base

FOLLOWING the general procedure of the National Bureau of Economic Research, the practice of many investment analysts, and a generally accepted procedure of accountants, the base is defined as the stated value of "capitalization" as indicated in the annual statements of the company. "Capitalization" for our purposes, then, includes the sum of preferred stock (for the period up to 1923), common stock, and surplus.[1] Since Sears's policy in recent years has been to carry substantial reserves for contingencies, it is suggested that these reserves are essentially surplus reserves and as such should be included in the capitalization figure. Short-term loans have been excluded on the basis that interest paid on such loans constitutes an operating expense and hence is already reflected in the annual net profit figure; and, further, that short-term loans do not represent risk capital.

The possibility of using the market value of outstanding shares is excluded as irrelevant, since the market value "represents" capitalization of prospective earnings. It is a function of anticipations, expectations, and the social psychology of traders and certainly does not constitute sunk investment in the company.

For our purposes "net profit" is simply the reported net income after taxes indicated on the annual Consolidated Income Account.[2] The use of the stated net income as the "profit" figure may be questioned, since the current year's profit may turn out, as a result of subsequent developments, to be either greater or less than currently stated. But the possibilities that adjustments made in the course of this study might err, and the tendency of compensatory results over a period of several years, suggest the use of the net earnings figure published in the annual statement. It is probably not the "best" figure, but it is the available figure and one which is used in other studies of industrial profits.

Since the net income earned during the fiscal year is generated by the invested capital available at the beginning of the year and that which accumulates during the year, the device used here is to take the average of the sum of the invested capital of the current year and the previous year. This is admittedly imperfect, but, in view of the availability of *annual* statements, it is suggested that the method provides the only feasible way of reflecting the additive effect of the gradual accretion of the current year's earnings.

In computing the return on average capital investment, the various figures used were obtained from the annual balance sheets as follows:

1. NET PROFIT. Net profit figures were taken, as stated, directly from the annual balance sheets of the company.
2. GROSS CAPITAL INVESTMENT. This figure includes capital stock issued, earned surplus at the end of the year before dividends or surplus deductions, and excess reserves over and above specifically known needs.
3. NET CAPITAL INVESTMENT. This figure includes capital stock issued, earned surplus after dividends have been paid and deductions from surplus made, and excess reserves over and above known needs.
4. AVERAGE CAPITAL INVESTMENT. This figure is an average of the capital investment at the beginning of a year (previous year's *net* capital investment) and that at the end of the year (this year's *gross* capital investment). It was hoped in this way to obtain a more accurate approximation of the actual capital investment attributable to any given year.
5. RETURN ON AVERAGE CAPITAL INVESTMENT. This figure is the ratio of net profit to average capital investment, expressed to the nearest tenth of a per cent.

Notes

Notes

CHAPTER I

Introduction: Sears, Roebuck as Mass Distributor

1. Benjamin Jowett, *The Dialogues of Plato*, Vol. V: *The Laws* (3d ed.; New York and London: Oxford University Press, 1892), Book XI, p. 306.
2. Committee on Distribution, Twentieth Century Fund, *Does Distribution Cost Too Much?* (New York: Twentieth Century Fund, 1939), p. 127.

CHAPTER II

American Economic Expansion

1. Louis M. Hacker and Benjamin B. Kendrick, *The United States since 1865* (3d ed.; New York: Crofts, 1939), p. 31.
2. Harold U. Faulkner, *Economic History of the United States* (New York: Harper & Bros., 1937), p. 209.
3. Chester Wright, *Economic History of the United States* (New York: McGraw-Hill Book Co., 1941), p. 612.
4. Faulkner, *op. cit.*, pp. 270 and 162.
5. Release of the Department of Commerce, Bureau of the Census (Washington, D.C., October 31, 1939).
6. Hacker and Kendrick, *op. cit.*, pp. 128–29.
7. *Ibid.*, pp. 105–66. Hacker and Kendrick also assert (p. 165) that repeal of the corn laws in England and passage of the Homestead Act in the United States were the two most important factors in transforming American agriculture in the last half of the nineteenth century.
8. Faulkner, *op. cit.*, p. 162.
9. Fred Albert Shannon, *The Farmer's Last Frontier* (New York: Farrar & Rinehart, Inc., 1945), p. 51 (quoting *Statistical Abstract of the United States, 1910* [Washington: Government Printing Office, 1911], p. 121). Faulkner (*op. cit.*, p. 270) sets the annual increase in this period at 15,000,000 acres but does not introduce supporting figures; Faulkner also says that the average annual increase from 1900 to 1910 dropped 4,000,000 acres.
10. Shannon, *op. cit.*, p. 51 (quoting *Statistical Abstract of the United States, 1910*, p. 128).
11. Hacker and Kendrick, *op. cit.*, p. 167.
12. Ida M. Tarbell, *The Nationalizing of Business, 1878–1898* (New York: Copyright 1936 by The Macmillan Company, and used with their permission), p. 262.
13. *Ibid.*, p. 268.
14. Faulkner, *op. cit.*, p. 263.
15. Shannon, *op. cit.*, p. 139 (quoting *Agricultural Yearbook, 1899*, p. 319).
16. Fred Albert Shannon, *America's Economic Growth* (New York: Copyright 1940 by The Macmillan Company, and used with their permission), p. 409.
17. *Ibid.*, p. 379.
18. *Ibid.*, p. 176.
19. Faulkner, *op. cit.*, pp. 162–63, 271.
20. *Ibid.*, pp. 174–76.
21. *Statistical Abstract of the United States, 1946* (Washington: Government Printing Office, 1946), p. 8.
22. Frank Presbrey, *The History and Development of Advertising* (New York: Doubleday & Company, 1929), p. 286.

23. Paul H. Nystrom, *The Economics of Retailing* (3d ed.; New York: Copyright 1930 by The Ronald Press Company), I, 194–95.

24. Daniel C. Roper (First Assistant Postmaster-General [1913–16]), *The United States Post Office* (New York: Funk & Wagnalls Co., 1917), pp. 177 and 80–81.

25. *Ibid.*, p. 141.

26. Clyde Kelly, *United States Postal Policy* (New York: D. Appleton & Co., 1931), pp. 112–13.

27. N. H. Egleston, *Villages and Village Life* (New York: Harper & Bros., 1878), p. 35.

28. Arthur M. Schlesinger, *The Rise of the City, 1878–1898* (New York: Copyright 1933 by The Macmillan Company and used with their permission), p. 58.

29. E. V. Smalley, "The Isolation of Life on Prairie Farms," *Atlantic Monthly*, LXXXII (1893), 378–81.

30. *Statistical Abstract of the United States, 1946*, p. 5.

31. Despite the dramatic rise of two great mail-order houses, the general store hung on tenaciously for many years. Nystrom (*op. cit.*, pp. 79–80), writing in 1930, says: "The general merchandise store was the most characteristic retail institution during the transition period from pioneer life down to full-fledged economic development and maturity. The general merchandise store remained the most common and the greatest outlet for goods to consumers even down to the twentieth century. It supplied practically all of the simple requirements of the early settlers, and as their incomes and prosperity grew the general merchandise stores also expanded to supply their needs up to recent years."

32. Irwin M. Heine, "The Influence of Geographic Factors on the Mail Order Business," *American Marketing Journal*, III, No. 2 (April, 1936), 128.

33. *Op. cit.*, p. 80.

34. For interesting details on the technique and implications of the credit operations of storekeepers in the rural South see Thomas D. Clark, *Pills, Petticoats and Plows* (Indianapolis: Copyright 1944, used by special permission of the publishers, The Bobbs-Merrill Company, Inc.), chap. x. Nystrom (*op. cit.*, p. 81) says: "Long-term credits were customary in the general merchandise trade in all parts of the country. During most of the nineteenth century settlements on accounts were usually made annually. In some sections this period was shortened to six months before the opening of the twentieth century."

35. *Op. cit.*, p. 82 cf. Clark (*op. cit.*, esp. chaps. i–iii), who says: "Everything of importance that ever happened either occurred at the store or was reported there immediately. If a man got shot he somehow arranged to have the shooting take place at the store, or if he wished to give an enemy a first-class flailing, he usually found him on the store porch along with a highly appreciative audience. When he wished to 'cuss' the government or to complain at the Lord because of the perfidy of politics and weather conditions, there was no place, not even excepting a country church ground, the polls or a saloon, ever offered quite the same golden opportunity to get drunk" (p. 32).

36. Clark, *op. cit.*, p. 316.

37. *Ibid.*, pp. 316–17.

38. Solon Justus Buck, *Harvard Historical Studies*, Vol. XIX: *The Granger Movement* (Cambridge: Harvard University Press, 1913), p. 16.

39. *Ibid.*, p. 18.

40. Nystrom, *op. cit.*, p. 175.

41. *Ibid.*, p. 176.

42. Frank Luther Mott, *A History of American Magazines, 1865–1885*, III (Cambridge: Harvard University Press, 1938), 37–39.

43. The authority for this and following details on Ward's life and the founding of his mail-order company is a copy of a one-page memorandum found among Ward's private papers at the time of his death, written in his own handwriting apparently around 1900 (quoted by Rae Elizabeth Rips, "An Introductory Study of the Role of the Mail-Order Business in American History, 1872–1914" [Master's thesis, University of Chicago, 1938], *passim*).

NOTES TO PAGES 20-25   721

44. Ward Catalogue No. 11 (1874) (quoted by Rips, *op. cit.*, pp. 15-16).
45. Ward catalogue (cited by Rips, *op. cit.*, pp. 16-18).
46. Letters from customers reprinted in *Among Ourselves*, Ward's house organ (cited by Rips, *op. cit.*, p. 63).
47. Cited by Rips, *op. cit.*, pp. 19-20.
48. Montgomery Ward and Company, *Almanac, 1897, a Book of Practical Information for the Farmer and Stock Raiser*, and *Almanac and Year Book, 1899, a Book of Practical Information for the People* (both cited by Rips, *op. cit.*, p. 20); both almanacs contain pictures and a description of the train.
49. "A Short History of the Oldest Mail Order House," *Forward* (a Ward house organ), IV (November, 1925), 2 (cited by Rips, *op. cit.*, p. 19).
50. Nystrom, *op. cit.*, pp. 185-86.
51. *Ibid.*, p. 186.
52. Wesley Briggs Phillips, *How Department Stores Are Carried On* (New York: Dodd, Mead & Co., 1901), *passim*.
53. Presbrey, *op. cit.*, p. 570.
54. Nystrom, *op. cit.*, p. 187.

CHAPTER III

Origins: Building a Business

1. *Dictionary of American Biography* (New York: Charles Scribner's Sons, 1935), XVI, 540. A. C. Roebuck, in Vol. I, p. 4, of his unpublished memoirs, "Early and Some Later History of Sears, Roebuck and Co." (2 vols., 1940), agrees with the information in the *Dictionary of American Biography*. Louis Asher (another long-time associate) and Edith Heal puts Sears's birth date exactly one year later, December 7, 1864, in *Send No Money* (Chicago: Argus Books, 1942), p. xi. M. R. Werner on p. 31 of *Julius Rosenwald. The Life of a Practical Humanitarian* (New York: Harper & Bros., 1939) chooses December 4, 1863. In his unpublished history of the company, W. E. Woodward simply states on p. 10 that Sears was twenty-three years old in 1886. Roebuck's final selection of December 7, 1863, as Sears's birth date represents a revision of a judgment made in 1918 and adhered to as late as 1925. In a letter to Julius Rosenwald in 1918, Roebuck declared: "Mr. Sears was born in December 1863. The date it seems to me was the 23rd, he being approximately twenty days older than I."
2. Asher and Heal, *op. cit.*, p. xii.
3. *Ibid.*, pp. xii ff. On p. xxv it is asserted that, after Richard Sears finally settled permanently in Chicago, he telephoned his mother nightly by long distance.
4. *Ibid.*, p. xiii.
5. *Op. cit.*, I, 4.
6. *Op. cit.*, p. 31.
7. Asher and Heal, *op. cit.*, p. xix.
8. Werner (*op. cit.*, p. 31) attributes this information to "Richard Sears' sister." Roebuck (*op. cit.*, I, 112) identifies the sister as Eva and quotes the same information as being contained in a letter from her to Julius Rosenwald, dated July 29, 1918.
9. Roebuck (*op. cit.*, I, 115) says: "Mr. Sears' first acquaintance with the general mail order business seemed to have come through his knowledge of the magnitude and nature of the business that was being done by Montgomery Ward and Company during 1887 to 1889 when he was operating the R. W. Sears Watch Co. business in Chicago. Thereafter, at various times, it was apparent that he had not lost sight of his ambition to some day be engaged in a business like it." Asher and Heal (*op cit.*, p. 21) say that Sears in 1890 enthusiastically brought his fist down upon a Montgomery Ward catalogue which lay on his desk and exclaimed, "That's the game I want to get into—the biggest game in the United States today."
10. *Op. cit.*, I, 4.
11. *Op. cit.*, p. xxii.
12. Roebuck, letter to Rosenwald, July 17, 1918.
13. Asher and Heal, *op. cit.*, p. 15.

14. Roebuck, letter to Julius Rosenwald, July 17, 1918. Roebuck adds: "One of these companies, I believe, was Kirtland Bros. & Co. located in New York City and some other company located, I believe, in Fredonia, N.Y."

15. Roebuck, *op. cit.*, I, 5. Roebuck was in a position to know how the jewelry business operated in that period, since he himself engaged in that business as an employee of Richard Sears and later bought one of Sears's watch companies and operated it.

16. *Ibid.*, Roebuck quoting a conversation years afterward with one of the station agents with whom Sears dealt in this particular enterprise.

17. Roebuck, letter to Julius Rosenwald, July 17, 1918, revised October 2, 1925. The "letter," written for Rosenwald's use on a trip to France, was actually a short draft of what eventually became the "Early and Some Later History of Sears, Roebuck and Co."

18. *Op. cit.*, I, 15.

19. Florence Kiper Frank, unpublished manuscript on life of Julius Rosenwald.

20. Roebuck, *op. cit.*, I, 6.

21. Roebuck, letter to Rosenwald, July 17, 1918.

22. Asher and Heal (*op. cit.*, p. 17) say that a deposit of fifty cents to a dollar was required in 1887, "as a guarantee of good faith and to cover express charges in case the watch was returned."

23. Roebuck, *op. cit.*, I, 6, 121–26. Details of Roebuck's life are given in understandably profuse detail in his "History."

24. Roebuck (*ibid.*, p. 7) says that this advertisement was reproduced in a full-page spread in the *Chicago Daily News* in October, 1934 (to emphasize the value of classified advertising in the *News*). Roebuck adds that the ad was copied and given a page by the *Los Angeles Times* on November 2, 1934, and that the *Boston Herald* and many other newspapers gave it from a quarter- to a half-page.

25. Frank, *op. cit.*, p. 12.

26. Roebuck, *op. cit.*, I, 6.

27. Roebuck, letter to Rosenwald, July 17, 1918.

28. Roebuck, *op. cit.*, I, 7.

29. *Ibid.*, p. 8.

30. *Ibid.*

31. Charles W. Moore, *Timing a Century: History of the Waltham Watch Company* (Cambridge: Harvard University Press, 1945), pp. 76–80.

32. Roebuck, *op. cit.*, I, 89–90.

33. *Ibid.*

34. *Ibid.*, p. 7.

35. *Ibid.*, p. 9.

36. Asher and Heal, *op. cit.*, pp. 42–43; Roebuck, *op. cit.*, I, 114.

37. Asher and Heal (*op. cit.*, p. 11 n.) quote an executive of Montgomery Ward as stating in later years: "We believe R. W. Sears was the first one to come out plainly with 'satisfaction or money refunded.'" It is possible that Sears was indeed the first to use this literal phrasing of the guaranty, but the attempt to credit Sears with initiating the guaranty skirts the facts (see n. 38).

38. Rae E. Rips ("An Introductory Study of the Role of the Mail-Order Business in American History, 1872–1914" [unpublished Master's thesis, University of Chicago, 1938], p. 13) quotes the Montgomery Ward catalogue of 1874 as stating that no sales were to be considered complete with the mere delivery of the goods; the customer had to be satisfied or he could return the goods with no cost to himself.

39. Asher and Heal (*op. cit.*, p. 10) quote Sears as saying time and again to his associates, "The mail order pot never has and never will boil without a red hot fire all the time."

40. Roebuck, *op. cit.*, I, 9.

41. *Ibid.*, pp. 162–63. Chapter titled "False Stories" quotes "History #1" (written by Sears, Roebuck and Company for newspaper publicity) as saying Sears "sold out for $60,000, a success at 25," etc. Roebuck quotes "History #2," written for the same purpose, as saying "Sears sold out with $100,000 to his credit, played with the idea of becoming a banker," etc. Roebuck further quotes the company's 1933 World's Fair

booklet as reverting to the earlier estimate with the statement, "Sears is offered $60,000 for his business [the R. W. Sears Watch Company] by an Eastern Syndicate." (Roebuck also points out that it was a Chicago concern, not an eastern syndicate.) Roebuck says that he talked in 1934 with a man to whom Sears had shown the check; that man's clear recollection was that the check was for $72,000. Roebuck also states that Sears told him he had invested $60,000 in farm mortgages in Iowa, which makes Roebuck think that Sears must have gotten $72,000 for the sale, since he probably would not have so invested his entire return.

42. *Ibid.*, p. 9.
43. *Ibid.*, p. 19.
44. Asher and Heal, *op. cit.*, p. 17.
45. Roebuck, *op. cit.*, I, 10.
46. *Ibid.*
47. *Ibid.*, p. 77.
48. *Ibid.*, pp. 13-14.
49. *Ibid.*
50. *Ibid.*, p. 14.
51. *Ibid.*, Vol. II, Exhibits 33-39, in which the articles of incorporation, filed in the county of Hennepin, in the state of Minnesota, at 11:10 o'clock on the eighth day of April, A.D. 1892, are reproduced.
52. *Ibid.*, Exhibit 40, in which stock certificate, signed by A. C. Roebuck, secretary, and Richard W. Sears, president, is reproduced.
53. *Ibid.*, I, 14.
54. *Ibid.*, p. 16. A. Curtis Company and Alvah Company were both derived from Roebuck's first and middle names. As with the Hoverson Company, Richard Sears often followed a practice of designating his enterprises by the names of his associates.
55. *Ibid.*, p. 17.
56. *Ibid.*, Vol. II, Exhibits 32-39, photostatic reproduction of articles of incorporation filed in Hennepin County, Minnesota, on April 8, 1892. The change of the company's name to "Sears, Roebuck and Company" did not alter the limitation on corporate indebtedness or liability nor, in fact, anything but the nomenclature.
57. *Ibid.*, I, 17. Roebuck (p. 25) states, however, that "in February, 1925 the First Retail Store was Established. It is located in the northeast corner of the Merchandise Building at Homan and Arthington Sts., Chicago." This indicates that Roebuck did not feel that the Minneapolis venture was a real retail store. Certainly the company does not.
58. *Ibid.*, p. 17.
59. *Ibid.*, p. 162.
60. *Ibid.*, p. 29.
61. *Ibid.*
62. *Ibid.*, p. 18.
63. *Ibid.*, p. 87.
64. Asher and Heal (*op. cit.*, pp. 58-59) tell of how Conkey capitalized upon Sears's need for catalogues and of the hard bargains driven by Conkey.
65. *Ibid.*, p. 162.
66. Frank Presbrey, *The History and Development of Advertising* (New York: Doubleday & Company, Inc., 1929), p. 383.
67. Asher and Heal (*op. cit.*, p. 40) say: "Sears did not even bother to key his ads," but, they continue (p. 41), "later on, when page and half-page copy was used, such ads were carefully keyed."
68. *Op. cit.*, I, 116.
69. Werner, *op. cit.*, p. 36 (reproduction of ad).
70. Louis Asher insisted in an interview with the authors that that advertisement appeared for only a very short while. But Roebuck (*op. cit.*, I, 118) goes out of his way to disassociate himself from the scheme by pointing out that the miniature furniture was offered by Sears "under the name of R. W. Sears & Co. in 1889 and sold for ninety-five cents. [Roebuck apparently meant the R. W. Sears Watch Company.] That was while I was engaged in business in Toronto, Canada. Mr. Sears told me it was first ad-

vertised as a miniature set and later as a bauble set. (The definition of a bauble is a toy.)" He may have told Roebuck, but apparently he did not extend himself to tell his customers.

71. Asher and Heal, *op. cit.*, p. 17.
72. Roebuck, *op. cit.*, I, 15.
73. It is noteworthy that in all his correspondence with Roebuck, which the latter reproduces in profusion in his history, Sears never called his partner by his first name. It was always "Friend Roebuck," "Mr. Roebuck," or just plain "Roebuck." And Roebuck in turn never refers to Sears a single time as other than "Mr. Sears." Sears also always wrote to Louis Asher as "Mr. Asher."
74. Roebuck (*op. cit.*, I, 113–14) calls Sears "a very agreeable chap to be associated with" and goes into some detail there and elsewhere on Sears's personality. Asher and Heal (*op. cit.*, p. xvi), discussing Sears's relations with his associates, assert that Sears made suggestions instead of giving orders and relied upon such openings as "Suppose we do this.... What do you think of this idea? Please—could you give me a few minutes' time?" Other veterans of Sears, Roebuck interviewed by the authors declare that, even when Sears had a door to his office, it was never closed—subordinates just walked in; and that Sears habitually walked to the office of the person he wanted to see instead of issuing a summons for that party. And (*ibid.*, p. 84) they insist that Sears always backed his subordinates to the hilt.
75. Roebuck, *op. cit.*, I, 15.
76. *Ibid.*, p. 19; Vol. II, Exhibit 72, photostatic copy of "Statement of Assets and Liabilities," dated August 19, 1895, and signed by Richard W. Sears, Aaron E. Nusbaum, and Julius Rosenwald, verifies these figures.
77. *Ibid.*, I, 19.

CHAPTER IV

Capital and Transition: Growing Pains and Financial Panic

1. Alvah C. Roebuck, "Early and Some Later History of Sears, Roebuck and Co." (2 vols., 1940), I, 23; Vol. II, Exhibits 89 and 90.
2. *Ibid.*, I, 20.
3. *Ibid.*, Vol. II, Exhibit 40. Photostatic copy of Roebuck's stockholdings shows he held 250 shares of par value of $100 each out of a total capital stock of $75,000.
4. M. R. Werner, *Julius Rosenwald: The Life of a Practical Humanitarian* (New York: Harper & Bros., 1939), p. 28.
5. *Ibid.*, p. 40.
6. *Ibid.*
7. "A little time prior to August 17, 1895, Mr. Sears said, 'It is apparent that a deal can be made with Mr. Rosenwald and Mr. Nusbaum a relative, to become affiliated with our Company, and that they will each invest $25,000.'" It is impossible to know just what Roebuck meant by "a little time" (Roebuck, *op. cit.*, I, 19).
8. Werner, *op. cit.*, p. 41.
9. Werner (*ibid.*) quotes Nusbaum's widow as saying Nusbaum took the initiative in the whole affair and approached Rosenwald only after being refused by Edward Stonehill (another brother-in-law) and Louis E. Eckstein. Florence Kiper Frank, however (unpublished manuscript on life of Julius Rosenwald), says that it was Rosenwald who suggested Nusbaum to Sears as a possible partner; even if this were so, it still would not preclude Nusbaum's later having come back to Rosenwald to persuade him to buy a quarter-interest in Sears, Roebuck.
10. *Op. cit.*, pp. 2–3.
11. *Ibid.*, pp. 4–5.
12. "Records I found in Mr. Julius Rosenwald's files indicate that the 375 shares of Sears, Roebuck and Co. stock eventually owned by Mr. Rosenwald, was accepted by Newborg, Rosenberg and Co., New York clothing manufacturers, to apply on the Sears, Roebuck and Co., account for clothing sold to them through Rosenwald and Co., Newborg, Rosenberg and Co.'s Chicago agents. May 15, 1897 that stock was purchased by Julius Rosenwald, M. S. Rosenwald and J. E. Weil. Seven notes of $5000 each, were

given in part payment. Later Mr. Julius Rosenwald acquired the interests of the other two" (Roebuck, *op. cit.,* I, 21). *Ibid.,* Vol. II, Exhibits 123-24: reproduced photostatic copies of foregoing agreements. *Ibid.,* Exhibits 86-88: photostatic copy of an "Agreement between Julius Rosenwald et al in re Capital Stock of Sears, Roebuck and Co.," negotiated by the law firm of Loeb and Adler, contains the statements: "WHEREAS said Julius Rosenwald is the owner of Three Hundred Seventy-five (375) shares of the capital stock of SEARS, ROEBUCK AND COMPANY . . ." and "WHEREAS said stock was purchased originally with the funds of Newborg, Rosenberg and Company. . . ."

13. *Ibid.,* I, 20.
14. Frank, *op. cit.,* p. 17.
15. Werner, *op. cit.,* p. 67.
16. Roebuck, *op. cit.,* Vol. II, Exhibit 123, par. C, photostat of one of more than two dozen memorandums of agreement from Rosenwald's files, refers to an agreement "between Richard W. Sears, Aaron E. Nusbaum, and said Julius Rosenwald, providing for the deposit of two shares of stock of Sears, Roebuck and Co. by said Sears, one share by said Nusbaum and one share by said Rosenwald, with Loeb and Adler in escrow." Frank (*op. cit.*) states that the four shares deposited with the law firm were to be voted in case of a deadlock. This appears to be a reasonable inference, but it is impossible to state categorically now what the rights of the holders of these shares were, since these rights would be determined by the terms of the agreement, which is not available.
17. Roebuck, *op. cit.,* I, 23-24. On September 6, 1895, Roebuck sold the company the right to use his name in an agreement of which this photostatic copy appears as Exhibit 84 (*ibid.,* Vol. II):

"KNOW ALL MEN BY THESE PRESENTS, That I, A. C. Roebuck . . . for and in consideration of One Dollar and other good and valuable considerations to me in hand paid by Richard W. Sears . . . do hereby release and forever discharge said Richard W. Sears from any and all claims or demand I may now have against him and from any and all claims or demand, right, title or interest in the business carried on by said Richard W. Sears in the name of Sears, Roebuck and Co., by reason of said Richard W. Sears having used my name in said business . . . and I do hereby give to the said Sears, Roebuck and Co., corporation, etc., full right, authority and privilege to use said name of 'Roebuck' in their said corporate name.

[Signed] ALVAH CURTIS ROEBUCK."

The company's right to use Roebuck's name in perpetuity was also specifically reinforced in the bill of sale of November 9, 1897 (*ibid.,* Vol. II, Exhibits 89 and 90), which served to conclude the agreement of 1895 whereby R. W. Sears had held Roebuck's shares in trust.

18. *Ibid.,* I, 21.
19. *Ibid.,* p. 20; *ibid.,* Vol. II, Exhibits 92-95, reproduces photostatic copy of terms of sale between Sears and Rosenwald; payments by Rosenwald were to be spread over a period of forty-four months. Terms between Sears and Nusbaum were presumably the same.
20. *Ibid.,* Vol. II, Exhibit 123, par. F. Copy of one of Rosenwald's memorandums shows that, simultaneous with his leaving Rosenwald and Company to join Sears, Roebuck in an active capacity, an agreement between those two companies covering purchase of clothing by Sears, Roebuck was canceled. This agreement (giving Rosenwald and Company a first option on all clothing purchased by Sears) had been effected on September 6, 1895, when Rosenwald bought into the mail-order firm; it was probably designed to help secure the capital which Newborg, Rosenberg and Company had put up through Rosenwald and Company to purchase Julius Rosenwald's quarter-interest in Sears, Roebuck.
21. Details on Rosenwald's early life are taken from Werner, *op. cit.,* and Frank, *op. cit.*
22. An interesting trio: Morgenthau became ambassador to Turkey; Goldman's company organized the syndicate that in 1906 underwrote the Sears, Roebuck's stock issue (recounted later in this chapter); and Moses Newborg was one of the founders

of Newborg, Rosenberg and Company and, with Rosenwald, cofounder of Rosenwald and Company.

23. "Rosenwald & Weil, a smaller firm, naturally conducted their trade in the manner of their competitors, and competition was fierce" (Werner, op. cit., pp. 25-26).

24. Frank, op. cit., p. 1.

25. Ibid., p. 30.

26. Letter from Asher to Florence Kiper Frank, December 2, 1935.

27. Louis Asher and Edith Heal, Send No Money (Chicago: Argus Books, 1942), p. 20.

28. "I believe it was in 1896 at Fulton and Des Plaines Streets, Mr. Sears said to me, 'Roebuck, if they would give me that――lot of clothing on the second floor, I would accept it for my interest, and get out, but they won't do it.' Several other times between 1895 and 1909 Mr. Sears told me of his desire and inability to sell his interest in the company" (op. cit., I, 115).

29. Ibid., p. 30.

30. Rosenwald's "emotional state" at this juncture is drawn from Frank, op. cit. In this connection, Mrs. Frank points out that the friction thus generated never affected Rosenwald's happy relationship with his wife.

31. Ibid.

32. Roebuck, op. cit., Vol. II, Exhibits 102-3 (photostatic copy of agreement between Nusbaum and Rosenwald and Sears, drawn by Albert Loeb). The money was to be paid in eighteen instalments, ranging in amount from $50,000 to $100,000 and staggered from May 7, 1901, to January 1, 1907. The promissory notes for all the money except the immediate cash payment of $75,000 were to carry interest at the rate of 4½ per cent per annum, payable quarterly. The terms of the agreement also specified that "said company will not, until all of said notes and interest thereon have been paid in full, declare or pay to any of the stockholders of said company any dividends on any stock, and will not pay to its officers or directors any salary or salaries in excess of the aggregate sum of One Hundred Thousand ($100,000.00) Dollars per annum for all said officers and directors." Nusbaum apparently felt that the company would have to scrape the barrel to meet its payments to him.

33. Ibid., I, 49.

34. At a special meeting of the board of directors (ibid., p. 48).

35. Photostatic copy of minutes (ibid., Vol. II, Exhibits 104-6). In the order of business as shown in these minutes, Nusbaum's resignation and the acceptance of the resignation *precede* his offer to sell his interest, the terms of the offer, and the acceptance of the offer.

36. Ibid., I, 49-50.

37. Ibid., p. 50 (paraphrasing minutes of meeting of board of directors held December 12, 1904).

38. Ibid.

39. Data on working capital and expenditures for real property are from financial statements prepared from the books of Sears, Roebuck and Company by Deloitte, Plender and Griffiths, auditors and accountants for Goldman, Sachs and Company in 1906.

40. Werner, op. cit., p. 74. Prior to this time Goldman, Sachs and Company handled commercial paper for Sears, Roebuck. The underwriting of issues was almost as new for the financial house as the public issue was to the mail-order house, for Sears was only the second investment banking operation of the Wall Street firm. Earlier in 1906 it had underwritten an issue for General Cigar Company.

41. Roebuck, op. cit., I, 50. Roebuck (ibid., p. 51) goes on to say: "It is probable that the consolidation above referred to was for the purpose of making the stock more attractive to prospective customers."

42. Copy of "Certificate of Incorporation and By-Laws."

43. Roebuck, op. cit., I, 51.

44. Ibid.

45. Ibid.

46. The circular quoted an auditor's statement dated August 28 and announced that

public subscription would open at 10:00 A.M. on Monday, September 17, indicating the undated circular was issued between those dates.

47. Roebuck, *op. cit.*, I, 31.

48. Werner, *op. cit.*, p. 75.

49. The 1906 offerings circular contained this statement: "The Company may redeem the entire issue of its Preferred Stock at any time at 125 per cent., and under its charter is permitted to buy its own stock in the open market, for Treasury Account, and when so purchased shall cancel the same."

50. Sears, Roebuck and Company, *Annual Report for Year Ending December 31, 1924.*

51. Werner, *op. cit.*, p. 75. Werner also says (pp. 74–75) that Rosenwald formed a Sears, Roebuck Stock Syndicate in June, 1906, to allow some of his relatives and friends to participate in the new stock flotation.

52. Sears, Roebuck and Company, Treasurer's Office. Application No. A-3299 to Committee on Stock List, New York Stock Exchange, dated November 12, 1906, indicates that the 1906 issue of Sears, Roebuck and Company preferred stock was approved for listing by the governing committee of the New York Stock Exchange December 12, 1906, one month after the company applied for listing of 100,000 shares of 7 per cent cumulative preferred aggregating $10,000,000 par value, all issued and subscribed. The application to the Exchange showed the following members of the board of directors of Sears, Roebuck and Company: A. Barton Hepburn, Henry Goldman, Philip Lehman, and Robert P. Sniffen, all of New York; John Higgins, Walker O. Lewis, Albert H. Loeb, Julius Rosenwald, and Richard W. Sears, all of Chicago. The common stock was not listed on the Exchange until 1910.

53. Wesley C. Mitchell, *Business Cycles: The Problem and Its Setting* (Berkeley: University of California Press, 1913), pp. 515 ff. Cf. O. M. W. Sprague, "History of Crisis under the National Banking System," *Publications of the National Monetary Commission* (Washington: Government Printing Office, 1910), chap. iii.

54. *Op. cit.*, pp. 82–83.

55. *Commercial and Financial Chronicle*, LXXXV, 863.

56. Sprague, *op. cit.*, pp. 251–52.

57. Report of the Secretary, *Yearbook of the Department of Agriculture, 1907* (Washington: Government Printing Office, 1908), p. 9.

58. Report of the Secretary, *Yearbook of the Department of Agriculture, 1908* (Washington: Government Printing Office, 1909), p. 9.

59. *Op. cit.*, p. 518; see pp. 518–21.

60. Asher and Heal, *op. cit.*, p. 104.

CHAPTER V

Sales Pressure and Promotion

1. Louis Asher and Edith Heal, *Send No Money* (Chicago: Argus Books, 1942), p. 32.

2. *Ibid.*, p. 40.

3. Ralph M. Hower, *The History of an Advertising Agency, N. W. Ayer & Son at Work, 1869–1939* (Cambridge: Harvard University Press, 1939), p. 98.

4. *Ibid.*, p. 37.

5. Asher and Heal, *op. cit.*, p. 31.

6. *Ibid.*, p. 40.

7. *Ibid.*, p. 49. Asher (*ibid.*, p. 33) asserts that the total cost of advertising in the mail-order publications by the company was $50,000–$60,000 a month.

8. M. R. Werner, *Julius Rosenwald: The Life of a Practical Humanitarian* (New York: Harper & Bros., 1939), p. 51.

9. These and similar variations appear in all Sears's ads in the April, 1898, issue of the *American Woman* and in many other publications of the same period.

10. Asher and Heal, *op cit.*, p. 32.

11. According to a story in the *Chicago Evening Post*, February 13, 1904, Sears was *the* largest advertiser.

12. Asher, "Notes"; Asher and Heal, *op. cit.*, p. 42.
13. Interview with Elmer Scott.
14. Asher and Heal (*op. cit.*, p. 9) quote an undated letter from Sears: "Get the orders *first*, don't worry about delays and the warehousing."
15. Asher, "Notes."
16. A. C. Roebuck, "Early and Some Later History of Sears, Roebuck and Co." (2 vols., 1940), I, 19: "It was found we could not pick up from the manufacturers and wholesalers more than a part of our daily requirements, as a result of which many substitutions were made, and many shipments were refused by customers." Roebuck adds (p. 21) that the magnitude of Sears's clothing sales was an important factor in influencing Rosenwald to purchase an interest in the company late in 1895. And Werner (*op. cit.*, pp. 43–44) quotes "an early employee of the clothing department" as saying of the 1895 promotion: "The whole stock consisted of possibly three or four hundred suits in three different classes of material. . . . I believe some 25,000 suits were sold, although we did not have one in stock when the ad went out. And at the beginning the buyer went downtown and bought up what he could and at night all of us, including Mr. Sears and Mr. Roebuck, filled the orders as far as the purchase went."
17. Roebuck, letter to Rosenwald, July 17, 1918.
18. Asher, "Notes."
19. Florence K. Frank, unpublished manuscript on the life of Julius Rosenwald, p. 28; Werner, *op. cit.*, p. 64.
20. Roebuck, letter to Rosenwald, July 17, 1916.
21. *Ibid.*
22. Werner (*op. cit.*, p. 64) says that, when the manufacturer dropped his price to $9.50, advertising cost one dollar and overhead cost another dollar, leaving one dollar profit on each machine.
23. Roebuck, letter to Rosenwald, July 17, 1918.
24. Asher, "Notes."
25. Asher and Heal, *op. cit.*, p. 51.
26. Arthur M. Schlesinger, *Political and Social Growth of the American People, 1865–1940* (New York: Copyright 1941 by The Macmillan Company, and used with their permission), pp. 217–18.
27. Frank L. Mott, *A History of American Magazines, 1865–1885*, III (Cambridge: Harvard University Press, 1938), 11. A dramatic instance of this practice had come to light in 1874, when the trustee in bankruptcy for Jay Cooke and Company brought an action against Henry C. Bowen to set aside a contract whereby the latter was to use the editorial columns of his *Independent* to help sell the bonds of the Northern Pacific Railroad on a percentage basis. Bowen had at the time already received $50,000 in bonds and $460,000 in stock.
28. Werner, *op. cit.*, p. 65.
29. All details of the Arney promotion episode are based upon Asher's "Notes."
30. Frank Presbrey, *The History and Development of Advertising* (New York: Doubleday & Company, Inc., 1929), p. 363.
31. *Ibid.*, pp. 410–12.
32. Roebuck, *op. cit.*, I, 29. One of the credit vouchers is reproduced as Exhibit 85 in *ibid.*, Vol. II.
33. As witness the many ads for patent medicines previously cited in the *Fireside Visitor* of 1894 and also in virtually every other "mail-order" publication of this period.
34. Roebuck (*op. cit.*, I, 26) says that Sears asked him to take over the electric-belt department in the latter part of 1899. Roebuck adds: "I tried one of the electric belts after the proposition was submitted to me, and found that while it developed a strong current of electricity, and produced a tingling sensation, it was so strong that if the battery cells became uncovered and touched the flesh it would burn and cauterize it, and as I did not have faith in it as a curative agent, I declined the offer." Asher and Heal (*op. cit.*, p. 38) seek to justify the belt by saying: "Other firms sold it. There was no law against it."
35. Asher and Heal, *op. cit.*, p. 62.
36. According to information supplied the authors by William Pettigrew and sub-

stantiated by Werner (*op. cit.*, p. 66), by Roebuck (*op. cit.*, I, 28), and by Asher's "Notes." Pettigrew also asserts that the company realized some 60 per cent by bringing in the merchandise and disposing of it. But he adds that the loss of 40 per cent (on $800,000–$900,000) was a sizable figure at that period.

37. No reference to the banking department appears in the 1899 catalogue; the 1900 catalogue is not available; the first reference found is that of 1901, but its tone and general handling do not comport fully with the treatment usually accorded the introduction of a new department. It is possible that the banking department was launched in 1900.

38. Asher and Heal, *op. cit.*, p. 88.

39. An unidentified manufacturer agreed to furnish 30,000 cream separators a year to Sears, Roebuck for five years at a price based on factory cost plus a profit of $2.00 per machine (*ibid.*, p. 89).

40. *Ibid.* In connection with the cream-separator promotion it should be pointed out, however, that, even prior to Sears's hunting trip, the company had stocked and listed a cream separator selling at $62.50 (*ibid.*, p. 87). Less than a hundred of them were sold in 1903 until the separator was dramatized to Richard Sears by the Dakota farmer.

41. *Ibid.*, p. 91.

42. Werner, *op. cit.*, pp. 65–66.

43. Roebuck (*op. cit.*, I, 38) quotes a letter from one W. O. Lewis, a former employee of the company, written in 1937: "As I remember it we opened around 1904 or somewhat earlier a store at Joliet and one at Elgin or Rockford. I rather think the latter. Took orders from catalog for customers. Took in butter and eggs, etc. After a trial we discovered it did not work out as expected." William Pettigrew vouches for the locations of Pontiac and Watseka.

44. Werner, *op. cit.*, pp. 65–66.

45. This was remedied later, as indicated by this excerpt from a letter Sears wrote Asher on October 27, 1906: "By the way now that our Profit Sharing certificates are good only for *one* year it is of the *greatest importance* that if they are not dated exact as they go out, they must *surely* by some mark show the month and year of issue, for 12 months hence that will become so very important . . ." (quoted in Asher and Heal, *op. cit.*, p. 167).

46. *Ibid.*, pp. 70–71.

47. This did not, however, seem to discourage Richard Sears. He wrote Asher on November 1, 1906, while at sea bound for Europe: "I enclose a couple of scratches, just ideas of what I would like to see in the Customers Profit Sharing line in our spring Catl. I am very anxious to see the Profit Sharing put up just right and with liberal space in our next Catl . . ." (quoted in *ibid.*, p. 167). And as late as January 19, 1907, Sears wrote Asher from London: "Our Profit Sharing is now so liberal we ought to be able to interest owners of small factories and superintendents of larger ones to take orders from employees and co-workers from our big catalogue. They should see inducement enough in our Profit Sharing goods and to get at them I would suggest the following: consider addressing the proprietors of all factories, mills and manufacturing places, perhaps a list of 300M, tell them if they are not interested please hand the letter to their superintendent about taking orders from and for all employees.

"Point out our Great Profit Sharing inducements, ask them to send for our Big Catalogue or Profit Sharing book or both. Take orders from all employees for all their needs, and in this way get Profit Sharing certificates" (quoted in *ibid.*, p. 176).

48. Report by Deloitte, Plender, Griffiths and Company, accountants and auditors, 49 Wall Street, New York City. This report preceded the Sears, Roebuck stock issue later that year by the New York bankers.

49. "Septs" and "Sepr" are Sears's abbreviations for (cream) separators. The De Laval referred to is a company which sued Sears, Roebuck for infringement of patent on the cream separators; according to correspondence between Sears and Asher, the litigation cost Sears, Roebuck from 10,000 to 15,000 sales of separators.

50. Letter from Scott to Louis Asher, February 12, 1940.

51. Statement by Elmer L. Scott, personal interview.

52. Werner, *op. cit.*, p. 44.

CHAPTER VI

Catalogue Appeals and Policies

1. M. R. Werner (*Julius Rosenwald: The Life of a Practical Humanitarian* [New York: Harper & Bros., 1939], p. 53) and A. C. Roebuck ("Early and Some Later History of Sears, Roebuck and Co." [2 vols., 1940], I, 116) state that in late 1895 or early 1896 Sears authorized the mailing of his photograph and a personal letter to each of the firm's customers, the substance of which was, "When you come to Chicago, be sure to call on me. I'd like to shake hands with you." Roebuck adds that Sears soon found he had given an order too large to fill. Werner (*op. cit.*, p. 53) says that a portly clerk later had to impersonate Sears to greet visitors.

2. The 1895 catalogue, for instance, says on p. 2: "We refer you to the Union National Bank, Minneapolis, or Atlas National Bank, Chicago, and you are at liberty, if you choose, to send your money to them with instructions not to turn it over to us unless they know us to be perfectly reliable. We refer you to any Express Company doing business in Chicago or Minneapolis, Adams, American, United States, Pacific, Great Northern and Northern Pacific and you can, if you choose, send your money to the agent of any one of these companies, either Chicago or Minneapolis, with instructions not to turn it over to us unless they know us to be perfectly reliable, or you can very likely find people in your own locality who know us."

3. Louis Asher and Edith Heal, *Send No Money* (Chicago: Argus Books, 1942), p. 110.

4. Memorandum from William Pettigrew.

5. Pettigrew, who is the source of much of the information on early catalogue production, and Elmer Scott told the authors that space allocation in the catalogue even after 1900 was based largely on what Richard Sears thought the merchandise "ought to have"; if he were pushing bicycles at the time, for example, that line received as much space as Sears felt would prove profitable. Judgment was based primarily on sales records and expected sales, which hinged on Sears's own merchandising sense; there were no hard-and-fast rules governing space allocation or position.

6. Asher and Heal, *op. cit.*, pp. 36–37.

7. *Ibid.*, p. 56.

8. Roebuck, *op. cit.*, I, 64.

9. Asher and Heal, *op. cit.*, p. 56. Asher says: "Actually, the 1000 page book cost Sears, Roebuck and Company about 50 cents to mail," but he fails to make it clear whether this was merely the cost of postage, or of printing, or both. Werner (*op. cit.*, p. 66) asserts: "The cost to the Company of printing and distributing it [the catalogue] always varied between sixty and eighty-five cents a copy."

10. Asher and Heal, *op. cit.*, p. 57.

11. Quoted by Asher and Heal, *op. cit.*, p. 165. (Italics ours.)

12. *Ibid.*

13. Werner, *op. cit.*, p. 66. Earlier in the same paragraph, however, Werner says that "Sears, Roebuck charged fifty cents a copy for its catalogue in 1901 and for several years thereafter."

14. To help keep matters confused, Roebuck (*op. cit.*, I, 64) says: "In 1905 the policy of sending the catalog free was again established."

15. Asher and Heal, *op. cit.*, pp. 57–58.

16. Sears, Roebuck and Company, Auditing Department, "Report" (1908).

17. Asher and Heal, *op. cit.*, pp. 67–69.

18. *Ibid.*, p. 69.

19. In a letter written to Asher on February 5, 1905, Sears said: "If our Iowa deal proves out o.k., we will be able to circulate big catalogues at 25¢ each or better, or say 3,000,000 books a season at say $750,000 or an average of 20M books every day . . ." (*ibid.*, p. 170).

20. *Ibid.*, p. 183.

21. *Ibid.*, p. 184.

22. *Ibid.*, p. 185.

23. Most of the information on catalogue production up to 1908 comes from notes of Pettigrew and Asher and from a report by Henry Case.

24. Based, like most of the rest of this section, on notes from Pettigrew; substantiated by Elmer Scott.

25. It is evident, however, from a letter Sears wrote Asher on January 31, 1902 (Asher and Heal, *op. cit.*, p. 163), that ink and paper presented problems even while Conkey had the printing contract: "I hope we can run our catalogue from April on, on 22 pound paper, but so we are not at the mercy of the paper mills and subject to Conkey's kicks on paper, (which no doubt are justified) when we know he can handle the light sheet, I think we always should have 15 to 20 cars stored at Hammond ahead before we get started on a season's run, then if any paper isn't right instead of running it and putting up with the delays caused by defects, we can ship the imperfect paper back to the mills and in this way they will learn to give us the proper paper." The same interest in ink and paper is reflected in another letter to Asher written by Sears on February 16, 1902: "Your letter and sample of forms on light paper, run heavy and light ink at hand. The only way is to run them light. These catalogues that we have paid a bonus to get rapidly are worth (in my opinion) *far* more to us *now* than in June or July, when we need a certain volume of business to keep our *total* expense down and the only way to do it is to get the *catalogues* out as fast as possible . . ." (*ibid.*).

26. Frank Presbrey (*The History and Development of Advertising* [New York: Doubleday & Company, 1929], p. 50) says: "The art of engraving on wood was kept alive by the mail order catalogue. It was a time-consuming, expensive method of illustration but no other cut served as well for cheap printing."

CHAPTER VII

Mail-Order Merchandise

1. A. C. Roebuck, "Early and Some Later History of Sears, Roebuck and Co." (2 vols., 1940), I, 22.

2. *Ibid.*, p. 32.

3. *Ibid.* Letter from J. Fletcher Skinner, general merchandise manager, to Richard Sears dated December 12, 1906, while Sears was in Berlin, Germany, is quoted in part: "As far as its [the grocery department's] being a paying proposition, I don't believe it is or ever will be. It is simply a question of our continuing the business at no profit or a very small profit, for the benefit of Sears, Roebuck and Company's entire business." Company records and correspondence from executives indicate clearly that Skinner's cautious hope for even "a very small profit" was optimistic.

4. Former key employees in the grocery department assert that they scoured the market to obtain the best-quality groceries they could find. One of these officials particularly recalls that hams and coffee sold by Sears ranked in quality with any available in the United States at the time.

5. Louis Asher and Edith Heal, *Send No Money* (Chicago: Argus Books, 1942), p. 186.

6. Frank Presbrey, *The History and Development of Advertising* (New York: Doubleday & Company, 1929), pp. 296, 364.

7. *Ibid.*, p. 362.

8. Ralph M. Hower, *The History of an Advertising Agency, N. W. Ayer & Son at Work, 1869–1939* (Cambridge: Harvard University Press, 1939), p. 56.

9. Asher and Heal, *op. cit.*, p. 92.

10. "Stock Foods was a dud. With the most professional treatment it failed to create a ripple" (*ibid.*, p. 96).

11. See *ibid.*, pp. 96–101, which quotes from voluminous correspondence with Sears, in which the latter outlined extensive promotion plans for stock food.

12. Information on the "Modern Homes" department is gleaned from A. W. Clark's undated "Report on Modern Homes, Norwood Sash and Door Manufacturing Company," prepared for Sears, Roebuck apparently in 1936. The Norwood Company was the Sears subsidiary handling the "Modern Homes" operation. For further details on "Modern Homes" in later periods see chap. xxvii.

13. Reprinted from David L. Cohn, *The Good Old Days* (by permission of Simon and Schuster, Publishers, Copyright, 1940, by David L. Cohn), p. 154.

14. Asher and Heal, *op. cit.*, p. 175.

15. As witness the emphasis in the catalogue on farm implements and goods; the advertising mediums Sears employed at this time; the company's relative lack of interest in urbanites is amply reflected in the fact that no retail stores were opened until 1925; and the early customer indexes of the company, which show a marked emphasis on farm and rural community residents.

16. Norman Beasley, *Main Street Merchant* (New York: Whittlesey House, 1948), p. 45.

17. Roebuck (*op. cit.*, I, 90) tells of watches people showed him as late as 1935 which had been purchased as much as forty-one years earlier; he asserts that they were still keeping time.

18. Information supplied by Pettigrew.

19. Statement by Asher.

20. As indicated earlier, Sears had stressed his guaranty ever since 1887. By 1895, virtually every individual item listed in the catalogue carried its own specially phrased guaranty. By 1901, a general guaranty in the catalogue read: "WE GUARANTEE SATISFACTION and safe delivery on everything you order or refund your money." And by 1906 it was: "Your Money Back if You Are Not Satisfied." This statement was followed by a more detailed exposition: "*Every order you send us is accepted* with the understanding and agreement that if the goods we send you are not found perfectly satisfactory they can be returned to us at our expense and the money sent us, together with any freight or express charges paid, will be immediately refunded. Accompanying every shipment are these plainly printed conditions: '*If these goods please you*, you cannot do us a greater favor than to tell your neighbors and allow them to use your catalog to send us orders. *If they don't please you*, you cannot do us a greater favor than to return the goods at our expense and get your money back, together with any transportation charges you may have paid.'"

21. Asher and Heal (*op. cit.*, p. 124) quote a possibly apocryphal conversation between two department managers of Sears who were bragging about the amounts of their respective business. One reportedly said to the other: "Why we get more returned goods back in a day than your department ships out in a week." Asher also states (*ibid.*, p. 125) that Department R (returned goods) once occupied 50,000 square feet of space, while the six sections devoted to outgoing shipments required a total of only 60,000. It is also asserted, on the same page, that at one time Sears, Roebuck was shipping 10,000 women's hats daily and getting 1,500 back each day.

22. *Ibid.*, p. 78.

23. Letter to I. S. Rosenfels, advertising manager, Sears, Roebuck and Company, from R. Buckner, former head of the clothing department, dated August 6, 1918.

24. Paul H. Nystrom, *The Economics of Retailing* (3d ed.; New York: Copyright 1930 by The Ronald Press Company), I, 161–62.

25. Asher, "Notes."

26. Roebuck, *op. cit.*, I, 27.

27. *Ibid.*, p. 19. Roebuck cites the clothing department as "an outstanding example of the inconsistency of that theory."

28. This inventory figure is as of February 1, 1897. Dates applicable to inventory figures in succeeding years are indicated in Table 10.

29. It is true that by 1905, when this article appeared, Sears, Roebuck's inventory policy had been considerably improved. But in the article Richard Sears blandly indicated that his policy had *always* been just that indicated by the title. And, even in 1905, inventory control was more a hope than an actuality with Sears, Roebuck.

30. Asher and Heal, *op. cit.*, p. 28.

31. *Ibid.*, pp. 26–28.

32. *Ibid.*, pp. 28–29.

33. Roebuck, *op. cit.*, I, 80.

34. Asher and Heal, *op. cit.*, p. 24.

35. *Ibid.*, pp. 23–24.

CHAPTER VIII

Management and Methods: Order Out of Chaos

1. M. R. Werner, *Julius Rosenwald: The Life of a Practical Humanitarian* (New York: Harper & Bros., 1939), pp. 70–74.
2. *Ibid.*, p. 74.
3. Asher, "Notes."
4. Another separate department, established in 1896 as an ostensibly separate business, was the American Woolen Mills, which sold Sears, Roebuck clothing through agents. This enterprise was sold (at a profit) in 1906 when it was felt to be in competition with the company's own direct-to-consumer sales (A. C. Roebuck, "Early and Some Later History of Sears, Roebuck and Co." [2 vols., 1940], I, 22–23).
5. Louis Asher and Edith Heal, *Send No Money* (Chicago: Argus Books, 1942), pp. 82–84.
6. Florence K. Frank, unpublished manuscript on the life of Julius Rosenwald. Louis Asher's "Notes" confirm Frank's evaluation.
7. Quoted by Roebuck, *op. cit.*, I, 194.
8. Asher and Heal, *op. cit.*, p. 124.
9. Interview.
10. Asher and Heal, *op. cit.*, p. 124.
11. *Ibid.*, p. 172.

CHAPTER IX

Working Conditions, Welfare, and Wages

1. A. C. Roebuck, letter to Julius Rosenwald, July 17, 1918.
2. Louis Asher and Edith Heal, *Send No Money* (Chicago: Argus Books, 1942), p. 130.
3. *Ibid.*, pp. 129–30.
4. M. R. Werner, *Julius Rosenwald: The Life of a Practical Humanitarian* (New York: Harper & Bros., 1939), p. 49.
5. Editorial, *Seroco Topics*, Vol. I, No. 1 (January 21, 1899).
6. *Ibid.*
7. E. L. Shuey, *Factory People and Their Employers* (New York: Lenihan & Co., 1900), p. 63.
8. Gordon S. Watkins and P. A. Dodd, *The Management of Labor Relations* (New York: McGraw-Hill Book Co., 1941), p. 446: "The National Cash Register Company appears to be the first firm to publish an employee magazine—Factory News, which appeared in 1890. 'From this beginning the use of periodical publications for employees spread, although slowly at first'" (*Employee Magazines in the United States* [New York: National Industrial Conference Board, 1925], p. 2).
9. Asher and Heal, *op. cit.*, p. 132.
10. W. H. Lange, *Trends in Personnel Health Service* ("General Management Series," No. 85 [New York: American Management Association, 1925]), p. 8.
11. Asher and Heal, *op. cit.*, pp. 131–32.
12. *Ibid.*, pp. 133–34.
13. Several former employees hired during the period 1895–1900 state that they received starting wages of $5.00–$10.00 per week "depending on experience."
14. The 1907 manual was evidently not the first publication of this sort, since some 1905 issues of *The Skylight* refer to a pamphlet entitled *Sears, Roebuck & Co. and Their Employes*.
15. *Sears, Roebuck and Company and Their Employes*, p. 49.
16. *Ibid.*, p. 34.
17. *Ibid.*, pp. 34–35.
18. Quoted in Harry A. Millis and Royal E. Montgomery, *Economics of Labor* (New York: McGraw-Hill Book Co., 1938), I, 470.

19. *Ritchie* v. *People*, 155 Ill. 98 (1895).

20. Elizabeth Brandeis (in J. R. Commons and Associates, *History of Labor in the United States* [New York: Macmillan Co., 1935], III, 469) states that Massachusetts had an earlier mercantile hour law from 1883 to 1884.

21. *Muller* v. *Oregon*, 208 U.S. 412 (1908).

22. Brandeis, *op. cit.*, pp. 316 ff.

23. *Ibid.*

24. *Welfare Work for Employees in Industrial Establishments in the United States* (U.S. Bureau of Labor Statistics Bull. 250, "Miscellaneous Series" [Washington, 1919]), pp. 12–13.

CHAPTER X

Opposition and Competition

1. A. C. Roebuck, "Early and Some Later History of Sears, Roebuck and Co." (2 vols., 1940), I, 166–72.

2. Louis Asher and Edith Heal, *Send No Money* (Chicago: Argus Books, 1942), p. 105.

3. A fruitless even if harassing tactic, according to Asher and Heal, who assert that "the mail sacks the next day were brimming over with postcards addressed to the mail order firm asking for another catalogue" (*ibid.*).

4. M. R. Werner, *Julius Rosenwald: The Life of a Practical Humanitarian* (New York: Harper & Bros., 1939), p. 60.

5. Asher and Heal, *op. cit.*, p. 105.

6. Quoted by Rae E. Rips, "An Introductory Study of the Role of the Mail-Order Business in American History, 1872–1914" (unpublished Master's thesis, University of Chicago, 1938), pp. 76–77.

7. Letter to the authors. Cox adds a comment which indicates Sears, Roebuck's sensitiveness to public relations even at that time: "Another incident occurred when we were replacing an old, frame rural church with a brick one. My uncle asked this town merchant for a contribution for the new building. The merchant said, 'Why don't you ask Rears and Soreback?' My uncle replied that it was an excellent idea. He wrote and to his own surprise got a check back for $10.00. The merchant was chagrined."

8. From Asher's correspondence file.

9. Roebuck, *op. cit.*, I, 38.

10. Rips, *op. cit.*, p. 86.

11. *Ibid.*, p. 93.

12. *Ibid.*, p. 84.

13. Roebuck, *op. cit.*, I, 166–67.

14. Reproduced in part in Asher and Heal, *op. cit.*, p. 72.

15. Roebuck (*op. cit.*, I, 100) quotes Richard Sears as once having told him that "he had been told by the transportation companies that we passed our competitors [Montgomery Ward] during 1899." And Werner (*op. cit.*, p. 65) states, "In 1899, when the annual sales were $8,505,577, it [Sears, Roebuck] surpassed its nearest competitor." Records of the two firms show that not until 1900 did Sears outstrip Ward's.

16. R. M. Hower, *The History of Macy's* (Cambridge: Harvard University Press, 1946), pp. 332–33.

CHAPTER XI

End of an Era

1. M. R. Werner, *Julius Rosenwald: The Life of a Practical Humanitarian* (New York: Harper & Bros., 1939), p. 76.

2. Cf. Paul H. Nystrom, *The Economics of Retailing* (3d ed.; New York: Ronald Press Co., 1930), pp. 180 ff.

3. It is interesting to note here the general similarity between the policies of R. H. Macy and R. W. Sears. Hower says: "From the very beginning Rowland Macy pursued

certain rather definite patterns of action or business policies which have come down to the present with little modification and which are of basic importance. The major policies are four: dealing for cash only; selling at one price to all customers alike, regardless of bargaining ability; selling at very low prices (in today's terminology, underselling competitors); and aggressive advertising" (R. M. Hower, *The History of Macy's* [Cambridge: Harvard University Press, 1946], p. 48).

4. *Your United States: Impressions of a First Visit* (New York: Harper & Bros., 1912), pp. 93–94.

5. Hower, *op. cit.*, p. 394.

6. While Sears, Roebuck shows substantially higher advertising expense than does Macy's, the advantage of the former is substantial in the categories of wage and rent expense, which is clear from the data on Macy's reproduced below from Hower, *op. cit.*:

Year	Salaries	Rent	Advertising	Delivery	Total Expense
1902	9.51	2.11	2.11	1.94	19.06
1903	10.07	3.25	1.91	1.67	21.10
1904	0.05	2.05	1.05	1.81	20.80
1905	9.80	2.67	1.57	1.72	19.96

7. Louis Asher and Edith Heal, *Send No Money* (Chicago: Argus Books, 1942), p. 178. Richard Sears refers to "general expense" as including all operating expense other than advertising.

8. Florence K. Frank's unpublished manuscript on the life of Julius Rosenwald is the authority for this and the following two paragraphs.

9. "His [Richard Sears's] object was to bridge time, to insure a continued stream of orders, to create a vast mail order catalogue business in the shortest possible time. Supposing there were thirty complaints a day on the $12.75 bicycle. There were 1000 orders to offset the dissatisfied 3%. To make 97 new boosters for Sears, Roebuck & Company, it was necessary to disappoint 3" (Asher and Heal, *op. cit.*, p. 9). And Elmer Scott stated in an interview: "Sears said he'd have 100 ideas and discard 80 of them; of the remaining 20, seven would be good." Sears was thus apparently willing to let a favorable percentage yardstick apply to his own schemes as well as to his customers' satisfaction or dissatisfaction.

10. Asher's correspondence file.

11. Asher and Heal (*op. cit.*, p. 90) assert that the plan to promote separators through this plan was formulated by the advertising manager and the manager of the separator department in Sears's absence from the country.

12. *Ibid.*

13. *Ibid.*, p. 91.

14. *Ibid.*, p. 90.

15. *Ibid.*, p. 91.

16. Letters of R. W. Sears in the collection of Louis Asher.

17. Asher and Heal, *op. cit.*, pp. 186–87.

18. This metaphor occurs again and again when interviewing former Sears's executives on the 1907 crisis. It was evidently of Rosenwald's own devising. Note R. W. Sears's reference to "Easy in the Boat or not" (*supra*).

19. Asher and Heal, *op. cit.*, pp. 157–58.

20. *Ibid.*, pp. 158–59.

21. *Ibid.*, p. 159.

22. "Memorandum to Department Managers, November 20, 1907."

23. Letter from A. H. Loeb to Henry Goldman, of Goldman, Sachs and Company, dated August 27, 1908.

24. A. C. Roebuck, "Early and Some Later History of Sears, Roebuck and Co." (2 vols., 1940), I, 118.

25. Asher and Heal, *op. cit.*, p. 160.

26. "Human Interest Story of Richard W. Sears," *Printers' Ink*, LXXXVIII (October 8, 1914), 21.

27. Asher and Heal, *op. cit.*, p. 159; Roebuck, *op. cit.*, I, 56.

28. After leaving the presidency of the mail-order house, Sears engaged in various other enterprises. He developed lumber and railroad interests in Florida, bought and sold farm land in Minnesota and the Dakotas, and sold livestock by mail. He also purchased an interest in the Emerson typewriter business and brought in his old reliable lieutenant, A. C. Roebuck, to iron some kinks out of that business (a new, single-shift typewriter, the Woodstock, resulted). Even before his resignation, Sears had begun to dispose of some of his common stock. Between June, 1906, and November 4, 1908, he reduced his holdings from 140,310 shares to 112,476. And between May 19 and December 15, 1909, he further reduced his stockholdings to 4,550 shares, which final amount was sold March 2, 1915, after his death (Roebuck, *op. cit.*, I, 111 3/4). Goldman, Sachs apparently purchased all or nearly all of the stock Sears liquidated in this period, as that banking house paid Richard Sears $10,000,000 for his interest in Sears, Roebuck (Werner, *op. cit.*, p. 75).

29. "Human Interest Story of Richard W. Sears," *op. cit.*, p. 25.

30. A. D. Porter, "Things Began To Happen When Sears Sent His Catalogue Free," *Printers' Ink*, CIII (May 16, 1918), 116.

CHAPTER XII

The Mail-Order Market

1. United States Post Office Department publicity "throwaway" distributed in 1938 to celebrate the twenty-fifth anniversary of parcel post.

2. Memorandums to the authors submitted by Michael Cremonesi and William Pettigrew, executives of the company in this period.

3. Frederick F. Ingram, "The Parcels Post," *Twentieth Century Magazine*, III (March, 1911), 518; quoted by Rae E. Rips, "An Introductory Study of the Role of the Mail-Order Business in American History, 1872–1914" (unpublished master's thesis, University of Chicago, 1938), p. 110.

4. *Hearings before the Subcommittee on Parcel Post of the Senate Committee on Post Offices and Post Roads under Sen. Res. 56, November, 1911–January, 1912* (Washington: Government Printing Office, 1912), pp. 882–85 (cited by Rips, *op. cit.*, p. 108).

5. From a letter from Postmaster-General Meyer to Senator Burnham (*Congressional Record*, XLII, Part III, 2954) in reply to a charge that extension of the parcel post would save "a certain mail order house" $40,000 a year on the cost of mailing its catalogues (cited by Rips, *op. cit.*, p. 105).

6. United States Post Office Department publicity "throwaway" (1938).

7. Daniel C. Roper, *The United States Post Office* (New York: Funk & Wagnalls, 1917), pp. 189–91.

8. *Ibid.*

9. Transcript of lecture delivered by Homer J. Buckley, September 22, 1942, on the occasion of a Sears, Roebuck and Company seminar conducted at Northwestern University.

10. Of the importance of the postal auxiliaries, Buckley says: "Take away the rural free delivery and the right to distribute catalogs and printed matter through the parcel post service of the Post Office Department, and the whole structure of mail order advertising and mail order buying and selling would be seriously impaired. Its very life rests ... on these two major and comparatively new features of the post office service ..." (*ibid.*).

11. Report of the Secretary, reprinted in *Yearbook of the United States Department of Agriculture, 1909* (Washington: Government Printing Office, 1910), pp. 9–10.

12. Chester Wright, *Economic History of the United States* (New York: McGraw-Hill Book Co., 1941), p. 634.

13. Harold U. Faulkner, *The Quest for Social Justice, 1898–1914* (New York: Copyright 1931 by The Macmillan Company, and used with their permission), pp. 3–4.

14. Preston W. Slosson, *The Great Crusade and After, 1914–1928* (New York: Copyright 1930 by The Macmillan Company, and used with their permission), p. 199.

15. *Ibid.*, p. 200.

16. *Ibid.*, pp. 202–3.

NOTES TO PAGES 193-215

17. Paul H. Nystrom, *The Economics of Retailing* (3d ed.; New York: Copyright 1930 by The Ronald Press Company), p. 210.
18. *World Almanac, 1948*, p. 668.
19. So extensive became the use of mechanical power that Slosson (*op. cit.*, p. 190) is led to say: "Motor traction and electric power on the farm increasingly made agriculture a form of applied engineering."
20. Wright, *op. cit.*, p. 631.
21. Nystrom, *op. cit.*, p. 231. See chap. xix below for further development of changes in retailing.

CHAPTER XIII

The Debacle of 1921

1. Sears, Roebuck and Company, *Annual Report, 1920*.
2. M. R. Werner, *Julius Rosenwald: The Life of a Practical Humanitarian* (New York: Harper & Bros., 1939), pp. 195–96.
3. Werner quotes a letter from the chairman of the Overseas Entertainment Section of the YMCA (*ibid.*, p. 209).
4. *Ibid.*, pp. 209–11.
5. *Ibid.*, pp. 216–25.
6. Warren M. Persons, "The Crisis of 1920 in the United States: A Quantitative Survey," *American Economic Review* (Supplement), XII, No. 1 (March, 1922), 5–19.
7. This activity of the Justice Department was pursuant to the broad powers granted to the President under the enabling legislation enacted into law when the Lever Bill was signed August 10, 1917. This legislation laid the basis for all the "controls" during the war period (see Paul W. Garrett, *Government Control over Prices* [Washington: Government Printing Office, 1920], *passim*).
8. Persons, *op. cit.*, pp. 5–19.
9. William N. Mitchell, "The Preparation and Use of the Merchandise Budget in Mail-Order Houses," (unpublished Master's thesis, University of Chicago, 1925), p. 20.
10. Midyear statement of Sears, Roebuck and Company.
11. Willard Thorp, *Business Annals* (New York: Bureau of Economic Research, Inc., 1926), p. 144.
12. Sears, Roebuck and Company, *Annual Report, 1920*.
13. Department of Agriculture, *Crops and Markets*, July, 1929, p. 253 (quoted by Werner, *op. cit.*, pp. 226–27).
14. *Op. cit.*, p. 6.
15. Financial statements of Sears, Roebuck and Company.
16. Werner, *op. cit.*, p. 227.
17. *Ibid.*
18. D. K. Middleton in *Wall Street Journal*, June 27, 1947.
19. Simon S. Kuznets, *Cyclical Fluctuations, Retail and Wholesale Trades, United States, 1919–1925* (New York: Adelphi Co., 1926), p. 149.
20. Paul H. Nystrom, *The Economics of Retailing* (3d ed.; New York: Copyright 1930 by The Ronald Press Company), p. 210.
21. Werner (*op. cit.*, p. 228) supports this figure on reduction of operating costs.
22. The following lines have here been classified as durable goods: furniture, jewelry, silverware, hardware, harness, vehicles, musical instruments, phonographs, stoves, cream separators, sewing machines, bicycles, automobile supply, paints, farm implements, carpets, plumbing, washing machines, pianos, gas engines, roofing, wallpaper, houses, lumber, etc., lighting plants, typewriters, *Encyclopaedia Britannica*, and millwork.
23. *Op. cit.*, p. 225.
24. Quoted in *ibid.*, p. 231.
25. *New York Times*, December 30, 1921.
26. Werner, *op. cit.*, pp. 231–32.
27. Thorp, *op. cit.*, p. 144.
28. *Statistical Abstract of the United States, 1946*, pp. 624 and 284.

29. Annual reports of Sears, Roebuck and Company, 1923–30. Some arrangement was apparently made between Rosenwald and the company to extend his three-year option to repurchase the five million shares at par; the original three-year period would have expired December 29, 1924.

30. Sears, Roebuck and Company, *Annual Report, 1932*.

31. *Ibid.*

CHAPTER XIV

Reorientation of Merchandising

1. Correspondence files and memorandums.

2. *Statistical Abstract of the United States, 1946*, p. 488.

3. Newton A. Fuessle, "Putting a Grand Air into Copy," *Printers' Ink*, XCVII (October 26, 1916), 54.

4. Sears, Roebuck and Company, *Annual Report, 1932*. It should be noted, however, that it was a "department" only from the promotional and administrative points of view until 1930; in that year the component merchandise items of homes, theretofore scattered among many departments, were brought together for the first time under "Modern Homes," which then became a department in the usual meaning of that term in Sears.

5. These and virtually all the following details are taken from a detailed "Report on Modern Homes, Norwood Sash and Door Manufacturing Company," prepared for the company in 1936 by A. W. Clark; and from interviews with F. W. Kushel, head of the "Modern Homes" department from 1906 to 1930, and other Sears's executives connected with this department.

6. Chester Wright, *Economic History of the United States* (New York: McGraw-Hill Book Co., 1941), p. 981.

7. Interview with A. V. H. Mory.

8. Statement prepared for the authors by D. M. Nelson.

9. *Ibid.*

10. "Annual Report of Testing Laboratories for 1922," by G. M. Hobbs, p. 2.

11. Memorandum prepared for Julius Rosenwald by R. P. Sniffen, August 5, 1918.

12. "Controlling the Quality of Sears' Merchandise," a paper by Elizabeth Weirick, in charge of testing laboratories, Sears, Roebuck and Company, March 22, 1935.

13. Louis Asher and Edith Heal, *Send No Money* (Chicago: Argus Books, 1942), p. 172.

14. Fred A. Shannon, *America's Economic Growth* (New York: Copyright 1940 by The Macmillan Company, and used with their permission), p. 391.

15. The company's own records of its factories and its relationship with sources in this middle period are so scanty that most of the information has to be pieced together from catalogues and interviews with former executives.

16. Taken from a speech made in 1923 by a company executive believed to be Donald M. Nelson.

CHAPTER XV

Changes in Catalogue Selling

1. Montgomery Ward in 1909–10 employed its own equivalent of the "2-4-6-8-cent" department, but it was not accorded the amount of space or position in Ward's catalogue that Sears gave it. Nor were the offerings made nearly as enticing. The department opened on page 14 of Ward's fall and winter 1909–10 book, with two- and four-cent specials sharing that one page. There was no item at six cents, goods appearing on page 15 at eight cents. The next group of offerings, on the following page, were priced at two for twenty-five cents. Page 17 was devoted to items selling at twenty-five cents each, and page 18 was occupied by thirty-three-cent items. By 1914 the department had disappeared from the Ward catalogue.

2. Robert S. Lynd and Alice C. Hanson, "The People as Consumers," in *Recent Social Trends in the United States: Report of the President's Research Committee on Social Trends* (New York: Whittlesey House, 1934), p. 873.

3. Reprinted from *The Good Old Days* by permission of Simon and Schuster, Publishers, Copyright 1940, by David L. Cohn, pp. xxiii–xxxiv.

4. H. N. Case, "Outline of Activities of H. N. Case and Associates, July 1, 1913, to 1945" (unpublished résumé of Case's research activities in more than three decades at Sears). Case's detailed account of the countless research activities he conducted for the company is the authority for most of the following material on this phase of catalogue production.

5. Frank Presbrey, *The History and Development of Advertising* (New York: Doubleday & Company, Inc., 1929), pp. 287–88.

6. "Building the Catalogue That Brings in $150,000,000 a Year by Mail," *Printers' Ink,* C (July 19, 1917), 8.

CHAPTER XVI

Selling on Instalments

1. Authority for this and much of the succeeding information on the company's credit history is a study, "Credit History," made by the company and issued over the name of R. W. Leonardson. The study is dated June, 1938, but was apparently added to after that time, as credit data for 1941 are shown. Much of what Leonardson says is verifiable in the catalogue.

2. Reavis Cox, *The Economics of Instalment Buying* (New York: Copyright 1948 by The Ronald Press Company), p. 62.

3. *Ibid.*

4. *Ibid.*, p. 63.

5. This amount represented receivables from customers due for shortages in remittances for merchandise or shipping charges and to some extent for casual sales on credit made despite company policy.

6. "Returned merchandise" refers to goods repossessed by the company from customers unable to meet their payments and to goods sent back by dissatisfied customers. "Policy allowance" refers to allowances made in response to claims by customers of various deficiencies, which the company felt it would be more advantageous to grant than to contest and investigate. "Uncollectible" represents total loss.

7. Cox (*op. cit.*, p. 72), however, says that Montgomery Ward inaugurated instalment selling in 1911.

8. It is not possible to calculate the ratio of credit sales to total sales prior to 1928, since the data available on credit sales for earlier years include only the Chicago and Philadelphia plants.

9. Cox, *op. cit.*, p. 72.

10. W. C. Plummer, "Social and Economic Consequences of Buying on the Instalment Plan," *Annals of the American Academy of Political and Social Science,* Vol. CXXIX, Supplement 2 (quoted by Preston W. Slosson, *The Great Crusade and After, 1914–1928* [New York: Copyright 1930 by The Macmillan Company, and used with their permission], p. 181).

11. *Op. cit.*, p. 181.

12. *Ibid.*, p. 182.

13. Cox, *op. cit.*, p. 64

14. *Ibid.*, p. 68.

CHAPTER XVII

Operating Methods and Employee Welfare

1. This and most of the following description of operations in this period are based largely upon a speech made by Donald M. Nelson in 1924, listing accomplishments through the preceding year; a résumé of traffic department activities prepared in 1946 by Mr. Cremonesi of that department; and interviews with executives associated with the company in this period.

2. Louis Asher and Edith Heal, *Send No Money* (Chicago: Argus Books, 1942), p. 140.
3. Letter dated November 25, 1906, from Nice, France.
4. O. C. Doering, memorandum to department managers dated March 15, 1909.
5. *Studies in Personnel Policy*, No. 11 (New York: National Industrial Conference Board, 1939), p. 3.
6. For details of profit-sharing see Appendix A.
7. Manuscript of Julius Rosenwald prepared for his visits to the United States troops in Europe.
8. Quoted in M. R. Werner, *Julius Rosenwald: The Life of a Practical Humanitarian* (New York: Harper & Bros., 1939), pp. 161–62.
9. Illinois Senate Committee, *Report on Vice* (Springfield, 1916), pp. 178 ff.
10. *Ibid.*, p. 37.
11. Testimony of J. R. Rosenwald before the Illinois Senate Vice Committee (*ibid.*, p. 183). It is interesting that about this same time a similar investigation took place in New York City. Ralph M. Hower (*The History of Macy's* [Cambridge: Harvard University Press, 1946], p. 387) says: "For a number of years sensational stories had circulated about immorality among department store employees, supposedly resulting from the low wages received by the sales girls. New York's Committee of Fourteen began to wonder whether there might be any connection between working conditions in department stores and commercialized vice."
12. *Op. cit.*, pp. 383–84.
13. Illinois Senate Vice Committee, *Hearings*, p. 183.
14. Interview with William Wallace.
15. Interview with Russell Reedy.
16. "Douglas estimated an average decrease for *all* industry from 53.5 per week in 1914 to 50.4 in 1920.... The Census reported that from 1914 to 1919 the percentage of manufacturing wage earners working 48 hours or less increased from 11.8 per cent to 48.6 per cent; and that the percentage working 54 and over decreased from 74.7 per cent to 29.6 per cent" (quoted in John R. Commons and Associates, *History of Labor in the United States, 1896–1932* [New York: Macmillan Co., 1935], III, 109).
17. Announcement published to employees May 25, 1916.
18. Statement posted March 29, 1917.
19. Cf. Daniel Bloomfield (ed.), *Employment Management* (New York: H. W. Wilson Co., 1920), p. 1, who states: "You may ransack the literature of industrial management written ten years ago and you will not find the phrase 'employment management' used or the work of the personnel or employment supervisor mentioned.... Neither the work of employment management nor the functions of an employment executive were recognized in the scheme of industrial organization as it was commonly carried out."
20. Cf. Commons and Associates, *op. cit.*, pp. 324 ff.

CHAPTER XVIII

The Period in Review

1. While there is an obvious danger in basing conclusions on year-end inventory figures, these are the only data available in the cases of both companies.
2. Macy data from Ralph M. Hower, *The History of Macy's* (Cambridge: Harvard University Press, 1946), p. 376.
3. M. R. Werner, *Julius Rosenwald: The Life of a Practical Humanitarian* (New York: Harper & Bros., 1939), p. 62.
4. Company publicity, "From a Wayside Station to the World's Largest Store" (1926). In this connection it is interesting to note that the 1923 Montgomery Ward catalogue asserted that that company had within the previous six months perfected a shipping system which enabled it to fill most orders within forty-eight hours after receipt.
5. For example, "Advances to and Investments in Factories" appears as a single item in the balance sheets.

6. For the method used in the present instance see Appendix B. For the years prior to 1909 the character of the available data suggests that the net worth figure be used—simply the sum of capital and surplus shown on the balance sheet.

7. These conjectures are based on the average price of the security on the New York Stock Exchange, the annual average being derived from the high, low, and closing prices for the years indicated: $17.90 in 1921, $46.74 in 1925, and $52.58 in 1926.

8. Preston W. Slosson, *The Great Crusade and After, 1914–1928* (New York: Copyright 1930 by The Macmillan Company, and used with their permission), pp. 183 and 186.

9. "General Robert E. Wood, President." Copyright 1938 by Time, Inc. Reprinted from the May, 1938, issue of *Fortune* magazine by special permission of the Editors.

10. *Op. cit.*, p. 215.

11. George Milburn, "Catalogues and Culture," *Good Housekeeping*, CXXII (March, 1946), 183.

CHAPTER XIX

Urban America

1. Chester Wright, *Economic History of the United States* (New York: McGraw-Hill Book Co., 1941), p. 579.

2. *Ibid.*

3. Preston W. Slosson, *The Great Crusade and After, 1914–1928* (New York: Copyright 1930 by The Macmillan Company, and used with their permission), p. 197.

4. J. H. Kolb and Edmund de S. Brunner, "Rural Life," in *Recent Social Trends in the United States: Report of the President's Research Committee on Social Trends* (New York: Whittlesey House, 1934), p. 504.

5. *Statistical Abstract of the United States, 1947,* p. 16. Dixon Wecter (*The Age of the Great Depression, 1929–1941* [New York: Copyright 1948 by The Macmillan Company, and used with their permission], p. 133) states: "The early depression years saw a reversal of the traditional flow of population from farm to city, which in the previous decade alone had netted an urban increase of six million persons. Between 1930 and 1933, for the first time in the annals of the United States, this current slackened abruptly and actually began to run the other way.... During the year 1932 the farm showed a net addition of nearly three hundred thousand individuals, and by 1935 some two million were living on farms who had not been there five years before."

6. Earl E. Muntz, *Urban Sociology* (New York: Copyright 1938 by The Macmillan Company, and used with their permission), p. 48.

7. Wecter, *op. cit.*, p. 130.

8. "The National Income and Its Distribution," in *Recent Economic Changes in the United States* (New York: McGraw-Hill Book Co., 1929), II, 838.

9. *Op. cit.*, p. 138.

10. *Op. cit.*, p. 708.

11. Foster R. Dulles, *Twentieth Century America* (Boston: Houghton Mifflin Co. [for Reynal & Hitchcock], 1945), p. 264.

12. Wright, *op. cit.*, p. 603.

13. Malcolm M. Willey and Stuart A. Rice, "The Agencies of Communication," in *Recent Social Trends in the United States*, p. 175.

14. *Statistical Abstract of the United States, 1947,* p. 490.

15. *Op. cit.*, p. 129.

16. Cf. R. C. McGrane, *The Economic Development of the American Nation* (New York: Ginn & Co., 1942), p. 568. Of the effect of the automobile on residential location, Wecter (*op. cit.*, p. 129) states: "Yet in certain ways the social force of the internal-combustion engine was quite contrary to that wrought by the age of steam, whose effect upon population had been powerfully centripetal. The era of the motor car, allied with that of electricity, wrought a diffusive influence, separating the spot where one worked from the place where he slept and played. The mounting volume of traffic, pouring into the canyons of the metropolis each morning and debouching upon the hills and dales of

suburbia at dusk, bore witness to this change and also posed its own problems in speed and regulation."

17. R. D. McKenzie, "The Rise of Metropolitan Communities," in *Recent Social Trends in the United States*, pp. 443–45.

18. Kolb and Brunner, *op. cit.*, pp. 522–23.

19. *Op. cit.*, p. 457.

20. Robert S. Lynd and Alice C. Hanson, "The People as Consumers," in *Recent Social Trends in the United States*, p. 870.

21. Edwin Gay and Leo Wolman, "Trends in Economic Organization," in *Recent Social Trends in the United States*, p. 242.

22. Paul H. Nystrom, *The Economics of Retailing* (3d ed.; New York: Copyright 1930 by The Ronald Press Company), p. 219.

23. *Ibid.*, p. 229. Nystrom earlier remarks: "The department stores of the country are known to have enjoyed a continuously increasing volume during the years preceding 1914. Their sales volume increased very rapidly from 1914 to 1918, owing in part to the changes in money values but also because of increased volumes of merchandise sold. With the exception of the period of business depression in 1921 and 1922, the upward trend continued to 1923. Since then, according to the Federal Reserve Index, department store sales have continued to grow, but not at the same annual rates as in preceding years. Thus, while department store volume as of 1928 had increased by 38% over the sales of 1919, the rate of increase since 1923 has averaged only about 1.5% per year, which happened to be the estimated rate of growth of population in the United States for that period" (pp. 153–54).

24. Further details on efforts at legislative suppression may be found in chap. xxx. The more recent manifestation of the old animus is introduced here only to show the success of chain-store organizations as competitors of the local independent retailers— and of Sears, Roebuck and Company.

25. Nystrom (*op. cit.*, p. 209) states: "The growth of the chain stores, particularly of the J. C. Penney, W. T. Grant, and Neisner types [shown in Table 54] has probably given the general mail order houses more serious, vital competition than any competition ever growing out of efforts of individuals or of associations of independent retailers. The rapid growth of these chain stores must have been a factor in the consideration which led to the establishment of the mail order house chain stores."

26. *Op. cit.*, p. 872. The authors of the monograph further remark: "It was not until 1916 that an advertiser first spent a million dollars in a single year in advertising in the 30 leading periodicals checked by the Crowell Publishing Company, and the number spending a million dollars or more in these media increased to 20 in 1930. The largest advertiser in these 30 leading periodicals in 1915 spent in these media only $738,000, while the largest advertiser in the 30 leading periodicals in 1930 spent $3,789,000."

27. *Ibid.*, pp. 877–78. Nystrom (*op. cit.*, p. 99) states: "From a merchandising standpoint, the outstanding movement during the past ten years has been the recognition of fashion as a factor in merchandising, the study of fashion movements, the employment of fashion specialists as assistants in merchandising, and the appeal to consumers by offers of fashion rather than the old-time offers of quality and price."

28. Cf. Kolb and Brunner, *op. cit.*, pp. 537–39.

CHAPTER XX

THE NEW MANAGEMENT: ASCENDANCY OF ROBERT E. WOOD

1. M. R. Werner, *Julius Rosenwald: The Life of a Practical Humanitarian* (New York: Harper & Bros., 1939), p. 30.

2. *Ibid.*, p. 225.

3. Werner's study (*ibid.*) contains a fairly detailed account of Rosenwald's philanthropies and is the source for much of the material in this section.

4. *Ibid.*, p. 80.

5. For details on the philosophy and operations of Rosenwald's philanthropies see Edwin Embree and Julia Waxman, *Investment in People: The Story of the Julius Rosen-*

wald Fund (New York: Harper & Bros., 1949). Rosenwald had a strong aversion to philanthropies being dominated by what he called "the dead hand" of the departed donor. This conviction was expressed in his proviso that all funds of the Julius Rosenwald Fund be expended within twenty-five years after his death; he had a firm belief that the generation contributing to the making of wealth should also be the generation profiting from its disbursement.

6. Werner, *op. cit.*, p. 232.

7. *Ibid.*, p. 234.

8. "General Robert E. Wood, President." Copyright 1938 by Time, Inc. Reprinted from the May, 1938, issue of *Fortune* magazine by special permission of the Editors.

9. *Op. cit.*, p. 236.

10. *Ibid.*, p. 366. A good example of Rosenwald's compulsive generosity came in 1929, when the stock-market crash threatened to wipe out the life-savings of many Sears, Roebuck employees who held stock in that and other companies. Lessing Rosenwald immediately offered to guarantee the stock accounts of Sears's employees with stockbrokers. The elder Rosenwald forthwith assumed the responsibility and borrowed $7,000,000 from the Chase National Bank to centralize the transaction by taking over employees' accounts from brokerage houses (*ibid*., pp. 239–42).

11. *Statistical Abstract of the United States, 1947*, p. 610.

12. In 1936, while Roebuck's act was still going strong, the company celebrated its golden jubilee. Roebuck was to appear at the Cincinnati store at a Founder's Day promotional celebration. Governor Ruby Laffoon, of Kentucky, breveted Alvah C. Roebuck a colonel. The honorific apparently greatly pleased the cofounder. The little sign on the table behind which he sat in his retail-store appearances was forthwith changed to read: "Meet Colonel A. C. Roebuck, Cofounder of Sears, Roebuck & Co." And the honorary rank appeared in virtually every newspaper story throughout his tour of the stores; the free publicity was, incidentally, immense in amount and all that could be desired in tone. The sales-promotion results seem to have been even more gratifying. Letters from many store managers, quoted in Roebuck's unpublished history, assert that the day of the Colonel's appearance marked the greatest sales volume their stores had ever experienced.

13. *New York Times*, June 30, 1942. It may, however, be well to take that statement *cum grano salis*, since the same story says Carney joined the firm in 1902 and put in forty-four years of service before his death in 1942, a mathematical impossibility beyond the reach of even a skilled operations man.

CHAPTER XXI

Learning Anew: The Retail Stores

1. *Business Week* (October 19, 1946, p. 8) asserted: "Besides his Ward experience, he applied to his new job a lifetime's accumulation of a hobby that might have been devised for its applicability to nationwide retailing. Even as a young lieutenant during construction of the Panama Canal, he preferred to pass up the parties and stay in his quarters studying the Statistical Abstract of the U.S., for the sheer love of figures. The Bureau of the Census has for years recognized his statistical achievements by using him as a consultant." And *Fortune* (May, 1938, p. 104) said of the General: "He can digest pages of figures at a glance. The green-backed dust-dry U.S. Census Reports, together with the U.S. *Statistical Abstract,* are his Book of Revelations. Virtually from memory he can supply a picture of buying power in any strategic Sears area, based on his knowledge of population trends, bank clearances, trade and government reports."

2. *Statistical Abstract of the United States, 1947*, pp. 610, 813.

3. "General Robert E. Wood, President." Copyright 1938 by Time, Inc. Reprinted from the May, 1938, issue of *Fortune* magazine by special permission of the Editors.

CHAPTER XXII

New Patterns of Organization

1. Quoted by C. B. Caldwell, Sears's director of personnel, in an address delivered Detroit, March 11, 1948.

CHAPTER XXIII
Some Aspects of Central Buying

1. From a study made by Social Research, Inc.
2. Speech by A. T. Chameroy, manager, Merchandising Testing and Development Laboratories, Sears, Roebuck and Company, to the Chicago District of the American Society for Testing Materials at the Stevens Hotel, Chicago, March 22, 1946.
3. Unpublished manuscript of W. N. Mitchell, p. 61. The manuscript included notes made by Mitchell in 1924 in the course of preparation of a Master's thesis to be presented to the University of Chicago.
4. *Ibid.*, p. 85.
5. "General Robert E. Wood, President." Copyright 1938 by Time, Inc. Reprinted from the May, 1938, issue of *Fortune* magazine by special permission of the Editors.
6. "Sears, Roebuck Uses Depression To Develop New Products," *Business Week*, March 18, 1931, pp. 7–8.
7. Address by T. V. Houser at the New England Sales Managers Conference, Boston, Massachusetts, January 8, 1943.
8. "Sears, Roebuck Uses Depression To Develop New Products," *op. cit.*, p. 8.
9. Cf. Dixon Wecter, *The Age of the Great Depression, 1929–1941* (New York: Copyright 1948 by The Macmillan Company, and used with their permission), p. 283.
10. *Wall Street Journal*, January 4, 1946. This appears actually to have been a resumption of a development held in abeyance by the war, for as early as 1939 Sears had marketed its own home freezing units in 10- and 15-foot sizes, as well as a combination freezer and refrigerator of 10 cubic feet.
11. Address by Houser at the New England Sales Managers Conference, Boston, Massachusetts, January 8, 1943.
12. Address by Houser before the Tri-State Conference on "Today's Management Problems," Cincinnati, Ohio, March 10–12, 1947.
13. Sears, Roebuck and Company, *Annual Report, 1938*.
14. Address by Houser at the New England Sales Managers Conference, Boston, Massachusetts, January 8, 1943.
15. "General Robert E. Wood, President." Copyright 1938 by Time, Inc. Reprinted from the May, 1938, issue of *Fortune* magazine by special permission of the Editors.
16. "Young Sears, Roebuck." Copyright 1948 by Time, Inc. Reprinted from the August, 1948, issue of *Fortune* magazine by special permission of the Editors.
17. Frank Presbrey, *The History and Development of Advertising* (New York: Doubleday & Company, Inc., 1929), *passim*.
18. Edward A. Filene, *The Model Stock Plan* (New York: McGraw-Hill Book Co., 1930), *passim*.

CHAPTER XXIV
Merchandising Influences and Adventures

1. Robert Littell, "The Great American Salesman." Copyright 1932 by Time, Inc. Reprinted from the February, 1932, issue of *Fortune* magazine by special permission of the Editors.
2. "Sears's War." Copyright 1942 by Time, Inc. Reprinted from the September, 1942, issue of *Fortune* magazine by special permission of the Editors.
3. *Ibid.*
4. *Ibid.*
5. *Ibid.*
6. "Drop Mail Insurance," *Business Week*, April 2, 1938.
7. *Journal of Commerce* (Chicago), March 26, 1938.
8. "Policy in Pictures," *Business Week*, May 17, 1947.
9. "Sears Insurance," *Business Week*, December 4, 1948, p. 96.
10. *New York Times*, January 21, 1943.
11. "New Encyclopedia," *Business Week*, March 6, 1948.

12. "Sears and Housing," *Business Week,* September 2, 1939. The same article asserted that the company was remaining in the housing business "to keep the two good-sized factories from losing a piece of the corporation's shirt." Sears then had some $3,500,000 invested in its lumber and millwork plants, Cincinnati and Port Newark, according to *Business Week.*

CHAPTER XXV

New Techniques of Mail-Order Selling

1. *Wall Street Journal,* December 24, 1932.
2. *New York Times,* July 11, 1930.
3. "New Mail Order Catalogs Show Special Sales Effort," *Business Week,* December 31, 1930, p. 9.
4. *Ibid.*
5. "Phone Order Selling," *Business Week,* November 17, 1934.
6. *Ibid.*
7. George Bijur, "Ten Mail-Order Americas," *Advertising and Selling,* XXXIII (September, 1940), 33. The addition of the eleventh branch plant in 1947 did not alter Bijur's thesis.
8. *Ibid.,* pp. 33–34, 54.
9. John D. C. Weldon, "Assaying Industrial Prospects for California and Mountain States," *Magazine of Wall Street,* LXXIX (March 15, 1947), 657, 659, 702.
10. *New York Herald Tribune,* July 18, 1942.
11. *Wall Street Journal,* November 26, 1946.
12. *Ibid.,* July 22, 1938.
13. *New York Herald Tribune,* July 22, 1938.
14. Survey made for Sears, Roebuck and Company by Social Research, Inc.

CHAPTER XXVI

Expanding Over-the-Counter Sales

1. "Young Sears, Roebuck." Copyright 1948 by Time, Inc. Reprinted from the August, 1948, issue of *Fortune* magazine by special permission of the Editors.
2. "Expanding South," *Business Week,* October 12, 1946, p. 75.
3. *Ibid.*
4. "Young Sears, Roebuck," *op. cit.,* p. 132.

CHAPTER XXVII

Easy Payments and "Modern Homes"

1. This section on Sears's instalment selling is based largely upon a company report, "Credit History" (June, 1938, 1941), issued over the name of R. W. Leonardson (see chap. xvi, n. 1, above).
2. Dixon Wecter, *The Age of the Great Depression, 1929–1941* (New York: Copyright 1948 by The Macmillan Company, and used with their permission), p. 7.
3. *Women's Wear Daily,* March 31, 1937. The same story asserts that Sears's net volume on time payments in 1936 was about $98,000,000, while Montgomery Ward's net for the same year was $91,000,000.
4. "General Robert E. Wood, President." Copyright 1938 by Time, Inc. Reprinted from the May, 1938, issue of *Fortune* magazine by special permission of the Editors.
5. C. D. Long, *Building Cycles and the Theory of Investment* (Princeton: Princeton University Press, 1940), pp. 5, 9.
6. A. W. Clark, "Report on Modern Homes, Norwood Sash and Door Manufacturing Company" (1936), p. 19.

CHAPTER XXVIII
Store Planning and Design

1. This chapter is based largely upon an unpublished report made in 1941 by L. S. Janes, director of Sears, Roebuck's Store Planning and Display Department, titled "The Development of Sears Retail Stores."
2. "Without Windows," *Architectural Forum*, LXII (March, 1935), 206–11.
3. "No Windows," *Architect and Engineer*, CXX (February, 1935), 35–38.
4. "Store Building, Los Angeles; with Construction Outline," *Architectural Forum*, LXXII (February, 1940), 70–76. *Architect and Engineer* also carried a photograph of the Los Angeles store, emphasizing the roof parking and pointing to other innovations, on p. 10 of its February, 1940, issue.
5. "5 Retail Stores Planned for a Motor Age," *Architectural Record*, LXXXVIII (September, 1940), 31–42.
6. *Ibid.*
7. "Three Retail Stores; Birmingham, Alabama, Honolulu, Washington, D.C.," *Architectural Forum*, LXXVI (April, 1942), 207–16.

CHAPTER XXIX
Personnel Management Matures

1. "Proceedings of the Personnel Conference, Chicago, October 24–28, 1933."
2. A fact made plain in any study of the proceedings of the 1937 personnel conference, the first such meeting after 1933.
3. "Personnel Conference Proceedings, Chicago, 1937," Sec. I, pp. 2–3.
4. Pages in the personnel manual corrected to 1937 indicate that some guides to be used were experience and stability of previous employment and residence.
5. "On to Chicago—Personnel Discussion" (1939), p. 16.
6. Cf. O. P. Robinson, *Retail Personnel Relations* (New York: Prentice-Hall, 1940), p. 163.
7. Sears, Roebuck and Company, Department 707, *The Retail Personnel Program for 1940*, pp. 18–19.
8. Cf. *Retail Personnel Program for 1939*, pp. 6 ff.
9. Department 707 data show the following breakdown:

Total number of tests administered	41,159
Persons tested by company divisions:	
Retail	2,690
Parent	5,028
Mail order	4,641
Miscellaneous	2,565
Total number of persons tested	14,924

10. *The Retail Personnel Program for 1940*, p. 4.
11. *Ibid.*, p. 9.
12. *Ibid.*, p. 13.
13. Department 707, "Progress Report, 1945–47," p. 6.
14. In line with the more mature character of postwar trainees and the tight labor market, in 1947 hiring rates for trainees averaged $49.65 per week (compared with $23 in 1940), according to Department 707's "Personnel Report No. 3" of April 1, 1948.
15. Memorandum from C. B. Caldwell to C. H. Kellstadt, dated June 25, 1948.
16. "Notices to Employes and Store Managers, 2–16–33, J. M. Barker, Vice-President."
17. "To All Store Managers from R. E. Wood, May 28, 1935."
18. Bulletin 0-399 had first been issued as a means of putting provisions of the NRA retail code into effect. Following the Schechter decision the original bulletin was revised. It is the revised bulletin that is referred to in the text.

19. Letter dated April 20, 1936, from T. J. Carney to all store managers.
20. Bulletin 0-399, Revised, May 19, 1937.
21. At about the same time that Bulletin 0-399 appeared many of the state legislatures were enacting statutes regarding wages and hours, particularly hours for women employees. Wherever state laws were more liberal than company policy, such laws governed of course.
22. Transcript of meeting June 16, 1937, p. 116.
23. *The Retail Personnel Program for 1940*, p. 33.
24. *Retail Personnel Manual*, par. 4001 (rev.).
25. *The Retail Personnel Program for 1940*, pp. 34–35.
26. "On to Chicago—Personnel Discussion" (1939), p. 34.
27. Memorandum in files of Department 707.
28. Correspondence file, C. B. Caldwell to Lessing Rosenwald, October 7, 1938. In addressing the personnel conference in 1939, a speaker further pointed out some of the general background of the experiment: "Managers have undoubtedly been noticing in the trade journals the efforts of industry to improve stabilization of work and wages to allay the hardships of layoffs, shut downs, and short time.... It has long been felt that employe morale in our own company could be improved by some form of guaranteed continuity of work or income."
29. Under both plans, salesmen of major appliances working on a drawing account against commission would receive their regular drawing account and one-half of the commission in excess of the draw and the other half was paid into a reserve used for paying the drawing account in off seasons when their services might not be needed, or when the volume of sales was so low that they "went into the red."
30. *The Retail Personnel Program for 1940*, p. 37.
31. Company correspondence dated December 23, 1948.
32. The four subscriptions were as follows:

Date Approved	No. Shares	Price
March 27, 1933	150,000	$25
April 27, 1936*	200,000	45
April 25, 1938	50,000	45
April 29, 1940	125,000	60

* In addition, employees participated in the purchase of shares issued in the number of 588,689 at $72 in this year.

33. The personnel manual specifies the following service requirements and procedure for continuing the insurance for retirees: "Any employe who is retired by the company at age 60 or thereafter, with ten or more years of continuous service, or any employe over age 60 and having 30 or more years of continuous service with the company who elects to retire, and who is insured under this Plan at the time of retirement, will be entitled to continue in the Plan without cost to himself after retirement.

"Each such retired employe will retain the full amount of insurance in effect at the time of retirement, except that any eligible employe insured for more than $7,500 will be insured for $7,500 upon retirement.

"Note that all employes being retired who are deemed eligible for this insurance will be notified by a personal letter from Department 707- —, at the time of retirement. Copy will be sent to store, to Department 765 and check list cashier (in case of certain check list employes who are paid through control store). Make no commitments locally."

34. The profit-sharing plan is analyzed in detail in Appendix A.
35. Sears, Roebuck and Company, *Annual Report, 1947*.
36. The costs of the benefit program as detailed in Table 83 are understated to the extent that they do not reflect at all the administrative costs involved.
37. Annual sales declined over $47,000,000 in 1942, and 1943 brought a further decline of over $15,000,000 more, owing to merchandise shortages in traditional Sears's lines.

38. It is interesting to note the status of conscientious objectors under the military benefits program. Conscientious objectors classified by Selective Service authorities as 1A-O, those refusing to bear arms but willing to aid in the war effort, received all benefits. Men classified 4E, those refusing to assist in any way in the prosecution of the war, were granted leaves of absence, but did not receive any of the financial benefits.

39. As of June, 1946.

40. Department 707, "Report to the President, February 18, 1948."

41. Department 707, "Special Report No. 95" (April 21, 1943). All turnover figures are based on the separations formula, i.e., Turnover = Separations/Average Employment.

42. Cf. Robinson, *op. cit.*, pp. 360 ff.

43. Department 707, "Special Report No. 95."

44. Company records.

45. While the figures presented above are for retail employees, the turnover in mail order was parallel. Mail-order figures have not been included, because the retail section offers more detailed classification of reasons for turnover.

46. Of some 40,000 male employees in 1944, 31,052 were of draft age. Up to this point the company had requested 1,482 deferments, of which over 1,000 were granted by Selective Service boards.

47. Department 707 made an extensive study of company-wide turnover in 1947, the results of which are available in "Personnel Report No. 2," April 1, 1948, and include the following summary percentage figures:

	Time-Card Employees	Executives
Retail	39.3	3.6
Mail order	37.9	8.9
Company-wide	39.3	5.6

48. Company records show the following data on amounts paid in suggestion awards: 1939, $17,906; 1940, $28,794; 1941, $32,620; 1942, $28,081; 1943, $20,425; 1944, $26,994; 1945, $26,791; 1946, $25,240; and 1947, $30,000.

49. Worker attitudes were evaluated in terms of their expressed reactions to such statements as: "There is no favoritism shown in this store"; and "If I had any cause for dissatisfaction, I would have a very good, or at least a reasonably good, chance of getting a square deal from the store executives."

50. An address by G. B. Hattersley delivered before the American Management Association Conference, February 15, 1940.

51. The process by which the new organization surveys came to be an important part of the personnel program of the company offers an interesting illustration of the significance of accident in the course of a firm's development. The present instance is one of the very few cases in which it has been possible accurately to identify the source of the particular policy. It was through a young man (D. G. Moore) holding a relatively inconspicuous position in the personnel department at Sears that Gardner came to be associated with the company. Moore had been taking some graduate work at the University of Chicago and had come into contact there with Gardner. According to C. B. Caldwell, the personnel director at Sears, "Moore rather insisted that we take more interest in this thing. As a result of his interest Dr. Gardner was introduced to those of us in Sears that have come to appreciate what he can do" ("Personnel Conference Record, Sears, Roebuck and Company, November 1946," p. 116).

52. "Discovering and Evaluating Employe Attitudes," an address before the American Management Association, New York, October 3, 1947.

53. Memorandum of May 16, 1947.

54. "Special Report No. 23," February 19, 1940, p. 11.

55. Quoted in Department 707's *The Retail Personnel Program for 1939*, p. 82, or see chap. xxii.

56. *The Retail Personnel Program for 1940*, Frontispiece.

NOTES TO PAGES 600-614

57. Harry A. Millis and Royal E. Montgomery, *Economics of Labor*, Vol. III: *Organized Labor* (New York: McGraw-Hill Book Co., 1945), pp. 188, 190.

58. For information on the general development of unionism in retailing, the writer is indebted to Mr. Robert Buchele, who is currently making a study of retail unionism as a part of Professor Robert Burns's research on "Organization of White-Collar Workers" for the Industrial Relations Center of the University of Chicago.

59. *Proceedings, Third Biennial Convention, United Retail, Wholesale and Department Store Employees of America (CIO)* (Chicago, 1942), p. 150.

CHAPTER XXX

THE NEW OPPOSITION

1. J. P. Nichols, *The Chain Store Tells Its Story* (New York: Institute of Distribution, Inc., 1940), p. 83.

2. *Ibid.*, p. 18.

3. Maurice W. Lee, *Anti-Chain-Store Tax Legislation* ("Studies in Business Administration," Vol. IX, No. 4 [Chicago: University of Chicago Press, 1939]), p. 5.

4. *Op. cit.*, p. 129.

5. Robert H. Givens, Jr., *Outlawry of Chainstores* (Tampa: Martello Publishers, Inc., 1936), p. 9.

6. *Ibid.*, p. 70.

7. The 1927 laws of Maryland (outright prohibition of chains) and North Carolina (flat tax on chains) had been held unconstitutional (cf. Lee, *op. cit.*, p. 11, and chap. iii).

8. 283 U.S. 527 (1931).

9. *Great Atlantic and Pacific Tea Company et al. v. Alice Lee Grosjean, Supervisor of Public Accounts*, 57 S. Ct. 722 (1937).

10. Cf. Nichols, *op. cit.*, pp. 152-54.

11. E. P. Learned and Nathan Isaacs, "The Robinson-Patman Law: Some Assumptions and Expectations," *Harvard Business Review*, XV (1937), 142-43.

12. Nichols, *op. cit.*, p. 162.

13. Lee, *op. cit.*, pp. 24-25.

14. Statement of Hon. Wright Patman, *Hearings before a Subcommittee of the Committee on Ways and Means, House of Representatives, Seventy-sixth Congress, Third Session, on H.R. 1, A Bill Providing for an Excise Tax on Retail Stores*, I, 19.

15. *Ibid.*, p. 188.

16. Federal Trade Commission, *Final Report on the Chain-Store Investigation* (Washington: Government Printing Office, 1935), pp. 91-92.

17. *Hearings . . . on H.R. 1*, I, 1129.

18. *Ibid.*, p. 1131.

19. *Ibid.*, pp. 2237-38.

20. *Ibid.*, pp. 1058-59.

21. *Ibid.*, p. 157.

22. *Ibid.*, p. 156.

23. That Congressman Patman has not yet given up his goal of hamstringing chains is evident from his continued insistence on introducing discriminatory legislation. In nearly every session since 1940 he has proposed bills ranging from slight modifications of his original tax plans to the more recent suggestion of modifying corporate tax legislation to the disadvantage of the chains.

24. Institute of Distribution, *Retail Tax Manual, Supplement No. 2* (New York, October 15, 1948), p. 34.

25. E. T. Grether, *Price Control under Fair Trade Legislation* (New York: Oxford University Press, 1939), p. 21.

26. *Ibid.*, pp. 7-8.

27. "General Robert E. Wood, President." Copyright 1938 by Time, Inc. Reprinted from the May, 1938, issue of *Fortune* magazine by special permission of the Editors.

28. The *Wall Street Journal*, February 9, 1934.

29. *New York Herald Tribune*, March 6, 1936.

30. The subsequent litigation dragged through the courts for years, finally reaching the Supreme Court of the United States, but the net result of all Goodyear's litigation had no effect on Sears, Roebuck's tire purchasing after the abrogation of the contract with Goodyear.

31. *Wall Street Journal*, July 17, 1936. The *Journal* added, the following day: "One of the attractive features of making tires for Sears is considered to be that each manufacturer can if he wishes make use in his plant of any improvement as to layout or otherwise which are [sic] developed in any other of the plants which are at the time making tires for the big merchandising concern."

32. *Women's Wear Daily*, April 28, 1937.

CHAPTER XXXI

Public Relations: Scholarships and Special Services

1. Quoted by E. J. Condon, Sears's public relations director, in his report to the board of directors of the company meeting in Los Angeles February 3, 1947.

2. Letter from Paul W. Chapman, dean of the College of Agriculture, University of Georgia, dated December 3, 1948.

3. From a report to the company directors by E. J. Condon, February 3, 1947, in Chicago.

4. Quoted by E. J. Condon in his report to the company's board of directors meeting in Chicago, February 3, 1947.

CHAPTER XXXII

The Period in Review

1. *Wall Street Journal*, February 6, 1933.

2. Gay and Wolman have commented: "The full extent of the merger movement is not recorded. A compilation of figures on mergers and acquisitions by Willard Thorp shows that it is no misnomer to characterize the post-war decade as the era of consolidations. The record of over 1,200 mergers in manufacturing and mining between 1919 and 1928, involving a net disappearance of over 6,000 independent enterprises by the end of 1928 and some 2,000 more by the end of 1930, is far from a complete record of mergers in all fields" (Edwin Gay and Leo Wolman, "Trends in Economic Organization," in *Recent Social Trends in the United States* [New York, 1934], pp. 240–41).

3. *New York Times*, September 1, 1931.

4. M. R. Werner, *Julius Rosenwald: The Life of a Practical Humanitarian* (New York: Harper & Bros., 1939), p. 237.

5. Norman Beasley, *Main Street Merchant* (New York: Whittlesey House, 1948), p. 222.

6. *Ibid.*, p. 130.

7. *Ibid.*, pp. 133–34.

8. Quoted in *ibid.*, p. 134.

9. Sears, Roebuck and Company, *Annual Report, 1936*.

10. Letter dated April 27, 1948, from C. E. Humm (vice-president of Sears, Roebuck and Company) to the authors.

11. "Young Sears, Roebuck." Copyright 1948 by Time, Inc. Reprinted from the August, 1948, issue of *Fortune* magazine by special permission of the Editors.

CHAPTER XXXIII

In Retrospect

1. Edwin R. Embree and Julia Waxman, *Investment in People: The Story of the Julius Rosenwald Fund* (New York: Harper & Bros., 1949), p. 8.

APPENDIX A

SHARING PROFITS WITH EMPLOYEES

1. Unless otherwise indicated all data on company and profit-sharing fund development and experience are based on original records of the company.
2. R. L. Dixon, "Profit Sharing," *Journal of Accountancy*, LXXXII, No. 1 (July, 1946), 10. Profit shares as, or in lieu of, wages are much older, of course, and still constitute an important source of income to workers in some industries, e.g., fishing (cf. N. B. Gilman, *Profit Sharing between Employer and Employee* [Boston: Houghton Mifflin Co., 1889]).
3. *Profit Sharing in the United States* (Bureau of Labor Statistics, Bull. 208, Misc. Series, No. 13 [Washington: Government Printing Office, 1916]), p. 9.
4. Interview with Mrs. J. T. Bowen, October, 1946. The text of Mrs. Bowen's letter was first published in M. R. Werner, *Julius Rosenwald: The Life of a Practical Humanitarian* (New York: Harper & Bros., 1939), p. 159.
5. *Report of the Senate Vice Committee (Illinois)*, 1916, p. 182.
6. According to O. C. Doering, the profit-sharing plan grew out of a discussion in "J. R.'s" office. An executive from Butler Brothers was discussing with "J. R.," Albert Loeb, and O. C. Doering, plans for employee security. Doering said that if Rosenwald was interested in giving employees a sense of security, he needed a pension plan. The details for the plan were developed largely by Albert Loeb, assisted by Doering and Adler.
7. C. C. Balderston, *Profit Sharing for Wage Earners* (New York: Industrial Relations Counselors, 1937), pp. 8, 9.
8. M. W. Latimer, *Industrial Pension Systems* (New York: Industrial Relations Counselors, 1932), I, 42, shows:

Period of Establishment	Number of Pension Plans
1874–1900	12
1901–5	24
1906–10	30
1911–15	101
1916–20	120
1921–25	72
1926–29	59
Date unknown	3
Total	421

9. The regulations provide that the chairman of the investment committee must be a trustee and an officer of Sears, Roebuck and Company.
10. *The Distribution of Ownership in the 200 Largest Non-financial Corporations* (TNEC Monograph No. 29 [Washington: Government Printing Office, 1940]), p. 176.
11. *Ibid.*, p. 1940. The 13.95 figure is apparently the result of adding the number of shares held by members of the family either directly or in trust for other members of the family and the 1.13 per cent held by the Julius Rosenwald Fund. See p. 1287 of *ibid.* for breakdown of the holdings of the largest holders of record.
12. As will be discussed below, most members who withdraw from the fund have less than five years' service (classified as Group A members). All credits in such accounts in excess of these employees' deposits and 5 per cent interest are known as "lapses" and are distributed to the accounts of the remaining members.
13. All regular employees, *regardless of position*, who have completed one year's continuous service are eligible to participate in the fund as a privilege of employment. Employees of such wholly owned subsidiaries as the company designates may participate on the same terms as employees of the parent-company. Regular employees of partially owned subsidiaries or affiliates of Sears working in any merchandising establishment of the company under the latter's supervision and management are eligible at the discretion of the fund trustees. Current practice decrees that at the expiration of one year of continuous employment, the employee is invited to become a member. Under present practice, if he chooses not to join, he signs a waiver indicating that he is aware

of his eligibility to become a depositor ("depositor" is here used as synonymous with membership in the profit-sharing fund). Having signed the waiver, however, the employee does not abrogate the privilege of becoming a depositor at a later date.

14. The stock was split four for one in 1925.
15. "Fund Executive Director's Special Reports, November 18, 1942."
16. From 1916 to 1924 the limit was $150; in 1924–25 there was no limit; from 1925 to 1934 the limit was $300.
17. Based on the company's 1940 contribution, the effect of creating Group D depositors is indicated below:

Group	Distribution before Group D	Distribution with Group D
A	$0.52	$0.508
B	1.04	1.016
C	1.56	1.524
D	. . . .	2.033

The definition of Group D is such that this group is small in number, and consequently siphons off little of the company's contribution at the expense of the "junior" groups. As of December 31, 1947, there were 2,016 Group D depositors out of 81,262 members.

18. The purchase of the annuity, however, is entirely at the discretion of the trustees, who may without liability disregard the member's request. This limitation is apparently necessitated by tax regulations.
19. "The proceeds from such liquidation . . . may be retained by the Trustees in cash at bank, or wholly or partially invested in capital stock of the Company, bonds or other obligations of the United States Government or other securities whether or not designated by law as suitable for the investment of trust funds; and such of said proceeds as shall be retained in cash, the securities, if any so purchase, and the income received therefrom by the Trustees shall be credited to such depositor's account in the Fund" (Art. VI, sec. 2, of revised rules).
20. Until 1946 interest on these accounts was compounded semiannually.
21. Details as to the occasions when fund trustees permitted reinstatement:

1. In 1919, for World War I veterans returning to the company.
2. From January 31, 1934, through August 31, 1934, an opportunity was given former members who withdrew due to vicissitudes of the depression years 1930–33.
3. From February 1, 1937, through April 13, 1937, reinstatement privileges were available. This was another opportunity open to those who withdrew on account of the depression.
4. From August 12, 1940, through October 31, 1940, reinstatement privileges were extended. This was also prompted by the depression of the 1930's—especially the recession of late 1937.
5. From August 1, 1945, through September 30, 1945, an opportunity for reinstatement was given employees who had felt it necessary to resign fund membership because of military service during World War II.

22. Depositors completing ten or more years' continuous service may apply to the trustees for withdrawal of amounts not to exceed in the aggregate one-half of the depositor's credits except that Group D members may apply for withdrawals of greater amount.
23. Actual market quotations.

APPENDIX B

Method for Calculating the Capital Base

1. This follows the definition and procedure of the NBER study, "Industrial Profits in the United States" (R. C. Epstein, 1934).
2. The National Bureau study referred to above uses net income before taxes.

Bibliography

Bibliography

I. BOOKS

ADAMS, SAMUEL H. *The Great American Fraud.* New York: P. F. Collier & Son, 1905.

AMERICAN ACADEMY OF SOCIAL AND POLITICAL SCIENCE. *The Ethics of the Professions and of Business.* (*The Annals....*) Philadelphia: The Academy, 1922.

———. *Personnel and Employment Problems.* Philadelphia: The Academy, 1916.

ANDERSON, WILBERT L. *The Country Town: A Study of Rural Evolution.* New York: Doubleday, Page & Co., 1914.

APPEL, JOSEPH H. *The Business Biography of John Wanamaker: Founder and Builder.* New York: Macmillan Co., 1930.

ASHER, LOUIS E., and HEAL, EDITH. *Send No Money.* Chicago: Argus Books, 1942.

ATHERTON, LEWIS E. *The Pioneer Merchant in America.* Columbia, Mo.: University of Missouri Press, 1939.

BAILEY, LIBERTY HYDE. *Cyclopedia of American Agriculture.* New York: Macmillan Co., 1907–9.

BALDERSTON, C. CANBY. *Profit Sharing for Wage Earners.* New York: Industrial Relations Counselors, 1937.

BARGER, HAROLD, and LANDSBERG, HANS. *American Agriculture, 1899–1939: A Study of Output, Employment and Productivity.* New York: National Bureau of Economic Research, Inc., 1942.

BARROLL, EDWARD C., et al. (eds.). *Making Money in the Mail Order Mint.* Boston: Rollins & Co., 1915.

BATES, CHARLES A. *The Art and Literature of Business.* New York: Bates Publishing Co., 1902.

BEASLEY, NORMAN. *Main Street Merchant.* New York: Whittlesey House, 1948.

BENNETT, [ENOCH] ARNOLD. *Your United States: Impressions of a First Visit.* New York: Harper & Bros., 1912.

BERKWITZ, W. L. *The Encyclopedia of the Mail Order Business.* New York, 1908.

———. *Reminiscences.* New York: W. L. Berkwitz, 1908.

BLOOMFIELD, DANIEL (ed.). *Employment Management.* New York: H. W. Wilson Co., 1920.

BLOOMFIELD, MEYER. *Labor and Compensation.* New York: Industrial Extension Institution, Inc., 1918.

BRANDEIS, ELIZABETH. "Labor Legislation," in *History of Labor in the United States, 1896–1932,* Vol. III, ed. JOHN R. COMMONS and ASSOCIATES. New York: Macmillan Co., 1935.

BRANN, W. L. *The Romance of Montgomery Ward and Company.* New York: Campbell, Starring & Co., 1929.

BRENISER, ROSS D. *The Schemes Back of the Ads.* Philadelphia: Privately printed, 1914.

BUCK, SOLON J. *The Agrarian Crusade: A Chronicle of the Farmer in Politics.* New Haven: Yale University Press, 1921.

———. *The Granger Movement: A Study of Agricultural Organization and Its Political, Economic, and Social Manifestations.* Cambridge: Harvard University Press, 1913.

BURNS, ARTHUR F. *Production Trends in the United States since 1870*. New York: National Bureau of Economic Research, 1934.

CLARK, THOMAS D. *Pills, Petticoats and Plows*. Indianapolis: Bobbs-Merrill Co., 1944.

COHN, DAVID L. *The Good Old Days*. New York: Simon & Schuster, 1940.

COMMITTEE ON RECENT ECONOMIC CHANGES OF THE PRESIDENT'S CONFERENCE ON UNEMPLOYMENT. *Recent Economic Changes in the United States*. New York: McGraw-Hill Book Co., 1929.

COPELAND, MORRIS. "The National Income and Its Distribution," in *Recent Economic Changes in the United States*, Vol. II. New York: McGraw-Hill Book Co., 1929.

COX, REAVIS. *The Economics of Instalment Buying*. New York: Ronald Press Co., 1948.

DANIELS, WILLIAM COOKE. *The Department Store System*. Denver: Privately printed, 1900.

DEWHURST, J. F., AND ASSOCIATES. *America's Needs and Resources*. New York: Twentieth Century Fund, 1947.

DEWING, ARTHUR S. *The Financial Policy of Corporations*. New York: Ronald Press Co., 1941.

Dictionary of American Biography, The, Vols. XVI and XIX. New York: Charles Scribner's Sons, 1935.

DOUGLAS, PAUL H. *Real Wages in the United States, 1890–1926*. Boston: Houghton Mifflin Co., 1930.

DULLES, FOSTER R. *Twentieth Century America*. Boston: Houghton Mifflin Co. (for Reynal & Hitchcock), 1945.

Economic Almanac for 1941–42, The. New York: National Industrial Conference Board, 1942.

EDGAR, ALBERT E. *How To Advertise a Retail Store*. Columbus: Advertising World, 1913.

EGLESTON, N. H. *Villages and Village Life*. New York: Harper & Bros., 1878.

EMBREE, EDWIN, and WAXMAN, JULIA. *Investment in People: The Story of the Julius Rosenwald Fund*. New York: Harper & Bros., 1949.

EYTINGE, LOUIS V. *Writing Business Letters Which Get the Business*. Chicago: Office Appliance Co., 1914.

FAULKNER, HAROLD U. *Economic History of the United States*. Rev. ed. New York: Macmillan Co., 1937.

———. *The Quest for Social Justice, 1898–1914*. New York: Macmillan Co., 1931.

FERBER, EDNA. *Fanny Herself*. New York: Frederick A. Stokes Co., 1917.

FILENE, EDWARD A. *The Model Stock Plan*. New York: McGraw-Hill Book Co., 1930.

FISHER, IRVING. *The Stock Market Crash—and After*. New York: Macmillan Co., 1930.

FLOWER, SIDNEY. *The Mail Order Business*. Chicago: S. Flower, 1902.

FRANK, FLORENCE KIPER. "Life of Julius Rosenwald." (Unpublished MS.)

GAY, EDWIN, and WOLMAN, LEO. "Trends in Economic Organization," in *Recent Social Trends in the United States: Report of the President's Research Committee on Social Trends*. New York: Whittlesey House, 1934.

GILMAN, N. B. *Profit Sharing between Employer and Employee*. Boston: Houghton Mifflin Co., 1889.

GIVENS, ROBERT H., JR. *Outlawry of Chainstores*. Tampa: Martello Publishers, Inc., 1936.

BIBLIOGRAPHY

Gras, N. S. B. "The Historical Background of Modern Price Regulation," in *Business and Modern Society*, ed. Malcolm Perrine McNair and Howard T. Lewis. Cambridge: Harvard University Press, 1938.

Grether, E. T. *Price Control under Fair Trade Legislation*. New York: Oxford University Press, 1939.

Guenther, Louis. *How To Make More Money, or Selling by Mail*. Chicago: LaSalle Publishing Co., 1907.

Hacker, Louis M., and Kendrick, Benjamin B. *The United States since 1865.* 3d ed. New York: Crofts & Co., 1939.

Hadley, Arthur T. *Standards of Public Morality*. New York: Macmillan Co., 1907.

Heacock, William A. *The Best Way To Start a Mail Order Business*. Lockport: Mail Order World, 1908.

Hermance, E. L. *The Ethics of Business*. New York and London: Harper & Bros., 1926.

The History and Progress of Montgomery Ward & Co. . . . the Romance of the Golden Rule and Some Interesting Facts about the Mail Order Business. Chicago: Montgomery Ward & Co., 1925.

How To Do Business by Mail. Philadelphia: Home Publication Society, 1915.

Howard, Edward. *The American Watchmaker*. New York: D. O. Haynes & Co., 1905.

Hower, Ralph M. *The History of an Advertising Agency, N. W. Ayer & Son at Work, 1869–1939*. Cambridge: Harvard University Press, 1939.

———. *The History of Macy's*. Cambridge: Harvard University Press, 1946.

Institute of Distribution, Inc. *Tax Manual, Supplement No. 2*. New York: The Institute, October 15, 1948.

Irving, George B. *My Town, or, Community Patriotism*. Chicago: Rogerson Press, 1912.

Jones, Fred M. *Middlemen in the Domestic Trade of the United States, 1800–1860*. Urbana: University of Illinois, 1937.

Kelly, Clyde. *United States Postal Policy*. New York: D. Appleton & Co., 1931.

Kolb, J. H., and Brunner, Edmund de S. "Rural Life," in *Recent Social Trends in the United States: Report of the President's Research Committee on Social Trends*. New York: Whittlesey House, 1934.

Kuznets, Simon S. *Cyclical Fluctuations, Retail and Wholesale Trades, United States, 1919–1925*. New York: Adelphi Co., 1926.

Lange, W. H. *Trends in Personnel Health Service*. ("General Management Series," No. 85.) New York: American Management Association, 1929.

Latimer, M. W. *Industrial Pension Systems in the United States and Canada*. New York: Industrial Relations Counselors, Inc., 1932.

Lee, James. *Twenty-five Years in the Mail Order Business*. Chicago: A. E. Swett, 1902.

Lee, Maurice W. *Anti-Chain-Store Tax Legislation*. ("Studies in Business Administration," Vol. IX, No. 4.) Chicago: University of Chicago Press, 1939.

Leroy-Beaulieu, Pierre. *The United States in the Twentieth Century*. Authorized translation by H. Addington Bruce. New York: Funk & Wagnalls Co., 1906.

Lescohier, Don D. "Working Conditions," in *History of Labor in the United States, 1896–1932*, Vol. III, ed. John R. Commons and Associates. New York: Macmillan Co., 1935.

Leven, Maurice. *Income in the Various States*. New York: National Bureau of Economic Research, Inc., 1925.

LINDGREN, CHARLES. *The New Salesmanship and How To Do Business.* Chicago: Laird & Lee, 1911.
LIPPINCOTT, ISAAC. *Economic Development of the United States.* 3d ed. New York: Appleton-Century Co., 1933.
LONG, C. D. *Building Cycles and the Theory of Investment.* Princeton: Princeton University Press, 1940.
LONGMAN, DONALD R. *Distribution Cost Analysis.* New York: Harper & Bros., 1941.
LYND, ROBERT S., and HANSON, ALICE C. "The People as Consumers," in *Recent Social Trends in the United States: Report of the President's Research Committee on Social Trends.* New York: Whittlesey House, 1934.
LYTLE, JOHN H. *Letters That Land Orders.* Detroit: Businessmen's Publishing Co., 1911.
MCGRANE, R. C. *The Economic Development of the American Nation.* New York: Ginn & Co., 1942.
MCKENZIE, R. D. "The Rise of Metropolitan Communities," in *Recent Social Trends in the United States: Report of the President's Research Committee on Social Trends.* New York: Whittlesey House, 1934.
MARTIN, ROBERT FITZ-RANDOLPH. *National Income in the United States, 1799–1938.* New York: National Industrial Conference Board, Inc., 1939.
MILLIS, HARRY A., and MONTGOMERY, ROYAL E. *Economics of Labor,* Vol. III: *Organized Labor.* New York: McGraw-Hill Book Co., 1945.
MILLS, FREDERICK. *Prices in Recession and Recovery.* New York: National Bureau of Economic Research, Inc., 1936.
MITCHELL, BROADUS. *Depression Decade: From New Era through New Deal.* New York: Rinehart & Co., Inc., 1947.
MITCHELL, BROADUS, and MITCHELL, LOUISE PEARSON. *American Economic History.* Boston: Houghton Mifflin Co., 1947.
MITCHELL, W. C. *Business Cycles: The Problem and Its Setting.* Berkeley: University of California Press, 1913.
MITCHELL, W. C., et al. *Income in the United States: Its Amount and Distribution, 1909–1919.* New York: Harcourt, Brace & Co., 1921.
MITCHELL, WILLIAM N. "The Preparation and Use of the Merchandise Budget in Mail-Order Houses." Unpublished Master's thesis, Department of Commerce and Administration, University of Chicago. March, 1925.
MOCK, HARRY EDGAR. *Medical Work and Sanitation: A Résumé of the Advancement along the Above Lines for the Benefit of the Employes of Sears, Roebuck & Co.* Chicago: Privately printed, 1911.
MOORE, CHARLES W. *Timing a Century: A History of the Waltham Watch Company.* Cambridge: Harvard University Press, 1945.
MOTT, FRANK LUTHER. *A History of American Magazines, 1865–1885,* Vol. III. Cambridge: Harvard University Press, 1938.
MUNTZ, EARL E. *Urban Sociology.* New York: Macmillan Co., 1938.
NEVINS, ALLAN. *The Emergence of Modern America.* New York: Macmillan Co., 1935.
NICHOLS, J. P. *The Chain Store Tells Its Story.* New York: Institute of Distribution, Inc., 1940.
NORVELL, SAUNDERS. *Forty Years of Hardware.* New York: Hardware Age, 1924.
NYSTROM, PAUL H. *The Economics of Retailing,* Vol. I. Rev. ed. New York: Ronald Press Co., 1930.
O'CONNOR, D. CHARLES. *A Treatise on Commercial Pharmacy.* Philadelphia: J. B. Lippincott Co., 1912.

PAGE, E. D. *Trade Morals.* New Haven: Yale University Press, 1914.
PENNEY, J. C. *J. C. Penney: The Man with a Thousand Partners.* New York: Harper & Bros., 1931.
PHILLIPS, WESLEY BRIGGS. *How Department Stores Are Carried On.* New York: Dodd, Mead & Co., 1901.
PRATT, V. E. *Selling by Mail.* New York: McGraw-Hill Book Co., 1924.
PRESBREY, FRANK. *The History and Development of Advertising.* New York: Doubleday & Company, 1929.
Report of the Commission on Country Life. New York: Sturgis & Walton Co., 1911.
Report upon Condition of Employees. New York: National Civic Federation, 1915.
RIPS, RAE ELIZABETH. "An Introductory Study of the Role of the Mail-Order Business in American History, 1872-1914." Unpublished Master's thesis, Department of History, University of Chicago. June, 1938.
ROBINSON, O. P. *Retail Personnel Relations.* New York: Prentice-Hall, Inc., 1940.
ROEBUCK, ALVAH C. "Early and Some Later History of Sears, Roebuck and Co." 2 vols. Chicago, 1940. (Unpublished MS.)
ROGERS, HARRY E. *The Principles of Selling Goods by Mail.* Boston: Boston Envelope Co., 1912.
ROPER, DANIEL C. *The United States Post Office.* New York: Funk & Wagnalls Co., 1917.
ROSENWALD, JULIUS. "Mail Order Merchandising," in FREDERIC W. WILE (ed.), *A Century of Industrial Progress.* New York: Doubleday, Doran & Co., 1928.
ROST, O. FRED. *Distribution Today.* New York: McGraw-Hill Book Co., 1933.
SCHLESINGER, ARTHUR M. *Political and Social Growth of the American People, 1865-1940.* 3d ed. New York: Macmillan Co., 1941.
———. *The Rise of the City, 1878-1898.* New York: Macmillan Co., 1933.
SCHMIDT, LOUIS BERNARD. *Topical Studies and References of the Economic History of American Agriculture.* Philadelphia: McKinley Publishing Co., 1923.
SCHMIDT, LOUIS BERNARD, and ROSS, EARLE DUDLEY. *Readings in the Economic History of American Agriculture.* New York: Macmillan Co., 1925.
SELIGMAN, E. R. A., and LOVE, ROBERT A. *Price Cutting and Price Maintenance.* New York: Harper & Bros., 1932.
SHANNON, FRED ALBERT. *America's Economic Growth.* New York: Macmillan Co., 1940.
———. *The Farmer's Last Frontier.* New York: Farrar & Rinehart, 1945.
SHAW, ALBERT. *The Outlook for the Average Man.* New York: Macmillan Co., 1907.
SHUEY, E. L. *Factory People and Their Employers.* New York: Lenihan & Co., 1900.
SLOSSON, PRESTON W. *The Great Crusade and After, 1914-1928.* New York: Macmillan Co., 1930.
SPAHR, C. B. *The Present Distribution of Wealth in the United States.* New York: T. Y. Crowell Co., 1896.
Studies in Personnel Policy, No. 11. New York: National Industrial Conference Board, 1939.
SULLIVAN, THOMAS J. *Merchants and Manufacturers on Trial.* Chicago: Sullivan Co., 1914.
TARBELL, IDA M. *The Nationalizing of Business, 1878-1898.* New York: Macmillan Co., 1936.
THOMPSON, WARREN S., and WHELPTON, P. K. *Population Trends in the United States.* New York: McGraw-Hill Book Co., 1933.

THOMPSON, WILLIAM S. (comp.). *A Directory of Mailing Lists.* New York and London: G. P. Putnam's Sons, 1917.
THORP, WILLARD LONG. *Business Annals.* New York: National Bureau of Economic Research, Inc., 1926.
Twentieth Century Business Encyclopedia. New York: Maywood Publishing Co., 1934.
Twenty-five Years of Retailing . . . 1916–1936. . . . New York: National Retail Dry Goods Association, 1936.
WATKINS, GORDON S. and DODD, P. A. *The Management of Labor Relations.* New York: McGraw-Hill Book Co., 1941.
WECTER, DIXON. *The Age of the Great Depression, 1929–1941.* New York: Macmillan Co., 1948.
WELLS, DAVID A. *Recent Economic Changes.* New York: Appleton, 1890.
WERNER, M. R. *Julius Rosenwald: The Life of a Practical Humanitarian.* New York: Harper & Bros., 1939.
WILLEY, MALCOLM M., and RICE, STUART A. "The Agencies of Communication," in *Recent Social Trends in the United States: Report of the President's Research Committee on Social Trends.* New York: Whittlesey House, 1934.
WRIGHT, CHESTER. *Economic History of the United States.* New York: McGraw-Hill Book Co., 1941.

II. ARTICLES

ADAMS, SAMUEL HOPKINS. "The Department Store," *Scribner's Magazine,* Vol. XXI (January, 1897).
"Advertising and the Farmer," *Scribner's Magazine,* XLI (May, 1907), 635–36.
ALFORD, L. P. "The Status of Industrial Relations," *Transactions of the American Society of Mechanical Engineers, 1919,* Vol. XLI (1920).
———. "Ten Years' Progress in Management," *Transactions of the American Society of Mechanical Engineers, 1922,* Vol. XLIV (1923).
ALLEN, LOUIS. "Turning Faith into Orders," *System,* XXVI (October, 1914), 287–89.
ALLYN, L. B. "Falling in Line," *Harper's Weekly,* LX (April 17, 1915), 370.
ANDERSON, M. D. "Economics of Business Fluctuation in the United States, 1919–1925," *American Economic Review,* XVII (June, 1927), 230–71.
ANDREWS, H. M. "Continental To Sell New Cars by Mail-Order Methods," *Printers' Ink,* CLXI (December 20, 1932), 10–11.
"Annual Report," *Commercial and Financial Chronicle,* CXLIV (April 10, 1937), 2499.
"Annual Report–Plus: Story of Sears," *Printers' Ink,* CXCV (April 25, 1941), 71–73.
"Another Look," *Magazine of Wall Street,* LXVIII (May 31, 1941), 211.
"Automobile Insurance Goes into the Mail Order Catalogue," *Business Week,* March 25, 1931, p. 8.
BACHELDER, N. J. "Parcel Post and Rural Merchant," *Postal Progress,* I (May, 1907), 4.
BALCH, FRANK O. "Individuality a Keynote of Mail-Order Success," *Judicious Advertising,* IX (September, 1911), 93–94.
BARRINGER, E. L. "Sears, Roebuck Enters Gas Business with Station in Atlanta," *National Petroleum News,* XXIII (August 12, 1931), 64–65.
BARROLL, EDWARD C. "Businessmen as Mail Order Buyers," *Advertisers' Magazine,* III (May, 1910), 44–46.
BEATTY, S. F. "Forty-seven Years of Selling by Mail," *Printers' Ink,* CLXVI (March 8, 1934), 70, 80–81.

BEATY, JOHN Y. "Meeting Customers I Never Saw," *System*, XXXVIII (December, 1920), 1059-61.
"Bids for Farm Trade with New Tractor," *Printers' Ink*, CLVIII (January 14, 1932), 48.
"Big Half Year," *Barron's*, XVI (August 31, 1936), 5.
BIGELOW, C. G. "Counter Display That Increased Sears, Roebuck Seat Cover Sales 500 Per Cent," *Printed Salesmanship*, LVIII (January, 1932), 380-82.
"The Biggest Thing in Business: Men," *Printers' Ink*, CVII (June 26, 1919), 3.
BIJUR, GEORGE. "Ten Mail Order Americas," *Advertising and Selling*, XXXIII (September, 1940), 33-34.
"Billion-Dollar General Store," *Business Week*, April 7, 1945, p. 96.
BLACK, JOHN. "Sears, Roebuck Laboratory, a Factor in Textile Development," *Textile World*, LXXX (August 15, 1931), 34.
BLACK, W. P. "Mail Order Companies Go to Town," *Barron's*, XX (February 26, 1940), 3.
BRADSHAW, T. F. "Superior Methods Created the Early Chain Stores," *Bulletin of the Business Historical Society*, XVII (April, 1943), 35-43.
"Brass Tacks for the Investor," *Barron's*, XXI (January 13, 1941), 44.
"Brass Tacks for the Investor; Brief Analysis," *Barron's*, XVIII (May 16, 1938), 20.
"Brass Tacks for the Investor, Brief Analysis," *Barron's*, XIX (June 26, 1939), 20.
BRENISER, ROSS D. "Mail Order People," *Advertisers' Magazine*, I (November, 1907), 6-7.
"Britannica Jr. Given Away for Distribution to Schools," *Publishers' Weekly*, CXXXVIII (December 7, 1940), 2123.
"Britannica's Atlas," *Business Week*, November 21, 1942, p. 24.
BROWN, ROBERT C. "Mail Order Honesty," *Advertisers' Magazine*, I (January, 1908), 18.
"Building the Catalog That Brings in $150,000,000 a Year by Mail," *Printers' Ink*, C (July 19, 1917), 3.
"Building for Sears, Roebuck & Co., Milwaukee; Views, Plans and Cost Data," *Architectural Forum*, LI (September, 1929), 305-8.
BUMSTEAD, ARTHUR. "Returning Prosperity and the Mail Order Man," *Advertisers' Magazine*, I (August, 1908), 19.
"The Business of Flower Seeds," *Fortune*, XI (April, 1935), 104-8.
CALLAHAN, JAMES E. "Some Timely Pointers on the Mail-Order Business," *Ad Sense*, XX (May, 1906), 414-17.
CASSADY, RALPH, JR., and HAAS, HAROLD M. "Analyzing the Market of Mail-Order House Retail Stores," *Harvard Business Review*, XIII (July, 1935), 493-502.
CASSON, HERBERT N. "The Marvelous Development of the Mail-Order Business," *Munsey's Magazine*, XXXVIII (January, 1908), 513-15.
"Catalog Innovations; Montgomery Ward, Sears Roebuck, and Chicago Mail Order Company," *Printers' Ink*, CXC (February 2, 1940), 45-46.
"Catalogues of Mail-Order Houses Affected by Price Rulings," *Printers' Ink*, CI (October 25, 1917), 25-27.
CHAMBERLIN, J. H. "Big Book," *Reader's Digest*, XXXIV (June, 1939), 70-73.
"City in a Store; Home Office and Chicago Mail Order Division," *Popular Mechanics*, LXXIX (May, 1943), 40-43.
CLIFFORD, J. C. "Comparative Investment Audit; Sears, Roebuck, Montgomery Ward," *Magazine of Wall Street*, LXXIV (April 15, 1944), 25-27.
———. "Mail Order Outlook," *ibid.*, LIV (October 13, 1934), 660-61.

CLIFFORD, J. C. "Montgomery Ward vs. Sears, Roebuck," *ibid.*, LXVII (November 16, 1940), 146–47.
COHN, D. L. "History Out of a Catalogue," *Saturday Review of Literature*, XXI (March 9, 1940), 11–13.
"Color That Injects Life into Sales Appeal of Mail Order Catalogs," *Printers' Ink*, CII (February 7, 1918), 19.
"Columns Closed to Mail Order Advertising," *Better Business*, I (October, 1917), 19–20.
"Companies Which Should Show Large Gains in Earnings," *Magazine of Wall Street*, LII (July 8, 1933), 279–80.
"Consolidated Income Account for Years Ended January 31, 1939–1942," *Commercial and Financial Chronicle*, CLVI (July 6, 1942), 86.
"Consolidated Income, Years Ended January 31, 1943–1945," *Commercial and Financial Chronicle*, CLXI (April 23, 1943), 1819.
COOLEY, S. "Monopolies and Monopolies," *Public*, XVII (June 6, 1914), 531–32.
COONS, HANNIBAL. "Bicycles Built for All," *Holiday*, IV (July, 1948), 88.
"Cost Plus What; Trade Commission Hearing on Goodyear Brings Up Same Basic Questions on Advertising Policy," *Printers' Ink*, CLXXIV (February 13, 1936), 58.
"The Cover," *Business Week*, October 19, 1946, p. 8.
CURTIS, I. G. "Housekeeping by Parcels Post," *Good Housekeeping*, LIII (July, 1911), 2–10.
DIEBOLD, G. H. "A Mail-Order Follow-up that Sold Automobiles," *Advertisers' Magazine*, I (February, 1908), 28–29
DIGNAM, J. B. "The Great Southwest as a Mail Order Territory," *Advertisers' Magazine*, III (November, 1909), 22–24.
"Distribution Charges and What They Mean to Your Business," *Modern Industry*, VIII (September, 1944), 48–50.
DIXON, R. L. "Profit Sharing," *Journal of Accountancy*, LXXXII, No. 1 (July, 1946), 10.
DOBBS, P. "Mail Order Prospects High," *Magazine of Wall Street*, LVI (September 28, 1935), 600–601.
DOBBS, S. C. "A National Movement for Better Advertising," *Advertisers' Magazine*, III (February, 1910), 32.
DONALD, W. J. and E. K. "Trends in Personnel Administration," *Harvard Business Review*, VII (January, 1929), 143–55.
DRAKE, M. "Setting Price Policies for Goods Sold by Mail," *Sales Management*, XXXIII (October 10, 1933), 377–78.
"Drop Mail Insurance," *Business Week*, April 2, 1938, p. 24.
DUFFUS, R. L. "1900–1925," *Century*, CIX (1925), 487.
"Earnings, January 31, 1937–January 31, 1940," *Commercial and Financial Chronicle*, CL (June 1, 1940), 3528.
"Earnings Report," *Barron's*, XIV (March 12, 1934), 10.
"Eastward the Empire," *Time*, XXVIII (September 7, 1936), 50.
EGNER, FRANK. "Mail-Order Testing," *Printers' Ink*, CLXXVI (July 9, 1936), 57–59.
"Encyclopaedia Britannica in Mail Order Edition," *Printers' Ink*, XCIII (December 9, 1915), 70.
"Encyclopedia Britannica to University of Chicago," *Commercial and Financial Chronicle*, CLVII (February 4, 1943), 2195.
ENDICOTT, WILLIAM. "Reminiscences of Seventy-five Years," *Massachusetts Historical Society Proceedings*, XLVI (1912–13), 208–33.

ENGELHARD, GEORGE P. "Parcels Post," *Outlook,* XCVI (December 3, 1910), 794.
"Enormous Mailing," *Business Week,* August 1, 1936, pp. 14–15.
ERBES, P. H., JR. "Catalog Comeback; Alleged To Have Been on Its Deathbed Ten Years Ago, Mail Order Thrives Today as Never Before," *Printers' Ink,* CXCI (April 5, 1940), 11–13.
———. "Catalog No. 126; Ward's 55th Anniversary Book," *ibid.,* CLXXVIII (January 28, 1937), 121–22.
———. "Catalog Progress; Study of Current Sears and Ward Books," *ibid.,* CLXXVI (August 6, 1936), 37.
———. "Newest New Catalog; Sears, Roebuck's Latest Offering Drastically Modernized," *ibid.,* CLXXXVI (January 26, 1939), 149–53.
"Expanding South," *Business Week,* October 12, 1946, p. 75.
"Extra Dividend; Additional Shares Offered to Stockholders; Listing of Additional Capital Stock," *Commercial and Financial Chronicle,* CXLIII (December 26, 1936), 4167.
"Farm Bill To Aid Sears," *Econostat,* I (July 15, 1933), 11, 23.
"Files with SEC," *Commercial and Financial Chronicle,* CXLIII (December 5, 1936), 3647.
"$500,000 a Day for Sears, Roebuck & Co.," *Printers' Ink,* XC (January 7, 1915), 89.
"5 Retail Stores Planned for a Motor Age," *Architectural Record,* LXXXVIII (September, 1910), 31–42.
"Four Pamphlets Given Customers To Advertise Sears Gasoline," *National Petroleum News,* XXIV (May 25, 1932), 40.
FREDERICK, J. GEORGE. "Direct or Indirect Mail-Order Advertising," *Advertisers' Magazine,* I (January, 1908), 26.
———. "Straight Mail Order Talk to Manufacturers," *ibid.* (December, 1907), pp. 6–7.
FROMAN, L. A. "The Cost of Instalment Buying," *Harvard Business Review,* XI (January, 1933), 233–34.
"FTC vs. Quantity Discounts," *Business Week,* September 21, 1935, p. 14.
FUESSLE, NEWTON A. "Putting the Grand Air into Copy," *Printers' Ink,* XCVII (October 26, 1916), 54.
GARDNER, ERNEST F. "Mail-Order Advertising Follow-up," *Advertisers' Magazine,* III (September, 1910), 35–37.
GATES, W. "Investment Opportunities in Stocks Which Can Pay Larger Dividends," *Magazine of Wall Street,* LVIII (July 18, 1936), 425.
———. "Merchandising Companies Stimulated by Wave of Public Buying," *Magazine of Wall Street,* LVII (December 7, 1935), 212–13.
"General Robert E. Wood, President," *Fortune,* XVII (May, 1938), 66–69.
GERKE, ROBERT H. "Specialization Required in the Mail-Order Business," *Advertisers' Magazine,* I (March, 1908), 13.
GIBSON, D. "Retailing Goods by Mail," *Harper's Weekly,* LVII (January 25, 1913), 16.
"Gift for Mexico," *Time,* XLV (February 26, 1945), 80.
"Good Position; Expansion Program Completion Should Release Greater Earnings for the Stock," *Barron's,* XI (February 23, 1931), 11.
"Good Showing; 5th Period Sales Hold," *Barron's,* XI (June 1, 1931), 19.
"Goods Face Severe Tests before Going on Market," *Chicago Herald-Examiner,* October 10, 1933.
"Goodyear Favors to Sears," *Printers' Ink,* CLXXII (September 19, 1935), 12.

"Goodyear Ordered To Desist; End of Price Discrimination on Sears, Roebuck Tires," *Printers' Ink,* CLXXIV (March 12, 1936), 75–76.

"Goodyear To Appeal from FTC Order Ending Sears, Roebuck Deal," *Sales Management,* XXXVIII (March 15, 1936), 376.

Gras, N. S. B., et al. "The Social Implications of Business Administration," *Bulletin of the Business Historical Society,* XVII (February, 1943), 1–31.

Haase, A. E. "How Sears, Roebuck Creates National Advertisers," *Printers' Ink,* CXLIII (June 14, 1928), 10.

"Handling Mail Orders," *System,* XXXI (April, 1917), 424–25.

Harrington, J. O. "Sears, Roebuck Overpriced?" *Magazine of Wall Street,* LXXI (January 9, 1943), 351–53.

Harris, H. L. "Economic Studies Are Basis for New Sears, Roebuck Home Building Service," *Sales Management,* XXII (April 12, 1930), 64–66.

Harrison, C. M. "Sears, Roebuck To Teach Farmers Lesson in Marketing," *Printers' Ink,* CXXV (December 6, 1923), 53–54.

Hartman, W. C. "Applications of Motion Study in Sears, Roebuck & Co.," *Society for the Advancement of Management Journal,* I (July–September, 1936), 118–22.

Harvard University, Graduate School of Business Administration, Bureau of Business Research. *Bulletins,* Nos. 1–125. Cambridge: Harvard University Press, 1913––.

Hecht, F. C. "How the Infotag Helps Sears Sell," *Printers' Ink Monthly,* XLI (August, 1940), 10–12.

–––. "How Sears, Roebuck Used Informative Labeling," *Industrial Standardization,* XII (May, 1941), 109–14.

Heine, I. M. "The Influence of Geographic Factors in the Development of the Mail Order Business," *American Marketing Journal,* III (April, 1936), 127–30.

Hische, George B. "Great Mail Order Successes," *Ad Sense,* XIX (July, 1905), 39–41.

"History of Sears in Annual Report," *American Business,* XI (April, 1941), 43.

Hodge, Harold. "Parcels Post, What It Means to the Mail Order Man and the Farmer," *Advertisers' Magazine,* I (June, 1908), 23–25.

Holman, W. C. "Keeping Retail Trade at Home," *System,* XXIII (January, 1913), 13–20.

Horne, A. M. "Close Communion Selling," *Printers' Ink,* CLXXI (May 16, 1935), 37.

–––. "Sears and Ward Drop Fair-Trade; Still Oppose National Brands," *ibid.,* CLXXXIV (September 8, 1938), 19–21.

Hoskins, C. "Montgomery Ward Rebuilds Business by Morale," *Forbes,* XXIX (April 15, 1932), 14–16.

Hotchkiss, W. E. "Industrial Relations Management," *Harvard Business Review,* I (July, 1923), 438–50.

"How the Mail-Order Companies Fared," *Barron's,* XIII (January 9, 1933), 9.

"How Sears, Roebuck Produces Mail-Order Copy That Sells," *Printers' Ink,* CCII (March 5, 1943), 72–74.

"How Sears and Tire Companies Make Their Drive-ins Pay," *National Petroleum News,* XXXVII (September 12, 1945), 46.

"How To Wrest Fashion Prestige Away from New York Mail Order Houses," *Printers' Ink,* XCVI (September 21, 1916), 28.

Howard, M. E. "Inner Workings of Mail Order Campaigns," *Judicious Advertising,* IX (December, 1910), 57–62.

HUBBARD, D. "New Sears, Roebuck Copy Mirrors 1924 Mail Order Trends," *Printers' Ink*, CXXVI (March 13, 1924), 17–19.
HUGHES, L. M. "Peerless May Discard Dealers and Sell Motors by Mail," *Sales Management*, XXVII (August 29, 1931), 310–11.
"Human Interest Story of Richard W. Sears," *Printers' Ink*, LXXXVIII (October 8, 1914), 21.
HUMPHREY, G. E. "Insurance To Be Only on Automobile at First," *Eastern Underwriter*, XXXII (March 20, 1931), 22.
"Income Accounts for Calendar Years, 1924–27," *Commercial and Financial Chronicle*, CXXVI (January 28, 1928), 570.
INGRAM, FREDERICK F. "The Parcels Post," *Twentieth Century Magazine*, III (March, 1911), 514–22.
"Insuring Tire-Buyers," *Business Week*, June 6, 1936, p. 43.
JERAN, J. "South Offers Greatest Economic Future of Any Section of the United States," *Manufacturers Record*, CXII (November, 1943), 32–33.
JOHNSON, VICTOR B. "Beating the Mail Order Houses at Their Own Game," *Advertising and Selling*, XXI (February, 1912), 85–87.
"Jubilee Catalogs Load 20 Trains," *Literary Digest*, CXXII (September 26, 1936), 44.
KAESSMANN, FRED G. "The Science of Mail Order Merchandising," *Advertisers' Magazine*, Vol. I–III (July, 1910).
LAING, W. T. "Third-Cover Bedfellows; Three Big Mail-Order Companies Experiment with Color Pages Shared in Common," *Printers' Ink*, CLXXVI (August 27, 1936), 52.
"Largest Mailable Parcel," *Literary Digest*, XLVII (August 9, 1913), 209.
LAWRENCE, H. "Base Earnings," *Barron's*, XXIII (April 5, 1943), 5.
———. "Outstanding Reports of the Week, *ibid.*, XIX (March 27, 1939), 20.
"Leaders in Diversified Industries with Favorable Prospects," *Magazine of Wall Street*, XLIX (November 14, 1931), 83.
LEARNED, E. P., and ISAACS, NATHAN. "The Robinson-Patman Law: Some Assumptions and Expectations," *Harvard Business Review*, XV (winter, 1936), 137–55.
"Lessening the Hazards of the Mail Order Business," *Printers' Ink*, CV (December 19, 1918), 58.
"Light in Patman Law Darkness; Termination of Goodyear-Sears Tire Contract," *Business Week*, July 25, 1936, pp. 14–15.
LITTELL, R. "Great American Salesman," *Fortune*, V (February, 1932), 42–47.
"Lost $2,543,651; Results in Period to January 28," *Barron's*, XIII (March 6, 1933), 8.
McALLISTER, T. W. "Retail Merchant; a Reply to the Views of T. H. Price on the Mail Order Business," *Outlook*, CXII (March 8, 1916), 580–84.
McMAHON, W. "Easy Money," *Collier's*, LI (August 16, 1913), 26.
"Mail Order Advertising 10 Years Ago," *Advertisers' Magazine*, III (December, 1909), 30–32.
"Mail-Order Basement; Agency Sales Plan," *Business Week*, September 30, 1933, p. 12.
"Mail-Order Books," *Business Week*, June 26, 1943, pp. 86–87.
"The Mail Order Catalogue and a Market Decline," *Printers' Ink*, CXII (September 16, 1920), 162.
"Mail Order House Advertises Homes in Newspapers," *Printers' Ink*, CXIX (June 29, 1922), 96.
"Mail Order House Invades Chain Service Station Field," *Business Week*, August 12, 1931, p. 9.

"Mail Order House Links Up Realtors," *Business Week*, April 23, 1930, p. 16.

"Mail Order Houses Building Up Installment Sales," *Printers' Ink*, CVI (February 27, 1919), 34.

"Mail Order Houses Make Bid for More Urban Business," *Printers' Ink*, CC (July 31, 1942), 20.

"Mail Order Houses Turn State Fairs into Advertising Laboratories," *Printers' Ink*, XCVII (October 19, 1916), 108.

"Mail Order Invades Cities; Telephone Now Enables Urban Residents To Order from Sears and Ward Catalogs," *Printers' Ink*, CLXIX (November 15, 1934), 20.

"The Mail Order Man and His Letters," *Advertisers' Magazine*, I (November, 1907), 14–15.

"Mail Order Soliciting for the Manufacturer," *Advertisers' Magazine*, I (May, 1908), 18–19.

"Mail Order Store Building in Los Angeles, Cal.," *Architectural Record*, LXIV (July, 1928), 65–69.

"The Making of a Mail Order Menace," *Printers' Ink*, CII (January 17, 1918), 66.

MANN, LAWRENCE. "The Importance of Retail Trade in the United States," *American Economic Review*, XIII (December, 1923), 609–17.

MARSTON, C. B. "Mail Order Plans That Won My Store," *System*, XXIX (April, 1916), 397–402.

MARTIN, C. H. "How Dealers in Small Cities Compete with Mail Order Houses," *World's Work*, XIII (November, 1906), 8246–48.

"The Marvel of the Silent Salesman," *Harper's Weekly*, LVII (January 25, 1913), 24.

"Merchandising Stocks in Strong Position," *Magazine of Wall Street*, XLVII (March 7, 1931), 627.

MERRITT, ALBERT N. "Governmental Functions and the Express Business," *Journal of Political Economy*, XVI (July, 1908), 417–35.

MERTZ, PAUL A. "Personnel Practices of Sears, Roebuck & Co.," *Personnel Journal*, XVIII (June, 1939), 74.

MILBURN, GEORGE. "Catalogues and Culture," *Good Housekeeping*, CXXII (March, 1946), 183.

MILLS, F. C. "Movements of Mail Order Prices," *Journal of the American Statistical Association*, XXXII (March, 1937), 131.

MILLS, J. "How I Meet Mail-Order Competition," *System*, XXVIII (December, 1915), 642–44.

"Modern Homes Division Is Back Again in the Home Building Business," *Brick and Clay Record*, XCV (October, 1939), 20.

"Montgomery Ward Pulls Ahead of Sears, Roebuck," *Magazine of Wall Street*, LXII (October 8, 1938), 732–35.

MOORE, F. HOMER. "Canada a Mecca for Mail-Orders," *Advertisers' Magazine*, II (March, 1909), 14.

MOWRY, D. E. "Spends $30,000,000 a Year in the South," *Manufacturers Record*, CIV (November, 1935), 23.

"Must the Small Town Storekeeper Go?" *Annalist*, I (March 3, 1913), 196–98.

"Moving from Red to Black Ink," *Magazine of Wall Street*, LII (September 16, 1933), 530.

"Net To Be Halved," *Barron's*, X (November 17, 1930), 10.

"New Encyclopedia," *Business Week*, May 6, 1948, p. 103.

"New Installment Plan for Home Building," *Business Week*, January 29, 1930, p. 10.

"New Mail Order Catalogs Show Special Sales Effort," *Business Week*, December 31, 1930, p. 9.

"The New and Unusual in the Mail Order Field," *Advertisers' Magazine*, I (October, 1907), 6–12.

"Newspaper Campaign Presages Tilt between Mail-Order House and Phonograph Industry," *Printers' Ink*, XCVII (December 28, 1916), 12.

NICHOLS, G. A. "Can Retailer or Jobber Afford To Own Factories," *Printers' Ink*, CXXXV (April 15, 1926), 3–4.

NIMMONS, G. C. "Eastern Store of Sears, Roebuck & Co. at Philadelphia," *Architectural Record*, L (August, 1921), 118–32.

———. "New Renaissance in Architecture as Seen in the Design of Buildings for Mail Order Houses," *American Architect and the Architectural Review*, CXXXIV (August 5, 1928), 141–49.

———. "Sears, Roebuck & Co.'s Plant—Chicago," *Architectural Record*, XLVIII (June, 1919), 506–25.

NIMMONS and FELLOWS. "Designing a Great Mercantile Plant," *Architectural Record*, XIX (June, 1906), 403–11.

"1932 Loss," *Barron's*, XIII (January 2, 1933), 14.

"No Windows," *Architect and Engineer*, CXX (February, 1935), 35–38.

NYSTROM, PAUL. "An Estimate of the Volume of Retail Trade in the United States," *Harvard Business Review*, III (January, 1925), 150–59.

ODELL, C. L. "Sears, Roebuck Agents Are Now Marketing Life and Automobile Insurance," *National Underwriter*, XXXIX (February 7, 1935), 1.

OLIVIER, WARNER. "160 Miles of Words," *Saturday Evening Post*, CCXVIII (July 21, 1945), 9–73.

"One Way To Help Your Industry," *Printers' Ink*, CVII (April 3, 1919), 154.

OSBORNE, R. L. "Regional Sales of General Merchandise," *Survey of Current Business*, XVI (September, 1936), 14–17.

"The Parcels Post and Mail Order Business," *Outlook*, XCVI (December 31, 1910), 1033.

PERSONS, WARREN M. "The Crisis of 1920 in the United States," *American Economic Review* (Supplement), XII (March, 1922), 5–19.

"Philadelphia Plant," *American Architect and Architectural Review*, CXVII (January 7, 1920), 7–9.

"Phone Order Selling," *Business Week*, November 17, 1934, p. 6.

"Policy in Pictures," *Business Week*, May 17, 1947, p. 38.

PORTER, A. D. "Things Began To Happen When Sears Sent His Catalog Free," *Printers' Ink*, CIII (May 16, 1918), 114.

PRICE, T. H. "Mail Order Business," *Outlook*, CXII (January 26, 1916), 227–32.

"Prices Are Cut in the New Farmers' Bible," *Newsweek*, IV (August 25, 1934), 36.

"Profit-sharing Meets the Test of Depression," *Business Week*, March 23, 1932, p. 14.

"Purchasing Tests Save Money for Sears," *American Business*, VII (October, 1937), 41–48.

PURITON, E. E. "Satisfaction or Your Money Back," *Independent and Weekly Review*, CI (February 21, 1920), 275–77, 294–99.

PUTNAM, M. R. "Workers and Farmers Boost Sears Sales," *Barron's*, XXI (September 8, 1941), 5.

"Putting the Woman in the Job for Which She Is Fitted," *Printers' Ink*, CIV (September 26, 1918), 4.

"Rapid Development of the Mail Order Business," *Printers' Ink*, XCV (April 13, 1916), 80.

READ, F. "Why Kroger Is Selling Groceries in Sears, Roebuck Stores," *Printers' Ink,* CLII (September 4, 1930), 70.
"Record Sales," *Business Week,* March 26, 1939, p. 16.
"Report Is Made as to the Sears, Roebuck Insurance Companies," *National Underwriter,* XXXIX (June 27, 1935), 36.
"Report for 1931," *Barron's,* XII (February 8, 1932), 16.
"Report of Sub-committee on Administration: The Present State of the Art of Industrial Management," *Transactions of the American Society of Mechanical Engineers, 1912,* Vol. XXXIV (1913).
"Report for the Year, 1929," *Barron's,* X (February 3, 1930), 4.
"Retail Mail-Order Houses Make the Real Fight for Business," *Printers' Ink,* CXIV (January 27, 1921), 113.
"Retail Sales by Parcel Post," *System,* XXIII (April, 1913), 374–78.
"Review of Mail-Order Conditions," *Advertisers' Magazine,* I (March, 1908), 4–5.
REYNOLDS, BRUCE. "How Stores Sell by Mail without a Catalogue," *Judicious Advertising,* IX (March, 1911), 113–14.
RICHMOND, H., JR. "Prospects Favor Sears, Roebuck," *Magazine of Wall Street,* LXII (August 13, 1938), 500–502.
RIDER, FREMONT. "The Parcels Post and the Retailer," *World's Work,* XXI (April, 1911), 14248-51.
"Rights to Stockholders," *Commercial and Financial Chronicle,* CXLIV (January 2, 1937), 119.
ROBINSON, HENRY M. "Mail-Order Romantic Realism," *Bookman,* LXXI (July, 1930), 396–99.
"Robinson-Patman Act Forces Goodyear Co. To Terminate Sears-Roebuck Tire Contract," *Rubber Age,* XXXIX (August, 1936), 287.
"Roof Parking on Sears-Roebuck Building," *Architect and Engineer,* CXL (February, 1940), 10.
ROSENWALD, JULIUS. "What We Have Learned from 6,000,000 Customers," *American Magazine,* LXVI (August 21, 1920), 80–82.
———. "Why You Can't Do Too Much for Customers," *System,* XLVI (December, 1924), 709–12.
"Rotogravure Sections in Mail Order Catalogue," *Printers' Ink,* CXVI (July 28, 1921), 104.
RUSS, GEORGE A. "The Farmer as a Mail-Order Trader," *Advertisers' Magazine,* I (November, 1907), 22.
"Sales, February–August 1933–36, and Listing," *Commercial and Financial Chronicle,* CXLIII (August 22, 1936), 1247.
"Sales May Turn Up," *Barron's,* XXIV (February 7, 1944), 7.
"Sears Abroad; New Subsidiary," *Business Week,* December 22, 1934, p. 22.
"Sears Agency Plan," *Business Week,* February 29, 1936, p. 6.
"Sears Aims High," *Business Week,* March 10, 1934, p. 28.
"Sears Constant Wage," *Business Week,* April 22, 1939, pp. 30–32.
"Sears Continues Drive for Rich Metropolitan Markets," *Business Week,* November 9, 1932, p. 10.
"Sears Entering Super Service," *Petroleum Age,* XXV (September, 1931), 36–37.
"Sears Ersatz; Long List of Products Using Substitute Materials," *Business Week,* April 18, 1942, pp. 52–54.
"Sears Fiftieth," *Printers' Ink,* CLXXIV (January 23, 1936), 60.
"Sears Gives Old Tires a New Push," *Business Week,* March 23, 1940, p. 40.
"Sears Goes South; Opens Buying Office in Atlanta," *Business Week,* May 22, 1943, pp. 91–92.

"Sears House Plan; General Houses, Inc. Makes Houses; Sears Sells Things To Go in Them," *Business Week,* May 2, 1936, pp. 17–18.

"Sears and Housing," *Business Week,* September 2, 1939, pp. 27–28.

"Sears Improves Operating Profit Margin," *Barron's,* XXI (March 31, 1941), 13.

"Sears Insurance," *Business Week,* December 4, 1948, p. 96.

"Sears Offers Art; Catalog for Fall and Winter," *Business Week,* July 8, 1944, p. 94.

"Sears Offers Insurance Policy with Tires," *National Petroleum News,* XXVIII (June 3, 1936), 41.

"Sears Prefabricates," *Business Week,* August 31, 1935, p. 16.

"Sears Roebuck Boards the Prefabrication Bandwagon with Plywood Houses," *Architectural Forum,* LXIII (October, 1935), 452.

"Sears, Roebuck Broadens Offer To Finance Home Modernization," *Business Week,* October 22, 1930, p. 18.

"Sears, Roebuck & Co. Are Building a Paper Mill in Chicago for Manufacturing Wall Paper Out of Old Catalogs and the Waste Paper from Their Printing Plant" (news note), *Printers' Ink,* XCIV (March 23, 1916), 122.

"Sears, Roebuck & Co. Chicago, and Their Use of Printing Press," *Graphic Arts,* III (February, 1912), 121–36.

"Sears, Roebuck & Co. Resumes Display Advertising," *Printers' Ink,* CXXIV (July 26, 1923), 10.

"Sears, Roebuck & Co. Try Out Sampling Methods with Silvertone Phonograph," *Printers' Ink,* CIX (October 23, 1919), 25.

"Sears, Roebuck Companies Argue for Licenses in Ohio," *National Underwriter,* XXXIX (October 24, 1935), 1.

"Sears Roebuck Has Completed Major Expansion Program," *Barron's,* X (January 6, 1930), 21.

"Sears, Roebuck Initiates Monthly People's [sic] Book Club by Mail Order," *Printers' Ink,* CCIV (July 9, 1943), 44.

"Sears Roebuck Joins Promoters To Erect Group of 100 Houses," *Business Week,* September 10, 1930, p. 7.

"Sears, Roebuck Launches Great Expansion Program," *Business Week,* August 13, 1930, p. 11.

"Sears, Roebuck Profit-sharing Plan," *Survey,* XXXVI (July 22, 1916), 426–27.

"Sears, Roebuck Profit-sharing Plan Wins Cooperation of Employees," *Printers' Ink,* CVII (April 10, 1919), 57.

"Sears Roebuck Retail Stores Planned To Increase Mail Order Sales," *Sales Management,* VIII (March 21, 1925), 454.

"Sears, Roebuck Sells a Hat," *Advertising and Selling,* XXXI (April, 1938), 30–31.

"Sears, Roebuck To Develop Over the Counter Trade," *Printers' Ink,* CXXIX (December 25, 1924), 86.

"Sears, Roebuck To Make Fight on Advertising Issue," *Printers' Ink,* CIV (September 12, 1918), 53.

"Sears, Roebuck Uses Depression To Develop New Products," *Business Week,* March 18, 1931, pp. 7–8.

"Sears, Roebuck–Ward Merger Off," *Barron's,* XI (September 7, 1931), 24.

"Sears, Roebuck, Ward Merger Talk Again Revives," *Business Week,* September 2, 1931, pp. 13–14.

"Sears, Roebuck's Old Fashioned Copy Sells the Goods," *Printers' Ink,* CXIII (November 11, 1920), 202.

"Sears Sells Some Time Accounts to National City Bank," *Business Week,* June 17, 1939, pp. 44–45.
"Sears Slash; Lower Price Quotations—Spring Catalog," *Business Week,* February 16, 1935, p. 23.
"Sears Standardizing Wage Plans," *Business Week,* April 27, 1940, pp. 26–28.
"Sears Store Policy; Denies It Will Add More Associated and Agency Outlets," *Business Week,* September 16, 1939, pp. 41–43.
"Sears Surprises; as Prices Generally Rise Sales Flyer Reduces Them," *Business Week,* January 2, 1937, p. 20.
"Sears Tries Tab," *Business Week,* November 14, 1942, pp. 77–78.
"Sears' Two Bosses Are Buddies; Organization Plan Gives Carney and Nelson Equal Authority," *Business Week,* April 8, 1939, p. 18.
"Sears' War; World's Greatest Merchant Sees Sales Falling and Problems Mounting and Makes the Best of It," *Fortune,* XXVI (September, 1942), 78–83.
"Sears and Ward Fight Advertised Merchandising; State Fair Trade Acts Bring about Open Warfare against Nationally Known Drugs and Cosmetics," *Printers' Ink,* CLXXX (August 12, 1937), 14–17, 20.
"Sears and Wards; Watch Them Run," *Business Week,* April 1, 1939, pp. 34–35.
"Searspaper; Sears, Roebuck & Co. Newspaper," *Business Week,* April 7, 1934, p. 18.
"Selling Power in the Catalog Wrapper," *Printers' Ink,* XCVII (October 5, 1916), 53.
Sisland, A. G. "Perfecting a Mailing System," *System,* XXXVI (October, 1919), 710.
"Six Stocks in Strong Position To Resist Depression," *Magazine of Wall Street,* XLV (November 30, 1929), 105.
Smalley, E. V. "The Isolation of Life on Prairie Farms," *Atlantic Monthly,* LXXII (September, 1893), 378–81.
Smith, S. C. "Parcels Post Again," *Independent,* LXX (January 26, 1911), 185.
"Some Policies behind the Selling Work of Sears, Roebuck & Co.," *Printers' Ink,* LXXXVII (May 28, 1914), 17.
"Sound Position and Prospects of Largest Retail Merchandiser," *Magazine of Wall Street,* XLII (July 14, 1928), 480.
"Special Offerings," *Commercial and Financial Chronicle,* CXLVI (October 5, 1942), 1244.
"Speculative Audit; Favorable and Unfavorable Factors Affecting Common Stock Values," *Barron's,* XIII (August 21, 1933), 12.
"Standards for Gasoline Sears, Roebuck Is To Sell," *National Petroleum News,* XXIII (April 20, 1932), 17.
Starrett, J. "Building a Great Mercantile Plant," *Architectural Record,* XIX (April, 1906), 265–74.
"Statistics of Income, Capital, Stock Earnings, etc. 1929–38," *Annalist,* LII (September 21, 1938), 405.
"Statistics of Income, Capital, Stock Earnings, etc. Years Ended January 29, 1935–36," *Annalist,* XLVIII (July 3, 1936), 10.
Stern, L. "Fifty Years Old and Still Growing," *Magazine of Wall Street,* LVII (March 28, 1936), 700–702.
Stewart, R. P. "Sears, Roebuck in War and Peace," *Barron's,* XXII (June 1, 1942), 7–8.
———. "Why Sears-Ward Profit Trails Diverge," *ibid.,* May 3, 1937, p. 6.
"Stocks for Income Today and Profits Tomorrow," *Magazine of Wall Street,* LXIV (July 15, 1939), 345.

"Stocks Selling Close To Net Quick Asset Value," *Magazine of Wall Street,* LI (November 12, 1932), 107.

STOOPS, H. R. "Mail Order Strategy; Technique Rather than Delicate Finesse Builds Up Country-wide Sales, with Repeat Business as Base," *Printers' Ink,* CLXXII (July 11, 1935), 31–33.

"Store Building, Los Angeles; with Construction Outline," *Architectural Forum,* LXXII (February, 1940), 70–76.

"Store for Sears, Roebuck & Co., Kansas City, Mo.," *American Architect and the Architectural Review,* CXXIX (January 5, 1926), 24.

"Stores and the Catalogue," *Fortune,* XI (January, 1935), 69–74.

STOW, CHARLES H. "The Parcels Post and the Mail Order Man," *Advertisers' Magazine,* I (December, 1907), 12–14.

"A Striking Success in Selling Women's Apparel by Mail," *Advertisers' Magazine,* I (April, 1908), 46.

"Studies of Individual Stocks," *Barron's,* XVI (April 13, 1936), 18.

"Studies of Individual Stocks," *Barron's,* XVI (November 16, 1936), 15.

"Suit Filed against 1936 Revenue Act," *Commercial and Financial Chronicle,* CXLIII (October 24, 1936), 2611.

"Ten Outstanding Investments of 1931," *Magazine of Wall Street,* XLVII (January 10, 1931), 355.

TETLOW, HARRY. "Who Said 'eheu Fugaces?'" *Commonweal,* XXIX (January 6, 1939), 294–95.

THOMPSON, L. "Eden in Easy Payments; Sears Roebuck Catalogue; Spring and Summer 1937," *Saturday Review of Literature,* XV (April 3, 1937), 15–16.

THORNDIKE, E. L. "The Relation between the Quantity Purchased and the Price per Unit; Quantity Discounts of Representative Mail-Order Houses, Department Stores and Dealers in Specialties," *Harvard Business Review,* XVII (January, 1939), 209–21.

"Those Mail Order Tires; Goodyear Contract with Sears, Roebuck & Co.," *Business Week,* January 27, 1934, p. 12.

"Three Retail Stores; Birmingham, Alabama, Honolulu, Washington, D.C.," *Architectural Forum,* LXXVI (April, 1942), 207–16.

"Tires, Trade-ins, Trouble; Mail Order Tires," *Business Week,* March 17, 1934, p. 12.

"To Acquire Affiliate," *Commercial and Financial Chronicle,* CLVIII (December 20, 1943), 2475.

"To Discontinue Stock Dividends," *Barron's,* XI (February 2, 1931), 23.

"To Pare Down Its Notes," *Barron's,* X (February 17, 1930), 12.

"To Pay Extra Dividend; To Increase Capital Stock and To Offer Stock to Employees," *Commercial and Financial Chronicle,* CXLIII (October 31, 1936), 2859.

"Trade Commission Hearings in Goodyear Case Reveal Details of Sears, Roebuck Contracts," *Rubber Age,* XXXIV (February–March, 1934), 229, 280.

"Traffic in Names," *Literary Digest,* XLVII (December 27, 1913), 1321.

"Two More Sears Roebuck Stores Open in Chicago," *Sales Management,* IX (November 14, 1925), 682–83.

VAN VLISSINGEN, A. "52 Pay Checks a Year; Sears, Roebuck's New Standard Income Plan," *Factory Management,* XCVII (January, 1939), 65–67.

"Views of Insurance Men on Sears, Roebuck Mail Order Plan," *National Underwriter,* XXXV (March 20, 1931), 3.

WALKER, JOHN BRISBEN. "Who Will Be Benefited by a Parcels Post?" *Cosmopolitan,* XXXVI (February, 1904), 499–501.

"War Adding to Mailing Problem of Catalogue Houses," *Printers' Ink,* CIV (August 8, 1918), 17.
"Ward's Export Trade," *Nation's Business,* IV (October, 1916), 3–6.
WATSON, T. W. "Sears, Roebuck To Operate Stations with Its Retail Stores," *National Petroleum News,* XXIV (May 18, 1932), 41–42.
WEISS, E. B., and CUMMING, J. C. "How To Sell through Department-Store Chains; Retail Organization of Sears, Roebuck & Co.," *Printers' Ink Monthly,* XLI (July, 1940), 6–7.
WELDON, JOHN D. C. "Assaying Industrial Prospects for California and Mountain States," *Magazine of Wall Street,* LXXIX (March 15, 1947), 657–703.
WESTERFIELD, RAY BERT. "Middlemen in English Business, Particularly between 1660 and 1760," *Transactions of the Connecticut Academy of Arts and Sciences,* XIX (May, 1915), 111–445.
"What Advertising and Weeding Out Have Done for Mail Order," *Printers' Ink,* CXXV (October 11, 1923), 126.
"What the 'Buyers' Strike' Taught Retail Mail Order Houses," *Printers' Ink,* CXVIII (February 2, 1922), 25.
"What Is the Investment Outlook for This Company?" *Magazine of Wall Street,* L (July 9, 1932), 368–69.
WHITMORE, E. "Why Sears Is Pushing Southern Industrial Development," *American Business,* XII (January, 1942), 12–14.
WICKWARE, FRANCIS SILL. "The Life and Times of Sears, Roebuck," *Collier's,* December 3, 10, 17, and 24, 1949.
WILLIAMS, ALFRED. "Metamorphoses of the Mail Order Field," *Judicious Advertising,* IX (September, 1911), 43–48.
WILLIAMS, G. "Meet the Co-founder," *Reader's Digest,* XXXIV (January, 1939), 29–32.
WILLIAMS, J. S. "Balanced Portfolio of Stocks," *Magazine of Wall Street,* LXVI (July 27, 1940), 459.
———. "Examining the Future of Five Seasoned Common Stocks," *ibid.,* LXVIII (August 9, 1941), 452.
"Without Windows," *Architectural Forum,* LXII (March, 1935), 206–11.
"World's Largest Chain Merchandiser: An Audit," *Barron's,* XVI (June 8, 1936), 16.
WORSHAM, J. A. "Mail Order and Chains," *Printers' Ink,* CLXXII (July 11, 1935), 54.
WRIGHT, J. L.; STEELE, J. S.; and KIRKPATRICK, S. R. "The Department Store in the East," *Arena,* Vol. XX (August, 1899).
———. "The Department Store in the West," *ibid.,* Vol. XX (September, 1899).
"Young Sears, Roebuck," *Fortune,* XXXVIII (August, 1948), 84–132.
ZIMMERMAN, W. S. "How Retailers Use the Parcel Post," *System,* XXIII (March–May, 1913), 271–77.

III. GOVERNMENT DOCUMENTS

ABEL, JAMES F., and BOND, NORMAN J. *Illiteracy in the Several Countries of the World.* (Department of Interior Bull., No. 4.) Washington: Government Printing Office, 1929.
BUREAU OF THE CENSUS. *A Century of Population Growth. . . . 1790–1900.* Washington: Government Printing Office, 1909.
———. *Decennial Censuses of the United States—Population.* Washington: Government Printing Office, 1791––.

BIBLIOGRAPHY

———. *Topical Index of Population Census Reports, 1900–1930*. (Cooperation of the Committee on Social Statistics of the Social Science Research Council and the Institute of Social and Religious Research.) Washington: Government Printing Office, 1934.

BUREAU OF EDUCATION. *Bulletin No. 20*. Washington: Government Printing Office, 1913.

BUREAU OF LABOR STATISTICS. *Welfare Work for Employees in Industrial Establishments in the United States*. (Bull. No. 250; Misc. Series.) Washington: Government Printing Office, 1919.

DEPARTMENT OF AGRICULTURE. *Yearbook for 1907*. Washington: Government Printing Office, 1908.

———. *Yearbook for 1908*. Washington: Government Printing Office, 1909.

———. *Yearbook for 1909*. Washington: Government Printing Office, 1910.

DEPARTMENT OF COMMERCE. *Statistical Abstract of the United States, 1946*. Washington: Government Printing Office, 1946.

———. *Statistical Abstract of the United States, 1947*. Washington: Government Printing Office, 1947.

———. *Survey of Current Business, National Income Supplement*. Washington: Government Printing Office, July, 1947.

———. *Survey of Current Business*. Washington: Government Printing Office, February, 1948.

———. *Survey of Current Business*. Washington: Government Printing Office, July, 1948.

EMMET, BORIS. *Profit Sharing in the United States*. (Bureau of Labor Statistics Bull. No. 208; Misc. Series No. 13.) Washington: Government Printing Office, 1916.

FEDERAL TRADE COMMISSION. *Final Report on the Chain Store Investigation*. Washington: Government Printing Office, 1935.

GARRETT, PAUL W. *Government Control over Prices*. Washington: Government Printing Office, 1920.

SPRAGUE, O. M. W. *History of Crises under the National Banking System*. ("Publications of the National Monetary Commission.") Washington: Government Printing Office, 1910.

WOOD, R. E. "Statement before the Herring Committee Advocating Profit Sharing," *Congressional Digest*, XVIII (January, 1939), 21–22.

IV. ADDRESSES AND HEARINGS

Hearing before Illinois Senate Vice Committee. Springfield, Ill., 1913.

Hearings before a Subcommittee of the Committee on Ways and Means, House of Representatives, Seventy-sixth Congress, 3d Session, on H.R. 1, A Bill Providing for an Excise Tax on Retail Stores, I, 19. Washington: Government Printing Office, 1940.

Report on Vice: Hearings before Illinois Senate Committee. Springfield, Ill., 1916.

SELIGMAN, ISAAC N. "Address on Ethics of Business (Clinton Hall, New York, December 17, 1909)." New York, 1909. (Typewritten.)

WORTHY, JAMES C. "Discovering and Evaluating Employe Attitudes: An Address before the American Management Association, New York, October 3, 1947."

———. "Methods and Techniques for Building a Cooperative Organization: An Address in the Executive Seminar Series on Industrial Relations, Industrial Relations Center, University of Chicago, April 1, 1947."

Index

Index

"A" customer, 90, 132
"A" stores, 343–46, 348–51, 360–61, 363–64, 367, 369, 386, 432, 482–99, 512, 531, 543, 544–45, 551, 553, 561, 562, 563, 572, 589, 655
Abilene (Texas) *Farmers Journal,* 158, 159
Absenteeism, 137, 199, 522
Addams, Jane, 138, 598
Adler, Max, 234, 239, 265, 297, 329–30, 352, 358, 384, 624
Administration, 124, 358–73, 371–73, 675–76
"Advance Domino III," 636
Advertising, 39, 42–46, 59–63, 68–69, 82–83, 85, 88–89, 114, 174, 321, 382, 420, 450–58, 464–68, 475, 478–81, 490, 491–92, 495, 496, 670; of bicycles, 70–72; competition of, to mail-order selling, 321–22; of cream separators, 75; of electric belts, 72–73; expenditures on, 174–76; by four-color printing in catalogue, 98, 99, 104; of patent medicines, 102–4; reforms in, 114; respectability of, 245–58; of sewing machines, 67–69; of stoves, 69–70; *see also* Catalogue; Contests
Advertising Guide, 97, 477, 478
Agricultural Adjustment Administration, 614
Agricultural decline of 1919, 193
Agricultural education, 623–40
Agricultural Foundation, The, 623–24, 628–29, 631–42
Aids for Selecting Division Managers, 554–55
Alden's, 3
Alexander, Gilbert, 440
Alexander, W. H., 352
Allen, E. C., 19
Allstate Fire Insurance Company, 438–42
Allstate Insurance Company, 436–42, 455, 616
Allstate tires, 351, 390, 394–95, 397, 416–17, 478, 617
Allstate's "Illustrator Policy," 441–42
Almanacs, 21
Alvah Company, 36
American Agriculturist, 19
American Federation of Labor, 149, 600
American Fireside, 467
American Gas Association, 379
American Institute of Public Opinion, 448
American Management Association, 586, 588

American Medical Association, 249, 382, 478, 640
American Peoples Encyclopedia, 446–47
American Society of Heating and Ventilating Engineers, 379
American Society of Refrigerating Engineers, 379
American Society for Testing Materials, 379
American Woman, 64, 70
American Woolen Mills Department, 116
Among Ourselves, 21
Andrews, Ira R., 548–49, 550
Anniversary checks, 281, 290
Annual reports, 649–50, 655, 656
Anthony Adverse, 426
Appleby, John F., 11
Architect and Engineer, 540
Architectural Forum, 535, 539, 543, 545
Architectural Record, 535, 544
Architecture of stores, 531
Armour and Company, 633
Army Transport Service, 326
Arney, Harry, 71, 72
Asher, Louis, 51, 65, 66, 68, 88, 89, 92, 95, 96, 97, 109, 115, 134, 137, 143, 151, 162, 181–82, 451, 721–24 n., 726–35 n., 738 n., 740 n.
Asher, Max, 128
Atlanta Constitution, 122
Atlanta farmer's market, 637–38
Atlanta plant, 256, 328
Atlantic Monthly, 14
Atlantic and Pacific Tea Company; *see* Great Atlantic and Pacific Tea Company
Austin, C. N., 352
Automobile, effect of, on mail-order business, 317–18
Automobile Magazine, 108
Automobiles, 108, 220–21
Avery, Sewell, 499
Ayer, N. W., and Son, 60

"B" stores, 343–46, 348–51, 363–64, 369, 386, 482–99, 511, 545, 572, 589
"D and O" store, 182, 400
Baker, Newton D., 197, 198, 291
Balderston, C. C., 751 n.
Baltimore and Ohio Railroad, 325
Barker, J. M., 359, 360, 362–64, 440, 509, 550, 553, 568
Barron, C. W., 212
Barrows, Arthur S., 336, 364, 445, 497, 546

777

Basic buying program, 397–99, 405, 411, 420, 489, 490, 501, 674–76
Beasley, Norman, 732 n., 750 n.
Beker, A. G., and Company, 201
Benefits to employees, 141; *see also* Personnel policy
Bennett, Arnold, characterization of American businessman by, 174
Benton, William, 445
"Best on Earth," 34
Better Business Bureaus, 382, 478
Bicycles, 100, 101, 103, 427
"Big tickets," 110, 385, 387, 398, 400, 428–29, 430, 436, 482, 485, 486, 490, 497, 499, 513, 563, 654, 673, 674
Bijur, George, 745 n.
Bishop, C. H., 637
Blair, Walter, 447
Bloomfield, Daniel, 740 n.
Blue Cross Plan, 577
Bonus payments, 576
Boston News Bureau, 212
Boston plant, 256
Bowen, Mrs. Joseph T., 679–80, 681
Boy Scouts, 644
Bradley, David, factory, bought by Sears, Roebuck and Company, 241
Branch offices, 30, 217, 218–19, 255, 256, 307, 328
Brand names, 397, 414–20
Brandeis, Elizabeth, 734 n.
Brennan, L. J., 107
Briggs Auto Company, 396
Brunner, Edmund deS., 741 n., 742 n.
Buck, Solon Justus, 17, 720 n.
Buckley, Homer, 190
Buckner, R., 732 n.
Bulletin O-399, 570–71
Bunn, P. V., study of correspondence problem by, 131
Burns, Arthur, 521
Burroughs, Edgar Rice, 425
Burrows, F. E., 550
Business Corporations Law, of New York, 56
Business ethics, 110, 112, 114
Business Week, 392, 442, 448, 453, 458, 500, 523, 524
"Buyer's strike" of 1920, 200
Buyers, 119–21, 127–28, 432
Buying, 364, 365, 371, 374–420; *see also* Basic buying program

"C" stores, 343–46, 348–51, 386, 482–99, 511, 589
Cain, James M., 426, 479
Caldwell, C. B., 551, 553, 559, 561, 567, 574, 593

Caldwell, Erskine, 479
Camp Fire Girls, 644
Capital investment, 499–501, 654–56, 658
Capitalization, 54, 55–56, 57, 303–7, 715–16
Carlisle (Ark.) *Tribune*, 153, 155, 156, 157
Carney, Thomas J., 219, 291, 328, 334–36, 344–45, 381, 437, 549, 550, 551, 569, 571, 573, 574, 598, 671–72
Carriage trade, 1
Carrying charges, 508, 509, 511, 512
Carson, Pirie, Scott and Company, 381, 533
Case, Frank, 97
Case, H. N., 731 n., 739 n.
Cash Buyers Union, 68
"Catalog, The," by Edgar Guest, 456
Catalogue, 245–63, 450–58; addressing of, 278; as basis of Sears's advertising, 59–62; binding of, 260; and brand names, 419; charge for, 41; circulation of, 132, 254, 255, 262–63, 307, 432–34; cost of, 475–76; of Dallas branch, 81, 82; as editorial "mouthpiece," 614–16, 620–21; emphasis of, on quality, 309; establishment of plant for printing of, 98; first, of Sears, Roebuck, 36–41; illustrations in, 99, 100, 102, 258–59; indexing of, 88; influence of, in raising living standards, 310; instalment selling by, 506, 507, 511, 512; "lineup" of, 97; manufacture of, 256–62; "Modern Homes," 522–24; of Montgomery Ward, 20; more conservative copy of, 300; of 1906, 119; of 1907, 415; of 1908, 119; of 1910, 119; of 1946, 396; paper problem of, 99, 257–58; pictures of factories in, 242; policy of, 85–99; problem of four-color printing of, 98–99; regional, 468–72; respectability of, 479; space allocation of, 104, 220, 222–23, 422–27; value of, compared to magazine advertising, 68; during war, 430, 434–36; of the Warren Company, 33, 35
Catalogue circulation, research in, 460–68
Catalogue copy, guide to preparation of, 251–54
Catalogue order offices, 458, 460, 477, 478
"Chain-litter movement," 634–36
Chain Store Age, 535
Chain stores, 195, 308, 319–20, 339–40, 349, 554, 606–21
Chain-tax statutes, 607–12
Chapman, Paul W., 633, 639, 750 n.
Charge accounts, 492
Chicago Daily News, 27
Chicago Fireside Friend, 19

INDEX

Chicago Journal of Commerce, 214, 453, 617, 651
Chicago Public Library, 142
Chicago Stock Exchange Restaurant and Buffet, 48
Chicago Tribune, 151, 152
Chicago Vice Commission, 283
Chicago's Century of Progress, Sears, Roebuck building at, 629
Christian Herald, 448
Christianson, Theodore, 610
Clark, A. W., 731, 745
Clark, Alfred C., 155, 157
Clark, Thomas D., 17, 720 n.
Clayton Act, 609, 617
C.O.D. shipments, 33, 34, 35, 66, 74, 264, 459
Cohn, David L., 254, 732 n., 739 n.
Coldspot refrigerators, 390–92, 397, 414, 417, 430, 513, 517
Collections, on instalment accounts, 270–72, 274
College scholarship plan, 631–34
Collier's Weekly, 104
Columbian Exposition, 21, 47
Comfort, 19, 61
Commercial Investment Trust Corporation, 508
Commission men, 18
Committee on Human Relations of the University of Chicago, 582
Commons, John R., 740
Community Chest, 644
Community Fund, 643, 644
Community projects of Sears, Roebuck, 630–31
Community State Bank; *see* Sears'—Community State Bank
Companion, 19
Comparative shoppers, 232, 380, 564
Comparison of volume, Sears, Roebuck and Montgomery Ward, 203–05, 303–4, 337, 430, 664–65
Complaints, 130; *see also* Correspondence; Returns
Condon, E. J., 629, 637, 642, 750 n.
Congress of Industrial Organizations, 600
Conkey, W. B., 42, 98, 256
Consolidated Book Publishing Company, 448
Consumer Education Division, 641
"Consumer Shopping Guide," 457
"Consumer's Guide, The," 59
Contests, 456, 479, 629–30, 634, 637, 638, 642
Continental and Commercial Trust and Savings Bank (Chicago), 201
Conversion to war production, 413, 434

Coolidge, Calvin, 340
Cooper, James Fenimore, 63
Copeland, Morris, 314
Correspondence, 130–31, 159, 278–79
Cosmopolitan, 60, 64
Council of National Defense, 196, 197
"Cow-hog-hen" program, 631, 634–36, 643, 644
Cox, Garfield V., 152
Cox, Reavis, 265, 739 n.
Crawford, L. H., 218, 226, 250, 297
Cream separators, 100, 110, 179–80, 266, 269, 384, 388, 414–15
Credit policy, 15, 16, 18, 505–19; *see also* Instalment selling
Credit unions, 577, 707
Cremonesi, Michael, 736 n.
"Crop Improvement" plan, 622–23
Cultivator and Country Gentleman, 19
Cuneo, John F., 256
Cuneo Press, 256, 448
Curtis, A., Company, 36
Curtis, Cyrus, 89
Customer classification, 461–68
Customer index, 507
Customer service, 127
Customers' profit-sharing, 77–80, 94, 166

Dallas branch, 79–84, 126–27, 217
Dell, Ethel M., 426
Depression: of 1907, 57–58, 179; of 1920–21, 204–5, 304, 604, 623, 672; of 1929, 308, 323, 331, 346, 362–63, 452–55, 604
Dickson, W. J., 387
Dictionary of American Biography, 23
Dies, Representative Martin, of Texas, 609
Dionne quintuplets, 425
Discharge of personnel, 551
Discount, 38
Disney, Walt, 425
Display, 386; problems of, in retail stores, 353, 354–55; windows, 492, 534, 536, 541, 545
Distribution costs, 400–402
Division 400, 433, 458, 500
Dodd, Alvin, 548–49
Dodd, P. A., 733 n.
Doering, Otto C., 132, 134–36, 170, 234, 265, 276–79, 280, 292, 297, 329–31, 358, 363, 598, 624, 671
Donnelley, R. R., and Sons Company, 256
Dressed Poultry Marketing Service, 628
Duff-Gordon, Lady, stylist for Sears, Roebuck, 225, 299, 309
Dulles, Foster R., 741 n.
Dupont de Nemours, E. I., Company, 326
Durable goods; *see* Hard lines
Duryea, C. E., 194, 195

Eastman Kodak Company, 149
Easy-payment terms; see Instalment selling
Edison, Thomas Alva, 108
Egleston, N. H., 720 n.
"Electric belt," 104, 395, 414
"Electric ring," 104
Elliott Machinery Company, 279
Embree, Edwin R., 670, 750 n.
Emmet, Boris, 679
Employees, 137–49, 280–92, 547–603; discount to, 579, 581; Group Hospitalization Plan, 577; number of, 289, 290; Savings Department, 142; training of, 289, 548, 551, 554, 558–67, 587, 588, 592–93, 596–97; see also Employment; Personnel policy; Profit-sharing fund; Wages and hours
Employment, 182, 205, 289, 547, 548, 551, 554, 555–58, 560, 565, 573–75, 588
Encyclopaedia Britannica, 217, 266, 443–46
Esquire magazine, 479
Ethics, business, 110, 112, 114
Expansion, 30, 217, 218–19, 255, 256, 307, 308; of foreign business, 500–502, 655; of tire business of Wards, under Wood; 326; Sears on, 80, 218; Wood on, 546; see also "A" stores; "B" stores; "C" stores; Retail stores
Export trade, 500–502
Express shipments, 188

Factory ownership, policy of, 411–12
Fair, The, 381
Fair-trade legislation, 48, 613, 614, 620
Farm Service Division of the Agricultural Foundation, 624
Farmer's Market in Atlanta, 637–38
Farmer's Review, 21
Farrell, J. T., 479
Fashion, influence of, 322
Faulkner, Harold W., 719 n., 736 n.
Federal Communications Commission, 626
Federal Deposit Insurance Corporation, 443
Federal Housing Administration, 508, 512
Federal Reserve Bank of New York, 519, 520
Federal Reserve Board, 200
Federal Reserve System, 443; regulations of, 513
Federal Trade Commission, 251, 382, 394, 477, 478, 613, 617–20
Fentress, Calvin, Jr., 440
Field, Marshall, 2

Filene, Edward A., 420, 674, 744 n.
Filene's, 164
Finian's Rainbow, 254
Fireside Companion, 19
Fireside Visitor, 19, 41, 62, 63, 74
Firestone Tire and Rubber Company, 618
First Trust and Savings Bank (Chicago), 201
Fisk tires, 618
Florida Recovery Act, 608
Food stores, 76; see also Grocery department
Forbes, Winslow, Dr., 108
Ford, Henry, 136, 322
Foreign business, 500–502, 655
Forever Amber, 479
Fortune magazine, 309, 349, 409–10, 427, 430, 431, 432, 433, 499, 501, 512, 616, 659
4-H Clubs, 629–30, 635, 638, 642, 644
Fowler, G. F., 97
Frank, Florence Kiper, 48, 67, 129, 722 n., 725 n., 726 n., 728 n., 735 n.
Freedom of Opportunity Foundation, 610
Freight, 87, 101, 188
Fryberg, Andrew, 118
Fuessle, Newton A., 738
Future Farmers of America, 636, 639

Gallup, George, 448
Gardner, Burleigh B., 588
Gay, Edwin, 742 n., 750 n.
General Asphalt Company, 326
General Houses, Inc., 448–49
General Motors Corporation, 4
General store, 15, 16
George Lane Stores, 339
Gillam, Manly M., 43
Gilman, N. B., 714
Gimbel's, 381
Girl Scouts, 644
Givens, Robert H., Jr., 749 n.
Globe Building, 35, 37
Golden Egg, The, 639
Goldman, Harry, 82
Goldman, Henry, 51, 54–55, 56, 82, 126, 735 n.
Goldman, Sachs and Company, 51, 55, 78, 201
Goldsmith, J., 352
"Good–Better–Best" technique, 386–87, 420
Good Stories, 64
Goodrich tires, 618
Goodyear Tire and Rubber Company, 389, 394–95, 617–20
Grange, the, 17, 20, 21, 173

INDEX

Grant, W. T., Company, 320
Great Atlantic and Pacific Tea Company, The, 320, 339–40, 606
Great Crusade, The, 193
Green Grass of Wyoming, The, 448
Green Hand, The, 639
Grether, E. T., 614, 749 n.
Grey, Zane, 426
Grocery department, 101–2, 223, 228, 255, 297, 298, 338, 384, 453
Group insurance, 577, 580, 590
Guaranty, 36, 87, 102, 173, 245, 250–51, 309, 441, 454, 478, 492, 670
Guest, Edgar A., 456

Hacker, Louis M., 719 n.
Hall, W. F., Printing Company, 256
Hammerslaugh Brothers, 50
Hammett, Dashiell, 426
"Handy Volume" of *Encyclopaedia Britannica,* 443–44
Hanson, Alice C., 321, 322, 738 n., 742 n.
Happy Hours, 64
Hard lines, 385, 387–88, 400, 428–29, 430, 474, 482, 486, 497, 498, 513, 673
"Harmony House," 396–97, 425
Harper's Bazaar, 69, 322
Harper's Weekly, 64
Harris Trust and Savings Bank (Chicago), 681
Harvard Graduate School of Business, 587, 588
Harvard University Press, 587
Hatch Act, 9
Hattersley, G. B., 365
Hawthorne experiments, 587
Heal, Edith, 721–24 n., 726–35 n., 738 n., 740 n.
Health education, 142
Health service, inauguration of, 141
Hearth and Home, 64
Heine, Irwin M., 720 n.
Henie, Sonja, 425
Henry Rose Stores, Inc., 489–90
Hercules Life Insurance Company, 439–40
Higgins, John, 56, 184, 265
Hill, Grace Livingston, 420
Hobbs, Dr., 234
Hoch, William, 394
Home Construction Division, 525–30
Home Monthly, 61
Home Owners Loan Corporation, 528, 529, 530
"Home-Trade Clubs," 155–57
Home Trade League of America, 156
Homefolks, 69
Homestead Acts, 9, 191

"Honor-Bilt" homes, 522–24
Hooper, Franklin Horace, 443, 444, 445
Hope of Earth, 448
Hormel, George A., and Company, 574
Hospitalization, for employees, 142, 577, 579
Hours and wages, 144–45, 148, 283–87, 291, 346, 357, 568–76, 603
House organs, 141
Houser, T. V., 359, 376, 395, 398, 399, 400, 402, 403, 405, 409, 416
Hoverson, Henry, and Company, 33
How To Prepare Catalogue Copy, 97, 251
Hower, Ralph M., 103, 285, 727 n., 731 n., 734 n., 735 n., 740 n.
Hoyle's *Book of Games,* 426
Hucksters, 184
Hughes, La Fayette, 636
Hull House, 138, 683
Humm, C. E., 683, 750 n.
Humphrey, G. E., 437
Hutchins, Robert M., 445, 446

Illinois Central Railroad, 327
Illinois National Guard, 287, 288
Illinois Senate Vice Committee, 283–84, 680
Illinois Trust and Savings Bank (Chicago), 201
Incentive methods, 286
Industrial health service, 142
Industrial medicine, 148–49
Ingram, Frederick F., 736 n.
Inness, George, 480
Inspection of merchandise, 230–39, 377, 380–82
Instalment selling, 217, 264–75, 300, 310, 387, 441, 443, 444, 447, 453, 459, 460, 466, 505–19, 514–16, 522, 523, 524
Institute of Paper Chemistry, 258
Insull, Samuel, 625
Insurance: for employees, 141; sale of, by mail, 436–42
Internal Revenue Act, 683
International Harvester Company, 149
Interstate Commerce Commission, 12
Inventory, 115, 117, 201, 295, 332, 374, 375, 376–77, 420
Iowa State College, 633
"Iowaization" plan, 92, 132, 179, 463–64
Isaacs, Nathan, 749 n.
It Can't Happen Here, 426

Jackson, Walter, 443
Janes, L. S., 354, 481, 495, 534, 539, 546
Johnson, Albert, 134
Jones, Marvin, 642

Journal (Kansas City), 68
Jowett, Benjamin, 719 n.

Kansas City branch, 307, 328
Kansas State College, 639
Keene, Fred, 97
Kelly, Clyde, 720 n.
Kendrick, Benjamin B., 719 n.
Kildee, dean of Iowa State College, 633
Kingsley, H. W., 360
Kingston (N.Y.) *Leader*, 152
Kittle, Charles M., 330, 331, 341, 624, 625, 650, 672; death of, 329; financial ability of, 328–29; opposition to, 327; prosperity of Sears, Roebuck under, 329; ruthlessness of, 328; as successor to Julius Rosenwald, 327; support of, to retail stores, 328
Kiwanis International, 643, 644
Knickerbocker Trust Company, 57
Kolb, J. H., 741 n., 742 n.
Kresge, S. S., Company, 151
Kresl, Carl, 683
Kress's, 494
Kushel, F. W., 108
Kuznets, Simon S., 737 n.
Kyne, Peter B., 426

Labor turnover, 137, 522
Labor unions, 587
Laboratories; see Testing laboratories
Ladies' Home Journal, 89, 103–4, 322
La Follette, Robert M., Jr., 683
Lange, W. H., 142, 733 n.
Langeloh, W. W., 683
Larkin Company, 22
Latimer, M. W., 751 n.
Latin-American outlets, 655
Lawrence, Arthur, 26, 30, 33
Learned, E. P., 749 n.
Leclaire, M., 714
Lee, Maurice W., 606, 749 n.
Lehar, Franz, 222
Lehman, Philip, 56
Lehman Brothers, 55, 56, 78
Leinsdorf, Erich, 448
Leonardson, R. W., 739 n., 745 n.
Leslie's Weekly, 73, 164, 168
Lewis, D., 153, 158
Lewis, W. O., 56, 729 n.
Library, 379–80
Lions Clubs, 643, 644
Littell, Robert, 744 n.
Loeb, Albert, 50, 53, 75, 117, 130, 153, 219, 229, 230, 241, 249, 283, 292, 297, 671, 682, 735 n.; administrative responsibilities of, 125; as *de facto* president, 198; ill-health and death of, 325; personal characteristics of, 125; salary of, 56, 84; as secretary, 53, 54, 56; as vice-president and treasurer, 184
Loeb and Adler, law firm of, 50, 124
Loewy, Raymond, 391
Long, C. D., 745 n.
Los Angeles plant, 256, 328
Lowe, W. N., 437
Lynd, Robert S., 321, 738 n., 742 n.

McClure's magazine, 60
McConnell, Fowler B., 336–37, 373, 551, 553, 563, 571, 589, 590, 593
McCormick and Company, 574
McGrane, R. C., 741 n.
McKenzie, R. D., 318, 319, 742 n.
McKinley, William, 141
Macy, R. H., and Company, 22, 164–68, 174, 200, 234, 274, 285, 295, 297–98, 674
Madsen, Louis L., 636
Magnificent Obsession, 426
Mail-order business: advertisements of, in *New Yorker*, 3; in Colonial days, 2; effects of technology upon, 195; with Europe, 18; failure of, after 1919, 193; magazines of, 44, 59–61, 85; number of firms in, 2, 3, 320; rise of, 15, 18
Mail Order Journal, 61
Mailing lists, 41
Management, 123–36
Management and the Worker, 587
Manufacturing sources, 118–22, 238–44, 398
Markdowns, 674
Market Bulletin (Georgia), 637
"Marsh Harvester," 11
Marshall Field and Company, 201, 226, 381
Mass-production methods, 2
May Company, 543
Mayo, Elton, 587
Mayo, Dr. William, 23
Medical services, 288, 547
Meier, John, 134
Meine, Franklin J., 446
Memphis plant, 256, 328
Merchandise: quality of, 112–14; regional variations of, 468–72; selection of, 173
Merchandise management, 295–310
Merchandising, 216–44
Merchants and Manufacturers on Trial, 156
Mergenthaler Company, 98
Merger, rumors of: with J. C. Penney, 652–53; with Ward's, 651–52

INDEX

Merseles, Theodore, 326, 339, 340, 343
Mertz, Paul, 574
Metropolitan Life Insurance Company, 527, 528
Metropolitan Press Syndicate, 98
Middleton, D. K., 737 n.
Milburn, George, 741 n.
Military duty, company attitude toward, 287-88
Military personnel policy, 580-83
Miller, G. H., 284
Miller-Tydings Act, 613, 614, 615, 621
Millis, Harry A., 733 n., 749 n.
Mills, R. H., 157
Minneapolis office, 26-27, 35, 37, 137
Minneapolis plant, 256
Minneapolis and St. Louis Railroad, 24
Miracle of the Bells, The, 448
Mitchell, Wesley C., 57, 727 n.
Mitchell, William N., 383, 737 n., 744 n.
"Modern Homes" department, 226-28, 242, 268, 300, 448, 519-30
Montgomery, Royal E., 733 n., 749 n.
Montgomery Ward and Company; and automobile sales, 389; beginning of, in 1892, 19-22; and charge for catalogue, 92; and CIO, 600; and C.O.D. shipment, 267; comparison with Sears, 293-95, 303-4, 430, 664-65; as competitor to Sears, 163-64; and credit terms, 506, 511, 512; and Customer Dividend Certificates, 78; as customer of Roebuck, 101; and documentation of quality, 309; and expansion of tire business under Robert E. Wood, 326; and instalment selling, 267-68, 274; "mail-order agencies" of, 342-43; merger with J. C. Penney, 652-53; merger with Sears, Roebuck, 651-52; opposition of local merchants to, 150-51, 160; and parcel post, 187, 188; and patent medicine, 247, 249-50; and prefabricated houses, 523-24; and prepayment of postage and freight, 451; proportion of mail-order sales of, 3; and reduction in prices, 452-53, 474; and retail stores, 338-39; and telephone service of, 458-59
Moore, Charles W., 29, 722 n.
Moore, J. F., 365
Moore, Harry A., 346
Moore and Evans Company, 32
Morale, 280, 563, 575, 579, 586-90
Morgan, J. P., and Company, 651
Morgenthau, Henry, 51
Morrill Act of 1862, 9
Mory, A. V. H., 229-34, 248
Mott, Frank Luther, 720 n., 728 n.

Movies, 638-40, 644
Mullen, John, 686
Munsey's magazine, 60
Muntz, Earl E., 741 n.
Murphy, H. F., 365

National Association of Jobbers in American Watches, 29
National Association of Retail Druggists, 610, 611
National Bellas Hess Company, 22, 171, 204, 338, 551, 554
National Bureau of Standards, 379
National Cash Register Company, 149
National City Bank (New York), 510
National Cloak and Suit Company; see National Bellas Hess Company
National Electrical Manufacturers Association, 380
National Fertilizer Association, 629
National Formulary, 249
National fur show, 627
National Industrial Recovery Act, 599
National Labor Relations Act, 599
National Life Insurance Company of the United States, 438-39
National Livestock Loss Prevention Board, 639, 640
National Recovery Administration, 455, 569-70, 599, 614
National Safety Council, 639
National Tribune, 68
National Underwriters Laboratory, 379, 382
Negri, Pola, 310
Nelson, Donald M., 201, 203, 217, 230-32, 243, 249, 329, 331, 334, 377, 381, 385, 391, 403, 404, 409, 551, 563, 612, 614, 638
New Deal, effect of, on Sears, Roebuck, 333-34, 656
New Haven Clock Company, 414
New York Herald Tribune, 619
New York Stock Exchange, 688-89, 695
New York Times, 200, 201, 211-12, 213, 429, 430, 432, 445, 452
New York Weekly, 19
New Yorker, 3
Newborg, Moses, 51, 214
Newborg, Rosenwald and Company, 49
News-Graphic, 567-68, 581, 646
Newspaper advertising, 464
Nichols, J. P., 607, 608, 749 n.
Night work, elimination of, in 1902, 143
North to the Orient, 426
Northwestern Agriculturist, 160

Nostrums, 102–4, 247–50; *see also* Patent medicines
Nourse, Edwin G., 173
Nunn-Bush, 574
Nusbaum, Aaron E., 47, 123, 138; buys half-interest in Sears's business, 48; joins firm, 49; personality of, 51; sells out, 53
Nusbaum, Augusta, 51
Nystrom, Paul H., 13, 15, 114, 320, 720 n., 721 n., 732 n., 734 n., 737 n., 742 n.

O'Connor, J. H., 522
O'Connor, J. J., 268, 269
Odell, Carl, 436, 437, 440
Office of Price Administration, 431, 472–74
O'Hara, Barratt, 680
Omissions in catalogue, 198–99
One Thousand Pointers for Stock Raisers, 107
Operational methods, 276–92
Opinion Research Corporation, 621
Opposition: to chain stores, 606–21; to mail order, 150–68, 187; *see also* Suppressive legislation
Order handling, method of, 135–36
Organization, 124, 358–73, 675–76
Organs, 105
Ounce of Prevention, An, 639, 640
Outlet stores, 339
Overtime work, 143–44

Paid vacations, 693; *see also* Vacations
Palmer, C. D., 130, 131, 279
Panama Railroad and Steamship Line, 326
Parcel post, 13, 157–58, 187–91, 298, 299, 307
Patent medicines, 102–4, 236, 247–50, 299, 414, 671; *see also* "Electric belt"; "Electric ring"
Patman, Wright, 609, 610
Patrons of Husbandry; *see* Grange, the
Penney, J. C., Company, 2, 112, 195, 320, 353, 398, 551, 554, 652; attempted merger with Sears and Ward's, 652–53
Pension plans, 577–79, 681; abuses of, 682; *see also* Retirement plan
Peoples Book Club, 426, 447–48, 479
People's Literary Companion, 19
Personnel department, establishment of, 353
Personnel policy, 138, 280–92, 352–53, 356, 362, 547–603, 676, 713; manuals of, 145–47, 548, 549, 554–55, 594

Persons, Warren M., 737 n.
Pettigrew, William, 88, 97, 116, 176, 237, 251, 731 n., 736 n.
Philadelphia branch, 218–19, 256, 307
Phillips, Wesley Briggs, 721 n.
Pianos, 105
"Pican," 626
Piece work, 144, 286
Plato, *The Laws*, 2
Plummer, W. C., 739 n.
Poling, Daniel, 448
Pollack, E. J., 331, 359, 443, 509, 551
Population, shift of, from rural to urban concentration, 313
Porter, A. D., 736 n.
Porter, Gene Stratton, 425
Post, Emily, 426
Powell, E. H., 445
Prairie Farmer magazine, 625; purchases radio station WLS from Sears, 625–26
Pratt Institute, 234
Pre-emption Act of 1841, 9
Prefabricated homes, 448–49, 530
Prepayment: of freight, 451–52; of postage, 451–52
Presbrey, Frank, 43, 72, 259, 719 n., 721 n., 723 n., 728 n., 731 n., 739 n., 744 n.
Press and Printer (Boston), 103
Press relations, 646
Preventive medicine, 141
Price, Herman, 391
Printers' Ink, 184, 246
Proctor and Gamble Company, 149
Profit-sharing fund, 281–83, 288, 290, 291, 576, 578, 579, 580, 581, 590, 598, 671; actual cases of, cited, 711; annuity feature of, 703–4; company contribution to, 690, 699, 701–3; earnings of, 692; eligibility for, 696–97; employee contributions to, 700; evaluation of, 712–13; history of, 679, 681, 714; influence of stock-market fluctuations upon, 708; investment policy of, 686–88; mechanics of, 683–86; membership of, 693–96; origin of 681; as pension program, 682; purpose of, 693, 703; retirement regulations of 703–5; stock acquisition of, 689–90; withdrawals from, 697–99, 705–7
Profits and earnings, 53–54, 169, 170, 293–95, 300–307, 715–16
Promotions, 289–90, 292, 548, 554, 559
Prudential Life Insurance Company, 527
Public relations, 127, 171, 477, 622–47
Publisher and Advertiser, 117

INDEX

Purdue University, 639
Pure Food and Drug Act, 104, 153, 154, 229, 230, 233, 246, 247, 478

Quarter Century of Sears Mail Order Advertising Tests and Studies, A, 461

Radio advertising, 624-26
Railway Mail Service, 262, 277
Raw Fur Marketing Service, 626-27
Raw Wool Marketing Service, 627-28
Recent Social Trends in the United States, 318
Reconversion Committee, 497-99
Recreation program for employees, 547
Recruitment of personnel from colleges, 554, 559
Red Cross, 473, 643, 644
Refunds, 198, 435, 459, 474
Reserve-group training program, 554, 562
Retail clerks' unions, 600
Retail code, 569
Retail Personnel Organization, 549
Retail stores, 77, 308, 328, 331, 338-57, 397, 421-22, 429, 436, 457, 482-504, 505; consolidation of, 346-47; expansion of, 343-47, 648-50, 653-55, 660, 666-67; first opened, 341; problems of, 348-57; sales volume, of Montgomery Ward's, 344-46; sales volume, of Sears, Roebuck, 341-42, 344-46; *see also* "A" stores; "B" stores; "C" stores
Retirement plan, 577-79, 681
Return policy, 173
Returns, 113, 116, 132, 297-98, 382, 460, 508, 674
Revitalizing a National Selling Machine, 418
Rice, Stuart A., 741 n.
Rips, Rae Elizabeth, 720 n., 721 n., 722 n., 723 n., 734 n.
Robe, The, 448
Roberts, C. B., 360, 365
Robinson, O. P., 746 n., 748 n.
Robinson-Patman Act, 609-13, 614, 615, 619, 620
Rockefeller, John D., Jr., 212
Roebuck, Alvah Curtis, 35, 50, 66, 68, 116, 123, 124, 151, 669, 721-35 n.; answers Sears's ad for a watchmaker, 27; birth and parentage of, 27; buys out Sears, 33, 34; buys Warren Company from Sears, 34; death of, 334; employed by Sears, 28; health of, 46; liabilities of, 47; return of, to company, 334; sells out to Sears, 47; watch business of, 27
Roethlisberger, F. J., 587

Roosevelt, Franklin D., 615, 616, 621
Roosevelt, Mrs. Franklin D., 346
Roosevelt, Theodore, 87
Roper, Daniel C., 13, 190, 720 n., 736 n.
Rose, Henry, 489, 508; *see also* Henry Rose Stores, Inc.
Rosenfels, I. S., 247, 263, 732 n.
Rosenwald, Julius, 48, 49, 64, 65, 76, 79, 81-82, 84, 96, 97, 107, 117, 123, 124, 125, 130, 138, 151, 162, 176-78, 196, 199, 201, 203, 232, 241, 243, 246, 280, 283-84, 290, 292, 296-97, 307, 324, 325, 328, 347, 382, 443, 520, 548, 598, 622, 625, 650, 652, 669, 670-72, 679-80, 682, 721 n.-40 n.; birth and parentage of, 50; buys out Nusbaum, 53; career of, 51; and choice of successor, 327; as committee chairman of Council of National Defense, 197; death of, 215, 332; decision of, to break with Nusbaum and side with Sears, 52-53; financial arrangements of, in event of death, 215; joins Sears in 1896, 50; marriage of, to Nusbaum's sister, 51; opposition of, to advertising during crisis, 181, opposition of, to parcel post, 188; personal fortune of, 170-71; philanthropies of, 324-25; pledges personal fortune to save company, 209-13; as president, 184; rift of, with Sears, 127; salary of, and agreement with Sears, 56; sells stockholdings, 56; stops manufacturing own catalogues, 256; testimony of, in hearings of Illinois Senate Vice Committee, 680-81; as treasurer and vice-president, 53; as YMCA representative to France in 1918, 197
Rosenwald, Mrs. Julius, 330, 332
Rosenwald, Lessing J., 115, 134, 218, 289, 292, 325, 346, 350, 359, 384, 437, 549, 574, 598; becomes chairman of the board, 332-33; birth of, 51; as chairman of the board of Allstate Insurance Company, 437; desire of, for presidency of Sears, Roebuck, 330-31; personal characteristics of, 332-33; prejudice of, toward Charles Kittle, 328; retirement of, 334
Rosenwald, Samuel, 50
Rosenwald and Company, 49, 66
Rosenwald and Weil, 49, 51, 66
Rotary International, 643, 644
Rural Electrification Administration, 195
Rural free delivery, 14

Salaries, 144-45, 148, 283-87, 291, 346, 357, 568-76, 608

Sales volume, 3, 4, 5, 57, 110, 196, 293–95, 329, 335, 336–37, 432, 476–77, 604
Salvation Army, 644
Sams, C. E., 652, 653
"Savings and Profit Sharing Pension Fund," 679–714
Schechter case, 569
"Schedule system" for shipment of merchandise, 133
Schlesinger, Arthur M., 14, 720 n., 728n.
Scholarships, 642, 643, 644
Schulte-United, 554
Schwinn, Arnold, 118
Scott, Elmer L., 134, 143, 145, 149, 178, 279–80, 500, 549, 598, 729 n.; employee-training plan of, 140; experiments of, with business in Mexico, 82, 88, 97; interest of, in employee relations, 138; introduction by, of piece work, 286
Scott, J. R., 97, 229, 230
Scott, Walter Dill, 446
Scrip, 202, 304
Sears, Eva, 26, 35
Sears, Kate, 26
Sears, Richard Warren: adds diamonds and jewelry to watch business, 30; advertising methods of, 30, 39–44, 64, 86; article by, in *Publisher and Advertiser*, 117; attempts retailing, 37; author of "War to the Knife," 30; becomes station agent of Minneapolis and St. Louis Railroad, 24; begins selling on instalment plan, 28; begins watch business, 20, 25; birth and parentage of, 23; boyhood of, 24; as buyer, 116; buys out Nusbaum, 53; conflict of, with Rosenwald, 115, 127; death of, in 1914, 184; devotion of, to wife, 183; difficulty of, with Nusbaum, 51–52; disposes of Toronto business, 34; domination of catalogue policy by, 88–89; early interest of, in mail order, 24; education of, 24; establishes branch office in Chicago, 37; establishes second watch business, 33; establishes the Warren Company, 33; on expansion, 80, 218; on factory ownership, 244; founds R. W. Sears Watch Company, 26; guaranty of merchandise by, 31; health of, 46, 183; and instalment buying, 79; interest of, in merchandise, 109; "Iowaization" plan of, 92–96; liabilities of, 46; major decisions made by, 123; opens A. Curtis Company and Alvah Company, 36; opens office in Toronto, 30; opposition of, to Rosenwald over policies in Panic of 1907, 182; personal fortune of, 170–71; preoccupation of, with low prices, 32, 238; promotion of bicycles by, 70–72; promotion of cream separators by, 75; promotion of "Customers' Profit-sharing Premium Plan" by, 77–79; promotion of electric belts by, 72–73; promotion habit of, without adequate stock, 113; promotion of men's suits by, 66; promotion of sewing machines by, 67; provides capital for his manufacturers, 118; pursues advertising after reorganization of 1895, 59; relationship with Rosenwald, 48, 49; reliance of, on mail-order magazines, 60–63; resigns directorship of board in 1913, 184; resigns presidency, 183; retirement of, from mail-order business, 33; return of, to business with Roebuck, 35; salary of, 56; sells half-interest to Nusbaum, 48; sells half-interest to Roebuck, 34; sells out to Moore and Evans Company, 32; sells stockholdings, 56; sells Warren Company, 34; sources of business of, 37; talent of, as promoter, 82–84; as telegraph operator, 24; volume of business of, 39
"Sears Adult Farmer's Short Course," 634
Sears–Community State Bank, 442–43
Sears Finance Corporation, 508
Sears Forum, 568
Sears International, Inc., 500–502
Sears Mutual Benefit Association, 280–81
Sears, Roebuck and Company, Ltd., 500
Sears, Roebuck and Company and Their Employees, 145
Sears, Roebuck Foundation, 627, 642–47
Sears Watch Company, R. W., 26, 28, 31, 32, 33, 123
Seattle branch, 217, 255, 307
Securities and Exchange Commission, 683
Semi-weekly Journal (Atlanta), 69
"Send No Money," 74
Separations; *see* Turnover
Seroco Club, 139, 140, 279–80
Seroco Mutual Benefit Association, 141
Seroco Topics, 104, 139
Service Division, 260–61
Sewing machines, 66–67, 100, 101
Shannon, Fred Albert, 719 n., 738 n.
"Shears and Robust," in *Finian's Rainbow*, 254
Sherman Antitrust Act, 613
Shipping facilities, 298–99
Shop Management, 286
"Shoppers," 232, 380, 564

INDEX

Shuey, E. L., 733 n.
Sick allowances, 693
Simon and Schuster, 448
Simonson, Hans, 390
Singer Sewing Machine Company, 265
Sizing of clothing, 232, 235–36, 239
Skinner, J. Fletcher, 75, 97, 109, 115, 117, 127, 134, 169, 216, 229, 239, 246, 249, 255, 297, 383, 384, 731 n.
Skylight, The, 140–41, 279, 568
Slosson, Preston W., 193, 736 n., 741 n.
Smalley, E. V., 720 n.
Smith, Adam, 431
Smith, Charles E., 14
Sniffen, Robert P., 56, 124, 235, 237, 239, 738 n.; in charge of New York buying office, 128
Social Research, Inc., 503
Social Security Administration, 701
Soft lines, 387–89, 402, 429–30, 473, 482, 486, 487, 489–90, 496, 497, 498, 509, 510, 541, 673
Space and Sales Guide, The, 496
Spangler, Charles C., 42
Specification buying; *see* Basic buying
Spiegel, May, Stern Company (Spiegel's), 3, 22, 274
Sprague, O. M. W., 727 n.
Standard Oil Company of Indiana, 522
Starkey, A. L., 278
State Board of Tax Commissioners of Indiana v. Jackson, 608
Statistical Abstract of the United States, 340
Stitch in Time, A, 639
Stock control system, 115
Stockholdings, 53, 196, 202, 203, 307
Store Planning and Display Department, 357, 490–91, 492–96, 498, 531–46
Strauss, J. I., 200
Strauss, J. W., 543
Strawn, Silas H., 651
Style considerations, 421, 489; *see also* Duff-Gordon, Lady
Substitute materials, 432; *see also* Synthetics, use of
Suburban movement, 314
Sullivan, Thomas J., 156
Suppressive legislation, 605–21
Swift and Company, 633
Synthetics, use of, 413, 422

Taft, William Howard, 189
Talmadge, Eugene, 254
Tarbell, Ida M., 10, 719 n.
Taxes of Sears, Roebuck, 659, 661–62

Taylor, Frederick W., 276, 287
Tchaikovsky, Pëtr Ilich, 448
Telephone orders, 458–60, 500, 668
Telethrift service, 458–60, 476, 477, 500
Temple, Shirley, 425
Temporary National Economic Committee, 688
$10.00 Cash for a Very Little Work, 94
Territorial officers, 359–62, 365, 367
Testimonials, 35, 36, 37, 61, 62, 86
Testing of applicants, 555–56, 565; under direction of L. L. Thurstone, 557–58
Testing laboratories, 230–36, 239, 248, 249, 250–51, 299–300, 309, 377–80, 383, 389, 392–93, 394, 403, 478, 671
Textile Laboratory of Sears, Roebuck, 231
Thompson-Starrett Company, 126
Thorne, George R., 20
Thorne, William, 188
Thorp, Willard, 737 n.
Thurstone, L. L., 557
Tiffany and Company, 22
Time-payment plan; *see* Instalment selling
Tippett, W. M., 242
Tips to Trappers, 626–27
Tires, 389–90
Top management, organization of, in 1948, 365–71
Topeka (Kan.) *State Journal*, 635
Training of personnel, 289, 548, 551, 554, 558–67, 587, 588, 592–93, 596–97
Tribune Farmer (New York), 69
Truman, President Harry S., 474
Turnover of personnel, 137, 292, 522, 556, 575, 683–85
Twentieth Century Fund, 2, 611
"Twine-binder," 11
"2-4-6-8-cent" department, 106, 107, 220, 246, 384

Under the 4-H Flag, 638–39
Unemployment insurance, 573, 574, 575
Unemployment in 1921, 203
Unionism, 600–601
United Cigar Stores Company, 320
United Mine Workers, 601
United Service Organizations (USO), 473
United States Bureau of Entomology and Plant Quarantine, 379
United States Bureau of Labor Statistics, 679
United States Bureau of Mines, 379
United States Bureau of Standards, 394
United States Department of Agriculture, 624, 629, 639
United States Forestry Service, 630

United States Office of Education, 640
United States Pharmacopoeia, 249
United States Rubber Company, 618
United States Soil Conservation Service, 639
United States Steel Corporation, 4
University of Chicago, 445, 557, 582, 588
University of Georgia, 633
Utah State College, 636

Vacation policy, 148, 149, 287, 579, 590, 693
Valentino, Rudolph, 310
Vice-presidents of Sears, Roebuck, functions of, 358
Vickery, P. O., 19
Victory gardens, 642–43
Vocational training, 567, 640–41
Vogue, 322
Volume of business, 3, 4, 5, 57, 110, 196, 293–95, 329, 335, 336–37, 432, 476–77, 604
Voorhis, Elmer J., 226, 235, 239

Wages and hours, 144–45, 148, 283–87, 291, 346, 357, 568–76, 608
Wall Street Journal, 213, 304, 328, 329, 435, 437, 452, 474, 480, 525, 526, 530
Wallace, Henry A., 615
Wallace, William, 686, 693, 714 n.
Waltham Watch Company, 29
Wanamaker, John, 2, 13, 22, 43, 164, 168, 200, 674
War, effect of, 413–14, 428–36, 472–74
War Manpower Commission, 566
War Production Board, 431
Ward, Aaron Montgomery, 2
"Wardway" homes, 524
Ware, Caroline, 611
Warren Company, the, 33, 34, 35
Washington National Life Insurance Company of Evanston, Illinois, 440
Watches, 100, 105, 116
Watkins, Gordon S., 733 n.
Watson, B. F., 352
Waxman, Julia, 750 n.
Wecter, Dixon, 315, 506, 741 n., 744 n., 745 n.
Weil, Julius, 51
Weirick, Elizabeth, 234, 235
Weldon, John D. C., 745 n.
Welfare and social activities of employees, 149, 279–92
WENR, radio station, 625
Werner, M. R., 67, 324, 328, 651, 721 n., 723–30 n., 733 n., 734 n., 736 n., 737 n., 740 n., 742 n., 743 n., 750 n.

Western Electric Company, 141
Westervelt, W. I., 377, 391, 614
Westrich, "Jack," 221
Westward migration, 9
What Sears Owners Say, 221
Where the Road Turns Right, 639
White, Pearl, 310
White's Class Advertising, 65
Willard, Daniel, 325
Willey, Malcolm M., 741 n.
Williams, "Bill," 97
Wilson, Woodrow, 196
WLS, radio station, 235, 624–26
Wolman, Leo, 742 n., 750 n.
Women's Farm Journal, 21
Wood, Robert Elkington, 324–37, 672–73; as assistant to president of General Asphalt Company, 326; as assistant to vice-president of E. I. Dupont de Nemours Company, 326; birth of, 325; as chairman of the board of Sears, 334; clash of, with Merseles, 327; continuity of management provided by, 337; decentralization policy of, 358–60, 365, 373; as director of Panama Railroad and Steamship Line, 326; elected president of Sears, 329–31; experience and career of, 325–27; gamble of, on postwar expansion, 546; interest of, in tires, 389; leadership of, 666–67; as merchandise manager of Montgomery Ward, 326–27; originated outlet stores, 339–41; in Panama Canal Service, 325–26; and personnel policy, 598; relationship of, to sources, 404–9; on retail stores, 346–50; return of, to active duty in World War I, 326; social consciousness of, 643, 647; support of New Deal by, 615–17; as vice-president of Sears, 327
Woolworth, F. W., Company, 151, 320
Working conditions, in early days of company, 137–38
World War II, effect of, on company, 413–14, 428–36, 472–74
Wright, Chester, 316, 317, 719 n., 736 n., 737 n., 738 n., 741 n.
Wright, Harold Bell, 426
WSB, radio station, 625

Yeomans, Lucien I., 229, 230
YMCA, 197, 644
Youth's Companion, 64
Yust, Walter, 445
YWCA, 644

Zone officers, 364
Zone system, 369